PETERSON'S GUIDE TO DISTANCE LEARNING PROGRAMS

2005

THOMSON
PETERSON'S™

Australia • Canada • Mexico • Singapore • Spain • United Kingdom • United States

About Thomson Peterson's

Thomson Peterson's (www.petersons.com) is a leading provider of education information and advice, with books and online resources focusing on education search, test preparation, and financial aid. Its Web site offers searchable databases and interactive tools for contacting educational institutions, online practice tests and instruction, and planning tools for securing financial aid. Thomson Peterson's serves 110 million education consumers annually.

For more information, contact Thomson Peterson's, 2000 Lenox Drive, Lawrenceville, NJ 08648; 800-338-3282; or find us on the World Wide Web at www.petersons.com/about.

Editor: Fern A. Oram; Production Editor: Linda Seghers; Copy Editors: Bret Bollmann, Jim Colbert, Michele N. Firestone, Michael Haines, Sally Ross, Jill C. Schwartz, Pam Sullivan, Valerie Bolus Vaughan; Research Project Manager: Christine Lucas; Programmer: Phyllis Johnson; Manufacturing Manager: Ivona Skibicki; Composition Manager: Linda M. Williams; Client Relations Representatives: Mimi Kaufman, Lois Regina Milton, Mary Ann Murphy, Jim Swinarski, Eric Wallace.

ISSN 1546-590X
ISBN 0-7689-1398-5

Printed in the United States of America

10 9 8 7 6 5 4 3 2 1 06 05 04

Ninth Edition

CONTENTS

A NOTE FROM THE PETERSON'S EDITORS

For nearly ten years, Peterson's has given students and parents the most comprehensive, up-to-date information on distance learning programs in the United States and abroad. *Peterson's Guide to Distance Learning Programs 2005* features advice and tips on getting an education without setting foot in a classroom, with information on choosing and paying for a distance education, the importance of accreditation, and the latest developments in distance learning consortia. Peterson's researches the data published in *Peterson's Guide to Distance Learning Programs* each year. The information is furnished by the institutions and is accurate at the time of publishing.

Opportunities abound for students, and this guide can help you find what you want in a number of ways:

For step-by-step guidance in navigating the brave new world of distance learning, just turn the page for our **Welcome to Distance Learning** section. Providing a quick overview, "What Is Distance Learning?" is the perfect place to start. To choose a distance learning program that is right for you, "Selecting the Right Distance Learning Program to Fit Your Needs" and "Studying via Distance Learning" expand upon the program characteristics and options that you'll want to look for, along with the types of degrees offered. "Accreditation—What It Is and Why It Should Be Important to You" says it all—accreditation IS important and this article explains why. Distance learning is no different from traditional higher education in that someone has to pay for it. "Paying for Your Distance Education" outlines the financial aid options available to distance learners. Should you come across the term "consortium" in your search for distance learning, fear not, as "Consortia Demystified" explains what these powerful distance education models are all about. Finally, "Searching for Distance Learning Programs Online" outlines why you'll want to visit Petersons.com for even more distance learning search and selection resources.

Next, you'll want to read through "How to Use This Guide," which explains the information presented in the individual institution profiles, how we collect our data, and how we determine eligibility for inclusion in this guide. Following that are the **Profiles of Distance Learning Programs.** Here you'll find our expanded and unparalleled institution profiles, arranged alphabetically. They provide a complete picture of need-to-know information about accredited institutions offering distance learning programs—including the number of students enrolled in distance learning courses, availability of financial aid, services offered to distance learners, and degrees and awards offered.

And if you still thirst for even more information, nearly 200 two-page narrative descriptions appear in the **In-Depth Descriptions of Distance Learning Programs** and **In-Depth Descriptions of Distance Learning Consortia** sections of the book. These descriptions are prepared by the institutions and provide great detail about each institution's distance learning programs. They are edited to provide a consistent format across entries for your ease of comparison.

For easy reference on all the distance learning buzzwords, the **Appendix** offers a **Glossary** with everything from *accreditation* to *work-study award.*

If you already have specifics in mind, such as a particular institution or course, turn to the **Indexes**. Here you'll find indexes that allow you to search by degrees and certificate programs and by non-degree-related course subject areas offered. You'll also find the "Geographical Listing of Distance Learning Programs." Page numbers referring to all information presented about an institution are conveniently referenced.

Peterson's publishes a full line of resources to help you and your family with any information you need to guide you through your search for a distance learning program. Peterson's publications can be found at your local bookstore, library, and high school guidance office—or visit us on the Web at www.petersons.com.

Institutions will be pleased to know that Peterson's helped you in your selection. Admissions staff members are more than happy to answer questions, address specific problems, and help in any way they can. The editors at Peterson's wish you great success in your distance learning program search.

WELCOME TO DISTANCE LEARNING

WHAT IS DISTANCE LEARNING?

One student is a professional who needs to update work-related skills. Another is a working mother who never finished her bachelor's degree and would love to have that diploma and get a better job. A third student attends a local community college but would like to get a degree offered by a four-year institution halfway across the country—without moving.

For this diverse group of students, disrupting family and work by commuting to sometimes distant on-campus classes on a rigid schedule is simply not a workable option. Many people are discovering that distance learning is a blessing—you can get the education you need, which might otherwise be difficult or impossible to obtain in the traditional manner.

Broadly defined, distance learning is the delivery of educational programs to students who are off-site.

In distance learning courses, the instructor is not in the same place as the student. The students may be widely separated by geography and time, and the instructor and students communicate with each other using various means, from U.S. mail to the Internet. You can be a distance learner whether you live 300 miles from the university or across the street.

Distance learning courses are categorized according to the primary technologies they use to deliver instruction: print-based, audio-based, video-based, and Internet-based. The audio, video, and Internet courses all have variations that are synchronous—classes take place at specific times only—and asynchronous—classes occur at flexible times.

Print-based courses (correspondence courses) use print materials as the medium of instruction. Students receive the materials by mail at the start of the course and return completed assignments by mail. Sometimes fax machines speed up the delivery of assignments, and the telephone can be used if communication between instructor and student is necessary.

Audio-based courses may involve two-way communication, as in audio or phone conferencing; or they may involve one-way communication, including radio broadcast and prerecorded audiotapes sent to students. Audio technologies may be used to supplement the main technology used in the course. For example, in an Internet-based distance education course, students and professors may call one another periodically.

Video-based technologies include two-way interactive videoconferencing, one-way video with two-way audio, one-way live video, and one-way prerecorded videotapes provided to students. Of these, two-way interactive video and prerecorded videotapes are the most popular.

Two-way Interactive Video courses take place simultaneously in two or more sites. The instructor is located in the home site with a group of students, and other students are located in satellite locations, often with a facilitator to help out. Each site has TV monitors or large screens on which the instructor and students can be viewed. The course is conducted as a lecture. When students speak in class, they press a button on an apparatus on their desks, which makes the camera point to them as they speak and allows their voices to be transmitted to the other location. Quizzes and exams are faxed to the satellite location and back or mailed by an assistant when they are completed. Two-way interactive video bridges geographical distances but not time. Students must be in a particular place at a particular time to take the course.

Prerecorded Video courses are videotaped and mailed to off-site students. To supplement this, the course may have a Web site where notes and assignments are posted, or these may be mailed to the off-site students along with the tapes. If students have questions, they can call or e-mail the instructor after they view the tape.

Internet-based courses (also called online courses or e-learning) are offered over the Internet. Some online courses use synchronous, real-time instruction based primarily on interactive computer conferencing or chat rooms. However, most Internet-based courses use asynchronous instruction, making use of online course management systems, Web sites, e-mail, electronic mailing lists, newsgroups, bulletin boards, and messaging programs.

In asynchronous online courses, instructors post instructional material and assignments, including text, images, video, audio, and even interactive simulations, on the course Web site. Using messaging systems, newsgroups, or bulletin boards, they can start online discussions by posting a comment or question; students can log on using a password and join the discussion at their convenience. In some courses there may be periodic real-time interaction in chat rooms or interactive environments like MUDS (multiple-user dungeons) and MOOS (multiple-object orientations). Feedback and guidance to individual students can be done by e-mail or telephone. Note that most of the interaction in an online course is text-based; instructors and students communicate primarily through the keyboarded word.

Obviously, students must have a computer with the appropriate software and Internet access in order to take an Internet-based course. The cost of technology aside, online distance learning programs have considerable advantages. Because the course material stays online for a period of time, students can log on at their own convenience.

To ensure that students keep up, many instructors structure the learning environment by setting weekly deadlines for reading lectures and completing assignments, requiring group projects, and making participation in online discussions mandatory. In online courses with participation requirements, the amount of interaction between the faculty and students is far greater than in a large lecture class held on campus. There's no lying low in the back of the classroom in a well-run online course.

Mixing the Technologies

Many courses combine technologies with print materials. For example, a course can begin with a videoconference, with the instructor introducing himself or herself and outlining the course requirements. A printed study guide with all assigned readings and activities is distributed to all participants at the first session. Students who cannot get to a videoconferencing site are sent a videocassette of the first session along with the study guide.

After the first session, the course moves online. Using chat rooms, threaded discussions, and e-mail, participants do their assignments and group projects and interact online. Assignments are snail-mailed to the faculty member. Finally, the class concludes with another synchronous videoconference or recorded videotape.

Future Trends

Today, online instruction, two-way interactive video, and one-way prerecorded video are the most popular instructional technologies in distance education. According to the Department of Education's National Center for Education Statistics, colleges and universities are planning to increase their use of Internet-based instruction and two-way interactive video. Prerecorded video is likely to decrease in popularity.

The explosive growth in distance learning has come primarily from online courses and is likely to continue. With better databases and other sources of information continuing to appear on the Internet, ease of access to reliable data will increase. As high-bandwidth connections to the Internet replace phone connections, the capacity to quickly transmit large amounts of data increases dramatically. Eventually, high-bandwidth technologies will make individualized, customized, and live video interactions possible, with lengthy video programming available.

Degree and Certificate Programs

Many institutions of higher learning simply offer a smorgasbord of distance education courses that can be taken for credit. An increasing number of institutions, however, have taken distance education to the next step; they have begun to offer undergraduate and graduate certificate and degree programs that can be completed entirely by distance education. For example, a student with an associate degree from a local community college can go on to earn a baccalaureate degree from a four-year institution by distance learning, without relocating. Or a working professional can earn a master's degree or professional certificate on a part-time basis through distance learning.

Who Offers Distance Learning?

The better question might be, "Who doesn't?" With lifelong learning becoming commonplace and communications technologies improving rapidly, the demand for distance education has grown dramatically, as well as the number and variety of providers.

The first group of providers consists of traditional colleges, universities, graduate schools, community colleges, technical schools, and vocational schools. These providers range from schools that only their neighbors have heard of to household names like Stanford, Virginia Tech, and the University of California.

The challenges posed by distance education have forced colleges and universities to be creative in their approaches. Some schools have formed partnerships with cable companies, public broadcasting services, satellite broadcasters, and online education companies to deliver high-quality distance education. Colleges and universities also partner with corporations to deliver courses and degree programs to employees.

Finally, there are many online purveyors of noncredit distance education courses on subjects that range from candlemaking and beauty secrets to C++ programming and Spanish. These courses may be fun and even instructive, but do not contribute to your formal educational credentials.

SELECTING THE RIGHT DISTANCE LEARNING PROGRAM TO FIT YOUR NEEDS

As a prospective distance learning student, you should evaluate distance learning programs as much as you would any campus-based, traditional program. To start, ask yourself: "Does the curriculum meet my educational and professional goals?" If it doesn't, there's not much point in looking into that program any further, however flexible and convenient it seems. If the program does meet your educational needs, then the real work of evaluating it must begin. Distance education students need to be especially concerned about the quality of the programs they are considering for two main reasons.

First, with the proliferation of distance learning degree programs spurred by the Internet, there are a lot of diploma mills out there. Second, you must be especially careful about quality, because in many disciplines distance degrees are still considered the poor relations of degrees earned on campus.

Basically, you must do a lot of research by gathering information from the program, the university, accrediting agencies, professional associations, the faculty, current and former students, and colleagues. Only then can you make an informed decision about whether a program is right for you.

Reputation

For many students, the reputation of the school is the paramount factor in selecting a program. Not only should you consider the reputation of a university in general, but you should consider the reputation of a distance degree from a university in your field.

Program and Academic Quality

If you are pursuing a graduate degree or know your field of interest as an undergraduate, it is important to separate the reputation of the program or department in which you are interested from the reputation of the university to which it belongs.

One way to assess the quality of a program is to find out whether or not it is accredited by a specialized agency—if that applies in your field. But there are other ways to assess a program's academic quality. First, look at the curriculum. Does it cover what you need to learn? Is the syllabus up-to-date? Next, check some of the program's student data. For example, what percentage of students who enroll actually complete the degree? What percentage of students are employed in a field relating to their studies?

Faculty

Check out the faculty members. What are their credentials? What are their areas of expertise? Are they well regarded in their field? If the program is professional in nature, look for faculty members with a blend of academic background and professional experience. If the program is academic, you should find out whether tenure-track professors with Ph.D.'s teach both the on-campus and distance courses or if distance courses are relegated to part-time adjunct faculty members and/or assistants.

The Technology

Not only will you depend on your own computer, VCR, or television, but you will also depend on the institution's technology. Ask current students what their experiences have been. Does the server often go down? Are there frequent problems with camera equipment or satellite transmissions? Find out what technical support is offered to students. The best setup is free technical support accessed via a toll-free number 24 hours a day, seven days a week.

Student-Faculty Interaction

Will you be expected to log on to an online course at specific times or at your convenience? Will you be expected to participate in online discussions a certain number of times during the course? Some programs do little to overcome the distance learner's social isolation; others rely on group work to forge a community of learning. Still others use a cohort format, in which a group of students enrolls in a program at the same time and proceeds through it together at the same pace. Pay particular attention to the student-faculty ratio in online courses. If there are more than 30 students per instructor, you're not likely to get much individual attention.

Advising and Other Services

Academic advising is one of the most important student services for distance learners, especially if you are seeking to transfer credits or earn credits through examinations or from life experience to apply to a degree. Check what advising services are offered to distance learners and see how easy they are to access. Advising is also of particular concern to students in a consortium. If you are interested in a program that is part of a consortium, find out if the consortium offers advising or mentoring to help you navigate among institutions and guide your overall progress.

Has the institution kept up with an innovative degree program? For example, at many universities, distance learning courses and programs originate in a couple of departments eager to pursue new ways of educating. However, the university's centralized academic and administrative services may lag behind, leaving distance students to struggle with a system not designed for their needs.

Time Frames

Check to see how much time you have to complete a certificate or degree program, and decide whether or not the time frame meets your needs. Some programs have a generous upper limit on the number of years you may take to complete a degree, which allows you to proceed at your own pace. Other programs may be structured on an accelerated or cohort model, with a timetable and interim deadlines. If that's the case, make sure your own schedule can accommodate this.

Cost

The cost of a distance education degree or certificate program is often the same for on-campus and distance students. However, there are some things you should look out for. If you enroll in a consortium, member institutions may charge tuition at different rates. If you enroll in a public university, you will probably be charged out-of-state tuition if you are not a state resident. Some institutions charge an extra technology fee to cover the costs associated with distance education.

STUDYING VIA DISTANCE LEARNING

If you are interested in pursuing your education by distance learning, you are not limited to a few specialized courses or degree programs. Actually, almost every course, certificate, and degree program that you can take on campus is also available in a distance learning format. There are exceptions, however. Degree programs in subjects that require laboratory work or performance, for example, cannot usually be done completely at a distance. Still, distance education spans a wide range of offerings, from accredited graduate-level degree programs to self-help and hobby courses. Although some programs and courses are limited to residents of certain states or regions, many are available nationwide and internationally.

Today you can earn an associate or bachelor's degree entirely by distance learning. You also may be able to shorten the time it takes to earn a degree if you transfer college credits from other institutions of higher learning, earn credits through equivalency exams, or present a portfolio of your accomplishments. For adults, earning credits for past academic and other work can cut a year or more off the time it takes to earn an undergraduate degree. So don't be shy about negotiating for credits with the school in which you plan to enroll—the time and money you save may be considerable.

Undergraduate Degree Programs

ASSOCIATE DEGREE

Distance learning associate degrees are offered in a wide range of fields, including liberal arts, business, computer science, and health professions. Many students who have earned an associate degree go on to apply those credits toward a bachelor's degree.

BACHELOR'S DEGREE

Distance learning bachelor's degrees are offered in many fields, including business, computer science, economics, engineering, English, history, nursing, psychology, and telecommunications. Some colleges and universities offer interdisciplinary degrees, such as environmental studies or arts management, and some permit students to design their own interdisciplinary program.

Graduate Degree Programs

MASTER'S DEGREE

Distance learning master's degree programs outnumber other distance learning degree programs by a considerable margin. Most of these degree programs are professional in nature and are designed for working adults with experience in the field. If you are interested in a master's degree in library science, business, or education, you are in luck. These are fields in which there are many distance master's degree programs from which to choose. However, if you are looking for a distance learning master's degree program in an academic field, such as English language and literature, chemistry, or ethnic and cultural studies, your choices are far more limited. Most master's programs in academic fields are campus based.

Another type of master's degree that is offered via distance learning is the interdisciplinary degree. Some are offered in liberal studies or humanities and are granted for advanced study and a culminating project or thesis. Others combine academic and professional areas of study. Still others are offered in broad subject areas like environmental studies, in which students are expected to design their own course of study based on their particular interests.

DOCTORAL DEGREE

Most distance learning doctoral programs, even those offered by virtual universities, have a brief residency requirement. There are far fewer distance learning doctoral programs than master's programs. However, you can find programs in a wide range of fields, although the number of programs within each field may be limited. You can earn a distance learning doctoral degree in fields as diverse as business, computer science, counseling psychology, education, engineering, English literature, human services, instructional technology, library science, management, pharmacy, and public policy. As with distance learning master's degrees, distance learning doctoral degrees tend to be professional rather than academic in orientation. Many of these degree programs are designed with the professional working adult in mind.

Certificate Programs

Distance learning certificate programs can train you for a new career or give you a foundation in a new subject even if you've already earned a college degree in an entirely different field. Some schools now offer a portion of a master's or other degree as a certificate. This allows you to take part of the full degree curriculum and either stop at the certification level or proceed through for the entire degree. If this is an option that interests you, be sure to consider the admissions requirements carefully. If you think you may matriculate through to the entire degree, be sure you understand the admissions requirements for each program, as they may differ.

Professional Certificate Programs

Professional certificate programs are often designed with the help of professional associations and licensing boards, and thus encompass real-world, practical knowledge. Many are designed to prepare students for professional certification or licensure. At the end of the program, the student sits for an exam and earns a state-recognized certificate from a certifying agency or licensing board. If this is your goal, you should make sure that the certification program you want to take meets the certifying agency or licensing board's requirements. That way, you won't waste your time or money completing a program that won't help you meet your ultimate professional goals.

To give you just a few examples of professional certificate programs offered via distance learning, within the engineering profession there are certificates in computer-integrated manufacturing, systems engineering, and fire-protection engineering. In business, there are distance learning certificate programs in information technology and health services management. In education, distance learning certificates include early reading instruction, children's literature, and English as a second language. In health care, certificates include medical assisting, home health nursing, and health-care administration. In law, distance learning certificates are offered in paralegal/legal assistant studies and legal issues for business professionals.

Certificate Programs in Academic Subjects

Less common, but still available via distance learning, are undergraduate and graduate certificate programs in academic subjects. At the undergraduate level, you can earn a certificate in areas such as American studies, Chinese language and literature, English composition, creative writing, ethnic and cultural studies, general studies, humanities, and liberal arts and sciences. If you later enroll in an undergraduate degree program, you may be able to apply the credits earned in a certificate program toward your degree. At the graduate level, you can earn a certificate via distance learning in subjects such as biology, English language and literature, geography, physiological psychology, religious studies, and statistics.

ACCREDITATION—WHAT IT IS AND WHY IT SHOULD BE IMPORTANT TO YOU

The accreditation status of a college, university, or program can give you an indication of its general quality and reputation. But just what does accreditation mean and how does it affect distance learners?

In the United States, authority over postsecondary educational institutions is decentralized. The states, not the federal government, have the authority to regulate educational institutions within their borders, and as a consequence, standards and quality vary considerably for state-approved schools. You will find many state-approved schools that are not accredited and many that are. In order to ensure a basic level of quality, the practice of accrediting institutions arose. Private, nongovernmental educational agencies with a regional or national scope have adopted standards to evaluate whether or not colleges and universities provide educational programs at basic levels of quality.

Institutions that seek accreditation conduct an in-depth self-study to measure their performance against the standards. The accrediting agency then conducts an on-site evaluation and either awards accreditation or pre-accreditation status—or denies accreditation. Periodically the agency reevaluates each institution to make sure its continued accreditation is warranted. So accreditation is not a one-shot deal—an institution must maintain high standards or it runs the risk of jeopardizing its accreditation status as a result of one of the periodic evaluations.

Seeking accreditation is entirely voluntary on the part of the institution of higher education. The initial accreditation process takes a long time—as much as five or ten years—and it costs money. Of course, being awarded candidacy status does not ensure that an institution will eventually be fully accredited.

Institutional Accreditation

Institutional accreditation is awarded to an institution by one of six regional accrediting agencies and many national accrediting agencies, such as the Distance Education and Training Council. The regional accrediting agencies play the largest role in institutional accreditation. If a college or university is regionally accredited, that means that the institution as a whole has met the accrediting agency's standards. Within the institution, particular programs and departments contribute to the institution's objectives at varying levels of quality.

Specialized Accreditation

In contrast to institutional accreditation, specialized accreditation usually applies to a single department, program, or school that is part of a larger institution of higher education. The accredited unit may be as big as a college within a university or as small as a curriculum within a field of study. Most specialized accrediting agencies review units within institutions that are regionally accredited, although some also accredit freestanding institutions. There are specialized accrediting agencies in nearly fifty fields, including allied health, art and design, Bible college education, business, engineering, law, marriage and family therapy, nursing, psychology, and theology.

Specialized accreditation may or may not be a consideration for you when you evaluate distance education programs. That's because the role of specialized accreditation varies considerably depending on the field of study. In some professional fields, you must have a degree or certificate from a program with specialized accreditation in order to take qualifying exams or practice the profession. In other fields, specialized accreditation has little or no effect on your ability to work. Thus, it's especially important that you find out what role accreditation plays in your field since it may affect your professional future as well as the quality of your education.

Researching a School and Its Accreditors

It's important to find out what role accreditation plays in your field, since it may affect your professional future as well as the quality of your education. Since accreditation is awarded by private organizations, any group can hang out a shingle and proclaim itself an accrediting agency. Some diploma mills, for example, have been known to create their own accrediting agency and then proclaim themselves "accredited."

So how can you tell if the school or college in which you are interested is regionally accredited, if the program has the specialized accreditation you need, and if the agencies that have accredited the school and program are legitimate?

Of course, you can simply ask the school or program, but since accreditation is so important, it's probably a lot wiser to check elsewhere. First, check with the regional accrediting agency that covers the state in which the school is located. Then check with any specialized accrediting agency that may assess the particular program in which you are interested. To find out if an accrediting agency is legitimate and nationally recognized, you can consult the Council for Higher Education Accreditation (CHEA), a private agency that accredits the accreditors (http://www.chea.org). Or you can check with the U.S. Department of Education (USDE). Their Web site has a complete list of institutional and specialized accrediting agencies recognized by the federal government (http://www.ed.gov/admins/finaid/accred.html?src=qc). This Web site will also tell you whether or not accreditation by a particular agency makes the school eligible to participate in federal financial aid programs.

Researching Canadian Institutions of Higher Education

In Canada, as in the United States, there is no centralized governmental accrediting agency. Instead, the provincial governments evaluate the quality of university programs in each province, with a few nationwide agencies evaluating professional programs. To check on a Canadian university, you can contact the appropriate provincial department of education. To get general information about accreditation in Canada, visit the Web site of the Council of Ministers of Education at http://www.cmec.ca. Their Web site also has contact information and links to the provincial departments of education.

Researching an Unaccredited Institution

Seeking accreditation is a voluntary process, which some legitimate schools choose not to undertake. In addition, the newer virtual universities may not have been around long enough to be accredited. So what can you do to make sure a school is legitimate if it is not accredited?

First, you can call the state agency with jurisdiction over higher education in the state in which the school is located. The agency can at least tell you whether or not the school is operating with a legitimate charter, and it may be able to tell you if any complaints have been lodged or legal action taken against it.

Second, you can call the school and ask why it is not accredited and whether the school has plans to seek accreditation. If the school tells you it has applied for accreditation, double-check its status with the agency it names.

Third, you can consult with people in your field about the school's reputation and the value of its degree. Remember, in some fields a degree from an unaccredited school or program will bar you from professional licensure and practice. Keep in mind that enrolling in an unaccredited school or program can be risky. If you can avoid it, do so.

Accreditation Issues Relating to Distance Education

In the United States, controversy has arisen over the accreditation of online programs within traditional universities and the accreditation of completely virtual universities. On the one hand, many felt that online degree programs should be evaluated using the same criteria as other degree programs within institutions of higher education. Others thought that new standards were needed to properly evaluate distance education. Although this issue has not yet been settled, the six regional accrediting agencies have proposed uniform guidelines for evaluating distance education.

The impetus for this move is the fact that many distance education programs cross regional borders; the agencies want to ensure that similar standards are adopted across the country. Among the proposed criteria specific to accrediting distance education are faculty control of course content, technical and program support for both faculty members and students, and evaluation and assessment methods for measuring student learning. However, until these or other guidelines are accepted, distance education programs continue to be evaluated using the same criteria as on-campus programs.

What Does Accreditation Mean to You?

There are several benefits of enrolling in a program at a regionally accredited college or university. You are assured of a basic level of quality education and services. Any credits you earn are more likely to be transferable to other regionally accredited institutions, although each institution makes its own decisions on transfer credits on a case-by-case basis.

Any certificate or degree you earn is more likely to be recognized by other colleges and universities and by employers as a legitimate credential. You may qualify for federal loans and grants because regionally accredited institutions, such as nationally accredited institutions, are eligible to participate in Title IV financial aid programs.

Recognized Accrediting Bodies and Categories of Accreditation

Below is a list of all forms of accreditation awarded by accrediting bodies recognized by the U.S. Department of Education or the Council for Higher Education Accreditation.

GENERAL ACCREDITATION

General accreditation applies to an institution as a whole and is not limited to institutions or programs in a particular field of specialization.

REGIONAL

Regional accreditation denotes accreditation of an institution as a whole by one of the six regional associations of schools and colleges, each of which covers a specified portion of the United States and its territories as indicated in the following listings.

MIDDLE STATES

Degree-granting institutions that offer one or more postsecondary educational programs of at least one academic year in length in Delaware, the District of Columbia, Maryland, New Jersey, New York, Pennsylvania, Puerto Rico, and the U.S. Virgin Islands are covered by:

Middle States Association of Colleges and Schools (MSA)
Commission on Higher Education (CHE)
3624 Market Street
Philadelphia, PA 19104

Jean Avnet Morse, Executive Director
Telephone: 267-284-5025
Fax: 215-662-5501
E-mail: info@msache.org
URL: http://www.msache.org

NEW ENGLAND

Institutions in Connecticut, Maine, Massachusetts, New Hampshire, Rhode Island, and Vermont.

Colleges and universities that offer programs leading to the baccalaureate or higher degrees and institutions that award only the associate degree but include in their offerings degree programs in liberal arts or general studies are covered by:

New England Association of Schools and Colleges (NEASC)
Commission on Institutions of Higher Education (CIHE)
209 Burlington Road
Bedford, MA 01730-1433

Dr. Charles M. Cook, Director
Telephone: 781-271-0022 Ext. 313
Fax: 781-271-0950
E-mail: ccook@neasc.org
URL: http://www.neasc.org/cihe/cihe.htm

Colleges and institutions that offer programs leading to the associate degree but do not offer programs leading to a degree in liberal arts or general studies are covered by:

New England Association of Schools and Colleges (NEASC)
Commission on Technical and Career Institutions (CTCI)
209 Burlington Road
Bedford, MA 01730-1433
Paul Bento, Director
Telephone: 781-271-0022 Ext. 316
Fax: 781-271-0950
E-mail: pbento@neasc.org
URL: http://www.neasc.org/ctci/ctci.htm

NORTH CENTRAL

Institutions in Arizona, Arkansas, Colorado, Illinois, Indiana, Iowa, Kansas, Michigan, Minnesota, Missouri, Nebraska, New Mexico, North Dakota, Ohio, Oklahoma, South Dakota, West Virginia, Wisconsin, and Wyoming that offer at least one undergraduate program of two or more academic years in length or at least one graduate program of one or more academic years in length if no undergraduate programs are offered.

North Central Association of Colleges and Schools (NCA)
Higher Learning Commission
30 North LaSalle Street, Suite 2400
Chicago, IL 60602-2504

Dr. Steven D. Crow, Executive Director
Telephone: 312-263-0456 Ext. 102
Fax: 312-263-7462
E-mail: scrow@hlcommission.org
URL: http://www.ncahigherlearningcommission.org

NORTHWEST

Postsecondary institutions with programs of at least one academic year in length in Alaska, Idaho, Montana, Nevada, Oregon, Utah, and Washington.

Northwest Commission on Colleges and Universities
8060 165th Avenue, NE, Suite 100
Redmond, WA 98052

Dr. Sandra E. Elman, Executive Director
Telephone: 425-558-4224
Fax: 425-376-0596
E-mail: selman@nwccu.org
URL: http://www.nwccu.org

SOUTHERN

Institutions in Alabama, Florida, Georgia, Kentucky, Louisiana, Mississippi, North Carolina, South Carolina, Tennessee, Texas, and Virginia.

Institutions that offer one or more degree programs of at least two academic years at the associate level, at least four academic years at the baccalaureate level, or at least one academic year at the postbaccalaureate level are covered by the following:

Southern Association of Colleges and Schools (SACS)
Commission on Colleges (COC)
1866 Southern Lane
Decatur, GA 30033

Dr. James T. Rogers, Executive Director
Telephone: 404-679-4512
Fax: 404-679-4558
E-mail: jrogers@sacscoc.org
URL: http://www.sacscoc.org/

WESTERN

Institutions in American Samoa, California, Guam, Hawaii, Republic of Palau, the Republic of the Marshall Islands, the Federated States of Micronesia, and the Commonwealth of the Northern Mariana Islands.

Institutions that offer one or more educational programs of at least one academic year in length at the postsecondary level are covered by the following:

Western Association of Schools and Colleges (WASC)
Accrediting Commission for Community and Junior Colleges (ACCJC)
10 Commercial Boulevard
Novato, CA 94949

Dr. Barbara A. Beno, Executive Director
Telephone: 415-506-0234
Fax: 415-506-0238
E-mail: accjc1@pacbell.net
URL: http://www.accjc.org

Institutions that offer one or more educational programs of at least one academic year in length beyond the first two years of college are covered by the following:

Western Association of Schools and Colleges (WASC)
Senior College Commission
985 Atlantic Avenue, Suite 100
Alameda, CA 94501

Ralph A. Wolff, Executive Director
Telephone: 510-748-9001
Fax: 510-748-9797
E-mail: rwolff@wascsenior.org
URL: http://www.wascweb.org/senior/index.htm

State Program Registration

Registration of collegiate degree-granting programs or curricula offered by institutions of higher education and of credit-bearing certificate and diploma programs offered by degree-granting institutions of higher education.

New York State Board of Regents
State Education Department
Education Building
Room 110
Albany, NY 12234

Robert M. Bennett, Chancellor
Telephone: 518-474-5889
URL: http://www.regents.nysed.gov/

PAYING FOR YOUR DISTANCE EDUCATION

Pursuing a certificate or degree can be expensive, but it is usually money well spent. On average, people with undergraduate and graduate degrees earn far more than those who do not have these credentials. Still the question remains: How are you going to pay for school and support yourself (and your family) at the same time? The good news is that there is financial aid available for students in distance education programs.

Federal Financial Aid

Most of your financial aid is likely to come from the federal government, which provides need-based aid in the form of grants, work-study programs, and loans. Up-to-date information about federal financial aid programs can be found at the U.S. Department of Education's Web site, http://www.ed.gov/studentaid, or by calling 1-800-4-FEDAID. The U.S. Department of Education's booklet *The Student Guide* is an excellent resource on all federal aid programs, and is available online (http://studentaid.ed.gov/students/publications/student_guide/index.html) or from any institution's financial aid office.

To apply for federal financial aid, you must file the Free Application for Federal Student Aid (FAFSA). You can apply online at http://www.fafsa.ed.gov or by filing the paper application available from any financial aid office. You will need to obtain an electronic signature PIN number to file on the Web, easily obtainable at http://www.pin.ed.gov.

Are You Eligible for Federal Financial Aid?

Financial need is just one criterion used to determine whether or not you are eligible to receive "need-based" aid from the federal government. In addition, you must:

- have a high school diploma or GED or pass a test approved by the Department of Education,
- be enrolled in a degree or certificate program,
- be enrolled in an eligible institution,
- be a U.S. citizen or eligible noncitizen,
- have a Social Security number,
- register with the Selective Service, if required, and
- maintain satisfactory academic progress once you are in school.

Institutional Eligibility: An Issue Pertinent to Distance Learners

In order to participate in federal financial aid programs, an institution of higher learning must fulfill certain criteria established by Congress. There are many regulations that establish institutional eligibility. For more information, you should contact the college directly or check on the U.S. Department of Education's Web site, http://www.fafsa.ed.gov. The federal government has recently relaxed some of the regulations governing distance education programs, and more changes are likely to occur in the next few years as these programs continue to grow.

An institution's accreditation status affects its eligibility to participate in federal financial aid programs. If you plan to enroll in a regionally accredited traditional college or university, you can safely assume that the institution as a whole is eligible to participate in the federal aid programs, since distance certificates and degrees are likely to be a very small proportion of its overall offerings. However, because institutions have the discretion to exclude specific programs, check to see if the school disperses federal aid to students enrolled in programs that interest you.

Federal Aid Programs

Once you've confirmed the eligibility of the institution and program in which you are interested, check the federal aid programs in which they participate. Not all schools participate in all the federal aid programs. The following is a summary of the federal aid programs.

- **Pell Grants** These grants do not have to be repaid and are awarded to undergraduate students (with no prior degree) on the basis of need, even if they are enrolled less than half-time. Full-time is usually considered as 12 credits per term; half-time as 6 or more credits per term.
- **Federal Supplemental Educational Opportunity Grants** These are awarded to undergraduates (with no prior

degree) with exceptional financial need, even if they are enrolled less than half-time.

- **Federal Work-Study Program** This program provides part-time jobs in public and private nonprofit organizations to both undergraduate and graduate students who demonstrate financial need. The government pays up to 75 percent of the student's wages, and the employer pays the balance.
- **The Federal Family Education Loan (FFEL) Program** and the **William D. Ford Direct Loan Program** (commonly called **Stafford Loans**) These two major loan programs are sponsored by the federal government. You are eligible to borrow under these loan programs if you are enrolled at least half-time and have remaining costs after the Pell Grant and aid from other sources are subtracted from your annual cost of attendance. Depending on your remaining financial need, these loans may be subsidized (no interest while in school) or unsubsidized (interest accrues while in school). There are overall loan limits in place for the federal loan programs, based on your year in school.
- **Perkins Loan Program** These loans are available to both undergraduate and graduate students who demonstrate exceptional financial need, whether enrolled full-time or part-time.

State Aid Programs

Many states limit their financial aid to state residents who attend school in-state. But some states offer aid to residents who attend school in-state or elsewhere, and some offer aid to students who attend school in their state regardless of their residency status. Contact your state higher education office directly to find out what's available and whether you are eligible to apply (most states use the FAFSA to determine eligibility).

Institutional and Private Sources of Financial Aid

COLLEGES AND UNIVERSITIES

Second only to the federal government in the amount of financial aid disbursed yearly are colleges and universities. Many of these institutions award both need-based and merit-based aid to deserving students. To find out more about the types of aid that the school offers, contact the financial aid office.

NATIONAL AND LOCAL ORGANIZATIONS

Foundations, nonprofit organizations, churches, service and fraternal organizations, professional associations, corporations, unions, and many other national and local organizations offer scholarships, grants, and low-interest loans to students.

ALTERNATIVE LOAN PROGRAMS

In addition to the federal loan programs, there are many private alternative loan programs designed to help students. Most private loan programs disburse funds based on your creditworthiness rather than your financial need. The college's financial aid office is the best source of information on alternative loan programs.

- **Home Equity Loans** A home equity loan or line of credit can be an attractive financing alternative to private loan programs. Some of these loans are offered at low rates and allow you to defer payment of the principal for years, while also offering attractive tax advantages.
- **Credit Cards** Whatever you do, do not use your credit cards to borrow money for school on a long-term basis. The interest rates and finance charges will be high, and the balance will grow astronomically. Credit cards are useful to pay tuition and fees if you can pay the balance in full, expect a student loan to come through shortly, or expect your employer to reimburse your costs. Otherwise, avoid them, and contact the financial aid office for advice.
- **Internships and Cooperative Education Programs** Internships with organizations outside the university can provide money as well as practical experience in your field. As an intern, you are usually paid by the outside organization, and you may or may not get college credit for the work you do.
- **Employer Reimbursement** If you work full-time and attend school part-time, your employer may reimburse you for part or all of your tuition. This is often one of the most attractive features for adult students returning to school and thinking of enrolling in a distance education program. Check with your Human Resources office for more information.

Tax Benefits for Students

Whether or not you receive financial aid, there are many recently enacted tax benefits for adults who want to return to school. In effect, these tax cuts provide financial aid support indirectly through the tax system. For more detailed information, check out the National Association of Student Financial Aid (NASFAA) Web site at http://www.nasfaa.org/AnnualPubs/TaxBenefitsGuideIntrofaa.html.

- **The HOPE Scholarship Tax Credit** Students whose adjusted gross income falls within certain limits receive a 100 percent tax credit for the first $1000 of tuition and required fees and a 50 percent credit on the second $1000 for the first two years of college. The maximum credit is $1500 per year.

- **The Lifetime Learning Tax Credit** A family may receive a 20 percent tax credit for the first $10,000 of tuition and required fees paid each year. The maximum credit is $2000 per year, available for an unlimited number of years.
- **The Tuition and Fees Tax Deducation** This deduction can reduce the amount of your taxable income by as much as $4000 per year in 2004. You do not need to itemize your deductions to take advantage of this program. In general, eligibility is limited to Adjusted Gross Incomes of under $65,000 for single individuals and $130,000 for married taxpayers.
- **Individual Retirement Accounts** Taxpayers can withdraw funds from an IRA, without penalty, for their own higher education expenses or those of their spouse, child, or even grandchild.
- **State Tuition Plans** When a family uses a qualified state-sponsored tuition plan to save for college, no tax is due in connection with the plan until the time of withdrawal.
- **Tax-Deductible Student Loan Interest** The new student loan interest deduction allows students or their families to take a tax deduction for interest paid in the first sixty months of repayment on student loans.
- **Tax-Deductible Employer Reimbursements** If you take undergraduate courses and your employer reimburses you for education-related expenses, you may be able to exclude up to $5250 of employer-provided education benefits from your income.
- **Community Service Loan Forgiveness** This provision excludes from your income any student loan amounts forgiven by nonprofit, tax-exempt charitable, or educational institutions for borrowers who take community-service jobs that address unmet community needs.

CONSORTIA DEMYSTIFIED

Types of Consortia

Over the last few years, several types of consortia have emerged as the most successful and most popular distance education models. Among them are statewide consortia of public colleges and universities, statewide consortia of public and private institutions, regional consortia, consortia of peer institutions of higher education, and specialized consortia.

STATEWIDE CONSORTIA OF PUBLIC COLLEGES AND UNIVERSITIES

On the tightly focused side of the spectrum, a consortium may consist of the campuses of a single state university system. Students access the distance learning offerings of the various state colleges through a portal sometimes referred to as a virtual university.

A good example of a public statewide consortium is the University of Texas TeleCampus collaboration, consisting of fifteen UT campuses (http://www.telecampus.utsystem.edu). In collaborative degree plans offered via the TeleCampus, you may apply to one school, take courses from several partner institutions, use centralized support services, and receive a fully accredited degree from the home campus to which you originally applied. The TeleCampus serves as both a portal to distance education offerings in the Texas system and as a centralized point of service.

Many other states operate or develop consortia of their public colleges and universities, including Colorado, Connecticut, Illinois, Kentucky, New Jersey, New York, Ohio, Texas, and Utah. All have arrangements in place whereby students can take some transferable credits online from more than one institution and apply them to a degree at their home institution.

STATEWIDE CONSORTIA OF PUBLIC AND PRIVATE COLLEGES AND UNIVERSITIES

Broadening the scope a bit is the statewide consortium that includes both public and private institutions of higher education. Students in the state can use a single Web site to select distance education courses offered by member colleges and universities. If you are enrolled in a degree program at one member institution, you have access to distance learning courses given by other member institutions. Although the consortia members typically work together to maximize the transferability of credits from one college or university to another, it is still usually up to you to ensure that credits earned elsewhere can be applied to your home institution's degree.

For example, Kentucky Virtual University (KYVU) encompasses more than twenty-five institutions in the state of Kentucky, ranging from universities to technical colleges (http://www.kcvu.org). Each member institution charges its own tuition rates for in-state and out-of-state students. In addition to maintaining a centralized Internet directory of all distance learning courses offered in Kentucky, KYVU offers exceptional student support services. For example, you can fill out a common form to apply online to any of the member institutions. Once you are admitted to the KYVU system, you have centralized online access to every library book in the system, as well as online access to the full text of thousands of journals. If you wish to check out a book, it is sent to the nearest public library, where you can pick it up free of charge. If there is no library nearby, the book is sent by courier to your home or office. Your academic records are maintained by each institution at which you take a course, but also by KYVU, which keeps your complete records from all institutions.

REGIONAL CONSORTIA

Regional consortia include institutions of higher education from more than one state. Such consortia may involve public institutions, private institutions, or a mix of both. The Southern Regional Education Board (SREB) launched the Southern Regional Electronic Campus (SREC) in 1998 and now offers courses from nearly 200 colleges and universities in sixteen states (http://www.electroniccampus.org). SREC attempts to guarantee a standard of quality in the courses it lists by reviewing them to make sure they are well set up and supported by adequate services. It does not judge curriculum (it leaves that to member institutions) nor does it list courses in their first year of instruction.

From the Electronic Campus Web site, you can identify distance learning programs and courses that are available from all member institutions. For more detailed information, you can search the site by college or university, discipline, level, and state, including course descriptions and how the programs and courses are delivered. You can also connect directly to a particular college or university to learn about registration, enrollment, and cost. To improve its student services, the Electronic Campus has formed a partnership with the University System of Georgia to create Ways In (http://www.waysin.org), whereby students are able to apply for admission, register for classes, get information about and apply for financial aid, make payments, purchase textbooks, and use new online library services.

The SREC system is administratively decentralized. The acceptance of transfer credits and the use of credits for program requirements are determined by the college or university in which the student is enrolled. Likewise, all institutions set their own levels for in-state and out-of-state tuition, maintain individual student records, and determine policy with respect to access to their own student services. Therefore, if you take three classes from three different institutions you might have to be admitted to all three, pay three different tuition rates, and contact all three institutions for your academic records.

A unique model of regional distance education collaboration, consisting of institutions from nineteen states and Canada, is Western Governors University (http://www.wgu.edu). Unlike most other virtual universities that serve as the hub of a consortium, WGU enrolls its own students and grants its own degrees by assessing students' knowledge through competency-based examinations. WGU does not teach its own courses, but it provides its students with access to courses from member institutions. WGU, established in 1998, is regionally accredited, although its unusual degree model may account for WGU's relatively low enrollment of degree-seeking students.

Other regional consortia include the National Universities Degree Consortium, a collaboration of eleven accredited universities from across the United States (http://www.nudc.org); and the Canadian Virtual University, which includes ten universities across Canada (http://www.cvu-uvc.ca). Today, students can even choose to participate in a global consortium like CREAD (http://cread.outreach.psu.edu), the Inter-American network of institutions throughout North, Central, and South America.

CONSORTIA OF PEER INSTITUTIONS OF HIGHER EDUCATION

Groups of institutions sometimes form consortia because they have a common orientation or complementary strengths from which students might benefit.

For example, the Jesuit Distance Education Network of the Association of Jesuit Colleges and Universities seeks to expand the array of learning options for students on its twenty-five campuses in nineteen states (http://www.jesuitnet.com). Administrators hope to develop the JesuitNET system so that a student enrolled at any member institution will be able to take fully transferable online courses at any other member institution. Tuition rates will be set by individual colleges and universities. Through its Web site, JesuitNET promotes these schools' online degree and certificate programs as well as individual courses.

Another private college and university consortium uses a team teaching approach to deliver courses to students on multiple campuses. Sixteen institutions in the Associated Colleges of the South have created a virtual classics department (http://www.sunoikisis.org). SUNOIKISIS, the "ACS Virtual Classics Department," was created as part of the Mellon-ACS Pilot Project in Classics. Funded by the Mellon Foundation, the goal of the initiative was to build a digital infrastructure that would support a wide range of collaborative efforts among the sixteen institutions of the Associated Colleges of the South. By creating a virtual department of classics, ACS students would have access to the best instruction and scholarly resources.

SPECIALIZED CONSORTIA

Some consortia are formed by institutions that focus on a particular field. For example, National Technological University (NTU) is one of the oldest technology-based consortia (http://www.ntu.edu). A global university, NTU, arranges for its member colleges and universities across the country to deliver advanced technical education and training, usually to employees of corporate clients. Currently, more than 1,400 courses are available through NTU's participating universities, which provides fourteen master's degree programs. An unusual aspect of the NTU consortium is that the consortium itself, rather than the member institutions, is the degree-granting body.

Pros and Cons of Consortia Learning Models

One obvious advantage of consortia is the pooling of resources. More university partners translates to more choices in curriculum, and often a shared expense in developing instructional design and technology. Consortia can offer a centralized database or course schedule that allows you to find members' courses easily rather than having to search many institutions' materials and Web sites for what you need. You may also have the chance to choose from among a group of respected faculty members from within the consortia, which allows you to find the teachers with expertise most closely suited to your academic and professional interests. This large sampling of faculty members tends to offer a more diverse worldview in the classroom. In addition, a consortium can often provide essential student services on a scale not fiscally achievable by a single university. For example, a dozen universities can pool resources for a much broader digital library than any single school could supply on its own.

However, from the student's point of view, consortia can have problems, many of which can be attributed to their relative newness. The most critical are problems with transferring credits. Other drawbacks may include large class sizes and problems in communication.

TRANSFERRING CREDITS

One problem that sometimes comes up for students trying to earn an entire degree, or part of a degree, online is that their home institution may require a minimum number of home credits, yet it may not offer enough courses via distance learning for a student to meet that minimum.

Increasingly, this problem is less likely to arise, for several reasons. First, as distance education degree programs become more common and well known, students are likely to search them out and apply directly to the institution that offers them. Second, individual institutions will continue to add to their distance education offerings, broadening the course choices for their home students. And third, some state systems and other consortia may eventually decide to liberalize their rules on transfer credit maximums within the consortium as the demand for distance degrees increases.

Indeed, some consortia have already succeeded in solving credit transfer problems, and others are addressing the challenge of reconciling differing credit transfer policies and logistics. However, to ensure that any courses you take will successfully transfer from one institution to another (and ultimately toward your degree), you should secure an academic adviser at the start of your program and investigate the transferrability of credits before you register for courses at other institutions within the consortium. Serving as your own adviser brings the risk that some courses may ultimately not transfer toward your degree.

LARGE CLASS SIZE

Because so many students have access to courses in a consortium, online classes may reach an unmanageable size if limits are not placed on the student-to-teacher ratio. Many schools now adopt a ceiling on the number of students allowed in an online class, with teaching assistants or subsections of the course added for each additional set of students. This is vital to the processing of information and interaction required in a successful online course. Faculty members often find that a class of 25 students is quite manageable, but more becomes problematic.

MISCOMMUNICATION

Communication may be difficult in a consortium. The larger the consortium, the more likely that many universities or university systems are involved, and therefore you may need to communicate with several institutions that have differing policies and procedures. Additional communication snags can arise when you try to move your student records from one campus to another. Some consortia have spent considerable time, effort, and money to make this tedious and laborious process appear seamless to you as a student. For those that have not, you should be prepared to take a proactive stance to see that your records are successfully moved from one department, college, or university to another.

Comparing the Single University to the Consortium

A student who is looking for a learning community with school pride and a great deal of local loyalty may find the multicampus environment of a consortium less desirable than the collegiality of the single-university environment. In today's workplace and economy, however, many students opt for the flexibility and increased curriculum choices of a consortium over an individual school. Many consortia have succeeded in creating a sense of community for learners. The high level of dialogue in the online environment can often build friendships, connections, and communities not achieved in a traditional environment. A single university can offer you the chance to immerse yourself in one department (of your major, for example), but a consortium can offer a wider variety of choices in mentors and philosophies. As a student, you should think about your preference.

SEARCHING FOR DISTANCE LEARNING PROGRAMS ONLINE

Thinking about distance learning? The Internet can be a great tool for gathering information about institutions and their distance learning programs. There are many worthwhile sites that are ready to help guide you through the various aspects of the selection process, including Peterson's Distance Learning Channel at www.petersons.com/distancelearning.

How Peterson's Distance Learning Channel Can Help

Whether you are completing your degree or continuing your education, Peterson's has everything you need to know and connects you with some of the most respected providers of online education.

Choosing a distance learning program involves a serious commitment of time and resources. Therefore, it is important to have the most up-to-date information about prospective institutions and their programs at your fingertips. That is why Peterson's Distance Learning Channel is a great place to start the process!

DISTANCE LEARNING PROGRAMS DETAILED SEARCH

Explore more than 1,000 programs in IT, business, and other areas. Find a program by selecting from any of the criteria below or search by Name or Keyword. To select multiple criteria, hold down the Ctrl or Cmd key while making your selections.

- *Course of Study*
- *Degree/Award Level*
- *On-Campus Requirements*

Once you have found the program of your choice, simply click on it to get information about the institution and its programs, including delivery media, credit options, faculty, tuition and fees, accreditation, and application information and contacts.

E-MAIL THE SCHOOL

If, after looking at the information provided on Peterson's Distance Learning Channel, you still have questions, you can send an e-mail directly to the admissions department of the school. Just click on the "E-mail the School" button and send your message. In most instances, if you keep your questions short and to the point, you will receive an answer in no time at all.

VISIT SCHOOL WEB SITE

For institutions that have provided information about their Web sites, simply click on the "School Web Site" button and you will be taken directly to that institution's Web page. Once you arrive at the school's Web site, look around and get a feel for the place. Often, schools offer virtual tours of the campus, complete with photos and commentary. If you have specific questions about the school, a visit to a school's Web site will often yield an answer.

MICROSITE

Several educational institutions provide students access to microsites, where more information about the types of resources and services offered can be found. In addition, students can take campus tours, apply for admission, and explore academic majors.

GET RECRUITED

With so many distance learning programs to choose from nowadays, it's hard to know where to begin. Whether you are a recent college grad, an adult learner, or considering a career change, DistanceLearningWantsYou[SM] is the first step in finding the perfect distance learning program.

DistanceLearningWantsYou[SM] (www.distancelearningwantsyou.com) is the new approach to finding the right program, and DistanceLearningWantsYou[SM] registration is free! All you need to do is complete a short student profile with information on your educational and personal background and your preferred field of study, learning medium, and career goals. Then just sit back and have distance learning programs come to you!

OTHER RESOURCES

What kind of learning environment is best for you—a traditional setting or a distance learning program? Check out

Peterson's Distance Learning Channel's Assessment Test to see if distance learning is right for you. You'll also find information on Preferred Partners, companies who offer flexible loan options designed specifically for working students like you, and Featured Consortia, groups of institutions that can offer you even more flexibility, such as greater variety in course selection and exposure to faculty members, and often a choice of campus location. Peterson's Distance Learning Channel even offers a FREE practice CLEP Test!

Use the Tools to Your Advantage

Choosing a distance learning program is an involved and complicated process. The tools available to you at www.petersons.com/distancelearning can help you to be more productive in this process. So, what are you waiting for? Fire up your computer; your distance learning future may be just a click away!

HOW TO USE THIS GUIDE

Profiles of Distance Learning Programs

Here, in alphabetical order, you'll find more than 1,000 institutions offering postsecondary education at a distance. Each profile covers such items as accreditation information, availability of financial aid, degrees and awards offered, course subject areas offered outside of degree programs, and the person or office to contact for program information. In addition, there are **Special Messages** from institutions about new programs or special events.

For each institution, specific degrees and award programs are listed, followed by a list of subjects for which individual courses (undergraduate, graduate, and non-credit) are offered.

INSTITUTIONAL INFORMATION

The sections here describe overall characteristics of an institution and its distance learning offerings, featuring key facts and figures about the institutions, including:

- institution Web site,
- background information on the institution,
- the type of accreditation held by the institution,
- when distance learning courses were first offered at the institution,
- the number of students enrolled in distance learning courses in fall 2003,
- the availability of financial aid,
- services available to distance learners, and
- the person or office to contact for more information about the institution's distance learning courses.

DEGREES AND AWARDS

This part of the profile lists each program leading to a degree or certificate that can be completed entirely at a distance. Programs are grouped by the level of award: associate degrees, baccalaureate degrees, graduate degrees, undergraduate certificates, and graduate certificates.

COURSE SUBJECT AREAS OFFERED OUTSIDE OF DEGREE PROGRAMS

Listed here are the general subject areas in which the institution offers courses at a distance. Subjects are divided into those offered for undergraduate credit and for graduate credit and those that are non-credit. Note that this is not a listing of course titles; you will need to contact the institution for a detailed list of courses offered.

In-Depth Descriptions of Distance Learning Programs

Additional details on distance learning offerings are provided by participating institutions and consortia. Each two-page entry provides details on delivery media, programs of study, special programs, credit options, faculty, students, admission, tuition and fees, financial aid, and applying.

An institution's absence from this section does not constitute an editorial decision on the part of Peterson's. Rather, this section is an open forum for institutions to expand upon information provided in the **Profiles of Distance Learning Programs** section of the book. The descriptions are arranged alphabetically by institution name.

In-Depth Descriptions of Distance Learning Consortia

The organizations listed in this section represent consortia of institutions offering distance learning programs. Each consortium has been formed so that an expanded set of distance learning options can be offered beyond the resources available through any single member institution. These consortia do not have a central application process and/or do not directly award credits and degrees. Applications are processed, and credits and conferred degrees are awarded, through one of the member institutions. Further, consortia generally are not directly granted accreditations; rather, credits and degrees reflect the accreditation of the awarding institution. The reader should obtain specific information directly from the consortium.

Appendix

With the **Glossary** found here, you'll be able to learn all the pertinent terms from A to Z.

Indexes

If you are interested in locating a certificate or degree program in a specific field of study, refer to the index of

Institutions Offering Degree and Certificate Programs. Here you'll find institutions offering everything from accounting to theological and ministerial studies.

If it is individual courses you're looking for, the index of **Non-Degree-Related Course Subject Areas** will guide you to institutions offering credit and noncredit courses at either the undergraduate or graduate level.

The **Geographical Listing of Distance Learning Programs** lets you find programs that are offered by institutions that are located near you. Keep in mind that most institutions' offerings are available nationally, and sometimes internationally. See individual listings for details.

Data Collection Procedures

The information provided in these profiles was collected during the summer of 2004 by way of a survey posted online for colleges and universities. With minor exceptions, all data included in this edition have been submitted by officials at the schools themselves. For a few schools that failed to respond to Peterson's Web-based survey in time to meet the deadline, information was drawn from their Web sites. In addition, many of the institutions that submitted data were contacted directly by the Peterson's research staff to verify unusual figures, resolve discrepancies, and obtain additional data. All usable information received in time for publication has been included. The omission of any particular item from an index or profile listing signifies that the item is either not applicable to that institution or that data were not available. Although Peterson's has every reason to believe that the information presented in this guide is accurate, students should check with each college or university to verify such figures as tuition and fees, which may have changed since the publication of this guide.

Criteria for Inclusion in This Book

In the research for this guide, the following definition of distance learning was used: a planned teaching/learning experience in which teacher and students are separated by physical distance and use any of a wide spectrum of media. This definition is based on the one developed by the University of Wisconsin Extension.

Peterson's Guide to Distance Learning Programs profiles more than 1,000 institutions of higher education currently offering courses or entire programs at a distance. To be included, all U.S. institutions must have full accreditation or candidate-for-accreditation (preaccreditation) status granted by an institutional or specialized accrediting body recognized by the U.S. Department of Education or the Council for Higher Education Accreditation. The six U.S. regional accrediting associations are: the New England Association of Schools and Colleges, Middle States Association of Colleges and Schools, North Central Association of Colleges and Schools, Northwest Commission on Colleges and Universities, Southern Association of Colleges and Schools, and Western Association of Schools and Colleges. Approval by state educational agencies is conferred separately on some distance education courses. Canadian institutions must be chartered and authorized to grant degrees by the provincial government, be affiliated with a chartered institution, or be accredited by a recognized U.S. accrediting body.

PROFILES OF DISTANCE LEARNING PROGRAMS

ABILENE CHRISTIAN UNIVERSITY

Abilene, Texas

Instructional Technology

http://www.acu.edu/distanceeducation

Abilene Christian University was founded in 1906. It is accredited by Southern Association of Colleges and Schools. It first offered distance learning courses in 1996. In fall 2003, there were 100 students enrolled in distance learning courses. Institutionally administered financial aid is available to distance learners.

Services Distance learners have accessibility to academic advising, bookstore, campus computer network, career placement assistance, e-mail services, library services, tutoring.

Contact Carol Williams, PhD, Assistant Provost of Research and Services, Abilene Christian University, 1600 Campus Court, ACU Box 29140, Abilene, TX 79699-9201. *Telephone:* 325-674-2223. *Fax:* 325-674-6717. *E-mail:* carol.williams@acu.edu.

DEGREES AND AWARDS

Programs offered do not lead to a degree or other formal award.

COURSE SUBJECT AREAS OFFERED OUTSIDE OF DEGREE PROGRAMS

Undergraduate—bible/biblical studies; communications, general; English language and literature, general; sociology.

Graduate—bible/biblical studies.

ACADIA UNIVERSITY

Wolfville, Nova Scotia, Canada

Division of Continuing and Distance Education

http://conted.acadiau.ca

Acadia University was founded in 1838. It is provincially chartered. It first offered distance learning courses in 1968. In fall 2003, there were 1,000 students enrolled in distance learning courses. Institutionally administered financial aid is available to distance learners.

Services Distance learners have accessibility to academic advising, bookstore, campus computer network, e-mail services, library services, tutoring.

Contact Ms. Sarah Murphy, Student Services Representative, Acadia University, 38 Crowell Drive, Wolfville, NS B4P 2R6, Canada. *Telephone:* 800-565-6568. *Fax:* 902-585-1068. *E-mail:* sarah.murphy@acadiau.ca.

DEGREES AND AWARDS

Certificate Business Administration; Computer Science
MEd Curriculum Studies in Learning and Technology

COURSE SUBJECT AREAS OFFERED OUTSIDE OF DEGREE PROGRAMS

Undergraduate—accounting; art history; biology, general; business; chemistry; computer programming; computer science; economics; educational/instructional media design; education, general; English composition; English language and literature, general; English language and literature/letters, other; experimental psychology; foods and nutrition studies; foreign languages and literatures; geological and related sciences; gerontology; history; marketing management and research; mathematics; microbiology/bacteriology; multi/interdisciplinary studies, other; parks, recreation and leisure facilities management; philosophy; physics; political science and government; psychology; sociology; special education.

Graduate—educational/instructional media design; education, other.

Non-credit—mathematics.

ADAMS STATE COLLEGE

Alamosa, Colorado

Division of Extended Studies

http://exstudies.adams.edu

Adams State College was founded in 1921. It is accredited by North Central Association of Colleges and Schools. It first offered distance learning courses in 1978. In fall 2003, there were 590 students enrolled in distance learning courses. Institutionally administered financial aid is available to distance learners.

Services Distance learners have accessibility to academic advising, bookstore, library services.

Contact Jesse Jaramillo, Assistant Program Manager, Adams State College, Extended Studies, 208 Edgemont Boulevard, Alamosa, CO 81102. *Telephone:* 800-548-6679. *Fax:* 719-587-7974. *E-mail:* ascextend@adams.edu.

DEGREES AND AWARDS

AA General Education Requirements
AS General Education Requirements
BA Business Administration; Interdisciplinary Studies; Sociology
BS Business Administration

COURSE SUBJECT AREAS OFFERED OUTSIDE OF DEGREE PROGRAMS

Undergraduate—accounting; business; business/managerial economics; developmental/child psychology; English composition; environmental science; finance; law and legal studies related; management information systems/business data processing; mathematical statistics; radio/television broadcasting; sociology.

Graduate—biology, general; educational evaluation, research and statistics; educational/instructional media design; education, general; physical sciences, other; teacher education, specific academic and vocational programs.

Non-credit—accounting; business; business and personal services marketing operations; computer software and media applications; data processing technology; English composition; English creative writing; English language and literature, general; entrepreneurship; foreign languages and literatures; general retailing/wholesaling; gerontology; legal studies.

See full description on page 342.

ADIRONDACK COMMUNITY COLLEGE

Queensbury, New York

http://www.sunyacc.edu/

Adirondack Community College was founded in 1960. It is accredited by Middle States Association of Colleges and Schools. It first offered distance learning courses in 1999. In fall 2003, there were 349 students enrolled in distance learning courses. Institutionally administered financial aid is available to distance learners.

Adirondack Community College (continued)

Services Distance learners have accessibility to academic advising, bookstore, career placement assistance, e-mail services, library services, tutoring.

Contact Mr. Douglas Gaulin, Distance Learning Advisor, Adirondack Community College, 640 Bay Road, Queensbury, NY 12804. *Telephone:* 518-743-2253. *E-mail:* gaulind@acc.sunyacc.edu.

DEGREES AND AWARDS

AAS Business Administration; Marketing

AS Business Administration; Criminal Justice (Police Science)

COURSE SUBJECT AREAS OFFERED OUTSIDE OF DEGREE PROGRAMS

Undergraduate—accounting; business; business administration and management; business communications; computer software and media applications; criminal justice and corrections; criminology; developmental and child psychology; economics; English composition; English language and literature, general; English technical and business writing; fine arts and art studies; foods and nutrition studies; health and physical education/fitness; marketing management and research; mathematics; philosophy; psychology; sociology.

AIB COLLEGE OF BUSINESS

Des Moines, Iowa

http://www.aib.edu/onlineEducation

AIB College of Business was founded in 1921. It is accredited by North Central Association of Colleges and Schools. It first offered distance learning courses in 2001. In fall 2003, there were 135 students enrolled in distance learning courses. Institutionally administered financial aid is available to distance learners.

Services Distance learners have accessibility to academic advising, bookstore, campus computer network, career placement assistance, e-mail services, library services, tutoring.

Contact Dale Engle, Admissions Representative, AIB College of Business, 2500 Fleur Drive, Des Moines, IA 50321. *Telephone:* 800-444-1921. *Fax:* 515-244-6773. *E-mail:* engled@aib.edu.

DEGREES AND AWARDS

AA Business Administration and Leadership

COURSE SUBJECT AREAS OFFERED OUTSIDE OF DEGREE PROGRAMS

Undergraduate—accounting; administrative and secretarial services; advertising; applied mathematics; business; business administration and management; business management and administrative services, other; computer software and media applications; data entry/microcomputer applications; economics; English composition; English language and literature, general; English technical and business writing; entrepreneurship; financial management and services; human resources management; industrial and organizational psychology; international business; marketing management and research; mathematics; psychology; sociology.

ALASKA PACIFIC UNIVERSITY

Anchorage, Alaska

RANA (Rural Alaska Native Adult) Program

http://rana.alaskapacific.edu

Alaska Pacific University was founded in 1959. It first offered distance learning courses in 1999. In fall 2003, there were 30 students enrolled in distance learning courses. Institutionally administered financial aid is available to distance learners.

Services Distance learners have accessibility to academic advising, bookstore, campus computer network, career placement assistance, e-mail services, library services, tutoring.

Contact Ms. Annette J. Zella, Associate Director, Alaska Pacific University, 4101 University Drive, Anchorage, AK 99508. *Telephone:* 907-564-8213. *Fax:* 907-564-8317. *E-mail:* ajzella@alaskapacific.edu.

DEGREES AND AWARDS

AA Accounting; Business; Education (K-8); Human Services; Liberal Studies

BA Accounting; Education (K-8); Human Services; Liberal Studies; Organizational Management with a Nonprofit Emphasis; Organizational Management with an emphasis in Healthcare Administration

Certificate Education (K-8)

ALBUQUERQUE TECHNICAL VOCATIONAL INSTITUTE

Albuquerque, New Mexico

http://planet.tvi.edu/distancelearn

Albuquerque Technical Vocational Institute was founded in 1965. It is accredited by North Central Association of Colleges and Schools. It first offered distance learning courses in 1997. In fall 2003, there were 1,229 students enrolled in distance learning courses. Institutionally administered financial aid is available to distance learners.

Services Distance learners have accessibility to academic advising, bookstore, campus computer network, e-mail services, library services.

Contact Dr. Diane R. Johnson, Director, Distance Learning, Albuquerque Technical Vocational Institute, 5600 Eagle Rock Road, NE, Albuquerque, NM 87113. *Telephone:* 505-224-5271. *Fax:* 505-224-5273. *E-mail:* drjohnson@tvi.edu.

DEGREES AND AWARDS

AAS Office Administration

COURSE SUBJECT AREAS OFFERED OUTSIDE OF DEGREE PROGRAMS

Undergraduate—accounting; administrative and secretarial services; biology, general; business; business administration and management; business management and administrative services, other; business/managerial economics; communications, general; computer and information sciences, general; computer programming; construction management; criminal justice and corrections; culinary arts and related services; data processing technology; economics; English composition; English creative writing; English language and literature, general; entrepreneurship; fire protection; information sciences and systems; institutional food workers and administrators; international business; legal studies; marketing operations/marketing and distribution, other; mathematics; medical laboratory technology; microbiology/bacteriology; nursing; philosophy; psychology; real estate; sociology; speech and rhetorical studies.

ALCORN STATE UNIVERSITY

Alcorn State, Mississippi
Office of Academic Technologies
http://www.blackboard.alcorn.edu

Alcorn State University was founded in 1871. It is accredited by Southern Association of Colleges and Schools. It first offered distance learning courses in 1997. In fall 2003, there were 149 students enrolled in distance learning courses. Institutionally administered financial aid is available to distance learners.

Services Distance learners have accessibility to academic advising, e-mail services, library services.

Contact Mrs. Candice Santell, Director of Academic Technology, Alcorn State University, 1000 ASU Drive, #539, Alcorn State, MS 39096-7500. *Telephone:* 601-877-2479. *Fax:* 601-877-6350. *E-mail:* csantell@lorman.alcorn.edu.

DEGREES AND AWARDS

MSN Nursing

COURSE SUBJECT AREAS OFFERED OUTSIDE OF DEGREE PROGRAMS

Undergraduate—curriculum and instruction; nursing; teacher education, specific academic and vocational programs.
Graduate—environmental health.

ALLAN HANCOCK COLLEGE

Santa Maria, California
http://www.hancockcollege.edu

Allan Hancock College was founded in 1920. It is accredited by Western Association of Schools and Colleges. It first offered distance learning courses in 1974. In fall 2003, there were 1,299 students enrolled in distance learning courses. Institutionally administered financial aid is available to distance learners.

Services Distance learners have accessibility to academic advising, bookstore, library services, tutoring.

Contact Anna Rice, Multimedia Technician, Allan Hancock College, Learning Resources Center, 800 South College Drive, Santa Maria, CA 93454-6399. *Telephone:* 805-922-6966 Ext. 3320. *Fax:* 805-922-3763. *E-mail:* arice@hancockcollege.edu.

DEGREES AND AWARDS

Programs offered do not lead to a degree or other formal award.

COURSE SUBJECT AREAS OFFERED OUTSIDE OF DEGREE PROGRAMS

Undergraduate—accounting; business; computer and information sciences, general; computer/information technology administration and management; computer science; data entry/microcomputer applications; economics; electrical and electronics equipment installers and repairers; English composition; English language and literature, general; fine arts and art studies; fire protection; food sciences and technology; health and physical education/fitness; history; mathematics; music; philosophy; political science and government; sociology.

ALLEN COLLEGE

Waterloo, Iowa
http://www.allencollege.edu/

Allen College was founded in 1989. It is accredited by North Central Association of Colleges and Schools. It first offered distance learning courses in 2000. In fall 2003, there were 70 students enrolled in distance learning courses. Institutionally administered financial aid is available to distance learners.

Services Distance learners have accessibility to academic advising, bookstore, campus computer network, career placement assistance, e-mail services, library services.

Contact Lisa D. Brodersen, Associate Professor of Nursing & Coordinator of Distance Education, Allen College, 1825 Logan Avenue, Waterloo, IA 50703. *Telephone:* 319-226-2034. *Fax:* 319-226-2070. *E-mail:* broderld@ihs.org.

DEGREES AND AWARDS

Programs offered do not lead to a degree or other formal award.

COURSE SUBJECT AREAS OFFERED OUTSIDE OF DEGREE PROGRAMS

Undergraduate—nursing.
Graduate—nursing.
Non-credit—nursing.

ALLEN COUNTY COMMUNITY COLLEGE

Iola, Kansas
http://www.allencc.net/

Allen County Community College was founded in 1923. It is accredited by North Central Association of Colleges and Schools. It first offered distance learning courses in 2000. In fall 2003, there were 226 students enrolled in distance learning courses. Institutionally administered financial aid is available to distance learners.

Services Distance learners have accessibility to academic advising, bookstore, career placement assistance, e-mail services, library services.

Contact Regena M. Bailey Aye, Academic Advisor, Allen County Community College, PO Box 66, Burlingame, KS 66413. *Telephone:* 785-654-2416 Ext. 212. *E-mail:* rbailey@allencc.edu.

DEGREES AND AWARDS

Programs offered do not lead to a degree or other formal award.

COURSE SUBJECT AREAS OFFERED OUTSIDE OF DEGREE PROGRAMS

Undergraduate—agriculture/agricultural sciences; business; computer software and media applications; economics; English composition; health and physical education/fitness; history; mathematics; music; physical sciences, general; political science and government; psychology.

ALLIANCE UNIVERSITY COLLEGE

Calgary, Alberta, Canada
http://www.auc-nuc.ca/student_information/extension_education/index.html

Alliance University College was founded in 1941. It is provincially chartered. It first offered distance learning courses in 1991. In fall

Alliance University College (continued)

2003, there were 47 students enrolled in distance learning courses. Institutionally administered financial aid is available to distance learners.

Services Distance learners have accessibility to academic advising, career placement assistance, library services.

Contact Mrs. Eunice Emilson, Administrative Assistant for Extension Education, Alliance University College, #630, 833 4th Avenue SW, Calgary, AB T2P 3T5, Canada. *Telephone:* 403-410-2907. *Fax:* 403-571-2556. *E-mail:* extension@auc-nuc.ca.

DEGREES AND AWARDS

Programs offered do not lead to a degree or other formal award.

COURSE SUBJECT AREAS OFFERED OUTSIDE OF DEGREE PROGRAMS

Undergraduate—bible/biblical studies; biblical and other theological languages and literatures; business; classical and ancient Near Eastern languages and literatures; education, other; family and community studies; history; mathematics and computer science; philosophy and religion; theological and ministerial studies.

Graduate—bible/biblical studies; biblical and other theological languages and literatures; education, other; history; missions/missionary studies and missiology; theological and ministerial studies.

ALLIANT INTERNATIONAL UNIVERSITY

San Diego, California

http://www.alliant.edu

Alliant International University was founded in 1952. It is accredited by Western Association of Schools and Colleges. It first offered distance learning courses in 2000. In fall 2003, there were 200 students enrolled in distance learning courses. Institutionally administered financial aid is available to distance learners.

Services Distance learners have accessibility to academic advising, bookstore, campus computer network, career placement assistance, e-mail services, library services.

Contact Dr. Andrea Henne, Director of Distributed Learning, Alliant International University, 10455 Pomerado Road, San Diego, CA 92131. *Telephone:* 858-635-4873. *Fax:* 858-635-4699. *E-mail:* ahenne@alliant.edu.

DEGREES AND AWARDS

Certificate Behavioral Interventions for ADHD; Pre-MBA Certificate of Completion; Technology

MAE Teaching Emphasis

MS Clinical Psychopharmacology (Post-Doctoral)

COURSE SUBJECT AREAS OFFERED OUTSIDE OF DEGREE PROGRAMS

Undergraduate—accounting; business; business administration and management; business/managerial economics; computer and information sciences, general; economics; financial management and services; marketing management and research.

Graduate—business; computer and information sciences, general; education administration and supervision; education, general; psychology.

Non-credit—psychology; teacher education, specific academic and vocational programs.

ALPENA COMMUNITY COLLEGE

Alpena, Michigan

http://www.alpenacc.edu

Alpena Community College was founded in 1952. It is accredited by North Central Association of Colleges and Schools. It first offered distance learning courses in 1997. In fall 2003, there were 70 students enrolled in distance learning courses. Institutionally administered financial aid is available to distance learners.

Services Distance learners have accessibility to bookstore, e-mail services, library services.

Contact Dr. Mary Ann Carlson, Vice President of Instruction and Student/Community Services, Alpena Community College, 666 Johnson Street, Alpena, MI 49707. *Telephone:* 989-358-7233. *Fax:* 989-358-7561. *E-mail:* carlsonm@alpenacc.edu.

DEGREES AND AWARDS

Programs offered do not lead to a degree or other formal award.

COURSE SUBJECT AREAS OFFERED OUTSIDE OF DEGREE PROGRAMS

Undergraduate—computer/information technology administration and management; computer systems networking and telecommunications; criminal justice and corrections; electrical and electronic engineering-related technology; English composition; fine arts and art studies; health and medical administrative services; philosophy; political science and government.

ALVIN COMMUNITY COLLEGE

Alvin, Texas

Instructional Services

http://www.alvincollege.edu/de

Alvin Community College was founded in 1949. It is accredited by Southern Association of Colleges and Schools. It first offered distance learning courses in 1995. In fall 2003, there were 900 students enrolled in distance learning courses. Institutionally administered financial aid is available to distance learners.

Services Distance learners have accessibility to academic advising, bookstore, library services.

Contact Mr. Patrick M. Sanger, Director of Distance Education, Alvin Community College, 3110 Mustang Road, Alvin, TX 77511. *Telephone:* 281-756-3728. *Fax:* 281-756-3880. *E-mail:* psanger@alvincollege.edu.

DEGREES AND AWARDS

Programs offered do not lead to a degree or other formal award.

COURSE SUBJECT AREAS OFFERED OUTSIDE OF DEGREE PROGRAMS

Undergraduate—administrative and secretarial services; American literature (United States); applied mathematics; biology; biology, general; business; business administration and management; business communications; computer and information sciences, general; computer and information sciences, other; computer/information technology administration and management; computer programming; computer science; English composition; English creative writing; English language and literature, general; English language and literature/letters, other; geography; history; Internet and World Wide Web; liberal arts and sciences, general studies and humanities; mathematics;

mathematics and computer science; mathematics, other; miscellaneous health professions; psychology; psychology, other.
Non-credit—administrative and secretarial services; computer and information sciences, general; computer and information sciences, other.

AMBERTON UNIVERSITY

Garland, Texas

http://www.amberton.edu/

Amberton University was founded in 1971. It is accredited by Southern Association of Colleges and Schools. It first offered distance learning courses in 1992. In fall 2003, there were 675 students enrolled in distance learning courses. Institutionally administered financial aid is available to distance learners.

Services Distance learners have accessibility to academic advising, bookstore, library services.
Contact Dr. Jo Lynn Loyd, Vice President for Strategic Services, Amberton University, 1700 Eastgate Drive, Garland, TX 75041. *Telephone:* 972-279-6511 Ext. 126. *Fax:* 972-279-9773. *E-mail:* jloyd@amberton.edu.

DEGREES AND AWARDS

BA Professional Development
BBA Management
MA Professional Development
MBA Management
MS Human Relations and Business

AMERICAN ACADEMY OF NUTRITION, COLLEGE OF NUTRITION

Knoxville, Tennessee

http://www.nutritioneducation.com/

American Academy of Nutrition, College of Nutrition was founded in 1984. It is accredited by Distance Education and Training Council. It first offered distance learning courses in 1985. In fall 2003, there were 300 students enrolled in distance learning courses. Institutionally administered financial aid is available to distance learners.

Contact Cheryl Freeman, Student Services, American Academy of Nutrition, College of Nutrition, 1204 Kenesaw Avenue, Knoxville, TN 37919. *Telephone:* 865-524-8079. *Fax:* 865-524-8339. *E-mail:* aantn@aol.com.

DEGREES AND AWARDS

AS Nutrition

COURSE SUBJECT AREAS OFFERED OUTSIDE OF DEGREE PROGRAMS

Undergraduate—anatomy; biological and physical sciences; biology; business marketing and marketing management; chemistry; developmental/child psychology; English language and literature, general; environmental health; foods and nutrition studies; mathematics; organic chemistry; physiology; psychology.
Non-credit—foods and nutrition studies; health professions and related sciences, other.

THE AMERICAN COLLEGE

Bryn Mawr, Pennsylvania

http://www.amercoll.edu/

The American College was founded in 1927. It is accredited by Middle States Association of Colleges and Schools. In fall 2003, there were 20,000 students enrolled in distance learning courses. Institutionally administered financial aid is available to distance learners.

Services Distance learners have accessibility to academic advising, bookstore, library services.
Contact Office of Student Services, The American College, 270 South Bryn Mawr Avenue, Bryn Mawr, PA 19010. *Telephone:* 888-263-7265. *Fax:* 610-526-1465. *E-mail:* studentservices@amercoll.edu.

DEGREES AND AWARDS

Certificate CFP(r) Certification Curriculum; Pensions and Executive Compensation

Diploma Chartered Advisor for Senior Living (CASL) Designation; Chartered Financial Consultant (ChFC(r)) Designation; Chartered Leadership Fellow(r) (CLF(r)) Designation; Chartered Life Underwriter (CLU(r)) Designation; LUTC Fellow Designation; Registered Employee Benefits Consultant(r) (REBC(r)) Designation; Registered Health Underwriter(r) (RHU(r)) Designation

Advanced Graduate Diploma Chartered Advisor in Philanthropy(r)(CAP) Designation

Graduate Certificate Asset Management; Business Succession Planning; Charitable Planning; Estate Planning and Taxation; Graduate Financial Planning Track

MSFS Financial Services

COURSE SUBJECT AREAS OFFERED OUTSIDE OF DEGREE PROGRAMS

Undergraduate—business; business administration and management; finance; financial management and services; financial services marketing operations; gerontology; health products and services marketing operations; human resources management; insurance/risk management; investments and securities; social psychology.
Graduate—business; business administration and management; financial management and services; human resources management; insurance/risk management; investments and securities.

AMERICAN COLLEGE OF COMPUTER & INFORMATION SCIENCES

Birmingham, Alabama

http://www.accis.edu/

American College of Computer & Information Sciences was founded in 1988. It is accredited by Distance Education and Training Council. It first offered distance learning courses in 1988. In fall 2003, there were 4,000 students enrolled in distance learning courses. Institutionally administered financial aid is available to distance learners.

Services Distance learners have accessibility to academic advising, bookstore, campus computer network, e-mail services, library services.

American College of Computer & Information Sciences (continued)

Contact David Lenhart, Admissions Coordinator, American College of Computer & Information Sciences, 2101 Magnolia Avenue, Birmingham, AL 35205. *Telephone:* 205-323-6191. *Fax:* 205-328-2229. *E-mail:* admiss@accis.edu.

DEGREES AND AWARDS

BS Business Administration; Computer Science; Information Systems; Management Information Systems
MBA Business Administration
MCS Computer Science
MS Information Systems

COURSE SUBJECT AREAS OFFERED OUTSIDE OF DEGREE PROGRAMS

Undergraduate—accounting; applied mathematics; biology, general; business; business administration and management; business communications; business information and data processing services; business quantitative methods and management science; chemistry; communications, other; computer and information sciences, general; computer programming; computer science; computer systems analysis; computer systems networking and telecommunications; economics; educational psychology; English composition; English creative writing; history; human resources management; information sciences and systems; mathematics and computer science; psychology; science, technology and society.
Graduate—accounting; applied mathematics; business; business administration and management; business quantitative methods and management science; computer and information sciences, general; computer and information sciences, other; computer programming; computer science; computer software and media applications; information sciences and systems; mathematics and computer science.

See full description on page 344.

AMERICAN GRADUATE UNIVERSITY

Covina, California

http://www.agu.edu/

American Graduate University was founded in 1969. It is accredited by Distance Education and Training Council. It first offered distance learning courses in 1975. In fall 2003, there were 320 students enrolled in distance learning courses. Institutionally administered financial aid is available to distance learners.

Services Distance learners have accessibility to academic advising, bookstore, library services.
Contact Ms. Marie J. Sirney, Vice President, Administration and Accreditation, American Graduate University, 733 North Dodsworth Avenue, Covina, CA 91724. *Telephone:* 626-966-4576. *Fax:* 626-915-1709. *E-mail:* mariesirney@agu.edu.

DEGREES AND AWARDS

MA Acquisition Management–Master of Acquisition Management; Contract Management–Master of Contract Management; Project Management–Master of Project Management

COURSE SUBJECT AREAS OFFERED OUTSIDE OF DEGREE PROGRAMS

Graduate—accounting; business administration and management; business communications; business/managerial economics.

AMERICAN INTERCONTINENTAL UNIVERSITY ONLINE

Hoffman Estates, Illinois

http://www.aiuonline.edu

American InterContinental University Online was founded in 1970. It is accredited by Southern Association of Colleges and Schools. It first offered distance learning courses in 2001. In fall 2003, there were 12,000 students enrolled in distance learning courses. Institutionally administered financial aid is available to distance learners.

Services Distance learners have accessibility to academic advising, career placement assistance, e-mail services, library services.
Contact Steve Fireng, First Vice President of Admissions and Marketing, American InterContinental University Online, 5550 Prairie Stone Parkway, Suite 400, Hoffman Estates, IL 60192. *Telephone:* 877-701-3800. *Fax:* 866-647-9403. *E-mail:* info@aiuonline.edu.

DEGREES AND AWARDS

ABA Business Administration–Business Concentration (13-month program); Business Administration–Information Systems Concentration (13-month program)
BA Visual Communication–Digital Design (13-month program)
BBA Accounting and Finance Concentration (13-month program); Business Administration (13-month program); Healthcare Management Concentration (13-month program); Human Resources Concentration (13-month program); Management Concentration (13-month program); Marketing Concentration (13-month program)
BS Criminal Justice (13-month program); Information Technology–BIT (13-month program)
MBA Accounting and Finance Concentration (10-month program); Business Administration (10-month program); Healthcare Management Concentration (10-month program); Human Resources Concentration (10-month program); Marketing Concentration (10-month program)
MEd Education (10-month program)
MIT Information Technology (10-month program)

See full description on page 346.

AMERICAN PUBLIC UNIVERSITY SYSTEM

Charles Town, West Virginia

http://www.apus.edu/

American Public University System was founded in 1991. It is accredited by Distance Education and Training Council. It first offered distance learning courses in 1993. In fall 2003, there were 6,500 students enrolled in distance learning courses. Institutionally administered financial aid is available to distance learners.

Services Distance learners have accessibility to academic advising, bookstore, campus computer network, e-mail services, library services, tutoring.
Contact Ms. Beth LaGuardia, Director of Marketing, American Public University System, 111 West Congress Street, Charles Town, WV 25414. *Telephone:* 877-468-6268 Ext. 6421. *E-mail:* blaguardia@apus.edu.

DEGREES AND AWARDS

AA General Studies

BA African and African American Studies; American Studies; Asian Studies; Corrections Management; Criminal Justice; Emergency and Disaster Management; English; Fire Science Management; History; Homeland Security; Interdisciplinary Studies; International Peace and Conflict Resolution; International Relations; Management; Marketing; Military History, Military Management, Intelligence Studies; Philosophy; Political Science; Psychology; Religion; Security Management; Sociology; Women's Studies
BBA Business Administration
BS Aerospace Studies
MA Criminal Justice; International Peace and Conflict Resolution; Military History, Military Management, Intelligence Studies; Military Studies; National Security Studies; Political Science; Strategic Intelligence; Transportation Management
MAM Management
MBA Business Administration
MPA Public Administration
MS Space Studies

COURSE SUBJECT AREAS OFFERED OUTSIDE OF DEGREE PROGRAMS

Undergraduate—area studies; business administration and management; business information and data processing services; child care and guidance workers and managers; computer/information technology administration and management; criminal justice and corrections; criminology; English composition; English language and literature, general; health and medical administrative services; history; human resources management; international business; international relations and affairs; liberal arts and sciences, general studies and humanities; military studies; military technologies; philosophy; philosophy and religion; political science and government; psychology; public administration; public policy analysis.
Graduate—business; criminal justice and corrections; cultural studies; history; international relations and affairs; military studies; military technology; public administration and services, other.

See full description on page 348.

AMERICAN RIVER COLLEGE

Sacramento, California
Open Learning
http://www.arc.losrios.edu

American River College was founded in 1955. It is accredited by Western Association of Schools and Colleges. It first offered distance learning courses in 1975. In fall 2003, there were 1,000 students enrolled in distance learning courses. Institutionally administered financial aid is available to distance learners.

Services Distance learners have accessibility to academic advising, e-mail services, library services, tutoring.
Contact Ms. Marsha Conley, Instructional Technology Coordinator, American River College, 4700 College Oak Drive, Sacramento, CA 95841. *Telephone:* 916-484-8996. *E-mail:* conleym@arc.losrios.edu.

DEGREES AND AWARDS

Programs offered do not lead to a degree or other formal award.

COURSE SUBJECT AREAS OFFERED OUTSIDE OF DEGREE PROGRAMS

Undergraduate—biology; business; business administration and management; business communications; business/managerial economics; business marketing and marketing management; computer and information sciences, general; computer programming; computer software and media applications; computer systems networking and telecommunications; counseling psychology; design and applied arts; English composition; English language and literature, general; English technical and business writing; entrepreneurship; geography; gerontology; history; physical sciences, general; social sciences and history, other; sociology; telecommunications.

ANDERSON UNIVERSITY

Anderson, Indiana
http://www.anderson.edu/

Anderson University was founded in 1917. It is accredited by North Central Association of Colleges and Schools. It first offered distance learning courses in 1999.

Contact Anderson University.

DEGREES AND AWARDS

Programs offered do not lead to a degree or other formal award.

ANDREW JACKSON UNIVERSITY

Birmingham, Alabama
http://www.aju.edu/

Andrew Jackson University was founded in 1994. It is accredited by Distance Education and Training Council. It first offered distance learning courses in 1994. In fall 2003, there were 500 students enrolled in distance learning courses. Institutionally administered financial aid is available to distance learners.

Services Distance learners have accessibility to academic advising.
Contact Ms. Bell N. Woods, Director of Admissions, Andrew Jackson University, 10 Old Montgomery Highway, Suite 225, Birmingham, AL 35209. *Telephone:* 205-871-9288. *Fax:* 205-871-9294. *E-mail:* admissions@aju.edu.

DEGREES AND AWARDS

AA Communication; General Studies
AS Business; Communication; Criminal Justice
BA Communications
BS Business; Criminal Justice
MBA Business/Management
MPA Public Administration
MS Criminal Justice

COURSE SUBJECT AREAS OFFERED OUTSIDE OF DEGREE PROGRAMS

Undergraduate—business; communications, general; criminal justice and corrections.
Graduate—business administration and management; criminal justice and corrections; public administration.

ANDREWS UNIVERSITY

Berrien Springs, Michigan
http://www.andrews.edu/dlit

Andrews University was founded in 1874. It is accredited by North Central Association of Colleges and Schools. It first offered distance

Andrews University (continued)

learning courses in 1997. In fall 2003, there were 60 students enrolled in distance learning courses. Institutionally administered financial aid is available to distance learners.

Services Distance learners have accessibility to academic advising, campus computer network, e-mail services, library services, tutoring.
Contact Mrs. Marsha Jean Beal, Director of The Center for Distance Learning and Instructional Technology, Andrews University, Room #304, James White Library, Berrien Springs, MI 49104-0074. *Telephone:* 269-471-6200. *Fax:* 269-471-6166. *E-mail:* bealmj@andrews.edu.

DEGREES AND AWARDS

AA Liberal Arts, General Studies, Humanities
BA Liberal Arts, General Studies, Humanities; Theological Studies
BS Liberal Arts, General Studies, Humanities

COURSE SUBJECT AREAS OFFERED OUTSIDE OF DEGREE PROGRAMS

Undergraduate—American studies; astronomy; bible/biblical studies; developmental/child psychology; English composition; French; geography; history; mathematics related; religion/religious studies; social psychology; sociology.

ANNE ARUNDEL COMMUNITY COLLEGE

Arnold, Maryland
Distance Learning Center
http://www.aacc.edu/diseduc

Anne Arundel Community College was founded in 1961. It is accredited by Middle States Association of Colleges and Schools. It first offered distance learning courses in 1981. In fall 2003, there were 3,540 students enrolled in distance learning courses. Institutionally administered financial aid is available to distance learners.

Services Distance learners have accessibility to academic advising, bookstore, campus computer network, career placement assistance, e-mail services, library services, tutoring.
Contact Mrs. Patty McCarthy-O'Neill, Distance Learning Center Program Coordinator, Anne Arundel Community College, Distance Learning Center, 101 College Parkway, Arnold, MD 21012-1895. *Telephone:* 410-777-2514. *Fax:* 410-777-2691. *E-mail:* pmmccarthyoneill@aacc.edu.

DEGREES AND AWARDS

AA General Studies
AAS Business Management
AS Business Administration

COURSE SUBJECT AREAS OFFERED OUTSIDE OF DEGREE PROGRAMS

Undergraduate—accounting; American history; applied mathematics; biological and physical sciences; business administration and management; business management and administrative services, other; business/managerial economics; business marketing and marketing management; chemistry; communications, general; computer and information sciences, general; computer science; developmental/child psychology; economics; English composition; finance; geography; health and physical education/fitness; history; law and legal studies related; mathematical statistics; mathematics related; oceanography; paralegal/legal assistant; philosophy; social psychology; social sciences and history, other; sociology.

AQUINAS INSTITUTE OF THEOLOGY

St. Louis, Missouri
http://www.ai.edu/

Aquinas Institute of Theology was founded in 1925. It is accredited by North Central Association of Colleges and Schools. It first offered distance learning courses in 1995. In fall 2003, there were 31 students enrolled in distance learning courses. Institutionally administered financial aid is available to distance learners.

Services Distance learners have accessibility to campus computer network, e-mail services, library services.
Contact Mrs. Sharon McKinnis, Assistant to the Program Directors, Aquinas Institute of Theology, 3642 Lindell Boulevard, St. Louis, MO 63108. *Telephone:* 314-977-7022. *Fax:* 314-977-7225. *E-mail:* mckinnis@slu.edu.

DEGREES AND AWARDS

Programs offered do not lead to a degree or other formal award.

COURSE SUBJECT AREAS OFFERED OUTSIDE OF DEGREE PROGRAMS

Graduate—theological and ministerial studies.

ARAPAHOE COMMUNITY COLLEGE

Littleton, Colorado
Educational Technology
http://www.arapahoe.edu

Arapahoe Community College was founded in 1965. It is accredited by North Central Association of Colleges and Schools. It first offered distance learning courses in 1985. In fall 2003, there were 2,562 students enrolled in distance learning courses. Institutionally administered financial aid is available to distance learners.

Services Distance learners have accessibility to academic advising, bookstore, campus computer network, e-mail services, library services.
Contact Kim Ostrowski, Director of Student Outreach, Arapahoe Community College, 5900 South Santa Fe Drive, Littleton, CO 80120. *Telephone:* 303-797-5601. *Fax:* 303-797-5935. *E-mail:* kostrowski@arapahoe.edu.

DEGREES AND AWARDS

AA General Studies–Transfer
AAS Convergent Technologies; Medical Office Technology; Mortuary Science

COURSE SUBJECT AREAS OFFERED OUTSIDE OF DEGREE PROGRAMS

Undergraduate—accounting; architecture and related programs, other; business administration and management; business information and data processing services; business management and administrative services, other; communications technologies; computer and information sciences, general; computer software and media applications; computer systems networking and telecommunications; criminal justice and corrections; economics; electrical and electronic engineering-related technology; engineering-related technologies, other; health and medical administrative services; medical laboratory technology; nursing; pharmacy; political science and government; sociology; tourism/travel marketing.

ARKANSAS STATE UNIVERSITY-BEEBE

Beebe, Arkansas

http://www.asub.edu

Arkansas State University–Beebe was founded in 1927. It is accredited by North Central Association of Colleges and Schools. It first offered distance learning courses in 1999. In fall 2003, there were 575 students enrolled in distance learning courses. Institutionally administered financial aid is available to distance learners.

Services Distance learners have accessibility to academic advising, bookstore, career placement assistance, e-mail services, library services, tutoring.

Contact Chris Boyett, Director of Distance Learning, Arkansas State University–Beebe, PO Box 1000, Beebe, AR 72012. *Telephone:* 501-882-4442. *Fax:* 501-882-4403. *E-mail:* jcboyett@asub.edu.

DEGREES AND AWARDS

Programs offered do not lead to a degree or other formal award.

COURSE SUBJECT AREAS OFFERED OUTSIDE OF DEGREE PROGRAMS

Undergraduate—accounting; biological and physical sciences; biology, general; business; business communications; chemistry; communications, general; computer and information sciences, general; computer programming; developmental and child psychology; English composition; English creative writing; history; mathematics; microbiology/bacteriology; political science and government; psychology.

ARKANSAS STATE UNIVERSITY-MOUNTAIN HOME

Mountain Home, Arkansas

http://www.asumh.edu

Arkansas State University–Mountain Home is accredited by North Central Association of Colleges and Schools. It first offered distance learning courses in 2000. In fall 2003, there were 115 students enrolled in distance learning courses. Institutionally administered financial aid is available to distance learners.

Services Distance learners have accessibility to academic advising, bookstore, campus computer network, e-mail services, library services.

Contact Ms. Sherry D. Ewart, Registrar, Arkansas State University–Mountain Home, 1600 South College Street, Mountain Home, AR 72653. *Telephone:* 870-508-6104. *Fax:* 870-508-6287. *E-mail:* sewart@asumh.edu.

DEGREES AND AWARDS

AAS Hearing Healthcare; Opticianry

COURSE SUBJECT AREAS OFFERED OUTSIDE OF DEGREE PROGRAMS

Undergraduate—computer science; mathematics.

ARKANSAS TECH UNIVERSITY

Russellville, Arkansas

Virtual Learning Center

http://ccc.atu.edu

Arkansas Tech University was founded in 1909. It is accredited by North Central Association of Colleges and Schools. It first offered distance learning courses in 1996. In fall 2003, there were 660 students enrolled in distance learning courses. Institutionally administered financial aid is available to distance learners.

Services Distance learners have accessibility to academic advising, bookstore, campus computer network, career placement assistance, e-mail services, library services.

Contact Student Information, Arkansas Tech University, Russellville, AR 72801. *Telephone:* 479-968-0343. *E-mail:* ccc@mail.atu.edu.

DEGREES AND AWARDS

Programs offered do not lead to a degree or other formal award.

COURSE SUBJECT AREAS OFFERED OUTSIDE OF DEGREE PROGRAMS

Undergraduate—agricultural business and management; biological sciences/life sciences, other; biology, general; business administration and management; chemistry; computer and information sciences, general; education, other; electrical and electronic engineering-related technology; English language and literature, general; history; hospitality services management; journalism and mass communications; mathematics; music; natural resources management and protective services; nursing; parks, recreation and leisure facilities management; parks, recreation and leisure studies; physical sciences, general; political science and government; psychology; sociology.

Graduate—educational/instructional media design; education, general; education, other; English language and literature, general; information sciences and systems; journalism and mass communications; liberal arts and sciences, general studies and humanities; mathematics; physical sciences, general.

ARLINGTON BAPTIST COLLEGE

Arlington, Texas

Distance Education Department

http://www.abconline.edu/

Arlington Baptist College was founded in 1939. It is accredited by Accrediting Association of Bible Colleges. It first offered distance learning courses in 1994. In fall 2003, there were 20 students enrolled in distance learning courses. Institutionally administered financial aid is available to distance learners.

Services Distance learners have accessibility to academic advising, bookstore.

Contact Janie Hall, Registrar, Arlington Baptist College, 3001 West Division, Arlington, TX 76012. *Telephone:* 817-461-8741 Ext. 105. *Fax:* 817-274-1138.

Arlington Baptist College (continued)

DEGREES AND AWARDS

Programs offered do not lead to a degree or other formal award.

COURSE SUBJECT AREAS OFFERED OUTSIDE OF DEGREE PROGRAMS

Undergraduate—bible/biblical studies; theological and ministerial studies.

Non-credit—bible/biblical studies; theological and ministerial studies.

THE ART INSTITUTE ONLINE

Pittsburgh, Pennsylvania

http://www.aionline.edu

The Art Institute Online is accredited by Accrediting Council for Independent Colleges and Schools. It first offered distance learning courses in 2000. In fall 2003, there were 1,500 students enrolled in distance learning courses. Institutionally administered financial aid is available to distance learners.

Services Distance learners have accessibility to academic advising, bookstore, career placement assistance, e-mail services, library services.

Contact Mr. Ken Boutelle, Director of Admissions, The Art Institute Online, 420 Boulevard of the Allies, Pittsburgh, PA 15219. *Telephone:* 877-872-8869. *Fax:* 412-291-7238. *E-mail:* aioadm@aii.edu.

DEGREES AND AWARDS

AS Graphic Design; Interactive Media Design

BS Advertising; Culinary Management Degree Completion Program; Game Art and Design; Graphic Design; Interactive Media Design; Interior Design

Diploma Digital Design; Residential Planning; Web Design

COURSE SUBJECT AREAS OFFERED OUTSIDE OF DEGREE PROGRAMS

Undergraduate—advertising; culinary arts and related services; design and applied arts; Internet and World Wide Web; liberal arts and sciences, general studies and humanities.

See full description on page 350.

ASHEVILLE-BUNCOMBE TECHNICAL COMMUNITY COLLEGE

Asheville, North Carolina

http://www.abtech.edu

Asheville-Buncombe Technical Community College was founded in 1959. It is accredited by Southern Association of Colleges and Schools. It first offered distance learning courses in 1999. In fall 2003, there were 680 students enrolled in distance learning courses. Institutionally administered financial aid is available to distance learners.

Services Distance learners have accessibility to academic advising, bookstore, campus computer network, e-mail services, library services.

Contact L. B. Holmes, Director of Distance Learning, Asheville-Buncombe Technical Community College, 340 Victoria Road, Asheville, NC 28801. *Telephone:* 828-254-1921 Ext. 835. *Fax:* 828-281-9831. *E-mail:* rholmes@abtech.edu.

DEGREES AND AWARDS

Programs offered do not lead to a degree or other formal award.

COURSE SUBJECT AREAS OFFERED OUTSIDE OF DEGREE PROGRAMS

Undergraduate—accounting; applied mathematics; biology, general; business administration and management; child care and guidance workers and managers; computer and information sciences, general; computer programming; data entry/microcomputer applications; economics; foreign languages and literatures; health and physical education/fitness; history; mathematical statistics; mathematics; philosophy and religion; psychology; sociology; speech and rhetorical studies.

Non-credit—business administration and management; business communications; computer programming; computer systems networking and telecommunications; construction management; data entry/microcomputer applications; entrepreneurship; family/consumer resource management; film/video and photographic arts; foreign languages and literatures; home/office products marketing; human resources management; individual and family development studies; legal studies; marketing management and research; quality control and safety technologies.

ASHLAND COMMUNITY AND TECHNICAL COLLEGE

Ashland, Kentucky

http://www.ashland.kctcs.edu/

Ashland Community and Technical College was founded in 1937. It is accredited by Council on Occupational Education. It first offered distance learning courses in 1980. In fall 2003, there were 100 students enrolled in distance learning courses. Institutionally administered financial aid is available to distance learners.

Services Distance learners have accessibility to academic advising, campus computer network, e-mail services, library services.

Contact Dr. Carol M. Greene, Coordinator, Distance Learning, Ashland Community and Technical College, 1400 College Drive, Ashland, KY 41101. *Telephone:* 606-326-2142. *Fax:* 606-324-2186. *E-mail:* carol.greene@kctcs.edu.

DEGREES AND AWARDS

AA General Education

COURSE SUBJECT AREAS OFFERED OUTSIDE OF DEGREE PROGRAMS

Undergraduate—American literature (United States); criminal justice and corrections; economics; education, other; English composition; English creative writing; English language and literature/letters, other; sociology.

ASHWORTH COLLEGE

Norcross, Georgia

http://www.ashworthcollege.edu

Ashworth College is accredited by Distance Education and Training Council. It first offered distance learning courses in 2000. In fall 2003, there were 30,000 students enrolled in distance learning courses. Institutionally administered financial aid is available to distance learners.

Services Distance learners have accessibility to academic advising, e-mail services, library services, tutoring.

Contact John Graves, Dean, Ashworth College, 430 Technology Parkway, Norcross, GA 30092. *Fax:* 770-729-9389. *E-mail:* jgraves@pcdi.com.

DEGREES AND AWARDS

AD Accounting; Computer Information Management; Criminal Justice; Early Childhood Education; Health Information Management; Human Resource Management; Management; Paralegal; Psychology

MBA Business Administration

MCJ Criminal Justice

COURSE SUBJECT AREAS OFFERED OUTSIDE OF DEGREE PROGRAMS

Non-credit—accounting; animal sciences; business administration and management; carpenters; child care and guidance workers and managers; computer and information sciences, general; computer programming; culinary arts and related services; English as a second language; entrepreneurship; financial management and services; floristry marketing operations; health and medical assistants; heating, air conditioning and refrigeration mechanics and repairers; hospitality services management; landscape architecture; natural resources conservation; protective services, other; taxation; teacher assistant/aide; tourism/travel marketing.

ASPEN UNIVERSITY

Denver, Colorado

http://www.aspen.edu/

Aspen University was founded in 1987. It is accredited by Distance Education and Training Council. It first offered distance learning courses in 1992. In fall 2003, there were 200 students enrolled in distance learning courses. Institutionally administered financial aid is available to distance learners.

Services Distance learners have accessibility to academic advising, bookstore, e-mail services.

Contact Ms. Kristine Kari Larson, Registrar, Aspen University, 501 South Cherry Street, #350, Denver, CO 80246. *Telephone:* 303-333-4224 Ext. 172. *Fax:* 303-336-1144. *E-mail:* klarson@aspen.edu.

DEGREES AND AWARDS

BBA Business Administration–Bachelor of Science in Business Administration

EMBA Business Administration

MBA Business Administration

MEd Education

MIT Science in Information Technology

MS Information Management

MSIS Information Systems

COURSE SUBJECT AREAS OFFERED OUTSIDE OF DEGREE PROGRAMS

Graduate—accounting; business administration and management; business/managerial economics; information sciences and systems; telecommunications.

Non-credit—professional studies.

ASSEMBLIES OF GOD THEOLOGICAL SEMINARY

Springfield, Missouri

Office of Continuing Education

http://www.agts.edu

Assemblies of God Theological Seminary was founded in 1972. It is accredited by North Central Association of Colleges and Schools. It first offered distance learning courses in 1980. In fall 2003, there were 23 students enrolled in distance learning courses. Institutionally administered financial aid is available to distance learners.

Services Distance learners have accessibility to academic advising, bookstore, campus computer network, e-mail services, library services, tutoring.

Contact Randy C. Walls, Director, Assemblies of God Theological Seminary, 1435 North Glenstone Avenue, Springfield, MO 65802. *Telephone:* 800-467-2487 Ext. 1046. *Fax:* 417-268-1009. *E-mail:* rwalls@agts.edu.

DEGREES AND AWARDS

Programs offered do not lead to a degree or other formal award.

COURSE SUBJECT AREAS OFFERED OUTSIDE OF DEGREE PROGRAMS

Graduate—bible/biblical studies; biblical and other theological languages and literatures; history; missions/missionary studies and missiology; pastoral counseling and specialized ministries; philosophy and religion; religion/religious studies; theological and ministerial studies; theological studies and religious vocations, other.

ATHABASCA UNIVERSITY

Athabasca, Alberta, Canada

http://www.athabascau.ca

Athabasca University was founded in 1970. It is provincially chartered. It first offered distance learning courses in 1972. In fall 2003, there were 26,691 students enrolled in distance learning courses. Institutionally administered financial aid is available to distance learners.

Services Distance learners have accessibility to academic advising, bookstore, campus computer network, e-mail services, library services, tutoring.

Contact Information Centre, Athabasca University, 1 University Drive, Athabasca, AB T9S 3A3, Canada. *Telephone:* 800-788-9041. *Fax:* 780-675-6437. *E-mail:* inquire@athabascau.ca.

DEGREES AND AWARDS

BA Anthropology (4 year); Anthropology Concentration (3 year); Canadian Studies (4 year); English (4 year); English Concentration (3 year); French (4 year); French Concentration (3 year); General 3 year Program; History (4 year); History Concentration (3 year); Human Resources and Labour Relations; Humanities (4 year); Humanities Concentration (3 year); Information Systems (4 year); Information Systems Concentration (3 year); Labour Studies (4 year); Labour Studies Concentration (3 year); Management (3 year); Management (4 year); Management Post-Diploma (3 year); Management Post-Diploma (4 year); Nursing–Post-LPN; Political Economy (4 year); Political Economy Concentration (3 year); Psychology (4 year);

Athabasca University (continued)

Psychology Concentration (3 year); Sociology (4 year); Sociology Concentration (3 year); Women's Studies (4 year); Women's Studies Concentration (3 year)

BBA Administration–Bachelor of Administration (with Concentration); Administration–Bachelor of Administration Post-Diploma (with Concentration)

BComm Commerce (4 year); E-Commerce

BGS General Studies with Designation (Arts/Science or Applied Studies)

BN Nursing–Post-RN

BPA Communication Studies; Criminal Justice; Governance, Law, and Management; Human Services

BS Computing and Information Systems (4 year); Computing and Information Systems–Post-Diploma; General 4 year Program; General Post-Diploma; Human Science–Post-Diploma; Human Science

Certificate Accounting; Administration; Advanced Accounting; Career Development; Computers and Management Information Systems; Computing and Information Systems; Counseling Women; English Language Studies; French Language Proficiency; Health Development Administration; Labour Studies; Nursing–Home Health Nursing; Public Administration

Diploma Arts; Inclusive Education

Advanced Graduate Diploma Distance Education Technology; Management; Nursing–Advanced Nursing Practice

MA Integrated Studies

MBA Business Administration; Information Technology Management; Project Management

MCDCC Counselling (Collaborative)

MCH Health Studies–Master of Health Studies

MDE Distance Education

MSIS Information Systems

COURSE SUBJECT AREAS OFFERED OUTSIDE OF DEGREE PROGRAMS

Undergraduate—accounting; advertising; anthropology; astronomy; biological and physical sciences; biological sciences/life sciences, other; biology, general; business; business administration and management; business communications; business information and data processing services; business management and administrative services, other; business/managerial economics; chemistry; child care and guidance workers and managers; communication disorders sciences and services; communications, general; communications, other; communications technologies; community health services; community organization, resources and services; community psychology; comparative literature; computer and information sciences, general; computer and information sciences, other; computer/information technology administration and management; computer programming; computer science; computer software and media applications; computer systems analysis; computer systems networking and telecommunications; counseling psychology; criminal justice and corrections; criminology; data processing technology; demography/population studies; developmental and child psychology; economics; educational evaluation, research and statistics; English as a second language; English composition; English creative writing; English language and literature, general; environmental control technologies; family and community studies; financial management and services; fine arts and art studies; foods and nutrition studies; foreign languages and literatures; geography; geological and related sciences; health and medical administrative services; health and medical preparatory programs; health professions and related sciences, other; history; human resources management; human services; individual and family development studies; industrial and organizational psychology; international relations and affairs; journalism and mass communications; legal studies; marketing management and research; marketing operations/marketing and distribution, other; mathematical statistics; mathematics; mathematics and computer science; mental health services; music; natural resources conservation; natural resources management and protective services; nursing; philosophy; philosophy and religion; physical sciences, general; physiological psychology/psychobiology; plant sciences; political science and government; professional studies; psychology; psychology, other; public administration; public health; public policy analysis; public relations and organizational communications; social sciences, general; sociology.

Graduate—accounting; agricultural business and management; business administration and management; business and personal services marketing operations; business communications; business information and data processing services; business management and administrative services, other; business/managerial economics; business quantitative methods and management science; child care and guidance workers and managers; community health services; community organization, resources and services; community psychology; computer and information sciences, general; computer and information sciences, other; computer/information technology administration and management; computer science; computer systems analysis; counseling psychology; curriculum and instruction; developmental and child psychology; economics; education administration and supervision; educational evaluation, research and statistics; educational psychology; education, other; family and community studies; financial services marketing operations; health and medical preparatory programs; health professions and related sciences, other; history; human resources management; human services; industrial and organizational psychology; information sciences and systems; international business; international relations and affairs; marketing management and research; marketing operations/marketing and distribution, other; mathematics and computer science; mental health services; nursing; philosophy; political science and government; psychology; public administration; public administration and services, other; public health; public policy analysis; public relations and organizational communications; social sciences and history, other; social sciences, general; social work; sociology; special education; taxation.

Non-credit—accounting; administrative and secretarial services; anthropology; astronomy; biology, general; business; business administration and management; business and personal services marketing operations; business communications; business information and data processing services; business management and administrative services, other; business/managerial economics; business quantitative methods and management science; chemistry; child care and guidance workers and managers; city/urban, community and regional planning; clinical psychology; communication disorders sciences and services; communications, general; communications technologies; community health services; community organization, resources and services; community psychology; computer and information sciences, general; computer/information technology administration and management; computer programming; computer science; computer software and media applications; computer systems analysis; construction management; counseling psychology; criminal justice and corrections; criminology; cultural studies; data entry/microcomputer applications; data processing technology; developmental and child psychology; economics; education administration and supervision; educational evaluation, research and statistics; educational/instructional media design; educational psychology; education, other; English as a second language; English composition; English language and literature, general; environmental control technologies; family and community studies; financial management and services; financial services marketing operations; fine arts and art studies; foods and nutrition studies; foreign languages and literatures; geological and related sciences; gerontology; health professions and related sciences, other; history; human resources management; human services; individual and family development studies; industrial and organizational psychology; international business; international relations and affairs; journalism and mass communications; legal studies; liberal arts and sciences, general studies and humanities; marketing management and research; marketing operations/ marketing and distribution, other; mathematical statistics; mathematics; mathematics and computer science; medical basic sciences; mental health services; miscellaneous health professions; music; nursing; philosophy; philosophy and religion; physical sciences, general; political science and government; professional studies; psychology; public administration; public administration and services, other; public health; public policy analysis; public relations and organizational communications; radio and television broadcasting; school psychology; science technologies, other; science, technology and society; social and philosophical foundations of education; social psychology; social sciences and history, other; social sciences, general; social work; sociology; taxation; teaching English as a second language/foreign language.

See full description on page 352.

ATHENS TECHNICAL COLLEGE

Athens, Georgia

http://www.athenstech.edu

Athens Technical College was founded in 1958. It is accredited by Southern Association of Colleges and Schools. It first offered distance learning courses in 1995. In fall 2003, there were 700 students enrolled in distance learning courses. Institutionally administered financial aid is available to distance learners.

Services Distance learners have accessibility to academic advising, bookstore, campus computer network, career placement assistance, e-mail services, library services, tutoring.

Contact Mr. Jason Ritchie, Webmaster, Athens Technical College, 800 US Highway 29 North, Athens, GA 30601-1500. *Telephone:* 706-355-5134. *E-mail:* jritchie@athenstech.edu.

DEGREES AND AWARDS

Programs offered do not lead to a degree or other formal award.

COURSE SUBJECT AREAS OFFERED OUTSIDE OF DEGREE PROGRAMS

Undergraduate—accounting; business; computer and information sciences, general; economics; electrical and electronics equipment installers and repairers; English composition; English technical and business writing; legal studies; mathematics; psychology.

ATLANTIC SCHOOL OF THEOLOGY

Halifax, Nova Scotia, Canada

http://www.astheology.ns.ca/

Atlantic School of Theology was founded in 1971. It is provincially chartered. It first offered distance learning courses in 1999. In fall 2003, there were 45 students enrolled in distance learning courses. Institutionally administered financial aid is available to distance learners.

Services Distance learners have accessibility to academic advising, bookstore, e-mail services, library services.

Contact Dr. Thomas McIllwraith, Director of Distributed Education, Atlantic School of Theology, 660 Francklyn Street, Halifax, NS B3H 3B5, Canada. *Telephone:* 902-496-7945. *Fax:* 902-492-4048. *E-mail:* tmcillwraith@astheology.ns.ca.

DEGREES AND AWARDS

Programs offered do not lead to a degree or other formal award.

COURSE SUBJECT AREAS OFFERED OUTSIDE OF DEGREE PROGRAMS

Graduate—bible/biblical studies; religion/religious studies; religious education; religious/sacred music; theological and ministerial studies; theological studies and religious vocations, other.

Non-credit—bible/biblical studies; religion/religious studies; religious education; theological and ministerial studies; theological studies and religious vocations, other.

ATLANTIC UNIVERSITY

Virginia Beach, Virginia

http://www.atlanticuniv.edu/

Atlantic University was founded in 1930. It is accredited by Distance Education and Training Council. It first offered distance learning courses in 1985. In fall 2003, there were 121 students enrolled in distance learning courses. Institutionally administered financial aid is available to distance learners.

Services Distance learners have accessibility to e-mail services, library services.

Contact Mr. Gregory Deming, Director of Admissions, Atlantic University, 215 67th Street, Virginia Beach, VA 23451. *Telephone:* 757-631-8101 Ext. 210. *Fax:* 757-631-8096. *E-mail:* admissions@atlanticuniv.edu.

DEGREES AND AWARDS

MA Transpersonal Studies

COURSE SUBJECT AREAS OFFERED OUTSIDE OF DEGREE PROGRAMS

Graduate—art history; bible/biblical studies; creative writing; education, other; fine arts and art studies; philosophy and religion related; psychology, other; religion/religious studies; women's studies.

Non-credit—art history; bible/biblical studies; creative writing; education, other; fine arts and art studies; philosophy and religion related; psychology, other; religion/religious studies; women's studies.

AUBURN UNIVERSITY

Auburn University, Alabama

Distance Learning/Outreach Technology

http://www.auburn.edu/auonline

Auburn University was founded in 1856. It is accredited by Southern Association of Colleges and Schools. It first offered distance learning courses in 1975. In fall 2003, there were 1,000 students enrolled in distance learning courses. Institutionally administered financial aid is available to distance learners.

Services Distance learners have accessibility to academic advising, bookstore, campus computer network, career placement assistance, e-mail services, library services.

Auburn University (continued)

Contact Ms. E. La'Shaun Seay, Outreach Assistant II, Auburn University, 305. O. D. Smith Hall, Auburn University, AL 36849-5611. *Telephone:* 334-844-3110. *Fax:* 334-844-3118. *E-mail:* seayear@auburn.edu.

DEGREES AND AWARDS

Certificate Community Employment Services; Dietary Management; Early Childhood Intervention
EMBA Business Administration; Physicians Executive MBA
MA Rehabilitation Counseling
MAE Aerospace Engineering; Foreign Language
MBA Business Administration
MBA/M Acc Accountancy
MBA/MSMIS Management Information Systems
MCE Chemical Engineering; Civil Engineering
MCSE Computer Science and Engineering
MEd Collaborative Teacher and Early Childhood Education; Music
MISE Industrial and Systems Engineering
MME Materials Engineering; Mechanical Engineering
MS Hotel and Restaurant Management
PharmD Pharmacy

COURSE SUBJECT AREAS OFFERED OUTSIDE OF DEGREE PROGRAMS

Undergraduate—agriculture/agricultural sciences; communications, general; film/video and photographic arts; geography.
Non-credit—architectural environmental design; architectural urban design and planning; architecture; education, general; engineering, general; foods and nutrition studies; pharmacy; veterinary medicine (DVM).

See full description on page 354.

AUBURN UNIVERSITY MONTGOMERY

Montgomery, Alabama

http://www.aum.edu/

Auburn University Montgomery was founded in 1967. It is accredited by Southern Association of Colleges and Schools. It first offered distance learning courses in 1999. In fall 2003, there were 200 students enrolled in distance learning courses. Institutionally administered financial aid is available to distance learners.

Services Distance learners have accessibility to academic advising, bookstore, campus computer network, e-mail services, library services.
Contact Dean Alan S. Hackel, School of Continuing Education, Auburn University Montgomery, PO Box 244023, Montgomery, AL 36124-4023. *Telephone:* 334-244-3338. *Fax:* 334-244-3865. *E-mail:* ahackel@mail.aum.edu.

DEGREES AND AWARDS

Programs offered do not lead to a degree or other formal award.

COURSE SUBJECT AREAS OFFERED OUTSIDE OF DEGREE PROGRAMS

Undergraduate—criminal justice and corrections; education administration and supervision; education, other.
Graduate—criminal justice and corrections; education administration and supervision; educational evaluation, research and statistics.
Non-credit—administrative and secretarial services; business administration and management; computer software and media applications; health and medical administrative services.

AUGUSTA TECHNICAL COLLEGE

Augusta, Georgia

http://www.augusta.tec.ga.us/

Augusta Technical College was founded in 1961. It is accredited by Southern Association of Colleges and Schools. It first offered distance learning courses in 1996. In fall 2003, there were 400 students enrolled in distance learning courses. Institutionally administered financial aid is available to distance learners.

Services Distance learners have accessibility to academic advising, campus computer network, career placement assistance, e-mail services, library services.
Contact Ms. Stormy G. Grygo, Continuing Education Specialist, Augusta Technical College, 3200 Augusta Tech Drive, Augusta, GA 30906. *Telephone:* 706-771-4025. *Fax:* 706-771-4016. *E-mail:* sgrygo@augustatech.edu.

DEGREES AND AWARDS

Programs offered do not lead to a degree or other formal award.

COURSE SUBJECT AREAS OFFERED OUTSIDE OF DEGREE PROGRAMS

Non-credit—administrative and secretarial services; business administration and management; child care and guidance workers and managers; computer software and media applications; electrical and electronic engineering-related technology; heating, air conditioning and refrigeration mechanics and repairers; plumbers and pipefitters.

AUSTIN PEAY STATE UNIVERSITY

Clarksville, Tennessee

http://www.apsu.edu/

Austin Peay State University was founded in 1927. It is accredited by Southern Association of Colleges and Schools. It first offered distance learning courses in 1996. In fall 2003, there were 3,500 students enrolled in distance learning courses. Institutionally administered financial aid is available to distance learners.

Services Distance learners have accessibility to academic advising, bookstore, campus computer network, e-mail services, library services, tutoring.
Contact Dr. Stanley Groppel, Dean of Extended and Distance Education, Austin Peay State University, PO Box 4678, Clarksville, TN 37044. *Telephone:* 931-221-7816. *Fax:* 931-221-7748. *E-mail:* groppels@apsu.edu.

DEGREES AND AWARDS

AAS Police Science and Administration
BPS Organizational Leadership; Regents Online Degree Program; Technology Studies
MA Corporate Communication

COURSE SUBJECT AREAS OFFERED OUTSIDE OF DEGREE PROGRAMS

Undergraduate—astronomy; health and physical education/fitness; mathematics and computer science; psychology; public administration; sociology; speech and rhetorical studies.

Graduate—communications, other; health and physical education/fitness.

AZUSA PACIFIC UNIVERSITY

Azusa, California

http://online.apu.edu/

Azusa Pacific University was founded in 1899. It is accredited by Western Association of Schools and Colleges. It first offered distance learning courses in 1999. In fall 2003, there were 850 students enrolled in distance learning courses. Institutionally administered financial aid is available to distance learners.

Services Distance learners have accessibility to bookstore, e-mail services, library services.
Contact Dr. Bruce Simmerok, Director of Distance Learning and Continuing Education, Azusa Pacific University, 901 East Alosta Avenue, Azusa, CA 91702-7000. *Telephone:* 626-815-5038. *E-mail:* bsimmerok@apu.edu.

DEGREES AND AWARDS

Certificate Library Media Teaching
MA Educational Technology
MAE School Librarianship

COURSE SUBJECT AREAS OFFERED OUTSIDE OF DEGREE PROGRAMS

Undergraduate—computer science; history; religion/religious studies.
Graduate—computer science; education administration and supervision; educational evaluation, research and statistics; educational/instructional media design; nursing; teacher education, specific academic and vocational programs; theological and ministerial studies.

BAINBRIDGE COLLEGE

Bainbridge, Georgia

http://www.bainbridge.edu

Bainbridge College was founded in 1972. It is accredited by Southern Association of Colleges and Schools. It first offered distance learning courses in 2000. Institutionally administered financial aid is available to distance learners.

Services Distance learners have accessibility to academic advising, bookstore, career placement assistance, e-mail services, library services, tutoring.
Contact Ms. Connie B. Snyder, Director of Admissions and Records, Bainbridge College, 2500 East Shotwell Street, PO Box 990, Bainbridge, GA 39818-0990. *Telephone:* 229-248-2504. *Fax:* 229-248-2623. *E-mail:* csnyder@bainbridge.edu.

DEGREES AND AWARDS

Programs offered do not lead to a degree or other formal award.

COURSE SUBJECT AREAS OFFERED OUTSIDE OF DEGREE PROGRAMS

Undergraduate—accounting; administrative and secretarial services; applied mathematics; business; computer and information sciences, general; liberal arts and sciences, general studies and humanities; mathematical statistics.
Non-credit—business administration and management; communications, general; computer software and media applications; computer systems networking and telecommunications; foreign languages and literatures; health and medical assistants; legal studies; real estate.

BAKER COLLEGE OF FLINT

Flint, Michigan

Baker College OnLine

http://online.baker.edu

Baker College of Flint was founded in 1911. It is accredited by North Central Association of Colleges and Schools. It first offered distance learning courses in 1994. In fall 2003, there were 10,211 students enrolled in distance learning courses. Institutionally administered financial aid is available to distance learners.

Services Distance learners have accessibility to academic advising, bookstore, campus computer network, e-mail services, library services, tutoring.
Contact Mr. Chuck J. Gurden, Vice President of Graduate and Online Admissions, Baker College of Flint, 1116 West Bristol Road, Flint, MI 48507. *Telephone:* 810-766-4390. *Fax:* 810-766-4399. *E-mail:* cgurde01@baker.edu.

DEGREES AND AWARDS

ABA Business Administration
BBA Business Administration
MBA Business Administration

COURSE SUBJECT AREAS OFFERED OUTSIDE OF DEGREE PROGRAMS

Undergraduate—business administration and management; computer/information technology administration and management.

See full description on page 356.

BAKER COLLEGE OF JACKSON

Jackson, Michigan

http://online.baker.edu

Baker College of Jackson was founded in 1994. It is accredited by North Central Association of Colleges and Schools. It first offered distance learning courses in 1995. In fall 2003, there were 14,900 students enrolled in distance learning courses. Institutionally administered financial aid is available to distance learners.

Services Distance learners have accessibility to academic advising, bookstore, campus computer network, career placement assistance, e-mail services, library services, tutoring.
Contact Mr. Chuck J. Gurden, Vice President for Graduate and Online Admissions, Baker College of Jackson, 1116 West Bristol Road, Flint, MI 48507. *Telephone:* 800-469-3165. *Fax:* 810-766-4399. *E-mail:* chuck@baker.edu.

DEGREES AND AWARDS

BBA Business Administration

BALL STATE UNIVERSITY

Muncie, Indiana

School of Continuing Education and Public Service

http://www.bsu.edu/distance

Ball State University was founded in 1918. It is accredited by North Central Association of Colleges and Schools. It first offered distance

Ball State University (continued)

learning courses in 1984. In fall 2003, there were 2,318 students enrolled in distance learning courses. Institutionally administered financial aid is available to distance learners.

Services Distance learners have accessibility to academic advising, bookstore, campus computer network, career placement assistance, e-mail services, library services.

Contact Ms. Diane K. Watters, Marketing Manager, Ball State University, School of Extended Education, Carmichael Hall, Room 200, Muncie, IN 47306. *Telephone:* 765-285-9042. *Fax:* 765-285-7161. *E-mail:* dbuck@bsu.edu.

DEGREES AND AWARDS

AA General Program

BSN Nursing

MA Career and Technical Education; Physical Education–Coaching Specialization; Technology Education

MAE Educational Administration and Supervision; Elementary Education; Special Education

MBA Business Administration

MSN Nursing

BALTIMORE CITY COMMUNITY COLLEGE

Baltimore, Maryland

http://www.bccc.edu

Baltimore City Community College was founded in 1947. It is accredited by Middle States Association of Colleges and Schools. It first offered distance learning courses in 1992. In fall 2003, there were 597 students enrolled in distance learning courses. Institutionally administered financial aid is available to distance learners.

Services Distance learners have accessibility to bookstore, e-mail services, library services, tutoring.

Contact Karen McClaskey, Student Support Manager, Baltimore City Community College, 2901 Liberty Heights Avenue, Baltimore, MD 21215. *Telephone:* 410-462-7625. *Fax:* 410-462-8252. *E-mail:* kmcclaskey@bccc.edu.

DEGREES AND AWARDS

AA Dietetic Technician; Law Enforcement

COURSE SUBJECT AREAS OFFERED OUTSIDE OF DEGREE PROGRAMS

Undergraduate—accounting; bilingual/bicultural education; biological and physical sciences; biology, general; business; business administration and management; computer software and media applications; criminal justice and corrections; curriculum and instruction; economics; English composition; English technical and business writing; hospitality services management; microbiology/bacteriology; oceanography; psychology; sociology; special education.

Non-credit—accounting; business administration and management; computer software and media applications; personal and miscellaneous services, other.

BAPTIST BIBLE COLLEGE OF PENNSYLVANIA

Clarks Summit, Pennsylvania

http://academics.bbc.edu

Baptist Bible College of Pennsylvania was founded in 1932. It is accredited by Accrediting Association of Bible Colleges. It first offered distance learning courses in 1998. In fall 2003, there were 40 students enrolled in distance learning courses. Institutionally administered financial aid is available to distance learners.

Services Distance learners have accessibility to academic advising, bookstore, e-mail services, library services.

Contact Mr. Kai-Chun Cheng, Distance Learning Facilitator, Baptist Bible College of Pennsylvania, 538 Venard Road, Clarks Summit, PA 18411. *Telephone:* 570-585-9408. *Fax:* 570-585-4057. *E-mail:* kccheng@bbc.edu.

DEGREES AND AWARDS

Programs offered do not lead to a degree or other formal award.

COURSE SUBJECT AREAS OFFERED OUTSIDE OF DEGREE PROGRAMS

Graduate—bible/biblical studies; counseling psychology; education, general; missions/missionary studies and missiology; religion/religious studies; theological and ministerial studies; theological studies and religious vocations, other.

THE BAPTIST COLLEGE OF FLORIDA

Graceville, Florida

Division of Distance Learning

http://www.baptistcollege.edu

The Baptist College of Florida was founded in 1943. It is accredited by Southern Association of Colleges and Schools. It first offered distance learning courses in 1999. In fall 2003, there were 75 students enrolled in distance learning courses. Institutionally administered financial aid is available to distance learners.

Services Distance learners have accessibility to academic advising, bookstore, campus computer network, career placement assistance, e-mail services, library services, tutoring.

Contact Jack Cunningham, Director of Distance Learning, The Baptist College of Florida, 5400 College Drive, Graceville, FL 32440. *Telephone:* 850-263-3261 Ext. 433. *Fax:* 850-263-7506. *E-mail:* jrcunningham@baptistcollege.edu.

DEGREES AND AWARDS

AD Divinity

BS Biblical Studies

COURSE SUBJECT AREAS OFFERED OUTSIDE OF DEGREE PROGRAMS

Undergraduate—bible/biblical studies; counseling psychology; philosophy and religion.

BAPTIST MISSIONARY ASSOCIATION THEOLOGICAL SEMINARY

Jacksonville, Texas

http://bmats.edu

Baptist Missionary Association Theological Seminary was founded in 1955. It is accredited by Southern Association of Colleges and Schools. It first offered distance learning courses in 2000. In fall 2003, there were 20 students enrolled in distance learning courses. Institutionally administered financial aid is available to distance learners.

Services Distance learners have accessibility to academic advising, bookstore, library services.
Contact Dr. Philip W. Attebery, Dean/Registrar, Baptist Missionary Association Theological Seminary, 1530 East Pine Street, Jacksonville, TX 75766. *Telephone:* 903-586-2501. *Fax:* 903-586-0378. *E-mail:* bmatsem@bmats.edu.

DEGREES AND AWARDS

Programs offered do not lead to a degree or other formal award.

COURSE SUBJECT AREAS OFFERED OUTSIDE OF DEGREE PROGRAMS

Undergraduate—theological and ministerial studies; theological studies and religious vocations, other.
Graduate—theological and ministerial studies; theological studies and religious vocations, other.
Non-credit—theological and ministerial studies; theological studies and religious vocations, other.

BAPTIST THEOLOGICAL SEMINARY AT RICHMOND

Richmond, Virginia

http://www.btsr.edu

Baptist Theological Seminary at Richmond was founded in 1991. It is accredited by Association of Theological Schools in the United States and Canada. It first offered distance learning courses in 2000. In fall 2003, there were 80 students enrolled in distance learning courses. Institutionally administered financial aid is available to distance learners.

Services Distance learners have accessibility to academic advising, bookstore, e-mail services, library services.
Contact Dr. James Peak, Associate Dean for Continuing Education, Baptist Theological Seminary at Richmond, 3400 Brook Road, Richmond, VA 23227. *Telephone:* 804-204-1240. *E-mail:* jpeak@btsr.edu.

DEGREES AND AWARDS

Programs offered do not lead to a degree or other formal award.

COURSE SUBJECT AREAS OFFERED OUTSIDE OF DEGREE PROGRAMS

Graduate—bible/biblical studies; biblical and other theological languages and literatures; education, other; foreign languages and literatures; Greek languages and literatures (modern); religion/religious studies; religious education; religious/sacred music.
Non-credit—bible/biblical studies; biblical and other theological languages and literatures; miscellaneous health professions; philosophy and religion; religion/religious studies; religious education; theological and ministerial studies; theological studies and religious vocations, other.

BARCLAY COLLEGE

Haviland, Kansas

Home College Program

http://www.barclaycollege.edu

Barclay College was founded in 1917. It is accredited by Accrediting Association of Bible Colleges. It first offered distance learning courses in 1993. In fall 2003, there were 60 students enrolled in distance learning courses. Institutionally administered financial aid is available to distance learners.

Services Distance learners have accessibility to academic advising, bookstore, e-mail services, library services.
Contact Dr. Glenn Leppert, Academic Dean, Barclay College, 607 North Kingman, Haviland, KS 67059-0288. *Telephone:* 620-862-5252 Ext. 46. *Fax:* 620-862-5403. *E-mail:* lepgl@barclaycollege.edu.

DEGREES AND AWARDS

Programs offered do not lead to a degree or other formal award.

COURSE SUBJECT AREAS OFFERED OUTSIDE OF DEGREE PROGRAMS

Undergraduate—bible/biblical studies; education, other; English composition; English language and literature, general; missions/missionary studies and missiology; physical sciences, general; psychology; religious/sacred music; sociology; theological and ministerial studies.

BEAUFORT COUNTY COMMUNITY COLLEGE

Washington, North Carolina

Distance Education Center

http://www.beaufort.cc.nc.us/

Beaufort County Community College was founded in 1967. It is accredited by Southern Association of Colleges and Schools. It first offered distance learning courses in 1995. In fall 2003, there were 500 students enrolled in distance learning courses. Institutionally administered financial aid is available to distance learners.

Services Distance learners have accessibility to academic advising, bookstore, campus computer network, career placement assistance, e-mail services, library services.
Contact Penny Sermons, Director of Learning Resources Center, Beaufort County Community College, PO Box 1069, Washington, NC 27889. *Telephone:* 252-940-6243. *Fax:* 252-946-9575. *E-mail:* pennys@email.beaufort.cc.nc.us.

DEGREES AND AWARDS

Programs offered do not lead to a degree or other formal award.

Beaufort County Community College (continued)

COURSE SUBJECT AREAS OFFERED OUTSIDE OF DEGREE PROGRAMS

Undergraduate—accounting; business administration and management; business information and data processing services; computer and information sciences, general; English language and literature, general; liberal arts and sciences, general studies and humanities; psychology; social psychology; sociology.
Non-credit—accounting; business communications; computer and information sciences, general; Internet and World Wide Web.

BELLEVUE COMMUNITY COLLEGE

Bellevue, Washington
Telecommunications Program–Distance Learning Department
http://distance-ed.bcc.ctc.edu

Bellevue Community College was founded in 1966. It is accredited by Northwest Commission on Colleges and Universities. It first offered distance learning courses in 1980. In fall 2003, there were 2,400 students enrolled in distance learning courses. Institutionally administered financial aid is available to distance learners.

Services Distance learners have accessibility to academic advising, bookstore, library services.
Contact Liz Anderson, Co-Director of Distance Learning, Bellevue Community College, 3000 Landerholm Circle, SE, Bellevue, WA 98007-6484. *Telephone:* 425-564-2438. *Fax:* 425-564-6186. *E-mail:* landerso@bcc.ctc.edu.

DEGREES AND AWARDS

AA General Studies; Graphics and Animation–2-D Web Animation Specialty; Web/Multimedia Authoring
AAS Transfer Degree for Business Students; Transfer Degree
Certificate of Achievement Web/Multimedia Authoring
Certificate Business Software Specialist–Business Technology Systems

COURSE SUBJECT AREAS OFFERED OUTSIDE OF DEGREE PROGRAMS

Undergraduate—accounting; adult/continuing education; American literature (United States); American studies; anthropology; archaeology; astronomy; atmospheric sciences and meteorology; biology; botany; business; chemistry; communications, general; developmental and child psychology; English composition; English creative writing; English literature (British and Commonwealth); environmental science; fire protection; geography; geological and related sciences; history; Internet and World Wide Web; management information systems/business data processing; mathematics related; philosophy; psychology; social sciences and history, other; sociology; speech and rhetorical studies.

BELLEVUE UNIVERSITY

Bellevue, Nebraska
Online Programs
http://www.bellevue.edu

Bellevue University was founded in 1965. It is accredited by North Central Association of Colleges and Schools. It first offered distance learning courses in 1996. In fall 2003, there were 2,300 students enrolled in distance learning courses. Institutionally administered financial aid is available to distance learners.

Services Distance learners have accessibility to academic advising, campus computer network, e-mail services.
Contact Roberta Mersch, Online Admissions, Bellevue University, 1000 Galvin Road South, Bellevue, NE 68005. *Telephone:* 800-756-7920. *Fax:* 402-293-3730. *E-mail:* mm@bellevue.edu.

DEGREES AND AWARDS

BA Leadership
BS Business Administration of Technical Studies; Business Information Systems; Correctional Administration and Management; Criminal Justice Administration; E-Business; Global Business Management; Health Care Administration; Internet Systems and Software Technology; Management Information Systems; Management of Human Resources; Management; Marketing Management
MA Leadership; Management
MBA Business Administration
MS Computer Information Systems; Health Care Administration

COURSE SUBJECT AREAS OFFERED OUTSIDE OF DEGREE PROGRAMS

Undergraduate—business; business administration and management; business and personal services marketing operations; business information and data processing services; business management and administrative services, other; business/managerial economics; business quantitative methods and management science.
Graduate—business; business administration and management; business and personal services marketing operations; business communications; business information and data processing services; business management and administrative services, other; business/managerial economics; business quantitative methods and management science.

See full description on page 358.

BELLINGHAM TECHNICAL COLLEGE

Bellingham, Washington
http://www.btc.ctc.edu/

Bellingham Technical College is accredited by Northwest Commission on Colleges and Universities. It first offered distance learning courses in 2000. In fall 2003, there were 60 students enrolled in distance learning courses. Institutionally administered financial aid is available to distance learners.

Services Distance learners have accessibility to academic advising, library services.
Contact Ms. Sharon Carpenter, Dean of Professional and Technical Education, Bellingham Technical College, 3028 Lindbergh Avenue, Bellingham, WA 98225-1599. *Telephone:* 360-738-3105 Ext. 331. *Fax:* 360-676-2798. *E-mail:* scarpent@btc.ctc.edu.

DEGREES AND AWARDS

AAS Technical Sales

COURSE SUBJECT AREAS OFFERED OUTSIDE OF DEGREE PROGRAMS

Undergraduate—accounting; business; business administration and management; business communications; computer and information

sciences, other; computer science; computer systems networking and telecommunications; medical basic sciences.
Non-credit—accounting; computer and information sciences, general; computer engineering; computer/information technology administration and management; computer software and media applications; health and medical preparatory programs.

BEMIDJI STATE UNIVERSITY

Bemidji, Minnesota
Center for Extended Learning
http://www.bemidjistate.edu

Bemidji State University was founded in 1919. It is accredited by North Central Association of Colleges and Schools. It first offered distance learning courses in 1977. In fall 2003, there were 1,200 students enrolled in distance learning courses. Institutionally administered financial aid is available to distance learners.

Services Distance learners have accessibility to academic advising, bookstore, career placement assistance, e-mail services, library services, tutoring.
Contact Robert J. Griggs, Dean of Distance Learning and Summer School, Bemidji State University, 1500 Birchmont Drive, NE, Bemidji, MN 56601-2699. *Telephone:* 218-755-2068. *Fax:* 218-755-4048. *E-mail:* rgriggs@bemidjistate.edu.

DEGREES AND AWARDS

AS Criminal Justice
BS Criminal Justice; Elementary Education
MS Industrial Technology
MSE Education

COURSE SUBJECT AREAS OFFERED OUTSIDE OF DEGREE PROGRAMS

Undergraduate—anthropology; business administration and management; criminal justice and corrections; criminology; economics; English composition; general teacher education; geography; health and physical education/fitness; history; industrial production technologies; philosophy; philosophy and religion; psychology; social work; sociology; teacher education, specific academic and vocational programs.
Graduate—educational/instructional media design; education, general; industrial production technologies.

BENEDICT COLLEGE

Columbia, South Carolina
http://www.benedict.edu

Benedict College was founded in 1870. It is accredited by Southern Association of Colleges and Schools. Institutionally administered financial aid is available to distance learners.

Contact Mr. Gary Knight, Vice President of Institutional Effectiveness, Benedict College, 1600 Harden Street, Columbia, SC 29204. *Telephone:* 803-253-5275. *Fax:* 803-252-5215. *E-mail:* knightg@benedict.edu.

DEGREES AND AWARDS

Programs offered do not lead to a degree or other formal award.

BERKELEY COLLEGE

West Paterson, New Jersey
http://www.berkeleycollege.edu/

Berkeley College was founded in 1931. It is accredited by Middle States Association of Colleges and Schools. It first offered distance learning courses in 2001. In fall 2003, there were 390 students enrolled in distance learning courses. Institutionally administered financial aid is available to distance learners.

Services Distance learners have accessibility to academic advising, bookstore, campus computer network, career placement assistance, e-mail services, library services, tutoring.
Contact Ms. Susan Mandra, Director, Online Admissions, Berkeley College, 44 Rifle Camp Road, West Paterson, NJ 07424. *Telephone:* 973-278-5400 Ext. 1213. *Fax:* 973-278-9141. *E-mail:* srm@berkeleycollege.edu.

DEGREES AND AWARDS

AAS Business Administration
BS Business Administration

COURSE SUBJECT AREAS OFFERED OUTSIDE OF DEGREE PROGRAMS

Undergraduate—accounting; advertising; apparel and accessories marketing operations; business; business administration and management; business management and administrative services, other; business/managerial economics; business quantitative methods and management science; computer software and media applications; economics; English composition; English language and literature/letters, other; entrepreneurship; general retailing/wholesaling; history; human resources management; industrial and organizational psychology; international business; legal studies; marketing operations/marketing and distribution, other; philosophy; political science and government; psychology; social sciences and history, other; sociology.

See full description on page 360.

BERKELEY COLLEGE-NEW YORK CITY CAMPUS

New York, New York
http://www.berkeleycollege.edu/

Berkeley College-New York City Campus was founded in 1936. It is accredited by Middle States Association of Colleges and Schools. It first offered distance learning courses in 1998. In fall 2003, there were 222 students enrolled in distance learning courses. Institutionally administered financial aid is available to distance learners.

Services Distance learners have accessibility to academic advising, bookstore, campus computer network, career placement assistance, e-mail services, library services, tutoring.
Contact Ms. Susan Mandra, Director, Online Admissions, Berkeley College-New York City Campus, 3 East 43rd Street, New York, NY 10017. *Telephone:* 800-446-5400. *Fax:* 212-818-1079. *E-mail:* srm@berkeleycollege.edu.

DEGREES AND AWARDS

BBA Business Administration–Management

Berkeley College-New York City Campus (continued)

COURSE SUBJECT AREAS OFFERED OUTSIDE OF DEGREE PROGRAMS

Undergraduate—accounting; advertising; area, ethnic and cultural studies, other; business; business administration and management; business management and administrative services, other; business/managerial economics; business quantitative methods and management science; computer software and media applications; conservation and renewable natural resources, other; economics; English composition; English language and literature/letters, other; entrepreneurship; general retailing/wholesaling; geography; history; human resources management; industrial and organizational psychology; international business; marketing operations/marketing and distribution, other; mathematics, other; philosophy; political science and government; psychology; social sciences and history, other.

See full description on page 360.

BERKELEY COLLEGE-WESTCHESTER CAMPUS

White Plains, New York

http://www.berkeleycollege.edu/

Berkeley College-Westchester Campus was founded in 1945. It is accredited by Middle States Association of Colleges and Schools. It first offered distance learning courses in 1998. In fall 2003, there were 104 students enrolled in distance learning courses.

Services Distance learners have accessibility to academic advising, bookstore, campus computer network, e-mail services, library services.

Contact Ms. Susan Mandra, Director, Online Admissions, Berkeley College-Westchester Campus, 44 Rifle Camp Road, West Paterson, NJ 07424. *Telephone:* 973-278-5400 Ext. 1213. *Fax:* 973-278-9141. *E-mail:* srm@berkeleycollege.edu.

DEGREES AND AWARDS

Programs offered do not lead to a degree or other formal award.

COURSE SUBJECT AREAS OFFERED OUTSIDE OF DEGREE PROGRAMS

Undergraduate—accounting; advertising; area, ethnic and cultural studies, other; business; business administration and management; business management and administrative services, other; business/managerial economics; business quantitative methods and management science; computer software and media applications; economics; English composition; English language and literature/letters, other; entrepreneurship; geography; history; human resources management; industrial and organizational psychology; international business; legal studies; marketing operations/marketing and distribution, other; philosophy; political science and government; psychology; social sciences and history, other.

See full description on page 360.

BETHANY COLLEGE OF THE ASSEMBLIES OF GOD

Scotts Valley, California

External Degree Program

http://bethany.edu/edp/

Bethany College of the Assemblies of God was founded in 1919. It is accredited by Western Association of Schools and Colleges. It first offered distance learning courses in 1992. In fall 2003, there were 120 students enrolled in distance learning courses. Institutionally administered financial aid is available to distance learners.

Services Distance learners have accessibility to academic advising, bookstore, campus computer network, e-mail services, library services, tutoring.

Contact Ms. Julia J. Garcia, Assistant Director, Bethany College of the Assemblies of God, 800 Bethany Drive, Scotts Valley, CA 95066. *Telephone:* 800-843-9410. *Fax:* 831-430-0953. *E-mail:* edp@fc.bethany.edu.

DEGREES AND AWARDS

AA Church Ministries; Early Child Development; General Studies
BA Addiction Studies; Applied Professional Studies; Biblical and Theological Studies; Church Leadership; Early Child Development; General Ministries; Liberal Arts; Psychology
Certificate Addiction Counseling Certification Program
MA Arts

COURSE SUBJECT AREAS OFFERED OUTSIDE OF DEGREE PROGRAMS

Undergraduate—anthropology; applied mathematics; archaeology; area, ethnic and cultural studies, other; bible/biblical studies; biblical and other theological languages and literatures; bilingual/bicultural education; biological and physical sciences; biological sciences/life sciences, other; biology, general; child care and guidance workers and managers; classical and ancient Near Eastern languages and literatures; clinical psychology; communications, general; communications technologies; community psychology; counseling psychology; cultural studies; demography/population studies; developmental and child psychology; English composition; English language and literature, general; family and community studies; fine arts and art studies; foreign languages and literatures; geography; Greek languages and literatures (modern); history; liberal arts and sciences, general studies and humanities; mathematical statistics; missions/missionary studies and missiology; pastoral counseling and specialized ministries; philosophy and religion; physical sciences, general; political science and government; psychology; religion/religious studies; religious education; social psychology; social sciences and history, other; social sciences, general; sociology; theological and ministerial studies.

Special Message

Bethany College (BC) was founded in 1919. Now, each semester, through its External Degree Program (EDP), BC offers more than eighty courses that lead to a dozen AA and BA degrees. The School of Distributed Learning also offers one-night-a-week degree completion programs in San Jose, California; Las Vegas, Nevada, and Santa Cruz County, California. (These programs require physical attendance). Regionally accredited by the Western Association of Schools and Colleges, Bethany offers its students an excellent education. BC has helped hundreds of students to complete their degrees since 1992. EDP is designed for people who want to complete an accredited Bachelor of Arts degree conveniently and quickly, without relocating to a college campus. The program is offered electronically, with shared and collaborative learning facilitated by instructors who are involved in today's corporate environment and thoroughly understand it. Campus visits are thus not required. Interaction takes place via computer, telephone, or fax. Students have the convenience and ease that user-friendly technology can bring to education, without the struggles of a manual, correspondence-driven system. Students have online access to orientation information, library services, registration, and the College's bookstore. With electronically mediated classes there are no classes to attend, no commuting, no late-night or other travel. Goals can be achieved and students can complete their degrees and move ahead in their career with increased skills and insight through this unique approach to a traditional college education. For further information, interested students should contact the School of Distributed Learning (telephone: 800-843-9410 (toll-free); fax: 831-430-0953; e-mail: edp@fc.bethany.edu) or visit the Web site at http://www.bethany.edu/edp.

BETHANY THEOLOGICAL SEMINARY

Richmond, Indiana

http://www.bethanyseminary.edu

Bethany Theological Seminary was founded in 1905. It is accredited by North Central Association of Colleges and Schools. It first offered distance learning courses in 2003. In fall 2003, there were 20 students enrolled in distance learning courses. Institutionally administered financial aid is available to distance learners.

Services Distance learners have accessibility to academic advising, bookstore, e-mail services, library services.
Contact Dr. Daniel W. Ulrich, Associate Dean and Director of Distributed Education, Bethany Theological Seminary, 615 National Road West, Richmond, IN 47374. *Telephone:* 765-983-1800. *Fax:* 765-983-1840. *E-mail:* enroll@bethanyseminary.edu.

DEGREES AND AWARDS

MDiv Ministry Training

COURSE SUBJECT AREAS OFFERED OUTSIDE OF DEGREE PROGRAMS

Undergraduate—religion/religious studies.
Graduate—religion/religious studies; religious education.

BETHUNE-COOKMAN COLLEGE

Daytona Beach, Florida

http://www.bethune.cookman.edu/

Bethune-Cookman College was founded in 1904. It is accredited by Southern Association of Colleges and Schools. It first offered distance learning courses in 2004. In fall 2003, there were 200 students enrolled in distance learning courses. Institutionally administered financial aid is available to distance learners.

Services Distance learners have accessibility to academic advising, campus computer network, e-mail services.
Contact Dr. Deborah Marie Henson-Governor, EdD, Director of Continuing Education, Bethune-Cookman College, 640 Dr. Mary McLeod Bethune Boulevard, Daytona Beach, FL 32114. *Telephone:* 386-481-2342. *Fax:* 386-481-2380. *E-mail:* governord@cookman.edu.

DEGREES AND AWARDS

Programs offered do not lead to a degree or other formal award.

COURSE SUBJECT AREAS OFFERED OUTSIDE OF DEGREE PROGRAMS

Undergraduate—bible/biblical studies; foreign languages and literatures; history; psychology.

BISHOP STATE COMMUNITY COLLEGE

Mobile, Alabama

http://www.bishop.edu

Bishop State Community College was founded in 1965. It is accredited by Southern Association of Colleges and Schools. It first offered distance learning courses in 2000. In fall 2003, there were 600 students enrolled in distance learning courses. Institutionally administered financial aid is available to distance learners.

Services Distance learners have accessibility to academic advising, library services, tutoring.
Contact Josh Gilliam, Coordinator of Instructional Design, Bishop State Community College, Mobile, AL 36603. *E-mail:* jgilliam@bscc.cc.al.us.

DEGREES AND AWARDS

Programs offered do not lead to a degree or other formal award.

COURSE SUBJECT AREAS OFFERED OUTSIDE OF DEGREE PROGRAMS

Undergraduate—accounting; applied mathematics; business administration and management; computer and information sciences, general; economics; electrical and electronic engineering-related technology; English language and literature, general; nursing; psychology; social psychology; social sciences and history, other; sociology.

BISMARCK STATE COLLEGE

Bismarck, North Dakota

EPCE

http://www.bismarckstate.edu/elpw/

Bismarck State College was founded in 1939. It is accredited by North Central Association of Colleges and Schools. It first offered distance learning courses in 1998. Institutionally administered financial aid is available to distance learners.

Services Distance learners have accessibility to academic advising, bookstore, campus computer network, career placement assistance, e-mail services, library services, tutoring.
Contact Lane Huber, Director of Distance Learning, Bismarck State College, 1500 Edwards Avenue, PO Box 5587, Bismarck, ND 58506-5587. *Telephone:* 701-224-5714. *Fax:* 701-224-5719. *E-mail:* lahuber@gwmail.nodak.edu.

DEGREES AND AWARDS

AAS Electric Power Technology

Bismarck State College (continued)

COURSE SUBJECT AREAS OFFERED OUTSIDE OF DEGREE PROGRAMS

Undergraduate—applied mathematics; business communications; computer and information sciences, general; electrical and electronic engineering-related technology; electrical and power transmission installers; electromechanical instrumentation and maintenance technology; engineering-related technologies, other; industrial equipment maintenance and repairers; nuclear and industrial radiologic technologies; quality control and safety technologies; technology education/industrial arts.

BISMARCK STATE COLLEGE

Bismarck, North Dakota

http://www.bismarckstate.edu

Bismarck State College was founded in 1939. It is accredited by North Central Association of Colleges and Schools. It first offered distance learning courses in 1991. In fall 2003, there were 950 students enrolled in distance learning courses. Institutionally administered financial aid is available to distance learners.

Services Distance learners have accessibility to academic advising, bookstore, campus computer network, career placement assistance, e-mail services, library services, tutoring.

Contact Lane Huber, Director of Distance Education, Bismarck State College, PO Box 5587, Bismarck, ND 58506-5587. *Telephone:* 701-224-5714. *Fax:* 701-224-5719. *E-mail:* lane.huber@bsc.nodak.edu.

DEGREES AND AWARDS

AA Criminal Justice
AAS Criminal Justice; Electric Power Technology; Electric Transmission System Technology; Human Services; Nuclear Power Technology; Power Plant Technology; Process Plant Technology
Certificate of Completion Electric Power Technology; Information Processing Specialist; Power Plant Technology; Process Plant Technology
Certificate Electric Transmission System Technology

COURSE SUBJECT AREAS OFFERED OUTSIDE OF DEGREE PROGRAMS

Undergraduate—biology, general; business; computer science; computer software and media applications; criminal justice and corrections; English composition; English technical and business writing; history; human services; information sciences and systems; Internet and World Wide Web; marketing operations/marketing and distribution, other; mathematics; philosophy; psychology; sociology.
Non-credit—electrical and electronic engineering-related technology; industrial equipment maintenance and repairers; industrial production technologies; nuclear engineering; plant sciences.

BLACKHAWK TECHNICAL COLLEGE

Janesville, Wisconsin

http://www.blackhawk.edu

Blackhawk Technical College was founded in 1968. It is accredited by North Central Association of Colleges and Schools. It first offered distance learning courses in 2000. In fall 2003, there were 257 students enrolled in distance learning courses. Institutionally administered financial aid is available to distance learners.

Services Distance learners have accessibility to academic advising, bookstore, career placement assistance, e-mail services.

Contact Connie Richards, Registration Supervisor, Blackhawk Technical College, 6004 Prairie Road, PO Box 5009, Janesville, WI 53547. *Telephone:* 608-757-7654. *Fax:* 608-743-4407. *E-mail:* crichards@blackhawk.edu.

DEGREES AND AWARDS

Programs offered do not lead to a degree or other formal award.

COURSE SUBJECT AREAS OFFERED OUTSIDE OF DEGREE PROGRAMS

Undergraduate—accounting; administrative and secretarial services; dental services.
Non-credit—administrative and secretarial services; child care and guidance workers and managers; clothing/apparel and textile studies; computer software and media applications; consumer and homemaking education; crafts, folk art and artisanry; criminal justice and corrections; drafting; English as a second language; English creative writing; film/video and photographic arts; fire protection; floristry marketing operations; foreign languages and literatures, other; institutional food workers and administrators; insurance marketing operations; leatherworking/upholstery; real estate; woodworkers.

BLACK HILLS STATE UNIVERSITY

Spearfish, South Dakota

Extended Services and Instructional Technology

http://www.bhsu.edu/academics/distlrn/

Black Hills State University was founded in 1883. It is accredited by North Central Association of Colleges and Schools. It first offered distance learning courses in 1994. In fall 2003, there were 578 students enrolled in distance learning courses. Institutionally administered financial aid is available to distance learners.

Services Distance learners have accessibility to academic advising, bookstore, campus computer network, career placement assistance, e-mail services, library services.

Contact Sheila R. Aaker, Extended Services Coordinator, Black Hills State University, Extended Services, 1200 University Street, Unit 9508, Spearfish, SD 57799-9508. *Telephone:* 605-642-6771. *Fax:* 605-642-6031. *E-mail:* sheilaaaker@bhsu.edu.

DEGREES AND AWARDS

Advanced Graduate Diploma Curriculum and Instruction

COURSE SUBJECT AREAS OFFERED OUTSIDE OF DEGREE PROGRAMS

Undergraduate—accounting; American literature (United States); biblical and other theological languages and literatures; business; business management and administrative services, other; developmental/child psychology; economics; education, other; English composition; English language and literature, general; English technical and business writing; financial management and services; fine arts and art studies; geography; human resources management; international business; library science, other; psychology; psychology, other; sociology.
Graduate—developmental/child psychology; educational evaluation, research and statistics; educational/instructional media design; education, general; education, other; hospitality services management.

BLOOMFIELD COLLEGE

Bloomfield, New Jersey

http://www.bloomfield.edu/

Bloomfield College was founded in 1868. It is accredited by Middle States Association of Colleges and Schools. It first offered distance learning courses in 1997. In fall 2003, there were 47 students enrolled in distance learning courses. Institutionally administered financial aid is available to distance learners.

Services Distance learners have accessibility to campus computer network, e-mail services, library services.

Contact Ms. Martha LaBare, Interim Vice President for Academic Affairs, Bloomfield College, 467 Franklin Street, Bloomfield, NJ 07003. *Telephone:* 973-748-9000 Ext. 326. *Fax:* 973-743-3998. *E-mail:* martha_labare@bloomfield.edu.

DEGREES AND AWARDS

Programs offered do not lead to a degree or other formal award.

COURSE SUBJECT AREAS OFFERED OUTSIDE OF DEGREE PROGRAMS

Undergraduate—business administration and management.

BLOOMSBURG UNIVERSITY OF PENNSYLVANIA

Bloomsburg, Pennsylvania

School of Graduate Studies

http://www.bloomu.edu

Bloomsburg University of Pennsylvania was founded in 1839. It is accredited by Middle States Association of Colleges and Schools. It first offered distance learning courses in 1983. In fall 2003, there were 94 students enrolled in distance learning courses. Institutionally administered financial aid is available to distance learners.

Services Distance learners have accessibility to academic advising, bookstore, campus computer network, career placement assistance, e-mail services, library services.

Contact Dr. James Matta, Dean, Bloomsburg University of Pennsylvania, 400 East 2nd Street, Bloomsburg, PA 17815-1301. *Telephone:* 570-389-4015. *Fax:* 570-389-3054. *E-mail:* jmatta@bloomu.edu.

DEGREES AND AWARDS

MS Instructional Technology Education Specialist

COURSE SUBJECT AREAS OFFERED OUTSIDE OF DEGREE PROGRAMS

Undergraduate—business management and administrative services, other; nursing.

Graduate—business management and administrative services, other; curriculum and instruction; educational/instructional media design.

BLUE MOUNTAIN COMMUNITY COLLEGE

Pendleton, Oregon

Distance Education–Extended Programs

http://www.bluecc.edu/

Blue Mountain Community College was founded in 1962. It is accredited by Northwest Commission on Colleges and Universities. It first offered distance learning courses in 1982. In fall 2003, there were 375 students enrolled in distance learning courses. Institutionally administered financial aid is available to distance learners.

Services Distance learners have accessibility to academic advising, bookstore, campus computer network, library services, tutoring.

Contact Mr. Bruce Kauss, Distance Education Specialist, Blue Mountain Community College, PO Box 100, Pendleton, OR 97801. *Telephone:* 541-278-5763 Ext. 5763. *Fax:* 541-278-5841. *E-mail:* bkauss@bluecc.edu.

DEGREES AND AWARDS

Programs offered do not lead to a degree or other formal award.

COURSE SUBJECT AREAS OFFERED OUTSIDE OF DEGREE PROGRAMS

Undergraduate—accounting; administrative and secretarial services; American literature (United States); anthropology; applied mathematics; archaeology; biology, general; business; business management and administrative services, other; criminology; developmental/child psychology; teacher assistant/aide.

BOISE BIBLE COLLEGE

Boise, Idaho

http://www.boisebible.edu

Boise Bible College was founded in 1945. It is accredited by Accrediting Association of Bible Colleges. It first offered distance learning courses in 2000. In fall 2003, there were 7 students enrolled in distance learning courses. Institutionally administered financial aid is available to distance learners.

Services Distance learners have accessibility to academic advising, e-mail services.

Contact Mrs. Beth Duffel, Admissions Counselor, Boise Bible College, 8695 West Marigold Street, Boise, ID 83714. *Telephone:* 208-376-7731. *Fax:* 208-376-7743. *E-mail:* bethd@boisebible.edu.

DEGREES AND AWARDS

Programs offered do not lead to a degree or other formal award.

COURSE SUBJECT AREAS OFFERED OUTSIDE OF DEGREE PROGRAMS

Undergraduate—bible/biblical studies; religion/religious studies; religious education; theological and ministerial studies; theological studies and religious vocations, other.

BOISE STATE UNIVERSITY

Boise, Idaho

Division of Extended Studies

http://www.boisestate.edu/distance

Boise State University was founded in 1932. It is accredited by Northwest Commission on Colleges and Universities. It first offered distance learning courses in 1980. In fall 2003, there were 2,777 students enrolled in distance learning courses. Institutionally administered financial aid is available to distance learners.

Services Distance learners have accessibility to academic advising, bookstore, career placement assistance, e-mail services, library services, tutoring.

Boise State University (continued)

Contact Joann Swanson, Coordinator of Distance Education Student Services, Boise State University, 1910 University Drive, Boise, ID 83725-1120. *Telephone:* 208-426-5622. *Fax:* 208-426-3467. *E-mail:* joannswanson@boisestate.edu.

DEGREES AND AWARDS

MS Instructional and Performance Technology

MSE Educational Technology

COURSE SUBJECT AREAS OFFERED OUTSIDE OF DEGREE PROGRAMS

Undergraduate—accounting; anthropology; biological and physical sciences; business management and administrative services, other; chemistry; economics; English composition; English technical and business writing; health and medical administrative services; history; human resources management; mathematics; music; nursing; philosophy; physics; psychology; sociology; Spanish; theater arts/drama.

Graduate—educational/instructional media design; education, other; health and medical administrative services; human resources management.

BOISE STATE UNIVERSITY

Boise, Idaho

Department in Educational Technology

http://education.boisestate.edu/edtech2

Boise State University was founded in 1932. It is accredited by Northwest Commission on Colleges and Universities. It first offered distance learning courses in 1999. In fall 2003, there were 220 students enrolled in distance learning courses. Institutionally administered financial aid is available to distance learners.

Services Distance learners have accessibility to academic advising, bookstore, career placement assistance, e-mail services, library services, tutoring.

Contact Jerry Foster, Admissions Counselor and Academic Advisor, Boise State University, Department of Educational Technology, E-304, 1910 University Drive, MS-1747, Boise, ID 83725-1747. *Telephone:* 208-426-1966. *Fax:* 208-426-1451. *E-mail:* jfoster@boisestate.edu.

DEGREES AND AWARDS

MSE Educational Technology Emphasis

COURSE SUBJECT AREAS OFFERED OUTSIDE OF DEGREE PROGRAMS

Undergraduate—computer software and media applications; educational/instructional media design; education, other; Internet and World Wide Web; teacher education, specific academic and vocational programs.

Graduate—computer software and media applications; educational/instructional media design; education, other; Internet and World Wide Web; teacher education, specific academic and vocational programs.

BOISE STATE UNIVERSITY

Boise, Idaho

Program in Instructional and Performance Technology

http://ipt.boisestate.edu

Boise State University was founded in 1932. It is accredited by Northwest Commission on Colleges and Universities. It first offered distance learning courses in 1989. In fall 2003, there were 155 students enrolled in distance learning courses. Institutionally administered financial aid is available to distance learners.

Services Distance learners have accessibility to academic advising, bookstore, campus computer network, career placement assistance, e-mail services, library services, tutoring.

Contact Ms. Jo Ann Fenner, Associate Program Developer, Boise State University, ET-338, 1910 University Drive, Boise, ID 83725. *Telephone:* 208-424-5135. *Fax:* 208-426-1970. *E-mail:* bsuipt@boisestate.edu.

DEGREES AND AWARDS

MS Instructional and Performance Technology

COURSE SUBJECT AREAS OFFERED OUTSIDE OF DEGREE PROGRAMS

Graduate—computer software and media applications; curriculum and instruction; educational evaluation, research and statistics; educational/instructional media design; human resources management.

BOSSIER PARISH COMMUNITY COLLEGE

Bossier City, Louisiana

BPCC Distance Learning Program/Institutional Advancement

http://www.bpcc.edu

Bossier Parish Community College was founded in 1967. It is accredited by Southern Association of Colleges and Schools. It first offered distance learning courses in 1995. In fall 2003, there were 1,084 students enrolled in distance learning courses. Institutionally administered financial aid is available to distance learners.

Services Distance learners have accessibility to academic advising, bookstore, campus computer network, career placement assistance, e-mail services, library services, tutoring.

Contact Kathleen Gay, Director of Educational Technology, Bossier Parish Community College, 2719 Airline Drive, Bossier City, LA 71111. *Telephone:* 318-741-7391. *Fax:* 318-741-7393. *E-mail:* kgay@bpcc.edu.

DEGREES AND AWARDS

AAS Computer Information Systems

AD Criminal Justice

AGS General Studies

COURSE SUBJECT AREAS OFFERED OUTSIDE OF DEGREE PROGRAMS

Undergraduate—American history; applied mathematics; art history; biological and physical sciences; biological sciences/life sciences, other; computer and information sciences, general; computer and

information sciences, other; computer science; computer software and media applications; criminal justice and corrections; curriculum and instruction; developmental/child psychology; education, general; education, other; English composition; English language and literature, general; European history; film/video and photographic arts; fire science; food sciences and technology; foreign languages and literatures; health and medical administrative services; health and medical assistants; history; mathematics; mathematics related; pharmacy; psychology, other; sociology; telecommunications.
Non-credit—business and personal services marketing operations; carpenters; computer and information sciences, general; computer programming; computer software and media applications; computer systems analysis; crafts, folk art and artisanry; culinary arts and related services; custodial, housekeeping and home services workers and managers; dance; design and applied arts; education, general; English as a second language; English creative writing; film/video and photographic arts; fishing and fisheries sciences and management; floristry marketing operations; gaming/sports officiating; hospitality/recreation marketing; hospitality services management; human resources management; legal studies; miscellaneous health aides; real estate; religious education.

BOSTON UNIVERSITY

Boston, Massachusetts
BU Interactive
http://www.bu.edu/disted

Boston University was founded in 1839. It is accredited by New England Association of Schools and Colleges. It first offered distance learning courses in 2001. In fall 2003, there were 500 students enrolled in distance learning courses. Institutionally administered financial aid is available to distance learners.

Services Distance learners have accessibility to academic advising, bookstore, campus computer network, career placement assistance, e-mail services, library services.
Contact Susan Kryczka, Director of Distance Education, Boston University, Office of Distance Education, 940 Commonwealth Avenue West, Boston, MA 02215. *Telephone:* 617-358-1962. *Fax:* 617-358-1961. *E-mail:* kryczka@bu.edu.

DEGREES AND AWARDS

BLS Executive Bachelor's Degree Completion Program
Graduate Certificate Clinical Investigation; Instructional Technology
MCJ Criminal Justice
MSCS Computer Information Systems–Master of Science in Computer Information Systems
MSHRM Human Resource Management
MSM Insurance Management–Master of Science in Insurance Management
DPT Physical Therapy

COURSE SUBJECT AREAS OFFERED OUTSIDE OF DEGREE PROGRAMS

Graduate—curriculum and instruction; educational/instructional media design.
Non-credit—financial management and services.

Special Message

Boston University's Office of Distance Education was established in 2000 to meet the educational needs of today's busy professionals. Using various technologies, Boston University offers courses and programs from a variety of departments and colleges at the University through videotape, CD-ROM, and online programs via the Internet. These programs represent the University's commitment to high-quality programming for distance learners and brings the classroom to the student's office, company, or home.

The Office of Distance Education allows students to take selected courses, complete a graduate certificate, and even pursue a complete graduate degree program via the Internet. The courses are highly interactive and challenging, and they are developed and taught by Boston University faculty members. Also offered are a variety of noncredit programs available on videotape or CD-ROM. Recent seminars on optics, e-business, communications, manufacturing, computer languages, and project management have been offered. New topics and programs are regularly developed, based on industry needs.

For additional information on all Boston University distance education programs, interested students should visit the Web site at http://www.bu.edu/disted or contact the Office of Distance Education (telephone: 617-358-1960).

BOSTON UNIVERSITY

Boston, Massachusetts
Metropolitan College
http://www.bu.edu/disted

Boston University was founded in 1839. It is accredited by New England Association of Schools and Colleges. It first offered distance learning courses in 2002. In fall 2003, there were 600 students enrolled in distance learning courses. Institutionally administered financial aid is available to distance learners.

Services Distance learners have accessibility to academic advising, bookstore, campus computer network, career placement assistance, e-mail services, library services.
Contact Deanna Learman, Assistant Program Manager, Boston University, 940 Commonwealth Avenue West, 2nd Floor, Boston, MA 02215. *Telephone:* 617-358-1960. *Fax:* 617-358-1961. *E-mail:* online@bu.edu.

DEGREES AND AWARDS

BLS Executive Undergraduate Degree Completion
Graduate Certificate Clinical Investigation; Instructional Technology
MCJ Criminal Justice
MSCS Computer Science

BOWLING GREEN STATE UNIVERSITY

Bowling Green, Ohio
http://ideal.bgsu.edu

Bowling Green State University was founded in 1910. It is accredited by North Central Association of Colleges and Schools. It first offered distance learning courses in 1998. In fall 2003, there were 2,500 students enrolled in distance learning courses. Institutionally administered financial aid is available to distance learners.

Bowling Green State University (continued)

Services Distance learners have accessibility to academic advising, bookstore, campus computer network, career placement assistance, e-mail services, library services, tutoring.

Contact Terry Herman, Director of Online Learning, Bowling Green State University, 47 College Park, CEE, Bowling Green, OH 43403. *Telephone:* 419-372-8181. *Fax:* 419-372-8667. *E-mail:* hermant@bgnet.bgsu.edu.

DEGREES AND AWARDS

BS Advanced Technological Education
PhD Technology Management

COURSE SUBJECT AREAS OFFERED OUTSIDE OF DEGREE PROGRAMS

Undergraduate—American literature (United States); applied mathematics; communications, general; computer and information sciences, general; computer science; cultural studies; education administration and supervision; English composition; English creative writing; English language and literature, general; English literature (British and Commonwealth); English technical and business writing; environmental control technologies; environmental/environmental health engineering; family and community studies; foods and nutrition studies; geography; geological and related sciences; health and medical administrative services; history; information sciences and systems; Internet and World Wide Web; library science, other; mathematics; music; nursing; philosophy; philosophy and religion; political science and government; psychology; public health; social work; technology education/industrial arts; telecommunications.

Graduate—American literature (United States); construction/building technology; construction management; English creative writing; English language and literature, general; English literature (British and Commonwealth); English technical and business writing; gerontology; Internet and World Wide Web; psychology; Romance languages and literatures; special education; speech and rhetorical studies; technology education/industrial arts.

Non-credit—computer software and media applications.

BRADLEY UNIVERSITY

Peoria, Illinois

Division of Continuing Education and Professional Development

http://www.bradley.edu/continue

Bradley University was founded in 1897. It is accredited by North Central Association of Colleges and Schools. It first offered distance learning courses in 1985. In fall 2003, there were 20 students enrolled in distance learning courses. Institutionally administered financial aid is available to distance learners.

Services Distance learners have accessibility to academic advising, bookstore, campus computer network, e-mail services, library services.

Contact Susan Manley, Program Director, Bradley University, 1501 West Bradley Avenue, Peoria, IL 61625. *Telephone:* 309-677-2820. *Fax:* 309-677-3321. *E-mail:* susank@bradley.edu.

DEGREES AND AWARDS

MSEE Electrical Engineering
MSME Mechanical Engineering

COURSE SUBJECT AREAS OFFERED OUTSIDE OF DEGREE PROGRAMS

Undergraduate—communications, general.
Graduate—electrical engineering; mechanical engineering.

BRAZOSPORT COLLEGE

Lake Jackson, Texas

http://www.brazosport.edu/

Brazosport College was founded in 1968. It is accredited by Southern Association of Colleges and Schools. It first offered distance learning courses in 1997. In fall 2003, there were 200 students enrolled in distance learning courses. Institutionally administered financial aid is available to distance learners.

Services Distance learners have accessibility to academic advising, bookstore, e-mail services, library services.

Contact Mr. Terry Comingore, Director, Learning Assistance and Instructional Media, Brazosport College, 500 College Drive, Lake Jackson, TX 77566. *Telephone:* 979-230-3318. *Fax:* 979-230-3443. *E-mail:* tcomingo@brazosport.edu.

DEGREES AND AWARDS

Programs offered do not lead to a degree or other formal award.

COURSE SUBJECT AREAS OFFERED OUTSIDE OF DEGREE PROGRAMS

Undergraduate—accounting; chemistry; education, general; English composition; fine arts and art studies; history; mathematics; political science and government; psychology.

BRENAU UNIVERSITY

Gainesville, Georgia

Department of Distance Learning

http://online.brenau.edu

Brenau University was founded in 1878. It is accredited by Southern Association of Colleges and Schools. It first offered distance learning courses in 1998. In fall 2003, there were 326 students enrolled in distance learning courses. Institutionally administered financial aid is available to distance learners.

Services Distance learners have accessibility to academic advising, bookstore, career placement assistance, e-mail services, library services.

Contact Dr. Heather Snow Gibbons, Director of the Online College, Brenau University, 1 Centennial Circle, Gainesville, GA 30501. *Telephone:* 770-718-5327. *Fax:* 770-718-5329. *E-mail:* hgibbons@lib.brenau.edu.

DEGREES AND AWARDS

BA Public Administration (Criminal Justice)
BBA Management
BS Public Administration (Criminal Justice)
BSN Nursing–RN-BSN Bridge Degree
Graduate Certificate Conflict Resolution
MBA Accounting; Advanced Management Studies; Healthcare Management; Leadership Development
MEd Early Childhood Education; Middle Grades Education

COURSE SUBJECT AREAS OFFERED OUTSIDE OF DEGREE PROGRAMS

Undergraduate—accounting; business; business administration and management; business and personal services marketing operations; business communications; business information and data processing services; business management and administrative services, other; business/managerial economics; business quantitative methods and management science; communications, general; computer and information sciences, general; criminal justice and corrections; criminology; design and applied arts; economics; education, general; English language and literature, general; foreign languages and literatures; general teacher education; health and medical assistants; health and medical preparatory programs; health professions and related sciences, other; history; human resources management; information sciences and systems; international business; journalism and mass communications; legal studies; marketing management and research; mathematics; miscellaneous health professions; museology/museum studies; nursing; political science and government; psychology; public relations and organizational communications; visual and performing arts, other.

Graduate—accounting; business; business administration and management; business and personal services marketing operations; business communications; business information and data processing services; business management and administrative services, other; business/managerial economics; business quantitative methods and management science; computer and information sciences, general; economics; education administration and supervision; educational evaluation, research and statistics; educational psychology; education, general; education, other; financial management and services; health and medical administrative services; health and medical diagnostic and treatment services; health professions and related sciences, other; international business; marketing management and research; marketing operations/marketing and distribution, other; miscellaneous health professions; nursing; rehabilitation/therapeutic services; taxation.

See full description on page 362.

BREVARD COMMUNITY COLLEGE

Cocoa, Florida
Distance Learning
http://www.brevardcc.edu

Brevard Community College was founded in 1960. It is accredited by Southern Association of Colleges and Schools. It first offered distance learning courses in 1974. In fall 2003, there were 4,000 students enrolled in distance learning courses. Institutionally administered financial aid is available to distance learners.

Services Distance learners have accessibility to academic advising, bookstore, campus computer network, career placement assistance, e-mail services, library services, tutoring.

Contact Ms. Jennifer Blalock, Dean of Educational Services, Brevard Community College, 1519 Clearlake Road, Cocoa, FL 32922. *Telephone:* 321-433-7096. *Fax:* 321-433-7648. *E-mail:* robertsra@brevardcc.edu.

DEGREES AND AWARDS

AA General Studies
AAS Business
AS Business; Computer Information Systems–MIS option; Legal Studies

COURSE SUBJECT AREAS OFFERED OUTSIDE OF DEGREE PROGRAMS

Undergraduate—accounting; administrative and secretarial services; advertising; animal sciences; applied mathematics; astronomy; biological and physical sciences; biological sciences/life sciences, other; business; business administration and management; business and personal services marketing operations; business communications; business information and data processing services; business management and administrative services, other; business/managerial economics; chemistry; communications, general; communications, other; computer and information sciences, general; computer and information sciences, other; computer/information technology administration and management; computer programming; computer software and media applications; computer systems networking and telecommunications; criminology; cultural studies; developmental/child psychology; economics; educational/instructional media design; educational psychology; education, general; education, other; English creative writing; English language and literature, general; English technical and business writing; film/video and photographic arts; health and medical assistants; health professions and related sciences, other; history; information sciences and systems; international business; international relations and affairs; Internet and World Wide Web; journalism; legal studies; liberal arts and sciences, general studies and humanities; mathematics; mathematics and computer science; music; philosophy and religion; physical sciences, general; physical sciences, other; psychology; Romance languages and literatures; social psychology; social sciences and history, other; sociology; speech and rhetorical studies; taxation; visual and performing arts.

BRIDGEWATER STATE COLLEGE

Bridgewater, Massachusetts
Distance Learning and Technology Programs
http://www.bridgew.edu/distance

Bridgewater State College was founded in 1840. It is accredited by New England Association of Schools and Colleges. It first offered distance learning courses in 1996. In fall 2003, there were 550 students enrolled in distance learning courses. Institutionally administered financial aid is available to distance learners.

Services Distance learners have accessibility to bookstore, campus computer network, e-mail services, library services.

Contact Dr. Mary W. Fuller, Director of Distance Learning and Technology Programs, Bridgewater State College, John Joseph Moakley Center for Technological Applications, Burrill Avenue, Bridgewater, MA 02325. *Telephone:* 508-531-6145. *Fax:* 508-531-6121. *E-mail:* mfuller@bridgew.edu.

DEGREES AND AWARDS

Programs offered do not lead to a degree or other formal award.

COURSE SUBJECT AREAS OFFERED OUTSIDE OF DEGREE PROGRAMS

Undergraduate—anthropology; business communications; business/managerial economics; communication disorders sciences and services; communications, general; computer/information technology administration and management; criminology; cultural studies; curriculum and instruction; education administration and supervision; educational evaluation, research and statistics; education, general; English composition; English technical and business writing; entrepreneurship; geography; history; music; political science and government; psychology; sociology; special education.

Bridgewater State College (continued)

Graduate—communications, general; economics; education administration and supervision; foreign languages and literatures; psychology; special education.

Non-credit—accounting; administrative and secretarial services; business; business administration and management; business management and administrative services, other; business/managerial economics; communications, general; computer systems analysis; English creative writing; financial management and services; health and medical administrative services; health and medical assistants; information sciences and systems; tourism/travel marketing.

BRIERCREST DISTANCE LEARNING

Caronport, Saskatchewan, Canada

http://www.briercrest.ca/bdl/

Briercrest Distance Learning was founded in 1980. It is provincially chartered. It first offered distance learning courses in 1981. In fall 2003, there were 800 students enrolled in distance learning courses. Institutionally administered financial aid is available to distance learners.

Services Distance learners have accessibility to academic advising, bookstore, career placement assistance, library services, tutoring.

Contact Amy Kaiser, Enrollment Coordinator, Briercrest Distance Learning, 510 College Drive, Caronport, SK S0H 0S0, Canada. *Telephone:* 800-667-5199. *Fax:* 800-667-2329. *E-mail:* distance-info@briercrest.ca.

DEGREES AND AWARDS

AA Christian Studies
BA Christian Studies
Certificate Bible

COURSE SUBJECT AREAS OFFERED OUTSIDE OF DEGREE PROGRAMS

Undergraduate—bible/biblical studies; business administration and management; counseling psychology; English language and literature, general; history; missions/missionary studies and missiology; religion/religious studies; religious education; teaching English as a second language/foreign language; theological and ministerial studies; theological studies and religious vocations, other.

Graduate—bible/biblical studies; biblical and other theological languages and literatures; history; religion/religious studies; religious education; theological and ministerial studies; theological studies and religious vocations, other.

Non-credit—bible/biblical studies; history; religion/religious studies.

BRIGHAM YOUNG UNIVERSITY

Provo, Utah

Independent Study

http://elearn.byu.edu

Brigham Young University was founded in 1875. It is accredited by Northwest Commission on Colleges and Universities. It first offered distance learning courses in 1961. Institutionally administered financial aid is available to distance learners.

Services Distance learners have accessibility to academic advising, bookstore, e-mail services, library services.

Contact Sarah Gay, Registrar, Brigham Young University, 206 Harman Building, PO Box 21514, Provo, UT 84602-1514. *Telephone:* 800-914-8931. *Fax:* 801-422-0102. *E-mail:* indstudy@byu.edu.

DEGREES AND AWARDS

Programs offered do not lead to a degree or other formal award.

COURSE SUBJECT AREAS OFFERED OUTSIDE OF DEGREE PROGRAMS

Undergraduate—accounting; American history; American literature (United States); anthropology; archaeology; art history; astronomy; biological sciences/life sciences, other; biology; biology, general; botany; business administration and management; business communications; business management and administrative services, other; business marketing and marketing management; chemical engineering; chemistry; civil engineering; communication disorders sciences and services; communications, general; curriculum and instruction; dance; developmental/child psychology; economics; education administration and supervision; educational psychology; education, general; education, other; English composition; European history; film studies; food sciences and technology; geography; geological and related sciences; Germanic languages and literatures; health and physical education/fitness; Hebrew; history; information sciences and systems; liberal arts and sciences, general studies and humanities; mathematical statistics; mathematics related; microbiology/bacteriology; music; nursing; organizational behavior; philosophy; philosophy and religion related; physical sciences, general; physics; political science and government; psychology; religion/religious studies; religious education; social work; sociology; Spanish; special education; speech and rhetorical studies; technology education/industrial arts; theater arts/drama; visual and performing arts; zoology.

Non-credit—computer and information sciences, general; computer software and media applications; English creative writing; English language and literature/letters, other; family and community studies; history; religion/religious studies.

BRISTOL COMMUNITY COLLEGE

Fall River, Massachusetts

Distance Learning

http://dl.mass.edu

Bristol Community College was founded in 1965. It is accredited by New England Association of Schools and Colleges. It first offered distance learning courses in 1990. In fall 2003, there were 439 students enrolled in distance learning courses. Institutionally administered financial aid is available to distance learners.

Services Distance learners have accessibility to bookstore, campus computer network, e-mail services, library services.

Contact Candy M. Center, Director of Distance Learning, Bristol Community College, 777 Elsbree Street, Fall River, MA 02720. *Telephone:* 508-678-2811 Ext. 2304. *Fax:* 508-730-3270. *E-mail:* ccenter@bristol.mass.edu.

DEGREES AND AWARDS

AS Computer Information Systems/Computer Programming; Computer Information Systems/Multimedia and Internet

Certificate Basic Web Page Development; Computer Programming; Desktop Publishing Technology; Information Technology Fluency; Multimedia Communications

COURSE SUBJECT AREAS OFFERED OUTSIDE OF DEGREE PROGRAMS

Undergraduate—accounting; anthropology; business; business information and data processing services; computer and information sciences, general; computer and information sciences, other; computer/information technology administration and management; computer programming; computer science; computer software and media applications; computer systems analysis; computer systems networking and telecommunications; data entry/microcomputer applications; data processing technology; English composition; English literature (British and Commonwealth); English technical and business writing; environmental science; European history; geography; history; information sciences and systems; mathematical statistics; mathematics; mathematics, other; mathematics related; psychology; psychology, other; social sciences and history, other; sociology.

Non-credit—accounting; administrative and secretarial services; business; business administration and management; business and personal services marketing operations; business communications; business information and data processing services; business management and administrative services, other; business quantitative methods and management science; communications, general; communications, other; computer and information sciences, general; computer and information sciences, other; computer engineering; computer/information technology administration and management; computer programming; computer science; computer software and media applications; computer systems analysis; computer systems networking and telecommunications; data entry/microcomputer applications; data processing technology; electrical and electronic engineering-related technology; electrical and electronics equipment installers and repairers; electrical and power transmission installers; electrical, electronics and communications engineering; electromechanical instrumentation and maintenance technology; engineering/industrial management; engineering-related technologies, other; human resources management; information sciences and systems; Internet and World Wide Web; legal studies; marketing management and research; marketing operations/marketing and distribution, other; mathematics; mechanical engineering-related technologies; mechanics and repairers, other; miscellaneous engineering-related technologies; precision production trades, other; systems engineering; technology education/industrial arts; telecommunications; vehicle and mobile equipment mechanics and repairers; vehicle/equipment operation.

BROCK UNIVERSITY

St. Catharines, Ontario, Canada
Centre for Adult Studies and Distance Learning, Faculty of Education
http://adult.ed.brocku.ca

Brock University was founded in 1964. It is provincially chartered. It first offered distance learning courses in 1994. In fall 2003, there were 500 students enrolled in distance learning courses. Institutionally administered financial aid is available to distance learners.

Services Distance learners have accessibility to academic advising, bookstore, campus computer network, career placement assistance, e-mail services, library services, tutoring.

Contact Sandra Plavinskis, Coordinator of B.Ed. in Adult Education Degree and Certificate Programs, Brock University, Centre for Adult Studies and Distance Learning, Faculty of Education, St. Catharines, ON L2S 3A1, Canada. *Telephone:* 905-688-5550 Ext. 4308. *Fax:* 905-984-4842. *E-mail:* sandra@ed.brocku.ca.

DEGREES AND AWARDS

BEd Adult Education
Certificate Adult Education

COURSE SUBJECT AREAS OFFERED OUTSIDE OF DEGREE PROGRAMS

Undergraduate—education, general; education, other.

BROOKDALE COMMUNITY COLLEGE

Lincroft, New Jersey
Telecourse Program–Division of Arts and Communication
http://www.brookdalecc.edu

Brookdale Community College was founded in 1967. It is accredited by Middle States Association of Colleges and Schools. It first offered distance learning courses in 1974. In fall 2003, there were 1,000 students enrolled in distance learning courses. Institutionally administered financial aid is available to distance learners.

Services Distance learners have accessibility to bookstore, campus computer network, e-mail services, library services, tutoring.

Contact Norah Kerr-McCurry, Manager, Brookdale Community College, Distance Education Applications, 765 Newman Springs Road, Lincroft, NJ 07738. *Telephone:* 732-224-2628. *Fax:* 732-224-2001. *E-mail:* nmccurry@brookdalecc.edu.

DEGREES AND AWARDS

AA Business Administration; Liberal Arts; Social Sciences

COURSE SUBJECT AREAS OFFERED OUTSIDE OF DEGREE PROGRAMS

Undergraduate—accounting; American literature (United States); anthropology; biology; business administration and management; business marketing and marketing management; chemistry; creative writing; developmental/child psychology; English composition; English language and literature, general; mathematics; philosophy and religion related; social psychology; social sciences and history, other; sociology; theater arts/drama.

BROOME COMMUNITY COLLEGE

Binghamton, New York
http://www.sunybroome.edu/

Broome Community College was founded in 1946. It is accredited by Middle States Association of Colleges and Schools. It first offered distance learning courses in 1998. In fall 2003, there were 785 students enrolled in distance learning courses. Institutionally administered financial aid is available to distance learners.

Services Distance learners have accessibility to academic advising, bookstore, campus computer network, career placement assistance, e-mail services, library services, tutoring.

Contact Martin J. Guzzi, Assistant Registrar, Broome Community College, PO Box 1017, Binghamton, NY 13902. *Telephone:* 607-778-5527. *Fax:* 607-778-5294. *E-mail:* guzzi_m@sunybroome.edu.

DEGREES AND AWARDS

Programs offered do not lead to a degree or other formal award.

Broome Community College (continued)

COURSE SUBJECT AREAS OFFERED OUTSIDE OF DEGREE PROGRAMS

Undergraduate—accounting; astronomy; business; chemistry; computer/information technology administration and management; computer science; English composition; geological and related sciences; health and medical administrative services; history; human services; international business; Internet and World Wide Web; marketing operations/marketing and distribution, other; mathematical statistics; mathematics; pharmacy; physical sciences, general; physics; political science and government; psychology; social work.

Non-credit—accounting; business administration and management; computer and information sciences, general; computer programming; computer software and media applications; data entry/microcomputer applications.

BROWARD COMMUNITY COLLEGE

Fort Lauderdale, Florida
Instructional Technology
http://www.broward.edu

Broward Community College was founded in 1960. It is accredited by Southern Association of Colleges and Schools. It first offered distance learning courses in 1978. In fall 2003, there were 6,500 students enrolled in distance learning courses. Institutionally administered financial aid is available to distance learners.

Services Distance learners have accessibility to academic advising, bookstore, e-mail services, library services.

Contact Gladys Dubon, Flexible Learning Specialist, Broward Community College, 3501 Southwest Davie Road, Davie, FL 33314. *Telephone:* 954-201-6564. *Fax:* 954-201-6398. *E-mail:* gdubon@broward.edu.

DEGREES AND AWARDS

Programs offered do not lead to a degree or other formal award.

COURSE SUBJECT AREAS OFFERED OUTSIDE OF DEGREE PROGRAMS

Undergraduate—accounting; American history; anthropology; biology; business; business marketing and marketing management; computer science; developmental/child psychology; economics; education, other; English composition; entrepreneurship; European history; geography; geological and related sciences; health and physical education/fitness; law and legal studies related; mathematical statistics; mathematics related; nursing; philosophy; philosophy and religion related; psychology; sociology; Spanish.

BRUNSWICK COMMUNITY COLLEGE

Supply, North Carolina
http://www.brunswick.cc.nc.us/

Brunswick Community College was founded in 1979. It is accredited by Southern Association of Colleges and Schools. It first offered distance learning courses in 1999. In fall 2003, there were 350 students enrolled in distance learning courses. Institutionally administered financial aid is available to distance learners.

Services Distance learners have accessibility to academic advising, bookstore, career placement assistance, library services, tutoring.

Contact Ann Harrison, Distance Learning Coordinator, Brunswick Community College, PO Box 30, Supply, NC 28462. *Telephone:* 910-755-7303. *Fax:* 910-754-6995. *E-mail:* harrisona@mail.brunswick.cc.nc.us.

DEGREES AND AWARDS

Programs offered do not lead to a degree or other formal award.

COURSE SUBJECT AREAS OFFERED OUTSIDE OF DEGREE PROGRAMS

Undergraduate—administrative and secretarial services; agricultural business and production, other; business administration and management; chemistry; child care and guidance workers and managers; computer software and media applications; criminal justice and corrections; economics; health professions and related sciences, other; philosophy and religion; psychology.

BRYANT AND STRATTON ONLINE

Lackawanna, New York
http://www.bryantstratton.edu

Bryant and Stratton Online is accredited by Middle States Association of Colleges and Schools. It first offered distance learning courses in 1997. In fall 2003, there were 231 students enrolled in distance learning courses. Institutionally administered financial aid is available to distance learners.

Services Distance learners have accessibility to academic advising, bookstore, e-mail services, library services, tutoring.

Contact Admissions, Bryant and Stratton Online, 1234 Abbott Road, Rear Building, Lackawanna, NY 14218. *Telephone:* 716-821-5556 Ext. 241. *Fax:* 716-821-5518. *E-mail:* online@bryantstratton.edu.

DEGREES AND AWARDS

AD Business Online; Information Technology Online

COURSE SUBJECT AREAS OFFERED OUTSIDE OF DEGREE PROGRAMS

Undergraduate—accounting; business; business administration and management; business communications; computer/information technology administration and management; computer programming; computer software and media applications; computer systems networking and telecommunications; Internet and World Wide Web.

BUCKS COUNTY COMMUNITY COLLEGE

Newtown, Pennsylvania
Distance Learning Office
http://www.bucks.edu/distance

Bucks County Community College was founded in 1964. It is accredited by Middle States Association of Colleges and Schools. It first offered distance learning courses in 1994. In fall 2003, there were 1,800 students enrolled in distance learning courses. Institutionally administered financial aid is available to distance learners.

Services Distance learners have accessibility to academic advising, bookstore, campus computer network, career placement assistance, e-mail services, library services, tutoring.
Contact Ms. Georglyn Davidson, Director of Distance Learning, Bucks County Community College, 275 Swamp Road, Newtown, PA 18940. *Telephone:* 215-968-8052. *Fax:* 215-968-8148. *E-mail:* learning@bucks.edu.

DEGREES AND AWARDS

AA Business Administration; Liberal Arts; Management; Marketing; Science
Certificate Entrepreneurship; Management; Microsoft Office; Retailing; Supervision; Web Designer

COURSE SUBJECT AREAS OFFERED OUTSIDE OF DEGREE PROGRAMS

Undergraduate—accounting; American history; art history; astronomy; biological sciences/life sciences, other; biology; biology, general; business; business administration and management; business communications; business information and data processing services; business management and administrative services, other; business marketing and marketing management; communications, general; computer and information sciences, general; computer programming; computer software and media applications; criminal justice and corrections; criminology; developmental and child psychology; developmental/child psychology; education, general; English composition; English creative writing; English language and literature, general; English technical and business writing; European history; fire protection; general teacher education; health and medical administrative services; health and physical education/fitness; historic preservation, conservation and architectural history; history; journalism and mass communications; law and legal studies related; legal studies; liberal arts and sciences, general studies and humanities; mathematical statistics; mathematics; music; nursing; philosophy; philosophy and religion; philosophy and religion related; physical sciences, general; psychology; real estate; social psychology; social sciences and history, other; social sciences, general; sociology; Spanish; taxation; teacher education, specific academic and vocational programs; women's studies.
Non-credit—fire protection.

BUENA VISTA UNIVERSITY

Storm Lake, Iowa
Centers
http://centers.bvu.edu

Buena Vista University was founded in 1891. It is accredited by North Central Association of Colleges and Schools. It first offered distance learning courses in 1975. In fall 2003, there were 1,371 students enrolled in distance learning courses. Institutionally administered financial aid is available to distance learners.

Services Distance learners have accessibility to academic advising, bookstore, campus computer network, career placement assistance, e-mail services, library services.
Contact Dr. Janet K. Stremel, Dean of Centers, Buena Vista University, 610 West 4th Street, Storm Lake, IA 50588. *Telephone:* 712-749-2250. *Fax:* 712-749-1470. *E-mail:* centers@bvu.edu.

DEGREES AND AWARDS

BA Business; Elementary Education; English; History; Information Management; Political Science–Criminal Justice; Social Sciences
Certification Middle School Education; Secondary Education; Special Education–Instructional Specialist I
MSE Educational Administration and Leadership; School Guidance and Counseling

COURSE SUBJECT AREAS OFFERED OUTSIDE OF DEGREE PROGRAMS

Undergraduate—education, other; special education.
Graduate—education, other.

BUFFALO STATE COLLEGE, STATE UNIVERSITY OF NEW YORK

Buffalo, New York
http://www.buffalostate.edu/offices/elearning

Buffalo State College, State University of New York was founded in 1867. It is accredited by Middle States Association of Colleges and Schools. It first offered distance learning courses in 1998. In fall 2003, there were 224 students enrolled in distance learning courses. Institutionally administered financial aid is available to distance learners.

Services Distance learners have accessibility to bookstore, campus computer network, e-mail services, library services.
Contact Melaine Kenyon, Electronic Learning Specialist, Buffalo State College, State University of New York, 1300 Elmwood Avenue, Buffalo, NY 14222. *Telephone:* 716-878-6829. *Fax:* 716-878-3417. *E-mail:* elearning@buffalostate.edu.

DEGREES AND AWARDS

CAGS Adult Education; Creativity, Change Leadership, and Creative Problem Solving; Human Resource Development
MS Adult Education; Creative Studies

BURLINGTON COUNTY COLLEGE

Pemberton, New Jersey
Distance Learning Office
http://www.bcc.edu/

Burlington County College was founded in 1966. It is accredited by Middle States Association of Colleges and Schools. It first offered distance learning courses in 1978. In fall 2003, there were 1,383 students enrolled in distance learning courses. Institutionally administered financial aid is available to distance learners.

Services Distance learners have accessibility to bookstore, library services.
Contact Sue Espenshade, Coordinator of Distance Learning, Burlington County College, 601 Pemberton-Browns Mills Road, Pemberton, NJ 08068. *Telephone:* 609-894-9311 Ext. 7790. *Fax:* 609-894-4189. *E-mail:* sespensh@bcc.edu.

DEGREES AND AWARDS

AA Liberal Arts and Sciences
AS Business Management

COURSE SUBJECT AREAS OFFERED OUTSIDE OF DEGREE PROGRAMS

Undergraduate—American history; anthropology; art history; biology; business marketing and marketing management; developmental/

Burlington County College (continued)

child psychology; ecology; English composition; European history; film studies; French; mathematical statistics; sociology; Spanish.

BUTLER COUNTY COMMUNITY COLLEGE

El Dorado, Kansas

http://www.butlercc.edu/

Butler County Community College was founded in 1927. It is accredited by North Central Association of Colleges and Schools. It first offered distance learning courses in 1998. In fall 2003, there were 836 students enrolled in distance learning courses. Institutionally administered financial aid is available to distance learners.

Services Distance learners have accessibility to academic advising, bookstore, e-mail services, library services.

Contact Ms. Kaye Meyer, Director, Instructional Technology, Butler County Community College, 901 South Haverhill, El Dorado, KS 67042. *Telephone:* 316-322-3345. *Fax:* 316-322-3315. *E-mail:* km-eyer@butlercc.edu.

DEGREES AND AWARDS

Programs offered do not lead to a degree or other formal award.

COURSE SUBJECT AREAS OFFERED OUTSIDE OF DEGREE PROGRAMS

Undergraduate—accounting; applied mathematics; astronomy; business management and administrative services, other; chemistry; computer programming; criminal justice and corrections; criminology; data entry/microcomputer applications; drafting; economics; English composition; family and community studies; fine arts and art studies; gerontology; health and physical education/fitness; history; human resources management; mathematics; music; nursing; philosophy; physical sciences, general; physics; psychology; social sciences, general; sociology; speech and rhetorical studies.

BUTLER COUNTY COMMUNITY COLLEGE

Butler, Pennsylvania

http://www.bc3.edu/distlearn

Butler County Community College was founded in 1965. It is accredited by Middle States Association of Colleges and Schools. It first offered distance learning courses in 1998. In fall 2003, there were 600 students enrolled in distance learning courses. Institutionally administered financial aid is available to distance learners.

Services Distance learners have accessibility to academic advising, bookstore, career placement assistance, library services, tutoring.

Contact Deborah Ayers, Director of Distance Education, Butler County Community College, PO Box 1203, Butler, PA 16003. *Telephone:* 888-826-2829 Ext. 279. *E-mail:* deborah.ayers@bc3.edu.

DEGREES AND AWARDS

AA General Studies

COURSE SUBJECT AREAS OFFERED OUTSIDE OF DEGREE PROGRAMS

Undergraduate—accounting; applied mathematics; biology, general; business administration and management; chemistry; communications, general; computer science; criminology; data entry/microcomputer applications; economics; educational psychology; education, general; English composition; English creative writing; English technical and business writing; financial management and services; fire protection; foods and nutrition studies; health and medical assistants; health and physical education/fitness; history; marketing management and research; mathematics; music; philosophy; philosophy and religion; political science and government; psychology; sociology.

CALDWELL COLLEGE

Caldwell, New Jersey

Center for Continuing Education

http://www.caldwell.edu/adult-admissions/index.html

Caldwell College was founded in 1939. It is accredited by Middle States Association of Colleges and Schools. It first offered distance learning courses in 1979. In fall 2003, there were 800 students enrolled in distance learning courses. Institutionally administered financial aid is available to distance learners.

Services Distance learners have accessibility to academic advising, bookstore, campus computer network, career placement assistance, e-mail services, library services, tutoring.

Contact Mr. Jack Albalah, Director, Adult Undergraduate Admissions, Caldwell College, 9 Ryerson Avenue, Caldwell, NJ 07006. *Telephone:* 973-618-3285. *Fax:* 973-618-3660. *E-mail:* jalbalah@caldwell.edu.

DEGREES AND AWARDS

BA Communication Arts; Criminal Justice; English; Foreign Language; History; Multidisciplinary Studies/ Social Science/ Fire Science; Multidisciplinary Studies/Humanities; Multidisciplinary Studies/Social Sciences; Political Science; Psychology; Sociology; Theology
BS Accounting; Business; Computer Information Systems; International Business; Management; Marketing

COURSE SUBJECT AREAS OFFERED OUTSIDE OF DEGREE PROGRAMS

Undergraduate—accounting; biology, general; business administration and management; chemistry; communications, other; computer and information sciences, other; criminal justice and corrections; economics; education, general; fine arts and art studies; general teacher education; information sciences and systems; mathematics and computer science; music; political science and government; psychology; religion/religious studies; sociology.

See full description on page 364.

CALDWELL COMMUNITY COLLEGE AND TECHNICAL INSTITUTE

Hudson, North Carolina

http://www.cccti.edu

Caldwell Community College and Technical Institute was founded in 1964. It is accredited by Southern Association of Colleges and

Schools. It first offered distance learning courses in 1989. In fall 2003, there were 850 students enrolled in distance learning courses. Institutionally administered financial aid is available to distance learners.

Services Distance learners have accessibility to academic advising, bookstore, career placement assistance, library services, tutoring.

Contact Nancy M. Risch, Director, Distance Learning, Caldwell Community College and Technical Institute, 2855 Hickory Boulevard, Hudson, NC 28638-2397. *Telephone:* 828-726-2236. *Fax:* 828-726-2489. *E-mail:* nancyr@cccti.edu.

DEGREES AND AWARDS

AA College Transfer
AAS Emergency Preparedness Technology

COURSE SUBJECT AREAS OFFERED OUTSIDE OF DEGREE PROGRAMS

Undergraduate—accounting; administrative and secretarial services; biological and physical sciences; biological sciences/life sciences, other; biology, general; business; business administration and management; business communications; child care and guidance workers and managers; communications, general; computer and information sciences, general; educational psychology; English composition; English language and literature, general; English technical and business writing; fine arts and art studies; fire protection; history; liberal arts and sciences, general studies and humanities; marketing management and research; mathematics; music; physical sciences, general; psychology; social sciences, general; sociology.
Non-credit—accounting; administrative and secretarial services; business administration and management; business and personal services marketing operations; business communications; business/managerial economics; computer and information sciences, other; computer/information technology administration and management; computer software and media applications; criminal justice and corrections; English creative writing; English technical and business writing; financial management and services; foreign languages and literatures; health and medical preparatory programs; peace and conflict studies.

CALIFORNIA INSTITUTE OF INTEGRAL STUDIES

San Francisco, California
Transformative Learning and Change
http://www.ciis.edu

California Institute of Integral Studies was founded in 1968. It is accredited by Western Association of Schools and Colleges. It first offered distance learning courses in 1993. In fall 2003, there were 117 students enrolled in distance learning courses. Institutionally administered financial aid is available to distance learners.

Services Distance learners have accessibility to academic advising, bookstore, campus computer network, e-mail services, library services, tutoring.

Contact Ms. Allyson Werner, Admissions Counselor for School of Consciousness and Transformation, California Institute of Integral Studies, 1453 Mission Street, San Francisco, CA 94103. *Telephone:* 415-575-6155. *Fax:* 415-575-1268. *E-mail:* awerner@ciis.edu.

DEGREES AND AWARDS

MA Transformative Leadership
PhD Humanities–Transformative Learning and Change

COURSE SUBJECT AREAS OFFERED OUTSIDE OF DEGREE PROGRAMS

Graduate—adult/continuing education; anthropology; Asian studies; ecology; health professions and related sciences, other; organizational behavior; philosophy and religion; social psychology; sociology; women's studies.
Non-credit—adult/continuing education; anthropology; Asian studies; ecology; organizational behavior; philosophy and religion; social psychology; sociology; women's studies.

See full description on page 366.

CALIFORNIA NATIONAL UNIVERSITY FOR ADVANCED STUDIES

Northridge, California
http://www.cnuas.edu/

California National University for Advanced Studies was founded in 1993. It is accredited by Distance Education and Training Council. It first offered distance learning courses in 1993. In fall 2003, there were 450 students enrolled in distance learning courses. Institutionally administered financial aid is available to distance learners.

Services Distance learners have accessibility to academic advising, bookstore, campus computer network, e-mail services, library services.

Contact Dr. Lolly Horn, CEO and Vice President for Academic Affairs, California National University for Advanced Studies, 8550 Balboa Boulevard, Suite 210, Northridge, CA 91325. *Telephone:* 800-782-2422. *Fax:* 818-830-2418. *E-mail:* lhorn@mail.cnuas.edu.

DEGREES AND AWARDS

BS Business Administration; Computer Science; Engineering; Quality Assurance Science
Certificate Human Resource Management Practice
MBA Business Administration
MHRM Human Resources
MS Engineering

COURSE SUBJECT AREAS OFFERED OUTSIDE OF DEGREE PROGRAMS

Undergraduate—accounting; business administration and management; business communications; business/managerial economics; business marketing and marketing management; computer and information sciences, general; economics; electrical engineering; engineering, general; environmental engineering; finance; human resources management; international business; management information systems/business data processing; mechanical engineering; organizational behavior; quality control and safety technologies.
Graduate—accounting; business administration and management; business marketing and marketing management; computer and information sciences, general; computer engineering; electrical engineering; engineering, general; environmental engineering; human resources management; management information systems/business data processing; mechanical engineering; organizational behavior.
Non-credit—accounting; applied mathematics; business administration and management; business communications; business management and administrative services, other; business/managerial economics; business quantitative methods and management science; computer and information sciences, general; computer engineering;

California National University for Advanced Studies (continued)

computer programming; computer science; computer systems networking and telecommunications; electrical and electronic engineering-related technology; engineering, general; engineering, other; engineering physics; English creative writing; human resources management; international business; marketing operations/marketing and distribution, other; mechanical engineering; quality control and safety technologies; systems engineering.

CALIFORNIA STATE UNIVERSITY, CHICO

Chico, California
Center for Regional and Continuing Education
http://rce.csuchico.edu/online

California State University, Chico was founded in 1887. It is accredited by Western Association of Schools and Colleges. It first offered distance learning courses in 1975. In fall 2003, there were 800 students enrolled in distance learning courses. Institutionally administered financial aid is available to distance learners.

Services Distance learners have accessibility to academic advising, bookstore, campus computer network, career placement assistance, e-mail services, library services.

Contact Mr. Jeffrey S. Layne, Program Director, California State University, Chico, Chico, CA 95929-0250. *Telephone:* 530-898-6105. *Fax:* 530-898-4020. *E-mail:* jlayne@csuchico.edu.

DEGREES AND AWARDS

BA Jewish Studies; Liberal Studies; Social Sciences
BS Computer Science
BSN Nursing
MS Computer Science

COURSE SUBJECT AREAS OFFERED OUTSIDE OF DEGREE PROGRAMS

Undergraduate—accounting; anthropology; area, ethnic and cultural studies, other; community health services; curriculum and instruction; dance; education, general; family and community studies; health and medical administrative services; history; Judaic studies; liberal arts and sciences, general studies and humanities; music; nursing; psychology; social sciences, general; sociology.
Graduate—computer science.

CALIFORNIA STATE UNIVERSITY, DOMINGUEZ HILLS

Carson, California
Distance Learning
http://dominguezonline.csudh.edu

California State University, Dominguez Hills was founded in 1960. It is accredited by Western Association of Schools and Colleges. It first offered distance learning courses in 1974. In fall 2003, there were 4,000 students enrolled in distance learning courses. Institutionally administered financial aid is available to distance learners.

Services Distance learners have accessibility to academic advising, bookstore, e-mail services, library services, tutoring.

Contact Registration Office, California State University, Dominguez Hills, Division of Extended Education, 1000 East Victoria Street, Carson, CA 90747. *Telephone:* 877-GO-HILLS. *Fax:* 310-516-3971. *E-mail:* eereg@csudh.edu.

DEGREES AND AWARDS

BS Nursing Completion Program; Quality Assurance
Certificate of Completion Quality Assurance
Certificate Assistive Technology; Community College Teaching; Production and Inventory Control; Purchasing
MA Humanities; Negotiation and Conflict Management
MS Nursing; Quality Assurance

COURSE SUBJECT AREAS OFFERED OUTSIDE OF DEGREE PROGRAMS

Undergraduate—education administration and supervision; education, general; education, other; nursing; quality control and safety technologies.
Graduate—business; liberal arts and sciences, general studies and humanities; nursing; peace and conflict studies; public administration; quality control and safety technologies.
Non-credit—accounting; business and personal services marketing operations; business communications; business management and administrative services, other; computer and information sciences, general; computer/information technology administration and management; education, general; financial management and services; health and medical administrative services; human resources management; legal studies; marketing operations/marketing and distribution, other; music.

See full description on page 368.

CALIFORNIA STATE UNIVERSITY, DOMINGUEZ HILLS

Carson, California
Program in Nursing
http://www.csudh.edu/soh/don/index.htm

California State University, Dominguez Hills was founded in 1960. It is accredited by Western Association of Schools and Colleges. It first offered distance learning courses in 1981. In fall 2003, there were 1,310 students enrolled in distance learning courses. Institutionally administered financial aid is available to distance learners.

Services Distance learners have accessibility to academic advising, bookstore, campus computer network, e-mail services, library services.

Contact Tonie Mills, Coordinator, HHS Student Services Center, California State University, Dominguez Hills, Student Services Center, College of Health and Human Services, 1000 East Victoria Street, Carson, CA 90747. *Telephone:* 800-344-5484. *Fax:* 310-217-6800. *E-mail:* tomills@csudh.edu.

DEGREES AND AWARDS

BSN Nursing
Graduate Certificate Post-master's Family Nurse Practitioner; Public Health Nurse; Quality Improvement for Nursing
MSN Nursing

COURSE SUBJECT AREAS OFFERED OUTSIDE OF DEGREE PROGRAMS

Undergraduate—nursing.
Graduate—nursing.

CALIFORNIA STATE UNIVERSITY, FULLERTON

Fullerton, California
Distributed/Distance Learning Program
http://distance-ed.fullerton.edu/

California State University, Fullerton was founded in 1957. It is accredited by Western Association of Schools and Colleges. It first offered distance learning courses in 1978. In fall 2003, there were 1,500 students enrolled in distance learning courses. Institutionally administered financial aid is available to distance learners.

Services Distance learners have accessibility to academic advising, bookstore, campus computer network, career placement assistance, e-mail services, library services, tutoring.
Contact Distance Education, California State University, Fullerton, Department of Distance Education—PLS45, 800 North State College Boulevard, Fullerton, CA 92834. *Telephone:* 714-278-4752. *Fax:* 714-278-4619. *E-mail:* distance-ed@fullerton.edu.

DEGREES AND AWARDS

BSN Nursing
MS Instructional Design and Technology; Software Engineering
MSEE Electrical Engineering

COURSE SUBJECT AREAS OFFERED OUTSIDE OF DEGREE PROGRAMS

Undergraduate—business; communications, general; computer programming; education, general; sociology.
Graduate—accounting; advertising; educational/instructional media design; electrical engineering.
Non-credit—bilingual/bicultural education; business; communications technologies; computer programming; computer software and media applications; computer systems networking and telecommunications; criminology; curriculum and instruction; education, general; education, other; English creative writing; teacher education, specific academic and vocational programs.

CALIFORNIA STATE UNIVERSITY, HAYWARD

Hayward, California
Division of Extended and Continuing Education
http://www.online.csuhayward.edu

California State University, Hayward was founded in 1957. It is accredited by Western Association of Schools and Colleges. It first offered distance learning courses in 1998. In fall 2003, there were 200 students enrolled in distance learning courses. Institutionally administered financial aid is available to distance learners.

Services Distance learners have accessibility to academic advising, bookstore, campus computer network, e-mail services, library services.

Contact Nan Chico, Director of Online Programs, California State University, Hayward, Hayward, CA 94542. *Telephone:* 510-885-4384. *Fax:* 510-885-4498. *E-mail:* nchico@csuhayward.edu.

DEGREES AND AWARDS

Certificate Education
MSE Education

COURSE SUBJECT AREAS OFFERED OUTSIDE OF DEGREE PROGRAMS

Undergraduate—computer software and media applications; fine arts and art studies; hospitality/recreation marketing.
Graduate—education, other.
Non-credit—professional studies.

CALIFORNIA STATE UNIVERSITY, MONTEREY BAY

Seaside, California
http://csumb.edu/online

California State University, Monterey Bay was founded in 1994. It is accredited by Western Association of Schools and Colleges. It first offered distance learning courses in 2000. In fall 2003, there were 625 students enrolled in distance learning courses. Institutionally administered financial aid is available to distance learners.

Services Distance learners have accessibility to academic advising, bookstore, campus computer network, e-mail services, library services, tutoring.
Contact Lina Richburg, Distributed Learning Support, California State University, Monterey Bay, Distributed Learning and Extended Education, Seaside, CA 93955. *Telephone:* 831-582-4500. *Fax:* 831-582-4502. *E-mail:* extended@csumb.edu.

DEGREES AND AWARDS

BA Liberal Studies Degree Completion

COURSE SUBJECT AREAS OFFERED OUTSIDE OF DEGREE PROGRAMS

Undergraduate—business administration and management; computer and information sciences, general; computer software and media applications; cultural studies; educational/instructional media design; education, general; entrepreneurship; foreign languages and literatures; gaming/sports officiating; geological and related sciences; international business; Internet and World Wide Web; marketing management and research; marketing operations/marketing and distribution, other; social and philosophical foundations of education; special education.
Non-credit—computer and information sciences, other; legal studies.

CALIFORNIA STATE UNIVERSITY, NORTHRIDGE

Northridge, California
Educational Technologies and Distance Learning
http://www.csun.edu/exl/distance.htm

California State University, Northridge was founded in 1958. It is accredited by Western Association of Schools and Colleges. It first offered distance learning courses in 1982. In fall 2003, there were 170

California State University, Northridge (continued)
students enrolled in distance learning courses. Institutionally administered financial aid is available to distance learners.

Services Distance learners have accessibility to academic advising, bookstore, campus computer network, career placement assistance, e-mail services, library services.

Contact Barbra L. Frye, Senior Program Coordinator, Distance Learning Systems Group, California State University, Northridge, College of Extended Learning, 18111 Nordhoff Street, Mail Code 8401, Northridge, CA 91330-8401. *Telephone:* 818-677-6404. *Fax:* 818-677-6408. *E-mail:* barb.frye@csun.edu.

DEGREES AND AWARDS

MS Speech Pathology
MSE Engineering Management
MST Communication Disorders and Sciences

COURSE SUBJECT AREAS OFFERED OUTSIDE OF DEGREE PROGRAMS

Non-credit—communication disorders sciences and services.

CALIFORNIA STATE UNIVERSITY, SACRAMENTO

Sacramento, California
Distance and Distributed Education
http://www.csus.edu/distance

California State University, Sacramento was founded in 1947. It is accredited by Western Association of Schools and Colleges. It first offered distance learning courses in 1986. In fall 2003, there were 3,200 students enrolled in distance learning courses. Institutionally administered financial aid is available to distance learners.

Services Distance learners have accessibility to academic advising, bookstore, campus computer network, e-mail services, library services, tutoring.

Contact Dr. Rose Leigh Vines, Director of Distance and Distributed Education, California State University, Sacramento, 6000 J Street, Sacramento, CA 95819. *Telephone:* 916-278-7948. *Fax:* 916-278-5644.

DEGREES AND AWARDS

Programs offered do not lead to a degree or other formal award.

COURSE SUBJECT AREAS OFFERED OUTSIDE OF DEGREE PROGRAMS

Undergraduate—accounting; anthropology; business communications; business management and administrative services, other; computer and information sciences, general; criminal justice and corrections; economics; electrical engineering; family and community studies; foods and nutrition studies; French; geological and related sciences; gerontology; health and physical education/fitness; history; Internet and World Wide Web; journalism and mass communications; management information systems/business data processing; marketing operations/marketing and distribution, other; mathematical statistics; mathematics; medical laboratory technology; medieval and Renaissance studies; music; nursing; psychology; real estate; sociology; special education.

Graduate—business management and administrative services, other; educational evaluation, research and statistics; educational/instructional media design; electrical, electronics and communications engineering; nursing; public policy analysis.

CALIFORNIA UNIVERSITY OF PENNSYLVANIA

California, Pennsylvania
http://www.cup.edu/graduate

California University of Pennsylvania was founded in 1852. It is accredited by Middle States Association of Colleges and Schools. It first offered distance learning courses in 2004. In fall 2003, there were 70 students enrolled in distance learning courses. Institutionally administered financial aid is available to distance learners.

Services Distance learners have accessibility to academic advising, bookstore, campus computer network, career placement assistance, e-mail services, library services.

Contact Ms. Suzanne Czilzer Powers, Director of Graduate Admissions and Recruitment, California University of Pennsylvania, School of Graduate Studies and Research, 250 University Avenue, California, PA 15419. *Telephone:* 724-938-4187. *Fax:* 724-938-5712. *E-mail:* powers_s@cup.edu.

DEGREES AND AWARDS

MEd Administrative Principal Program
MS Exercise Science and Health Promotion–Performance Enhancement and Injury Prevention; Legal Studies–Law and Public Policy

COURSE SUBJECT AREAS OFFERED OUTSIDE OF DEGREE PROGRAMS

Graduate—criminal justice and corrections; education administration and supervision; health and physical education/fitness; health professions and related sciences, other; legal studies; public administration.

CALVIN THEOLOGICAL SEMINARY

Grand Rapids, Michigan
http://www.calvinseminary.edu

Calvin Theological Seminary was founded in 1876. It first offered distance learning courses in 2001. In fall 2003, there were 4 students enrolled in distance learning courses. Institutionally administered financial aid is available to distance learners.

Services Distance learners have accessibility to academic advising, e-mail services, library services.

Contact Mr. David J. DeBoer, Director of Recruitment and Financial Aid, Calvin Theological Seminary, 3233 Burton Street, SE, Grand Rapids, MI 49546. *Telephone:* 616-957-7035. *Fax:* 616-957-8621. *E-mail:* ddeboer@calvinseminary.edu.

DEGREES AND AWARDS

MA New Church Development

COURSE SUBJECT AREAS OFFERED OUTSIDE OF DEGREE PROGRAMS

Graduate—bible/biblical studies; biblical and other theological languages and literatures; missions/missionary studies and missiology; pastoral counseling and specialized ministries; religion/religious studies; religious education; religious/sacred music; theological and ministerial studies; theological studies and religious vocations, other.

CAMPBELL UNIVERSITY

Buies Creek, North Carolina
http://www.campbell.edu

Campbell University was founded in 1887. It is accredited by Southern Association of Colleges and Schools. It first offered distance learning courses in 2000. In fall 2003, there were 360 students enrolled in distance learning courses. Institutionally administered financial aid is available to distance learners.

Services Distance learners have accessibility to bookstore, campus computer network, e-mail services, library services.

Contact Mr. Frank Signorile, Jr., Program Coordinator, Distance Education, Campbell University, PO Box 4366, Building As-212, Station Education, MCAS New River, Jacksonville, NC 28540. *Telephone:* 910-449-6600. *Fax:* 910-346-4273. *E-mail:* signorile@mailcenter.campbell.edu.

DEGREES AND AWARDS

Programs offered do not lead to a degree or other formal award.

COURSE SUBJECT AREAS OFFERED OUTSIDE OF DEGREE PROGRAMS

Undergraduate—accounting; American literature (United States); bible/biblical studies; business administration and management; business communications; English composition; fine arts and art studies; geography; mathematical statistics; mathematics and computer science; political science and government.

CAPE COD COMMUNITY COLLEGE

West Barnstable, Massachusetts
Distance and Learning Technology
http://learning.capecod.mass.edu

Cape Cod Community College was founded in 1961. It is accredited by New England Association of Schools and Colleges. It first offered distance learning courses in 1993. In fall 2003, there were 500 students enrolled in distance learning courses. Institutionally administered financial aid is available to distance learners.

Services Distance learners have accessibility to academic advising, bookstore, campus computer network, career placement assistance, e-mail services, library services.

Contact Greg Masterson, Director of Distance Learning, Cape Cod Community College, 2240 Iyanough Road, West Barnstable, MA 02668. *Telephone:* 508-375-4040 Ext. 4345. *Fax:* 508-375-4041. *E-mail:* gmasters@capecod.mass.edu.

DEGREES AND AWARDS

Programs offered do not lead to a degree or other formal award.

COURSE SUBJECT AREAS OFFERED OUTSIDE OF DEGREE PROGRAMS

Undergraduate—business administration and management; computer software and media applications; developmental and child psychology; fine arts and art studies; history; mathematics; psychology; sociology.

CAPE FEAR COMMUNITY COLLEGE

Wilmington, North Carolina
http://cfcc.edu

Cape Fear Community College was founded in 1959. It is accredited by Southern Association of Colleges and Schools. It first offered distance learning courses in 1988. In fall 2003, there were 700 students enrolled in distance learning courses. Institutionally administered financial aid is available to distance learners.

Services Distance learners have accessibility to academic advising, bookstore, campus computer network, career placement assistance, e-mail services, library services, tutoring.

Contact Dr. Larolyn Zylicz, Chair, Distance Learning Department, Cape Fear Community College, 411 North Front Street, Wilmington, NC 28401. *Telephone:* 910-362-7245. *Fax:* 910-362-7152. *E-mail:* lzylicz@cfcc.edu.

DEGREES AND AWARDS

Programs offered do not lead to a degree or other formal award.

COURSE SUBJECT AREAS OFFERED OUTSIDE OF DEGREE PROGRAMS

Undergraduate—accounting; American literature (United States); business; business administration and management; chemistry; communications, general; economics; English composition; English technical and business writing; fine arts and art studies; health and physical education/fitness; history; Internet and World Wide Web; legal studies; marketing operations/marketing and distribution, other; mathematics; philosophy; psychology; religion/religious studies; sociology.
Non-credit—business.

CAPELLA UNIVERSITY

Minneapolis, Minnesota
http://www.capellauniversity.edu/

Capella University was founded in 1993. It is accredited by North Central Association of Colleges and Schools. It first offered distance learning courses in 1993. In fall 2003, there were 9,500 students enrolled in distance learning courses. Institutionally administered financial aid is available to distance learners.

Services Distance learners have accessibility to academic advising, bookstore, library services.

Contact Enrollment Services, Capella University, 222 South 9th Street, 20th Floor, Minneapolis, MN 55402. *Telephone:* 888-227-3552 Ext. 8. *Fax:* 612-339-8022. *E-mail:* info@capella.edu.

DEGREES AND AWARDS

BS Business; Information Technology
MBA Business Administration
MS Education; Human Services; Information Technology; Organization and Management; Psychology
PhD Education; Human Services; Organization and Management; Psychology

COURSE SUBJECT AREAS OFFERED OUTSIDE OF DEGREE PROGRAMS

Undergraduate—business; computer/information technology administration and management; computer systems networking and tele-

Capella University (continued)

communications; human resources management; Internet and World Wide Web; marketing operations/marketing and distribution, other. **Graduate**—business; business administration and management; business and personal services marketing operations; business communications; business information and data processing services; business management and administrative services, other; business quantitative methods and management science; clinical psychology; community organization, resources and services; computer/information technology administration and management; computer programming; computer systems networking and telecommunications; counseling psychology; criminal justice and corrections; developmental and child psychology; education administration and supervision; educational/instructional media design; educational psychology; education, general; education, other; entrepreneurship; general teacher education; human resources management; human services; industrial and organizational psychology; international business; Internet and World Wide Web; marketing management and research; marketing operations/marketing and distribution, other; miscellaneous health professions; psychology; psychology, other; public health; quality control and safety technologies; school psychology; social work.
Non-credit—business; business administration and management; business communications; business management and administrative services, other; clinical psychology; computer/information technology administration and management; computer programming; counseling psychology; criminal justice and corrections; education administration and supervision; educational/instructional media design; educational psychology; education, general; education, other; entrepreneurship; human resources management; human services; industrial and organizational psychology; international business; Internet and World Wide Web; marketing management and research; marketing operations/marketing and distribution, other; psychology; psychology, other; school psychology; social psychology; social work.

CAPITOL COLLEGE

Laurel, Maryland

http://www.capitol-college.edu/academicprograms/graduateprograms/index.shtml

Capitol College was founded in 1964. It is accredited by Middle States Association of Colleges and Schools. It first offered distance learning courses in 1998. In fall 2003, there were 400 students enrolled in distance learning courses. Institutionally administered financial aid is available to distance learners.

Services Distance learners have accessibility to academic advising, bookstore, career placement assistance, e-mail services, library services.

Contact Mr. Ken S. Crockett, Director of Graduate Admissions, Capitol College, Capitol College Graduate Programs, Laurel, MD 20708. *Telephone:* 301-369-2800 Ext. 3026. *Fax:* 301-953-3876. *E-mail:* gradschool@capitol-college.edu.

DEGREES AND AWARDS

MBA Business Administration
MS Computer Science; Electrical Engineering; Information Architecture; Information and Telecommunication Systems Management; Network Security

COURSE SUBJECT AREAS OFFERED OUTSIDE OF DEGREE PROGRAMS

Graduate—business quantitative methods and management science; computer and information sciences, general; computer and information sciences, other; computer/information technology administration and management; computer science; computer systems networking and telecommunications; engineering, general; information sciences and systems; Internet and World Wide Web; management information systems/business data processing; systems engineering; systems science and theory; telecommunications.

CARDEAN UNIVERSITY

Deerfield, Illinois

http://www.cardean.edu/

Cardean University was founded in 1997. It is accredited by Distance Education and Training Council. It first offered distance learning courses in 2000. In fall 2003, there were 1,200 students enrolled in distance learning courses. Institutionally administered financial aid is available to distance learners.

Services Distance learners have accessibility to academic advising, bookstore, library services.

Contact Mr. Tom Fitzgibbon, Director of Admissions, Cardean University, 500 Lake Cook Road, Suite 150, Deerfield, IL 60015. *Telephone:* 866-948-1289. *E-mail:* admissions@cardean.edu.

DEGREES AND AWARDS

MBA Accounting and Information Systems; Ecommerce; Finance; General Program; Global Management; Health Care Administration; Human Resources Management; Leadership; Management of Information Systems; Management of Technology; Marketing; Professional Accounting; Project Management; Risk Management; Strategy and Economics

COURSE SUBJECT AREAS OFFERED OUTSIDE OF DEGREE PROGRAMS

Graduate—accounting; business; business communications; business information and data processing services; business/managerial economics; business quantitative methods and management science.

CARL ALBERT STATE COLLEGE

Poteau, Oklahoma

http://www.carlalbert.edu

Carl Albert State College was founded in 1934. It is accredited by North Central Association of Colleges and Schools. It first offered distance learning courses in 1996. In fall 2003, there were 200 students enrolled in distance learning courses. Institutionally administered financial aid is available to distance learners.

Services Distance learners have accessibility to academic advising, bookstore, library services.

Contact Ms. Kathy A. Harrell, Dean of Instruction, Carl Albert State College, 1507 South McKenna, Poteau, OK 74953. *Telephone:* 918-647-1230. *Fax:* 918-647-1201. *E-mail:* kharrell@carlalbert.edu.

DEGREES AND AWARDS

AA Business Administration; Psychology/Sociology; Social Sciences

COURSE SUBJECT AREAS OFFERED OUTSIDE OF DEGREE PROGRAMS

Undergraduate—accounting; administrative and secretarial services; business administration and management; business information and data processing services; computer and information sciences, general;

criminal justice and corrections; data entry/microcomputer applications; English composition; health and physical education/fitness; history; mathematics; nursing; political science and government; psychology; telecommunications.

CARLETON UNIVERSITY

Ottawa, Ontario, Canada
Instructional Television
http://www.carleton.ca/cutv/

Carleton University was founded in 1942. It is provincially chartered. It first offered distance learning courses in 1978. In fall 2003, there were 4,577 students enrolled in distance learning courses. Institutionally administered financial aid is available to distance learners.

Services Distance learners have accessibility to academic advising, bookstore, campus computer network, e-mail services, library services.
Contact Jeff Cohen, Manager, Course Production and Broadcast, Carleton University, Tory Building, Room 430, 1125 Colonel By Drive, Ottawa, ON K1S 5B6, Canada. *Telephone:* 613-520-2600 Ext. 8105. *Fax:* 613-520-4456. *E-mail:* jeff_cohen@carleton.ca.

DEGREES AND AWARDS

Programs offered do not lead to a degree or other formal award.

COURSE SUBJECT AREAS OFFERED OUTSIDE OF DEGREE PROGRAMS

Undergraduate—accounting; anthropology; astronomy; biology; chemistry; developmental/child psychology; earth sciences; economics; English language and literature, general; geography; history; legal studies; political science and government; psychology; religion/religious studies; social psychology; social work.
Graduate—economics; fire protection.

CARROLL COMMUNITY COLLEGE

Westminster, Maryland
http://www.carrollcc.edu

Carroll Community College was founded in 1993. It is accredited by Middle States Association of Colleges and Schools. It first offered distance learning courses in 1993. In fall 2003, there were 494 students enrolled in distance learning courses. Institutionally administered financial aid is available to distance learners.

Services Distance learners have accessibility to academic advising, bookstore, library services.
Contact Ms. Edie Hemingway, Coordinator of Admissions, Carroll Community College, 1601 Washington Road, Westminster, MD 21157. *Telephone:* 410-386-8405. *Fax:* 410-386-8446. *E-mail:* ehemingway@carrollcc.edu.

DEGREES AND AWARDS

Programs offered do not lead to a degree or other formal award.

COURSE SUBJECT AREAS OFFERED OUTSIDE OF DEGREE PROGRAMS

Undergraduate—astronomy; biology, general; business administration and management; computer and information sciences, general; computer/information technology administration and management; computer systems networking and telecommunications; criminal justice and corrections; economics; English composition; English technical and business writing; geography; history; marketing management and research; mathematical statistics; philosophy; psychology; social psychology; sociology.
Non-credit—administrative and secretarial services; business; business administration and management; computer software and media applications; computer systems networking and telecommunications; English creative writing; English technical and business writing; financial management and services.

CASCADIA COMMUNITY COLLEGE

Bothell, Washington
http://www.cascadia.ctc.edu/

Cascadia Community College was founded in 1999. It first offered distance learning courses in 2001. In fall 2003, there were 250 students enrolled in distance learning courses. Institutionally administered financial aid is available to distance learners.

Services Distance learners have accessibility to academic advising, bookstore, campus computer network, e-mail services, library services.
Contact Sharon Buck, EdD, Interim Associate Dean for Student Learning, Cascadia Community College, 18345 Campus Way, NE, Bothell, WA 98011. *Telephone:* 425-352-8168. *E-mail:* sbuck@cascadia.ctc.edu.

DEGREES AND AWARDS

Programs offered do not lead to a degree or other formal award.

COURSE SUBJECT AREAS OFFERED OUTSIDE OF DEGREE PROGRAMS

Undergraduate—accounting; astronomy; biological and physical sciences; chemistry; communications, other; comparative literature; economics; English composition; geological and related sciences; history; mathematics.

CASPER COLLEGE

Casper, Wyoming
http://www.caspercollege.edu/

Casper College was founded in 1945. It is accredited by North Central Association of Colleges and Schools. It first offered distance learning courses in 1986. In fall 2003, there were 885 students enrolled in distance learning courses. Institutionally administered financial aid is available to distance learners.

Services Distance learners have accessibility to academic advising, bookstore, career placement assistance, library services, tutoring.
Contact Paul J. Marquard, Director of Distance Education, Casper College, 125 College Drive, Casper, WY 82601-4699. *Telephone:* 307-268-2250. *Fax:* 307-268-2224. *E-mail:* marquard@caspercollege.edu.

DEGREES AND AWARDS

Programs offered do not lead to a degree or other formal award.

COURSE SUBJECT AREAS OFFERED OUTSIDE OF DEGREE PROGRAMS

Undergraduate—accounting; anthropology; astronomy; biological and physical sciences; biological sciences/life sciences, other; biology,

Casper College (continued)

general; business; business administration and management; business management and administrative services, other; chemistry; computer and information sciences, general; computer programming; computer science; computer software and media applications; economics; educational psychology; education, general; education, other; engineering, general; engineering science; English composition; English creative writing; fine arts and art studies; geography; mathematical statistics; mathematics; music; psychology; sociology; special education; teacher assistant/aide; zoology.

THE CATHOLIC DISTANCE UNIVERSITY

Hamilton, Virginia

http://www.cdu.edu/

The Catholic Distance University was founded in 1983. It is accredited by Distance Education and Training Council. It first offered distance learning courses in 1983. In fall 2003, there were 950 students enrolled in distance learning courses. Institutionally administered financial aid is available to distance learners.

Services Distance learners have accessibility to academic advising, bookstore, e-mail services, library services.

Contact Dr. Ivanna Richardson, Graduate Registrar, The Catholic Distance University, 120 East Colonial Highway, Hamilton, VA 20158. *Telephone:* 540-338-2700 Ext. 712. *Fax:* 540-338-4788. *E-mail:* masters@cdu.edu.

DEGREES AND AWARDS

Certification Advanced Catechist Certificate
Diploma Apostolic Catechetical Diploma
Advanced Graduate Diploma Master Apostolic Catechetical Diploma
MA Religious Studies
MCT Religious Studies–Catholic Theology (MRS)

COURSE SUBJECT AREAS OFFERED OUTSIDE OF DEGREE PROGRAMS

Undergraduate—religion/religious studies; religious education; theological studies and religious vocations, other.
Graduate—religion/religious studies; religious education; theological studies and religious vocations, other.
Non-credit—religion/religious studies; religious education; theological and ministerial studies; theological studies and religious vocations, other.

CAYUGA COUNTY COMMUNITY COLLEGE

Auburn, New York

http://www.cayuga-cc.edu/

Cayuga County Community College was founded in 1953. It is accredited by Middle States Association of Colleges and Schools. It first offered distance learning courses in 1998. In fall 2003, there were 300 students enrolled in distance learning courses. Institutionally administered financial aid is available to distance learners.

Services Distance learners have accessibility to academic advising, bookstore, career placement assistance, e-mail services, library services, tutoring.

Contact Ed Kowalski, Director of Evening and Special Programs, Cayuga County Community College, 197 Franklin Street, Auburn, NY 13021. *Telephone:* 315-255-1743. *Fax:* 315-255-2117. *E-mail:* kowalskie@cayuga-cc.edu.

DEGREES AND AWARDS

AA Liberal Arts and Humanities
AAS Business Administration
AS Business Administration; Liberal Arts and Sciences/Mathematics and Sciences

COURSE SUBJECT AREAS OFFERED OUTSIDE OF DEGREE PROGRAMS

Undergraduate—accounting; anthropology; biology, general; business; computer science; economics; English language and literature, general; health and physical education/fitness; history; mathematics; political science and government; psychology; telecommunications.

CECIL COMMUNITY COLLEGE

North East, Maryland

http://www.cecilcc.edu

Cecil Community College was founded in 1968. It is accredited by Middle States Association of Colleges and Schools. It first offered distance learning courses in 1999. In fall 2003, there were 54 students enrolled in distance learning courses. Institutionally administered financial aid is available to distance learners.

Services Distance learners have accessibility to bookstore, campus computer network, e-mail services.

Contact Carrie S. Ray-Sturgill, Operations Technician, Cecil Community College, One Seahawk Drive, North East, MD 21901. *Telephone:* 410-287-6060 Ext. 552. *Fax:* 410-287-1001. *E-mail:* cray@cecilcc.edu.

DEGREES AND AWARDS

Programs offered do not lead to a degree or other formal award.

COURSE SUBJECT AREAS OFFERED OUTSIDE OF DEGREE PROGRAMS

Undergraduate—astronomy; business; chemistry; mathematics; physics; psychology; sociology.

CEDARVILLE UNIVERSITY

Cedarville, Ohio

http://www.cedarville.edu/

Cedarville University was founded in 1887. It is accredited by North Central Association of Colleges and Schools. It first offered distance learning courses in 1999. In fall 2003, there were 50 students enrolled in distance learning courses. Institutionally administered financial aid is available to distance learners.

Services Distance learners have accessibility to academic advising, campus computer network, career placement assistance, e-mail services, library services.

Contact Chuck Allport, Assistant to the Academic Vice President, Cedarville University, 251 North Main Street, Cedarville, OH 45314. *Telephone:* 937-766-7681. *Fax:* 937-766-3217. *E-mail:* chuckallport@cedarville.edu.

DEGREES AND AWARDS

Programs offered do not lead to a degree or other formal award.

COURSE SUBJECT AREAS OFFERED OUTSIDE OF DEGREE PROGRAMS

Undergraduate—anthropology; biology; business communications; English language and literature, general; history; journalism and mass communications; social sciences, general; sociology; soil sciences; special education.

CENTRAL BAPTIST THEOLOGICAL SEMINARY

Kansas City, Kansas
Long Distance Learning
http://www.cbts.edu

Central Baptist Theological Seminary was founded in 1901. It is accredited by North Central Association of Colleges and Schools. It first offered distance learning courses in 1989. In fall 2003, there were 20 students enrolled in distance learning courses. Institutionally administered financial aid is available to distance learners.

Services Distance learners have accessibility to academic advising, bookstore, career placement assistance, e-mail services, library services.

Contact Ms. MaryBeth Robertson, Director of Enrollment Services, Central Baptist Theological Seminary, 741 North 31st Street, Kansas City, KS 66102. *Telephone:* 913-371-5313 Ext. 102. *Fax:* 913-371-8110. *E-mail:* mbrobertson@cbts.edu.

DEGREES AND AWARDS

Programs offered do not lead to a degree or other formal award.

COURSE SUBJECT AREAS OFFERED OUTSIDE OF DEGREE PROGRAMS

Graduate—bible/biblical studies; biblical and other theological languages and literatures; pastoral counseling and specialized ministries; religion/religious studies; religious education; theological and ministerial studies; theological studies and religious vocations, other.

Non-credit—bible/biblical studies; biblical and other theological languages and literatures; pastoral counseling and specialized ministries; religion/religious studies; religious education; theological and ministerial studies; theological studies and religious vocations, other.

CENTRAL BIBLE COLLEGE

Springfield, Missouri
http://www.cbcag.edu/

Central Bible College was founded in 1922. It is accredited by Accrediting Association of Bible Colleges. It first offered distance learning courses in 2001. In fall 2003, there were 100 students enrolled in distance learning courses. Institutionally administered financial aid is available to distance learners.

Services Distance learners have accessibility to academic advising, bookstore, campus computer network, e-mail services, library services.

Contact Dr. Leo Theriot, Director, Center for LifeLong Learning, Central Bible College, 3000 North Grant Avenue, Springfield, MO 65803. *Telephone:* 417-833-2551 Ext. 1800. *Fax:* 417-833-0854. *E-mail:* ltheriot@cbcag.edu.

DEGREES AND AWARDS

Programs offered do not lead to a degree or other formal award.

COURSE SUBJECT AREAS OFFERED OUTSIDE OF DEGREE PROGRAMS

Undergraduate—bible/biblical studies; education, general.

Non-credit—bible/biblical studies; biblical and other theological languages and literatures.

CENTRAL CONNECTICUT STATE UNIVERSITY

New Britain, Connecticut
http://www.ccsu.edu/

Central Connecticut State University was founded in 1849. It is accredited by New England Association of Schools and Colleges. It first offered distance learning courses in 1992. In fall 2003, there were 70 students enrolled in distance learning courses. Institutionally administered financial aid is available to distance learners.

Services Distance learners have accessibility to campus computer network, e-mail services, library services.

Contact Leroy E. Temple, PhD, Director, Media Services, Central Connecticut State University, 1615 Stanley Street, New Britain, CT 06050-4010. *Telephone:* 860-832-2032. *Fax:* 860-832-2039. *E-mail:* templer@ccsu.edu.

DEGREES AND AWARDS

Programs offered do not lead to a degree or other formal award.

COURSE SUBJECT AREAS OFFERED OUTSIDE OF DEGREE PROGRAMS

Undergraduate—nursing.

CENTRAL MICHIGAN UNIVERSITY

Mount Pleasant, Michigan
Distance/Distributed Learning
http://DDLcampus.cmich.edu

Central Michigan University was founded in 1892. It is accredited by North Central Association of Colleges and Schools. It first offered distance learning courses in 1970. In fall 2003, there were 2,041 students enrolled in distance learning courses. Institutionally administered financial aid is available to distance learners.

Services Distance learners have accessibility to academic advising, bookstore, campus computer network, e-mail services, library services, tutoring.

Contact Ms. Connie Detwiler, Distance Learning, Central Michigan University, College of Extended Learning, Mount Pleasant , MI 48859. *Telephone:* 800-688-4268. *Fax:* 989-774-1822. *E-mail:* celinfo@mail.cel.cmich.edu.

Central Michigan University (continued)

DEGREES AND AWARDS

BAA Health Administration

BS Administration; Community Development

Advanced Graduate Diploma Audiology; Health Administration–DHA

MS Administration, general; Information Resource Management

See full description on page 370.

CENTRAL MISSOURI STATE UNIVERSITY

Warrensburg, Missouri
Department of Nursing
http://www.cmsu.edu/extcamp

Central Missouri State University was founded in 1871. It is accredited by North Central Association of Colleges and Schools. It first offered distance learning courses in 1993. In fall 2003, there were 1,100 students enrolled in distance learning courses. Institutionally administered financial aid is available to distance learners.

Services Distance learners have accessibility to academic advising, bookstore, campus computer network, career placement assistance, e-mail services, library services, tutoring.

Contact Dr. Michael R. Penrod, Outreach Coordinator for Distance Learning, Central Missouri State University, Office of Extended Campus, 410 Humphreys, Warrensburg, MO 64093. *Telephone:* 800-729-2678 Ext. 22. *Fax:* 660-543-8480. *E-mail:* penrod@cmsu1.cmsu.edu.

DEGREES AND AWARDS

BSN Nursing

MSN Nursing–Rural Family Nursing

COURSE SUBJECT AREAS OFFERED OUTSIDE OF DEGREE PROGRAMS

Undergraduate—computer science; criminal justice and corrections; curriculum and instruction; educational evaluation, research and statistics; educational psychology; engineering/industrial management; foods and nutrition studies; library science/librarianship; teacher education, specific academic and vocational programs; technology education/industrial arts.

Graduate—criminal justice and corrections; curriculum and instruction; educational evaluation, research and statistics; educational psychology; engineering/industrial management; library science/librarianship; nursing; special education; technology education/industrial arts.

Non-credit—accounting; computer programming; computer software and media applications; computer systems networking and telecommunications; enterprise management and operation; Internet and World Wide Web.

See full description on page 372.

CENTRAL MISSOURI STATE UNIVERSITY

Warrensburg, Missouri
Extended Campus–Distance Learning
http://www.cmsu.edu/extcamp

Central Missouri State University was founded in 1871. It is accredited by North Central Association of Colleges and Schools. It first offered distance learning courses in 1993. In fall 2003, there were 1,100 students enrolled in distance learning courses. Institutionally administered financial aid is available to distance learners.

Services Distance learners have accessibility to academic advising, bookstore, campus computer network, career placement assistance, e-mail services, library services, tutoring.

Contact Dr. Michael R. Penrod, Outreach Coordinator for Distance Learning, Central Missouri State University, Office of Extended Campus, 410 Humphreys, Warrensburg, MO 64093. *Telephone:* 800-729-2678 Ext. 22. *Fax:* 660-543-8480. *E-mail:* penrod@cmsu1.cmsu.edu.

DEGREES AND AWARDS

BSN Nursing

MS Criminal Justice; Industrial Management; Library Information Technology; Library Science and Information Services

MSN Nursing–Rural Family Nursing

PhD Technology Management

COURSE SUBJECT AREAS OFFERED OUTSIDE OF DEGREE PROGRAMS

Undergraduate—computer science; criminal justice and corrections; curriculum and instruction; educational evaluation, research and statistics; educational psychology; engineering/industrial management; foods and nutrition studies; library science/librarianship; teacher education, specific academic and vocational programs; technology education/industrial arts.

Graduate—criminal justice and corrections; curriculum and instruction; educational evaluation, research and statistics; educational psychology; engineering/industrial management; library science/librarianship; nursing; special education; technology education/industrial arts.

Non-credit—accounting; computer programming; computer software and media applications; computer systems networking and telecommunications; enterprise management and operation; Internet and World Wide Web.

CENTRAL MISSOURI STATE UNIVERSITY

Warrensburg, Missouri
Department of Library Science and Information Services
http://www.cmsu.edu/extcamp

Central Missouri State University was founded in 1871. It is accredited by North Central Association of Colleges and Schools. It first offered distance learning courses in 1993. In fall 2003, there were 1,100 students enrolled in distance learning courses. Institutionally administered financial aid is available to distance learners.

Services Distance learners have accessibility to academic advising, bookstore, campus computer network, career placement assistance, e-mail services, library services, tutoring.
Contact Dr. Michael R. Penrod, Outreach Coordinator for Distance Learning, Central Missouri State University, Office of Extended Campus, 410 Humphreys, Warrensburg, MO 64093. *Telephone:* 800-729-2678 Ext. 22. *Fax:* 660-543-8480. *E-mail:* penrod@cmsu1.cmsu.edu.

DEGREES AND AWARDS

MS Library Information Technology; Library Science and Information Services

COURSE SUBJECT AREAS OFFERED OUTSIDE OF DEGREE PROGRAMS

Undergraduate—computer science; criminal justice and corrections; curriculum and instruction; educational evaluation, research and statistics; educational psychology; engineering/industrial management; foods and nutrition studies; library science/librarianship; technology education/industrial arts.
Graduate—criminal justice and corrections; curriculum and instruction; educational evaluation, research and statistics; educational psychology; engineering/industrial management; library science/librarianship; nursing; special education; technology education/industrial arts.
Non-credit—accounting; computer programming; computer software and media applications; computer systems networking and telecommunications; enterprise management and operation; Internet and World Wide Web.

See full description on page 374.

CENTRAL MISSOURI STATE UNIVERSITY

Warrensburg, Missouri
Department of Criminal Justice
http://www.cmsu.edu/extcamp

Central Missouri State University was founded in 1871. It is accredited by North Central Association of Colleges and Schools. It first offered distance learning courses in 1993. In fall 2003, there were 1,100 students enrolled in distance learning courses. Institutionally administered financial aid is available to distance learners.

Services Distance learners have accessibility to academic advising, bookstore, campus computer network, career placement assistance, e-mail services, library services, tutoring.
Contact Dr. Michael R. Penrod, Outreach Coordinator for Distance Learning, Central Missouri State University, Office of Extended Campus, 410 Humphreys, Warrensburg, MO 64093. *Telephone:* 800-729-2678 Ext. 22. *Fax:* 660-543-8480. *E-mail:* penrod@cmsu1.cmsu.edu.

DEGREES AND AWARDS

MS Criminal Justice

COURSE SUBJECT AREAS OFFERED OUTSIDE OF DEGREE PROGRAMS

Undergraduate—computer science; criminal justice and corrections; curriculum and instruction; educational evaluation, research and statistics; educational psychology; engineering/industrial management; foods and nutrition studies; library science/librarianship; teacher education, specific academic and vocational programs; technology education/industrial arts.
Graduate—criminal justice and corrections; curriculum and instruction; educational evaluation, research and statistics; educational psychology; engineering/industrial management; library science/librarianship; nursing; special education; technology education/industrial arts.
Non-credit—accounting; computer programming; computer software and media applications; computer systems networking and telecommunications; enterprise management and operation; Internet and World Wide Web.

See full description on page 376.

CENTRAL MISSOURI STATE UNIVERSITY

Warrensburg, Missouri
Department of Industrial Technology
http://www.cmsu.edu/extcamp

Central Missouri State University was founded in 1871. It is accredited by North Central Association of Colleges and Schools. It first offered distance learning courses in 1993. In fall 2003, there were 1,100 students enrolled in distance learning courses. Institutionally administered financial aid is available to distance learners.

Services Distance learners have accessibility to academic advising, bookstore, campus computer network, career placement assistance, e-mail services, library services, tutoring.
Contact Dr. Michael R. Penrod, Outreach Coordinator for Distance Learning, Central Missouri State University, Office of Extended Campus, 410 Humphreys, Warrensburg, MO 64093. *Telephone:* 800-729-2678 Ext. 22. *Fax:* 660-543-8480. *E-mail:* penrod@cmsu1.cmsu.edu.

DEGREES AND AWARDS

MS Industrial Management
PhD Technology Management

COURSE SUBJECT AREAS OFFERED OUTSIDE OF DEGREE PROGRAMS

Undergraduate—computer science; criminal justice and corrections; curriculum and instruction; educational evaluation, research and statistics; educational psychology; engineering/industrial management; foods and nutrition studies; library science/librarianship; teacher education, specific academic and vocational programs; technology education/industrial arts.
Graduate—criminal justice and corrections; curriculum and instruction; educational evaluation, research and statistics; educational psychology; engineering/industrial management; library science/librarianship; nursing; special education; technology education/industrial arts.
Non-credit—accounting; computer programming; computer software and media applications; computer systems networking and telecommunications; enterprise management and operation; Internet and World Wide Web.

See full description on page 378.

CENTRAL OREGON COMMUNITY COLLEGE

Bend, Oregon
Open Campus Distance Learning Program
http://www.cocc.edu/opencampus

Central Oregon Community College was founded in 1949. It is accredited by Northwest Commission on Colleges and Universities. It first offered distance learning courses in 1996. Institutionally administered financial aid is available to distance learners.

Services Distance learners have accessibility to academic advising, bookstore, campus computer network, e-mail services, library services, tutoring.

Contact Barbara Klett, Instructional Technology Coordinator, Central Oregon Community College, 2600 Northwest College Way, Bend, OR 97701. *Telephone:* 541-383-7785. *E-mail:* bklett@cocc.edu.

DEGREES AND AWARDS

AA Oregon Transfer

COURSE SUBJECT AREAS OFFERED OUTSIDE OF DEGREE PROGRAMS

Undergraduate—biological and physical sciences; business administration and management; chemistry; communications, general; computer and information sciences, general; criminal justice and corrections; developmental and child psychology; foods and nutrition studies; geography; history; information sciences and systems; liberal arts and sciences, general studies and humanities; mathematics; psychology.

CENTRAL TEXAS COLLEGE

Killeen, Texas
Distance Education and Educational Technology
http://online.ctcd.edu

Central Texas College was founded in 1967. It is accredited by Southern Association of Colleges and Schools. It first offered distance learning courses in 1972. In fall 2003, there were 8,000 students enrolled in distance learning courses. Institutionally administered financial aid is available to distance learners.

Services Distance learners have accessibility to academic advising, bookstore, career placement assistance, library services, tutoring.

Contact Laura Ann Forest, System Registrar, Central Texas College, PO Box 1800, Killeen, TX 76540. *Telephone:* 254-526-1114. *Fax:* 254-526-1481. *E-mail:* systems.registrar@ctcd.edu.

DEGREES AND AWARDS

AAS Applied Technology; Business Management; Business Management; Computer Science–Information Technology; Criminal Justice; Hospitality Management
AGS General Studies
ASAST Applied Science

COURSE SUBJECT AREAS OFFERED OUTSIDE OF DEGREE PROGRAMS

Undergraduate—accounting; administrative and secretarial services; alcohol/drug abuse counseling; American history; anthropology; applied mathematics; area, ethnic and cultural studies, other; bible/biblical studies; business administration and management; business communications; business information and data processing services; business management and administrative services, other; communications, general; community psychology; computer and information sciences, general; computer and information sciences, other; computer programming; computer science; computer systems analysis; computer systems networking and telecommunications; counseling psychology; criminal justice and corrections; criminology; culinary arts and related services; cultural studies; developmental and child psychology; economics; English composition; English language and literature, general; English technical and business writing; entrepreneurship; fine arts and art studies; fire protection; health and physical education/fitness; history; hospitality/recreation marketing; hospitality services management; human resources management; institutional food workers and administrators; Internet and World Wide Web; law and legal studies related; marketing management and research; mathematical statistics; mathematics; mathematics related; mental health services; military studies; multi/interdisciplinary studies, other; nursing; philosophy; philosophy and religion; political science and government; psychology; psychology, other; real estate; religion/religious studies; social sciences and history, other; social sciences, general; sociology; tourism/travel marketing.

CENTRAL VIRGINIA COMMUNITY COLLEGE

Lynchburg, Virginia
Learning Resources
http://www.cvcc.vccs.edu

Central Virginia Community College was founded in 1966. It is accredited by Southern Association of Colleges and Schools. It first offered distance learning courses in 1984. In fall 2003, there were 955 students enrolled in distance learning courses. Institutionally administered financial aid is available to distance learners.

Services Distance learners have accessibility to academic advising, bookstore, campus computer network, e-mail services, library services, tutoring.

Contact Susan S. Beasley, Media Specialist, Central Virginia Community College, 3506 Wards Road, Lynchburg, VA 24502. *Telephone:* 434-832-7742. *Fax:* 434-832-7746. *E-mail:* beasleys@cvcc.vccs.edu.

DEGREES AND AWARDS

AAS Medical Laboratory Technology

COURSE SUBJECT AREAS OFFERED OUTSIDE OF DEGREE PROGRAMS

Undergraduate—accounting; administrative and secretarial services; applied mathematics; astronomy; biology; business marketing and marketing management; chemistry; computer and information sciences, general; economics; English composition; English language and literature, general; English technical and business writing; history; information sciences and systems; library science, other; marketing management and research; music; philosophy; political science and government; psychology; sociology; speech and rhetorical studies; visual and performing arts, other.

CENTRAL WASHINGTON UNIVERSITY

Ellensburg, Washington
Center for Learning Technologies
http://www.cwu.edu/~media/

Central Washington University was founded in 1891. It is accredited by Northwest Commission on Colleges and Universities. It first offered distance learning courses in 1996. In fall 2003, there were 886 students enrolled in distance learning courses. Institutionally administered financial aid is available to distance learners.

Services Distance learners have accessibility to academic advising, bookstore, campus computer network, e-mail services, library services.
Contact Tracy Terrell, Registrar, Central Washington University, Mitchell Hall, 400 East University Way, Ellensburg, WA 98926-7465. *Telephone:* 509-963-3076. *Fax:* 509-963-3022. *E-mail:* terrell@cwu.edu.

DEGREES AND AWARDS

MS Physical Education, Health, and Leisure Studies

COURSE SUBJECT AREAS OFFERED OUTSIDE OF DEGREE PROGRAMS

Undergraduate—accounting; business; computer/information technology administration and management; criminal justice and corrections; psychology.
Graduate—accounting; health and physical education/fitness.
Non-credit—education, general.

CENTRAL WYOMING COLLEGE

Riverton, Wyoming
Distance Education and Extended Studies
http://www.cwc.edu

Central Wyoming College was founded in 1966. It is accredited by North Central Association of Colleges and Schools. It first offered distance learning courses in 1983. In fall 2003, there were 885 students enrolled in distance learning courses. Institutionally administered financial aid is available to distance learners.

Services Distance learners have accessibility to academic advising, bookstore, e-mail services, library services.
Contact Jason Harris, Research Analyst, Central Wyoming College, 2660 Peck Avenue, Riverton, WY 82501. *Telephone:* 307-855-2270. *Fax:* 307-855-2092. *E-mail:* jharris@cwc.edu.

DEGREES AND AWARDS

Programs offered do not lead to a degree or other formal award.

COURSE SUBJECT AREAS OFFERED OUTSIDE OF DEGREE PROGRAMS

Undergraduate—accounting; anthropology; area, ethnic and cultural studies, other; biology; business; chemistry; computer and information sciences, general; criminal justice and corrections; economics; English composition; family and marriage counseling; foreign languages and literatures, other; geography; health and physical education/fitness; history; mathematics; political science and government; psychology; religion/religious studies; social sciences, general; sociology; teacher education, specific academic and vocational programs.
Non-credit—business; business information and data processing services; communications, general; computer and information sciences, general; cultural studies; dance; data entry/microcomputer applications; design and applied arts; electrical and power transmission installers; family and community studies; financial management and services; foreign languages and literatures; health and medical assistants; health and medical diagnostic and treatment services; health and physical education/fitness; history; Internet and World Wide Web; mental health services; music; precision metal workers; psychology.

CENTURY COLLEGE

White Bear Lake, Minnesota
Customized Training Division
http://www.centurycollege.mnscu.edu/cect

Century College was founded in 1970. It is accredited by North Central Association of Colleges and Schools. It first offered distance learning courses in 1998. In fall 2003, there were 200 students enrolled in distance learning courses. Institutionally administered financial aid is available to distance learners.

Services Distance learners have accessibility to bookstore, e-mail services, library services.
Contact Lynette Podritz, Customer Service Representative, Century College, 3300 Century Avenue, North, White Bear Lake, MN 55110. *Telephone:* 651-779-3904. *Fax:* 651-779-5082. *E-mail:* l.podritz@century.mnscu.edu.

DEGREES AND AWARDS

Programs offered do not lead to a degree or other formal award.

COURSE SUBJECT AREAS OFFERED OUTSIDE OF DEGREE PROGRAMS

Undergraduate—health and medical administrative services; health and medical preparatory programs.
Non-credit—accounting; anatomy; applied mathematics; business administration and management; communications, general; computer and information sciences, general; data entry/microcomputer applications; English composition; health and medical administrative services; health and medical assistants; mathematics.

CERRITOS COLLEGE

Norwalk, California
Distributed Education Program
http://www.cerritos.edu/de

Cerritos College was founded in 1956. It is accredited by Western Association of Schools and Colleges. It first offered distance learning courses in 1985. In fall 2003, there were 4,000 students enrolled in distance learning courses. Institutionally administered financial aid is available to distance learners.

Services Distance learners have accessibility to bookstore, e-mail services, library services.
Contact Yvette Juarez, Program Assistant for Distance Education, Cerritos College, 11110 Alondra Boulevard, Norwalk, CA 90650. *Telephone:* 562-860-2451 Ext. 2405. *E-mail:* yjuarez@cerritos.edu.

DEGREES AND AWARDS

Programs offered do not lead to a degree or other formal award.

Cerritos College (continued)

COURSE SUBJECT AREAS OFFERED OUTSIDE OF DEGREE PROGRAMS

Undergraduate—administrative and secretarial services; American history; anthropology; business; curriculum and instruction; data entry/microcomputer applications; English composition; journalism; law and legal studies related; management information systems/ business data processing; radio/television broadcasting; sociology.

CHADRON STATE COLLEGE

Chadron, Nebraska
Extended Campus Programs
http://www.csc.edu

Chadron State College was founded in 1911. It is accredited by North Central Association of Colleges and Schools. It first offered distance learning courses in 1991. In fall 2003, there were 700 students enrolled in distance learning courses. Institutionally administered financial aid is available to distance learners.

Services Distance learners have accessibility to academic advising, bookstore, campus computer network, e-mail services, library services, tutoring.

Contact Mr. Steve Taylor, Assistant Vice President for Extended Campus Programs, Chadron State College, 1000 Main Street, Chadron, NE 69337. *Telephone:* 308-432-6211. *Fax:* 308-432-6473. *E-mail:* staylor@csc.edu.

DEGREES AND AWARDS

MBA Business Administration
MSE Math

COURSE SUBJECT AREAS OFFERED OUTSIDE OF DEGREE PROGRAMS

Undergraduate—accounting; biological and physical sciences; business; business administration and management; business and personal services marketing operations; business communications; business information and data processing services; business management and administrative services, other; business/managerial economics; business quantitative methods and management science; criminology; developmental and child psychology; developmental/child psychology; economics; educational psychology; education, general; education, other; English composition; English literature (British and Commonwealth); English technical and business writing; family and community studies; general retailing/wholesaling; general teacher education; geography; history; home economics, general; home economics, other; housing studies; human resources management; human services; individual and family development studies; industrial and organizational psychology; information sciences and systems; legal studies; liberal arts and sciences, general studies and humanities; library science/librarianship; library science, other; marketing management and research; marketing operations/marketing and distribution, other; mathematical statistics; mathematics; mathematics and computer science; mathematics, other; philosophy; philosophy and religion; physical sciences, general; physical sciences, other; psychology; psychology, other; real estate; social sciences and history, other; social sciences, general; social work; sociology; special education; teacher education, specific academic and vocational programs.

Graduate—accounting; business administration and management; business and personal services marketing operations; business information and data processing services; business management and administrative services, other; business/managerial economics; business quantitative methods and management science; counseling psychology; curriculum and instruction; education administration and supervision; educational evaluation, research and statistics; educational/ instructional media design; educational psychology; education, general; education, other; English language and literature, general; history; human resources management; industrial and organizational psychology; marketing management and research; marketing operations/ marketing and distribution, other; mathematical statistics; mathematics; mathematics and computer science; mathematics, other; psychology; psychology, other; school psychology; special education; teacher education, specific academic and vocational programs; technology education/industrial arts.

CHAMINADE UNIVERSITY OF HONOLULU

Honolulu, Hawaii
http://www.chaminade.edu/

Chaminade University of Honolulu was founded in 1955. It is accredited by Western Association of Schools and Colleges. It first offered distance learning courses in 1997. In fall 2003, there were 605 students enrolled in distance learning courses. Institutionally administered financial aid is available to distance learners.

Services Distance learners have accessibility to academic advising, bookstore, campus computer network, e-mail services, library services.

Contact Skip Lee, Director of Accelerated Undergraduate Program, Chaminade University of Honolulu, 3140 Waialae Avenue, Honolulu, HI 96816-1578. *Telephone:* 808-735-4851. *Fax:* 808-735-4766. *E-mail:* slee@chaminade.edu.

DEGREES AND AWARDS

Programs offered do not lead to a degree or other formal award.

COURSE SUBJECT AREAS OFFERED OUTSIDE OF DEGREE PROGRAMS

Undergraduate—accounting; anthropology; business administration and management; criminal justice and corrections; dramatic/theater arts and stagecraft; economics; education, general; English composition; English creative writing; English language and literature, general; finance; history; mathematics; music; philosophy; philosophy and religion related; physics; political science and government; psychology; religion/religious studies; sociology.

Graduate—business administration and management; education, general; religion/religious studies.

CHAMPLAIN COLLEGE

Burlington, Vermont
Continuing Education Division
http://www.champlain.edu/coce

Champlain College was founded in 1878. It is accredited by New England Association of Schools and Colleges. It first offered distance learning courses in 1993. In fall 2003, there were 585 students enrolled in distance learning courses. Institutionally administered financial aid is available to distance learners.

Services Distance learners have accessibility to academic advising, bookstore, career placement assistance, library services, tutoring.

Contact R.J. Sweeney, Recruitment Specialist, Champlain College, Center for OnLine and Continuing Education, 163 South Willard Street, Burlington, VT 05401. *Telephone:* 800-545-3459. *Fax:* 802-865-6447. *E-mail:* coce@champlain.edu.

DEGREES AND AWARDS

AS Accounting; Business; Global Networks and Telecommunications; Management; Software Development; Web Site Development and Management
BS Business; Computer Information Systems; Professional Studies; Software Engineering
Certificate Accounting; Business; E-Business and Commerce; Global Networks and Telecommunications; International Business; Management; Software Development; Web Site Development and Management
MS Managing Innovation and Information Technology

COURSE SUBJECT AREAS OFFERED OUTSIDE OF DEGREE PROGRAMS

Undergraduate—accounting; advertising; business; business administration and management; business communications; chemistry; communications, general; communications, other; computer and information sciences, general; computer and information sciences, other; computer/information technology administration and management; computer programming; computer software and media applications; computer systems networking and telecommunications; economics; English composition; English creative writing; English language and literature, general; entrepreneurship; financial management and services; geography; history; human resources management; international business; Internet and World Wide Web; liberal arts and sciences, general studies and humanities; mathematics; mathematics and computer science; physical sciences, general; professional studies; psychology; sociology; telecommunications.
Graduate—information sciences and systems.

See full description on page 380.

CHARTER OAK STATE COLLEGE

New Britain, Connecticut

http://www.charteroak.edu/

Charter Oak State College was founded in 1973. It is accredited by New England Association of Schools and Colleges. It first offered distance learning courses in 1992. In fall 2003, there were 700 students enrolled in distance learning courses. Institutionally administered financial aid is available to distance learners.

Services Distance learners have accessibility to academic advising, bookstore, career placement assistance, library services, tutoring.
Contact Peggy Intravia, Assistant for Distance Learning Program, Charter Oak State College, 55 Paul J. Manafort Drive, New Britain, CT 06053-2142. *Telephone:* 860-832-3837. *Fax:* 860-832-3999. *E-mail:* mintravia@charteroak.edu.

DEGREES AND AWARDS

AA General Studies
AS General Studies
BA General Studies
BS General Studies
Diploma General Studies

COURSE SUBJECT AREAS OFFERED OUTSIDE OF DEGREE PROGRAMS

Undergraduate—anthropology; art history; astronomy; biology; business; chemistry; economics; English composition; English language and literature, general; entrepreneurship; film/video and photographic arts; geography; health products and services marketing operations; history; human resources management; journalism and mass communication related; mathematics; nursing; philosophy; political science and government; psychology; social psychology; social sciences, general; sociology.
Non-credit—nursing; pharmacy.

See full description on page 382.

CHATTANOOGA STATE TECHNICAL COMMUNITY COLLEGE

Chattanooga, Tennessee

Distance Learning Program

http://www.chattanoogastate.edu/cde/

Chattanooga State Technical Community College was founded in 1965. It is accredited by Southern Association of Colleges and Schools. It first offered distance learning courses in 1985. In fall 2003, there were 1,500 students enrolled in distance learning courses. Institutionally administered financial aid is available to distance learners.

Services Distance learners have accessibility to academic advising, bookstore, career placement assistance, library services, tutoring.
Contact Tim Dills, Assistant Director, Center for Distributed Education, Chattanooga State Technical Community College, 4501 Amnicola Highway, Chattanooga, TN 37406-1097. *Telephone:* 423-697-4408. *Fax:* 423-697-4479. *E-mail:* tim.dills@chattanoogastate.edu or cde@chattanoogastate.edu.

DEGREES AND AWARDS

Programs offered do not lead to a degree or other formal award.

COURSE SUBJECT AREAS OFFERED OUTSIDE OF DEGREE PROGRAMS

Undergraduate—accounting; biology, general; business; business administration and management; communications, general; computer and information sciences, general; computer science; construction management; developmental/child psychology; economics; education, general; English composition; English language and literature, general; English literature (British and Commonwealth); English technical and business writing; financial management and services; fire science; geography; health and medical administrative services; health and medical assistants; health and medical preparatory programs; health professions and related sciences, other; history; liberal arts and sciences, general studies and humanities; mathematical statistics; mathematics; miscellaneous health professions; music; philosophy and religion; physics; political science and government; psychology; religion/religious studies; sociology; speech and rhetorical studies.

CHEMEKETA COMMUNITY COLLEGE

Salem, Oregon

Chemeketa Online

http://online.chemeketa.edu

Chemeketa Community College was founded in 1955. It is accredited by Northwest Commission on Colleges and Universities. It first offered distance learning courses in 1979. In fall 2003, there were 5,000 students enrolled in distance learning courses. Institutionally administered financial aid is available to distance learners.

Services Distance learners have accessibility to academic advising, bookstore, e-mail services, library services, tutoring.

Contact Ms., Distance Education, Chemeketa Community College, 4000 Lancaster Drive, NE, PO Box 14007, Salem, OR 97309-7070. *Telephone:* 503-399-7873. *Fax:* 503-589-7628. *E-mail:* col@chemeketa.edu.

DEGREES AND AWARDS

AA Oregon Transfer

AAS Fire Protection Technology–Fire Prevention; Fire Protection Technology–Fire Suppression; Hospitality and Tourism Management

AGS General Studies

Certificate of Completion Computer Assisted Drafting (CAD)

Certificate Business Technology

COURSE SUBJECT AREAS OFFERED OUTSIDE OF DEGREE PROGRAMS

Undergraduate—accounting; administrative and secretarial services; American literature (United States); anthropology; applied mathematics; archaeology; area, ethnic and cultural studies, other; astronomy; biological and physical sciences; biological sciences/life sciences, other; biology, general; business; business administration and management; business communications; business information and data processing services; business management and administrative services, other; chemistry; computer and information sciences, general; computer and information sciences, other; computer programming; computer science; computer software and media applications; computer systems networking and telecommunications; criminal justice and corrections; criminology; cultural studies; curriculum and instruction; data entry/microcomputer applications; developmental and child psychology; drafting; economics; education, general; education, other; English composition; English creative writing; English technical and business writing; family and community studies; fine arts and art studies; fire protection; foods and nutrition studies; geography; geological and related sciences; health and medical assistants; health and physical education/fitness; health professions and related sciences, other; history; hospitality/recreation marketing; hospitality services management; information sciences and systems; liberal arts and sciences, general studies and humanities; marketing operations/marketing and distribution, other; mathematical statistics; mathematics; mathematics and computer science; mathematics, other; music; philosophy; philosophy and religion; physical sciences, general; physical sciences, other; political science and government; psychology; psychology, other; real estate; religion/religious studies; social sciences and history, other; social sciences, general; sociology; speech and rhetorical studies; tourism/travel marketing.

CHESAPEAKE COLLEGE

Wye Mills, Maryland

http://www.chesapeake.edu/distance

Chesapeake College was founded in 1965. It is accredited by Middle States Association of Colleges and Schools. It first offered distance learning courses in 1994. In fall 2003, there were 895 students enrolled in distance learning courses. Institutionally administered financial aid is available to distance learners.

Services Distance learners have accessibility to bookstore, library services, tutoring.

Contact Mary Celeste Alexander, Director, Chesapeake College, 1000 College Circle, Wye Mills, MD 21679. *Telephone:* 410-822-5400 Ext. 263. *Fax:* 410-827-5875. *E-mail:* mcalexander@chesapeake.edu.

DEGREES AND AWARDS

Programs offered do not lead to a degree or other formal award.

COURSE SUBJECT AREAS OFFERED OUTSIDE OF DEGREE PROGRAMS

Undergraduate—accounting; business; business administration and management; child care and guidance workers and managers; computer and information sciences, general; criminology; English composition; English creative writing; English technical and business writing; history; mathematics; medical laboratory technology; physical sciences, general; psychology; rehabilitation/therapeutic services; sociology.

CINCINNATI STATE TECHNICAL AND COMMUNITY COLLEGE

Cincinnati, Ohio

http://www.cincinnatistate.edu

Cincinnati State Technical and Community College was founded in 1966. It is accredited by North Central Association of Colleges and Schools. It first offered distance learning courses in 1994. In fall 2003, there were 529 students enrolled in distance learning courses. Institutionally administered financial aid is available to distance learners.

Services Distance learners have accessibility to academic advising, bookstore, e-mail services, library services.

Contact Ms. Gaby Boeckermann, Director of Admissions, Cincinnati State Technical and Community College, 3520 Central Parkway, Cincinnati, OH 45223. *Telephone:* 513-569-1550. *E-mail:* gaby.boeckermann@cincinnatistate.edu.

DEGREES AND AWARDS

Programs offered do not lead to a degree or other formal award.

COURSE SUBJECT AREAS OFFERED OUTSIDE OF DEGREE PROGRAMS

Undergraduate—accounting; administrative and secretarial services; business; business administration and management; business information and data processing services; civil engineering/civil technology; computer and information sciences, general; computer/information technology administration and management; computer software and media applications; computer systems networking and telecommunications; data entry/microcomputer applications; data processing technology; engineering-related technologies, other; health and medical administrative services; health and medical assistants; health professions and related sciences, other; horticulture services operations and management; information sciences and systems; Internet and World Wide Web; legal studies; mechanical engineering-related technologies; miscellaneous health professions.

CITRUS COLLEGE

Glendora, California
Distance Education
http://www.citruscollege.com

Citrus College was founded in 1915. It is accredited by Western Association of Schools and Colleges. It first offered distance learning courses in 1996. In fall 2003, there were 1,736 students enrolled in distance learning courses. Institutionally administered financial aid is available to distance learners.

Services Distance learners have accessibility to academic advising, bookstore, campus computer network, e-mail services, library services, tutoring.

Contact Ms. Lari Kirby, Distance Education Supervisor, Citrus College, 1000 West Foothill Boulevard, Glendora, CA 91741-1899. *Telephone:* 626-914-8569. *E-mail:* online@citruscollege.edu.

DEGREES AND AWARDS

AA Liberal Arts

COURSE SUBJECT AREAS OFFERED OUTSIDE OF DEGREE PROGRAMS

Undergraduate—anthropology; biological and physical sciences; business; communications, general; computer and information sciences, general; economics; English composition; history; journalism and mass communications; liberal arts and sciences, general studies and humanities; mathematics; philosophy; psychology; sociology.

CITY UNIVERSITY

Bellevue, Washington
Distance Learning Option
http://www.cityu.edu

City University was founded in 1973. It first offered distance learning courses in 1985. Institutionally administered financial aid is available to distance learners.

Services Distance learners have accessibility to academic advising, library services.

Contact Office of Admissions, City University, 11900 NE First Street, Bellevue, WA 98005. *Telephone:* 800-426-5596. *Fax:* 425-709-5361. *E-mail:* info@cityu.edu.

DEGREES AND AWARDS

AS General Studies Emphasis

BA Applied Psychology; Education–Elementary Education; Education–Special Education

BS Accounting; Business Administration (E-Commerce Emphasis); Business Administration (Europe); Business Administration (General Management Emphasis); Business Administration (Human Resource Emphasis); Business Administration (Information Systems/Technology Emphasis); Business Administration (Marketing Emphasis); Business Administration (Project Management Emphasis); Business Administration–E-Commerce Emphasis (Bulgaria); Business Administration–General Management Emphasis (Bulgaria); Business Administration–Individualized Study Emphasis; Business Administration–Information Systems/Technology Emphasis (Bulgaria); Computer Systems (Networking/Telecommunications Emphasis); Computer Systems (Programming in C++ Emphasis); Computer Systems (Web Design Emphasis); Computer Systems–Database Technology Emphasis; Computer Systems–Individualized Study Emphasis; Computer Systems–Information Technology Security Emphasis; Computer Systems–Web Languages Emphasis; General Studies; Mass Communication and Journalism

Certificate Accounting; Marketing; Networking/Telecommunications; Programming in C++; Project Management; Web Design; Web Languages

Graduate Certificate C++ Programming; E-Commerce; Educational Leadership and Principal Certification; Financial Management; General Management; Information Systems; Marketing; Personal Financial Planning; Professional Certification for Teachers; Project Management; Technology Management; Web Development; Web Programming in E-Commerce

MA Counseling Psychology (Canada); Counseling Psychology (US); Management–General Management Emphasis; Management–Human Resource Management Emphasis; Management–Individualized Study Emphasis

MAT Teacher Certification–Master of Teaching

MBA Accounting Emphasis; Financial Management Emphasis; General Management Emphasis; Information Systems Emphasis; Marketing Emphasis; Personal Financial Planning; Project Management Emphasis

MEd Curriculum and Instruction Specialized Study; Curriculum, Technology, and Instruction (Canada); Education Leadership and Principal Certification; Educational Leadership (Alberta, Canada); Educational Leadership (British Columbia, Canada); Educational Leadership; Guidance and Counseling; Integrated Technology and Learning; Integrating Arts and Performance Learning; Reading and Literacy

MPA General Management Emphasis; Human Resource Management Emphasis; Managerial Leadership Emphasis

MS Computer Systems–C++ Programming Emphasis; Computer Systems–Individualized Study Emphasis; Computer Systems–Technology Management Emphasis; Computer Systems–Web Development Emphasis; Computer Systems–Web Programming in E-Commerce Emphasis; Project Management

See full description on page 384.

CLACKAMAS COMMUNITY COLLEGE

Oregon City, Oregon
Learning Resources
http://dl.clackamas.edu

Clackamas Community College was founded in 1966. It first offered distance learning courses in 1997. In fall 2003, there were 1,772 students enrolled in distance learning courses. Institutionally administered financial aid is available to distance learners.

Services Distance learners have accessibility to academic advising, bookstore, campus computer network, e-mail services, library services.

Contact Cynthia R. Andrews, Director of Distance Learning, Title III and Library, Clackamas Community College, 19600 South Molalla Avenue, Oregon City, OR 97045. *Telephone:* 503-657-6958 Ext. 2417. *Fax:* 503-655-8925. *E-mail:* cyndia@clackamas.cc.or.us.

Clackamas Community College (continued)

DEGREES AND AWARDS

Programs offered do not lead to a degree or other formal award.

COURSE SUBJECT AREAS OFFERED OUTSIDE OF DEGREE PROGRAMS

Undergraduate—accounting; administrative and secretarial services; adult/continuing education; American history; anthropology; biology; business; business administration and management; business and personal services marketing operations; business communications; business information and data processing services; business management and administrative services, other; chemistry; communications, other; computer and information sciences, general; computer and information sciences, other; computer science; computer software and media applications; computer systems networking and telecommunications; criminal justice and corrections; criminology; drafting; education, general; English as a second language; English composition; English literature (British and Commonwealth); English technical and business writing; environmental/environmental health engineering; European history; family and community studies; fine arts and art studies; foods and nutrition studies; health and physical education/fitness; horticulture services operations and management; marketing management and research; mathematics; music; philosophy; psychology; sociology; speech and rhetorical studies.

CLARION UNIVERSITY OF PENNSYLVANIA

Clarion, Pennsylvania
Extended Studies and Distance Learning Department
http://www.clarion.edu/academic/distance/index.shtml

Clarion University of Pennsylvania was founded in 1867. It is accredited by Middle States Association of Colleges and Schools. It first offered distance learning courses in 1996. In fall 2003, there were 614 students enrolled in distance learning courses. Institutionally administered financial aid is available to distance learners.

Services Distance learners have accessibility to academic advising, bookstore, campus computer network, e-mail services, library services.

Contact Lynne M. Lander Fleisher, Assistant Director, Clarion University of Pennsylvania, 840 Wood Street, Clarion, PA 16214. *Telephone:* 814-393-2778. *Fax:* 814-393-2779. *E-mail:* lfleisher@clarion.edu.

DEGREES AND AWARDS

AA Arts and Sciences; Early Childhood Education
MA Rehabilitative Science
MLS Library Science
MSN Nursing–Family Nurse Practitioner

COURSE SUBJECT AREAS OFFERED OUTSIDE OF DEGREE PROGRAMS

Undergraduate—communications, general; economics; education, other; English composition; foreign languages and literatures, other; health and physical education/fitness; library science/librarianship; music; nursing; philosophy; psychology; real estate.

Graduate—education, general; library science/librarianship; nursing; rehabilitation/therapeutic services.
Non-credit—real estate.

CLARK COLLEGE

Vancouver, Washington
http://www.clark.edu/

Clark College was founded in 1933. It is accredited by Northwest Commission on Colleges and Universities. It first offered distance learning courses in 1982.

Services Distance learners have accessibility to bookstore, library services.

Contact Joy Horning, Administrative Assistant, Clark College, 1800 East McLoughlin Boulevard, Vancouver, WA 98663. *Telephone:* 360-992-2293. *Fax:* 360-992-2881. *E-mail:* jhorning@clark.edu.

DEGREES AND AWARDS

Programs offered do not lead to a degree or other formal award.

COURSE SUBJECT AREAS OFFERED OUTSIDE OF DEGREE PROGRAMS

Undergraduate—business administration and management; education, other; English composition; entrepreneurship; financial management and services; health and physical education/fitness; mathematics; psychology.

CLARKSON COLLEGE

Omaha, Nebraska
Office of Distance Education
http://www.clarksoncollege.edu

Clarkson College was founded in 1888. It is accredited by North Central Association of Colleges and Schools. It first offered distance learning courses in 1986. In fall 2003, there were 582 students enrolled in distance learning courses. Institutionally administered financial aid is available to distance learners.

Services Distance learners have accessibility to academic advising, bookstore, campus computer network, career placement assistance, e-mail services, library services, tutoring.

Contact Admissions, Clarkson College, 101 South 42nd Street, Omaha, NE 68131. *Telephone:* 800-647-5500. *Fax:* 402-552-6057. *E-mail:* admiss@clarksoncollege.edu.

DEGREES AND AWARDS

AD Health Information Management
BS Health Care Business Management; Medical Imaging
BSN Nursing–RN/BSN
Certificate Health Information Management; Nursing–Master of Science in Nursing Family Nurse Practitioner
MS Health Care Business Leadership
MSN Nursing–Administration; Nursing–Education; Nursing–Family Nurse Practitioning Major

CLATSOP COMMUNITY COLLEGE

Astoria, Oregon
http://www.clatsopcc.edu

Clatsop Community College was founded in 1958. It first offered distance learning courses in 1986. In fall 2003, there were 99 students enrolled in distance learning courses. Institutionally administered financial aid is available to distance learners.

Services Distance learners have accessibility to library services.
Contact Kirsten Horning, Telecommunications Specialist, Clatsop Community College, 1680 Lexington, Astoria, OR 97103. *Telephone:* 503-338-2341. *Fax:* 503-338-2387. *E-mail:* khorning@clatsopcc.edu.

DEGREES AND AWARDS

Programs offered do not lead to a degree or other formal award.

COURSE SUBJECT AREAS OFFERED OUTSIDE OF DEGREE PROGRAMS

Undergraduate—accounting; anthropology; business; computer and information sciences, general; criminology; English composition; English creative writing; English language and literature, general; geography; health and physical education/fitness; history; mathematical statistics; mathematics; philosophy and religion; political science and government; psychology; sociology.

CLEMSON UNIVERSITY

Clemson, South Carolina
Distance Education, Educational Technology Services
http://www.ets.clemson.edu/

Clemson University was founded in 1889. It is accredited by Southern Association of Colleges and Schools. It first offered distance learning courses in 1988. In fall 2003, there were 1,000 students enrolled in distance learning courses. Institutionally administered financial aid is available to distance learners.

Services Distance learners have accessibility to academic advising, bookstore, campus computer network, career placement assistance, e-mail services, library services.
Contact Dr. Paul E. Adams, Coordinator, Distance Education Programs, ETS, Clemson University, 445 Brackett Hall, PO Box 342803, Clemson, SC 29634-2803. *Telephone:* 864-656-4188. *Fax:* 864-656-0183. *E-mail:* pauladm@clemson.edu.

DEGREES AND AWARDS

BSN Nursing
MCSM Construction Science and Management
MS Human Resource Development
MSEE Electrical Engineering
MSN Nursing
PhD Educational Leadership

COURSE SUBJECT AREAS OFFERED OUTSIDE OF DEGREE PROGRAMS

Undergraduate—astronomy; business; communications, general; economics; English composition; parks, recreation and leisure studies; physics.
Graduate—business administration and management; human resources management.
Non-credit—administrative and secretarial services; business; communications, general; computer and information sciences, general; construction/building technology; construction management; data entry/microcomputer applications; English composition; English creative writing.

CLEVELAND COMMUNITY COLLEGE

Shelby, North Carolina
Distance Learning Program
http://www.cleveland.cc.nc.us

Cleveland Community College was founded in 1965. It is accredited by Southern Association of Colleges and Schools. It first offered distance learning courses in 1999. In fall 2003, there were 500 students enrolled in distance learning courses. Institutionally administered financial aid is available to distance learners.

Services Distance learners have accessibility to library services.
Contact Jody Ledford, Distance Learning Coordinator, Cleveland Community College, 137 South Post Road, Shelby, NC 28152. *Telephone:* 704-484-4000. *Fax:* 704-484-4036. *E-mail:* ledford@cleveland.cc.nc.us.

DEGREES AND AWARDS

Programs offered do not lead to a degree or other formal award.

COURSE SUBJECT AREAS OFFERED OUTSIDE OF DEGREE PROGRAMS

Undergraduate—biology, general; business/managerial economics; carpenters; child care and guidance workers and managers; computer/information technology administration and management; computer programming.

CLEVELAND STATE UNIVERSITY

Cleveland, Ohio
Off-Campus Academic Programs
http://www.csuohio.edu/offcampus

Cleveland State University was founded in 1964. It is accredited by North Central Association of Colleges and Schools. It first offered distance learning courses in 1994. In fall 2003, there were 783 students enrolled in distance learning courses. Institutionally administered financial aid is available to distance learners.

Services Distance learners have accessibility to academic advising, bookstore, campus computer network, career placement assistance, e-mail services, library services.
Contact Dr. Barbara E. Hanniford, Dean of Continuing Studies, Cleveland State University, Division of Continuing Education, 3100 Chester Avenue, Cleveland, OH 44114-2214. *Telephone:* 216-687-2149. *Fax:* 216-687-5299. *E-mail:* b.hanniford@csuohio.edu.

DEGREES AND AWARDS

Endorsement Computer/Technology
Graduate Certificate Adult Learning and Development; Bioethics
MS Health Science
MSE Adult Learning and Development; Educational Technology
MSW Social Work

COURSE SUBJECT AREAS OFFERED OUTSIDE OF DEGREE PROGRAMS

Undergraduate—biological sciences/life sciences, other; chemistry; city/urban, community and regional planning; computer programming; computer systems analysis; engineering/industrial management; engineering-related technologies, other; English language and literature, general; geography; geological and related sciences; health

Cleveland State University (continued)

professions and related sciences, other; information sciences and systems; nursing; philosophy and religion related; political science and government; psychology; public administration; social work; sociology; telecommunications; urban affairs/studies; women's studies.

Graduate—adult/continuing education; area, ethnic and cultural studies, other; chemical engineering; city/urban, community and regional planning; computer/information technology administration and management; computer software and media applications; computer systems networking and telecommunications; curriculum and instruction; education, other; electrical engineering; engineering/industrial management; engineering-related technologies, other; English language and literature, general; health and medical administrative services; health professions and related sciences, other; industrial engineering; industrial/manufacturing engineering; Internet and World Wide Web; miscellaneous engineering-related technologies; philosophy and religion related; public administration; social work; technology education/industrial arts; telecommunications; urban affairs/studies.

Non-credit—accounting; business; business administration and management; business and personal services marketing operations; business communications; business information and data processing services; computer software and media applications; computer systems networking and telecommunications; data entry/microcomputer applications; education, other; entrepreneurship; family and community studies; family/consumer resource management; film/video and photographic arts; foods and nutrition studies; foreign languages and literatures, other; health and physical education/fitness; health professions and related sciences, other; individual and family development studies; Internet and World Wide Web; journalism and mass communications; miscellaneous health professions; public health; technology education/industrial arts; telecommunications.

CLINTON COMMUNITY COLLEGE

Plattsburgh, New York

http://clinton.edu

Clinton Community College was founded in 1969. It is accredited by Middle States Association of Colleges and Schools. It first offered distance learning courses in 2000. In fall 2003, there were 190 students enrolled in distance learning courses. Institutionally administered financial aid is available to distance learners.

Services Distance learners have accessibility to academic advising, bookstore, campus computer network, career placement assistance, e-mail services, library services, tutoring.

Contact Prof. Vicky Sloan, Distance Learning Coordinator, Clinton Community College, 136 Clinton Point Drive, Plattsburgh, NY 12901. *Telephone:* 518-562-4281. *E-mail:* sloavl@clintoncc.suny.edu.

DEGREES AND AWARDS

AA Liberal Arts/Humanities and Social Science
AS Business Administration

COURSE SUBJECT AREAS OFFERED OUTSIDE OF DEGREE PROGRAMS

Undergraduate—accounting; applied mathematics; biological and physical sciences; business administration and management; business communications; computer and information sciences, general; computer programming; criminal justice and corrections; economics; English composition; English language and literature, general; history; liberal arts and sciences, general studies and humanities; mathematical statistics; medical laboratory technology; music; psychology; sociology.

CLOVIS COMMUNITY COLLEGE

Clovis, New Mexico

http://www.clovis.edu/

Clovis Community College was founded in 1990. It is accredited by North Central Association of Colleges and Schools. It first offered distance learning courses in 1990. In fall 2003, there were 500 students enrolled in distance learning courses. Institutionally administered financial aid is available to distance learners.

Services Distance learners have accessibility to academic advising, bookstore, library services.

Contact Ms. Susan M. Veronikas, Educational Technologist, Clovis Community College, 417 Schepps Boulevard, Clovis, NM 88101. *Telephone:* 505-769-4903. *E-mail:* susan.veronikas@clovis.edu.

DEGREES AND AWARDS

AAS Criminal Justice

COURSE SUBJECT AREAS OFFERED OUTSIDE OF DEGREE PROGRAMS

Undergraduate—American history; art history; bible/biblical studies; biology; business administration and management; communications, general; computer and information sciences, general; criminal justice and corrections; developmental/child psychology; economics; English composition; mathematics; mathematics related; sociology; Spanish.

COASTAL BEND COLLEGE

Beeville, Texas

http://vct.coastalbend.edu/content/index.cfm/fa/viewpage/category_id/125.htm

Coastal Bend College was founded in 1965. It is accredited by Southern Association of Colleges and Schools. It first offered distance learning courses in 1997. In fall 2003, there were 544 students enrolled in distance learning courses. Institutionally administered financial aid is available to distance learners.

Services Distance learners have accessibility to academic advising, campus computer network, career placement assistance, e-mail services, library services, tutoring.

Contact Ms. Alma Adamez, Director of Educational Services, Coastal Bend College, 3800 Charco Road, Beeville, TX 78102. *Telephone:* 361-354-2268. *Fax:* 361-354-2269. *E-mail:* adamez@coastalbend.edu.

DEGREES AND AWARDS

Programs offered do not lead to a degree or other formal award.

COURSE SUBJECT AREAS OFFERED OUTSIDE OF DEGREE PROGRAMS

Undergraduate—astronomy; business administration and management; business/managerial economics; computer science; criminal justice and corrections; English composition; geological and related sciences; history; marketing management and research; mathematics; music; philosophy; physics; political science and government; psychology; social work; sociology.

COCONINO COMMUNITY COLLEGE

Flagstaff, Arizona

http://www.coconino.edu/extended/online.html

Coconino Community College was founded in 1991. It is accredited by North Central Association of Colleges and Schools. It first offered distance learning courses in 1999. In fall 2003, there were 800 students enrolled in distance learning courses. Institutionally administered financial aid is available to distance learners.

Services Distance learners have accessibility to bookstore, library services.
Contact Mr. Rick McDonald, Instructional Technology Coordinator, Coconino Community College, Flagstaff, AZ 86001. *E-mail:* rick.mcdonald@coconino.edu.

DEGREES AND AWARDS

AA Elementary Education
AAB Business (ABus)

COURSE SUBJECT AREAS OFFERED OUTSIDE OF DEGREE PROGRAMS

Undergraduate—business; communications, general; computer and information sciences, general; criminal justice and corrections; education, general; English composition; geography; health professions and related sciences, other; history; mathematics; philosophy; psychology; sociology.
Non-credit—computer software and media applications; English composition; English creative writing; foreign languages and literatures; music.

COLEMAN COLLEGE

La Mesa, California

http://www.coleman.edu

Coleman College was founded in 1963. It is accredited by Accrediting Council for Independent Colleges and Schools. It first offered distance learning courses in 2001. In fall 2003, there were 250 students enrolled in distance learning courses. Institutionally administered financial aid is available to distance learners.

Services Distance learners have accessibility to academic advising, bookstore, career placement assistance, e-mail services, library services.
Contact Debbie Coleman, Director of Admissions, Coleman College, 7380 Parkway Drive, La Mesa, CA 91942. *Telephone:* 619-465-3990 Ext. 101. *E-mail:* debcoleman@coleman.edu.

DEGREES AND AWARDS

MS Business Technology Management–Master of Science in Business Technology Management

COURSE SUBJECT AREAS OFFERED OUTSIDE OF DEGREE PROGRAMS

Undergraduate—accounting; business administration and management; computer and information sciences, general; computer/information technology administration and management; computer programming; English composition; English creative writing; English technical and business writing; history; human resources management; marketing management and research; mathematical statistics; mathematics; philosophy; physical sciences, general; psychology; sociology.
Graduate—business; business administration and management; business communications; marketing management and research.

COLLEGE FOR LIFELONG LEARNING

Concord, New Hampshire

http://www.cll.edu

College for Lifelong Learning was founded in 1972. It is accredited by New England Association of Schools and Colleges. It first offered distance learning courses in 1999. In fall 2003, there were 239 students enrolled in distance learning courses. Institutionally administered financial aid is available to distance learners.

Services Distance learners have accessibility to academic advising, bookstore, e-mail services, library services.
Contact Ms. Karen R. King, Registrar, College for Lifelong Learning, 125 North State Street, Concord, NH 03301. *Telephone:* 603-228-3000 Ext. 312. *Fax:* 603-229-0964. *E-mail:* karen.king@cll.edu.

DEGREES AND AWARDS

AA General Studies
BS Information Technology

COURSE SUBJECT AREAS OFFERED OUTSIDE OF DEGREE PROGRAMS

Undergraduate—adult/continuing education; business administration and management; communications, general; computer/information technology administration and management; criminal justice and corrections; family and community studies; financial management and services; health services administration; liberal arts and sciences, general studies and humanities; management information systems/business data processing; multi/interdisciplinary studies, other; social sciences, general; special education.

COLLEGE OF DUPAGE

Glen Ellyn, Illinois

Alternative Learning Division

http://www.cod.edu/cil

College of DuPage was founded in 1967. It is accredited by North Central Association of Colleges and Schools. It first offered distance learning courses in 1980. In fall 2003, there were 6,000 students enrolled in distance learning courses. Institutionally administered financial aid is available to distance learners.

Services Distance learners have accessibility to academic advising, bookstore, campus computer network, e-mail services, library services, tutoring.
Contact Ron Schiesz, Counselor for Alternative Learning Program, College of DuPage, Center for Independent Learning, 425 Fawell Street, Glen Ellyn, IL 60137-6599. *Telephone:* 630-942-3326 Ext. 3326. *Fax:* 630-942-3764. *E-mail:* schiesz@cdnet.cod.edu.

College of DuPage (continued)

DEGREES AND AWARDS

Programs offered do not lead to a degree or other formal award.

COURSE SUBJECT AREAS OFFERED OUTSIDE OF DEGREE PROGRAMS

Undergraduate—accounting; American history; anthropology; biology; business administration and management; chemistry; communications, general; computer programming; computer software and media applications; computer systems networking and telecommunications; criminal justice and corrections; developmental/child psychology; earth sciences; economics; educational psychology; English as a second language; English composition; history; human services; journalism and mass communications; liberal arts and sciences, general studies and humanities; library assistant; library science/librarianship; marketing operations/marketing and distribution, other; mathematics; music; philosophy and religion; physics; psychology; religion/religious studies; social psychology; social sciences and history, other; social sciences, general; sociology; Spanish.

COLLEGE OF EMMANUEL AND ST. CHAD

Saskatoon, Saskatchewan, Canada

College of Emmanuel and St. Chad was founded in 1879. It is provincially chartered. Institutionally administered financial aid is available to distance learners.

Services Distance learners have accessibility to academic advising, bookstore, campus computer network, library services.

Contact Ms. Colleen Walker, Registrar, College of Emmanuel and St. Chad, 1337 College Drive, Saskatoon, SK S7N 0W6, Canada. *Telephone:* 306-975-1558. *Fax:* 306-934-2683. *E-mail:* colleen.walker@usask.ca.

DEGREES AND AWARDS

Programs offered do not lead to a degree or other formal award.

COURSE SUBJECT AREAS OFFERED OUTSIDE OF DEGREE PROGRAMS

Graduate—theological and ministerial studies; theological studies and religious vocations, other.

COLLEGE OF MENOMINEE NATION

Keshena, Wisconsin

http://www.menominee.edu

College of Menominee Nation is accredited by North Central Association of Colleges and Schools. It first offered distance learning courses in 2002. In fall 2003, there were 30 students enrolled in distance learning courses.

Services Distance learners have accessibility to e-mail services.

Contact Mr. David Heup, Distance Education Coordinator, College of Menominee Nation, PO Box 1179, N172 Hwy 47 & 55, Keshena, WI 54135. *Telephone:* 715-799-6226 Ext. 3059. *E-mail:* dheup@menominee.edu.

DEGREES AND AWARDS

Programs offered do not lead to a degree or other formal award.

COURSE SUBJECT AREAS OFFERED OUTSIDE OF DEGREE PROGRAMS

Undergraduate—accounting; business; education, general.

COLLEGE OF MOUNT ST. JOSEPH

Cincinnati, Ohio

http://www.msj.edu/

College of Mount St. Joseph was founded in 1920. It is accredited by North Central Association of Colleges and Schools. It first offered distance learning courses in 1997. In fall 2003, there were 84 students enrolled in distance learning courses. Institutionally administered financial aid is available to distance learners.

Services Distance learners have accessibility to academic advising, bookstore, campus computer network, career placement assistance, e-mail services, library services, tutoring.

Contact Ms. Peggy Minnich, Director of Admissions, College of Mount St. Joseph, 5701 Delhi Road, Cincinnati, OH 45233. *Telephone:* 513-244-4814. *E-mail:* peggy_minnich@mail.msj.edu.

DEGREES AND AWARDS

Programs offered do not lead to a degree or other formal award.

COURSE SUBJECT AREAS OFFERED OUTSIDE OF DEGREE PROGRAMS

Undergraduate—biology; business administration and management; computer and information sciences, general; education, general; music; paralegal/legal assistant; political science and government; religion/religious studies; social psychology.

Graduate—education, general.

Non-credit—religion/religious studies.

THE COLLEGE OF ST. SCHOLASTICA

Duluth, Minnesota

Graduate Studies

http://grad.css.edu

The College of St. Scholastica was founded in 1912. It is accredited by North Central Association of Colleges and Schools. It first offered distance learning courses in 1986. In fall 2003, there were 217 students enrolled in distance learning courses. Institutionally administered financial aid is available to distance learners.

Services Distance learners have accessibility to academic advising, bookstore, campus computer network, career placement assistance, e-mail services, library services, tutoring.

Contact Tonya J. Roth, Graduate Recruitment Counselor, The College of St. Scholastica, 1200 Kenwood Avenue, Duluth, MN 55811. *Telephone:* 218-723-6285. *Fax:* 218-733-2275. *E-mail:* gradstudies@css.edu.

DEGREES AND AWARDS

BA Health Information Management Degree Completion
Certificate Health Informatics

MA Health Information Management; Nursing–Family Nurse Practitioner
MEd Curriculum and Instruction; Educational Media and Technology

COURSE SUBJECT AREAS OFFERED OUTSIDE OF DEGREE PROGRAMS

Undergraduate—biology, general; economics; gerontology; health and medical administrative services; music; nursing; psychology.
Graduate—curriculum and instruction; health and medical administrative services; library science, other; music; nursing.

COLLEGE OF SAN MATEO

San Mateo, California
http://www.collegeofsanmateo.edu

College of San Mateo was founded in 1922. It is accredited by Western Association of Schools and Colleges. It first offered distance learning courses in 1977. In fall 2003, there were 1,300 students enrolled in distance learning courses. Institutionally administered financial aid is available to distance learners.

Services Distance learners have accessibility to academic advising, bookstore, campus computer network, career placement assistance, e-mail services, library services, tutoring.
Contact Betty Fleming, Distance Learning Coordinator, College of San Mateo, 1700 West Hillsdale Boulevard, San Mateo, CA 94402-3784. *Telephone:* 650-524-6933. *Fax:* 650-574-6345. *E-mail:* fleming@smccd.net.

DEGREES AND AWARDS

Programs offered do not lead to a degree or other formal award.

COURSE SUBJECT AREAS OFFERED OUTSIDE OF DEGREE PROGRAMS

Undergraduate—accounting; anthropology; astronomy; business; business communications; business marketing and marketing management; chemistry; computer programming; English composition; film studies; French; health and physical education/fitness; Italian; law and legal studies related; mathematics; philosophy; political science and government; psychology; sociology; Spanish.

COLLEGE OF THE ALBEMARLE

Elizabeth City, North Carolina
Distance Education
http://www.albemarle.edu

College of The Albemarle was founded in 1960. It is accredited by Southern Association of Colleges and Schools. It first offered distance learning courses in 1993. In fall 2003, there were 1,000 students enrolled in distance learning courses. Institutionally administered financial aid is available to distance learners.

Services Distance learners have accessibility to academic advising, bookstore, career placement assistance, e-mail services, library services.
Contact Jerry Oliver, Distance Education Coordinator, College of The Albemarle, PO Box 2327, Elizabeth City, NC 27906-2327. *Telephone:* 252-335-0821 Ext. 2313. *Fax:* 252-337-6710. *E-mail:* joliver@albemarle.edu.

DEGREES AND AWARDS

AAS Business Administration; Criminal Justice

COURSE SUBJECT AREAS OFFERED OUTSIDE OF DEGREE PROGRAMS

Undergraduate—accounting; art history; biology, general; business; business administration and management; business communications; business marketing and marketing management; child care and guidance workers and managers; computer and information sciences, general; computer science; economics; education related; electrical and electronic engineering-related technology; English composition; English literature (British and Commonwealth); health and physical education/fitness; history; law and legal studies related; mathematics related; psychology; sociology.
Non-credit—accounting; administrative and secretarial services; business; business administration and management; business communications; business information and data processing services; business management and administrative services, other; communications, general; computer and information sciences, general; computer engineering; computer/information technology administration and management; computer programming; computer science; computer software and media applications; computer systems networking and telecommunications; data entry/microcomputer applications; data processing technology; education administration and supervision; English composition; English language and literature, general; English technical and business writing; gerontology; hospitality/recreation marketing; human services; information sciences and systems; mental health services; public administration; public administration and services, other; telecommunications.

COLLEGE OF THE CANYONS

Santa Clarita, California
Learning Resources
http://www.canyons.edu

College of the Canyons was founded in 1969. It is accredited by Western Association of Schools and Colleges. It first offered distance learning courses in 1987. In fall 2003, there were 1,000 students enrolled in distance learning courses. Institutionally administered financial aid is available to distance learners.

Services Distance learners have accessibility to bookstore, campus computer network, e-mail services, library services.
Contact Ms. Renee Drake, Instructional Media Technician II for Distance Learning, College of the Canyons, 26455 Rockwell Canyon Road, Santa Clarita, CA 91355. *Telephone:* 661-362-3600. *Fax:* 661-259-3421. *E-mail:* renee.drake@canyons.edu.

DEGREES AND AWARDS

Programs offered do not lead to a degree or other formal award.

COURSE SUBJECT AREAS OFFERED OUTSIDE OF DEGREE PROGRAMS

Undergraduate—administrative and secretarial services; anthropology; astronomy; biological and physical sciences; business communications; chemistry; computer and information sciences, general; computer and information sciences, other; computer programming; computer science; developmental and child psychology; economics; English composition; English language and literature, general; family and community studies; film/video and photographic arts; health and physical education/fitness; history; hospitality services management; institutional food workers and administrators; Internet and World

College of the Canyons (continued)
Wide Web; music; philosophy; philosophy and religion; political science and government; psychology; sociology; speech and rhetorical studies.

COLLEGE OF THE SISKIYOUS

Weed, California

Distance Learning

http://www.siskiyous.edu/distancelearning/

College of the Siskiyous was founded in 1957. It is accredited by Western Association of Schools and Colleges. It first offered distance learning courses in 1975. In fall 2003, there were 550 students enrolled in distance learning courses. Institutionally administered financial aid is available to distance learners.

Services Distance learners have accessibility to academic advising, career placement assistance, e-mail services, library services, tutoring.
Contact Nancy Shepard, Telecommunications Specialist, College of the Siskiyous, 800 College Avenue, Weed, CA 96094. *Telephone:* 530-938-5520. *Fax:* 530-938-5238. *E-mail:* shepard@siskiyous.edu.

DEGREES AND AWARDS

Programs offered do not lead to a degree or other formal award.

COURSE SUBJECT AREAS OFFERED OUTSIDE OF DEGREE PROGRAMS

Undergraduate—accounting; business; business communications; computer science; English composition; English language and literature/letters, other; English literature (British and Commonwealth); family/consumer resource management; health and physical education/fitness; history; liberal arts and sciences, general studies and humanities; mathematics; nursing; political science and government; psychology; social sciences, general; student counseling and personnel services; teacher assistant/aide.

COLLEGE OF THE SOUTHWEST

Hobbs, New Mexico

http://www.csw.edu/

College of the Southwest was founded in 1962. It is accredited by North Central Association of Colleges and Schools. It first offered distance learning courses in 1994. In fall 2003, there were 200 students enrolled in distance learning courses. Institutionally administered financial aid is available to distance learners.

Services Distance learners have accessibility to academic advising, bookstore, campus computer network, e-mail services, library services.
Contact Glenna Ohaver, Registrar, College of the Southwest, 6610 Lovington Highway, Hobbs, NM 88240. *Telephone:* 505-392-6561. *Fax:* 505-392-6006. *E-mail:* gohaver@csw.edu.

DEGREES AND AWARDS

BS Criminal Justice
MSE Educational Administration and Counseling; Educational Diagnostician

COURSE SUBJECT AREAS OFFERED OUTSIDE OF DEGREE PROGRAMS

Undergraduate—accounting; advertising; biology; business administration and management; computer science; creative writing; criminal justice and corrections; developmental/child psychology; economics; educational psychology; education, general; English as a second language; English composition; history; marketing management and research; organizational psychology; psychology; religion/religious studies; social psychology; sociology.
Graduate—counseling psychology; curriculum and instruction; education administration and supervision; educational evaluation, research and statistics.

COLLIN COUNTY COMMUNITY COLLEGE DISTRICT

Plano, Texas

Distance Learning Center

http://www.ccccd.edu

Collin County Community College District was founded in 1985. It is accredited by Southern Association of Colleges and Schools. It first offered distance learning courses in 1987. In fall 2003, there were 3,000 students enrolled in distance learning courses. Institutionally administered financial aid is available to distance learners.

Services Distance learners have accessibility to academic advising, bookstore, campus computer network, career placement assistance, e-mail services, library services, tutoring.
Contact Hector de Luna, Coordinator of Distance Education, Collin County Community College District, 2800 East Spring Creek Parkway, Plano, TX 75074. *Telephone:* 972-881-5828. *Fax:* 972-881-5626. *E-mail:* hdeluna@ccccd.edu.

DEGREES AND AWARDS

Programs offered do not lead to a degree or other formal award.

COURSE SUBJECT AREAS OFFERED OUTSIDE OF DEGREE PROGRAMS

Undergraduate—accounting; business; communications, general; communications, other; economics; English composition; geography; history; journalism and mass communications; music; social psychology; social sciences, general; sociology.

COLORADO CHRISTIAN UNIVERSITY

Lakewood, Colorado

Academic Technologies Group

http://www.ccuonline.org

Colorado Christian University was founded in 1914. It is accredited by North Central Association of Colleges and Schools. It first offered distance learning courses in 1999. In fall 2003, there were 1,154 students enrolled in distance learning courses. Institutionally administered financial aid is available to distance learners.

Services Distance learners have accessibility to academic advising, bookstore, campus computer network, e-mail services, library services.

Contact Mr. Jan Bybee, Manager of Academic Technologies, Colorado Christian University, 180 South Garrison Street, Lakewood, CO 80226. *Telephone:* 303-963-3385. *Fax:* 303-963-3381. *E-mail:* jbybee@ccu.edu.

DEGREES AND AWARDS

MBA Business Administration

COURSE SUBJECT AREAS OFFERED OUTSIDE OF DEGREE PROGRAMS

Undergraduate—biblical and other theological languages and literatures; business administration and management; computer and information sciences, general; computer software and media applications; history; marketing management and research; philosophy and religion; physiological psychology/psychobiology; technology education/industrial arts.
Graduate—business administration and management; business marketing and marketing management; educational evaluation, research and statistics; financial management and services.

COLORADO MOUNTAIN COLLEGE DISTRICT SYSTEM

Glenwood Springs, Colorado
Educational Technology
http://www.coloradomtn.edu/distlearn/

Colorado Mountain College District System first offered distance learning courses in 1985. In fall 2003, there were 800 students enrolled in distance learning courses. Institutionally administered financial aid is available to distance learners.

Services Distance learners have accessibility to bookstore, library services.
Contact Mr. Daryl D. Yarrow, Division Director for Distance Learning, Colorado Mountain College District System, 831 Grand Avenue, Glenwood Springs, CO 81601. *Telephone:* 800-621-8559 Ext. 8336. *Fax:* 970-947-8307. *E-mail:* dyarrow@coloradomtn.edu.

DEGREES AND AWARDS

Programs offered do not lead to a degree or other formal award.

COURSE SUBJECT AREAS OFFERED OUTSIDE OF DEGREE PROGRAMS

Undergraduate—accounting; anthropology; archaeology; art history; astronomy; biology; business; business communications; business marketing and marketing management; chemistry; computer science; computer software and media applications; construction trades, other; developmental/child psychology; earth sciences; economics; education, other; English composition; geography; health professions and related sciences, other; history; hospitality services management; library science, other; mathematical statistics; mathematics related; philosophy; physics; psychology; social psychology; sociology; Spanish.
Non-credit—computer software and media applications.

COLORADO STATE UNIVERSITY

Fort Collins, Colorado
Division of Continuing Education
http://www.learn.colostate.edu

Colorado State University was founded in 1870. It is accredited by North Central Association of Colleges and Schools. It first offered distance learning courses in 1967. In fall 2003, there were 1,000 students enrolled in distance learning courses. Institutionally administered financial aid is available to distance learners.

Services Distance learners have accessibility to academic advising, bookstore, library services.
Contact Debi Colbert, Distance Degrees, Colorado State University, 1040 Campus Delivery, Fort Collins, CO 80523-1040. *Telephone:* 970-491-5288. *Fax:* 970-491-7885. *E-mail:* dcolbert@learn.colostate.edu.

DEGREES AND AWARDS

BA Liberal Arts–Social Science
Certificate of Completion Veterinary Professionals
Certificate Apparel and Merchandising; Applied Statistics and Data Analysis; Finance; Information Science and Technology; Natural Resources and the Environment; Postsecondary Teaching; Statistical Theory and Methods; Telecommunications
Graduate Certificate Post-Secondary Teaching
MAg Agricultural Sciences
MBA Business Administration
MCS Computer Science
ME Civil Engineering; Electrical and Computer Engineering; Engineering Management; Mechanical Engineering
MEd Adult Education and Training
MS Engineering Management; Engineering Management; Industrial Engineering; Mechanical Engineering; Rangeland Ecosystem Science; Statistics
PhD Electrical Engineering; Industrial Engineering; Mechanical Engineering; Systems Engineering

COURSE SUBJECT AREAS OFFERED OUTSIDE OF DEGREE PROGRAMS

Undergraduate—agriculture/agricultural sciences; animal sciences; computer science; consumer and homemaking education; design and applied arts; developmental/child psychology; economics; educational psychology; foods and nutrition studies; history; horticulture services operations and management; individual and family development studies; psychology; sociology.
Graduate—business marketing and marketing management; chemical engineering; electrical engineering; engineering/industrial management; engineering mechanics; environmental engineering; finance; industrial engineering; mechanical engineering.
Non-credit—accounting; business; computer programming; economics; legal studies; medical basic sciences; music; teacher education, specific academic and vocational programs; tourism/travel marketing.

See full description on page 388.

COLORADO STATE UNIVERSITY

Fort Collins, Colorado
College of Business
http://www.csumba.com

Colorado State University was founded in 1870. It is accredited by North Central Association of Colleges and Schools. It first offered distance learning courses in 1975. In fall 2003, there were 370 students enrolled in distance learning courses. Institutionally administered financial aid is available to distance learners.

Services Distance learners have accessibility to academic advising, bookstore, campus computer network, career placement assistance, e-mail services, library services.

Colorado State University (continued)

Contact Ms. Rachel Stoll, Graduate Admissions Coordinator, Colorado State University, College of Business, 164 Rockwell Hall, Fort Collins, CO 80523-1270. *Telephone:* 800-491-4MBA Ext. 2. *Fax:* 970-491-2348. *E-mail:* rachel.stoll@business.colostate.edu.

DEGREES AND AWARDS

MBA Distance MBA

See full description on page 386.

COLORADO STATE UNIVERSITY-PUEBLO

Pueblo, Colorado
Division of Continuing Education
http://coned.colostate-pueblo.edu

Colorado State University-Pueblo was founded in 1933. It is accredited by North Central Association of Colleges and Schools. It first offered distance learning courses in 1970. In fall 2003, there were 1,500 students enrolled in distance learning courses. Institutionally administered financial aid is available to distance learners.

Services Distance learners have accessibility to academic advising, bookstore, library services.

Contact Angela Healy, Program Manager, Colorado State University-Pueblo, 2200 Bonforte Boulevard, Pueblo, CO 81001-4901. *Telephone:* 800-388-6154. *Fax:* 719-549-2438. *E-mail:* coned@colostate-pueblo.edu.

DEGREES AND AWARDS

BS Social Sciences; Sociology; Sociology/Criminology
Certificate Paralegal Studies

COURSE SUBJECT AREAS OFFERED OUTSIDE OF DEGREE PROGRAMS

Undergraduate—anthropology; biological sciences/life sciences, other; business; chemistry; economics; education, general; English composition; English language and literature, general; geography; geological and related sciences; history; liberal arts and sciences, general studies and humanities; mathematics; nursing; political science and government; psychology.
Graduate—education, general.
Non-credit—administrative and secretarial services; business administration and management; business information and data processing services; computer software and media applications; data entry/microcomputer applications; enterprise management and operation; health and medical administrative services; tourism/travel marketing.

COLORADO TECHNICAL UNIVERSITY

Colorado Springs, Colorado
http://www.ctuonline.edu

Colorado Technical University was founded in 1965. It is accredited by North Central Association of Colleges and Schools. It first offered distance learning courses in 2003. Institutionally administered financial aid is available to distance learners.

Services Distance learners have accessibility to academic advising, bookstore, campus computer network, career placement assistance, e-mail services, library services.

Contact Admissions Department, Colorado Technical University, 4435 North Chestnut Street, Suite E, Colorado Springs, CO 80907. *Telephone:* 800-416-8904. *E-mail:* info@ctuonline.edu.

DEGREES AND AWARDS

BS Criminal Justice (BSCJ)
BSBA Human Resource Management Concentration; Information Technology Concentration; Management Concentration; Marketing Concentration
EMBA Business Administration
MSM Business Management Concentration; Information Systems Security Concentration; Information Technology Management Concentration; Project Management Concentration

See full description on page 390.

COLUMBIA BASIN COLLEGE

Pasco, Washington
http://www.columbiabasin.edu/distance/

Columbia Basin College was founded in 1955. It is accredited by Northwest Commission on Colleges and Universities. It first offered distance learning courses in 1985. In fall 2003, there were 3,000 students enrolled in distance learning courses. Institutionally administered financial aid is available to distance learners.

Services Distance learners have accessibility to academic advising, bookstore, career placement assistance, e-mail services, library services, tutoring.

Contact Dr. Deborah R. Meadows, Dean for Business/Information Technology and Social Science/Foreign Language, Columbia Basin College, 2600 North 20th Avenue, Pasco, WA 99301. *Telephone:* 509-547-0511 Ext. 2373. *Fax:* 509-546-0401. *E-mail:* dmeadows@columbiabasin.edu.

DEGREES AND AWARDS

AAS Business, Humanities, Social Sciences

COURSE SUBJECT AREAS OFFERED OUTSIDE OF DEGREE PROGRAMS

Undergraduate—accounting; administrative and secretarial services; anthropology; art history; business; business administration and management; communications, general; computer and information sciences, other; computer programming; computer science; counseling psychology; cultural studies; economics; English composition; English language and literature, general; English technical and business writing; geography; health and physical education/fitness; history; Internet and World Wide Web; mathematics; mathematics related; political science and government; psychology; sociology.
Non-credit—business.

COLUMBIA COLLEGE

Columbia, Missouri
http://www.ccis.edu/online

Columbia College was founded in 1851. It is accredited by North Central Association of Colleges and Schools. It first offered distance learning courses in 2000. In fall 2003, there were 4,000 students enrolled in distance learning courses. Institutionally administered financial aid is available to distance learners.

Services Distance learners have accessibility to academic advising, bookstore, campus computer network, career placement assistance, e-mail services, library services.

Contact Ms. Sara Farris, Assistant Director, Columbia College, 1001 Rogers Street, Columbia, MO 65216. *Telephone:* 573-875-7459. *Fax:* 573-875-7444. *E-mail:* sbfarris@ccis.edu.

DEGREES AND AWARDS

AA General Studies
AGS General Studies
AS Business Administration; Criminal Justice; Fire Science Administration
BA Business Administration; Criminal Justice; General Studies; Interdisciplinary Studies; Psychology
BS Business Administration

COURSE SUBJECT AREAS OFFERED OUTSIDE OF DEGREE PROGRAMS

Undergraduate—accounting; American literature (United States); biological sciences/life sciences, other; business administration and management; computer and information sciences, general; criminal justice and corrections; curriculum and instruction; education, general; English literature (British and Commonwealth); enterprise management and operation; history; marketing operations/marketing and distribution, other; mathematics; mathematics and computer science; multi/interdisciplinary studies, other; philosophy and religion; political science and government; psychology; social sciences and history, other; social work; sociology.

COLUMBIA SOUTHERN UNIVERSITY

Orange Beach, Alabama

http://www.columbiasouthern.edu

Columbia Southern University is accredited by Distance Education and Training Council. It first offered distance learning courses in 1993. In fall 2003, there were 5,200 students enrolled in distance learning courses. Institutionally administered financial aid is available to distance learners.

Services Distance learners have accessibility to academic advising, bookstore, library services.

Contact Admissions Department, Columbia Southern University, 24847 Commercial Avenue, Orange Beach, AL 36561. *Telephone:* 251-981-3771. *Fax:* 251-981-3815. *E-mail:* admissions@columbiasouthern.edu.

DEGREES AND AWARDS

AAS Business
BS Business Administration; Criminal Justice Administration; Environmental Management; Health Care Administration; Information Technology; Occupational Safety and Health
MBA Business Administration
MS Occupational Safety and Health

COLUMBIA UNION COLLEGE

Takoma Park, Maryland

http://www.cuc.edu/

Columbia Union College was founded in 1904. It is accredited by Middle States Association of Colleges and Schools. It first offered distance learning courses in 1969. In fall 2003, there were 73 students enrolled in distance learning courses. Institutionally administered financial aid is available to distance learners.

Services Distance learners have accessibility to academic advising, bookstore, campus computer network, career placement assistance, e-mail services, library services, tutoring.

Contact Dr. Oliver Koh, Coordinator for External Programs, Columbia Union College, 12501 Old Columbia Pike, Silver Spring, MD 20904. *Telephone:* 301-680-6590. *Fax:* 301-680-5157. *E-mail:* okoh@hsi.edu.

DEGREES AND AWARDS

AA General Studies
AS General Studies
BA General Studies; Psychology; Religion; Theology
BS Business Administration; General Studies; Information Systems

COURSE SUBJECT AREAS OFFERED OUTSIDE OF DEGREE PROGRAMS

Undergraduate—accounting; bible/biblical studies; biblical and other theological languages and literatures; biology, general; business; business administration and management; communications, general; computer and information sciences, general; economics; education, general; English composition; English language and literature, general; foods and nutrition studies; foreign languages and literatures; geography; health professions and related sciences, other; history; marketing management and research; mathematical statistics; mathematics; music; physics; political science and government; psychology; religion/religious studies; social sciences, general; sociology; theological and ministerial studies.

COLUMBIA UNIVERSITY

New York, New York

Columbia Video Network

http://www.cvn.columbia.edu

Columbia University was founded in 1754. It is accredited by Middle States Association of Colleges and Schools. It first offered distance learning courses in 1986. In fall 2003, there were 470 students enrolled in distance learning courses. Institutionally administered financial aid is available to distance learners.

Services Distance learners have accessibility to academic advising, campus computer network, career placement assistance, e-mail services, library services.

Contact Evan Jacobs, Online Recruiter, Columbia University, 540 Mudd Building, MC 4719, 500 West 120th Street, New York, NY 10027. *Telephone:* 212-854-6447. *Fax:* 212-854-0466. *E-mail:* info@cvn.columbia.edu.

DEGREES AND AWARDS

Certificate of Achievement Applied Mathematics; Business and Technology; Civil Engineering; Financial Engineering; Finite Element Method/Computational Fluid Dynamics; Genomic Engineering; Industrial Engineering; Information Systems; Intelligent Systems; Manufacturing Engineering; Materials Science and Engineering; Multimedia Networking; Networking and Systems; New Media Engineering; Operations Research; Telecommunications; Wireless and Mobile Communications
MS Civil Engineering–Construction Engineering and Management; Computer Science; Engineering and Management Systems; Materials Science and Engineering

Columbia University (continued)

MSEE Electrical Engineering
MSME Mechanical Engineering
PMC Computer Science; Electrical Engineering; Mechanical Engineering

COURSE SUBJECT AREAS OFFERED OUTSIDE OF DEGREE PROGRAMS

Undergraduate—computer science.
Graduate—applied mathematics; bioengineering and biomedical engineering; business; civil engineering; computer science; electrical engineering; engineering/industrial management; environmental engineering; industrial engineering; journalism; materials science; mechanical engineering.
Non-credit—applied mathematics; bioengineering and biomedical engineering; business; civil engineering; computer science; electrical engineering; engineering/industrial management; environmental engineering; industrial engineering; journalism; materials science; mechanical engineering.

COLUMBUS STATE COMMUNITY COLLEGE

Columbus, Ohio
Global Campus
http://www.cscc.edu

Columbus State Community College was founded in 1963. It is accredited by North Central Association of Colleges and Schools. It first offered distance learning courses in 1980. In fall 2003, there were 6,000 students enrolled in distance learning courses. Institutionally administered financial aid is available to distance learners.

Services Distance learners have accessibility to academic advising, bookstore, campus computer network, e-mail services, library services.

Contact Tom Erney, Director of Instructional Services, Columbus State Community College, Box 1609, Columbus, OH 43216-1609. *Telephone:* 614-287-2532. *Fax:* 614-287-5123. *E-mail:* terney@cscc.edu.

DEGREES AND AWARDS

AA General Studies
AAS Business Management; Marketing
CCCPE E-Commerce; Geographic Information Systems

COURSE SUBJECT AREAS OFFERED OUTSIDE OF DEGREE PROGRAMS

Undergraduate—accounting; American literature (United States); anthropology; biological sciences/life sciences, other; business administration and management; business communications; business marketing and marketing management; chemistry; comparative literature; computer programming; computer software and media applications; cultural studies; economics; English composition; English creative writing; English language and literature, general; English literature (British and Commonwealth); English technical and business writing; finance; foods and nutrition studies; general retailing/wholesaling; geography; health and medical administrative services; health professions and related sciences, other; history; human resources management; Internet and World Wide Web; law and legal studies related; marketing operations/marketing and distribution, other; mathematics; mechanical engineering-related technologies; nursing; organizational behavior; philosophy; psychology; science technologies, other; sociology; Spanish; speech and rhetorical studies; visual and performing arts, other.

Special Message

Columbus State Community College is accredited by the Higher Learning Commission of the North Central Association of Colleges and Schools. The College, located in central Ohio, serves more than 22,000 students each quarter. In the 2003 autumn quarter, more than 6,000 students enrolled in distance learning courses through Columbus State's Global Campus.

Columbus State's Global Campus (http://global.cscc.edu/index.asp) offers more than 220 Web-based courses. Its three online degrees comprise an Associate of Arts leading to a bachelor's degree and Associate of Applied Science degrees in business management and in marketing. Two certificate programs are offered: E-commerce and Geographic Information Systems (GIS). An associate degree in nursing is planned to be offered in 2004. Global Campus also features interactive videoconferencing courses and 20 video telecourses shown on the local educational access channel on cable television. Telecourse tapes can be rented from the Columbus State bookstore (http://bookstore.cscc.edu). Testing for out-of-state distance learning students can be arranged through the Columbus State Student Success Testing Center (http://www.cscc.edu/sstc/index.htm).

Columbus State is a member of the Ohio Learning Network (OLN), a consortium of Ohio colleges that promote distance learning (http://www.oln.org). Opportunities to gain access to courses or degrees from other Ohio institutions are available. Students may also access courses via distance learning through the Regional Learning Network (RLN), a membership agreement between Columbus State, Clark State, Edison State, and Southern State Community Colleges.

Online student services are: registration, orientation, academic advising, career counseling, and fee payment. Tuition per credit hour is $69 for residents and $152 for nonresidents. Financial aid is available. For more information on Columbus State programs and services, applicants should call 800-621-6407 (toll-free) or visit the Web site at http://www.cscc.edu.

COLUMBUS STATE UNIVERSITY

Columbus, Georgia
Instructional Technology Services
http://www.colstate.edu

Columbus State University was founded in 1958. It is accredited by Southern Association of Colleges and Schools. It first offered distance learning courses in 1991. In fall 2003, there were 950 students enrolled in distance learning courses. Institutionally administered financial aid is available to distance learners.

Services Distance learners have accessibility to academic advising, bookstore, career placement assistance, library services.

Contact Sandra K. Stratford, Instructional Technology Services Coordinator, Columbus State University, 4225 University Avenue, Columbus, GA 31907. *Telephone:* 706-568-2043. *Fax:* 706-568-2459. *E-mail:* stratford_sandra@colstate.edu.

DEGREES AND AWARDS

MS Applied Computer Science

COURSE SUBJECT AREAS OFFERED OUTSIDE OF DEGREE PROGRAMS

Undergraduate—computer science; education, general.

Graduate—computer programming; education administration and supervision; gerontology; teacher education, specific academic and vocational programs.

THE COMMUNITY COLLEGE OF BALTIMORE COUNTY

Baltimore, Maryland
Office of Distance/Extended Learning
http://www.ccbcmd.edu/distance/index.html

The Community College of Baltimore County was founded in 1957. It is accredited by Middle States Association of Colleges and Schools. It first offered distance learning courses in 1997. In fall 2003, there were 2,700 students enrolled in distance learning courses. Institutionally administered financial aid is available to distance learners.

Services Distance learners have accessibility to academic advising, bookstore, campus computer network, e-mail services, library services, tutoring.

Contact Tinnie A. Ward, Senior Director of Distance Learning, The Community College of Baltimore County, 7201 Rossville Boulevard, Baltimore, MD 21237. *Telephone:* 410-780-6504. *Fax:* 410-780-6144. *E-mail:* tward@ccbcmd.edu.

DEGREES AND AWARDS

AA Business Administration

AAS E-Business Management; E-Business Management; E-Business Technology; E-Business Technology; General Information Technology

AGS General Studies

COURSE SUBJECT AREAS OFFERED OUTSIDE OF DEGREE PROGRAMS

Undergraduate—accounting; administrative and secretarial services; applied mathematics; astronomy; biology, general; business; business administration and management; business communications; cell and molecular biology; communications, general; computer and information sciences, general; computer/information technology administration and management; computer programming; computer science; computer systems analysis; computer systems networking and telecommunications; criminal justice and corrections; criminology; data processing technology; economics; English composition; English technical and business writing; entrepreneurship; geography; history; human resources management; legal studies; marketing management and research; mathematical statistics; mathematics; parks, recreation and leisure studies; parks, recreation, leisure and fitness studies, other; physical sciences, general; political science and government; psychology; sociology.

Non-credit—computer and information sciences, general; computer and information sciences, other; computer programming; computer software and media applications.

COMMUNITY COLLEGE OF DENVER

Denver, Colorado
Distance Learning
http://www.ccd.edu/OnlineLearning/index.html

Community College of Denver was founded in 1970. It is accredited by North Central Association of Colleges and Schools. It first offered distance learning courses in 1986. In fall 2003, there were 1,200 students enrolled in distance learning courses. Institutionally administered financial aid is available to distance learners.

Services Distance learners have accessibility to academic advising, bookstore, e-mail services, library services, tutoring.

Contact Jeanne Stroh, Director for Online, Evening, and Weekend College, Community College of Denver, Campus Box CCD West, PO Box 173363, Denver, CO 80211-3363. *Telephone:* 303-477-3154. *Fax:* 303-477-5894. *E-mail:* jeanne.stroh@ccd.edu.

DEGREES AND AWARDS

AA Business Administration; Economics Emphasis; English/Literature Emphasis; History Emphasis; Humanities/Philosophy Emphasis; Psychology Emphasis; Sociology Emphasis

AAS Business Administration, Management Emphasis; Business Generalist Emphasis; International Business Emphasis; Management Emphasis, General Management; Marketing Emphasis

AGS Elementary Education; Generalist

AS Generalist

Certificate Business Administration; Business Administration, Entrepreneurship; Business Administration, International Business; Early Childhood Education, Group/Leader/Child Development Associate–Infant/Toddler; Early Childhood Education, Group/Leader/Child Development Associate–Preschool; Medical Office Technology, Health Information Specialist–Medical Records Emphasis; Teacher Education, Paraeducator

Diploma Business Administration

COURSE SUBJECT AREAS OFFERED OUTSIDE OF DEGREE PROGRAMS

Undergraduate—accounting; anthropology; art history; astronomy; bible/biblical studies; biology; biology, general; business administration and management; business communications; business management and administrative services, other; chemistry; child care and guidance workers and managers; comparative literature; computer/information technology administration and management; computer software and media applications; computer systems networking and telecommunications; economics; English composition; English creative writing; English language and literature, general; English technical and business writing; entrepreneurship; general teacher education; geography; geological and related sciences; health and medical preparatory programs; history; international business; liberal arts and sciences, general studies and humanities; marketing operations/marketing and distribution, other; mathematics; microbiology/bacteriology; nursing; philosophy; philosophy and religion related; physics; political science and government; psychology; religion/religious studies; sociology; speech and rhetorical studies; teacher assistant/aide; teacher education, specific academic and vocational programs.

CONCORDIA COLLEGE

Bronxville, New York

CUENET (Concordia University Education Network)

http://www.concordia-ny.edu

Concordia College was founded in 1881. It is accredited by Middle States Association of Colleges and Schools. It first offered distance learning courses in 1995. In fall 2003, there were 60 students enrolled in distance learning courses. Institutionally administered financial aid is available to distance learners.

Contact Dr. David C. Jacobson, Provost, Concordia College, 171 White Plains Road, Bronxville, NY 10708. *Telephone:* 914-337-9300 Ext. 2126. *Fax:* 914-395-4500. *E-mail:* dcj@concordia-ny.edu.

DEGREES AND AWARDS

Programs offered do not lead to a degree or other formal award.

COURSE SUBJECT AREAS OFFERED OUTSIDE OF DEGREE PROGRAMS

Undergraduate—bible/biblical studies; business communications; psychology; religion/religious studies; sociology.

CONCORDIA UNIVERSITY

Irvine, California

School of Education

http://www.cui.edu

Concordia University was founded in 1972. It is accredited by Western Association of Schools and Colleges. It first offered distance learning courses in 2003. In fall 2003, there were 15 students enrolled in distance learning courses. Institutionally administered financial aid is available to distance learners.

Services Distance learners have accessibility to academic advising, bookstore, library services.

Contact Dr. Joseph Bordeaux, Associate Dean, School of Education, Concordia University, 1530 Concordia West, Irvine, CA 92612-3299. *Telephone:* 949-854-8002 Ext. 1345. *Fax:* 949-854-6878. *E-mail:* joseph.bordeaux@cui.edu.

DEGREES AND AWARDS

MAE Education

CONCORDIA UNIVERSITY AT AUSTIN

Austin, Texas

Center for Distance Education

http://www.concordia.edu

Concordia University at Austin was founded in 1926. It is accredited by Southern Association of Colleges and Schools. It first offered distance learning courses in 1992. In fall 2003, there were 110 students enrolled in distance learning courses. Institutionally administered financial aid is available to distance learners.

Services Distance learners have accessibility to academic advising, bookstore, campus computer network, career placement assistance, e-mail services, library services, tutoring.

Contact Rev. Dr. David Kluth, Vice President of University Services, Concordia University at Austin, 3400 I.H. 35 North, Austin, TX 78705. *Telephone:* 512-486-1176. *Fax:* 512-486-1373. *E-mail:* david.kluth@concordia.edu.

DEGREES AND AWARDS

Programs offered do not lead to a degree or other formal award.

COURSE SUBJECT AREAS OFFERED OUTSIDE OF DEGREE PROGRAMS

Undergraduate—American history; biology; criminal justice and corrections; developmental/child psychology; English language and literature/letters, other; mathematics; religion/religious studies.
Graduate—education administration and supervision.
Non-credit—American history; biology; English language and literature/letters, other; journalism and mass communication related; mathematics; psychology; religion/religious studies; sociology.

CONCORDIA UNIVERSITY, ST. PAUL

St. Paul, Minnesota

College of Graduate and Continuing Studies

http://www.csp.edu

Concordia University, St. Paul was founded in 1893. It is accredited by North Central Association of Colleges and Schools. It first offered distance learning courses in 1998. In fall 2003, there were 2,051 students enrolled in distance learning courses. Institutionally administered financial aid is available to distance learners.

Services Distance learners have accessibility to academic advising, bookstore, campus computer network, e-mail services, library services, tutoring.

Contact Ms. Gail Ann Wells, Enrollment Representative, Concordia University, St. Paul, 275 Syndicate Street, North, St. Paul, MN 55104. *Telephone:* 800-333-4705 Ext. 6186. *Fax:* 651-603-6320. *E-mail:* cshs@csp.edu.

DEGREES AND AWARDS

AA General Program
BA Child Development; Criminal Justice; Family Life Education; Marketing Management; Organizational Management and Communications; School Aged Child Development; Youth Development
MA Human Services Criminal Justice for Juvenile Justice Practitioners; Human Services–Criminal Justice; Human Services–Family Life Education; Youth Development Alternative Education
MAE Community Education; Congregational Leadership; Differentiated Learning; Early Childhood; School Age Child Development; Youth Development

COURSE SUBJECT AREAS OFFERED OUTSIDE OF DEGREE PROGRAMS

Undergraduate—business; developmental and child psychology; education, general; family and community studies; sociology.
Graduate—business; developmental and child psychology; education, general; family and community studies; sociology.
Non-credit—business; communications, general; fine arts and art studies; mathematics and computer science; social sciences, general.

CONCORDIA UNIVERSITY WISCONSIN

Mequon, Wisconsin
Continuing Education Division
http://www.cuw.edu

Concordia University Wisconsin was founded in 1881. It is accredited by North Central Association of Colleges and Schools. It first offered distance learning courses in 1994. In fall 2003, there were 400 students enrolled in distance learning courses. Institutionally administered financial aid is available to distance learners.

Services Distance learners have accessibility to academic advising, bookstore, campus computer network, career placement assistance, e-mail services, library services, tutoring.
Contact Sarah Weaver Pecor, Director, Concordia University Wisconsin, 12800 North Lake Shore Drive, Mequon, WI 53097. *Telephone:* 262-243-4257. *Fax:* 262-243-4459. *E-mail:* sarah.weaver@cuw.edu.

DEGREES AND AWARDS

MBA Business Administration
MS Curriculum and Instruction; Education Administration; Education Counseling; Reading
MSN Nursing

COURSE SUBJECT AREAS OFFERED OUTSIDE OF DEGREE PROGRAMS

Undergraduate—accounting; business management and administrative services, other; business quantitative methods and management science; economics; financial management and services; history; marketing management and research; nursing.
Graduate—business administration and management; curriculum and instruction; education administration and supervision; educational psychology; education, other; nursing.

CONNECTICUT STATE UNIVERSITY SYSTEM

Hartford, Connecticut
OnlineCSU
http://www.onlinecsu.net

Connecticut State University System is accredited by New England Association of Schools and Colleges. It first offered distance learning courses in 1998. In fall 2003, there were 1,000 students enrolled in distance learning courses. Institutionally administered financial aid is available to distance learners.

Services Distance learners have accessibility to academic advising, bookstore, e-mail services, library services, tutoring.
Contact Ms. Rebecca L. Putt, Marketing and Planning Manager, Connecticut State University System, 39 Woodland Street, Hartford, CT 06105-2337. *Telephone:* 860-493-0039. *E-mail:* puttr@so.ct.edu.

DEGREES AND AWARDS

Certificate Sixth Year in Educational Foundations
MLS Library Science
MS Data Mining; Educational Technology

COURSE SUBJECT AREAS OFFERED OUTSIDE OF DEGREE PROGRAMS

Undergraduate—accounting; adult/continuing education; anthropology; Asian studies; business marketing and marketing management; communications, general; computer science; criminal justice and corrections; curriculum and instruction; economics; English composition; information sciences and systems; management information systems/business data processing; mathematical statistics; mechanical engineering; nursing; organizational behavior; philosophy; sociology; theater arts/drama.
Graduate—accounting; adult/continuing education; anthropology; Asian studies; business marketing and marketing management; computer systems networking and telecommunications; curriculum and instruction; educational/instructional media design; English composition; management information systems/business data processing; mathematical statistics; mechanical engineering; organizational behavior; social work; sociology.

See full description on page 392.

COPIAH-LINCOLN COMMUNITY COLLEGE–NATCHEZ CAMPUS

Natchez, Mississippi
http://www.colin.edu

Copiah-Lincoln Community College–Natchez Campus was founded in 1972. It is accredited by Southern Association of Colleges and Schools. It first offered distance learning courses in 1998. In fall 2003, there were 600 students enrolled in distance learning courses. Institutionally administered financial aid is available to distance learners.

Services Distance learners have accessibility to academic advising, bookstore, campus computer network, career placement assistance, e-mail services, library services, tutoring.
Contact Mrs. Gwen S. McCalip, Director of Admissions and Records, Copiah-Lincoln Community College–Natchez Campus, 11 Co-Lin Circle, Natchez, MS 39120-8446. *Telephone:* 601-446-1224. *Fax:* 601-446-1222. *E-mail:* gwen.mccalip@colin.edu.

DEGREES AND AWARDS

AA General Program

COURSE SUBJECT AREAS OFFERED OUTSIDE OF DEGREE PROGRAMS

Undergraduate—accounting; administrative and secretarial services; American literature (United States); biology, general; business; economics; English composition; English literature (British and Commonwealth); geography; history; mathematics; psychology; sociology.

CORNING COMMUNITY COLLEGE

Corning, New York
Open Learning Program
http://corning-cc.edu/distancelearning

Corning Community College was founded in 1956. It is accredited by Middle States Association of Colleges and Schools. It first offered distance learning courses in 1996. In fall 2003, there were 495 students enrolled in distance learning courses. Institutionally administered financial aid is available to distance learners.

Corning Community College (continued)

Services Distance learners have accessibility to academic advising, bookstore, campus computer network, career placement assistance, e-mail services, library services, tutoring.

Contact Barry Garrison, Executive Assistant to the President, Corning Community College, 1 Academic Drive, Corning, NY 14830. *Telephone:* 607-962-9527. *Fax:* 607-962-9485. *E-mail:* garrisbb@coning-cc.edu.

DEGREES AND AWARDS

Programs offered do not lead to a degree or other formal award.

COURSE SUBJECT AREAS OFFERED OUTSIDE OF DEGREE PROGRAMS

Undergraduate—accounting; administrative and secretarial services; business administration and management; business/managerial economics; chemistry; computer programming; computer systems networking and telecommunications; education, general; English composition; health and physical education/fitness; history; human services; philosophy; psychology; sociology; tourism/travel marketing.

COSSATOT COMMUNITY COLLEGE OF THE UNIVERSITY OF ARKANSAS

De Queen, Arkansas

Division of Distance Education

http://cccua.edu

Cossatot Community College of the University of Arkansas was founded in 1991. It is accredited by North Central Association of Colleges and Schools. It first offered distance learning courses in 1997. In fall 2003, there were 525 students enrolled in distance learning courses. Institutionally administered financial aid is available to distance learners.

Services Distance learners have accessibility to academic advising, bookstore, e-mail services, library services, tutoring.

Contact Steve L. Cole, Esq., Division Chair of Distance Education, Cossatot Community College of the University of Arkansas, PO Box 960, DeQueen, AR 71832. *Telephone:* 870-584-4471. *Fax:* 870-642-3320. *E-mail:* scole@cccua.edu.

DEGREES AND AWARDS

AA University Transfer

AGS General Studies

COURSE SUBJECT AREAS OFFERED OUTSIDE OF DEGREE PROGRAMS

Undergraduate—accounting; agricultural business and management; biology, general; botany; business; business communications; business/managerial economics; child care and guidance workers and managers; communications, general; computer and information sciences, general; computer programming; economics; education, general; English as a second language; English composition; English language and literature/letters, other; English technical and business writing; fine arts and art studies; fire protection; health and physical education/fitness; history; mathematics; nursing; psychology; sociology.

Non-credit—accounting; administrative and secretarial services; business; business administration and management; business and personal services marketing operations; business communications; business information and data processing services; business management and administrative services, other; business/managerial economics; business quantitative methods and management science; computer and information sciences, general; computer and information sciences, other; computer engineering; computer/information technology administration and management; computer programming; computer science; computer software and media applications; electrical and electronic engineering-related technology; electrical and electronics equipment installers and repairers; electrical and power transmission installers; electrical, electronics and communications engineering; electromechanical instrumentation and maintenance technology; marketing management and research; marketing operations/marketing and distribution, other; special education.

COUNTY COLLEGE OF MORRIS

Randolph, New Jersey

Professional Programs and Distance Education

http://www.ccm.edu

County College of Morris was founded in 1966. It is accredited by Middle States Association of Colleges and Schools. It first offered distance learning courses in 1979. In fall 2003, there were 1,000 students enrolled in distance learning courses. Institutionally administered financial aid is available to distance learners.

Services Distance learners have accessibility to bookstore, e-mail services, library services.

Contact Ms. Sheri Ventura, Coordinator of Distance Learning Services, County College of Morris, 214 Center Grove Road, Randolph, NJ 07869-2086. *Telephone:* 973-328-5184. *Fax:* 973-328-5082. *E-mail:* sventura@ccm.edu.

DEGREES AND AWARDS

Programs offered do not lead to a degree or other formal award.

COURSE SUBJECT AREAS OFFERED OUTSIDE OF DEGREE PROGRAMS

Undergraduate—applied mathematics; biological sciences/life sciences, other; biology, general; business; computer science; economics; English composition; English creative writing; health and physical education/fitness; history; horticulture services operations and management; mathematics; psychology; sociology.

COVENANT THEOLOGICAL SEMINARY

St. Louis, Missouri

External Studies Office

http://access.covenantseminary.edu

Covenant Theological Seminary was founded in 1956. It is accredited by North Central Association of Colleges and Schools. It first offered distance learning courses in 1989. In fall 2003, there were 132 students enrolled in distance learning courses. Institutionally administered financial aid is available to distance learners.

Services Distance learners have accessibility to academic advising, bookstore, campus computer network, e-mail services, library services, tutoring.

Contact Mr. Eric Richards, Director of Covenant Seminary Admissions, Covenant Theological Seminary, 12330 Conway Road, St. Louis, MO 63141. *Telephone:* 800-264-8064 Ext. 450. *Fax:* 314-434-4819. *E-mail:* admissions@covenantseminary.edu.

DEGREES AND AWARDS

Graduate Certificate Theology
MA Theology

COURSE SUBJECT AREAS OFFERED OUTSIDE OF DEGREE PROGRAMS

Graduate—bible/biblical studies; missions/missionary studies and missiology; philosophy and religion; religion/religious studies; theological and ministerial studies; theological studies and religious vocations, other.
Non-credit—bible/biblical studies; missions/missionary studies and missiology; philosophy and religion; religion/religious studies; theological and ministerial studies; theological studies and religious vocations, other.

CREIGHTON UNIVERSITY

Omaha, Nebraska
School of Pharmacy and Health Professions
http://spahp.creighton.edu

Creighton University was founded in 1878. It is accredited by North Central Association of Colleges and Schools. It first offered distance learning courses in 1995. In fall 2003, there were 250 students enrolled in distance learning courses. Institutionally administered financial aid is available to distance learners.

Services Distance learners have accessibility to academic advising, bookstore, campus computer network, career placement assistance, e-mail services, library services.
Contact Marie E. Bensman, Director of Admissions, Creighton University, 2500 California Plaza, Omaha, NE 68178. *Telephone:* 800-325-2830 Ext. 1. *Fax:* 402-280-5739. *E-mail:* mbensman@creighton.edu.

DEGREES AND AWARDS

DPT Physical Therapy
PharmD Pharmacy

COURSE SUBJECT AREAS OFFERED OUTSIDE OF DEGREE PROGRAMS

Graduate—health and medical administrative services; health professions and related sciences, other; pharmacy.

CROWN COLLEGE

St. Bonifacius, Minnesota
Crown College Online
http://www.crownonline.org

Crown College was founded in 1916. It is accredited by Northwest Commission on Colleges and Universities. It first offered distance learning courses in 2000. In fall 2003, there were 48 students enrolled in distance learning courses. Institutionally administered financial aid is available to distance learners.

Services Distance learners have accessibility to academic advising, bookstore, campus computer network, career placement assistance, e-mail services, library services, tutoring.
Contact Dr. William J. Hyndman, Crown College Online, Crown College, 6425 County Road 30, St. Bonifacius, MN 55375. *Telephone:* 952-446-4153. *Fax:* 952-446-4149. *E-mail:* cconline@crown.edu.

DEGREES AND AWARDS

AS Christian Ministries
BS Christian Ministry
MA Intercultural Studies; Ministry Leadership

COURSE SUBJECT AREAS OFFERED OUTSIDE OF DEGREE PROGRAMS

Undergraduate—missions/missionary studies and missiology; pastoral counseling and specialized ministries; philosophy and religion; religion/religious studies; religious education.
Graduate—bible/biblical studies; missions/missionary studies and missiology; philosophy and religion; theological and ministerial studies.

CULVER-STOCKTON COLLEGE

Canton, Missouri
http://www.culver.edu/

Culver-Stockton College was founded in 1853. It is accredited by North Central Association of Colleges and Schools. It first offered distance learning courses in 2002. In fall 2003, there were 43 students enrolled in distance learning courses. Institutionally administered financial aid is available to distance learners.

Services Distance learners have accessibility to academic advising, bookstore, campus computer network, career placement assistance, e-mail services, library services, tutoring.
Contact Dr. David W. Wilson, Dean of Academic Affairs, Culver-Stockton College, One College Hill, Canton, MO 63435. *Telephone:* 217-231-6325. *Fax:* 217-231-6614. *E-mail:* dwilson@culver.edu.

DEGREES AND AWARDS

Programs offered do not lead to a degree or other formal award.

COURSE SUBJECT AREAS OFFERED OUTSIDE OF DEGREE PROGRAMS

Undergraduate—astronomy; biology, general; computer and information sciences, general; nursing.

CUMBERLAND COLLEGE

Williamsburg, Kentucky
http://www.cumberlandcollege.edu

Cumberland College was founded in 1889. It is accredited by Southern Association of Colleges and Schools. It first offered distance learning courses in 2004. In fall 2003, there were 10 students enrolled in distance learning courses. Institutionally administered financial aid is available to distance learners.

Contact Dr. Betty Herron, Professor of Education, Cumberland College, Education Department, Cumberland College Station, Will-

Cumberland College (continued)

iamsburg, KY 40769. *Telephone:* 606-539-4398 Ext. 4398. *Fax:* 606-539-4014. *E-mail:* bherron@cumberlandcollege.edu.

DEGREES AND AWARDS

Programs offered do not lead to a degree or other formal award.

COURSE SUBJECT AREAS OFFERED OUTSIDE OF DEGREE PROGRAMS

Graduate—special education.

CUMBERLAND COUNTY COLLEGE

Vineland, New Jersey
Multimedia and Distance Learning Services
http://www.cccnj.edu

Cumberland County College was founded in 1963. It is accredited by Middle States Association of Colleges and Schools. It first offered distance learning courses in 1990. In fall 2003, there were 450 students enrolled in distance learning courses. Institutionally administered financial aid is available to distance learners.

Services Distance learners have accessibility to academic advising, bookstore, campus computer network, career placement assistance, e-mail services, library services, tutoring.

Contact Amar Madineni, Assistant Dean of Instruction for Information Technology, Cumberland County College, College Drive, PO Box 1500, Vineland, NJ 08362-0517. *Telephone:* 856-691-8600 Ext. 341. *Fax:* 856-691-9489. *E-mail:* amar@cccnj.net.

DEGREES AND AWARDS

Programs offered do not lead to a degree or other formal award.

COURSE SUBJECT AREAS OFFERED OUTSIDE OF DEGREE PROGRAMS

Undergraduate—adult/continuing education; anthropology; business; business administration and management; creative writing; economics; English composition; foreign languages and literatures; history; journalism and mass communication related; psychology; psychology, other; sociology.

CUMBERLAND UNIVERSITY

Lebanon, Tennessee
Master of Arts in Education
http://www.cumberland.edu/

Cumberland University was founded in 1842. It is accredited by Southern Association of Colleges and Schools. It first offered distance learning courses in 1999. In fall 2003, there were 395 students enrolled in distance learning courses.

Services Distance learners have accessibility to academic advising, e-mail services, library services.

Contact Debbie Whitaker, Program Coordinator, Cumberland University, MAE Graduate Admissions Office, One Cumberland Square, Lebanon, TN 37087-3408. *Telephone:* 800-467-0562 Ext. 1217. *Fax:* 877-217-5284. *E-mail:* dwhitaker@cumberland.edu.

DEGREES AND AWARDS

MEd Education

COURSE SUBJECT AREAS OFFERED OUTSIDE OF DEGREE PROGRAMS

Graduate—education, general.

CUYAMACA COLLEGE

El Cajon, California
Telecourse Program
http://www.cuyamaca.net

Cuyamaca College was founded in 1978. It is accredited by Western Association of Schools and Colleges. It first offered distance learning courses in 1985. In fall 2003, there were 309 students enrolled in distance learning courses. Institutionally administered financial aid is available to distance learners.

Services Distance learners have accessibility to e-mail services, library services.

Contact Mrs. Nancy Asbury, Administrative Secretary for Telecourse Office, Cuyamaca College, 900 Rancho San Diego Parkway, El Cajon, CA 92019-4304. *Telephone:* 619-660-4401. *Fax:* 619-660-4493. *E-mail:* nancy.asbury@gcccd.net.

DEGREES AND AWARDS

Programs offered do not lead to a degree or other formal award.

COURSE SUBJECT AREAS OFFERED OUTSIDE OF DEGREE PROGRAMS

Undergraduate—anthropology; astronomy; business; developmental and child psychology; developmental/child psychology; economics; English language and literature, general; entrepreneurship; geological and related sciences; health and physical education/fitness; history; political science and government; psychology; sociology.

DAEMEN COLLEGE

Amherst, New York
http://distance.daemen.edu

Daemen College was founded in 1947. It is accredited by Middle States Association of Colleges and Schools. It first offered distance learning courses in 1999. In fall 2003, there were 325 students enrolled in distance learning courses. Institutionally administered financial aid is available to distance learners.

Services Distance learners have accessibility to academic advising, bookstore, campus computer network, e-mail services, library services.

Contact Ms. Cheryl Littlejohn, Distance Learning Coordinator, Daemen College, 4380 Main Street, BC211A, Amherst, NY 14226. *Telephone:* 716-839 8532. *Fax:* 716-839 8261. *E-mail:* clittlej@daemen.edu.

DEGREES AND AWARDS

Programs offered do not lead to a degree or other formal award.

COURSE SUBJECT AREAS OFFERED OUTSIDE OF DEGREE PROGRAMS

Undergraduate—business; education, general; English composition; entrepreneurship; foreign languages and literatures; health and medical administrative services; health and medical preparatory programs; health professions and related sciences, other; nursing.
Graduate—medical clinical sciences (M.S., Ph.D.); nursing.

DAKOTA COUNTY TECHNICAL COLLEGE

Rosemount, Minnesota
http://www.dctc.edu

Dakota County Technical College was founded in 1970. It is accredited by North Central Association of Colleges and Schools. It first offered distance learning courses in 1999. In fall 2003, there were 500 students enrolled in distance learning courses. Institutionally administered financial aid is available to distance learners.

Services Distance learners have accessibility to academic advising, bookstore, career placement assistance, e-mail services, library services, tutoring.

Contact Patrick Lair, Admissions Coordinator, Dakota County Technical College, 1300 145th Street East, County Road 42, Rosemount, MN 55068. *Telephone:* 651-423-8301. *Fax:* 651-423-8775. *E-mail:* patrick.lair@dctc.mnscu.edu.

DEGREES AND AWARDS

Programs offered do not lead to a degree or other formal award.

COURSE SUBJECT AREAS OFFERED OUTSIDE OF DEGREE PROGRAMS

Undergraduate—advertising; architecture; biological sciences/life sciences, other; biology, general; business administration and management; business management and administrative services, other; child care and guidance workers and managers; computer software and media applications; computer systems networking and telecommunications; design and applied arts; economics; engineering-related technologies, other; English composition; English creative writing; English language and literature, general; English technical and business writing; entrepreneurship; history; liberal arts and sciences, general studies and humanities; marketing management and research; mathematics; psychology; social sciences and history, other; social sciences, general; sociology.

DAKOTA STATE UNIVERSITY

Madison, South Dakota
E-Education Services
http://www.departments.dsu.edu/disted/

Dakota State University was founded in 1881. It is accredited by North Central Association of Colleges and Schools. It first offered distance learning courses in 1990. In fall 2003, there were 529 students enrolled in distance learning courses. Institutionally administered financial aid is available to distance learners.

Services Distance learners have accessibility to academic advising, bookstore, campus computer network, career placement assistance, e-mail services, library services, tutoring.

Contact Dr. Deb Gearhart, Director of E-Education Services, Dakota State University, 820 North Washington Avenue, Madison, SD 57042-1799. *Telephone:* 800-641-4309. *Fax:* 605-256-5095. *E-mail:* dsuinfo@dsu.edu.

DEGREES AND AWARDS

BS Health Information Administration Degree Completion Program
MS Educational Technology
MSIS Information Systems

COURSE SUBJECT AREAS OFFERED OUTSIDE OF DEGREE PROGRAMS

Undergraduate—accounting; computer and information sciences, general; computer and information sciences, other; computer programming; computer science; computer systems analysis; education, other; English composition; English language and literature, general; health services administration; human resources management; information sciences and systems; mathematics; music; psychology; sociology.

Graduate—computer and information sciences, other; educational/instructional media design; education, other; information sciences and systems.

Non-credit—computer and information sciences, general; computer programming.

DALLAS BAPTIST UNIVERSITY

Dallas, Texas
Dallas Baptist University Online (DBU Online)
http://online.dbu.edu

Dallas Baptist University was founded in 1965. It is accredited by Southern Association of Colleges and Schools. It first offered distance learning courses in 1998. In fall 2003, there were 873 students enrolled in distance learning courses. Institutionally administered financial aid is available to distance learners.

Services Distance learners have accessibility to academic advising, bookstore, campus computer network, career placement assistance, e-mail services, library services, tutoring.

Contact Ms. Amy Walker, Online Student Coordinator, Dallas Baptist University, Online Education, 3000 Mountain Creek Parkway, Dallas, TX 75211-9299. *Telephone:* 800-460-8188. *Fax:* 214-333-5373. *E-mail:* online@dbu.edu.

DEGREES AND AWARDS

BA Biblical Studies; Christian Ministries; Psychology
BBA Management Information Systems; Management
BS Business Administration; Management Information Systems; Management
Certificate E-Business
MAM Human Resource Management; Management, general
MBA E-Business; Finance; Management Information Systems; Management
MEd Educational Organization and Administration; Higher Education

COURSE SUBJECT AREAS OFFERED OUTSIDE OF DEGREE PROGRAMS

Undergraduate—accounting; atmospheric sciences and meteorology; bible/biblical studies; biology, general; business administration and management; communications, general; computer and information sciences, general; criminal justice and corrections; economics; education, general; English language and literature, general; financial management and services; fine arts and art studies; geological and related sciences; health and physical education/fitness; history; marketing management and research; mathematics; psychology; sociology.

Graduate—accounting; business administration and management; business quantitative methods and management science; computer/information technology administration and management; criminal justice and corrections; curriculum and instruction; economics; education administration and supervision; educational evaluation, research

Dallas Baptist University (continued)

and statistics; education, other; enterprise management and operation; entrepreneurship; financial management and services; human resources management; information sciences and systems; international business; liberal arts and sciences, general studies and humanities; marketing management and research; marketing operations/marketing and distribution, other; religious education.

See full description on page 394.

DALLAS COUNTY COMMUNITY COLLEGE DISTRICT

Dallas, Texas
Dallas TeleCollege
http://www.telecollege.dcccd.edu

Dallas County Community College District is accredited by Southern Association of Colleges and Schools. It first offered distance learning courses in 1972. Institutionally administered financial aid is available to distance learners.

Services Distance learners have accessibility to academic advising, bookstore, campus computer network, e-mail services, library services, tutoring.

Contact Mrs. Angela Auzenne, Public Information Director, Dallas County Community College District, 9596 Walnut Street, Dallas, TX 75243-2112. *Telephone:* 972-669-6657. *Fax:* 972-669-6409. *E-mail:* aauzenne@dcccd.edu.

DEGREES AND AWARDS

AA Liberal Arts and General Studies
AS Business; General Studies

COURSE SUBJECT AREAS OFFERED OUTSIDE OF DEGREE PROGRAMS

Undergraduate—accounting; administrative and secretarial services; anthropology; astronomy; biology; business marketing and marketing management; child care and guidance workers and managers; computer and information sciences, general; computer and information sciences, other; computer engineering; computer/information technology administration and management; computer programming; computer science; computer software and media applications; computer systems analysis; computer systems networking and telecommunications; creative writing; data entry/microcomputer applications; data processing technology; developmental/child psychology; drafting; economics; education, general; education, other; English as a second language; English composition; health and medical administrative services; health professions and related sciences, other; history; human resources management; journalism and mass communications; liberal arts and sciences, general studies and humanities; mathematics; mathematics and computer science; mathematics related; music; philosophy; philosophy and religion; physical sciences, general; physical sciences, other; psychology; real estate; social sciences and history, other; social sciences, general; sociology; speech and rhetorical studies; telecommunications.

See full description on page 396.

DANIEL WEBSTER COLLEGE

Nashua, New Hampshire
http://www.dwc.edu/de

Daniel Webster College was founded in 1965. It is accredited by New England Association of Schools and Colleges. It first offered distance learning courses in 2000. In fall 2003, there were 600 students enrolled in distance learning courses. Institutionally administered financial aid is available to distance learners.

Services Distance learners have accessibility to academic advising, bookstore, campus computer network, career placement assistance, e-mail services, library services, tutoring.

Contact Jan Donahue, Academic Advisor, Daniel Webster College, 20 University Drive, Nashua, NH 03063. *Telephone:* 603-577-6500. *Fax:* 603-577-6503. *E-mail:* donahue@dwc.edu.

DEGREES AND AWARDS

ABA Business Administration
AGS General Studies
BS Business and Management; Social Sciences
Certificate C/UNIX Programming; Client-Server Application Development; MS Windows Programming; PC Networking; UNIX Systems Administration; Webmaster Technology

COURSE SUBJECT AREAS OFFERED OUTSIDE OF DEGREE PROGRAMS

Undergraduate—accounting; advertising; applied mathematics; business; business administration and management; business/managerial economics; computer programming; English composition; English language and literature, general; entrepreneurship; history; human resources management; Internet and World Wide Web; mathematical statistics; mathematics; mathematics and computer science; psychology; sociology.

Special Message

Daniel Webster College (DWC) is constantly growing and changing, yet it does so while maintaining its classic New England character. The College features the Eaton-Richmond Center, its newest academic building, and the Harvey Woods baseball field, which opened in 2003. It also maintains seven state-of-the-art computer labs, designed to support the College's reputation as a regional leader in computer information systems and information technology education.

During the 2003 academic year the College added new certificate programs in .NET, Microsoft Certified Systems Engineer (MCSE), and Microsoft Certified Systems Administrator (MCSA). Undergraduate degree programs in social science and marketing were also added. In addition, the College had a tremendous kick-off with its new MBA program.

The College continues to pay significant attention to its online students. The distance education program grew more than 200 percent in 2003, added additional library services, and implemented the Student Online Access to Records (SOAR) program, giving its distance education (DE) students full access to their grades, schedules, and student account records online. The College's goal is to offer quality classes that go wherever its students go.

The faculty and staff members of DWC are dedicated to supporting the educational needs of students regionally, nationally, and internationally with the highest quality services and programs available anywhere. That effort requires constant change. Yet, for all this, DWC is still a classic New England college.

See full description on page 398.

DANVILLE AREA COMMUNITY COLLEGE

Danville, Illinois
Distance Learning Department
http://www.dacc.edu

Danville Area Community College was founded in 1946. It is accredited by North Central Association of Colleges and Schools. It first offered distance learning courses in 1994. In fall 2003, there were 500 students enrolled in distance learning courses. Institutionally administered financial aid is available to distance learners.

Services Distance learners have accessibility to academic advising, bookstore, campus computer network, career placement assistance, e-mail services, library services, tutoring.

Contact Jon Spors, Director, Danville Area Community College, Instructional Media, 2000 East Main Street, Danville, IL 61832. *Telephone:* 217-443-8577. *Fax:* 217-443-3178. *E-mail:* jspors@dacc.edu.

DEGREES AND AWARDS

AAS Criminology

COURSE SUBJECT AREAS OFFERED OUTSIDE OF DEGREE PROGRAMS

Undergraduate—accounting; agriculture/agricultural sciences, other; anthropology; applied mathematics; astronomy; biological sciences/life sciences, other; business administration and management; business information and data processing services; communications, other; criminal justice and corrections; data processing technology; economics; electrical, electronics and communications engineering; English composition; environmental/environmental health engineering; geography; health professions and related sciences, other; history; Internet and World Wide Web; mathematical statistics; mathematics; music; physics; psychology; sociology.

DANVILLE COMMUNITY COLLEGE

Danville, Virginia
Learning Resource Center
http://www.dcc.vccs.edu

Danville Community College was founded in 1967. It is accredited by Southern Association of Colleges and Schools. It first offered distance learning courses in 1990. In fall 2003, there were 500 students enrolled in distance learning courses. Institutionally administered financial aid is available to distance learners.

Services Distance learners have accessibility to academic advising, bookstore, career placement assistance, e-mail services, library services, tutoring.

Contact Dr. Max Glass, Interim Vice President of Instruction, Danville Community College, 1008 South Main Street, Danville, VA 24541. *Telephone:* 434-797-8410. *Fax:* 434-797-8415. *E-mail:* mglass@dcc.vccs.edu.

DEGREES AND AWARDS

Programs offered do not lead to a degree or other formal award.

COURSE SUBJECT AREAS OFFERED OUTSIDE OF DEGREE PROGRAMS

Undergraduate—accounting; administrative and secretarial services; biological sciences/life sciences, other; business; business administration and management; business marketing and marketing management; child care and guidance workers and managers; communications, general; community health services; computer programming; computer science; computer software and media applications; criminal justice and corrections; criminology; dental clinical sciences/graduate dentistry (M.S., Ph.D.); dental services; design and applied arts; drafting; educational/instructional media design; English composition; English language and literature, general; English literature (British and Commonwealth); foods and nutrition studies; graphic and printing equipment operators; health and physical education/fitness; mathematics; music; nursing.

DARTON COLLEGE

Albany, Georgia
Office of Distance Learning
http://www.darton.edu

Darton College was founded in 1965. It is accredited by Southern Association of Colleges and Schools. It first offered distance learning courses in 1993. In fall 2003, there were 1,190 students enrolled in distance learning courses. Institutionally administered financial aid is available to distance learners.

Services Distance learners have accessibility to academic advising, bookstore, campus computer network, career placement assistance, e-mail services, library services, tutoring.

Contact Ms. Kathryn D. Bishop, Director of Instructional Technology and Distance Learning, Darton College, 2400 Gillionville Road, Albany, GA 31707. *Telephone:* 229-430-6838. *Fax:* 229-430-6910. *E-mail:* bishopk@darton.edu.

DEGREES AND AWARDS

AA Art; English; Foreign Language; History; Journalism and Mass Communication; Music

AAS Accounting; Business Computer Specialist Option; Governmental Services; Histologic Technology; Management; Office Administration

AS Anthropology; Biological Science; Business Administration; Business Education; Computer Information Systems; Criminal Justice; Economics; General Studies; Health and Physical Ed–Teacher Ed Option; Industrial Distribution Technology; Medical Laboratory Technology; Nursing; Office Administration; Physical Therapy Assistant; Political Science; Pre-Dentistry; Pre-Law; Pre-Optometry; Psychology; Respiratory Therapy; Social Work; Sociology; Teacher Education–Early Childhood; Teacher Education–Middle Grades; Teacher Education–Secondary; Teacher Education–Special Education; Trade and Industrial Education

COURSE SUBJECT AREAS OFFERED OUTSIDE OF DEGREE PROGRAMS

Undergraduate—accounting; American literature (United States); applied mathematics; biological sciences/life sciences, other; business; business administration and management; communications, general; computer software and media applications; computer systems networking and telecommunications; criminal justice and corrections; East and Southeast Asian languages and literatures; economics; education, general; education, other; English composition; English language and literature, general; English literature (British and Commonwealth); financial management and services; foreign languages and literatures; foreign languages and literatures, other; general teacher education; Germanic languages and literatures; health and medical administrative services; health and medical assistants; health and

Darton College (continued)

medical preparatory programs; health and physical education/fitness; health professions and related sciences, other; history; liberal arts and sciences, general studies and humanities; mathematical statistics; mathematics; medical laboratory technology; miscellaneous physical sciences; music; philosophy; philosophy and religion; physical sciences, general; political science and government; psychology; Romance languages and literatures; sociology; speech and rhetorical studies.
Non-credit—business administration and management; business and personal services marketing operations; business communications; business management and administrative services, other; English creative writing; English technical and business writing; financial management and services; Internet and World Wide Web; real estate.

DAVENPORT UNIVERSITY ONLINE

Grand Rapids, Michigan

http://www.davenport.edu

Davenport University Online is accredited by North Central Association of Colleges and Schools. It first offered distance learning courses in 1999. In fall 2003, there were 5,500 students enrolled in distance learning courses. Institutionally administered financial aid is available to distance learners.

Services Distance learners have accessibility to academic advising, bookstore, career placement assistance, e-mail services, library services, tutoring.
Contact Enrollment Services Specialist, Davenport University Online, 415 East Fulton Street, Grand Rapids, MI 49503. *Telephone:* 800-203-5323. *Fax:* 800-811-2658. *E-mail:* duonline@davenport.edu.

DEGREES AND AWARDS

AAS Health Information Technology; Information and Computer Security
ABA Accounting; Administrative Office Technology–Executive Office Administration Specialty; Entrepreneurship; Management; Marketing; Systems Application Development
BAA Applied Business
BBA Accounting Information Management–Management Accounting Specialty; Accounting Information Management–Public Accounting Specialty; Business Professional Studies; E-Business–Web Development Specialty; Entrepreneurship; Health Services Administration; Information and Computer Security; Integrative Professional Studies; Management–Financial Administration Specialty; Management–Human Resource Management Specialty; Management–Manufacturing Management Specialty; Marketing–Advertising/Promotion Specialty; Marketing–Business to Business Specialty; Marketing–E-Business Specialty; Marketing–Marketing Management Specialty
BS Nursing Completion Program
Certificate Forensic Accounting; Information and Computer Security
Diploma Accounting Assistant; Business Management; Desktop Applications; Medical Billing; Medical Coding; Web Applications
MBA Accounting Specialty; Entrepreneurial Specialty; Health Care Management; Human Resource Management Specialty; Strategic Management Specialty

COURSE SUBJECT AREAS OFFERED OUTSIDE OF DEGREE PROGRAMS

Undergraduate—accounting; administrative and secretarial services; advertising; biology, general; business; business administration and management; business information and data processing services; business management and administrative services, other; business/managerial economics; business marketing and marketing management; business quantitative methods and management science; communications, general; computer and information sciences, general; computer/information technology administration and management; computer programming; computer systems networking and telecommunications; economics; English composition; entrepreneurship; financial management and services; foods and nutrition studies; health and medical administrative services; health professions and related sciences, other; history; human resources management; international business; marketing management and research; marketing operations/marketing and distribution, other; mathematical statistics; mathematics; nursing; physics; political science and government; psychology; sociology; taxation; telecommunications.
Graduate—accounting; business; business administration and management; business management and administrative services, other; economics; entrepreneurship; financial management and services; health and medical administrative services; human resources management; marketing management and research.

See full description on page 400.

DAVIS COLLEGE

Bible School Park, New York

Davis College was founded in 1900. It is accredited by Accrediting Association of Bible Colleges. It first offered distance learning courses in 2004. In fall 2003, there were 1 students enrolled in distance learning courses. Institutionally administered financial aid is available to distance learners.

Services Distance learners have accessibility to academic advising, bookstore, e-mail services, library services, tutoring.
Contact Ms. Karen Francis, Assistant Registrar, Davis College, 400 Riverside Drive, Johnson City, NY 13790. *Telephone:* 607-729-1581 Ext. 306. *Fax:* 607-729-2962. *E-mail:* registrar@davisny.edu.

DEGREES AND AWARDS

Programs offered do not lead to a degree or other formal award.

DAWSON COMMUNITY COLLEGE

Glendive, Montana

Continuing and Extension Education Department

http://www.dawson.edu

Dawson Community College was founded in 1940. It first offered distance learning courses in 1990. In fall 2003, there were 60 students enrolled in distance learning courses. Institutionally administered financial aid is available to distance learners.

Services Distance learners have accessibility to academic advising, bookstore, career placement assistance, library services.
Contact Jolene Myers, Director of Admissions, Dawson Community College, 300 College Drive, Glendive, MT 59330. *Telephone:* 406-377-9410. *Fax:* 406-377-8132. *E-mail:* myers@dawson.edu.

DEGREES AND AWARDS

AAS Business Management; Human Services

COURSE SUBJECT AREAS OFFERED OUTSIDE OF DEGREE PROGRAMS

Undergraduate—agricultural business and management; agriculture/agricultural sciences; American literature (United States); anthropology; biology; business administration and management; communications, general; computer software and media applications; creative writing; criminal justice and corrections; developmental/child psychology; English composition; fine arts and art studies; human services; psychology; sociology.

DEFIANCE COLLEGE

Defiance, Ohio
Design for Leadership
http://www.defiance.edu

Defiance College was founded in 1850. It is accredited by North Central Association of Colleges and Schools. It first offered distance learning courses in 1971. In fall 2003, there were 35 students enrolled in distance learning courses. Institutionally administered financial aid is available to distance learners.

Services Distance learners have accessibility to academic advising, bookstore, campus computer network, career placement assistance, e-mail services, library services, tutoring.

Contact Dr. Kenneth Edward Christiansen, Co-Coordinator, Design for Leadership, Defiance College, 701 North Clinton Street, Defiance, OH 43512. *Telephone:* 419-783-2465. *Fax:* 419-784-0426. *E-mail:* design@defiance.edu.

DEGREES AND AWARDS

AA Religious Education
BA Religious Education
Certificate African American Ministry Leadership; Church Education; Youth Ministry Leadership

COURSE SUBJECT AREAS OFFERED OUTSIDE OF DEGREE PROGRAMS

Undergraduate—bible/biblical studies; religious education.

DELAWARE COUNTY COMMUNITY COLLEGE

Media, Pennsylvania
Distance Learning
http://www.dccc.edu/dl

Delaware County Community College was founded in 1967. It is accredited by Middle States Association of Colleges and Schools. It first offered distance learning courses in 1980. In fall 2003, there were 2,000 students enrolled in distance learning courses. Institutionally administered financial aid is available to distance learners.

Services Distance learners have accessibility to academic advising, bookstore, campus computer network, e-mail services, library services, tutoring.

Contact Alexander Plachuta, Assistant Director of Distance Learning, Delaware County Community College, 901 South Media Line Road, Media, PA 19063. *Telephone:* 610-359-5158. *E-mail:* distance@dccc.edu.

DEGREES AND AWARDS

AA General Studies

COURSE SUBJECT AREAS OFFERED OUTSIDE OF DEGREE PROGRAMS

Undergraduate—accounting; administrative and secretarial services; advertising; American literature (United States); anthropology; area, ethnic and cultural studies, other; area studies; astronomy; atmospheric sciences and meteorology; biological and physical sciences; biology, general; business; business administration and management; business and personal services marketing operations; business communications; business information and data processing services; business management and administrative services, other; business/managerial economics; business quantitative methods and management science; clinical psychology; community psychology; comparative literature; computer and information sciences, general; computer and information sciences, other; computer engineering; computer/information technology administration and management; computer programming; computer science; computer software and media applications; computer systems networking and telecommunications; construction/building technology; construction trades, other; counseling psychology; criminal justice and corrections; cultural studies; data entry/microcomputer applications; data processing technology; demography/population studies; developmental and child psychology; developmental/child psychology; economics; educational psychology; English composition; English creative writing; English language and literature, general; family and community studies; financial management and services; food sciences and technology; geography; history; home economics, general; human resources management; information sciences and systems; journalism and mass communications; law and legal studies related; legal studies; liberal arts and sciences, general studies and humanities; marketing management and research; marketing operations/marketing and distribution, other; mathematics; mathematics and computer science; nursing; pharmacy; philosophy; philosophy and religion; physics; psychology; psychology, other; religion/religious studies; science technologies, other; science, technology and society; social psychology; social sciences and history, other; social sciences, general; sociology.

Non-credit—computer and information sciences, general; computer and information sciences, other; computer engineering; computer programming; computer science; computer software and media applications; computer systems analysis; computer systems networking and telecommunications.

DELAWARE TECHNICAL & COMMUNITY COLLEGE, JACK F. OWENS CAMPUS

Georgetown, Delaware
http://www.dtcc.edu/

Delaware Technical & Community College, Jack F. Owens Campus was founded in 1967. It is accredited by Middle States Association of Colleges and Schools. It first offered distance learning courses in 1985. In fall 2003, there were 2,000 students enrolled in distance learning courses.

Services Distance learners have accessibility to academic advising, bookstore, career placement assistance, e-mail services, library services, tutoring.

Delaware Technical & Community College, Jack F. Owens Campus (continued)

Contact Michael A. Mills, Director of Distance Education, Delaware Technical & Community College, Jack F. Owens Campus, PO Box 897, Dover, DE 19903. *Telephone:* 302-857-1750. *E-mail:* mmills@college.dtcc.edu.

DEGREES AND AWARDS

AAS Office Administration

COURSE SUBJECT AREAS OFFERED OUTSIDE OF DEGREE PROGRAMS

Undergraduate—accounting; agricultural business and management; agricultural business and production, other; agriculture/agricultural sciences; applied mathematics; business administration and management; computer science; criminal justice and corrections; economics; educational/instructional media design; English as a second language; English composition; English technical and business writing; human services; mathematical statistics; mathematics; psychology; sociology.

DELAWARE TECHNICAL & COMMUNITY COLLEGE, STANTON/WILMINGTON CAMPUS

Newark, Delaware
Distance Learning Programs and Outreach
http://www.dtcc.edu

Delaware Technical & Community College, Stanton/Wilmington Campus was founded in 1968. It is accredited by Middle States Association of Colleges and Schools. It first offered distance learning courses in 1985. In fall 2003, there were 2,000 students enrolled in distance learning courses. Institutionally administered financial aid is available to distance learners.

Services Distance learners have accessibility to academic advising, bookstore, career placement assistance, e-mail services, library services, tutoring.

Contact Mr. Michael A. Mills, Director of Distance Education, Delaware Technical & Community College, Stanton/Wilmington Campus, PO Box 897, Dover, DE 19903. *Telephone:* 302-857-1750. *E-mail:* mmills@college.dtcc.edu.

DEGREES AND AWARDS

AAS Office Administration

COURSE SUBJECT AREAS OFFERED OUTSIDE OF DEGREE PROGRAMS

Undergraduate—accounting; agricultural business and management; agricultural business and production, other; agriculture/agricultural sciences; applied mathematics; business administration and management; computer science; criminal justice and corrections; economics; educational/instructional media design; English as a second language; English composition; English technical and business writing; human services; mathematical statistics; mathematics; psychology; sociology.

DELTA COLLEGE

University Center, Michigan
Distance Learning Office and Telelearning
http://www.delta.edu/distancelearning

Delta College was founded in 1961. It is accredited by North Central Association of Colleges and Schools. It first offered distance learning courses in 1982. In fall 2003, there were 1,500 students enrolled in distance learning courses. Institutionally administered financial aid is available to distance learners.

Services Distance learners have accessibility to academic advising, bookstore, campus computer network, career placement assistance, e-mail services, library services, tutoring.

Contact Ms. Jane M. Adams, Senior Administrative Secretary, Delta College, 1961 Delta Road, University Center, MI 48710. *Telephone:* 989-686-9088. *E-mail:* jmadams@alpha.delta.edu.

DEGREES AND AWARDS

AA General Studies

COURSE SUBJECT AREAS OFFERED OUTSIDE OF DEGREE PROGRAMS

Undergraduate—American history; American literature (United States); biological technology; biology; business communications; business marketing and marketing management; computer and information sciences, general; computer programming; criminal justice and corrections; developmental/child psychology; economics; English composition; English language and literature, general; English technical and business writing; film/video and photographic arts; fine arts and art studies; health and physical education/fitness; industrial production technologies; Internet; law and legal studies related; materials engineering; materials science; mathematical statistics; mathematics; mathematics related; metallurgical engineering; microbiology/bacteriology; philosophy; political science and government; psychology; sociology; Spanish; speech and rhetorical studies; visual and performing arts.

DENVER SEMINARY

Denver, Colorado
http://www.denverseminary.edu

Denver Seminary was founded in 1950. It is accredited by North Central Association of Colleges and Schools. It first offered distance learning courses in 1988. In fall 2003, there were 114 students enrolled in distance learning courses. Institutionally administered financial aid is available to distance learners.

Services Distance learners have accessibility to academic advising, bookstore, career placement assistance.

Contact Ms. Venita Doughty, Director of Educational Technology, Denver Seminary, PO Box 100000, Denver, CO 80250. *Telephone:* 303-762-6933. *Fax:* 303-761-8060. *E-mail:* venita.doughty@denverseminary.edu.

DEGREES AND AWARDS

Programs offered do not lead to a degree or other formal award.

COURSE SUBJECT AREAS OFFERED OUTSIDE OF DEGREE PROGRAMS

Graduate—bible/biblical studies; history; philosophy and religion related; theological and ministerial studies.

DEPAUL UNIVERSITY

Chicago, Illinois

School of Computer Science, Telecommunications, and Information Systems

http://www.cti.depaul.edu/admissions

DePaul University was founded in 1898. It is accredited by North Central Association of Colleges and Schools. It first offered distance learning courses in 1995. In fall 2003, there were 575 students enrolled in distance learning courses. Institutionally administered financial aid is available to distance learners.

Services Distance learners have accessibility to academic advising, bookstore, career placement assistance, e-mail services, library services, tutoring.

Contact Maureen Garvey, Director of Admissions, DePaul University, DePaul CTI, 243 South Wabash Avenue, Chicago, IL 60604. *Telephone:* 312-362-8714. *Fax:* 312-362-6116. *E-mail:* distance-learning@cs.depaul.edu.

DEGREES AND AWARDS

MA Information Technology

MS Computer Science; Computer, Information, and Network Security; Distributed Systems; E-Commerce Technology; Information Systems; Instructional Technology Systems; Software Engineering; Telecommunication Systems

COURSE SUBJECT AREAS OFFERED OUTSIDE OF DEGREE PROGRAMS

Undergraduate—computer programming.

Graduate—communications technologies; computer and information sciences, general; computer and information sciences, other; computer/information technology administration and management; computer programming; computer science; computer software and media applications; computer systems analysis; computer systems networking and telecommunications; educational/instructional media design; information sciences and systems; telecommunications.

See full description on page 404.

DEPAUL UNIVERSITY

Chicago, Illinois

School for New Learning

http://www.snlonline.net

DePaul University was founded in 1898. It is accredited by North Central Association of Colleges and Schools. It first offered distance learning courses in 1996. In fall 2003, there were 700 students enrolled in distance learning courses. Institutionally administered financial aid is available to distance learners.

Services Distance learners have accessibility to academic advising, bookstore, campus computer network, career placement assistance, e-mail services, library services, tutoring.

Contact Mr. Kenn Skorupa, Senior Academic Advisor, DePaul University, Center for Distance Education, 25 East Jackson Boulevard, 2nd Floor, Chicago, IL 60604. *Telephone:* 866-765-3678. *Fax:* 312-362-5053. *E-mail:* support@snlonline.net.

DEGREES AND AWARDS

BA Business Administration; Liberal Arts and Sciences; Individually Designed Focus Area

COURSE SUBJECT AREAS OFFERED OUTSIDE OF DEGREE PROGRAMS

Undergraduate—business; business administration and management; liberal arts and sciences, general studies and humanities; professional studies.

See full description on page 402.

DES MOINES AREA COMMUNITY COLLEGE

Ankeny, Iowa

Distance Learning/Continuing Education

http://www.dmacc.edu/online

Des Moines Area Community College was founded in 1966. It is accredited by North Central Association of Colleges and Schools. It first offered distance learning courses in 1970. In fall 2003, there were 5,500 students enrolled in distance learning courses. Institutionally administered financial aid is available to distance learners.

Services Distance learners have accessibility to academic advising, bookstore, career placement assistance, e-mail services, library services, tutoring.

Contact Pat Thieben, Director of Distance Learning, Des Moines Area Community College, 2006 South Ankeny Boulevard, Ankeny, IA 50021. *Telephone:* 515-965-7086. *Fax:* 515-965-6002. *E-mail:* pathieben@dmacc.edu.

DEGREES AND AWARDS

AAS Business Administration

Certification Microcomputers

COURSE SUBJECT AREAS OFFERED OUTSIDE OF DEGREE PROGRAMS

Undergraduate—accounting; administrative and secretarial services; biological and physical sciences; biology, general; business; business administration and management; business and personal services marketing operations; business communications; business information and data processing services; business management and administrative services, other; business/managerial economics; business quantitative methods and management science; chemistry; comparative literature; computer and information sciences, general; computer and information sciences, other; computer programming; computer science; criminal justice and corrections; criminology; data entry/microcomputer applications; data processing technology; developmental/child psychology; economics; educational psychology; English composition; English language and literature, general; English technical and business writing; entrepreneurship; fire protection; foods and nutrition studies; geography; health and medical administrative services; history; hospitality services management; library science, other; mathematics; miscellaneous health professions; music; philosophy; philosophy and religion; psychology; religion/religious studies; social sciences and history, other; social sciences, general; sociology.

Non-credit—computer software and media applications.

DEVRY UNIVERSITY ONLINE

Oakbrook Terrace, Illinois

http://www.devry.edu/online

DeVry University Online was founded in 2000. It is accredited by North Central Association of Colleges and Schools. Institutionally administered financial aid is available to distance learners.

DeVry University Online (continued)

Services Distance learners have accessibility to academic advising, bookstore, career placement assistance, library services.

Contact Mr. Michael Alexander, Vice President of Online Operations, DeVry University Online, One Tower Lane, Oakbrook Terrace, IL 60181. *Telephone:* 630-574-1957. *E-mail:* malexander@keller.edu.

DEGREES AND AWARDS

BS Business Administration; Computer Information Systems; Information Technology; Technical Management
MBA Business Administration
MPA Public Administration
MPM Project Management
MS Accounting and Financial Management; Human Resource Management; Information Systems Management; Telecommunications Management

COURSE SUBJECT AREAS OFFERED OUTSIDE OF DEGREE PROGRAMS

Undergraduate—accounting; area, ethnic and cultural studies, other; biological sciences/life sciences, other; business; communications, general; computer and information sciences, general; economics; English composition; English creative writing; English technical and business writing; legal studies; liberal arts and sciences, general studies and humanities; marketing management and research; mathematics; taxation.

Graduate—accounting; business; communications, general; communications technologies; computer and information sciences, general; economics; entrepreneurship; financial management and services; health professions and related sciences, other; human resources management; marketing management and research; mathematics; public administration; taxation; telecommunications.

See full description on page 406.

DICKINSON STATE UNIVERSITY

Dickinson, North Dakota

http://www.dsu.nodak.edu/

Dickinson State University was founded in 1918. It is accredited by North Central Association of Colleges and Schools. It first offered distance learning courses in 1998. In fall 2003, there were 500 students enrolled in distance learning courses. Institutionally administered financial aid is available to distance learners.

Services Distance learners have accessibility to academic advising, bookstore, campus computer network, career placement assistance, e-mail services, library services, tutoring.

Contact Ms. Marty Odermann-Gardner, Director, Dickinson State University, 291 Campus Drive, CB 183, Dickinson, ND 58601. *Telephone:* 701-483-2129. *Fax:* 701-483-2028. *E-mail:* marty.odermann.gardner@dsu.nodak.edu.

DEGREES AND AWARDS

AA General Program
BSAST Applied Science in Technology (BAST)
BUS University Studies

COURSE SUBJECT AREAS OFFERED OUTSIDE OF DEGREE PROGRAMS

Undergraduate—accounting; business; business administration and management; business communications; geography; history; liberal arts and sciences, general studies and humanities; nursing; psychology.

DRAKE UNIVERSITY

Des Moines, Iowa

Distance Learning Program

http://www.onlinelearning.drake.edu/summer/

Drake University was founded in 1881. It is accredited by North Central Association of Colleges and Schools. It first offered distance learning courses in 1997. In fall 2003, there were 2,195 students enrolled in distance learning courses. Institutionally administered financial aid is available to distance learners.

Services Distance learners have accessibility to academic advising, bookstore, campus computer network, e-mail services, library services.

Contact Ms. Sandra K. Smeltzer, Assistant to the Provost, Drake University, Office of the Provost, 25th and University, Des Moines, IA 50311. *Telephone:* 515-271-4985. *Fax:* 515-271-2954. *E-mail:* sandra.smeltzer@drake.edu.

DEGREES AND AWARDS

Programs offered do not lead to a degree or other formal award.

COURSE SUBJECT AREAS OFFERED OUTSIDE OF DEGREE PROGRAMS

Undergraduate—accounting; advertising; biochemistry and biophysics; biology, general; business; business administration and management; business information and data processing services; business/managerial economics; business quantitative methods and management science; communications, general; communications, other; computer and information sciences, general; economics; education, general; education, other; English composition; English creative writing; English language and literature, general; fine arts and art studies; health professions and related sciences, other; history; human resources management; information sciences and systems; international relations and affairs; journalism and mass communications; liberal arts and sciences, general studies and humanities; mathematics and computer science; peace and conflict studies; pharmacy; political science and government; psychology; psychology, other; social sciences and history, other; sociology; special education; visual and performing arts, other.

Graduate—advertising; business; business administration and management; economics; education, general; English language and literature, general; health professions and related sciences, other; history; human resources management; information sciences and systems; journalism and mass communications; liberal arts and sciences, general studies and humanities; peace and conflict studies; pharmacy; political science and government; psychology; public administration; public administration and services, other; public health.

Special Message

Distance education at Drake University includes a thriving summer online program. Each summer Drake offers a wide array of fully online courses that students can complete without having to attend a face-to-face class meeting. During summer 2004, nearly 60 courses are scheduled for both undergraduate and graduate credit, which can easily be transferred to other institutions.

Many of Drake's courses are suitable for advanced high school students and/or students about to enter college. In addition, Drake offers a sample Web course for prospective students, as well as extensive online support and training for enrolled online students.

Students must register online for Web-based courses at http://www.multimedia.drake.edu/summer/ beginning in early April. A list of 2004 courses, as well as details about the registration process, can be found at http://www.onlinelearning/drake.edu/summer/.

Experienced Drake faculty members teach every online course; courses are generally limited to 20–25 students. In student evaluations of Drake's program, about two thirds of the students say that they learn equally well or better in an online environment than in a traditional classroom. Drake's online program also provides access to on-campus library sources, as well as tuition and fees, advising, and ordering books.

Drake's online program is particularly suited to independent and self-motivated learners whose schedules require flexibility.

Drake's online program began in 1997 and serves registrants throughout the world. For more information on the Web-based program, students should contact Summer Programming at 800-44-DRAKE Ext. 4368 (toll-free) or via e-mail at onlinelearning@drake.edu.

DREW UNIVERSITY

Madison, New Jersey

Drew University was founded in 1867. It is accredited by Middle States Association of Colleges and Schools. It first offered distance learning courses in 1998. In fall 2003, there were 60 students enrolled in distance learning courses. Institutionally administered financial aid is available to distance learners.

Services Distance learners have accessibility to academic advising, campus computer network, e-mail services, library services.

Contact Dr. Carl Savage, Associate Director, Doctor of Ministry Program, Drew University, 36 Madison Avenue, Madison, NJ 07940. *Telephone:* 973-408-3586. *Fax:* 973-408-3178. *E-mail:* csavage@drew.edu.

DEGREES AND AWARDS

Programs offered do not lead to a degree or other formal award.

COURSE SUBJECT AREAS OFFERED OUTSIDE OF DEGREE PROGRAMS

Graduate—theological and ministerial studies.

DREXEL UNIVERSITY

Philadelphia, Pennsylvania

College of Business and Administration

http://mbaonline.lebow.drexel.edu

Drexel University was founded in 1891. It is accredited by Middle States Association of Colleges and Schools. It first offered distance learning courses in 1998. In fall 2003, there were 300 students enrolled in distance learning courses. Institutionally administered financial aid is available to distance learners.

Services Distance learners have accessibility to academic advising, bookstore, career placement assistance, e-mail services, library services.

Contact David Stewart, Senior Director, Graduate Programs, Drexel University, LeBow College of Business, 105 Matheson Hall, 3141 Chestnut Street, Philadelphia, PA 19104. *Telephone:* 215-895-1506. *Fax:* 215-895-1997. *E-mail:* david.m.stewart@drexel.edu.

DEGREES AND AWARDS

MBA Business

COURSE SUBJECT AREAS OFFERED OUTSIDE OF DEGREE PROGRAMS

Undergraduate—accounting; business; business administration and management; business communications; business/managerial economics; business quantitative methods and management science; marketing management and research; marketing operations/marketing and distribution, other; taxation.

Graduate—accounting; business administration and management; business management and administrative services, other; business/managerial economics; business quantitative methods and management science; computer/information technology administration and management; marketing management and research; marketing operations/marketing and distribution, other.

DUKE UNIVERSITY

Durham, North Carolina

Executive MBA Programs

http://www.fuqua.duke.edu/admin/gemba

Duke University was founded in 1838. It is accredited by Southern Association of Colleges and Schools. It first offered distance learning courses in 1996. In fall 2003, there were 279 students enrolled in distance learning courses. Institutionally administered financial aid is available to distance learners.

Services Distance learners have accessibility to academic advising, bookstore, campus computer network, e-mail services, library services.

Contact Kelli Kilpatrick, Director of Recruiting and Admissions, Executive MBA Programs, Duke University, 1 Towerview Drive, Durham, NC 27708. *Telephone:* 919-660-7804. *Fax:* 919-660-2940. *E-mail:* kelli.kilpatrick@duke.edu.

DEGREES AND AWARDS

MBA The Duke MBA–Cross Continent; The Duke MBA–Global Executive

COURSE SUBJECT AREAS OFFERED OUTSIDE OF DEGREE PROGRAMS

Graduate—accounting; business marketing and marketing management; finance; international business; mathematical statistics; organizational behavior.

Non-credit—financial management and services; marketing management and research.

See full description on page 408.

DUKE UNIVERSITY

Durham, North Carolina

Nicholas School of the Environment and Earth Sciences

http://www.nicholas.duke.edu/del

Duke University was founded in 1838. It is accredited by Southern Association of Colleges and Schools. Institutionally administered financial aid is available to distance learners.

Duke University (continued)

Contact Sara Ashenburg, Director, Duke Environmental Leadership Program, Duke University, Nicholas School of the Environment and Earth Sciences, Box 90328, Durham, NC 27708-0328. *Telephone:* 919-613-8082. *Fax:* 919-613-9002. *E-mail:* del@env.duke.edu.

DEGREES AND AWARDS

MEM Duke Environmental Leadership Program

See full description on page 410.

DUQUESNE UNIVERSITY

Pittsburgh, Pennsylvania
Center for Distance Learning
http://www.distancelearning.duq.edu

Duquesne University was founded in 1878. It is accredited by Middle States Association of Colleges and Schools. It first offered distance learning courses in 1996. In fall 2003, there were 743 students enrolled in distance learning courses. Institutionally administered financial aid is available to distance learners.

Services Distance learners have accessibility to academic advising, bookstore, career placement assistance, e-mail services, library services, tutoring.

Contact Ruth Newberry, Director, Educational Technology, Duquesne University, Rockwell Hall, 600 Forbes Avenue, Pittsburgh, PA 15282. *Telephone:* 412-396-1813. *Fax:* 412-396-5144. *E-mail:* virtualcampus@duq.edu.

DEGREES AND AWARDS

BS Degree Completion
BSN Nursing–RN-BSN/MSN
Certificate Nursing–Post-BSN
Graduate Certificate Nursing–Post-Masters
MA Leadership and Liberal Studies
MEM Environmental Management
MS Leadership and Business Ethics; Music Education–Masters in Music Education
MSN Nursing
PhD Nursing
PharmD Pharmacy–Nontraditional Doctor of Pharmacy

COURSE SUBJECT AREAS OFFERED OUTSIDE OF DEGREE PROGRAMS

Undergraduate—art history; educational psychology; environmental science; philosophy and religion related.

Graduate—computer software and media applications; curriculum and instruction; educational/instructional media design; environmental science; philosophy and religion related.

EARLHAM SCHOOL OF RELIGION

Richmond, Indiana
http://esr.earlham.edu

Earlham School of Religion was founded in 1960. It first offered distance learning courses in 2001. In fall 2003, there were 30 students enrolled in distance learning courses. Institutionally administered financial aid is available to distance learners.

Services Distance learners have accessibility to academic advising, bookstore, campus computer network, e-mail services, library services.

Contact Ms. Susan G. Axtell, Director of Recruitment and Admissions, Earlham School of Religion, 228 College Avenue, Richmond, IN 47374. *Telephone:* 800-432-1377. *Fax:* 765-983-1688. *E-mail:* axtelsu@earlham.edu.

DEGREES AND AWARDS

MA ESR Access
MDiv ESR Access

COURSE SUBJECT AREAS OFFERED OUTSIDE OF DEGREE PROGRAMS

Graduate—bible/biblical studies; biblical and other theological languages and literatures; pastoral counseling and specialized ministries; peace and conflict studies; religion/religious studies; theological and ministerial studies; theological studies and religious vocations, other.

EAST ARKANSAS COMMUNITY COLLEGE

Forrest City, Arkansas
http://www.eacc.edu

East Arkansas Community College was founded in 1974. It is accredited by North Central Association of Colleges and Schools. In fall 2003, there were 100 students enrolled in distance learning courses. Institutionally administered financial aid is available to distance learners.

Services Distance learners have accessibility to academic advising, bookstore, career placement assistance, library services, tutoring.

Contact Mrs. Becca Whitehead, Distance Learning Coordinator, East Arkansas Community College, 1700 Newcastle Road, Forrest City, AR 72335. *Telephone:* 870-699-4480 Ext. 201. *Fax:* 870-633-7222. *E-mail:* distancelearning@eacc.edu.

DEGREES AND AWARDS

Programs offered do not lead to a degree or other formal award.

COURSE SUBJECT AREAS OFFERED OUTSIDE OF DEGREE PROGRAMS

Undergraduate—business/managerial economics; English composition; Internet and World Wide Web; mathematics; political science and government.

EAST CAROLINA UNIVERSITY

Greenville, North Carolina
Division of Continuing Studies
http://www.options.ecu.edu

East Carolina University was founded in 1907. It is accredited by Southern Association of Colleges and Schools. It first offered distance learning courses in 1947. In fall 2003, there were 3,266 students enrolled in distance learning courses. Institutionally administered financial aid is available to distance learners.

Services Distance learners have accessibility to academic advising, bookstore, campus computer network, e-mail services, library services.

Contact Carolyn Dunn, Marketing Coordinator, East Carolina University, Erwin Building, Room 215, Greenville, NC 27858. *Telephone:* 800-398-9275. *Fax:* 252-328-1600. *E-mail:* dunnca@mail.ecu.edu.

DEGREES AND AWARDS

BS Birth-Kindergarten Education; Communication/Public Relations/Journalism Concentration; Health Information Management; Health Services Management; Industrial Technology; Information Technologies
BSN Nursing–RN to BSN
Graduate Certificate Assistive Technology; Computer Network Professional; Professional Communication; Security Studies; Substance Abuse; Tele-Learning; Virtual Reality in Education and Training; Website Developer
MA English–Professional and Technical Communication Concentration; Psychology, general
MAE Art Education; Health/Teacher Education; Science Teacher Education; Special Education
MBA Business Administration
MLS Library Science
MS Criminal Justice; Industrial Technology–Computer Networking Management; Industrial Technology–Digital Communication Technology; Industrial Technology–Distribution and Logistics; Industrial Technology–Information Security; Industrial Technology–Manufacturing; Industrial Technology–Performance Improvement; Instructional Technology; Nutrition and Dietetics; Occupational Safety; Physician Assistant; Speech Language and Auditory Pathology; Vocational Education–Information Technologies
MSE Instructional Technology; Music Education
MSN Nurse Midwifery; Nursing Education; Nursing–Family Nurse Practitioner

COURSE SUBJECT AREAS OFFERED OUTSIDE OF DEGREE PROGRAMS

Undergraduate—administrative and secretarial services; biology, general; business; business communications; business information and data processing services; business management and administrative services, other; chemistry; child care and guidance workers and managers; communications, general; communications, other; computer and information sciences, general; curriculum and instruction; data entry/microcomputer applications; data processing technology; educational psychology; education, general; engineering/industrial management; hospitality/recreation marketing; hospitality services management; industrial/manufacturing engineering; industrial production technologies; information sciences and systems; journalism and mass communications; philosophy; philosophy and religion; philosophy and religion related; teacher education, specific academic and vocational programs; technology education/industrial arts.

Graduate—accounting; business; business administration and management; business management and administrative services, other; communication disorders sciences and services; computer/information technology administration and management; computer science; computer systems networking and telecommunications; criminal justice and corrections; criminology; data processing technology; educational/instructional media design; education, general; English technical and business writing; fine arts and art studies; foods and nutrition studies; industrial/manufacturing engineering; industrial production technologies; Internet and World Wide Web; library science/librarianship; psychology; psychology, other; quality control and safety technologies; rehabilitation/therapeutic services; special education.

See full description on page 412.

EAST CENTRAL COLLEGE

Union, Missouri

http://www.eastcentral.edu

East Central College was founded in 1959. It is accredited by North Central Association of Colleges and Schools. It first offered distance learning courses in 1982. In fall 2003, there were 332 students enrolled in distance learning courses. Institutionally administered financial aid is available to distance learners.

Services Distance learners have accessibility to academic advising, bookstore, career placement assistance, e-mail services, library services, tutoring.
Contact Karen Klos, Instructional Design Coordinator, East Central College, 1964 Prairie Dell Road, Union, MO 63084. *Telephone:* 636-583-5195 Ext. 2387. *Fax:* 636-583-6637. *E-mail:* klosk@eastcentral.edu.

DEGREES AND AWARDS

Programs offered do not lead to a degree or other formal award.

COURSE SUBJECT AREAS OFFERED OUTSIDE OF DEGREE PROGRAMS

Undergraduate—biology, general; business; computer and information sciences, general; computer software and media applications; economics; English composition; English language and literature, general; environmental/environmental health engineering; fine arts and art studies; health professions and related sciences, other; history; industrial/manufacturing engineering; Internet and World Wide Web; marketing operations/marketing and distribution, other; psychology; speech and rhetorical studies.

EASTERN ILLINOIS UNIVERSITY

Charleston, Illinois

School of Continuing Education

http://www.eiu.edu/~adulted

Eastern Illinois University was founded in 1895. It is accredited by North Central Association of Colleges and Schools. It first offered distance learning courses in 1994. In fall 2003, there were 600 students enrolled in distance learning courses. Institutionally administered financial aid is available to distance learners.

Services Distance learners have accessibility to academic advising, bookstore, campus computer network, career placement assistance, e-mail services, library services.
Contact Dr. L. Kaye Woodward, Director of Board of Trustees BA Program, Eastern Illinois University, 600 Lincoln Avenue, Charleston, IL 61920. *Telephone:* 217-581-5618. *Fax:* 217-581-7076. *E-mail:* bogta@www.eiu.edu.

DEGREES AND AWARDS

BA General Studies

COURSE SUBJECT AREAS OFFERED OUTSIDE OF DEGREE PROGRAMS

Undergraduate—biological and physical sciences; biological sciences/life sciences, other; biology, general; consumer and homemaking education; education, general; family/consumer resource management; individual and family development studies; industrial produc-

Eastern Illinois University (continued)

tion technologies; mathematics, other; psychology; social sciences and history, other; teacher education, specific academic and vocational programs.

Graduate—accounting; business administration and management; child care and guidance workers and managers; computer and information sciences, general; construction management; education administration and supervision; family and community studies; family/consumer resource management; industrial/manufacturing engineering; marketing management and research.

Non-credit—legal studies.

EASTERN KENTUCKY UNIVERSITY

Richmond, Kentucky
Continuing Education and Outreach
http://www.eku.edu/onlinelearning/

Eastern Kentucky University was founded in 1906. It is accredited by Southern Association of Colleges and Schools. It first offered distance learning courses in 1995. In fall 2003, there were 2,300 students enrolled in distance learning courses. Institutionally administered financial aid is available to distance learners.

Services Distance learners have accessibility to academic advising, bookstore, campus computer network, career placement assistance, e-mail services, library services, tutoring.

Contact William St. Pierre, Director of Distance Education, Eastern Kentucky University, 202 Perkins, 521 Lancaster Avenue, Richmond, KY 40475. *Telephone:* 859-622-8342. *Fax:* 859-622-6205. *E-mail:* bill.stpierre@eku.edu.

DEGREES AND AWARDS

MS Loss Prevention and Safety

COURSE SUBJECT AREAS OFFERED OUTSIDE OF DEGREE PROGRAMS

Undergraduate—American history; anthropology; art history; biology; business marketing and marketing management; curriculum and instruction; educational psychology; English composition; family and marriage counseling; geography; health professions and related sciences, other; journalism and mass communication related; mathematics related; philosophy and religion related; political science and government; radio/television broadcasting; sign language interpretation; social work; sociology.

Graduate—computer science; counseling psychology; criminal justice and corrections; curriculum and instruction; education administration and supervision; health and medical diagnostic and treatment services; library science/librarianship; nursing; special education.

EASTERN MENNONITE UNIVERSITY

Harrisonburg, Virginia
Eastern Mennonite Seminary
http://www.emu.edu/seminary

Eastern Mennonite University was founded in 1917. It is accredited by Southern Association of Colleges and Schools. It first offered distance learning courses in 1997. In fall 2003, there were 24 students enrolled in distance learning courses. Institutionally administered financial aid is available to distance learners.

Services Distance learners have accessibility to academic advising, bookstore, campus computer network, career placement assistance, e-mail services, library services.

Contact Don Yoder, Director of Admissions, Seminary and Graduate Programs, Eastern Mennonite University, 1200 Park Road, Harrisonburg, VA 22802-2462. *Telephone:* 540-432-4257. *Fax:* 540-432-4444. *E-mail:* semadmiss@emu.edu.

DEGREES AND AWARDS

Programs offered do not lead to a degree or other formal award.

COURSE SUBJECT AREAS OFFERED OUTSIDE OF DEGREE PROGRAMS

Graduate—bible/biblical studies; theological and ministerial studies.

EASTERN MICHIGAN UNIVERSITY

Ypsilanti, Michigan
Distance Education
http://www.ce.emich.edu

Eastern Michigan University was founded in 1849. It is accredited by North Central Association of Colleges and Schools. It first offered distance learning courses in 1997. In fall 2003, there were 2,400 students enrolled in distance learning courses. Institutionally administered financial aid is available to distance learners.

Services Distance learners have accessibility to academic advising, bookstore, campus computer network, career placement assistance, e-mail services, library services, tutoring.

Contact Jody Cebina, Distance Education, Eastern Michigan University, Continuing Education, 101 Boone Hall, Ypsilanti, MI 48197. *Telephone:* 734-487-1081. *Fax:* 734-487-6695. *E-mail:* distance.education@emich.edu.

DEGREES AND AWARDS

BS Dietetics; Technology Management (Degree Completion)
Graduate Certificate Educational Media and Technology
MS Educational Media and Technology; Engineering; Human Nutrition; Quality

COURSE SUBJECT AREAS OFFERED OUTSIDE OF DEGREE PROGRAMS

Undergraduate—African-American studies; American history; apparel and accessories marketing operations; applied mathematics; Army R.O.T.C.; biology, general; business; business administration and management; business communications; chemistry; communications, general; communications, other; English composition; English language and literature, general; fine arts and art studies; food products retailing and wholesaling operations; foods and nutrition studies; food sciences and technology; geography; history; hospitality services management; human resources management; investments and securities; law and legal studies related; legal studies; marketing management and research; marketing operations/marketing and distribution, other; mathematics; medical genetics; philosophy; philosophy and religion; political science and government; psychology; sociology; special education; technology education/industrial arts; theater arts/drama; women's studies.

Graduate—African-American studies; business administration and management; business communications; education administration and supervision; educational evaluation, research and statistics;

educational/instructional media design; educational psychology; education, general; education, other; engineering, general; engineering/industrial management; engineering, other; engineering-related technologies, other; engineering science; foods and nutrition studies; food sciences and technology; general teacher education; human resources management; Internet and World Wide Web; law and legal studies related; marketing management and research; marketing operations/marketing and distribution, other; miscellaneous health professions; nursing; psychology, other; quality control and safety technologies; school psychology; teacher education, specific academic and vocational programs; technology education/industrial arts.
Non-credit—accounting; education, general; education, other; human resources management.

See full description on page 414.

EASTERN OREGON UNIVERSITY

La Grande, Oregon
Division of Distance Education
http://www.eou.edu/dde/

Eastern Oregon University was founded in 1929. It first offered distance learning courses in 1978. In fall 2003, there were 1,800 students enrolled in distance learning courses. Institutionally administered financial aid is available to distance learners.

Services Distance learners have accessibility to academic advising, bookstore, campus computer network, career placement assistance, e-mail services, library services, tutoring.
Contact Melanie Rowley, Inquiry Coordinator, Eastern Oregon University, Zabel Hall, Room 222, 1 University Boulevard, La Grande, OR 97850-2899. *Telephone:* 800-544-2195. *Fax:* 541-962-3627. *E-mail:* dde@eou.edu.

DEGREES AND AWARDS

BA Philosophy, Politics and Economics
BS Business Administration; Business and Economics; Fire Services Administration; Liberal Studies; Physical Education/Health; Psychology

COURSE SUBJECT AREAS OFFERED OUTSIDE OF DEGREE PROGRAMS

Undergraduate—accounting; agricultural business and management; anthropology; biology, general; botany; business; chemistry; dramatic/theater arts and stagecraft; economics; English language and literature, general; geography; health and physical education/fitness; music; philosophy; physics; political science and government; psychology.

Special Message

Founded in 1929, Eastern Oregon University is a state-supported, comprehensive institution. Eastern is accredited by the Northwest Association of Schools and Colleges. The Division of Distance Education is the distance learning arm of the institution, with a long history of experience delivering both courses and degrees (the first courses were offered in 1978). In 2004–05, Eastern offers more than 500 courses at a distance and 6 different BA/BS distance degree programs: the multidisciplinary liberal studies degree; the philosophy, politics, and economics degree; the business/economics degree; the business administration degree; the physical education and health degree; and the fire services administration degree. A new psychology degree is pending. Distance learning courses are to be offered on-site or online to accommodate the requirements of each degree program. All students are required to have e-mail access and Web-browsing capabilities.

More than 1,850 students are currently enrolled in the distance learning degree programs. The courses and degrees are available to students in the United States and Canada and to armed services personnel abroad. Eastern does not charge extra out-of-state tuition. Most of the courses are taught by the same faculty members who teach on-campus courses; the distance learning degrees are the same as those available on campus. Degree-seeking students receive close advising support and have online access to full library services at a distance. The admission requirements for students entering the distance learning degree programs are the same as those for on-campus programs; Eastern is not an open admission university.

Students may take up to 8 quarter course units per term without being admitted. Specific information about enrollment is available at the online class registration site (http://webster.eou.edu/). For more information about courses or degree programs, students should e-mail dde@eou.edu or visit the Division of Distance Education Web site (http://www.eou.edu/dde/) and fill out an online inquiry form.

EASTERN SHORE COMMUNITY COLLEGE

Melfa, Virginia
Academic Division
http://www.es.vccs.edu/

Eastern Shore Community College was founded in 1971. It is accredited by Southern Association of Colleges and Schools. It first offered distance learning courses in 1991. In fall 2003, there were 125 students enrolled in distance learning courses. Institutionally administered financial aid is available to distance learners.

Services Distance learners have accessibility to academic advising, bookstore, campus computer network, e-mail services, library services.
Contact Ms. MaryKay Mulligan, Dean of Instruction, Eastern Shore Community College, 29300 Lankford Highway, Melfa, VA 23410. *Telephone:* 757-789-1748. *E-mail:* mmulligan@es.vccs.edu.

DEGREES AND AWARDS

Programs offered do not lead to a degree or other formal award.

COURSE SUBJECT AREAS OFFERED OUTSIDE OF DEGREE PROGRAMS

Undergraduate—advertising; anthropology; biological sciences/life sciences, other; business administration and management; criminal justice and corrections; history; music; psychology; sociology.

EASTERN WASHINGTON UNIVERSITY

Cheney, Washington
Division of Continuing Education, Summer Session and Outreach
http://www.deo.ewu.edu

Eastern Washington University was founded in 1882. It is accredited by Northwest Commission on Colleges and Universities. It first

Eastern Washington University (continued)

offered distance learning courses in 1970. In fall 2003, there were 600 students enrolled in distance learning courses. Institutionally administered financial aid is available to distance learners.

Services Distance learners have accessibility to bookstore, library services.

Contact Michele Opsal, Program Coordinator, Eastern Washington University, 219 Hargreaves Hall, Cheney, WA 99004-2414. *Telephone:* 509-359-2268. *Fax:* 509-359-6257. *E-mail:* gothedistance@mail.ewu.edu.

DEGREES AND AWARDS

Programs offered do not lead to a degree or other formal award.

COURSE SUBJECT AREAS OFFERED OUTSIDE OF DEGREE PROGRAMS

Undergraduate—accounting; African-American studies; American history; business; creative writing; education, general; English language and literature, general; history; human resources management; mathematics; psychology, other; social psychology; women's studies.

EASTERN WYOMING COLLEGE

Torrington, Wyoming
Outreach
http://ewc.wy.edu

Eastern Wyoming College was founded in 1948. It is accredited by North Central Association of Colleges and Schools. It first offered distance learning courses in 1990. In fall 2003, there were 169 students enrolled in distance learning courses. Institutionally administered financial aid is available to distance learners.

Services Distance learners have accessibility to academic advising, bookstore, library services, tutoring.

Contact Dee Ludwig, Associate Dean of Instruction, Eastern Wyoming College, 3200 West C Street, Torrington, WY 82240. *Telephone:* 307-532-8221. *Fax:* 307-532-8222. *E-mail:* dludwig@ewc.wy.edu.

DEGREES AND AWARDS

Programs offered do not lead to a degree or other formal award.

COURSE SUBJECT AREAS OFFERED OUTSIDE OF DEGREE PROGRAMS

Undergraduate—accounting; biology, general; business; business administration and management; computer and information sciences, general; computer software and media applications; criminal justice and corrections; economics; English composition; English language and literature, general; geological and related sciences; health and physical education/fitness; physiological psychology/psychobiology; political science and government; sociology; zoology.

EAST LOS ANGELES COLLEGE

Monterey Park, California
http://www.elac.edu

East Los Angeles College was founded in 1945. It is accredited by Western Association of Schools and Colleges. It first offered distance learning courses in 1998. In fall 2003, there were 1,000 students enrolled in distance learning courses. Institutionally administered financial aid is available to distance learners.

Services Distance learners have accessibility to academic advising, e-mail services, library services.

Contact Ms. Kerrin McMahan, Distance Education Coordinator, East Los Angeles College, 1301 Avenida Cesar Chavez, Monterey Park, CA 91754. *Telephone:* 323-265-8774. *E-mail:* mcmahakm@elac.edu.

DEGREES AND AWARDS

Programs offered do not lead to a degree or other formal award.

COURSE SUBJECT AREAS OFFERED OUTSIDE OF DEGREE PROGRAMS

Undergraduate—accounting; administrative and secretarial services; business information and data processing services; computer and information sciences, general; English composition; family/consumer resource management; fine arts and art studies; foods and nutrition studies; health and physical education/fitness; history; liberal arts and sciences, general studies and humanities; mathematics; philosophy; psychology; speech and rhetorical studies; visual and performing arts.

EDGECOMBE COMMUNITY COLLEGE

Tarboro, North Carolina
http://www.edgecombe.edu

Edgecombe Community College was founded in 1968. It is accredited by Southern Association of Colleges and Schools. It first offered distance learning courses in 1988. In fall 2003, there were 176 students enrolled in distance learning courses. Institutionally administered financial aid is available to distance learners.

Services Distance learners have accessibility to academic advising, bookstore, campus computer network, career placement assistance, e-mail services, library services, tutoring.

Contact Mr. Richard Greene, Distance Learning Coordinator, Edgecombe Community College, 225 Tarboro Street, Rocky Mount, NC 27801. *Telephone:* 252-823-5166 Ext. 340. *Fax:* 252-985-2212. *E-mail:* greener@edgecombe.edu.

DEGREES AND AWARDS

Programs offered do not lead to a degree or other formal award.

COURSE SUBJECT AREAS OFFERED OUTSIDE OF DEGREE PROGRAMS

Undergraduate—accounting; business; business administration and management; business communications; business information and data processing services; business management and administrative services, other; child care and guidance workers and managers; computer and information sciences, general; computer and information sciences, other; computer/information technology administration and management; computer programming; computer software and media applications; computer systems analysis; computer systems networking and telecommunications; cultural studies; data entry/microcomputer applications; English composition; English technical and business writing; health and medical administrative services; health and medical preparatory programs; history; psychology; sociology; teacher education, specific academic and vocational programs.

Non-credit—accounting; administrative and secretarial services; area, ethnic and cultural studies, other; business; business administration and management; business and personal services marketing operations; business communications; business information and data processing services; business management and administrative services, other; business/managerial economics; communications, general; community health services; computer and information sciences, general; computer and information sciences, other; computer/information technology administration and management; computer programming; computer science; computer software and media applications; consumer and homemaking education; data entry/microcomputer applications; English as a second language; English language and literature, general; health and medical administrative services.

EDISON COMMUNITY COLLEGE

Fort Myers, Florida
Distance Learning
http://www.edison.edu

Edison Community College was founded in 1962. It is accredited by Southern Association of Colleges and Schools. It first offered distance learning courses in 1993. In fall 2003, there were 2,000 students enrolled in distance learning courses. Institutionally administered financial aid is available to distance learners.

Services Distance learners have accessibility to bookstore, campus computer network, library services.

Contact Lori Kremski-Bronder, Distance Learning Coordinator, Edison Community College, PO Box 60210, Fort Myers, FL 33906-6210. *Telephone:* 239-489-9080. *Fax:* 239-433-8000. *E-mail:* lbronder@edison.edu.

DEGREES AND AWARDS

AA General Education

COURSE SUBJECT AREAS OFFERED OUTSIDE OF DEGREE PROGRAMS

Undergraduate—astronomy; business administration and management; communications, general; computer programming; computer software and media applications; criminal justice and corrections; data entry/microcomputer applications; developmental and child psychology; developmental/child psychology; economics; educational psychology; education, general; English composition; mathematical statistics; psychology; sociology.

EDISON STATE COMMUNITY COLLEGE

Piqua, Ohio
http://www.edisonohio.edu/

Edison State Community College was founded in 1973. It is accredited by North Central Association of Colleges and Schools. It first offered distance learning courses in 1987. In fall 2003, there were 500 students enrolled in distance learning courses. Institutionally administered financial aid is available to distance learners.

Services Distance learners have accessibility to career placement assistance, library services, tutoring.

Contact Ann Marie Miller, Internet Instructional Administrator, Edison State Community College, 1973 Edison Drive, Piqua, OH 45356. *Telephone:* 937-778-7882. *E-mail:* amiller@edisonohio.edu.

DEGREES AND AWARDS

AAB Medical Office Assistant

COURSE SUBJECT AREAS OFFERED OUTSIDE OF DEGREE PROGRAMS

Undergraduate—accounting; administrative and secretarial services; advertising; anthropology; art history; biology; business; business administration and management; business communications; business information and data processing services; business marketing and marketing management; cell biology; chemistry; child care and guidance workers and managers; computer and information sciences, general; computer engineering; computer/information technology administration and management; computer programming; computer science; computer software and media applications; computer systems analysis; computer systems networking and telecommunications; design and applied arts; ecology; economics; engineering design; engineering/industrial management; English composition; fine arts and art studies; human resources management; industrial/manufacturing engineering; industrial production technologies; Internet and World Wide Web; mathematical statistics; mathematics; mathematics and computer science; nursing; philosophy; philosophy and religion; philosophy and religion related; physics; sociology; theater arts/drama.

Non-credit—accounting; administrative and secretarial services; business; business administration and management; computer and information sciences, general; computer/information technology administration and management; computer software and media applications; human resources management; Internet and World Wide Web.

EDMONDS COMMUNITY COLLEGE

Lynnwood, Washington
Continuing Education
http://online.edcc.edu

Edmonds Community College was founded in 1967. It first offered distance learning courses in 1995. In fall 2003, there were 2,500 students enrolled in distance learning courses. Institutionally administered financial aid is available to distance learners.

Services Distance learners have accessibility to academic advising, bookstore, campus computer network, career placement assistance, library services, tutoring.

Contact Tina Torres, Distance Learning Program Assistant, Edmonds Community College, 20000 68th Avenue West, Lynnwood, WA 98036-5999. *Telephone:* 425-640-1098. *Fax:* 425-640-1704. *E-mail:* ttorres@edcc.edu.

DEGREES AND AWARDS

AA Business Administration; Business Education; Business Information Technology; Business Management; Family Support Studies/Human Development; Social Sciences

Certificate Computer Game Development

COURSE SUBJECT AREAS OFFERED OUTSIDE OF DEGREE PROGRAMS

Undergraduate—accounting; business administration and management; computer programming; developmental/child psychology; English language and literature, general; mathematics.

EDUCATION DIRECT CENTER FOR DEGREE STUDIES

Scranton, Pennsylvania
Center for Degree Studies
http://www.EducationDirect.com

Education Direct Center for Degree Studies was founded in 1975. It is accredited by Distance Education and Training Council. It first offered distance learning courses in 1975. Institutionally administered financial aid is available to distance learners.

Services Distance learners have accessibility to academic advising, e-mail services, library services, tutoring.
Contact Ms. Linda K. Smith, Manager of Data Processing, Education Direct Center for Degree Studies, 925 Oak Street, Scranton, PA 18515. *Telephone:* 570-342-7701. *E-mail:* linda.smith@thomson.com.

DEGREES AND AWARDS

AD Accounting ASB; Applied Computer Science ASB; Business Management ASB; Business Management with Finance Option ASB; Business Management with Marketing Option ASB; Civil Engineering Technology; Criminal Justice ASB; Early Childhood Education ASB; Electrical Engineering Technology AST; Electronics Technology AST; Hospitality Management ASB; Industrial Engineering Technology AST; Internet Technology Multimedia and Design AST; Internet Technology Web Programming AST; Internet Technology–E-Commerce Administration AST; Mechanical Engineering Technology AST; Paralegal Studies; Veterinary Technician AST

COURSE SUBJECT AREAS OFFERED OUTSIDE OF DEGREE PROGRAMS

Non-credit—accounting; administrative and secretarial services; carpenters; child care and guidance workers and managers; computer programming; foods and nutrition studies; health and medical administrative services; health and medical assistants; journalism and mass communications; teacher assistant/aide.

See full description on page 416.

EL CAMINO COLLEGE

Torrance, California
Distance Education
http://www.elcamino.edu/Library/DistanceEd

El Camino College was founded in 1947. It is accredited by Western Association of Schools and Colleges. It first offered distance learning courses in 1970. In fall 2003, there were 1,327 students enrolled in distance learning courses. Institutionally administered financial aid is available to distance learners.

Services Distance learners have accessibility to academic advising, campus computer network, career placement assistance, e-mail services, library services, tutoring.
Contact Ms. Joanie M. Shannon, Program Coordinator, El Camino College, Distance Education, 16007 Crenshaw Boulevard, Torrance, CA 90506. *Telephone:* 310-660.6453. *Fax:* 310-660.3513. *E-mail:* jshannon@elcamino.edu.

DEGREES AND AWARDS

Programs offered do not lead to a degree or other formal award.

COURSE SUBJECT AREAS OFFERED OUTSIDE OF DEGREE PROGRAMS

Undergraduate—anthropology; astronomy; biological sciences/life sciences, other; child care and guidance workers and managers; economics; English composition; geological and related sciences; health and physical education/fitness; journalism and mass communications; music; philosophy; political science and government; psychology; social sciences and history, other; sociology.

ELGIN COMMUNITY COLLEGE

Elgin, Illinois
http://www.elgin.edu

Elgin Community College was founded in 1949. It is accredited by North Central Association of Colleges and Schools. It first offered distance learning courses in 1980. In fall 2003, there were 1,611 students enrolled in distance learning courses. Institutionally administered financial aid is available to distance learners.

Services Distance learners have accessibility to academic advising, bookstore, campus computer network, e-mail services, library services, tutoring.
Contact Billie B. Barnett, Distance Learning Program Developer, Elgin Community College, 1700 Spartan Drive, Elgin, IL 60123. *Telephone:* 847-214-7945. *Fax:* 847-608-5479. *E-mail:* bbarnett@elgin.edu.

DEGREES AND AWARDS

Programs offered do not lead to a degree or other formal award.

COURSE SUBJECT AREAS OFFERED OUTSIDE OF DEGREE PROGRAMS

Undergraduate—accounting; administrative and secretarial services; anthropology; business; computer and information sciences, general; education, other; English composition; English language and literature, general; legal studies; mathematics.

ELIZABETH CITY STATE UNIVERSITY

Elizabeth City, North Carolina
http://www.ecsu.edu

Elizabeth City State University was founded in 1891. It is accredited by Southern Association of Colleges and Schools. It first offered distance learning courses in 1998. In fall 2003, there were 152 students enrolled in distance learning courses. Institutionally administered financial aid is available to distance learners.

Services Distance learners have accessibility to academic advising, bookstore, campus computer network, e-mail services, library services, tutoring.
Contact Mrs. Kimberley N. Stevenson, Director of the Virtual College, Elizabeth City State University, 1704 Weeksville Road, 208 Information Technology Center, Elizabeth City, NC 27909. *Telephone:* 252-335-3699. *Fax:* 252-335-3426. *E-mail:* knstevenson@mail.ecsu.edu.

DEGREES AND AWARDS

Programs offered do not lead to a degree or other formal award.

COURSE SUBJECT AREAS OFFERED OUTSIDE OF DEGREE PROGRAMS

Undergraduate—accounting; business; business administration and management; business communications; business management and administrative services, other; business/managerial economics; business quantitative methods and management science; criminal justice and corrections; educational/instructional media design; educational psychology; education, general; English composition; history; human resources management; marketing operations/marketing and distribution, other; mathematical statistics; music; psychology; public administration; public policy analysis; sociology; special education; taxation; teacher education, specific academic and vocational programs.

ELIZABETHTOWN COLLEGE

Elizabethtown, Pennsylvania

Center for Continuing Education and Distance Learning

http://www.etown.edu/cce

Elizabethtown College was founded in 1899. It is accredited by Middle States Association of Colleges and Schools. It first offered distance learning courses in 2001. In fall 2003, there were 50 students enrolled in distance learning courses. Institutionally administered financial aid is available to distance learners.

Services Distance learners have accessibility to academic advising, bookstore, campus computer network, e-mail services, library services.

Contact Dr. John Kokolus, Dean of Continuing Education and Distance Learning, Elizabethtown College, 1 Alpha Drive, Elizabethtown, PA 17022. *Telephone:* 717-361-1291. *Fax:* 717-361-1466. *E-mail:* kokolusj@etown.edu.

DEGREES AND AWARDS

Programs offered do not lead to a degree or other formal award.

COURSE SUBJECT AREAS OFFERED OUTSIDE OF DEGREE PROGRAMS

Undergraduate—accounting; American literature (United States); area, ethnic and cultural studies, other; business; business administration and management; business communications; communications, general; communications, other; English language and literature, general; history; human resources management; medieval and Renaissance studies.

EMBRY-RIDDLE AERONAUTICAL UNIVERSITY

Daytona Beach, Florida

Distance Learning

http://www.erau.edu/db/degrees/ma-mbaaonline.html

Embry-Riddle Aeronautical University was founded in 1926. It is accredited by Southern Association of Colleges and Schools. It first offered distance learning courses in 2003. In fall 2003, there were 96 students enrolled in distance learning courses. Institutionally administered financial aid is available to distance learners.

Services Distance learners have accessibility to academic advising, bookstore, career placement assistance, e-mail services, library services.

Contact Mr. William Hampton, Director of Graduate Admissions, Embry-Riddle Aeronautical University, 600 South Clyde Morris Boulevard, Daytona Beach, FL 32114. *Telephone:* 386-226-6115. *Fax:* 386-226-7111. *E-mail:* gradadm@erau.edu.

DEGREES AND AWARDS

MBA Business Administration in Aviation

COURSE SUBJECT AREAS OFFERED OUTSIDE OF DEGREE PROGRAMS

Undergraduate—aerospace, aeronautical and astronautical engineering; business administration and management; business/managerial economics; business marketing and marketing management; business quantitative methods and management science; English composition; finance; law and legal studies related; mathematical statistics; mathematics related; organizational behavior.

Graduate—business administration and management; business quantitative methods and management science; labor/personnel relations; management information systems/business data processing.

Non-credit—air transportation workers.

EMBRY-RIDDLE AERONAUTICAL UNIVERSITY, EXTENDED CAMPUS

Daytona Beach, Florida

Distance Learning Enrollment Office

http://www.erau.edu/ec/dleo/index.html

Embry-Riddle Aeronautical University, Extended Campus was founded in 1970. It is accredited by Southern Association of Colleges and Schools. It first offered distance learning courses in 1983. In fall 2003, there were 1,149 students enrolled in distance learning courses. Institutionally administered financial aid is available to distance learners.

Services Distance learners have accessibility to academic advising, bookstore, career placement assistance, library services.

Contact Ms. Marsha Lewis, Recruitment Advisor, Embry-Riddle Aeronautical University, Extended Campus, 600 South Clyde Morris Boulevard, Daytona Beach, FL 32114-3900. *Telephone:* 386-226-6363. *Fax:* 386-226-7627. *E-mail:* dleo.student.recruiter@erau.edu.

DEGREES AND AWARDS

AS Aircraft Maintenance; Professional Aeronautics; Technical Management

BS Aviation Maintenance Management; Professional Aeronautics; Technical Management

MAS Aeronautical Science

MS Management

COURSE SUBJECT AREAS OFFERED OUTSIDE OF DEGREE PROGRAMS

Undergraduate—applied mathematics; business; computer science; economics; English language and literature, general; English technical and business writing; legal studies; mathematical statistics; social sciences, general.

Embry-Riddle Aeronautical University, Extended Campus (continued)

Graduate—air transportation workers; business; business administration and management; psychology.
Non-credit—air transportation workers.

See full description on page 418.

EMMANUEL BIBLE COLLEGE

Kitchener, Ontario, Canada
http://www.ebcollege.on.ca

Emmanuel Bible College was founded in 1940. It is provincially chartered. It first offered distance learning courses in 1993. In fall 2003, there were 103 students enrolled in distance learning courses. Institutionally administered financial aid is available to distance learners.

Services Distance learners have accessibility to academic advising.
Contact Ms. Carol Blake, Director of Distance Education, Emmanuel Bible College, 100 Fergus Avenue, Kitchener, ON N2A 2H2, Canada. *Telephone:* 519-894-8900 Ext. 256. *E-mail:* cblake@ebcollege.on.ca.

DEGREES AND AWARDS

Programs offered do not lead to a degree or other formal award.

COURSE SUBJECT AREAS OFFERED OUTSIDE OF DEGREE PROGRAMS

Undergraduate—anthropology; bible/biblical studies; philosophy and religion; psychology; religion/religious studies; sociology; theological and ministerial studies.

EMORY UNIVERSITY

Atlanta, Georgia
The Rollins School of Public Health
http://www.sph.emory.edu/CMPH

Emory University was founded in 1836. It is accredited by Southern Association of Colleges and Schools. It first offered distance learning courses in 1997. In fall 2003, there were 120 students enrolled in distance learning courses. Institutionally administered financial aid is available to distance learners.

Services Distance learners have accessibility to academic advising, bookstore, campus computer network, career placement assistance, e-mail services, library services.
Contact Kara Brown Robinson, Assistant Director of Academic Programs, Emory University, 1518 Clifton Road-RSPH, Office 148, Atlanta, GA 30322. *Telephone:* 404-727-3317. *Fax:* 404-727-3996. *E-mail:* klbrow2@sph.emory.edu.

DEGREES AND AWARDS

MPH Career Master of Public Health Program

COURSE SUBJECT AREAS OFFERED OUTSIDE OF DEGREE PROGRAMS

Graduate—public health.

Special Message

The Career Master of Public Health (CMPH) program at the Rollins School of Public Health of Emory University is an innovative new way for public health professionals to prepare themselves as leaders in the 21st century. The CMPH is a 42-credit-hour Master of Public Health (MPH) degree program designed for those who have completed a bachelor's degree and who have a minimum of 5 years of professional experience.

The CMPH program runs for 7 semesters in a mixed format of on-campus face-to-face sessions and an Internet-based community learning environment, providing working professionals the opportunity to earn an MPH without interrupting their career. Courses begin and end with on-campus face-to-face sessions; between the on-campus sessions, learners interact with classmates and instructors in an Internet-based learning community. The mixed format ensures that students, regardless of location, receive the quality education Emory is known for, while gaining a familiarity with emerging technologies and developing close, rewarding relationships with faculty members and classmates.

The CMPH program combines a curriculum relevant in today's public health environment with computer and Web-based skills critical for today's successful professionals. The CMPH curriculum is based on the goals and objectives of the "Ten Essential Public Health Services" as stated in the *Public Health Workforce: An Agenda for the 21st Century* and the Core Competencies developed by the Council on Linkages Between Academia and Public Health Practice.

The rich learning environment of the CMPH program is due in part from the diversity of knowledge and experience learners bring to the program, as well as the knowledge and experience of Emory's high-quality faculty members, who are both practitioners as well as teachers.

ENDICOTT COLLEGE

Beverly, Massachusetts
http://www.endicott.edu/

Endicott College was founded in 1939. It is accredited by New England Association of Schools and Colleges. It first offered distance learning courses in 2000. In fall 2003, there were 30 students enrolled in distance learning courses. Institutionally administered financial aid is available to distance learners.

Services Distance learners have accessibility to academic advising, bookstore, campus computer network, e-mail services, library services.
Contact Paul Squarcia, Vice President and Dean of School of Graduate and Professional Studies, Endicott College, 376 Hale Street, Beverly, MA 01915. *Telephone:* 978-232-2084. *Fax:* 978-232-3000. *E-mail:* psquarci@endicott.edu.

DEGREES AND AWARDS

MBA Business Administration
MEd Integrated Studies; Organizational Management

COURSE SUBJECT AREAS OFFERED OUTSIDE OF DEGREE PROGRAMS

Undergraduate—business; education, general.
Graduate—business; education, general.

Non-credit—business; education, general.

ERIE COMMUNITY COLLEGE

Buffalo, New York

http://www.ecc.edu/

Erie Community College was founded in 1971. It is accredited by Middle States Association of Colleges and Schools. It first offered distance learning courses in 1992. In fall 2003, there were 2,387 students enrolled in distance learning courses. Institutionally administered financial aid is available to distance learners.

Services Distance learners have accessibility to academic advising, bookstore, campus computer network, career placement assistance, e-mail services, library services, tutoring.

Contact Prof. Jason L Steinitz, Acting Coordinator of Distance Learning, Erie Community College, 4041 Southwestern Boulevard, Orchard Park, NY 14127. *Telephone:* 716-851-1305. *Fax:* 716-851-1629. *E-mail:* steinitz@ecc.edu.

DEGREES AND AWARDS

Programs offered do not lead to a degree or other formal award.

COURSE SUBJECT AREAS OFFERED OUTSIDE OF DEGREE PROGRAMS

Undergraduate—business administration and management; computer software and media applications; English composition; geography.

EUGENE BIBLE COLLEGE

Eugene, Oregon

External Studies Department

http://www.ebc.edu

Eugene Bible College was founded in 1925. It is accredited by Accrediting Association of Bible Colleges. It first offered distance learning courses in 1987. In fall 2003, there were 50 students enrolled in distance learning courses. Institutionally administered financial aid is available to distance learners.

Services Distance learners have accessibility to academic advising, e-mail services.

Contact Mr. David Earl Sinclair, Director of External Studies, Eugene Bible College, 2155 Bailey Hill Road, Eugene, OR 97405. *Telephone:* 541-485-1780 Ext. 115. *Fax:* 541-343-5801. *E-mail:* distance-ed@ebc.edu.

DEGREES AND AWARDS

Certificate One Year Bible Certificate

COURSE SUBJECT AREAS OFFERED OUTSIDE OF DEGREE PROGRAMS

Undergraduate—applied mathematics; bible/biblical studies; biblical and other theological languages and literatures; biological and physical sciences; biology, general; computer and information sciences, general; educational psychology; education, general; English composition; English literature (British and Commonwealth); Greek languages and literatures (modern); history; mathematics; missions/missionary studies and missiology; music; religion/religious studies; religious education; religious/sacred music; school psychology; sociology; speech and rhetorical studies.

EVERETT COMMUNITY COLLEGE

Everett, Washington

Library/Media/Arts and Distance Learning

http://www.everettcc.edu/distance

Everett Community College was founded in 1941. It first offered distance learning courses in 1997. In fall 2003, there were 900 students enrolled in distance learning courses. Institutionally administered financial aid is available to distance learners.

Services Distance learners have accessibility to academic advising, bookstore, library services.

Contact Sara Frizelle, Director of Distance Learning, Everett Community College, 2000 Tower Street, Everett, WA 98201. *Telephone:* 425-388-9585. *Fax:* 425-388-9144. *E-mail:* sfrizelle@everettcc.edu.

DEGREES AND AWARDS

AAS Direct Transfer
AGS General Studies

COURSE SUBJECT AREAS OFFERED OUTSIDE OF DEGREE PROGRAMS

Undergraduate—accounting; anthropology; applied mathematics; archaeology; business; child care and guidance workers and managers; computer and information sciences, general; English composition; history; journalism and mass communications; liberal arts and sciences, general studies and humanities; library science, other; mathematics; music; philosophy; physical sciences, general; psychology; psychology, other; science technologies, other; science, technology and society; social sciences, general; sociology; visual and performing arts.

Non-credit—business information and data processing services; computer and information sciences, general; computer software and media applications.

EVERGLADES UNIVERSITY

Boca Raton, Florida

http://www.evergladesuniversity.edu

Everglades University was founded in 1989. It is accredited by Northwest Commission on Colleges and Universities. Institutionally administered financial aid is available to distance learners.

Services Distance learners have accessibility to academic advising, bookstore, career placement assistance, library services.

Contact Department of Admissions, Everglades University, 1500 Northwest 49th Street, Fort Lauderdale, FL 33309. *Telephone:* 954-772-2655. *Fax:* 954-772-2695. *E-mail:* evergladesadmissions@evergladesuniversity.edu.

DEGREES AND AWARDS

BS Applied Management; Business Administration; Information Technology
MBA Business Administration

COURSE SUBJECT AREAS OFFERED OUTSIDE OF DEGREE PROGRAMS

Undergraduate—aerospace, aeronautical and astronautical engineering; business administration and management; business management and administrative services, other; information sciences and systems.

Everglades University (continued)

Graduate—aerospace, aeronautical and astronautical engineering; business administration and management; information sciences and systems.

EVERGREEN VALLEY COLLEGE

San Jose, California
Telecourse Program
http://www.evc.edu

Evergreen Valley College was founded in 1975. It is accredited by Western Association of Schools and Colleges. It first offered distance learning courses in 1981. In fall 2003, there were 818 students enrolled in distance learning courses. Institutionally administered financial aid is available to distance learners.

Services Distance learners have accessibility to library services, tutoring.

Contact Janice Tomisaka, Program Specialist, Evergreen Valley College, 3095 Yerba Buena Road, San Jose, CA 95135-1598. *Telephone:* 408-270-6422. *Fax:* 408-532-1858. *E-mail:* jan.tomisaka@sjeccd.org.

DEGREES AND AWARDS

Programs offered do not lead to a degree or other formal award.

COURSE SUBJECT AREAS OFFERED OUTSIDE OF DEGREE PROGRAMS

Undergraduate—anthropology; astronomy; business; computer and information sciences, general; consumer and homemaking education; English composition; history; library science, other; music; political science and government; psychology; sociology; Spanish.

EXCELSIOR COLLEGE

Albany, New York
Learning Services
http://www.excelsior.edu

Excelsior College was founded in 1970. It is accredited by Middle States Association of Colleges and Schools. It first offered distance learning courses in 1970. In fall 2003, there were 25,880 students enrolled in distance learning courses. Institutionally administered financial aid is available to distance learners.

Services Distance learners have accessibility to academic advising, bookstore, library services.

Contact Dr. Linda Jolly, Provost and Chief Academic Officer, Excelsior College, 7 Columbia Circle, Albany, NY 12203. *Telephone:* 518-464-8500. *Fax:* 518-464-8777. *E-mail:* ljolly@excelsior.edu.

DEGREES AND AWARDS

AA Liberal Arts
AAS Administrative/Management Studies; Aviation Studies; Nursing; Technical Studies
AS Business; Computer Software; Electronics Technology; Liberal Arts; Nuclear Technology; Nursing; Technology
BA Liberal Arts; Liberal Studies
BS Accounting; Business, general; Computer Information Systems; Computer Software; Computer Technology; Criminal Justice; Electronics Technology; Finance; International Business; Liberal Arts; Liberal Studies; Management Information Systems; Management of Human Resources; Marketing; Nuclear Technology; Operations Management; Risk Management; Technology
BSN Nursing
MA Liberal Studies
MS Nursing

See full description on page 420.

FAIRLEIGH DICKINSON UNIVERSITY, METROPOLITAN CAMPUS

Teaneck, New Jersey
Office of Educational Technology
http://www.fdu.edu/

Fairleigh Dickinson University, Metropolitan Campus was founded in 1942. It is accredited by Middle States Association of Colleges and Schools. It first offered distance learning courses in 1990. In fall 2003, there were 500 students enrolled in distance learning courses.

Services Distance learners have accessibility to bookstore, e-mail services, library services.

Contact Sandra Selick, Director of Educational Technology, Fairleigh Dickinson University, Metropolitan Campus, 1000 River Road, H-DH2-15, Teaneck, NJ 07666. *Telephone:* 201-692-7060. *Fax:* 201-692-7273. *E-mail:* selick@fdu.edu.

DEGREES AND AWARDS

Certificate English as a Second Language; Information Systems; Psychopharmacology
MS Electrical Engineering

COURSE SUBJECT AREAS OFFERED OUTSIDE OF DEGREE PROGRAMS

Undergraduate—anthropology; biology; business marketing and marketing management; chemistry; communications, general; computer science; criminal justice and corrections; culinary arts and related services; economics; English as a second language; English composition; English language and literature, general; fine arts and art studies; foreign languages and literatures; history; nursing; philosophy; philosophy and religion related; political science and government; psychology; sociology; taxation.
Graduate—accounting; biology, general; business; computer programming; computer science; education, general; electrical engineering; English language and literature, general; information sciences and systems; nursing; psychology.
Non-credit—accounting; business; computer programming; computer science; computer software and media applications; education, general; information sciences and systems; psychology.

FAIRMONT STATE UNIVERSITY

Fairmont, West Virginia
http://www.fscwv.edu/

Fairmont State University was founded in 1865. It is accredited by North Central Association of Colleges and Schools. It first offered distance learning courses in 1974. In fall 2003, there were 730 students enrolled in distance learning courses. Institutionally administered financial aid is available to distance learners.

Services Distance learners have accessibility to academic advising, bookstore, campus computer network, career placement assistance, e-mail services, library services, tutoring.
Contact Jennifer Weist, Program Manager, Fairmont State University, 1201 Locust Avenue, Fairmont , WV 26554. *Telephone:* 304-367-4503. *Fax:* 304-367-4881. *E-mail:* jweist@mail.fscwv.edu.

DEGREES AND AWARDS

Programs offered do not lead to a degree or other formal award.

COURSE SUBJECT AREAS OFFERED OUTSIDE OF DEGREE PROGRAMS

Undergraduate—business; business communications; economics; education, general; education, other; English composition; foods and nutrition studies; general teacher education; geography; history; information sciences and systems; Internet and World Wide Web; liberal arts and sciences, general studies and humanities; multi/interdisciplinary studies, other; sociology.
Graduate—education administration and supervision; educational evaluation, research and statistics; educational/instructional media design; educational psychology; education, general; education, other.
Non-credit—computer/information technology administration and management; computer systems networking and telecommunications.

FASHION INSTITUTE OF TECHNOLOGY

New York, New York

http://www.fitnyc.edu/onlinecourses

Fashion Institute of Technology was founded in 1944. It is accredited by Middle States Association of Colleges and Schools. It first offered distance learning courses in 1998. In fall 2003, there were 500 students enrolled in distance learning courses. Institutionally administered financial aid is available to distance learners.

Services Distance learners have accessibility to campus computer network, e-mail services, library services.
Contact Beth Harris, Academic Coordinator, Fashion Institute of Technology, 7th Avenue at 27th Street, New York, NY 10001. *Telephone:* 212-217-3601. *Fax:* 212-217-7639. *E-mail:* fitonline@fitnyc.edu.

DEGREES AND AWARDS

Programs offered do not lead to a degree or other formal award.

COURSE SUBJECT AREAS OFFERED OUTSIDE OF DEGREE PROGRAMS

Undergraduate—advertising; business; business marketing and marketing management; English as a second language; fine arts and art studies; law and legal studies related; management information systems/business data processing; mathematics; photography.
Non-credit—accounting; business; marketing management and research; mathematics.

Special Message

The Fashion Institute of Technology (FIT) offers a variety of industry-specific courses including Advertising and Promotion, Introduction to the Fashion Industry, Product Development, Merchandise Planning and Control, Import Buying, Fashion Business Practices, and Fundamentals of Textiles, as well as liberal arts courses such as History of Western Art and Civilization, Modern Art, and English as a Second Language. Other online offerings include Starting a Small Business, Introduction to Business Law, Photography Portfolio Development for the World Wide Web, and Information Systems in Business Management. For detailed descriptions of each course, as well as a complete list of online course offerings, students should visit the FIT Web site at http://www.fitnyc.edu/onlinecourses.

Students who are currently enrolled at FIT can enroll for online courses through FIT's regular enrollment procedures. For anyone who is not currently enrolled at FIT, registration and enrollment forms are available on the FIT Web site. For registration information, students should visit the FIT Web site or e-mail registrar@fitsuny.edu. All credit courses can be applied toward an FIT degree. Students who are interested in obtaining degree status should contact the Office of Admissions at 212-217-7755 or e-mail fitinfo@fitsuny.edu.

Using groupware and the Internet, FIT and the SUNY Learning Network (SLN) have created an electronic forum where students and professors--working at a distance from each other--learn collaboratively. For information about the SUNY Learning Network and to preview a course, students should visit the SLN Web site at http://www.sln.suny.edu. For information on general online courses, students can e-mail fitonline@fitsuny.edu.

FAYETTEVILLE STATE UNIVERSITY

Fayetteville, North Carolina

http://www.uncfsu.edu/conted

Fayetteville State University was founded in 1867. It is accredited by Southern Association of Colleges and Schools. It first offered distance learning courses in 1999. In fall 2003, there were 300 students enrolled in distance learning courses. Institutionally administered financial aid is available to distance learners.

Services Distance learners have accessibility to academic advising, bookstore, campus computer network, career placement assistance, e-mail services, library services.
Contact Mrs. Barbara Ragland Jones, Director, Extended Learning, Fayetteville State University, Continuing Education Building, 1200 Murchison Road, Fayetteville, NC 28301. *Telephone:* 910-672-1227. *Fax:* 910-672-2115. *E-mail:* bjones@uncfsu.edu.

DEGREES AND AWARDS

Programs offered do not lead to a degree or other formal award.

COURSE SUBJECT AREAS OFFERED OUTSIDE OF DEGREE PROGRAMS

Undergraduate—business; criminal justice and corrections; general teacher education; history; psychology; sociology; special education.
Graduate—business administration and management; education, general; history; special education.

FEATHER RIVER COMMUNITY COLLEGE DISTRICT

Quincy, California

http://www.frc.edu

Feather River Community College District was founded in 1968. It is accredited by Western Association of Schools and Colleges. It first

Feather River Community College District (continued)

offered distance learning courses in 2002. In fall 2003, there were 35 students enrolled in distance learning courses. Institutionally administered financial aid is available to distance learners.

Services Distance learners have accessibility to academic advising, bookstore, campus computer network, e-mail services, library services, tutoring.

Contact Dr. Michael Norman Bagley, Dean of Instruction, Feather River Community College District, 570 Golden Eagle Avenue, Quincy, CA 95971. *Telephone:* 530-283-0202 Ext. 342. *Fax:* 530-283-3757. *E-mail:* mbagley@frc.edu.

DEGREES AND AWARDS

Programs offered do not lead to a degree or other formal award.

COURSE SUBJECT AREAS OFFERED OUTSIDE OF DEGREE PROGRAMS

Undergraduate—administrative and secretarial services; biological sciences/life sciences, other; data processing technology; English composition; history; mathematics; psychology.

Non-credit—accounting; bible/biblical studies; biopsychology; botany; business; business administration and management; business communications; business information and data processing services; child care and guidance workers and managers; community health services; community organization, resources and services; computer and information sciences, general; computer programming; computer software and media applications; crafts, folk art and artisanry; culinary arts and related services; cultural studies; East and Southeast Asian languages and literatures; East European languages and literatures; education, general; English as a second language; English composition; English creative writing; English technical and business writing; entrepreneurship; family/consumer resource management; film/video and photographic arts; financial management and services; financial services marketing operations; foods and nutrition studies; foreign languages and literatures; general retailing/wholesaling; general teacher education; gerontology; health and medical administrative services; historic preservation, conservation and architectural history; history; home economics, general; horticulture services operations and management; human resources management; journalism and mass communications; legal studies; Middle Eastern languages and literatures; museology/museum studies; music; philosophy; philosophy and religion; psychology; public administration; radio and television broadcasting; real estate; teaching English as a second language/foreign language; tourism/travel marketing.

FERRIS STATE UNIVERSITY

Big Rapids, Michigan

http://www.ferris.edu/

Ferris State University was founded in 1884. It is accredited by North Central Association of Colleges and Schools. It first offered distance learning courses in 1991. In fall 2003, there were 100 students enrolled in distance learning courses. Institutionally administered financial aid is available to distance learners.

Services Distance learners have accessibility to academic advising, bookstore, campus computer network, career placement assistance, e-mail services, library services, tutoring.

Contact Mr. Steve Cox, Producer and Director, Ferris State University, 1010 Campus Drive, FLITE 460C, Big Rapids, MI 49307. *Telephone:* 231-591-2721. *Fax:* 231-591-2785. *E-mail:* coxs@ferris.edu.

DEGREES AND AWARDS

Programs offered do not lead to a degree or other formal award.

COURSE SUBJECT AREAS OFFERED OUTSIDE OF DEGREE PROGRAMS

Undergraduate—international business; mathematics; nursing.

Graduate—optometry (OD); pharmacy.

Non-credit—community organization, resources and services; curriculum and instruction; educational evaluation, research and statistics; international relations and affairs; public policy analysis.

FIELDING GRADUATE INSTITUTE

Santa Barbara, California

http://www.fielding.edu/

Fielding Graduate Institute was founded in 1974. It is accredited by Western Association of Schools and Colleges. It first offered distance learning courses in 1974. In fall 2003, there were 1,551 students enrolled in distance learning courses. Institutionally administered financial aid is available to distance learners.

Services Distance learners have accessibility to academic advising, bookstore, campus computer network, e-mail services, library services.

Contact Marine Dumas, Admissions Manager, Fielding Graduate Institute, 2112 Santa Barbara Street, Santa Barbara, CA 93105. *Telephone:* 805-898-4039. *Fax:* 805-687-9793. *E-mail:* mdumas@fielding.edu.

DEGREES AND AWARDS

Certificate Neuropsychology

Certification Organization Development and Organizational Management

MA Collaborative Educational Leadership; Organizational Management; Organizational Development

EdD Educational Leadership and Change

PhD Clinical Psychology; Human and Organizational Development; Media Psychology

FLATHEAD VALLEY COMMUNITY COLLEGE

Kalispell, Montana

Education Services

http://www.fvcc.edu

Flathead Valley Community College was founded in 1967. It is accredited by Northwest Commission on Colleges and Universities. It first offered distance learning courses in 1992. In fall 2003, there were 177 students enrolled in distance learning courses. Institutionally administered financial aid is available to distance learners.

Services Distance learners have accessibility to e-mail services, library services.

Contact Faith Hodges, Director of Enrollment Planning and Research, Flathead Valley Community College, 777 Grandview Drive, Kalispell, MT 59901. *Telephone:* 406-756-3812. *Fax:* 406-756-3815. *E-mail:* fhodges@fvcc.edu.

DEGREES AND AWARDS

Programs offered do not lead to a degree or other formal award.

COURSE SUBJECT AREAS OFFERED OUTSIDE OF DEGREE PROGRAMS

Undergraduate—biological and physical sciences; computer software and media applications; English composition; English language and literature, general; film/video and photographic arts; heating, air conditioning and refrigeration mechanics and repairers.
Non-credit—computer software and media applications.

FLORIDA ATLANTIC UNIVERSITY

Boca Raton, Florida
University Resource Management
http://www.itss.fau.edu

Florida Atlantic University was founded in 1961. It is accredited by Southern Association of Colleges and Schools. It first offered distance learning courses in 1965. In fall 2003, there were 32,000 students enrolled in distance learning courses. Institutionally administered financial aid is available to distance learners.

Services Distance learners have accessibility to academic advising, bookstore, campus computer network, e-mail services, library services.
Contact ITSS ITSS, Instructional Technology Support Services, Florida Atlantic University, 777 Glades Road, Boca Raton, FL 33431. *Telephone:* 561-297-2054. *E-mail:* itss@fau.edu.

DEGREES AND AWARDS

Certificate Gerontology
MBA Accounting; Executive Master of Taxation; Management
MFA Virtual Fine Arts

COURSE SUBJECT AREAS OFFERED OUTSIDE OF DEGREE PROGRAMS

Undergraduate—accounting; business; chemistry; computer science; educational/instructional media design; education, general; electrical, electronics and communications engineering; foreign languages and literatures, other; health professions and related sciences, other; marketing management and research; nursing; ocean engineering; political science and government.
Graduate—accounting; business administration and management; business/managerial economics; computer science; education administration and supervision; educational evaluation, research and statistics; educational/instructional media design; education, other; engineering, general; financial management and services; fine arts and art studies; foreign languages and literatures; health professions and related sciences, other; information sciences and systems; marketing management and research; mechanical engineering; ocean engineering; social work.

FLORIDA COMMUNITY COLLEGE AT JACKSONVILLE

Jacksonville, Florida
Open Campus
http://www.distancelearning.org

Florida Community College at Jacksonville was founded in 1963. It is accredited by Southern Association of Colleges and Schools. It first offered distance learning courses in 1979. In fall 2003, there were 7,500 students enrolled in distance learning courses. Institutionally administered financial aid is available to distance learners.

Services Distance learners have accessibility to academic advising, bookstore, campus computer network, career placement assistance, e-mail services, library services, tutoring.
Contact Advisor, Florida Community College at Jacksonville, Learner Support Center, 601 West State Street, Jacksonville, FL 32202. *Telephone:* 904-646-2300. *Fax:* 904-633-5955. *E-mail:* advisor@fccj.edu.

DEGREES AND AWARDS

AAS Applied Science; Arts and Sciences
AS Business, Accelerated Degree

COURSE SUBJECT AREAS OFFERED OUTSIDE OF DEGREE PROGRAMS

Undergraduate—accounting; anthropology; biological and physical sciences; business administration and management; chemistry; computer science; computer software and media applications; economics; education, general; English composition; finance; geography; history; liberal arts and sciences, general studies and humanities; mathematics related; philosophy and religion; psychology; sociology; speech and rhetorical studies.

FLORIDA GULF COAST UNIVERSITY

Fort Myers, Florida
Enrollment Services
http://www.fgcu.edu

Florida Gulf Coast University was founded in 1991. It is accredited by Southern Association of Colleges and Schools. It first offered distance learning courses in 1997. Institutionally administered financial aid is available to distance learners.

Services Distance learners have accessibility to academic advising, bookstore, campus computer network, career placement assistance, e-mail services, library services, tutoring.
Contact Undergraduate Admissions or Graduate Admissions, Florida Gulf Coast University, 10501 FGCU Boulevard, South, Fort Myers, FL 33965-6565. *Telephone:* 239-590-7878. *Fax:* 239-590-7894. *E-mail:* admissions@fgcu.edu.

DEGREES AND AWARDS

BS Criminal Justice; Health Services Administration
MA Curriculum and Instruction
MBA Business Administration
MEd Curriculum and Instruction
MPA Public Administration
MS Health Professions Education; Health Services Administration

COURSE SUBJECT AREAS OFFERED OUTSIDE OF DEGREE PROGRAMS

Undergraduate—accounting; business quantitative methods and management science; computer science; criminal justice and corrections; education administration and supervision; education, other; English as a second language; environmental/environmental health engineering; financial management and services; gerontology; health and medical administrative services; history; human services; marketing management and research; mathematics; nursing; psychology; public administration.

Florida Gulf Coast University (continued)

Graduate—education, other; English as a second language; public administration.

See full description on page 422.

FLORIDA HOSPITAL COLLEGE OF HEALTH SCIENCES

Orlando, Florida
Distance Learning Programs
http://www.fhchsimaging.com

Florida Hospital College of Health Sciences is accredited by Southern Association of Colleges and Schools. Institutionally administered financial aid is available to distance learners.

Services Distance learners have accessibility to academic advising, bookstore, e-mail services, library services.

Contact Florida Hospital College of Health Sciences, 7226 West Colonial Drive, PMB 400, Orlando, FL 32818-6731. *Fax:* 407-573-6731. *E-mail:* info@compassknowledge.com.

DEGREES AND AWARDS

BS Nursing–RN-BS
BSRS Radiologic Sciences

COURSE SUBJECT AREAS OFFERED OUTSIDE OF DEGREE PROGRAMS

Undergraduate—biological sciences/life sciences, other; legal studies; liberal arts and sciences, general studies and humanities; mathematics.

FLORIDA INSTITUTE OF TECHNOLOGY

Melbourne, Florida
Extended Campus
http://www.ec.fit.edu

Florida Institute of Technology was founded in 1958. It is accredited by Southern Association of Colleges and Schools. It first offered distance learning courses in 1995. In fall 2003, there were 600 students enrolled in distance learning courses. Institutionally administered financial aid is available to distance learners.

Services Distance learners have accessibility to academic advising, bookstore, career placement assistance, e-mail services, library services.

Contact Vicky W. Knerly, Senior Resident Administrator, Florida Institute of Technology, PO Box 22115, St. Simons Island, GA 31522-8515. *Telephone:* 912-634-6336. *Fax:* 912-634-7783. *E-mail:* vgc@fit.edu.

DEGREES AND AWARDS

MBA Professional Master of Business Administration
MPA Public Administration
MS Acquisition and Contract Management; Human Resources Management; Logistics Management; Material Acquisition Management; Operations Research; Project Management; Systems Management
MSM Management

COURSE SUBJECT AREAS OFFERED OUTSIDE OF DEGREE PROGRAMS

Graduate—accounting; business; business administration and management; business/managerial economics; business quantitative methods and management science; engineering/industrial management; human resources management; information sciences and systems; marketing management and research; public administration; systems engineering; systems science and theory.
Non-credit—financial management and services.

See full description on page 424.

FLORIDA INTERNATIONAL UNIVERSITY

Miami, Florida
Office of Distance Learning
http://www.fiu.edu

Florida International University was founded in 1965. It is accredited by Southern Association of Colleges and Schools. It first offered distance learning courses in 1995. In fall 2003, there were 6,000 students enrolled in distance learning courses. Institutionally administered financial aid is available to distance learners.

Services Distance learners have accessibility to bookstore, campus computer network, e-mail services, library services.

Contact Debra Williams, Program Assistant, Florida International University, 3000 Northeast 151 Street, KCC 334, North Miami, FL 33181. *Telephone:* 305-919-5217. *Fax:* 305-919-5484. *E-mail:* williamd@fiu.edu.

DEGREES AND AWARDS

BS International Business
Certificate Gerontology; Health Promotion
MBA Business Administration
MS Computer Engineering; Construction Management; Electrical Engineering; Forensic Science; Hospitality Management; Occupational Therapy; Public Health

COURSE SUBJECT AREAS OFFERED OUTSIDE OF DEGREE PROGRAMS

Undergraduate—business; business administration and management; engineering, general; engineering/industrial management; engineering mechanics; geological and related sciences.
Graduate—education administration and supervision; engineering, general; engineering mechanics; engineering, other.
Non-credit—legal studies.

FLORIDA METROPOLITAN UNIVERSITY–BRANDON CAMPUS

Tampa, Florida
http://www.onlinecci.com

Florida Metropolitan University–Brandon Campus was founded in 1890. It is accredited by Accrediting Council for Independent Colleges and Schools. It first offered distance learning courses in 1999. In fall 2003, there were 400 students enrolled in distance learning courses. Institutionally administered financial aid is available to distance learners.

Services Distance learners have accessibility to academic advising, bookstore, career placement assistance, library services.
Contact Madeline Lock, Online Learning Coordinator, Florida Metropolitan University–Brandon Campus, 3924 Coconut Palm Drive, Tampa, FL 33619. *Telephone:* 813-621-0041 Ext. 153. *E-mail:* mlock@cci.edu.

DEGREES AND AWARDS

AS Accounting; Business Administration; Criminal Justice; Legal Assistant/Paralegal
BS Accounting; Business Administration; Criminal Justice
MBA Business Administration
MS Criminal Justice

COURSE SUBJECT AREAS OFFERED OUTSIDE OF DEGREE PROGRAMS

Undergraduate—accounting; American literature (United States); business; business communications; computer software and media applications; criminal justice and corrections; criminology; economics; English composition; health and medical preparatory programs; history; human resources management; international business; Internet and World Wide Web; legal studies; marketing management and research; marketing operations/marketing and distribution, other; mathematics; political science and government; psychology; public relations and organizational communications; social psychology; sociology.
Graduate—business; business administration and management; business and personal services marketing operations; business information and data processing services; business/managerial economics; criminal justice and corrections; criminology; economics.

FLORIDA METROPOLITAN UNIVERSITY–TAMPA CAMPUS

Tampa, Florida

http://www.fmu.edu

Florida Metropolitan University–Tampa Campus was founded in 1890. It is accredited by Accrediting Council for Independent Colleges and Schools. It first offered distance learning courses in 1999. In fall 2003, there were 635 students enrolled in distance learning courses. Institutionally administered financial aid is available to distance learners.

Services Distance learners have accessibility to academic advising, campus computer network, career placement assistance, e-mail services, library services.
Contact Mr. Donnie Broughton, Director of Admissions, Florida Metropolitan University–Tampa Campus, 3319 West Hillsborough Avenue, Tampa, FL 33614. *Telephone:* 813-879-6000 Ext. 129. *Fax:* 813-871-2483. *E-mail:* dbrought@cci.edu.

DEGREES AND AWARDS

AS Accounting; Accounting

FLORIDA NATIONAL COLLEGE

Hialeah, Florida

http://www.vc.fnc.edu

Florida National College was founded in 1982. It is accredited by Southern Association of Colleges and Schools. It first offered distance learning courses in 2002. In fall 2003, there were 300 students enrolled in distance learning courses. Institutionally administered financial aid is available to distance learners.

Services Distance learners have accessibility to academic advising, bookstore, campus computer network, career placement assistance, e-mail services, library services, tutoring.
Contact Mr. Jose Ibarra, Distance Learning Administrator, Florida National College, 4425 West 20th Avenue, Hialeah, FL 33012. *Telephone:* 305-821-3333 Ext. 1047. *E-mail:* webmaster@vc.fnc.edu.

DEGREES AND AWARDS

Programs offered do not lead to a degree or other formal award.

COURSE SUBJECT AREAS OFFERED OUTSIDE OF DEGREE PROGRAMS

Undergraduate—accounting; administrative and secretarial services; business; business administration and management; business management and administrative services, other; business/managerial economics; computer and information sciences, general; computer programming; computer software and media applications; computer systems networking and telecommunications; education, general; English language and literature, general; health and medical administrative services; health and medical assistants; health professions and related sciences, other; liberal arts and sciences, general studies and humanities.

FLORIDA STATE UNIVERSITY

Tallahassee, Florida

Office for Distributed and Distance Learning

http://online.fsu.edu

Florida State University was founded in 1851. It is accredited by Southern Association of Colleges and Schools. It first offered distance learning courses in 1987. In fall 2003, there were 1,700 students enrolled in distance learning courses. Institutionally administered financial aid is available to distance learners.

Services Distance learners have accessibility to academic advising, bookstore, campus computer network, career placement assistance, e-mail services, library services, tutoring.
Contact Student Support Services, Florida State University, C3500 University Center, Tallahassee, FL 32306-2550. *Telephone:* 877-357-8283. *Fax:* 850-644-5803. *E-mail:* inquiries@oddl.fsu.edu.

DEGREES AND AWARDS

BS Computer and Information Science–Computer Science or Software Engineering Majors; Nursing; Social Science–Interdisciplinary Social Science
MBA Professional Master of Business Administration
MS Adult Education–Human Resource Development Major; Criminology–Criminal Justice Studies Major; Information Studies; Instructional Systems–Distance Learning Major; Mathematics Education; Science Education
MSM Risk Management/Insurance
MSN Nurse Educator Track
MSW Social Work

COURSE SUBJECT AREAS OFFERED OUTSIDE OF DEGREE PROGRAMS

Graduate—educational/instructional media design; human resources management.

See full description on page 426.

FLOYD COLLEGE

Rome, Georgia

Department of Extended Learning

http://www.floyd.edu/extendedlearning/

Floyd College was founded in 1970. It is accredited by Southern Association of Colleges and Schools. It first offered distance learning courses in 1977. In fall 2003, there were 548 students enrolled in distance learning courses. Institutionally administered financial aid is available to distance learners.

Services Distance learners have accessibility to academic advising, bookstore, campus computer network, e-mail services, library services.

Contact Jeff Brown, Director of Extended Learning, Floyd College, PO Box 1864, Rome, GA 30162. *Telephone:* 706-802-5300. *Fax:* 706-802-5997. *E-mail:* jbrown@floyd.edu.

DEGREES AND AWARDS

Programs offered do not lead to a degree or other formal award.

COURSE SUBJECT AREAS OFFERED OUTSIDE OF DEGREE PROGRAMS

Undergraduate—American history; anatomy; chemistry; developmental/child psychology; English composition; European history; health and physical education/fitness; mathematics related; physiology; sign language interpretation; sociology.

FONTBONNE UNIVERSITY

St. Louis, Missouri

http://www.fontbonne.edu/

Fontbonne University was founded in 1917. It is accredited by North Central Association of Colleges and Schools. It first offered distance learning courses in 2000. In fall 2003, there were 591 students enrolled in distance learning courses. Institutionally administered financial aid is available to distance learners.

Services Distance learners have accessibility to academic advising, bookstore, campus computer network, e-mail services, library services, tutoring.

Contact Tony Teoli, Distance Learning Coordinator, Fontbonne University, 6800 Wydown Boulevard, St. Louis, MO 63105-3098. *Telephone:* 314-889-1499. *Fax:* 314-889-1451. *E-mail:* tteoli@fontbonne.edu.

DEGREES AND AWARDS

Programs offered do not lead to a degree or other formal award.

COURSE SUBJECT AREAS OFFERED OUTSIDE OF DEGREE PROGRAMS

Undergraduate—biological and physical sciences; communications, general; computer software and media applications; economics; English composition; health professions and related sciences, other; mathematics; philosophy; psychology; religion/religious studies.

Graduate—communication disorders sciences and services; computer software and media applications; teacher education, specific academic and vocational programs.

FORREST JUNIOR COLLEGE

Anderson, South Carolina

http://www.forrestcollege.com

Forrest Junior College was founded in 1946. It is accredited by Accrediting Council for Independent Colleges and Schools. It first offered distance learning courses in 2000. In fall 2003, there were 173 students enrolled in distance learning courses. Institutionally administered financial aid is available to distance learners.

Services Distance learners have accessibility to academic advising, campus computer network, career placement assistance, e-mail services, library services, tutoring.

Contact Mrs. Brenda P. Cooley, Vice President of Administration and Programs, Forrest Junior College, 601 East River Street, Anderson, SC 29624. *Telephone:* 864-225-7653 Ext. 204. *Fax:* 864-261-7471. *E-mail:* brendacooley@forrestcollege.com.

DEGREES AND AWARDS

Programs offered do not lead to a degree or other formal award.

COURSE SUBJECT AREAS OFFERED OUTSIDE OF DEGREE PROGRAMS

Undergraduate—accounting; administrative and secretarial services; business; business administration and management; business and personal services marketing operations; business communications; business information and data processing services; business management and administrative services, other; business/managerial economics; computer and information sciences, general; computer and information sciences, other; computer/information technology administration and management; computer software and media applications; computer systems networking and telecommunications; health and medical administrative services; health and medical assistants; human resources management; legal studies; miscellaneous health aides; miscellaneous health professions.

Non-credit—computer and information sciences, general; computer and information sciences, other; computer/information technology administration and management; computer systems networking and telecommunications; health professions and related sciences, other.

FORT HAYS STATE UNIVERSITY

Hays, Kansas

Virtual College

http://www.fhsu.edu/virtualcollege

Fort Hays State University was founded in 1902. It is accredited by North Central Association of Colleges and Schools. It first offered distance learning courses in 1987. In fall 2003, there were 3,294 students enrolled in distance learning courses. Institutionally administered financial aid is available to distance learners.

Services Distance learners have accessibility to academic advising, bookstore, campus computer network, career placement assistance, e-mail services, library services, tutoring.

Contact Cynthia Elliott, Dean of Virtual College, Fort Hays State University, 600 Park Street, Hays, KS 67601-4099. *Telephone:* 785-628-4291. *Fax:* 785-628-4037. *E-mail:* virtualcollege@fhsu.edu.

DEGREES AND AWARDS

AGS Business; History; Human Services; Information Networking and Telecommunications; Organizational Leadership; Sociology
BA Sociology

BGS Business; Gerontology; History; Human Services; Information Networking and Telecommunications; Justice Studies; Military Specialties; Organizational Leadership; Sociology
BS Information Networking and Telecommunications; Justice Studies; Technology Leadership
BSN Nursing–RN to BSN
Certificate Internetworking; Justice Studies Information Networking
Certification Cisco Certified Network Associate Preparation, Accelerated; Cisco Certified Network Associate Preparation, Military
MA Liberal Studies
MSN Nursing Administration Track; Nursing Education Track

COURSE SUBJECT AREAS OFFERED OUTSIDE OF DEGREE PROGRAMS

Undergraduate—accounting; administrative and secretarial services; area, ethnic and cultural studies, other; business; business administration and management; business communications; business information and data processing services; business management and administrative services, other; communication disorders sciences and services; communications, general; communications, other; community health services; computer and information sciences, general; computer and information sciences, other; computer/information technology administration and management; computer programming; computer science; computer software and media applications; computer systems analysis; computer systems networking and telecommunications; criminal justice and corrections; criminology; cultural studies; economics; education administration and supervision; educational evaluation, research and statistics; educational/instructional media design; educational psychology; education, general; education, other; English composition; English creative writing; English language and literature, general; general teacher education; health and medical administrative services; health and physical education/fitness; health professions and related sciences, other; history; human services; information sciences and systems; Internet and World Wide Web; liberal arts and sciences, general studies and humanities; marketing management and research; marketing operations/marketing and distribution, other; military studies; multi/interdisciplinary studies, other; nursing; social sciences and history, other; social sciences, general; social work; sociology; student counseling and personnel services; teacher education, specific academic and vocational programs; technology education/industrial arts.
Graduate—educational/instructional media design; education, general; education, other; multi/interdisciplinary studies, other; nursing; teacher assistant/aide; teacher education, specific academic and vocational programs.

THE FRANCISCAN UNIVERSITY

Clinton, Iowa

http://www.tfu.edu

The Franciscan University was founded in 1918. It is accredited by North Central Association of Colleges and Schools. It first offered distance learning courses in 2002. In fall 2003, there were 95 students enrolled in distance learning courses. Institutionally administered financial aid is available to distance learners.

Services Distance learners have accessibility to academic advising, bookstore, e-mail services, library services, tutoring.
Contact Ms. Waunita Sullivan, Director of Enrollment, The Franciscan University, 400 North Bluff Boulevard, PO Box 2967, Clinton, IA 52733-2967. *Telephone:* 563-242-4023 Ext. 3400. *Fax:* 563-242-6102. *E-mail:* admissions@tfu.edu.

DEGREES AND AWARDS

Programs offered do not lead to a degree or other formal award.

COURSE SUBJECT AREAS OFFERED OUTSIDE OF DEGREE PROGRAMS

Graduate—education, other.

FRANCISCAN UNIVERSITY OF STEUBENVILLE

Steubenville, Ohio

Distance Learning

http://www.franciscan.edu/distancelearning

Franciscan University of Steubenville was founded in 1946. It is accredited by North Central Association of Colleges and Schools. It first offered distance learning courses in 1995. In fall 2003, there were 229 students enrolled in distance learning courses. Institutionally administered financial aid is available to distance learners.

Services Distance learners have accessibility to academic advising, bookstore.
Contact Ms. Virginia Garrison, Coordinator, Franciscan University of Steubenville, 1235 University Boulevard, Steubenville, OH 43952. *Telephone:* 740-283-6517 Ext. 4611. *Fax:* 740-284-7037. *E-mail:* distance@franciscan.edu.

DEGREES AND AWARDS

MA Theology

COURSE SUBJECT AREAS OFFERED OUTSIDE OF DEGREE PROGRAMS

Undergraduate—philosophy; theological and ministerial studies.
Graduate—theological and ministerial studies.
Non-credit—philosophy; theological and ministerial studies.

FRANKLIN PIERCE COLLEGE

Rindge, New Hampshire

http://www.fpc.edu/

Franklin Pierce College was founded in 1962. It is accredited by New England Association of Schools and Colleges. It first offered distance learning courses in 2004. Institutionally administered financial aid is available to distance learners.

Services Distance learners have accessibility to academic advising, bookstore, campus computer network, career placement assistance, e-mail services, library services, tutoring.
Contact Loraine Hobausz, Campus Director, Franklin Pierce College, 12 Industrial Way, Salem, NH 03079. *Telephone:* 603-898-1263. *E-mail:* hobauszl@fpc.edu.

DEGREES AND AWARDS

AA General Studies; Management; Marketing
BS General Studies; Management; Marketing
MBA Leadership
MS Information Technology Management for Law Enforcement

Franklin Pierce College (continued)

COURSE SUBJECT AREAS OFFERED OUTSIDE OF DEGREE PROGRAMS

Undergraduate—accounting; business administration and management; business/managerial economics; computer and information sciences, general; computer/information technology administration and management; criminal justice and corrections; economics; financial management and services; liberal arts and sciences, general studies and humanities; professional studies.

FRANKLIN UNIVERSITY

Columbus, Ohio
Technical and Non-Campus-Based Programs
http://www.franklin.edu

Franklin University was founded in 1902. It is accredited by North Central Association of Colleges and Schools. It first offered distance learning courses in 1996. In fall 2003, there were 3,339 students enrolled in distance learning courses. Institutionally administered financial aid is available to distance learners.

Services Distance learners have accessibility to academic advising, bookstore, campus computer network, career placement assistance, e-mail services, library services, tutoring.

Contact Admissions, Franklin University, 201 South Grant Avenue, Columbus, OH 43215. *Telephone:* 614-797-4700. *Fax:* 614-797-4799. *E-mail:* info@franklin.edu.

DEGREES AND AWARDS

AS Accounting; Business Administration; Computer Science; Information Technology

BS Accounting; Applied Management; Business Administration; Computer Science; Digital Communication; Health Care Management; Information Technology; Management Information Sciences; Management; Public Safety Management

MBA Online MBA

COURSE SUBJECT AREAS OFFERED OUTSIDE OF DEGREE PROGRAMS

Undergraduate—accounting; business administration and management; communications, general; computer science; economics; financial management and services; health services administration; human resources management; information sciences and systems; marketing management and research; mathematical statistics; mathematics and computer science.

Graduate—business administration and management.

See full description on page 428.

FREDERICK COMMUNITY COLLEGE

Frederick, Maryland
http://frederick.edu/

Frederick Community College was founded in 1957. It is accredited by Middle States Association of Colleges and Schools. It first offered distance learning courses in 1998. In fall 2003, there were 1,015 students enrolled in distance learning courses. Institutionally administered financial aid is available to distance learners.

Services Distance learners have accessibility to academic advising, bookstore, career placement assistance, e-mail services, library services, tutoring.

Contact Dr. Deborah McClellan, Director of Student Advising, Frederick Community College, 7932 Opossumtown Pike, Frederick, MD 21702. *Telephone:* 301-846-2477. *Fax:* 301-846-2498. *E-mail:* dmcclellan@frederick.edu.

DEGREES AND AWARDS

AA Business Administration; General Studies

COURSE SUBJECT AREAS OFFERED OUTSIDE OF DEGREE PROGRAMS

Undergraduate—accounting; astronomy; biological technology; biology, general; business administration and management; business communications; communications, general; computer and information sciences, general; economics; English composition; English creative writing; health and medical assistants; health and physical education/fitness; history; human services; liberal arts and sciences, general studies and humanities; mathematics; philosophy; sociology; speech and rhetorical studies; visual and performing arts.

Non-credit—accounting; business; business communications; business/managerial economics; communications, general; computer and information sciences, general; computer programming; computer software and media applications; computer systems networking and telecommunications; data entry/microcomputer applications; data processing technology; electrical and electronic engineering-related technology; English technical and business writing; health and physical education/fitness; home economics, general; Internet and World Wide Web; marketing management and research; public relations and organizational communications; real estate; vehicle/equipment operation.

FULTON-MONTGOMERY COMMUNITY COLLEGE

Johnstown, New York
http://fmcc.suny.edu/

Fulton-Montgomery Community College was founded in 1964. It is accredited by Middle States Association of Colleges and Schools. It first offered distance learning courses in 2002. In fall 2003, there were 20 students enrolled in distance learning courses. Institutionally administered financial aid is available to distance learners.

Contact Mr. Reid J Smalley, Director of Workforce Development, Fulton-Montgomery Community College, 2805 State Highway 67, Johnstown, NY 12095. *Telephone:* 518-762-4651 Ext. 8102. *Fax:* 518-762-4334. *E-mail:* rsmalley@fmcc.suny.edu.

DEGREES AND AWARDS

Programs offered do not lead to a degree or other formal award.

COURSE SUBJECT AREAS OFFERED OUTSIDE OF DEGREE PROGRAMS

Undergraduate—accounting; business administration and management; computer software and media applications; economics; English composition; history; public administration; sociology.

Non-credit—accounting; business; business administration and management; computer software and media applications; computer systems networking and telecommunications; entrepreneurship; health professions and related sciences, other; legal studies.

GADSDEN STATE COMMUNITY COLLEGE

Gadsden, Alabama
Distance Learning
http://www.gadsdenstate.edu/dl/

Gadsden State Community College was founded in 1965. It is accredited by Southern Association of Colleges and Schools. It first offered distance learning courses in 1978. In fall 2003, there were 450 students enrolled in distance learning courses. Institutionally administered financial aid is available to distance learners.

Services Distance learners have accessibility to academic advising, bookstore, campus computer network, career placement assistance, library services, tutoring.
Contact Ms. Sandra J. Roberts, Distance Learning Coordinator, Gadsden State Community College, PO Box 227, 1001 Wallace Drive, Allen Hall, Gadsden, AL 35902. *Telephone:* 256-549-8355. *Fax:* 256-549-8404. *E-mail:* swells@gadsdenstate.edu.

DEGREES AND AWARDS

AGS General Studies
AS Education, general

GANNON UNIVERSITY

Erie, Pennsylvania
Center for Adult Learning
http://www.gannon.edu

Gannon University was founded in 1925. It is accredited by Middle States Association of Colleges and Schools. It first offered distance learning courses in 1976. In fall 2003, there were 100 students enrolled in distance learning courses. Institutionally administered financial aid is available to distance learners.

Services Distance learners have accessibility to academic advising, bookstore, campus computer network, career placement assistance, e-mail services, library services.
Contact Judy van Rheenen, Adult Enrollment Advisor, Gannon University, 109 University Square, Erie, PA 16541. *Telephone:* 814-871-7474. *Fax:* 814-871-5827. *E-mail:* cfal@gannon.edu.

DEGREES AND AWARDS

Programs offered do not lead to a degree or other formal award.

COURSE SUBJECT AREAS OFFERED OUTSIDE OF DEGREE PROGRAMS

Undergraduate—bible/biblical studies; business; business communications; criminal justice and corrections; criminology; developmental and child psychology; economics; English composition; English creative writing; legal studies; marketing management and research; music; philosophy; psychology; religion/religious studies.

GASTON COLLEGE

Dallas, North Carolina
http://www.gaston.cc.nc.us

Gaston College was founded in 1963. It is accredited by Southern Association of Colleges and Schools. It first offered distance learning courses in 1997. In fall 2003, there were 1,230 students enrolled in distance learning courses. Institutionally administered financial aid is available to distance learners.

Services Distance learners have accessibility to academic advising, bookstore, campus computer network, career placement assistance, library services, tutoring.
Contact Mrs. Kimberly C. Gelsinger, Director of Distance Education, Gaston College, 201 Highway 321 South, Dallas, NC 28034. *Telephone:* 704-922-6515. *Fax:* 704-922-6443. *E-mail:* gelsinger.kim@gaston.cc.nc.us.

DEGREES AND AWARDS

AAS Criminal Justice Technology; Dietetics
AD Education, general

COURSE SUBJECT AREAS OFFERED OUTSIDE OF DEGREE PROGRAMS

Undergraduate—accounting; American literature (United States); biological sciences/life sciences, other; business; business communications; business information and data processing services; business management and administrative services, other; chemistry; child care and guidance workers and managers; communications, general; communications technologies; computer and information sciences, general; computer programming; computer software and media applications; computer systems networking and telecommunications; criminal justice and corrections; criminology; English composition; English language and literature, general; English literature (British and Commonwealth); geography; geological and related sciences; health and medical assistants; information sciences and systems; Internet and World Wide Web; legal studies; liberal arts and sciences, general studies and humanities; mathematics; psychology; psychology, other; teacher education, specific academic and vocational programs.

GATEWAY COMMUNITY COLLEGE

New Haven, Connecticut
http://www.gwcc.commnet.edu/

Gateway Community College was founded in 1992. It is accredited by New England Association of Schools and Colleges. It first offered distance learning courses in 1999. In fall 2003, there were 73 students enrolled in distance learning courses. Institutionally administered financial aid is available to distance learners.

Services Distance learners have accessibility to academic advising, career placement assistance, e-mail services, library services, tutoring.
Contact Ms. Catherine Surface, Director of Admissions, Gateway Community College, 60 Sargent Drive, New Haven, CT 06511. *Telephone:* 203-285-2013. *Fax:* 203-285-2018. *E-mail:* csurface@gwcc.commnet.com.

DEGREES AND AWARDS

Programs offered do not lead to a degree or other formal award.

COURSE SUBJECT AREAS OFFERED OUTSIDE OF DEGREE PROGRAMS

Undergraduate—business; English as a second language; microbiology/bacteriology; philosophy; political science and government; social sciences, general.
Non-credit—computer software and media applications; Internet and World Wide Web; personal and miscellaneous services, other.

GEORGE C. WALLACE COMMUNITY COLLEGE

Dothan, Alabama

http://wallace.edu

George C. Wallace Community College was founded in 1949. It is accredited by Southern Association of Colleges and Schools. It first offered distance learning courses in 2001. In fall 2003, there were 760 students enrolled in distance learning courses. Institutionally administered financial aid is available to distance learners.

Services Distance learners have accessibility to e-mail services, library services.

Contact Mr. Frank Barefield, Jr., Director of MIS, George C. Wallace Community College, Eufaula, AL 36072. *Telephone:* 334-619-1500. *Fax:* 334-687-0255. *E-mail:* fbarefield@wallace.edu.

DEGREES AND AWARDS

Programs offered do not lead to a degree or other formal award.

COURSE SUBJECT AREAS OFFERED OUTSIDE OF DEGREE PROGRAMS

Undergraduate—accounting; biological and physical sciences; biology, general; business; business administration and management; chemistry; computer and information sciences, general; data entry/microcomputer applications; economics; English composition; English literature (British and Commonwealth); fine arts and art studies; history; mathematics; physical sciences, general; psychology.

GEORGE MASON UNIVERSITY

Fairfax, Virginia

http://www.gmu.edu/

George Mason University was founded in 1957. It is accredited by Southern Association of Colleges and Schools. It first offered distance learning courses in 1990. In fall 2003, there were 500 students enrolled in distance learning courses. Institutionally administered financial aid is available to distance learners.

Services Distance learners have accessibility to academic advising, bookstore, campus computer network, e-mail services, library services.

Contact Miss Cheryl Choy, Special Assistant for Distance and Technical Education in the Office of the Provost, George Mason University, 4400 University Drive, MSN 1D6, Fairfax, VA 22030. *E-mail:* cchoy@gmu.edu.

DEGREES AND AWARDS

Graduate Certificate Computer Networking; Nonprofit Management; Quality Improvement and Outcomes Management
MA Transportation Policy, Operations, and Logistics
MS Bioscience Management
MS/MPH Commonwealth Master of Public Health

COURSE SUBJECT AREAS OFFERED OUTSIDE OF DEGREE PROGRAMS

Undergraduate—computer and information sciences, other; computer science; English composition; English technical and business writing; geography.

Graduate—biological sciences/life sciences, other; business management and administrative services, other; computer science; computer systems networking and telecommunications; health professions and related sciences, other; public administration and services, other.

GEORGIA INSTITUTE OF TECHNOLOGY

Atlanta, Georgia

Center for Distance Learning

http://www.cdl.gatech.edu

Georgia Institute of Technology was founded in 1885. It is accredited by Southern Association of Colleges and Schools. It first offered distance learning courses in 1977. In fall 2003, there were 485 students enrolled in distance learning courses. Institutionally administered financial aid is available to distance learners.

Services Distance learners have accessibility to academic advising, bookstore, campus computer network, e-mail services, library services.

Contact Ms. Tanya Krawiec, Student Support Services Manager, Georgia Institute of Technology, 84 5th Street, NW, Room 013, Atlanta, GA 30308-1031. *Telephone:* 404-894-3378. *Fax:* 404-894-8924. *E-mail:* tanya.krawiec@dlpe.gatech.edu.

DEGREES AND AWARDS

MS Aerospace Engineering; Civil Engineering; Electrical Engineering; Environmental Engineering; Industrial and Systems Engineering; Mechanical Engineering; Medical Physics

COURSE SUBJECT AREAS OFFERED OUTSIDE OF DEGREE PROGRAMS

Graduate—aerospace engineering; bioengineering and biomedical engineering; civil engineering; computer engineering; electrical engineering; engineering design; engineering/industrial management; environmental engineering; industrial engineering; mathematics; mechanical engineering.

Non-credit—aerospace engineering; civil engineering; computer engineering; electrical engineering; environmental engineering; industrial engineering; mathematics; mechanical engineering.

See full description on page 430.

GEORGIA SOUTHERN UNIVERSITY

Statesboro, Georgia

Distance Learning Center

http://academics.georgiasouthern.edu/dlc/

Georgia Southern University was founded in 1906. It is accredited by Southern Association of Colleges and Schools. It first offered distance learning courses in 1992. In fall 2003, there were 1,432 students enrolled in distance learning courses. Institutionally administered financial aid is available to distance learners.

Services Distance learners have accessibility to academic advising, bookstore, campus computer network, career placement assistance, e-mail services, library services, tutoring.

Contact Mrs. Christie A. Pittman, Administrative Secretary, Georgia Southern University, PO Box 8018, Statesboro, GA 30460. *Telephone:* 912-681-0882. *Fax:* 912-871-1424. *E-mail:* cpittman@georgiasouthern.edu.

DEGREES AND AWARDS

BBA Business Administration
MBA Business Administration
MPA Public Administration

COURSE SUBJECT AREAS OFFERED OUTSIDE OF DEGREE PROGRAMS

Undergraduate—accounting; business administration and management; business quantitative methods and management science; education administration and supervision; engineering mechanics; English composition; marketing management and research; mathematics; nursing; political science and government; sociology.
Graduate—accounting; business management and administrative services, other; curriculum and instruction; education administration and supervision; educational/instructional media design; educational psychology; nursing; public administration and services, other.

GLENVILLE STATE COLLEGE

Glenville, West Virginia
http://www.glenville.edu/

Glenville State College was founded in 1872. It is accredited by North Central Association of Colleges and Schools. It first offered distance learning courses in 1995. In fall 2003, there were 475 students enrolled in distance learning courses. Institutionally administered financial aid is available to distance learners.

Services Distance learners have accessibility to academic advising, bookstore, campus computer network, career placement assistance, e-mail services, library services.
Contact Kathy Butler, Vice President For Academic Affairs, Glenville State College, 200 High Street, Glenville, WV 26351. *Telephone:* 304-462-4100 Ext. 7100. *Fax:* 304-462-4407. *E-mail:* kathy.butler@glenville.edu.

DEGREES AND AWARDS

Programs offered do not lead to a degree or other formal award.

COURSE SUBJECT AREAS OFFERED OUTSIDE OF DEGREE PROGRAMS

Undergraduate—accounting; agricultural business and management; agricultural engineering; agriculture/agricultural sciences; agriculture/agricultural sciences, other; Air Force R.O.T.C.; biology, general; business; business and personal services marketing operations; business management and administrative services, other; conservation and renewable natural resources, other; criminal justice and corrections; criminology; economics; education, general; education, other; English composition; environmental/environmental health engineering; fine arts and art studies; forestry and related sciences; general teacher education; health and physical education/fitness; mathematics, other; military technologies; psychology, other; social sciences, general.
Non-credit—mathematics, other.

GLOBAL UNIVERSITY OF THE ASSEMBLIES OF GOD

Springfield, Missouri
http://www.globaluniversity.edu/

Global University of the Assemblies of God was founded in 1948. It is accredited by Distance Education and Training Council. It first offered distance learning courses in 1948. In fall 2003, there were 8,394 students enrolled in distance learning courses. Institutionally administered financial aid is available to distance learners.

Services Distance learners have accessibility to academic advising, library services.
Contact Mrs. Jessica Dorn, Director of Enrollment Services/Registrar, Global University of the Assemblies of God, 1211 South Glenstone Avenue, Springfield, MO 65804. *Telephone:* 417-862-9533. *Fax:* 417-862-0863. *E-mail:* jdorn@globaluniversity.edu.

DEGREES AND AWARDS

AA Bible and Theology; Ministerial Studies; Religious Studies
BA Bible and Theology; Bible/Pastoral Ministries; Missions; Religious Education
Diploma Ministry; Theology
MA Biblical Studies; Ministerial Studies
MDiv Divinity

COURSE SUBJECT AREAS OFFERED OUTSIDE OF DEGREE PROGRAMS

Non-credit—bible/biblical studies; biblical and other theological languages and literatures; missions/missionary studies and missiology; pastoral counseling and specialized ministries; philosophy and religion; religion/religious studies; religious education; religious/sacred music; theological and ministerial studies; theological studies and religious vocations, other.

GODDARD COLLEGE

Plainfield, Vermont
Distance Learning Programs
http://www.goddard.edu

Goddard College was founded in 1938. It is accredited by New England Association of Schools and Colleges. It first offered distance learning courses in 1981. In fall 2003, there were 498 students enrolled in distance learning courses. Institutionally administered financial aid is available to distance learners.

Services Distance learners have accessibility to academic advising, bookstore, campus computer network, e-mail services, library services.
Contact Brenda Hawkins, Director of Admissions, Goddard College, 123 Pitkin Road, Plainfield, VT 05667. *Telephone:* 800-468-4888 Ext. 240. *Fax:* 802-454-1029. *E-mail:* hawkinsb@goddard.edu.

DEGREES AND AWARDS

Programs offered do not lead to a degree or other formal award.

COURSE SUBJECT AREAS OFFERED OUTSIDE OF DEGREE PROGRAMS

Undergraduate—area, ethnic and cultural studies, other; area studies; classical and ancient Near Eastern languages and literatures; communications, general; communications, other; comparative literature; counseling psychology; dance; developmental and child psychology; dramatic/theater arts and stagecraft; education, general; education, other; English composition; English creative writing; English language and literature, general; fine arts and art studies; foreign languages and literatures; general teacher education; geography; history; liberal arts and sciences, general studies and humanities; music; peace and conflict studies; philosophy; physical sciences, general; psychology; psychology, other; social sciences, general; sociology.

Goddard College (continued)

Graduate—dance; developmental and child psychology; dramatic/theater arts and stagecraft; educational psychology; education, general; education, other; English creative writing; entrepreneurship; experimental psychology; fine arts and art studies; general teacher education; liberal arts and sciences, general studies and humanities; natural resources conservation; peace and conflict studies; philosophy; psychology; psychology, other; school psychology; social psychology; teacher education, specific academic and vocational programs.

GOGEBIC COMMUNITY COLLEGE

Ironwood, Michigan

http://www.gogebic.edu

Gogebic Community College was founded in 1932. It is accredited by North Central Association of Colleges and Schools. It first offered distance learning courses in 1992. In fall 2003, there were 350 students enrolled in distance learning courses. Institutionally administered financial aid is available to distance learners.

Services Distance learners have accessibility to academic advising, bookstore, library services.

Contact Mr. James Lorenson, Dean of Instruction, Gogebic Community College, East 4946 Jackson Road, Ironwood, MI 49938. *Telephone:* 906-932-4231 Ext. 215. *E-mail:* jiml@admin.gogebic.cc.mi.us.

DEGREES AND AWARDS

Programs offered do not lead to a degree or other formal award.

COURSE SUBJECT AREAS OFFERED OUTSIDE OF DEGREE PROGRAMS

Undergraduate—accounting; biological and physical sciences; business; business management and administrative services, other; computer and information sciences, general; computer/information technology administration and management; ecology; English composition; health and medical administrative services; history; liberal arts and sciences, general studies and humanities; mathematics; miscellaneous health professions; psychology; social sciences and history, other; sociology.

GOLDEN GATE UNIVERSITY

San Francisco, California

Cyber Campus

http://www.ggu.edu/cybercampus

Golden Gate University was founded in 1853. It is accredited by Western Association of Schools and Colleges. It first offered distance learning courses in 1997. In fall 2003, there were 1,600 students enrolled in distance learning courses.

Services Distance learners have accessibility to bookstore.

Contact Alan Roper, Director of Administration, Golden Gate University, 536 Mission Street, San Francisco, CA 94105. *Telephone:* 415-369-5263. *Fax:* 415-227-4502. *E-mail:* cybercampus@ggu.edu.

DEGREES AND AWARDS

BA Management
BBA Business Administration; Computer Information Systems; Finance; Telecommunications Management
BS Information Technology
Certificate Finance
Graduate Certificate Accounting; Estate Planning; Finance; Financial Planning; International Taxation; Marketing; Taxation; Taxation
MBA Business Administration; Finance; Human Resource Management; Information Technology; International Business; Management; Marketing; Operations and Supply Chain Management
MBA/M Acc Accounting; Accounting
MS Enterprise Systems Management; Finance; Finance; Financial Planning; Human Resource Management; Information Technology; Integrated Marketing Communications; Marketing; Systems and Network Management; Taxation

COURSE SUBJECT AREAS OFFERED OUTSIDE OF DEGREE PROGRAMS

Undergraduate—accounting; computer and information sciences, general; English composition; finance; management information systems/business data processing; mathematics; telecommunications.
Graduate—accounting; business marketing and marketing management; computer and information sciences, general; English composition; finance; health services administration; management information systems/business data processing; taxation; telecommunications.

GOLDEN WEST COLLEGE

Huntington Beach, California

http://www.gwc.cccd.edu/

Golden West College was founded in 1966. It is accredited by Western Association of Schools and Colleges. It first offered distance learning courses in 1999. In fall 2003, there were 2,435 students enrolled in distance learning courses. Institutionally administered financial aid is available to distance learners.

Services Distance learners have accessibility to bookstore, library services, tutoring.

Contact GWC Online Help Desk, Golden West College. *Telephone:* 714-895-8389. *E-mail:* helpdesk@onlinegwc.cccd.edu.

DEGREES AND AWARDS

Programs offered do not lead to a degree or other formal award.

COURSE SUBJECT AREAS OFFERED OUTSIDE OF DEGREE PROGRAMS

Undergraduate—accounting; anthropology; biology, general; business; computer software and media applications; criminal justice and corrections; developmental and child psychology; English composition; foreign languages and literatures; history; mathematics; philosophy; political science and government; psychology; real estate; sociology.

GONZAGA UNIVERSITY

Spokane, Washington

School of Professional Studies

http://www.gonzaga.edu/

Gonzaga University was founded in 1887. It is accredited by Northwest Commission on Colleges and Universities. It first offered distance learning courses in 1976. In fall 2003, there were 220 students enrolled in distance learning courses. Institutionally administered financial aid is available to distance learners.

Services Distance learners have accessibility to academic advising, bookstore, campus computer network, e-mail services, library services, tutoring.
Contact Ms. Shannon Zaranski, Assistant to the Dean of Professional Studies, Gonzaga University, 502 East Boone, MSC 2616, Spokane, WA 99258. *Telephone:* 509-323-3569. *Fax:* 509-323-3566. *E-mail:* zaranski@gu.gonzaga.edu.

DEGREES AND AWARDS

BSN Nursing
MA Organizational Leadership
MN Nursing

COURSE SUBJECT AREAS OFFERED OUTSIDE OF DEGREE PROGRAMS

Undergraduate—educational psychology; education, general; liberal arts and sciences, general studies and humanities; music; nursing; philosophy; religion/religious studies; visual and performing arts.
Graduate—business management and administrative services, other; educational psychology; education, general; education, other; human resources management; human services; liberal arts and sciences, general studies and humanities; nursing; philosophy and religion; visual and performing arts, other.

GONZAGA UNIVERSITY

Spokane, Washington
Department of Nursing
http://www.gonzaga.edu/nursing

Gonzaga University was founded in 1887. It is accredited by Northwest Commission on Colleges and Universities. It first offered distance learning courses in 1978. In fall 2003, there were 200 students enrolled in distance learning courses. Institutionally administered financial aid is available to distance learners.

Services Distance learners have accessibility to academic advising, bookstore, campus computer network, career placement assistance, e-mail services, library services.
Contact Jane A. Tiedt, Community Liaison, Gonzaga University, 502 East Boone Avenue, Spokane, WA 99258. *Telephone:* 509-323-6643. *Fax:* 509-323-5827. *E-mail:* tiedt@gu.gonzaga.edu.

DEGREES AND AWARDS

MSN Nursing–BSN/MSN

COURSE SUBJECT AREAS OFFERED OUTSIDE OF DEGREE PROGRAMS

Undergraduate—nursing.
Graduate—nursing.

GOUCHER COLLEGE

Baltimore, Maryland
Center for Graduate and Professional Studies
http://www.goucher.edu

Goucher College was founded in 1885. It is accredited by Middle States Association of Colleges and Schools. It first offered distance learning courses in 1995. In fall 2003, there were 320 students enrolled in distance learning courses. Institutionally administered financial aid is available to distance learners.

Services Distance learners have accessibility to academic advising, bookstore, campus computer network, e-mail services, library services.
Contact Noreen P. Mack, Director for Marketing and Program Development, Goucher College, 1021 Dulaney Valley Road, Baltimore, MD 21204. *Telephone:* 410-337-6200. *Fax:* 410-337-6085. *E-mail:* nmack@goucher.edu.

DEGREES AND AWARDS

Programs offered do not lead to a degree or other formal award.

COURSE SUBJECT AREAS OFFERED OUTSIDE OF DEGREE PROGRAMS

Graduate—education, general.

GRAND VIEW COLLEGE

Des Moines, Iowa
Camp Dodge Campus
http://www.gvc.edu

Grand View College was founded in 1896. It is accredited by North Central Association of Colleges and Schools. It first offered distance learning courses in 1994. In fall 2003, there were 10 students enrolled in distance learning courses. Institutionally administered financial aid is available to distance learners.

Services Distance learners have accessibility to academic advising, bookstore, campus computer network, career placement assistance, e-mail services, library services.
Contact Ms. Lora Kelly-Benck, Director of Camp Dodge Campus, Grand View College, 1200 Grandview Avenue, Des Moines, IA 50316. *Telephone:* 515-245-4546. *Fax:* 515-252-4753. *E-mail:* lkelly-benck@gvc.edu.

DEGREES AND AWARDS

Programs offered do not lead to a degree or other formal award.

COURSE SUBJECT AREAS OFFERED OUTSIDE OF DEGREE PROGRAMS

Undergraduate—business management and administrative services, other; business/managerial economics; criminal justice and corrections; English composition; English language and literature, general; history; psychology; social psychology; sociology; speech and rhetorical studies.

GRANTHAM UNIVERSITY

Slidell, Louisiana
http://www.grantham.edu/

Grantham University was founded in 1951. It is accredited by Distance Education and Training Council. It first offered distance learning courses in 1951. In fall 2003, there were 5,000 students enrolled in distance learning courses. Institutionally administered financial aid is available to distance learners.

Services Distance learners have accessibility to academic advising, bookstore, career placement assistance.
Contact Mr. George Colon, Director of Recruitment, Grantham University, 34641 Grantham College Road, Slidell, LA 70460-6815. *Telephone:* 800-955-2527. *Fax:* 985-649-1812. *E-mail:* admissions@grantham.edu.

Grantham University (continued)

DEGREES AND AWARDS

AS Business Administration; Computer Engineering Technology; Computer Science; Criminal Justice–Computer Science; Criminal Justice–Homeland Security; Criminal Justice; Electronics Engineering Technology; Engineering Management; Information Systems; Software Engineering Technology

BS Business Administration; Computer Engineering Technology; Computer Science; Criminal Justice–Computer Science; Criminal Justice–Homeland Security; Criminal Justice; Electronics Engineering Technology; Engineering Management; Information Systems; Software Engineering Technology

MBA Business Administration; Information Management; Project Management

MS Information Management Technology; Information Management–Project Management; Information Technology

COURSE SUBJECT AREAS OFFERED OUTSIDE OF DEGREE PROGRAMS

Undergraduate—accounting; business; business administration and management; business/managerial economics; chemistry; computer and information sciences, general; computer engineering; computer/information technology administration and management; computer programming; computer science; computer software and media applications; computer systems analysis; computer systems networking and telecommunications; criminal justice and corrections; data entry/microcomputer applications; economics; electrical and electronic engineering-related technology; electrical, electronics and communications engineering; electrical engineering; English composition; English technical and business writing; history; human resources management; information sciences and systems; Internet and World Wide Web; legal studies; marketing operations/marketing and distribution, other; mathematics and computer science; mathematics related; physics; psychology; sociology.

See full description on page 432.

GRATZ COLLEGE

Melrose Park, Pennsylvania

http://www.gratz.edu

Gratz College was founded in 1895. It is accredited by Middle States Association of Colleges and Schools. It first offered distance learning courses in 2000. In fall 2003, there were 50 students enrolled in distance learning courses. Institutionally administered financial aid is available to distance learners.

Services Distance learners have accessibility to academic advising, bookstore, e-mail services, library services.

Contact Ms. Nancy N. Waldman, Distance Learning Coordinator, Gratz College, 7605 Old York Road, Melrose Park, PA 19027. *Telephone:* 215-635-7300 Ext. 115. *Fax:* 215-635-7399. *E-mail:* nwaldman@gratz.edu.

DEGREES AND AWARDS

Programs offered do not lead to a degree or other formal award.

GREENFIELD COMMUNITY COLLEGE

Greenfield, Massachusetts

http://www.gcc.mass.edu/

Greenfield Community College was founded in 1962. It is accredited by New England Association of Schools and Colleges. It first offered distance learning courses in 2002. In fall 2003, there were 45 students enrolled in distance learning courses. Institutionally administered financial aid is available to distance learners.

Services Distance learners have accessibility to campus computer network, e-mail services, library services.

Contact Doug Wilkins, Professor, Greenfield Community College, Greenfield, MA 01301. *E-mail:* online@gcc.mass.edu.

DEGREES AND AWARDS

Programs offered do not lead to a degree or other formal award.

COURSE SUBJECT AREAS OFFERED OUTSIDE OF DEGREE PROGRAMS

Undergraduate—anthropology; computer/information technology administration and management; education, general; English composition; sociology.

GREENVILLE TECHNICAL COLLEGE

Greenville, South Carolina

Distance Learning

http://www.college-online.com

Greenville Technical College was founded in 1962. It is accredited by Southern Association of Colleges and Schools. It first offered distance learning courses in 1991. In fall 2003, there were 4,000 students enrolled in distance learning courses. Institutionally administered financial aid is available to distance learners.

Services Distance learners have accessibility to academic advising, bookstore, campus computer network, career placement assistance, e-mail services, library services.

Contact Karen Baldwin, Advisor, Online and Nontraditional Programs, Greenville Technical College, PO Box 5616, Greenville, SC 29606-5616. *Telephone:* 864-250-8393. *Fax:* 864-250-8502. *E-mail:* karen.baldwin@gvltec.edu.

DEGREES AND AWARDS

AA Liberal Arts

COURSE SUBJECT AREAS OFFERED OUTSIDE OF DEGREE PROGRAMS

Undergraduate—accounting; art history; biology; computer software and media applications; developmental/child psychology; English composition; law and legal studies related; social psychology; sociology; Spanish.

Non-credit—nursing.

GROSSMONT COLLEGE

El Cajon, California

http://www.grossmont.edu

Grossmont College was founded in 1961. It is accredited by Western Association of Schools and Colleges. It first offered distance learning courses in 1997. In fall 2003, there were 1,300 students enrolled in distance learning courses. Institutionally administered financial aid is available to distance learners.

Services Distance learners have accessibility to academic advising, bookstore, campus computer network, e-mail services, library services, tutoring.
Contact Dean Kats Gustafson, Associate Dean, Instructional and Technology Resources, Grossmont College, 8800 Grossmont College Drive, El Cajon, CA 92020. *Telephone:* 619-644.7390. *Fax:* 619-644.7053. *E-mail:* kats.gustafson@gcccd.net.

DEGREES AND AWARDS

Programs offered do not lead to a degree or other formal award.

COURSE SUBJECT AREAS OFFERED OUTSIDE OF DEGREE PROGRAMS

Undergraduate—accounting; astronomy; child care and guidance workers and managers; communications, general; computer systems networking and telecommunications; criminal justice and corrections; educational/instructional media design; English composition; health and medical assistants; history; political science and government.
Non-credit—teacher assistant/aide.

HAGERSTOWN COMMUNITY COLLEGE

Hagerstown, Maryland

http://www.hagerstowncc.edu/

Hagerstown Community College was founded in 1946. It is accredited by Middle States Association of Colleges and Schools. It first offered distance learning courses in 1998. In fall 2003, there were 150 students enrolled in distance learning courses. Institutionally administered financial aid is available to distance learners.

Services Distance learners have accessibility to bookstore.
Contact Mr. Jack A. Drooger, Jr., Computer Training Coordinator, Hagerstown Community College, Continuing Education, 11400 Robinwood Drive, Hagerstown, MD 21742. *Telephone:* 301-790-2800 Ext. 453. *Fax:* 301-733-4229. *E-mail:* jack_d@hagerstowncc.edu.

DEGREES AND AWARDS

Programs offered do not lead to a degree or other formal award.

COURSE SUBJECT AREAS OFFERED OUTSIDE OF DEGREE PROGRAMS

Non-credit—computer programming; computer software and media applications; computer systems networking and telecommunications.

HALIFAX COMMUNITY COLLEGE

Weldon, North Carolina

Distance Learning

http://www.halifaxcc.edu

Halifax Community College was founded in 1967. It is accredited by Southern Association of Colleges and Schools. It first offered distance learning courses in 1999. In fall 2003, there were 821 students enrolled in distance learning courses. Institutionally administered financial aid is available to distance learners.

Services Distance learners have accessibility to career placement assistance, e-mail services, library services.
Contact Beth Gray-Robertson, Director of Distance Learning, Halifax Community College, PO Drawer 809, Weldon , NC 27890. *Telephone:* 252-536-7299. *Fax:* 252-536-6347. *E-mail:* robertsonb@halifaxcc.edu.

DEGREES AND AWARDS

Programs offered do not lead to a degree or other formal award.

COURSE SUBJECT AREAS OFFERED OUTSIDE OF DEGREE PROGRAMS

Undergraduate—accounting; business; communications, general; computer and information sciences, other; computer science; developmental and child psychology; economics; English composition; English literature (British and Commonwealth); fine arts and art studies; mathematics; religion/religious studies; teacher assistant/aide.
Non-credit—business administration and management; computer software and media applications; computer systems networking and telecommunications; data entry/microcomputer applications; general teacher education.

HAMLINE UNIVERSITY

St. Paul, Minnesota

http://www.hamline.edu/

Hamline University was founded in 1854. It is accredited by North Central Association of Colleges and Schools. It first offered distance learning courses in 1998. In fall 2003, there were 124 students enrolled in distance learning courses. Institutionally administered financial aid is available to distance learners.

Services Distance learners have accessibility to campus computer network, career placement assistance, e-mail services, library services.
Contact Annette McNamara, Program Administrator, Hamline University, 1536 Hewitt Avenue, A1720, St. Paul, MN 55104-1284. *Telephone:* 651-523-2175. *Fax:* 651-523-2489. *E-mail:* amcnamara@gw.hamline.edu.

DEGREES AND AWARDS

Programs offered do not lead to a degree or other formal award.

COURSE SUBJECT AREAS OFFERED OUTSIDE OF DEGREE PROGRAMS

Undergraduate—history.
Graduate—bilingual/bicultural education; educational/instructional media design; education, general; education, other; English as a second language; general teacher education; mathematics; public administration and services, other; special education; teacher education, specific academic and vocational programs; teaching English as a second language/foreign language.
Non-credit—education administration and supervision; educational/instructional media design; education, general; education, other; English as a second language; public administration; public administration and services, other; teacher education, specific academic and vocational programs; teaching English as a second language/foreign language; urban affairs/studies.

HARFORD COMMUNITY COLLEGE

Bel Air, Maryland

http://www.harford.edu/distlearn/

Harford Community College was founded in 1957. It is accredited by Middle States Association of Colleges and Schools. It first offered distance learning courses in 1999. In fall 2003, there were 1,010 students enrolled in distance learning courses. Institutionally administered financial aid is available to distance learners.

Services Distance learners have accessibility to academic advising, bookstore, campus computer network, career placement assistance, e-mail services, library services.

Contact Christel Vonderscheer, Distance Learning Coordinator, Harford Community College, 401 Thomas Run Road, Bel Air, MD 21015. *Telephone:* 410-836-4145. *Fax:* 410-836-4481. *E-mail:* cvonders@harford.edu.

DEGREES AND AWARDS

AA General Studies
AS Business Administration

COURSE SUBJECT AREAS OFFERED OUTSIDE OF DEGREE PROGRAMS

Undergraduate—computer and information sciences, general; computer programming; computer systems networking and telecommunications; educational psychology; English composition; English language and literature, general; foreign languages and literatures; mathematics; psychology; social sciences and history, other.
Non-credit—computer and information sciences, general; computer programming; computer systems networking and telecommunications.

HARRISBURG AREA COMMUNITY COLLEGE

Harrisburg, Pennsylvania
Distance Education Office

http://www.hacc.edu/programs/disted/disted.cfm

Harrisburg Area Community College was founded in 1964. It is accredited by Middle States Association of Colleges and Schools. It first offered distance learning courses in 1987. In fall 2003, there were 1,500 students enrolled in distance learning courses. Institutionally administered financial aid is available to distance learners.

Services Distance learners have accessibility to academic advising, bookstore, career placement assistance, library services, tutoring.

Contact Ms. Wanda Page, Distance Learning Technician, Harrisburg Area Community College, 1 HACC Drive, Harrisburg, PA 17110. *Telephone:* 717-780-1122. *Fax:* 717-780-1925. *E-mail:* distance@hacc.edu.

DEGREES AND AWARDS

Programs offered do not lead to a degree or other formal award.

COURSE SUBJECT AREAS OFFERED OUTSIDE OF DEGREE PROGRAMS

Undergraduate—accounting; American literature (United States); anthropology; applied mathematics; astronomy; biological and physical sciences; business; business administration and management; business management and administrative services, other; business/managerial economics; computer programming; computer science; computer software and media applications; criminal justice and corrections; developmental and child psychology; economics; education, general; engineering, general; English composition; English language and literature, general; English literature (British and Commonwealth); English technical and business writing; environmental/environmental health engineering; foods and nutrition studies; geography; geological and related sciences; health and medical assistants; history; information sciences and systems; Internet and World Wide Web; library science, other; mathematical statistics; mathematics; mathematics and computer science; microbiology/bacteriology; philosophy; physical sciences, general; psychology; public health; sociology.

HARTFORD SEMINARY

Hartford, Connecticut

http://www.hartsem.edu/academic/distance.htm

Hartford Seminary was founded in 1834. It is accredited by New England Association of Schools and Colleges. It first offered distance learning courses in 2002. In fall 2003, there were 15 students enrolled in distance learning courses. Institutionally administered financial aid is available to distance learners.

Services Distance learners have accessibility to academic advising, bookstore, library services, tutoring.

Contact Dr. Scott Thumma, Director of Distance Education, Hartford Seminary, 77 Sherman Street, Hartford, CT 06105. *Telephone:* 860-509-9571. *E-mail:* sthumma@hartsem.edu.

DEGREES AND AWARDS

Programs offered do not lead to a degree or other formal award.

COURSE SUBJECT AREAS OFFERED OUTSIDE OF DEGREE PROGRAMS

Graduate—pastoral counseling and specialized ministries; religion/religious studies; sociology.
Non-credit—religion/religious studies.

HEARTLAND COMMUNITY COLLEGE

Normal, Illinois

http://www.hcc-online.org

Heartland Community College was founded in 1990. It is accredited by North Central Association of Colleges and Schools. It first offered distance learning courses in 1991. In fall 2003, there were 600 students enrolled in distance learning courses. Institutionally administered financial aid is available to distance learners.

Services Distance learners have accessibility to academic advising, career placement assistance, library services, tutoring.

Contact Mr. Padriac Sean Shinville, Division Chair of Alternative Learning and Developmental Education, Heartland Community College, 1500 West Raab Road, Normal, IL 61761. *Telephone:* 309-268-8414. *Fax:* 309-268-7986. *E-mail:* padriac.shinville@hcc.cc.il.us.

DEGREES AND AWARDS

Programs offered do not lead to a degree or other formal award.

COURSE SUBJECT AREAS OFFERED OUTSIDE OF DEGREE PROGRAMS

Undergraduate—accounting; American literature (United States); business; child care and guidance workers and managers; communications, general; economics; English composition; foods and nutrition studies; history; psychology.

HEART OF GEORGIA TECHNICAL COLLEGE

Dublin, Georgia

http://www.hgtc.org

Heart of Georgia Technical College was founded in 1984. It is accredited by Northwest Commission on Colleges and Universities. It first offered distance learning courses in 1993. In fall 2003, there were 62 students enrolled in distance learning courses. Institutionally administered financial aid is available to distance learners.

Services Distance learners have accessibility to academic advising, bookstore, campus computer network, career placement assistance, e-mail services, tutoring.

Contact Ms. Lisa Kelly, Admissions Director, Heart of Georgia Technical College, 560 Pinehill Road, Dublin, GA 31021. *Telephone:* 478-274-7837. *Fax:* 478-275-6642. *E-mail:* lisak@hgtc.org.

DEGREES AND AWARDS

Programs offered do not lead to a degree or other formal award.

COURSE SUBJECT AREAS OFFERED OUTSIDE OF DEGREE PROGRAMS

Undergraduate—applied mathematics; business administration and management; business information and data processing services; computer and information sciences, other; computer systems analysis; computer systems networking and telecommunications; education administration and supervision; education, other; electrical and electronic engineering-related technology; engineering-related technologies, other; English language and literature, general; English technical and business writing; health professions and related sciences, other; mathematics; psychology; teacher assistant/aide; technology education/industrial arts.

HEBREW COLLEGE

Newton Centre, Massachusetts

http://www.hebrewcollege.edu/online

Hebrew College was founded in 1921. It is accredited by New England Association of Schools and Colleges. It first offered distance learning courses in 1995. In fall 2003, there were 94 students enrolled in distance learning courses. Institutionally administered financial aid is available to distance learners.

Services Distance learners have accessibility to academic advising, campus computer network, career placement assistance, library services, tutoring.

Contact Nathan Ehrlich, Dean, Hebrew College Online, Hebrew College, 160 Herrick Road, Newton Centre, MA 02459. *Telephone:* 617-559-8672. *Fax:* 617-559-8601. *E-mail:* nathan@hebrewcollege.edu.

DEGREES AND AWARDS

MA Jewish Studies

COURSE SUBJECT AREAS OFFERED OUTSIDE OF DEGREE PROGRAMS

Undergraduate—bible/biblical studies; biblical and other theological languages and literatures; education, other; foreign languages and literatures; Judaic studies; Middle Eastern languages and literatures; philosophy and religion; religion/religious studies.

Graduate—bible/biblical studies; biblical and other theological languages and literatures; education, other; foreign languages and literatures; Judaic studies; Middle Eastern languages and literatures; philosophy and religion; religion/religious studies.

Non-credit—bible/biblical studies; biblical and other theological languages and literatures; education, other; foreign languages and literatures; Judaic studies; Middle Eastern languages and literatures; philosophy and religion; religion/religious studies.

HENRY FORD COMMUNITY COLLEGE

Dearborn, Michigan

http://www.hfcc.edu

Henry Ford Community College was founded in 1938. It is accredited by North Central Association of Colleges and Schools. It first offered distance learning courses in 2004. Institutionally administered financial aid is available to distance learners.

Services Distance learners have accessibility to bookstore, e-mail services, library services.

Contact Dr. Vivian Beaty, Director of Instructional Technology, Henry Ford Community College, Instructional Technology, 5101 Evergreen Road, Dearborn, MI 48128-1495. *Telephone:* 313-845-9663 Ext. 3. *Fax:* 313-845-9844. *E-mail:* vbeaty@hfcc.edu.

DEGREES AND AWARDS

Programs offered do not lead to a degree or other formal award.

COURSE SUBJECT AREAS OFFERED OUTSIDE OF DEGREE PROGRAMS

Undergraduate—anthropology; astronomy; computer and information sciences, general; computer software and media applications; criminal justice and corrections; educational/instructional media design; English composition; English language and literature, general; English technical and business writing; journalism and mass communications; Middle Eastern languages and literatures; political science and government; religion/religious studies.

HIBBING COMMUNITY COLLEGE

Hibbing, Minnesota

http://www.hcc.mnscu.edu/

Hibbing Community College was founded in 1916. It is accredited by North Central Association of Colleges and Schools. It first offered distance learning courses in 1967. In fall 2003, there were 750 students enrolled in distance learning courses. Institutionally administered financial aid is available to distance learners.

Hibbing Community College (continued)

Services Distance learners have accessibility to academic advising, bookstore, campus computer network, career placement assistance, e-mail services, library services, tutoring.

Contact James Antilla, Director of Instructional Technology, Hibbing Community College, 1515 East 25th Street, Hibbing, MN 55746-3300. *Telephone:* 218-262-7250. *Fax:* 218-262-6717. *E-mail:* jamesantilla@hcc.mnscu.edu.

DEGREES AND AWARDS

AA Medical Lab Tech

COURSE SUBJECT AREAS OFFERED OUTSIDE OF DEGREE PROGRAMS

Undergraduate—accounting; applied mathematics; area, ethnic and cultural studies, other; biological and physical sciences; business administration and management; computer and information sciences, general; computer programming; computer science; computer software and media applications; data entry/microcomputer applications; drafting; economics; English composition; fine arts and art studies; foods and nutrition studies; health and medical preparatory programs; history; information sciences and systems; Internet and World Wide Web; liberal arts and sciences, general studies and humanities; mathematics; medical laboratory technology; multi/interdisciplinary studies, other; nursing; political science and government; psychology; social sciences, general.

Non-credit—accounting; computer and information sciences, general; computer software and media applications; Internet and World Wide Web; real estate.

See full description on page 434.

HILLSBOROUGH COMMUNITY COLLEGE

Tampa, Florida

Distance Learning Office

http://www.hccfl.edu/eCampus

Hillsborough Community College was founded in 1968. It is accredited by Southern Association of Colleges and Schools. It first offered distance learning courses in 1971. In fall 2003, there were 1,460 students enrolled in distance learning courses. Institutionally administered financial aid is available to distance learners.

Services Distance learners have accessibility to academic advising, bookstore, career placement assistance, library services, tutoring.

Contact Michael Comins, Director of Academic Technology, Hillsborough Community College, 39 Columbia Drive, Tampa, FL 33606. *Telephone:* 813-253-7017. *Fax:* 813-259-6018. *E-mail:* mcomins@hccfl.edu.

DEGREES AND AWARDS

AS Opticiarny

COURSE SUBJECT AREAS OFFERED OUTSIDE OF DEGREE PROGRAMS

Undergraduate—American literature (United States); applied mathematics; astronomy; business; business marketing and marketing management; computer and information sciences, general; computer/information technology administration and management; computer programming; computer science; developmental/child psychology; economics; English composition; English creative writing; English language and literature, general; family and community studies; finance; foods and nutrition studies; geological and related sciences; health professions and related sciences, other; Internet and World Wide Web; legal studies; ophthalmic/optometric services; psychology; sociology.

HILLSDALE FREE WILL BAPTIST COLLEGE

Moore, Oklahoma

Department of External Studies

http://www.hc.edu/

Hillsdale Free Will Baptist College was founded in 1959. It is accredited by Transnational Association of Christian Colleges and Schools. It first offered distance learning courses in 1975. In fall 2003, there were 100 students enrolled in distance learning courses. Institutionally administered financial aid is available to distance learners.

Services Distance learners have accessibility to academic advising, bookstore, e-mail services, library services.

Contact Edwin L. Wade, Director of Distance Learning, Hillsdale Free Will Baptist College, PO Box 7208, Moore, OK 73153-1208. *Telephone:* 405-912-9000 Ext. 9018. *Fax:* 405-912-9050. *E-mail:* xstudies@hc.edu.

DEGREES AND AWARDS

Programs offered do not lead to a degree or other formal award.

HOLY APOSTLES COLLEGE AND SEMINARY

Cromwell, Connecticut

http://www.holyapostles.edu

Holy Apostles College and Seminary was founded in 1956. It is accredited by New England Association of Schools and Colleges. It first offered distance learning courses in 1998. In fall 2003, there were 80 students enrolled in distance learning courses. Institutionally administered financial aid is available to distance learners.

Services Distance learners have accessibility to academic advising, e-mail services, library services, tutoring.

Contact Mr. Robert Mish, Distance Learning Coordinator, Holy Apostles College and Seminary, 33 Prospect Hill Road, Cromwell, CT 06416. *Telephone:* 860-632-3015. *Fax:* 860-632-3075. *E-mail:* distancelearn@holyapostles.edu.

DEGREES AND AWARDS

MA Philosophy; Theology

COURSE SUBJECT AREAS OFFERED OUTSIDE OF DEGREE PROGRAMS

Graduate—philosophy and religion.

HOLY NAMES UNIVERSITY

Oakland, California

Holy Names University was founded in 1868. It is accredited by Western Association of Schools and Colleges. It first offered distance learning courses in 1995. In fall 2003, there were 133 students enrolled in distance learning courses. Institutionally administered financial aid is available to distance learners.

Services Distance learners have accessibility to academic advising, bookstore, e-mail services, library services.

Contact Office of Admissions, Holy Names University, 3500 Mountain Boulevard, Oakland, CA 94619-1699. *Telephone:* 510-436-1351. *Fax:* 510-436-1325. *E-mail:* admissions@hnu.edu.

DEGREES AND AWARDS

BN Nursing–Accelerated RN-BSN

HONOLULU COMMUNITY COLLEGE

Honolulu, Hawaii
Distance Learning
http://honolulu.hawaii.edu/distance

Honolulu Community College was founded in 1920. It is accredited by Western Association of Schools and Colleges. It first offered distance learning courses in 1991. In fall 2003, there were 500 students enrolled in distance learning courses. Institutionally administered financial aid is available to distance learners.

Services Distance learners have accessibility to academic advising, bookstore, campus computer network, career placement assistance, e-mail services, library services.

Contact Sherrie Rupert, Distance Learning Coordinator, Honolulu Community College, 874 Dillingham Boulevard, Honolulu, HI 96817. *Telephone:* 808-845-9151. *Fax:* 808-847-9829. *E-mail:* srupert@hcc.hawaii.edu.

DEGREES AND AWARDS

Programs offered do not lead to a degree or other formal award.

COURSE SUBJECT AREAS OFFERED OUTSIDE OF DEGREE PROGRAMS

Undergraduate—anthropology; architectural engineering technology; astronomy; chemistry; English as a second language; English composition; English language and literature, general; fire science; foods and nutrition studies; geological and related sciences; history; microbiology/bacteriology; philosophy; political science and government; psychology; social sciences and history, other; speech and rhetorical studies.

HOPE INTERNATIONAL UNIVERSITY

Fullerton, California
Distance Learning Department
http://www.hiu.edu

Hope International University was founded in 1928. It is accredited by Western Association of Schools and Colleges. It first offered distance learning courses in 1994. In fall 2003, there were 289 students enrolled in distance learning courses. Institutionally administered financial aid is available to distance learners.

Services Distance learners have accessibility to academic advising, bookstore, career placement assistance, library services.

Contact Wende J. Holtzen, Distance Learning Assistant, Hope International University, 2500 East Nutwood Avenue, Fullerton, CA 92831. *Telephone:* 714-879-3901 Ext. 1246. *Fax:* 714-681-7230. *E-mail:* wholtzen@hiu.edu.

DEGREES AND AWARDS

AA Biblical Studies; Christian Ministry
BS Business Administration and Management; Christian Ministry; Human Development
Certificate Biblical Studies; Christian Ministry
MBA International Development; Management; Nonprofit Management
MSM International Development

COURSE SUBJECT AREAS OFFERED OUTSIDE OF DEGREE PROGRAMS

Undergraduate—bible/biblical studies; history; psychology; religion/religious studies.
Graduate—bible/biblical studies; cultural studies; psychology; religion/religious studies.
Non-credit—bible/biblical studies; cultural studies; history; psychology; religion/religious studies.

HOPKINSVILLE COMMUNITY COLLEGE

Hopkinsville, Kentucky
http://www.hopkinsville.kctcs.edu

Hopkinsville Community College was founded in 1965. It is accredited by Southern Association of Colleges and Schools. It first offered distance learning courses in 1990. In fall 2003, there were 300 students enrolled in distance learning courses. Institutionally administered financial aid is available to distance learners.

Services Distance learners have accessibility to academic advising, bookstore, campus computer network, e-mail services, library services, tutoring.

Contact Mr. Jonnie C. Blair, Associate Dean for Academic Affairs, Hopkinsville Community College, North Drive, PO Box 2100, Hopkinsville, KY 42241-2100. *Telephone:* 270-886-3921 Ext. 6125. *Fax:* 270-886-5755. *E-mail:* jonnie.blair@kctcs.edu.

DEGREES AND AWARDS

AA Accounting Transfer Option; Business Marketing and Marketing Management Transfer Framework; Business Transfer Framework; Communications Transfer Framework; Secretarial Science Transfer Framework
AAS Criminal Justice, Law Enforcement; Information Technology Networking Option; Occupational/Technical Studies, general
License A+ Certificate

COURSE SUBJECT AREAS OFFERED OUTSIDE OF DEGREE PROGRAMS

Undergraduate—accounting; administrative and secretarial services; agriculture/agricultural sciences; American history; astronomy; biological and physical sciences; biological sciences/life sciences, other; business; business administration and management; chemistry; communications, general; computer systems networking and telecommunications; criminal justice and corrections; English language and literature, general; liberal arts and sciences, general studies and humanities; mathematics; philosophy; psychology; social sciences and history, other; sociology.

HORRY-GEORGETOWN TECHNICAL COLLEGE

Conway, South Carolina
Department of Distance Learning
http://www.hgtc.edu/DistanceLearning/

Horry-Georgetown Technical College was founded in 1966. It is accredited by Southern Association of Colleges and Schools. It first offered distance learning courses in 1995. In fall 2003, there were 1,000 students enrolled in distance learning courses. Institutionally administered financial aid is available to distance learners.

Services Distance learners have accessibility to academic advising, bookstore, career placement assistance, e-mail services, library services, tutoring.

Contact John W. Sharpe, Distance Learning Technician, Horry-Georgetown Technical College, 2050 Highway 501 East, PO Box 261966, Conway, SC 29528. *Telephone:* 843-349-7554. *Fax:* 843-349-7533. *E-mail:* john.sharpe@hgtc.edu.

DEGREES AND AWARDS

Programs offered do not lead to a degree or other formal award.

COURSE SUBJECT AREAS OFFERED OUTSIDE OF DEGREE PROGRAMS

Undergraduate—accounting; administrative and secretarial services; agriculture/agricultural sciences; American literature (United States); astronomy; biological and physical sciences; business; business administration and management; business and personal services marketing operations; business communications; cognitive psychology and psycholinguistics; communications, other; computer science; criminal justice and corrections; developmental and child psychology; English composition; history; hospitality services management; individual and family development studies; Internet and World Wide Web; marketing management and research; mathematics related; philosophy; Romance languages and literatures; sociology.

HOUSTON COMMUNITY COLLEGE SYSTEM

Houston, Texas
Distance Education Department
http://www.distance.hccs.edu

Houston Community College System was founded in 1971. It is accredited by Southern Association of Colleges and Schools. It first offered distance learning courses in 1985. In fall 2003, there were 5,981 students enrolled in distance learning courses. Institutionally administered financial aid is available to distance learners.

Services Distance learners have accessibility to academic advising, bookstore, e-mail services, library services, tutoring.

Contact Eva Gonzalez, Distance Education Associate, Houston Community College System, 3100 Main, MC1740, Houston, TX 77002. *Telephone:* 713-718-5152. *Fax:* 713-718-5388. *E-mail:* eva.gonzalez@hccs.edu.

DEGREES AND AWARDS

Programs offered do not lead to a degree or other formal award.

COURSE SUBJECT AREAS OFFERED OUTSIDE OF DEGREE PROGRAMS

Undergraduate—accounting; American history; American literature (United States); anthropology; art history; astronomy; biology, general; business administration and management; business marketing and marketing management; chemistry; child care and guidance workers and managers; community health services; computer/information technology administration and management; computer science; criminology; developmental/child psychology; earth sciences; economics; English composition; English literature (British and Commonwealth); environmental science; European history; fire protection; foods and nutrition studies; geography; history; human resources management; human services; management information systems/business data processing; mathematics; mathematics related; philosophy; photography; physical sciences, general; political science and government; psychology; real estate; Romance languages and literatures; sociology; Spanish.

HOWARD COLLEGE

Big Spring, Texas
http://www.howardcollege.edu/

Howard College was founded in 1945. It is accredited by Southern Association of Colleges and Schools. It first offered distance learning courses in 1997. In fall 2003, there were 350 students enrolled in distance learning courses. Institutionally administered financial aid is available to distance learners.

Services Distance learners have accessibility to campus computer network, e-mail services, library services.

Contact Stan D. Solis, Director of Distance Learning, Howard College, 1001 Birdwell Lane, Big Spring, TX 79720. *Telephone:* 432-264-5124. *Fax:* 432-264-5146. *E-mail:* ssolis@howardcollege.edu.

DEGREES AND AWARDS

Programs offered do not lead to a degree or other formal award.

COURSE SUBJECT AREAS OFFERED OUTSIDE OF DEGREE PROGRAMS

Undergraduate—accounting; business; economics; English composition; English literature (British and Commonwealth); foods and nutrition studies; mathematics; nursing; psychology; sociology.

HOWARD COMMUNITY COLLEGE

Columbia, Maryland
Office of Distance Learning
http://www.howardcc.edu/

Howard Community College was founded in 1966. It is accredited by Middle States Association of Colleges and Schools. It first offered distance learning courses in 1995. In fall 2003, there were 1,000 students enrolled in distance learning courses. Institutionally administered financial aid is available to distance learners.

Services Distance learners have accessibility to academic advising, bookstore, campus computer network, e-mail services, library services, tutoring.

Contact Virginia Kirk, Director of Distance Learning, Howard Community College, 10901 Little Patuxent Parkway, Columbia, MD 21044. *Telephone:* 410-772-4911. *Fax:* 410-772-4401. *E-mail:* vkirk@howardcc.edu.

DEGREES AND AWARDS

AA General Studies
AAS General Program

COURSE SUBJECT AREAS OFFERED OUTSIDE OF DEGREE PROGRAMS

Undergraduate—accounting; American literature (United States); applied mathematics; astronomy; atmospheric sciences and meteorology; business; business administration and management; business communications; business information and data processing services; business management and administrative services, other; communications, general; computer and information sciences, general; criminology; educational evaluation, research and statistics; education, general; English composition; English creative writing; English language and literature, general; geological and related sciences; health and physical education/fitness; history; international business; liberal arts and sciences, general studies and humanities; mathematical statistics; mathematics; music; psychology; social psychology; social sciences and history, other; visual and performing arts.

HUDSON COUNTY COMMUNITY COLLEGE

Jersey City, New Jersey

http://www.hudson.cc.nj.us/

Hudson County Community College was founded in 1974. It is accredited by Middle States Association of Colleges and Schools. It first offered distance learning courses in 1998. In fall 2003, there were 100 students enrolled in distance learning courses. Institutionally administered financial aid is available to distance learners.

Services Distance learners have accessibility to e-mail services, library services.

Contact Mr. Donald C Miklas, Director of Computers, Technology, Leadership and Business Programs, Hudson County Community College, Division of Continuing Education and Community Affairs, 25 Journal Square, Jersey City, NJ 07306. *Telephone:* 201-714-7300 Ext. 7300. *Fax:* 201-653-1351. *E-mail:* dmiklas@hccc.edu.

DEGREES AND AWARDS

Programs offered do not lead to a degree or other formal award.

COURSE SUBJECT AREAS OFFERED OUTSIDE OF DEGREE PROGRAMS

Undergraduate—accounting; administrative and secretarial services; apparel and accessories marketing operations; business; business management and administrative services, other; child care and guidance workers and managers; clothing, apparel and textile workers and managers; communications, general; community health services; community organization, resources and services; computer and information sciences, general; computer and information sciences, other; computer software and media applications; consumer and homemaking education; custodial, housekeeping and home services workers and managers; dance; health and medical administrative services; vocational home economics, other.

Non-credit—accounting; administrative and secretarial services; business communications; business information and data processing services; communication disorders sciences and services; communications technologies; community organization, resources and services; computer and information sciences, general; computer programming; curriculum and instruction; education, other; foreign languages and literatures, other; health and medical assistants; hospitality services management; Internet and World Wide Web; public administration; quality control and safety technologies; teacher education, specific academic and vocational programs; technology education/industrial arts; telecommunications.

ILLINOIS EASTERN COMMUNITY COLLEGES, FRONTIER COMMUNITY COLLEGE

Fairfield, Illinois

http://www.iecc.cc.il.us./fcc

Illinois Eastern Community Colleges, Frontier Community College was founded in 1976. It is accredited by North Central Association of Colleges and Schools. It first offered distance learning courses in 1994. In fall 2003, there were 60 students enrolled in distance learning courses. Institutionally administered financial aid is available to distance learners.

Services Distance learners have accessibility to academic advising, campus computer network, career placement assistance, e-mail services, tutoring.

Contact Mr. Jerry Hefley, Dean of the College, Illinois Eastern Community Colleges, Frontier Community College, 2 Frontier Drive, Fairfield, IL 62837. *Telephone:* 618-842-3711 Ext. 4005. *Fax:* 618-842-6340. *E-mail:* hefleyj@iecc.edu.

DEGREES AND AWARDS

Programs offered do not lead to a degree or other formal award.

COURSE SUBJECT AREAS OFFERED OUTSIDE OF DEGREE PROGRAMS

Undergraduate—business; foods and nutrition studies; health and physical education/fitness; marketing management and research.

ILLINOIS EASTERN COMMUNITY COLLEGES, LINCOLN TRAIL COLLEGE

Robinson, Illinois

http://www.iecc.cc.il.us/ltc

Illinois Eastern Community Colleges, Lincoln Trail College was founded in 1969. It is accredited by North Central Association of Colleges and Schools. It first offered distance learning courses in 1994. In fall 2003, there were 493 students enrolled in distance learning courses. Institutionally administered financial aid is available to distance learners.

Services Distance learners have accessibility to academic advising, campus computer network, career placement assistance, e-mail services, tutoring.

Contact Ms. Penny Quinn, Dean of Instruction, Illinois Eastern Community Colleges, Lincoln Trail College, 11220 State Highway 1, Robinson, IL 62454. *Telephone:* 618-544-8657 Ext. 1144. *Fax:* 618-544-7423. *E-mail:* quinnp@iecc.edu.

DEGREES AND AWARDS

Programs offered do not lead to a degree or other formal award.

Illinois Eastern Community Colleges, Lincoln Trail College (continued)

COURSE SUBJECT AREAS OFFERED OUTSIDE OF DEGREE PROGRAMS

Undergraduate—astronomy; business; computer and information sciences, general; computer software and media applications; English composition; health professions and related sciences, other; mathematics; psychology, other.

ILLINOIS EASTERN COMMUNITY COLLEGES, OLNEY CENTRAL COLLEGE

Olney, Illinois
http://www.iecc.cc.il.us/occ/

Illinois Eastern Community Colleges, Olney Central College was founded in 1962. It is accredited by North Central Association of Colleges and Schools. It first offered distance learning courses in 1994. In fall 2003, there were 188 students enrolled in distance learning courses. Institutionally administered financial aid is available to distance learners.

Services Distance learners have accessibility to academic advising, campus computer network, career placement assistance, e-mail services, tutoring.

Contact Ms. Jennifer Mathes, Dean of Instruction, Illinois Eastern Community Colleges, Olney Central College, 305 North West Street, Olney, IL 62450. *Telephone:* 618-395-7777 Ext. 2002. *Fax:* 618-395-5212. *E-mail:* mathesj@iecc.edu.

DEGREES AND AWARDS

Programs offered do not lead to a degree or other formal award.

COURSE SUBJECT AREAS OFFERED OUTSIDE OF DEGREE PROGRAMS

Undergraduate—accounting; business; communications, general; computer and information sciences, general; economics; English composition; liberal arts and sciences, general studies and humanities; psychology; sociology.

ILLINOIS EASTERN COMMUNITY COLLEGES, WABASH VALLEY COLLEGE

Mount Carmel, Illinois
http://www.iecc.cc.il.us/wvc

Illinois Eastern Community Colleges, Wabash Valley College was founded in 1960. It is accredited by North Central Association of Colleges and Schools. It first offered distance learning courses in 1994. In fall 2003, there were 109 students enrolled in distance learning courses. Institutionally administered financial aid is available to distance learners.

Services Distance learners have accessibility to academic advising, campus computer network, career placement assistance, e-mail services, tutoring.

Contact Mr. Matt Fowler, Dean of Instruction, Illinois Eastern Community Colleges, Wabash Valley College, 2200 College Drive, Mt. Carmel, IL 62863. *Telephone:* 618-262-8641 Ext. 3213. *Fax:* 618-262-5614. *E-mail:* fowlerm@iecc.edu.

DEGREES AND AWARDS

Programs offered do not lead to a degree or other formal award.

COURSE SUBJECT AREAS OFFERED OUTSIDE OF DEGREE PROGRAMS

Undergraduate—accounting; business; chemistry; history; liberal arts and sciences, general studies and humanities; mathematical statistics; mathematics; mathematics related.

ILLINOIS INSTITUTE OF TECHNOLOGY

Chicago, Illinois
IIT Online
http://www.iit-online.iit.edu

Illinois Institute of Technology was founded in 1890. It is accredited by North Central Association of Colleges and Schools. It first offered distance learning courses in 1976. In fall 2003, there were 934 students enrolled in distance learning courses. Institutionally administered financial aid is available to distance learners.

Services Distance learners have accessibility to academic advising, bookstore, campus computer network, career placement assistance, e-mail services, library services.

Contact Ms. Holli Pryor-Harris, Director of Client Services, Illinois Institute of Technology, Office of Academic Affairs, Graduate College, 3300 South Federal, Room 110A, Chicago, IL 60616-3793. *Telephone:* 312-567-3167. *Fax:* 312-567-7140. *E-mail:* pryor@iit.edu.

DEGREES AND AWARDS

Graduate Certificate Advanced Electronics; Analytical Method Development; Analytical Spectroscopy; Characterization of Organic and Inorganic Materials; Chromatography; Computer Engineering; Computer and Network Security Technologies; Control Systems; Current Energy Issues; Electricity Markets; Hazardous Waste Engineering; Indoor Air Quality; Intelligent Information Systems; Internet; Networking and Telecommunications; Particle Processing; Pharmaceutical Processing; Power Engineering; Process Operations Management; Signal Processing; Software Engineering; Synthesis and Characterization of Inorganic Material; Synthesis and Characterization of Organic Materials; Water and Wastewater Treatment; Wireless Communications

M Ch E Chemical Engineering
MB Biology
ME Computer Engineering; Telecommunications and Software Engineering
MECE Electrical and Computer Engineering
MEE Environmental Engineering
MEM Electricity Markets
MGE Gas Engineering
MHP Health Physics
MITM Information Technology Management
MITO Industrial Technology and Operations
MMAE Mechanical and Aerospace Engineering
MME Manufacturing Engineering
MMSE Materials and Science Engineering
MS Chemical Engineering; Computer Science; Electrical Engineering; Mechanical and Aerospace Engineering

COURSE SUBJECT AREAS OFFERED OUTSIDE OF DEGREE PROGRAMS

Undergraduate—applied mathematics; biochemistry and biophysics; biological and physical sciences; cell and molecular biology; chemical engineering; computer and information sciences, general; computer engineering; computer programming; computer science; electrical engineering; engineering mechanics; mechanical engineering.
Graduate—aerospace engineering; analytical chemistry; biochemistry and biophysics; bioengineering and biomedical engineering; biological and physical sciences; biological sciences/life sciences, other; cell and molecular biology; chemical engineering; chemistry; computer engineering; computer science; electrical engineering; engineering mechanics; environmental engineering; food sciences and technology; industrial engineering; inorganic chemistry; materials engineering; mechanical engineering; metallurgical engineering; organic chemistry; telecommunications.

ILLINOIS STATE UNIVERSITY

Normal, Illinois
Extended University
http://www.exu.ilstu.edu

Illinois State University was founded in 1857. It is accredited by North Central Association of Colleges and Schools. It first offered distance learning courses in 1994. In fall 2003, there were 200 students enrolled in distance learning courses. Institutionally administered financial aid is available to distance learners.

Services Distance learners have accessibility to academic advising, bookstore, campus computer network, career placement assistance, e-mail services, library services.
Contact Susan Deason, Program Coordinator, Extended Learning, Illinois State University, Campus Box 4090, Normal, IL 61790. *Telephone:* 309-438-5288. *Fax:* 309-438-5069. *E-mail:* sjvankl@ilstu.edu.

DEGREES AND AWARDS

BSN Nursing
Certification Visual Impairment and Blindness

COURSE SUBJECT AREAS OFFERED OUTSIDE OF DEGREE PROGRAMS

Undergraduate—education, other; English language and literature, general; foreign languages and literatures; health professions and related sciences, other; history; nursing; technology education/industrial arts.
Graduate—curriculum and instruction; education administration and supervision; foreign languages and literatures; nursing; special education; technology education/industrial arts.

IMMACULATA UNIVERSITY

Immaculata, Pennsylvania
http://www.immaculata.edu/

Immaculata University was founded in 1920. It is accredited by Middle States Association of Colleges and Schools. It first offered distance learning courses in 1999. In fall 2003, there were 2,700 students enrolled in distance learning courses. Institutionally administered financial aid is available to distance learners.

Services Distance learners have accessibility to academic advising, bookstore, campus computer network, career placement assistance, e-mail services, library services, tutoring.
Contact Dr. Elke Franke, Dean of College of LifeLong Learning, Immaculata University, Box 300, Immaculata, PA 19345-0300. *Telephone:* 610-647-4400 Ext. 3235. *Fax:* 610-647-0215. *E-mail:* efranke@immaculata.edu.

DEGREES AND AWARDS

Programs offered do not lead to a degree or other formal award.

COURSE SUBJECT AREAS OFFERED OUTSIDE OF DEGREE PROGRAMS

Undergraduate—accounting; advertising; apparel and accessories marketing operations; applied mathematics; area, ethnic and cultural studies, other; bible/biblical studies; biblical and other theological languages and literatures; biological and physical sciences; biological sciences/life sciences, other; biology, general; business; business administration and management; business communications; business information and data processing services; business quantitative methods and management science; chemistry; clothing/apparel and textile studies; cognitive psychology and psycholinguistics; communications, general; computer and information sciences, general; computer and information sciences, other; computer/information technology administration and management; computer programming; computer software and media applications; computer systems analysis; English composition; entrepreneurship; environmental control technologies; family/consumer resource management; foods and nutrition studies; foreign languages and literatures; history; international business; Internet and World Wide Web; mathematics; microbiology/bacteriology; music; nursing; physics; psychology; religion/religious studies; sociology; systems science and theory; theological studies and religious vocations, other.
Graduate—clinical psychology; curriculum and instruction; educational evaluation, research and statistics; educational/instructional media design; education, general; foods and nutrition studies; general teacher education; music; nursing; psychology, other.
Non-credit—education, general; foods and nutrition studies.

INDEPENDENCE COMMUNITY COLLEGE

Independence, Kansas
Center for Distance Learning
http://www.indycc.edu/

Independence Community College was founded in 1925. It is accredited by North Central Association of Colleges and Schools. It first offered distance learning courses in 1998. In fall 2003, there were 60 students enrolled in distance learning courses. Institutionally administered financial aid is available to distance learners.

Services Distance learners have accessibility to academic advising, bookstore, campus computer network, e-mail services, library services, tutoring.
Contact Stoney Gaddy, Instructor, Independence Community College, PO Box 708, Independence, KS 67301. *Telephone:* 620-331-4100 Ext. 4306. *Fax:* 620-331-5344. *E-mail:* sgaddy@indycc.edu.

DEGREES AND AWARDS

Programs offered do not lead to a degree or other formal award.

Independence Community College (continued)

COURSE SUBJECT AREAS OFFERED OUTSIDE OF DEGREE PROGRAMS

Undergraduate—astronomy; biological and physical sciences; computer and information sciences, general; computer systems networking and telecommunications; English composition; fine arts and art studies; political science and government; sociology.

INDIANA INSTITUTE OF TECHNOLOGY

Fort Wayne, Indiana
Independent Study
http://www.indianatech.edu

Indiana Institute of Technology was founded in 1930. It is accredited by North Central Association of Colleges and Schools. It first offered distance learning courses in 1982. In fall 2003, there were 300 students enrolled in distance learning courses. Institutionally administered financial aid is available to distance learners.

Services Distance learners have accessibility to academic advising, bookstore, e-mail services.

Contact Ms. Jill A. Wright, Admissions Counselor, Indiana Institute of Technology, 1600 East Washington Boulevard, Fort Wayne, IN 46803. *Telephone:* 888-666-8324 Ext. 2258. *Fax:* 260-422-1518. *E-mail:* jawright@indianatech.edu.

DEGREES AND AWARDS

AS Accounting; Business Administration; Management
BS Accounting; Business Administration
BSBA Accounting and Business Administration; Human Resources; Management; Marketing

COURSE SUBJECT AREAS OFFERED OUTSIDE OF DEGREE PROGRAMS

Undergraduate—accounting; business; business administration and management; computer and information sciences, general; English composition; psychology; social sciences, general.

INDIANA STATE UNIVERSITY

Terre Haute, Indiana
Division of Lifelong Learning
http://indstate.edu/distance

Indiana State University was founded in 1865. It is accredited by North Central Association of Colleges and Schools. It first offered distance learning courses in 1969. In fall 2003, there were 2,000 students enrolled in distance learning courses. Institutionally administered financial aid is available to distance learners.

Services Distance learners have accessibility to academic advising, bookstore, campus computer network, career placement assistance, e-mail services, library services.

Contact Chrys Ford, Assistant Director of Distance Support Services, Indiana State University, Office of Distance Support Services, Erickson Hall, Room 210-211, Terre Haute, IN 47809. *Telephone:* 888-237-8080. *Fax:* 812-237-8540. *E-mail:* studentservices@indstate.edu.

DEGREES AND AWARDS

AS Aviation Flight Technology, general
BS Business Administration; Career and Technical Education; Community Health; Criminology; Electronics Technology; Human Resource Development; Industrial Supervision; Industrial Technology; Insurance; Mechanical Design Technology; Nursing
Certificate Corrections; Law Enforcement; Library Media Services; Private Security and Loss Prevention
Endorsement Driver Education
License School Administration
Graduate Certificate Library Media Services; Public Administration
MS Criminology; Electronics and Computer Technology; Health and Safety; Human Resource Development; Nursing; Student Affairs and Higher Education
PhD Technology Management

COURSE SUBJECT AREAS OFFERED OUTSIDE OF DEGREE PROGRAMS

Undergraduate—accounting; aerospace, aeronautical and astronautical engineering; business; business administration and management; business management and administrative services, other; construction/building technology; criminal justice and corrections; criminology; curriculum and instruction; economics; educational/instructional media design; education, general; education, other; electrical, electronics and communications engineering; English composition; English language and literature, general; fine arts and art studies; geography; history; human resources management; insurance/risk management; library science, other; mathematical statistics; mathematics related; music; nursing; psychology; sociology; technology education/industrial arts.

Graduate—criminal justice and corrections; criminology; curriculum and instruction; education administration and supervision; educational/instructional media design; educational psychology; education, other; electrical and electronic engineering-related technology; health and physical education/fitness; library science, other; nursing; political science and government; public administration; public administration and services, other; special education; student counseling and personnel services; technology education/industrial arts.

Non-credit—social work.

Special Message

The DegreeLink Program offers eligible individuals an opportunity to transfer college credit to Indiana State University and complete selected Bachelor of Science degrees via distance education. Individuals who have completed designated degrees from Ivy Tech State College and Vincennes University may transfer credit as a 2-year block into one or more DegreeLink programs. In addition, individuals who have earned credits or an associate degree from any accredited collegiate institution are eligible for and encouraged to transfer credit on a course-by-course basis and complete a Bachelor of Science degree via distance technologies.

Baccalaureate degree-completion programs offered include business administration, career and technical education, community health, criminology, electronics technology, industrial technology, human resource development, industrial supervision, insurance, mechanical design technology, and nursing.

A unique feature of the DegreeLink Program is a statewide network of area learning centers that offer free access to Internet-connected computers and student services coordinators who provide one-on-one assistance to in-state and out-of-state students and all individuals interested in DegreeLink.

Degree-completion courses are offered primarily via the Internet, print-based correspondence, videotape, and live televised courses accessible at receive sites. Most DegreeLink programs can be completed via distance education within Indiana. Selected DegreeLink programs are accessible globally via the Internet.

For more information, students should call the Office of Distance Support Services at 888-237-8080 (toll-free) or visit the Web site (http://web.indstate.edu/degreelink).

See full description on page 436.

INDIANA UNIVERSITY OF PENNSYLVANIA

Indiana, Pennsylvania

School of Continuing Education

http://www.iup.edu/continuing-ed/

Indiana University of Pennsylvania was founded in 1875. It is accredited by Middle States Association of Colleges and Schools. It first offered distance learning courses in 1990. In fall 2003, there were 563 students enrolled in distance learning courses. Institutionally administered financial aid is available to distance learners.

Services Distance learners have accessibility to academic advising, bookstore, career placement assistance, e-mail services, library services.

Contact Mr. George Rogers, Assistant Dean, College of Continuing Education, Indiana University of Pennsylvania, 104 Keith Hall, 390 Pratt Drive, Indiana, PA 15705. *Telephone:* 724-357-2292. *Fax:* 724-357-7597. *E-mail:* grogers@iup.edu.

DEGREES AND AWARDS

Certification Physics (WINPC)
Graduate Certificate Safety Sciences

COURSE SUBJECT AREAS OFFERED OUTSIDE OF DEGREE PROGRAMS

Undergraduate—accounting; business; business management and administrative services, other; communications technologies; criminology; English technical and business writing; foods and nutrition studies; geological and related sciences; hospitality services management; information sciences and systems; liberal arts and sciences, general studies and humanities; marketing management and research; mathematics; physics; political science and government; psychology.
Graduate—educational psychology; education, other; engineering-related technologies, other; physics.

INDIANA UNIVERSITY–PURDUE UNIVERSITY FORT WAYNE

Fort Wayne, Indiana

http://www.ipfw.edu/dlearning

Indiana University–Purdue University Fort Wayne was founded in 1917. It is accredited by North Central Association of Colleges and Schools. It first offered distance learning courses in 1996. In fall 2003, there were 2,097 students enrolled in distance learning courses. Institutionally administered financial aid is available to distance learners.

Services Distance learners have accessibility to bookstore, campus computer network, e-mail services, library services.

Contact IPFW Distance Learning, Indiana University–Purdue University Fort Wayne, 2101 East Coliseum Boulevard, Fort Wayne, IN 46805. *Telephone:* 260-481-6111. *Fax:* 260-481-6949. *E-mail:* dlearn@ipfw.edu.

DEGREES AND AWARDS

Programs offered do not lead to a degree or other formal award.

COURSE SUBJECT AREAS OFFERED OUTSIDE OF DEGREE PROGRAMS

Undergraduate—accounting; biology, general; business; communications, general; comparative literature; computer science; economics; education, general; engineering/industrial management; English composition; history; journalism and mass communications; mathematics; nursing; philosophy; political science and government; psychology; sociology.
Graduate—business administration and management; education administration and supervision; nursing.
Non-credit—administrative and secretarial services; business communications; business management and administrative services, other; computer software and media applications; computer systems networking and telecommunications.

INDIANA UNIVERSITY SYSTEM

Bloomington, Indiana

School of Continuing Studies

http://scs.indiana.edu

Indiana University System is accredited by North Central Association of Colleges and Schools. In fall 2003, there were 3,600 students enrolled in distance learning courses. Institutionally administered financial aid is available to distance learners.

Services Distance learners have accessibility to academic advising, bookstore, campus computer network, e-mail services, library services.

Contact Peer Advisor, Indiana University System, Owen Hall 001, 790 East Kirkwood Avenue, Bloomington, IN 47405-7101. *Telephone:* 800-334-1011. *Fax:* 812-855-8680. *E-mail:* scs@indiana.edu.

DEGREES AND AWARDS

AA General Studies
BA General Studies
Certificate Distance Education; Healthcare Accounting and Financial Management
Diploma General Studies
MS Adult Education

COURSE SUBJECT AREAS OFFERED OUTSIDE OF DEGREE PROGRAMS

Undergraduate—liberal arts and sciences, general studies and humanities.
Graduate—education, other.

See full description on page 438.

INDIANA WESLEYAN UNIVERSITY

Marion, Indiana

Center for Distributed Learning

http://www.IWUonline.com

Indiana Wesleyan University was founded in 1920. It is accredited by North Central Association of Colleges and Schools. It first offered distance learning courses in 1996. In fall 2003, there were 1,200 students enrolled in distance learning courses. Institutionally administered financial aid is available to distance learners.

Services Distance learners have accessibility to academic advising, bookstore, library services, tutoring.

Contact Adult Education Services, Indiana Wesleyan University, 4301 South Washington Street, Marion, IN 46953. *Telephone:* 888-IWU-2day. *Fax:* 765-677-2601. *E-mail:* info@iwuonline.com.

DEGREES AND AWARDS

AAB Business (ASB)
BS Business Information Systems–Bachelor Completion Program; Management–Bachelor Completion Program; Nursing–RNBS Adult Completion Program
Certificate Exceptional Needs with Mild Interventions (licensure)
MA Ministry–Ministerial Leadership and Youth Ministry Concentrations
MBA Business Administration
MEd Education
MSM Management

COURSE SUBJECT AREAS OFFERED OUTSIDE OF DEGREE PROGRAMS

Undergraduate—anthropology; bible/biblical studies; biblical and other theological languages and literatures; communications, general; computer and information sciences, general; criminal justice and corrections; criminology; earth sciences; English composition; fine arts and art studies; history; Internet and World Wide Web; mathematics; music; philosophy and religion related; psychology.
Graduate—educational psychology.

See full description on page 440.

INSTITUTE FOR CHRISTIAN STUDIES

Toronto, Ontario, Canada

http://www.icscanada.edu

Institute for Christian Studies was founded in 1967. It is provincially chartered. It first offered distance learning courses in 1990. In fall 2003, there were 13 students enrolled in distance learning courses. Institutionally administered financial aid is available to distance learners.

Services Distance learners have accessibility to academic advising, bookstore, e-mail services, library services.

Contact Ms. Ansley Tucker, Associate Academic Dean, Institute for Christian Studies, 229 College Street, Toronto, ON M5T 1R4, Canada. *Telephone:* 888-326-5347 Ext. 243. *Fax:* 416-979-2331. *E-mail:* registrar@icscanada.edu.

DEGREES AND AWARDS

Programs offered do not lead to a degree or other formal award.

COURSE SUBJECT AREAS OFFERED OUTSIDE OF DEGREE PROGRAMS

Graduate—bible/biblical studies; education, other; philosophy; philosophy and religion; political science and government; theological and ministerial studies.

INTER AMERICAN UNIVERSITY OF PUERTO RICO, SAN GERMÁN CAMPUS

San Germán, Puerto Rico

http://www.sg.inter.edu/

Inter American University of Puerto Rico, San Germán Campus was founded in 1912. It is accredited by Middle States Association of Colleges and Schools. It first offered distance learning courses in 1997. In fall 2003, there were 250 students enrolled in distance learning courses. Institutionally administered financial aid is available to distance learners.

Services Distance learners have accessibility to campus computer network, e-mail services, library services.

Contact Prof. Luis M. Zornosa, Distance Learning Coordinator, Inter American University of Puerto Rico, San Germán Campus, PO Box 5100, Department of Management and Entrepreneurial Sciences, San Germán, PR 00683, Puerto Rico. *Telephone:* 787-264-1912 Ext. 7543. *E-mail:* marcolom@alpha.sg.inter.edu.

DEGREES AND AWARDS

Programs offered do not lead to a degree or other formal award.

COURSE SUBJECT AREAS OFFERED OUTSIDE OF DEGREE PROGRAMS

Undergraduate—biological sciences/life sciences, other; business administration and management; business information and data processing services; computer science; engineering, general; English as a second language; general teacher education; health professions and related sciences, other; music; philosophy and religion; social sciences, general.
Graduate—business administration and management; business information and data processing services; education, general; library science/librarianship.

IOWA STATE UNIVERSITY OF SCIENCE AND TECHNOLOGY

Ames, Iowa

Continuing Education and Communication Services

http://www.lifelearner.iastate.edu

Iowa State University of Science and Technology was founded in 1858. It is accredited by North Central Association of Colleges and Schools. It first offered distance learning courses in 1969. In fall 2003, there were 1,144 students enrolled in distance learning courses. Institutionally administered financial aid is available to distance learners.

Services Distance learners have accessibility to academic advising, bookstore, campus computer network, career placement assistance, e-mail services, library services.

Contact Lynette Spicer, Communication Specialist, Iowa State University of Science and Technology, Extension Youth 4-H Building, Ames, IA 50011-3630. *Telephone:* 515-294-1327. *Fax:* 515-294-7767. *E-mail:* lspicer@iastate.edu.

DEGREES AND AWARDS

Certificate Information Assurance; Power Systems Engineering
MAg Agriculture
ME Systems Engineering
MS Agronomy; Computer Engineering; Electrical Engineering; Mechanical Engineering; Statistics

COURSE SUBJECT AREAS OFFERED OUTSIDE OF DEGREE PROGRAMS

Undergraduate—agriculture/agricultural sciences; atmospheric sciences and meteorology; biochemistry and biophysics; biology; economics; entomology; food sciences and technology; individual and family development studies.
Graduate—agricultural economics; agriculture/agricultural sciences; atmospheric sciences and meteorology; biochemistry and biophysics; computer engineering; electrical engineering; family/consumer resource management; foods and nutrition studies; food sciences and technology; industrial/manufacturing engineering; mathematical statistics; mechanical engineering.

IOWA WESTERN COMMUNITY COLLEGE

Council Bluffs, Iowa

http://iwcc.edu

Iowa Western Community College was founded in 1966. It is accredited by North Central Association of Colleges and Schools. It first offered distance learning courses in 1983. In fall 2003, there were 925 students enrolled in distance learning courses. Institutionally administered financial aid is available to distance learners.

Services Distance learners have accessibility to academic advising, bookstore, campus computer network, e-mail services, library services, tutoring.
Contact Barb Vredeveld, Dean, Iowa Western Community College, 2700 College Road, Box 4-C, Council Bluffs, IA 51502. *Telephone:* 712-325-3400. *Fax:* 712-325-3717. *E-mail:* bvredeveld@iwcc.edu.

DEGREES AND AWARDS

AS Liberal Arts and Studies

COURSE SUBJECT AREAS OFFERED OUTSIDE OF DEGREE PROGRAMS

Undergraduate—accounting; advertising; agricultural business and management; American literature (United States); anthropology; applied mathematics; astronomy; biological sciences/life sciences, other; biology, general; business; business administration and management; business communications; chemistry; child care and guidance workers and managers; communications, general; computer and information sciences, general; computer software and media applications; criminal justice and corrections; criminology; data entry/microcomputer applications; dramatic/theater arts and stagecraft; economics; education, general; electrical and electronic engineering-related technology; English composition; English language and literature, general; English language and literature/letters, other; entrepreneurship; financial management and services; fine arts and art studies; geography; health and medical assistants; health and physical education/fitness; history; legal studies; liberal arts and sciences, general studies and humanities; marketing operations/marketing and distribution, other; mathematical statistics; mathematics; mathematics, other; philosophy; philosophy and religion; physical sciences, general; physical sciences, other; political science and government; psychology; social sciences, general; sociology; speech and rhetorical studies.

IRVINE VALLEY COLLEGE

Irvine, California

http://www.ivc.edu

Irvine Valley College was founded in 1979. It is accredited by Western Association of Schools and Colleges. It first offered distance learning courses in 1996. In fall 2003, there were 1,400 students enrolled in distance learning courses. Institutionally administered financial aid is available to distance learners.

Services Distance learners have accessibility to academic advising, bookstore, e-mail services, library services.
Contact Mr. Ruben Guzman, Registrar, Irvine Valley College, 5500 Irvine Center Drive, Office of Admissions, Records and Enrollment Management, Irvine, CA 92618. *Telephone:* 949-451-5461. *Fax:* 949-451-5433. *E-mail:* rguzman@ivc.edu.

DEGREES AND AWARDS

Programs offered do not lead to a degree or other formal award.

COURSE SUBJECT AREAS OFFERED OUTSIDE OF DEGREE PROGRAMS

Undergraduate—accounting; administrative and secretarial services; American literature (United States); applied mathematics; business; business administration and management; business information and data processing services; computer and information sciences, general; computer programming; computer software and media applications; computer systems networking and telecommunications; criminal justice and corrections; data entry/microcomputer applications; English creative writing; English language and literature, general; fine arts and art studies; foreign languages and literatures; Internet and World Wide Web; marketing operations/marketing and distribution, other; mathematics; mathematics, other; music; political science and government; psychology; sociology; student counseling and personnel services; teaching English as a second language/foreign language; visual and performing arts.

IVY TECH STATE COLLEGE–BLOOMINGTON

Bloomington, Indiana

http://www.ivytech.edu/bloomington/

Ivy Tech State College–Bloomington was founded in 2001. It is accredited by North Central Association of Colleges and Schools. In fall 2003, there were 568 students enrolled in distance learning courses. Institutionally administered financial aid is available to distance learners.

Services Distance learners have accessibility to academic advising, bookstore, career placement assistance, e-mail services, library services, tutoring.
Contact Neil Frederick, Assistant Director of Admissions, Ivy Tech State College–Bloomington, 3116 Canterbury Court, Bloomington,

Ivy Tech State College–Bloomington (continued)

IN 47404-0393. *Telephone:* 812-332-1559 Ext. 4118. *Fax:* 812-332-8147. *E-mail:* nfrederi@ivytech.edu.

DEGREES AND AWARDS

AAS Accounting; Business Administration; Computer Information Systems; Design Technology; Early Childhood Education; Human Services; Paralegal
AS Computer Information Systems; Human Services; Paralegal
Technical Certificate Early Childhood Education

COURSE SUBJECT AREAS OFFERED OUTSIDE OF DEGREE PROGRAMS

Undergraduate—accounting; administrative and secretarial services; computer and information sciences, general; computer programming; computer systems analysis; computer systems networking and telecommunications; criminal justice and corrections; electrical and electronic engineering-related technology.

IVY TECH STATE COLLEGE–CENTRAL INDIANA

Indianapolis, Indiana

http://www.ivytech.edu/indianapolis/

Ivy Tech State College–Central Indiana was founded in 1963. It is accredited by North Central Association of Colleges and Schools. It first offered distance learning courses in 1995. In fall 2003, there were 835 students enrolled in distance learning courses. Institutionally administered financial aid is available to distance learners.

Services Distance learners have accessibility to academic advising, bookstore, career placement assistance, e-mail services, library services, tutoring.
Contact Sonia Dickerson, Admissions, Ivy Tech State College–Central Indiana, One West 26th Street, Indianapolis, IN 46208-4777. *Telephone:* 317-921-4612. *Fax:* 317-921-4753. *E-mail:* sdickers@ivytech.edu.

DEGREES AND AWARDS

AAS Accounting; Business Administration; Computer Information Systems; Design Technology; Early Childhood Education; Human Services; Paralegal
AS Computer Information Systems; Human Services; Paralegal
Technical Certificate Early Childhood Education

COURSE SUBJECT AREAS OFFERED OUTSIDE OF DEGREE PROGRAMS

Undergraduate—accounting; administrative and secretarial services; child care and guidance workers and managers; communications, general; fire science; hospitality services management; human services; legal studies.

IVY TECH STATE COLLEGE–COLUMBUS

Columbus, Indiana

http://www.ivytech.edu/columbus/

Ivy Tech State College–Columbus was founded in 1963. It is accredited by North Central Association of Colleges and Schools. It first offered distance learning courses in 1995. In fall 2003, there were 362 students enrolled in distance learning courses. Institutionally administered financial aid is available to distance learners.

Services Distance learners have accessibility to academic advising, bookstore, career placement assistance, e-mail services, library services, tutoring.
Contact Neil S. Bagadiong, Director of Admissions/Assistant to the Dean of Student Affairs, Ivy Tech State College–Columbus, 4475 Central Avenue, Columbus, IN 47203-1868. *Telephone:* 812-372-9925 Ext.. *Fax:* 812-372-0311. *E-mail:* nbagadio@ivytech.edu.

DEGREES AND AWARDS

AAS Accounting; Business Administration; Computer Information Systems; Design Technology; Early Childhood Education; Human Services; Paralegal
AS Computer Information Systems; Human Services; Paralegal
Technical Certificate Early Childhood Education

COURSE SUBJECT AREAS OFFERED OUTSIDE OF DEGREE PROGRAMS

Undergraduate—accounting; administrative and secretarial services; biology, general; business administration and management; computer and information sciences, general; computer programming; computer software and media applications; computer systems analysis; computer systems networking and telecommunications; English composition; human services; marketing operations/marketing and distribution, other; mathematics; physical sciences, general; visual and performing arts.

IVY TECH STATE COLLEGE–EASTCENTRAL

Muncie, Indiana

http://www.ivytech.edu/muncie/

Ivy Tech State College–Eastcentral was founded in 1968. It is accredited by North Central Association of Colleges and Schools. It first offered distance learning courses in 1995. In fall 2003, there were 654 students enrolled in distance learning courses. Institutionally administered financial aid is available to distance learners.

Services Distance learners have accessibility to academic advising, bookstore, career placement assistance, e-mail services, library services, tutoring.
Contact Corey A. Sharp, Recruitment/Outreach Specialist, Ivy Tech State College–Eastcentral, 4301 South Cowan Road, Muncie, IN 47302-9448. *Telephone:* 765-289-2291. *Fax:* 765-289-2292. *E-mail:* csharp@ivytech.edu.

DEGREES AND AWARDS

AAS Accounting; Business Administration; Computer Information Systems; Design Technology; Early Childhood Education; Human Services; Paralegal
AS Computer Information Systems; Human Services; Paralegal
Technical Certificate Early Childhood Education

COURSE SUBJECT AREAS OFFERED OUTSIDE OF DEGREE PROGRAMS

Undergraduate—administrative and secretarial services; business administration and management; child care and guidance workers and managers; criminal justice and corrections; human services; legal studies; mathematics; psychology.

IVY TECH STATE COLLEGE–KOKOMO

Kokomo, Indiana

http://www.ivytech.edu/kokomo/

Ivy Tech State College–Kokomo was founded in 1968. It is accredited by North Central Association of Colleges and Schools. It first offered distance learning courses in 1995. In fall 2003, there were 305 students enrolled in distance learning courses. Institutionally administered financial aid is available to distance learners.

Services Distance learners have accessibility to academic advising, bookstore, career placement assistance, e-mail services, library services, tutoring.

Contact Alayne Cook, Director of Admissions Coordinator, Ivy Tech State College–Kokomo, 1815 East Morgan Street, Kokomo, IN 46903-1373. *Telephone:* 765-459-0561 Ext. 318. *Fax:* 765-454-5111. *E-mail:* acook@ivytech.edu.

DEGREES AND AWARDS

AAS Accounting; Business Administration; Computer Information Systems; Design Technology; Early Childhood Education; Human Services; Paralegal

AS Computer Information Systems; Human Services; Paralegal

Technical Certificate Early Childhood Education

COURSE SUBJECT AREAS OFFERED OUTSIDE OF DEGREE PROGRAMS

Undergraduate—accounting; administrative and secretarial services; business administration and management; computer and information sciences, general; computer programming; computer science; computer software and media applications; computer systems analysis; computer systems networking and telecommunications; criminal justice and corrections; English composition; history; quality control and safety technologies.

IVY TECH STATE COLLEGE–LAFAYETTE

Lafayette, Indiana

http://www.ivytech.edu/lafayette/

Ivy Tech State College–Lafayette was founded in 1968. It is accredited by North Central Association of Colleges and Schools. It first offered distance learning courses in 1995. In fall 2003, there were 305 students enrolled in distance learning courses. Institutionally administered financial aid is available to distance learners.

Services Distance learners have accessibility to academic advising, bookstore, career placement assistance, e-mail services, library services, tutoring.

Contact Judy Doppelfeld, Director of Admissions, Ivy Tech State College–Lafayette, 3101 South Creasy Lane, Lafayette, IN 47903. *Telephone:* 765-772-9116. *Fax:* 765-772-9107. *E-mail:* jdoppelf@ivytech.edu.

DEGREES AND AWARDS

AAS Accounting; Business Administration; Computer Information Systems; Design Technology; Early Childhood Education; Human Services; Paralegal

AS Computer Information Systems; Human Services; Paralegal

Technical Certificate Early Childhood Education

COURSE SUBJECT AREAS OFFERED OUTSIDE OF DEGREE PROGRAMS

Undergraduate—computer and information sciences, general; computer programming; computer science; computer software and media applications; computer systems analysis; computer systems networking and telecommunications.

IVY TECH STATE COLLEGE–NORTH CENTRAL

South Bend, Indiana

Instructional Technology

http://www.ivytech.edu/southbend/

Ivy Tech State College–North Central was founded in 1968. It is accredited by North Central Association of Colleges and Schools. It first offered distance learning courses in 1993. In fall 2003, there were 691 students enrolled in distance learning courses. Institutionally administered financial aid is available to distance learners.

Services Distance learners have accessibility to academic advising, bookstore, career placement assistance, e-mail services, library services, tutoring.

Contact Pam Decker, Director of Admissions, Ivy Tech State College–North Central, 220 Dean Johnson Boulevard, South Bend, IN 46601. *Telephone:* 219-289-7001. *Fax:* 219-236-7177. *E-mail:* pdecker@ivytech.edu.

DEGREES AND AWARDS

AAS Accounting; Business Administration; Computer Information Systems; Design Technology; Early Childhood Education; Human Services; Paralegal

AS Computer Information Systems; Human Services; Paralegal

Technical Certificate Early Childhood Education

COURSE SUBJECT AREAS OFFERED OUTSIDE OF DEGREE PROGRAMS

Undergraduate—accounting; administrative and secretarial services; biology, general; business administration and management; computer and information sciences, general; computer programming; computer software and media applications; computer systems analysis; computer systems networking and telecommunications; economics; English composition; human services; legal studies; marketing operations/marketing and distribution, other; philosophy; political science and government; psychology; sociology; visual and performing arts, other.

IVY TECH STATE COLLEGE–NORTHEAST

Fort Wayne, Indiana

http://www.ivytech.edu/fortwayne/

Ivy Tech State College–Northeast was founded in 1969. It is accredited by North Central Association of Colleges and Schools. It first offered distance learning courses in 1995. In fall 2003, there were 526 students enrolled in distance learning courses. Institutionally administered financial aid is available to distance learners.

Services Distance learners have accessibility to academic advising, bookstore, campus computer network, career placement assistance, library services, tutoring.

Ivy Tech State College–Northeast (continued)

Contact Steve Scheer, Director of Admissions, Ivy Tech State College–Northeast, 3800 North Anthony Boulevard, Fort Wayne, IN 46805-1489. *Telephone:* 219-482-9171. *Fax:* 219-480-4252. *E-mail:* sscheer@ivytech.edu.

DEGREES AND AWARDS

AAS Accounting; Business Administration; Computer Information Systems; Design Technology; Early Childhood Education; Human Services; Paralegal

AS Computer Information Systems; Human Services; Human Services; Paralegal

Technical Certificate Early Childhood Education

COURSE SUBJECT AREAS OFFERED OUTSIDE OF DEGREE PROGRAMS

Undergraduate—administrative and secretarial services; child care and guidance workers and managers; construction/building technology; fire protection; human services.

IVY TECH STATE COLLEGE–NORTHWEST

Gary, Indiana

http://www.ivytech.edu/gary

Ivy Tech State College–Northwest was founded in 1963. It is accredited by North Central Association of Colleges and Schools. It first offered distance learning courses in 1995. In fall 2003, there were 974 students enrolled in distance learning courses. Institutionally administered financial aid is available to distance learners.

Services Distance learners have accessibility to academic advising, bookstore, career placement assistance, e-mail services, library services, tutoring.

Contact Twilla Lewis, Associate Dean of Student Affairs, Ivy Tech State College–Northwest, 1440 East 35th Avenue, Gary, IN 46409-1499. *Telephone:* 219-981-1111 Ext. 273. *Fax:* 219-981-4415. *E-mail:* tlewis@ivytech.edu.

DEGREES AND AWARDS

AAS Accounting; Business Administration; Computer Information Systems; Design Technology; Early Childhood Education; Human Services; Paralegal Studies; Paralegal

AS Computer Information Systems; Human Services; Paralegal

COURSE SUBJECT AREAS OFFERED OUTSIDE OF DEGREE PROGRAMS

Undergraduate—accounting; administrative and secretarial services; business administration and management; business marketing and marketing management; child care and guidance workers and managers; communications, general; computer programming; computer software and media applications; computer systems analysis; computer systems networking and telecommunications; economics; English composition; environmental science; fire science; history; hospitality services management; human services; mathematics; nursing; physical sciences, general; psychology; sociology.

IVY TECH STATE COLLEGE–SOUTHCENTRAL

Sellersburg, Indiana

http://www.ivytech.edu/sellersburg/

Ivy Tech State College–Southcentral was founded in 1968. It is accredited by North Central Association of Colleges and Schools. It first offered distance learning courses in 1995. In fall 2003, there were 350 students enrolled in distance learning courses. Institutionally administered financial aid is available to distance learners.

Services Distance learners have accessibility to academic advising, bookstore, career placement assistance, e-mail services, library services, tutoring.

Contact Mindy B. Steinberg, Director of Admission, Ivy Tech State College–Southcentral, 8204 Highway 311, Sellersburg, IN 47172-1897. *Telephone:* 812-246-4137. *Fax:* 812-246-9905. *E-mail:* msteinbe@ivytech.edu.

DEGREES AND AWARDS

AAS Accounting; Business Administration; Computer Information Systems; Design Technology; Early Childhood Education; Human Services; Paralegal

AS Computer Information Systems; Human Services; Paralegal

Technical Certificate Early Childhood Education

COURSE SUBJECT AREAS OFFERED OUTSIDE OF DEGREE PROGRAMS

Undergraduate—accounting; administrative and secretarial services; business administration and management; economics; history; marketing management and research; mathematics; physical sciences, general; sociology.

IVY TECH STATE COLLEGE–SOUTHEAST

Madison, Indiana

http://www.ivytech.edu/madison/

Ivy Tech State College–Southeast was founded in 1963. It is accredited by North Central Association of Colleges and Schools. It first offered distance learning courses in 1995. In fall 2003, there were 332 students enrolled in distance learning courses. Institutionally administered financial aid is available to distance learners.

Services Distance learners have accessibility to academic advising, bookstore, career placement assistance, e-mail services, library services, tutoring.

Contact Cindy Hutcherson, Assistant Director of Admissions and Career Counselor, Ivy Tech State College–Southeast, 590 Ivy Tech Drive, Madison, IN 47250-1881. *Telephone:* 812-265-2580. *Fax:* 812-265-4028. *E-mail:* chutcher@ivytech.edu.

DEGREES AND AWARDS

AAS Accounting; Business Administration; Computer Information Systems; Design Technology; Early Childhood Education; Human Services; Paralegal

AS Computer Information Systems; Human Services; Paralegal

Technical Certificate Early Childhood Education

COURSE SUBJECT AREAS OFFERED OUTSIDE OF DEGREE PROGRAMS

Undergraduate—administrative and secretarial services; computer and information sciences, general; computer programming; computer software and media applications; computer systems analysis; computer systems networking and telecommunications; environmental control technologies.

IVY TECH STATE COLLEGE–SOUTHWEST

Evansville, Indiana

http://www.ivytech.edu/evansville/

Ivy Tech State College–Southwest was founded in 1963. It is accredited by North Central Association of Colleges and Schools. It first offered distance learning courses in 1995. In fall 2003, there were 375 students enrolled in distance learning courses. Institutionally administered financial aid is available to distance learners.

Services Distance learners have accessibility to academic advising, bookstore, career placement assistance, e-mail services, library services, tutoring.

Contact Denise Johnson-Kincade, Assistant Director, Ivy Tech State College–Southwest, 3501 First Avenue, Evansville, IN 47710-3398. *Telephone:* 812-429-1430. *Fax:* 812-246-9905 Ext.. *E-mail:* ajohnson@ivytech.edu.

DEGREES AND AWARDS

AAS Accounting; Business Administration; Computer Information Systems; Design Technology; Early Childhood Education; Human Services; Paralegal
AS Computer Information Systems; Human Services; Paralegal
Technical Certificate Early Childhood Education

COURSE SUBJECT AREAS OFFERED OUTSIDE OF DEGREE PROGRAMS

Undergraduate—accounting; business administration and management; child care and guidance workers and managers; computer and information sciences, general; computer programming; computer software and media applications; computer systems analysis; computer systems networking and telecommunications; design and applied arts; human services; marketing management and research; mathematics.

IVY TECH STATE COLLEGE–WABASH VALLEY

Terre Haute, Indiana

http://www.ivytech.edu/terrehaute/

Ivy Tech State College–Wabash Valley was founded in 1966. It is accredited by North Central Association of Colleges and Schools. It first offered distance learning courses in 1996. In fall 2003, there were 1,284 students enrolled in distance learning courses. Institutionally administered financial aid is available to distance learners.

Services Distance learners have accessibility to academic advising, bookstore, career placement assistance, e-mail services, library services, tutoring.

Contact Michael Fisher, Assessment Coordinator, Ivy Tech State College–Wabash Valley, 7999 US Highway 41, Terre Haute, IN 47802-4898. *Telephone:* 812-299-1121. *Fax:* 812-299-5723. *E-mail:* mfisher@ivytech.edu.

DEGREES AND AWARDS

AAS Accounting; Business Administration; Computer Information Systems; Design Technology; Early Childhood Education; Human Services; Paralegal
AS Computer Information Systems; Human Services; Paralegal
Technical Certificate Accounting; Business Administration; Design; Early Childhood Education

COURSE SUBJECT AREAS OFFERED OUTSIDE OF DEGREE PROGRAMS

Undergraduate—accounting; administrative and secretarial services; biology, general; business administration and management; communications, general; computer and information sciences, general; computer programming; computer software and media applications; computer systems analysis; computer systems networking and telecommunications; design and applied arts; drafting; economics; electrical and electronic engineering-related technology; English composition; history; human services; marketing management and research; mathematics; physical sciences, general; physics; psychology; sociology.

IVY TECH STATE COLLEGE–WHITEWATER

Richmond, Indiana

http://www.ivytech.edu/richmond/

Ivy Tech State College–Whitewater was founded in 1963. It is accredited by North Central Association of Colleges and Schools. It first offered distance learning courses in 1995. In fall 2003, there were 552 students enrolled in distance learning courses. Institutionally administered financial aid is available to distance learners.

Services Distance learners have accessibility to academic advising, bookstore, career placement assistance, e-mail services, library services, tutoring.

Contact Jeff Plasterer, Director of Admissions, Ivy Tech State College–Whitewater, 2325 Chester Boulevard, Richmond, IN 47374-1298. *Telephone:* 765-966-2656 Ext. 320. *Fax:* 765-962-8741. *E-mail:* jplaster@ivytech.edu.

DEGREES AND AWARDS

AAS Accounting; Business Administration; Computer Information Systems; Design Technology; Early Childhood Education; Human Services; Paralegal
AS Computer Information Systems; Human Services; Paralegal
Technical Certificate Early Childhood Education

COURSE SUBJECT AREAS OFFERED OUTSIDE OF DEGREE PROGRAMS

Undergraduate—accounting; administrative and secretarial services; biology, general; business administration and management; communications, general; computer and information sciences, general; computer programming; computer software and media applications; computer systems analysis; computer systems networking and telecommunications; economics; English composition; history; human services; industrial equipment maintenance and repairers; marketing management and research; mathematics; psychology; sociology.

JACKSONVILLE STATE UNIVERSITY

Jacksonville, Alabama

Department of Distance Education

http://distance.jsu.edu

Jacksonville State University was founded in 1883. It is accredited by Southern Association of Colleges and Schools. It first offered distance learning courses in 1994. In fall 2003, there were 5,000 students enrolled in distance learning courses. Institutionally administered financial aid is available to distance learners.

Services Distance learners have accessibility to academic advising, bookstore, campus computer network, career placement assistance, e-mail services, library services, tutoring.

Contact Dr. Franklin L. King, Director of Distance Education, Jacksonville State University, 700 Pelham Road North, Jacksonville, AL 36265-1602. *Telephone:* 256-782-5616. *Fax:* 256-782-8128. *E-mail:* fking@jsucc.jsu.edu.

DEGREES AND AWARDS

BS Emergency Management (Public Safety Communications minor)
MPA Emergency Management; Spatial Analysis and Management Concentration
MS Emergency Management

COURSE SUBJECT AREAS OFFERED OUTSIDE OF DEGREE PROGRAMS

Undergraduate—accounting; American literature (United States); anthropology; applied mathematics; atmospheric sciences and meteorology; biological and physical sciences; biological sciences/life sciences, other; biology, general; business; business administration and management; business and personal services marketing operations; business information and data processing services; business management and administrative services, other; business/managerial economics; business quantitative methods and management science; child care and guidance workers and managers; community health services; computer and information sciences, general; computer and information sciences, other; computer/information technology administration and management; computer programming; computer science; computer software and media applications; computer systems analysis; computer systems networking and telecommunications; criminal justice and corrections; criminology; curriculum and instruction; data processing technology; developmental and child psychology; developmental/child psychology; economics; education administration and supervision; educational evaluation, research and statistics; educational psychology; education, general; education, other; engineering, general; English composition; English language and literature, general; English language and literature/letters, other; English literature (British and Commonwealth); environmental control technologies; financial management and services; foods and nutrition studies; general teacher education; geography; geological and related sciences; health and physical education/fitness; health professions and related sciences, other; history; information sciences and systems; marketing management and research; marketing operations/marketing and distribution, other; mathematical statistics; mathematics; mathematics and computer science; mathematics, other; medical basic sciences; medical residency programs; music; nursing; physics; political science and government; protective services, other; psychology; psychology, other; public administration; public administration and services, other; quality control and safety technologies; school psychology; social sciences, general; social work; sociology; special education; student counseling and personnel services; teacher education, specific academic and vocational programs; technology education/industrial arts.

Graduate—accounting; business; business administration and management; business and personal services marketing operations; business communications; business information and data processing services; business management and administrative services, other; business/managerial economics; business quantitative methods and management science; computer and information sciences, general; computer and information sciences, other; computer engineering; computer/information technology administration and management; computer programming; computer science; computer software and media applications; computer systems analysis; computer systems networking and telecommunications; criminal justice and corrections; criminology; curriculum and instruction; developmental and child psychology; economics; education administration and supervision; educational evaluation, research and statistics; educational/instructional media design; educational psychology; education, general; education, other; environmental control technologies; family and community studies; financial management and services; financial services marketing operations; fire protection; geography; geological and related sciences; health and physical education/fitness; health professions and related sciences, other; human resources management; individual and family development studies; information sciences and systems; marketing management and research; marketing operations/marketing and distribution, other; mathematical statistics; mathematics and computer science; medical basic sciences; medical residency programs; miscellaneous health professions; nursing; political science and government; professional studies; protective services, other; public administration; public administration and services, other; quality control and safety technologies; school psychology; social sciences, general; social work; sociology; special education; teacher education, specific academic and vocational programs.

JAMES MADISON UNIVERSITY

Harrisonburg, Virginia

Distance Learning Center, Office of Continuing Education

http://jmuonline.jmu.edu

James Madison University was founded in 1908. It is accredited by Southern Association of Colleges and Schools. It first offered distance learning courses in 1996. In fall 2003, there were 250 students enrolled in distance learning courses. Institutionally administered financial aid is available to distance learners.

Services Distance learners have accessibility to academic advising, bookstore, career placement assistance, e-mail services, library services.

Contact Jim Mazoue, PhD, Distance Learning Coordinator, Distributed and Distance Learning, James Madison University, 111A Carrier Library, MSC 1702, Harrisonburg, VA 22807. *Telephone:* 540-568-2591. *Fax:* 540-568-6734. *E-mail:* mazouejg@jmu.edu.

DEGREES AND AWARDS

MBA Information Security
MCC Information Security

COURSE SUBJECT AREAS OFFERED OUTSIDE OF DEGREE PROGRAMS

Undergraduate—accounting; adult/continuing education; biological technology; business; communications, general; communications technologies; English composition; English technical and business writ-

ing; foreign languages and literatures; health and physical education/fitness; health professions and related sciences, other; human resources management; mathematical statistics; philosophy; psychology.
Graduate—special education.
Non-credit—American literature (United States); applied mathematics; archaeology; architecture; astronomy; astrophysics; biological and physical sciences; biological sciences/life sciences, other; business; business and personal services marketing operations; business communications; business management and administrative services, other; business quantitative methods and management science; communication disorders sciences and services; communications, other; computer programming; computer science; computer systems networking and telecommunications; conservation and renewable natural resources, other; construction/building technology; construction management; construction trades, other; consumer and homemaking education; cosmetic services; counseling psychology; crafts, folk art and artisanry; criminal justice and corrections; culinary arts and related services; data entry/microcomputer applications; education, general; English as a second language; English composition; English creative writing; English language and literature, general; entrepreneurship; film/video and photographic arts; financial services marketing operations; fine arts and art studies; fire protection; food products retailing and wholesaling operations; foods and nutrition studies; foreign languages and literatures; forestry and related sciences; gaming/sports officiating; general teacher education; geography; geological and related sciences; Germanic languages and literatures; health and medical diagnostic and treatment services; health and medical preparatory programs; health and physical education/fitness; history; home economics, general; hospitality/recreation marketing; human resources management; human services; information sciences and systems; international business; journalism and mass communications; landscape architecture; liberal arts and sciences, general studies and humanities; library assistant; marketing management and research; marketing operations/marketing and distribution, other; mathematics and computer science; miscellaneous biological specializations; miscellaneous health aides; miscellaneous health professions; miscellaneous mechanics and repairers; miscellaneous physical sciences; museology/museum studies; music; nursing; parks, recreation, leisure and fitness studies, other; physical sciences, general; physical sciences, other; physics; plant sciences; political science and government; public administration; public health; public relations and organizational communications; quality control and safety technologies; radio and television broadcasting; real estate; Romance languages and literatures; social sciences, general; special education; speech and rhetorical studies; student counseling and personnel services; systems engineering; taxation; telecommunications; transportation and materials moving workers, other; urban affairs/studies; visual and performing arts.

JAMESTOWN COMMUNITY COLLEGE

Jamestown, New York

Distance Education

http://www.sunyjcc.edu/online

Jamestown Community College was founded in 1950. It is accredited by Middle States Association of Colleges and Schools. It first offered distance learning courses in 1995. In fall 2003, there were 150 students enrolled in distance learning courses. Institutionally administered financial aid is available to distance learners.

Services Distance learners have accessibility to academic advising, bookstore, campus computer network, career placement assistance, e-mail services, library services, tutoring.

Contact Admissions Director, Admissions Office, Jamestown Community College, 525 Falconer Street, PO Box 20, Jamestown, NY 14702-0020. *Telephone:* 800-388-8557 Ext. 2476. *Fax:* 716-664-9592. *E-mail:* admissions@mail.sunyjcc.edu.

DEGREES AND AWARDS

AAS Computer Information Systems
AS Computer Science

COURSE SUBJECT AREAS OFFERED OUTSIDE OF DEGREE PROGRAMS

Non-credit—accounting; administrative and secretarial services; business; business administration and management; business communications; communications, general; computer and information sciences, general; computer and information sciences, other; computer software and media applications; computer systems networking and telecommunications; English composition; English creative writing; enterprise management and operation; financial management and services; food sciences and technology; foreign languages and literatures; health and medical administrative services; human resources management; human services; Internet and World Wide Web; journalism and mass communications; legal studies; liberal arts and sciences, general studies and humanities; marketing management and research; psychology, other; real estate; sociology.

JEFFERSON COLLEGE

Hillsboro, Missouri

Learning Resources

http://www.jeffco.edu/

Jefferson College was founded in 1963. It is accredited by North Central Association of Colleges and Schools. It first offered distance learning courses in 1984. In fall 2003, there were 540 students enrolled in distance learning courses. Institutionally administered financial aid is available to distance learners.

Services Distance learners have accessibility to academic advising, bookstore, campus computer network, career placement assistance, e-mail services, library services.
Contact Mr. Allan A. Wamsley, Director of Instructional Support Center, Jefferson College, 1000 Viking Drive, Hillsboro, MO 63050. *Telephone:* 636-797-3000 Ext. 342. *Fax:* 636-789-5801. *E-mail:* awamsley@jeffco.edu.

DEGREES AND AWARDS

Programs offered do not lead to a degree or other formal award.

COURSE SUBJECT AREAS OFFERED OUTSIDE OF DEGREE PROGRAMS

Undergraduate—American history; biological and physical sciences; biology, general; business; computer software and media applications; economics; English composition; European history; geography; Germanic languages and literatures; health and physical education/fitness; mathematics; music; philosophy; physics; psychology; sociology; speech and rhetorical studies; visual and performing arts.

JEFFERSON COLLEGE OF HEALTH SCIENCES

Roanoke, Virginia

http://www.jchs.edu/

Jefferson College of Health Sciences was founded in 1982. It is accredited by Southern Association of Colleges and Schools. It first

Jefferson College of Health Sciences (continued)

offered distance learning courses in 1999. In fall 2003, there were 300 students enrolled in distance learning courses. Institutionally administered financial aid is available to distance learners.

Services Distance learners have accessibility to academic advising, bookstore, e-mail services, library services.

Contact Jennifer Becker, Educational Resource Associate, Jefferson College of Health Sciences, PO Box 13186, Roanoke, VA 24031. *Telephone:* 540-985-8573. *Fax:* 540-985-8512. *E-mail:* jhbecker@jchs.edu.

DEGREES AND AWARDS

Programs offered do not lead to a degree or other formal award.

COURSE SUBJECT AREAS OFFERED OUTSIDE OF DEGREE PROGRAMS

Undergraduate—community health services; computer software and media applications; English composition; English technical and business writing; foods and nutrition studies; gerontology; health and medical diagnostic and treatment services; health and medical preparatory programs; health and physical education/fitness; health professions and related sciences, other; human resources management; mathematical statistics; miscellaneous health professions; nursing; philosophy; psychology; public health; sociology.

Non-credit—health and medical diagnostic and treatment services; nursing.

JEFFERSON COMMUNITY COLLEGE

Watertown, New York

Division of Continuing Education

http://www.sunyjefferson.edu

Jefferson Community College was founded in 1961. It is accredited by Middle States Association of Colleges and Schools. It first offered distance learning courses in 1995. In fall 2003, there were 500 students enrolled in distance learning courses. Institutionally administered financial aid is available to distance learners.

Services Distance learners have accessibility to academic advising, bookstore, career placement assistance, e-mail services, library services, tutoring.

Contact MaKeever Clarke, Distance Learning Coordinator, Jefferson Community College, 1220 Coffeen Street, Watertown, NY 13601. *Telephone:* 315-786-6527. *Fax:* 315-786-0158. *E-mail:* mclarke@sunyjefferson.edu.

DEGREES AND AWARDS

AA Individual Studies; Liberal Arts–Humanities and Social Science
AAS Individual Studies
AS Business Administration; Criminal Justice; Individual Studies

COURSE SUBJECT AREAS OFFERED OUTSIDE OF DEGREE PROGRAMS

Undergraduate—business administration and management; business management and administrative services, other; economics; English composition; English technical and business writing; history; mathematics related; psychology; sociology.

JEFFERSON DAVIS COMMUNITY COLLEGE

Brewton, Alabama

http://www.jdcc.edu

Jefferson Davis Community College was founded in 1965. It is accredited by Southern Association of Colleges and Schools. It first offered distance learning courses in 1994. In fall 2003, there were 137 students enrolled in distance learning courses. Institutionally administered financial aid is available to distance learners.

Services Distance learners have accessibility to library services.

Contact Kathleen Hall, Dean of Instruction, Jefferson Davis Community College, PO Box 958, Brewton, AL 36427. *Telephone:* 251-809-1500. *Fax:* 251-809-1527. *E-mail:* kathleen.hall@jdcc.edu.

DEGREES AND AWARDS

Programs offered do not lead to a degree or other formal award.

COURSE SUBJECT AREAS OFFERED OUTSIDE OF DEGREE PROGRAMS

Undergraduate—accounting; computer software and media applications; economics; English composition; health and physical education/fitness; mathematical statistics; political science and government.

THE JEWISH THEOLOGICAL SEMINARY

New York, New York

http://courses.jtsa.edu/

The Jewish Theological Seminary was founded in 1886. It is accredited by Middle States Association of Colleges and Schools. It first offered distance learning courses in 1996. In fall 2003, there were 60 students enrolled in distance learning courses. Institutionally administered financial aid is available to distance learners.

Services Distance learners have accessibility to academic advising, career placement assistance, e-mail services, library services, tutoring.

Contact Department of Distance Learning, The Jewish Theological Seminary, 3080 Broadway, Mailbox 90, New York, NY 10027. *Telephone:* 212-678-8897. *Fax:* 212-749-9085. *E-mail:* dlp@jtsa.edu.

DEGREES AND AWARDS

MA Interdepartmental Studies–Judaic Studies; Jewish Education

COURSE SUBJECT AREAS OFFERED OUTSIDE OF DEGREE PROGRAMS

Undergraduate—archaeology; bible/biblical studies; biblical and other theological languages and literatures; classical and ancient Near Eastern languages and literatures; history; Middle Eastern languages and literatures; philosophy; philosophy and religion; religion/religious studies; religious education; teacher education, specific academic and vocational programs.

Graduate—archaeology; bible/biblical studies; biblical and other theological languages and literatures; classical and ancient Near Eastern languages and literatures; history; Middle Eastern languages and literatures; philosophy; philosophy and religion; religion/religious studies; religious education; teacher education, specific academic and vocational programs.

Non-credit—archaeology; bible/biblical studies; biblical and other theological languages and literatures; classical and ancient Near Eastern languages and literatures; history; Middle Eastern languages and literatures; philosophy; philosophy and religion; religion/religious studies; religious education; teacher education, specific academic and vocational programs.

JOHN A. LOGAN COLLEGE

Carterville, Illinois
Learning Resources
http://www.jalc.edu

John A. Logan College was founded in 1967. It is accredited by North Central Association of Colleges and Schools. It first offered distance learning courses in 1979. In fall 2003, there were 589 students enrolled in distance learning courses. Institutionally administered financial aid is available to distance learners.

Services Distance learners have accessibility to academic advising, campus computer network, career placement assistance, library services, tutoring.

Contact Robert Fester, Advisor and Counselor, John A. Logan College, 700 Logan College Road, Carterville, IL 62918. *Telephone:* 618-985-2828 Ext. 8385. *E-mail:* bob.fester@jal.cc.il.us.

DEGREES AND AWARDS

Programs offered do not lead to a degree or other formal award.

COURSE SUBJECT AREAS OFFERED OUTSIDE OF DEGREE PROGRAMS

Undergraduate—accounting; biological and physical sciences; business; computer and information sciences, general; English composition; English creative writing; fine arts and art studies; history; liberal arts and sciences, general studies and humanities; political science and government; psychology.

JOHN F. KENNEDY UNIVERSITY

Pleasant Hill, California
http://www.jfku.edu

John F. Kennedy University was founded in 1964. It is accredited by Western Association of Schools and Colleges. Institutionally administered financial aid is available to distance learners.

Contact Ellena Bloedorn, Director of Admissions, John F. Kennedy University, 100 Ellinwood Way, Pleasant Hill, CA 94523-4817. *Telephone:* 925-969-3330. *Fax:* 925-969-3331. *E-mail:* bloedorn@jfku.edu.

DEGREES AND AWARDS

Programs offered do not lead to a degree or other formal award.

COURSE SUBJECT AREAS OFFERED OUTSIDE OF DEGREE PROGRAMS

Undergraduate—area, ethnic and cultural studies, other; business; business administration and management; cultural studies; education, general; liberal arts and sciences, general studies and humanities; philosophy and religion; physical sciences, general; psychology.

Graduate—area, ethnic and cultural studies, other; biological sciences/life sciences, other; business administration and management; clinical psychology; counseling psychology; criminology; cultural studies; design and applied arts; developmental and child psychology; fine arts and art studies; general teacher education; legal studies; museology/museum studies; peace and conflict studies; philosophy and religion; psychology; visual and performing arts.

JOHN JAY COLLEGE OF CRIMINAL JUSTICE OF THE CITY UNIVERSITY OF NEW YORK

New York, New York
http://www.jjay.cuny.edu

John Jay College of Criminal Justice of the City University of New York was founded in 1964. It is accredited by Middle States Association of Colleges and Schools. It first offered distance learning courses in 1999. In fall 2003, there were 5,000 students enrolled in distance learning courses. Institutionally administered financial aid is available to distance learners.

Services Distance learners have accessibility to e-mail services, library services.

Contact Prof. Robert James Hong, Director of Educational Technology, John Jay College of Criminal Justice of the City University of New York, 445 West 59th Street, Room 3410 North Hall, New York, NY 10019-1107. *Telephone:* 212-237-8849. *Fax:* 212-237-8919. *E-mail:* rhong@jjay.cuny.edu.

DEGREES AND AWARDS

Programs offered do not lead to a degree or other formal award.

COURSE SUBJECT AREAS OFFERED OUTSIDE OF DEGREE PROGRAMS

Undergraduate—computer/information technology administration and management; criminal justice and corrections; economics; English technical and business writing; health and physical education/fitness; legal studies; public administration.

Graduate—protective services, other; public administration.

THE JOHNS HOPKINS UNIVERSITY

Baltimore, Maryland
School of Continuing Studies, Electronic and Distance Education
http://webapps.jhu.edu/jhuniverse/academics/distance_education/

The Johns Hopkins University was founded in 1876. It is accredited by Middle States Association of Colleges and Schools. It first offered distance learning courses in 1998. In fall 2003, there were 300 students enrolled in distance learning courses. Institutionally administered financial aid is available to distance learners.

Services Distance learners have accessibility to academic advising, bookstore, campus computer network, e-mail services, library services, tutoring.

Contact Dr. Candice V. Dalrymple, Associate Dean and Director of Center for Educational Resources, The Johns Hopkins University, Administration Office, Milton S. Eisenhower Library, 3400 North Charles Street, Baltimore, MD 21218. *Telephone:* 410-516-8848. *Fax:* 410-516-5080. *E-mail:* cdalrymple@jhu.edu.

The Johns Hopkins University (continued)

DEGREES AND AWARDS

Programs offered do not lead to a degree or other formal award.

JOHNSON BIBLE COLLEGE

Knoxville, Tennessee
Distance Learning Office
http://www.jbc.edu/mastersnt/

Johnson Bible College was founded in 1893. It is accredited by Accrediting Association of Bible Colleges. It first offered distance learning courses in 1988. In fall 2003, there were 61 students enrolled in distance learning courses. Institutionally administered financial aid is available to distance learners.

Services Distance learners have accessibility to academic advising, bookstore, campus computer network, e-mail services, library services.

Contact Dr. John C. Ketchen, Director of Distance Learning, Johnson Bible College, 7900 Johnson Drive, Knoxville, TN 37998. *Telephone:* 865-251-2254. *Fax:* 865-251-2285. *E-mail:* mketchen@jbc.edu.

DEGREES AND AWARDS

MA New Testament

COURSE SUBJECT AREAS OFFERED OUTSIDE OF DEGREE PROGRAMS

Graduate—bible/biblical studies.

JOHNSON COUNTY COMMUNITY COLLEGE

Overland Park, Kansas
http://www.jccc.net

Johnson County Community College was founded in 1967. It is accredited by North Central Association of Colleges and Schools. It first offered distance learning courses in 1975. In fall 2003, there were 2,500 students enrolled in distance learning courses. Institutionally administered financial aid is available to distance learners.

Services Distance learners have accessibility to academic advising, bookstore, campus computer network, career placement assistance, e-mail services, library services, tutoring.

Contact Dr. Bill Lamb, Dean of Liberal Arts and Distance Learning, Johnson County Community College, 12345 College Boulevard, Overland Park, KS 66210-1299. *Telephone:* 913-469-8500 Ext. 2339. *Fax:* 913-469-2585. *E-mail:* blamb@jccc.net.

DEGREES AND AWARDS

AA Multidisciplinary Study
AGS General Studies

COURSE SUBJECT AREAS OFFERED OUTSIDE OF DEGREE PROGRAMS

Undergraduate—accounting; American history; anthropology; biology; business marketing and marketing management; chemistry; computer software and media applications; computer systems networking and telecommunications; economics; English composition; English literature (British and Commonwealth); English technical and business writing; environmental science; mathematics; oceanography; paralegal/legal assistant; psychology; sociology; speech and rhetorical studies.

Non-credit—computer software and media applications; health and medical administrative services; health and medical preparatory programs; real estate.

JOHN TYLER COMMUNITY COLLEGE

Chester, Virginia
http://www.jtcc.edu/DistanceEd

John Tyler Community College was founded in 1967. It is accredited by Southern Association of Colleges and Schools. It first offered distance learning courses in 1997. In fall 2003, there were 729 students enrolled in distance learning courses. Institutionally administered financial aid is available to distance learners.

Services Distance learners have accessibility to bookstore, e-mail services, library services.

Contact Mrs. Angela Branch, Instructional Center Technician, John Tyler Community College, 13101 Jefferson Davis Highway, Chester, VA 23831-5316. *Telephone:* 804-594-1625. *Fax:* 804-594-1591. *E-mail:* distanceed@jtcc.edu.

DEGREES AND AWARDS

AAS Arts and Sciences for Transfer

COURSE SUBJECT AREAS OFFERED OUTSIDE OF DEGREE PROGRAMS

Undergraduate—accounting; administrative and secretarial services; applied mathematics; architectural engineering technology; biology, general; business administration and management; business management and administrative services, other; chemistry; child care and guidance workers and managers; community health services; computer and information sciences, general; computer and information sciences, other; computer/information technology administration and management; computer systems networking and telecommunications; criminal justice and corrections; data entry/microcomputer applications; developmental and child psychology; drafting; economics; education, general; English composition; English creative writing; English language and literature, general; fine arts and art studies; foreign languages and literatures, other; funeral services and mortuary science; liberal arts and sciences, general studies and humanities; mechanics and repairers, other; music; nursing; philosophy; physical sciences, general; physics; psychology; public administration and services, other; Romance languages and literatures; social psychology; social sciences and history, other; sociology; soil sciences; teacher assistant/aide; teacher education, specific academic and vocational programs.

JOHN WOOD COMMUNITY COLLEGE

Quincy, Illinois
Alternative and Distance Learning Center
http://www.jwcc.edu/instruct/

John Wood Community College was founded in 1974. It is accredited by North Central Association of Colleges and Schools. It first offered distance learning courses in 1987. In fall 2003, there were 400 students enrolled in distance learning courses. Institutionally administered financial aid is available to distance learners.

Services Distance learners have accessibility to academic advising, bookstore, career placement assistance, e-mail services, library services, tutoring.

Contact Mark McNett, Director of Admissions, John Wood Community College, 1301 South 48th Street, Quincy, IL 62305. *Telephone:* 217-224-6500 Ext. 4339. *Fax:* 217-224-4208. *E-mail:* mcnett@jwcc.edu.

DEGREES AND AWARDS

Programs offered do not lead to a degree or other formal award.

COURSE SUBJECT AREAS OFFERED OUTSIDE OF DEGREE PROGRAMS

Undergraduate—accounting; American history; anatomy; anthropology; Army R.O.T.C.; art history; astronomy; business; business administration and management; computer and information sciences, general; criminal justice and corrections; data entry/microcomputer applications; developmental/child psychology; economics; educational psychology; English composition; health and physical education/fitness; Internet and World Wide Web; liberal arts and sciences, general studies and humanities; mathematical statistics; mathematics; military studies; music; philosophy; philosophy and religion; philosophy and religion related; physical sciences, general; physics; plant sciences; political science and government; protective services, other; psychology; religion/religious studies; social psychology; social sciences, general; sociology; special education.

Non-credit—computer and information sciences, general; insurance/risk management.

JONES COLLEGE

Jacksonville, Florida

http://www.jones.edu/

Jones College was founded in 1918. It is accredited by Accrediting Council for Independent Colleges and Schools. It first offered distance learning courses in 1998. In fall 2003, there were 400 students enrolled in distance learning courses. Institutionally administered financial aid is available to distance learners.

Services Distance learners have accessibility to academic advising, bookstore, campus computer network, career placement assistance, e-mail services, library services, tutoring.

Contact Mr. Thomas A. Clift, Dean of Distance Learning, Jones College, 5353 Arlington Expressway, Jacksonville, FL 32211-5588. *Telephone:* 904-743-1122 Ext. 134. *Fax:* 904-743-4446. *E-mail:* tclift@jones.edu.

DEGREES AND AWARDS

AS Business Administration; Computer Information Systems
BS Business Administration; Computer Information Systems

COURSE SUBJECT AREAS OFFERED OUTSIDE OF DEGREE PROGRAMS

Undergraduate—accounting; business; business administration and management; business communications; business information and data processing services; business/managerial economics; communications, general; community psychology; computer and information sciences, general; computer and information sciences, other; computer programming; computer systems analysis; data processing technology; economics; English composition; English language and literature, general; English language and literature/letters, other; English technical and business writing; health and medical assistants; information sciences and systems; international business; international relations and affairs; Internet and World Wide Web; legal studies; liberal arts and sciences, general studies and humanities; marketing operations/marketing and distribution, other; mathematics; mathematics, other; social sciences and history, other; social sciences, general; sociology; taxation.

See full description on page 442.

JONES INTERNATIONAL UNIVERSITY

Englewood, Colorado

http://www.jonesinternational.edu/

Jones International University was founded in 1995. It is accredited by North Central Association of Colleges and Schools. It first offered distance learning courses in 1995. In fall 2003, there were 1,050 students enrolled in distance learning courses. Institutionally administered financial aid is available to distance learners.

Services Distance learners have accessibility to academic advising, bookstore, library services.

Contact Ms. Candice Morrissey, Associate Director of Admissions, Jones International University, 9697 East Mineral Avenue, Englewood, CO 80112. *Telephone:* 800-811-5663. *Fax:* 303-799-0966. *E-mail:* admissions@jonesinternational.edu.

DEGREES AND AWARDS

BA Business Communication
BBA Business Administration
BS Information Technology
MA Business Communication
MBA Business Administration
MEd E-Learning; K-12 Educators and Administration

COURSE SUBJECT AREAS OFFERED OUTSIDE OF DEGREE PROGRAMS

Undergraduate—business administration and management; business communications; communications technologies; computer/information technology administration and management; English technical and business writing; entrepreneurship; human resources management; international business; Internet and World Wide Web; multi/interdisciplinary studies, other; telecommunications.

Graduate—business communications; business management and administrative services, other; communications, other; educational/instructional media design; education, other; entrepreneurship; international business; Internet and World Wide Web; library science, other; multi/interdisciplinary studies, other; peace and conflict studies; public relations and organizational communications; telecommunications.

See full description on page 444.

JUDSON COLLEGE

Marion, Alabama

Distance Learning Program

http://www.judson.edu

Judson College was founded in 1838. It is accredited by Southern Association of Colleges and Schools. It first offered distance learning

Judson College (continued)

courses in 1976. In fall 2003, there were 100 students enrolled in distance learning courses. Institutionally administered financial aid is available to distance learners.

Services Distance learners have accessibility to academic advising, bookstore, campus computer network, career placement assistance, e-mail services, library services.

Contact Angie M. Teague, Director of Distance Learning, Judson College, PO Box 120, Marion, AL 36756. *Telephone:* 800-447-9472 Ext. 169. *Fax:* 334-683-5147. *E-mail:* ateague@judson.edu.

DEGREES AND AWARDS

BA Business; Criminal Justice; English; History; Music; Psychology; Religious Studies; Secondary Education
BMin Ministry Studies
BS Business; Criminal Justice; Education; Psychology

COURSE SUBJECT AREAS OFFERED OUTSIDE OF DEGREE PROGRAMS

Undergraduate—bible/biblical studies; biological and physical sciences; business administration and management; criminal justice and corrections; education, general; English composition; English language and literature, general; history; music; political science and government; psychology; sociology.

Special Message

Judson College, located in Marion, Alabama, has provided quality academic programs in an environment supportive of Christian principles for more than 165 years. The College's educational programs have evolved through the years to meet the needs of each new generation. Fully accredited by the Commission on Colleges of the Southern Association of Colleges and Schools, Judson offers students the opportunity to work out flexible degree plans leading to complete bachelor's degrees through the Distance Learning Program. Majors include business, criminal justice, education, English, history, music, psychology, and religious studies.

Courses are delivered through a variety of methods, including Internet, e-mail, telephone, video, general mail, and facsimile. Students can take up to 18 semester hours in a six-month enrollment period that can begin at any time.

The Distance Learning Program at Judson offers the unique opportunity to earn a maximum of 30 semester hours of credit based on experiential learning. This learning can be evidenced by submission of a thoroughly documented portfolio, satisfactory performance on institutional administered challenge exams, CLEP exams, and DANTES exams.

For more information, interested students may visit the Judson College Web site at http://www.judson.edu. The Distance Learning Office may be contacted by telephone at 800-447-9472 Ext. 169 (toll-free) or 866-4-JUDSON (458-3766) or by e-mail at ateague@future.judson.edu.

JUDSON COLLEGE

Elgin, Illinois
Division of Continuing Education
http://www.judsoncollege.edu

Judson College was founded in 1963. It is accredited by North Central Association of Colleges and Schools. It first offered distance learning courses in 1998. In fall 2003, there were 250 students enrolled in distance learning courses. Institutionally administered financial aid is available to distance learners.

Services Distance learners have accessibility to academic advising, bookstore, campus computer network, career placement assistance, e-mail services, library services, tutoring.

Contact Robert Lindahl, Student Specialist for Customized Learning Center, Judson College, 1151 North State Street, Elgin, IL 60123. *Telephone:* 847-628-1547. *Fax:* 847-695-4880. *E-mail:* rlindahl@judsoncollege.edu.

DEGREES AND AWARDS

BA Management and Leadership

COURSE SUBJECT AREAS OFFERED OUTSIDE OF DEGREE PROGRAMS

Undergraduate—advertising; astronomy; bible/biblical studies; communications, general; computer software and media applications; criminal justice and corrections; English composition; English language and literature, general; English technical and business writing; environmental control technologies; fine arts and art studies; history; liberal arts and sciences, general studies and humanities; mathematics; political science and government; psychology; sociology.

JUNIATA COLLEGE

Huntingdon, Pennsylvania
http://www.juniata.edu/

Juniata College was founded in 1876. It is accredited by Middle States Association of Colleges and Schools. It first offered distance learning courses in 2000.

Services Distance learners have accessibility to campus computer network.

Contact Dr. Loren K. Rhodes, Professor of Information Technology, Juniata College, Brumbaugh Science Center, 1700 Moore Street, Huntingdon, PA 16652. *Telephone:* 814-641-3620. *Fax:* 814-641-3685. *E-mail:* rhodes@juniata.edu.

DEGREES AND AWARDS

Programs offered do not lead to a degree or other formal award.

COURSE SUBJECT AREAS OFFERED OUTSIDE OF DEGREE PROGRAMS

Undergraduate—information sciences and systems.

KANSAS CITY KANSAS COMMUNITY COLLEGE

Kansas City, Kansas
Distance Education
http://www.kckcc.edu

Kansas City Kansas Community College was founded in 1923. It is accredited by North Central Association of Colleges and Schools. It first offered distance learning courses in 1989. In fall 2003, there were 1,900 students enrolled in distance learning courses. Institutionally administered financial aid is available to distance learners.

Services Distance learners have accessibility to academic advising, bookstore, campus computer network, e-mail services, library services.

Contact Tamara Miller, Director of Distance Learning, Kansas City Kansas Community College, 7250 State Avenue, Kansas City, KS 66112. *Telephone:* 913-288-7136. *Fax:* 913-288-7663. *E-mail:* tmiller@toto.net.

DEGREES AND AWARDS

Programs offered do not lead to a degree or other formal award.

COURSE SUBJECT AREAS OFFERED OUTSIDE OF DEGREE PROGRAMS

Undergraduate—accounting; administrative and secretarial services; American literature (United States); anthropology; archaeology; bilingual/bicultural education; biological and physical sciences; biology, general; business; business administration and management; business management and administrative services, other; child care and guidance workers and managers; computer and information sciences, general; computer and information sciences, other; computer science; computer software and media applications; computer systems networking and telecommunications; data entry/microcomputer applications; economics; English composition; English language and literature, general; fire protection; foreign languages and literatures; history; liberal arts and sciences, general studies and humanities; marketing operations/marketing and distribution, other; mathematics; miscellaneous health professions; personal and miscellaneous services, other; philosophy; physical sciences, general; psychology; social sciences, general; sociology.

KANSAS STATE UNIVERSITY

Manhattan, Kansas
Division of Continuing Education, Continuing Learning
http://www.dce.ksu.edu/distance

Kansas State University was founded in 1863. It is accredited by North Central Association of Colleges and Schools. It first offered distance learning courses in 1971. In fall 2003, there were 6,000 students enrolled in distance learning courses. Institutionally administered financial aid is available to distance learners.

Services Distance learners have accessibility to academic advising, bookstore, campus computer network, career placement assistance, e-mail services, library services.

Contact Daniel Butcher, Bachelor Degree Completion Program Coordinator, Kansas State University, 13 College Court Building, Manhattan, KS 66506. *Telephone:* 785-532-5575. *Fax:* 785-532-5637. *E-mail:* degrees@dce.ksu.edu.

DEGREES AND AWARDS

BS Animal Science and Industry; Business, general; Dietetics; Food Science and Industry; Interdisciplinary Social Sciences

Certificate of Completion Early Childhood Education Administration Credential

Certificate Drama Therapy; Food Science; Occupational Health; Personal Financial Planning

Graduate Certificate Academic Advising; Food Science

MS Agribusiness; Chemical Engineering; Civil Engineering; Electrical Engineering; Engineering Management; Food Science; Gerontology; Industrial/Organizational Psychology; Mechanical Engineering; Personal Financial Planning; Software Engineering; Youth Development

COURSE SUBJECT AREAS OFFERED OUTSIDE OF DEGREE PROGRAMS

Undergraduate—accounting; agricultural business and management; agricultural business and production, other; agriculture/agricultural sciences; agriculture/agricultural sciences, other; American history; animal sciences; biochemistry; business; business administration and management; business management and administrative services, other; business marketing and marketing management; child care and guidance workers and managers; computer and information sciences, general; English language and literature, general; finance; financial management and services; foods and nutrition studies; food sciences and technology; horticulture science; labor/personnel relations; management information systems/business data processing; mathematical statistics; organizational behavior; psychology; sociology; women's studies.

Graduate—agricultural business and management; chemical engineering; civil engineering; computer engineering; computer science; computer software and media applications; engineering, general; engineering/industrial management; engineering mechanics; engineering, other; engineering science; financial management and services; horticulture science; human resources management; industrial and organizational psychology; industrial engineering; labor/personnel relations; mechanical engineering; psychology; public administration; quality control and safety technologies.

Non-credit—financial management and services; food sciences and technology.

See full description on page 446.

KAUAI COMMUNITY COLLEGE

Lihue, Hawaii
University Center-Kauai
http://www.kauaicc.hawaii.edu

Kauai Community College was founded in 1965. It is accredited by Western Association of Schools and Colleges. It first offered distance learning courses in 1988. In fall 2003, there were 51 students enrolled in distance learning courses. Institutionally administered financial aid is available to distance learners.

Services Distance learners have accessibility to academic advising, bookstore, e-mail services, library services.

Contact Ms. Alison Shigematsu, Educational Specialist, Kauai Community College, 3-1901 Kaumualii Highway, Lihue, HI 96766-9591. *Telephone:* 808-245-8330. *Fax:* 808-245-8232. *E-mail:* ashigema@hawaii.edu.

DEGREES AND AWARDS

Programs offered do not lead to a degree or other formal award.

COURSE SUBJECT AREAS OFFERED OUTSIDE OF DEGREE PROGRAMS

Undergraduate—computer and information sciences, general; English literature (British and Commonwealth); journalism and mass communications; nursing.

KEISER COLLEGE

Fort Lauderdale, Florida

http://online.keisercollege.edu

Keiser College was founded in 1977. It is accredited by Northwest Commission on Colleges and Universities. It first offered distance learning courses in 1999. In fall 2003, there were 1,000 students enrolled in distance learning courses. Institutionally administered financial aid is available to distance learners.

Services Distance learners have accessibility to academic advising, bookstore, campus computer network, career placement assistance, e-mail services, library services, tutoring.

Contact Admissions Counselor, Keiser College, 1500 NW 49th Street, Fort Lauderdale, FL 33309. *Telephone:* 800-534-7371. *Fax:* 954-351-4030. *E-mail:* admissions@keisercollege.edu.

DEGREES AND AWARDS

AA Accounting; Business; Health Service Administration; Paralegal Studies
AS Computer Science and Technology; Cyber Security; Medical Assisting (ASMA)
BA Business Administration
BS Management of Information Systems

COURSE SUBJECT AREAS OFFERED OUTSIDE OF DEGREE PROGRAMS

Undergraduate—accounting; business administration and management; computer/information technology administration and management; computer systems networking and telecommunications; criminal justice and corrections; health and medical administrative services; health and medical assistants; legal studies.

See full description on page 448.

KELLOGG COMMUNITY COLLEGE

Battle Creek, Michigan

Distributed Learning

http://www.kellogg.edu

Kellogg Community College was founded in 1956. It is accredited by North Central Association of Colleges and Schools. It first offered distance learning courses in 1990. In fall 2003, there were 700 students enrolled in distance learning courses. Institutionally administered financial aid is available to distance learners.

Services Distance learners have accessibility to academic advising, bookstore, e-mail services, library services, tutoring.

Contact Linda Blekking, Secretary, Distance Learning, Kellogg Community College, 450 North Avenue, Battle Creek, MI 49017. *Telephone:* 269-965-3931 Ext. 2383. *E-mail:* blekkingl@kellogg.edu.

DEGREES AND AWARDS

AAS Social Work

COURSE SUBJECT AREAS OFFERED OUTSIDE OF DEGREE PROGRAMS

Undergraduate—accounting; advertising; American history; anthropology; biological and physical sciences; business; business communications; business marketing and marketing management; computer and information sciences, general; computer software and media applications; economics; English composition; law and legal studies related; mathematics related; philosophy and religion related; sociology.

KENT STATE UNIVERSITY

Kent, Ohio

Master of Public Administration Program

http://www.kent.edu/mpa

Kent State University was founded in 1910. It is accredited by North Central Association of Colleges and Schools. It first offered distance learning courses in 2001. In fall 2003, there were 40 students enrolled in distance learning courses. Institutionally administered financial aid is available to distance learners.

Services Distance learners have accessibility to academic advising, bookstore, campus computer network, e-mail services, library services, tutoring.

Contact Prof. Joseph Drew, PhD, Coordinator, Kent-MPA Program, Kent State University, Political Science, Kent, OH 44242-0001. *Telephone:* 330-672-3239. *Fax:* 330-672-3362. *E-mail:* jdrew@kent.edu.

DEGREES AND AWARDS

MPA Public Administration

COURSE SUBJECT AREAS OFFERED OUTSIDE OF DEGREE PROGRAMS

Undergraduate—educational/instructional media design; industrial production technologies; information sciences and systems; library science/librarianship; nursing.

Graduate—public administration; public administration and services, other.

See full description on page 450.

KENTUCKY STATE UNIVERSITY

Frankfort, Kentucky

KSU Distance Learning

http://www.kysu.edu

Kentucky State University was founded in 1886. It is accredited by Southern Association of Colleges and Schools. It first offered distance learning courses in 1997. In fall 2003, there were 259 students enrolled in distance learning courses. Institutionally administered financial aid is available to distance learners.

Services Distance learners have accessibility to academic advising, e-mail services, library services.

Contact Ms. Diane Garrison, Coordinator of Online Learning and Support Services, Kentucky State University, 400 East Main, Academic Services Building, Room 503, Frankfort, KY 40601. *Telephone:* 502-597-6938. *Fax:* 502-597-5046. *E-mail:* dgarrison@gwmail.kysu.edu.

DEGREES AND AWARDS

Programs offered do not lead to a degree or other formal award.

COURSE SUBJECT AREAS OFFERED OUTSIDE OF DEGREE PROGRAMS

Undergraduate—accounting; biological and physical sciences; business information and data processing services; computer and information sciences, general; computer programming; drafting; economics; English composition; English language and literature, general; foreign languages and literatures; marketing operations/marketing and distribution, other; psychology; public administration and services, other; social work; sociology.
Graduate—biological and physical sciences; public administration and services, other.

KETTERING UNIVERSITY

Flint, Michigan
Graduate School
http://graduate.kettering.edu

Kettering University was founded in 1919. It is accredited by North Central Association of Colleges and Schools. It first offered distance learning courses in 1982. In fall 2003, there were 1,350 students enrolled in distance learning courses. Institutionally administered financial aid is available to distance learners.

Services Distance learners have accessibility to academic advising, bookstore, campus computer network, e-mail services, library services.
Contact Joanne Allen, Publications Coordinator, Kettering University, 1700 West Third Avenue, Flint, MI 48504-4898. *Telephone:* 866-584-7237 Ext. 5. *Fax:* 810-762-9935. *E-mail:* gradoff@kettering.edu.

DEGREES AND AWARDS

MS Engineering; Information Technology; Manufacturing Management; Operations Management

See full description on page 452.

THE KING'S COLLEGE AND SEMINARY

Van Nuys, California
http://www.kingscollege.edu

The King's College and Seminary is accredited by Accrediting Association of Bible Colleges. It first offered distance learning courses in 1998. In fall 2003, there were 250 students enrolled in distance learning courses. Institutionally administered financial aid is available to distance learners.

Services Distance learners have accessibility to academic advising, bookstore, career placement assistance, library services.
Contact Marilyn J. Chappell, Director of Admissions, The King's College and Seminary, 14800 Sherman Way, Van Nuys, CA 91405. *Telephone:* 818-779-8040. *Fax:* 818-779-8429. *E-mail:* admissions@kingscollege.edu or admissions@kingsseminary.edu.

DEGREES AND AWARDS

AD Christian Ministries–Associate of Christian Ministries
BTh Theological Studies–Bachelor of Theological Studies
MA Practical Theology–Master of Practical Theology
MDiv Divinity
DMin Ministry

COURSE SUBJECT AREAS OFFERED OUTSIDE OF DEGREE PROGRAMS

Undergraduate—bible/biblical studies; biblical and other theological languages and literatures; communications, general; computer and information sciences, general; counseling psychology; developmental and child psychology; English composition; individual and family development studies; liberal arts and sciences, general studies and humanities; missions/missionary studies and missiology; music; pastoral counseling and specialized ministries; religion/religious studies; religious education; religious/sacred music; theological and ministerial studies; theological studies and religious vocations, other; urban affairs/studies.
Graduate—bible/biblical studies; biblical and other theological languages and literatures; computer and information sciences, general; counseling psychology; missions/missionary studies and missiology; music; pastoral counseling and specialized ministries; religion/religious studies; religious education; religious/sacred music; theological and ministerial studies; theological studies and religious vocations, other; urban affairs/studies.
Non-credit—bible/biblical studies; biblical and other theological languages and literatures; communications, general; computer and information sciences, general; counseling psychology; developmental and child psychology; English composition; individual and family development studies; liberal arts and sciences, general studies and humanities; missions/missionary studies and missiology; music; pastoral counseling and specialized ministries; religion/religious studies; religious education; religious/sacred music; theological and ministerial studies; theological studies and religious vocations, other; urban affairs/studies.

KIRKWOOD COMMUNITY COLLEGE

Cedar Rapids, Iowa
http://www.kirkwood.edu

Kirkwood Community College was founded in 1966. It is accredited by North Central Association of Colleges and Schools. It first offered distance learning courses in 1980. In fall 2003, there were 4,000 students enrolled in distance learning courses. Institutionally administered financial aid is available to distance learners.

Services Distance learners have accessibility to academic advising, bookstore, campus computer network, career placement assistance, e-mail services, library services.
Contact Wendell Maakestad, Director of Distance Learning, Kirkwood Community College, 6301 Kirkwood Boulevard, SW, 214 Linn Hall, Cedar Rapids, IA 52406. *Telephone:* 319-398-5565. *Fax:* 319-398-5492. *E-mail:* wmaakes@kirkwood.edu.

DEGREES AND AWARDS

AA General Programs; Liberal Arts

COURSE SUBJECT AREAS OFFERED OUTSIDE OF DEGREE PROGRAMS

Undergraduate—accounting; administrative and secretarial services; business administration and management; business information and data processing services; criminology; health and medical preparatory programs; human services; journalism and mass communications; miscellaneous health professions; teacher education, specific academic and vocational programs.

Kirkwood Community College (continued)

Non-credit—business; computer and information sciences, general; computer software and media applications; computer systems analysis; computer systems networking and telecommunications; data entry/microcomputer applications; data processing technology.

LACKAWANNA COLLEGE

Scranton, Pennsylvania
Distance Learning Center
http://www.lackawanna.edu

Lackawanna College was founded in 1894. It is accredited by Middle States Association of Colleges and Schools. It first offered distance learning courses in 1994. Institutionally administered financial aid is available to distance learners.

Contact Mr. Griffith R. Lewis, Senior Director, MIS, Lackawanna College, 501 Vine Street, Scranton, PA 18509. *Telephone:* 570-961-7853. *Fax:* 570-961-7877. *E-mail:* lewisg@lackawanna.edu.

DEGREES AND AWARDS

Programs offered do not lead to a degree or other formal award.

COURSE SUBJECT AREAS OFFERED OUTSIDE OF DEGREE PROGRAMS

Undergraduate—medical basic sciences; miscellaneous health professions.

Non-credit—medical basic sciences; miscellaneous health professions.

LAKELAND COLLEGE

Sheboygan, Wisconsin
Lakeland College Online
http://www.lakeland.edu/online

Lakeland College was founded in 1862. It is accredited by North Central Association of Colleges and Schools. It first offered distance learning courses in 1997. In fall 2003, there were 800 students enrolled in distance learning courses. Institutionally administered financial aid is available to distance learners.

Services Distance learners have accessibility to academic advising, bookstore, e-mail services, library services, tutoring.

Contact Carol Butzen, Academic Counselor, Lakeland College, PO Box 359, Sheboygan, WI 53082-0359. *Telephone:* 800-569-1293. *Fax:* 920-565-1341. *E-mail:* butzencl@lakeland.edu.

DEGREES AND AWARDS

BA Accounting; Business Administration; Computer Science; Marketing
MA Theology
MBA Business Administration
MEd Education

COURSE SUBJECT AREAS OFFERED OUTSIDE OF DEGREE PROGRAMS

Undergraduate—accounting; business; computer science; marketing operations/marketing and distribution, other.

Graduate—business administration and management.

See full description on page 454.

LAKELAND COMMUNITY COLLEGE

Kirtland, Ohio
Instructional Technology
http://www.lakelandcc.edu/dl

Lakeland Community College was founded in 1967. It is accredited by North Central Association of Colleges and Schools. It first offered distance learning courses in 1980. In fall 2003, there were 1,500 students enrolled in distance learning courses. Institutionally administered financial aid is available to distance learners.

Services Distance learners have accessibility to academic advising, bookstore, campus computer network, career placement assistance, e-mail services, library services, tutoring.

Contact Ms. Sherry Kocevar, Instructional Materials Coordinator, Lakeland Community College, 7700 Clocktower Drive, Kirtland, OH 44094-5198. *Telephone:* 440-525-7130. *Fax:* 440-525-7602. *E-mail:* skocevar@lakelandcc.edu.

DEGREES AND AWARDS

Programs offered do not lead to a degree or other formal award.

COURSE SUBJECT AREAS OFFERED OUTSIDE OF DEGREE PROGRAMS

Undergraduate—accounting; applied mathematics; art history; biology; business marketing and marketing management; computer and information sciences, general; economics; entrepreneurship; film/video and photographic arts; geography; health and physical education/fitness; history; mathematical statistics; sociology.

Non-credit—accounting; administrative and secretarial services; advertising; business and personal services marketing operations; business communications; business information and data processing services; business management and administrative services, other; business/managerial economics; business quantitative methods and management science; communication disorders sciences and services; communications, general; communications, other; communications technologies; community health services; community organization, resources and services; computer and information sciences, general; computer and information sciences, other; computer engineering; computer/information technology administration and management; computer programming; data entry/microcomputer applications; data processing technology; engineering, other; enterprise management and operation; entrepreneurship; environmental control technologies; environmental/environmental health engineering; family and community studies; family/consumer resource management; film/video and photographic arts; financial management and services; financial services marketing operations; fine arts and art studies; floristry marketing operations; general retailing/wholesaling; gerontology; health and physical education/fitness; health products and services marketing operations; health professions and related sciences, other; heating, air conditioning and refrigeration mechanics and repairers; historic preservation, conservation and architectural history; history; horticulture services operations and management; hospitality/recreation marketing; hospitality services management; quality control and safety technologies; real estate; soil sciences; South Asian languages and literatures; special education; taxation; tourism/travel marketing; veterinary clinical sciences (M.S., Ph.D.); wildlife and wildlands management.

LAKE REGION STATE COLLEGE

Devils Lake, North Dakota

http://www.lrsc.nodak.edu

Lake Region State College was founded in 1941. It is accredited by North Central Association of Colleges and Schools. It first offered distance learning courses in 1980. Institutionally administered financial aid is available to distance learners.

Services Distance learners have accessibility to academic advising, bookstore, career placement assistance, e-mail services, library services, tutoring.

Contact Grace A. Kurtz, Director of Continuing Education, Lake Region State College, 1801 College Drive North, Devils Lake, ND 58301. *Telephone:* 701-662-1508. *E-mail:* grace.kurtz@lrsc.nodak.edu.

DEGREES AND AWARDS

AA Liberal Arts

COURSE SUBJECT AREAS OFFERED OUTSIDE OF DEGREE PROGRAMS

Undergraduate—accounting; biological sciences/life sciences, other; biology, general; business administration and management; business and personal services marketing operations; chemistry; health and physical education/fitness; history; mathematics; psychology; social work.

LAKE SUPERIOR COLLEGE

Duluth, Minnesota

http://www.lsc.mnscu.edu/online/

Lake Superior College was founded in 1995. It is accredited by North Central Association of Colleges and Schools. It first offered distance learning courses in 1997. In fall 2003, there were 1,500 students enrolled in distance learning courses. Institutionally administered financial aid is available to distance learners.

Services Distance learners have accessibility to academic advising, bookstore, career placement assistance, e-mail services, library services, tutoring.

Contact Melissa Leno, Enrollment Services Specialist, Lake Superior College, 2101 Trinity Road, Duluth, MN 55811. *Telephone:* 218-733-5903. *E-mail:* m.leno@lsc.mnscu.edu.

DEGREES AND AWARDS

AA Liberal Education
AAS Accountant
AS Business Administration; Business and Technology
Certificate Microcomputer Office Specialist; Professional Bookkeeper

COURSE SUBJECT AREAS OFFERED OUTSIDE OF DEGREE PROGRAMS

Undergraduate—accounting; administrative and secretarial services; anthropology; astronomy; biological and physical sciences; business; business communications; communications, general; computer and information sciences, general; computer software and media applications; economics; English composition; English technical and business writing; fine arts and art studies; geography; geological and related sciences; health and medical preparatory programs; health professions and related sciences, other; history; liberal arts and sciences, general studies and humanities; mathematics; philosophy and religion; physical sciences, general; political science and government; psychology; sociology.

LAMAR STATE COLLEGE–PORT ARTHUR

Port Arthur, Texas

Academic Division

http://www.pa.lamar.edu/

Lamar State College–Port Arthur was founded in 1909. It is accredited by Southern Association of Colleges and Schools. It first offered distance learning courses in 1996. In fall 2003, there were 100 students enrolled in distance learning courses. Institutionally administered financial aid is available to distance learners.

Services Distance learners have accessibility to academic advising, campus computer network, e-mail services, library services.

Contact Dr. Charles Gongre, Dean of Academic Programs, Lamar State College–Port Arthur, PO Box 310, Port Arthur, TX 77641. *Telephone:* 409-984-6229. *Fax:* 409-984-6000. *E-mail:* charles.gongre@lamarpa.edu.

DEGREES AND AWARDS

Programs offered do not lead to a degree or other formal award.

COURSE SUBJECT AREAS OFFERED OUTSIDE OF DEGREE PROGRAMS

Undergraduate—astronomy; biblical and other theological languages and literatures; business administration and management; computer and information sciences, general; computer programming; computer science; computer software and media applications; computer systems networking and telecommunications; consumer and homemaking education; data entry/microcomputer applications; foods and nutrition studies; health professions and related sciences, other; mathematics; philosophy; philosophy and religion; psychology.

Non-credit—administrative and secretarial services; advertising; business; business administration and management; business and personal services marketing operations; business information and data processing services; business management and administrative services, other; business/managerial economics; computer and information sciences, general; computer/information technology administration and management; computer programming; computer science; computer software and media applications; computer systems analysis; computer systems networking and telecommunications; data entry/microcomputer applications; data processing technology; English creative writing; English technical and business writing; enterprise management and operation; entrepreneurship; financial management and services; financial services marketing operations; general retailing/wholesaling; human resources management; information sciences and systems; Internet and World Wide Web; marketing management and research; miscellaneous health aides.

LAMAR UNIVERSITY

Beaumont, Texas

Division of Continuing and Distance Education

http://dept.lamar.edu/cde

Lamar University was founded in 1923. It is accredited by Southern Association of Colleges and Schools. It first offered distance learning

Lamar University (continued)

courses in 1994. In fall 2003, there were 1,800 students enrolled in distance learning courses. Institutionally administered financial aid is available to distance learners.

Services Distance learners have accessibility to academic advising, bookstore, campus computer network, career placement assistance, e-mail services, library services.

Contact Ms. Orvelle Brown, Coordinator of Student Services, Lamar University, PO Box 10008, Beaumont, TX 77710. *Telephone:* 409-880-8431. *Fax:* 409-880-8683. *E-mail:* brownok@hal.lamar.edu.

DEGREES AND AWARDS

Programs offered do not lead to a degree or other formal award.

COURSE SUBJECT AREAS OFFERED OUTSIDE OF DEGREE PROGRAMS

Undergraduate—English language and literature, general; history; mathematics.

LANDER UNIVERSITY

Greenwood, South Carolina
http://www.lander.edu/ucg

Lander University was founded in 1872. It is accredited by Southern Association of Colleges and Schools. It first offered distance learning courses in 2002. In fall 2003, there were 50 students enrolled in distance learning courses. Institutionally administered financial aid is available to distance learners.

Services Distance learners have accessibility to academic advising, bookstore, campus computer network, career placement assistance, e-mail services, library services.

Contact Ms. Claire M. Cappio, Coordinator, UCG Programs, Lander University, University Center of Greenville, 225 South Pleasantburg Drive, Greenville, SC 29607. *Telephone:* 864-250-8920. *Fax:* 864-250-8924. *E-mail:* ccappio@lander.edu.

DEGREES AND AWARDS

Programs offered do not lead to a degree or other formal award.

COURSE SUBJECT AREAS OFFERED OUTSIDE OF DEGREE PROGRAMS

Undergraduate—counseling psychology; criminal justice and corrections; political science and government; psychology; public administration; sociology.

LANSING COMMUNITY COLLEGE

Lansing, Michigan
Virtual College
http://www.lcc.edu/online/

Lansing Community College was founded in 1957. It is accredited by North Central Association of Colleges and Schools. It first offered distance learning courses in 1979. In fall 2003, there were 3,029 students enrolled in distance learning courses. Institutionally administered financial aid is available to distance learners.

Services Distance learners have accessibility to academic advising, bookstore, campus computer network, e-mail services, library services, tutoring.

Contact Mr. Jim Moran, Online Course Quality Coordinator, Lansing Community College, PO Box 40010, Lansing, MI 48901-7210. *Telephone:* 517-483-5267. *Fax:* 517-483-1758. *E-mail:* moranj@lcc.edu.

DEGREES AND AWARDS

AD 2+2 Transfer to Central Michigan University; Business; Criminal Justice, Law Enforcement; E-Business; General Studies; International Business; Transfer to Walsh College
Certificate of Achievement E-Business; Internet for Business; Microcomputer Database Specialist
Certificate of Completion Information Technology Basics; Internet for Business

COURSE SUBJECT AREAS OFFERED OUTSIDE OF DEGREE PROGRAMS

Undergraduate—accounting; architecture; astronomy; biology, general; chemistry; computer and information sciences, general; computer programming; creative writing; design and applied arts; earth sciences; English composition; foreign languages and literatures; geography; history; law and legal studies related; marketing operations/marketing and distribution, other; mathematics; mathematics related; music; natural resources conservation; psychology; social psychology; sociology; speech and rhetorical studies; theater arts/drama.

LA SIERRA UNIVERSITY

Riverside, California
http://www.lasierra.edu/distance

La Sierra University was founded in 1922. It is accredited by Western Association of Schools and Colleges. It first offered distance learning courses in 1999. Institutionally administered financial aid is available to distance learners.

Services Distance learners have accessibility to academic advising, bookstore, campus computer network, e-mail services, library services, tutoring.

Contact Dean W. Hunt, EdD, Director of Distance Learning, La Sierra University, 4700 Pierce Street, Riverside, CA 92515. *Telephone:* 951-785-2223. *Fax:* 951-785-2205. *E-mail:* dhunt@lasierra.edu.

DEGREES AND AWARDS

MA Curriculum and Instruction–Instructional Technology
MAT Teaching

COURSE SUBJECT AREAS OFFERED OUTSIDE OF DEGREE PROGRAMS

Undergraduate—general teacher education; religion/religious studies; teacher education, specific academic and vocational programs.
Graduate—educational/instructional media design; education, other; general teacher education; teacher education, specific academic and vocational programs.

LAWRENCE TECHNOLOGICAL UNIVERSITY

Southfield, Michigan
http://www.ltu.edu/

Lawrence Technological University was founded in 1932. It is accredited by North Central Association of Colleges and Schools. It first offered distance learning courses in 1998. In fall 2003, there were 317 students enrolled in distance learning courses. Institutionally administered financial aid is available to distance learners.

Services Distance learners have accessibility to academic advising, campus computer network, career placement assistance, e-mail services, library services, tutoring.

Contact Dr. Pam Lowry, Director of Instructional Technology, Lawrence Technological University, 21000 West Ten Mile Road, Southfield, MI 48075. *Telephone:* 248-204-3653. *E-mail:* lowry@ltu.edu.

DEGREES AND AWARDS

Programs offered do not lead to a degree or other formal award.

COURSE SUBJECT AREAS OFFERED OUTSIDE OF DEGREE PROGRAMS

Undergraduate—business administration and management; communications technologies; marketing management and research.

Graduate—business administration and management; human resources management; information sciences and systems; international business; marketing management and research; teacher education, specific academic and vocational programs.

LAWSON STATE COMMUNITY COLLEGE

Birmingham, Alabama
Distance Education
http://www.lawsonstate.edu

Lawson State Community College was founded in 1949. It is accredited by Southern Association of Colleges and Schools. It first offered distance learning courses in 1995. In fall 2003, there were 325 students enrolled in distance learning courses. Institutionally administered financial aid is available to distance learners.

Services Distance learners have accessibility to bookstore, campus computer network, career placement assistance, e-mail services, library services.

Contact Henry Nance, Director, Lawson State Community College, 3060 Wilson Road, SW, Birmingham, AL 35221. *Telephone:* 205-929-6427. *Fax:* 205-929-6428. *E-mail:* hnance@cougar.ls.cc.al.us.

DEGREES AND AWARDS

Programs offered do not lead to a degree or other formal award.

COURSE SUBJECT AREAS OFFERED OUTSIDE OF DEGREE PROGRAMS

Undergraduate—accounting; biology; computer and information sciences, general; developmental/child psychology; educational psychology; organizational psychology; radio/television broadcasting; social psychology; social work.

LEHIGH UNIVERSITY

Bethlehem, Pennsylvania
Office of Distance Learning
http://www.distance.lehigh.edu

Lehigh University was founded in 1865. It is accredited by Middle States Association of Colleges and Schools. It first offered distance learning courses in 1992. In fall 2003, there were 456 students enrolled in distance learning courses. Institutionally administered financial aid is available to distance learners.

Services Distance learners have accessibility to academic advising, bookstore, campus computer network, e-mail services, library services.

Contact Lisa Moughan, Marketing Coordinator, Lehigh University, 436 Brodhead Avenue, Bethlehem, PA 18015. *Telephone:* 610-758-4372. *Fax:* 610-758-4190. *E-mail:* lim2@lehigh.edu.

DEGREES AND AWARDS

Certificate Supply Chain Management
MBA Business Administration
ME Chemical Engineering; Polymer Science and Engineering
MS Chemistry; Manufacturing Systems Engineering; Molecular Biology; Pharmaceutical Chemistry; Polymer Science and Engineering; Quality Engineering

COURSE SUBJECT AREAS OFFERED OUTSIDE OF DEGREE PROGRAMS

Graduate—biological and physical sciences; business administration and management; cell and molecular biology; chemical engineering; chemistry; industrial/manufacturing engineering; polymer/plastics engineering.

Non-credit—business administration and management; business communications; chemical engineering; chemistry; engineering/industrial management; polymer/plastics engineering.

Special Message

To enable working professionals to pursue graduate and continuing education at work, Lehigh University's Educational Satellite Network (LESN) carries live, on-campus classes that are broadcast by satellite to students at multiple corporate sites. Companies partner with Lehigh to offer their employees the opportunity to earn master's degrees in chemistry, chemical engineering, manufacturing systems engineering, molecular biology, pharmaceutical chemistry, polymer science and engineering, quality engineering, and business administration (MBA).

Students express great satisfaction with Lehigh's distance education, particularly its convenience, quality instruction, and the University's responsiveness. This distance education enables students to receive the closest substitute to actual classroom participation possible—all on-campus courses are broadcast live to corporate sites so that students can interact on a real-time basis with instructors. All courses are archived, and students have access to Lehigh's state-of-the-art computer and electronic library systems. Lehigh distance students completing a credit program receive the same degree as on-campus students. Noncredit courses are also available.

In addition, LESN-Online offers distance education courses using streaming video technology so students can simultaneously view the instructor and course graphics. Lehigh's online programs include a full MS in Pharmaceutical Chemistry, an executive education program offering a certificate in Supply Chain Management, and a selection of individual business courses. Most courses can be taken individually for credit or noncredit, or as part of a degree or certificate program.

Since Lehigh began offering distance education in 1992, LESN has grown to serve more than 1,400 students at more than 40 corporate sites, including companies such as 3M, Air Products, Bristol-Myers Squibb, GlaxoSmithKline, and Merck & Company.

LENOIR COMMUNITY COLLEGE

Kinston, North Carolina

Distance Learning Services

http://sun2.lenoir.cc.nc.us/~disted/index.html

Lenoir Community College was founded in 1960. It is accredited by Southern Association of Colleges and Schools. It first offered distance learning courses in 1997. In fall 2003, there were 666 students enrolled in distance learning courses. Institutionally administered financial aid is available to distance learners.

Services Distance learners have accessibility to academic advising, bookstore, e-mail services, library services.

Contact Distance Education Coordinator, Lenoir Community College, Kinston, NC 28502-0188. *E-mail:* csm316@lenoircc.edu.

DEGREES AND AWARDS

AAS Court Reporting and Captioning; Global Logistics

COURSE SUBJECT AREAS OFFERED OUTSIDE OF DEGREE PROGRAMS

Undergraduate—art history; biology, general; education, other; English language and literature, general; foreign languages and literatures; history; mathematics, other; psychology.

LESLEY UNIVERSITY

Cambridge, Massachusetts

http://www.lesley.edu/online_learning/tie/index.html

Lesley University was founded in 1909. It is accredited by New England Association of Schools and Colleges. It first offered distance learning courses in 1996. In fall 2003, there were 350 students enrolled in distance learning courses. Institutionally administered financial aid is available to distance learners.

Services Distance learners have accessibility to academic advising, campus computer network, career placement assistance, e-mail services, library services.

Contact Dr. Maureen Yoder, Program Director for Online Technology in Education Program, Lesley University, 29 Everett Street, Cambridge, MA 02138. *Telephone:* 617-349-8421. *Fax:* 617-349-8169. *E-mail:* myoder@mail.lesley.edu.

DEGREES AND AWARDS

MEd Technology in Education

COURSE SUBJECT AREAS OFFERED OUTSIDE OF DEGREE PROGRAMS

Graduate—curriculum and instruction; educational/instructional media design; education, general; technology education/industrial arts.

LETOURNEAU UNIVERSITY

Longview, Texas

Graduate and Adult Continuing Studies

http://www.letu.edu/

LeTourneau University was founded in 1946. It is accredited by Southern Association of Colleges and Schools. It first offered distance learning courses in 1999. In fall 2003, there were 768 students enrolled in distance learning courses. Institutionally administered financial aid is available to distance learners.

Services Distance learners have accessibility to academic advising, bookstore, campus computer network, e-mail services, library services.

Contact James Townsend, Director of Admissions, LeTourneau University, PO Box 7001, Longview, TX 75607-7001. *Telephone:* 903-233-3400. *Fax:* 903-233-3411. *E-mail:* jamestownsend@letu.edu.

DEGREES AND AWARDS

Programs offered do not lead to a degree or other formal award.

COURSE SUBJECT AREAS OFFERED OUTSIDE OF DEGREE PROGRAMS

Undergraduate—bible/biblical studies; biology, general; communications, general; computer science; education, general; English composition; English language and literature, general; history; psychology.
Non-credit—engineering-related technologies, other.

LEWIS-CLARK STATE COLLEGE

Lewiston, Idaho

Center for Individualized Programs

http://www.lcsc.edu/dl

Lewis-Clark State College was founded in 1893. It is accredited by Northwest Commission on Colleges and Universities. It first offered distance learning courses in 1995. In fall 2003, there were 835 students enrolled in distance learning courses. Institutionally administered financial aid is available to distance learners.

Services Distance learners have accessibility to academic advising, bookstore, campus computer network, career placement assistance, e-mail services, library services.

Contact Kathy L. Martin, Dean, Community Programs, Lewis-Clark State College, 500 Eighth Avenue, Lewiston, ID 83501. *Telephone:* 208-799-2358. *Fax:* 208-799-2444. *E-mail:* kmartin@lcsc.edu.

DEGREES AND AWARDS

Programs offered do not lead to a degree or other formal award.

COURSE SUBJECT AREAS OFFERED OUTSIDE OF DEGREE PROGRAMS

Undergraduate—administrative and secretarial services; business administration and management; business information and data processing services; child care and guidance workers and managers; communications, general; computer and information sciences, general; education, general; English composition; geological and related sciences; liberal arts and sciences, general studies and humanities; mathematics; psychology; social sciences, general; teaching English as a second language/foreign language.
Non-credit—business management and administrative services, other; computer software and media applications; data entry/microcomputer applications; nursing; personal and miscellaneous services, other.

LIBERTY UNIVERSITY

Lynchburg, Virginia

Distance Learning Program

http://www.liberty.edu

Liberty University was founded in 1971. It is accredited by Southern Association of Colleges and Schools. It first offered distance learning courses in 1985. In fall 2003, there were 7,936 students enrolled in distance learning courses. Institutionally administered financial aid is available to distance learners.

Services Distance learners have accessibility to academic advising, bookstore, campus computer network, career placement assistance, e-mail services, library services, tutoring.

Contact Mr. Lee Beaumont, Director of Administrative Affairs, Liberty University, 1971 University Boulevard, Lynchburg, VA 24502-2269. *Telephone:* 800-424-9595. *Fax:* 800-628-7977. *E-mail:* edpadmissions@liberty.edu.

DEGREES AND AWARDS

AA General Studies; Religion
BS Business; Multidisciplinary Studies; Psychology; Religion
BSN Nursing–RN to BSN
MA Counseling, Human Relations Track; Counseling, Marriage and Family Therapy Track; Professional Counseling
MAR Religion
MBA Business Administration
MDiv Divinity
MEd Education
Post-Master's Certificate Education Specialist
EdD Education
PhD Counseling

COURSE SUBJECT AREAS OFFERED OUTSIDE OF DEGREE PROGRAMS

Undergraduate—accounting; bible/biblical studies; biology, general; business; business marketing and marketing management; developmental and child psychology; economics; educational psychology; education, general; English composition; gerontology; philosophy; psychology; social psychology; taxation; theological studies and religious vocations, other.
Graduate—bible/biblical studies; business administration and management; counseling psychology; curriculum and instruction; education administration and supervision; education, other; psychology; religion/religious studies; school psychology; special education; theological and ministerial studies; theological studies and religious vocations, other.

See full description on page 456.

LIFE PACIFIC COLLEGE

San Dimas, California
School of Distance Learning
http://www.lifepacific.edu/distance

Life Pacific College was founded in 1923. It is accredited by Northwest Commission on Colleges and Universities. It first offered distance learning courses in 1941. In fall 2003, there were 300 students enrolled in distance learning courses. Institutionally administered financial aid is available to distance learners.

Services Distance learners have accessibility to academic advising, bookstore, career placement assistance, library services.

Contact Brian Tomhave, Director, Life Pacific College, 1100 West Covina Boulevard, San Dimas, CA 91773. *Telephone:* 909-599-5433 Ext. 359. *Fax:* 909-599-6690. *E-mail:* distance@lifepacific.edu.

DEGREES AND AWARDS

AA Biblical Studies

COURSE SUBJECT AREAS OFFERED OUTSIDE OF DEGREE PROGRAMS

Undergraduate—bible/biblical studies; philosophy and religion related.
Non-credit—bible/biblical studies; biblical and other theological languages and literatures; religion/religious studies.

LIMESTONE COLLEGE

Gaffney, South Carolina
The Block Program
http://www.limestonevirtualcampus.net

Limestone College was founded in 1845. It is accredited by Southern Association of Colleges and Schools. It first offered distance learning courses in 1997. In fall 2003, there were 1,312 students enrolled in distance learning courses. Institutionally administered financial aid is available to distance learners.

Services Distance learners have accessibility to academic advising, bookstore, career placement assistance, e-mail services, library services.

Contact Mr. C. R. Horton, Director of the Virtual Campus, Limestone College, 1115 College Drive, Gaffney, SC 29340-3799. *Telephone:* 864-488-4586. *Fax:* 864-487-8706. *E-mail:* chorton@limestone.edu.

DEGREES AND AWARDS

AA Business Administration; Computer Science Internet Management; Computer Science Management Information Systems; Computer Science Programming; Liberal Studies
BA Human Resource Development; Liberal Studies; Psychology
BS Business Administration; Computer Science Internet Management; Computer Science Management Information Systems; Computer Science Programming; Liberal Studies

COURSE SUBJECT AREAS OFFERED OUTSIDE OF DEGREE PROGRAMS

Undergraduate—accounting; American literature (United States); bible/biblical studies; biology, general; business; business administration and management; business communications; business information and data processing services; business quantitative methods and management science; comparative literature; computer and information sciences, general; computer and information sciences, other; computer/information technology administration and management; computer programming; computer science; computer software and media applications; computer systems analysis; computer systems networking and telecommunications; criminal justice and corrections; data entry/microcomputer applications; data processing technology; dramatic/theater arts and stagecraft; economics; English composition; English creative writing; English language and literature, general; English language and literature/letters, other; English technical and business writing; financial management and services; general retailing/wholesaling; general teacher education; geography; gerontology; history; human resources management; human services; information sciences and systems; international business; Internet and World Wide Web; legal studies; marketing management and research; mathematical statistics; mathematics; military studies; music; philosophy; political science and government; psychology; psychology, other; religion/religious studies; social psychology; social work; sociology.

LINN-BENTON COMMUNITY COLLEGE

Albany, Oregon
Media Services
http://www.linnbenton.edu

Linn-Benton Community College was founded in 1966. It is accredited by Northwest Commission on Colleges and Universities. It first offered distance learning courses in 1979. In fall 2003, there were 735 students enrolled in distance learning courses. Institutionally administered financial aid is available to distance learners.

Services Distance learners have accessibility to academic advising, bookstore, e-mail services, library services.

Contact Christine Baker, Outreach Coordinator, Linn-Benton Community College, Admissions and Records, 6500 Pacific Boulevard, SW, Albany, OR 97321. *Telephone:* 541-917-4811. *Fax:* 541-917-4868. *E-mail:* admissions@linnbenton.edu.

DEGREES AND AWARDS

Programs offered do not lead to a degree or other formal award.

COURSE SUBJECT AREAS OFFERED OUTSIDE OF DEGREE PROGRAMS

Undergraduate—advertising; American literature (United States); applied mathematics; business; business administration and management; business/managerial economics; child care and guidance workers and managers; criminal justice and corrections; economics; English as a second language; English creative writing; English technical and business writing; health and medical administrative services; health and physical education/fitness; Internet and World Wide Web; journalism and mass communications; liberal arts and sciences, general studies and humanities; mathematics.

Non-credit—English as a second language; mathematics; personal and miscellaneous services, other.

LIPSCOMB UNIVERSITY

Nashville, Tennessee
http://www.lipscomb.edu/

Lipscomb University was founded in 1891. It is accredited by Southern Association of Colleges and Schools. It first offered distance learning courses in 1999. In fall 2003, there were 120 students enrolled in distance learning courses. Institutionally administered financial aid is available to distance learners.

Services Distance learners have accessibility to bookstore, campus computer network, career placement assistance, e-mail services, library services.

Contact Mr. Al Austelle, Director of the Center for Instructional Technology, Lipscomb University, 3901 Granny White Pike, Nashville, TN 37204-3951. *Telephone:* 615-279-5703. *Fax:* 615-279-6559. *E-mail:* al.austelle@lipscomb.edu.

DEGREES AND AWARDS

Programs offered do not lead to a degree or other formal award.

COURSE SUBJECT AREAS OFFERED OUTSIDE OF DEGREE PROGRAMS

Undergraduate—bible/biblical studies; biological sciences/life sciences, other; business administration and management; educational/instructional media design; education, general.

Graduate—bible/biblical studies; business administration and management; educational/instructional media design; education, general.

LOCK HAVEN UNIVERSITY OF PENNSYLVANIA

Lock Haven, Pennsylvania
http://www.lhup.edu/cde

Lock Haven University of Pennsylvania was founded in 1870. It is accredited by Middle States Association of Colleges and Schools. It first offered distance learning courses in 1995. Institutionally administered financial aid is available to distance learners.

Services Distance learners have accessibility to academic advising, bookstore, campus computer network, e-mail services, library services.

Contact Dr. Ellen P. O'Hara-Mays, Director of Learning Technologies and Distance Education, Lock Haven University of Pennsylvania, Court House Annex 311, Lock Haven, PA 17745. *Telephone:* 570-893-2072. *Fax:* 570-893-2638. *E-mail:* poharama@lhup.edu.

DEGREES AND AWARDS

AS Nursing
MEd Alternative Education; Teaching and Learning
MHS Physician Assistant

COURSE SUBJECT AREAS OFFERED OUTSIDE OF DEGREE PROGRAMS

Undergraduate—applied mathematics; comparative literature; computer programming; criminology; English composition; history.

Graduate—education, general.

Non-credit—education, general.

LONG BEACH CITY COLLEGE

Long Beach, California
http://de.lbcc.edu

Long Beach City College was founded in 1927. It is accredited by Western Association of Schools and Colleges. It first offered distance learning courses in 1980. In fall 2003, there were 2,200 students enrolled in distance learning courses. Institutionally administered financial aid is available to distance learners.

Services Distance learners have accessibility to academic advising, bookstore, library services, tutoring.

Contact Ms. Carmen Chestnut, Distance Learning Program Specialist, Long Beach City College, 4901 East Carson Street, Long Beach, CA 90808. *Telephone:* 562-938-4025. *Fax:* 562-938-4814. *E-mail:* cchestnut@lbcc.edu.

DEGREES AND AWARDS

Programs offered do not lead to a degree or other formal award.

COURSE SUBJECT AREAS OFFERED OUTSIDE OF DEGREE PROGRAMS

Undergraduate—accounting; anthropology; astronomy; biology, general; business administration and management; child care and guidance workers and managers; computer and information sciences, general; computer programming; computer science; computer software and media applications; computer systems networking and telecommunications; English as a second language; English composition; English creative writing; film/video and photographic arts; foods and nutrition studies; geography; history; international business; liberal arts and sciences, general studies and humanities; library science/librarianship; marketing management and research; mathematics; music; nursing; pharmacy; philosophy; political science and government; psychology; social psychology; sociology.

LONG ISLAND UNIVERSITY, C.W. POST CAMPUS

Brookville, New York

School of Continuing Studies

http://www.ed2go.com/cwp/

Long Island University, C.W. Post Campus was founded in 1954. It is accredited by Middle States Association of Colleges and Schools. It first offered distance learning courses in 1998. In fall 2003, there were 100 students enrolled in distance learning courses. Institutionally administered financial aid is available to distance learners.

Services Distance learners have accessibility to academic advising, e-mail services.

Contact Mr. Carl P. Bishop, Distance Learning Coordinator, Long Island University, C.W. Post Campus, 720 Northern Boulevard, Brookville, NY 11548. *Telephone:* 516-299-2237. *Fax:* 516-299-2066. *E-mail:* carl.bishop@liu.edu.

DEGREES AND AWARDS

Programs offered do not lead to a degree or other formal award.

COURSE SUBJECT AREAS OFFERED OUTSIDE OF DEGREE PROGRAMS

Non-credit—administrative and secretarial services; business administration and management; business management and administrative services, other; computer/information technology administration and management; computer programming; computer science; computer software and media applications; computer systems analysis; computer systems networking and telecommunications; Internet and World Wide Web; personal and miscellaneous services, other.

LORAIN COUNTY COMMUNITY COLLEGE

Elyria, Ohio

Instructional Television

http://www.lorainccc.edu

Lorain County Community College was founded in 1963. It is accredited by North Central Association of Colleges and Schools. It first offered distance learning courses in 1978. In fall 2003, there were 2,300 students enrolled in distance learning courses. Institutionally administered financial aid is available to distance learners.

Services Distance learners have accessibility to academic advising, bookstore, career placement assistance, library services, tutoring.

Contact Ms. Mary Jane Palmer, Coordinator of Distance Learning, Lorain County Community College, 1005 Abbe Road North, Elyria, OH 44035. *Telephone:* 440-366-7684. *Fax:* 440-366-4150. *E-mail:* mpalmer@lorainccc.edu.

DEGREES AND AWARDS

AA Universal Degree

COURSE SUBJECT AREAS OFFERED OUTSIDE OF DEGREE PROGRAMS

Undergraduate—accounting; computer and information sciences, general; creative writing; English as a second language; English composition; mathematics; psychology; science technologies, other; social psychology; sociology.

Non-credit—business; computer software and media applications; health professions and related sciences, other.

LORD FAIRFAX COMMUNITY COLLEGE

Middletown, Virginia

http://www.lf.vccs.edu

Lord Fairfax Community College was founded in 1969. It is accredited by Southern Association of Colleges and Schools. It first offered distance learning courses in 1995. In fall 2003, there were 450 students enrolled in distance learning courses. Institutionally administered financial aid is available to distance learners.

Services Distance learners have accessibility to bookstore, campus computer network, e-mail services, library services.

Contact Mrs. Susan Olmsted, Distance Learning Office Support Specialist, Lord Fairfax Community College, 173 Skirmisher Lane, PO Box 47, Middletown, VA 22645. *Telephone:* 540-868-7190. *Fax:* 540-868-7100. *E-mail:* lfolmss@lf.vccs.edu.

DEGREES AND AWARDS

Programs offered do not lead to a degree or other formal award.

COURSE SUBJECT AREAS OFFERED OUTSIDE OF DEGREE PROGRAMS

Undergraduate—accounting; applied mathematics; biology, general; business; business marketing and marketing management; computer software and media applications; computer systems networking and telecommunications; economics; English composition; financial services marketing operations; fine arts and art studies; history; legal studies; liberal arts and sciences, general studies and humanities; materials engineering; mathematics; miscellaneous physical sciences; nursing; physical sciences, general; physical science technologies; physiological psychology/psychobiology; social psychology; sociology.

Non-credit—business; business administration and management; business and personal services marketing operations; business communications; business information and data processing services; business management and administrative services, other; business/managerial economics; communications, general; communications, other; computer and information sciences, general; computer and information sciences, other; computer/information technology administration and management; computer software and media applications; computer systems analysis; computer systems networking and telecommunications; culinary arts and related services; data processing technology; electrical and electronic engineering-related technology; electrical and electronics equipment installers and repairers; English as a second language; English technical and business writing; enterprise management and operation; industrial equipment maintenance and repairers; marketing operations/marketing and distribution, other; precision production trades, other; protective services, other; telecommunications.

LOS ANGELES HARBOR COLLEGE

Wilmington, California
Distance Education Programs
http://www.lahc.cc.ca.us/acad.htm#onlinecourses

Los Angeles Harbor College was founded in 1949. It is accredited by Western Association of Schools and Colleges. It first offered distance learning courses in 1996. In fall 2003, there were 838 students enrolled in distance learning courses. Institutionally administered financial aid is available to distance learners.

Services Distance learners have accessibility to bookstore, e-mail services.

Contact Dr. Robert Richards, Associate Dean, Academic Affairs, Los Angeles Harbor College, 1111 Figueroa Place, Wilmington, CA 90744. *Telephone:* 310-233-4021. *Fax:* 310-233-4488. *E-mail:* richarr@lahc.edu.

DEGREES AND AWARDS

Programs offered do not lead to a degree or other formal award.

COURSE SUBJECT AREAS OFFERED OUTSIDE OF DEGREE PROGRAMS

Undergraduate—accounting; business; computer and information sciences, general; computer programming; criminal justice and corrections; criminology; economics; English composition; English language and literature, general; political science and government.

LOS ANGELES PIERCE COLLEGE

Woodland Hills, California
http://www.piercecollege.com

Los Angeles Pierce College was founded in 1947. It is accredited by Western Association of Schools and Colleges. It first offered distance learning courses in 1997. In fall 2003, there were 720 students enrolled in distance learning courses. Institutionally administered financial aid is available to distance learners.

Services Distance learners have accessibility to academic advising, campus computer network, e-mail services, library services.

Contact Carlos Martinez, Dean of Academic Affairs, Los Angeles Pierce College, 6201 Winnetka Avenue, Woodland Hills, CA 91371. *Telephone:* 818-710-4224. *Fax:* 818-710-9844. *E-mail:* martinc@piercecollege.edu.

DEGREES AND AWARDS

Programs offered do not lead to a degree or other formal award.

COURSE SUBJECT AREAS OFFERED OUTSIDE OF DEGREE PROGRAMS

Undergraduate—accounting; chemistry; computer and information sciences, general; computer science; computer software and media applications; economics; English composition; English language and literature, general; English language and literature/letters, other; fine arts and art studies; mathematics; mathematics, other; music; philosophy; philosophy and religion; physiological psychology/psychobiology; political science and government; psychology; psychology, other; social sciences and history, other; sociology.

LOS ANGELES TRADE-TECHNICAL COLLEGE

Los Angeles, California
http://www.lattc.edu/lattc/on_line_classes.htm

Los Angeles Trade-Technical College was founded in 1925. It is accredited by Western Association of Schools and Colleges. It first offered distance learning courses in 1986. In fall 2003, there were 175 students enrolled in distance learning courses. Institutionally administered financial aid is available to distance learners.

Services Distance learners have accessibility to academic advising, bookstore, campus computer network.

Contact Linda Delzeit-McIntyre, Los Angeles Trade-Technical College, 400 West Washington Boulevard, Los Angeles, CA 90015. *Telephone:* 213-763-3733. *Fax:* 213-763-5381. *E-mail:* delzeil@lattc.edu.

DEGREES AND AWARDS

AA General Studies

LOS ANGELES VALLEY COLLEGE

Van Nuys, California
http://www.lavc.cc.ca.us/

Los Angeles Valley College was founded in 1949. It is accredited by Western Association of Schools and Colleges. It first offered distance learning courses in 1999. In fall 2003, there were 250 students enrolled in distance learning courses. Institutionally administered financial aid is available to distance learners.

Services Distance learners have accessibility to academic advising, bookstore, campus computer network, e-mail services, tutoring.

Contact Ms. Marion G. Heyn, Director of Academic Computing & Distance Learning, Los Angeles Valley College, 5800 Fulton Avenue, Valley Glen, CA 91401. *Telephone:* 818-947-2532. *Fax:* 818-947-2620. *E-mail:* heynmg@lavc.edu.

DEGREES AND AWARDS

Programs offered do not lead to a degree or other formal award.

COURSE SUBJECT AREAS OFFERED OUTSIDE OF DEGREE PROGRAMS

Undergraduate—business; child care and guidance workers and managers; computer and information sciences, general; computer software and media applications; English composition.

LOUISIANA STATE UNIVERSITY AND AGRICULTURAL AND MECHANICAL COLLEGE

Baton Rouge, Louisiana
Independent Study
http://www.is.lsu.edu

Louisiana State University and Agricultural and Mechanical College was founded in 1860. It is accredited by Southern Association of Colleges and Schools. It first offered distance learning courses in 1941.

In fall 2003, there were 6,500 students enrolled in distance learning courses. Institutionally administered financial aid is available to distance learners.

Services Distance learners have accessibility to bookstore, e-mail services, library services.
Contact Student Services, Louisiana State University and Agricultural and Mechanical College, Office of Independent Study, 106E Pleasant Hall, Baton Rouge, LA 70803. *Telephone:* 800-234-5046. *Fax:* 225-578-3090. *E-mail:* iservices@doce.lsu.edu.

DEGREES AND AWARDS

Programs offered do not lead to a degree or other formal award.

COURSE SUBJECT AREAS OFFERED OUTSIDE OF DEGREE PROGRAMS

Undergraduate—accounting; adult/continuing education; American history; anatomy; anthropology; biology; business administration and management; business marketing and marketing management; communications, general; community health services; criminology; cultural studies; curriculum and instruction; developmental/child psychology; economics; educational psychology; English composition; English language and literature, general; English language and literature/letters, other; English literature (British and Commonwealth); English technical and business writing; environmental health; environmental science; European history; finance; fine arts and art studies; fire science; foreign languages and literatures; French; geography; geological and related sciences; Germanic languages and literatures; health and physical education/fitness; history; journalism; labor/personnel relations; Latin (ancient and medieval); law and legal studies related; library science, other; management information systems/business data processing; mathematical statistics; mathematics; mathematics related; mechanical engineering; music; organizational behavior; philosophy; philosophy and religion related; physical sciences, general; physics; physiology; political science and government; psychology; psychology, other; social sciences and history, other; social sciences, general; sociology; Spanish; theater arts/drama; women's studies.
Graduate—human services.
Non-credit—accounting; biology, general; English composition; mathematics.

LOUISIANA STATE UNIVERSITY AT EUNICE

Eunice, Louisiana
Continuing Education
http://www.lsue.edu/elearning

Louisiana State University at Eunice was founded in 1967. It is accredited by Southern Association of Colleges and Schools. It first offered distance learning courses in 1996. In fall 2003, there were 321 students enrolled in distance learning courses. Institutionally administered financial aid is available to distance learners.

Services Distance learners have accessibility to academic advising, bookstore, campus computer network, career placement assistance, e-mail services, library services.
Contact Mr. Dustin Hebert, Assistant to the Director of Continuing Education, Louisiana State University at Eunice, PO Box 1129, Eunice, LA 70535. *Telephone:* 337-550-1390. *Fax:* 337-550-1393. *E-mail:* dhebert@lsue.edu.

DEGREES AND AWARDS

Programs offered do not lead to a degree or other formal award.

COURSE SUBJECT AREAS OFFERED OUTSIDE OF DEGREE PROGRAMS

Undergraduate—administrative and secretarial services; American literature (United States); business administration and management; computer software and media applications; education, general; English composition; fire science; hospitality services management; information sciences and systems; marketing management and research; psychology.
Non-credit—computer software and media applications.

LOUISIANA STATE UNIVERSITY IN SHREVEPORT

Shreveport, Louisiana
Division of Continuing Education and Public Service
http://www.lsus.edu

Louisiana State University in Shreveport was founded in 1965. It is accredited by Southern Association of Colleges and Schools. It first offered distance learning courses in 1995. In fall 2003, there were 190 students enrolled in distance learning courses. Institutionally administered financial aid is available to distance learners.

Services Distance learners have accessibility to campus computer network, career placement assistance, e-mail services, library services.
Contact Dr. Donna A. Austin, Dean, Continuing Education and Public Service, Louisiana State University in Shreveport, One University Place, Shreveport, LA 71115. *Telephone:* 318-797-5021. *Fax:* 318-797-5395. *E-mail:* daustin@pilot.lsus.edu.

DEGREES AND AWARDS

Programs offered do not lead to a degree or other formal award.

COURSE SUBJECT AREAS OFFERED OUTSIDE OF DEGREE PROGRAMS

Undergraduate—business administration and management; computer software and media applications; English language and literature, general; financial management and services; health and physical education/fitness; history; psychology; social sciences and history, other; sociology.
Graduate—health and medical administrative services; library science/librarianship; social sciences, general.

LOUISIANA TECH UNIVERSITY

Ruston, Louisiana
Center for Instructional Technology and Distance Learning
http://www.latech.edu/citdl

Louisiana Tech University was founded in 1894. It is accredited by Southern Association of Colleges and Schools. It first offered distance learning courses in 1998. In fall 2003, there were 606 students enrolled in distance learning courses. Institutionally administered financial aid is available to distance learners.

Louisiana Tech University (continued)

Services Distance learners have accessibility to academic advising, bookstore, campus computer network, e-mail services, library services.

Contact Mr. David R. Cargill, Director of Center for Instructional Technology and Distance Learning, Louisiana Tech University, PO Box 10408, Ruston, LA 71272. *Telephone:* 318-257-2912. *Fax:* 318-257-2731. *E-mail:* david@latech.edu.

DEGREES AND AWARDS

Programs offered do not lead to a degree or other formal award.

COURSE SUBJECT AREAS OFFERED OUTSIDE OF DEGREE PROGRAMS

Undergraduate—architecture; biological sciences/life sciences, other; consumer and homemaking education; economics; education administration and supervision; English technical and business writing; forestry and related sciences; health professions and related sciences, other; journalism and mass communications; mathematics; political science and government.

Graduate—bioengineering and biomedical engineering; education administration and supervision; English language and literature, general; family and community studies; foods and nutrition studies; history.

LOYOLA UNIVERSITY NEW ORLEANS

New Orleans, Louisiana
Off-Campus Learning Program
http://www.loyno.edu/citycollege

Loyola University New Orleans was founded in 1912. It is accredited by Southern Association of Colleges and Schools. It first offered distance learning courses in 1991. In fall 2003, there were 100 students enrolled in distance learning courses. Institutionally administered financial aid is available to distance learners.

Services Distance learners have accessibility to academic advising, bookstore, campus computer network, career placement assistance, e-mail services, library services, tutoring.

Contact Michelle Carmouche, Off-Campus Learning Program Coordinator, Loyola University New Orleans, 6363 St. Charles Avenue, Campus Box 14, New Orleans, LA 70118. *Telephone:* 504-865-3250. *Fax:* 504-865-3254. *E-mail:* macarmou@loyno.edu.

DEGREES AND AWARDS

BSN Nursing–RN-BSN
MSN Nursing–Health Care Systems Management

COURSE SUBJECT AREAS OFFERED OUTSIDE OF DEGREE PROGRAMS

Undergraduate—English composition; mathematical statistics; nursing; philosophy and religion; sociology.
Graduate—nursing.

LUTHERAN THEOLOGICAL SEMINARY AT GETTYSBURG

Gettysburg, Pennsylvania
http://www.ltsg.edu/

Lutheran Theological Seminary at Gettysburg was founded in 1826. It is accredited by Middle States Association of Colleges and Schools. It first offered distance learning courses in 2000. In fall 2003, there were 40 students enrolled in distance learning courses. Institutionally administered financial aid is available to distance learners.

Services Distance learners have accessibility to e-mail services, library services.

Contact Mrs. Diane Mickley, Registrar, Lutheran Theological Seminary at Gettysburg, Gettysburg, PA 17325, United States Minor Outlying Islands. *Telephone:* 717-334-6286. *Fax:* 717-334-3469. *E-mail:* dmickley@ltsg.edu.

DEGREES AND AWARDS

Programs offered do not lead to a degree or other formal award.

COURSE SUBJECT AREAS OFFERED OUTSIDE OF DEGREE PROGRAMS

Graduate—bible/biblical studies; biblical and other theological languages and literatures; religion/religious studies; religious education; religious/sacred music; theological and ministerial studies; theological studies and religious vocations, other.

LYNN UNIVERSITY

Boca Raton, Florida
The Institute for Distance Learning
http://www.lynn.edu/distancelearning

Lynn University was founded in 1962. It is accredited by Southern Association of Colleges and Schools. It first offered distance learning courses in 1998. In fall 2003, there were 1,000 students enrolled in distance learning courses. Institutionally administered financial aid is available to distance learners.

Services Distance learners have accessibility to academic advising, bookstore, campus computer network, career placement assistance, e-mail services, library services.

Contact Juliet Singh, Distance Learning Support, Lynn University, 3601 North Military Trail, Boca Raton, FL 33431. *Telephone:* 561-237-7850. *Fax:* 561-237-7899. *E-mail:* jsingh@lynn.edu.

DEGREES AND AWARDS

BA Behavioral Science
BS Business; Criminal Justice; Health Care Administration
MBA Business Administration
MS Criminal Justice Administration

See full description on page 458.

MADISON AREA TECHNICAL COLLEGE

Madison, Wisconsin
Instructional Media/Distance Education Department
http://www.matcmadison.edu

Madison Area Technical College was founded in 1911. It is accredited by North Central Association of Colleges and Schools. It first offered distance learning courses in 1994. In fall 2003, there were 2,789 students enrolled in distance learning courses. Institutionally administered financial aid is available to distance learners.

Services Distance learners have accessibility to bookstore, e-mail services, library services.

Contact Lisa Franklin, Administrative Assistant for Distance Learning, Madison Area Technical College, 3550 Anderson Street, Madison, WI 53704. *Telephone:* 608-246-6288. *Fax:* 608-246-6287. *E-mail:* lfranklin@matcmadison.edu.

DEGREES AND AWARDS

AD Accounting
AS Administrative Assistant
ASM Supervisory Management/Leadership Development
Certificate Quality Management
Specialized diploma Optometric Technician

COURSE SUBJECT AREAS OFFERED OUTSIDE OF DEGREE PROGRAMS

Undergraduate—administrative and secretarial services; architectural environmental design; bioengineering and biomedical engineering; business administration and management; business information and data processing services; business marketing and marketing management; child care and guidance workers and managers; computer and information sciences, general; computer/information technology administration and management; computer programming; computer software and media applications; computer systems networking and telecommunications; construction/building technology; cosmetic services; criminal justice and corrections; dental services; design and applied arts; drafting; English composition; fire protection; hospitality/recreation marketing; industrial equipment maintenance and repairers; liberal arts and sciences, general studies and humanities; marketing operations/marketing and distribution, other; mathematical statistics; mathematics related; medical laboratory technology; nursing; ophthalmic/optometric services; parks, recreation and leisure studies; plumbers and pipefitters; protective services, other; real estate; teaching English as a second language/foreign language; tourism/travel marketing; vehicle and mobile equipment mechanics and repairers; woodworkers.

MADONNA UNIVERSITY

Livonia, Michigan
College of Continuing and Professional Studies
http://www.madonna.edu

Madonna University was founded in 1947. It is accredited by North Central Association of Colleges and Schools. It first offered distance learning courses in 1983. In fall 2003, there were 500 students enrolled in distance learning courses. Institutionally administered financial aid is available to distance learners.

Services Distance learners have accessibility to academic advising, bookstore, campus computer network, career placement assistance, e-mail services, library services, tutoring.

Contact Dr. James Novak, Dean, Madonna University, 36600 Schoolcraft Road, Livonia, MI 48150. *Telephone:* 800-852-4951 Ext. 5371. *Fax:* 734-432-5364. *E-mail:* jnovak@madonna.edu.

DEGREES AND AWARDS

BGS Individualized/Interdisciplinary Major
BSBA Business Administration and Management
BSN Nursing–RN to BSN Degree Completion
BSW Social Work
MSBA Leadership Studies–Healthcare; Leadership Studies; Medical and Dental Practice Administration
MSN Nursing Administration

COURSE SUBJECT AREAS OFFERED OUTSIDE OF DEGREE PROGRAMS

Undergraduate—advertising; alcohol/drug abuse counseling; English composition; gerontology; history; liberal arts and sciences, general studies and humanities; nursing; psychology; religion/religious studies.

Non-credit—criminal justice and corrections; gerontology; liberal arts and sciences, general studies and humanities.

MAHARISHI UNIVERSITY OF MANAGEMENT

Fairfield, Iowa
Distance MBA Program
http://www.mum.edu

Maharishi University of Management was founded in 1971. It is accredited by North Central Association of Colleges and Schools. It first offered distance learning courses in 1995. In fall 2003, there were 200 students enrolled in distance learning courses. Institutionally administered financial aid is available to distance learners.

Services Distance learners have accessibility to academic advising, e-mail services.

Contact Dr. Dennis Heaton, Coordinator of Distance Education, Maharishi University of Management, 1000 North Fourth Street, Fairfield, IA 52557. *Telephone:* 641-472-1128. *Fax:* 641-472-1128. *E-mail:* distance@mum.edu.

DEGREES AND AWARDS

MBA Business Administration

COURSE SUBJECT AREAS OFFERED OUTSIDE OF DEGREE PROGRAMS

Undergraduate—accounting; financial management and services; human resources management; marketing management and research.

Graduate—accounting; business marketing and marketing management; finance; international business; investments and securities; management information systems/business data processing.

Non-credit—accounting; business marketing and marketing management; finance; international business; investments and securities; management information systems/business data processing.

MANATEE COMMUNITY COLLEGE

Bradenton, Florida
Distance Education
http://www.mccfl.edu/

Manatee Community College was founded in 1957. It is accredited by Southern Association of Colleges and Schools. It first offered distance learning courses in 1973. In fall 2003, there were 850 students enrolled in distance learning courses. Institutionally administered financial aid is available to distance learners.

Services Distance learners have accessibility to academic advising, campus computer network, career placement assistance, library services, tutoring.

Contact Ms. Kathy Biggs, Director of Instructional Technology and Distance Learning, Manatee Community College, PO Box 1849, Bradenton, FL 34206. *Telephone:* 941-752-5645. *Fax:* 941-727-6050. *E-mail:* biggsk@mccfl.edu.

Manatee Community College (continued)

DEGREES AND AWARDS

Programs offered do not lead to a degree or other formal award.

COURSE SUBJECT AREAS OFFERED OUTSIDE OF DEGREE PROGRAMS

Undergraduate—accounting; American history; American literature (United States); anthropology; applied mathematics; art history; biology; biology, general; business; business administration and management; business and personal services marketing operations; business communications; business information and data processing services; business management and administrative services, other; business/managerial economics; business marketing and marketing management; developmental/child psychology; English composition; management information systems/business data processing; mathematical statistics; mathematics related; microbiology/bacteriology; paralegal/legal assistant; philosophy and religion related; sociology.

MANCHESTER COMMUNITY COLLEGE

Manchester, Connecticut

http://www.mcc.commnet.edu/

Manchester Community College was founded in 1963. It is accredited by New England Association of Schools and Colleges. It first offered distance learning courses in 1989. In fall 2003, there were 353 students enrolled in distance learning courses. Institutionally administered financial aid is available to distance learners.

Services Distance learners have accessibility to academic advising, bookstore, career placement assistance, library services, tutoring.

Contact Cathy Manly, Director of Distance Learning, Manchester Community College, Great Path, MS 15, PO Box 1046, Manchester, CT 06045-1046. *Telephone:* 860-512-3442. *E-mail:* cmanly@mcc.commnet.edu.

DEGREES AND AWARDS

Programs offered do not lead to a degree or other formal award.

COURSE SUBJECT AREAS OFFERED OUTSIDE OF DEGREE PROGRAMS

Undergraduate—American history; business administration and management; business communications; business quantitative methods and management science; computer and information sciences, general; computer systems networking and telecommunications; English composition; English language and literature, general; Internet and World Wide Web; mathematics; medical basic sciences; professional studies; sociology.

Non-credit—accounting; business; business administration and management; communications, general; computer and information sciences, general; computer programming; computer software and media applications; computer systems networking and telecommunications; education, other; English as a second language; English technical and business writing; financial management and services; health and medical diagnostic and treatment services; history; Internet and World Wide Web; professional studies.

MANSFIELD UNIVERSITY OF PENNSYLVANIA

Mansfield, Pennsylvania

Center for Lifelong Learning

http://cll.mansfield.edu

Mansfield University of Pennsylvania was founded in 1857. It is accredited by Middle States Association of Colleges and Schools. It first offered distance learning courses in 1995. In fall 2003, there were 500 students enrolled in distance learning courses. Institutionally administered financial aid is available to distance learners.

Services Distance learners have accessibility to academic advising, bookstore, campus computer network, career placement assistance, e-mail services, library services, tutoring.

Contact Karen Norton, Director of Credit Programs, Mansfield University of Pennsylvania, 204 Memorial Hall, Mansfield, PA 16933. *Telephone:* 570-662-4850. *Fax:* 570-662-4120. *E-mail:* knorton@mansfield.edu.

DEGREES AND AWARDS

BA Art History
BSN Nursing–RN to BSN
MEd Art Education
MSE School Library and Information Technologies
MSN Nursing Education

COURSE SUBJECT AREAS OFFERED OUTSIDE OF DEGREE PROGRAMS

Undergraduate—accounting; business administration and management; computer and information sciences, general; criminal justice and corrections; economics; English language and literature, general; mathematics; nursing; social work; sociology.

MARIAN COLLEGE OF FOND DU LAC

Fond du Lac, Wisconsin

http://www.mariancollege.edu/

Marian College of Fond du Lac was founded in 1936. It is accredited by North Central Association of Colleges and Schools. It first offered distance learning courses in 2000. In fall 2003, there were 85 students enrolled in distance learning courses. Institutionally administered financial aid is available to distance learners.

Services Distance learners have accessibility to academic advising, bookstore, campus computer network, career placement assistance, e-mail services, library services.

Contact Ms. Cheryl Shell, Registrar, Marian College of Fond du Lac, 45 South National Avenue, Fond du Lac, WI 54935. *Telephone:* 800-262-7426 Ext. 7618. *Fax:* 920-926-6708. *E-mail:* cshell@mariancollege.edu.

DEGREES AND AWARDS

Programs offered do not lead to a degree or other formal award.

COURSE SUBJECT AREAS OFFERED OUTSIDE OF DEGREE PROGRAMS

Undergraduate—business/managerial economics; communications, general; criminal justice and corrections; English language and literature, general; Germanic languages and literatures.

Graduate—education, general.

MARION TECHNICAL COLLEGE

Marion, Ohio

http://www.mtc.edu

Marion Technical College was founded in 1971. It is accredited by North Central Association of Colleges and Schools. It first offered distance learning courses in 1995. In fall 2003, there were 45 students enrolled in distance learning courses. Institutionally administered financial aid is available to distance learners.

Services Distance learners have accessibility to academic advising, campus computer network, e-mail services, library services.
Contact Vicky Wood, Dean of Business and Instructional Technologies, Marion Technical College, 1467 Mount Vernon Avenue, Marion, OH 43302. *Telephone:* 740-389-4636 Ext. 265. *Fax:* 740-389-6136. *E-mail:* woodv@mtc.edu.

DEGREES AND AWARDS

Programs offered do not lead to a degree or other formal award.

COURSE SUBJECT AREAS OFFERED OUTSIDE OF DEGREE PROGRAMS

Undergraduate—administrative and secretarial services; business information and data processing services; English composition; legal studies; mathematics; medical laboratory technology.

MARIST COLLEGE

Poughkeepsie, New York

School of Management

http://www.marist.edu/management

Marist College was founded in 1929. It is accredited by Middle States Association of Colleges and Schools. It first offered distance learning courses in 1998. In fall 2003, there were 350 students enrolled in distance learning courses. Institutionally administered financial aid is available to distance learners.

Services Distance learners have accessibility to academic advising, bookstore, campus computer network, career placement assistance, e-mail services, library services.
Contact Robert J. Walsh, Dean, Marist College, School of Management, Poughkeepsie, NY 12601. *Telephone:* 845-575-3225. *Fax:* 845-575-3640. *E-mail:* robert.walsh@marist.edu.

DEGREES AND AWARDS

MBA Business Administration
MPA Public Administration

COURSE SUBJECT AREAS OFFERED OUTSIDE OF DEGREE PROGRAMS

Graduate—accounting; business administration and management; business and personal services marketing operations; business management and administrative services, other; business/managerial economics; business quantitative methods and management science.

See full description on page 460.

MARIST COLLEGE

Poughkeepsie, New York

School of Communication and the Arts

http://www.marist.edu/graduate

Marist College was founded in 1929. It is accredited by Middle States Association of Colleges and Schools. Institutionally administered financial aid is available to distance learners.

Services Distance learners have accessibility to bookstore, campus computer network, e-mail services, library services.
Contact Ms. Anu R. Ailawadhi, Director of Graduate Admission, Marist College, Poughkeepsie, NY 12601-1387. *Telephone:* 845-575-3800. *E-mail:* graduate@marist.edu.

DEGREES AND AWARDS

MA Organizational Communication and Leadership

COURSE SUBJECT AREAS OFFERED OUTSIDE OF DEGREE PROGRAMS

Undergraduate—communications, general; journalism and mass communications; liberal arts and sciences, general studies and humanities.
Graduate—business administration and management; communications, general; information sciences and systems; public administration.

MARQUETTE UNIVERSITY

Milwaukee, Wisconsin

http://www.marquette.edu/online

Marquette University was founded in 1881. It is accredited by North Central Association of Colleges and Schools. It first offered distance learning courses in 1997. In fall 2003, there were 200 students enrolled in distance learning courses. Institutionally administered financial aid is available to distance learners.

Services Distance learners have accessibility to academic advising, bookstore, campus computer network, e-mail services, library services.
Contact Heidi Schweizer, Director of Center for Electronic Learning, Marquette University, PO Box 1881, Schroeder Health Complex Room 198, School of Education, Milwaukee, WI 53201. *Telephone:* 414-288-1423. *Fax:* 414-288-3945. *E-mail:* heidi.schweizer@marquette.edu.

DEGREES AND AWARDS

Certification 6-12 Alternative Certification
MA Education–Instructional Leadership

COURSE SUBJECT AREAS OFFERED OUTSIDE OF DEGREE PROGRAMS

Undergraduate—educational/instructional media design; education, general; education, other.
Graduate—education, general; technology education/industrial arts.
Non-credit—education administration and supervision; educational evaluation, research and statistics; educational/instructional media design; educational psychology; education, general; education, other.

MARSHALL UNIVERSITY

Huntington, West Virginia

Distributed Education Technology

http://www.marshall.edu/muonline

Marshall University was founded in 1837. It is accredited by North Central Association of Colleges and Schools. It first offered distance learning courses in 1986. In fall 2003, there were 3,526 students enrolled in distance learning courses. Institutionally administered financial aid is available to distance learners.

Marshall University (continued)

Services Distance learners have accessibility to academic advising, bookstore, campus computer network, e-mail services, library services.

Contact Crystal Stewart, Program Specialist, Marshall University, One John Marshall Drive, CB 216, Huntington, WV 25755-2140. *Telephone:* 304-696-2970. *Fax:* 304-696-2973. *E-mail:* stewar14@marshall.edu.

DEGREES AND AWARDS

AGS General Studies

COURSE SUBJECT AREAS OFFERED OUTSIDE OF DEGREE PROGRAMS

Undergraduate—accounting; business administration and management; business/managerial economics; business marketing and marketing management; chemistry; communications, general; communications, other; computer and information sciences, general; computer and information sciences, other; computer engineering; developmental/child psychology; economics; educational psychology; English composition; geography; history; journalism; management information systems/business data processing; mathematical statistics; mathematics; mathematics and computer science; mathematics, other; nursing; philosophy; psychology; social work; sociology; visual and performing arts.

Graduate—accounting; computer and information sciences, general; marketing management and research; social work; sociology; technology education/industrial arts; visual and performing arts.

MARTIN COMMUNITY COLLEGE

Williamston, North Carolina

http://www.martin.cc.nc.us

Martin Community College was founded in 1968. It is accredited by Southern Association of Colleges and Schools. It first offered distance learning courses in 2000. In fall 2003, there were 280 students enrolled in distance learning courses. Institutionally administered financial aid is available to distance learners.

Services Distance learners have accessibility to campus computer network, e-mail services.

Contact Mr. Tim Cooper, Instructor/ Distance Learning Coordinator, Martin Community College, 1161 Kehukee Park Road, Williamston, NC 27892. *Telephone:* 252-792-1521 Ext. 285. *Fax:* 252-792-0826. *E-mail:* tcooper@martin.cc.nc.us.

DEGREES AND AWARDS

Programs offered do not lead to a degree or other formal award.

COURSE SUBJECT AREAS OFFERED OUTSIDE OF DEGREE PROGRAMS

Undergraduate—accounting; business; child care and guidance workers and managers; communications, general; computer and information sciences, general; data processing technology; dental services; economics; health and medical assistants; Internet and World Wide Web; marketing management and research; mathematics; psychology.

Non-credit—mathematics.

MARTIN LUTHER COLLEGE

New Ulm, Minnesota

http://www.mlc-wels.edu/

Martin Luther College was founded in 1995. It is accredited by North Central Association of Colleges and Schools. In fall 2003, there were 75 students enrolled in distance learning courses. Institutionally administered financial aid is available to distance learners.

Contact Prof. John William Paulsen, Director of Special Services, Martin Luther College, 1995 Luther Court, New Ulm, MN 56073. *Telephone:* 507-354-8221 Ext. 352. *Fax:* 507-354-8225. *E-mail:* paulsejw@mlc-wels.edu.

DEGREES AND AWARDS

Programs offered do not lead to a degree or other formal award.

COURSE SUBJECT AREAS OFFERED OUTSIDE OF DEGREE PROGRAMS

Undergraduate—bible/biblical studies; computer/information technology administration and management; geography.

Graduate—education, general.

MARYGROVE COLLEGE

Detroit, Michigan

Master in the Art of Teaching Program

http://www.marygrove.edu

Marygrove College was founded in 1905. It is accredited by North Central Association of Colleges and Schools. It first offered distance learning courses in 1989. In fall 2003, there were 5,000 students enrolled in distance learning courses. Institutionally administered financial aid is available to distance learners.

Services Distance learners have accessibility to academic advising, bookstore, campus computer network, e-mail services, library services, tutoring.

Contact Dr. Eunice Jordan, Director, Marygrove College, Detroit, MI 48221. *Telephone:* 313-927-1507. *Fax:* 313-927-1530. *E-mail:* ejordan@marygrove.edu.

DEGREES AND AWARDS

MA Educational Administration
MAT Teacher Education

COURSE SUBJECT AREAS OFFERED OUTSIDE OF DEGREE PROGRAMS

Undergraduate—teacher education, specific academic and vocational programs.

Graduate—teacher education, specific academic and vocational programs.

MARYLAND INSTITUTE COLLEGE OF ART

Baltimore, Maryland

MICA On-Line

http://www.mica.edu

Maryland Institute College of Art was founded in 1826. It is accredited by Middle States Association of Colleges and Schools. It first offered distance learning courses in 1997. In fall 2003, there were 1,100 students enrolled in distance learning courses. Institutionally administered financial aid is available to distance learners.

Services Distance learners have accessibility to academic advising, bookstore, campus computer network, library services.

Contact Peter Dubeau, Associate Dean, Division of Continuing Studies, Maryland Institute College of Art, Division of Continuing Studies, Baltimore, MD 21217. *Telephone:* 410-225-2219. *Fax:* 410-225-2229. *E-mail:* cs@mica.edu.

DEGREES AND AWARDS

Programs offered do not lead to a degree or other formal award.

COURSE SUBJECT AREAS OFFERED OUTSIDE OF DEGREE PROGRAMS

Undergraduate—fine arts and art studies; graphic design/commercial art/illustration.
Non-credit—fine arts and art studies.

MARYLHURST UNIVERSITY

Marylhurst, Oregon
Department of Distance Learning
http://online.marylhurst.edu

Marylhurst University was founded in 1893. It is accredited by Northwest Commission on Colleges and Universities. It first offered distance learning courses in 1996. In fall 2003, there were 420 students enrolled in distance learning courses. Institutionally administered financial aid is available to distance learners.

Services Distance learners have accessibility to academic advising, bookstore, campus computer network, career placement assistance, library services.
Contact Nancy Thompson, Assitant Director for Online Programs, Marylhurst University, 17600 Pacific Highway, PO Box 261, Marylhurst, OR 97036. *Telephone:* 800-634-9982 Ext. 6319. *Fax:* 503-699-6249. *E-mail:* learning@marylhurst.edu.

DEGREES AND AWARDS

BA Interdisciplinary Studies; Organizational Communications
BS Management; Real Estate
MBA Business Administration

COURSE SUBJECT AREAS OFFERED OUTSIDE OF DEGREE PROGRAMS

Undergraduate—American history; American literature (United States); biological sciences/life sciences, other; biology; business communications; business marketing and marketing management; child care and guidance workers and managers; creative writing; educational psychology; English composition; film studies; finance; liberal arts and sciences, general studies and humanities; mathematical statistics; mathematics related; philosophy and religion related; real estate; religious education; urban affairs/studies.
Graduate—business marketing and marketing management; community psychology; finance; liberal arts and sciences, general studies and humanities; marketing management and research; multi/interdisciplinary studies, other; philosophy and religion related; theological and ministerial studies.
Non-credit—communications, general; cultural studies; mathematics; philosophy and religion; psychology, other; social and philosophical foundations of education.

MARYMOUNT UNIVERSITY

Arlington, Virginia
http://www.marymount.edu

Marymount University was founded in 1950. It is accredited by Southern Association of Colleges and Schools. It first offered distance learning courses in 1999. In fall 2003, there were 162 students enrolled in distance learning courses. Institutionally administered financial aid is available to distance learners.

Services Distance learners have accessibility to academic advising, bookstore, campus computer network, career placement assistance, e-mail services, library services, tutoring.
Contact Ms. Francesca Reed, Director, Graduate Admissions, Marymount University, 2807 North Glebe Road, Arlington, VA 22207. *Telephone:* 703-284-5901. *Fax:* 703-527-3815. *E-mail:* francesca.reed@marymount.edu.

DEGREES AND AWARDS

MEd Catholic School Leadership

COURSE SUBJECT AREAS OFFERED OUTSIDE OF DEGREE PROGRAMS

Graduate—business; business management and administrative services, other; computer science; information sciences and systems.

MARYVILLE UNIVERSITY OF SAINT LOUIS

St. Louis, Missouri
http://www.maryville.edu/

Maryville University of Saint Louis was founded in 1872. It is accredited by North Central Association of Colleges and Schools. It first offered distance learning courses in 2000. In fall 2003, there were 300 students enrolled in distance learning courses. Institutionally administered financial aid is available to distance learners.

Services Distance learners have accessibility to campus computer network, e-mail services.
Contact Mr. Donald Perry, Director, CEDL, Maryville University of Saint Louis, St. Louis, MO 63141. *E-mail:* dperry@maryville.edu.

DEGREES AND AWARDS

Programs offered do not lead to a degree or other formal award.

COURSE SUBJECT AREAS OFFERED OUTSIDE OF DEGREE PROGRAMS

Undergraduate—data processing technology; information sciences and systems.
Non-credit—accounting; advertising; business administration and management; business information and data processing services; communications technologies; computer and information sciences, general; computer software and media applications; computer systems analysis; computer systems networking and telecommunications; crafts, folk art and artisanry; data entry/microcomputer applications; data processing technology; English creative writing; enterprise management and operation; entrepreneurship; family and community studies; human resources management; information sciences and systems; Internet and World Wide Web; journalism and mass communications.

MASSASOIT COMMUNITY COLLEGE

Brockton, Massachusetts

http://www.massasoit.mass.edu/acad_depts/dist_learn/dist_learn.htm

Massasoit Community College was founded in 1966. It is accredited by New England Association of Schools and Colleges. It first offered distance learning courses in 1998. In fall 2003, there were 500 students enrolled in distance learning courses. Institutionally administered financial aid is available to distance learners.

Services Distance learners have accessibility to bookstore, e-mail services, library services.

Contact Linda McAlpine, Coordinator of Instructional Technology & e-learning, Massasoit Community College, 1 Massasoit Boulevard, Brockton, MA 02302. *Telephone:* 508-588-9100 Ext. 1613. *Fax:* 508-427-1250. *E-mail:* lmcalpine@massasoit.mass.edu.

DEGREES AND AWARDS

Programs offered do not lead to a degree or other formal award.

COURSE SUBJECT AREAS OFFERED OUTSIDE OF DEGREE PROGRAMS

Undergraduate—accounting; anthropology; biological and physical sciences; business; business administration and management; business communications; chemistry; child care and guidance workers and managers; computer and information sciences, general; film/video and photographic arts; geography; history; international business; Internet and World Wide Web; mathematical statistics; mathematics; music; philosophy; physical sciences, general; psychology; psychology, other; sociology; tourism/travel marketing.

Non-credit—business; business and personal services marketing operations; communications, general; computer and information sciences, general; English creative writing; gerontology; health professions and related sciences, other; home/office products marketing; human resources management; Internet and World Wide Web; journalism and mass communications; marketing operations/marketing and distribution, other; miscellaneous health professions; miscellaneous mechanics and repairers; peace and conflict studies; social sciences, general; taxation.

MASTER'S COLLEGE AND SEMINARY

Toronto, Ontario, Canada

http://www.mcs.edu/

Master's College and Seminary was founded in 1939. It is provincially chartered. It first offered distance learning courses in 1996. In fall 2003, there were 307 students enrolled in distance learning courses. Institutionally administered financial aid is available to distance learners.

Services Distance learners have accessibility to academic advising, bookstore, e-mail services, library services.

Contact Rev. Luc Lombardi, Director of Distance Education, Master's College and Seminary, 3080 Yonge Street, Box 70, Suite 3040, Toronto, ON M4N 3N1, Canada. *Telephone:* 800-295-6368 Ext. 224. *E-mail:* llombardi@mcs.edu.

DEGREES AND AWARDS

AA Religious Education–Bachelor of Religious Education
BTh Theology
CWC Christian Ministry Certificate–Pastoral Leadership

COURSE SUBJECT AREAS OFFERED OUTSIDE OF DEGREE PROGRAMS

Undergraduate—bible/biblical studies; biblical and other theological languages and literatures; counseling psychology; cultural studies; missions/missionary studies and missiology; pastoral counseling and specialized ministries; philosophy and religion; psychology, other; religion/religious studies; religious education; theological and ministerial studies; theological studies and religious vocations, other.

MAUI COMMUNITY COLLEGE

Kahului, Hawaii

Distance Learning Program

http://www.umaui.net/

Maui Community College was founded in 1967. It is accredited by Western Association of Schools and Colleges. It first offered distance learning courses in 1989. In fall 2003, there were 300 students enrolled in distance learning courses.

Services Distance learners have accessibility to academic advising, e-mail services.

Contact LeeAnn Pena-Araki, Secretary, Maui Community College, 310 West Kaahumanu Avenue, Kahului, HI 96732. *Telephone:* 808-984-3525. *Fax:* 808-244-6595. *E-mail:* penaarak@hawaii.edu.

DEGREES AND AWARDS

AA Liberal Arts
AAS Administration of Justice
BA Applied Social Sciences; Business Administration; English; Hawaiian Studies; Information and Computer Sciences; Interdisciplinary Studies, Human Relations in Organizations; Interdisciplinary Studies, Information Resource Management; Liberal Studies; Marine Science; Psychology
BEd Elementary Education; Elementary Education/Special Education
BS Computer Science
BSN Nursing
Certificate Business; Substance Abuse
Graduate Certificate Telecommunication and Information Resource Management; Travel Industry Management
MBA Business Administration
MEd Counseling and Guidance, Rehabilitation Counseling; Educational Administration; Educational Foundations
MLIS Library and Information Science
MS Information and Computer Sciences; Nursing
MSW Social Work

COURSE SUBJECT AREAS OFFERED OUTSIDE OF DEGREE PROGRAMS

Undergraduate—accounting; agriculture/agricultural sciences; astronomy; biology; business; business administration and management; business communications; carpenters; chemistry; clothing/apparel and textile studies; communications, general; computer and information sciences, general; computer engineering; computer science; construction trades, other; criminal justice and corrections; dance; dental services; developmental/child psychology; drafting; economics; electrical and electronic engineering-related technology; English composition; English literature (British and Commonwealth); English technical and business writing; food sciences and technology; foreign languages and literatures; health and medical assistants; history; information sciences and systems; Internet and World Wide Web; landscape architecture; mathematics; mathematics and computer science; miscellaneous mechanics and repairers; nursing; philosophy; physics; psychology; religion/religious studies; social psychology; social work; sociology; vehicle and mobile equipment mechanics and repairers; visual and performing arts; zoology.

MAYSVILLE COMMUNITY COLLEGE

Maysville, Kentucky
http://www.maycc.kctcs.net/

Maysville Community College was founded in 1967. It is accredited by Southern Association of Colleges and Schools. It first offered distance learning courses in 1997. In fall 2003, there were 400 students enrolled in distance learning courses. Institutionally administered financial aid is available to distance learners.

Services Distance learners have accessibility to academic advising, bookstore, campus computer network, career placement assistance, e-mail services, library services, tutoring.
Contact Mrs. Kimberly D. Bloomfield, Coordinator of Outreach and Distance Learning, Maysville Community College, 1755 US 68, Maysville, KY 41056. *Telephone:* 606-759-7141 Ext. 6130. *Fax:* 606-759-9601. *E-mail:* kim.bloomfield@kctcs.edu.

DEGREES AND AWARDS

AA Humanities

COURSE SUBJECT AREAS OFFERED OUTSIDE OF DEGREE PROGRAMS

Undergraduate—accounting; American history; biology, general; business; chemistry; communications, general; computer and information sciences, general; developmental and child psychology; economics; education, general; electrical and electronic engineering-related technology; English composition; English creative writing; English language and literature, general; environmental science; European history; finance; fine arts and art studies; geography; history; industrial/manufacturing engineering; marketing management and research; mathematical statistics; mathematics; medical genetics; nursing; philosophy and religion; psychology; real estate; social sciences, general; sociology.
Non-credit—business administration and management; business and personal services marketing operations; computer software and media applications; financial management and services; foreign languages and literatures; legal studies; medical basic sciences; psychology.

MAYVILLE STATE UNIVERSITY

Mayville, North Dakota
Enrollment Services Office
http://www.mayvillestate.edu

Mayville State University was founded in 1889. It is accredited by North Central Association of Colleges and Schools. It first offered distance learning courses in 1999. In fall 2003, there were 171 students enrolled in distance learning courses. Institutionally administered financial aid is available to distance learners.

Services Distance learners have accessibility to academic advising, bookstore, campus computer network, career placement assistance, e-mail services, library services.
Contact Dr. Gary Hagen, Vice President for Academic Affairs, Mayville State University, 330 Third Street, NE, Mayville, ND 58257. *Telephone:* 701-788-4787. *Fax:* 701-788-4748. *E-mail:* gary_hagen@mail.masu.nodak.edu.

DEGREES AND AWARDS

BA Early Childhood Education
BS Business Administration (Bachelor of Applied Science); Computer Information Systems (Bachelor of Applied Science)

COURSE SUBJECT AREAS OFFERED OUTSIDE OF DEGREE PROGRAMS

Undergraduate—accounting; biology, general; business administration and management; chemistry; child care and guidance workers and managers; education, general; English composition; library science/librarianship.

MCDANIEL COLLEGE

Westminster, Maryland
Graduate and Professional Studies
http://www.mcdaniel.edu

McDaniel College was founded in 1867. It is accredited by Middle States Association of Colleges and Schools. It first offered distance learning courses in 1999. In fall 2003, there were 64 students enrolled in distance learning courses. Institutionally administered financial aid is available to distance learners.

Services Distance learners have accessibility to academic advising, bookstore, e-mail services, library services.
Contact Crystal L. Perry, Administrator of Graduate Records, McDaniel College, 2 College Hill, Westminster, MD 21157. *Telephone:* 410-857-2513. *Fax:* 410-857-2515. *E-mail:* cperry@mcdaniel.edu.

DEGREES AND AWARDS

Programs offered do not lead to a degree or other formal award.

COURSE SUBJECT AREAS OFFERED OUTSIDE OF DEGREE PROGRAMS

Undergraduate—communications, general.
Graduate—educational evaluation, research and statistics; educational/instructional media design; education, other.

MEDICAL COLLEGE OF WISCONSIN

Milwaukee, Wisconsin
Master of Public Health Degree Programs
http://instruct.mcw.edu/prevmed

Medical College of Wisconsin was founded in 1913. It is accredited by North Central Association of Colleges and Schools. It first offered distance learning courses in 1986. In fall 2003, there were 137 students enrolled in distance learning courses. Institutionally administered financial aid is available to distance learners.

Medical College of Wisconsin (continued)

Services Distance learners have accessibility to academic advising, bookstore, campus computer network, career placement assistance, e-mail services, library services.

Contact Beverly Carlson, Program Coordinator, MPH Degree Programs, Medical College of Wisconsin, Division of Public Health, 8701 Watertown Plank Road, Milwaukee, WI 53226. *Telephone:* 414-456-4510. *Fax:* 414-456-6160. *E-mail:* mph@mcw.edu.

DEGREES AND AWARDS

MPH Occupational Medicine; Preventive Medicine, general

MEMORIAL UNIVERSITY OF NEWFOUNDLAND

St. John's, Newfoundland and Labrador, Canada
School of Continuing Education
http://www.distance.mun.ca

Memorial University of Newfoundland was founded in 1925. It is provincially chartered. It first offered distance learning courses in 1969. In fall 2003, there were 4,700 students enrolled in distance learning courses. Institutionally administered financial aid is available to distance learners.

Services Distance learners have accessibility to academic advising, bookstore, e-mail services, library services.

Contact Vieva Edison, Customer Services, Memorial University of Newfoundland, G. A. Hickman Building, ED-2000, St. John's, NF A1B 3X8, Canada. *Telephone:* 709-737-8700. *Fax:* 709-737-4070. *E-mail:* distance@mun.ca.

DEGREES AND AWARDS

BBA Business Administration

BComm Commerce (General)

BN Nursing–Post-Basic RN

BS Maritime Studies–Bachelor of Maritime Studies (BMS); Technology–Bachelor of Technology (BTech)

Certificate Business Administration; Career Development; Criminology; Library Studies; Municipal Administration; Newfoundland Studies; Public Administration

Diploma Business Administration

MEd Information Technology; Leadership Studies; Post-Secondary Studies; Teaching and Learning

MN Nursing

COURSE SUBJECT AREAS OFFERED OUTSIDE OF DEGREE PROGRAMS

Undergraduate—anthropology; biology; business administration and management; computer science; economics; education, general; education, other; engineering, general; English language and literature, general; geography; history; library science/librarianship; mathematical statistics; mathematics; medical clinical sciences (M.S., Ph.D.); nursing; philosophy; political science and government; psychology; religion/religious studies; social work; sociology; women's studies.

Graduate—criminology; education, other; library science/librarianship; nursing; social work.

MERCY COLLEGE

Dobbs Ferry, New York
MerLIN
http://merlin.mercy.edu

Mercy College was founded in 1951. It is accredited by Middle States Association of Colleges and Schools. It first offered distance learning courses in 1990. In fall 2003, there were 2,300 students enrolled in distance learning courses. Institutionally administered financial aid is available to distance learners.

Services Distance learners have accessibility to academic advising, bookstore, campus computer network, career placement assistance, e-mail services, library services, tutoring.

Contact Dr. Frank Bryce McCluskey, Dean of Online Education, Mercy College, 555 Broadway, Dobbs Ferry, NY 10522. *Telephone:* 914-674-7521. *Fax:* 914-674-7729. *E-mail:* fmccluskey@mercy.edu.

DEGREES AND AWARDS

AA Liberal Arts and Sciences

AS Liberal Arts and Sciences

BA Psychology

BS Business Administration; Computer Science; Psychology

MA English

MBA Business Administration

MPA Health Sciences

MS Banking; Counseling; Direct Marketing; Internet Business Systems; Organizational Leadership

COURSE SUBJECT AREAS OFFERED OUTSIDE OF DEGREE PROGRAMS

Undergraduate—accounting; American history; area, ethnic and cultural studies, other; art history; biology; business; business administration and management; business marketing and marketing management; communications technologies; community organization, resources and services; comparative literature; developmental/child psychology; education administration and supervision; educational psychology; English composition; English creative writing; English language and literature, general; English literature (British and Commonwealth); European history; international business; law and legal studies related; management information systems/business data processing; mathematical statistics; mathematics related; public administration and services, other; public health; social psychology; sociology.

Graduate—American literature (United States); business; business administration and management; business and personal services marketing operations; business communications; business information and data processing services; business management and administrative services, other; business/managerial economics; business marketing and marketing management; business quantitative methods and management science; community health services; comparative literature; computer and information sciences, general; computer and information sciences, other; computer/information technology administration and management; computer science; computer systems analysis; English language and literature, general; English language and literature/letters, other; English literature (British and Commonwealth); Internet and World Wide Web; management information systems/business data processing; marketing management and research; peace and conflict studies; psychology; psychology, other; social sciences and history, other.

MESA COMMUNITY COLLEGE

Mesa, Arizona

http://www.mc.maricopa.edu/other/distance/

Mesa Community College was founded in 1965. It is accredited by North Central Association of Colleges and Schools. It first offered distance learning courses in 1996. In fall 2003, there were 2,400 students enrolled in distance learning courses. Institutionally administered financial aid is available to distance learners.

Services Distance learners have accessibility to academic advising, bookstore, campus computer network, e-mail services, library services, tutoring.

Contact Distance Learning Office, Mesa Community College, 1833 West Southern Avenue, Mesa, AZ 85233. *E-mail:* distance.learning@mcmail.maricopa.edu.

DEGREES AND AWARDS

Programs offered do not lead to a degree or other formal award.

COURSE SUBJECT AREAS OFFERED OUTSIDE OF DEGREE PROGRAMS

Undergraduate—biology, general; business administration and management; communications, general; computer/information technology administration and management; computer programming; computer science; computer software and media applications; criminal justice and corrections; economics; English composition; English creative writing; English language and literature, general; English technical and business writing; foods and nutrition studies; foreign languages and literatures; health and medical preparatory programs; health professions and related sciences, other; history; home economics, other; mathematics; nursing; physiological psychology/psychobiology; political science and government; religion/religious studies; school psychology.

MESALANDS COMMUNITY COLLEGE

Tucumcari, New Mexico

http://www.mesalands.edu

Mesalands Community College was founded in 1979. It is accredited by North Central Association of Colleges and Schools. It first offered distance learning courses in 1997. In fall 2003, there were 125 students enrolled in distance learning courses. Institutionally administered financial aid is available to distance learners.

Services Distance learners have accessibility to academic advising, bookstore, library services, tutoring.

Contact Ms. Nancy C. Nydam, Distance Education Coordinator, Mesalands Community College, 911 South Tenth Street, Tucumcari, NM 88401. *Telephone:* 505-461-4413 Ext. 118. *Fax:* 505-461-1901. *E-mail:* nancyn@mesalands.edu.

DEGREES AND AWARDS

Programs offered do not lead to a degree or other formal award.

COURSE SUBJECT AREAS OFFERED OUTSIDE OF DEGREE PROGRAMS

Undergraduate—accounting; agricultural business and management; animal sciences; astronomy; business; computer and information sciences, general; computer science; economics; education, general; English language and literature, general; geography; geological and related sciences; history; human resources management; marketing management and research; mathematics; music; physical sciences, general; sociology; teacher assistant/aide.

METROPOLITAN COMMUNITY COLLEGE

Omaha, Nebraska

Student and Instructional Services

http://www.mccneb.edu

Metropolitan Community College was founded in 1974. It is accredited by North Central Association of Colleges and Schools. It first offered distance learning courses in 1985. In fall 2003, there were 6,430 students enrolled in distance learning courses. Institutionally administered financial aid is available to distance learners.

Services Distance learners have accessibility to academic advising, bookstore, career placement assistance, e-mail services, library services.

Contact Arlene Jordan, Director of Enrollment Management, Metropolitan Community College, PO Box 3777, Omaha, NE 68103-0777. *Telephone:* 402-457-2418. *Fax:* 402-457-2564. *E-mail:* ajordan@mccneb.edu.

DEGREES AND AWARDS

AA Liberal Arts
AAS Professional Studies
AD General Program

COURSE SUBJECT AREAS OFFERED OUTSIDE OF DEGREE PROGRAMS

Undergraduate—accounting; anthropology; biology, general; business; child care and guidance workers and managers; computer programming; criminal justice and corrections; economics; English composition; financial management and services; history; legal studies; mathematics; psychology; sociology.

METROPOLITAN STATE UNIVERSITY

St. Paul, Minnesota

http://www.metrostate.edu

Metropolitan State University was founded in 1971. It is accredited by North Central Association of Colleges and Schools. It first offered distance learning courses in 1994. In fall 2003, there were 741 students enrolled in distance learning courses. Institutionally administered financial aid is available to distance learners.

Services Distance learners have accessibility to bookstore, career placement assistance, e-mail services, library services.

Contact Ms. Rosa Rodriguez, Interim Director of Admissions, Metropolitan State University, 700 East 7th Street, St. Paul, MN 55106. *Telephone:* 651-793-1300. *Fax:* 651-793-1310. *E-mail:* rosa.rodriguez@metrostate.edu.

DEGREES AND AWARDS

BA Individualized
BS Business Administration; Management; Marketing
CCCPE Law Enforcement

Metropolitan State University (continued)

COURSE SUBJECT AREAS OFFERED OUTSIDE OF DEGREE PROGRAMS

Undergraduate—accounting; anthropology; business administration and management; business marketing and marketing management; communications, other; criminal justice and corrections; economics; English composition; financial management and services; human resources management; human services; information sciences and systems; international business; legal studies; management information systems/business data processing; marketing management and research; mathematics; music; nursing; philosophy; psychology; public administration.

Graduate—business marketing and marketing management; legal studies; management information systems/business data processing; marketing management and research; nursing.

MGH INSTITUTE OF HEALTH PROFESSIONS

Boston, Massachusetts

http://www.mghihp.edu

MGH Institute of Health Professions was founded in 1977. It is accredited by New England Association of Schools and Colleges. It first offered distance learning courses in 2000. In fall 2003, there were 184 students enrolled in distance learning courses. Institutionally administered financial aid is available to distance learners.

Services Distance learners have accessibility to academic advising, bookstore, campus computer network, e-mail services, library services, tutoring.

Contact Ms. Terry Lavin, Director of Admissions, MGH Institute of Health Professions, 36 1st Avenue, Boston, MA 02129-4557. *Telephone:* 617-726-6069. *Fax:* 617-726-8010. *E-mail:* tlavin@mghihp.edu.

DEGREES AND AWARDS

Graduate Certificate Clinical Investigation
MS Clinical Investigations
DPT Transitional Doctor of Physical Therapy

COURSE SUBJECT AREAS OFFERED OUTSIDE OF DEGREE PROGRAMS

Graduate—communication disorders sciences and services; health professions and related sciences, other; nursing.

MIAMI DADE COLLEGE

Miami, Florida

Virtual College

http://www.mdc.edu/vcollege/

Miami Dade College was founded in 1960. It is accredited by Southern Association of Colleges and Schools. It first offered distance learning courses in 1997. In fall 2003, there were 3,000 students enrolled in distance learning courses. Institutionally administered financial aid is available to distance learners.

Services Distance learners have accessibility to academic advising, bookstore, library services.

Contact Lloyd Hollingsworth, Student Services Coordinator and Webmaster, Miami Dade College, 950 Northwest 20th Street, Miami, FL 33127-4693. *Telephone:* 305-237-4222. *Fax:* 305-237-4081. *E-mail:* lholling@mdc.edu.

DEGREES AND AWARDS

Programs offered do not lead to a degree or other formal award.

COURSE SUBJECT AREAS OFFERED OUTSIDE OF DEGREE PROGRAMS

Undergraduate—accounting; American literature (United States); atmospheric sciences and meteorology; bible/biblical studies; biological and physical sciences; biological sciences/life sciences, other; biology, general; computer and information sciences, general; economics; education, general; English composition; English language and literature, general; health and medical administrative services; individual and family development studies; international relations and affairs; liberal arts and sciences, general studies and humanities; library science, other; mathematics; philosophy and religion; physical sciences, other; political science and government; psychology; religion/religious studies; social sciences, general; speech and rhetorical studies; taxation.

Non-credit—health professions and related sciences, other.

MICHIGAN TECHNOLOGICAL UNIVERSITY

Houghton, Michigan

Sponsored Educational Programs

http://www.admin.mtu.edu/sep

Michigan Technological University was founded in 1885. It is accredited by North Central Association of Colleges and Schools. It first offered distance learning courses in 1984. In fall 2003, there were 484 students enrolled in distance learning courses. Institutionally administered financial aid is available to distance learners.

Services Distance learners have accessibility to academic advising, bookstore, campus computer network, career placement assistance, e-mail services, library services, tutoring.

Contact Ms. Lynn A. Artman, Program Manager, Michigan Technological University, Sponsored Educational Programs, 1400 Townsend Drive, Houghton, MI 49931. *Telephone:* 800-405-4678. *Fax:* 906-487-2463. *E-mail:* laartman@mtu.edu.

DEGREES AND AWARDS

AAS Engineering Technology
BS Engineering; Surveying
Certificate Engineering Design
MS Electrical Engineering; Mechanical Engineering
PhD Electrical Engineering; Mechanical Engineering

COURSE SUBJECT AREAS OFFERED OUTSIDE OF DEGREE PROGRAMS

Undergraduate—civil engineering; economics; engineering mechanics; engineering-related technologies, other; mathematics; mechanical engineering; surveying.

Graduate—electrical engineering; mechanical engineering.

Non-credit—engineering mechanics; engineering-related technologies, other; mathematics; mechanical engineering.

MID-AMERICA CHRISTIAN UNIVERSITY

Oklahoma City, Oklahoma
TELOS Degree Completion
http://www.macu.edu/telos

Mid-America Christian University was founded in 1953. It is accredited by North Central Association of Colleges and Schools. It first offered distance learning courses in 1999. In fall 2003, there were 350 students enrolled in distance learning courses. Institutionally administered financial aid is available to distance learners.

Services Distance learners have accessibility to academic advising, bookstore, campus computer network, e-mail services, library services.

Contact Rev. Deanne Curtis-Mowry, Director of TELOS Degree Completion Program, Mid-America Christian University, 3500 SW 119th Street, Oklahoma City, OK 73170. *Telephone:* 405-692-3198. *Fax:* 405-692-3165. *E-mail:* dmowry@macu.edu.

DEGREES AND AWARDS

Programs offered do not lead to a degree or other formal award.

COURSE SUBJECT AREAS OFFERED OUTSIDE OF DEGREE PROGRAMS

Undergraduate—bible/biblical studies; pastoral counseling and specialized ministries; religion/religious studies; theological and ministerial studies.

Non-credit—bible/biblical studies; pastoral counseling and specialized ministries; religion/religious studies; theological and ministerial studies.

Special Message

Mid-America Christian University (MACU), now located in Oklahoma City, Oklahoma, was founded in 1953 and is in its twelfth year of offering a degree completion program (TELOS) for ministers and lay leaders. (TELOS is a Greek word meaning the end result or ultimate goal toward which one strives.)

The TELOS program allows students to achieve their goals through several expanded educational methods, such as Internet courses; contract learning (directed learning overseen by an individual professor); highly focused on-campus events; CLEP, DANTES, and other standardized proficiency tests; transfer of college credits from other institutions; and credit through prior learning experiences.

The TELOS degree, a Bachelor of Science in Professional Ministries, is a 124-hour degree. The TELOS program is a 57-hour program that focuses upon biblical/theological and pastoral leadership skills. In order to enter, the program requires that the students have approximately 2 years prior college and are at least 22 years of age. Students needing additional hours to complete the degree need to speak to their TELOS adviser about ways of achieving those hours (credit for prior learning, correspondence courses, contract learning courses, CLEP, DANTES, etc.).

MACU recognizes that not all persons desiring higher learning, and who are answering God's call to ministry, have prior college hours. All courses are available for those not seeking a degree at the same time of enrollment. Courses may, at a later date, be applied towards the TELOS degree.

The cost (excluding books and fees) is $600 per 3-hour course. For more information, applicants may contact MACU by phone at 877-569-3198 (toll-free) or e-mail at dmowry@macu.edu. Prospective students should visit the MACU Web site at http://www.macu.edu for full cost structure and degree requirements. MACU is accredited through the Higher Learning Commission, North Central Association, 30 North LaSalle Street, Suite 2400, Chicago, Illinois 60602-2504.

MIDDLESEX COMMUNITY COLLEGE

Bedford, Massachusetts
http://online.middlesex.mass.edu

Middlesex Community College was founded in 1970. It is accredited by New England Association of Schools and Colleges. It first offered distance learning courses in 1997. In fall 2003, there were 1,150 students enrolled in distance learning courses. Institutionally administered financial aid is available to distance learners.

Services Distance learners have accessibility to academic advising, bookstore, campus computer network, e-mail services, library services, tutoring.

Contact Mr. Sanford A. Arbogast, Instructional Technology Analyst, Middlesex Community College, Academic Resources Building, Springs Road, Bedford, MA 01730. *Telephone:* 781-280-3739. *Fax:* 781-280-3771. *E-mail:* arbogasts@middlesex.mass.edu.

DEGREES AND AWARDS

AA Liberal Arts and Sciences
AAS Liberal Studies
ABA Business Administration Career
AS Business Administration Transfer; Fire Protection
Certificate Small Business Management; Web Publishing

COURSE SUBJECT AREAS OFFERED OUTSIDE OF DEGREE PROGRAMS

Undergraduate—accounting; advertising; area, ethnic and cultural studies, other; biological sciences/life sciences, other; biology, general; business; business administration and management; business communications; business/managerial economics; communications technologies; community psychology; computer and information sciences, general; computer and information sciences, other; computer programming; computer science; computer software and media applications; criminal justice and corrections; cultural studies; data entry/microcomputer applications; dental services; developmental and child psychology; economics; educational psychology; English composition; English language and literature, general; English language and literature/letters, other; English literature (British and Commonwealth); English technical and business writing; fine arts and art studies; fire protection; foods and nutrition studies; foreign languages and literatures; foreign languages and literatures, other; geography; history; human resources management; Internet and World Wide Web; legal studies; liberal arts and sciences, general studies and humanities; marketing management and research; mathematical statistics; mathematics; mathematics and computer science; mathematics, other; philosophy; philosophy and religion; physical sciences, general; political science and government; psychology; social psychology; social sciences and history, other; social sciences, general; sociology; taxation.

Non-credit—business; business administration and management; computer software and media applications; computer systems analysis; English creative writing; English technical and business writing; financial management and services; fine arts and art studies; gerontology; Internet and World Wide Web.

MIDDLE TENNESSEE STATE UNIVERSITY

Murfreesboro, Tennessee
Division of Continuing Studies
http://www.mtsu.edu/learn

Middle Tennessee State University was founded in 1911. It is accredited by Southern Association of Colleges and Schools. It first offered distance learning courses in 1994. In fall 2003, there were 2,100 students enrolled in distance learning courses. Institutionally administered financial aid is available to distance learners.

Services Distance learners have accessibility to academic advising, bookstore, campus computer network, e-mail services, library services, tutoring.

Contact Dianna Rust, Director of Academic Outreach and Distance Learning, Middle Tennessee State University, 1301 East Main Street, PO Box X109, Murfreesboro, TN 37132. *Telephone:* 615-898-5611. *Fax:* 615-896-7925. *E-mail:* dzeh@mtsu.edu.

DEGREES AND AWARDS

BS Liberal Studies; Professional Studies, Concentration in Information Technology; Professional Studies, Concentration in Organizational Leadership
BSN Nursing
MEd Advanced Studies in Teaching and Learning
MS Mathematics
MSN Nursing

COURSE SUBJECT AREAS OFFERED OUTSIDE OF DEGREE PROGRAMS

Undergraduate—accounting; aerospace, aeronautical and astronautical engineering; agricultural business and management; American literature (United States); area, ethnic and cultural studies, other; astronomy; business administration and management; business communications; communications, general; criminal justice and corrections; economics; educational psychology; education, general; English composition; English language and literature, general; food sciences and technology; geological and related sciences; health and physical education/fitness; human resources management; journalism and mass communications; liberal arts and sciences, general studies and humanities; marketing operations/marketing and distribution, other; mathematics; nursing; political science and government; radio and television broadcasting; social sciences, general; social work; sociology.
Graduate—aerospace, aeronautical and astronautical engineering; economics; educational evaluation, research and statistics; marketing management and research; mathematics; nursing.
Non-credit—area, ethnic and cultural studies, other; bilingual/bicultural education; business; business administration and management; business and personal services marketing operations; business communications; business information and data processing services; business management and administrative services, other; business/managerial economics; city/urban, community and regional planning; computer and information sciences, general; computer/information technology administration and management; computer programming; computer science; computer software and media applications; computer systems networking and telecommunications; crafts, folk art and artisanry; culinary arts and related services; dance; dramatic/theater arts and stagecraft; engineering/industrial management; English as a second language; financial services marketing operations; fine arts and art studies; foreign languages and literatures; health and medical assistants; human resources management; industrial and organizational psychology; industrial/manufacturing engineering; miscellaneous health professions; nursing; real estate; wildlife and wildlands management.

Special Message

Middle Tennessee State University (MTSU) now offers accredited classes through a variety of technologies for students who may not be able to come to the campus.

Compressed video courses are instructed at one site and simultaneously sent to distant sites in Tennessee. Students and instructors can see one another on television monitors and talk to one another using microphones. Telecourses are offered via cable television or videotape. Students can view course segments on the MTSU cable channel or the local PBS affiliate or at the MTSU McWherter Learning Resources Center. Students consult with their instructors during telephone office hours or through e-mail. Students are required to attend an orientation, a midterm exam, and a final exam on campus.

Correspondence courses involve individual instruction of a student by an instructor. Typically, students study at home. Interaction between correspondence course faculty members and students consists of written assignments, testing, and assistance via such media as print/written word, telephone, fax, e-mail, and the World Wide Web. After registration, students receive a packet in the mail from the correspondence course coordinator, containing information about assignments and directions for completing and submitting them.

Online courses are taught primarily over the Internet through e-mail, newsgroups, distribution lists, and the World Wide Web. MTSU offers online Bachelor of Science degree programs in liberal studies and in professional studies with concentrations in information technology and organizational leadership as well as a Master of Education degree. These various distance learning programs are closing the gap between students and the campus.

MID-SOUTH COMMUNITY COLLEGE

West Memphis, Arkansas

Mid-South Community College was founded in 1993. It is accredited by North Central Association of Colleges and Schools. It first offered distance learning courses in 1997. In fall 2003, there were 90 students enrolled in distance learning courses. Institutionally administered financial aid is available to distance learners.

Services Distance learners have accessibility to campus computer network, e-mail services.

Contact Karly Vardaman, EOC Counselor, Mid-South Community College, 2000 West Broadway, West Memphis, AR 72301. *Telephone:* 870-733-6705. *E-mail:* kvardaman@midsouthcc.edu.

DEGREES AND AWARDS

Programs offered do not lead to a degree or other formal award.

COURSE SUBJECT AREAS OFFERED OUTSIDE OF DEGREE PROGRAMS

Undergraduate—computer and information sciences, general; liberal arts and sciences, general studies and humanities.
Non-credit—business communications; computer and information sciences, general; legal studies.

MIDSTATE COLLEGE

Peoria, Illinois

http://www.midstate.edu/

Midstate College was founded in 1888. It is accredited by North Central Association of Colleges and Schools. It first offered distance learning courses in 1999. In fall 2003, there were 198 students enrolled in distance learning courses. Institutionally administered financial aid is available to distance learners.

Services Distance learners have accessibility to academic advising, e-mail services, library services.

Contact Ms. Jessica Auer, Director of Admissions, Midstate College, 411 West Northmoor Road, Peoria, IL 61614. *Telephone:* 309-692-4092 Ext. 1090. *Fax:* 309-692-3893. *E-mail:* admissions@midstate.edu.

DEGREES AND AWARDS

BBA Business Administration

COURSE SUBJECT AREAS OFFERED OUTSIDE OF DEGREE PROGRAMS

Undergraduate—accounting; computer software and media applications; English composition.

MID-STATE TECHNICAL COLLEGE

Wisconsin Rapids, Wisconsin

Information Services

http://www.mstc.edu/academics/distance/cbt.htm

Mid-State Technical College was founded in 1917. It is accredited by North Central Association of Colleges and Schools. It first offered distance learning courses in 1996. Institutionally administered financial aid is available to distance learners.

Services Distance learners have accessibility to academic advising, bookstore, e-mail services, library services.

Contact Steve Thomas, Dean, Business Division, Mid-State Technical College, 500 32nd Street North, Wisconsin Rapids, WI 54494. *Telephone:* 715-422-5356. *Fax:* 715-422-5609.

DEGREES AND AWARDS

AD Supervisory Management

COURSE SUBJECT AREAS OFFERED OUTSIDE OF DEGREE PROGRAMS

Undergraduate—business administration and management; computer and information sciences, general; computer and information sciences, other; sociology; systems engineering.

MILLERSVILLE UNIVERSITY OF PENNSYLVANIA

Millersville, Pennsylvania

MU Online

http://muweb.millersville.edu/~muonline

Millersville University of Pennsylvania was founded in 1855. It is accredited by Middle States Association of Colleges and Schools. It first offered distance learning courses in 1998. In fall 2003, there were 75 students enrolled in distance learning courses. Institutionally administered financial aid is available to distance learners.

Services Distance learners have accessibility to academic advising, bookstore, campus computer network, career placement assistance, e-mail services, library services.

Contact Ms. Loreal L. Maguire, Assistant Director, Professional Training and Education, Millersville University of Pennsylvania, PO Box 1002, Millersville, PA 17551. *Telephone:* 717-872-3030. *Fax:* 717-871-2022. *E-mail:* loreal.maguire@millersville.edu.

DEGREES AND AWARDS

Programs offered do not lead to a degree or other formal award.

COURSE SUBJECT AREAS OFFERED OUTSIDE OF DEGREE PROGRAMS

Undergraduate—atmospheric sciences and meteorology; business administration and management; communications, general; economics; education, general; English composition; foreign languages and literatures; health and physical education/fitness; sociology; special education; teacher education, specific academic and vocational programs.

Graduate—education, general; foreign languages and literatures; health and physical education/fitness; special education; teacher education, specific academic and vocational programs; technology education/industrial arts.

MILWAUKEE SCHOOL OF ENGINEERING

Milwaukee, Wisconsin

MSOE-TV

http://www.msoe.edu/admiss

Milwaukee School of Engineering was founded in 1903. It is accredited by North Central Association of Colleges and Schools. It first offered distance learning courses in 1989. In fall 2003, there were 69 students enrolled in distance learning courses. Institutionally administered financial aid is available to distance learners.

Services Distance learners have accessibility to academic advising, bookstore, campus computer network, career placement assistance, e-mail services, library services.

Contact Mr. Kent Peterson, Manager of Internet Services, Milwaukee School of Engineering, 1025 North Broadway, Milwaukee, WI 53202-3109. *Telephone:* 414-277-7176. *Fax:* 414-277-7453. *E-mail:* peterson@msoe.edu.

DEGREES AND AWARDS

Programs offered do not lead to a degree or other formal award.

COURSE SUBJECT AREAS OFFERED OUTSIDE OF DEGREE PROGRAMS

Graduate—organizational behavior.

MINNEAPOLIS COLLEGE OF ART AND DESIGN

Minneapolis, Minnesota

MCAD Distance Learning

http://online.mcad.edu

Minneapolis College of Art and Design was founded in 1886. It is accredited by North Central Association of Colleges and Schools. It

Minneapolis College of Art and Design (continued)

first offered distance learning courses in 1995. In fall 2003, there were 191 students enrolled in distance learning courses. Institutionally administered financial aid is available to distance learners.

Services Distance learners have accessibility to bookstore, e-mail services, library services.

Contact Rebecca J. Alm, Director of Distance Learning, Minneapolis College of Art and Design, 2501 Stevens Avenue, South, Minneapolis, MN 55404. *Telephone:* 612-874-3658. *Fax:* 612-874-3704. *E-mail:* rebecca_alm@mcad.edu.

DEGREES AND AWARDS

Programs offered do not lead to a degree or other formal award.

COURSE SUBJECT AREAS OFFERED OUTSIDE OF DEGREE PROGRAMS

Undergraduate—American literature (United States); architecture and related programs, other; art history; design and applied arts; film studies; fine arts and art studies.

Non-credit—design and applied arts; fine arts and art studies.

MINNESOTA SCHOOL OF BUSINESS–BROOKLYN CENTER

Brooklyn Center, Minnesota

Minnesota School of Business–Brooklyn Center was founded in 1989. It is accredited by Accrediting Council for Independent Colleges and Schools. It first offered distance learning courses in 2001. In fall 2003, there were 325 students enrolled in distance learning courses. Institutionally administered financial aid is available to distance learners.

Services Distance learners have accessibility to e-mail services, library services.

Contact Jeff Georgeson, Director of Admissions, Minnesota School of Business–Brooklyn Center, 5910 Shingle Creek Parkway, Brooklyn Center, MN 55430. *Telephone:* 763-585-5206. *E-mail:* jgeorgeson@msbcollege.edu.

DEGREES AND AWARDS

Programs offered do not lead to a degree or other formal award.

COURSE SUBJECT AREAS OFFERED OUTSIDE OF DEGREE PROGRAMS

Undergraduate—accounting; administrative and secretarial services; advertising; American literature (United States); applied mathematics; area, ethnic and cultural studies, other; biological and physical sciences; biology, general; business; business administration and management; business communications; communications, general; computer and information sciences, general; computer engineering; economics; English composition; English language and literature, general; health and medical assistants; legal studies; mathematical statistics; psychology.

MINNESOTA SCHOOL OF BUSINESS-RICHFIELD

Richfield, Minnesota

http://www.msbcollege.edu

Minnesota School of Business-Richfield was founded in 1877. It is accredited by Accrediting Council for Independent Colleges and Schools. It first offered distance learning courses in 2000. In fall 2003, there were 990 students enrolled in distance learning courses. Institutionally administered financial aid is available to distance learners.

Services Distance learners have accessibility to academic advising, campus computer network, career placement assistance, e-mail services, library services, tutoring.

Contact Patricia Murray, Director of Admissions, Minnesota School of Business-Richfield, 1401 West 76th Street, Suite 500, Richfield, MN 55423. *Telephone:* 612-861-2000. *Fax:* 800-752-4223. *E-mail:* pmurray@msbcollege.edu.

DEGREES AND AWARDS

Programs offered do not lead to a degree or other formal award.

COURSE SUBJECT AREAS OFFERED OUTSIDE OF DEGREE PROGRAMS

Undergraduate—accounting; biology, general; business administration and management; communications, general; computer science; English technical and business writing; entrepreneurship; health and medical administrative services; international business; legal studies; liberal arts and sciences, general studies and humanities; mathematics; psychology.

MINNESOTA STATE COLLEGE–SOUTHEAST TECHNICAL

Winona, Minnesota

http://www.southeastmn.edu

Minnesota State College–Southeast Technical was founded in 1992. It is accredited by North Central Association of Colleges and Schools. It first offered distance learning courses in 1999. In fall 2003, there were 458 students enrolled in distance learning courses. Institutionally administered financial aid is available to distance learners.

Services Distance learners have accessibility to academic advising, bookstore, campus computer network, career placement assistance, e-mail services, library services, tutoring.

Contact Ms. Pat Buxengard, Project Director, Minnesota State College–Southeast Technical, 1200 Storrs Pond Road, PO Box 409, Winona, MN 55987. *Telephone:* 507-453-2419. *Fax:* 507-453-2424. *E-mail:* pbuxengard@southeastmn.edu.

DEGREES AND AWARDS

AAS Computer Programming, Web Applications Emphasis; Medical Administrative Secretary; Microcomputer Support Specialist; Professional Nanny/Family Child Care; Web Design and Development

Certificate C++ Client-Server Programming; C++ Windows Programming; Child Care Basics; Medical Secretary Transcriptionist; Microsoft Office Certificate; Web Applications Programming

Diploma Business Microcomputing; Medical Secretary

COURSE SUBJECT AREAS OFFERED OUTSIDE OF DEGREE PROGRAMS

Non-credit—accounting; business; business administration and management; business and personal services marketing operations; communications, general; computer software and media applications; English as a second language; general retailing/wholesaling; human resources management; journalism and mass communications; marketing management and research; personal and miscellaneous services, other; public relations and organizational communications.

MINOT STATE UNIVERSITY–BOTTINEAU CAMPUS

Bottineau, North Dakota

http://www.misu-b.nodak.edu

Minot State University–Bottineau Campus was founded in 1906. It is accredited by North Central Association of Colleges and Schools. It first offered distance learning courses in 2000. In fall 2003, there were 75 students enrolled in distance learning courses. Institutionally administered financial aid is available to distance learners.

Services Distance learners have accessibility to bookstore, library services.
Contact Jan Nahinurk, Director, Minot State University–Bottineau Campus, 105 Simrall Boulevard, Bottineau, ND 58318. *Telephone:* 888-918-5623. *E-mail:* nahinurk@misu.nodak.edu.

DEGREES AND AWARDS

AA Liberal Arts
AAS Accounting Technician; Administrative Assistant; Medical Assistant; Medical Secretary; Paraeducation
Certificate of Completion Advanced Medical Transcription; Basic Grounds Worker Skills; Medical Coding and Insurance Specialist
Diploma Medical Assistant; Reception Services

COURSE SUBJECT AREAS OFFERED OUTSIDE OF DEGREE PROGRAMS

Undergraduate—administrative and secretarial services; biological sciences/life sciences, other; business management and administrative services, other; health and medical administrative services; health and medical assistants; horticulture services operations and management; liberal arts and sciences, general studies and humanities; medical basic sciences; teacher assistant/aide.

MIRACOSTA COLLEGE

Oceanside, California

MiraCosta CyberCollege

http://www.miracosta.edu/cybercosta/

MiraCosta College was founded in 1934. It is accredited by Western Association of Schools and Colleges. It first offered distance learning courses in 1998. In fall 2003, there were 2,200 students enrolled in distance learning courses. Institutionally administered financial aid is available to distance learners.

Services Distance learners have accessibility to academic advising, bookstore, library services, tutoring.
Contact Mr. Brad Hinson, Open Learning Coordinator, MiraCosta College, One Barnard Drive, Oceanside, CA 92056. *Telephone:* 760-795-6745. *Fax:* 760-795-6723. *E-mail:* bhinson@miracosta.edu.

DEGREES AND AWARDS

Programs offered do not lead to a degree or other formal award.

COURSE SUBJECT AREAS OFFERED OUTSIDE OF DEGREE PROGRAMS

Undergraduate—accounting; biological sciences/life sciences, other; business; communications, general; computer and information sciences, general; computer software and media applications; economics; English as a second language; English composition; entrepreneurship; film studies; fine arts and art studies; geological and related sciences; history; hospitality services management; Internet and World Wide Web; mathematics; music; philosophy; philosophy and religion; real estate; sociology.
Non-credit—accounting; business administration and management; business management and administrative services, other; child care and guidance workers and managers; computer programming; computer software and media applications; consumer and homemaking education; English as a second language; English creative writing; health professions and related sciences, other; home economics, general; legal studies; mathematics; philosophy.

MISSISSIPPI DELTA COMMUNITY COLLEGE

Moorhead, Mississippi

http://www.msdelta.edu/distanceLearning/home.htm

Mississippi Delta Community College was founded in 1926. It is accredited by Southern Association of Colleges and Schools. It first offered distance learning courses in 2000. In fall 2003, there were 540 students enrolled in distance learning courses. Institutionally administered financial aid is available to distance learners.

Services Distance learners have accessibility to academic advising, bookstore, campus computer network, library services.
Contact Mrs. Jackie Bailey-Hall, Distance Learning Coordinator, Mississippi Delta Community College, PO Box 668, Moorhead, MS 38761. *Telephone:* 662-246-6392. *Fax:* 662-246-6296. *E-mail:* jbailey@msdelta.edu.

DEGREES AND AWARDS

AA General Program

COURSE SUBJECT AREAS OFFERED OUTSIDE OF DEGREE PROGRAMS

Undergraduate—accounting; astronomy; biological and physical sciences; biological sciences/life sciences, other; biology, general; botany; business; chemistry; criminal justice and corrections; economics; English composition; English language and literature, general; English literature (British and Commonwealth); family and community studies; geography; history; home economics, general; mathematics; music; physical sciences, general; physical sciences, other; political science and government; psychology; sociology; speech and rhetorical studies.

MISSISSIPPI STATE UNIVERSITY

Mississippi State, Mississippi

Division of Continuing Education

http://www.distance.msstate.edu

Mississippi State University was founded in 1878. It is accredited by Southern Association of Colleges and Schools. It first offered distance learning courses in 1987. In fall 2003, there were 800 students enrolled in distance learning courses. Institutionally administered financial aid is available to distance learners.

Services Distance learners have accessibility to academic advising, bookstore, career placement assistance, e-mail services, library services.
Contact Dr. Laura A. Crittenden, Manager of Credit Studies, Mississippi State University, Distance Education, 1 Barr Avenue, PO

Mississippi State University (continued)

Box 5247, Mississippi State, MS 39762-5247. *Telephone:* 662-325-2677. *Fax:* 662-325-0930. *E-mail:* lcrittenden@ce.msstate.edu.

DEGREES AND AWARDS

BS Elementary Education; Interdisciplinary Studies
Certificate Discovery Teacher Training
License Vocational Teacher Licensure
MAT Community College Leadership
MBA Business Administration
MC Sc Computer Science
MS Chemical Engineering; Civil Engineering; Computational Engineering; Electrical and Computer Engineering; Industrial Engineering; Mechanical Engineering; Physical Education–Health Education/Health Promotion Emphasis; Public Policy Administration; Workforce Education Leadership
MSE Elementary Education
PhD Community College Leadership

COURSE SUBJECT AREAS OFFERED OUTSIDE OF DEGREE PROGRAMS

Undergraduate—accounting; biological and physical sciences; biology, general; child care and guidance workers and managers; communications, general; counseling psychology; curriculum and instruction; developmental and child psychology; educational/instructional media design; educational psychology; education, other; fine arts and art studies; general teacher education; landscape architecture; mathematical statistics; multi/interdisciplinary studies, other; physical sciences, other; physics; teacher education, specific academic and vocational programs; zoology.
Graduate—agriculture/agricultural sciences; business; business administration and management; business/managerial economics; chemical engineering; civil engineering; computer engineering; computer science; counseling psychology; curriculum and instruction; education administration and supervision; educational evaluation, research and statistics; educational/instructional media design; educational psychology; engineering, general; engineering mechanics; engineering-related technologies, other; health professions and related sciences, other; public administration; teacher education, specific academic and vocational programs.

Special Message

Mississippi State University was founded as a land-grant institution in 1878 to meet the needs of the people, institutions, and organizations of the state and nation through undergraduate and graduate education. Mississippi State University enrolls more than 16,000 students on the main campus, branch campus, and off-campus centers and through distance learning.

Mississippi State University is a Doctoral I university and is placed among the top 100 universities in the nation to receive federal research support. The University is fully accredited by the Southern Association of Colleges and Schools.

The Division of Continuing Education is an academic service arm of the University and is committed to meeting the academic needs of nontraditional adult learners who are not able to attend classes on campus due to geographic location and/or career and personal commitments. With expertise in advanced telecommunication technology and its application in education, the Division of Continuing Education continues to be a leader in distance learning by utilizing the following delivery mediums: the Internet, videotapes, the Mississippi Interactive Video Network (MIVN), and intensive weekend seminars.

The Division coordinates distance learning courses and degree programs in the following disciplines: child development and interdisciplinary studies (bachelor's); elementary education (bachelor's and master's); agricultural and extension education, architecture (fall 2004), business administration, civil engineering, community college leadership (spring 2004), computer science, counselor education, electrical and computer engineering, industrial engineering, K-12 administration (educational specialist), mechanical engineering, physical education–health education/health promotion emphasis, public policy and administration, public program evaluation, workforce education leadership (master's); and community college leadership and K-12 administration (Ph.D.). In addition, the following programs are offered: Discovery Teacher Training, Insurance Summer Insitute Program (summer 2004), Special Programs for Academically Talented Students, and the Vocational Teacher Licensure Program. For more information, interested students should visit the Distance Learning Web site (http://www.distance.msstate.edu).

MISSISSIPPI UNIVERSITY FOR WOMEN

Columbus, Mississippi
Continuing Education
http://www.muw.edu/

Mississippi University for Women was founded in 1884. It is accredited by Southern Association of Colleges and Schools. It first offered distance learning courses in 1994. In fall 2003, there were 20 students enrolled in distance learning courses. Institutionally administered financial aid is available to distance learners.

Services Distance learners have accessibility to academic advising, bookstore, career placement assistance, e-mail services, library services.

Contact Kathy McShane, Coordinator, Mississippi University for Women, Advanced Placement Option, 1918 Briar Ridge Road, Tupelo, MS 38804. *Telephone:* 662-844-0284. *Fax:* 662-844-1927. *E-mail:* kmshane@muw.edu.

DEGREES AND AWARDS

BSN Nursing

COURSE SUBJECT AREAS OFFERED OUTSIDE OF DEGREE PROGRAMS

Undergraduate—nursing.

MISSOURI BAPTIST UNIVERSITY

St. Louis, Missouri
http://www.mobap.edu/distancelearning

Missouri Baptist University was founded in 1964. It is accredited by North Central Association of Colleges and Schools. It first offered distance learning courses in 2000. In fall 2003, there were 144 students enrolled in distance learning courses. Institutionally administered financial aid is available to distance learners.

Services Distance learners have accessibility to academic advising, bookstore, campus computer network, career placement assistance, e-mail services, library services.

Contact Mr. Eric J. Pitts, Technical Director of Distance Learning, Missouri Baptist University, One College Park Drive, St. Louis, MO 63141. *Telephone:* 314-744-5353 Ext. 5353. *Fax:* 314-434-7596. *E-mail:* distancelearning@mobap.edu.

DEGREES AND AWARDS

Programs offered do not lead to a degree or other formal award.

COURSE SUBJECT AREAS OFFERED OUTSIDE OF DEGREE PROGRAMS

Undergraduate—business administration and management; education administration and supervision; library science/librarianship; religion/religious studies; teacher education, specific academic and vocational programs.
Graduate—education administration and supervision; library science/librarianship; teacher education, specific academic and vocational programs.

MISSOURI SOUTHERN STATE UNIVERSITY

Joplin, Missouri
Continuing Education
http://www.mssu.edu/lifelonglearning

Missouri Southern State University was founded in 1937. It is accredited by North Central Association of Colleges and Schools. It first offered distance learning courses in 1986. In fall 2003, there were 1,850 students enrolled in distance learning courses. Institutionally administered financial aid is available to distance learners.

Services Distance learners have accessibility to academic advising, bookstore, campus computer network, career placement assistance, e-mail services, library services, tutoring.
Contact Dr. Jerry Williams, Director of Continuing Education, Missouri Southern State University, 3950 East Newman Road, Joplin, MO 64801. *Telephone:* 417-625-9384. *Fax:* 417-625-3024. *E-mail:* williams-r@mssu.edu.

DEGREES AND AWARDS

AA General Studies
AS General Business; Law Enforcement
BA Business; General Studies
BS Criminal Justice

COURSE SUBJECT AREAS OFFERED OUTSIDE OF DEGREE PROGRAMS

Undergraduate—accounting; biology, general; communications, general; criminal justice and corrections; developmental/child psychology; international business; journalism and mass communication related; physics; political science and government; psychology; radio/television broadcasting; social psychology; sociology; visual and performing arts.

MISSOURI TECH

St. Louis, Missouri
http://www.motech.edu/

Missouri Tech was founded in 1932. It is accredited by Accrediting Commission of Career Schools and Colleges of Technology.

Contact Mr. Bob Honaker, Director of Admissions, Missouri Tech, 1167 Corporate Lake Drive, St. Louis, MO 63132. *Telephone:* 314-569-3600. *Fax:* 314-569-1167. *E-mail:* bhonaker@motech.edu.

DEGREES AND AWARDS

Programs offered do not lead to a degree or other formal award.

MITCHELL TECHNICAL INSTITUTE

Mitchell, South Dakota
http://mti.tec.sd.us/

Mitchell Technical Institute was founded in 1968. It is accredited by North Central Association of Colleges and Schools. It first offered distance learning courses in 1994. In fall 2003, there were 300 students enrolled in distance learning courses. Institutionally administered financial aid is available to distance learners.

Services Distance learners have accessibility to academic advising, career placement assistance, e-mail services.
Contact John J. Heemstra, Telecommunications Coordinator, Mitchell Technical Institute, 821 North Capital, Mitchell, SD 57301. *Telephone:* 605-995-3065. *Fax:* 605-995-3067. *E-mail:* heemstraj@mti.tec.sd.us.

DEGREES AND AWARDS

Programs offered do not lead to a degree or other formal award.

COURSE SUBJECT AREAS OFFERED OUTSIDE OF DEGREE PROGRAMS

Undergraduate—computer and information sciences, general; culinary arts and related services; curriculum and instruction.
Non-credit—administrative and secretarial services; business management and administrative services, other; computer and information sciences, general; computer software and media applications; data entry/microcomputer applications; enterprise management and operation; entrepreneurship; health professions and related sciences, other; heating, air conditioning and refrigeration mechanics and repairers; quality control and safety technologies.

MOBERLY AREA COMMUNITY COLLEGE

Moberly, Missouri
http://www.macc.edu/

Moberly Area Community College was founded in 1927. It is accredited by North Central Association of Colleges and Schools. It first offered distance learning courses in 1995. In fall 2003, there were 350 students enrolled in distance learning courses. Institutionally administered financial aid is available to distance learners.

Services Distance learners have accessibility to academic advising, bookstore, campus computer network, career placement assistance, e-mail services, library services.
Contact Dr. James Grant, Dean of Student Services, Moberly Area Community College, 101 College Avenue, Moberly, MO 65270. *Telephone:* 660-263-4110 Ext. 239. *Fax:* 660-263-2406. *E-mail:* jamesg@macc.edu.

DEGREES AND AWARDS

AAS Computer Information Systems

Moberly Area Community College (continued)

COURSE SUBJECT AREAS OFFERED OUTSIDE OF DEGREE PROGRAMS

Undergraduate—accounting; biology, general; business administration and management; child care and guidance workers and managers; computer science; electrical and electronic engineering-related technology; English language and literature, general; fine arts and art studies; geography; history; industrial/manufacturing engineering; mathematics; psychology; social sciences and history, other; sociology; speech and rhetorical studies.

MODESTO JUNIOR COLLEGE

Modesto, California
Instruction
http://www.gomjc.org

Modesto Junior College was founded in 1921. It is accredited by Western Association of Schools and Colleges. It first offered distance learning courses in 1989. In fall 2003, there were 4,500 students enrolled in distance learning courses. Institutionally administered financial aid is available to distance learners.

Services Distance learners have accessibility to academic advising, bookstore, campus computer network, career placement assistance, library services.

Contact Kathy Haskin, Support Staff III, Modesto Junior College, Telecourse Office, 435 College Avenue, Modesto, CA 95350. *Telephone:* 209-575-6236. *Fax:* 209-575-6669. *E-mail:* haskink@yosemite.cc.ca.us.

DEGREES AND AWARDS

Programs offered do not lead to a degree or other formal award.

COURSE SUBJECT AREAS OFFERED OUTSIDE OF DEGREE PROGRAMS

Undergraduate—accounting; anthropology; business; business administration and management; business and personal services marketing operations; business management and administrative services, other; computer programming; computer science; computer software and media applications; criminal justice and corrections; developmental and child psychology; economics; English composition; family and community studies; geography; geological and related sciences; health and physical education/fitness; history; human resources management; library science, other; mathematics; music; philosophy; political science and government; psychology; psychology, other; social psychology; sociology.

Non-credit—student counseling and personnel services.

MONROE COMMUNITY COLLEGE

Rochester, New York
http://www.monroecc.edu/

Monroe Community College was founded in 1961. It is accredited by Middle States Association of Colleges and Schools. It first offered distance learning courses in 1997. In fall 2003, there were 1,850 students enrolled in distance learning courses. Institutionally administered financial aid is available to distance learners.

Services Distance learners have accessibility to academic advising, campus computer network, career placement assistance, e-mail services, library services, tutoring.

Contact Records and Registration, Monroe Community College, 1000 East Henrietta Road, Rochester, NY 14623-5780. *Telephone:* 585-292-2300. *E-mail:* registrationoffice@monroecc.edu.

DEGREES AND AWARDS

AAS Criminal Justice
AS Business Administration; Liberal Arts; Physical Education Studies
Certificate of Completion New York State Coaching Certification
Certificate Dental Assisting

COURSE SUBJECT AREAS OFFERED OUTSIDE OF DEGREE PROGRAMS

Undergraduate—accounting; advertising; American literature (United States); biology, general; business; communications, general; criminal justice and corrections; dental services; English composition; liberal arts and sciences, general studies and humanities; mathematics; psychology; social sciences, general.

MONROE COUNTY COMMUNITY COLLEGE

Monroe, Michigan
http://www.monroeccc.edu

Monroe County Community College was founded in 1964. It is accredited by North Central Association of Colleges and Schools. It first offered distance learning courses in 2000. In fall 2003, there were 400 students enrolled in distance learning courses. Institutionally administered financial aid is available to distance learners.

Services Distance learners have accessibility to academic advising, campus computer network, career placement assistance, e-mail services, library services, tutoring.

Contact Mr. Randy Daniels, Director of Admissions and Guidance Services, Monroe County Community College, 1555 South Raisinville Road, Monroe, MI 48161. *Telephone:* 734-384-4261 Ext. 4261. *Fax:* 734-242-9711. *E-mail:* rdaniels@monroeccc.edu.

DEGREES AND AWARDS

Programs offered do not lead to a degree or other formal award.

COURSE SUBJECT AREAS OFFERED OUTSIDE OF DEGREE PROGRAMS

Undergraduate—business; computer and information sciences, general; economics; English composition; English technical and business writing; mathematics; nursing; political science and government; psychology.

MONTANA STATE UNIVERSITY–BILLINGS

Billings, Montana
http://www.msubonline.org

Montana State University–Billings was founded in 1927. It is accredited by Northwest Commission on Colleges and Universities. It first offered distance learning courses in 1998. In fall 2003, there were 1,000 students enrolled in distance learning courses. Institutionally administered financial aid is available to distance learners.

Services Distance learners have accessibility to academic advising, bookstore, career placement assistance, e-mail services, library services, tutoring.

Contact Cindi Goffena, Academic Advisor for MSU-B Online University, Montana State University–Billings, McMullen Hall 100, 1500 North 30th Street, Billings, MT 59101. *Telephone:* 406-657-2206. *Fax:* 406-657-2206. *E-mail:* inquiry@msubonline.org.

DEGREES AND AWARDS

BA Communication/Organizational Communications/Mass Communication/Public Relations
BS Liberal Studies–Management and Communication Concentration
MHA Health Administration
MS Public Relations

COURSE SUBJECT AREAS OFFERED OUTSIDE OF DEGREE PROGRAMS

Undergraduate—accounting; art history; biology; business; business administration and management; business communications; business marketing and marketing management; communications, general; communications technologies; curriculum and instruction; economics; education, general; English composition; geography; history; industrial and organizational psychology; liberal arts and sciences, general studies and humanities; mathematical statistics; mathematics; organizational behavior; organizational psychology; physics; psychology; public relations and organizational communications; special education; theater arts/drama.
Graduate—communications, general; curriculum and instruction; education, general; health services administration; public relations and organizational communications.

See full description on page 462.

MONTANA STATE UNIVERSITY–BOZEMAN

Bozeman, Montana
The Burns Telecommunications Center/Extended Studies
http://www.montana.edu/distance

Montana State University–Bozeman was founded in 1893. It is accredited by Northwest Commission on Colleges and Universities. It first offered distance learning courses in 1992. In fall 2003, there were 1,000 students enrolled in distance learning courses. Institutionally administered financial aid is available to distance learners.

Services Distance learners have accessibility to academic advising, bookstore, e-mail services, library services.

Contact Kelly Boyce, Program Manager, Montana State University–Bozeman, EPS 128, Bozeman, MT 59717. *Telephone:* 406-994-6812. *Fax:* 406-994-7856. *E-mail:* kboyce@montana.edu.

DEGREES AND AWARDS

MN Nursing
MS Family and Financial Planning; Mathematics; Science Education
MSE Education

COURSE SUBJECT AREAS OFFERED OUTSIDE OF DEGREE PROGRAMS

Undergraduate—teacher education, specific academic and vocational programs.
Graduate—biological and physical sciences; biology; chemistry; earth sciences; health and physical education/fitness; mathematical statistics; mathematics; microbiology/bacteriology; physics; teacher education, specific academic and vocational programs.

MONTANA STATE UNIVERSITY–GREAT FALLS COLLEGE OF TECHNOLOGY

Great Falls, Montana
Outreach Department
http://www.msugf.edu

Montana State University–Great Falls College of Technology was founded in 1969. It is accredited by Northwest Commission on Colleges and Universities. It first offered distance learning courses in 1997. In fall 2003, there were 531 students enrolled in distance learning courses. Institutionally administered financial aid is available to distance learners.

Services Distance learners have accessibility to academic advising, bookstore, career placement assistance, e-mail services, library services, tutoring.

Contact Ms. Karen K. Vosen, Distance Education Student Support Coordinator, Montana State University–Great Falls College of Technology, 2100 16th Avenue South, Great Falls, MT 59405. *Telephone:* 406-771-4440. *Fax:* 406-771-4317. *E-mail:* kvosen@msugf.edu.

DEGREES AND AWARDS

AA General Education
AAS Health Information Technology
AS Montana University System General Core
Certificate Health Information Coding Specialist; Medical Billing Specialist; Medical Transcription

MONTANA TECH OF THE UNIVERSITY OF MONTANA

Butte, Montana
Office of Extended Studies
http://www.mtech.edu

Montana Tech of The University of Montana was founded in 1895. It is accredited by Northwest Commission on Colleges and Universities. It first offered distance learning courses in 1996. In fall 2003, there were 482 students enrolled in distance learning courses. Institutionally administered financial aid is available to distance learners.

Services Distance learners have accessibility to academic advising, bookstore, campus computer network, career placement assistance, e-mail services, library services.

Contact Administrative Support, Montana Tech of The University of Montana, 1300 West Park Street, Butte, MT 59701-8997. *Telephone:* 800-445-8324 Ext. 2. *Fax:* 406-496-4710. *E-mail:* admissions@mtech.edu.

DEGREES AND AWARDS

BS Occupational Safety and Health
MPM Project Engineering and Management
MS Industrial Hygiene

Montana Tech of the University of Montana (continued)

COURSE SUBJECT AREAS OFFERED OUTSIDE OF DEGREE PROGRAMS

Undergraduate—business; computer software and media applications; English composition; English technical and business writing; health professions and related sciences, other; nursing; philosophy; sociology.
Graduate—engineering/industrial management; health professions and related sciences, other; public health.

MONTGOMERY COMMUNITY COLLEGE

Troy, North Carolina
http://www.montgomery.cc.nc.us/

Montgomery Community College was founded in 1967. It is accredited by Southern Association of Colleges and Schools. It first offered distance learning courses in 2000. In fall 2003, there were 175 students enrolled in distance learning courses. Institutionally administered financial aid is available to distance learners.

Services Distance learners have accessibility to academic advising, bookstore, campus computer network, career placement assistance, library services, tutoring.
Contact Thomas M. Sargent, Director of Distance Learning, Montgomery Community College, 1011 Page Street, Troy, NC 27371. *Telephone:* 910-576-6222 Ext. 217. *Fax:* 910-576-2176. *E-mail:* sargentt@montgomery.edu.

DEGREES AND AWARDS

Programs offered do not lead to a degree or other formal award.

COURSE SUBJECT AREAS OFFERED OUTSIDE OF DEGREE PROGRAMS

Undergraduate—administrative and secretarial services; American literature (United States); business; business administration and management; computer and information sciences, general; computer software and media applications; criminal justice and corrections; English composition; English language and literature, general; English technical and business writing; human resources management; liberal arts and sciences, general studies and humanities; medical basic sciences; psychology; sociology.
Non-credit—bible/biblical studies; business administration and management; business communications; computer and information sciences, general; computer software and media applications; English composition; English language and literature, general; health and medical assistants.

MONTGOMERY COUNTY COMMUNITY COLLEGE

Blue Bell, Pennsylvania
Learning Resources Unit
http://www.mc3.edu/aa/DISTLRN/DISTLRN.htm

Montgomery County Community College was founded in 1964. It is accredited by Middle States Association of Colleges and Schools. It first offered distance learning courses in 1992. In fall 2003, there were 2,000 students enrolled in distance learning courses. Institutionally administered financial aid is available to distance learners.

Services Distance learners have accessibility to academic advising, bookstore, campus computer network, career placement assistance, e-mail services, library services, tutoring.
Contact Mr. John Mastroni, Director of Distance Learning, Montgomery County Community College, 340 DeKalb Pike, Blue Bell, PA 19422. *Telephone:* 215-641-6589. *Fax:* 215-619-7182. *E-mail:* jmastron@mc3.edu.

DEGREES AND AWARDS

AA Social Science
AGS General Studies
AS Business Administration; Liberal Studies
Certificate International Studies

COURSE SUBJECT AREAS OFFERED OUTSIDE OF DEGREE PROGRAMS

Undergraduate—accounting; anthropology; biology; business; business administration and management; computer and information sciences, general; computer programming; computer science; computer software and media applications; criminology; dental services; developmental/child psychology; economics; education, general; engineering, general; English composition; English literature (British and Commonwealth); English technical and business writing; fine arts and art studies; foreign languages and literatures; geography; geological and related sciences; health and physical education/fitness; history; liberal arts and sciences, general studies and humanities; mathematical statistics; mathematics; nursing; philosophy; psychology; social psychology; sociology; Spanish.

MOODY BIBLE INSTITUTE

Chicago, Illinois
Moody Bible Institute External Studies Division
http://www.moody.edu/

Moody Bible Institute was founded in 1886. It is accredited by Accrediting Association of Bible Colleges. It first offered distance learning courses in 1941. In fall 2003, there were 5,000 students enrolled in distance learning courses. Institutionally administered financial aid is available to distance learners.

Services Distance learners have accessibility to academic advising, e-mail services, library services.
Contact Customer Service, Moody Bible Institute, 820 North LaSalle Boulevard, Chicago, IL 60610. *Telephone:* 800-758-6352. *Fax:* 312-329-2081. *E-mail:* mdlc@moody.edu.

DEGREES AND AWARDS

ABS Biblical Studies
BS Biblical Studies
Certificate Biblical Studies

COURSE SUBJECT AREAS OFFERED OUTSIDE OF DEGREE PROGRAMS

Undergraduate—bible/biblical studies; biblical and other theological languages and literatures; classical and ancient Near Eastern languages and literatures; counseling psychology; educational psychology; English composition; philosophy; philosophy and religion; physical sciences, general; psychology; religion/religious studies; religious education; theological and ministerial studies; theological studies and religious vocations, other.

Graduate—bible/biblical studies; religion/religious studies; theological and ministerial studies; theological studies and religious vocations, other.
Non-credit—bible/biblical studies; religion/religious studies; theological and ministerial studies.

MOTLOW STATE COMMUNITY COLLEGE

Tullahoma, Tennessee
Academic Affairs
http://www.mscc.edu

Motlow State Community College was founded in 1969. It is accredited by Southern Association of Colleges and Schools. It first offered distance learning courses in 1996. In fall 2003, there were 500 students enrolled in distance learning courses. Institutionally administered financial aid is available to distance learners.

Services Distance learners have accessibility to academic advising, bookstore, campus computer network, career placement assistance, e-mail services, library services, tutoring.
Contact Dr. Mary McLemore, Vice President for Academic Affairs, Motlow State Community College, PO Box 8500, Lynchburg, TN 37352. *Telephone:* 931-393-1696. *Fax:* 931-393-1681. *E-mail:* mmclemore@mscc.edu.

DEGREES AND AWARDS

Programs offered do not lead to a degree or other formal award.

COURSE SUBJECT AREAS OFFERED OUTSIDE OF DEGREE PROGRAMS

Undergraduate—accounting; business administration and management; business information and data processing services; computer and information sciences, general; economics; mathematics.

MOTT COMMUNITY COLLEGE

Flint, Michigan
Distance Learning Office
http://www.cwp.mcc.edu

Mott Community College was founded in 1923. It is accredited by North Central Association of Colleges and Schools. It first offered distance learning courses in 1981. In fall 2003, there were 2,300 students enrolled in distance learning courses. Institutionally administered financial aid is available to distance learners.

Services Distance learners have accessibility to academic advising, bookstore, campus computer network, career placement assistance, e-mail services, library services, tutoring.
Contact Lori France, Distance Learning Coordinator, Mott Community College, College in the Workplace, 1401 East Court Street, CM 2210, Flint, MI 48503. *Telephone:* 800-398-2715. *Fax:* 810-762-0282. *E-mail:* lfrance@mcc.edu.

DEGREES AND AWARDS

AA General Studies (for transferring)
AAS Business, general
AGS General Studies (for transferring)
AS Transfer, general
Certificate of Achievement Computer Science
Certificate Quality Assurance

COURSE SUBJECT AREAS OFFERED OUTSIDE OF DEGREE PROGRAMS

Undergraduate—accounting; business; business communications; computer and information sciences, general; computer programming; English composition; English technical and business writing; geography; history; mathematics; psychology; quality control and safety technologies; social psychology; sociology.

MOUNTAIN EMPIRE COMMUNITY COLLEGE

Big Stone Gap, Virginia
Office of Continuing and Distance Education
http://www.me.vccs.edu/distance/index.html

Mountain Empire Community College was founded in 1972. It is accredited by Southern Association of Colleges and Schools. It first offered distance learning courses in 1979. In fall 2003, there were 538 students enrolled in distance learning courses. Institutionally administered financial aid is available to distance learners.

Services Distance learners have accessibility to academic advising, bookstore, campus computer network, e-mail services, library services, tutoring.
Contact Susan Kennedy, Coordinator of Distance Education, Mountain Empire Community College, 3441 Mountain Empire Road, Big Stone Gap, VA 24219. *Telephone:* 276-523-7488. *Fax:* 276-523-7486. *E-mail:* skennedy@me.vccs.edu.

DEGREES AND AWARDS

AAS Business Administration; Education; General Studies; Liberal Arts; Water/Wastewater Specialization

COURSE SUBJECT AREAS OFFERED OUTSIDE OF DEGREE PROGRAMS

Undergraduate—accounting; American history; art history; astronomy; atmospheric sciences and meteorology; biology; biology, general; business; business marketing and marketing management; child care and guidance workers and managers; communications, general; computer and information sciences, general; criminal justice and corrections; criminology; developmental/child psychology; economics; English composition; environmental science; foreign languages and literatures; geological and related sciences; health and physical education/fitness; history; law and legal studies related; mathematics; music; psychology; religion/religious studies; sociology; Spanish; speech and rhetorical studies.

MOUNTAIN STATE UNIVERSITY

Beckley, West Virginia
The School of Extended and Distance Learning
http://www.mountainstate.edu

Mountain State University was founded in 1933. It is accredited by North Central Association of Colleges and Schools. It first offered distance learning courses in 1992. In fall 2003, there were 1,200 students enrolled in distance learning courses. Institutionally administered financial aid is available to distance learners.

Mountain State University (continued)

Services Distance learners have accessibility to academic advising, bookstore, e-mail services, library services, tutoring.

Contact Karen McKee, Curriculum Coordinator, Mountain State University, PO Box 9003, Beckley, WV 25802-9003. *Telephone:* 304-253-7351 Ext. 1397. *Fax:* 304-929-1604. *E-mail:* kmckee@mountainstate.edu.

DEGREES AND AWARDS

AA Elementary Teacher Preparation; General Studies; Secondary Teacher Preparation

AS Aviation Technology; Banking and Finance; Business Administration–Accounting; Business Administration–Business Law; Business Administration–General Business; Business Administration–Management; Business Administration–Office Management; Computer Information Technology; Computer Networking Technology; Criminal Justice; Emergency Medical Services; Environmental Studies; General Studies; Marketing; Medical Assisting; Secretarial Science–Administrative; Secretarial Science–Legal; Secretarial Science–Medical; Travel

BA Interdisciplinary Studies–Psychology; Interdisciplinary Studies–Social and Behavioral Sciences

BS Aviation Management; Business Administration–Accounting; Business Administration–Business Law; Business Administration–General Business; Business Administration–Management; Business Administration–Office Management; Computer Networking; Criminal Justice; Health Care Management–Health Care Administration; Health Care Management–Health Care Informatics; Interdisciplinary Studies–Biology; Interdisciplinary Studies–Environmental Studies; Interdisciplinary Studies–Health Services Management; Interdisciplinary Studies–Natural Sciences; Interdisciplinary Studies–Pre-Medicine; Internet and E-Commerce; Marketing

BSN Nursing–RN to BSN

Certificate Aviation Technology; General Business; Office Technology–Secretarial Skills; Office Technology–Word Processing; Travel and Tourism

COURSE SUBJECT AREAS OFFERED OUTSIDE OF DEGREE PROGRAMS

Undergraduate—accounting; advertising; American history; anatomy; art history; astronomy; biochemistry; biology; biology, general; botany; business; business administration and management; business management and administrative services, other; business marketing and marketing management; chemistry; criminal justice and corrections; criminology; developmental/child psychology; earth sciences; ecology; economics; English composition; English language and literature/letters, other; environmental health; environmental science; European history; family and marriage counseling; finance; geography; gerontology; health services administration; history; insurance/risk management; international business; labor/personnel relations; law and legal studies related; liberal arts and sciences, general studies and humanities; management information systems/business data processing; mathematical statistics; mathematics; mathematics related; microbiology/bacteriology; music; nursing; organic chemistry; organizational behavior; philosophy; philosophy and religion related; physical sciences, general; physics; physiology; psychology; social psychology; social sciences and history, other; social sciences, general; social work; sociology.

Graduate—criminal justice and corrections; health and medical administrative services; multi/interdisciplinary studies, other; nursing.

MOUNTAIN STATE UNIVERSITY

Beckley, West Virginia
Online Programs
http://www.adcj.com

Mountain State University was founded in 1933. It is accredited by North Central Association of Colleges and Schools. It first offered distance learning courses in 2000. In fall 2003, there were 228 students enrolled in distance learning courses. Institutionally administered financial aid is available to distance learners.

Services Distance learners have accessibility to academic advising, bookstore, campus computer network, e-mail services, library services, tutoring.

Contact Off-Site Admissions Center Enrollment Advisor, Mountain State University, 7226 West Colonial Drive, PMB 400, Orlando, FL 32818-6731. *Telephone:* 800-645-5078. *Fax:* 407-573-2015. *E-mail:* info@adcj.com.

DEGREES AND AWARDS

BS Administration of Criminal Justice

COURSE SUBJECT AREAS OFFERED OUTSIDE OF DEGREE PROGRAMS

Undergraduate—criminal justice and corrections; criminology.

MOUNT ALLISON UNIVERSITY

Sackville, New Brunswick, Canada
Continuing and Distance Education
http://www.mta.ca/conted/index.html

Mount Allison University was founded in 1839. It is provincially chartered. It first offered distance learning courses in 1965. In fall 2003, there were 400 students enrolled in distance learning courses. Institutionally administered financial aid is available to distance learners.

Services Distance learners have accessibility to academic advising, bookstore, campus computer network, e-mail services, library services.

Contact Heather Patterson, Director, Mount Allison University, 65 York Street, Sackville, NB E4L 1E4, Canada. *Telephone:* 506-364-2266. *Fax:* 506-364-2272. *E-mail:* hpatters@mta.ca.

DEGREES AND AWARDS

Programs offered do not lead to a degree or other formal award.

COURSE SUBJECT AREAS OFFERED OUTSIDE OF DEGREE PROGRAMS

Undergraduate—American history; economics; English language and literature, general; English literature (British and Commonwealth); European history; history; mathematical statistics; mathematics; physical sciences, general; political science and government; psychology; religion/religious studies.

MT. HOOD COMMUNITY COLLEGE

Gresham, Oregon
http://www.mhcc.edu

Mt. Hood Community College was founded in 1966. It is accredited by Northwest Commission on Colleges and Universities. It first offered distance learning courses in 1998. In fall 2003, there were 350 students enrolled in distance learning courses. Institutionally administered financial aid is available to distance learners.

Services Distance learners have accessibility to academic advising, bookstore, campus computer network, library services, tutoring.
Contact Ms. Catherine Vogt, Program Specialist, Mt. Hood Community College, 26000 SE Stark Street, Gresham, OR 97030. *Telephone:* 503-491-6995. *Fax:* 503-491-7618. *E-mail:* vogtc@mhcc.edu.

DEGREES AND AWARDS

Programs offered do not lead to a degree or other formal award.

COURSE SUBJECT AREAS OFFERED OUTSIDE OF DEGREE PROGRAMS

Undergraduate—accounting; administrative and secretarial services; American literature (United States); astronomy; business administration and management; chemistry; child care and guidance workers and managers; computer and information sciences, general; computer software and media applications; economics; English composition; English creative writing; English technical and business writing; funeral services and mortuary science; health and medical administrative services; psychology.

MOUNT SAINT MARY COLLEGE

Newburgh, New York

http://my.msmc.edu/

Mount Saint Mary College was founded in 1960. It is accredited by Middle States Association of Colleges and Schools. It first offered distance learning courses in 2001. In fall 2003, there were 700 students enrolled in distance learning courses. Institutionally administered financial aid is available to distance learners.

Services Distance learners have accessibility to bookstore, campus computer network, e-mail services, library services.
Contact Robert A. Thabet, Director of Distance Education, Mount Saint Mary College, 330 Powell Avenue, Newburgh, NY 12550. *Telephone:* 845-569-3543. *Fax:* 845-562-6762. *E-mail:* thabet@msmc.edu.

DEGREES AND AWARDS

Programs offered do not lead to a degree or other formal award.

COURSE SUBJECT AREAS OFFERED OUTSIDE OF DEGREE PROGRAMS

Undergraduate—accounting; business; communications, general; computer and information sciences, general; educational psychology; education, general; general teacher education; geography; liberal arts and sciences, general studies and humanities; philosophy; psychology; sociology; special education.
Graduate—business administration and management; education, general; special education.
Non-credit—financial management and services.

MOUNT SAINT VINCENT UNIVERSITY

Halifax, Nova Scotia, Canada

Distance Learning and Continuing Education

http://www.msvu.ca/distance

Mount Saint Vincent University was founded in 1873. It is provincially chartered. It first offered distance learning courses in 1980. In fall 2003, there were 2,500 students enrolled in distance learning courses. Institutionally administered financial aid is available to distance learners.

Services Distance learners have accessibility to academic advising, bookstore, campus computer network, career placement assistance, e-mail services, library services, tutoring.
Contact Ms. Kerine Archibald, Receptionist, Mount Saint Vincent University, 166 Bedford Highway, Halifax, NS B3M 2J6, Canada. *Telephone:* 902-457-6511. *Fax:* 902-443-2135. *E-mail:* distance@msvu.ca.

DEGREES AND AWARDS

BA Liberal Arts and General Studies
BBA Business Administration
BTHM Tourism and Hospitality Management
Certificate Business Administration; French; Gerontology; Information Technology Management
MEd Education

COURSE SUBJECT AREAS OFFERED OUTSIDE OF DEGREE PROGRAMS

Undergraduate—accounting; advertising; biological and physical sciences; biology, general; business; business administration and management; business and personal services marketing operations; business/managerial economics; child care and guidance workers and managers; computer/information technology administration and management; cultural studies; developmental and child psychology; English language and literature, general; French; general teacher education; history; human resources management; mathematics; philosophy; psychology; sociology; women's studies.
Graduate—adult/continuing education; family and community studies.
Non-credit—business; communications, general; computer and information sciences, general; English creative writing; gerontology; housing studies; individual and family development studies; mathematics.

MT. SAN ANTONIO COLLEGE

Walnut, California

Distance Learning

http://vclass.mtsac.edu

Mt. San Antonio College was founded in 1946. It is accredited by Western Association of Schools and Colleges. It first offered distance learning courses in 1993. In fall 2003, there were 1,478 students enrolled in distance learning courses. Institutionally administered financial aid is available to distance learners.

Services Distance learners have accessibility to academic advising, bookstore, campus computer network, e-mail services, library services, tutoring.
Contact Kerry C. Stern, Dean, Mt. San Antonio College, Learning Resources, 1100 North Grand Avenue, Walnut, CA 91789. *Telephone:* 909-594-5611 Ext. 5658. *Fax:* 909-468-3992. *E-mail:* kstern@mtsac.edu.

DEGREES AND AWARDS

Programs offered do not lead to a degree or other formal award.

COURSE SUBJECT AREAS OFFERED OUTSIDE OF DEGREE PROGRAMS

Undergraduate—accounting; anthropology; biology, general; business administration and management; business and personal services

Mt. San Antonio College (continued)

marketing operations; chemistry; computer and information sciences, general; creative writing; economics; English as a second language; English composition; English creative writing; journalism; law and legal studies related; philosophy; psychology; real estate; religion/religious studies; sociology.

Non-credit—computer software and media applications.

MOUNT WACHUSETT COMMUNITY COLLEGE

Gardner, Massachusetts
Division of Continuing Education
http://www.mwcc.edu

Mount Wachusett Community College was founded in 1963. It is accredited by New England Association of Schools and Colleges. It first offered distance learning courses in 1994. In fall 2003, there were 620 students enrolled in distance learning courses. Institutionally administered financial aid is available to distance learners.

Services Distance learners have accessibility to academic advising, bookstore, career placement assistance, e-mail services, library services, tutoring.

Contact Ms. Debora Brennan, Distance Learning Administrative Assistant, Mount Wachusett Community College, 444 Green Street, Gardner, MA 01440. *Telephone:* 978-630-9275. *Fax:* 978-630-9537. *E-mail:* dbrennan@mwcc.mass.edu.

DEGREES AND AWARDS

AS Business Administration; Computer Information Systems; General Studies; Human Services; Paralegal Studies

COURSE SUBJECT AREAS OFFERED OUTSIDE OF DEGREE PROGRAMS

Undergraduate—advertising; American history; biology; business administration and management; business information and data processing services; business marketing and marketing management; computer programming; computer software and media applications; criminal justice and corrections; criminology; economics; English composition; family and marriage counseling; human services; mathematical statistics; mathematics; mathematics related; natural resources conservation; political science and government; psychology; sociology.

Non-credit—computer software and media applications; forest production and processing.

MURRAY STATE UNIVERSITY

Murray, Kentucky
Continuing Education
http://ceao.murraystate.edu

Murray State University was founded in 1922. It is accredited by Southern Association of Colleges and Schools. It first offered distance learning courses in 1990. In fall 2003, there were 3,714 students enrolled in distance learning courses. Institutionally administered financial aid is available to distance learners.

Services Distance learners have accessibility to academic advising, bookstore, campus computer network, e-mail services, library services.

Contact Crystal Riley, Coordinator of Distance Learning, Murray State University, 303 Sparks Hall, CEAO, Murray, KY 42071-0009. *Telephone:* 800-669-7654. *Fax:* 270-762-3593. *E-mail:* crystal.riley@murraystate.edu.

DEGREES AND AWARDS

BBA Business–Bachelor of Science in Business
BGS Independent Studies–Bachelor of Independent Studies/General Studies
BS Telecommunications Systems Management
Endorsement English as a Second Language; Gifted and Talented

COURSE SUBJECT AREAS OFFERED OUTSIDE OF DEGREE PROGRAMS

Undergraduate—agricultural business and management; agricultural business and production, other; agricultural economics; agriculture/agricultural sciences; American history; animal sciences; anthropology; business; business administration and management; communication disorders sciences and services; computer and information sciences, general; computer programming; computer science; computer systems networking and telecommunications; education, general; English composition; family and community studies; geography; geological and related sciences; graphic and printing equipment operators; history; journalism; journalism and mass communications; law and legal studies related; legal studies; mathematics related; music; nursing; philosophy; philosophy and religion; philosophy and religion related; public relations and organizational communications; radio/television broadcasting; social sciences and history, other; social sciences, general; social work; sociology.

Graduate—bilingual/bicultural education; communication disorders sciences and services; education administration and supervision; English as a second language; human services; marketing management and research; nursing; quality control and safety technologies; special education; teaching English as a second language/foreign language; telecommunications.

NAROPA UNIVERSITY

Boulder, Colorado
Outreach Office
http://www.naropa.edu/distance

Naropa University was founded in 1974. It is accredited by North Central Association of Colleges and Schools. It first offered distance learning courses in 1999. In fall 2003, there were 100 students enrolled in distance learning courses. Institutionally administered financial aid is available to distance learners.

Services Distance learners have accessibility to academic advising, bookstore, career placement assistance, e-mail services, library services.

Contact Kate Levene, Registration Coordinator, Naropa University, 2130 Arapahoe Avenue, Boulder, CO 80302. *Telephone:* 303-245-4657. *E-mail:* registrar@ecampus.naropa.edu.

DEGREES AND AWARDS

MA Transpersonal Psychology with Ecopsychology Concentration; Transpersonal Psychology
MAE Contemplative Education
MFA Creative Writing

COURSE SUBJECT AREAS OFFERED OUTSIDE OF DEGREE PROGRAMS

Undergraduate—American literature (United States); anthropology; area, ethnic and cultural studies, other; clinical psychology; community psychology; comparative literature; counseling psychology; cultural studies; developmental and child psychology; English creative writing; experimental psychology; gerontology; liberal arts and sciences, general studies and humanities; multi/interdisciplinary studies, other; peace and conflict studies; philosophy and religion; psychology; religion/religious studies.

Graduate—anthropology; area, ethnic and cultural studies, other; East and Southeast Asian languages and literatures; education, general; English language and literature, general; liberal arts and sciences, general studies and humanities; multi/interdisciplinary studies, other; psychology, other; religious education.

Non-credit—area, ethnic and cultural studies, other; area studies; cultural studies; educational psychology; education, general; education, other; English creative writing; individual and family development studies; peace and conflict studies; philosophy; philosophy and religion; psychology; psychology, other; religion/religious studies; religious education; religious/sacred music; theological and ministerial studies; theological studies and religious vocations, other.

NASSAU COMMUNITY COLLEGE

Garden City, New York
College of the Air
http://www.ncc.edu

Nassau Community College was founded in 1959. It is accredited by Middle States Association of Colleges and Schools. It first offered distance learning courses in 1991. In fall 2003, there were 1,100 students enrolled in distance learning courses. Institutionally administered financial aid is available to distance learners.

Services Distance learners have accessibility to academic advising, campus computer network, e-mail services, library services.

Contact Prof. Arthur L. Friedman, Coordinator, College of the Air, Nassau Community College, 1 Education Drive, Garden City, NY 11530-6793. *Telephone:* 516-572-7883. *Fax:* 516-572-0690. *E-mail:* friedma@ncc.edu.

DEGREES AND AWARDS

Programs offered do not lead to a degree or other formal award.

COURSE SUBJECT AREAS OFFERED OUTSIDE OF DEGREE PROGRAMS

Undergraduate—accounting; anthropology; astronomy; atmospheric sciences and meteorology; biology, general; business; business administration and management; business marketing and marketing management; communications, other; developmental/child psychology; economics; English language and literature/letters, other; entrepreneurship; film/video and photographic arts; French; geological and related sciences; health and physical education/fitness; history; Italian; journalism and mass communication related; law and legal studies related; mathematical statistics; mathematics; mathematics related; music; physical sciences, other; psychology; psychology, other; sociology; Spanish.

Non-credit—mathematics.

NATIONAL UNIVERSITY

La Jolla, California
NU Online
http://www.online.nu.edu

National University was founded in 1971. It is accredited by Western Association of Schools and Colleges. It first offered distance learning courses in 1994. In fall 2003, there were 7,333 students enrolled in distance learning courses. Institutionally administered financial aid is available to distance learners.

Services Distance learners have accessibility to academic advising, bookstore, campus computer network, career placement assistance, e-mail services, library services.

Contact Ms. Susan Bachman, Online Admissions Advisor, National University, 4141 Camino del Rio South, San Diego, CA 92108. *Telephone:* 800-NAT UNIV Ext. 7290. *Fax:* 858-563 7211. *E-mail:* sbachman@nu.edu.

DEGREES AND AWARDS

BA English; Global Studies
BBA Business Administration
BS Accountancy; Criminal Justice Administration; Information Systems; Information Technology; Nursing
Certificate Accountancy; Criminal Justice Professional Certificate; E-Business; Educational Technology; Finance; International Business; Marketing; Sports Management; Teachers Using Technology
Certification CLAD Multiple or Single Subject Certificate; Preliminary Level 1 Education Specialist–Mild/Moderate with Concurrent CLD/BCLAD; Preliminary Level I Education Specialist Credential: Mild/Mod; Preliminary Level I Education Specialist Credential: Mod/Severe; Preliminary Multiple Subject Teaching Credential with TED or BCLAD Emphasis; Preliminary Single Subject Teaching Credential with TED or BCLAD Emphasis; Professional Level II Education Specialist Credential: Mild/Mod; Professional Level II Education Specialist Credential: Mod/Severe; Professional Tier I Administrative Services; Professional Tier II Administrative Services Credential; Pupil Personnel Services–School Counseling Specialization
Diploma the Arts
EMBA Business Administration
MA English; Human Resource Management and Organizational Development; Management
MAT Teaching/Education with Credential Options
MBA Business Administration
MEd Cross Cultural Education with Credential Options
MFA Creative Writing
MPA Public Administration
MS Computer Science; Educational Administration; Educational Technology; Electronic Business; Forensic Sciences–Master of Forensic Sciences; Information Systems; Instructional Technology; Organizational Leadership; Special Education with Credential Options; Technology Management

COURSE SUBJECT AREAS OFFERED OUTSIDE OF DEGREE PROGRAMS

Undergraduate—accounting; biological and physical sciences; business; business administration and management; business quantitative methods and management science; communications technologies; computer software and media applications; construction/building technology; construction management; counseling psychology; criminal justice and corrections; education, general; English language and literature, general; information sciences and systems; nursing; psychology.

National University (continued)

Graduate—accounting; business; business administration and management; computer and information sciences, general; criminology; education administration and supervision; educational/instructional media design; education, general; English creative writing; human resources management; public administration; special education; teacher education, specific academic and vocational programs; technology education/industrial arts.

See full description on page 464.

NAUGATUCK VALLEY COMMUNITY COLLEGE

Waterbury, Connecticut

http://www.nvcc.commnet.edu

Naugatuck Valley Community College was founded in 1992. It is accredited by New England Association of Schools and Colleges. It first offered distance learning courses in 2003. Institutionally administered financial aid is available to distance learners.

Services Distance learners have accessibility to academic advising, campus computer network, e-mail services, library services.

Contact Ms. Eileen Medinger, Distance Learning Coordinator, Naugatuck Valley Community College, 750 Chase Parkway, Waterbury, CT 06708. *Telephone:* 203-575-8182. *E-mail:* emedinger@nvcc.commnet.edu.

DEGREES AND AWARDS

Programs offered do not lead to a degree or other formal award.

COURSE SUBJECT AREAS OFFERED OUTSIDE OF DEGREE PROGRAMS

Undergraduate—accounting; administrative and secretarial services; business administration and management; child care and guidance workers and managers; computer and information sciences, general; criminal justice and corrections; culinary arts and related services; fine arts and art studies; health professions and related sciences, other; liberal arts and sciences, general studies and humanities; music; nursing; social work; tourism/travel marketing; vehicle and mobile equipment mechanics and repairers; visual and performing arts, other.

Non-credit—accounting; crafts, folk art and artisanry; custodial, housekeeping and home services workers and managers; dance; data entry/microcomputer applications; data processing technology; English as a second language; health and medical preparatory programs; health and physical education/fitness; real estate.

NEBRASKA METHODIST COLLEGE

Omaha, Nebraska

http://www.methodistcollege.edu/

Nebraska Methodist College was founded in 1891. It is accredited by North Central Association of Colleges and Schools. It first offered distance learning courses in 1996. In fall 2003, there were 35 students enrolled in distance learning courses. Institutionally administered financial aid is available to distance learners.

Services Distance learners have accessibility to academic advising, bookstore, campus computer network, career placement assistance, e-mail services, library services, tutoring.

Contact Dr. Bill Lambrecht, Educational Technologist, Nebraska Methodist College, 8501 West Dodge Road, Omaha, NE 68114. *Telephone:* 402-354-6174. *Fax:* 402-354-8893. *E-mail:* blambre@methodistcollege.edu.

DEGREES AND AWARDS

MSN Nursing–Education Emphasis

COURSE SUBJECT AREAS OFFERED OUTSIDE OF DEGREE PROGRAMS

Undergraduate—computer and information sciences, other; health professions and related sciences, other; mathematics; nursing.

Graduate—computer and information sciences, other; health professions and related sciences, other; nursing.

Non-credit—education, general.

NEUMANN COLLEGE

Aston, Pennsylvania

neumannonline.org

http://www.neumann.edu/

Neumann College was founded in 1965. It is accredited by Middle States Association of Colleges and Schools. It first offered distance learning courses in 1998. In fall 2003, there were 200 students enrolled in distance learning courses. Institutionally administered financial aid is available to distance learners.

Services Distance learners have accessibility to academic advising, bookstore, campus computer network, career placement assistance, e-mail services, library services, tutoring.

Contact Dr. Patricia Szymurski, Dean, Division of Continuing Adult and Professional Studies, Neumann College, One Neumann Drive, Aston, PA 19014-1298. *Telephone:* 610-558-5530. *Fax:* 610-361-5490. *E-mail:* szymurst@neumann.edu.

DEGREES AND AWARDS

Programs offered do not lead to a degree or other formal award.

COURSE SUBJECT AREAS OFFERED OUTSIDE OF DEGREE PROGRAMS

Undergraduate—criminology; English language and literature, general; English literature (British and Commonwealth); English technical and business writing; human resources management; mathematics, other; psychology; religion/religious studies.

NEW ENGLAND INSTITUTE OF TECHNOLOGY

Warwick, Rhode Island

http://blackboard.neit.edu

New England Institute of Technology was founded in 1940. It is accredited by New England Association of Schools and Colleges. It first offered distance learning courses in 1996. In fall 2003, there were 80 students enrolled in distance learning courses. Institutionally administered financial aid is available to distance learners.

Services Distance learners have accessibility to academic advising, e-mail services, library services.

Contact Mr. Michael Caruso, Admissions Officer, New England Institute of Technology, 2500 Post Road, Warwick, RI 02886. *Telephone:* 401-739-5000 Ext. 3411. *E-mail:* mcaruso@neit.edu.

DEGREES AND AWARDS

Programs offered do not lead to a degree or other formal award.

COURSE SUBJECT AREAS OFFERED OUTSIDE OF DEGREE PROGRAMS

Undergraduate—English composition; mathematics; physics; psychology.

NEW HAMPSHIRE COMMUNITY TECHNICAL COLLEGE SYSTEM

Concord, New Hampshire

http://www.nhctc.edu/content/onlinelearning.htm

New Hampshire Community Technical College System is accredited by New England Association of Schools and Colleges. It first offered distance learning courses in 1999. In fall 2003, there were 700 students enrolled in distance learning courses. Institutionally administered financial aid is available to distance learners.

Services Distance learners have accessibility to academic advising, bookstore, campus computer network, career placement assistance, e-mail services, library services, tutoring.

Contact Mr. Paul Ambrose, Director of Distance Education, New Hampshire Community Technical College System, 26 College Drive, Concord, NH 03301. *Telephone:* 603-271-2740. *Fax:* 603-271-2725. *E-mail:* pambrose@nhctc.edu.

DEGREES AND AWARDS

Programs offered do not lead to a degree or other formal award.

COURSE SUBJECT AREAS OFFERED OUTSIDE OF DEGREE PROGRAMS

Undergraduate—accounting; biology, general; business administration and management; business and personal services marketing operations; comparative literature; computer and information sciences, general; computer and information sciences, other; computer programming; computer science; computer software and media applications; computer systems networking and telecommunications; education, general; education, other; English composition; entrepreneurship; history; information sciences and systems; mathematical statistics; mathematics; mathematics and computer science; mathematics, other; psychology; psychology, other; social psychology; sociology; special education; teacher education, specific academic and vocational programs; telecommunications.

Non-credit—business; business administration and management; business and personal services marketing operations; business communications; business information and data processing services; business management and administrative services, other; business/managerial economics; business quantitative methods and management science; computer and information sciences, general; computer and information sciences, other; computer programming; computer science; computer software and media applications; computer systems analysis; computer systems networking and telecommunications.

NEW JERSEY CITY UNIVERSITY

Jersey City, New Jersey

Continuing Education

http://newlearning.njcu.edu

New Jersey City University was founded in 1927. It is accredited by Middle States Association of Colleges and Schools. It first offered distance learning courses in 1997. In fall 2003, there were 126 students enrolled in distance learning courses. Institutionally administered financial aid is available to distance learners.

Services Distance learners have accessibility to e-mail services, library services.

Contact Marie A. Fosello, Director of Special Programs, New Jersey City University, 2039 Kennedy Boulevard, Jersey City, NJ 07305-1597. *Telephone:* 201-200-3449. *Fax:* 201-200-2188. *E-mail:* conted@njcu.edu.

DEGREES AND AWARDS

MS Accounting

COURSE SUBJECT AREAS OFFERED OUTSIDE OF DEGREE PROGRAMS

Undergraduate—accounting; business; criminal justice and corrections; economics; international relations and affairs; mathematics; physics; political science and government; public health.

Graduate—accounting; business administration and management; criminology; education administration and supervision; educational/instructional media design; public health; special education.

NEW JERSEY INSTITUTE OF TECHNOLOGY

Newark, New Jersey

Continuing Professional Education

http://cpe.njit.edu/

New Jersey Institute of Technology was founded in 1881. It is accredited by Middle States Association of Colleges and Schools. It first offered distance learning courses in 1985. In fall 2003, there were 5,000 students enrolled in distance learning courses. Institutionally administered financial aid is available to distance learners.

Services Distance learners have accessibility to academic advising, campus computer network, career placement assistance, e-mail services, library services, tutoring.

Contact Ellen Schreihoffer, Director of Extended Learning Delivery, New Jersey Institute of Technology, University Heights, Newark, NJ 07102. *Telephone:* 973-596-6093. *Fax:* 973-596-3288. *E-mail:* el@njit.edu.

DEGREES AND AWARDS

BA Information Systems

BS Computer Science; Information Technology–Bachelor of Science in Information Technology (BSIT)

Certificate Business Fundamentals; Information Systems Design; Information Systems Implementation; Internet Applications Development; Practice of Technical Communications; Project Management; Telecommunications Networking

MBA/Certificate Management Essentials; Management of Technology

New Jersey Institute of Technology (continued)

MS Engineering Management; Professional and Technical Communications

COURSE SUBJECT AREAS OFFERED OUTSIDE OF DEGREE PROGRAMS

Undergraduate—computer and information sciences, general; computer science; information sciences and systems.
Graduate—business administration and management; business management and administrative services, other; communications, other; computer science; engineering-related technologies, other; information sciences and systems.
Non-credit—computer programming; environmental control technologies; information sciences and systems.

See full description on page 466.

NEWMAN THEOLOGICAL COLLEGE

Edmonton, Alberta, Canada
http://www.newman.edu

Newman Theological College was founded in 1969. It is provincially chartered. It first offered distance learning courses in 1987. In fall 2003, there were 76 students enrolled in distance learning courses.

Services Distance learners have accessibility to bookstore, campus computer network, library services.
Contact Sharon Gauthier, Registrar, Newman Theological College, 15611 St. Albert Trail, Edmonton, AB T6V 1H3, Canada. *Telephone:* 780-447-2993. *Fax:* 780-447-2685. *E-mail:* registrar@newman.edu.

DEGREES AND AWARDS

BTh Theology
Certificate Theological Studies
Advanced Graduate Diploma Religious Education

COURSE SUBJECT AREAS OFFERED OUTSIDE OF DEGREE PROGRAMS

Undergraduate—theological and ministerial studies.
Graduate—religious education.

NEWMAN UNIVERSITY

Wichita, Kansas
Community Education
http://www.newmanu.edu

Newman University was founded in 1933. It is accredited by North Central Association of Colleges and Schools. It first offered distance learning courses in 1987. In fall 2003, there were 250 students enrolled in distance learning courses. Institutionally administered financial aid is available to distance learners.

Services Distance learners have accessibility to bookstore, campus computer network, e-mail services, library services.
Contact Norman Correll, Director of Distance Learning, Newman University, 3100 McCormick Avenue, Wichita, KS 67213. *Telephone:* 316-942-4291 Ext. 2222. *Fax:* 316-942-4483. *E-mail:* cornelln@newmanu.edu.

DEGREES AND AWARDS

BA Pastoral Ministry
BS Teacher Education
MSE Graduate Teacher Education

NEW MEXICO INSTITUTE OF MINING AND TECHNOLOGY

Socorro, New Mexico
Distance Education Department
http://www.nmt.edu/~eodi

New Mexico Institute of Mining and Technology was founded in 1889. It is accredited by North Central Association of Colleges and Schools. It first offered distance learning courses in 2000. In fall 2003, there were 70 students enrolled in distance learning courses. Institutionally administered financial aid is available to distance learners.

Services Distance learners have accessibility to academic advising, bookstore, campus computer network, career placement assistance, e-mail services, library services, tutoring.
Contact Mrs. Wendi Rae Carrillo, Student Support Specialist, New Mexico Institute of Mining and Technology, 801 Leroy Place, Socorro, NM 87801. *Telephone:* 505-835-5511. *Fax:* 505-835-5541. *E-mail:* wcarrillo@admin.nmt.edu.

DEGREES AND AWARDS

Programs offered do not lead to a degree or other formal award.

COURSE SUBJECT AREAS OFFERED OUTSIDE OF DEGREE PROGRAMS

Graduate—environmental/environmental health engineering; mathematics; mechanical engineering; mining and mineral engineering; petroleum engineering; teacher education, specific academic and vocational programs.

NEW MEXICO STATE UNIVERSITY

Las Cruces, New Mexico
Office of Distance Education and Weekend College
http://www.nmsu.edu/distance

New Mexico State University was founded in 1888. It is accredited by North Central Association of Colleges and Schools. It first offered distance learning courses in 1989. In fall 2003, there were 1,500 students enrolled in distance learning courses. Institutionally administered financial aid is available to distance learners.

Services Distance learners have accessibility to academic advising, bookstore, campus computer network, career placement assistance, e-mail services, library services.
Contact Carmen Gonzales, Vice Provost for Distance Education, New Mexico State University, Box 3WEC, Las Cruces, NM 88003. *Telephone:* 505-646-4692. *Fax:* 505-646-2044. *E-mail:* carmen@nmsu.edu.

DEGREES AND AWARDS

BA Human and Community Services–Bachelor of Human and Community Services; Sociology
BBA Business Administration
Endorsement Bilingual Endorsement–College of Education
MA Education–Learning Technologies

MCJ Criminal Justice
EdD Educational Administration–Community College Leadership Emphasis
PhD Curriculum and Instruction with a Learning Technologies Emphasis

COURSE SUBJECT AREAS OFFERED OUTSIDE OF DEGREE PROGRAMS

Undergraduate—business; business administration and management; community health services; human services; sociology.
Graduate—criminal justice and corrections; education, other; industrial/manufacturing engineering; mechanical engineering.

See full description on page 468.

NEW SCHOOL UNIVERSITY

New York, New York
Robert J. Milano Graduate School of Management and Urban Policy

New School University was founded in 1919. It is accredited by Middle States Association of Colleges and Schools. Institutionally administered financial aid is available to distance learners.

Contact Joseph K. Encarnacion, Associate Director of Admissions, New School University, 72 Fifth Avenue, 3rd Floor, New York, NY 10014. *Telephone:* 212-229-5462 Ext. 1110. *Fax:* 212-229-5354. *E-mail:* encarnaj@newschool.edu.

DEGREES AND AWARDS

Programs offered do not lead to a degree or other formal award.

COURSE SUBJECT AREAS OFFERED OUTSIDE OF DEGREE PROGRAMS

Graduate—business administration and management; business/managerial economics; city/urban, community and regional planning; community health services; community organization, resources and services; financial management and services; human resources management; political science and government; public health; public policy analysis.

See full description on page 470.

NEW YORK INSTITUTE OF TECHNOLOGY

Old Westbury, New York
On-Line Campus
http://www.nyit.edu

New York Institute of Technology was founded in 1955. It is accredited by Middle States Association of Colleges and Schools. It first offered distance learning courses in 1984. In fall 2003, there were 1,227 students enrolled in distance learning courses. Institutionally administered financial aid is available to distance learners.

Services Distance learners have accessibility to academic advising, bookstore, campus computer network, career placement assistance, e-mail services, library services.
Contact Ms. Kathleen Lyons, Assistant Director of Admissions, New York Institute of Technology, Carleton Avenue, PO Box 9029, Central Islip, NY 11729-9029. *Telephone:* 631-348-3200. *Fax:* 631-348-0912. *E-mail:* klyons@nyit.edu.

DEGREES AND AWARDS

BA Interdisciplinary Studies
BPS Hospitality Management; Interdisciplinary Studies
BS Business Administration; Community Mental Health; Criminal Justice; Interdisciplinary Studies; Psychology; Sociology
MBA Business
MS Energy Management; Instructional Technology

COURSE SUBJECT AREAS OFFERED OUTSIDE OF DEGREE PROGRAMS

Undergraduate—accounting; anthropology; biology, general; business administration and management; business management and administrative services, other; business marketing and marketing management; communications, general; criminal justice and corrections; economics; English composition; English creative writing; English language and literature, general; English language and literature/letters, other; environmental control technologies; finance; industrial engineering; interior design; journalism and mass communications; legal studies; mathematical statistics; mechanical engineering; philosophy; philosophy and religion related; political science and government; social psychology; social work; sociology; speech and rhetorical studies.
Graduate—accounting; business administration and management; business information and data processing services; business marketing and marketing management; educational/instructional media design.
Non-credit—computer and information sciences, general; computer and information sciences, other; computer/information technology administration and management; computer software and media applications; culinary arts and related services.

NEW YORK INSTITUTE OF TECHNOLOGY

Old Westbury, New York
Ellis College
http://www.ellis.nyit.edu

New York Institute of Technology was founded in 1955. It is accredited by Middle States Association of Colleges and Schools. It first offered distance learning courses in 2003. In fall 2003, there were 1,245 students enrolled in distance learning courses. Institutionally administered financial aid is available to distance learners.

Services Distance learners have accessibility to academic advising, bookstore, career placement assistance, library services.
Contact Mr. Thomas P. Fitzgibbon, Director of Sales, New York Institute of Technology, PO Box 345, Old Westbury, NY 11568. *Telephone:* 847-282-2410. *Fax:* 847-444-8155. *E-mail:* admissions@ellis.nyit.edu.

DEGREES AND AWARDS

BA Interdisciplinary Studies/Behavioral Sciences; Interdisciplinary Studies/Business; Interdisciplinary Studies/Communication Arts; Interdisciplinary Studies/Computer Science; Interdisciplinary Studies/English; Interdisciplinary Studies/Hospitality Management; Interdisciplinary Studies/Humanities; Interdisciplinary Studies/Labor Relations; Interdisciplinary Studies/Math–Physics; Interdisciplinary Studies/Social Sciences; Interdisciplinary Studies/Technical Writing; Interdisciplinary Studies/Technology; Interdisciplinary Studies/Telecommunications Management

New York Institute of Technology (continued)

BPS Interdisciplinary Studies/Behavioral Sciences; Interdisciplinary Studies/Business; Interdisciplinary Studies/Communication Arts; Interdisciplinary Studies/Computer Science; Interdisciplinary Studies/English; Interdisciplinary Studies/Hospitality Management; Interdisciplinary Studies/Humanities; Interdisciplinary Studies/Labor Relations; Interdisciplinary Studies/Math–Physics; Interdisciplinary Studies/Social Sciences; Interdisciplinary Studies/Technical Writing; Interdisciplinary Studies/Technology; Interdisciplinary Studies/Telecommunications Management

BS Interdisciplinary Studies/Behavioral Sciences; Interdisciplinary Studies/Business; Interdisciplinary Studies/Communication Arts; Interdisciplinary Studies/Computer Science; Interdisciplinary Studies/English; Interdisciplinary Studies/Hospitality Management; Interdisciplinary Studies/Humanities; Interdisciplinary Studies/Labor Relations; Interdisciplinary Studies/Math–Physics; Interdisciplinary Studies/Social Sciences; Interdisciplinary Studies/Technical Writing; Interdisciplinary Studies/Technology; Interdisciplinary Studies/Telecommunications Management; Managerial Accounting; Professional Accounting

BSBA Finance; General Management; Human Resources Management; International Business; Management of Information Systems; Marketing; Small Business and Entrepreneurship

MBA/Diploma Accounting and Information Systems; E-Commerce; Finance; General Program; Global Management; Health Care Administration; Human Resources Management; Leadership; Management of Information Systems; Management of Technology; Marketing; Professional Accounting; Project Management; Risk Management; Strategy and Economics

COURSE SUBJECT AREAS OFFERED OUTSIDE OF DEGREE PROGRAMS

Undergraduate—accounting; business; business administration and management; communications, general; computer science; entrepreneurship; health and medical administrative services; hospitality services management; human resources management; international business; marketing operations/marketing and distribution, other; mathematics; social sciences, general; telecommunications.

Graduate—accounting; economics; health and medical administrative services; human resources management; information sciences and systems; marketing operations/marketing and distribution, other.

NIPISSING UNIVERSITY

North Bay, Ontario, Canada
Center for Continuing Business Education
http://www.nipissingu.ca/ccbe

Nipissing University was founded in 1992. It is provincially chartered. It first offered distance learning courses in 1997. In fall 2003, there were 185 students enrolled in distance learning courses. Institutionally administered financial aid is available to distance learners.

Services Distance learners have accessibility to academic advising, bookstore, e-mail services, library services, tutoring.

Contact Sara Tonks, Program Administrator, Nipissing University, 100 College Drive, Box 5002, North Bay, ON P1B 8L7, Canada. *Telephone:* 705-474-3450 Ext. 4219. *Fax:* 705-475-0264. *E-mail:* ccbe@nipissingu.ca.

DEGREES AND AWARDS

BComm Financial Services

COURSE SUBJECT AREAS OFFERED OUTSIDE OF DEGREE PROGRAMS

Undergraduate—accounting; business administration and management; business quantitative methods and management science; economics; financial management and services; human resources management; international business; marketing management and research.

NORMANDALE COMMUNITY COLLEGE

Bloomington, Minnesota
Telecommunications and Media Services
http://www.normandale.edu

Normandale Community College was founded in 1968. It is accredited by North Central Association of Colleges and Schools. It first offered distance learning courses in 1981. In fall 2003, there were 500 students enrolled in distance learning courses. Institutionally administered financial aid is available to distance learners.

Services Distance learners have accessibility to bookstore, e-mail services, library services.

Contact Cheryl Zachman, Administrative Assistant in Business, Technology and Continuing Education, Normandale Community College, 9700 France Avenue, South, Bloomington, MN 55431. *Telephone:* 952-487-8163. *Fax:* 952-487-8101. *E-mail:* cheryl.zachman@normandale.edu.

DEGREES AND AWARDS

Programs offered do not lead to a degree or other formal award.

COURSE SUBJECT AREAS OFFERED OUTSIDE OF DEGREE PROGRAMS

Undergraduate—accounting; business administration and management; communications, other; computer software and media applications; economics; English composition; English language and literature, general; hospitality services management; human resources management; marketing management and research; mathematics; miscellaneous engineering-related technologies.

Non-credit—business administration and management; business information and data processing services; computer/information technology administration and management; entrepreneurship.

NORTHAMPTON COUNTY AREA COMMUNITY COLLEGE

Bethlehem, Pennsylvania
College-at-Home Program
http://www.northampton.edu

Northampton County Area Community College was founded in 1967. It is accredited by Middle States Association of Colleges and Schools. It first offered distance learning courses in 1974. In fall 2003, there were 2,064 students enrolled in distance learning courses. Institutionally administered financial aid is available to distance learners.

Services Distance learners have accessibility to academic advising, bookstore, e-mail services, library services, tutoring.

Contact Ms. Kim Kortze, Assistant Director of Distance Learning, Northampton County Area Community College, College Center

481, 3835 Green Pond Road, Bethlehem, PA 18020. *Telephone:* 610-861-4154. *Fax:* 610-861-5373. *E-mail:* kkortze@northampton.edu.

DEGREES AND AWARDS

AA Business Administration; General Studies; Individualized Transfer Studies; Social Work; Social Work

AAS Accounting; Early Childhood Education

AS Business Management

Specialized diploma Family Child Care; Home-based Early Childhood Education; Library Technical Services; School Age Child Care

COURSE SUBJECT AREAS OFFERED OUTSIDE OF DEGREE PROGRAMS

Undergraduate—accounting; anthropology; astronomy; biological sciences/life sciences, other; biology, general; business; business administration and management; business communications; business management and administrative services, other; business/managerial economics; child care and guidance workers and managers; computer science; developmental and child psychology; economics; education, general; education, other; engineering physics; English composition; English creative writing; English literature (British and Commonwealth); geography; geological and related sciences; health and physical education/fitness; Internet and World Wide Web; journalism and mass communications; library assistant; mathematics; music; nursing; philosophy; psychology; social sciences, general; social work; sociology; special education.

Non-credit—education, other; nursing.

Special Message

Northampton Community College (NCC) has 8 degrees that can be completely achieved through distance learning, over 100 Internet courses available to students, and articulation agreements with 8 other colleges and universities for seamless transfer to more than 20 bachelor's degree programs. In addition to Internet courses, there are multimedia courses (Tele-Webs) that have a video component. Courses are developed using asynchronous communication, which allows student to access their courses and instructors at flexible times during the week. Most courses are offered in a 16-week format.

Currently, degrees are available in accounting, business administration, business management, early childhood education, general studies, individual transfer studies, liberal arts, and social work. In addition, a certificate program is available in early childhood education, and specialized diplomas are available in library technical assistant and early childhood family child care. For information about courses and programs, students should go to http://www.northampton.edu and click on distance learning.

NCC and St. Luke's Health Network have collaborated to create a Perioperative Academy, offering training for registered nurses wishing to gain certification for working in operating rooms.

Starting in spring 2004, NCC is the first in the nation to offer online courses in RV maintenance.

Accredited by the Commission on Higher Education of the Middle States Association of Colleges and Schools, NCC has been providing distance learning since 1970, but added the high-tech Internet and Tele-Web courses in 1998. The distance learning program serves over 4,000 students per year.

NORTH CAROLINA STATE UNIVERSITY

Raleigh, North Carolina
Distance Education
http://distance.ncsu.edu

North Carolina State University was founded in 1887. It is accredited by Southern Association of Colleges and Schools. It first offered distance learning courses in 1976. In fall 2003, there were 2,215 students enrolled in distance learning courses. Institutionally administered financial aid is available to distance learners.

Services Distance learners have accessibility to academic advising, bookstore, campus computer network, career placement assistance, e-mail services, library services, tutoring.

Contact Lily Leegstra, Program Coordinator, North Carolina State University, Campus Box 7113, Raleigh, NC 27695-7113. *Telephone:* 919-515-9030. *Fax:* 919-515-6668. *E-mail:* lily_leegstra@ncsu.edu.

DEGREES AND AWARDS

Certificate Computer Programming; HACCP/Food Safety Managers

Graduate Certificate Geographic Information Systems; Training and Development

MCE Civil Engineering

MCS Computer Science

ME Engineering Online

MEd Training and Development

MS Wood and Paper Science

MSAE Aerospace Engineering

MSME Mechanical Engineering

MT Textile Off-Campus Televised Education (TOTE)

COURSE SUBJECT AREAS OFFERED OUTSIDE OF DEGREE PROGRAMS

Undergraduate—accounting; agricultural and food products processing; American literature (United States); anthropology; biological and physical sciences; business; chemistry; clothing/apparel and textile studies; communications, general; computer programming; economics; English composition; English language and literature, general; English technical and business writing; film/video and photographic arts; forestry and related sciences; health and physical education/fitness; history; mathematics; multi/interdisciplinary studies, other; music; parks, recreation and leisure facilities management; philosophy; physics; political science and government; psychology; soil sciences; South Asian languages and literatures; teacher education, specific academic and vocational programs; teaching English as a second language/foreign language; textile sciences and engineering; zoology.

Graduate—agricultural and food products processing; agricultural business and production, other; agriculture/agricultural sciences; chemical engineering; civil engineering; computer engineering; curriculum and instruction; education administration and supervision; engineering, general; information sciences and systems; teacher education, specific academic and vocational programs; textile sciences and engineering.

NORTH CENTRAL TEXAS COLLEGE

Gainesville, Texas
http://www.nctc.edu

North Central Texas College was founded in 1924. It is accredited by Southern Association of Colleges and Schools. It first offered distance

North Central Texas College (continued)

learning courses in 1999. In fall 2003, there were 250 students enrolled in distance learning courses. Institutionally administered financial aid is available to distance learners.

Services Distance learners have accessibility to academic advising, campus computer network, e-mail services, library services.

Contact Dr. Eddie C. Hadlock, Vice President of Instruction, North Central Texas College, 1525 West California, Gainesville, TX 76240. *Telephone:* 940-668-4234. *Fax:* 940-668-4258. *E-mail:* ehadlock@nctc.edu.

DEGREES AND AWARDS

Programs offered do not lead to a degree or other formal award.

COURSE SUBJECT AREAS OFFERED OUTSIDE OF DEGREE PROGRAMS

Undergraduate—administrative and secretarial services; biological sciences/life sciences, other; English composition; English literature (British and Commonwealth); history; mathematics; political science and government.

NORTHCENTRAL UNIVERSITY

Prescott, Arizona

http://www.ncu.edu/

Northcentral University is accredited by North Central Association of Colleges and Schools. It first offered distance learning courses in 1997. In fall 2003, there were 1,101 students enrolled in distance learning courses. Institutionally administered financial aid is available to distance learners.

Services Distance learners have accessibility to academic advising, bookstore, campus computer network, library services.

Contact Sue Johnson, Admissions Counselor, Northcentral University, 505 West Whipple Street, Prescott, AZ 86301. *Telephone:* 888-327-2877. *Fax:* 928-541-7817. *E-mail:* info@ncu.edu.

DEGREES AND AWARDS

BA Psychology
BBA Business Administration
MA Psychology
MBA Business Administration
PhD Business Administration; Psychology

COURSE SUBJECT AREAS OFFERED OUTSIDE OF DEGREE PROGRAMS

Undergraduate—business administration and management; computer science; psychology.

Graduate—business administration and management; computer and information sciences, other; engineering/industrial management; financial management and services; human resources management; industrial and organizational psychology; international business; psychology, other; public administration.

See full description on page 472.

NORTH CENTRAL UNIVERSITY

Minneapolis, Minnesota

Carlson Institute of Church Leadership

http://www.northcentral.edu/start/distance.html

North Central University was founded in 1930. It is accredited by North Central Association of Colleges and Schools. It first offered distance learning courses in 1991. In fall 2003, there were 275 students enrolled in distance learning courses. Institutionally administered financial aid is available to distance learners.

Services Distance learners have accessibility to academic advising, bookstore, library services.

Contact Carlson Institute for Church Leadership, North Central University, 910 Elliot Avenue, South, Minneapolis, MN 55404. *Telephone:* 800-446-1176. *Fax:* 612-343-4435. *E-mail:* carlinst@northcentral.edu.

DEGREES AND AWARDS

AA Theology
BA Church Ministries; Interdisciplinary Studies
BS Church Ministries; Interdisciplinary Studies
Certificate Bible
Diploma Church Ministries

COURSE SUBJECT AREAS OFFERED OUTSIDE OF DEGREE PROGRAMS

Undergraduate—bible/biblical studies; liberal arts and sciences, general studies and humanities; theological and ministerial studies; theological studies and religious vocations, other.

Non-credit—bible/biblical studies; liberal arts and sciences, general studies and humanities; theological and ministerial studies; theological studies and religious vocations, other.

NORTH COUNTRY COMMUNITY COLLEGE

Saranac Lake, New York

http://www.nccc.edu/

North Country Community College was founded in 1967. It is accredited by Middle States Association of Colleges and Schools. It first offered distance learning courses in 1998. In fall 2003, there were 210 students enrolled in distance learning courses. Institutionally administered financial aid is available to distance learners.

Services Distance learners have accessibility to campus computer network, library services.

Contact Mr. Thomas J. Finch, Dean of Academic Affairs, North Country Community College, 23 Santinoni Avenue, PO Box 89, Saranac Lake, NY 12983-0089. *Telephone:* 518-891-2915 Ext. 203. *Fax:* 518-891-5029. *E-mail:* acdean@nccc.edu.

DEGREES AND AWARDS

Programs offered do not lead to a degree or other formal award.

COURSE SUBJECT AREAS OFFERED OUTSIDE OF DEGREE PROGRAMS

Undergraduate—advertising; anthropology; art history; business communications; business marketing and marketing management; computer and information sciences, general; developmental/child psychology; earth sciences; economics; English composition; environmental science; geography; human resources management; psychology; sociology.

NORTH DAKOTA STATE COLLEGE OF SCIENCE

Wahpeton, North Dakota

http://www.ndscs.edu/

North Dakota State College of Science was founded in 1903. It is accredited by North Central Association of Colleges and Schools. It first offered distance learning courses in 1968. In fall 2003, there were 155 students enrolled in distance learning courses. Institutionally administered financial aid is available to distance learners.

Services Distance learners have accessibility to academic advising, bookstore, career placement assistance, library services, tutoring.
Contact Ms. Margaret Wall, Distance Education Director, North Dakota State College of Science, 800 Sixth Street North, Wahpeton, ND 58076-0002. *Telephone:* 701-671-2430. *Fax:* 701-671-2529. *E-mail:* margaret.wall@ndscs.nodak.edu.

DEGREES AND AWARDS

AAS Architectural Drafting and Estimating Technology; Health Information Technician
AS Nursing–Practical Nursing
Certificate Computer Information Systems–Web Design; Medical Transcription

COURSE SUBJECT AREAS OFFERED OUTSIDE OF DEGREE PROGRAMS

Undergraduate—accounting; chemistry; computer and information sciences, general; computer programming; developmental/child psychology; drafting; English composition; health and medical administrative services; health and physical education/fitness; mathematics; microbiology/bacteriology; sociology.

NORTH DAKOTA STATE UNIVERSITY

Fargo, North Dakota
Division of Distance and Continuing Education
http://www.ndsu.edu/dce

North Dakota State University was founded in 1890. It is accredited by North Central Association of Colleges and Schools. It first offered distance learning courses in 1974. In fall 2003, there were 300 students enrolled in distance learning courses. Institutionally administered financial aid is available to distance learners.

Contact Nancy Olson, Education Program Coordinator, North Dakota State University, PO Box 5819, University Station, Fargo, ND 58105. *Telephone:* 701-231-7015. *Fax:* 701-231-7016. *E-mail:* ndsu.dce@ndsu.nodak.edu.

DEGREES AND AWARDS

MBA/MSG Gerontology
MSFS Family Financial Planning

COURSE SUBJECT AREAS OFFERED OUTSIDE OF DEGREE PROGRAMS

Undergraduate—applied mathematics; child care and guidance workers and managers; clinical psychology; communications, general; computer and information sciences, general; computer engineering; data entry/microcomputer applications; developmental and child psychology; education, general; electrical and electronic engineering-related technology; foods and nutrition studies; hospitality services management; mathematics; psychology; sociology.
Graduate—clinical psychology; communications, general; computer engineering; curriculum and instruction; education administration and supervision; educational evaluation, research and statistics; educational/instructional media design; education, general; electrical and electronic engineering-related technology; family and community studies; family/consumer resource management; general teacher education; individual and family development studies; psychology; special education.
Non-credit—administrative and secretarial services; aerospace, aeronautical and astronautical engineering; business; child care and guidance workers and managers; clinical psychology; computer and information sciences, general; computer programming; computer science; data entry/microcomputer applications; health and medical assistants; Internet and World Wide Web; miscellaneous health professions.

NORTHEASTERN OKLAHOMA AGRICULTURAL AND MECHANICAL COLLEGE

Miami, Oklahoma
http://www.neoam.edu

Northeastern Oklahoma Agricultural and Mechanical College was founded in 1919. It is accredited by North Central Association of Colleges and Schools. It first offered distance learning courses in 1989. In fall 2003, there were 409 students enrolled in distance learning courses. Institutionally administered financial aid is available to distance learners.

Services Distance learners have accessibility to academic advising, bookstore, campus computer network, career placement assistance, e-mail services, library services.
Contact G. C. Manders, Coordinator of Continuing and Distance Education, Northeastern Oklahoma Agricultural and Mechanical College, 200 I Street, NE, Miami, OK 74354. *Telephone:* 918-540-6204. *Fax:* 918-540-6946. *E-mail:* distanceed@neoam.edu.

DEGREES AND AWARDS

Programs offered do not lead to a degree or other formal award.

COURSE SUBJECT AREAS OFFERED OUTSIDE OF DEGREE PROGRAMS

Undergraduate—accounting; agricultural business and management; business; business administration and management; business communications; business quantitative methods and management science; child care and guidance workers and managers; computer and information sciences, general; criminal justice and corrections; economics; education, general; engineering physics; English composition; film/video and photographic arts; fine arts and art studies; geography; health and medical preparatory programs; history; liberal arts and sciences, general studies and humanities; mathematics; music; political science and government; psychology; sociology.
Non-credit—accounting; administrative and secretarial services; computer programming; computer systems analysis; design and applied arts; health and medical administrative services; health professions and related sciences, other; information sciences and systems; Internet and World Wide Web; legal studies; miscellaneous health professions; pharmacy; tourism/travel marketing.

NORTHEASTERN UNIVERSITY

Boston, Massachusetts
Distance Learning Center
http://www.nuol.edu

Northeastern University was founded in 1898. It is accredited by New England Association of Schools and Colleges. It first offered distance

Northeastern University (continued)

learning courses in 1983. In fall 2003, there were 500 students enrolled in distance learning courses. Institutionally administered financial aid is available to distance learners.

Services Distance learners have accessibility to academic advising, bookstore, campus computer network, career placement assistance, e-mail services, library services.

Contact Demet Yener, Assistant Director, Northeastern University, 360 Huntington Avenue, 328 CP, Boston, MA 02115. *Telephone:* 617-373-5622. *Fax:* 617-373-5625. *E-mail:* d.yener@neu.edu.

DEGREES AND AWARDS

AS Arts and Sciences; Business Administration; Management Information Systems; Supply Chain Management

BS Health Management; Liberal Arts with Business Minor; Operations Technology; Technical Communications

Certificate Advanced Web Design; Business Administration; C++/Unix Programming; Computer Programming; Database Design and Administration; Electronic Publishing; English for Nurses; Information Networks Professional; Internet Technologies; Software Quality Assurance; Supply Chain Management; Technical Writing; Unix and Linux for Business

Certification Business English

Graduate Certificate International Regulatory Affairs; Knowledge Management; Nonprofit Management; Pharmacogenetics Essentials; Vaccines: Technologies, Trends, and Bioterrorism

MSEE Electrical and Computer Engineering

MSIS Information Systems

COURSE SUBJECT AREAS OFFERED OUTSIDE OF DEGREE PROGRAMS

Undergraduate—business administration and management; computer/information technology administration and management; computer programming; English technical and business writing; environmental control technologies; health professions and related sciences, other; Internet and World Wide Web; liberal arts and sciences, general studies and humanities; mathematics related; music; nursing; science technologies, other.

Graduate—business administration and management; electrical engineering; engineering/industrial management; environmental control technologies; industrial engineering; information sciences and systems; mechanical engineering; nursing; pharmacy.

Non-credit—communications technologies; computer programming; computer systems networking and telecommunications; English technical and business writing; environmental control technologies; Internet and World Wide Web; nursing; science technologies, other; telecommunications.

NORTHEAST STATE TECHNICAL COMMUNITY COLLEGE

Blountville, Tennessee
Evening and Distance Education
http://northeaststate.edu

Northeast State Technical Community College was founded in 1966. It is accredited by Southern Association of Colleges and Schools. It first offered distance learning courses in 1996. In fall 2003, there were 2,200 students enrolled in distance learning courses. Institutionally administered financial aid is available to distance learners.

Services Distance learners have accessibility to academic advising, bookstore, campus computer network, career placement assistance, e-mail services, library services.

Contact Ms. Tammy B. Street, Coordinator of Distance Education Programs and Services, Northeast State Technical Community College, PO Box 246, Blountville , TN 37617. *Telephone:* 423-354-2497. *Fax:* 423-323-0224. *E-mail:* tbstreet@northeaststate.edu.

DEGREES AND AWARDS

Programs offered do not lead to a degree or other formal award.

COURSE SUBJECT AREAS OFFERED OUTSIDE OF DEGREE PROGRAMS

Undergraduate—accounting; astronomy; biological and physical sciences; business administration and management; chemistry; computer and information sciences, general; economics; education, general; English composition; English language and literature, general; history; mathematics; music; political science and government; psychology; social sciences, general; speech and rhetorical studies.

NORTHERN ARIZONA UNIVERSITY

Flagstaff, Arizona
NAU Distance Learning
http://www.distance.nau.edu

Northern Arizona University was founded in 1899. It is accredited by North Central Association of Colleges and Schools. It first offered distance learning courses in 1977. In fall 2003, there were 5,950 students enrolled in distance learning courses. Institutionally administered financial aid is available to distance learners.

Services Distance learners have accessibility to academic advising, bookstore, campus computer network, career placement assistance, e-mail services, library services, tutoring.

Contact Distance Learning Service Center, Northern Arizona University, PO Box 4117, Flagstaff, AZ 86011-4117. *Telephone:* 800-426-8315. *Fax:* 928-523-1169. *E-mail:* distance.programs@nau.edu.

DEGREES AND AWARDS

BA Psychology; Spanish

BEd Career and Technical Education (BS Ed.); Elementary Education (BS Ed.); Secondary Education (BS Ed.); Special and Elementary Education (BS Ed.)

BLS BAILS Arts and Letters; BAILS Criminal Justice; BAILS Enterprise in Society; BAILS Learning and Pedagogy; BAILS Mathematics/Statistics; BAILS Organizational Communication; BAILS Parks and Recreation Management; BAILS Psychology; BAILS Sociology; Environmental Sciences

BS BAILS Environmental Sciences; Criminal Justice; Dental Hygiene Completion Program; Health Promotion; Hotel and Restaurant Management; Interior Design; Management (BSBA); Nursing–Accelerated Option; Nursing; Parks and Recreation Management

BSAST Computer Technology (BAS); Early Childhood (BAS); Health Promotion (BAS); Justice Systems and Policy Planning (BAS); Public Agency Services (BAS)

BSN Nursing–RN to BSN

BSW Social Work

Certificate Educational Technology; Elementary Education Postdegree; International Tourism Management; Parks and Recreation Management; Restaurant Management; Secondary Education Postdegree; Special Education Postdegree

Certification Principalship; Professional Writing; Superintendency; Supervisory
Endorsement Bilingual Education Endorsement; English as a Second Language; Gifted Education; Middle School Education; Reading
Graduate Certificate Public Management
MA Applied Communication; Counseling; English
MAT Mathematics; Teaching English as a Second Language
MEd Bilingual/Multicultural Education; Career and Technical Education; Counseling/Human Relations; Counseling/School Counseling; Early Childhood Education; Educational Leadership; Educational Technology; Elementary Education; Secondary Education with Certification Emphasis; Secondary Education; Special Education
MEngr Engineering
MS Nursing
EdD Educational Leadership

COURSE SUBJECT AREAS OFFERED OUTSIDE OF DEGREE PROGRAMS

Undergraduate—art history; biology, general; business marketing and marketing management; chemistry; communication disorders sciences and services; communications, other; computer and information sciences, general; computer and information sciences, other; construction management; criminal justice and corrections; curriculum and instruction; dental services; engineering, general; English language and literature, general; English language and literature/letters, other; English technical and business writing; environmental engineering; environmental science; forestry and related sciences; geography; geological and related sciences; health and medical assistants; health and medical preparatory programs; health professions and related sciences, other; history; hospitality services management; liberal arts and sciences, general studies and humanities; marketing management and research; miscellaneous health professions; music; natural resources conservation; natural resources management and protective services; nursing; parks, recreation and leisure facilities management; philosophy; philosophy and religion; political science and government; social sciences, general; social work; sociology; special education.
Graduate—bilingual/bicultural education; business administration and management; community health services; curriculum and instruction; education administration and supervision; educational evaluation, research and statistics; educational/instructional media design; educational psychology; education, other; electrical and electronic engineering-related technology; health and medical administrative services; human resources management; mathematical statistics; physical therapy; public administration; public administration and services, other; public health; vocational home economics, other.

Special Message

Northern Arizona University (NAU) is an accredited state university that has expanded its distance learning opportunities to include Web-based degree programs. A leader in distance education for more than 25 years, NAU has tried to meet the needs of place-bound students pursuing a degree. Serving more than 20,000 students, including more than 6,000 off campus, NAU is home to award-winning degree programs in hotel and restaurant management and ecosystem science management, and it continues to be a leader in teacher education with more than a century of experience and dedication to the training and advancement of America's educators.

NAU provides a learner-centered approach to education with small class sizes and qualified instructors. NAU students benefit from the knowledge and experience of professors continually involved in their field of expertise. Whether attending classes at one of the statewide campuses or taking classes via distance learning, including interactive television or online, each student receives personal attention and class interaction. NAU continues to be a quality-assured and dynamically driven institution with a dedication to being a premier residential campus as well as a leader in technologically advanced distance education.

See full description on page 474.

NORTHERN KENTUCKY UNIVERSITY

Highland Heights, Kentucky
Educational Outreach
http://dl.nku.edu

Northern Kentucky University was founded in 1968. It is accredited by Southern Association of Colleges and Schools. It first offered distance learning courses in 1983. In fall 2003, there were 553 students enrolled in distance learning courses. Institutionally administered financial aid is available to distance learners.

Services Distance learners have accessibility to academic advising, bookstore, campus computer network, e-mail services, library services.

Contact Debbie Poweleit, Coordinator of Distance Learning, Northern Kentucky University, Educational Outreach, OS 305A, Highland Heights, KY 41099-5700. *Telephone:* 859-572-1447. *Fax:* 859-572-5174. *E-mail:* dl@nku.edu.

DEGREES AND AWARDS

BA Organizational Leadership
BSN Nursing–RN-BSN Completion
Certification Nursing–Post-Masters Certification
Graduate Certificate Nurse Practitioner Advancement
MSN Nursing

COURSE SUBJECT AREAS OFFERED OUTSIDE OF DEGREE PROGRAMS

Undergraduate—administrative and secretarial services; biological sciences/life sciences, other; business; communications, general; construction management; English language and literature, general; financial management and services; health professions and related sciences, other; journalism and mass communications; liberal arts and sciences, general studies and humanities; music; nursing; political science and government; psychology.
Graduate—engineering-related technologies, other; nursing.
Non-credit—computer and information sciences, general; Internet and World Wide Web.

NORTHERN NEW MEXICO COMMUNITY COLLEGE

Española, New Mexico
http://wwww.nnmcc.edu

Northern New Mexico Community College was founded in 1909. It is accredited by North Central Association of Colleges and Schools. It first offered distance learning courses in 2001. In fall 2003, there were

Northern New Mexico Community College (continued)

192 students enrolled in distance learning courses. Institutionally administered financial aid is available to distance learners.

Services Distance learners have accessibility to academic advising, bookstore, campus computer network, e-mail services, library services.

Contact Mr. Michael L. Costello, Enrollment Manager, Northern New Mexico Community College, 921 Paseo de Onate, Espanola, NM 87532. *Telephone:* 505-747-2193. *Fax:* 505-747-2191. *E-mail:* mikec@nnmcc.edu.

DEGREES AND AWARDS

Programs offered do not lead to a degree or other formal award.

COURSE SUBJECT AREAS OFFERED OUTSIDE OF DEGREE PROGRAMS

Undergraduate—accounting; business administration and management; computer science; economics; English composition; fine arts and art studies; history; liberal arts and sciences, general studies and humanities; mathematical statistics; mathematics; nursing; psychology; sociology.

NORTHERN VIRGINIA COMMUNITY COLLEGE

Annandale, Virginia
Extended Learning Institute
http://eli.nvcc.edu

Northern Virginia Community College was founded in 1965. It is accredited by Southern Association of Colleges and Schools. It first offered distance learning courses in 1975. In fall 2003, there were 6,000 students enrolled in distance learning courses. Institutionally administered financial aid is available to distance learners.

Services Distance learners have accessibility to academic advising, bookstore, e-mail services, library services.

Contact Jayne Townend, Admissions and Records, Northern Virginia Community College, 8333 Little River Turnpike, Annandale, VA 22003-3796. *Telephone:* 703-323-3368. *Fax:* 703-323-3392. *E-mail:* jtownend@nvcc.edu.

DEGREES AND AWARDS

AA Liberal Arts
AAS Business Management; Business Management, Public Management Specialization
AS Business Administration; General Studies
Specialized diploma Information Systems Technology

COURSE SUBJECT AREAS OFFERED OUTSIDE OF DEGREE PROGRAMS

Undergraduate—accounting; advertising; American history; art history; biology; business marketing and marketing management; creative writing; developmental/child psychology; English composition; film studies; finance; French; geography; journalism; law and legal studies related; management information systems/business data processing; mathematical statistics; mathematics related; mechanical engineering; organizational behavior; philosophy and religion related; sociology; Spanish; theater arts/drama.

NORTH GEORGIA COLLEGE & STATE UNIVERSITY

Dahlonega, Georgia
E-Learning/Opportunity Services
http://www.ngcsu.edu

North Georgia College & State University was founded in 1873. It is accredited by Southern Association of Colleges and Schools. It first offered distance learning courses in 1995. In fall 2003, there were 700 students enrolled in distance learning courses. Institutionally administered financial aid is available to distance learners.

Services Distance learners have accessibility to academic advising, bookstore, career placement assistance, e-mail services, library services, tutoring.

Contact Scott Marshall, Coordinator of Student E-Learning Environments, North Georgia College & State University, Health and Natural Sciences Building—435, 82 College Circle, Dahlonega, GA 30597. *Telephone:* 706-864-1535. *Fax:* 706-864-1886.

DEGREES AND AWARDS

Programs offered do not lead to a degree or other formal award.

COURSE SUBJECT AREAS OFFERED OUTSIDE OF DEGREE PROGRAMS

Undergraduate—Army R.O.T.C.; computer and information sciences, general; engineering, other; foreign languages and literatures; general teacher education; gerontology; international and comparative education; international relations and affairs; military studies; nursing; psychology; sociology; teacher education, specific academic and vocational programs.
Graduate—education administration and supervision; educational evaluation, research and statistics; general teacher education; gerontology; international and comparative education; nursing; psychology; public administration; public administration and services, other; sociology; teacher education, specific academic and vocational programs.
Non-credit—communications technologies; computer and information sciences, general; computer software and media applications; educational/instructional media design; food products retailing and wholesaling operations; foods and nutrition studies; food sciences and technology; general teacher education; health professions and related sciences, other; institutional food workers and administrators; Internet and World Wide Web; mathematics; military studies; miscellaneous health professions; teacher education, specific academic and vocational programs.

NORTH HARRIS MONTGOMERY COMMUNITY COLLEGE DISTRICT

Houston, Texas
The Center for Teaching and Distance Learning
http://www.nhmccd.edu

North Harris Montgomery Community College District was founded in 1972. It first offered distance learning courses in 1993. In fall 2003, there were 5,900 students enrolled in distance learning courses. Institutionally administered financial aid is available to distance learners.

Services Distance learners have accessibility to academic advising, bookstore, e-mail services, library services, tutoring.

Contact Linda Bilides, Coordinator of Distance Learning Student Development Services, North Harris Montgomery Community College District, 5000 Research Forest Drive, The Woodlands, TX 77381-4399. *Telephone:* 832-813-6758. *Fax:* 832-813-6753. *E-mail:* linda.l.bilides@nhmccd.edu.

DEGREES AND AWARDS

AA General Studies
AAS E-Business Web Developer; Legal Office; Management; Mid-range Computing; Programming Specialist
AS General Studies

COURSE SUBJECT AREAS OFFERED OUTSIDE OF DEGREE PROGRAMS

Undergraduate—accounting; administrative and secretarial services; biology; business administration and management; computer and information sciences, general; computer software and media applications; computer systems networking and telecommunications; English composition; English creative writing; English language and literature, general; English technical and business writing; history; marketing management and research; mathematics; music; philosophy; social psychology; sociology; visual and performing arts.

NORTH HENNEPIN COMMUNITY COLLEGE

Brooklyn Park, Minnesota

http://www.nh.cc.mn.us/

North Hennepin Community College was founded in 1966. It is accredited by North Central Association of Colleges and Schools. It first offered distance learning courses in 2000. Institutionally administered financial aid is available to distance learners.

Services Distance learners have accessibility to academic advising, bookstore, career placement assistance, e-mail services, library services, tutoring.
Contact Information, North Hennepin Community College, 7411 85th Avenue North, Brooklyn Park, MN 55445. *Telephone:* 763-424-0702. *Fax:* 763-424-0929. *E-mail:* info@nhcc.mnscu.edu.

DEGREES AND AWARDS

Programs offered do not lead to a degree or other formal award.

COURSE SUBJECT AREAS OFFERED OUTSIDE OF DEGREE PROGRAMS

Undergraduate—accounting; biology, general; business; chemistry; communications, general; computer and information sciences, general; construction/building technology; economics; education, general; engineering, general; English language and literature, general; English technical and business writing; fine arts and art studies; foreign languages and literatures; legal studies; liberal arts and sciences, general studies and humanities; marketing management and research; mathematics and computer science; nursing; philosophy; physics; psychology; sociology; visual and performing arts.
Non-credit—business administration and management; communications, other; computer software and media applications; computer systems networking and telecommunications; information sciences and systems; professional studies.

NORTH IDAHO COLLEGE

Coeur d'Alene, Idaho

http://www.nic.edu

North Idaho College was founded in 1933. It first offered distance learning courses in 1997. In fall 2003, there were 500 students enrolled in distance learning courses. Institutionally administered financial aid is available to distance learners.

Services Distance learners have accessibility to academic advising, bookstore, e-mail services, library services.
Contact Dr. Candace Wheeler, Director of Distance Education, North Idaho College, 1000 West Garden Avenue, Coeur d'Alene, ID 83814. *Telephone:* 208-769-3436. *Fax:* 208-769-7728. *E-mail:* candace_wheeler@nic.edu.

DEGREES AND AWARDS

AS General Program

COURSE SUBJECT AREAS OFFERED OUTSIDE OF DEGREE PROGRAMS

Undergraduate—accounting; American literature (United States); anthropology; area, ethnic and cultural studies, other; biology, general; business; chemistry; child care and guidance workers and managers; communications, general; English composition; fine arts and art studies; health and medical assistants; mathematics; philosophy; political science and government; psychology; sociology.

NORTHWEST ARKANSAS COMMUNITY COLLEGE

Bentonville, Arkansas

Northwest Arkansas Distance Education

http://www.nwacc.edu/disted

NorthWest Arkansas Community College was founded in 1989. It is accredited by North Central Association of Colleges and Schools. It first offered distance learning courses in 1997. In fall 2003, there were 400 students enrolled in distance learning courses. Institutionally administered financial aid is available to distance learners.

Services Distance learners have accessibility to academic advising, library services, tutoring.
Contact Mr. Clint Brooks, Distance Learning Coordinator, NorthWest Arkansas Community College, BH 2414, One College Drive, Bentonville, AR 72712. *Telephone:* 479-619-4382. *Fax:* 479-619-4383. *E-mail:* cbrooks@nwacc.edu.

DEGREES AND AWARDS

AA General Program

COURSE SUBJECT AREAS OFFERED OUTSIDE OF DEGREE PROGRAMS

Undergraduate—accounting; agricultural and food products processing; agriculture/agricultural sciences; applied mathematics; biology, general; business communications; chemistry; clothing/apparel and textile studies; communications, general; computer and information sciences, general; computer and information sciences, other; computer systems networking and telecommunications; criminal justice and corrections; economics; English composition; English language and literature, general; fine arts and art studies; health and medical diagnostic and treatment services; health and physical education/fitness; history; Internet and World Wide Web; liberal arts and

NorthWest Arkansas Community College (continued)

sciences, general studies and humanities; mathematics; medical basic sciences; miscellaneous health professions; philosophy; psychology; psychology, other; social sciences and history, other; social sciences, general; sociology.
Non-credit—English composition; mathematics.

NORTHWEST CHRISTIAN COLLEGE

Eugene, Oregon
http://www.nwcc.edu/

Northwest Christian College was founded in 1895. It first offered distance learning courses in 1999. In fall 2003, there were 28 students enrolled in distance learning courses. Institutionally administered financial aid is available to distance learners.

Services Distance learners have accessibility to academic advising, e-mail services, library services.
Contact Dr. Stuart B. Tennant, Provost, Northwest Christian College, 828 East 11th Avenue, Eugene, OR 97401. *Telephone:* 541-684-7214. *Fax:* 541-684-7323. *E-mail:* stuart@nwcc.edu.

DEGREES AND AWARDS

Programs offered do not lead to a degree or other formal award.

COURSE SUBJECT AREAS OFFERED OUTSIDE OF DEGREE PROGRAMS

Undergraduate—bible/biblical studies; general teacher education.

NORTHWESTERN COLLEGE

St. Paul, Minnesota
Center for Distance Education
http://distance.nwc.edu

Northwestern College was founded in 1902. It is accredited by North Central Association of Colleges and Schools. It first offered distance learning courses in 1994. In fall 2003, there were 400 students enrolled in distance learning courses. Institutionally administered financial aid is available to distance learners.

Services Distance learners have accessibility to academic advising, bookstore, campus computer network, career placement assistance, e-mail services, library services, tutoring.
Contact Betty Piper, Assistant Director, Northwestern College, 3003 Snelling Avenue North, Saint Paul, MN 55113. *Telephone:* 800-308-5495. *Fax:* 651-631-5133. *E-mail:* distance@nwc.edu.

DEGREES AND AWARDS

AA Biblical Studies
BA Biblical Studies; Intercultural Ministries Degree Completion
Certificate Bible

COURSE SUBJECT AREAS OFFERED OUTSIDE OF DEGREE PROGRAMS

Undergraduate—archaeology; astronomy; bible/biblical studies; chemistry; communications, general; computer software and media applications; cultural studies; Greek languages and literatures (modern); history; liberal arts and sciences, general studies and humanities; mathematics; missions/missionary studies and missiology; philosophy and religion; psychology; religion/religious studies; religious/sacred music; speech and rhetorical studies; theological and ministerial studies; theological studies and religious vocations, other.

See full description on page 476.

NORTHWESTERN MICHIGAN COLLEGE

Traverse City, Michigan
Distance Education Services
http://www.nmc.edu/flo/

Northwestern Michigan College was founded in 1951. It is accredited by North Central Association of Colleges and Schools. It first offered distance learning courses in 1982. In fall 2003, there were 893 students enrolled in distance learning courses. Institutionally administered financial aid is available to distance learners.

Services Distance learners have accessibility to academic advising, bookstore, campus computer network, career placement assistance, e-mail services, library services, tutoring.
Contact Janet Oliver, Director, Northwestern Michigan College, Educational Media Technologies, 1701 East Front Street, Traverse City, MI 49686. *Telephone:* 231-955-1075. *Fax:* 231-955-1080. *E-mail:* joliver@nmc.edu.

DEGREES AND AWARDS

AAS General Education Transfer
AD Nursing

COURSE SUBJECT AREAS OFFERED OUTSIDE OF DEGREE PROGRAMS

Undergraduate—accounting; American history; anthropology; biology; biology, general; business administration and management; business communications; business information and data processing services; chemistry; computer and information sciences, general; computer and information sciences, other; computer programming; computer software and media applications; computer systems networking and telecommunications; creative writing; criminal justice and corrections; English composition; English technical and business writing; European history; history; Internet and World Wide Web; legal studies; mathematical statistics; mathematics related; music; nursing; philosophy; physics; psychology; psychology, other; sociology.

NORTHWESTERN OKLAHOMA STATE UNIVERSITY

Alva, Oklahoma
http://www.nwalva.edu/

Northwestern Oklahoma State University was founded in 1897. It is accredited by North Central Association of Colleges and Schools. It first offered distance learning courses in 2004. Institutionally administered financial aid is available to distance learners.

Services Distance learners have accessibility to bookstore, campus computer network, e-mail services, library services.
Contact Dr. Nancy J. Knous, Coordinator of Distance Learning, Northwestern Oklahoma State University, 709 Oklahoma Boule-

vard, Alva, OK 73717. *Telephone:* 580-327-8443. *Fax:* 580-327-8431. *E-mail:* njknous@nwosu.edu.

DEGREES AND AWARDS

Programs offered do not lead to a degree or other formal award.

COURSE SUBJECT AREAS OFFERED OUTSIDE OF DEGREE PROGRAMS

Undergraduate—accounting; advertising; business; business administration and management; business communications; English language and literature, general; sociology.
Graduate—education administration and supervision; education, other.

NORTHWESTERN STATE UNIVERSITY OF LOUISIANA

Natchitoches, Louisiana
http://www.nsula.edu/ece

Northwestern State University of Louisiana was founded in 1884. It is accredited by Southern Association of Colleges and Schools. It first offered distance learning courses in 1997. In fall 2003, there were 2,649 students enrolled in distance learning courses. Institutionally administered financial aid is available to distance learners.

Services Distance learners have accessibility to academic advising, bookstore, campus computer network, career placement assistance, e-mail services, library services, tutoring.
Contact Mrs. Darlene Williams, Director of Electronic and Continuing Education, Northwestern State University of Louisiana, Electronic and Continuing Education, 201 Williamson Hall, Natchitoches, LA 71497. *Telephone:* 318-357-6355. *Fax:* 318-357-5573. *E-mail:* darlene@nsula.edu.

DEGREES AND AWARDS

AA Criminal Justice
AGS General Studies
BSN Nursing
BSRS Radiologic Technology
Certification School Media Specialist
Advanced Graduate Diploma Education Specialist
MA Adult Education
MAE Educational Technology
MSE Health and Human Performance

COURSE SUBJECT AREAS OFFERED OUTSIDE OF DEGREE PROGRAMS

Undergraduate—accounting; biological and physical sciences; business administration and management; chemistry; computer and information sciences, general; computer software and media applications; creative writing; criminal justice and corrections; educational/instructional media design; education, other; English composition; English language and literature, general; English technical and business writing; fine arts and art studies; general teacher education; health and physical education/fitness; history; journalism and mass communications; library science, other; marketing management and research; mathematics; nursing; physical sciences, general; psychology; social work; zoology.
Graduate—education administration and supervision; educational evaluation, research and statistics; educational/instructional media design; educational psychology; education, other; psychology; special education.

NORTHWESTERN TECHNICAL COLLEGE

Rock Springs, Georgia
http://www.nwtcollege.org

Northwestern Technical College was founded in 1966. It is accredited by Northwest Commission on Colleges and Universities. It first offered distance learning courses in 1998. In fall 2003, there were 500 students enrolled in distance learning courses. Institutionally administered financial aid is available to distance learners.

Services Distance learners have accessibility to academic advising, bookstore, campus computer network, career placement assistance, e-mail services, library services.
Contact Dr. Dorenda McConnell, Dean of Distance Education, Northwestern Technical College, 265 Bicentennial Trail, Rock Springs, GA 30739. *Telephone:* 706-764-3593. *Fax:* 706-764-3566. *E-mail:* dmcconne@nwtcollege.org.

DEGREES AND AWARDS

Programs offered do not lead to a degree or other formal award.

COURSE SUBJECT AREAS OFFERED OUTSIDE OF DEGREE PROGRAMS

Undergraduate—administrative and secretarial services; applied mathematics; biological sciences/life sciences, other; biology, general; child care and guidance workers and managers; computer and information sciences, general; computer science; computer software and media applications; data entry/microcomputer applications; English language and literature, general; English technical and business writing; liberal arts and sciences, general studies and humanities; mathematics; miscellaneous health professions; psychology.

NORTHWESTERN UNIVERSITY

Evanston, Illinois
Communication Systems Strategy and Management Program
http://www.communication.northwestern.edu/mscstrategy

Northwestern University was founded in 1851. It is accredited by North Central Association of Colleges and Schools. It first offered distance learning courses in 2004. Institutionally administered financial aid is available to distance learners.

Services Distance learners have accessibility to academic advising, bookstore, campus computer network, e-mail services, library services.
Contact Ms. Donna J. Weirich, Director, Northwestern University, Frances Searle Building, 2240 Campus Drive, 2-118, Evanston, IL 60208. *Telephone:* 847-491-3848. *Fax:* 847-467-1036. *E-mail:* dweirich@northwestern.edu.

DEGREES AND AWARDS

MSC Business Strategy

COURSE SUBJECT AREAS OFFERED OUTSIDE OF DEGREE PROGRAMS

Graduate—business; communications technologies.
Non-credit—English as a second language.

Northwestern University (continued)

Special Message

This two-year master's degree is uniquely designed for the working professional. It addresses the ever-increasing demands placed on managers who are responsible for the investment, productivity, and performance of information/communication technologies and systems in business--including those responsible for the development of products and services in both the old economy and the new Internet economy.

The program is interdisciplinary, and it provides the advanced skills and expertise to help managers effectively bridge the "understanding gap" that occurs between a company's technical support staff and its non-technical executive decision-makers.

The program is a complete, fourteen-course curriculum. It focuses on business and management expertise and is often described by graduates as incorporating the essential elements of an M.B.A. Yet, the curriculum incorporates an effective foundation in technology and systems principles. Overall, the program is a progression in the development of related, advanced skills. In the first year, course topics include science and technology of information systems, the management and general application of communication and technology systems, and technological innovation.

The second year extends this interdisciplinary framework into course topics from market assessment/strategy, business finance, legal/political issues and process, and network management. Given that the program emphasizes the larger managerial perspective, a wide variety of undergraduate degrees are accepted; having an engineering degree or technical background is not required.

See full description on page 478.

NORTHWEST GRADUATE SCHOOL OF THE MINISTRY

Seattle, Washington

Northwest Graduate School of the Ministry was founded in 1990. It is accredited by Transnational Association of Christian Colleges and Schools. Institutionally administered financial aid is available to distance learners.

Services Distance learners have accessibility to academic advising, e-mail services.

Contact Mrs. Judi Melton, Registrar, Northwest Graduate School of the Ministry, 1013 Eighth Avenue, Seattle, WA 98104. *Telephone:* 206-264-9100 Ext. 14. *Fax:* 206-264-8828. *E-mail:* judim@nwgs.edu.

DEGREES AND AWARDS

Programs offered do not lead to a degree or other formal award.

COURSE SUBJECT AREAS OFFERED OUTSIDE OF DEGREE PROGRAMS

Graduate—bible/biblical studies; religion/religious studies; theological and ministerial studies; theological studies and religious vocations, other.

NORTHWEST MISSOURI STATE UNIVERSITY

Maryville, Missouri

Center for Information Technology in Education

http://www.NorthwestOnline.org

Northwest Missouri State University was founded in 1905. It is accredited by North Central Association of Colleges and Schools. It first offered distance learning courses in 1999. In fall 2003, there were 650 students enrolled in distance learning courses. Institutionally administered financial aid is available to distance learners.

Services Distance learners have accessibility to academic advising, bookstore, campus computer network, career placement assistance, e-mail services, library services.

Contact Dr. Roger Lee Von Holzen, Director of Center for Information Technology in Education, Northwest Missouri State University, OL 246, Maryville, MO 64468. *Telephone:* 660-562-1532. *Fax:* 660-562-1049. *E-mail:* rvh@mail.nwmissouri.edu.

DEGREES AND AWARDS

BS Accounting; Business Management; Computer Science
MS Geographic Information Science
MSE Special Education

COURSE SUBJECT AREAS OFFERED OUTSIDE OF DEGREE PROGRAMS

Undergraduate—American history; communications, general; computer and information sciences, general; earth sciences; foreign languages and literatures; geography; mathematics; music; philosophy; political science and government; psychology; theater arts/drama.
Graduate—education, general; geography; special education.

NORTHWOOD UNIVERSITY

Midland, Michigan

University College

http://www.northwoodonline.org

Northwood University was founded in 1959. It is accredited by North Central Association of Colleges and Schools. It first offered distance learning courses in 1965. In fall 2003, there were 280 students enrolled in distance learning courses. Institutionally administered financial aid is available to distance learners.

Services Distance learners have accessibility to academic advising, bookstore, career placement assistance, e-mail services, library services, tutoring.

Contact Marcella A. Matzke, Program Center Manager, Northwood University, 4000 Whiting Drive, Midland, MI 48640. *Telephone:* 800-445-5873. *Fax:* 989-837-4457. *E-mail:* matzke@northwood.edu.

DEGREES AND AWARDS

Programs offered do not lead to a degree or other formal award.

COURSE SUBJECT AREAS OFFERED OUTSIDE OF DEGREE PROGRAMS

Undergraduate—business administration and management.

NORWALK COMMUNITY COLLEGE

Norwalk, Connecticut

http://www.ncc.commnet.edu/

Norwalk Community College was founded in 1961. It is accredited by New England Association of Schools and Colleges. It first offered distance learning courses in 2001. In fall 2003, there were 100 students enrolled in distance learning courses. Institutionally administered financial aid is available to distance learners.

Services Distance learners have accessibility to e-mail services, library services.

Contact Admissions Office, Norwalk Community College, Admissions Office, 188 Richards Avenue, Norwalk, CT 06854-1655. *Telephone:* 203-857-7060. *Fax:* 203-857-3335. *E-mail:* admissions@ncc.commnet.edu.

DEGREES AND AWARDS

Programs offered do not lead to a degree or other formal award.

COURSE SUBJECT AREAS OFFERED OUTSIDE OF DEGREE PROGRAMS

Undergraduate—business information and data processing services; chemistry; English composition; English language and literature, general.

NORWICH UNIVERSITY

Northfield, Vermont

Online Graduate Programs

http://www3.norwich.edu/grad

Norwich University was founded in 1819. It is accredited by New England Association of Schools and Colleges. It first offered distance learning courses in 1997. In fall 2003, there were 400 students enrolled in distance learning courses. Institutionally administered financial aid is available to distance learners.

Services Distance learners have accessibility to academic advising, bookstore, campus computer network, career placement assistance, e-mail services, library services.

Contact Jane Joslin, Administrative Assistant, Norwich University, 158 Harmon Drive, Northfield, VT 05663. *Telephone:* 802-485-2730. *Fax:* 802-485-2533. *E-mail:* jdaniels@norwich.edu.

DEGREES AND AWARDS

MBA Certificate of Advanced Graduate Study
MCE Civil Engineering
MS Diplomacy; Information Assurance; Justice Administration

See full description on page 480.

NOVA SCOTIA AGRICULTURAL COLLEGE

Truro, Nova Scotia, Canada

Center for Continuing and Distance Education

http://www.nsac.ns.ca

Nova Scotia Agricultural College was founded in 1905. It is provincially chartered. It first offered distance learning courses in 1996. In fall 2003, there were 60 students enrolled in distance learning courses. Institutionally administered financial aid is available to distance learners.

Services Distance learners have accessibility to academic advising, bookstore, library services.

Contact Mrs. Pamela Doyle, Administrative Assistant, Nova Scotia Agricultural College, PO Box 550, 23 Sheep Hill Lane, Truro, NS B2N 5E3, Canada. *Telephone:* 902-893-6666. *Fax:* 902-895-5528. *E-mail:* cde@nsac.ns.ca.

DEGREES AND AWARDS

Programs offered do not lead to a degree or other formal award.

COURSE SUBJECT AREAS OFFERED OUTSIDE OF DEGREE PROGRAMS

Undergraduate—agricultural economics; agriculture/agricultural sciences; animal sciences; plant sciences.

Non-credit—agriculture/agricultural sciences; animal sciences; plant sciences.

NOVA SOUTHEASTERN UNIVERSITY

Fort Lauderdale, Florida

Graduate School of Computer and Information Sciences

http://www.scis.nova.edu/

Nova Southeastern University was founded in 1964. It is accredited by Southern Association of Colleges and Schools. It first offered distance learning courses in 1983. In fall 2003, there were 1,400 students enrolled in distance learning courses. Institutionally administered financial aid is available to distance learners.

Services Distance learners have accessibility to academic advising, bookstore, campus computer network, career placement assistance, e-mail services, library services.

Contact Sherese Young, Coordinator, Nova Southeastern University, 3301 College Avenue, Marketing Department, Fort Lauderdale, FL 33314-4416. *Telephone:* 800-986-2247 Ext. 2005. *Fax:* 954-262-3915. *E-mail:* scisinfo@nova.edu.

DEGREES AND AWARDS

MS Computer Information Systems; Computer Science; Computing Technology in Education; Information Security; Management Information Systems
EdD Computing Technology in Education
PhD Computer Information Systems; Computer Science; Computing Technology in Education; Information Sciences; Information Systems

COURSE SUBJECT AREAS OFFERED OUTSIDE OF DEGREE PROGRAMS

Graduate—business administration and management; business information and data processing services; computer and information sciences, general; computer and information sciences, other; computer/information technology administration and management; computer programming; computer science; computer software and media applications; computer systems analysis; computer systems networking and telecommunications; educational/instructional media design; education, general; education, other; information sciences and systems;

Nova Southeastern University (continued)

Internet and World Wide Web; library science/librarianship; library science, other; systems science and theory; technology education/industrial arts.

See full description on page 482.

OAKLAND CITY UNIVERSITY

Oakland City, Indiana

http://www.oak.edu/

Oakland City University was founded in 1885. It is accredited by North Central Association of Colleges and Schools. It first offered distance learning courses in 1999. In fall 2003, there were 25 students enrolled in distance learning courses. Institutionally administered financial aid is available to distance learners.

Services Distance learners have accessibility to academic advising, bookstore, library services.

Contact Mr. Michael Badgley, Director of Online Learning, Oakland City University, 143 North Lucretia Street, Oakland City, IN 47660. *Telephone:* 812-749-1248. *Fax:* 812-749-1233. *E-mail:* mbadgley@oak.edu.

DEGREES AND AWARDS

Programs offered do not lead to a degree or other formal award.

COURSE SUBJECT AREAS OFFERED OUTSIDE OF DEGREE PROGRAMS

Undergraduate—business; business communications; English composition; English language and literature, general; fine arts and art studies; geography; history; psychology; religion/religious studies.

OCEAN COUNTY COLLEGE

Toms River, New Jersey

http://www.ocean.edu

Ocean County College was founded in 1964. It is accredited by Middle States Association of Colleges and Schools. It first offered distance learning courses in 2000. Institutionally administered financial aid is available to distance learners.

Services Distance learners have accessibility to campus computer network, e-mail services, library services.

Contact Mrs. Barbara Schradin, Executive Assistant Vice President, Technology and Campus Services, Ocean County College, College Drive, PO Box 2001, Toms River, NJ 08754-2001. *Telephone:* 732-255-0400 Ext. 2239. *Fax:* 732-255-0444. *E-mail:* bschradin@ocean.edu.

DEGREES AND AWARDS

Programs offered do not lead to a degree or other formal award.

COURSE SUBJECT AREAS OFFERED OUTSIDE OF DEGREE PROGRAMS

Undergraduate—accounting; business administration and management; business and personal services marketing operations; business/managerial economics; computer and information sciences, general; economics; English composition; fine arts and art studies; health and physical education/fitness; history; mathematics; nursing; philosophy.

ODESSA COLLEGE

Odessa, Texas

Division of Distance Education

http://www.odesssa.edu

Odessa College was founded in 1946. It is accredited by Southern Association of Colleges and Schools. It first offered distance learning courses in 1986. In fall 2003, there were 2,000 students enrolled in distance learning courses. Institutionally administered financial aid is available to distance learners.

Services Distance learners have accessibility to academic advising, bookstore, campus computer network, career placement assistance, e-mail services, library services.

Contact Wilma Chastain, Director of Distance Learning, Odessa College, 201 West University, Odessa, TX 79764. *Telephone:* 432-335-6317. *Fax:* 432-335-6667. *E-mail:* wchastian@odessa.edu.

DEGREES AND AWARDS

ASAST Occupational Safety and Health Technology

COURSE SUBJECT AREAS OFFERED OUTSIDE OF DEGREE PROGRAMS

Undergraduate—accounting; administrative and secretarial services; biology; business; computer and information sciences, general; developmental/child psychology; English composition; environmental control technologies; environmental/environmental health engineering; mathematics; social psychology; sociology.

Non-credit—business administration and management; business management and administrative services, other; computer software and media applications; English creative writing; financial services marketing operations; foreign languages and literatures; Internet and World Wide Web; legal studies.

OHIO NORTHERN UNIVERSITY

Ada, Ohio

Raabe College of Pharmacy

http://www.onu.edu/pharmacy/ntpd/default.asp

Ohio Northern University was founded in 1871. It is accredited by North Central Association of Colleges and Schools. It first offered distance learning courses in 1997. In fall 2003, there were 42 students enrolled in distance learning courses. Institutionally administered financial aid is available to distance learners.

Services Distance learners have accessibility to academic advising, bookstore, campus computer network, career placement assistance, e-mail services, library services.

Contact Dr. Karen Kier, Director of Non-Traditional Pharm.D Program, Ohio Northern University, 525 South Main Street, Ada, OH 45810. *Telephone:* 419-772-2282. *Fax:* 419-772-2289. *E-mail:* k-kier@onu.edu.

DEGREES AND AWARDS

PharmD Pharmacy

COURSE SUBJECT AREAS OFFERED OUTSIDE OF DEGREE PROGRAMS

Undergraduate—pharmacy.

Graduate—pharmacy.

THE OHIO STATE UNIVERSITY

Columbus, Ohio
Technology Enhanced Learning and Research (TELR)
http://telr.ohio-state.edu

The Ohio State University was founded in 1870. It is accredited by North Central Association of Colleges and Schools. It first offered distance learning courses in 1995. In fall 2003, there were 3,000 students enrolled in distance learning courses. Institutionally administered financial aid is available to distance learners.

Services Distance learners have accessibility to academic advising, bookstore, campus computer network, e-mail services, library services, tutoring.

Contact Dr. Catherine M. Gynn, Assistant Director, Technology Enhanced Learning and Research (TELR), The Ohio State University, 480 Baker Systems, 1971 Neil Avenue, Columbus, OH 43210. *Telephone:* 614-247-7280. *Fax:* 614-292-7081. *E-mail:* gynn.1@osu.edu.

DEGREES AND AWARDS

EMBA Business Administration
PharmD NonTraditional PharmD

COURSE SUBJECT AREAS OFFERED OUTSIDE OF DEGREE PROGRAMS

Undergraduate—business; engineering, other; family/consumer resource management; foreign languages and literatures; forestry; horticulture science; political science and government; social work; visual and performing arts, other.

Graduate—business administration and management; education administration and supervision; education, other; engineering, other; horticulture science; mechanical engineering; nuclear engineering; nursing; social work.

Non-credit—gerontology; mental health services; special education.

OHIO UNIVERSITY

Athens, Ohio
Lifelong Learning
http://www.ohio.edu/independent/

Ohio University was founded in 1804. It is accredited by North Central Association of Colleges and Schools. It first offered distance learning courses in 1941. In fall 2003, there were 1,700 students enrolled in distance learning courses. Institutionally administered financial aid is available to distance learners.

Services Distance learners have accessibility to academic advising, bookstore, career placement assistance, e-mail services, library services.

Contact Independent and Distance Learning Programs, Ohio University, 222 Haning Hall, Athens, OH 45701. *Telephone:* 800-444-2910. *Fax:* 740-593-2901. *E-mail:* independent.study@ohio.edu.

DEGREES AND AWARDS

AA Arts and Humanities; Social Sciences
AIS Individualized Studies
AS Mathematics; Natural Science
BGS Specialized Studies

COURSE SUBJECT AREAS OFFERED OUTSIDE OF DEGREE PROGRAMS

Undergraduate—accounting; administrative and secretarial services; American literature (United States); anthropology; biological and physical sciences; biology; business; chemistry; communications, general; creative writing; criminology; developmental/child psychology; economics; educational psychology; English composition; English language and literature, general; English technical and business writing; foreign languages and literatures; geography; history; human resources management; journalism; journalism and mass communications; marketing management and research; mathematics; philosophy and religion; psychology; sociology; tourism/travel marketing; women's studies.

See full description on page 484.

OKALOOSA-WALTON COLLEGE

Niceville, Florida
Distance Learning
http://www.owc.edu

Okaloosa-Walton College was founded in 1963. It is accredited by Southern Association of Colleges and Schools. It first offered distance learning courses in 1994. In fall 2003, there were 2,016 students enrolled in distance learning courses. Institutionally administered financial aid is available to distance learners.

Services Distance learners have accessibility to academic advising, bookstore, career placement assistance, library services, tutoring.

Contact Mrs. Anne Southard, EdD, Director of Distance Learning, Okaloosa-Walton College, 100 College Boulevard, Niceville, FL 32578-1295. *Telephone:* 850-729-6040. *Fax:* 850-729-5295. *E-mail:* southara@owc.edu.

DEGREES AND AWARDS

Programs offered do not lead to a degree or other formal award.

COURSE SUBJECT AREAS OFFERED OUTSIDE OF DEGREE PROGRAMS

Undergraduate—accounting; advertising; biological and physical sciences; biology, general; business administration and management; business communications; business management and administrative services, other; chemistry; computer and information sciences, general; criminal justice and corrections; economics; educational psychology; English composition; general retailing/wholesaling; Internet and World Wide Web; philosophy; physical sciences, general; political science and government; psychology; quality control and safety technologies; religion/religious studies; social sciences, general; sociology; technology education/industrial arts.

OKLAHOMA STATE UNIVERSITY

Stillwater, Oklahoma
Distance Learning
http://ueied.ue.okstate.edu/dl/index.htm

Oklahoma State University was founded in 1890. It is accredited by North Central Association of Colleges and Schools. It first offered distance learning courses in 1945. In fall 2003, there were 3,507 students enrolled in distance learning courses. Institutionally administered financial aid is available to distance learners.

Oklahoma State University (continued)

Services Distance learners have accessibility to academic advising, bookstore, campus computer network, career placement assistance, e-mail services, library services, tutoring.

Contact Cecilia Boardman, Senior Office Assistant, Oklahoma State University, 001 Classroom Building, Stillwater, OK 74078. *Telephone:* 405-744-6390. *Fax:* 405-744-3420. *E-mail:* ext-dl@okstate.edu.

DEGREES AND AWARDS

MAg Agricultural Education
MBA Business Administration
MS Agricultural Education; Computer Science; Control Systems Engineering; Electrical and Computer Engineering; Engineering Technology Management; Environmental Science/Management; Fire and Emergency Management Administration; Mechanical Engineering; Telecommunications Management
MSHA Health Care Administration

COURSE SUBJECT AREAS OFFERED OUTSIDE OF DEGREE PROGRAMS

Undergraduate—accounting; agricultural economics; agriculture/agricultural sciences, other; American history; American literature (United States); animal sciences; anthropology; business administration and management; business communications; business marketing and marketing management; communication disorders sciences and services; counseling psychology; creative writing; developmental/child psychology; economics; educational evaluation, research and statistics; educational psychology; education, other; electrical and electronic engineering-related technology; engineering-related technologies, other; engineering science; English composition; English literature (British and Commonwealth); English technical and business writing; family and community studies; finance; fire science; foods and nutrition studies; French; geography; geological and related sciences; Germanic languages and literatures; health and physical education/fitness; history; horticulture services operations and management; individual and family development studies; journalism; law and legal studies related; management information systems/business data processing; marketing operations/marketing and distribution, other; mathematical statistics; mathematics related; music; organizational behavior; philosophy; political science and government; psychology; sociology; Spanish.
Graduate—chemical engineering; educational evaluation, research and statistics; electrical engineering; environmental engineering; fire science; industrial engineering; mechanical engineering.
Non-credit—communications, other; community health services; computer programming; English technical and business writing; fire protection; real estate; special education.

OKLAHOMA WESLEYAN UNIVERSITY

Bartlesville, Oklahoma

http://www.okwu.edu

Oklahoma Wesleyan University was founded in 1909. It is accredited by North Central Association of Colleges and Schools. It first offered distance learning courses in 1998. In fall 2003, there were 100 students enrolled in distance learning courses. Institutionally administered financial aid is available to distance learners.

Services Distance learners have accessibility to academic advising, bookstore, e-mail services, library services, tutoring.

Contact Dr. Darek Jarmola, Dean, Adult and Graduate Studies, Oklahoma Wesleyan University, 2201 Silver Lake Road, Bartlesville, OK 74006. *Telephone:* 918-335-6259. *Fax:* 918-335-6244. *E-mail:* ags@okwu.edu.

DEGREES AND AWARDS

Programs offered do not lead to a degree or other formal award.

COURSE SUBJECT AREAS OFFERED OUTSIDE OF DEGREE PROGRAMS

Undergraduate—history; Internet and World Wide Web.

OLD DOMINION UNIVERSITY

Norfolk, Virginia

Office of Distance Learning and Extended Education

http://www.dl.odu.edu

Old Dominion University was founded in 1930. It is accredited by Southern Association of Colleges and Schools. It first offered distance learning courses in 1984. In fall 2003, there were 5,350 students enrolled in distance learning courses. Institutionally administered financial aid is available to distance learners.

Services Distance learners have accessibility to academic advising, bookstore, campus computer network, career placement assistance, e-mail services, library services.

Contact Dr. Jeanie Kline, Assistant Vice President of Distance Learning, Old Dominion University, Gornto TELETECHNET Center, Norfolk, VA 23529. *Telephone:* 757-683-3163. *Fax:* 757-683-5492. *E-mail:* jkline@odu.edu.

DEGREES AND AWARDS

BA Criminal Justice
BHS Health Sciences
BS Computer Science; Criminal Justice; Education–Teacher Preparation; Human Services Counseling; Occupational and Technical Studies
BSBA Business Administration
BSET Civil Engineering Technology; Electrical Engineering Technology; Mechanical Engineering Technology
BSN Nursing
MEM Engineering Management
MS Education–Pre-K Through 6; Occupational and Technical Studies; Special Education
MSN Nursing–Nurse Leader and Nurse Educator Options

COURSE SUBJECT AREAS OFFERED OUTSIDE OF DEGREE PROGRAMS

Undergraduate—accounting; business communications; business information and data processing services; business/managerial economics; business marketing and marketing management; business quantitative methods and management science; communications, general; community health services; computer and information sciences, general; computer science; computer systems networking and telecommunications; criminal justice and corrections; education, other; engineering-related technologies, other; finance; journalism; management information systems/business data processing; nursing; organizational psychology; philosophy; social psychology; sociology.
Graduate—accounting; aerospace engineering; business marketing and marketing management; education, other; electrical engineering;

engineering/industrial management; environmental engineering; finance; management information systems/business data processing; mechanical engineering; nursing.

See full description on page 486.

ORAL ROBERTS UNIVERSITY

Tulsa, Oklahoma

http://www.oru.edu/

Oral Roberts University was founded in 1963. It is accredited by North Central Association of Colleges and Schools. It first offered distance learning courses in 1975. In fall 2003, there were 470 students enrolled in distance learning courses. Institutionally administered financial aid is available to distance learners.

Services Distance learners have accessibility to academic advising, bookstore, campus computer network, career placement assistance, e-mail services, library services, tutoring.

Contact Mrs. Kathryn Neal, Assistant Director of Recruitment, Oral Roberts University, Adult Learning Service Center, 7777 South Lewis Avenue, Tulsa, OK 74171. *Telephone:* 800-643-7976. *Fax:* 918-495-7965. *E-mail:* kneal@oru.edu.

DEGREES AND AWARDS

BS Business Administration; Christian Care and Counseling; Church Ministries; Elementary Education with Certification; Liberal Studies
Certificate Nonprofit Management
MA Practical Theology
MAE Christian School Administration; Christian School Curriculum; Christian School Postsecondary Administration; Early Childhood Education; Public School Administration; Teaching English as a Second Language (TESL); Teaching with Certification
MAM Nonprofit Management
MDiv Divinity
DMin Ministry
EdD Christian School Administration (PK-12); Postsecondary School Administration; Public School Administration

COURSE SUBJECT AREAS OFFERED OUTSIDE OF DEGREE PROGRAMS

Non-credit—bible/biblical studies; theological and ministerial studies.

ORANGE COAST COLLEGE

Costa Mesa, California

http://www.orangecoastcollege.com

Orange Coast College was founded in 1947. It is accredited by Western Association of Schools and Colleges. It first offered distance learning courses in 1998. In fall 2003, there were 1,829 students enrolled in distance learning courses. Institutionally administered financial aid is available to distance learners.

Services Distance learners have accessibility to bookstore, library services.

Contact Dr. Nancy Kidder, Administrative Dean of Admissions and Records and International Programs, Orange Coast College, 2701 Fairview Road, Costa Mesa, CA 92626. *Telephone:* 714-432-0202. *E-mail:* nkidder@mail.occ.cccd.edu.

DEGREES AND AWARDS

Programs offered do not lead to a degree or other formal award.

COURSE SUBJECT AREAS OFFERED OUTSIDE OF DEGREE PROGRAMS

Undergraduate—accounting; administrative and secretarial services; anthropology; architecture; biology, general; business management and administrative services, other; child care and guidance workers and managers; clothing/apparel and textile studies; computer and information sciences, general; computer/information technology administration and management; computer programming; computer software and media applications; construction/building technology; dance; drafting; electrical and electronics equipment installers and repairers; electromechanical instrumentation and maintenance technology; English composition; foods and nutrition studies; food sciences and technology; health and medical administrative services; health and medical assistants; health professions and related sciences, other; heating, air conditioning and refrigeration mechanics and repairers; hospitality/recreation marketing; hospitality services management; music; real estate.

OREGON INSTITUTE OF TECHNOLOGY

Klamath Falls, Oregon

http://www.oit.edu/dist

Oregon Institute of Technology was founded in 1947. It is accredited by Northwest Commission on Colleges and Universities. It first offered distance learning courses in 1997. In fall 2003, there were 365 students enrolled in distance learning courses. Institutionally administered financial aid is available to distance learners.

Services Distance learners have accessibility to academic advising, bookstore, campus computer network, e-mail services, library services.

Contact Beth Murphy, Director, Distance Education, Oregon Institute of Technology, 3201 Campus Drive, Klamath Falls, OR 97601. *Telephone:* 503-885-1141. *E-mail:* murphyb@oit.edu.

DEGREES AND AWARDS

BS Dental Hygiene–Degree Completion in Dental Hygiene; Radiological Science–Degree Completion in Radiological Science; Respiratory Care; Ultrasound–Degree Completion in Ultrasound with Option in Echocardiography; Ultrasound–Degree Completion in Ultrasound with Option in Vascular Technology

COURSE SUBJECT AREAS OFFERED OUTSIDE OF DEGREE PROGRAMS

Undergraduate—accounting; anthropology; business; business administration and management; computer/information technology administration and management; dental clinical sciences/graduate dentistry (M.S., Ph.D.); engineering/industrial management; health and medical diagnostic and treatment services; miscellaneous health professions.

OREGON STATE UNIVERSITY

Corvallis, Oregon

Extended Campus

http://ecampus.oregonstate.edu

Oregon State University was founded in 1868. It is accredited by Northwest Commission on Colleges and Universities. It first offered

Oregon State University (continued)

distance learning courses in 1986. In fall 2003, there were 1,495 students enrolled in distance learning courses. Institutionally administered financial aid is available to distance learners.

Services Distance learners have accessibility to academic advising, bookstore, campus computer network, career placement assistance, e-mail services, library services, tutoring.

Contact Ecampus Student Services, Oregon State University, OSU Extended Campus, 4943 The Valley Library, Corvallis, OR 97331-4504. *Telephone:* 800-667-1465. *Fax:* 541-737-2734. *E-mail:* ecampus@oregonstate.edu.

DEGREES AND AWARDS

BA Liberal Studies

BS Agriculture, general; Environmental Sciences; Liberal Studies; Natural Resources

COURSE SUBJECT AREAS OFFERED OUTSIDE OF DEGREE PROGRAMS

Undergraduate—agricultural economics; agriculture/agricultural sciences; agriculture/agricultural sciences, other; American history; American literature (United States); anthropology; area, ethnic and cultural studies, other; atmospheric sciences and meteorology; botany; business; business communications; chemistry; communications, general; conservation and renewable natural resources, other; creative writing; ecology; economics; education, general; English composition; English creative writing; English language and literature, general; English technical and business writing; environmental science; European history; fishing and fisheries sciences and management; forestry; forestry and related sciences; geological and related sciences; health and medical administrative services; history; history of science and technology; liberal arts and sciences, general studies and humanities; marketing operations/marketing and distribution, other; mathematical statistics; mathematics related; natural resources conservation; natural resources management and protective services; oceanography; philosophy; philosophy and religion related; plant sciences; political science and government; psychology; science, technology and society; social sciences and history, other; sociology; soil sciences; wildlife and wildlands management; women's studies.

Graduate—adult/continuing education; agriculture/agricultural sciences; education administration and supervision; education, general; education, other; environmental/environmental health engineering; foods and nutrition studies; general teacher education; health and medical administrative services; natural resources conservation; nuclear and industrial radiologic technologies; nuclear engineering; public health; teacher education, specific academic and vocational programs; wildlife and wildlands management.

Non-credit—business and personal services marketing operations; business management and administrative services, other; communications, general; computer software and media applications; English as a second language; English language and literature, general; family/consumer resource management; film/video and photographic arts; fine arts and art studies; foreign languages and literatures; health and medical administrative services; Internet and World Wide Web; psychology; Romance languages and literatures.

See full description on page 488.

OWENSBORO COMMUNITY AND TECHNICAL COLLEGE

Owensboro, Kentucky

http://www.octc.kctcs.edu

Owensboro Community and Technical College was founded in 1986. It is accredited by Northwest Commission on Colleges and Universities. In fall 2003, there were 315 students enrolled in distance learning courses. Institutionally administered financial aid is available to distance learners.

Services Distance learners have accessibility to e-mail services, library services.

Contact Ms. Barbara Tipmore, Admissions Counselor, Owensboro Community and Technical College, 4800 New Hartford Road, Owensboro, KY 42303. *Telephone:* 270-686-4527. *E-mail:* barb.tipmore@kctcs.edu.

DEGREES AND AWARDS

Programs offered do not lead to a degree or other formal award.

COURSE SUBJECT AREAS OFFERED OUTSIDE OF DEGREE PROGRAMS

Undergraduate—accounting; business; business administration and management; child care and guidance workers and managers; communications, general; computer and information sciences, general; English language and literature, general; history; psychology.

OXNARD COLLEGE

Oxnard, California

http://www.oxnardcollege.edu

Oxnard College was founded in 1975. It is accredited by Western Association of Schools and Colleges. It first offered distance learning courses in 1997. In fall 2003, there were 98 students enrolled in distance learning courses. Institutionally administered financial aid is available to distance learners.

Services Distance learners have accessibility to academic advising, bookstore, e-mail services, library services.

Contact Dr. Jaime Casillas, Dean, Economic Development and Community Initiatives, Oxnard College, 4000 South Rose Avenue, Oxnard, CA 93033. *Telephone:* 805-986-5888. *Fax:* 805-986-5988. *E-mail:* jcasillas@vcccd.net.

DEGREES AND AWARDS

Programs offered do not lead to a degree or other formal award.

COURSE SUBJECT AREAS OFFERED OUTSIDE OF DEGREE PROGRAMS

Undergraduate—accounting; administrative and secretarial services; advertising; American literature (United States); anthropology; applied mathematics; area, ethnic and cultural studies, other; area studies; astronomy; bilingual/bicultural education; biological sciences/life sciences, other; biology, general; botany; business; business administration and management; business communications; business management and administrative services, other; chemistry; child care and guidance workers and managers; clinical psychology; communications, general; computer and information sciences, general; computer engineering; computer/information technology administration and management; computer programming; computer science; computer systems analysis; computer systems networking and telecommunications; criminal justice and corrections; culinary arts and related services; data entry/microcomputer applications; dental services; developmental and child psychology; dramatic/theater arts and stagecraft; economics; education, general; English as a second language; English composition; English creative writing; English language and literature, general; English technical and business writing; environmental control technologies; film/video and photographic arts; fine arts and art studies; fire protection; foreign languages and literatures, other; geological and related sciences; heating, air conditioning and refrigeration mechanics and repairers; history; human services; international business; Internet and World Wide Web; journalism and mass communications; legal studies; library science, other; marketing management and research; mathematics; mechanics and repairers, other; microbiology/bacteriology; music; philosophy; physical sciences, general; physics; political science and government; psychology; public health; radio and television broadcasting; social psychology; sociology; special education; speech and rhetorical studies; taxation; tourism/travel marketing.

PACE UNIVERSITY

New York, New York
Online Pace
http://www.online.pace.edu

Pace University was founded in 1906. It is accredited by Middle States Association of Colleges and Schools. It first offered distance learning courses in 1995. In fall 2003, there were 2,599 students enrolled in distance learning courses. Institutionally administered financial aid is available to distance learners.

Services Distance learners have accessibility to academic advising, bookstore, campus computer network, career placement assistance, e-mail services, library services, tutoring.

Contact Mr. James Stenerson, Director of Center for Instructional Technology, Pace University, 861 Bedford Road, Pleasantville , NY 10590. *Telephone:* 914-773-3317. *E-mail:* jstenerson@pace.edu.

DEGREES AND AWARDS

BS Professional Communication Studies; Professional Technology Studies

Specialized diploma Computing–Doctor of Professional Studies in Computing

Graduate Certificate Business Aspects of Publishing; Internet Technologies; Internet Technology; Telecommunications

MBA e.MBA

MS Internet Technology for E-Commerce; Publishing

COURSE SUBJECT AREAS OFFERED OUTSIDE OF DEGREE PROGRAMS

Undergraduate—accounting; anthropology; biology, general; business; business administration and management; communications, general; computer and information sciences, other; computer programming; computer science; criminal justice and corrections; criminology; education, general; English language and literature, general; financial management and services; fine arts and art studies; foreign languages and literatures; history; international business; Internet and World Wide Web; legal studies; marketing management and research; mathematical statistics; mathematics, other; nursing; political science and government; psychology; science, technology and society; sociology; teacher education, specific academic and vocational programs; telecommunications; visual and performing arts.

Graduate—bilingual/bicultural education; business; business administration and management; computer and information sciences, general; computer and information sciences, other; computer/information technology administration and management; computer programming; computer software and media applications; computer systems analysis; computer systems networking and telecommunications; education administration and supervision; educational/instructional media design; education, general; education, other; Internet and World Wide Web; marketing management and research; nursing.

Non-credit—business; computer and information sciences, general; education, general; liberal arts and sciences, general studies and humanities; nursing; personal and miscellaneous services, other.

See full description on page 490.

PACIFIC GRADUATE SCHOOL OF PSYCHOLOGY

Palo Alto, California
Master's Degree (M.S.) in Psychology
http://www.pgsp.edu/distance.htm

Pacific Graduate School of Psychology was founded in 1975. It is accredited by Western Association of Schools and Colleges. It first offered distance learning courses in 1999. In fall 2003, there were 35 students enrolled in distance learning courses. Institutionally administered financial aid is available to distance learners.

Services Distance learners have accessibility to academic advising, e-mail services, library services.

Contact Mrs. Elizabeth Hilt, Vice President of Enrollment Management, Pacific Graduate School of Psychology, 935 East Meadow Drive, Palo Alto, CA 94303. *Telephone:* 800-818-6136. *Fax:* 650-843-3418. *E-mail:* ehit@pgsp.edu.

DEGREES AND AWARDS

MS Psychology

COURSE SUBJECT AREAS OFFERED OUTSIDE OF DEGREE PROGRAMS

Graduate—psychology.

PACIFIC OAKS COLLEGE

Pasadena, California
Distance Learning
http://www.pacificoaks.edu

Pacific Oaks College was founded in 1945. It is accredited by Western Association of Schools and Colleges. It first offered distance learning courses in 1996. In fall 2003, there were 202 students enrolled in distance learning courses. Institutionally administered financial aid is available to distance learners.

Services Distance learners have accessibility to academic advising, bookstore, library services.

Contact Betty Jones, Co-Director of Distance Learning, Pacific Oaks College, 5 Westmoreland Place, Pasadena, CA 91103. *Telephone:* 800-613-0300. *Fax:* 626-397-1317. *E-mail:* bjones@pacificoaks.edu.

Pacific Oaks College (continued)

DEGREES AND AWARDS

BA Human Development
MA Human Development

COURSE SUBJECT AREAS OFFERED OUTSIDE OF DEGREE PROGRAMS

Undergraduate—education, other; individual and family development studies.
Graduate—education, other; individual and family development studies.

PACIFIC UNION COLLEGE

Angwin, California

http://www.puc.edu/

Pacific Union College was founded in 1882. It is accredited by Western Association of Schools and Colleges. It first offered distance learning courses in 2001. In fall 2003, there were 53 students enrolled in distance learning courses. Institutionally administered financial aid is available to distance learners.

Services Distance learners have accessibility to academic advising, bookstore, campus computer network, e-mail services, library services, tutoring.
Contact Rosemary H. Dibben, Distance Learning Coordinator, Pacific Union College, Resource Learning Center, One Angwin Avenue, Angwin, CA 94508. *Telephone:* 707-965-6694. *E-mail:* rdibben@puc.edu.

DEGREES AND AWARDS

Programs offered do not lead to a degree or other formal award.

COURSE SUBJECT AREAS OFFERED OUTSIDE OF DEGREE PROGRAMS

Undergraduate—chemistry; mathematics.

PALM BEACH COMMUNITY COLLEGE

Lake Worth, Florida

http://www.pbcc.edu/dl

Palm Beach Community College was founded in 1933. It is accredited by Southern Association of Colleges and Schools. It first offered distance learning courses in 1997. In fall 2003, there were 5,000 students enrolled in distance learning courses. Institutionally administered financial aid is available to distance learners.

Services Distance learners have accessibility to academic advising, bookstore, career placement assistance, library services.
Contact Ms. Anne Guiler, Distance Learning Coordinator, Palm Beach Community College, 3000 Saint Lucie Avenue, Boca Raton, FL 33431. *Telephone:* 561-862-4402. *E-mail:* guilera@pbcc.edu.

DEGREES AND AWARDS

AA General Studies

COURSE SUBJECT AREAS OFFERED OUTSIDE OF DEGREE PROGRAMS

Undergraduate—accounting; anthropology; astronomy; biological and physical sciences; business; chemistry; communications, general; computer and information sciences, general; developmental and child psychology; economics; education, general; electrical and electronic engineering-related technology.

PALOMAR COLLEGE

San Marcos, California
Educational Television

http://www.palomar.edu

Palomar College was founded in 1946. It is accredited by Western Association of Schools and Colleges. It first offered distance learning courses in 1975. In fall 2003, there were 4,000 students enrolled in distance learning courses. Institutionally administered financial aid is available to distance learners.

Services Distance learners have accessibility to academic advising, bookstore, campus computer network, e-mail services, library services, tutoring.
Contact Mrs. Michelle Grace, Educational TV Senior Office Specialist, Palomar College, 1140 West Mission Road, San Marcos, CA 92069. *Telephone:* 760-744-1150 Ext. 2431. *Fax:* 760-761-3519. *E-mail:* mgrace@palomar.edu.

DEGREES AND AWARDS

Programs offered do not lead to a degree or other formal award.

COURSE SUBJECT AREAS OFFERED OUTSIDE OF DEGREE PROGRAMS

Undergraduate—accounting; anthropology; area, ethnic and cultural studies, other; biology; botany; business; chemistry; computer and information sciences, general; computer software and media applications; developmental/child psychology; economics; English composition; family/consumer resource management; finance; fine arts and art studies; fire protection; foods and nutrition studies; journalism and mass communication related; law and legal studies related; liberal arts and sciences, general studies and humanities; library science, other; music; philosophy; psychology; sign language interpretation; sociology; Spanish.

THE PARALEGAL INSTITUTE, INC.

Phoenix, Arizona

http://www.theparalegalinstitute.com/

The Paralegal Institute, Inc. was founded in 1974. It is accredited by Distance Education and Training Council. It first offered distance learning courses in 1979. In fall 2003, there were 600 students enrolled in distance learning courses. Institutionally administered financial aid is available to distance learners.

Services Distance learners have accessibility to academic advising, e-mail services, tutoring.
Contact Robert Jerry, Director of Admissions, The Paralegal Institute, Inc., 2933 West Indian School Road, Drawer 11408, Phoenix, AZ 85061-1408. *Telephone:* 800-354-1254. *Fax:* 602-212-0502. *E-mail:* paralegalinst@mindspring.com.

DEGREES AND AWARDS

AA Criminal Justice; Paralegal

COURSE SUBJECT AREAS OFFERED OUTSIDE OF DEGREE PROGRAMS

Undergraduate—criminal justice and corrections; legal studies; medical basic sciences; nursing.

PARK UNIVERSITY

Parkville, Missouri
School for Extended Learning
http://www.park.edu/online

Park University was founded in 1875. It is accredited by North Central Association of Colleges and Schools. It first offered distance learning courses in 1996. Institutionally administered financial aid is available to distance learners.

Services Distance learners have accessibility to academic advising, bookstore, career placement assistance, e-mail services, library services, tutoring.

Contact Office of Admissions, Park University, 8700 Northwest River Park Drive, Parkville, MO 64152-3795. *Telephone:* 800-745-7275. *E-mail:* admissions@park.edu.

DEGREES AND AWARDS

BS Criminal Justice Administration; Management; Management/Computer Information Systems; Management/Human Resources; Management/Marketing; Social Psychology
MBA Business Administration; Health Care/Health Services Management; International Business
MEd General Education; Multi-Cultural Education; School Law; Teaching At-Risk Students
MPA Government–Business Relations; Nonprofit and Community Services Management; Public Management

COURSE SUBJECT AREAS OFFERED OUTSIDE OF DEGREE PROGRAMS

Undergraduate—accounting; American history; American literature (United States); area, ethnic and cultural studies, other; bible/biblical studies; biology; business; business administration and management; business communications; business information and data processing services; business management and administrative services, other; business marketing and marketing management; communications, general; communications, other; computer and information sciences, general; computer programming; creative writing; criminal justice and corrections; criminology; economics; education, other; English composition; English creative writing; English language and literature, general; finance; geography; geological and related sciences; health services administration; history; human resources management; labor/personnel relations; marketing management and research; marketing operations/marketing and distribution, other; mathematical statistics; mathematics; organizational behavior; philosophy and religion related; political science and government; psychology; social psychology.
Graduate—business administration and management; business management and administrative services, other; computer and information sciences, general; education administration and supervision; education, general; international business; public administration; public administration and services, other.

See full description on page 492.

PASCO-HERNANDO COMMUNITY COLLEGE

New Port Richey, Florida
http://www.phcc.edu

Pasco-Hernando Community College was founded in 1972. It is accredited by Southern Association of Colleges and Schools. It first offered distance learning courses in 1993. In fall 2003, there were 1,037 students enrolled in distance learning courses. Institutionally administered financial aid is available to distance learners.

Services Distance learners have accessibility to campus computer network, library services.

Contact Mr. Michael Malizia, Director of Admissions and Student Records, Pasco-Hernando Community College, 10230 Ridge Road, New Port Richey, FL 34654-5199. *Telephone:* 727-816-3261. *Fax:* 727-816-3389. *E-mail:* malizim@phcc.edu.

DEGREES AND AWARDS

Programs offered do not lead to a degree or other formal award.

COURSE SUBJECT AREAS OFFERED OUTSIDE OF DEGREE PROGRAMS

Undergraduate—biology, general; business; business administration and management; computer programming; computer systems networking and telecommunications; English composition; English literature (British and Commonwealth); general teacher education; health and physical education/fitness; history; Internet and World Wide Web; physical sciences, general; psychology; social sciences and history, other; sociology; speech and rhetorical studies.
Non-credit—business and personal services marketing operations; business communications; computer and information sciences, general; computer software and media applications; English technical and business writing; family/consumer resource management; health professions and related sciences, other; Internet and World Wide Web; personal and miscellaneous services, other.

PASSAIC COUNTY COMMUNITY COLLEGE

Paterson, New Jersey
http://www.pccc.cc.nj.us/

Passaic County Community College was founded in 1968. It is accredited by Middle States Association of Colleges and Schools. It first offered distance learning courses in 1998. In fall 2003, there were 700 students enrolled in distance learning courses. Institutionally administered financial aid is available to distance learners.

Services Distance learners have accessibility to academic advising, bookstore, library services, tutoring.

Contact Mr. Rick Perdew, Coordinator of Instructional Technology, Passaic County Community College, 1 College Boulevard, Paterson, NJ 07505-1179. *Telephone:* 973-684-5790. *Fax:* 973-684-4079. *E-mail:* rperdew@pccc.edu.

DEGREES AND AWARDS

AAS Health Information Technology

COURSE SUBJECT AREAS OFFERED OUTSIDE OF DEGREE PROGRAMS

Undergraduate—business; communications, general; computer and information sciences, general; English language and literature, gen-

Passaic County Community College (continued)

eral; health professions and related sciences, other; mathematical statistics; mathematics, other; physical sciences, general.

PATRICK HENRY COLLEGE

Purcellville, Virginia

http://www.phc.edu/distancelearning

Patrick Henry College was founded in 1999. It is accredited by American Academy for Liberal Education. It first offered distance learning courses in 2001. In fall 2003, there were 130 students enrolled in distance learning courses. Institutionally administered financial aid is available to distance learners.

Services Distance learners have accessibility to academic advising, bookstore, library services.

Contact Mr. Richard Shipe, Director of Distance Learning, Patrick Henry College, One Patrick Henry Circle, Purcellville, VA 20132. *Telephone:* 540-338-5600. *Fax:* 540-338-8705. *E-mail:* rgshipe@phc.edu.

DEGREES AND AWARDS

Programs offered do not lead to a degree or other formal award.

COURSE SUBJECT AREAS OFFERED OUTSIDE OF DEGREE PROGRAMS

Undergraduate—bible/biblical studies; biology, general; economics; English composition; history; liberal arts and sciences, general studies and humanities; philosophy; political science and government.

PATRICK HENRY COMMUNITY COLLEGE

Martinsville, Virginia

Learning Resource Center

http://www.ph.vccs.edu

Patrick Henry Community College was founded in 1962. It is accredited by Southern Association of Colleges and Schools. It first offered distance learning courses in 1981. In fall 2003, there were 875 students enrolled in distance learning courses. Institutionally administered financial aid is available to distance learners.

Services Distance learners have accessibility to academic advising, bookstore, campus computer network, e-mail services, library services, tutoring.

Contact Mark Nelson, Distance Learning Webmaster, Patrick Henry Community College, PO Box 5311, Martinsville, VA 24115. *Telephone:* 276-656-0275. *Fax:* 276-656-0353. *E-mail:* mnelson@ph.vccs.edu.

DEGREES AND AWARDS

AAS Information Systems Technology

Certificate Career Studies–Allied Health; Career Studies–Management Assistant; Career Studies–Medical Transcriptionist; Career Studies–Office Assisting; Career Studies–Wellness; Clerical Studies

COURSE SUBJECT AREAS OFFERED OUTSIDE OF DEGREE PROGRAMS

Undergraduate—accounting; American history; art history; biological and physical sciences; business administration and management; business information and data processing services; communications, general; computer/information technology administration and management; computer systems networking and telecommunications; developmental/child psychology; economics; English composition; English literature (British and Commonwealth); health and physical education/fitness; mathematics; psychology; religion/religious studies; sociology.

PAUL D. CAMP COMMUNITY COLLEGE

Franklin, Virginia

http://www.pc.vccs.edu

Paul D. Camp Community College was founded in 1971. It is accredited by Southern Association of Colleges and Schools. It first offered distance learning courses in 1986. In fall 2003, there were 384 students enrolled in distance learning courses. Institutionally administered financial aid is available to distance learners.

Services Distance learners have accessibility to academic advising, bookstore, campus computer network, career placement assistance, e-mail services, library services.

Contact Shelia M. Hobbs, Distance Learning Instructional Technologist, Paul D. Camp Community College, 100 North College Drive, Franklin, VA 23851. *Telephone:* 757-569-6739 Ext. 6739. *Fax:* 757-569-6775. *E-mail:* shobbs@pc.vccs.edu.

DEGREES AND AWARDS

Programs offered do not lead to a degree or other formal award.

COURSE SUBJECT AREAS OFFERED OUTSIDE OF DEGREE PROGRAMS

Undergraduate—accounting; advertising; biology, general; business administration and management; business communications; business information and data processing services; business management and administrative services, other; business/managerial economics; child care and guidance workers and managers; computer/information technology administration and management; computer programming; data entry/microcomputer applications; English language and literature, general; health and physical education/fitness; history; psychology; social psychology.

PEIRCE COLLEGE

Philadelphia, Pennsylvania

Peirce College Non-Traditional Education

http://www.peirce.edu

Peirce College was founded in 1865. It is accredited by Middle States Association of Colleges and Schools. It first offered distance learning courses in 1997. In fall 2003, there were 452 students enrolled in distance learning courses. Institutionally administered financial aid is available to distance learners.

Services Distance learners have accessibility to academic advising, bookstore, career placement assistance, library services, tutoring.

Contact Online Program Advisors, Peirce College, 1420 Pine Street, Philadelphia, PA 19102. *Telephone:* 877-670-9190 Ext. 9800. *Fax:* 215-670-9101. *E-mail:* online@peirce.edu.

DEGREES AND AWARDS

AS Business Administration with Business Law Concentration; Business Administration with Management Concentration; Business Administration with Marketing Concentration; Information Technology with Business Information Systems Concentration; Information Technology with Networking Concentration; Information Technology with Technology Management Concentration; Paralegal Studies
BS Business Administration with Business Law Concentration; Business Administration with Management Concentration; Business Administration with Marketing Concentration; Business Administration with Real Estate Management Concentration; Information Technology with Networking Concentration; Information Technology with Technology Management Concentration; Paralegal Studies
Certificate Business Administration–Business Law; Business Administration–Management; Information Technology–Help Desk Technician; Information Technology–Windows Networking Operating Systems; Paralegal Studies

COURSE SUBJECT AREAS OFFERED OUTSIDE OF DEGREE PROGRAMS

Undergraduate—business; business administration and management; business information and data processing services; business management and administrative services, other; computer/information technology administration and management; computer systems networking and telecommunications; economics; information sciences and systems; Internet and World Wide Web; legal studies; marketing management and research; marketing operations/marketing and distribution, other; mathematics; real estate.

PENINSULA COLLEGE

Port Angeles, Washington

http://pc.ctc.edu/

Peninsula College was founded in 1961. It first offered distance learning courses in 1994. In fall 2003, there were 408 students enrolled in distance learning courses. Institutionally administered financial aid is available to distance learners.

Services Distance learners have accessibility to academic advising, bookstore, library services, tutoring.
Contact Vicki Sievert, TeleLearning Coordinator, Peninsula College, 1502 East Lauridsen Boulevard, A-11, Port Angeles, WA 98362. *Telephone:* 360-417-6272. *Fax:* 360-417-6295. *E-mail:* vickis@pcadmin.ctc.edu.

DEGREES AND AWARDS

AA General Program

COURSE SUBJECT AREAS OFFERED OUTSIDE OF DEGREE PROGRAMS

Undergraduate—accounting; American literature (United States); anthropology; applied mathematics; astronomy; business administration and management; chemistry; child care and guidance workers and managers; computer and information sciences, general; computer/information technology administration and management; criminal justice and corrections; developmental and child psychology; economics; English composition; English language and literature, general; entrepreneurship; family and community studies; geological and related sciences; health and physical education/fitness; history; mathematics; music; philosophy; psychology; sociology.

PENNSYLVANIA COLLEGE OF OPTOMETRY

Elkins Park, Pennsylvania

http://www.pco.edu/

Pennsylvania College of Optometry was founded in 1919. It is accredited by Middle States Association of Colleges and Schools. It first offered distance learning courses in 1990. In fall 2003, there were 100 students enrolled in distance learning courses. Institutionally administered financial aid is available to distance learners.

Services Distance learners have accessibility to academic advising, bookstore, campus computer network, career placement assistance, e-mail services, library services.
Contact Dr. George S. Osborne, Dean of School of Audiology, Pennsylvania College of Optometry, 8360 Old York Road, Elkins Park, PA 19027. *Telephone:* 215-780-1238. *Fax:* 215-780-1259. *E-mail:* gosborne@pco.edu.

DEGREES AND AWARDS

Certificate of Completion Low Vision Rehabilitation; Orientation and Mobility; Rehabilitation Teaching; Teacher of Children who are Blind or Visually Impaired
MEd Teacher of Children who are Blind or Visually Impaired
MS Low Vision Rehabilitation; Orientation and Mobility; Rehabilitation Teaching

COURSE SUBJECT AREAS OFFERED OUTSIDE OF DEGREE PROGRAMS

Graduate—education, other; special education.

PENNSYLVANIA COLLEGE OF TECHNOLOGY

Williamsport, Pennsylvania

http://www.pct.edu/

Pennsylvania College of Technology was founded in 1965. It is accredited by Middle States Association of Colleges and Schools. It first offered distance learning courses in 1996. In fall 2003, there were 310 students enrolled in distance learning courses. Institutionally administered financial aid is available to distance learners.

Services Distance learners have accessibility to academic advising, bookstore, campus computer network, career placement assistance, e-mail services, library services, tutoring.
Contact Paula Neal, Distance Learning Services Assistant, Pennsylvania College of Technology, 1 College Avenue, Williamsport, PA 17701. *Telephone:* 570-320-8019. *Fax:* 570-321-5559. *E-mail:* pneal@pct.edu.

DEGREES AND AWARDS

BS Applied Health Studies; Automotive Technology Management; Dental Hygiene; Residential Construction Technology and Management; Technology Management
BSN Nursing

COURSE SUBJECT AREAS OFFERED OUTSIDE OF DEGREE PROGRAMS

Undergraduate—accounting; architecture; art history; biological sciences/life sciences, other; biology; business; business marketing and marketing management; chemistry; computer and information sci-

Pennsylvania College of Technology (continued)

ences, general; construction management; dental services; English language and literature/letters, other; environmental/environmental health engineering; finance; health professions and related sciences, other; history of science and technology; international business; marketing management and research; mathematical statistics; nursing; organizational behavior; philosophy and religion related; science, technology and society; social sciences, general.

See full description on page 494.

THE PENNSYLVANIA STATE UNIVERSITY UNIVERSITY PARK CAMPUS

State College, Pennsylvania
Department of Distance Education/World Campus
http://www.worldcampus.psu.edu

The Pennsylvania State University University Park Campus was founded in 1855. It is accredited by Middle States Association of Colleges and Schools. In fall 2003, there were 1,000 students enrolled in distance learning courses. Institutionally administered financial aid is available to distance learners.

Services Distance learners have accessibility to academic advising, bookstore, campus computer network, e-mail services, library services.

Contact World Campus Advising Office, The Pennsylvania State University University Park Campus, 207 Mitchell Building, University Park, PA 16802. *Telephone:* 800-252-3592. *Fax:* 814-865-3290. *E-mail:* psuwd@psu.edu.

DEGREES AND AWARDS

AA Letters, Arts, and Sciences

AS Business Administration; Dietetic Food Systems Management; Hotel, Restaurant, and Institutional Management; Human Development and Family Studies

BA Letters, Arts, and Sciences

BS Organizational Leadership

Certificate of Completion Architectural Lighting Design; Communications Studies; Retail Management I; Supervisory Leadership

Certificate Adult Development and Aging Services; Advanced Business Management; Advanced Turfgrass Management; Business Management; Children, Youth and Family Services; Dietary Manager; Dietetics and Aging; Family Literacy; Food Service Supervision; General Business; Hospitality Management; Human Resources; Information Science and Technology; Marketing Management; Retail Management II; Retail Management; Small Business Management; Turfgrass Management; Writing Social Commentary

Certification Geographic Information Systems; Labor Studies and Industrial Relations

Graduate Certificate Addictions Studies; Community and Economic Development; Distance Education; Educational Technology Integration; Family Literacy; Logistics and Supply Chain Management; Noise Control Engineering

MBA-EP iMBA

MEd Adult Education; Curriculum and Instruction

MEngr Oil and Natural Gas Engineering Management

COURSE SUBJECT AREAS OFFERED OUTSIDE OF DEGREE PROGRAMS

Undergraduate—accounting; American history; animal sciences; anthropology; art history; biological and physical sciences; biology; business; business administration and management; business communications; business marketing and marketing management; chemistry; communications, general; comparative literature; creative writing; criminal justice and corrections; cultural studies; earth sciences; economics; educational evaluation, research and statistics; English composition; English creative writing; English technical and business writing; enterprise management and operation; environmental science; finance; fine arts and art studies; foods and nutrition studies; foreign languages and literatures; French; Germanic languages and literatures; gerontology; health and physical education/fitness; health services administration; history; hospitality services management; human resources management; individual and family development studies; industrial and organizational psychology; information sciences and systems; institutional food workers and administrators; investments and securities; journalism; journalism and mass communications; labor/personnel relations; management information systems/business data processing; marketing operations/marketing and distribution, other; mathematical statistics; mathematics; mathematics related; music; organic chemistry; organizational behavior; philosophy; physics; physiology; plant sciences; political science and government; psychology; religion/religious studies; Romance languages and literatures; science, technology and society; sociology; Spanish; speech and rhetorical studies; visual and performing arts; wildlife and wildlands management.

Graduate—alcohol/drug abuse counseling; architectural environmental design; business administration and management; business/managerial economics; business quantitative methods and management science; city/urban, community and regional planning; communications, other; curriculum and instruction; educational/instructional media design; electrical engineering; electromechanical instrumentation and maintenance technology; engineering/industrial management; environmental control technologies; marketing operations/marketing and distribution, other; mathematical statistics; transportation and materials moving workers, other.

Non-credit—architectural environmental design; business administration and management; business communications; engineering, other; geography; human resources management; wildlife and wildlands management.

PHILADELPHIA UNIVERSITY

Philadelphia, Pennsylvania
http://www.philau.edu/

Philadelphia University was founded in 1884. It is accredited by Middle States Association of Colleges and Schools. It first offered distance learning courses in 1998. In fall 2003, there were 120 students enrolled in distance learning courses. Institutionally administered financial aid is available to distance learners.

Services Distance learners have accessibility to academic advising, campus computer network, career placement assistance, e-mail services, library services, tutoring.

Contact Dr. Judith McKee, Associate Vice President for Academic Affairs/Dean of Graduate Studies, Philadelphia University, School House Lane and Henry Avenue, Philadelphia, PA 19144. *Telephone:* 215-951-2705. *E-mail:* mckeej@philau.edu.

DEGREES AND AWARDS

MBA Textile and Apparel Marketing

MS Midwifery

PIERCE COLLEGE

Puyallup, Washington
Developmental Education
http://www.pierce.ctc.edu/distance

Pierce College was founded in 1967. It is accredited by Northwest Commission on Colleges and Universities. It first offered distance learning courses in 1982. In fall 2003, there were 850 students enrolled in distance learning courses. Institutionally administered financial aid is available to distance learners.

Services Distance learners have accessibility to academic advising, bookstore, campus computer network, e-mail services, library services.

Contact Martha Makaneole, Programs Assistant, Pierce College, 9401 Farwest Drive SW, Lakewood, WA 98498. *Telephone:* 253-964-6244. *Fax:* 253-964-6299. *E-mail:* mmakaneole@pierce.etc.edu.

DEGREES AND AWARDS

Programs offered do not lead to a degree or other formal award.

COURSE SUBJECT AREAS OFFERED OUTSIDE OF DEGREE PROGRAMS

Undergraduate—American literature (United States); anthropology; applied mathematics; astronomy; biology; business communications; computer and information sciences, general; computer and information sciences, other; developmental/child psychology; earth sciences; engineering design; English composition; English creative writing; English language and literature, general; French; geological and related sciences; history; mathematics; mental health services; philosophy and religion related; physics; political science and government; psychology.
Non-credit—health professions and related sciences, other.

PITT COMMUNITY COLLEGE

Greenville, North Carolina
Distance Education Department
http://www.pittcc.edu

Pitt Community College was founded in 1961. It is accredited by Southern Association of Colleges and Schools. It first offered distance learning courses in 1996. In fall 2003, there were 1,561 students enrolled in distance learning courses. Institutionally administered financial aid is available to distance learners.

Services Distance learners have accessibility to academic advising, bookstore, library services, tutoring.

Contact Mr. Jamie Byrd, Associate Vice President of Distance Learning, Pitt Community College, Highway 11 South, PO Drawer 7007, Greenville, NC 27835-7007. *Telephone:* 252-493-7608. *Fax:* 252-493-7613. *E-mail:* jbyrd@email.pittcc.edu.

DEGREES AND AWARDS

AAS Business Administration; Computer Programming; Health Information Technology; Healthcare Management Technology; Information Systems Generalist
Certificate Basic Accounting Certification; Basic Office Technology Skills; Business Administration–Human Resources Management; Computer Software Applications; Healthcare Accounting; Healthcare Leadership and Management; Healthcare Management; Information Systems Technology; Leadership; Management Application and Principles; Managerial/Small Business Accounting; Marketing; Object Oriented Programming; Starting Your Own Business; Technology for Educators

COURSE SUBJECT AREAS OFFERED OUTSIDE OF DEGREE PROGRAMS

Undergraduate—accounting; advertising; alcohol/drug abuse counseling; biochemistry; biology; business marketing and marketing management; English composition; international business; law and legal studies related; philosophy and religion related; sociology.
Non-credit—adult/continuing education; creative writing; finance.

POLYTECHNIC UNIVERSITY, LONG ISLAND GRADUATE CENTER

Melville, New York
http://www.poly.edu

Polytechnic University, Long Island Graduate Center was founded in 1854. It is accredited by Middle States Association of Colleges and Schools. It first offered distance learning courses in 1999. In fall 2003, there were 29 students enrolled in distance learning courses. Institutionally administered financial aid is available to distance learners.

Services Distance learners have accessibility to bookstore, campus computer network, career placement assistance, e-mail services, library services.

Contact Dr. I-Tai Lu, Professor, Polytechnic University, Long Island Graduate Center, Graduate Center, 105 Maxess Road, Melville, NY 11747. *Telephone:* 631-755-4226. *Fax:* 631-755-4404. *E-mail:* itailu@poly.edu.

DEGREES AND AWARDS

Programs offered do not lead to a degree or other formal award.

COURSE SUBJECT AREAS OFFERED OUTSIDE OF DEGREE PROGRAMS

Graduate—electrical, electronics and communications engineering.

PORTLAND STATE UNIVERSITY

Portland, Oregon
Independent Study
http://www.istudy.pdx.edu

Portland State University was founded in 1946. It is accredited by Northwest Commission on Colleges and Universities. In fall 2003, there were 731 students enrolled in distance learning courses. Institutionally administered financial aid is available to distance learners.

Services Distance learners have accessibility to academic advising, bookstore, campus computer network, e-mail services, library services, tutoring.

Contact Rebecca Robinson, Independent Study Program Manager, Portland State University, PO Box 1491, Portland, OR 97207-1491. *Telephone:* 800-547-8887 Ext. 8485. *Fax:* 503-725-4880. *E-mail:* robinsonr@pdx.edu.

DEGREES AND AWARDS

Programs offered do not lead to a degree or other formal award.

Portland State University (continued)

COURSE SUBJECT AREAS OFFERED OUTSIDE OF DEGREE PROGRAMS

Undergraduate—chemistry; criminal justice and corrections; economics; English composition; English language and literature, general; geological and related sciences; history; mathematical statistics; mathematics related; psychology; religion/religious studies; sociology.

DEGREES AND AWARDS

Programs offered do not lead to a degree or other formal award.

COURSE SUBJECT AREAS OFFERED OUTSIDE OF DEGREE PROGRAMS

Undergraduate—accounting; business; business communications; computer and information sciences, general.
Non-credit—business administration and management; entrepreneurship; real estate.

PRAIRIE BIBLE COLLEGE

Three Hills, Alberta, Canada
Prairie Distance Education
http://www.prairie.edu/distanceed

Prairie Bible College was founded in 1922. It is provincially chartered. It first offered distance learning courses in 1950. In fall 2003, there were 750 students enrolled in distance learning courses. Institutionally administered financial aid is available to distance learners.

Services Distance learners have accessibility to academic advising, bookstore, campus computer network, career placement assistance, e-mail services, library services.
Contact Mrs. Connie Nyman, Student Services Coordinator, Prairie Bible College, Prairie Distance Education, Box 4000, Three Hills, AB T0M 2N0, Canada. *Telephone:* 800-785-4226. *Fax:* 403-443-3099. *E-mail:* distance.ed@prairie.edu.

DEGREES AND AWARDS

AA Religious Studies
BA Bible, Theology, Ministry
Certificate Bible
Diploma Theological Studies (Graduate)
Graduate Certificate Theological Studies

COURSE SUBJECT AREAS OFFERED OUTSIDE OF DEGREE PROGRAMS

Undergraduate—anthropology; bible/biblical studies; biblical and other theological languages and literatures; English composition; European history; missions/missionary studies and missiology; music; philosophy and religion related; psychology; theological and ministerial studies.
Graduate—anthropology; bible/biblical studies; missions/missionary studies and missiology; theological and ministerial studies.

PRAIRIE STATE COLLEGE

Chicago Heights, Illinois
Learning Resources Center
http://www.prairiestate.edu/

Prairie State College was founded in 1958. It is accredited by North Central Association of Colleges and Schools. It first offered distance learning courses in 1981. In fall 2003, there were 350 students enrolled in distance learning courses.

Services Distance learners have accessibility to academic advising, bookstore, e-mail services, library services.
Contact Mary Welsh, Director of Admissions, Prairie State College, 202 South Halsted Street, Chicago Heights, IL 60411. *Telephone:* 708-709-3513. *Fax:* 708-755-2587. *E-mail:* mwelsh@prairiestate.edu.

PRATT COMMUNITY COLLEGE

Pratt, Kansas
http://www.prattcc.edu

Pratt Community College was founded in 1938. It is accredited by North Central Association of Colleges and Schools. It first offered distance learning courses in 1999. In fall 2003, there were 350 students enrolled in distance learning courses. Institutionally administered financial aid is available to distance learners.

Services Distance learners have accessibility to academic advising, bookstore, campus computer network, career placement assistance, e-mail services, library services, tutoring.
Contact Pam M. Dietz, Assistant Dean of Instruction, Pratt Community College, 348 NE SR 61, Pratt, KS 67124. *Telephone:* 620-672-9800 Ext. 238. *Fax:* 620-672-5288. *E-mail:* pamd@prattcc.edu.

DEGREES AND AWARDS

AS General Studies

COURSE SUBJECT AREAS OFFERED OUTSIDE OF DEGREE PROGRAMS

Undergraduate—accounting; biology, general; business administration and management; chemistry; communications, general; criminology; economics; education, general; geography; history; liberal arts and sciences, general studies and humanities; mathematics; miscellaneous health aides; music; political science and government; psychology; social sciences and history, other; sociology.

PRESCOTT COLLEGE

Prescott, Arizona
http://www.prescott.edu/

Prescott College was founded in 1966. It is accredited by North Central Association of Colleges and Schools. It first offered distance learning courses in 1978. In fall 2003, there were 500 students enrolled in distance learning courses. Institutionally administered financial aid is available to distance learners.

Services Distance learners have accessibility to academic advising, career placement assistance, e-mail services, library services.
Contact Melanie Lefever, Admissions Counselor, Prescott College, Admissions, 220 Grove Avenue, Prescott, AZ 86301. *Telephone:* 800-628-6364 Ext. 2106. *Fax:* 928-776-5242. *E-mail:* admissions@prescott.edu.

DEGREES AND AWARDS

BA Adventure Education; Counseling Psychology/Human Services; Education; Environmental Studies; Humanities; Management; Sustainable Community Development
Certification Teacher Certification

MA Adventure Education; Counseling and Psychology; Education; Environmental Studies; Humanities

COURSE SUBJECT AREAS OFFERED OUTSIDE OF DEGREE PROGRAMS

Undergraduate—communications, general; counseling psychology; cultural studies; demography/population studies; education, general; English creative writing; English language and literature, general; family and community studies; history; human resources management; human services; liberal arts and sciences, general studies and humanities; multi/interdisciplinary studies, other; natural resources conservation; parks, recreation and leisure studies; peace and conflict studies; philosophy and religion; psychology; visual and performing arts; wildlife and wildlands management.

Graduate—area, ethnic and cultural studies, other; communications, general; conservation and renewable natural resources, other; cultural studies; education, general; English language and literature, general; family and community studies; history; human services; liberal arts and sciences, general studies and humanities; multi/interdisciplinary studies, other; natural resources management and protective services; parks, recreation and leisure facilities management; peace and conflict studies; philosophy and religion; psychology; visual and performing arts; wildlife and wildlands management.

See full description on page 496.

PULASKI TECHNICAL COLLEGE

North Little Rock, Arkansas

http://www.pulaskitech.edu

Pulaski Technical College was founded in 1945. It is accredited by North Central Association of Colleges and Schools. It first offered distance learning courses in 1999. In fall 2003, there were 700 students enrolled in distance learning courses. Institutionally administered financial aid is available to distance learners.

Services Distance learners have accessibility to academic advising, bookstore, library services.

Contact Ms. Amy Baldwin, Distance Education Coordinator, Pulaski Technical College, 3000 West Scenic Drive, North Little Rock, AR 72118. *Telephone:* 501-812-2262. *Fax:* 501-812-2340. *E-mail:* abaldwin@pulaskitech.edu.

DEGREES AND AWARDS

AA General Program

COURSE SUBJECT AREAS OFFERED OUTSIDE OF DEGREE PROGRAMS

Undergraduate—American literature (United States); biology, general; business; computer and information sciences, general; computer systems analysis; computer systems networking and telecommunications; English composition; English creative writing; English literature (British and Commonwealth); journalism and mass communications; psychology.

PURDUE UNIVERSITY

West Lafayette, Indiana

Krannert Executive Education Programs

http://www2.krannert.purdue.edu/

Purdue University was founded in 1869. It is accredited by North Central Association of Colleges and Schools. It first offered distance learning courses in 1983. In fall 2003, there were 201 students enrolled in distance learning courses. Institutionally administered financial aid is available to distance learners.

Services Distance learners have accessibility to academic advising, bookstore, campus computer network, tutoring.

Contact Erika C. Steuterman, Director, Executive Masters Programs, Purdue University, KCTR 206, 425 West State Street, West Lafayette, IN 47907-2056. *Telephone:* 765-494-7700. *Fax:* 765-494-0862. *E-mail:* keepinfo@mgmt.purdue.edu.

DEGREES AND AWARDS

MBA Executive Master of Business Administration; International Masters in Management Program (IMM)

See full description on page 498.

QUEEN'S UNIVERSITY AT KINGSTON

Kingston, Ontario, Canada

Continuing and Distance Studies

http://www.queensu.ca/cds

Queen's University at Kingston was founded in 1841. It is provincially chartered. In fall 2003, there were 2,500 students enrolled in distance learning courses. Institutionally administered financial aid is available to distance learners.

Services Distance learners have accessibility to academic advising, bookstore, campus computer network, career placement assistance, e-mail services, library services, tutoring.

Contact Wilma Fernetich, Distance Education Advisor, Queen's University at Kingston, Kingston, ON K7L 2N6, Canada. *Telephone:* 613-533-6000 Ext. 77770. *Fax:* 613-533-6805. *E-mail:* fernetic@post.queensu.ca.

DEGREES AND AWARDS

Programs offered do not lead to a degree or other formal award.

COURSE SUBJECT AREAS OFFERED OUTSIDE OF DEGREE PROGRAMS

Undergraduate—English composition; English creative writing; English literature (British and Commonwealth); geography; Germanic languages and literatures; history; mathematical statistics; microbiology/bacteriology; psychology; religion/religious studies; sociology; Spanish; theater arts/drama; women's studies.

QUINEBAUG VALLEY COMMUNITY COLLEGE

Danielson, Connecticut

http://www.qvcc.commnet.edu/

Quinebaug Valley Community College was founded in 1971. It is accredited by New England Association of Schools and Colleges. It first offered distance learning courses in 1998. In fall 2003, there were 112 students enrolled in distance learning courses. Institutionally administered financial aid is available to distance learners.

Services Distance learners have accessibility to academic advising, library services, tutoring.

Quinebaug Valley Community College (continued)

Contact Dr. Toni T. Moumouris, Enrollment and Transition Counselor, Quinebaug Valley Community College, 742 Upper Maple Street, Danielson, CT 06239. *Telephone:* 860-774-1130 Ext. 318. *Fax:* 860-779-2998. *E-mail:* tmoumouris@qvcc.commnet.edu.

DEGREES AND AWARDS

AS General Studies
Certificate Health Information Management Technology

COURSE SUBJECT AREAS OFFERED OUTSIDE OF DEGREE PROGRAMS

Undergraduate—astronomy; health and medical administrative services; history; liberal arts and sciences, general studies and humanities; sociology.

QUINNIPIAC UNIVERSITY

Hamden, Connecticut

http://www.quinnipiac.edu/quonline

Quinnipiac University was founded in 1929. It is accredited by New England Association of Schools and Colleges. It first offered distance learning courses in 2001. In fall 2003, there were 100 students enrolled in distance learning courses. Institutionally administered financial aid is available to distance learners.

Services Distance learners have accessibility to academic advising, bookstore, campus computer network, career placement assistance, e-mail services, library services, tutoring.
Contact Cindy Gallatin, Dean, Distance Learning, Quinnipiac University, 275 Mount Carmel Avenue, Hamden, CT 06518. *Telephone:* 203-582-5669. *E-mail:* quonline@quinnipiac.edu.

DEGREES AND AWARDS

Programs offered do not lead to a degree or other formal award.

COURSE SUBJECT AREAS OFFERED OUTSIDE OF DEGREE PROGRAMS

Undergraduate—accounting; biological and physical sciences; biological sciences/life sciences, other; business; business administration and management; chemistry; communications technologies; computer science; computer systems analysis; economics; education, general; history; journalism and mass communications; marketing management and research; mathematics; philosophy; teacher education, specific academic and vocational programs.
Graduate—accounting; business management and administrative services, other; business/managerial economics; business quantitative methods and management science; computer science; economics; education, general; financial management and services; journalism and mass communications; marketing management and research; marketing operations/marketing and distribution, other; nursing; teacher education, specific academic and vocational programs.
Non-credit—mathematics.

RANDOLPH COMMUNITY COLLEGE

Asheboro, North Carolina

Virtual Campus

http://www.virtualrandolph.org

Randolph Community College was founded in 1962. It is accredited by Southern Association of Colleges and Schools. It first offered distance learning courses in 1998. In fall 2003, there were 1,200 students enrolled in distance learning courses. Institutionally administered financial aid is available to distance learners.

Services Distance learners have accessibility to academic advising, bookstore, e-mail services, library services.
Contact Deborah M. Kennedy, Administrative Assistant, Distance Education & Instructional Technology, Randolph Community College, 629 Industrial Park Avenue, PO Box 1009, Asheboro, NC 27205. *Telephone:* 336-633-0263. *Fax:* 336-629-4695. *E-mail:* dmkennedy@randolph.edu.

DEGREES AND AWARDS

AA College Transfer
AAS Accounting; Business Administration; Criminal Justice; Information Systems; Office Systems Technology

COURSE SUBJECT AREAS OFFERED OUTSIDE OF DEGREE PROGRAMS

Undergraduate—accounting; business marketing and marketing management; child care and guidance workers and managers; computer and information sciences, general; computer software and media applications; criminal justice and corrections; cultural studies; economics; English composition; European history; finance; health and medical assistants; history; law and legal studies related; music; philosophy and religion related; psychology; sociology; teacher education, specific academic and vocational programs.
Non-credit—accounting; administrative and secretarial services; computer software and media applications; gerontology; health and medical assistants; health and medical diagnostic and treatment services; medical basic sciences; medical laboratory technology; pharmacy.

RAPPAHANNOCK COMMUNITY COLLEGE

Glenns, Virginia

Flexible Learning Opportunities (FLO)

http://www.rcc.vccs.edu

Rappahannock Community College was founded in 1970. It is accredited by Southern Association of Colleges and Schools. It first offered distance learning courses in 1995. In fall 2003, there were 1,000 students enrolled in distance learning courses. Institutionally administered financial aid is available to distance learners.

Services Distance learners have accessibility to academic advising, bookstore, campus computer network, career placement assistance, e-mail services, library services, tutoring.
Contact Kristy Walker, Assistant for Distance Learning and Technology, Rappahannock Community College, 52 Campus Drive, Warsaw, VA 22572. *Telephone:* 804-333-6786. *Fax:* 804-333-6784. *E-mail:* kwalker@rcc.vccs.edu.

DEGREES AND AWARDS

AAS Business Management; General Studies
ABA Business Administration
Certificate Administrative Support; Bookkeeping/Accounting; E-Commerce; Leadership in Organizations; Microcomputer Applications Career Studies

COURSE SUBJECT AREAS OFFERED OUTSIDE OF DEGREE PROGRAMS

Undergraduate—accounting; American literature (United States); business administration and management; business communications; community health services; criminal justice and corrections; English composition; fine arts and art studies; health and physical education/fitness; history; mathematics; psychology; religion/religious studies; sociology.

RARITAN VALLEY COMMUNITY COLLEGE

Somerville, New Jersey
Distance Learning
http://www.raritanval.edu/newhometest/frameset/virtualcampus.html

Raritan Valley Community College was founded in 1965. It is accredited by Middle States Association of Colleges and Schools. It first offered distance learning courses in 1997. In fall 2003, there were 1,600 students enrolled in distance learning courses. Institutionally administered financial aid is available to distance learners.

Services Distance learners have accessibility to academic advising, bookstore, campus computer network, career placement assistance, e-mail services, library services, tutoring.

Contact Chuck Chulvick, Vice President of Learning and Technology Services, Raritan Valley Community College, PO Box 3300, Somerville, NJ 08876. *Telephone:* 908-526-1200 Ext. 8409. *Fax:* 908-429 0034. *E-mail:* cchulvic@raritanval.edu.

DEGREES AND AWARDS

AS Business Administration; Management Information Systems

COURSE SUBJECT AREAS OFFERED OUTSIDE OF DEGREE PROGRAMS

Undergraduate—American literature (United States); anthropology; applied mathematics; area, ethnic and cultural studies, other; astronomy; business administration and management; business management and administrative services, other; computer and information sciences, general; computer and information sciences, other; computer/information technology administration and management; computer programming; computer software and media applications; computer systems networking and telecommunications; criminal justice and corrections; criminology; economics; English composition; English creative writing; English language and literature, general; English language and literature/letters, other; family and community studies; history; legal studies; marketing management and research; marketing operations/marketing and distribution, other; mathematical statistics; mathematics; mathematics, other; nursing; psychology; psychology, other; social sciences, general; social work; sociology.

READING AREA COMMUNITY COLLEGE

Reading, Pennsylvania
http://www.racc.edu

Reading Area Community College was founded in 1971. It is accredited by Middle States Association of Colleges and Schools. It first offered distance learning courses in 1986. In fall 2003, there were 377 students enrolled in distance learning courses. Institutionally administered financial aid is available to distance learners.

Services Distance learners have accessibility to e-mail services, library services.

Contact Mrs. Carol A. Alspach, Coordinator of Special Programs, Reading Area Community College, 10 South Second Street, PO Box 1706, Reading, PA 19603. *Telephone:* 610-607 6219. *Fax:* 610-372 4264. *E-mail:* calspach@racc.edu.

DEGREES AND AWARDS

Programs offered do not lead to a degree or other formal award.

COURSE SUBJECT AREAS OFFERED OUTSIDE OF DEGREE PROGRAMS

Undergraduate—accounting; anthropology; biological sciences/life sciences, other; business; business administration and management; computer and information sciences, general; developmental and child psychology; economics; English composition; family and community studies; mathematics; psychology; sociology.

REGENT UNIVERSITY

Virginia Beach, Virginia
Distance Education
http://www.regent.edu

Regent University was founded in 1977. It is accredited by Southern Association of Colleges and Schools. It first offered distance learning courses in 1989. In fall 2003, there were 1,157 students enrolled in distance learning courses. Institutionally administered financial aid is available to distance learners.

Services Distance learners have accessibility to academic advising, bookstore, campus computer network, e-mail services, library services.

Contact Central Enrollment Management, Regent University, 1000 Regent University Drive, Virginia Beach, VA 23464. *Telephone:* 800-373-5504. *Fax:* 757-226-4381. *E-mail:* admissions@regent.edu.

DEGREES AND AWARDS

Certificate TESOL
CAGS Education; Organizational Leadership; Public Policy
EMBA Business Administration
Graduate Certificate Business (various); Leadership (Graduate Studies Certificate)
MA Communication; English Bible Concentration; Government; Human Services Counseling; Journalism; Organizational Leadership; Organizational Leadership; Practical Theology
MAM Management
MBA Professional Master of Business Administration
MDiv Divinity
MEd Christian School Program; Individualized Degree Plan; TESOL
DSL Strategic Leadership
EdD Education
PhD Communication; Counselor Education and Supervision; Organizational Leadership

COURSE SUBJECT AREAS OFFERED OUTSIDE OF DEGREE PROGRAMS

Non-credit—pastoral counseling and specialized ministries.

Regent University (continued)

Special Message

Regent University has been offering classes since 1978 and began distance education in 1989. Today, Regent offers more than 20 degree programs online and is considered a worldwide model for online education. The Regent online Worldwide Campus combines technology and practical application with instant access to learning resources, professors, and other students via the Internet. Designed for busy career professionals, nonresidential students, military personnel, professionals who travel, and stay-at-home parents, the Worldwide Campus is ideal for anyone who needs flexibility in their scheduling. In addition to this distinction, Regent prepares leaders to make a positive impact upon society through degree programs taught from a Judeo-Christian perspective. Regent students typically share these commitments toward faith and values and represent a wide variety of Christian denominations. Regent offers study in eight professional fields: business, communication and the arts, divinity, education, government, law (although currently unavailable online), leadership, and psychology and counseling. Regent University also offers programs on the Virginia Beach campus, the Washington, D.C., campus (near the nation's capitol), and through a combination of on-campus and online learning.

See full description on page 500.

REGIS UNIVERSITY

Denver, Colorado
School for Professional Studies and Distance Learning
http://www.regisonline.org

Regis University was founded in 1877. It is accredited by North Central Association of Colleges and Schools. It first offered distance learning courses in 1992. In fall 2003, there were 5,000 students enrolled in distance learning courses. Institutionally administered financial aid is available to distance learners.

Services Distance learners have accessibility to academic advising, bookstore, campus computer network, career placement assistance, e-mail services, library services, tutoring.

Contact Kathy Rank, Associate Director of SPS Online Enrollment, Regis University, Adult Learning Center, Mail Code M-6, 3333 Regis Boulevard, Denver, CO 80221. *Telephone:* 303-458-4315. *Fax:* 303-9645274. *E-mail:* krank@regis.edu.

DEGREES AND AWARDS

BS Business Administration; Computer Information Systems; Computer Networking; Computer Science; Finance; Marketing; Public Administration

BSN Nursing–RN to BSN

Certificate of Completion Computer Networking; Irish Studies; Java Programming; Management Information Systems; UNIX (Solaris)

Certificate Public Administration

Graduate Certificate Database Technologies (MSCIT); E-Commerce Engineering (MSCIT); Executive International Management (MSM); Executive Leadership (MSM); Executive Project Management (MSM); Humane and Environmental Studies (MNM); Leadership (MNM); Management of Technology (MSCIT); Networking Technologies (MSCIT); Object-Oriented Technologies (MSCIT); Program Management (MNM); Resource Development (MNM); Strategic Business Management (MSM)

MBA Business Administration

MEd Education

MS Computer Information Technology; Nonprofit Management

MSM Management

COURSE SUBJECT AREAS OFFERED OUTSIDE OF DEGREE PROGRAMS

Undergraduate—accounting; business administration and management; business/managerial economics; business marketing and marketing management; communications, general; computer/information technology administration and management; computer programming; computer science; computer systems networking and telecommunications; finance; history; information sciences and systems; marketing management and research; marketing operations/marketing and distribution, other; mathematical statistics; organizational behavior; philosophy and religion related; public administration; religion/religious studies; social psychology; sociology.

Graduate—accounting; adult/continuing education; anthropology; business communications; business management and administrative services, other; business/managerial economics; business marketing and marketing management; computer and information sciences, general; computer and information sciences, other; computer/information technology administration and management; computer programming; computer science; computer systems networking and telecommunications; curriculum and instruction; education administration and supervision; education, other; finance; international business; management information systems/business data processing; management science; organizational behavior; philosophy and religion related; public administration; public administration and services, other.

REND LAKE COLLEGE

Ina, Illinois
Learning Resource Center
http://www.rlc.edu

Rend Lake College was founded in 1967. It is accredited by North Central Association of Colleges and Schools. It first offered distance learning courses in 1995. In fall 2003, there were 600 students enrolled in distance learning courses. Institutionally administered financial aid is available to distance learners.

Services Distance learners have accessibility to academic advising, bookstore, campus computer network, career placement assistance, e-mail services, library services, tutoring.

Contact Karla J. Lewis, Coordinator of Distance Learning & Media Technology, Rend Lake College, Learning Resource Center, 468 North Ken Gray Parkway, Ina, IL 62846. *Telephone:* 618-437-5321 Ext. 1299. *Fax:* 618-437-5598. *E-mail:* klewis@rlc.edu.

DEGREES AND AWARDS

Programs offered do not lead to a degree or other formal award.

COURSE SUBJECT AREAS OFFERED OUTSIDE OF DEGREE PROGRAMS

Undergraduate—anthropology; astronomy; biology, general; business; computer science; health and physical education/fitness; history; horticulture science; mathematics; microbiology/bacteriology; music;

nursing; philosophy and religion; political science and government; psychology; real estate; sociology; speech and rhetorical studies.
Non-credit—accounting; administrative and secretarial services; business administration and management; computer software and media applications; entrepreneurship; human resources management; marketing operations/marketing and distribution, other.

THE RICHARD STOCKTON COLLEGE OF NEW JERSEY

Pomona, New Jersey
Office of Distance Education
http://www.stockton.edu

The Richard Stockton College of New Jersey was founded in 1969. It is accredited by Middle States Association of Colleges and Schools. It first offered distance learning courses in 1996. In fall 2003, there were 1,200 students enrolled in distance learning courses. Institutionally administered financial aid is available to distance learners.

Services Distance learners have accessibility to campus computer network, e-mail services, library services.
Contact Dennis Fotia, Distance Education Coordinator, The Richard Stockton College of New Jersey, PO Box 195, Pomona, NJ 08240-0195. *Telephone:* 609-652-4580. *Fax:* 609-748-5562. *E-mail:* dennis.fotia@stockton.edu.

DEGREES AND AWARDS

Programs offered do not lead to a degree or other formal award.

COURSE SUBJECT AREAS OFFERED OUTSIDE OF DEGREE PROGRAMS

Undergraduate—anthropology; applied mathematics; business administration and management; business marketing and marketing management; English composition; film/video and photographic arts; gerontology; health professions and related sciences, other; journalism and mass communication related; liberal arts and sciences, general studies and humanities; nursing; photography; psychology; sociology; women's studies.
Graduate—information sciences and systems; nursing.

RICHLAND COMMUNITY COLLEGE

Decatur, Illinois
Lifelong Learning Division

Richland Community College was founded in 1971. It is accredited by North Central Association of Colleges and Schools. It first offered distance learning courses in 1994. In fall 2003, there were 375 students enrolled in distance learning courses. Institutionally administered financial aid is available to distance learners.

Services Distance learners have accessibility to academic advising, campus computer network, career placement assistance, e-mail services, library services.
Contact Ms. Catherine L. Sebok, Director, Recruitment and Outreach Services, Richland Community College, One College Park, Decatur, IL 62521. *Telephone:* 217-875-7200 Ext. 558. *Fax:* 217-875-7783. *E-mail:* csebok@richland.cc.edu.

DEGREES AND AWARDS

Programs offered do not lead to a degree or other formal award.

COURSE SUBJECT AREAS OFFERED OUTSIDE OF DEGREE PROGRAMS

Undergraduate—accounting; art history; business communications; creative writing; developmental/child psychology; English composition; European history; Internet and World Wide Web; psychology; social psychology; sociology.

RIO HONDO COLLEGE

Whittier, California
http://www.riohondo.edu/

Rio Hondo College was founded in 1960. It is accredited by Western Association of Schools and Colleges. It first offered distance learning courses in 1998. In fall 2003, there were 3,200 students enrolled in distance learning courses. Institutionally administered financial aid is available to distance learners.

Services Distance learners have accessibility to academic advising, bookstore, campus computer network, library services, tutoring.
Contact Antonio Flores, Dean of Admissions and Records, Rio Hondo College, 3600 Workman Mill Road, Whittier, CA 90601. *Telephone:* 562-692-0921 Ext. 3146. *E-mail:* aflores@riohondo.edu.

DEGREES AND AWARDS

Programs offered do not lead to a degree or other formal award.

COURSE SUBJECT AREAS OFFERED OUTSIDE OF DEGREE PROGRAMS

Undergraduate—accounting; anthropology; business management and administrative services, other; computer and information sciences, general; computer programming; economics; education, other; English composition; English language and literature, general; fine arts and art studies; fire protection; geological and related sciences; health and medical administrative services; health and physical education/fitness; history; international business; library science, other; mathematics; political science and government; psychology; Romance languages and literatures; sociology.

RIVERLAND COMMUNITY COLLEGE

Austin, Minnesota
http://www.riverland.cc.mn.us

Riverland Community College was founded in 1940. It is accredited by North Central Association of Colleges and Schools. In fall 2003, there were 325 students enrolled in distance learning courses. Institutionally administered financial aid is available to distance learners.

Services Distance learners have accessibility to academic advising, bookstore, career placement assistance, e-mail services, library services.
Contact Mr. Willliam Dowden, Instructional Support Manager, Riverland Community College, 1900 Eighth Avenue NW, Austin, MN 55912. *Telephone:* 507-434-7384. *Fax:* 507-433-0515. *E-mail:* wdowden@river.cc.mn.us.

DEGREES AND AWARDS

Programs offered do not lead to a degree or other formal award.

Riverland Community College (continued)

COURSE SUBJECT AREAS OFFERED OUTSIDE OF DEGREE PROGRAMS

Undergraduate—accounting; administrative and secretarial services; American history; American literature (United States); biological and physical sciences; biological sciences/life sciences, other; business; business administration and management; computer/information technology administration and management; computer systems networking and telecommunications; developmental/child psychology; English composition; English creative writing; English language and literature, general; English language and literature/letters, other; geography; history; Internet and World Wide Web; legal studies; mathematical statistics; psychology; sociology.

RIVERSIDE COMMUNITY COLLEGE

Riverside, California
Open Campus
http://www.opencampus.com

Riverside Community College was founded in 1916. It is accredited by Western Association of Schools and Colleges. It first offered distance learning courses in 1982. In fall 2003, there were 6,000 students enrolled in distance learning courses. Institutionally administered financial aid is available to distance learners.

Services Distance learners have accessibility to academic advising, bookstore, campus computer network, career placement assistance, e-mail services, library services.

Contact Col. Glen Brady, Director, Distance Education, Riverside Community College, Open Campus, 4800 Magnolia Avenue, Riverside, CA 92506-1299. *Telephone:* 909-222-8094. *Fax:* 909-328-3596. *E-mail:* glen.brady@rcc.edu.

DEGREES AND AWARDS

Programs offered do not lead to a degree or other formal award.

COURSE SUBJECT AREAS OFFERED OUTSIDE OF DEGREE PROGRAMS

Undergraduate—accounting; anthropology; astronomy; business; business administration and management; computer and information sciences, general; economics; English language and literature, general; foreign languages and literatures; geography; graphic and printing equipment operators; history; marketing management and research; mathematics; music; oceanography; philosophy; political science and government; psychology; religion/religious studies; sociology; telecommunications.

Non-credit—business administration and management; computer and information sciences, general; computer programming; economics; English creative writing; foreign languages and literatures; graphic and printing equipment operators; health professions and related sciences, other; Internet and World Wide Web.

ROCHESTER INSTITUTE OF TECHNOLOGY

Rochester, New York
Graduate Enrollment Services
http://www.rit.edu/online

Rochester Institute of Technology was founded in 1829. It is accredited by Middle States Association of Colleges and Schools. It first offered distance learning courses in 1979. In fall 2003, there were 1,600 students enrolled in distance learning courses. Institutionally administered financial aid is available to distance learners.

Services Distance learners have accessibility to academic advising, bookstore, campus computer network, e-mail services, library services.

Contact Mr. Joseph T. Nairn, Senior Associate Director, Office of Part-time Enrollment Services, Rochester Institute of Technology, Bausch & Lomb Center, 58 Lomb Memorial Drive, Rochester, NY 14623. *Telephone:* 716-475-2229. *Fax:* 716-475-7164. *E-mail:* opes@rit.edu.

DEGREES AND AWARDS

BS Applied Arts and Science; Electrical/Mechanical Engineering Technology; Safety Technology; Telecommunications Technology

Certificate Advanced Technical Communications; Basic Quality Management; Basic Technical Communications; Disaster and Emergency Management; Environmental Management and Technology; Health Systems Administration; Industrial Environmental Management; Introduction to Programming; Public Relations–Professional Writing; Quality Implementation; Reliability Maintenance; Safety and Health Technology; Structural Design; Telecommunications–Data Communications; Telecommunications–Network Management; Telecommunications–Voice Communications

Graduate Certificate Health Systems Finance; Integrated Health Systems; Statistical Methods for Product and Process Improvement; Statistical Quality; Technical Information Design

MS Applied Statistics; Cross Disciplinary Professional Studies; Environmental Health and Safety Management; Health Systems Administration; Imaging Science; Information Technology; Microelectronics Manufacturing Engineering; Print Media; Software Development and Management; Telecommunications Engineering Technology

COURSE SUBJECT AREAS OFFERED OUTSIDE OF DEGREE PROGRAMS

Undergraduate—electrical engineering; engineering/industrial management; engineering mechanics; English composition; environmental science; mechanical engineering; sociology.

Graduate—electrical engineering.

See full description on page 502.

ROCKLAND COMMUNITY COLLEGE

Suffern, New York
Telecourse and Distance Learning Department
http://www.sunyrockland.edu/virtualrcc

Rockland Community College was founded in 1959. It is accredited by Middle States Association of Colleges and Schools. It first offered distance learning courses in 1985. In fall 2003, there were 600 students enrolled in distance learning courses. Institutionally administered financial aid is available to distance learners.

Services Distance learners have accessibility to academic advising, bookstore, campus computer network, career placement assistance, e-mail services, library services, tutoring.

Contact Lynne Koplik, Distance Education Supervisor, Rockland Community College, 145 College Road, Room 4124, Suffern, NY 10901. *Telephone:* 845-574-4780. *Fax:* 845-356-5811. *E-mail:* lkoplik@sunyrockland.edu.

DEGREES AND AWARDS

AA Liberal Arts and Sciences

COURSE SUBJECT AREAS OFFERED OUTSIDE OF DEGREE PROGRAMS

Undergraduate—anthropology; biology, general; business; chemistry; computer science; economics; English composition; English language and literature, general; financial management and services; fine arts and art studies; geography; health and medical preparatory programs; health professions and related sciences, other; history; liberal arts and sciences, general studies and humanities; marketing management and research; mathematics; medical basic sciences; nursing; philosophy; physical sciences, general; political science and government; psychology; social sciences and history, other.
Non-credit—nursing.

ROGER WILLIAMS UNIVERSITY

Bristol, Rhode Island
School of Continuing Studies
http://www.rwu.edu/Academics/Academic+Programs/School+of+Continuing+Studies/

Roger Williams University was founded in 1956. It is accredited by New England Association of Schools and Colleges. It first offered distance learning courses in 1974. In fall 2003, there were 101 students enrolled in distance learning courses. Institutionally administered financial aid is available to distance learners.

Services Distance learners have accessibility to academic advising, bookstore, campus computer network, career placement assistance, e-mail services, library services.
Contact John Stout, Dean, School of Continuing Studies, Roger Williams University, 150 Washington Street, Providence, RI 02903. *Telephone:* 401-254-3530. *Fax:* 401-254-3560. *E-mail:* jstout@rwu.edu.

DEGREES AND AWARDS

BGS Industrial Technology
BS Criminal Justice; Public Administration

COURSE SUBJECT AREAS OFFERED OUTSIDE OF DEGREE PROGRAMS

Undergraduate—criminal justice and corrections; criminology; engineering/industrial management; history of science and technology; industrial/manufacturing engineering; investments and securities; law and legal studies related; public administration; public administration and services, other; sociology.

See full description on page 504.

ROOSEVELT UNIVERSITY

Chicago, Illinois
Distance Learning
http://www.roosevelt.edu/ruonline

Roosevelt University was founded in 1945. It is accredited by North Central Association of Colleges and Schools. It first offered distance learning courses in 2001. In fall 2003, there were 600 students enrolled in distance learning courses. Institutionally administered financial aid is available to distance learners.

Services Distance learners have accessibility to academic advising, bookstore, campus computer network, career placement assistance, e-mail services, library services.
Contact Karen S. Gersten, Associate Dean and Managing Director of Distance Learning, Roosevelt University, University College, 430 South Michigan Avenue, Chicago, IL 60605. *Telephone:* 312-281-3129. *Fax:* 312-281-3132. *E-mail:* kgersten@roosevelt.edu.

DEGREES AND AWARDS

Certificate Organizational Leadership
Graduate Certificate E-Learning; Instructional Design; Training and Development
MA Training and Development

COURSE SUBJECT AREAS OFFERED OUTSIDE OF DEGREE PROGRAMS

Undergraduate—accounting; business; business administration and management; business communications; education, general; hospitality services management; law and legal studies related; legal studies; liberal arts and sciences, general studies and humanities; multi/interdisciplinary studies, other; physical sciences, general; psychology; social sciences, general.
Graduate—communications technologies; education, general.

See full description on page 506.

ROSALIND FRANKLIN UNIVERSITY OF MEDICINE AND SCIENCE

North Chicago, Illinois
http://www.rosalindfranklin.edu

Rosalind Franklin University of Medicine and Science was founded in 1912. It is accredited by North Central Association of Colleges and Schools. It first offered distance learning courses in 1993. In fall 2003, there were 119 students enrolled in distance learning courses. Institutionally administered financial aid is available to distance learners.

Services Distance learners have accessibility to academic advising, bookstore, e-mail services, tutoring.
Contact Ms. Laura Nehls, Administrative Assistant, Rosalind Franklin University of Medicine and Science, 3333 Green Bay Road, North Chicago, IL 60064-3095. *Telephone:* 847-578-3408. *E-mail:* distance.education@rosalindfranklin.edu.

DEGREES AND AWARDS

MS Clinical Nutrition/Nutrition Education; Healthcare Management
DPT Transition Doctor of Physical Therapy

COURSE SUBJECT AREAS OFFERED OUTSIDE OF DEGREE PROGRAMS

Graduate—biological sciences/life sciences, other; business administration and management; education, other; financial management and services; foods and nutrition studies; health professions and related sciences, other; human resources management; Internet and World Wide Web.
Non-credit—biological sciences/life sciences, other; business administration and management; education, other; financial management

Rosalind Franklin University of Medicine and Science (continued)

and services; foods and nutrition studies; health professions and related sciences, other; human resources management; Internet and World Wide Web.

ROWAN TECHNICAL COLLEGE

Morehead, Kentucky

http://www.maycc.kctcs.edu

Rowan Technical College was founded in 1984. It is accredited by Northwest Commission on Colleges and Universities. It first offered distance learning courses in 2004. Institutionally administered financial aid is available to distance learners.

Services Distance learners have accessibility to academic advising, bookstore, campus computer network, career placement assistance, e-mail services, library services, tutoring.

Contact Mrs. Kimberly D. Bloomfield, Coordinator of Outreach and Distance Learning, Rowan Technical College, 1755 US 68, Maysville, KY 41056. *Telephone:* 606-759-7141 Ext. 66130. *Fax:* 606-759-9601. *E-mail:* kim.bloomfield@kctcs.edu.

DEGREES AND AWARDS

AA General Program; General Program

COURSE SUBJECT AREAS OFFERED OUTSIDE OF DEGREE PROGRAMS

Undergraduate—accounting; business management and administrative services, other; educational psychology; education, general; history; psychology; sociology.

ROYAL ROADS UNIVERSITY

Victoria, British Columbia, Canada

http://www.royalroads.ca/

Royal Roads University was founded in 1996. It is provincially chartered. It first offered distance learning courses in 1996. In fall 2003, there were 3,000 students enrolled in distance learning courses. Institutionally administered financial aid is available to distance learners.

Services Distance learners have accessibility to academic advising, bookstore, campus computer network, career placement assistance, e-mail services, library services.

Contact Mr. Todd Orchard, Programs Liaison, Royal Roads University, 2005 Sooke Road, Victoria, BC V9B 5Y2, Canada. *Telephone:* 250-391-2600 Ext. 4155. *Fax:* 250-391-2548. *E-mail:* todd.orchard@royalroads.ca.

DEGREES AND AWARDS

BA Applied Communication; Justice Studies
BComm Entrepreneurial Management
BS Environmental Management
MA Applied Communications; Conflict Analysis and Management; Distributed Learning; Environment and Management; Environmental Education and Communication; Human Security and Peacebuilding; Leadership and Training
MBA Digital Technologies Management; Executive Management; Human Resources Management; Public Relations and Communication Management
MS Environment and Management

COURSE SUBJECT AREAS OFFERED OUTSIDE OF DEGREE PROGRAMS

Undergraduate—business administration and management; communications, general; environmental/environmental health engineering; legal studies.

Graduate—business administration and management; business communications; business information and data processing services; business management and administrative services, other; communications, general; communications, other; education administration and supervision; educational/instructional media design; human resources management; information sciences and systems; public administration and services, other; public relations and organizational communications.

RYERSON UNIVERSITY

Toronto, Ontario, Canada

Distance Education

http://www.ryerson.ca/ce/de

Ryerson University was founded in 1948. It is provincially chartered. It first offered distance learning courses in 1999. In fall 2003, there were 2,532 students enrolled in distance learning courses. Institutionally administered financial aid is available to distance learners.

Services Distance learners have accessibility to academic advising, bookstore, campus computer network, career placement assistance, e-mail services, library services, tutoring.

Contact Martha Ireland, Manager, Support Services, Ryerson University, G. Raymond Chang School of Continuing Education, Distance Education, 350 Victoria Street, Toronto, ON M5B 2K3, Canada. *Telephone:* 416-979-5000 Ext. 7874. *Fax:* 416-595-9602. *E-mail:* mireland@ryerson.ca.

DEGREES AND AWARDS

Programs offered do not lead to a degree or other formal award.

COURSE SUBJECT AREAS OFFERED OUTSIDE OF DEGREE PROGRAMS

Undergraduate—accounting; business; business administration and management; business communications; business information and data processing services; business/managerial economics; business quantitative methods and management science; child care and guidance workers and managers; communications, general; community health services; criminal justice and corrections; economics; English language and literature, general; entrepreneurship; family and community studies; foods and nutrition studies; general retailing/wholesaling; geography; gerontology; health professions and related sciences, other; history; hospitality services management; human resources management; legal studies; liberal arts and sciences, general studies and humanities; marketing management and research; nursing; philosophy; psychology; public administration; public relations and organizational communications; social sciences, general; sociology.

SACRAMENTO CITY COLLEGE

Sacramento, California

Courses by Television

http://www.scc.losrios.edu/de

Sacramento City College was founded in 1916. It is accredited by Western Association of Schools and Colleges. It first offered distance learning courses in 1986. In fall 2003, there were 1,073 students enrolled in distance learning courses. Institutionally administered financial aid is available to distance learners.

Services Distance learners have accessibility to academic advising, bookstore, campus computer network, career placement assistance, e-mail services, library services, tutoring.

Contact Jane Phillips, Student Coordinator of Distance Education, Sacramento City College, Learning Resources, Sacramento, CA 95822. *Telephone:* 916-558-2361. *E-mail:* phillije@exi.scc.losrios.edu.

DEGREES AND AWARDS

Programs offered do not lead to a degree or other formal award.

COURSE SUBJECT AREAS OFFERED OUTSIDE OF DEGREE PROGRAMS

Undergraduate—anthropology; computer and information sciences, general; computer and information sciences, other; computer programming; computer software and media applications; English composition; English creative writing; foreign languages and literatures; geography; gerontology; health professions and related sciences, other; history; journalism and mass communications; library science, other; music; philosophy and religion; psychology; sociology.

SACRED HEART MAJOR SEMINARY

Detroit, Michigan

Sacred Heart Major Seminary was founded in 1919. It is accredited by North Central Association of Colleges and Schools. It first offered distance learning courses in 2003. In fall 2003, there were 16 students enrolled in distance learning courses.

Services Distance learners have accessibility to academic advising, bookstore, e-mail services, library services.

Contact Ms. Debi Piontkowski, Institute for Ministry, Sacred Heart Major Seminary, 2701 Chicago Boulevard, Detroit, MI 48206. *Telephone:* 313-883-8520. *E-mail:* piontkowski.debi@shms.edu.

DEGREES AND AWARDS

Programs offered do not lead to a degree or other formal award.

COURSE SUBJECT AREAS OFFERED OUTSIDE OF DEGREE PROGRAMS

Undergraduate—theological and ministerial studies.

SACRED HEART UNIVERSITY

Fairfield, Connecticut

University College/ Continuing Education

http://onlinelearning.sacredheart.edu

Sacred Heart University was founded in 1963. It is accredited by New England Association of Schools and Colleges. It first offered distance learning courses in 1997. In fall 2003, there were 350 students enrolled in distance learning courses. Institutionally administered financial aid is available to distance learners.

Services Distance learners have accessibility to academic advising, bookstore, campus computer network, career placement assistance, e-mail services, library services, tutoring.

Contact Edward Donato, Associate Dean of University College, Sacred Heart University, 5151 Park Avenue, Fairfield, CT 06825. *Telephone:* 203-371-7836. *Fax:* 203-365-7500. *E-mail:* donatoe@sacredheart.edu.

DEGREES AND AWARDS

BSN Nursing
MSHA Geriatric Rehabilitation and Wellness
MSN Nursing–Patient Care Services Administration–Family Nurse Practitioner

COURSE SUBJECT AREAS OFFERED OUTSIDE OF DEGREE PROGRAMS

Undergraduate—biological and physical sciences; business administration and management; chemistry; communications, general; computer and information sciences, general; computer science; English composition; English language and literature/letters, other; fine arts and art studies; foreign languages and literatures; foreign languages and literatures, other; health professions and related sciences, other; history; international business; liberal arts and sciences, general studies and humanities; marketing management and research; music; philosophy; philosophy and religion; physical sciences, general; political science and government; religion/religious studies; religious education; social sciences and history, other.

Graduate—accounting; business administration and management; computer science; economics; education, general; financial management and services; gerontology; health professions and related sciences, other; marketing management and research; mathematics; nursing.

Special Message

Sacred Heart University offers 3 online degree programs and numerous undergraduate courses in art, business, chemistry, communications, computer science, English, history, mathematics, media studies, music, philosophy, political science, psychology, religion, Spanish, and sports management.

For nurses wishing to complete their undergraduate degree, the RN to BSN Program, accredited by the National League for Nursing Accrediting Commission, requires 57 credits in nursing; up to 30 credits may be awarded for previous nursing work. An undergraduate certificate program in home health care management for RNs is available online. For information, students should contact Alma Haluch (telephone: 203-371-7715, e-mail: halucha@sacredheart.edu).

Through online work, students can meet all graduate degree requirements for the MSN in patient care services and about 40 percent of the requirements for the MSN family nurse practitioner or may just work on an MSN. For information, students should contact Tatum Krause (telephone: 203-365-4750, e-mail: krauset@sacredheart.edu).

Online MS in geriatric rehabilitation and wellness students may choose either a 24- or 36-month study plan. Students should contact Michelle Lusardi (telephone: 203-365-4721, e-mail: lusardim@sacredheart.edu).

Meeting the need for computer-literate teachers, Sacred Heart offers an education technology program with a cross-endorsement in computer technology. MBA prerequisites are available online. The Sports Business University provides business training in leadership skills for the sports industry.

Benefits for online students include full online or in-person use of the University library, small classes, personal online-help advisers to assist with technical questions or problems, a free Internet e-mail account, online book-ordering privileges, and free e-portfolio server space and software.

Sacred Heart University (continued)

Courses are offered year-round, on a semester-based calendar. There is also an intensive program for those who want to earn credits on a faster schedule.

Founded in 1963, Sacred Heart is a high-quality, independent, locally oriented University led and staffed by laity serving a regional, national, and international purpose. With a dynamic link to adult and corporate communities, it serves adults in their quest for knowledge, continuous learning, and personal, professional, and spiritual growth.

For further information or assistance, students should contact Edward Donato, Associate Dean, University College, Sacred Heart University (telephone: 203-371-7836, e-mail: donatoe@sacredheart.edu).

SADDLEBACK COLLEGE

Mission Viejo, California
Office of Instruction
http://www.saddlebackcollege.edu

Saddleback College was founded in 1967. It is accredited by Western Association of Schools and Colleges. It first offered distance learning courses in 1975. In fall 2003, there were 2,000 students enrolled in distance learning courses. Institutionally administered financial aid is available to distance learners.

Services Distance learners have accessibility to academic advising, bookstore, career placement assistance, e-mail services, library services.

Contact Ms. Sheri L. Nelson, Senior Administrative Assistant, Saddleback College, AGB 117, 28000 Marguerite Parkway, Mission Viejo, CA 92692. *Telephone:* 949-582-4515. *Fax:* 949-347-0438. *E-mail:* snelson@saddleback.edu.

DEGREES AND AWARDS

Programs offered do not lead to a degree or other formal award.

COURSE SUBJECT AREAS OFFERED OUTSIDE OF DEGREE PROGRAMS

Undergraduate—accounting; American history; anthropology; business information and data processing services; business management and administrative services, other; business marketing and marketing management; computer science; developmental and child psychology; health and medical preparatory programs; individual and family development studies; international business; library science, other; marketing operations/marketing and distribution, other; music; nursing; political science and government; real estate; social sciences and history, other; sociology.

ST. AMBROSE UNIVERSITY

Davenport, Iowa
http://www.sau.edu/

St. Ambrose University was founded in 1882. It is accredited by North Central Association of Colleges and Schools. It first offered distance learning courses in 1990. In fall 2003, there were 36 students enrolled in distance learning courses. Institutionally administered financial aid is available to distance learners.

Services Distance learners have accessibility to academic advising, bookstore, campus computer network, career placement assistance, e-mail services, library services.

Contact Ms. Meg F. Halligan, Director of Admissions, St. Ambrose University, 518 West Locust Street, Davenport, IA 52803-2898. *Telephone:* 563-333-6311. *Fax:* 563-333-6321. *E-mail:* halliganmegf@sau.edu.

DEGREES AND AWARDS

Programs offered do not lead to a degree or other formal award.

COURSE SUBJECT AREAS OFFERED OUTSIDE OF DEGREE PROGRAMS

Undergraduate—business administration and management; computer and information sciences, general; journalism and mass communication related; philosophy.

Graduate—business administration and management; mathematical statistics; occupational therapy; physical therapy; special education.

ST. CLAIR COUNTY COMMUNITY COLLEGE

Port Huron, Michigan
http://www.SC4.edu/

St. Clair County Community College was founded in 1923. It is accredited by North Central Association of Colleges and Schools. It first offered distance learning courses in 2000. In fall 2003, there were 777 students enrolled in distance learning courses. Institutionally administered financial aid is available to distance learners.

Services Distance learners have accessibility to bookstore, library services, tutoring.

Contact Linda Davis, Coordinator of Distance Learning, St. Clair County Community College, 323 Erie Street, PO Box 5015, Port Huron, MI 48061-5015. *Telephone:* 810-989-5765. *E-mail:* ldavis@sc4.edu.

DEGREES AND AWARDS

Programs offered do not lead to a degree or other formal award.

COURSE SUBJECT AREAS OFFERED OUTSIDE OF DEGREE PROGRAMS

Undergraduate—astronomy; business administration and management; business communications; chemistry; communications, other; computer and information sciences, general; electrical and electronic engineering-related technology; English composition; English creative writing; general teacher education; geography; history; mathematical statistics; mathematics; nursing; political science and government; psychology; social sciences, general; sociology.

ST. CLOUD STATE UNIVERSITY

St. Cloud, Minnesota
Center for Continuing Studies
http://www.stcloudstate.edu/~ccs/

St. Cloud State University was founded in 1869. It is accredited by North Central Association of Colleges and Schools. It first offered distance learning courses in 1975. In fall 2003, there were 2,300 students enrolled in distance learning courses. Institutionally administered financial aid is available to distance learners.

Services Distance learners have accessibility to bookstore, campus computer network, e-mail services, library services.
Contact Ms. Patricia A. Aceves, Director of Distributed Learning, St. Cloud State University, 720 4th Avenue, South, St. Cloud, MN 56301. *Telephone:* 320-308-3081. *Fax:* 320-308-5041. *E-mail:* paceves@stcloudstate.edu.

DEGREES AND AWARDS

AA Liberal Arts
BGS Self Designed
MCM Marketing; Self Designed Studies; Speech Communication
MEd Educational Administration
MS Applied Psychology

COURSE SUBJECT AREAS OFFERED OUTSIDE OF DEGREE PROGRAMS

Undergraduate—aerospace, aeronautical and astronautical engineering; American literature (United States); anthropology; biology; business information and data processing services; chemistry; communications, general; counseling psychology; criminal justice and corrections; economics; education administration and supervision; education of the speech impaired; English as a second language; English composition; English creative writing; English language and literature, general; environmental/environmental health engineering; environmental science; history; mathematics; philosophy; psychology; social sciences and history, other; sociology; speech and rhetorical studies.
Graduate—English as a second language; journalism and mass communication related; psychology, other.

ST. CLOUD TECHNICAL COLLEGE

St. Cloud, Minnesota
Central Minnesota Distance Learning Network
http://www.sctc.edu

St. Cloud Technical College was founded in 1948. It is accredited by North Central Association of Colleges and Schools. It first offered distance learning courses in 1988. In fall 2003, there were 120 students enrolled in distance learning courses. Institutionally administered financial aid is available to distance learners.

Services Distance learners have accessibility to bookstore, career placement assistance, e-mail services, library services.
Contact Ms. Jodi Elness, Director of Enrollment Management, St. Cloud Technical College, 1540 Northway Drive, St. Cloud, MN 56303. *Telephone:* 320-308-5087. *Fax:* 320-308-5981. *E-mail:* jelness@sctc.edu.

DEGREES AND AWARDS

Programs offered do not lead to a degree or other formal award.

COURSE SUBJECT AREAS OFFERED OUTSIDE OF DEGREE PROGRAMS

Undergraduate—child care and guidance workers and managers; computer and information sciences, general; English technical and business writing.
Non-credit—accounting; administrative and secretarial services; advertising; applied mathematics; business; business communications; business management and administrative services, other; child care and guidance workers and managers; computer and information sciences, general; computer programming; computer science; financial management and services; medical basic sciences; visual and performing arts, other.

ST. EDWARD'S UNIVERSITY

Austin, Texas
New College
http://www.stedwards.edu

St. Edward's University was founded in 1885. It is accredited by Southern Association of Colleges and Schools. It first offered distance learning courses in 1994. In fall 2003, there were 200 students enrolled in distance learning courses. Institutionally administered financial aid is available to distance learners.

Services Distance learners have accessibility to academic advising, bookstore, campus computer network, career placement assistance, e-mail services, library services.
Contact Ms. Amy Bush, New College Recruitment Coordinator, St. Edward's University, Center for Academic Progress, 3001 South Congress Avenue, Austin, TX 78704-6489. *Telephone:* 512-448-8745. *Fax:* 512-428-1032. *E-mail:* amyb@admin.stedwards.edu.

DEGREES AND AWARDS

Programs offered do not lead to a degree or other formal award.

COURSE SUBJECT AREAS OFFERED OUTSIDE OF DEGREE PROGRAMS

Undergraduate—accounting; anthropology; business administration and management; business communications; business management and administrative services, other; business/managerial economics; communications, general; computer systems analysis; criminal justice and corrections; economics; education, general; English language and literature, general; geography; history; human resources management; human services; marketing operations/marketing and distribution, other; philosophy; philosophy and religion; public administration; social sciences and history, other.
Graduate—accounting; business administration and management; business communications; business/managerial economics; computer/information technology administration and management; computer systems analysis; counseling psychology; entrepreneurship; financial services marketing operations; human resources management; human services; liberal arts and sciences, general studies and humanities; marketing management and research; marketing operations/marketing and distribution, other; peace and conflict studies; public relations and organizational communications.
Non-credit—business administration and management; computer/information technology administration and management; computer systems analysis.

ST. JOHN'S UNIVERSITY

Jamaica, New York
http://www.stjohns.edu/distancelearning

St. John's University was founded in 1870. It is accredited by Middle States Association of Colleges and Schools. It first offered distance learning courses in 1994. In fall 2003, there were 368 students enrolled in distance learning courses. Institutionally administered financial aid is available to distance learners.

Services Distance learners have accessibility to academic advising, bookstore, campus computer network, career placement assistance, e-mail services, library services, tutoring.
Contact Elizabeth Alexander, Associate Vice President, St. John's University, 8000 Utopia Parkway, Jamaica, NY 11439. *Telephone:* 718-990-2353. *Fax:* 718-990-5689. *E-mail:* distancelearning@stjohns.edu.

St. John's University (continued)

DEGREES AND AWARDS

AA Liberal Arts
AS Business; Criminal Justice
MS Educational Administration
PMC Educational Administration

COURSE SUBJECT AREAS OFFERED OUTSIDE OF DEGREE PROGRAMS

Undergraduate—business administration and management; communications, other; criminal justice and corrections; economics; education, general; English language and literature, general; history; legal studies; marketing management and research; mathematics; physics; political science and government.
Graduate—business management and administrative services, other; economics; education administration and supervision; education, general; teacher education, specific academic and vocational programs.

SAINT JOSEPH'S COLLEGE OF MAINE

Standish, Maine
Graduate & Professional Studies
http://www.sjcme.edu/gps

Saint Joseph's College of Maine was founded in 1912. It is accredited by New England Association of Schools and Colleges. It first offered distance learning courses in 1976. In fall 2003, there were 4,500 students enrolled in distance learning courses. Institutionally administered financial aid is available to distance learners.

Services Distance learners have accessibility to academic advising, bookstore, campus computer network, career placement assistance, e-mail services, library services, tutoring.
Contact Lynne Robinson, Director of Admissions, Saint Joseph's College of Maine, 278 Whites Bridge Road, Standish, ME 04084-5263. *Telephone:* 800-752-4723. *Fax:* 207-892-7480. *E-mail:* info@sjcme.edu.

DEGREES AND AWARDS

AS Adult Education and Training; Business Administration; Criminal Justice; General Studies; Human Services; Information Technology Management; Management; Psychology
BA Adult Religious Education
BLS American Studies; Christian Tradition
BS Criminal Justice; General Studies; Health Care Administration; Long-Term Care Administration; Radiological Sciences
BSBA Business Administration
BSN Nursing
BSPA Professional Arts
Certificate Adult Education and Training; Advanced Health Care Management; Advanced Long-Term Care Administration; American Studies; Business Administration; Christian Tradition; Criminal Justice; Health Care Management; Information Technology Management; Long-Term Care Administration; Nursing–Parish Nursing; Professional Studies
Graduate Certificate Health Services Administration; International Health Care; Long-Term Care; Nursing Administration and Leadership; Nursing and Healthcare Education; Nursing–Parish Nursing; Pastoral Studies; Practice Management
MA Pastoral Ministry; Pastoral Studies; Pastoral Theology
MBA Quality Leadership; Resort Management
MBA/MSN Health Services Administration and Nursing Dual Degree
MHSA Health Services Administration
MSE Education
MSN Nursing

COURSE SUBJECT AREAS OFFERED OUTSIDE OF DEGREE PROGRAMS

Undergraduate—accounting; bible/biblical studies; business administration and management; communications, general; computer/information technology administration and management; criminology; developmental/child psychology; educational evaluation, research and statistics; educational psychology; English composition; health and medical administrative services; human services; marketing management and research; multi/interdisciplinary studies, other; nursing; organizational psychology; pastoral counseling and specialized ministries; philosophy and religion; religious education; social psychology; sociology; teacher education, specific academic and vocational programs.
Graduate—accounting; bible/biblical studies; business administration and management; business communications; business management and administrative services, other; business/managerial economics; business quantitative methods and management science; curriculum and instruction; education administration and supervision; educational evaluation, research and statistics; entrepreneurship; health and medical administrative services; health products and services marketing operations; marketing management and research; nursing; parks, recreation and leisure facilities management; pastoral counseling and specialized ministries; philosophy and religion; public administration; religion/religious studies; teacher education, specific academic and vocational programs; theological and ministerial studies; theological studies and religious vocations, other; tourism/travel marketing.
Non-credit—bible/biblical studies; pastoral counseling and specialized ministries; religion/religious studies.

See full description on page 508.

ST. JOSEPH'S COLLEGE, SUFFOLK CAMPUS

Patchogue, New York

St. Joseph's College, Suffolk Campus was founded in 1916. It is accredited by Middle States Association of Colleges and Schools. It first offered distance learning courses in 1999. In fall 2003, there were 250 students enrolled in distance learning courses. Institutionally administered financial aid is available to distance learners.

Services Distance learners have accessibility to campus computer network, e-mail services, library services.
Contact Dr. Mark Hessler, Coordinator of Creative Programming, St. Joseph's College, Suffolk Campus, 155 West Roe Boulevard, Patchogue, NY 11772. *Telephone:* 631-447-3284. *E-mail:* mhessler@sjcny.edu.

DEGREES AND AWARDS

Programs offered do not lead to a degree or other formal award.

COURSE SUBJECT AREAS OFFERED OUTSIDE OF DEGREE PROGRAMS

Undergraduate—biological and physical sciences; biology, general; business; business administration and management; business communications; business/managerial economics; education, general; English language and literature, general; health professions and related sciences, other; history; political science and government; psychology.

SAINT JOSEPH'S UNIVERSITY

Philadelphia, Pennsylvania

http://www.sju.edu

Saint Joseph's University was founded in 1851. It is accredited by Middle States Association of Colleges and Schools. It first offered distance learning courses in 2001. In fall 2003, there were 50 students enrolled in distance learning courses. Institutionally administered financial aid is available to distance learners.

Services Distance learners have accessibility to e-mail services, library services.
Contact Terese Waldron, Director of Graduate Business Distance Learning Programs, Saint Joseph's University, 5600 City Avenue, Philadelphia, PA 19083. *Telephone:* 610-660-3150. *Fax:* 610-660-3160. *E-mail:* twaldron@sju.edu.

DEGREES AND AWARDS

MBA Pharmaceutical Marketing

COURSE SUBJECT AREAS OFFERED OUTSIDE OF DEGREE PROGRAMS

Undergraduate—philosophy.

SAINT LEO UNIVERSITY

Saint Leo, Florida

Center for Distance Learning

http://www.saintleo.edu/col

Saint Leo University was founded in 1889. It is accredited by Southern Association of Colleges and Schools. It first offered distance learning courses in 1998. In fall 2003, there were 10,000 students enrolled in distance learning courses. Institutionally administered financial aid is available to distance learners.

Services Distance learners have accessibility to academic advising, bookstore, campus computer network, career placement assistance, e-mail services, library services, tutoring.
Contact Dr. Jody Conway, Assistant Director, Saint Leo University, Center for Online Learning, 9417 Princess Palm Avenue, Suite 150, Tampa, FL 33619-8317. *Telephone:* 813-626-6455 Ext. 225. *Fax:* 813-622-7440. *E-mail:* jody.conway@saintleo.edu.

DEGREES AND AWARDS

BA Accounting; Business Administration; Criminal Justice
BS Computer Information Systems

COURSE SUBJECT AREAS OFFERED OUTSIDE OF DEGREE PROGRAMS

Undergraduate—accounting; biological sciences/life sciences, other; business administration and management; business communications; business quantitative methods and management science; computer and information sciences, general; computer and information sciences, other; computer programming; computer systems analysis; computer systems networking and telecommunications; criminal justice and corrections; criminology; English composition; English language and literature, general; fine arts and art studies; human resources management; Internet and World Wide Web; liberal arts and sciences, general studies and humanities; marketing management and research; mathematics; philosophy; philosophy and religion; physical sciences, general; psychology; public administration; social sciences and history, other; taxation.
Graduate—business administration and management.

ST. LOUIS COMMUNITY COLLEGE SYSTEM

St. Louis, Missouri

Telelearning Services

http://stlcc.edu/distance

St. Louis Community College System is accredited by North Central Association of Colleges and Schools. It first offered distance learning courses in 1973. In fall 2003, there were 5,000 students enrolled in distance learning courses. Institutionally administered financial aid is available to distance learners.

Services Distance learners have accessibility to academic advising, bookstore, career placement assistance, library services.
Contact Daniel A. Bain, Director of Telelearning Services, St. Louis Community College System, 300 South Broadway, St. Louis, MO 63102. *Telephone:* 314-539-5056. *Fax:* 314-539-5125. *E-mail:* dbain@stlcc.edu.

DEGREES AND AWARDS

AA General Program; Transfer Studies, general

COURSE SUBJECT AREAS OFFERED OUTSIDE OF DEGREE PROGRAMS

Undergraduate—marketing management and research.
Graduate—business administration and management.
Non-credit—business; business administration and management; business information and data processing services; business management and administrative services, other.

SAINT LOUIS UNIVERSITY

St. Louis, Missouri

School of Nursing

http://www.slu.edu/colleges/NR

Saint Louis University was founded in 1818. It is accredited by North Central Association of Colleges and Schools. It first offered distance learning courses in 1997. In fall 2003, there were 90 students enrolled in distance learning courses. Institutionally administered financial aid is available to distance learners.

Services Distance learners have accessibility to academic advising, bookstore, campus computer network, career placement assistance, e-mail services, library services, tutoring.
Contact Director of Marketing and Recruitment, Saint Louis University, 3525 Caroline Street, St. Louis, MO 63104-1099. *Telephone:* 314-977-8995. *Fax:* 314-977-8949. *E-mail:* slunurse@slu.edu.

DEGREES AND AWARDS

MBA/Pharm D Nursing
MSN Nursing
PMC Nursing
PhD Nursing

Saint Louis University (continued)

Special Message

Saint Louis University School of Nursing is a leader in nursing distance education. It was the first nursing school in the US to offer complete master's degree programs in nursing online through the World Wide Web.

Currently, MSN, MSN (research), and post-master's certificate programs are available online for the acute care, adult, family, gerontological, pediatric, and psychiatric nurse practitioner tracks and for the adult, gerontological, perinatal, and psychiatric clinical nurse specialist tracks. Students complete all course work for the degree program through distance education. The online tracks are designed to follow the same curriculum and program objectives required of on-campus students. Faculty members work with students to help select clinical sites and preceptors that are compatible with the students' and the program's objectives. To participate, students must be comfortable using PC hardware and software and should have an e-mail account and be proficient in accessing the World Wide Web. Students enrolled in the online programs have access to the University's main and health sciences libraries and resources via the Internet.

On campus, the School offers several BSN programs; master's programs in adult nursing (CNS, NP), family and community health nursing (NP), gerontological nursing (CNS, NP), perinatal nursing (CNS), and psychiatric–mental health nursing (CNS); and a doctoral program in nursing.

Saint Louis University is accredited by the North Central Association of Colleges and Schools. The School of Nursing is fully accredited by the National League for Nursing Accrediting Commission and approved by the Missouri State Board of Nursing and has preliminary approval by the Committee on Collegiate Education of the American Association of Colleges of Nursing. The master's programs are accredited by the National League for Nursing Council for Baccalaureate and Higher Degree Programs.

SAINT MARY-OF-THE-WOODS COLLEGE

Saint Mary-of-the-Woods, Indiana
Women's External Degree Program
http://www.smwc.edu/

Saint Mary-of-the-Woods College was founded in 1840. It is accredited by North Central Association of Colleges and Schools. It first offered distance learning courses in 1973. In fall 2003, there were 1,300 students enrolled in distance learning courses. Institutionally administered financial aid is available to distance learners.

Services Distance learners have accessibility to academic advising, bookstore, career placement assistance, e-mail services, library services.

Contact Mrs. Linda Clark-Laffoon, Associate Director of Distance Education Admission, Saint Mary-of-the-Woods College, Office of Distance Education Admission, 122 Guerin Hall, Saint Mary-of-the-Woods, IN 47876. *Telephone:* 800-926-7692. *Fax:* 812-535-5010. *E-mail:* wedadms@smwc.edu.

DEGREES AND AWARDS

AA Humanities; Paralegal Studies
AS Accounting; Business, general; Early Childhood/Child Development; Gerontology
BA English; History and Political Studies; Humanities; Journalism; Mathematics; Paralegal Studies; Professional Writing; Social Science/History; Theology
BS Accounting Information Systems; Accounting; Business Administration; Computer Information Systems; Digital Media Communication; Equine Business Management; Gerontology; Human Resource Management; Human Services; Kindergarten-Elementary Education; Marketing; Middle School/High School Special Education; Not-for-Profit Child Care Administration; Not-for-Profit Financial Administration; Not-for-Profit Human Services; Not-for-Profit Public Relations; Occupational Therapy Applications; Preschool-Grade 3 Education/Mild Intervention; Psychology; Secondary Education–English; Secondary Education–Mathematics; Secondary Education–Social Studies
Certificate Gerontology; Paralegal Studies; Theology
MA Art Therapy; Earth Literacy; Music Therapy; Pastoral Theology

COURSE SUBJECT AREAS OFFERED OUTSIDE OF DEGREE PROGRAMS

Undergraduate—accounting; business; business administration and management; computer and information sciences, general; education, general; education, other; English creative writing; English technical and business writing; general teacher education; gerontology; history; human resources management; human services; journalism and mass communications; liberal arts and sciences, general studies and humanities; marketing management and research; mathematics; political science and government; psychology; social sciences and history, other; special education; teacher education, specific academic and vocational programs; theological studies and religious vocations, other.
Graduate—conservation and renewable natural resources, other; music; theological and ministerial studies.

See full description on page 510.

SAINT MARY-OF-THE-WOODS COLLEGE

Saint Mary-of-the-Woods, Indiana
Program in Pastoral Theology
http://www.smwc.edu

Saint Mary-of-the-Woods College was founded in 1840. It is accredited by North Central Association of Colleges and Schools. It first offered distance learning courses in 1974. In fall 2003, there were 1,200 students enrolled in distance learning courses. Institutionally administered financial aid is available to distance learners.

Services Distance learners have accessibility to academic advising.

Contact Ms. Jill Blunk, Director of Distance Education Admission, Saint Mary-of-the-Woods College, Saint Mary-of-the-Woods, IN 47876. *E-mail:* wedadms@smwc.edu.

DEGREES AND AWARDS

AD General Program
BA General Program

COURSE SUBJECT AREAS OFFERED OUTSIDE OF DEGREE PROGRAMS

Undergraduate—accounting; business administration and management; computer and information sciences, general; English creative writing; gerontology; history; human resources management; human services; journalism and mass communications; marketing operations/

marketing and distribution, other; mathematics; political science and government; social sciences, general; theological studies and religious vocations, other.
Graduate—theological studies and religious vocations, other.

ST. MARY'S UNIVERSITY OF SAN ANTONIO

San Antonio, Texas
Graduate School
http://www.stmarytx.edu

St. Mary's University of San Antonio was founded in 1852. It is accredited by Southern Association of Colleges and Schools. It first offered distance learning courses in 1997. In fall 2003, there were 40 students enrolled in distance learning courses. Institutionally administered financial aid is available to distance learners.

Services Distance learners have accessibility to academic advising, bookstore, campus computer network, career placement assistance, e-mail services, library services.
Contact St. Mary's University of San Antonio.

DEGREES AND AWARDS

MA Community Counseling; International Relations; Theology

See full description on page 512.

ST. NORBERT COLLEGE

De Pere, Wisconsin
Program in Education
http://www.snc.edu/mse

St. Norbert College was founded in 1898. It is accredited by North Central Association of Colleges and Schools. It first offered distance learning courses in 1996. In fall 2003, there were 20 students enrolled in distance learning courses. Institutionally administered financial aid is available to distance learners.

Services Distance learners have accessibility to academic advising, bookstore, campus computer network, career placement assistance, e-mail services, library services, tutoring.
Contact Mr. Daniel Meyer, Dean of Admissions, St. Norbert College, 100 Grant Street, De Pere, WI 54115. *Telephone:* 920-403-3005. *Fax:* 920-403-4072. *E-mail:* daniel.meyer@snc.edu.

DEGREES AND AWARDS

Programs offered do not lead to a degree or other formal award.

COURSE SUBJECT AREAS OFFERED OUTSIDE OF DEGREE PROGRAMS

Graduate—education, general.

SAINT PAUL COLLEGE–A COMMUNITY & TECHNICAL COLLEGE

St. Paul, Minnesota
http://www.saintpaul.edu

Saint Paul College–A Community & Technical College was founded in 1919. It is accredited by North Central Association of Colleges and Schools. It first offered distance learning courses in 1999. In fall 2003, there were 500 students enrolled in distance learning courses. Institutionally administered financial aid is available to distance learners.

Services Distance learners have accessibility to academic advising, bookstore, campus computer network, career placement assistance, e-mail services, library services.
Contact Office of Admissions, Saint Paul College–A Community & Technical College, 235 Marshall Avenue, St. Paul, MN 55102. *Telephone:* 800-227-6029. *Fax:* 651-221-1416. *E-mail:* admissions@saintpaul.edu.

DEGREES AND AWARDS

Certification Software Support Specialist/Help Desk
Technical Certificate Human Resources

COURSE SUBJECT AREAS OFFERED OUTSIDE OF DEGREE PROGRAMS

Undergraduate—administrative and secretarial services; business administration and management; business communications; business information and data processing services; computer software and media applications; education, general; human resources management.

ST. PETERSBURG COLLEGE

St. Petersburg, Florida
Electronic Campus
http://e.spcollege.edu

St. Petersburg College was founded in 1927. It is accredited by Southern Association of Colleges and Schools. It first offered distance learning courses in 1970. In fall 2003, there were 13,000 students enrolled in distance learning courses. Institutionally administered financial aid is available to distance learners.

Services Distance learners have accessibility to academic advising, bookstore, career placement assistance, e-mail services, library services, tutoring.
Contact Lynda Womer, Program Director, St. Petersburg College, PO Box 13489, St. Petersburg, FL 33733. *Telephone:* 727-394-6116. *Fax:* 727-394-6124. *E-mail:* womerl@spcollege.edu.

DEGREES AND AWARDS

AA General Program
AS Crime Scene Technology; Emergency Administration and Management; Funeral Services; Medical Laboratory Technology; Veterinary Technology
BA Dental Hygiene; Technology Management
Certificate Computer Related Crime Investigations; Crime Scene Technology; Critical Care (Advanced Technical Certification); Emergency Administration and Management; Fire Inspector I; Fire Inspector II; Fire Investigator I; Fire Investigator II; Fire Officer I; Fire Officer II; Nursing–Perioperative Nursing; Quality Assurance and Software Testing; Veterinary Hospital Management; Veterinary Hospital Manager

COURSE SUBJECT AREAS OFFERED OUTSIDE OF DEGREE PROGRAMS

Undergraduate—accounting; American literature (United States); anthropology; archaeology; area studies; astronomy; bible/biblical studies; biological and physical sciences; biology, general; business; business administration and management; business communications; chemistry; communications, general; computer science; economics;

St. Petersburg College (continued)

educational evaluation, research and statistics; educational/instructional media design; educational psychology; education, general; English as a second language; entrepreneurship; financial management and services; fine arts and art studies; foreign languages and literatures; funeral services and mortuary science; geography; history; liberal arts and sciences, general studies and humanities; mathematics; microbiology/bacteriology; music; philosophy; political science and government; psychology; social psychology.

ST. PHILIP'S COLLEGE

San Antonio, Texas

http://www.accd.edu/spc/

St. Philip's College was founded in 1898. It is accredited by Southern Association of Colleges and Schools. It first offered distance learning courses in 1991. In fall 2003, there were 2,000 students enrolled in distance learning courses. Institutionally administered financial aid is available to distance learners.

Services Distance learners have accessibility to academic advising, bookstore, library services, tutoring.

Contact Mr. David Bolton Mead, Coordinator of Distance Learning, St. Philip's College, 1801 Martin Luther King Drive, San Antonio, TX 78203. *Telephone:* 210-351-3442. *Fax:* 210-531-3513. *E-mail:* dmead@accd.edu.

DEGREES AND AWARDS

Programs offered do not lead to a degree or other formal award.

SALEM COMMUNITY COLLEGE

Carneys Point, New Jersey

http://www.salemcc.edu

Salem Community College was founded in 1972. It is accredited by Middle States Association of Colleges and Schools. It first offered distance learning courses in 1997. In fall 2003, there were 170 students enrolled in distance learning courses. Institutionally administered financial aid is available to distance learners.

Services Distance learners have accessibility to academic advising, bookstore, campus computer network, e-mail services, library services, tutoring.

Contact Mr. Mike Burbine, Associate Dean, Academic Affairs, Salem Community College, 460 Hollywood Avenue, Carneys Point, NJ 08069. *Telephone:* 856-351-2642. *E-mail:* burbine@salemcc.edu.

DEGREES AND AWARDS

Programs offered do not lead to a degree or other formal award.

COURSE SUBJECT AREAS OFFERED OUTSIDE OF DEGREE PROGRAMS

Undergraduate—business administration and management; computer/information technology administration and management; computer systems networking and telecommunications; economics; history; individual and family development studies; psychology; sociology; speech and rhetorical studies.

Non-credit—business communications; teacher education, specific academic and vocational programs.

SALVE REGINA UNIVERSITY

Newport, Rhode Island

Extension Study

http://www.salve.edu

Salve Regina University was founded in 1934. It is accredited by New England Association of Schools and Colleges. It first offered distance learning courses in 1985. In fall 2003, there were 300 students enrolled in distance learning courses. Institutionally administered financial aid is available to distance learners.

Services Distance learners have accessibility to academic advising, bookstore, campus computer network, career placement assistance, e-mail services, library services.

Contact Charles H. Reed, Director of Extension Studies, Salve Regina University, 100 Ochre Point Avenue, Newport, RI 02840-4192. *Telephone:* 401-341-2212. *Fax:* 401-341-2931. *E-mail:* reedc@salve.edu.

DEGREES AND AWARDS

BA Liberal Studies
BS Business
Certificate Management and Correctional Administration; Management
MA International Relations
MBA Business Administration
MS Management

COURSE SUBJECT AREAS OFFERED OUTSIDE OF DEGREE PROGRAMS

Graduate—business; business administration and management; health and medical administrative services; international relations and affairs; rehabilitation/therapeutic services.

Non-credit—business; health and medical administrative services; human resources management.

See full description on page 514.

SAM HOUSTON STATE UNIVERSITY

Huntsville, Texas

Correspondence Course Division

http://www.shsu.edu/~cor_www

Sam Houston State University was founded in 1879. It is accredited by Southern Association of Colleges and Schools. It first offered distance learning courses in 1953. In fall 2003, there were 1,900 students enrolled in distance learning courses. Institutionally administered financial aid is available to distance learners.

Services Distance learners have accessibility to academic advising, bookstore, campus computer network, e-mail services, library services, tutoring.

Contact Gail M. Wright, Correspondence Course Coordinator, Sam Houston State University, Box 2536, Huntsville, TX 77341-2536. *Telephone:* 936-294-1003. *Fax:* 936-294-3703. *E-mail:* cor_gmw@shsu.edu.

DEGREES AND AWARDS

Programs offered do not lead to a degree or other formal award.

COURSE SUBJECT AREAS OFFERED OUTSIDE OF DEGREE PROGRAMS

Undergraduate—accounting; American history; anthropology; business marketing and marketing management; creative writing; economics; family/consumer resource management; finance; geography; inorganic chemistry; insurance/risk management; law and legal studies related; mathematics related; organic chemistry; photography; sociology.

SAMUEL MERRITT COLLEGE

Oakland, California
Academic Affairs
http://www.samuelmerritt.edu

Samuel Merritt College was founded in 1909. It is accredited by Western Association of Schools and Colleges. It first offered distance learning courses in 2001. In fall 2003, there were 22 students enrolled in distance learning courses. Institutionally administered financial aid is available to distance learners.

Services Distance learners have accessibility to academic advising, e-mail services, library services, tutoring.

Contact Mr. John Garten-Shuman, Dean of Enrollment Services, Samuel Merritt College, Bechtel Hall, 370 Hawthorne Avenue, Oakland, CA 94609. *Telephone:* 800-607-6377. *Fax:* 510-869-6525. *E-mail:* jgartens@samuelmerritt.edu.

DEGREES AND AWARDS

MSN Nursing

SAN BERNARDINO VALLEY COLLEGE

San Bernardino, California
Distance Education Office
http://www.valleycollege.net

San Bernardino Valley College was founded in 1926. It is accredited by Western Association of Schools and Colleges. It first offered distance learning courses in 1986. In fall 2003, there were 1,202 students enrolled in distance learning courses. Institutionally administered financial aid is available to distance learners.

Services Distance learners have accessibility to bookstore, campus computer network, career placement assistance, e-mail services, library services, tutoring.

Contact Silvia Silvestrini, Secretary, Distributed Education, San Bernardino Valley College, 275 South Memorial Drive, Suite 129, San Bernardino, CA 92408. *Telephone:* 909-384-4325. *Fax:* 909-382-6085. *E-mail:* ssilvest@sbccd.cc.ca.us.

DEGREES AND AWARDS

AA Liberal Arts

COURSE SUBJECT AREAS OFFERED OUTSIDE OF DEGREE PROGRAMS

Undergraduate—accounting; anthropology; astronomy; biology, general; business; business administration and management; business management and administrative services, other; chemistry; communications, other; economics; English language and literature, general; family and community studies; fine arts and art studies; geography; geological and related sciences; liberal arts and sciences, general studies and humanities; mathematics, other; ocean engineering; philosophy; philosophy and religion; physical sciences, general; political science and government; psychology, other; radio and television broadcasting; religion/religious studies; social sciences and history, other; sociology; speech and rhetorical studies.

SAN JACINTO COLLEGE DISTRICT

Pasadena, Texas
Distance Learning
http://www.sjcd.edu

San Jacinto College District was founded in 1961. It is accredited by Southern Association of Colleges and Schools. It first offered distance learning courses in 1997. In fall 2003, there were 2,677 students enrolled in distance learning courses. Institutionally administered financial aid is available to distance learners.

Services Distance learners have accessibility to academic advising, bookstore, career placement assistance, library services, tutoring.

Contact Dr. Ken Dvorak, Director, Distance Learning, San Jacinto College District, 4111 Fairmont Parkway, Suite 110, Pasadena, TX 77504. *Telephone:* 281-998-6110. *Fax:* 281-998-6362. *E-mail:* ken.dvorak@sjcd.edu.

DEGREES AND AWARDS

Programs offered do not lead to a degree or other formal award.

COURSE SUBJECT AREAS OFFERED OUTSIDE OF DEGREE PROGRAMS

Undergraduate—accounting; advertising; American literature (United States); applied mathematics; business; child care and guidance workers and managers; computer and information sciences, general; computer software and media applications; criminology; English composition; English literature (British and Commonwealth); English technical and business writing; family and community studies; fine arts and art studies; fire protection; health professions and related sciences, other; Internet and World Wide Web; marketing management and research; mathematics; music; philosophy; psychology; public administration; real estate; social sciences and history, other; sociology.

SANTA FE COMMUNITY COLLEGE

Gainesville, Florida
http://www.sfcc.edu

Santa Fe Community College was founded in 1966. It is accredited by Southern Association of Colleges and Schools. It first offered distance learning courses in 1998. In fall 2003, there were 2,000 students enrolled in distance learning courses. Institutionally administered financial aid is available to distance learners.

Services Distance learners have accessibility to academic advising, bookstore, career placement assistance, library services.

Contact Harley Smith, Director, Santa Fe Community College, Education Media, 3000 Northwest 83rd Street, Gainesville, FL 32606. *Telephone:* 352-395-5427. *Fax:* 352-395-5945. *E-mail:* harley.smith@santafe.cc.fl.us.

DEGREES AND AWARDS

Programs offered do not lead to a degree or other formal award.

Santa Fe Community College (continued)

COURSE SUBJECT AREAS OFFERED OUTSIDE OF DEGREE PROGRAMS

Undergraduate—applied mathematics; archaeology; astronomy; business; clinical psychology; English language and literature, general; foreign languages and literatures; geological and related sciences; health and medical administrative services; music; physical sciences, general; sociology; visual and performing arts.

Non-credit—accounting; administrative and secretarial services; advertising; agricultural business and management; botany; business administration and management; business communications; business information and data processing services; child care and guidance workers and managers; communications, general; community health services; comparative literature; computer/information technology administration and management; computer programming; computer software and media applications; computer systems analysis; computer systems networking and telecommunications; construction management; crafts, folk art and artisanry; data entry/microcomputer applications; design and applied arts; dramatic/theater arts and stagecraft; East European languages and literatures; education administration and supervision; entrepreneurship; family and community studies; financial management and services; foreign languages and literatures; health and medical administrative services; health professions and related sciences, other; history; legal studies; marketing operations/marketing and distribution, other; miscellaneous health professions; parks, recreation, leisure and fitness studies, other; peace and conflict studies; plant sciences; public relations and organizational communications; special education; teaching English as a second language/foreign language.

SANTA ROSA JUNIOR COLLEGE

Santa Rosa, California

http://online.santarosa.edu/

Santa Rosa Junior College was founded in 1918. It is accredited by Western Association of Schools and Colleges. It first offered distance learning courses in 1989. In fall 2003, there were 4,600 students enrolled in distance learning courses. Institutionally administered financial aid is available to distance learners.

Services Distance learners have accessibility to academic advising, bookstore, campus computer network, e-mail services, library services.

Contact Dr. Richard Sapanaro, Director of Open Learning, Santa Rosa Junior College, 1501 Mendocino Avenue, Santa Rosa, CA 95401. *Telephone:* 707-524-1757. *Fax:* 707-521-7922. *E-mail:* rsapanaro@santarosa.edu.

DEGREES AND AWARDS

Programs offered do not lead to a degree or other formal award.

COURSE SUBJECT AREAS OFFERED OUTSIDE OF DEGREE PROGRAMS

Undergraduate—accounting; administrative and secretarial services; anthropology; astronomy; atmospheric sciences and meteorology; business; business administration and management; business communications; business marketing and marketing management; child care and guidance workers and managers; communications, general; communications, other; communications technologies; computer and information sciences, general; computer and information sciences, other; computer programming; computer science; computer software and media applications; computer systems networking and telecommunications; counseling psychology; criminal justice and corrections; criminology; culinary arts and related services; English composition; English creative writing; English language and literature, general; family and community studies; food sciences and technology; foreign languages and literatures, other; graphic and printing equipment operators; health and medical assistants; health professions and related sciences, other; journalism and mass communications; liberal arts and sciences, general studies and humanities; library science/librarianship; library science, other; philosophy; psychology; psychology, other; real estate; sociology; telecommunications; visual and performing arts.

Non-credit—English creative writing.

SANTIAGO CANYON COLLEGE

Orange, California

Santiago Canyon College was founded in 2000. It is accredited by Western Association of Schools and Colleges. In fall 2003, there were 1,500 students enrolled in distance learning courses. Institutionally administered financial aid is available to distance learners.

Services Distance learners have accessibility to academic advising, bookstore, campus computer network, career placement assistance, e-mail services, library services, tutoring.

Contact Ms. Bonnie Slager, Coordinator of Distance Learning, Santiago Canyon College, 8045 East Chapman Avenue, Orange, CA 92869. *Telephone:* 714-628-4753. *E-mail:* slager_bonnie@sccollege.edu.

DEGREES AND AWARDS

Programs offered do not lead to a degree or other formal award.

COURSE SUBJECT AREAS OFFERED OUTSIDE OF DEGREE PROGRAMS

Undergraduate—accounting; business; business administration and management; business and personal services marketing operations; business information and data processing services; business management and administrative services, other; computer and information sciences, general; human services; psychology; real estate.

SAUK VALLEY COMMUNITY COLLEGE

Dixon, Illinois

http://www.svcc.edu/

Sauk Valley Community College was founded in 1965. It is accredited by North Central Association of Colleges and Schools. It first offered distance learning courses in 1993. In fall 2003, there were 217 students enrolled in distance learning courses. Institutionally administered financial aid is available to distance learners.

Services Distance learners have accessibility to academic advising, bookstore, career placement assistance, e-mail services, library services, tutoring.

Contact Alan Pfeifer, Dean of Information Services, Sauk Valley Community College, 173 Illinois Route 2, Dixon, IL 61021. *Telephone:* 815-288-5511 Ext. 218. *Fax:* 815-288-5958. *E-mail:* pfeifer@svcc.edu.

DEGREES AND AWARDS

Programs offered do not lead to a degree or other formal award.

COURSE SUBJECT AREAS OFFERED OUTSIDE OF DEGREE PROGRAMS

Undergraduate—accounting; administrative and secretarial services; American history; biology; business; business administration and management; computer programming; criminal justice and corrections; criminology; economics; English composition; international business; mathematics related; psychology; sociology.
Non-credit—computer and information sciences, general.

SAVANNAH COLLEGE OF ART AND DESIGN

Savannah, Georgia

http://www.scad.edu

Savannah College of Art and Design was founded in 1978. It is accredited by Southern Association of Colleges and Schools. It first offered distance learning courses in 2003. In fall 2003, there were 24 students enrolled in distance learning courses. Institutionally administered financial aid is available to distance learners.

Services Distance learners have accessibility to academic advising, bookstore, campus computer network, career placement assistance, e-mail services, library services, tutoring.
Contact Ms. Eve Seibert, Director of Recruitment, Savannah College of Art and Design, PO Box 3146, Savannah, GA 31402-3146. *Telephone:* 912-525-5100. *Fax:* 912-525-5986. *E-mail:* eseibert@scad.edu.

DEGREES AND AWARDS

Certificate Digital Publishing
Graduate Certificate Digital Publishing; Historic Preservation; Interactive Design
MA Graphic Design; Historic Preservation

COURSE SUBJECT AREAS OFFERED OUTSIDE OF DEGREE PROGRAMS

Undergraduate—fine arts and art studies.
Graduate—fine arts and art studies.

See full description on page 516.

SAYBROOK GRADUATE SCHOOL AND RESEARCH CENTER

San Francisco, California

http://www.saybrook.edu/

Saybrook Graduate School and Research Center was founded in 1970. It is accredited by Western Association of Schools and Colleges. It first offered distance learning courses in 1971. In fall 2003, there were 525 students enrolled in distance learning courses. Institutionally administered financial aid is available to distance learners.

Services Distance learners have accessibility to academic advising, bookstore, campus computer network, library services.
Contact Mr. Geoffrey R. Smith, Dean of Admissions, Saybrook Graduate School and Research Center, 450 Pacific Avenue, San Francisco, CA 94133-4640. *Telephone:* 800-825-4480. *Fax:* 415-433-9271. *E-mail:* admissions@saybrook.edu.

DEGREES AND AWARDS

Graduate Certificate Building a Sustainable World; Community Health and Development; Creativity Studies; Expressive Arts for Healing and Social Change; Leading Organizational Transformation; Organizational Consulting; Peace and Conflict Resolution (International Focus); Socially Engaged Spirituality; Violence Prevention and Response
MA Human Science; Leadership and Organizational Transformation (Weekend Program); Marriage and Family Therapy; Organizational Systems; Psychology
PhD Doctoral Completion Program; Human Science; Organizational Studies; Police and Public Safety Psychology (CopDoc); Psychology

COURSE SUBJECT AREAS OFFERED OUTSIDE OF DEGREE PROGRAMS

Graduate—clinical psychology; cognitive psychology and psycholinguistics; community organization, resources and services; community psychology; counseling psychology; developmental and child psychology; family and community studies; gerontology; individual and family development studies; industrial and organizational psychology; peace and conflict studies; psychology; psychology, other; social psychology.
Non-credit—financial management and services; industrial and organizational psychology; psychology; psychology, other.

See full description on page 518.

SCHENECTADY COUNTY COMMUNITY COLLEGE

Schenectady, New York

http://www.sunysccc.edu

Schenectady County Community College was founded in 1969. It is accredited by Middle States Association of Colleges and Schools. It first offered distance learning courses in 1998. In fall 2003, there were 283 students enrolled in distance learning courses. Institutionally administered financial aid is available to distance learners.

Services Distance learners have accessibility to academic advising, bookstore, campus computer network, e-mail services, library services, tutoring.
Contact Mary Clare O'Connor, Associate for Continuing Education, Schenectady County Community College, 78 Washington Avenue, Schenectady, NY 12305. *Telephone:* 518-381-1315. *E-mail:* oconnomc@gw.sunysccc.edu.

DEGREES AND AWARDS

Programs offered do not lead to a degree or other formal award.

COURSE SUBJECT AREAS OFFERED OUTSIDE OF DEGREE PROGRAMS

Undergraduate—accounting; astronomy; business administration and management; child care and guidance workers and managers; computer software and media applications; culinary arts and related services; English composition; English technical and business writing; enterprise management and operation; fire protection; history; hospitality services management; legal studies; mathematics; music.

SCHILLER INTERNATIONAL UNIVERSITY

Dunedin, Florida

http://www.schiller.edu/

Schiller International University was founded in 1991. It is accredited by Accrediting Council for Independent Colleges and Schools. It first offered distance learning courses in 1999. In fall 2003, there were 94 students enrolled in distance learning courses. Institutionally administered financial aid is available to distance learners.

Services Distance learners have accessibility to academic advising, bookstore, career placement assistance, e-mail services, library services.

Contact Ms. Susan Russeff, Associate Director of Admissions, Schiller International University, 453 Edgewater Drive, Dunedin, FL 34698. *Telephone:* 727-736-5082 Ext. 239. *Fax:* 727-734-0359. *E-mail:* admissions@schiller.edu.

DEGREES AND AWARDS

MBA Management of Information Technology
MBAIB International Business and Management of Information Technology

COURSE SUBJECT AREAS OFFERED OUTSIDE OF DEGREE PROGRAMS

Undergraduate—accounting; business; business administration and management; business communications; business/managerial economics; English composition; history; human resources management; international business; international relations and affairs; marketing management and research; mathematical statistics; mathematics; physical sciences, general; psychology.
Graduate—accounting; business administration and management; business communications; business/managerial economics; computer/information technology administration and management; financial management and services; hospitality services management; human resources management; industrial and organizational psychology; international business; legal studies; marketing management and research; mathematical statistics; tourism/travel marketing.

See full description on page 520.

SCHOOLCRAFT COLLEGE

Livonia, Michigan

Distance Learning Office

http://www.schoolcraft.edu/distance

Schoolcraft College was founded in 1961. It is accredited by North Central Association of Colleges and Schools. It first offered distance learning courses in 1982. In fall 2003, there were 2,339 students enrolled in distance learning courses. Institutionally administered financial aid is available to distance learners.

Services Distance learners have accessibility to academic advising, bookstore, career placement assistance, library services, tutoring.
Contact Dr. William J. Rugg,, Director, Distance and Distributed Learning, Schoolcraft College, Distance Learning Office, 18600 Haggerty Road, Livonia, MI 48152-2696. *Telephone:* 734-462-4801. *Fax:* 734-462-4589. *E-mail:* wrugg@schoolcraft.edu.

DEGREES AND AWARDS

AA Liberal Arts; OMNIBUS
AGS Liberal Arts

COURSE SUBJECT AREAS OFFERED OUTSIDE OF DEGREE PROGRAMS

Undergraduate—accounting; advertising; American literature (United States); anthropology; astronomy; biological sciences/life sciences, other; business; communications, general; computer science; developmental/child psychology; economics; engineering, general; English composition; English language and literature/letters, other; fine arts and art studies; mathematics; music; philosophy and religion; psychology; sociology; speech and rhetorical studies.
Non-credit—community health services; computer programming; computer software and media applications.

SEATTLE CENTRAL COMMUNITY COLLEGE

Seattle, Washington

Distance Learning Program

http://www.seattlecentral.edu/distance

Seattle Central Community College was founded in 1966. It is accredited by Northwest Commission on Colleges and Universities. It first offered distance learning courses in 1990. In fall 2003, there were 600 students enrolled in distance learning courses. Institutionally administered financial aid is available to distance learners.

Services Distance learners have accessibility to academic advising, bookstore, campus computer network, e-mail services, library services.
Contact Ms. Queenie L. Baker, Director, Seattle Central Community College, 1701 Broadway, BE1142, Seattle, WA 98122-2400. *Telephone:* 800-510-1724. *Fax:* 206-287-5562. *E-mail:* qbaker@sccd.ctc.edu.

DEGREES AND AWARDS

AA General Program; Liberal Arts

COURSE SUBJECT AREAS OFFERED OUTSIDE OF DEGREE PROGRAMS

Undergraduate—accounting; American studies; anthropology; Asian studies; developmental/child psychology; English composition; environmental science; film studies; geography; journalism; journalism and mass communication related; mathematical statistics; mathematics related; medieval/Renaissance studies; oceanography; philosophy and religion related; sociology; Spanish.

Special Message

Since its founding in 1967, Seattle Central Community College has developed into a school with a national reputation for innovative educational programs. Located in Seattle, Washington, Seattle Central is one of the largest colleges in the state, with an enrollment of 10,000 students. The College is unique among the state's community colleges for its ethnic and cultural diversity. Each year, more students from Seattle Central go on to 4-year institutions than from any other community college in the state.

If the ultimate goal is a 4-year degree, the Associate of Arts (AA) degree via distance learning provides freshman- and sophomore-level classes recognized by most universities. For those not sure about college, distance learning may help them decide. Students can enroll via distance learning in an individual course that interests them or helps improve their knowledge and skills and earn credit toward an

AA degree, or they can earn a certificate in a specific technical area. There are several reasons why distance learning may work for students, including those with a work or home schedule conflict, disability or homebound situation, lifestyle preferences, traffic gridlock, or a residence too far from a college. It can also be a good match with the student's learning style or simply be more convenient.

Seattle Central's distance learning program offers courses in a variety of formats, including correspondence courses, telecourses, videocassette courses, and online courses.

For more information, students should contact the Distance Learning Program at 800-510-1724 (toll-free) or by e-mail (dislrn@sccd.ctc.edu) or visit the home page (http://seattlecentral.edu/distance).

SEATTLE PACIFIC UNIVERSITY

Seattle, Washington

School of Education

http://www.spu.edu/connection

Seattle Pacific University was founded in 1891. It is accredited by Northwest Commission on Colleges and Universities. It first offered distance learning courses in 1984. In fall 2003, there were 420 students enrolled in distance learning courses. Institutionally administered financial aid is available to distance learners.

Services Distance learners have accessibility to bookstore, campus computer network, e-mail services, library services.

Contact Megan Hamshar, Distance Learning Program Coordinator, Seattle Pacific University, 3307 Third Avenue West, Suite 215, Seattle, WA 98119-1950. *Telephone:* 800-482-3848. *Fax:* 206-281-2271. *E-mail:* connect@spu.edu.

DEGREES AND AWARDS

MEd Curriculum and Instruction–Online

COURSE SUBJECT AREAS OFFERED OUTSIDE OF DEGREE PROGRAMS

Graduate—American history; astronomy; bilingual/bicultural education; curriculum and instruction; education, general; general teacher education; geography; history; Internet and World Wide Web; library science/librarianship; parks, recreation and leisure studies; special education; teacher education, specific academic and vocational programs; teaching English as a second language/foreign language.

SEMINOLE COMMUNITY COLLEGE

Sanford, Florida

Distance Learning Department

http://www.scc-fl.edu/dl

Seminole Community College was founded in 1966. It is accredited by Southern Association of Colleges and Schools. It first offered distance learning courses in 1970. In fall 2003, there were 2,500 students enrolled in distance learning courses. Institutionally administered financial aid is available to distance learners.

Services Distance learners have accessibility to academic advising, bookstore, career placement assistance, e-mail services, library services.

Contact Mrs. Lillie Gibson, Distance Learning Support Specialist, Seminole Community College, 100 Weldon Boulevard, Sanford, FL 32773. *Telephone:* 407-328-2424. *Fax:* 407-328-2233. *E-mail:* gibsonl@scc-fl.edu.

DEGREES AND AWARDS

AS Computer Information Technology; Computer Programming and Analysis (C++ Programming Specialization); Computer Programming and Analysis

Certificate Microsoft Certified Systems Administrator

Technical Certificate Accounting Applications; Microsoft Certified Systems Engineer; Office Support

COURSE SUBJECT AREAS OFFERED OUTSIDE OF DEGREE PROGRAMS

Undergraduate—accounting; administrative and secretarial services; anthropology; applied mathematics; area, ethnic and cultural studies, other; astronomy; atmospheric sciences and meteorology; biological and physical sciences; biology, general; business administration and management; business communications; business information and data processing services; business management and administrative services, other; computer and information sciences, general; computer and information sciences, other; computer/information technology administration and management; computer programming; computer science; computer software and media applications; computer systems analysis; computer systems networking and telecommunications; criminal justice and corrections; criminology; data entry/microcomputer applications; data processing technology; developmental and child psychology; economics; education, general; electrical and electronic engineering-related technology; electrical and electronics equipment installers and repairers; English composition; English technical and business writing; family and community studies; geography; geological and related sciences; health and medical administrative services; health and medical assistants; health and medical preparatory programs; health professions and related sciences, other; history; legal studies; liberal arts and sciences, general studies and humanities; library science/librarianship; library science, other; mathematical statistics; mathematics; miscellaneous health professions; music; psychology; social psychology; social sciences, general; sociology; teacher education, specific academic and vocational programs.

Non-credit—health and medical administrative services; protective services, other.

SEQUOIA INSTITUTE

Fremont, California

http://www.sequoiainstitute.com/

Sequoia Institute was founded in 1966. It is accredited by Accrediting Commission of Career Schools and Colleges of Technology. It first offered distance learning courses in 2000. In fall 2003, there were 123 students enrolled in distance learning courses. Institutionally administered financial aid is available to distance learners.

Services Distance learners have accessibility to academic advising, e-mail services.

Contact Ms. Joseph L. File, Director of Admissions, Sequoia Institute, 200 Whitney Place, Fremont, CA 94539-7663. *Telephone:* 510-580-3507. *E-mail:* jfile@sequoiainstitute.com.

DEGREES AND AWARDS

Programs offered do not lead to a degree or other formal award.

SETON HALL UNIVERSITY

South Orange, New Jersey
SetonWorldWide
http://www.setonworldwide.net

Seton Hall University was founded in 1856. It is accredited by Middle States Association of Colleges and Schools. It first offered distance learning courses in 1998. In fall 2003, there were 350 students enrolled in distance learning courses. Institutionally administered financial aid is available to distance learners.

Services Distance learners have accessibility to academic advising, bookstore, campus computer network, career placement assistance, e-mail services, library services.

Contact Ms. Cindy Jimenez, Program Coordinator, Seton Hall University, Kozlowski Hall, 400 South Orange Avenue, South Orange, NJ 07079. *Telephone:* 973-761-9087. *Fax:* 973-761-9325. *E-mail:* setonworldwide@shu.edu.

DEGREES AND AWARDS

BSN Nursing–RN to BSN
MA Counseling; Educational Administration and Supervision; Strategic Communication and Leadership
MHA Healthcare Administration
MSN Nurse Practitioner

See full description on page 522.

SETON HILL UNIVERSITY

Greensburg, Pennsylvania
Academic Affairs
http://www.setonhill.edu

Seton Hill University was founded in 1883. It is accredited by Middle States Association of Colleges and Schools. It first offered distance learning courses in 1999. In fall 2003, there were 100 students enrolled in distance learning courses. Institutionally administered financial aid is available to distance learners.

Services Distance learners have accessibility to academic advising, bookstore, campus computer network, career placement assistance, e-mail services, library services, tutoring.

Contact Ms. Mary Kay Cooper, Director of Admissions and Adult Student Services, Seton Hill University, 1 Seton Hill Drive, Greensburg, PA 15601. *Telephone:* 724-830-4639. *Fax:* 724-830-1294. *E-mail:* mcooper@setonhill.edu.

DEGREES AND AWARDS

Programs offered do not lead to a degree or other formal award.

COURSE SUBJECT AREAS OFFERED OUTSIDE OF DEGREE PROGRAMS

Undergraduate—business; communications, other; computer and information sciences, general; history; human resources management; political science and government; psychology; religion/religious studies.
Graduate—accounting; communications technologies; educational/instructional media design; English creative writing.
Non-credit—hospitality/recreation marketing; human resources management.

SEWARD COUNTY COMMUNITY COLLEGE

Liberal, Kansas
http://www.sccc.edu

Seward County Community College was founded in 1969. It is accredited by North Central Association of Colleges and Schools. It first offered distance learning courses in 1992. In fall 2003, there were 115 students enrolled in distance learning courses. Institutionally administered financial aid is available to distance learners.

Services Distance learners have accessibility to academic advising, bookstore, e-mail services.

Contact Mr. Dale L. Reed, Associate Dean of Educational Services, Seward County Community College, PO Box 1137, Liberal, KS 67905. *Telephone:* 620-626-3137. *Fax:* 620-629-2715. *E-mail:* dreed@sccc.edu.

DEGREES AND AWARDS

Programs offered do not lead to a degree or other formal award.

COURSE SUBJECT AREAS OFFERED OUTSIDE OF DEGREE PROGRAMS

Undergraduate—accounting; advertising; agriculture/agricultural sciences; American literature (United States); biology, general; business information and data processing services; chemistry; communications, general; computer/information technology administration and management; computer software and media applications; economics; English composition; geography; history; mathematical statistics; mathematics; psychology.

SHASTA BIBLE COLLEGE

Redding, California
Individualized Distance Learning
http://www.shasta.edu

Shasta Bible College was founded in 1971. It is accredited by Transnational Association of Christian Colleges and Schools. It first offered distance learning courses in 1999. In fall 2003, there were 9 students enrolled in distance learning courses. Institutionally administered financial aid is available to distance learners.

Services Distance learners have accessibility to academic advising, bookstore, campus computer network, career placement assistance, e-mail services.

Contact Pastor George Gunn, Dean of Admissions and Records, Shasta Bible College, 2951 Goodwater Avenue, Redding, CA 96002. *Telephone:* 530-221-4275. *Fax:* 530-221-6929. *E-mail:* ggunn@shasta.edu.

DEGREES AND AWARDS

Programs offered do not lead to a degree or other formal award.

COURSE SUBJECT AREAS OFFERED OUTSIDE OF DEGREE PROGRAMS

Undergraduate—education, other; religion/religious studies.
Graduate—education administration and supervision.
Non-credit—bible/biblical studies.

SHAWNEE STATE UNIVERSITY

Portsmouth, Ohio
Department of Nursing
http://www.shawnee.edu/acadamics/hsc/nurs/index.html

Shawnee State University was founded in 1986. It is accredited by North Central Association of Colleges and Schools. In fall 2003, there were 42 students enrolled in distance learning courses. Institutionally administered financial aid is available to distance learners.

Services Distance learners have accessibility to bookstore, e-mail services, library services.
Contact Dr. Gayle Massie, Acting Chair, 4 Year Nursing Program, Shawnee State University, 940 Second Street, Health Sciences Building, Room 122, Portsmouth, OH 45662. *Telephone:* 740-351-3382. *E-mail:* gmassie@shawnee.edu.

DEGREES AND AWARDS

Programs offered do not lead to a degree or other formal award.

COURSE SUBJECT AREAS OFFERED OUTSIDE OF DEGREE PROGRAMS

Undergraduate—accounting; anthropology; biology, general; business administration and management; business information and data processing services; chemistry; computer and information sciences, general; computer engineering; computer programming; education, general; electromechanical instrumentation and maintenance technology; English as a second language; English language and literature, general; environmental control technologies; fine arts and art studies; foreign languages and literatures, other; geography; health and medical assistants; health and physical education/fitness; history; journalism and mass communications; legal studies; mathematics; medical laboratory technology; music; nursing; philosophy; physical sciences, general; political science and government; psychology; social sciences and history, other; social sciences, general; sociology; visual and performing arts.

SHELTON STATE COMMUNITY COLLEGE

Tuscaloosa, Alabama
http://www.sheltonstate.edu/sscc/info/distance/index.html

Shelton State Community College was founded in 1979. It is accredited by Southern Association of Colleges and Schools. It first offered distance learning courses in 2001. In fall 2003, there were 400 students enrolled in distance learning courses. Institutionally administered financial aid is available to distance learners.

Services Distance learners have accessibility to academic advising, bookstore, campus computer network, e-mail services, library services.
Contact Ms. Sara W. Brenizer, Coordinator, Distance Education, Shelton State Community College, 9500 Old Greensboro Road, Tuscaloosa, AL 35405. *Telephone:* 205-391-2296. *Fax:* 205-391-2205. *E-mail:* sbrenizer@sheltonstate.edu.

DEGREES AND AWARDS

Programs offered do not lead to a degree or other formal award.

COURSE SUBJECT AREAS OFFERED OUTSIDE OF DEGREE PROGRAMS

Undergraduate—biological sciences/life sciences, other; business; chemistry; computer and information sciences, general; geography; health professions and related sciences, other; history; legal studies; sociology.

SHENANDOAH UNIVERSITY

Winchester, Virginia
School of Continuing Education
http://www.su.edu/cont-ed

Shenandoah University was founded in 1875. It is accredited by Southern Association of Colleges and Schools. It first offered distance learning courses in 1988. In fall 2003, there were 1,500 students enrolled in distance learning courses. Institutionally administered financial aid is available to distance learners.

Services Distance learners have accessibility to academic advising, bookstore, career placement assistance, e-mail services, library services.
Contact Dr. Diane E. Melby, Director of Continuing Education, Shenandoah University, 1460 University Drive, Winchester, VA 22601. *Telephone:* 540-665-4643. *Fax:* 540-665-3496. *E-mail:* dmelby@su.edu.

DEGREES AND AWARDS

Programs offered do not lead to a degree or other formal award.

COURSE SUBJECT AREAS OFFERED OUTSIDE OF DEGREE PROGRAMS

Undergraduate—computer and information sciences, general; computer engineering; computer software and media applications; computer systems networking and telecommunications; legal studies; pharmacy; tourism/travel marketing.
Graduate—education administration and supervision; educational psychology; education, general; education, other.

SHIPPENSBURG UNIVERSITY OF PENNSYLVANIA

Shippensburg, Pennsylvania
Extended Studies
http://www.ship.edu/extended/

Shippensburg University of Pennsylvania was founded in 1871. It is accredited by Middle States Association of Colleges and Schools. It first offered distance learning courses in 1998. In fall 2003, there were 115 students enrolled in distance learning courses. Institutionally administered financial aid is available to distance learners.

Services Distance learners have accessibility to academic advising, bookstore, campus computer network, career placement assistance, e-mail services, library services, tutoring.
Contact Dr. Kathleen Howley, Dean of Extended Studies, Shippensburg University of Pennsylvania, 1871 Old Main Drive, Shippensburg, PA 17257-2299. *Telephone:* 717-477-1348. *Fax:* 717-477-4050. *E-mail:* extended@ship.edu.

Shippensburg University of Pennsylvania (continued)

DEGREES AND AWARDS

MBA Business Administration
MS Applied Gerontology
MSIS Information Systems

COURSE SUBJECT AREAS OFFERED OUTSIDE OF DEGREE PROGRAMS

Undergraduate—communications, general; criminal justice and corrections; economics; English language and literature, general; geography; gerontology; international business; marketing management and research; mathematics; philosophy; physics; psychology; social work; speech and rhetorical studies.
Graduate—accounting; business administration and management; business information and data processing services; communications, general; criminal justice and corrections; English creative writing; English language and literature, general; entrepreneurship; gerontology; information sciences and systems; international business; psychology.

SHORELINE COMMUNITY COLLEGE

Shoreline, Washington
http://success.shoreline.edu/distance/

Shoreline Community College was founded in 1964. It is accredited by Northwest Commission on Colleges and Universities. It first offered distance learning courses in 1997. In fall 2003, there were 755 students enrolled in distance learning courses. Institutionally administered financial aid is available to distance learners.

Services Distance learners have accessibility to academic advising, bookstore, career placement assistance, e-mail services, library services, tutoring.
Contact Dr. Ann Garnsey-Harter, Distance Learning Coordinator, Shoreline Community College, Distance Learning Services, 16101 Greenwood Avenue North, Shoreline, WA 98133. *Telephone:* 206-546-6966. *Fax:* 206-546-4604. *E-mail:* dl@shoreline.edu.

DEGREES AND AWARDS

Certificate of Completion Accounting Clerk; Accounts Receivable/Payable Clerk; Payroll Clerk
Certificate Accounting; Purchasing Management

COURSE SUBJECT AREAS OFFERED OUTSIDE OF DEGREE PROGRAMS

Undergraduate—accounting; area, ethnic and cultural studies, other; biological sciences/life sciences, other; business; business administration and management; business communications; computer and information sciences, general; criminal justice and corrections; English composition; geological and related sciences; health professions and related sciences, other; history; library science, other; mathematics; music; pharmacy; philosophy; psychology.
Non-credit—curriculum and instruction.

SIMPSON COLLEGE

Indianola, Iowa
Division of Adult Learning
http://www.simpson.edu/dal

Simpson College was founded in 1860. It is accredited by North Central Association of Colleges and Schools. It first offered distance learning courses in 1996. In fall 2003, there were 250 students enrolled in distance learning courses. Institutionally administered financial aid is available to distance learners.

Services Distance learners have accessibility to academic advising, bookstore, campus computer network, career placement assistance, e-mail services, library services.
Contact Walter Pearson, Director, Simpson College, 701 North C Street, Indianola, IA 50125. *Telephone:* 515-961-1615. *Fax:* 515-961-1498. *E-mail:* pearsonw@simpson.edu.

DEGREES AND AWARDS

Programs offered do not lead to a degree or other formal award.

COURSE SUBJECT AREAS OFFERED OUTSIDE OF DEGREE PROGRAMS

Undergraduate—accounting; communications, general; computer science; criminal justice and corrections; English language and literature, general; financial management and services; human resources management; journalism and mass communications; liberal arts and sciences, general studies and humanities; marketing management and research.
Graduate—teacher education, specific academic and vocational programs.

SINCLAIR COMMUNITY COLLEGE

Dayton, Ohio
Distance Learning Division
http://www.sinclair.edu/distance

Sinclair Community College was founded in 1887. It is accredited by North Central Association of Colleges and Schools. It first offered distance learning courses in 1979. In fall 2003, there were 5,000 students enrolled in distance learning courses. Institutionally administered financial aid is available to distance learners.

Services Distance learners have accessibility to academic advising, bookstore, career placement assistance, e-mail services, library services, tutoring.
Contact Ms. Dodie E. Munn, Academic Counselor, Sinclair Community College, Distance Learning and Instructional Support Division, Room 14222, 444 West Third Street, Dayton, OH 45402. *Telephone:* 937-512-2990. *Fax:* 937-512-2891. *E-mail:* distance@sinclair.edu.

DEGREES AND AWARDS

AA Liberal Arts and Sciences
AS Business Administration
Certificate Software Applications for the Professional
Certification Medical Office Coding Specialist; Radiologic Technology Continuing Education Units (CEUs)

COURSE SUBJECT AREAS OFFERED OUTSIDE OF DEGREE PROGRAMS

Undergraduate—accounting; administrative and secretarial services; anthropology; architectural engineering technology; art history; astronomy; business administration and management; business information and data processing services; business marketing and marketing management; chemistry; civil engineering/civil technology; communications, general; computer and information sciences, general; computer programming; computer software and media applications; computer systems networking and telecommunications; developmental/child psychology; drafting; economics; electrical engineering; English

as a second language; English composition; English creative writing; English technical and business writing; entrepreneurship; health and medical assistants; history; law and legal studies related; liberal arts and sciences, general studies and humanities; mathematics; miscellaneous health professions; photography; psychology; social psychology; sociology.
Non-credit—health professions and related sciences, other.

See full description on page 524.

SKIDMORE COLLEGE

Saratoga Springs, New York
University Without Walls
http://www.skidmore.edu/uww

Skidmore College was founded in 1903. It is accredited by Middle States Association of Colleges and Schools. It first offered distance learning courses in 1971. In fall 2003, there were 250 students enrolled in distance learning courses. Institutionally administered financial aid is available to distance learners.

Services Distance learners have accessibility to academic advising, bookstore, campus computer network, career placement assistance, e-mail services, library services, tutoring.
Contact Tracy Riley, Administrative Assistant, Skidmore College, University Without Walls, 815 North Broadway, Saratoga Springs, NY 12866. *Telephone:* 518-580-5450. *Fax:* 518-580-5449. *E-mail:* uww@skidmore.edu.

DEGREES AND AWARDS

BA Individualized Studies
BS Individualized Studies

COURSE SUBJECT AREAS OFFERED OUTSIDE OF DEGREE PROGRAMS

Undergraduate—accounting; American literature (United States); anthropology; archaeology; area, ethnic and cultural studies, other; biology; business administration and management; communications, general; creative writing; cultural studies; dance; developmental/child psychology; English composition; environmental health; French; geography; journalism; microbiology/bacteriology; social work; sociology.

See full description on page 526.

SKIDMORE COLLEGE

Saratoga Springs, New York
Graduate Programs
http://www.skidmore.edu/mals

Skidmore College was founded in 1903. It is accredited by Middle States Association of Colleges and Schools. It first offered distance learning courses in 1992. In fall 2003, there were 51 students enrolled in distance learning courses. Institutionally administered financial aid is available to distance learners.

Services Distance learners have accessibility to academic advising, bookstore, campus computer network, e-mail services, library services, tutoring.
Contact Dr. Daniel Coleman, Director of Master of Arts in Liberal Studies, Skidmore College, 850 Broadway, Saratoga Springs, NY 12866. *Telephone:* 518-580-5480. *Fax:* 518-580-5486. *E-mail:* dcoleman@skidmore.edu.

DEGREES AND AWARDS

Programs offered do not lead to a degree or other formal award.

COURSE SUBJECT AREAS OFFERED OUTSIDE OF DEGREE PROGRAMS

Graduate—liberal arts and sciences, general studies and humanities.

SLIPPERY ROCK UNIVERSITY OF PENNSYLVANIA

Slippery Rock, Pennsylvania
http://www.sru.edu/

Slippery Rock University of Pennsylvania was founded in 1889. It is accredited by Middle States Association of Colleges and Schools. It first offered distance learning courses in 1995. In fall 2003, there were 319 students enrolled in distance learning courses. Institutionally administered financial aid is available to distance learners.

Services Distance learners have accessibility to academic advising, bookstore, campus computer network, career placement assistance, e-mail services, library services, tutoring.
Contact Dr. James Kushner, Dean of Lifelong Learning, Slippery Rock University of Pennsylvania, 124 North Hall, Slippery Rock, PA 16057. *Telephone:* 724-738-4484. *Fax:* 724-738-2908. *E-mail:* james.kushner@sru.edu.

DEGREES AND AWARDS

BSN Nursing
MS Park and Resource Management
MSN Nursing–Family Nurse Practitioner Graduate Program

COURSE SUBJECT AREAS OFFERED OUTSIDE OF DEGREE PROGRAMS

Undergraduate—accounting; gerontology.
Graduate—educational/instructional media design; nursing; parks, recreation and leisure facilities management.

SNEAD STATE COMMUNITY COLLEGE

Boaz, Alabama
http://www.snead.edu/

Snead State Community College was founded in 1898. It is accredited by Southern Association of Colleges and Schools. It first offered distance learning courses in 1998. In fall 2003, there were 1,000 students enrolled in distance learning courses. Institutionally administered financial aid is available to distance learners.

Services Distance learners have accessibility to academic advising, bookstore, library services.
Contact Dr. Greg D. Chapman, EdD, Director of Instruction, Snead State Community College, PO Box 734, Boaz, AL 35957. *Telephone:* 256-840-4111. *Fax:* 256-593-7180. *E-mail:* gchapman@snead.edu.

DEGREES AND AWARDS

AS General Program

Snead State Community College (continued)

COURSE SUBJECT AREAS OFFERED OUTSIDE OF DEGREE PROGRAMS

Undergraduate—accounting; American literature (United States); atmospheric sciences and meteorology; bible/biblical studies; biological and physical sciences; biological sciences/life sciences, other; biology, general; business; business communications; chemistry; child care and guidance workers and managers; computer and information sciences, general; computer science; computer software and media applications; criminal justice and corrections; criminology; dramatic/theater arts and stagecraft; economics; English composition; English creative writing; English language and literature, general; English literature (British and Commonwealth); fine arts and art studies; foreign languages and literatures; geography; health and physical education/fitness; history; mathematical statistics; mathematics; mathematics and computer science; microbiology/bacteriology; miscellaneous physical sciences; music; nursing; physical sciences, general; physics; psychology; religion/religious studies; sociology; speech and rhetorical studies.

SONOMA STATE UNIVERSITY

Rohnert Park, California

Liberal Studies Special Sessions Degree Programs

http://www.sonoma.edu/exed/Degrees/dindex.html

Sonoma State University was founded in 1960. It is accredited by Western Association of Schools and Colleges. It first offered distance learning courses in 1996. In fall 2003, there were 120 students enrolled in distance learning courses. Institutionally administered financial aid is available to distance learners.

Services Distance learners have accessibility to academic advising, bookstore, campus computer network, career placement assistance, e-mail services, library services.

Contact Beth Warner, Administrative Coordinator, Sonoma State University, 1801 East Cotati Avenue, Rohnert Park, CA 94928-3609. *Telephone:* 707-664-3977. *Fax:* 707-664-2613. *E-mail:* beth.warner@sonoma.edu.

DEGREES AND AWARDS

BA Liberal Studies
MA Action for a Viable Future

COURSE SUBJECT AREAS OFFERED OUTSIDE OF DEGREE PROGRAMS

Undergraduate—educational/instructional media design.
Non-credit—business administration and management; business communications; business management and administrative services, other; computer/information technology administration and management; computer software and media applications; computer systems networking and telecommunications.

SOUTH CENTRAL TECHNICAL COLLEGE

North Mankato, Minnesota

http://southcentral.edu

South Central Technical College was founded in 1946. It is accredited by North Central Association of Colleges and Schools. It first offered distance learning courses in 2001. In fall 2003, there were 318 students enrolled in distance learning courses. Institutionally administered financial aid is available to distance learners.

Services Distance learners have accessibility to academic advising, bookstore, e-mail services, library services.

Contact Donna Marzolf, Registrar, South Central Technical College, 1920 Lee Boulevard, North Mankato, MN 56003. *Telephone:* 507-389-7351. *Fax:* 507-388-9951. *E-mail:* donna.marzolf@southcentral.edu.

DEGREES AND AWARDS

AAS Community Supports for People with Disabilities; Medical Laboratory Technician

COURSE SUBJECT AREAS OFFERED OUTSIDE OF DEGREE PROGRAMS

Undergraduate—accounting; business communications; chemistry; computer software and media applications; data entry/microcomputer applications; education, general; family and community studies; Internet and World Wide Web; marketing operations/marketing and distribution, other; medical laboratory technology; miscellaneous health professions; nursing.

SOUTH DAKOTA SCHOOL OF MINES AND TECHNOLOGY

Rapid City, South Dakota

http://www.sdsmt.edu

South Dakota School of Mines and Technology was founded in 1885. It is accredited by North Central Association of Colleges and Schools.

Services Distance learners have accessibility to academic advising, bookstore, campus computer network, e-mail services.

Contact South Dakota School of Mines and Technology.

DEGREES AND AWARDS

Programs offered do not lead to a degree or other formal award.

COURSE SUBJECT AREAS OFFERED OUTSIDE OF DEGREE PROGRAMS

Undergraduate—chemistry; geography.

SOUTHEAST ARKANSAS COLLEGE

Pine Bluff, Arkansas

http://www.seark.edu/

Southeast Arkansas College was founded in 1991. It is accredited by North Central Association of Colleges and Schools. It first offered distance learning courses in 1995. In fall 2003, there were 545 students enrolled in distance learning courses. Institutionally administered financial aid is available to distance learners.

Services Distance learners have accessibility to bookstore, e-mail services, library services.

Contact Kim Brown-King, Coordinator of Distance Learning, Southeast Arkansas College, 1900 Hazel Street, Pine Bluff, AR 71603. *Telephone:* 870-543-5992. *Fax:* 870-543-5937. *E-mail:* kbrown-king@seark.edu.

DEGREES AND AWARDS

Programs offered do not lead to a degree or other formal award.

COURSE SUBJECT AREAS OFFERED OUTSIDE OF DEGREE PROGRAMS

Undergraduate—anthropology; applied mathematics; business; business administration and management; business communications; business management and administrative services, other; business/managerial economics; computer/information technology administration and management; computer science; criminal justice and corrections; criminology; economics; English composition; entrepreneurship; fire protection; geography; health and physical education/fitness; health professions and related sciences, other; history; marketing management and research; mathematics; mathematics, other; psychology; real estate; sociology.

SOUTHEAST COMMUNITY COLLEGE, BEATRICE CAMPUS

Beatrice, Nebraska

http://online.scc.cc.ne.us

Southeast Community College, Beatrice Campus was founded in 1976. It is accredited by North Central Association of Colleges and Schools. It first offered distance learning courses in 1996. In fall 2003, there were 1,000 students enrolled in distance learning courses. Institutionally administered financial aid is available to distance learners.

Services Distance learners have accessibility to academic advising, bookstore, career placement assistance, library services.

Contact Bob Morgan, Assistant Campus Director and Director of Distance Learning, Southeast Community College, Beatrice Campus, 4771 West Scott Road, Beatrice, NE 68310. *Telephone:* 402-228-3468 Ext. 272. *Fax:* 402-228-2218. *E-mail:* bmorgan@southeast.edu.

DEGREES AND AWARDS

AAS Business Administration; Radiologic Technology Program; Respiratory Care; Surgical Technology

Certification Food Service Training Program

License Nursing Home Administration

COURSE SUBJECT AREAS OFFERED OUTSIDE OF DEGREE PROGRAMS

Undergraduate—accounting; biological sciences/life sciences, other; business; business administration and management; business and personal services marketing operations; business communications; economics; English composition; English language and literature, general; English technical and business writing; health and medical administrative services; health professions and related sciences, other; history; human services; institutional food workers and administrators; liberal arts and sciences, general studies and humanities; mathematics; miscellaneous health professions; philosophy; psychology; social psychology; speech and rhetorical studies.

Non-credit—business quantitative methods and management science; mathematics.

SOUTHEAST COMMUNITY COLLEGE, LINCOLN CAMPUS

Lincoln, Nebraska

Academic Education

http://www.southeast.edu/

Southeast Community College, Lincoln Campus was founded in 1973. It is accredited by North Central Association of Colleges and Schools. It first offered distance learning courses in 1994. In fall 2003, there were 2,000 students enrolled in distance learning courses. Institutionally administered financial aid is available to distance learners.

Services Distance learners have accessibility to academic advising, bookstore, campus computer network, career placement assistance, library services.

Contact Randy Hiatt, Director of Distance and Extended Education, Southeast Community College, Lincoln Campus, 8800 O Street, Lincoln, NE 68520. *Telephone:* 402-437-2705. *Fax:* 402-437-2541. *E-mail:* rhiatt@southeast.edu.

DEGREES AND AWARDS

AAS Business Administration; Respiratory Care; Surgical Technology

AS Radiological Technology

COURSE SUBJECT AREAS OFFERED OUTSIDE OF DEGREE PROGRAMS

Undergraduate—accounting; adult/continuing education; American history; anthropology; applied mathematics; business administration and management; earth sciences; English composition; European history; geography; law and legal studies related; philosophy and religion related; sociology; Spanish.

Non-credit—agricultural business and management; child care and guidance workers and managers; family and community studies; health professions and related sciences, other.

SOUTHEASTERN BAPTIST THEOLOGICAL SEMINARY

Wake Forest, North Carolina

http://www.sebts.edu

Southeastern Baptist Theological Seminary was founded in 1950. It is accredited by Southern Association of Colleges and Schools. It first offered distance learning courses in 2004. Institutionally administered financial aid is available to distance learners.

Services Distance learners have accessibility to academic advising, bookstore, campus computer network, career placement assistance, e-mail services, library services, tutoring.

Contact Mr. Jerry Lee Yandell, Director of Admissions, Southeastern Baptist Theological Seminary, PO Box 1889, Wake Forest, NC 27588. *Telephone:* 919-761-2280. *Fax:* 919-556-0998.

DEGREES AND AWARDS

Programs offered do not lead to a degree or other formal award.

COURSE SUBJECT AREAS OFFERED OUTSIDE OF DEGREE PROGRAMS

Graduate—theological and ministerial studies.

SOUTHEASTERN COLLEGE OF THE ASSEMBLIES OF GOD

Lakeland, Florida

http://www.secollege.edu/excel

Southeastern College of the Assemblies of God was founded in 1935. It is accredited by Southern Association of Colleges and Schools. It first offered distance learning courses in 2002. In fall 2003, there were 50 students enrolled in distance learning courses. Institutionally administered financial aid is available to distance learners.

Services Distance learners have accessibility to academic advising, bookstore, library services.

Contact Dr. Richard Harris, Coordinator of Distributed Learning, Southeastern College of the Assemblies of God, 1000 Longfellow Boulevard, Lakeland, FL 33801. *Telephone:* 863-667-5164. *E-mail:* rcharris@secollege.edu.

DEGREES AND AWARDS

Programs offered do not lead to a degree or other formal award.

COURSE SUBJECT AREAS OFFERED OUTSIDE OF DEGREE PROGRAMS

Undergraduate—bible/biblical studies; biological sciences/life sciences, other; communications, general; English composition; English literature (British and Commonwealth); fine arts and art studies; mathematics; psychology; sociology.

SOUTHEASTERN COMMUNITY COLLEGE

Whiteville, North Carolina

http://www.sccnc.edu/dislearn/index.htm

Southeastern Community College was founded in 1964. It is accredited by Southern Association of Colleges and Schools. It first offered distance learning courses in 1980. In fall 2003, there were 635 students enrolled in distance learning courses. Institutionally administered financial aid is available to distance learners.

Services Distance learners have accessibility to academic advising, bookstore, career placement assistance, e-mail services, library services, tutoring.

Contact Ms. Angela Spears, Distance Learning Specialist, Southeastern Community College, PO Box 151, Whiteville, NC 28472. *Telephone:* 910-642-7141 Ext. 229. *Fax:* 910-642-7141 Ext. 1267. *E-mail:* aspears@sccnc.edu.

DEGREES AND AWARDS

AA Business Administration; College Transfer; Elementary, Middle Grades, and Special Education

AAS Business Administration; Electronic Commerce

COURSE SUBJECT AREAS OFFERED OUTSIDE OF DEGREE PROGRAMS

Undergraduate—accounting; biology, general; business administration and management; chemistry; computer and information sciences, general; economics; English composition; English language and literature, general; history; mathematics; music; psychology; social sciences, general; sociology.

SOUTHEASTERN COMMUNITY COLLEGE, NORTH CAMPUS

West Burlington, Iowa

Distance Learning

http://www.secc.cc.ia.us/sccscripts/admcourseselect.asp

Southeastern Community College, North Campus was founded in 1968. It is accredited by North Central Association of Colleges and Schools. It first offered distance learning courses in 1982. In fall 2003, there were 336 students enrolled in distance learning courses. Institutionally administered financial aid is available to distance learners.

Services Distance learners have accessibility to academic advising, bookstore, library services.

Contact Rebecca Hannum, Coordinator of Distance Learning, Southeastern Community College, North Campus, 1500 West Agency Road, PO Box 180, West Burlington, IA 52655-0180. *Telephone:* 319-752-2731 Ext. 8166. *Fax:* 319-752-4957. *E-mail:* rhannum@scciowa.edu.

DEGREES AND AWARDS

AA Education, general

SOUTHERN CHRISTIAN UNIVERSITY

Montgomery, Alabama

Extended Learning Program

http://www.southernchristian.edu

Southern Christian University was founded in 1967. It is accredited by Southern Association of Colleges and Schools. It first offered distance learning courses in 1993. In fall 2003, there were 650 students enrolled in distance learning courses. Institutionally administered financial aid is available to distance learners.

Services Distance learners have accessibility to academic advising, library services.

Contact Rick Johnson, Director of Enrollment Management, Southern Christian University, 1200 Taylor Road, Montgomery, AL 36117-3553. *Telephone:* 800-351-4040 Ext. 213. *Fax:* 334-387-3878. *E-mail:* rickjohnson@southernchristian.edu.

DEGREES AND AWARDS

BA Biblical Studies

BS Human Development; Human Resource Leadership; Liberal Studies; Management Communication; Ministry/Bible; Public Safety and Human Justice

MA Biblical Studies; Marriage and Family Therapy; Practical Theology; Professional Counseling

MDiv Marriage and Family Therapy; Ministerial Leadership; Pastoral Counseling; Professional Counseling

MS Ministerial Leadership; Organizational Leadership; Pastoral Counseling

DMin Christian Ministry; Family Therapy

PhD Family Therapy

COURSE SUBJECT AREAS OFFERED OUTSIDE OF DEGREE PROGRAMS

Undergraduate—human services; liberal arts and sciences, general studies and humanities; missions/missionary studies and missiology;

organizational behavior; pastoral counseling and specialized ministries; philosophy and religion; religion/religious studies; theological and ministerial studies.

Graduate—human services; missions/missionary studies and missiology; organizational behavior; pastoral counseling and specialized ministries; philosophy and religion; religion/religious studies; theological and ministerial studies.

Non-credit—human services; liberal arts and sciences, general studies and humanities; missions/missionary studies and missiology; organizational behavior; pastoral counseling and specialized ministries; philosophy and religion; religion/religious studies; theological and ministerial studies.

See full description on page 528.

SOUTHERN ILLINOIS UNIVERSITY CARBONDALE

Carbondale, Illinois
Office of Distance Education
http://www.dce.siu.edu/siuconnected

Southern Illinois University Carbondale was founded in 1869. It is accredited by North Central Association of Colleges and Schools. It first offered distance learning courses in 1981. In fall 2003, there were 752 students enrolled in distance learning courses. Institutionally administered financial aid is available to distance learners.

Services Distance learners have accessibility to bookstore, campus computer network, e-mail services, library services, tutoring.
Contact Dr. Susan Edgren, Assistant Director, Southern Illinois University Carbondale, Washington Square C, Mailcode 6705, Carbondale, IL 62901-6705. *Telephone:* 618-453-5659. *Fax:* 618-453-5668. *E-mail:* sedgren@siu.edu.

DEGREES AND AWARDS

BS Electrical Engineering

COURSE SUBJECT AREAS OFFERED OUTSIDE OF DEGREE PROGRAMS

Undergraduate—advertising; agricultural business and management; agricultural mechanization; biological sciences/life sciences, other; biology, general; business; communications technologies; computer/information technology administration and management; criminal justice and corrections; criminology; East and Southeast Asian languages and literatures; education administration and supervision; educational psychology; education, other; geography; health and medical preparatory programs; history; information sciences and systems; journalism and mass communications; marketing management and research; marketing operations/marketing and distribution, other; mathematics; music; parks, recreation and leisure studies; philosophy; political science and government; quality control and safety technologies; radio and television broadcasting; real estate; rehabilitation/therapeutic services; religion/religious studies; sociology; telecommunications.

Graduate—educational/instructional media design; rehabilitation/therapeutic services.

Non-credit—marketing management and research.

SOUTHERN ILLINOIS UNIVERSITY EDWARDSVILLE

Edwardsville, Illinois
Office of Continuing Education
http://www.siue.edu/CE/

Southern Illinois University Edwardsville was founded in 1957. It is accredited by North Central Association of Colleges and Schools. It first offered distance learning courses in 1994. In fall 2003, there were 60 students enrolled in distance learning courses. Institutionally administered financial aid is available to distance learners.

Services Distance learners have accessibility to academic advising, bookstore, campus computer network, career placement assistance, e-mail services, library services, tutoring.
Contact Lynn Heidinger-Brown, Director of Continuing Education, Southern Illinois University Edwardsville, Campus Box 1084, Edwardsville, IL 62026. *Telephone:* 618-650-3210. *Fax:* 618-650-2629. *E-mail:* lhbrown@siue.edu.

DEGREES AND AWARDS

BSN Nursing

COURSE SUBJECT AREAS OFFERED OUTSIDE OF DEGREE PROGRAMS

Undergraduate—nursing.
Graduate—business; education, general; nursing.

SOUTHERN METHODIST UNIVERSITY

Dallas, Texas
School of Engineering–Distance Learning
http://www.engr.smu.edu

Southern Methodist University was founded in 1911. It is accredited by Southern Association of Colleges and Schools. It first offered distance learning courses in 1962. In fall 2003, there were 600 students enrolled in distance learning courses. Institutionally administered financial aid is available to distance learners.

Services Distance learners have accessibility to academic advising, bookstore, campus computer network, career placement assistance, library services.
Contact Stephanie Dye, Associate Director of Distance Education, Southern Methodist University, PO Box 750335, Dallas, TX 75275-0335. *Telephone:* 214-768-3232. *Fax:* 214-768-4482. *E-mail:* sdye@engr.smu.edu.

DEGREES AND AWARDS

MS Civil Engineering; Computer Engineering; Computer Science; Electrical Engineering; Engineering Management; Environmental Engineering; Environmental Science (Environmental Systems Management Major); Environmental Science (Hazardous and Waste Materials Management Major); Environmental Science; Facilities Management; Information Engineering and Management; Manufacturing Systems Management; Mechanical Engineering; Operations Research; Packaging of Electronic and Optical Devices; Software Engineering; Systems Engineering; Telecommunications

Southern Methodist University (continued)

COURSE SUBJECT AREAS OFFERED OUTSIDE OF DEGREE PROGRAMS

Graduate—civil engineering; computer and information sciences, general; computer and information sciences, other; computer engineering; computer/information technology administration and management; computer science; electrical and electronic engineering-related technology; electrical engineering; engineering/industrial management; environmental engineering; information sciences and systems; mechanical engineering; mechanical engineering-related technologies; systems engineering; telecommunications.

See full description on page 530.

SOUTHERN NEW HAMPSHIRE UNIVERSITY

Manchester, New Hampshire
Distance Education Program
http://www.snhu.edu/Prospective_Student/distance_ed.html

Southern New Hampshire University was founded in 1932. It is accredited by New England Association of Schools and Colleges. It first offered distance learning courses in 1996. In fall 2003, there were 1,200 students enrolled in distance learning courses. Institutionally administered financial aid is available to distance learners.

Services Distance learners have accessibility to academic advising, bookstore, campus computer network, career placement assistance, e-mail services, library services, tutoring.

Contact Ms. Voula Annas, Marketing Manager, Distance Education, Southern New Hampshire University, 2500 North River Road, Manchester, NH 03106. *Telephone:* 866-860-0449. *Fax:* 603-645-9706. *E-mail:* de@snhu.edu.

DEGREES AND AWARDS

AA Liberal Arts

AS Accounting; Business Administration; Information Technology; Marketing

BA English Language and Literature; Psychology; Social Science

BS Accounting; Accounting/Finance; Business Administration; Business Studies; Economics/Finance; Information Technology; International Business; Management Advisory Services; Marketing; Technical Management

Certificate Accounting; Human Resources Management; Software Development

Graduate Certificate International Business

MBA Business Administration

MS Business Education; Hospitality Administration; International Business; Organizational Leadership

Special Message

Established in 1932, Southern New Hampshire University (SNHU) is a private, regional university set on 300 acres along the banks of the Merrimack River in Manchester, New Hampshire. SNHU offers certificate and degree programs in business, community economic development, culinary arts, education, hospitality, and liberal arts, with degrees at the associate level through the doctoral level.

SNHU's Distance Education (DE) program offers undergraduate and graduate certificate and degree programs and is one of the largest and fastest-growing programs in New England. SNHU is a recognized leader in fully online asynchronous learning and Web-based education. Total distance education enrollments exceeded 10,000 for the 2003–04 academic year. DE classes normally are limited to 18 students, providing a significant measure of faculty-student interaction. Blackboard Learning System™ is the learning management software for all SNHU online courses.

The University offers six 8-week undergraduate and four 12-week graduate terms each year. The undergraduate residency requirement, which may be satisfied by taking distance education courses, is 30 semester hours (ten classes) through SNHU, including 12 credit hours in the area of study for the bachelor's or 9 credit hours in the area of study for the associate degree, through SNHU, to graduate. DE students are not required to come to campus. The final 24 semester hours must be taken through SNHU. The graduate program typically limits transfer credit to 6 semester hours.

SNHU is regionally and nationally accredited by the New England Association of Schools and Colleges, the Association of Collegiate Business Schools and Programs, the New England Postsecondary Education Commission, the New Hampshire State Department of Education for Teacher Certification, the American Culinary Federation Education Institute, and the North American Society for Sport Management.

See full description on page 532.

SOUTH PIEDMONT COMMUNITY COLLEGE

Polkton, North Carolina
http://www.spcc.edu

South Piedmont Community College was founded in 1962. It is accredited by Southern Association of Colleges and Schools. It first offered distance learning courses in 1982. In fall 2003, there were 697 students enrolled in distance learning courses. Institutionally administered financial aid is available to distance learners.

Services Distance learners have accessibility to academic advising, bookstore, campus computer network, career placement assistance, library services, tutoring.

Contact Ms. Julia Grace May, Director of Distance Learning, South Piedmont Community College, 680 Highway 74 West, PO Box 126, Polkton, NC 28135. *Telephone:* 704-272-7635 Ext. 260. *Fax:* 704-272-7542. *E-mail:* jmay@spcc.cc.nc.us.

DEGREES AND AWARDS

Programs offered do not lead to a degree or other formal award.

COURSE SUBJECT AREAS OFFERED OUTSIDE OF DEGREE PROGRAMS

Undergraduate—accounting; biology, general; computer and information sciences, general; computer/information technology administration and management; economics; education administration and supervision; English composition; family and community studies; financial management and services; health professions and related sciences, other; marketing operations/marketing and distribution, other; teacher education, specific academic and vocational programs.

SOUTHWESTERN ASSEMBLIES OF GOD UNIVERSITY

Waxahachie, Texas
School of Distance Education
http://www.sagu.edu

Southwestern Assemblies of God University was founded in 1927. It is accredited by Accrediting Association of Bible Colleges. It first offered distance learning courses in 1983. In fall 2003, there were 510 students enrolled in distance learning courses. Institutionally administered financial aid is available to distance learners.

Services Distance learners have accessibility to academic advising, bookstore, campus computer network, career placement assistance, e-mail services, library services, tutoring.
Contact Mr. Darrell Davis, Distance Education Enrollment Counselor, Southwestern Assemblies of God University, 1200 Sycamore, Waxahachie, TX 75165. *Telephone:* 972-937-4010 Ext. 2413. *Fax:* 972-923-2658. *E-mail:* ddavis@sagu.edu.

DEGREES AND AWARDS

AA Bible; Business Administration; Business, general; Early Childhood Education; Education; English; General Studies; Media; Psychology; Social Studies
BA Business; Church Ministries; Education; English; History; Professional Studies
BS Business; Church Ministries; Education; English; History; Professional Studies
MA Human Services Counseling; Theological Studies
MEd Education
MS Human Services Counseling; Theological Studies

COURSE SUBJECT AREAS OFFERED OUTSIDE OF DEGREE PROGRAMS

Undergraduate—accounting; Air Force R.O.T.C.; bible/biblical studies; biology; business; business administration and management; creative writing; curriculum and instruction; developmental/child psychology; education administration and supervision; education, general; education, other; English composition; history; human resources management; missions/missionary studies and missiology; multi/interdisciplinary studies, other; music; pastoral counseling and specialized ministries; psychology; religion/religious studies; religious education; religious/sacred music; social psychology; social sciences and history, other; social sciences, general; sociology; teacher education, specific academic and vocational programs; theological and ministerial studies; theological studies and religious vocations, other.
Graduate—bible/biblical studies; counseling psychology; education administration and supervision; education, general; education, other; missions/missionary studies and missiology; religion/religious studies; religious education; teacher education, specific academic and vocational programs; theological and ministerial studies; theological studies and religious vocations, other.

SOUTHWESTERN BAPTIST THEOLOGICAL SEMINARY

Fort Worth, Texas
Department of Continuing Education
http://swbts.edu

Southwestern Baptist Theological Seminary was founded in 1908. It is accredited by Southern Association of Colleges and Schools. It first offered distance learning courses in 1993. In fall 2003, there were 270 students enrolled in distance learning courses. Institutionally administered financial aid is available to distance learners.

Services Distance learners have accessibility to academic advising, bookstore, campus computer network, career placement assistance, e-mail services, library services.
Contact Gary Waller, PhD, Dean of Distance Learning, Southwestern Baptist Theological Seminary, PO Box 22487, Fort Worth, TX 76122. *Telephone:* 817-923-1921 Ext. 3510. *Fax:* 817-921-8753. *E-mail:* gwaller@swbts.edu.

DEGREES AND AWARDS

Programs offered do not lead to a degree or other formal award.

COURSE SUBJECT AREAS OFFERED OUTSIDE OF DEGREE PROGRAMS

Undergraduate—bible/biblical studies; religion/religious studies; religious education; theological and ministerial studies.
Graduate—bible/biblical studies; biblical and other theological languages and literatures; education administration and supervision; educational evaluation, research and statistics; educational/instructional media design; educational psychology; education, other; family and community studies; foreign languages and literatures; pastoral counseling and specialized ministries; philosophy and religion; psychology; psychology, other; religion/religious studies; religious education; religious/sacred music; theological and ministerial studies; theological studies and religious vocations, other.

SOUTHWESTERN COLLEGE

Winfield, Kansas
Southwestern College Online
http://www.sckans.edu/online

Southwestern College was founded in 1885. It is accredited by North Central Association of Colleges and Schools. It first offered distance learning courses in 2000. In fall 2003, there were 75 students enrolled in distance learning courses. Institutionally administered financial aid is available to distance learners.

Services Distance learners have accessibility to academic advising, bookstore, career placement assistance, library services.
Contact Candyce Duggan, Director of Professional Studies, Southwestern College, 2040 South Rock Road, Wichita, KS 67207. *Telephone:* 888-684-5335 Ext. 112. *Fax:* 316-688-5218. *E-mail:* online@sckans.edu.

DEGREES AND AWARDS

BA Pastoral Studies
BS Business Administration; Business Quality Management; Computer Programming Technology; Criminal Justice; Human Resource Development; Security Management

COURSE SUBJECT AREAS OFFERED OUTSIDE OF DEGREE PROGRAMS

Undergraduate—business; business administration and management; computer/information technology administration and management; computer programming; criminal justice and corrections; economics; English composition; English language and literature, general; human resources management; industrial production technologies; liberal arts and sciences, general studies and humanities; nursing; philosophy; religion/religious studies; social sciences, general.
Graduate—education, general.

SOUTHWESTERN COLLEGE

Chula Vista, California

http://www.swc.cc.ca.us/~swconline

Southwestern College was founded in 1961. It is accredited by Western Association of Schools and Colleges. It first offered distance learning courses in 1988. In fall 2003, there were 476 students enrolled in distance learning courses. Institutionally administered financial aid is available to distance learners.

Services Distance learners have accessibility to academic advising, bookstore, campus computer network, e-mail services, library services, tutoring.

Contact Mary Wylie, Interim Dean of Academic Information Services, Southwestern College, 900 Otay Lakes Road, Chula Vista, CA 91910. *Telephone:* 619-482-6347. *Fax:* 619-482-6417. *E-mail:* mwylie@swc.cc.ca.us.

DEGREES AND AWARDS

Programs offered do not lead to a degree or other formal award.

COURSE SUBJECT AREAS OFFERED OUTSIDE OF DEGREE PROGRAMS

Undergraduate—anthropology; astronomy; child care and guidance workers and managers; economics; English as a second language; health and medical preparatory programs; history; legal studies; political science and government; psychology; sociology.

Non-credit—English as a second language.

SOUTHWESTERN OREGON COMMUNITY COLLEGE

Coos Bay, Oregon

http://www.socc.edu

Southwestern Oregon Community College was founded in 1961. It first offered distance learning courses in 1999. In fall 2003, there were 150 students enrolled in distance learning courses. Institutionally administered financial aid is available to distance learners.

Services Distance learners have accessibility to academic advising, bookstore, e-mail services, library services.

Contact Karen Helland, Director of Distance and Community Education, Southwestern Oregon Community College, 1988 Newmark, Coos Bay, OR 97420. *Telephone:* 541-888-7212. *Fax:* 541-888-7601. *E-mail:* khelland@socc.edu.

DEGREES AND AWARDS

Programs offered do not lead to a degree or other formal award.

COURSE SUBJECT AREAS OFFERED OUTSIDE OF DEGREE PROGRAMS

Undergraduate—accounting; anthropology; business; child care and guidance workers and managers; communications, general; computer engineering; computer science; criminal justice and corrections; criminology; curriculum and instruction; developmental and child psychology; family and community studies; foreign languages and literatures; health and medical assistants; human services; psychology; psychology, other; social work; sociology; teacher assistant/aide.

SOUTHWEST MISSOURI STATE UNIVERSITY

Springfield, Missouri

College of Continuing Education and the Extended University

http://ce.smsu.edu

Southwest Missouri State University was founded in 1905. It is accredited by North Central Association of Colleges and Schools. It first offered distance learning courses in 1974. In fall 2003, there were 2,200 students enrolled in distance learning courses. Institutionally administered financial aid is available to distance learners.

Services Distance learners have accessibility to academic advising, bookstore, campus computer network, career placement assistance, e-mail services, library services.

Contact Dr. Diana Garland, Associate Director of Academic Outreach, Southwest Missouri State University, College of Continuing Education and the Extended University, Academic Outreach, 901 South National, Springfield, MO 65804. *Telephone:* 888-879-7678. *Fax:* 417-836-6016. *E-mail:* dianagarland@smsu.edu.

DEGREES AND AWARDS

BS Business Completion Program, general; Elementary Education; Industrial Technology–Bachelor of Applied Science in Industrial Technology (Two-Year Completion)

BSN Nursing

Graduate Certificate Instructional Technology Specialist; Project Management

MBA Business Administration

MS Administrative Studies; Computer Information Systems; Elementary Education

MSW Social Work

COURSE SUBJECT AREAS OFFERED OUTSIDE OF DEGREE PROGRAMS

Undergraduate—accounting; American history; anthropology; astronomy; business marketing and marketing management; chemistry; communications, other; computer and information sciences, general; economics; English creative writing; film studies; finance; health and physical education/fitness; mathematics related; music; nursing; physics; political science and government; social work; sociology; special education.

Graduate—accounting; business marketing and marketing management; curriculum and instruction; economics; education administration and supervision; education, general; finance; general teacher education; health products and services marketing operations; history; industrial production technologies; legal studies; nursing; psychology; religion/religious studies; social work; taxation; teacher education, specific academic and vocational programs.

Non-credit—alcohol/drug abuse counseling; business information and data processing services; information sciences and systems.

SOUTHWEST VIRGINIA COMMUNITY COLLEGE

Richlands, Virginia

Audiovisual and Distance Education Services

http://desweb.sw.edu

Southwest Virginia Community College was founded in 1968. It is accredited by Southern Association of Colleges and Schools. It first offered distance learning courses in 1991. In fall 2003, there were 1,800 students enrolled in distance learning courses. Institutionally administered financial aid is available to distance learners.

Services Distance learners have accessibility to academic advising, bookstore, campus computer network, career placement assistance, e-mail services, library services, tutoring.

Contact Thomas A. Cash, Coordinator of DES, Southwest Virginia Community College, PO Box SVCC, Richlands, VA 24641. *Telephone:* 276-964-7280. *Fax:* 276-964-7686. *E-mail:* tom.cash@sw.edu.

DEGREES AND AWARDS

AS General Studies
Certificate Network and Internet Administration

COURSE SUBJECT AREAS OFFERED OUTSIDE OF DEGREE PROGRAMS

Undergraduate—American history; creative writing; developmental/child psychology; educational psychology; English composition; mathematical statistics; mathematics related; sociology; Spanish.

SOUTHWEST WISCONSIN TECHNICAL COLLEGE

Fennimore, Wisconsin

http://www.swtc.edu/

Southwest Wisconsin Technical College was founded in 1967. It is accredited by North Central Association of Colleges and Schools. It first offered distance learning courses in 1989. In fall 2003, there were 700 students enrolled in distance learning courses. Institutionally administered financial aid is available to distance learners.

Services Distance learners have accessibility to bookstore, e-mail services, library services, tutoring.

Contact Susan Davis Allen, Facilitator of Center for Learning Innovation, Southwest Wisconsin Technical College, 1800 Bronson Boulevard, Fennimore, WI 53809. *Telephone:* 608-822-3262 Ext. 2322. *Fax:* 608-822-6019. *E-mail:* sallen@swtc.edu.

DEGREES AND AWARDS

Diploma Medical Transcription
Technical Certificate Dietary Manager; Medical Coding Specialist

COURSE SUBJECT AREAS OFFERED OUTSIDE OF DEGREE PROGRAMS

Undergraduate—accounting; applied mathematics; business communications; business information and data processing services; communications, general; communications, other; computer and information sciences, general; computer programming; computer software and media applications; computer systems networking and telecommunications; cosmetic services; culinary arts and related services; curriculum and instruction; economics; educational/instructional media design; foods and nutrition studies; health and medical assistants; health and medical preparatory programs; hospitality services management; human resources management; mathematical statistics; mathematics; nursing; psychology; social sciences, general; sociology.

SPARTANBURG TECHNICAL COLLEGE

Spartanburg, South Carolina

http://dl.stcsc.edu

Spartanburg Technical College was founded in 1961. It is accredited by Southern Association of Colleges and Schools. It first offered distance learning courses in 1997. In fall 2003, there were 610 students enrolled in distance learning courses. Institutionally administered financial aid is available to distance learners.

Services Distance learners have accessibility to academic advising, bookstore, e-mail services, library services.

Contact Mr. Mark Alan Roseveare, Director of Distance Learning, Spartanburg Technical College, PO Box 4386, Business I-85 and New Cut Road, Spartanburg, SC 29305-4386. *Telephone:* 864-591-3763. *Fax:* 864-591-3941. *E-mail:* rosevearem@stcsc.edu.

DEGREES AND AWARDS

Programs offered do not lead to a degree or other formal award.

COURSE SUBJECT AREAS OFFERED OUTSIDE OF DEGREE PROGRAMS

Undergraduate—accounting; applied mathematics; business; business administration and management; computer software and media applications; data entry/microcomputer applications; English composition; English language and literature, general; marketing operations/marketing and distribution, other; mathematical statistics; mathematics; psychology; sociology.

SPERTUS INSTITUTE OF JEWISH STUDIES

Chicago, Illinois

http://www.spertus.edu/

Spertus Institute of Jewish Studies was founded in 1924. It is accredited by North Central Association of Colleges and Schools. It first offered distance learning courses in 1994. In fall 2003, there were 250 students enrolled in distance learning courses. Institutionally administered financial aid is available to distance learners.

Services Distance learners have accessibility to academic advising, library services.

Contact Sue Levison, Admissions, Spertus Institute of Jewish Studies, 618 South Michigan Avenue, Chicago, IL 60605. *Telephone:* 888-322-1769. *Fax:* 312-922-6406. *E-mail:* college@spertus.edu.

DEGREES AND AWARDS

MS Jewish Education–Master of Science in Jewish Education (MSJE)
MSJS Jewish Studies
DJS Jewish Studies

Special Message

Accredited by the North Central Association of Colleges and Schools, Spertus currently offers 4 degree programs on a distance learning basis: the Master of Science in Jewish Studies (MSJS), the Master of Science in Jewish Education (MSJE), the Doctor of Jewish Studies (DJS), and the Doctor of Science in Jewish Studies (DSJS).

Spertus Institute of Jewish Studies (continued)

The MSJS and the MSJE are designed for students with an accredited undergraduate degree and a desire to enrich their Jewish education or acquire a professional credential in Jewish education or Jewish communal service. The MSJS and MSJE programs are identical, except that students in the MSJE must choose a concentration area in Jewish education. Courses are delivered in a variety of ways, including distance learning packages, intensive seminars, and independent study. The programs progress at the learner's individual rate. Distance learners are encouraged to spend a minimum of 6 days per year at Spertus's Chicago campus for intensive course work. Forty-eight quarter hours are required for the degrees. Tuition is currently $225 per quarter hour. Scholarships, in the form of partial tuition remission, are available.

The DJS is designed for in-service Jewish clergy, educators, and communal service workers who are interested in and committed to building upon and enhancing previously acquired Judaica knowledge and professional skills and who desire to make a cutting-edge contribution to their respective fields. Admission to the DJS program is highly selective. Eighteen courses are required for the degree: 7 reading courses, 7 intensive seminars, and 4 courses toward the completion of a Project Demonstrating Excellence.

The DSJS program has been designed primarily for students who already hold a master's degree in Jewish studies and who want to explore how the wisdom of the Jewish past--as embodied in its sacred and significant texts and in the diverse historical experiences of the Jewish people--can be utilized to address the perplexities and problems of Jewish life in the present--both communal and individual. The DSJS program requires 18 courses, including 7 core courses; 3 text courses; 5 courses on issues, problems, methodologies, and major intellectual or historical figures in Jewish history; and 3 research and writing courses related to a final project. (In some cases, additional prerequisite courses may also be required.) Tuition for both the DJS and DSJS programs is currently $250 per quarter hour.

For more information, students should contact the Office of the Registrar at 888-322-1769 (toll-free), fax: 312-922-6406, or e-mail: college@spertus.edu or visit the Web site at http://www.spertus.edu.

SPOON RIVER COLLEGE

Canton, Illinois

http://www.spoonrivercollege.edu/

Spoon River College was founded in 1959. It is accredited by North Central Association of Colleges and Schools. It first offered distance learning courses in 1994. In fall 2003, there were 420 students enrolled in distance learning courses. Institutionally administered financial aid is available to distance learners.

Services Distance learners have accessibility to academic advising, bookstore, career placement assistance, library services.

Contact Sharon Wrenn, Dean of Student Services, Spoon River College, 23235 North County 22, Canton, IL 61520. *Telephone:* 309-647-4645. *Fax:* 309-649-6235. *E-mail:* info@src.cc.il.us.

DEGREES AND AWARDS

AA General Programs

COURSE SUBJECT AREAS OFFERED OUTSIDE OF DEGREE PROGRAMS

Undergraduate—biology; biology, general; child care and guidance workers and managers; education, general; English composition; English language and literature, general; fine arts and art studies; health professions and related sciences, other; philosophy and religion.
Non-credit—computer software and media applications.

SPRING ARBOR UNIVERSITY

Spring Arbor, Michigan

http://www.arboronline.org

Spring Arbor University was founded in 1873. It is accredited by North Central Association of Colleges and Schools. It first offered distance learning courses in 1998. In fall 2003, there were 890 students enrolled in distance learning courses. Institutionally administered financial aid is available to distance learners.

Services Distance learners have accessibility to academic advising, bookstore, campus computer network, career placement assistance, e-mail services, library services, tutoring.

Contact Dr. John Nemecek, Assistant Dean of School of Adult Studies, Spring Arbor University, 106 East Main Street, Spring Arbor, MI 49283. *Telephone:* 517-750-6351. *Fax:* 517-750-6602. *E-mail:* jnemecek@arbor.edu.

DEGREES AND AWARDS

MIM Organizational Management

COURSE SUBJECT AREAS OFFERED OUTSIDE OF DEGREE PROGRAMS

Undergraduate—business administration and management; business marketing and marketing management; computer software and media applications; creative writing; criminal justice and corrections; English composition; financial management and services; history; human resources management; music; philosophy; psychology; sociology.
Graduate—business administration and management; business communications; business/managerial economics; business marketing and marketing management; financial management and services; international business.

STANFORD UNIVERSITY

Stanford, California

Stanford Center for Professional Development

http://scpd.stanford.edu

Stanford University was founded in 1891. It is accredited by Western Association of Schools and Colleges. It first offered distance learning courses in 1969. In fall 2003, there were 1,500 students enrolled in distance learning courses. Institutionally administered financial aid is available to distance learners.

Services Distance learners have accessibility to bookstore, campus computer network, e-mail services, library services.

Contact Leslie French, SCPD Customer Relations, Stanford University, 496 Lomita Hall, Room 300, Stanford, CA 94305-4036. *Telephone:* 650-725-6950. *Fax:* 650-725-2868. *E-mail:* lfrench@stanford.edu.

DEGREES AND AWARDS

Graduate Certificate Advanced Software Systems; Artificial Intelligence; Bioinformatics; Computational Fluid Dynamics (Aeronautics and Astronautics/Mechanical Engineering); Computational Genomics; Computer Architecture; Computer Hardware and VLSI Design; Computer Languages and Operating Systems; Control and System

Engineering; Data Mining and Applications (Statistics); Databases; Design for Customer Value and Market Success; Digital Communication; Electronic Circuits; Electronic Devices and Technology; Fluids (Aeronautics and Astronautics/Mechanical Engineering); Foundations in Computer Science; Guidance and Control (Aeronautics and Astronautics); International Security; Management Science and Engineering; Networking (Electrical Engineering); Optics, Imaging and Communications; Product Creation and Innovative Manufacturing; Quantitative Methods in Finance and Risk Management (Statistics); Risk Analysis (Management Science and Engineering); Signal Processing; Software Systems; Spacecraft Design and Operation Proficiency; Telecommunications; Thin Films and Nanomaterials; Wireless Personal Communication

MA Learning, Design and Technology

MS Aeronautics and Astronautics; BioMedical Informatics; Computer Science; Electrical Engineering; Management Science and Engineering; Mechanical Engineering

COURSE SUBJECT AREAS OFFERED OUTSIDE OF DEGREE PROGRAMS

Non-credit—bioengineering and biomedical engineering; biological sciences/life sciences, other; biological technology; business administration and management; business/managerial economics; business quantitative methods and management science; civil engineering; civil engineering/civil technology; communications technologies; computer/information technology administration and management; computer science; computer systems networking and telecommunications; construction/building technology; construction management; electrical, electronics and communications engineering; electrical engineering; engineering design; engineering/industrial management; entrepreneurship; financial management and services; industrial engineering; industrial/manufacturing engineering; materials science; mechanical engineering; miscellaneous engineering-related technologies; telecommunications.

STANLY COMMUNITY COLLEGE

Albemarle, North Carolina

http://www.stanly.edu

Stanly Community College was founded in 1971. It is accredited by Southern Association of Colleges and Schools. It first offered distance learning courses in 1990. In fall 2003, there were 400 students enrolled in distance learning courses. Institutionally administered financial aid is available to distance learners.

Services Distance learners have accessibility to academic advising, bookstore, campus computer network, career placement assistance, e-mail services, library services.

Contact Marlene Saunders, Director of Distance Learning, Stanly Community College, 141 College Drive, Albemarle, NC 28001. *Telephone:* 704-991-0258. *Fax:* 704-982-0819. *E-mail:* saundem@stanly.edu.

DEGREES AND AWARDS

AAS Criminal Justice

COURSE SUBJECT AREAS OFFERED OUTSIDE OF DEGREE PROGRAMS

Undergraduate—accounting; applied mathematics; biology, general; business administration and management; business information and data processing services; business marketing and marketing management; child care and guidance workers and managers; computer and information sciences, general; computer and information sciences, other; criminal justice and corrections; developmental/child psychology; English composition; human services; nursing; psychology; sociology.

STATE UNIVERSITY OF NEW YORK AT NEW PALTZ

New Paltz, New York

Center for Continuing and Professional Education

http://www.newpaltz.edu

State University of New York at New Paltz was founded in 1828. It is accredited by Middle States Association of Colleges and Schools. It first offered distance learning courses in 1995. In fall 2003, there were 175 students enrolled in distance learning courses. Institutionally administered financial aid is available to distance learners.

Services Distance learners have accessibility to bookstore, campus computer network, e-mail services, library services.

Contact Helise Winters, Director of Extension and Distance Learning, State University of New York at New Paltz, 75 South Manheim Boulevard, Suite 9, New Paltz, NY 12561-2443. *Telephone:* 845-257-2894. *Fax:* 845-257-2899. *E-mail:* edl@newpaltz.edu.

DEGREES AND AWARDS

Programs offered do not lead to a degree or other formal award.

COURSE SUBJECT AREAS OFFERED OUTSIDE OF DEGREE PROGRAMS

Undergraduate—advertising; American literature (United States); anthropology; astronomy; communications, general; comparative literature; computer science; curriculum and instruction; developmental and child psychology; economics; English composition; English literature (British and Commonwealth); geography; history; psychology; sociology.

Graduate—education, general.

STATE UNIVERSITY OF NEW YORK AT OSWEGO

Oswego, New York

Office of Distance Learning

http://www.oswego.edu

State University of New York at Oswego was founded in 1861. It is accredited by Middle States Association of Colleges and Schools. It first offered distance learning courses in 1995. In fall 2003, there were 750 students enrolled in distance learning courses. Institutionally administered financial aid is available to distance learners.

Services Distance learners have accessibility to academic advising, bookstore, campus computer network, career placement assistance, e-mail services, library services, tutoring.

Contact Allison Finsterwalder, Associate Director, State University of New York at Oswego, Advisement Coordinator, Continuing Education, 214 Swetman Hall, Oswego, NY 13126. *Telephone:* 315-312-2270. *Fax:* 315-312-3078. *E-mail:* ced@oswego.edu.

State University of New York at Oswego (continued)

DEGREES AND AWARDS

BA Communications
BS Vocational Teacher Preparation

COURSE SUBJECT AREAS OFFERED OUTSIDE OF DEGREE PROGRAMS

Undergraduate—anthropology; business/managerial economics; communications, general; counseling psychology; criminal justice and corrections; dramatic/theater arts and stagecraft; economics; history; information sciences and systems; journalism and mass communications; psychology; teacher education, specific academic and vocational programs; telecommunications.
Graduate—accounting; business administration and management; counseling psychology; curriculum and instruction; economics; education, general; gerontology; information sciences and systems; psychology; teacher education, specific academic and vocational programs.
Non-credit—business administration and management; professional studies.

See full description on page 534.

STATE UNIVERSITY OF NEW YORK AT PLATTSBURGH

Plattsburgh, New York
Distance Learning Office
http://www.plattsburgh.edu/cll

State University of New York at Plattsburgh was founded in 1889. It is accredited by Middle States Association of Colleges and Schools. It first offered distance learning courses in 1990. In fall 2003, there were 487 students enrolled in distance learning courses. Institutionally administered financial aid is available to distance learners.

Services Distance learners have accessibility to academic advising, bookstore, campus computer network, e-mail services, library services, tutoring.
Contact Ms. Anna Liem, Interim Coordinator of Distance Learning Office, State University of New York at Plattsburgh, 101 Broad Street, Kehoe Building, 413, Plattsburgh, NY 12901. *Telephone:* 518-564-4234. *Fax:* 518-564-4236. *E-mail:* distance-learning@plattsburgh.edu.

DEGREES AND AWARDS

Programs offered do not lead to a degree or other formal award.

COURSE SUBJECT AREAS OFFERED OUTSIDE OF DEGREE PROGRAMS

Undergraduate—anthropology; area, ethnic and cultural studies, other; biopsychology; business; computer and information sciences, general; cultural studies; economics; education, general; education, other; entrepreneurship; fine arts and art studies; health and physical education/fitness; library science, other; marketing management and research; mathematical statistics; nursing; political science and government; sociology; tourism/travel marketing.
Graduate—business administration and management; education administration and supervision; educational/instructional media design; education, general; education, other; entrepreneurship; special education.

STATE UNIVERSITY OF NEW YORK COLLEGE AT CORTLAND

Cortland, New York
http://www.cortland.edu/

State University of New York College at Cortland was founded in 1868. It is accredited by Middle States Association of Colleges and Schools. It first offered distance learning courses in 1996. In fall 2003, there were 38 students enrolled in distance learning courses. Institutionally administered financial aid is available to distance learners.

Services Distance learners have accessibility to bookstore, e-mail services, library services.
Contact Gradin Avery, Director of Admissions, State University of New York College at Cortland, PO Box 2000, Cortland, NY 13045. *Telephone:* 607-753-4711. *Fax:* 607-753-5998. *E-mail:* admissions@cortland.edu.

DEGREES AND AWARDS

Programs offered do not lead to a degree or other formal award.

STATE UNIVERSITY OF NEW YORK COLLEGE AT FREDONIA

Fredonia, New York
Office of Lifelong Learning/SUNY Learning Network
http://sln.suny.edu

State University of New York College at Fredonia was founded in 1826. It is accredited by Middle States Association of Colleges and Schools. It first offered distance learning courses in 1998. In fall 2003, there were 32 students enrolled in distance learning courses. Institutionally administered financial aid is available to distance learners.

Services Distance learners have accessibility to academic advising, bookstore, campus computer network, career placement assistance, e-mail services, library services.
Contact Mr. Grant Umberger, Associate Director of Lifelong Learning, State University of New York College at Fredonia, LoGrasso Hall, Fredonia, NY 14048. *Telephone:* 716-673-3177. *Fax:* 716-673-3175. *E-mail:* grant.umberger@fredonia.edu.

DEGREES AND AWARDS

Programs offered do not lead to a degree or other formal award.

COURSE SUBJECT AREAS OFFERED OUTSIDE OF DEGREE PROGRAMS

Undergraduate—biological sciences/life sciences, other; business management and administrative services, other; computer and information sciences, other; political science and government.

STATE UNIVERSITY OF NEW YORK COLLEGE AT POTSDAM

Potsdam, New York
http://www.potsdam.edu/

State University of New York College at Potsdam was founded in 1816. It is accredited by Middle States Association of Colleges and

Schools. It first offered distance learning courses in 2002. In fall 2003, there were 26 students enrolled in distance learning courses. Institutionally administered financial aid is available to distance learners.

Services Distance learners have accessibility to academic advising, bookstore, campus computer network, e-mail services, library services.

Contact Ms. Lee Ghostlaw, Staff Assistant, Continuing Education, State University of New York College at Potsdam, 44 Pierrepont Avenue, Potsdam, NY 13676. *Telephone:* 315-267-2166. *Fax:* 315-267-3088. *E-mail:* ghostllk@potsdam.edu.

DEGREES AND AWARDS

Programs offered do not lead to a degree or other formal award.

COURSE SUBJECT AREAS OFFERED OUTSIDE OF DEGREE PROGRAMS

Graduate—educational/instructional media design.
Non-credit—accounting; business; business administration and management; communications, general; computer and information sciences, general; computer programming; computer software and media applications; culinary arts and related services; data entry/microcomputer applications; English creative writing; entrepreneurship; financial management and services; foreign languages and literatures; Internet and World Wide Web; legal studies; Romance languages and literatures; tourism/travel marketing.

STATE UNIVERSITY OF NEW YORK EMPIRE STATE COLLEGE

Saratoga Springs, New York
Center for Distance Learning
http://www.esc.edu/cdl

State University of New York Empire State College was founded in 1971. It is accredited by Middle States Association of Colleges and Schools. It first offered distance learning courses in 1979. In fall 2003, there were 4,200 students enrolled in distance learning courses. Institutionally administered financial aid is available to distance learners.

Services Distance learners have accessibility to academic advising, bookstore, campus computer network, career placement assistance, e-mail services, library services, tutoring.

Contact Ms. Kathleen Schechner, Outreach Specialist, State University of New York Empire State College, 111 West Avenue, Saratoga Springs, NY 12866. *Telephone:* 518-587-2100 Ext. 556. *Fax:* 518-587-2660. *E-mail:* kathy.schechner@esc.edu.

DEGREES AND AWARDS

AA Business, Management and Economics; Community and Human Services; Cultural Studies; Educational Studies; Historical Studies; Human Development; Interdisciplinary Studies; Labor Studies; Science, Math and Technology; Social Theory, Social Structure and Change; the Arts
AS Business, Management and Economics; Community and Human Services; Cultural Studies; Educational Studies; Historical Studies; Human Development; Interdisciplinary Studies; Labor Studies; Science, Math and Technology; Social Theory, Social Structure and Change; the Arts
BA Business, Management and Economics; Community and Human Services; Cultural Studies; Educational Studies; Historical Studies; Human Development; Interdisciplinary Studies; Labor Studies; Science, Math and Technology; Social Theory, Social Structure and Change; the Arts
BPS Business, Management and Economics
BS Business, Management and Economics; Community and Human Services; Community and Human Services; Cultural Studies; Educational Studies; Historical Studies; Human Development; Interdisciplinary Studies; Labor Studies; Science, Math and Technology; Social Theory, Social Structure and Change; the Arts
MA Liberal Studies; Policy Studies
MBA Business Administration

COURSE SUBJECT AREAS OFFERED OUTSIDE OF DEGREE PROGRAMS

Undergraduate—accounting; American history; biology; English composition; finance; fire services administration; international business; labor/personnel relations; law and legal studies related; management information systems/business data processing; mathematical statistics; mathematics related; organizational behavior; social psychology; sociology.
Graduate—business; political science and government; social sciences, general.

See full description on page 536.

STATE UNIVERSITY OF NEW YORK INSTITUTE OF TECHNOLOGY

Utica, New York
SUNY Learning Network
http://sln.suny.edu

State University of New York Institute of Technology was founded in 1966. It is accredited by Middle States Association of Colleges and Schools. It first offered distance learning courses in 1998. In fall 2003, there were 462 students enrolled in distance learning courses. Institutionally administered financial aid is available to distance learners.

Services Distance learners have accessibility to academic advising, bookstore, campus computer network, career placement assistance, e-mail services, library services.

Contact Ms. Marybeth Lyons, Director of Admissions, State University of New York Institute of Technology, PO Box 3050, Utica, NY 13504-3050. *Telephone:* 315-792-7500. *Fax:* 315-792-7837. *E-mail:* smbl@sunyit.edu.

DEGREES AND AWARDS

MBA Technology Management
MS Accountancy; Health Services Administration

COURSE SUBJECT AREAS OFFERED OUTSIDE OF DEGREE PROGRAMS

Undergraduate—accounting; business; business administration and management; communications, general; health and medical administrative services; health professions and related sciences, other; human resources management; nursing.
Graduate—accounting; business; business administration and management; communications, general; health and medical administrative services; health professions and related sciences, other; human resources management; nursing; taxation.

STATE UNIVERSITY OF NEW YORK INSTITUTE OF TECHNOLOGY

Utica, New York
Program in Health Services Administration
http://www.sln.suny.edu

State University of New York Institute of Technology was founded in 1966. It is accredited by Middle States Association of Colleges and Schools. It first offered distance learning courses in 1998. In fall 2003, there were 462 students enrolled in distance learning courses. Institutionally administered financial aid is available to distance learners.

Services Distance learners have accessibility to academic advising, bookstore, campus computer network, career placement assistance, e-mail services, library services.

Contact Ms. Marybeth Lyons, Director of Admissions, State University of New York Institute of Technology, PO Box 3050, Utica, NY 13504-3050. *Telephone:* 315-792-7500. *Fax:* 315-792-7837. *E-mail:* smbl@sunyit.edu.

DEGREES AND AWARDS

MS Health Services Administration

COURSE SUBJECT AREAS OFFERED OUTSIDE OF DEGREE PROGRAMS

Undergraduate—accounting; business; business administration and management; communications, general; health and medical administrative services; health professions and related sciences, other; human resources management; nursing.

Graduate—accounting; business; business administration and management; communications, general; health and medical administrative services; health professions and related sciences, other; human resources management; nursing; taxation.

See full description on page 542.

STATE UNIVERSITY OF NEW YORK INSTITUTE OF TECHNOLOGY

Utica, New York
Online MBA
http://sln.suny.edu

State University of New York Institute of Technology was founded in 1966. It is accredited by Middle States Association of Colleges and Schools. It first offered distance learning courses in 1998. In fall 2003, there were 462 students enrolled in distance learning courses. Institutionally administered financial aid is available to distance learners.

Services Distance learners have accessibility to academic advising, bookstore, campus computer network, career placement assistance, e-mail services, library services.

Contact Mrs. Cynthiya Zegarelli, State University of New York Institute of Technology, School of Management, PO Box 3050, Utica, NY 13504-3050. *Telephone:* 315-792-7429. *Fax:* 315-792-7138. *E-mail:* scaz@sunyit.edu.

DEGREES AND AWARDS

Graduate Certificate Business Administration
MBA Technology Management

COURSE SUBJECT AREAS OFFERED OUTSIDE OF DEGREE PROGRAMS

Undergraduate—accounting; business; business administration and management; communications, general; health and medical administrative services; health professions and related sciences, other; human resources management; nursing.

Graduate—accounting; business; business administration and management; communications, general; health and medical administrative services; health professions and related sciences, other; human resources management; nursing; taxation.

See full description on page 538.

STATE UNIVERSITY OF NEW YORK INSTITUTE OF TECHNOLOGY

Utica, New York
Program in Accountancy
http://sln.suny.edu

State University of New York Institute of Technology was founded in 1966. It is accredited by Middle States Association of Colleges and Schools. It first offered distance learning courses in 1998. In fall 2003, there were 462 students enrolled in distance learning courses. Institutionally administered financial aid is available to distance learners.

Services Distance learners have accessibility to academic advising, bookstore, campus computer network, career placement assistance, e-mail services, library services.

Contact Ms. Marybeth Lyons, Director of Admissions, State University of New York Institute of Technology, PO Box 3050, Utica, NY 13504-3050. *Telephone:* 315-792-7500. *Fax:* 315-792-7837. *E-mail:* smbl@sunyit.edu.

DEGREES AND AWARDS

MS Accountancy

COURSE SUBJECT AREAS OFFERED OUTSIDE OF DEGREE PROGRAMS

Undergraduate—accounting; business; business administration and management; communications, general; health and medical administrative services; health professions and related sciences, other; human resources management; nursing.

Graduate—accounting; business; business administration and management; communications, general; health and medical administrative services; health professions and related sciences, other; human resources management; nursing; taxation.

See full description on page 540.

STEPHEN F. AUSTIN STATE UNIVERSITY

Nacogdoches, Texas
http://oit.sfasu.edu/

Stephen F. Austin State University was founded in 1923. It is accredited by Southern Association of Colleges and Schools. It first offered distance learning courses in 1993. In fall 2003, there were 1,000 students enrolled in distance learning courses. Institutionally administered financial aid is available to distance learners.

Services Distance learners have accessibility to academic advising, bookstore, campus computer network, career placement assistance, e-mail services, library services, tutoring.

Contact Andra Floyd, Distance Education Support Specialist, Stephen F. Austin State University, SFA Box 13038, Nacogdoches, TX 75962. *Telephone:* 936-468-1919. *Fax:* 936-468-1308. *E-mail:* de@sfasu.edu.

DEGREES AND AWARDS

Certificate Elementary Education (Post-Baccalaureate Certification)

MA Music Education

COURSE SUBJECT AREAS OFFERED OUTSIDE OF DEGREE PROGRAMS

Undergraduate—accounting; agriculture/agricultural sciences; apparel and accessories marketing operations; astronomy; business administration and management; business communications; curriculum and instruction; economics; educational psychology; English technical and business writing; family/consumer resource management; financial management and services; hospitality services management; music; psychology; social work; special education.

Graduate—education administration and supervision; educational psychology; education, other; forestry and related sciences; general teacher education; music; psychology; special education.

STEPHENS COLLEGE

Columbia, Missouri

School of Graduate and Continuing Education

http://www.stephens.edu/admission/nontraditional/

Stephens College was founded in 1833. It is accredited by North Central Association of Colleges and Schools. It first offered distance learning courses in 1971. In fall 2003, there were 200 students enrolled in distance learning courses. Institutionally administered financial aid is available to distance learners.

Services Distance learners have accessibility to academic advising, bookstore, e-mail services, library services.

Contact Ms. Rebekah A. Savage, Assistant Director of Admission, Stephens College, 1200 East Broadway, Box 2121, Columbia, MO 65215. *Telephone:* 800-388-7579. *Fax:* 573-876-7237. *E-mail:* sce@stephens.edu.

DEGREES AND AWARDS

BA Business Administration; English; Psychology

BS Health Care and Second Area; Health Information Administration; Health Science and Second Area

Certificate Health Information Administration

MBA Clinical Information Systems Management; Entrepreneurial Studies; Financial Services and Risk Management; Management

COURSE SUBJECT AREAS OFFERED OUTSIDE OF DEGREE PROGRAMS

Undergraduate—accounting; business; computer and information sciences, general; developmental and child psychology; economics; English creative writing; English language and literature, general; health and medical administrative services; history; mathematics; philosophy; psychology; religion/religious studies; social sciences, general.

Graduate—accounting; business marketing and marketing management; entrepreneurship; finance; marketing management and research; mathematical statistics.

STEVENS INSTITUTE OF TECHNOLOGY

Hoboken, New Jersey

Graduate School

http://www.webcampus.stevens.edu

Stevens Institute of Technology was founded in 1870. It is accredited by Middle States Association of Colleges and Schools. It first offered distance learning courses in 1999. In fall 2003, there were 2,500 students enrolled in distance learning courses. Institutionally administered financial aid is available to distance learners.

Services Distance learners have accessibility to academic advising, bookstore, campus computer network, career placement assistance, e-mail services, library services, tutoring.

Contact Robert Zotti, Program Director, Online Learning, Stevens Institute of Technology, Hoboken, NJ 07030. *Telephone:* 800-496-4935. *Fax:* 201-216-5011. *E-mail:* webcampus@stevens.edu.

DEGREES AND AWARDS

Graduate Certificate Atmospheric and Environmental Science and Engineering; Computer Graphics; Cyber Security; Database Systems; Digital Signal Processing; Elements of Computer Science; Financial Engineering; Human Resources Management; Management Information Systems; Multimedia Technology; Networked Information Systems; Pharmaceutical Manufacturing Practices; Professional Communications; Project Management; Quantitative Software Engineering; Secure Network Systems Design; Technology Management; Telecommunications Management; Wireless Communications

ME Networked Information Systems

MS Computer Science with CyberSecurity Concentration; Computer Science/Telecom Management w/ Consentration in Security; Management and Forensics; Microelectronics and Photonics; Project Management; Quantitative Software Engineering; Systems Engineering; Telecommunication Management

COURSE SUBJECT AREAS OFFERED OUTSIDE OF DEGREE PROGRAMS

Undergraduate—engineering/industrial management; mathematics.

Graduate—computer software and media applications; management information systems/business data processing; management science.

Non-credit—computer science; engineering, general; technology education/industrial arts.

See full description on page 544.

STONY BROOK UNIVERSITY, STATE UNIVERSITY OF NEW YORK

Stony Brook, New York

Electronic Extension Program

http://www.stonybrook.edu/spd/online/

Stony Brook University, State University of New York was founded in 1957. It is accredited by Middle States Association of Colleges and Schools. It first offered distance learning courses in 1996. In fall 2003, there were 950 students enrolled in distance learning courses. Institutionally administered financial aid is available to distance learners.

Services Distance learners have accessibility to academic advising, campus computer network, library services.

Stony Brook University, State University of New York (continued)

Contact Kim Garvin, Assistant Director, Stony Brook University, State University of New York, School of Professional Development, N 215 SBS Building, Stony Brook, NY 11794-4310. *Telephone:* 631-632-9484. *Fax:* 631-632-9046. *E-mail:* kim.garvin@stonybrook.edu.

DEGREES AND AWARDS

MA Liberal Studies

COURSE SUBJECT AREAS OFFERED OUTSIDE OF DEGREE PROGRAMS

Graduate—education, general; liberal arts and sciences, general studies and humanities; social sciences and history, other.

STRAYER UNIVERSITY

Washington, District of Columbia
Strayer Online
http://www.online.strayer.edu

Strayer University was founded in 1892. It is accredited by Middle States Association of Colleges and Schools. It first offered distance learning courses in 1997. In fall 2003, there were 11,500 students enrolled in distance learning courses. Institutionally administered financial aid is available to distance learners.

Services Distance learners have accessibility to academic advising, bookstore, campus computer network, e-mail services, library services, tutoring.

Contact Deepali Kala, Enrollment Manager, Strayer University, PO Box 487, Newington, VA 22122. *Telephone:* 888-360-1588 Ext. 1106. *Fax:* 703-339-1852. *E-mail:* dk@strayer.edu.

DEGREES AND AWARDS

AA Accounting; Acquisition and Contract Management; Business Administration; Computer Information Systems; Computer Networking; Economics; General Studies; Marketing
BS Accounting; Business Administration; Computer Information Systems; Computer Networking; Economics; International Business
Certificate Accounting; Acquisition and Contract Management; Computer and Information Systems
Diploma Accounting; Computer Information Systems
Graduate Certificate Accounting; Business Administration; Computer Information Systems
MBA Business Administration
MEd Education
MHA Health Services Administration
MPA Public Administration
MS Communications Technology; Information Systems; Management Information Systems; Professional Accounting

COURSE SUBJECT AREAS OFFERED OUTSIDE OF DEGREE PROGRAMS

Undergraduate—accounting; area, ethnic and cultural studies, other; business; economics; English composition; English language and literature, general; financial management and services; foreign languages and literatures; history; information sciences and systems; international business; legal studies; marketing operations/marketing and distribution, other; mathematics; political science and government; psychology; sociology.

Graduate—accounting; business; economics; information sciences and systems; legal studies; mathematics.

See full description on page 546.

SUFFOLK UNIVERSITY

Boston, Massachusetts
Suffolk MBA Online
http://www.suffolk.edu/mbaonline

Suffolk University was founded in 1906. It is accredited by New England Association of Schools and Colleges. It first offered distance learning courses in 1999. In fall 2003, there were 300 students enrolled in distance learning courses. Institutionally administered financial aid is available to distance learners.

Services Distance learners have accessibility to academic advising, bookstore, campus computer network, career placement assistance, e-mail services, library services, tutoring.

Contact Dr. Lillian Hallberg, Assistant Dean, Graduate Programs, Suffolk University, 8 Ashburton Place, S-823, Boston, MA 02108-2770. *Telephone:* 617-573-8306. *Fax:* 617-573-8653. *E-mail:* lhallber@suffolk.edu.

DEGREES AND AWARDS

MBA Accelerated MBA for Attorneys; Accelerated MBA for CPAs; Business Administration

COURSE SUBJECT AREAS OFFERED OUTSIDE OF DEGREE PROGRAMS

Graduate—accounting; finance; human resources management; information sciences and systems; international business; marketing management and research; taxation.

See full description on page 548.

SULLIVAN UNIVERSITY

Louisville, Kentucky
Program in Dispute Resolution
http://home.sullivan.edu/grad_school/graduate/curriculum/MSDR.htm

Sullivan University was founded in 1864. It is accredited by Southern Association of Colleges and Schools. It first offered distance learning courses in 2002. In fall 2003, there were 14 students enrolled in distance learning courses. Institutionally administered financial aid is available to distance learners.

Services Distance learners have accessibility to academic advising, bookstore, campus computer network, career placement assistance, e-mail services, library services.

Contact Mr. Ron Hinson, Director of Graduate Admissions, Sullivan University, The Graduate School, 3101 Bardstown Road, Louisville, KY 40205. *Telephone:* 800-844-1354 Ext. 477. *Fax:* 502-456-0016. *E-mail:* rhinson@sullivan.edu.

DEGREES AND AWARDS

Certificate Dispute Resolution
MS Dispute Resolution, Conflict Management

COURSE SUBJECT AREAS OFFERED OUTSIDE OF DEGREE PROGRAMS

Graduate—business administration and management; business management and administrative services, other; community organization, resources and services; construction management; education administration and supervision; engineering/industrial management; health and medical administrative services; hospitality services management; human resources management; human services; international business; legal studies; mental health services; nursing; peace and conflict studies; public administration and services, other; social work.

See full description on page 550.

SULLIVAN UNIVERSITY

Louisville, Kentucky

http://www.sullivan.edu/

Sullivan University was founded in 1864. It is accredited by Southern Association of Colleges and Schools. It first offered distance learning courses in 1999. In fall 2003, there were 950 students enrolled in distance learning courses. Institutionally administered financial aid is available to distance learners.

Services Distance learners have accessibility to academic advising, bookstore, career placement assistance, e-mail services, library services.
Contact Mr. Greg Cawthon, Director of Admissions, Sullivan University, 3101 Bardstown Road, Louisville, KY 40205. *Telephone:* 502-456-6505 Ext. 370. *Fax:* 502-456-0040. *E-mail:* gcawthon@sullivan.edu.

DEGREES AND AWARDS

Programs offered do not lead to a degree or other formal award.

COURSE SUBJECT AREAS OFFERED OUTSIDE OF DEGREE PROGRAMS

Undergraduate—administrative and secretarial services; business administration and management; business/managerial economics; child care and guidance workers and managers; computer science; construction management; culinary arts and related services; English composition; hospitality services management; legal studies; tourism/travel marketing; transportation and materials moving workers, other.
Graduate—accounting; business administration and management; business/managerial economics; computer/information technology administration and management; English technical and business writing; financial management and services; Internet and World Wide Web; marketing management and research.

SUL ROSS STATE UNIVERSITY

Alpine, Texas

School of Arts and Sciences

http://www.sulross.edu

Sul Ross State University was founded in 1920. It is accredited by Southern Association of Colleges and Schools. It first offered distance learning courses in 1992. In fall 2003, there were 150 students enrolled in distance learning courses. Institutionally administered financial aid is available to distance learners.

Services Distance learners have accessibility to academic advising, bookstore, campus computer network, career placement assistance, e-mail services, library services, tutoring.
Contact Marshall Eidson, Instructional and User Services Team Leader, Sul Ross State University, OIT Instructional Services, Alpine, TX 79832. *Telephone:* 432-837-8669. *Fax:* 432-837-8364. *E-mail:* meidson@sulross.edu.

DEGREES AND AWARDS

Programs offered do not lead to a degree or other formal award.

COURSE SUBJECT AREAS OFFERED OUTSIDE OF DEGREE PROGRAMS

Undergraduate—biology, general; communications, general; English composition; English language and literature, general; geography; history; mathematics; physical sciences, general; political science and government; psychology.
Graduate—teacher education, specific academic and vocational programs.

SUMMIT PACIFIC COLLEGE

Abbotsford, British Columbia, Canada

http://www.summitpacific.ca

Summit Pacific College was founded in 1941. It is provincially chartered. It first offered distance learning courses in 1999. In fall 2003, there were 225 students enrolled in distance learning courses. Institutionally administered financial aid is available to distance learners.

Services Distance learners have accessibility to academic advising, bookstore, career placement assistance, tutoring.
Contact Rev. Robert McIntyre, Director, Distance Education, Summit Pacific College, 35235 Straiton Road, PO Box 1700, Abbotsford, BC V2S 7E7, Canada. *Telephone:* 604-851-7228. *Fax:* 604-853-8951. *E-mail:* distanceed@summitpacific.ca.

DEGREES AND AWARDS

Programs offered do not lead to a degree or other formal award.

COURSE SUBJECT AREAS OFFERED OUTSIDE OF DEGREE PROGRAMS

Undergraduate—bible/biblical studies; pastoral counseling and specialized ministries; religion/religious studies; religious education; theological and ministerial studies.
Non-credit—bible/biblical studies; religion/religious studies; religious education; theological and ministerial studies.

SYRACUSE UNIVERSITY

Syracuse, New York

Division of Continuing Education

http://www.suce.syr.edu/distance

Syracuse University was founded in 1870. It is accredited by Middle States Association of Colleges and Schools. It first offered distance learning courses in 1966. In fall 2003, there were 1,000 students enrolled in distance learning courses. Institutionally administered financial aid is available to distance learners.

Syracuse University (continued)

Services Distance learners have accessibility to academic advising, bookstore, campus computer network, career placement assistance, e-mail services, library services.

Contact Mr. Robert Colley, Associate Dean, Continuing Education/ University College, Syracuse University, 700 University Avenue, Suite 326, Syracuse, NY 13244-2530. *Telephone:* 315-443-3225. *Fax:* 315-443-4174. *E-mail:* rmcolley@uc.syr.edu.

DEGREES AND AWARDS

AA Liberal Arts
BA Liberal Studies
MA Advertising Design; Illustration
MBA Business Administration
MS Communications Management; Information Management; Library and Information Science; Telecommunications and Network Management
MSS Social Sciences

COURSE SUBJECT AREAS OFFERED OUTSIDE OF DEGREE PROGRAMS

Undergraduate—anthropology; business administration and management; business communications; computer programming; cultural studies; English composition; English creative writing; English language and literature, general; English technical and business writing; entrepreneurship; fine arts and art studies; geography; history; international relations and affairs; philosophy; physical sciences, general; political science and government; psychology; religion/religious studies; sociology.

Graduate—anthropology; cultural studies; history; psychology; sociology.

Non-credit—financial management and services; history; military studies; textile sciences and engineering.

See full description on page 556.

SYRACUSE UNIVERSITY

Syracuse, New York

Martin J. Whitman School of Management

http://whitman.syr.edu/imba

Syracuse University was founded in 1870. It is accredited by Middle States Association of Colleges and Schools. It first offered distance learning courses in 1977. In fall 2003, there were 166 students enrolled in distance learning courses. Institutionally administered financial aid is available to distance learners.

Services Distance learners have accessibility to academic advising, bookstore, campus computer network, career placement assistance, e-mail services, library services.

Contact Paula C. O'Callaghan, Director, iMBA Program, Syracuse University, 900 South Crouse Avenue, Syracuse, NY 13244-2130. *Telephone:* 315-443-9216. *E-mail:* paula@som.syr.edu.

DEGREES AND AWARDS

MBA Business Administration

COURSE SUBJECT AREAS OFFERED OUTSIDE OF DEGREE PROGRAMS

Graduate—accounting; business; business administration and management; business information and data processing services; business/managerial economics; business quantitative methods and management science; entrepreneurship; financial management and services; marketing management and research; marketing operations/marketing and distribution, other.

Special Message

Founded in 1977, the Independent Study MBA (iMBA) Program at Syracuse University is the nation's longest-running AACSB International–accredited distance learning MBA program. The 1-week residency at the beginning of each trimester is the hallmark of this program. During the week on campus, or at one of the international sites, students are taught by the same faculty members who have taught in the full-time and part-time evening MBA program at Syracuse. The iMBA curriculum is identical to the full-time MBA program. The week is composed of intensive classes and informal time with faculty members and other students. The beginning of each course is the class time during the residency week. For new students the first day consists of an orientation program and the registration process, followed by a reception with faculty members and returning students. For continuing students the first day consists of exams for the classes taken in the last trimester, followed by the reception. Then all students take intensive classes in the Martin J. Whitman School of Management building over the next 5 days. Classes are small, typically 10–30 students per course. At the conclusion of the residency week, students leave Syracuse with an understanding of the requirements for completion of their courses. They communicate extensively between residencies with their professors and classmates via e-mail. The course ends with the exam, if required, at the following residency. Following the model, students typically take 2 courses each trimester per year, completing 18 credits toward the MBA each year. The MBA can be completed in as little as 2 years or as many as 7; 3 years is the average. Admission is conducted on a rolling basis year-round. New students who are accepted may begin at any of the residencies, which occur annually in January, May, and August. Basic requirements for admission consideration are a bachelor's degree from a regionally accredited institution, TOEFL score for international applicants, and the completed application, including 1 recommendation letter. The GMAT is required for international applicants and admission is competitive. An online application is available at http://www.PrincetonReview.com. The Admissions Office can be reached at 315-443-9214; e-mail: imba@som.syr.edu; Web site: http://www.som.syr.edu/imba.

See full description on page 552.

SYRACUSE UNIVERSITY

Syracuse, New York

School of Information Studies

http://www.ist.syr.edu

Syracuse University was founded in 1870. It is accredited by Middle States Association of Colleges and Schools. It first offered distance learning courses in 1993. In fall 2003, there were 350 students enrolled in distance learning courses. Institutionally administered financial aid is available to distance learners.

Services Distance learners have accessibility to academic advising, bookstore, campus computer network, career placement assistance, e-mail services, library services, tutoring.

Contact Kathryn Allen, Director, Distance Learning, Syracuse University, School of Information Studies, 4-206 Center for Science and

Technology, Syracuse, NY 13244. *Telephone:* 315-443-4251. *Fax:* 315-443-5673. *E-mail:* kallen02@syr.edu.

DEGREES AND AWARDS

CAGS Digital Libraries; Information Security Management; Information Systems and Telecommunications Management; School Media
MLIS Library and Information Science
MS Information Management; Telecommunications and Network Management

COURSE SUBJECT AREAS OFFERED OUTSIDE OF DEGREE PROGRAMS

Graduate—business information and data processing services; communications technologies; computer and information sciences, general; computer/information technology administration and management; computer systems analysis; computer systems networking and telecommunications; data processing technology; information sciences and systems; Internet and World Wide Web; library assistant; library science/librarianship; library science, other; systems science and theory; telecommunications.

See full description on page 554.

TACOMA COMMUNITY COLLEGE

Tacoma, Washington
Distance Learning Program
http://www.tacoma.ctc.edu/inst_dept/distancelearning/

Tacoma Community College was founded in 1965. It is accredited by Northwest Commission on Colleges and Universities. It first offered distance learning courses in 1975. In fall 2003, there were 2,286 students enrolled in distance learning courses. Institutionally administered financial aid is available to distance learners.

Services Distance learners have accessibility to academic advising, bookstore, library services.
Contact Mr. Andy Duckworth, Distance Learning Assistant, Tacoma Community College, 6501 South 19th Street, Building 7, Room 25, Tacoma, WA 98466. *Telephone:* 253-460-3958. *Fax:* 253-566-6077. *E-mail:* aduckwor@tcc.ctc.edu.

DEGREES AND AWARDS

Programs offered do not lead to a degree or other formal award.

COURSE SUBJECT AREAS OFFERED OUTSIDE OF DEGREE PROGRAMS

Undergraduate—accounting; anthropology; applied mathematics; biology, general; business; chemistry; child care and guidance workers and managers; computer and information sciences, general; computer science; criminal justice and corrections; data entry/microcomputer applications; design and applied arts; engineering, other; engineering physics; English composition; fine arts and art studies; foreign languages and literatures; geography; health and medical administrative services; health and medical assistants; health and medical diagnostic and treatment services; health professions and related sciences, other; human services; information sciences and systems; legal studies; library science/librarianship; library science, other; mathematics; music; nursing; physics; political science and government; psychology; sociology; speech and rhetorical studies.

Non-credit—business administration and management; business information and data processing services; computer and information sciences, general.

TAFT COLLEGE

Taft, California
http://www.taftcollege.edu

Taft College was founded in 1922. It is accredited by Western Association of Schools and Colleges. It first offered distance learning courses in 1997. In fall 2003, there were 700 students enrolled in distance learning courses. Institutionally administered financial aid is available to distance learners.

Services Distance learners have accessibility to academic advising, bookstore, campus computer network, e-mail services, library services, tutoring.
Contact Patti Bench, Coordinator of Distance Learning, Taft College, 29 Emmons Park Drive, Taft, CA 93268. *Telephone:* 661-763-7757. *Fax:* 661-763-7816. *E-mail:* pbench@taft.org.

DEGREES AND AWARDS

AA Criminal Justice Administration; Liberal Arts
AS Early Childhood Education; General Business

COURSE SUBJECT AREAS OFFERED OUTSIDE OF DEGREE PROGRAMS

Undergraduate—accounting; applied mathematics; biological and physical sciences; business; business administration and management; child care and guidance workers and managers; computer science; criminal justice and corrections; English composition; English creative writing; English language and literature, general; English language and literature/letters, other; geological and related sciences; history; mathematical statistics; mathematics; mathematics, other; psychology; psychology, other; social sciences and history, other; social sciences, general; sociology.

TARLETON STATE UNIVERSITY

Stephenville, Texas
Center for Instructional Technology and Distributed Education
http://online.tarleton.edu

Tarleton State University was founded in 1899. It is accredited by Southern Association of Colleges and Schools. It first offered distance learning courses in 1994. In fall 2003, there were 3,000 students enrolled in distance learning courses. Institutionally administered financial aid is available to distance learners.

Services Distance learners have accessibility to academic advising, bookstore, campus computer network, career placement assistance, e-mail services, library services, tutoring.
Contact Mrs. Gayla Renee Wright, Interim Director, Tarleton State University, Box T-0810, Stephenville, TX 76402. *Telephone:* 254-968-9060. *Fax:* 254-968-9540. *E-mail:* gwright@tarleton.edu.

DEGREES AND AWARDS

MBA Business Administration
MSHRM Human Resource Management
MSIS Information Sciences

Tarleton State University (continued)

COURSE SUBJECT AREAS OFFERED OUTSIDE OF DEGREE PROGRAMS

Undergraduate—accounting; agriculture/agricultural sciences, other; American literature (United States); applied mathematics; business; business management and administrative services, other; business/managerial economics; cognitive psychology and psycholinguistics; community health services; computer programming; computer software and media applications; counseling psychology; curriculum and instruction; economics; education administration and supervision; educational/instructional media design; educational psychology; education, general; English composition; English creative writing; English language and literature, general; English technical and business writing; general teacher education; health and physical education/fitness; history; home economics, other; mathematics, other; nursing; physical sciences, general; political science and government; psychology, other.

Graduate—business marketing and marketing management; computer and information sciences, general; computer and information sciences, other; computer/information technology administration and management; computer programming; computer science; computer software and media applications; computer systems analysis; computer systems networking and telecommunications; counseling psychology; curriculum and instruction; education administration and supervision; educational evaluation, research and statistics; educational psychology; education, general; education, other; general teacher education; health and physical education/fitness; history; human resources management; information sciences and systems; marketing management and research; physical sciences, general; psychology; social sciences, general; special education; teacher education, specific academic and vocational programs.

Non-credit—accounting; administrative and secretarial services; business; business communications; child care and guidance workers and managers; computer programming; computer software and media applications; data entry/microcomputer applications; English as a second language; English creative writing; foreign languages and literatures; foreign languages and literatures, other; human resources management; real estate.

See full description on page 558.

TARRANT COUNTY COLLEGE DISTRICT

Fort Worth, Texas
Center for Distance Learning
http://web.tccd.net/

Tarrant County College District was founded in 1967. It is accredited by Southern Association of Colleges and Schools. It first offered distance learning courses in 1973. In fall 2003, there were 8,000 students enrolled in distance learning courses. Institutionally administered financial aid is available to distance learners.

Services Distance learners have accessibility to e-mail services, library services.

Contact Dr. Kevin R. Eason, Assistant Director of Distance Learning, Tarrant County College District, 5301 Campus Drive, Fort Worth, TX 76119. *Telephone:* 817-515-4430. *Fax:* 817-515-4400. *E-mail:* kevin.eason@tccd.edu.

DEGREES AND AWARDS

AA General Studies

COURSE SUBJECT AREAS OFFERED OUTSIDE OF DEGREE PROGRAMS

Undergraduate—accounting; biology; creative writing; developmental/child psychology; engineering mechanics; English composition; liberal arts and sciences, general studies and humanities; mechanical engineering; social psychology; sociology.

TAYLOR UNIVERSITY

Fort Wayne, Indiana
Center for Lifelong Learning
http://cll.taylor.edu

Taylor University was founded in 1938. It is accredited by North Central Association of Colleges and Schools. It first offered distance learning courses in 1941. In fall 2003, there were 1,150 students enrolled in distance learning courses. Institutionally administered financial aid is available to distance learners.

Services Distance learners have accessibility to academic advising, bookstore, e-mail services, library services.

Contact Mr. Kevin J. Mahaffy, Director of Enrollment Services, Taylor University, Center for Lifelong Learning, 1025 West Rudisill Boulevard, Fort Wayne, IN 46807-2197. *Telephone:* 260-744-8750. *Fax:* 260-744-8796. *E-mail:* cllinfo@tayloru.edu.

DEGREES AND AWARDS

AA Biblical Studies; Justice Administration–Ministry Concentration; Justice Administration–Public Policy Concentration; Liberal Arts–History Concentration; Liberal Arts–Interdisciplinary Concentration; Liberal Arts–Social Science Concentration

Certificate Biblical Studies; Christian Worker; Justice and Ministry; Leadership Development; Missions Studies

COURSE SUBJECT AREAS OFFERED OUTSIDE OF DEGREE PROGRAMS

Undergraduate—American literature (United States); area studies; bible/biblical studies; biblical and other theological languages and literatures; biological and physical sciences; biology, general; business; business administration and management; business information and data processing services; business/managerial economics; computer and information sciences, general; computer/information technology administration and management; counseling psychology; criminal justice and corrections; developmental and child psychology; economics; educational/instructional media design; educational psychology; education, general; English composition; English language and literature, general; English literature (British and Commonwealth); fine arts and art studies; geography; history; information sciences and systems; journalism and mass communications; liberal arts and sciences, general studies and humanities; mathematics; medieval and Renaissance studies; missions/missionary studies and missiology; multi/interdisciplinary studies, other; music; pastoral counseling and specialized ministries; peace and conflict studies; philosophy; philosophy and religion; physical sciences, general; professional studies; psychology; religion/religious studies; religious education; religious/sacred music; social psychology; social sciences and history, other; social sciences, general; sociology; speech and rhetorical studies; theological and ministerial studies; theological studies and religious vocations, other; urban affairs/studies.

Non-credit—accounting; administrative and secretarial services; advertising; applied mathematics; bible/biblical studies; biblical and other theological languages and literatures; business; business administration and management; business and personal services marketing operations; business communications; business information and data processing services; business management and administrative services, other; communications, general; communications, other; computer and information sciences, general; computer and information sciences, other; computer/information technology administration and management; computer programming; computer software and media applications; computer systems networking and telecommunications; data entry/microcomputer applications; data processing technology; English composition; English creative writing; English technical and business writing; entrepreneurship; family and community studies; family/consumer resource management; human resources management; information sciences and systems; insurance marketing operations; Internet and World Wide Web; marketing management and research; marketing operations/marketing and distribution, other; mathematics; mathematics and computer science; public relations and organizational communications; religion/religious studies; theological and ministerial studies.

See full description on page 560.

TAYLOR UNIVERSITY

Upland, Indiana

http://cll.tayloru.edu/

Taylor University was founded in 1846. It is accredited by North Central Association of Colleges and Schools. It first offered distance learning courses in 1941. In fall 2003, there were 1,350 students enrolled in distance learning courses. Institutionally administered financial aid is available to distance learners.

Services Distance learners have accessibility to academic advising, bookstore, library services.

Contact Mrs. Cheri Zelenka, Operations Manager, Center for Lifelong Learning, Taylor University, 1025 W. Rudisill Boulevard, Fort Wayne, IN 46807. *Telephone:* 260-744-8750. *Fax:* 260-744-8796. *E-mail:* cllinfo@tayloru.edu.

DEGREES AND AWARDS

AA Biblical Studies; Justice Administration; Liberal Arts

Certificate of Completion Biblical Studies; Christian Worker; Justice and Ministry; Leadership Development; Missions Studies

COURSE SUBJECT AREAS OFFERED OUTSIDE OF DEGREE PROGRAMS

Undergraduate—American literature (United States); bible/biblical studies; biblical and other theological languages and literatures; biological and physical sciences; business; communications, general; criminal justice and corrections; developmental and child psychology; education, general; history; information sciences and systems; liberal arts and sciences, general studies and humanities; mathematics; missions/missionary studies and missiology; pastoral counseling and specialized ministries; philosophy and religion; psychology; religion/religious studies; religious education; social sciences, general; theological and ministerial studies; theological studies and religious vocations, other.

TEACHERS COLLEGE COLUMBIA UNIVERSITY

New York, New York

Distance Learning Project

http://dlp.tc.columbia.edu

Teachers College Columbia University was founded in 1887. It is accredited by Middle States Association of Colleges and Schools. It first offered distance learning courses in 1998. In fall 2003, there were 400 students enrolled in distance learning courses. Institutionally administered financial aid is available to distance learners.

Services Distance learners have accessibility to academic advising, bookstore, campus computer network, career placement assistance, e-mail services, library services, tutoring.

Contact Distance Learning Project, Teachers College Columbia University, 525 West 120th Street, Box 164, New York, NY 10027. *Telephone:* 888-633-6933. *Fax:* 212-678-3291. *E-mail:* dlp@columbia.edu.

DEGREES AND AWARDS

Programs offered do not lead to a degree or other formal award.

COURSE SUBJECT AREAS OFFERED OUTSIDE OF DEGREE PROGRAMS

Graduate—cognitive psychology and psycholinguistics; communications, other; communications technologies; community health services; computer software and media applications; cultural studies; educational evaluation, research and statistics; educational/instructional media design; educational psychology; education, other; health professions and related sciences, other; history; human resources management; mathematical statistics; science, technology and society.

Non-credit—cognitive psychology and psycholinguistics; communications, general; communications technologies; community health services; computer software and media applications; cultural studies; educational evaluation, research and statistics; educational/instructional media design; educational psychology; education, other; health professions and related sciences, other; history; human resources management; mathematical statistics; science, technology and society.

See full description on page 562.

TEIKYO POST UNIVERSITY

Waterbury, Connecticut

Accelerated Degree Programs

http://www.tpuonline.com

Teikyo Post University was founded in 1890. It is accredited by New England Association of Schools and Colleges. It first offered distance learning courses in 1997. In fall 2003, there were 700 students enrolled in distance learning courses. Institutionally administered financial aid is available to distance learners.

Services Distance learners have accessibility to academic advising, bookstore, career placement assistance, library services, tutoring.

Contact Mr. Stephen Bayley, e-Business Administrator, Teikyo Post University, 800 Country Club Road, Waterbury, CT 06723. *Telephone:* 203-596-4609. *Fax:* 203-596-4618. *E-mail:* sbayley@teikyopost.edu.

DEGREES AND AWARDS

AS Early Childhood Education; Legal Studies; Management; Marketing

Teikyo Post University (continued)

BS Business Administration; Computer Information Systems; Criminal Justice; International Business Administration; Legal Studies; Management; Marketing

Certificate Computer Information Skills; Early Childhood Administration; Early Childhood Education; International Business Administration; Legal Studies

COURSE SUBJECT AREAS OFFERED OUTSIDE OF DEGREE PROGRAMS

Undergraduate—accounting; biology, general; business administration and management; communications, general; computer and information sciences, general; computer and information sciences, other; computer science; economics; English composition; English creative writing; geography; history; legal studies; marketing management and research; mathematics; mathematics, other; music; philosophy; philosophy and religion; political science and government; psychology; psychology, other; social psychology; sociology.

TEMPLE COLLEGE

Temple, Texas
http://www.templejc.edu

Temple College was founded in 1926. It is accredited by Southern Association of Colleges and Schools. It first offered distance learning courses in 1995. In fall 2003, there were 400 students enrolled in distance learning courses. Institutionally administered financial aid is available to distance learners.

Services Distance learners have accessibility to bookstore, campus computer network, e-mail services, library services.

Contact Mr. Ray Lanford, Director of Distance Education, Temple College, 2600 South First Street, Temple, TX 76504. *E-mail:* rlanford@templejc.edu.

DEGREES AND AWARDS

Programs offered do not lead to a degree or other formal award.

COURSE SUBJECT AREAS OFFERED OUTSIDE OF DEGREE PROGRAMS

Undergraduate—administrative and secretarial services; astronomy; biology, general; business administration and management; computer and information sciences, general; criminal justice and corrections; economics; English composition; English creative writing; English literature (British and Commonwealth); English technical and business writing; geography; geological and related sciences; history; mathematics; philosophy; psychology.

TEXAS A&M INTERNATIONAL UNIVERSITY

Laredo, Texas
http://www.tamiu.edu/distance/

Texas A&M International University was founded in 1969. It is accredited by Southern Association of Colleges and Schools. It first offered distance learning courses in 2003. In fall 2003, there were 2,700 students enrolled in distance learning courses. Institutionally administered financial aid is available to distance learners.

Services Distance learners have accessibility to academic advising, career placement assistance, e-mail services, library services, tutoring.

Contact Ms. Barbara Lunce, Registrar, Texas A&M International University, 5201 University Boulevard, Laredo, TX 78041-1900. *Telephone:* 956-326-2250. *E-mail:* blunce@tamiu.edu.

DEGREES AND AWARDS

Programs offered do not lead to a degree or other formal award.

COURSE SUBJECT AREAS OFFERED OUTSIDE OF DEGREE PROGRAMS

Undergraduate—business information and data processing services; communications, other; criminal justice and corrections; education administration and supervision; education, general; health and medical preparatory programs; history; psychology; social work.

Graduate—criminal justice and corrections; education administration and supervision; teacher education, specific academic and vocational programs.

TEXAS A&M UNIVERSITY

College Station, Texas
Office of Distance Education
http://distance.tamu.edu

Texas A&M University was founded in 1876. It is accredited by Southern Association of Colleges and Schools. It first offered distance learning courses in 1973. In fall 2003, there were 950 students enrolled in distance learning courses. Institutionally administered financial aid is available to distance learners.

Services Distance learners have accessibility to academic advising, bookstore, campus computer network, e-mail services, library services, tutoring.

Contact Ms. Cheryl Kruse, Distance Education Contact, Texas A&M University, 510 Blocker, 1478 TAMU, College Station, TX 77843. *Telephone:* 979-845-4282. *Fax:* 979-845-4422. *E-mail:* distance-ed@tamu.edu.

DEGREES AND AWARDS

MAg Agricultural Development, Fisheries, Plant Science, Poultry Science, Natural Resource Development, or Wildlife

MEd Educational Administration; Educational Psychology with Bilingual Education Emphasis; Educational Technology

MEngr Petroleum Engineering

MS Educational Human Resource Development; Engineering Systems Management; Mathematics–Teaching Track

PhD Hispanic Studies

COURSE SUBJECT AREAS OFFERED OUTSIDE OF DEGREE PROGRAMS

Graduate—agriculture/agricultural sciences; education administration and supervision; educational/instructional media design; engineering/industrial management; engineering-related technologies, other; human resources management; international relations and affairs; mathematics; petroleum engineering; plant sciences; wildlife and wildlands management.

TEXAS A&M UNIVERSITY-COMMERCE

Commerce, Texas
Instructional Technology and Distance Learning
http://www7.tamu-commerce.edu/itde/

Texas A&M University–Commerce was founded in 1889. It is accredited by Southern Association of Colleges and Schools. It first offered distance learning courses in 1993. In fall 2003, there were 1,050 students enrolled in distance learning courses. Institutionally administered financial aid is available to distance learners.

Services Distance learners have accessibility to academic advising, bookstore, campus computer network, career placement assistance, e-mail services, library services, tutoring.
Contact Charlotte A. Larkin, Director of Instructional Technology and Distance Education, Texas A&M University–Commerce, PO Box 3011, Commerce, TX 75429. *Telephone:* 903-886-5511. *Fax:* 903-886-5991. *E-mail:* charlotte_larkin@tamu-commerce.edu.

DEGREES AND AWARDS

Programs offered do not lead to a degree or other formal award.

COURSE SUBJECT AREAS OFFERED OUTSIDE OF DEGREE PROGRAMS

Undergraduate—biology, general; business administration and management; computer science; creative writing; developmental/child psychology; educational psychology; English composition; English language and literature, general; journalism; social work; sociology.
Graduate—accounting; business marketing and marketing management; curriculum and instruction; economics; education administration and supervision; educational/instructional media design; educational psychology; engineering/industrial management; English composition; finance; library science, other; radio/television broadcasting; special education.

TEXAS A&M UNIVERSITY-CORPUS CHRISTI

Corpus Christi, Texas
http://www.tamucc.edu

Texas A&M University–Corpus Christi was founded in 1947. It is accredited by Southern Association of Colleges and Schools. It first offered distance learning courses in 1976. In fall 2003, there were 350 students enrolled in distance learning courses. Institutionally administered financial aid is available to distance learners.

Services Distance learners have accessibility to academic advising, bookstore, campus computer network, career placement assistance, e-mail services, library services.
Contact Ms. Margaret Dechant, Director of Admissions and Records, Texas A&M University–Corpus Christi, 6300 Ocean Drive, Corpus Christi, TX 78412-5503. *Telephone:* 361-825-2624. *Fax:* 361-825-5887. *E-mail:* margaret.dechant@mail.tamucc.edu.

DEGREES AND AWARDS

BSN Nursing
MSN Nursing Administration

COURSE SUBJECT AREAS OFFERED OUTSIDE OF DEGREE PROGRAMS

Undergraduate—English composition; mathematical statistics.
Graduate—accounting; education, other; marketing management and research.

TEXAS A&M UNIVERSITY-KINGSVILLE

Kingsville, Texas
Center for Distance Learning and Continuing Education
http://www.tamuk.edu/distancelearning

Texas A&M University–Kingsville was founded in 1925. It is accredited by Southern Association of Colleges and Schools. It first offered distance learning courses in 1992. In fall 2003, there were 535 students enrolled in distance learning courses. Institutionally administered financial aid is available to distance learners.

Services Distance learners have accessibility to academic advising, bookstore, campus computer network, career placement assistance, e-mail services, library services.
Contact Dr. Tadeo Reyna, Jr., Director, Texas A&M University–Kingsville, 700 University Boulevard, MSC 147, Kingsville, TX 78363-8202. *Telephone:* 361-593-2861 Ext. 2854. *Fax:* 361-593-2859. *E-mail:* t-reyna@tamuk.edu.

DEGREES AND AWARDS

Programs offered do not lead to a degree or other formal award.

COURSE SUBJECT AREAS OFFERED OUTSIDE OF DEGREE PROGRAMS

Undergraduate—physics.
Graduate—bilingual/bicultural education; education administration and supervision; English as a second language; environmental/environmental health engineering.

TEXAS A&M UNIVERSITY-TEXARKANA

Texarkana, Texas
http://www.tamut.edu/

Texas A&M University–Texarkana was founded in 1971. It is accredited by Southern Association of Colleges and Schools. It first offered distance learning courses in 1995. In fall 2003, there were 250 students enrolled in distance learning courses. Institutionally administered financial aid is available to distance learners.

Services Distance learners have accessibility to academic advising, career placement assistance, e-mail services, library services.
Contact Mrs. Patricia Black, Director of Admissions and Registrar, Texas A&M University–Texarkana, PO Box 5518, Texarkana, TX 75505-5518. *Telephone:* 903-223-3069. *Fax:* 903-223-3140. *E-mail:* pat.black@tamut.edu.

DEGREES AND AWARDS

Programs offered do not lead to a degree or other formal award.

Texas A&M University–Texarkana (continued)

COURSE SUBJECT AREAS OFFERED OUTSIDE OF DEGREE PROGRAMS

Undergraduate—business; criminal justice and corrections; education, general; English language and literature, general; information sciences and systems; international business; marketing operations/ marketing and distribution, other; political science and government; public administration; teacher education, specific academic and vocational programs.
Graduate—accounting; business information and data processing services; economics; education administration and supervision; education, other.

TEXAS CHRISTIAN UNIVERSITY

Fort Worth, Texas
Cyberlearning
http://www.tcuglobal.edu

Texas Christian University was founded in 1873. It is accredited by Southern Association of Colleges and Schools. It first offered distance learning courses in 1999. In fall 2003, there were 450 students enrolled in distance learning courses. Institutionally administered financial aid is available to distance learners.

Services Distance learners have accessibility to academic advising, bookstore, campus computer network, career placement assistance, e-mail services, library services, tutoring.
Contact Mrs. Romana J. Hughes, Director, eLearning Initiatives, Texas Christian University, Box 298970, Fort Worth, TX 76129. *Telephone:* 817-257-7434. *Fax:* 817-257-7393. *E-mail:* r.hughes@tcu.edu.

DEGREES AND AWARDS

Advanced Graduate Diploma Liberal Arts–Master of Liberal Arts
MSN Nursing

COURSE SUBJECT AREAS OFFERED OUTSIDE OF DEGREE PROGRAMS

Undergraduate—American history; art history; biology; theater arts/ drama.

TEXAS STATE TECHNICAL COLLEGE–WACO

Waco, Texas
http://www.waco.tstc.edu/

Texas State Technical College–Waco was founded in 1965. It is accredited by Southern Association of Colleges and Schools. It first offered distance learning courses in 1995. In fall 2003, there were 500 students enrolled in distance learning courses. Institutionally administered financial aid is available to distance learners.

Services Distance learners have accessibility to academic advising, bookstore, campus computer network, career placement assistance, e-mail services, library services, tutoring.
Contact Lance Zimmerman, Director of Distance Education, Texas State Technical College–Waco, 3801 Campus Drive, Waco, TX 76705-1696. *Telephone:* 800-792-8784 Ext. 3257. *Fax:* 254-867-3470. *E-mail:* lance.zimmerman@tstc.edu.

DEGREES AND AWARDS

AAS Webmaster
Certificate of Completion E-Commerce; Internet SQL; Webmaster

COURSE SUBJECT AREAS OFFERED OUTSIDE OF DEGREE PROGRAMS

Undergraduate—computer programming; computer science; computer software and media applications; computer systems analysis; computer systems networking and telecommunications; data entry/ microcomputer applications; English composition; Internet and World Wide Web; mathematics.
Non-credit—computer programming; computer software and media applications; Internet and World Wide Web; personal and miscellaneous services, other.

TEXAS STATE UNIVERSITY-SAN MARCOS

San Marcos, Texas
Correspondence and Extension Studies
http://www.ideal.swt.edu/correspondence/

Texas State University-San Marcos was founded in 1899. It is accredited by Southern Association of Colleges and Schools. It first offered distance learning courses in 1953. In fall 2003, there were 1,500 students enrolled in distance learning courses. Institutionally administered financial aid is available to distance learners.

Services Distance learners have accessibility to bookstore, campus computer network, e-mail services, library services, tutoring.
Contact Carolyn Bettelheim, Administrative Assistant, Texas State University-San Marcos, 302 ASB North, 601 University Drive, San Marcos, TX 78666. *Telephone:* 512-245-2322. *Fax:* 512-245-8934. *E-mail:* corrstudy@txstate.edu.

DEGREES AND AWARDS

Programs offered do not lead to a degree or other formal award.

COURSE SUBJECT AREAS OFFERED OUTSIDE OF DEGREE PROGRAMS

Undergraduate—art history; biological sciences/life sciences, other; biology; business; criminal justice and corrections; criminology; dance; English composition; English creative writing; English language and literature, general; English language and literature/letters, other; English literature (British and Commonwealth); geography; health and medical administrative services; health services administration; history; mathematics; mathematics and computer science; music; philosophy; political science and government; psychology; sociology; Spanish.
Graduate—geography; mathematics.
Non-credit—health and medical administrative services.

Special Message

Texas State University–San Marcos is located in the Texas Hill Country. Established in 1899, it has grown into a major doctoral-granting institution, nationally recognized in many areas, with more than 25,000 students, 1,000 faculty members, and more than 100,000 graduates. Texas State also offers a comprehensive extended and distance learning program to all students.

The Office of Extended and Distance Learning offers college credit and support services through the Internet, interactive TV, correspondence study, satellite teaching locations throughout central

Texas, and study-abroad programs. Faculty members incorporate a variety of distributed technologies into their instructional programs. More than 100 courses are available to help students balance busy schedules and meet educational goals.

Texas State has offered correspondence courses to students since 1954. Currently, the Office of Correspondence Studies offers more than sixty accredited undergraduate and graduate university courses in a variety of subjects. Correspondence courses are available for enrollment at any time during the year, and students may take up to one full year to complete a course. Print-based and online courses are available. Students may submit assignments by e-mail and receive free online tutoring for many courses. A student need not be admitted to Texas State to take a Texas State correspondence course. For more information about correspondence study at Texas State, students should visit the Web site at http://www.txstate.edu/correspondence/ or call the Office of Correspondence Studies at 800-511-8656 (toll-free).

TEXAS TECH UNIVERSITY

Lubbock, Texas

http://www.de.ttu.edu

Texas Tech University was founded in 1923. It is accredited by Southern Association of Colleges and Schools. It first offered distance learning courses in 1941. In fall 2003, there were 650 students enrolled in distance learning courses. Institutionally administered financial aid is available to distance learners.

Services Distance learners have accessibility to academic advising, bookstore, campus computer network, e-mail services, library services.

Contact Mrs. Michele L. Moskos, Marketing Director of Extended Studies, Texas Tech University, Box 42191, Lubbock, TX 79409-2191. *Telephone:* 806-742-7200 Ext. 276. *Fax:* 806-742-7277. *E-mail:* dldegrees.oes@ttu.edu.

DEGREES AND AWARDS

BGS General Studies
Certificate Educational Diagnostician; Orientation and Mobility; Special Education, generic; Visually Handicapped
MA Technical Communication
ME Engineering
MEd Instructional Technology–Distance Education Emphasis; Special Education
MS Petroleum Engineering; Restaurant, Hotel, and Institutional Management; Software Engineering; Systems and Engineering Management
EdD Agricultural Education

COURSE SUBJECT AREAS OFFERED OUTSIDE OF DEGREE PROGRAMS

Undergraduate—accounting; agricultural economics; agriculture/agricultural sciences; American history; American literature (United States); anthropology; business administration and management; business marketing and marketing management; developmental and child psychology; economics; educational psychology; English composition; English literature (British and Commonwealth); English technical and business writing; European history; foods and nutrition studies; food sciences and technology; history; horticulture services operations and management; journalism and mass communications; legal studies; liberal arts and sciences, general studies and humanities; mathematics, other; music; psychology; social psychology; sociology; Spanish; tourism/travel marketing.

Graduate—agriculture/agricultural sciences; animal sciences; architecture; chemical engineering; civil engineering; computer and information sciences, other; computer science; curriculum and instruction; education administration and supervision; educational/instructional media design; education, general; education, other; electrical and electronic engineering-related technology; engineering, general; engineering, other; English technical and business writing; environmental/environmental health engineering; family/consumer resource management; industrial/manufacturing engineering; mathematical statistics; mathematics; mechanical engineering; music; petroleum engineering; plant sciences; textile sciences and engineering; visual and performing arts.

Non-credit—agricultural economics; architecture; business administration and management; Spanish.

See full description on page 564.

TEXAS WOMAN'S UNIVERSITY

Denton, Texas

http://www.twuonline.com

Texas Woman's University was founded in 1901. It is accredited by Southern Association of Colleges and Schools. It first offered distance learning courses in 1994. In fall 2003, there were 2,400 students enrolled in distance learning courses. Institutionally administered financial aid is available to distance learners.

Services Distance learners have accessibility to academic advising, bookstore, career placement assistance, e-mail services, library services, tutoring.

Contact Dr. Lynda Murphy, Coordinator of Distance Education, Texas Woman's University, PO Box 425649, Denton, TX 76204. *Telephone:* 940-898-3411. *Fax:* 940-898-3416. *E-mail:* lmurphy@twu.edu.

DEGREES AND AWARDS

BGS General Studies
BS Health Studies
MA Occupational Therapy; Teaching
MBA Business Administration
MLS Library Science
MS Deaf Education; Family Studies; Speech-Language Pathology
PhD Nursing

COURSE SUBJECT AREAS OFFERED OUTSIDE OF DEGREE PROGRAMS

Undergraduate—bilingual/bicultural education; education, general; English language and literature, general; family/consumer resource management; health and physical education/fitness; health professions and related sciences, other; history; home economics, general; nursing; occupational therapy; sociology.

Graduate—bilingual/bicultural education; business; computer and information sciences, general; education, general; education, other; family/consumer resource management; health and physical education/fitness; library science/librarianship; mathematical statistics; nursing; occupational therapy; physical therapy; school psychology; sociology.

THOMAS COLLEGE

Waterville, Maine
Continuing Education Division
http://www.thomas.edu

Thomas College was founded in 1894. It is accredited by New England Association of Schools and Colleges. It first offered distance learning courses in 1995. In fall 2003, there were 100 students enrolled in distance learning courses. Institutionally administered financial aid is available to distance learners.

Services Distance learners have accessibility to academic advising, bookstore, campus computer network, e-mail services.

Contact Maria O'Connell, Student Enrollment Associate, Thomas College, 180 West River Road, Waterville, ME 04901. *Telephone:* 207-859-1102. *Fax:* 207-859-1114. *E-mail:* ced@thomas.edu.

DEGREES AND AWARDS

Programs offered do not lead to a degree or other formal award.

COURSE SUBJECT AREAS OFFERED OUTSIDE OF DEGREE PROGRAMS

Undergraduate—business.
Graduate—business.

THOMAS EDISON STATE COLLEGE

Trenton, New Jersey
DIAL–Distance and Independent Adult Learning
http://www.tesc.edu

Thomas Edison State College was founded in 1972. It is accredited by Middle States Association of Colleges and Schools. It first offered distance learning courses in 1972. In fall 2003, there were 10,233 students enrolled in distance learning courses. Institutionally administered financial aid is available to distance learners.

Services Distance learners have accessibility to academic advising, bookstore, library services.

Contact Mr. Gordon Holly, Director of Admissions, Thomas Edison State College, 101 West State Street, Trenton, NJ 08608-1176. *Telephone:* 888-442-8372. *Fax:* 609-984-8447. *E-mail:* admissions@tesc.edu.

DEGREES AND AWARDS

AA Liberal Arts/General Studies
AAS Administrative Studies; Applied Computer Studies; Applied Electronic Studies; Applied Health Studies; Mechanics and Maintenance; Occupational Studies
ASAST Air Traffic Control; Architectural Design; Aviation Flight Technology; Aviation Maintenance Technology; Biomedical Electronics; Civil and Construction Engineering Technology; Clinical Lab Science; Computer Science Technology; Electrical Technology; Electronic Engineering Technology; Engineering Graphics; Environmental Sciences; Fire Protection Science; Forestry; Horticulture; Laboratory Animal Science; Manufacturing Engineering Technology; Marine Engineering Technology; Mechanical Engineering Technology; Medical Imaging; Nondestructive Testing Technology; Nuclear Engineering Technology; Nuclear Medicine Technology; Radiation Protection; Radiation Therapy; Respiratory Care; Surveying
ASM Accounting; Administrative Office Management; Banking; Computer Information Systems; Finance; Hospital Health Care Administration; Hotel/Motel/Restaurant Management; Human Resource Management; Insurance; International Business; Management, general; Marketing; Operations Management; Procurement; Public Administration; Purchasing and Materials Management; Real Estate; Retailing Management; Small Business Management/Entrepreneurship; Transportation/Distribution Management
ASNSM Biology; Computer Science; Mathematics
ASPSS Administration of Justice; Child Development Services; Community Services; Emergency Disaster Management; Fitness and Wellness Services; Gerontology; Legal Services; Recreation Services; Social Services for Special Populations; Social Services
BA Anthropology; Art; Biology; Communications; Computer Science; Economics; English; Environmental Studies; Foreign Language; History; Humanities; Journalism; Labor Studies; Liberal Studies; Mathematics; Music; Natural Sciences/Mathematics; Philosophy; Political Science; Psychology; Religion; Social Sciences/History; Sociology; Theater Arts
BS Administration of Justice; Child Development Services; Community Services; Emergency Disaster Management; Gerontology; Health Services Administration; Health Services Education; Health Services; Health and Nutrition Counseling; Legal Services; Mental Health and Rehabilitation Services; Recreation Services; Social Services Administration; Social Services for Special Populations; Social Services
BSAST Air Traffic Control; Architectural Design; Aviation Flight Technology; Aviation Maintenance Technology; Biomedical Electronics; Civil Engineering Technology; Clinical Lab Science; Computer Science Technology; Construction; Cytotechnology; Dental Hygiene; Electrical Technology; Electronic Engineering Technology; Engineering Graphics; Environmental Sciences; Fire Protection Science; Forestry; Horticulture; Laboratory Animal Science; Manufacturing Engineering Technology; Marine Engineering Technology; Mechanical Engineering Technology; Medical Imaging; Nondestructive Testing Technology; Nuclear Engineering Technology; Nuclear Medicine Technology; Perfusion Technology; Radiation Protection; Radiation Therapy; Respiratory Care; Surveying
BSBA Accounting; Administrative Office Management; Advertising Management; Banking; Computer Information Systems; Finance; Hospital Health Care Administration; Hotel/Motel/Restaurant Management; Human Resources Management; Insurance; International Business; Logistics; Management, general; Marketing; Operations Management; Procurement; Public Administration; Purchasing and Materials Management; Real Estate; Retailing Management; Small Business Management/Entrepreneurship; Transportation/Distribution Management
BSN Nursing
MA Professional Studies
MS Human Resources Management
MSM Management

See full description on page 566.

THREE RIVERS COMMUNITY COLLEGE

Norwich, Connecticut
http://www.trcc.commnet.edu/

Three Rivers Community College was founded in 1963. It is accredited by New England Association of Schools and Colleges. It first offered distance learning courses in 2000. In fall 2003, there were 300 students enrolled in distance learning courses. Institutionally administered financial aid is available to distance learners.

Services Distance learners have accessibility to bookstore, library services, tutoring.

Contact Larry Davenport, Director of Distance Learning, Three Rivers Community College. *Telephone:* 860-885-2659. *E-mail:* ldavenport@trcc.commnet.edu.

DEGREES AND AWARDS

CCCPE Fiber Optics

COURSE SUBJECT AREAS OFFERED OUTSIDE OF DEGREE PROGRAMS

Undergraduate—accounting; business administration and management; computer and information sciences, general; environmental/environmental health engineering; history; mathematics; psychology.

THUNDERBIRD, THE GARVIN SCHOOL OF INTERNATIONAL MANAGEMENT

Glendale, Arizona

http://www.thunderbird.edu/globalmba/

Thunderbird, The Garvin School of International Management was founded in 1946. It is accredited by North Central Association of Colleges and Schools. It first offered distance learning courses in 1998. In fall 2003, there were 284 students enrolled in distance learning courses. Institutionally administered financial aid is available to distance learners.

Services Distance learners have accessibility to academic advising, bookstore, campus computer network, career placement assistance, e-mail services, library services, tutoring.

Contact Dr. Bert Valencia, Executive Director, Thunderbird, The Garvin School of International Management, 15249 North 59th Avenue, Glendale, AZ 85306-6000. *Telephone:* 602-978-7534. *Fax:* 602-978-7874. *E-mail:* globalmba@t-bird.edu.

DEGREES AND AWARDS

MBA Global Master of Business Administration for Latin American Managers

COURSE SUBJECT AREAS OFFERED OUTSIDE OF DEGREE PROGRAMS

Graduate—accounting; business administration and management; business and personal services marketing operations; business communications; business information and data processing services; business management and administrative services, other; international business.

TIFFIN UNIVERSITY

Tiffin, Ohio

School of Off-Campus Learning

http://www.tiffin-global.org

Tiffin University was founded in 1888. It is accredited by North Central Association of Colleges and Schools. It first offered distance learning courses in 2000. In fall 2003, there were 202 students enrolled in distance learning courses. Institutionally administered financial aid is available to distance learners.

Services Distance learners have accessibility to academic advising, bookstore, career placement assistance, e-mail services, library services.

Contact Melani Pratt, Director of Online Education, Tiffin University, 155 Miami Street, Tiffin, OH 44883. *Telephone:* 800-968-6446 Ext. 3369. *Fax:* 419-443-5002. *E-mail:* online@tiffin.edu.

DEGREES AND AWARDS

BBA Accelerated Degree Completion
MBA Business Administration
MCJ Criminal Justice

TOMPKINS CORTLAND COMMUNITY COLLEGE

Dryden, New York

Instructional and Learning Resources

http://www.sunytccc.edu/e-tc3/e-tc3.asp

Tompkins Cortland Community College was founded in 1968. It is accredited by Middle States Association of Colleges and Schools. It first offered distance learning courses in 1997. In fall 2003, there were 1,438 students enrolled in distance learning courses. Institutionally administered financial aid is available to distance learners.

Services Distance learners have accessibility to bookstore, career placement assistance, library services, tutoring.

Contact Eric Machan Howd, Educational Technology Associate, Tompkins Cortland Community College, 170 North Street, PO Box 139, Dryden, NY 13053. *Telephone:* 607-844-8211 Ext. 4297. *E-mail:* howde@sunytccc.edu.

DEGREES AND AWARDS

AAS Business Administration–Applied Management; Chemical Dependency Studies Counseling; Hotel and Restaurant Management; Paralegal Studies

COURSE SUBJECT AREAS OFFERED OUTSIDE OF DEGREE PROGRAMS

Undergraduate—accounting; alcohol/drug abuse counseling; business; business communications; business marketing and marketing management; business quantitative methods and management science; communications, general; computer and information sciences, general; computer programming; computer software and media applications; developmental and child psychology; English as a second language; English composition; English language and literature, general; fine arts and art studies; hospitality services management; international business; Internet and World Wide Web; law and legal studies related; legal studies; mathematics; nursing; psychology; psychology, other; social psychology; sociology; visual and performing arts.

Non-credit—administrative and secretarial services; business management and administrative services, other; computer software and media applications; computer systems networking and telecommunications; data processing technology.

TOURO UNIVERSITY INTERNATIONAL

Cypress, California

http://www.tourou.edu/

Touro University International is accredited by Middle States Association of Colleges and Schools. It first offered distance learning

Touro University International (continued)

courses in 1999. In fall 2003, there were 5,000 students enrolled in distance learning courses. Institutionally administered financial aid is available to distance learners.

Services Distance learners have accessibility to academic advising, bookstore, campus computer network, e-mail services, library services.

Contact Wei Ren, Registrar, Touro University International, 5665 Plaza Drive, 3rd Floor, Cypress, CA 90630. *Telephone:* 714-816-0366. *Fax:* 714-827-7407. *E-mail:* registration@tourou.edu.

DEGREES AND AWARDS

BS Business Administration; Computer Science; Health Sciences; Information Technology Management
MAE Education
MBA Business Administration
MS Information Technology Management
MSC Health Sciences
PhD Business Administration; Educational Leadership; Health Sciences

COURSE SUBJECT AREAS OFFERED OUTSIDE OF DEGREE PROGRAMS

Undergraduate—accounting; business; business administration and management; computer/information technology administration and management; computer science; criminal justice and corrections; economics; health professions and related sciences, other; mathematics and computer science; philosophy; political science and government; psychology.

Graduate—accounting; business; business administration and management; criminal justice and corrections; education, general; health professions and related sciences, other; international business; military studies; teacher education, specific academic and vocational programs.

See full description on page 568.

TOWSON UNIVERSITY

Towson, Maryland

Towson University was founded in 1866. It is accredited by Middle States Association of Colleges and Schools.

Services Distance learners have accessibility to bookstore, campus computer network, e-mail services, library services.

Contact Mona Weber, Distance Learning Coordinator, Towson University, Towson. *E-mail:* mweber@towson.edu.

DEGREES AND AWARDS

Programs offered do not lead to a degree or other formal award.

TREASURE VALLEY COMMUNITY COLLEGE

Ontario, Oregon
Division of Extended Learning
http://www.tvcc.cc

Treasure Valley Community College was founded in 1962. It first offered distance learning courses in 1985. In fall 2003, there were 400 students enrolled in distance learning courses. Institutionally administered financial aid is available to distance learners.

Services Distance learners have accessibility to academic advising, bookstore, campus computer network, e-mail services, library services.

Contact Linda C. Simmons, Director of Continuing and Distance Education, Treasure Valley Community College, 650 College Boulevard, Ontario, OR 97914. *Telephone:* 541-881-8822 Ext. 358. *Fax:* 541-881-2721. *E-mail:* lsimmons@tvcc.cc.

DEGREES AND AWARDS

Programs offered do not lead to a degree or other formal award.

COURSE SUBJECT AREAS OFFERED OUTSIDE OF DEGREE PROGRAMS

Undergraduate—biology, general; business; chemistry; computer and information sciences, other; computer programming; mathematics, other; music; physical sciences, general; psychology; sociology.

TRINITY BIBLE COLLEGE

Ellendale, North Dakota
http://www.trinitybiblecollege.edu

Trinity Bible College was founded in 1948. It is accredited by Accrediting Association of Bible Colleges. It first offered distance learning courses in 2004. In fall 2003, there were 15 students enrolled in distance learning courses. Institutionally administered financial aid is available to distance learners.

Services Distance learners have accessibility to academic advising, campus computer network, e-mail services, library services.

Contact John Ragsdale, Director of Distance Education, Trinity Bible College, 50 South Sixth Aveune, Ellendale, ND 58436. *Telephone:* 888-822-2329 Ext. 2421. *Fax:* 701-349-5443. *E-mail:* jragsdale@trinitybiblecollege.edu.

DEGREES AND AWARDS

Programs offered do not lead to a degree or other formal award.

COURSE SUBJECT AREAS OFFERED OUTSIDE OF DEGREE PROGRAMS

Undergraduate—bible/biblical studies.

TRINITY EPISCOPAL SCHOOL FOR MINISTRY

Ambridge, Pennsylvania

Trinity Episcopal School for Ministry was founded in 1975. It is accredited by Association of Theological Schools in the United States and Canada. It first offered distance learning courses in 1997. In fall 2003, there were 110 students enrolled in distance learning courses. Institutionally administered financial aid is available to distance learners.

Services Distance learners have accessibility to academic advising, campus computer network, e-mail services.

Contact Mrs. Katharine Frey, Executive Director of TEEM, Trinity Episcopal School for Ministry, 311 11th Street, Ambridge, PA 15003. *Telephone:* 724-266-3838 Ext. 228. *Fax:* 724-266-4617. *E-mail:* kfrey@tesm.edu.

DEGREES AND AWARDS

Programs offered do not lead to a degree or other formal award.

COURSE SUBJECT AREAS OFFERED OUTSIDE OF DEGREE PROGRAMS

Graduate—theological and ministerial studies; theological studies and religious vocations, other.
Non-credit—theological studies and religious vocations, other.

TRINITY WESTERN UNIVERSITY

Langley, British Columbia, Canada
http://www.twu.ca/glc

Trinity Western University was founded in 1962. It is provincially chartered. It first offered distance learning courses in 2001. In fall 2003, there were 100 students enrolled in distance learning courses. Institutionally administered financial aid is available to distance learners.

Services Distance learners have accessibility to campus computer network, career placement assistance, e-mail services, library services.
Contact Lucy Gerbrant, Director of Web, Trinity Western University, GLC, 7600 Glover Road, Langley, BC V2Y 1Y1, Canada. *Telephone:* 604-513-2067. *E-mail:* glc@twu.ca.

DEGREES AND AWARDS

Programs offered do not lead to a degree or other formal award.

COURSE SUBJECT AREAS OFFERED OUTSIDE OF DEGREE PROGRAMS

Undergraduate—anthropology; fine arts and art studies; psychology; sociology.
Graduate—business administration and management; religion/religious studies; religious education; teacher education, specific academic and vocational programs; teaching English as a second language/foreign language.

TRI-STATE UNIVERSITY

Angola, Indiana
http://www.tristate.edu/

Tri-State University was founded in 1884. It is accredited by North Central Association of Colleges and Schools. It first offered distance learning courses in 1995. In fall 2003, there were 95 students enrolled in distance learning courses. Institutionally administered financial aid is available to distance learners.

Services Distance learners have accessibility to bookstore, e-mail services.
Contact Ms. Sara Yarian, Director of Admission, Tri-State University, 1 University Avenue, Angola, IN 46703. *Telephone:* 260-665-4132. *Fax:* 260-665-4578. *E-mail:* admit@tristate.edu.

DEGREES AND AWARDS

Programs offered do not lead to a degree or other formal award.

COURSE SUBJECT AREAS OFFERED OUTSIDE OF DEGREE PROGRAMS

Undergraduate—accounting; business; business administration and management; economics; fine arts and art studies; geological and related sciences; history; legal studies; liberal arts and sciences, general studies and humanities; marketing management and research; social sciences, general.

TRITON COLLEGE

River Grove, Illinois
Alternative Learning at Triton
http://www.triton.edu

Triton College was founded in 1964. It is accredited by North Central Association of Colleges and Schools. It first offered distance learning courses in 1997. Institutionally administered financial aid is available to distance learners.

Services Distance learners have accessibility to academic advising, bookstore, campus computer network, e-mail services, library services, tutoring.
Contact Mr. Douglas Olson, Dean, Student Services, Triton College, 2000 Fifth Avenue, River Grove, IL 60171. *Telephone:* 708-456-0300 Ext. 3230. *Fax:* 708-582-3162. *E-mail:* dolson@triton.edu.

DEGREES AND AWARDS

Programs offered do not lead to a degree or other formal award.

COURSE SUBJECT AREAS OFFERED OUTSIDE OF DEGREE PROGRAMS

Undergraduate—accounting; American history; anthropology; architecture; art history; astronomy; biology; business marketing and marketing management; chemistry; developmental and child psychology; developmental/child psychology; drafting; dramatic/theater arts and stagecraft; economics; educational psychology; English composition; foreign languages and literatures; health and physical education/fitness; history; Latin American studies; law and legal studies related; liberal arts and sciences, general studies and humanities; mathematical statistics; medical laboratory technology; nursing; philosophy; philosophy and religion related; psychology; real estate; social psychology; social sciences, general; sociology; Spanish; speech and rhetorical studies; theater arts/drama.
Non-credit—computer and information sciences, general.

TROY UNIVERSITY

Troy, Alabama
Distance Learning Center
http://www.tsulearn.net

Troy University was founded in 1887. It is accredited by Southern Association of Colleges and Schools. It first offered distance learning courses in 1998. In fall 2003, there were 1,200 students enrolled in distance learning courses. Institutionally administered financial aid is available to distance learners.

Services Distance learners have accessibility to academic advising, bookstore, career placement assistance, e-mail services, library services.
Contact Dr. Barbara Echord, Director of Distance Learning, Troy University, 304 Wallace Hall, Troy, AL 36082. *Telephone:* 334-670-5875. *Fax:* 334-670-5679. *E-mail:* bechord@troyst.edu.

Troy University (continued)

DEGREES AND AWARDS

MEd Instructional Technology
MPA Public Administration
MS Criminal Justice; Human Resource Management; International Relations; Management

See full description on page 570.

TROY UNIVERSITY–FLORIDA REGION

Fort Walton Beach, Florida
Distance Learning
http://www.tsufl.edu/distancelearning

Troy University–Florida Region is accredited by Southern Association of Colleges and Schools. It first offered distance learning courses in 1992. In fall 2003, there were 1,000 students enrolled in distance learning courses. Institutionally administered financial aid is available to distance learners.

Services Distance learners have accessibility to academic advising, bookstore, campus computer network, career placement assistance, e-mail services, library services, tutoring.
Contact Ms. Veronica Mercado, Student Services Specialist, Troy University–Florida Region, 326 Green Acres Road, Fort Walton Beach, FL 32547. *Telephone:* 866-MY TSUDL. *Fax:* 850-863-2702. *E-mail:* distlearn@troyst.edu.

DEGREES AND AWARDS

AS Business Administration; Education, general
BS Computer Science; Criminal Justice; Management; Political Science; Psychology; Resources Management (BAS)

COURSE SUBJECT AREAS OFFERED OUTSIDE OF DEGREE PROGRAMS

Undergraduate—business; business information and data processing services; computer/information technology administration and management; computer programming; economics; education, general; English language and literature, general; family and community studies; mathematics; organizational behavior; social sciences and history, other; social sciences, general.
Non-credit—computer and information sciences, general; computer and information sciences, other; computer engineering; computer/information technology administration and management; computer programming; computer science; computer software and media applications; computer systems analysis; computer systems networking and telecommunications.

See full description on page 572.

TROY UNIVERSITY MONTGOMERY

Montgomery, Alabama
External Degree Program-Professional Studies
http://www.tsum.edu/DL/

Troy University Montgomery was founded in 1965. It is accredited by Southern Association of Colleges and Schools. It first offered distance learning courses in 1987. In fall 2003, there were 1,100 students enrolled in distance learning courses. Institutionally administered financial aid is available to distance learners.

Services Distance learners have accessibility to academic advising, bookstore, career placement assistance, library services.
Contact Mr. David W. Barham, MSC, External Degree Program Coordinator, Troy University Montgomery, PO Drawer 4419, Rosa Parks Library and Museum, Room 310, Montgomery, AL 36103. *Telephone:* 334-241-9553. *Fax:* 888-357-8843 Ext. 553. *E-mail:* dbarham@troyst.edu.

DEGREES AND AWARDS

AS Business Administration; Business, History, Political Science, Psychology, Social Science, and Child Care; General Education; History; Political Science; Psychology; Social Sciences
BA Business Administration; English; History; Political Science; Psychology; Resources Management (Business), English, History, Political Science, Psychology, and Social Science; Social Sciences
BS Business Administration; English; History; Political Science; Psychology; Resources Management (Business), English, History, Political Science, Psychology, and Social Science; Social Sciences

COURSE SUBJECT AREAS OFFERED OUTSIDE OF DEGREE PROGRAMS

Undergraduate—accounting; business marketing and marketing management; developmental/child psychology; economics; English composition; finance; geography; history; law and legal studies related; organizational behavior; philosophy; physical sciences, general; political science and government; sociology; Spanish.

TUFTS UNIVERSITY

Medford, Massachusetts
Fletcher School of Law and Diplomacy
http://www.fletcher.tufts.edu/gmap

Tufts University was founded in 1852. It is accredited by New England Association of Schools and Colleges. It first offered distance learning courses in 2000. In fall 2003, there were 42 students enrolled in distance learning courses. Institutionally administered financial aid is available to distance learners.

Services Distance learners have accessibility to academic advising, campus computer network, career placement assistance, e-mail services, library services.
Contact Gabriela M. Artavia, Admissions Manager, Tufts University, 160 Packard Avenue, Medford, MA 02155. *Telephone:* 617-627-4524. *Fax:* 617-627-3005. *E-mail:* gabriela.artavia@tufts.edu.

DEGREES AND AWARDS

MA International Affairs

COURSE SUBJECT AREAS OFFERED OUTSIDE OF DEGREE PROGRAMS

Graduate—international business; international relations and affairs.

TULANE UNIVERSITY

New Orleans, Louisiana
University College
http://www.tulane.edu/~uc

Tulane University was founded in 1834. It is accredited by Southern Association of Colleges and Schools. It first offered distance learning courses in 1999. In fall 2003, there were 200 students enrolled in distance learning courses. Institutionally administered financial aid is available to distance learners.

Services Distance learners have accessibility to academic advising, campus computer network, career placement assistance, e-mail services, library services.

Contact Dr. Julia Grace Houston, Director of Media Arts and Distance Education, Tulane University, New Orleans, LA 70118. *Telephone:* 504-862-8000 Ext. 1672. *Fax:* 504-865-5562. *E-mail:* jhousto@tulane.edu.

DEGREES AND AWARDS

Programs offered do not lead to a degree or other formal award.

COURSE SUBJECT AREAS OFFERED OUTSIDE OF DEGREE PROGRAMS

Undergraduate—accounting; business and personal services marketing operations; business communications; business/managerial economics; computer and information sciences, general; computer programming; English composition; Internet and World Wide Web.

TUNXIS COMMUNITY COLLEGE

Farmington, Connecticut

http://www.tunxis.commnet.edu/tole

Tunxis Community College was founded in 1969. It is accredited by New England Association of Schools and Colleges. It first offered distance learning courses in 1996. In fall 2003, there were 1,600 students enrolled in distance learning courses. Institutionally administered financial aid is available to distance learners.

Services Distance learners have accessibility to academic advising, bookstore, e-mail services, library services, tutoring.

Contact Peter McCluskey, Director of Admissions, Tunxis Community College, 271 Scott Swamp Road, Farmington, CT 06032. *Telephone:* 860-255-3563. *E-mail:* tx-admissions@txcc.commnet.edu.

DEGREES AND AWARDS

AA Criminal Justice; General Studies/Liberal Arts
Certificate Corrections Pre-Certification

COURSE SUBJECT AREAS OFFERED OUTSIDE OF DEGREE PROGRAMS

Undergraduate—anthropology; area, ethnic and cultural studies, other; business administration and management; business information and data processing services; communications, general; computer and information sciences, general; computer systems networking and telecommunications; criminal justice and corrections; criminology; dental services; developmental and child psychology; English composition; English language and literature, general; foreign languages and literatures; history; industrial and organizational psychology; music; philosophy; psychology; sociology.

Non-credit—business; computer and information sciences, general; criminal justice and corrections; education, other; information sciences and systems.

UMPQUA COMMUNITY COLLEGE

Roseburg, Oregon

Media Services Department

http://www.umpqua.edu

Umpqua Community College was founded in 1964. It first offered distance learning courses in 1980. In fall 2003, there were 300 students enrolled in distance learning courses. Institutionally administered financial aid is available to distance learners.

Services Distance learners have accessibility to academic advising, bookstore.

Contact Christopher Bingham, Director of Media Services, Umpqua Community College, 1140 College Road, PO Box 967, Roseburg, OR 97470. *Telephone:* 541-440-4717. *Fax:* 541-440-4665. *E-mail:* chris.bingham@umpqua.edu.

DEGREES AND AWARDS

Programs offered do not lead to a degree or other formal award.

COURSE SUBJECT AREAS OFFERED OUTSIDE OF DEGREE PROGRAMS

Undergraduate—accounting; American literature (United States); archaeology; business administration and management; computer and information sciences, general; computer programming; drafting; English composition; mathematics; mathematics and computer science; oceanography; philosophy; philosophy and religion; podiatry (D.P.M., D.P., Pod.D.); psychology; psychology, other; sociology.

UNION INSTITUTE & UNIVERSITY

Cincinnati, Ohio

http://www.tui.edu

Union Institute & University was founded in 1969. It is accredited by North Central Association of Colleges and Schools. It first offered distance learning courses in 1993. In fall 2003, there were 1,300 students enrolled in distance learning courses. Institutionally administered financial aid is available to distance learners.

Services Distance learners have accessibility to academic advising, e-mail services, library services, tutoring.

Contact Admissions, Union Institute & University, 440 East McMillan Street, Cincinnati, OH 45206. *Telephone:* 800-486-3116. *Fax:* 513-861-0779. *E-mail:* admissions@tui.edu.

DEGREES AND AWARDS

BA Liberal Arts and Sciences
BS Liberal Arts and Sciences
MA Interdisciplinary
PhD Interdisciplinary Studies

See full description on page 574.

UNION THEOLOGICAL SEMINARY AND PRESBYTERIAN SCHOOL OF CHRISTIAN EDUCATION

Richmond, Virginia

http://www.union-psce.edu

Union Theological Seminary and Presbyterian School of Christian Education was founded in 1812. It is accredited by Southern Association of Colleges and Schools. It first offered distance learning courses in 1988. In fall 2003, there were 75 students enrolled in distance learning courses. Institutionally administered financial aid is available to distance learners.

Services Distance learners have accessibility to academic advising, e-mail services, library services.

Union Theological Seminary and Presbyterian School of Christian Education (continued)

Contact Rev. James W. Dale, Director of Admissions, Union Theological Seminary and Presbyterian School of Christian Education, 3401 Brook Road, Richmond, VA 23227. *Telephone:* 804-355-0671 Ext. 222. *Fax:* 804-355-3919. *E-mail:* jdale@union-psce.edu.

DEGREES AND AWARDS

MACE Christian Education

COURSE SUBJECT AREAS OFFERED OUTSIDE OF DEGREE PROGRAMS

Graduate—education, other.
Non-credit—education, other.

UNION UNIVERSITY

Jackson, Tennessee
http://www.uu.edu

Union University was founded in 1823. It is accredited by Southern Association of Colleges and Schools. It first offered distance learning courses in 1999. In fall 2003, there were 50 students enrolled in distance learning courses. Institutionally administered financial aid is available to distance learners.

Services Distance learners have accessibility to academic advising, bookstore, campus computer network, career placement assistance, e-mail services, library services.

Contact Sam Myatt, Director of Online Programs, Union University, 1050 Union University Drive, Jackson, TN 38305. *Telephone:* 731-661-5370. *Fax:* 731-661-5187. *E-mail:* smyatt@uu.edu.

DEGREES AND AWARDS

Programs offered do not lead to a degree or other formal award.

COURSE SUBJECT AREAS OFFERED OUTSIDE OF DEGREE PROGRAMS

Undergraduate—religion/religious studies.
Graduate—education, general; religion/religious studies.
Non-credit—religion/religious studies.

UNITED STATES SPORTS ACADEMY

Daphne, Alabama
Continuing Education and Distance Learning
http://www.ussa.edu

United States Sports Academy was founded in 1972. It is accredited by Southern Association of Colleges and Schools. It first offered distance learning courses in 1995. In fall 2003, there were 500 students enrolled in distance learning courses. Institutionally administered financial aid is available to distance learners.

Services Distance learners have accessibility to academic advising, bookstore, campus computer network, e-mail services, library services.

Contact Mr. David Allen, Director of Admissions, United States Sports Academy, One Academy Drive, Daphne, AL 36526-7055. *Telephone:* 800-223-2668 Ext. 145. *E-mail:* dallen@ussa.edu.

DEGREES AND AWARDS

Certification Fitness Specialist; Golf Fitness Instructor; Group Fitness Instructor; Human Performance Coach; International Sport Diploma; National Coaching Certification; Personal Fitness Trainer; Sports Agency; Sports Coaching (International Certification); Sports Coaching; Sports Management (International Certification); Sports Management; Sports Medicine; Strength and Conditioning; Tennis Fitness Instructor
MSS Fitness Management; Sports Coaching; Sports Management; Sports Medicine; Sports Studies
DSM Sports Management–Sports Medicine Emphasis; Sports Management

COURSE SUBJECT AREAS OFFERED OUTSIDE OF DEGREE PROGRAMS

Graduate—entrepreneurship; health and physical education/fitness; marketing management and research; miscellaneous health professions; parks, recreation, leisure and fitness studies, other.
Non-credit—health and physical education/fitness; miscellaneous health professions; parks, recreation and leisure facilities management; parks, recreation and leisure studies; parks, recreation, leisure and fitness studies, other.

See full description on page 576.

UNIVERSITÉ SAINTE-ANNE

Church Point, Nova Scotia, Canada
http://www.usainteanne.ca

Université Sainte-Anne was founded in 1890. It is provincially chartered. It first offered distance learning courses in 1985. In fall 2003, there were 118 students enrolled in distance learning courses. Institutionally administered financial aid is available to distance learners.

Services Distance learners have accessibility to academic advising, bookstore, campus computer network, e-mail services, library services, tutoring.

Contact Mr. Michel Gignac, Dean of Professionals Programs, Université Sainte-Anne, Éducation Permanente, Church Point, NS B0W 1M0, Canada. *Telephone:* 902-769-2114 Ext. 255. *Fax:* 902-769-2930. *E-mail:* gimichel@ssocial.ccfne.ns.ca.

DEGREES AND AWARDS

MEd Maîtrise en éducation–enseignement du FLS

COURSE SUBJECT AREAS OFFERED OUTSIDE OF DEGREE PROGRAMS

Undergraduate—business administration and management; education, general; education, other; English language and literature, general; general teacher education; history.
Graduate—education, other.
Non-credit—human services; miscellaneous health professions; teacher assistant/aide.

UNIVERSITY COLLEGE OF CAPE BRETON

Sydney, Nova Scotia, Canada
http://www.uccb.ca/distance

University College of Cape Breton was founded in 1974. It is provincially chartered. In fall 2003, there were 407 students enrolled in distance learning courses. Institutionally administered financial aid is available to distance learners.

Services Distance learners have accessibility to academic advising, bookstore, career placement assistance, e-mail services, library services.

Contact Joanne Pyke, Coordinator of Distance Education, University College of Cape Breton, PO Box 5300, Sydney, NS B1P 6L2, Canada. *Telephone:* 902-563-1806. *Fax:* 902-563-1449. *E-mail:* distance_ed@uccb.ca.

DEGREES AND AWARDS

BA Community Studies
BES Environmental Science
BHS Environmental Health
BST Manufacturing
Certificate Public Administration
MBE Education Counseling; Education Curriculum; Education Technology

COURSE SUBJECT AREAS OFFERED OUTSIDE OF DEGREE PROGRAMS

Undergraduate—accounting; business marketing and marketing management; creative writing; developmental/child psychology; environmental engineering; environmental health; international business; mathematical statistics; social psychology.

Non-credit—computer programming; computer software and media applications.

THE UNIVERSITY OF AKRON

Akron, Ohio
Information Services
http://www.uakron.edu

The University of Akron was founded in 1870. It is accredited by North Central Association of Colleges and Schools. It first offered distance learning courses in 1994. In fall 2003, there were 12,905 students enrolled in distance learning courses. Institutionally administered financial aid is available to distance learners.

Services Distance learners have accessibility to academic advising, bookstore, campus computer network, career placement assistance, e-mail services, library services, tutoring.

Contact Holly Harris-Bane, Director of Strategic Initiatives, The University of Akron, Buchtel Hall 102, Akron, OH 44325-4703. *Telephone:* 330-972-7508. *Fax:* 330-972-8699. *E-mail:* harrisb@uakron.edu.

DEGREES AND AWARDS

Programs offered do not lead to a degree or other formal award.

COURSE SUBJECT AREAS OFFERED OUTSIDE OF DEGREE PROGRAMS

Undergraduate—accounting; administrative and secretarial services; archaeology; astronomy; biochemistry and biophysics; biological and physical sciences; biology, general; botany; business; business administration and management; business communications; business/managerial economics; chemistry; communications, general; communications, other; community health services; community organization, resources and services; computer and information sciences, general; computer science; computer software and media applications; criminal justice and corrections; criminology; curriculum and instruction; design and applied arts; economics; education administration and supervision; educational evaluation, research and statistics; educational/instructional media design; education, general; education, other; engineering, other; English composition; English creative writing; English technical and business writing; financial management and services; fire protection; general teacher education; geography; Germanic languages and literatures; health and medical administrative services; hospitality/recreation marketing; hospitality services management; human resources management; Japanese; journalism and mass communications; liberal arts and sciences, general studies and humanities; marketing operations/marketing and distribution, other; mathematical statistics; mathematics; mathematics and computer science; medical basic sciences; microbiology/bacteriology; music; nursing; pharmacy; philosophy; philosophy and religion; physical sciences, general; physical sciences, other; political science and government; polymer/plastics engineering; protective services, other; psychology; public administration; social and philosophical foundations of education; social work; sociology; speech and rhetorical studies; taxation; teacher education, specific academic and vocational programs; teaching English as a second language/foreign language; technology education/industrial arts; telecommunications; zoology.

Graduate—accounting; applied mathematics; business administration and management; computer and information sciences, general; counseling psychology; economics; education administration and supervision; educational evaluation, research and statistics; educational/instructional media design; educational psychology; education, general; education, other; engineering, general; general teacher education; health professions and related sciences, other; human resources management; human services; information sciences and systems; Internet and World Wide Web; legal studies; mathematical statistics; mathematics; mathematics and computer science; mathematics, other; nursing; political science and government; psychology; psychology, other; public administration; public health; school psychology; social and philosophical foundations of education; social psychology; social work; speech and rhetorical studies; teacher education, specific academic and vocational programs; technology education/industrial arts.

Non-credit—area, ethnic and cultural studies, other; communications technologies; computer and information sciences, general; computer and information sciences, other; computer/information technology administration and management; computer programming; computer science; computer software and media applications; computer systems analysis; computer systems networking and telecommunications; curriculum and instruction; data entry/microcomputer applications; data processing technology; educational/instructional media design; education, other; entrepreneurship; general teacher education; health and medical assistants; human resources management; information sciences and systems; nursing.

THE UNIVERSITY OF ALABAMA

Tuscaloosa, Alabama
College of Continuing Studies
http://academicoutreach.ua.edu

The University of Alabama was founded in 1831. It is accredited by Southern Association of Colleges and Schools. It first offered distance learning courses in 1991. In fall 2003, there were 5,000 students enrolled in distance learning courses. Institutionally administered financial aid is available to distance learners.

Services Distance learners have accessibility to bookstore, campus computer network, e-mail services, library services.

Contact Ms. Nina Smith, Program Manager, Adult Student Services, The University of Alabama, Division of Academic Outreach, Box 870388, Tuscaloosa, AL 35487-0388. *Telephone:* 205-348-0089. *Fax:* 205-348-0249. *E-mail:* nsmith@ccs.ua.edu.

The University of Alabama (continued)

DEGREES AND AWARDS

BA Interdisciplinary Studies
BS Human Environmental Sciences–General Studies Option; Human Environmental Sciences–Restaurant and Hospitality Management; Interdisciplinary Studies; Mechanical Engineering; Nursing
Certificate Personal Financial Planning and Counseling
MA Health Studies–Health Promotion; Health Studies–Sports Medicine Health Care; Rehabilitation Counseling
MS Human Environmental Sciences–Food and Nutrition; Human Environmental Sciences–Interactive Technology; Nursing Case Management
MSAE Aerospace Engineering

COURSE SUBJECT AREAS OFFERED OUTSIDE OF DEGREE PROGRAMS

Undergraduate—accounting; advertising; American literature (United States); astronomy; biological and physical sciences; biology, general; business; communications, general; computer and information sciences, general; computer science; criminal justice and corrections; economics; education, general; engineering, general; English composition; English creative writing; English language and literature, general; English language and literature/letters, other; English literature (British and Commonwealth); family and community studies; family/consumer resource management; financial management and services; financial services marketing operations; foods and nutrition studies; foreign languages and literatures; general teacher education; geography; health professions and related sciences, other; history; home economics business services; home economics, general; home economics, other; hospitality/recreation marketing; hospitality services management; individual and family development studies; journalism and mass communications; liberal arts and sciences, general studies and humanities; mathematics; philosophy; philosophy and religion; political science and government; psychology; religion/religious studies; Romance languages and literatures; social sciences and history, other; social sciences, general; telecommunications; tourism/travel marketing.
Graduate—accounting; advertising; aerospace engineering; computer and information sciences, other; consumer and homemaking education; engineering mechanics; family/consumer resource management; financial management and services; health professions and related sciences, other; journalism and mass communications; nursing.

See full description on page 578.

THE UNIVERSITY OF ALABAMA IN HUNTSVILLE

Huntsville, Alabama
Engineering Management Distance Learning Programs
http://www.engdl.uah.edu/

The University of Alabama in Huntsville was founded in 1950. It is accredited by Southern Association of Colleges and Schools. It first offered distance learning courses in 1992. In fall 2003, there were 150 students enrolled in distance learning courses. Institutionally administered financial aid is available to distance learners.

Services Distance learners have accessibility to academic advising, bookstore, library services.

Contact Dawn R. Utley, PhD, Associate Director of Distance Learning, The University of Alabama in Huntsville, N136 Technology Hall, ISEEM Department, Huntsville, AL 35899. *Telephone:* 256-824-6075. *Fax:* 256-824-6608. *E-mail:* utley@ise.uah.edu.

DEGREES AND AWARDS

MSE Engineering Management; Industrial Engineering; Systems Engineering
PhD Industrial and Systems Engineering

COURSE SUBJECT AREAS OFFERED OUTSIDE OF DEGREE PROGRAMS

Graduate—accounting; engineering/industrial management; environmental engineering; industrial engineering; mathematical statistics; quality control and safety technologies; systems engineering.

UNIVERSITY OF ALASKA FAIRBANKS

Fairbanks, Alaska
Center for Distance Education and Independent Learning
http://distance.uaf.edu

University of Alaska Fairbanks was founded in 1917. It is accredited by Northwest Commission on Colleges and Universities. It first offered distance learning courses in 1970. In fall 2003, there were 4,000 students enrolled in distance learning courses. Institutionally administered financial aid is available to distance learners.

Services Distance learners have accessibility to bookstore, campus computer network, e-mail services, library services, tutoring.
Contact Tina I. Johnson, Communication/Reception, University of Alaska Fairbanks, PO Box 756700, Fairbanks, AK 99775. *Telephone:* 907-474-5353. *Fax:* 907-474-5402. *E-mail:* distance@uaf.edu.

DEGREES AND AWARDS

Programs offered do not lead to a degree or other formal award.

COURSE SUBJECT AREAS OFFERED OUTSIDE OF DEGREE PROGRAMS

Undergraduate—advertising; American literature (United States); anthropology; applied mathematics; art history; biology; biology, general; business; business administration and management; computer and information sciences, general; computer science; computer software and media applications; cultural studies; drafting; dramatic/theater arts and stagecraft; economics; education administration and supervision; educational psychology; English composition; English language and literature, general; English language and literature/letters, other; English technical and business writing; family and community studies; film studies; foreign languages and literatures; geography; gerontology; health professions and related sciences, other; history; journalism; journalism and mass communications; Latin (ancient and medieval); liberal arts and sciences, general studies and humanities; library science/librarianship; marketing operations/marketing and distribution, other; mathematical statistics; mathematics; mathematics related; miscellaneous health professions; music; philosophy; philosophy and religion related; psychology; radio and television broadcasting; real estate; social sciences and history, other; social sciences, general; social work; sociology; women's studies.

Graduate—education administration and supervision; educational psychology; education, other; history.

See full description on page 580.

UNIVERSITY OF ALASKA SOUTHEAST

Juneau, Alaska
Distance Learning at UAS
http://www.uas.alaska.edu/distance

University of Alaska Southeast was founded in 1972. It first offered distance learning courses in 1986. In fall 2003, there were 860 students enrolled in distance learning courses. Institutionally administered financial aid is available to distance learners.

Services Distance learners have accessibility to academic advising, bookstore, campus computer network, e-mail services, library services, tutoring.

Contact Maria Moya, Assistant to the Provost, University of Alaska Southeast, 11120 Glacier Highway, Juneau, AK 99801. *Telephone:* 907-465-6148. *Fax:* 907-465-8468. *E-mail:* maria.moya@uas.alaska.edu.

DEGREES AND AWARDS

BBA Business Administration
BLS Liberal Arts
Endorsement Early Childhood Education; Educational Technology; Reading; Special Education
MAT Early Childhood Education; Elementary Education
MBA Business Administration
MEd Early Childhood Education; Educational Technology; Reading
MPA Public Administration

THE UNIVERSITY OF ARIZONA

Tucson, Arizona
Extended University, Distance Learning Program
http://www.ceao.arizona.edu/dist/

The University of Arizona was founded in 1885. It is accredited by North Central Association of Colleges and Schools. It first offered distance learning courses in 1972. In fall 2003, there were 900 students enrolled in distance learning courses. Institutionally administered financial aid is available to distance learners.

Services Distance learners have accessibility to academic advising, bookstore, campus computer network, e-mail services, library services.

Contact Pam Shack, Associate Director, Distance Learning Operations, The University of Arizona, PO Box 210158, University Services Building, Room 302, Tucson, AZ 85721-0158. *Telephone:* 520-626-4573. *Fax:* 520-626-1102. *E-mail:* distance@email.arizona.edu.

DEGREES AND AWARDS

Certificate Technical Engineering Management
Graduate Certificate Optical Sciences; Reliability and Quality Engineering; Systems Engineering (Professional Graduate Certificate)
MEngr Engineering
MS Optical Sciences

COURSE SUBJECT AREAS OFFERED OUTSIDE OF DEGREE PROGRAMS

Graduate—aerospace engineering; electrical engineering; engineering/industrial management; engineering mechanics; gerontology; industrial engineering; library science/librarianship; mechanical engineering; nursing; teacher education, specific academic and vocational programs.

Special Message

University of Arizona (UA) distance learning classes are taught by outstanding faculty members of the University of Arizona and incorporate the latest research and technological developments. Courses are delivered in a variety of formats; some are entirely Web-based and others are delivered on CD-ROM or are video streamed on the Web.

UA's program offers a wide range of upper-division and graduate engineering and optical sciences courses.

The Arizona Master of Engineering distance degree is designed by faculty members, with input from industry professionals, to meet the individual educational needs of practicing engineers, and to be completed totally at a distance.

Professional graduate certificate programs are offered in Systems Engineering, Reliability and Quality Engineering, Optical Sciences, and Technical Engineering Management. Courses completed for these programs can be applied to the Master of Engineering or other master's degrees.

Other featured areas include the Special Education and Rehabilitation Department's certificate of three courses: Behavior Principles and Disability, Advanced Positive Behavioral Support, and Observation and Participation in Special Education Programs. The School of Information Resources and Library Science offers Web-based courses leading toward a master's degree. The Agricultural Education Department offers graduate-level Web-based courses. The Finance Department offers an undergraduate Web-based course, Introduction to Finance.

New programs are under development. For the most up-to-date information, students should visit the UA distance learning Web site at http://www.ceao.arizona.edu/dist/.

UNIVERSITY OF ARKANSAS AT LITTLE ROCK

Little Rock, Arkansas
Off-Campus Programs
http://www.ualr.edu/occp/

University of Arkansas at Little Rock was founded in 1927. It is accredited by North Central Association of Colleges and Schools. It first offered distance learning courses in 1975. In fall 2003, there were 830 students enrolled in distance learning courses. Institutionally administered financial aid is available to distance learners.

Services Distance learners have accessibility to academic advising, bookstore, e-mail services, library services.

Contact Donna Rae Eldridge, Assistant Director/Media Courses, University of Arkansas at Little Rock, Off-Campus Programs, 2801 South University Avenue, Little Rock, AR 72204-1099. *Telephone:* 501-569-3003. *Fax:* 501-569-3089. *E-mail:* dreldridge@ualr.edu.

University of Arkansas at Little Rock (continued)

DEGREES AND AWARDS

BA Criminal Justice; Liberal Arts
MA Rehabilitation Counseling

COURSE SUBJECT AREAS OFFERED OUTSIDE OF DEGREE PROGRAMS

Undergraduate—accounting; anthropology; astronomy; business information and data processing services; communications, general; communications, other; creative writing; criminal justice and corrections; data entry/microcomputer applications; developmental and child psychology; English creative writing; English language and literature, general; English language and literature/letters, other; English technical and business writing; foods and nutrition studies; geography; geological and related sciences; gerontology; health and physical education/fitness; health professions and related sciences, other; history; journalism and mass communications; liberal arts and sciences, general studies and humanities; mathematics; mathematics, other; multi/interdisciplinary studies, other; music; nursing; philosophy; philosophy and religion; physical sciences, general; physical sciences, other; political science and government; psychology; psychology, other; sociology; speech and rhetorical studies.
Graduate—criminal justice and corrections; educational evaluation, research and statistics; educational/instructional media design; gerontology; history; political science and government; rehabilitation/therapeutic services; social work; special education.

UNIVERSITY OF ARKANSAS AT PINE BLUFF

Pine Bluff, Arkansas
http://www.uaex.edu/AQFI

University of Arkansas at Pine Bluff was founded in 1873. It is accredited by North Central Association of Colleges and Schools. It first offered distance learning courses in 1997. In fall 2003, there were 1 students enrolled in distance learning courses. Institutionally administered financial aid is available to distance learners.

Services Distance learners have accessibility to academic advising, campus computer network, e-mail services.
Contact Dr. Carole Engle, Director and Chair, University of Arkansas at Pine Bluff, 1200 North University Drive, Mail Slot 4912, Pine Bluff, AR 71601. *Telephone:* 870-575-8523. *Fax:* 870-575-4637. *E-mail:* cengle@uaex.edu.

DEGREES AND AWARDS

Programs offered do not lead to a degree or other formal award.

COURSE SUBJECT AREAS OFFERED OUTSIDE OF DEGREE PROGRAMS

Undergraduate—accounting; agricultural business and management; agriculture/agricultural sciences; American literature (United States); animal sciences; architectural engineering; bilingual/bicultural education; biological and physical sciences; biology, general; business administration and management; business communications; chemistry; clothing/apparel and textile studies; communications, general; computer and information sciences, general; computer science; economics; education, general; English language and literature, general; fishing and fisheries sciences and management.
Graduate—education, general; fishing and fisheries sciences and management.
Non-credit—administrative and secretarial services; Air Force R.O.T.C.; bilingual/bicultural education; carpenters; computer/information technology administration and management.

UNIVERSITY OF BALTIMORE

Baltimore, Maryland
UBOnline
http://www.ubonline.edu

University of Baltimore was founded in 1925. It is accredited by Middle States Association of Colleges and Schools. It first offered distance learning courses in 2000. Institutionally administered financial aid is available to distance learners.

Services Distance learners have accessibility to academic advising, bookstore, campus computer network, career placement assistance, e-mail services, library services, tutoring.
Contact Julia Pitman, Director of Admissions, University of Baltimore, 1420 North Charles Street, Baltimore, MD 21201. *Telephone:* 877-APPLY-UB. *Fax:* 410-837-4793. *E-mail:* admissions@ubmail.ubalt.edu.

DEGREES AND AWARDS

BS Business Administration
MBA Business Administration
MPA Public Administration

UNIVERSITY OF BRIDGEPORT

Bridgeport, Connecticut
Office of Distance Learning
http://www.bridgeport.edu/pages/50.asp

University of Bridgeport was founded in 1927. It is accredited by New England Association of Schools and Colleges. It first offered distance learning courses in 1997. In fall 2003, there were 180 students enrolled in distance learning courses. Institutionally administered financial aid is available to distance learners.

Services Distance learners have accessibility to academic advising, bookstore, campus computer network, e-mail services, library services.
Contact Claude A. Perrottet, Coordinator of Student Services, University of Bridgeport, 126 Park Avenue, Bridgeport, CT 06601. *Telephone:* 203-576-4853. *Fax:* 203-576-4537. *E-mail:* ubonline@bridgeport.edu.

DEGREES AND AWARDS

BS Dental Hygiene Online (degree completion program)
Certification Marriage Education (for credit); Marriage Education (non-credit)
MS Human Nutrition

COURSE SUBJECT AREAS OFFERED OUTSIDE OF DEGREE PROGRAMS

Undergraduate—area, ethnic and cultural studies, other; business; business management and administrative services, other; community health services; counseling psychology; dental services; developmental and child psychology; economics; education, general; enterprise management and operation; entrepreneurship; family and community studies; film/video and photographic arts; foods and nutrition studies; history; human services; legal studies; liberal arts and sciences, general

studies and humanities; marketing operations/marketing and distribution, other; mathematics, other; music; peace and conflict studies; philosophy; philosophy and religion; political science and government; psychology; public health; religion/religious studies; social psychology; social sciences, general; sociology; visual and performing arts.
Graduate—biochemistry and biophysics; botany; foods and nutrition studies.
Non-credit—education, other; family and community studies; individual and family development studies.

THE UNIVERSITY OF BRITISH COLUMBIA

Vancouver, British Columbia, Canada
Distance Education and Technology
http://det.ubc.ca

The University of British Columbia was founded in 1915. It is provincially chartered. It first offered distance learning courses in 1949. In fall 2003, there were 5,566 students enrolled in distance learning courses. Institutionally administered financial aid is available to distance learners.

Services Distance learners have accessibility to academic advising, bookstore, campus computer network, career placement assistance, e-mail services, library services, tutoring.
Contact Sonja Fragoso, Learner Support, The University of British Columbia, 2329 West Mall, University Services Building, Room 1170, Vancouver, BC V6T 1Z4, Canada. *Telephone:* 604-822-6500. *Fax:* 604-822-8636. *E-mail:* sonja.fragoso@ubc.ca.

DEGREES AND AWARDS

Graduate Certificate Rehabilitation Sciences; Technology-Based Distributed Learning; Technology-Based Learning for Schools
MA Educational Technology–Master of Educational Technology

COURSE SUBJECT AREAS OFFERED OUTSIDE OF DEGREE PROGRAMS

Undergraduate—agricultural economics; agriculture/agricultural sciences; animal sciences; Canadian studies; civil engineering; computer and information sciences, general; dental services; educational/instructional media design; education, general; English language and literature, general; environmental control technologies; film studies; foods and nutrition studies; forest production and processing; forestry; forestry and related sciences; French; geography; history; landscape architecture; library science, other; medieval/Renaissance studies; metallurgical engineering; music; nursing; oceanography; philosophy; psychology; rehabilitation/therapeutic services; social work; soil sciences; urban affairs/studies; women's studies.
Graduate—educational/instructional media design; education, general; rehabilitation/therapeutic services.
Non-credit—English composition.

UNIVERSITY OF CALGARY

Calgary, Alberta, Canada
Learning Commons
http://www.commons.ucalgary.ca

University of Calgary was founded in 1945. It is provincially chartered. It first offered distance learning courses in 1977.

Services Distance learners have accessibility to academic advising, bookstore, campus computer network, career placement assistance, e-mail services, library services.
Contact Joanne Carruthers, E-Learning Coordinator, University of Calgary, Learning Commons, 546 Bi Sci Building, 2500 University Drive North West, Calgary, AB T2N 1N4, Canada. *Telephone:* 403-220-7364. *Fax:* 403-282-0730. *E-mail:* carruthe@ucalgary.ca.

DEGREES AND AWARDS

BCR Community Rehabilitation
BN Nursing
Certificate Adult Learning; E-Learning; Environmental Management; Human Resource Management; Management, general; Security Management; Teacher Assistant
MCE Continuing Education
MEd Education–Master of Education at a Distance

COURSE SUBJECT AREAS OFFERED OUTSIDE OF DEGREE PROGRAMS

Undergraduate—nursing; social work.
Graduate—education administration and supervision; educational evaluation, research and statistics; educational/instructional media design; educational psychology; education, general; social work.
Non-credit—adult/continuing education.

UNIVERSITY OF CALIFORNIA, LOS ANGELES

Los Angeles, California
University Extension
http://www.uclaextension.edu

University of California, Los Angeles was founded in 1919. It is accredited by Western Association of Schools and Colleges. It first offered distance learning courses in 1996. In fall 2003, there were 2,500 students enrolled in distance learning courses. Institutionally administered financial aid is available to distance learners.

Services Distance learners have accessibility to academic advising, bookstore, e-mail services, tutoring.
Contact Mrs. Sandra Saika, Project Representative, University of California, Los Angeles, 10995 LeConte Avenue, Room 714, Los Angeles, CA 90024. *Telephone:* 310-825-2648. *Fax:* 310-267-4783. *E-mail:* ssaika@uclaextension.edu.

DEGREES AND AWARDS

Programs offered do not lead to a degree or other formal award.

COURSE SUBJECT AREAS OFFERED OUTSIDE OF DEGREE PROGRAMS

Graduate—archaeology; business; business administration and management; design and applied arts; economics; English technical and business writing; film/video and photographic arts; foreign languages and literatures, other; health and physical education/fitness; liberal arts and sciences, general studies and humanities; mathematics; philosophy and religion; psychology; social sciences, general; visual and performing arts.

University of California, Los Angeles (continued)

Special Message

The dynamic interface between the knowledge of the academy and the knowledge generated in the world of practice has enabled UCLA Extension to serve adult learners in uniquely effective ways for more than eight decades. Today, Extension counts about 100,000 enrollments in 4,500 courses held in more than 50 locations in southern California.

UCLA Extension Online continues in the same creative tradition established by its face-to-face learning community by serving thousands of individuals from all over the U.S. and from 80 countries. Participants in its certified programs and in more than 200 individual courses experience an intimate and in-depth learning environment online. All courses are instructor-led, and all participants belong to a cohort of learners, in which lively discussions and networking set the standard for effective adult education.

Instructors are drawn from all over the world, experts in their fields by virtue of a combination of practice and academic credentials. All instructors are required to complete an extensive training program before they teach an online class, and all students receive an orientation to the software platform in which their classes reside.

Adults who seek to enhance or change careers, learners who take delight in exploring subjects that intrigue them, and corporate trainers who are looking for customized programs to meet their employees' specific needs—all are served by the rich breadth of educational opportunities available through UCLA Extension Online.

Prospective students should visit the Web site at http://www.uclaextension.edu and the chance to give themselves some credit.

UNIVERSITY OF CALIFORNIA, RIVERSIDE

Riverside, California
University Extension
http://www.unex.ucr.edu

University of California, Riverside was founded in 1954. It is accredited by Western Association of Schools and Colleges. It first offered distance learning courses in 1994. In fall 2003, there were 150 students enrolled in distance learning courses. Institutionally administered financial aid is available to distance learners.

Services Distance learners have accessibility to academic advising, bookstore, library services.

Contact Jon Kindschy, Director of Sciences, University of California, Riverside, Riverside, CA 92507. *Telephone:* 909-787-5804 Ext. 1622. *E-mail:* jonk@ucx.ucr.edu.

DEGREES AND AWARDS

Programs offered do not lead to a degree or other formal award.

COURSE SUBJECT AREAS OFFERED OUTSIDE OF DEGREE PROGRAMS

Non-credit—agriculture/agricultural sciences, other; atmospheric sciences and meteorology; computer software and media applications; education, other; geography; horticulture services operations and management; nursing; plant sciences.

UNIVERSITY OF CENTRAL ARKANSAS

Conway, Arkansas
Division of Continuing Education
http://www.uca.edu/aoep

University of Central Arkansas was founded in 1907. It is accredited by North Central Association of Colleges and Schools. It first offered distance learning courses in 1992. In fall 2003, there were 336 students enrolled in distance learning courses. Institutionally administered financial aid is available to distance learners.

Services Distance learners have accessibility to bookstore, library services.

Contact Sondra Pugh, Extended Study Secretary, University of Central Arkansas, 201 Donaghey Avenue, Brewer-Hegeman Conference Center, Suite 102, Suite 102, Conway, AR 72035. *Telephone:* 501-450-3118. *Fax:* 501-450-5277. *E-mail:* sondrap@mail.uca.edu.

DEGREES AND AWARDS

Programs offered do not lead to a degree or other formal award.

COURSE SUBJECT AREAS OFFERED OUTSIDE OF DEGREE PROGRAMS

Undergraduate—accounting; American literature (United States); business marketing and marketing management; educational psychology; English composition; English creative writing; Germanic languages and literatures; history; marketing management and research; mathematics; political science and government; psychology; social psychology; sociology.

Graduate—computer and information sciences, other; curriculum and instruction; education, other; geography; health professions and related sciences, other; library science, other; nursing; occupational therapy; physical therapy.

Non-credit—business administration and management; computer and information sciences, general; English language and literature, general; journalism and mass communications.

UNIVERSITY OF CENTRAL FLORIDA

Orlando, Florida
Center for Distributed Learning
http://online.ucf.edu

University of Central Florida was founded in 1963. It is accredited by Southern Association of Colleges and Schools. It first offered distance learning courses in 1996. In fall 2003, there were 5,440 students enrolled in distance learning courses. Institutionally administered financial aid is available to distance learners.

Services Distance learners have accessibility to academic advising, bookstore, campus computer network, e-mail services, library services.

Contact Dr. Margaret Miller, Coordinator of Student Support, University of Central Florida, 12424 Research Parkway, Suite 256, Orlando, FL 32826-3269. *Telephone:* 407-823-4912. *Fax:* 407-207-4911. *E-mail:* pmiller@mail.ucf.edu.

DEGREES AND AWARDS

BA Liberal Studies

BS Health Information Management; Health Services Administration; Information Systems Technology; Liberal Studies; Technical Education and Industry Training
BSET Engineering Technology
BSN Nursing
Graduate Certificate Community College Education; Educational Media; Instructional/Educational Technology; Nonprofit Management; Nursing and Health Professional Education; Professional Writing
MA Exceptional Education; Instructional/Educational Technology
MEd Educational Media
MS Criminal Justice; Forensic Science; Nonprofit Management
MSN Nursing Leadership and Management

COURSE SUBJECT AREAS OFFERED OUTSIDE OF DEGREE PROGRAMS

Undergraduate—education, other; electrical engineering; health services administration; industrial engineering; mathematical statistics; nursing; sociology.
Graduate—educational/instructional media design; electrical engineering; English technical and business writing; health services administration; industrial engineering; mathematical statistics; mechanical engineering.

See full description on page 582.

UNIVERSITY OF CINCINNATI

Cincinnati, Ohio
Distance Learning Programs
http://www.uc.edu/distance

University of Cincinnati was founded in 1819. It is accredited by North Central Association of Colleges and Schools. It first offered distance learning courses in 1976. Institutionally administered financial aid is available to distance learners.

Services Distance learners have accessibility to academic advising, bookstore, campus computer network, e-mail services, library services, tutoring.
Contact Dr. Melody Clark, Academic Director, Distance Learning, University of Cincinnati, PO Box 210631, Cincinnati, OH 45221-0631. *Telephone:* 513-556-9154. *Fax:* 513-556-7861. *E-mail:* melody.clark@uc.edu.

DEGREES AND AWARDS

AD Early Childhood Education
BS Addiction Studies; Clinical Laboratory Science; Fire Science Administration
MEd Educational Administration
MS Criminal Justice
PharmD Pharmacy

COURSE SUBJECT AREAS OFFERED OUTSIDE OF DEGREE PROGRAMS

Undergraduate—accounting; business; communication disorders sciences and services; computer software and media applications; criminal justice and corrections; geography; geological and related sciences; history; library science, other; philosophy; philosophy and religion; psychology.
Non-credit—business; computer and information sciences, general.

UNIVERSITY OF CINCINNATI

Cincinnati, Ohio
Online Programs
http://www.uc.edu/

University of Cincinnati was founded in 1819. It is accredited by North Central Association of Colleges and Schools. Institutionally administered financial aid is available to distance learners.

Services Distance learners have accessibility to academic advising, e-mail services, library services.
Contact University of Cincinnati, 7226 West Colonial Drive, PMB 400, Orlando, FL 32818-6731. *Fax:* 407-573-2015. *E-mail:* info@compassknowledge.com.

DEGREES AND AWARDS

BS Clinical Laboratory Science
MEd Educational Administration

UNIVERSITY OF CINCINNATI RAYMOND WALTERS COLLEGE

Cincinnati, Ohio
Outreach and Continuing Education
http://www.rwc.uc.edu/maps/news/courses.htm

University of Cincinnati Raymond Walters College was founded in 1967. It is accredited by North Central Association of Colleges and Schools. It first offered distance learning courses in 1995. In fall 2003, there were 280 students enrolled in distance learning courses. Institutionally administered financial aid is available to distance learners.

Services Distance learners have accessibility to bookstore, campus computer network, e-mail services, library services.
Contact Janice Ooten, Program Manager, University of Cincinnati Raymond Walters College, 9555 Plainfield Road, Cincinnati, OH 45236-1096. *Telephone:* 513-936-1533. *Fax:* 513-745-8315. *E-mail:* ootenjc@ucrwcu.rwc.uc.edu.

DEGREES AND AWARDS

Programs offered do not lead to a degree or other formal award.

COURSE SUBJECT AREAS OFFERED OUTSIDE OF DEGREE PROGRAMS

Undergraduate—business; business administration and management; computer/information technology administration and management; computer software and media applications; English composition; film/video and photographic arts; foods and nutrition studies; health professions and related sciences, other; Internet and World Wide Web; library science/librarianship; sociology.
Graduate—foods and nutrition studies.

UNIVERSITY OF COLORADO AT BOULDER

Boulder, Colorado
Center for Advanced Engineering and Technology Education (CAETE)
http://caete.colorado.edu

University of Colorado at Boulder was founded in 1876. It is accredited by North Central Association of Colleges and Schools. It

University of Colorado at Boulder (continued)

first offered distance learning courses in 1983. In fall 2003, there were 400 students enrolled in distance learning courses. Institutionally administered financial aid is available to distance learners.

Services Distance learners have accessibility to academic advising, bookstore, campus computer network, e-mail services, library services.

Contact Robin M.W. McClanahan, Marketing Manager, University of Colorado at Boulder, CAETE, 435 UCB, Boulder, CO 80309. *Telephone:* 303-492-0212. *Fax:* 303-492-5987. *E-mail:* caete@colorado.edu.

DEGREES AND AWARDS

Graduate Certificate Engineering Management; Power Electronics; Project Management; Software Engineering
ME Aerospace Engineering; Computer Science; Electrical and Computer Engineering; Engineering Management; Telecommunications
MS Aerospace Engineering; Electrical and Computer Engineering; Telecommunications

COURSE SUBJECT AREAS OFFERED OUTSIDE OF DEGREE PROGRAMS

Graduate—aerospace, aeronautical and astronautical engineering; bioengineering and biomedical engineering; civil engineering; computer engineering; computer science; electrical and electronic engineering-related technology; engineering/industrial management; environmental/environmental health engineering; mechanical engineering; telecommunications.

Non-credit—aerospace, aeronautical and astronautical engineering; bioengineering and biomedical engineering; civil engineering; computer engineering; computer science; electrical and electronic engineering-related technology; engineering/industrial management; environmental/environmental health engineering; mechanical engineering; telecommunications.

UNIVERSITY OF COLORADO AT COLORADO SPRINGS

Colorado Springs, Colorado

http://www.uccs.edu/~online/

University of Colorado at Colorado Springs was founded in 1965. It is accredited by North Central Association of Colleges and Schools. It first offered distance learning courses in 1996. In fall 2003, there were 610 students enrolled in distance learning courses. Institutionally administered financial aid is available to distance learners.

Services Distance learners have accessibility to academic advising, campus computer network, e-mail services, library services.

Contact Dana Rocha, Director of Extended Studies, University of Colorado at Colorado Springs, 1420 Austin Bluffs Parkway, MH 316, ADM 15, Colorado Springs, CO 80933-7150. *Telephone:* 719-262-4662. *E-mail:* drocha@uccs.edu.

DEGREES AND AWARDS

MA Curriculum and Instruction–Educational Leadership
MBA Business Administration
ME Space Studies
MSN Nurse Practitioner and Clinical Specialist

COURSE SUBJECT AREAS OFFERED OUTSIDE OF DEGREE PROGRAMS

Undergraduate—American literature (United States); area, ethnic and cultural studies, other; biological sciences/life sciences, other; chemistry; communications, general; economics; English composition; geography; gerontology; health professions and related sciences, other; history; mathematics; mechanical engineering; Middle Eastern languages and literatures; military studies; nursing; psychology; sociology.

Graduate—aerospace, aeronautical and astronautical engineering; business; criminal justice and corrections; education administration and supervision; health professions and related sciences, other; mechanical engineering; nursing; public administration.

UNIVERSITY OF COLORADO AT DENVER

Denver, Colorado

CU Online

http://cuonline.edu/petersons

University of Colorado at Denver was founded in 1912. It is accredited by North Central Association of Colleges and Schools. It first offered distance learning courses in 1996. In fall 2003, there were 1,500 students enrolled in distance learning courses. Institutionally administered financial aid is available to distance learners.

Services Distance learners have accessibility to academic advising, bookstore, e-mail services, library services, tutoring.

Contact Program Assistant, University of Colorado at Denver, Campus Box 198, PO Box 173364, Denver, CO 80217-3364. *Telephone:* 303-556-6505. *Fax:* 303-556-6530. *E-mail:* inquiry@cuonline.edu.

DEGREES AND AWARDS

BA Sociology
Certificate of Achievement World History for Educators
Certificate Designing and Implementing Web-based Learning Environments
MBA Business Administration
MEngr Geographic Information Systems (GIS)
MPA Public Administration

COURSE SUBJECT AREAS OFFERED OUTSIDE OF DEGREE PROGRAMS

Undergraduate—accounting; American history; American literature (United States); anthropology; biochemistry and biophysics; biology; cell biology; civil engineering; communications, general; computer programming; creative writing; cultural studies; economics; engineering, general; engineering mechanics; engineering science; English composition; English creative writing; English language and literature, general; English technical and business writing; fine arts and art studies; foreign languages and literatures; geography; geological and related sciences; history; Latin (ancient and medieval); liberal arts and sciences, general studies and humanities; mathematical statistics; mathematics, other; mathematics related; mechanical engineering; medical genetics; music; organizational psychology; philosophy and religion related; physics; political science and government; psychology; social psychology; sociology; theater arts/drama.

Graduate—accounting; architecture; business; business administration and management; business and personal services marketing operations; business communications; business information and data processing services; business management and administrative services, other; business/managerial economics; business quantitative methods and management science; education, general; education, other; engineering design; engineering, general; engineering/industrial management; engineering mechanics; engineering, other; engineering-related technologies, other; history; management information systems/ business data processing; marketing management and research; marketing operations/marketing and distribution, other; political science and government; public administration; public administration and services, other; public policy analysis.

See full description on page 584.

UNIVERSITY OF CONNECTICUT

Storrs, Connecticut
College of Continuing Studies
http://continuingstudies.uconn.edu/onlinecourses

University of Connecticut was founded in 1881. It is accredited by New England Association of Schools and Colleges. It first offered distance learning courses in 2001. In fall 2003, there were 350 students enrolled in distance learning courses. Institutionally administered financial aid is available to distance learners.

Services Distance learners have accessibility to academic advising, bookstore, campus computer network, career placement assistance, e-mail services, library services, tutoring.

Contact Dr. Judy Buffolino, Director of Distance Education, University of Connecticut, College of Continuing Studies, Distance Education Office, One Bishop Circle, Unit 4056, Storrs, CT 06269-4056. *Telephone:* 860-486-1080. *Fax:* 860-486-0756. *E-mail:* judy.buffolino@uconn.edu.

DEGREES AND AWARDS

BGS Information Technology Focus; Occupational and Environmental Safety and Health Focus
Certificate Environmental Health and Safety; Himalayan Studies; Information Technology–Web Content Development; Information Technology–Web Systems Administration; Occupational Safety and Health
Graduate Certificate Humanitarian Services Administration
MPS Human Resource Management; Humanitarian Services Administration

COURSE SUBJECT AREAS OFFERED OUTSIDE OF DEGREE PROGRAMS

Undergraduate—anthropology; area, ethnic and cultural studies, other; communications, general; computer and information sciences, other; computer/information technology administration and management; computer programming; computer software and media applications; cultural studies; economics; English language and literature, general; fine arts and art studies; geography; health professions and related sciences, other; Internet and World Wide Web; liberal arts and sciences, general studies and humanities; miscellaneous health professions; philosophy; political science and government; sociology.
Graduate—health professions and related sciences, other; human resources management; human services.
Non-credit—health professions and related sciences, other; miscellaneous health professions.

See full description on page 586.

UNIVERSITY OF DALLAS

Irving, Texas
Center for Distance Education
http://www.thedallasmba.com

University of Dallas was founded in 1955. It is accredited by Southern Association of Colleges and Schools. It first offered distance learning courses in 1970. In fall 2003, there were 500 students enrolled in distance learning courses. Institutionally administered financial aid is available to distance learners.

Services Distance learners have accessibility to academic advising, bookstore, career placement assistance, library services, tutoring.

Contact Ms. Vanessa Cox, Associate Director of Online Learning, University of Dallas, 1845 East Northgate Drive, Irving, TX 75062-4736. *Telephone:* 877-408-2335. *Fax:* 972-721-5265. *E-mail:* vcox@gsm.udallas.edu.

DEGREES AND AWARDS

Graduate Certificate Corporate Finance; E-Business Management; Health Services Management; Information Assurance; Information Technology; Management, general; Marketing Management; Supply Chain Management/Market Logistics; Telecommunications Management
MBA Corporate Finance; Health Services Management; Information Assurance; Information Technology; Management, general; Marketing Management; Supply Chain Management/Market Logistics; Telecommunications Management
MBA/MS Information Assurance
MM Corporate Finance; E-Business Management; Health Services Management; Information Technology; Management, general; Marketing Management; Supply Chain Management/Market Logistics; Telecommunications Management

COURSE SUBJECT AREAS OFFERED OUTSIDE OF DEGREE PROGRAMS

Graduate—accounting; business administration and management; business and personal services marketing operations; business marketing and marketing management; computer and information sciences, general; computer and information sciences, other; computer systems analysis; engineering/industrial management; finance; financial management and services; health services administration; international business; management information systems/business data processing; marketing management and research; marketing operations/marketing and distribution, other; telecommunications.

See full description on page 588.

UNIVERSITY OF DELAWARE

Newark, Delaware
Division of Professional and Continuing Studies
http://www.continuingstudies.udel.edu/udonline/

University of Delaware was founded in 1743. It is accredited by Middle States Association of Colleges and Schools. It first offered distance learning courses in 1988. In fall 2003, there were 947 students enrolled in distance learning courses. Institutionally administered financial aid is available to distance learners.

Services Distance learners have accessibility to academic advising, bookstore, campus computer network, career placement assistance, e-mail services, library services, tutoring.

University of Delaware (continued)

Contact Dr. Dayle I. Thorpe, Director, University of Delaware, 211 Clayton Hall, Newark, DE 19716. *Telephone:* 302-831-6442. *Fax:* 302-831-3292. *E-mail:* dthorpe@udel.edu.

DEGREES AND AWARDS

BS Hotel, Restaurant, and Institutional Management; Nursing
MME Mechanical Engineering
MS Health Services Administration
MSEE Electrical Engineering
MSN Nursing–Health Services Administration; Nursing–RN to MSN

COURSE SUBJECT AREAS OFFERED OUTSIDE OF DEGREE PROGRAMS

Undergraduate—American history; animal sciences; biology; business marketing and marketing management; chemical engineering; chemistry; civil engineering; communications, general; criminal justice and corrections; economics; education, general; electrical engineering; engineering science; English composition; English language and literature, general; English language and literature/letters, other; English technical and business writing; foods and nutrition studies; hospitality services management; individual and family development studies; mathematics related; mechanical engineering; music; nursing; organizational behavior; philosophy and religion related; political science and government; sociology; urban affairs/studies.

Graduate—chemical engineering; civil engineering; education, general; electrical engineering; engineering mechanics; foods and nutrition studies; health professions and related sciences, other; mechanical engineering; nursing; public administration; urban affairs/studies.

Non-credit—business management and administrative services, other; electrical engineering; foods and nutrition studies; hospitality services management; mechanical engineering.

See full description on page 590.

UNIVERSITY OF DENVER

Denver, Colorado
University College
http://www.universitycollege.du.edu

University of Denver was founded in 1864. It is accredited by North Central Association of Colleges and Schools. It first offered distance learning courses in 1996. In fall 2003, there were 375 students enrolled in distance learning courses. Institutionally administered financial aid is available to distance learners.

Services Distance learners have accessibility to academic advising, bookstore, campus computer network, career placement assistance, e-mail services, library services.

Contact Mr. Mark Guthrie, Director of Enrollment and Advising, University of Denver, 2211 South Josephine, Denver, CO 80208. *Telephone:* 303-871-7582. *Fax:* 303-871-3070. *E-mail:* maguthri@du.edu.

DEGREES AND AWARDS

Graduate Certificate Broadband; Electronic Commerce; Environmental Health and Safety Management; Environmental Information Management; Environmental Management; Environmental Policy and Management; Environmental Policy; Environmental Project Management; Geographic Information Systems (GIS); Global Affairs; Leadership; Natural Resources Management; Organizational Security; Project Management; Technology Management; Telecommunications Management and Policy; Telecommunications Networks; Telecommunications Technology; Telecommunications
MEPM Environmental Policy and Management
MPS Computer Information Systems Specialization; E-Commerce Specialization; Environmental Policy and Management Specialization; Geographic Information Systems Specialization; Leadership Specialization; Organizational Security Specialization; Project Management Specialization; Technology Management Specialization; Telecommunications Specialization
MTEL Telecommunications
MoTM Technology Management

COURSE SUBJECT AREAS OFFERED OUTSIDE OF DEGREE PROGRAMS

Graduate—business administration and management; communications, general; computer and information sciences, general; computer and information sciences, other; computer/information technology administration and management; computer systems networking and telecommunications; creative writing; foreign languages and literatures; liberal arts and sciences, general studies and humanities; natural resources management and protective services; telecommunications.

See full description on page 592.

UNIVERSITY OF DUBUQUE

Dubuque, Iowa
http://www.dbq.edu/

University of Dubuque was founded in 1852. It is accredited by North Central Association of Colleges and Schools. It first offered distance learning courses in 1999. In fall 2003, there were 380 students enrolled in distance learning courses. Institutionally administered financial aid is available to distance learners.

Services Distance learners have accessibility to academic advising, campus computer network, e-mail services.

Contact Dr. John Jewell, UD Seminary Director of Instructional Technology and Distance Learning, University of Dubuque, 2000 University Avenue, Dubuque, IA 52001. *Telephone:* 563-589-3101. *Fax:* 563-589-3110. *E-mail:* jjewel@dbq.edu.

DEGREES AND AWARDS

Programs offered do not lead to a degree or other formal award.

COURSE SUBJECT AREAS OFFERED OUTSIDE OF DEGREE PROGRAMS

Non-credit—religion/religious studies.

THE UNIVERSITY OF FINDLAY

Findlay, Ohio
Global Campus
http://ufonline.findlay.edu

The University of Findlay was founded in 1882. It is accredited by North Central Association of Colleges and Schools. It first offered distance learning courses in 1998. In fall 2003, there were 998 students enrolled in distance learning courses. Institutionally administered financial aid is available to distance learners.

Services Distance learners have accessibility to academic advising, bookstore, campus computer network, career placement assistance, e-mail services, library services, tutoring.
Contact Dr. Doris L. Salis, Dean of Adult and Continuing Education, The University of Findlay, 1000 North Main Street, Findlay, OH 45840. *Telephone:* 419-434-4600. *Fax:* 419-434-4822. *E-mail:* salis@mail.findlay.edu.

DEGREES AND AWARDS

BS Business Management; Criminal Justice Administration; Environmental Management
MBA Business Administration
MS Environmental Management

COURSE SUBJECT AREAS OFFERED OUTSIDE OF DEGREE PROGRAMS

Undergraduate—accounting; bible/biblical studies; business; business administration and management; business/managerial economics; chemistry; communications, other; criminal justice and corrections; criminology; cultural studies; economics; fine arts and art studies; human resources management; international business; marketing management and research; mathematical statistics; mathematics; philosophy and religion; religion/religious studies; social sciences, general; sociology; visual and performing arts.
Graduate—accounting; business; business administration and management; business communications; business/managerial economics; educational evaluation, research and statistics; educational/instructional media design; environmental control technologies; human resources management; marketing management and research; marketing operations/marketing and distribution, other; public administration.
Non-credit—business information and data processing services; business management and administrative services, other; business/managerial economics; business quantitative methods and management science.

UNIVERSITY OF FLORIDA

Gainesville, Florida
Florida Campus Direct
http://www.distancelearning.ufl.edu

University of Florida was founded in 1853. It is accredited by Southern Association of Colleges and Schools. It first offered distance learning courses in 1996. In fall 2003, there were 4,600 students enrolled in distance learning courses. Institutionally administered financial aid is available to distance learners.

Services Distance learners have accessibility to academic advising, bookstore, campus computer network, career placement assistance, e-mail services, library services, tutoring.
Contact Christopher D. Sessums, Director of Distance Learning, University of Florida, 2209 NW 13th Street, Gainesville, FL 32609. *Telephone:* 352-392-1711. *Fax:* 352-392-6950. *E-mail:* csessum@doce.ufl.edu.

DEGREES AND AWARDS

Diploma Business Administration (BS); Fire and Emergency Services (BS)
Graduate Certificate Forensic Toxicology
MA Latin
MAg Agricultural Education
MBA Business Administration
MBS Audiology; Health Services Administration
MS Computer Engineering; Computer Engineering; Environmental Science; International Construction Management; Materials Science and Engineering; Mechanical and Aerospace Engineering; Pharmacy Concentration in Forensic Drug Chemistry; Pharmacy–Forensic DNA and Serology Concentration
MSHA Occupational Therapy
PharmD Pharmacy

COURSE SUBJECT AREAS OFFERED OUTSIDE OF DEGREE PROGRAMS

Undergraduate—advertising; anthropology; applied mathematics; astronomy; biology; chemistry; criminology; economics; English as a second language; English composition; foods and nutrition studies; geography; history; journalism and mass communications; liberal arts and sciences, general studies and humanities; mathematics; multi/interdisciplinary studies, other; philosophy; philosophy and religion; political science and government; psychology; public administration; social sciences and history, other; sociology.
Non-credit—business communications; computer programming; computer systems analysis; computer systems networking and telecommunications; foods and nutrition studies; legal studies.

UNIVERSITY OF FLORIDA

Gainesville, Florida
Working Professional Doctor of Pharmacy Program
http://www.ufpharmd.com

University of Florida was founded in 1853. It is accredited by Southern Association of Colleges and Schools. It first offered distance learning courses in 1994. In fall 2003, there were 500 students enrolled in distance learning courses. Institutionally administered financial aid is available to distance learners.

Services Distance learners have accessibility to academic advising, campus computer network, e-mail services, library services.
Contact Off-Site Admissions Center Enrollment Advisor, University of Florida, 7226 West Colonial Drive, PMB 400, Orlando, FL 32818-6731. *Telephone:* 800-431-6687. *Fax:* 407-573-2015. *E-mail:* info@pharmd.distancelearning.ufl.edu.

DEGREES AND AWARDS

PharmD Working Professional Doctor of Pharmacy Program

UNIVERSITY OF GEORGIA

Athens, Georgia
Georgia Center for Continuing Education
http://www.gactr.uga.edu/idl

University of Georgia was founded in 1785. It is accredited by Southern Association of Colleges and Schools. It first offered distance learning courses in 1950. In fall 2003, there were 5,000 students enrolled in distance learning courses. Institutionally administered financial aid is available to distance learners.

Services Distance learners have accessibility to bookstore, campus computer network, library services.
Contact Melissa Pettigrew, University of Georgia, 1197 South Lumpkin Street, Athens, GA 30602-3603. *Telephone:* 800-877-3243. *Fax:* 706-542-6635. *E-mail:* idl@gactr.uga.edu.

University of Georgia (continued)

DEGREES AND AWARDS

Programs offered do not lead to a degree or other formal award.

COURSE SUBJECT AREAS OFFERED OUTSIDE OF DEGREE PROGRAMS

Undergraduate—accounting; agricultural business and management; agricultural business and production, other; agriculture/agricultural sciences; American literature (United States); anthropology; apparel and accessories marketing operations; area, ethnic and cultural studies, other; astronomy; business; business administration and management; business communications; business/managerial economics; classical and ancient Near Eastern languages and literatures; communication disorders sciences and services; communications, general; comparative literature; developmental and child psychology; dramatic/theater arts and stagecraft; economics; education administration and supervision; education, general; English composition; English language and literature, general; English literature (British and Commonwealth); English technical and business writing; family and community studies; fine arts and art studies; foods and nutrition studies; foreign languages and literatures; geography; geological and related sciences; Germanic languages and literatures; history; horticulture services operations and management; journalism and mass communications; legal studies; liberal arts and sciences, general studies and humanities; marketing management and research; mathematical statistics; mathematics; medieval and Renaissance studies; music; parks, recreation and leisure studies; philosophy; philosophy and religion; plant sciences; political science and government; psychology; religion/religious studies; school psychology; sociology; soil sciences; special education; speech and rhetorical studies; teacher education, specific academic and vocational programs; veterinary medicine (DVM).
Non-credit—agriculture/agricultural sciences; human resources management; pharmacy; soil sciences; special education.

UNIVERSITY OF GREAT FALLS

Great Falls, Montana
Center for Distance Learning
http://www.ugf.edu/distancelearning/

University of Great Falls was founded in 1932. It first offered distance learning courses in 1979. In fall 2003, there were 192 students enrolled in distance learning courses. Institutionally administered financial aid is available to distance learners.

Services Distance learners have accessibility to academic advising, bookstore, career placement assistance, e-mail services, library services, tutoring.
Contact Jim Gretch, Production Manager, University of Great Falls, 1301 20th Street, South, Great Falls, MT 59405. *Telephone:* 406-791-5320. *Fax:* 406-791-5394. *E-mail:* jgretch@ugf.edu.

DEGREES AND AWARDS

BA Criminal Justice; Paralegal Studies; Psychology
BBA Business Administration
MSIS Information Systems

COURSE SUBJECT AREAS OFFERED OUTSIDE OF DEGREE PROGRAMS

Undergraduate—accounting; American literature (United States); biological and physical sciences; business administration and management; business/managerial economics; computer and information sciences, general; computer science; counseling psychology; criminal justice and corrections; developmental and child psychology; English language and literature, general; English technical and business writing; history; human services; Internet and World Wide Web; legal studies; liberal arts and sciences, general studies and humanities; marketing management and research; mathematics; mathematics, other; philosophy and religion; psychology; social sciences, general; sociology.
Graduate—computer and information sciences, general; general teacher education.

UNIVERSITY OF GUELPH

Guelph, Ontario, Canada
Office of Open Learning and Distance Education
http://www.open.uoguelph.ca/

University of Guelph was founded in 1964. It is provincially chartered. It first offered distance learning courses in 1995. In fall 2003, there were 4,000 students enrolled in distance learning courses. Institutionally administered financial aid is available to distance learners.

Services Distance learners have accessibility to academic advising, bookstore, campus computer network, e-mail services, library services.
Contact Ms. M. Smart, Open Learning Program Counsellor, University of Guelph, 160 Johnston Hall, Guelph, ON N1G 2W1, Canada. *Telephone:* 519-824-4120 Ext. 56050. *Fax:* 519-824-1112. *E-mail:* msmart@open.uoguelph.ca.

DEGREES AND AWARDS

Certificate of Achievement Agribusiness Sales and Marketing
Certificate of Completion Environmental Science
Certificate Food Science; Hospitality Studies
MA Leadership
MBA Hospitality and Tourism

COURSE SUBJECT AREAS OFFERED OUTSIDE OF DEGREE PROGRAMS

Undergraduate—agricultural business and management; anthropology; biology; cell biology; developmental/child psychology; ecology; English composition; environmental science; finance; French; geography; mathematical statistics; microbiology/bacteriology; organizational psychology; social psychology; sociology.
Graduate—business administration and management.
Non-credit—agricultural business and management; animal sciences.

UNIVERSITY OF HAWAII–WEST OAHU

Pearl City, Hawaii
http://www.uhwo.hawaii.edu/distanceed

University of Hawaii–West Oahu was founded in 1976. It is accredited by Western Association of Schools and Colleges. It first offered distance learning courses in 1996. In fall 2003, there were 150 students enrolled in distance learning courses. Institutionally administered financial aid is available to distance learners.

Services Distance learners have accessibility to academic advising, bookstore, campus computer network, e-mail services, library services, tutoring.

Contact Robyn Oshiro, Student Services Specialist, University of Hawaii–West Oahu, 96-129 Ala Ike, Student Services Office, Pearl City, HI 96782. *Telephone:* 808-454-4700. *Fax:* 808-453-6075. *E-mail:* robyn.oshiro@uhwo.hawaii.edu.

DEGREES AND AWARDS

BA Business Administration; Social Sciences–Applied Track

COURSE SUBJECT AREAS OFFERED OUTSIDE OF DEGREE PROGRAMS

Undergraduate—accounting; anthropology; business administration and management; business management and administrative services, other; counseling psychology; criminal justice and corrections; criminology; economics; history; human resources management; philosophy; political science and government; psychology; public administration; social sciences, general; sociology.

UNIVERSITY OF HOUSTON

Houston, Texas
Division of Educational Technology and Outreach
http://distance.uh.edu

University of Houston was founded in 1927. It is accredited by Southern Association of Colleges and Schools. It first offered distance learning courses in 1983. In fall 2003, there were 7,988 students enrolled in distance learning courses. Institutionally administered financial aid is available to distance learners.

Services Distance learners have accessibility to academic advising, bookstore, campus computer network, e-mail services, library services.

Contact Distance Education Adviser, University of Houston, Educational Technology and University Outreach, 111 C.N. Hilton, Houston, TX 77204-3051. *Telephone:* 713-743-8627. *Fax:* 713-743-3300. *E-mail:* deadvisor@uh.edu.

DEGREES AND AWARDS

Programs offered do not lead to a degree or other formal award.

COURSE SUBJECT AREAS OFFERED OUTSIDE OF DEGREE PROGRAMS

Undergraduate—anthropology; apparel and accessories marketing operations; communications, general; dance; English language and literature, general; health and physical education/fitness; history; hospitality services management; liberal arts and sciences, general studies and humanities; philosophy and religion.

Graduate—computer science; educational psychology; hospitality services management; mathematics.

See full description on page 594.

UNIVERSITY OF HOUSTON–CLEAR LAKE

Houston, Texas
Distance and Extended Education
http://www.uhcl.edu/disted

University of Houston–Clear Lake was founded in 1971. It is accredited by Southern Association of Colleges and Schools. It first offered distance learning courses in 1995. In fall 2003, there were 1,253 students enrolled in distance learning courses. Institutionally administered financial aid is available to distance learners.

Services Distance learners have accessibility to academic advising, bookstore, campus computer network, e-mail services, library services.

Contact Kate Finstad, Director of Distance and Off-Campus Education, University of Houston–Clear Lake, 2700 Bay Area Boulevard, Box 101, Houston, TX 77058-1098. *Telephone:* 281-283-3032. *Fax:* 281-283-2119. *E-mail:* disted@cl.uh.edu.

DEGREES AND AWARDS

MS Instructional Technology; Software Engineering

COURSE SUBJECT AREAS OFFERED OUTSIDE OF DEGREE PROGRAMS

Graduate—business administration and management; computer and information sciences, general; computer programming; computer science; computer software and media applications; economics; educational/instructional media design; health and medical administrative services; human resources management.

See full description on page 596.

UNIVERSITY OF HOUSTON–DOWNTOWN

Houston, Texas
http://www.uhd.edu/

University of Houston–Downtown was founded in 1974. It is accredited by Southern Association of Colleges and Schools. It first offered distance learning courses in 1994. In fall 2003, there were 2,200 students enrolled in distance learning courses. Institutionally administered financial aid is available to distance learners.

Services Distance learners have accessibility to academic advising, bookstore, campus computer network, e-mail services, library services.

Contact Dr. Gail Evans, Executive Director of Distance Education, University of Houston–Downtown, One Main Street, Houston, TX 77002. *Telephone:* 713-221-2735. *Fax:* 713-221-8922. *E-mail:* evansg@uhd.edu.

DEGREES AND AWARDS

Programs offered do not lead to a degree or other formal award.

COURSE SUBJECT AREAS OFFERED OUTSIDE OF DEGREE PROGRAMS

Undergraduate—accounting; biological and physical sciences; biological technology; business administration and management; business communications; business/managerial economics; business marketing and marketing management; computer/information technology administration and management; computer programming; computer science; computer software and media applications; computer systems analysis; computer systems networking and telecommunications; criminal justice and corrections; developmental/child psychology; education, general; English language and literature/letters, other; finance; history; international business; law and legal studies related; liberal arts and sciences, general studies and humanities; management information systems/business data processing; marketing operations/marketing and distribution, other; mathematical statistics; organizational psychology; political science and government; sociology.

University of Houston–Downtown (continued)

Graduate—criminal justice and corrections; general teacher education.

UNIVERSITY OF HOUSTON–VICTORIA

Victoria, Texas

http://www.uhv.edu/

University of Houston–Victoria was founded in 1973. It is accredited by Southern Association of Colleges and Schools. It first offered distance learning courses in 1996. Institutionally administered financial aid is available to distance learners.

Services Distance learners have accessibility to academic advising, bookstore, campus computer network, career placement assistance, e-mail services, library services, tutoring.

Contact Ms. Chari Norgard, Director of Instructional Support Services, University of Houston–Victoria, 3007 North Ben Wilson, Victoria, TX 77901-4450. *Telephone:* 361-570-4290. *Fax:* 361-570-4314. *E-mail:* norgardc@uhv.edu.

DEGREES AND AWARDS

BBA Business; Management; Marketing
MBA Business

COURSE SUBJECT AREAS OFFERED OUTSIDE OF DEGREE PROGRAMS

Undergraduate—accounting; biology, general; computer and information sciences, general; education, general; English composition; history; psychology.
Graduate—accounting; communications, general; education, general; psychology.

UNIVERSITY OF IDAHO

Moscow, Idaho

Engineering Outreach

http://www.uidaho.edu/eo/

University of Idaho was founded in 1889. It is accredited by Northwest Commission on Colleges and Universities. It first offered distance learning courses in 1976. In fall 2003, there were 424 students enrolled in distance learning courses. Institutionally administered financial aid is available to distance learners.

Services Distance learners have accessibility to academic advising, bookstore, campus computer network, e-mail services, library services.

Contact Ms. Diane Bancke, Administrative Manager, University of Idaho, Engineering Outreach, PO Box 441014, Moscow, ID 83844-1014. *Telephone:* 800-824-2889. *Fax:* 208-885-9249. *E-mail:* outreach@uidaho.edu.

DEGREES AND AWARDS

Certificate Advanced Material Design; Applied Geotechnics; Communication Systems; Electric Machines and Drives; Heating, Ventilation, and Air Conditioning (HVAC) Systems; Power System Protection and Relaying; Secure and Dependable Computing Systems; Structural Engineering; Water Resources Engineering
MAT Teaching Mathematics
MEngr Biological and Agricultural Engineering; Civil Engineering; Computer Engineering; Electrical Engineering; Engineering Management; Mechanical Engineering
MS Biological and Agricultural Engineering; Computer Engineering; Computer Science; Electrical Engineering; Geological Engineering; Psychology

COURSE SUBJECT AREAS OFFERED OUTSIDE OF DEGREE PROGRAMS

Undergraduate—agricultural engineering; biology; chemical engineering; civil engineering; computer engineering; computer programming; computer science; electrical engineering; engineering/industrial management; geography; mathematical statistics; mathematics related; mechanical engineering; psychology.
Graduate—agricultural engineering; business management and administrative services, other; chemical engineering; computer engineering; computer science; electrical engineering; engineering/industrial management; environmental/environmental health engineering; mathematical statistics; mathematics related; mechanical engineering; philosophy and religion related; psychology.
Non-credit—computer programming; electrical, electronics and communications engineering.

See full description on page 598.

UNIVERSITY OF IDAHO

Moscow, Idaho

Independent Study in Idaho

http://www.uidaho.edu/isi

University of Idaho was founded in 1889. It is accredited by Northwest Commission on Colleges and Universities. It first offered distance learning courses in 1973. In fall 2003, there were 538 students enrolled in distance learning courses. Institutionally administered financial aid is available to distance learners.

Services Distance learners have accessibility to bookstore, library services.

Contact Jeanne Workman, Registration Coordinator, University of Idaho, Independent Study in Idaho, PO Box 443225, Moscow, ID 83844-3225. *Telephone:* 877-464-3246. *Fax:* 208-885-5738. *E-mail:* indepst@uidaho.edu.

DEGREES AND AWARDS

Programs offered do not lead to a degree or other formal award.

COURSE SUBJECT AREAS OFFERED OUTSIDE OF DEGREE PROGRAMS

Undergraduate—accounting; agricultural business and management; anthropology; biology, general; business; consumer and homemaking education; criminal justice and corrections; dental services; economics; education, other; English composition; English language and literature, general; environmental/environmental health engineering; family and community studies; family/consumer resource management; financial management and services; foreign languages and literatures; health and medical administrative services; health and physical education/fitness; history; journalism and mass communications; library science/librarianship; library science, other; mathematics; microbiology/bacteriology; museology/museum studies; music; philosophy; physics; political science and government; psychology; real estate; social sciences and history, other; social sciences, general; sociology; special education.

Graduate—library science/librarianship; library science, other.

See full description on page 598.

UNIVERSITY OF ILLINOIS

Urbana, Illinois
University of Illinois Online
http://www.online.uillinois.edu

University of Illinois is accredited by North Central Association of Colleges and Schools. It first offered distance learning courses in 1997. In fall 2003, there were 6,000 students enrolled in distance learning courses. Institutionally administered financial aid is available to distance learners.

Services Distance learners have accessibility to academic advising, bookstore, campus computer network, career placement assistance, e-mail services, library services, tutoring.

Contact Jeff Harmon, Director of Marketing, University of Illinois, 807 South Wright Street, Suite 370, MC 307, Champaign, IL 61820. *Telephone:* 800-633-8465. *Fax:* 217-333-5040. *E-mail:* uiol-info@uillinois.edu.

DEGREES AND AWARDS

BA English; History; Liberal Studies
BS Computer Science; Mathematics
Certificate of Completion Graduate Medical Education Core Curriculum
Advanced Graduate Diploma The Continuation Curriculum Option (CCO) Pathway to the Doctor of Pharmacy
CCCPE Antithrombosis Therapy Management; Blood Bank Technology Specialist; Business English; Career Specialist Studies; Certified Fire Fighter II; E-Business Strategy; Electromagnetics Technology; Engineering Law and Management; Fund Development; GME Core Curriculum; Hazardous Waste Risk and Remediation; Health Informatics; Information Systems; Integrated Circuits; Marketing Strategy in the Digital Age; Materials Failure; Materials; Math Teacher Link; NetMath; Networks and Distributed Systems; Nonprofit Management; Nursing–School Nurse; Nursing–Teaching Certificate in Nursing Education; Online Secondary Math; Planning Commissioner; Power and Energy Systems; Professional Development Sequence in Community College Teaching and Learning; Professional Development Sequence in Dairy Science; Professional Development Sequence in Financial Engineering and Risk Management; Professional Development Sequence in Translation, French; Project Management Online; Renewing Public Housing; Software Engineering; Specialty Needs for Primary Care Physicians (CME Online); Strategic Technology; Systems Software; Telecommunications and Signal Processing; Veterinary Education Online; Wireless Communication Technology
MAE Education Leadership–Master of Arts in Education Leadership
MBA Business Administration
MCC Computer Science
ME Engineering
MEd Community College Teaching and Learning (Ed.M); Curriculum, Technology, and Education Reform; Global Human Resource Development
MHA Health Professions Education–Master of Health Professions Education
MLIS LEEP–Library and Information Science
MPH Public Health Informatics
MS Agricultural Education; Management Information Systems
MSME Mechanical Engineering

COURSE SUBJECT AREAS OFFERED OUTSIDE OF DEGREE PROGRAMS

Undergraduate—computer and information sciences, general; English language and literature, general; history; liberal arts and sciences, general studies and humanities; mathematics.

Graduate—agriculture/agricultural sciences; business administration and management; computer and information sciences, general; computer/information technology administration and management; computer science; computer systems networking and telecommunications; curriculum and instruction; education, general; engineering, general; health professions and related sciences, other; human resources management; international business; library science/librarianship; materials engineering; mathematics; mechanical engineering; medical laboratory technology; nursing; pharmacy; public administration; teacher education, specific academic and vocational programs; veterinary medicine (DVM).

Non-credit—business; computer programming; English composition; English creative writing; English language and literature, general; English technical and business writing; fine arts and art studies; fire protection; Internet and World Wide Web; marketing management and research; public administration; public health.

See full description on page 600.

UNIVERSITY OF ILLINOIS AT CHICAGO

Chicago, Illinois
Office of External Education
http://www.uic.edu/depts/uionline/

University of Illinois at Chicago was founded in 1946. It is accredited by North Central Association of Colleges and Schools. It first offered distance learning courses in 1998. In fall 2003, there were 4,974 students enrolled in distance learning courses. Institutionally administered financial aid is available to distance learners.

Services Distance learners have accessibility to academic advising, bookstore, campus computer network, e-mail services, library services.

Contact Kristen Hartz, Project Coordinator, University of Illinois at Chicago, MC 140, 1333 South Halsted Street, Suite 205, Chicago , IL 60607. *Telephone:* 312-355-1275. *Fax:* 312-413-9730. *E-mail:* khartz@uic.edu.

DEGREES AND AWARDS

Certificate of Completion Business English Online; Continuing Medical Education–Specialty Needs for PCPs; Culture of U.S. Business; E-Business Strategy; Graduate Medical Education Core Curriculum; Health Informatics; Marketing Strategy in the Digital Age; Nonprofit Management; Planning Commissioner Online; Project Management; Public Health Informatics; Renewing Public Housing
Certificate Antithrombosis Management Service; Blood Bank Specialist; Electromagnetics Technology; Engineering Law and Management; Nursing Education Teaching Certificate; Nursing–School Nursing; Public Health Preparedness; Wireless Communication Technology
MEngr Engineering
MPH Public Health Informatics
MS Health Professions Education

University of Illinois at Chicago (continued)

COURSE SUBJECT AREAS OFFERED OUTSIDE OF DEGREE PROGRAMS

Graduate—business; engineering, general; health professions and related sciences, other; marketing management and research; medical clinical sciences (M.S., Ph.D.); nursing; pharmacy; public health.

Non-credit—business; education, other; health and medical administrative services; health and medical diagnostic and treatment services; Internet and World Wide Web; marketing management and research; medical residency programs; nursing; pharmacy; public administration and services, other; public health; urban affairs/studies.

UNIVERSITY OF ILLINOIS AT SPRINGFIELD

Springfield, Illinois
Office of Technology-Enhanced Learning
http://online.uis.edu

University of Illinois at Springfield was founded in 1969. It is accredited by North Central Association of Colleges and Schools. It first offered distance learning courses in 1984. In fall 2003, there were 1,200 students enrolled in distance learning courses. Institutionally administered financial aid is available to distance learners.

Services Distance learners have accessibility to academic advising, bookstore, campus computer network, career placement assistance, e-mail services, library services, tutoring.

Contact Ray Schroeder, Director, University of Illinois at Springfield, HRB 79, One University Plaza, Springfield, IL 62703. *Telephone:* 217-206-7317. *Fax:* 217-206-7539. *E-mail:* schroeder.ray@uis.edu.

DEGREES AND AWARDS

BA English; History

BLS Liberal Studies

BS Computer Science

MEd Teaching Leadership–Master in Teaching Leadership Degree Concentration

MS Management Information Systems

COURSE SUBJECT AREAS OFFERED OUTSIDE OF DEGREE PROGRAMS

Undergraduate—accounting; biological and physical sciences; biology, general; botany; business administration and management; chemistry; communications, general; computer science; English composition; English creative writing; human resources management; mathematical statistics; mathematics; philosophy; psychology; public administration; public policy analysis; women's studies.

Graduate—communications, general; computer science; education, other; management information systems/business data processing; philosophy; public administration.

UNIVERSITY OF ILLINOIS AT URBANA-CHAMPAIGN

Champaign, Illinois
Curriculum, Technology, and Education Reform Program
http://www.cter.ed.uiuc.edu/

University of Illinois at Urbana–Champaign was founded in 1867. It is accredited by North Central Association of Colleges and Schools.

Contact Ms. Norma Scagnoli, Program Coordinator, University of Illinois at Urbana–Champaign, Educational Psychology, 188P Education Building, 1310 South Sixth Street, MC 708, Champaign, IL 61820. *Telephone:* 217-244-3315. *E-mail:* scagnoli@uiuc.edu.

DEGREES AND AWARDS

MEd Curriculum, Technology, and Education Reform (CTER)

See full description on page 602.

UNIVERSITY OF ILLINOIS AT URBANA-CHAMPAIGN

Champaign, Illinois
Human Resource Education Program
http://www.hre.uiuc.edu/online/

University of Illinois at Urbana–Champaign was founded in 1867. It is accredited by North Central Association of Colleges and Schools. It first offered distance learning courses in 1998.

Contact Department of Human Resource Education, University of Illinois at Urbana–Champaign, 351 Education Building, 1310 South Sixth Street, Champaign, IL 61820. *Telephone:* 217-333-0807. *Fax:* 217-244-5632. *E-mail:* hreonline@uiuc.edu.

DEGREES AND AWARDS

Graduate Certificate Community College Teaching and Learning (CCTL) Certificate of Professional Development

MEd Community College Teaching and Learning (CCTL); Global Human Resource Development (HRD)

See full description on page 606.

UNIVERSITY OF ILLINOIS AT URBANA-CHAMPAIGN

Champaign, Illinois
Graduate School of Library and Information Science
http://www.lis.uiuc.edu/

University of Illinois at Urbana–Champaign was founded in 1867. It is accredited by North Central Association of Colleges and Schools. It first offered distance learning courses in 1996. In fall 2003, there were 250 students enrolled in distance learning courses. Institutionally administered financial aid is available to distance learners.

Services Distance learners have accessibility to academic advising, bookstore, campus computer network, career placement assistance, e-mail services, library services, tutoring.

Contact Carol Devoss, Admissions Officer, University of Illinois at Urbana–Champaign, 501 East Daniel Street, Champaign, IL 61820. *Telephone:* 800-982-0914. *Fax:* 217-244-3302. *E-mail:* apply@alexia.lis.uiuc.edu.

DEGREES AND AWARDS

CAGS Library and Information Science
MS Library and Information Science

COURSE SUBJECT AREAS OFFERED OUTSIDE OF DEGREE PROGRAMS

Graduate—computer and information sciences, general; computer/information technology administration and management; educational/instructional media design; Internet and World Wide Web; library science/librarianship; science, technology and society.

See full description on page 604.

THE UNIVERSITY OF IOWA

Iowa City, Iowa
Center for Credit Programs
http://www.continuetolearn.uiowa.edu/ccp

The University of Iowa was founded in 1847. It is accredited by North Central Association of Colleges and Schools. In fall 2003, there were 3,000 students enrolled in distance learning courses. Institutionally administered financial aid is available to distance learners.

Services Distance learners have accessibility to academic advising, bookstore, career placement assistance, e-mail services, library services.
Contact Ms. Angela Ward, Pre-Admission Coordinator, The University of Iowa, 116 International Center, Iowa City, IA 52242. *Telephone:* 800-272-6430. *Fax:* 319-335-2740. *E-mail:* angela-ward@uiowa.edu.

DEGREES AND AWARDS

BLS Liberal Studies

COURSE SUBJECT AREAS OFFERED OUTSIDE OF DEGREE PROGRAMS

Undergraduate—African-American studies; American studies; education, general; English creative writing; environmental health; fine arts and art studies; French; gerontology; history; journalism; Latin (ancient and medieval); liberal arts and sciences, general studies and humanities; mathematics; nursing; psychology; religion/religious studies; social work; sociology; Spanish; women's studies.
Graduate—economics; English creative writing; environmental health; fine arts and art studies; general teacher education; gerontology; history; journalism; mathematics; nursing; psychology; religion/religious studies; social work; sociology; women's studies.

See full description on page 608.

UNIVERSITY OF LA VERNE

La Verne, California
Distance Learning Center
http://www.ulv.edu/dlc/dlc.html

University of La Verne was founded in 1891. It is accredited by Western Association of Schools and Colleges. It first offered distance learning courses in 1996. In fall 2003, there were 350 students enrolled in distance learning courses. Institutionally administered financial aid is available to distance learners.

Services Distance learners have accessibility to academic advising, bookstore, campus computer network, career placement assistance, e-mail services, library services, tutoring.
Contact Mrs. Alene Harrison, Distance Learning Center Registrar, University of La Verne, 1950 3rd Street, La Verne, CA 91750. *Telephone:* 909-985-0944 Ext. 5301. *Fax:* 909-981-8695. *E-mail:* harrisoa@ulv.edu.

DEGREES AND AWARDS

BS Organizational Management; Public Administration
MBA Business Administration

COURSE SUBJECT AREAS OFFERED OUTSIDE OF DEGREE PROGRAMS

Undergraduate—anthropology; biology, general; chemistry; communications, general; criminology; developmental and child psychology; English composition; English creative writing; financial management and services; history; liberal arts and sciences, general studies and humanities; music; philosophy; physical sciences, general; psychology; public administration; public administration and services, other; speech and rhetorical studies; teacher education, specific academic and vocational programs.
Graduate—business; business administration and management; education administration and supervision; health and medical administrative services.
Non-credit—anthropology; astronomy; atmospheric sciences and meteorology; biological and physical sciences; biological sciences/life sciences, other; conservation and renewable natural resources, other; counseling psychology; criminology; education, general; education, other; film/video and photographic arts; fine arts and art studies; geological and related sciences; gerontology; historic preservation, conservation and architectural history; history; miscellaneous physical sciences; museology/museum studies; music; natural resources conservation; parks, recreation, leisure and fitness studies, other; physical sciences, other; teacher education, specific academic and vocational programs.

THE UNIVERSITY OF LETHBRIDGE

Lethbridge, Alberta, Canada
http://www.uleth.ca/

The University of Lethbridge was founded in 1967. It is provincially chartered. It first offered distance learning courses in 2001. In fall 2003, there were 111 students enrolled in distance learning courses. Institutionally administered financial aid is available to distance learners.

Services Distance learners have accessibility to academic advising, bookstore, campus computer network, career placement assistance, e-mail services, library services, tutoring.
Contact The University of Lethbridge, 4401 University Drive, Lethbridge, AB T1K 3M4, Canada. *Telephone:* 403-329-2233.

DEGREES AND AWARDS

Programs offered do not lead to a degree or other formal award.

COURSE SUBJECT AREAS OFFERED OUTSIDE OF DEGREE PROGRAMS

Undergraduate—education, other; Internet and World Wide Web.

The University of Lethbridge (continued)

Graduate—educational evaluation, research and statistics; education, general; education, other.

UNIVERSITY OF LOUISVILLE

Louisville, Kentucky
Division of Distance and Continuing Education
http://www.delphi.louisville.edu

University of Louisville was founded in 1798. It is accredited by Southern Association of Colleges and Schools. It first offered distance learning courses in 1992. In fall 2003, there were 1,250 students enrolled in distance learning courses. Institutionally administered financial aid is available to distance learners.

Services Distance learners have accessibility to academic advising, bookstore, career placement assistance, e-mail services, library services, tutoring.

Contact Joni Allison, Assistant Director, Delphi Center for Teaching and Learning, University of Louisville, Delphi Center, Belknap Campus, Ekstrom Library, 2nd Floor, Room 244, Louisville, KY 40292. *Telephone:* 502-852-8565. *Fax:* 502-852-0393. *E-mail:* jallison@louisville.edu.

DEGREES AND AWARDS

BA Communication
BS Administration of Justice; Communication; Occupational Training and Development
Certificate Management Development; Purchasing and Supply Chain Professional
MA Higher Education
MEd Administration of Justice–Master of Science in the Administration of Justice
MS Human Resource Education

COURSE SUBJECT AREAS OFFERED OUTSIDE OF DEGREE PROGRAMS

Non-credit—criminal justice and corrections.

UNIVERSITY OF LOUISVILLE

Louisville, Kentucky
Program in Special Education
http://www.delphi.louisville.edu

University of Louisville was founded in 1798. It is accredited by Southern Association of Colleges and Schools. It first offered distance learning courses in 1992. In fall 2003, there were 1,250 students enrolled in distance learning courses. Institutionally administered financial aid is available to distance learners.

Services Distance learners have accessibility to academic advising, bookstore, career placement assistance, e-mail services, library services, tutoring.

Contact Joni Allison, Assistant Director, Delphi School for Teaching and Learning, University of Louisville, Delphi Center, Belknap Campus, Ekstrom Library, 2nd Floor, Room 244, Louisville, KY 40292. *Telephone:* 502-852-8565. *Fax:* 502-852-0393. *E-mail:* jallison@louisville.edu.

DEGREES AND AWARDS

MEd Autism; Med-Assistive Technology; Moderate/Severe Disabilities; Orientation and Mobility; Visual Impairment
MS Special Education–Master of Special Education

COURSE SUBJECT AREAS OFFERED OUTSIDE OF DEGREE PROGRAMS

Non-credit—criminal justice and corrections.

UNIVERSITY OF MAINE

Orono, Maine
Continuing Education Division
http://Learnonline.umaine.edu

University of Maine was founded in 1865. It is accredited by New England Association of Schools and Colleges. It first offered distance learning courses in 1989. In fall 2003, there were 1,600 students enrolled in distance learning courses. Institutionally administered financial aid is available to distance learners.

Services Distance learners have accessibility to academic advising, bookstore, campus computer network, e-mail services, library services.

Contact James F. Toner, Associate Director, University of Maine, 5713 Chadbourne Hall, Orono, ME 04469-5713. *Telephone:* 207-581-3142. *Fax:* 207-581-3141. *E-mail:* jim.toner@umit.maine.edu.

DEGREES AND AWARDS

BUS University Studies
Certificate Maine Studies

COURSE SUBJECT AREAS OFFERED OUTSIDE OF DEGREE PROGRAMS

Undergraduate—accounting; Asian studies; biology; civil engineering/civil technology; communication disorders sciences and services; computer and information sciences, other; creative writing; developmental/child psychology; educational psychology; electrical engineering; English as a second language; English composition; English technical and business writing; environmental health; foreign languages and literatures, other; horticulture science; mechanical engineering; music; nursing; psychology; public administration; social psychology; sociology; special education; surveying; teacher education, specific academic and vocational programs; teaching English as a second language/foreign language; visual and performing arts; women's studies.
Graduate—animal sciences; anthropology; business; civil engineering; education, general; electrical engineering; liberal arts and sciences, general studies and humanities; mechanical engineering; social work.
Non-credit—electrical engineering.

THE UNIVERSITY OF MAINE AT AUGUSTA

Augusta, Maine
University of Maine System Network for Education and Technology (UNET)
http://www.uma.maine.edu

The University of Maine at Augusta was founded in 1965. It is accredited by New England Association of Schools and Colleges. It first offered distance learning courses in 1986. In fall 2003, there were

2,300 students enrolled in distance learning courses. Institutionally administered financial aid is available to distance learners.

Services Distance learners have accessibility to academic advising, bookstore, campus computer network, e-mail services, library services, tutoring.

Contact Sheri Fraser, Interim Director of Admissions, The University of Maine at Augusta, 46 University Drive, Augusta, ME 04330. *Telephone:* 207-621-3390. *Fax:* 207-621-3116. *E-mail:* fraser@maine.edu.

DEGREES AND AWARDS

AA Liberal Arts; Social Services
AS Business Administration; Liberal Studies; Library and Information Services
BS Library and Information Services; Mental Health and Human Services

COURSE SUBJECT AREAS OFFERED OUTSIDE OF DEGREE PROGRAMS

Undergraduate—accounting; American literature (United States); anthropology; applied mathematics; business; business administration and management; business communications; business management and administrative services, other; child care and guidance workers and managers; communications, general; community health services; comparative literature; computer and information sciences, general; computer software and media applications; counseling psychology; criminal justice and corrections; developmental/child psychology; economics; English composition; English creative writing; English language and literature, general; English technical and business writing; financial management and services; history; human resources management; human services; liberal arts and sciences, general studies and humanities; library science, other; mathematical statistics; mathematics; mental health services; music; nursing; philosophy; physical sciences, general; political science and government; psychology; social sciences, general; sociology; taxation.

UNIVERSITY OF MANAGEMENT AND TECHNOLOGY

Arlington, Virginia
http://www.umtweb.edu

University of Management and Technology was founded in 1998. It is accredited by Distance Education and Training Council. It first offered distance learning courses in 1998. In fall 2003, there were 1,500 students enrolled in distance learning courses. Institutionally administered financial aid is available to distance learners.

Services Distance learners have accessibility to academic advising, bookstore, library services, tutoring.

Contact Dr. J. Davidson Frame, Academic Dean, University of Management and Technology, 1901 North Fort Myer Drive, Suite 700, Arlington, VA 22209. *Telephone:* 703-516-0035. *Fax:* 703-516-0985. *E-mail:* davidson.frame@umtweb.edu.

DEGREES AND AWARDS

ABA Business Administration
BBA Information Technology Management; International Management; Management; Marketing Management
Certificate Project Management
Graduate Certificate Project Management
MBA Management; Project Management
MSCS Computer Science; Management Information Systems; Multimedia Technology; Software Engineering
MSM Management, general; Project Management; Public Administration; Telecommunications Management

COURSE SUBJECT AREAS OFFERED OUTSIDE OF DEGREE PROGRAMS

Undergraduate—business administration and management; computer and information sciences, general; computer science; international business; marketing management and research.
Graduate—business administration and management; computer and information sciences, general; computer programming; computer software and media applications; computer systems networking and telecommunications; public administration.
Non-credit—business administration and management; business management and administrative services, other.

UNIVERSITY OF MARYLAND

Baltimore, Maryland
School of Nursing
http://nursing.umaryland.edu

University of Maryland was founded in 1807. It is accredited by Middle States Association of Colleges and Schools. It first offered distance learning courses in 1992. In fall 2003, there were 300 students enrolled in distance learning courses. Institutionally administered financial aid is available to distance learners.

Services Distance learners have accessibility to academic advising, bookstore, campus computer network, career placement assistance, e-mail services, library services, tutoring.

Contact Dr. Mary Etta C. Mills, Associate Dean, Academic Affairs, University of Maryland, 655 West Lombard Street, Room 505K, Baltimore, MD 21201. *Telephone:* 410-706-3975. *E-mail:* mills@son.umaryland.edu.

DEGREES AND AWARDS

BSN Nursing–RN to BSN

COURSE SUBJECT AREAS OFFERED OUTSIDE OF DEGREE PROGRAMS

Undergraduate—nursing.
Graduate—information sciences and systems; nursing.

UNIVERSITY OF MARYLAND, BALTIMORE COUNTY

Baltimore, Maryland
UMBC Continuing Education
http://www.umbc.edu

University of Maryland, Baltimore County was founded in 1963. It is accredited by Middle States Association of Colleges and Schools. It first offered distance learning courses in 1984. In fall 2003, there were 239 students enrolled in distance learning courses. Institutionally administered financial aid is available to distance learners.

Services Distance learners have accessibility to bookstore, campus computer network, e-mail services, library services.

Contact Angela Walton-Raji, Associate Director,Graduate School, University of Maryland, Baltimore County, Graduate School, 1000

University of Maryland, Baltimore County (continued)

Hilltop Circle, Baltimore, MD 21250. *Telephone:* 410-455-3514. *Fax:* 410-455-1917. *E-mail:* awalton@umbc.edu.

DEGREES AND AWARDS

Graduate Certificate Distance Learning; Instructional Systems Development
MA Instructional Systems Development–Training Systems
MS Emergency Health Services
MSIS Information Systems

COURSE SUBJECT AREAS OFFERED OUTSIDE OF DEGREE PROGRAMS

Graduate—educational/instructional media design; education, other; health professions and related sciences, other; information sciences and systems.
Non-credit—business administration and management; business communications.

UNIVERSITY OF MARYLAND, COLLEGE PARK

College Park, Maryland
E-Learning
http://www.onlinestudies.umd.edu

University of Maryland, College Park was founded in 1856. It is accredited by Middle States Association of Colleges and Schools. It first offered distance learning courses in 2000. In fall 2003, there were 100 students enrolled in distance learning courses. Institutionally administered financial aid is available to distance learners.

Services Distance learners have accessibility to academic advising, bookstore, library services.
Contact Paul E. Roche, Senior Project Manager, University of Maryland, College Park, 2103 Reckord Armory, OCEE, College Park, MD 20742. *Telephone:* 301-405-8989. *Fax:* 301-314-9572. *E-mail:* proche@umd.edu.

DEGREES AND AWARDS

Diploma Life Sciences
MEngr Professional Master of Engineering in Fire Protection

See full description on page 610.

UNIVERSITY OF MARYLAND UNIVERSITY COLLEGE

Adelphi, Maryland
Office of Distance Education and Lifelong Learning
http://www.umuc.edu

University of Maryland University College was founded in 1947. It is accredited by Middle States Association of Colleges and Schools. It first offered distance learning courses in 1972. In fall 2003, there were 25,000 students enrolled in distance learning courses. Institutionally administered financial aid is available to distance learners.

Services Distance learners have accessibility to academic advising, bookstore, campus computer network, career placement assistance, library services, tutoring.
Contact Enrollment Team, University of Maryland University College, 3501 University Boulevard East, Adelphi, MD 20783. *Telephone:* 800-888-UMUC. *E-mail:* umucinfo@umuc.edu.

DEGREES AND AWARDS

BA Communication Studies; English; Humanities
BS Accounting; Business Administration; Computer Studies; Computer and Information Science; Environmental Management; Fire Science; History; Human Resource Management; Information Systems Management; Legal Studies; Management Studies; Marketing; Psychology; Social Science
MBA Business Administration
MEd Education
MS Accounting and Financial Management; Biotechnology Studies; Computer Systems Management; E-Commerce; Environmental Management; Health Care Administration; Information Technology; Management; Software Engineering; Technology Management; Telecommunications Management

COURSE SUBJECT AREAS OFFERED OUTSIDE OF DEGREE PROGRAMS

Undergraduate—accounting; anthropology; area studies; biology, general; business administration and management; chemistry; communications, general; computer and information sciences, general; criminal justice and corrections; economics; fire protection; gerontology; human resources management; information sciences and systems; journalism and mass communications; marketing operations/marketing and distribution, other; mathematics; psychology; social sciences, general; sociology.
Graduate—accounting; business administration and management; business management and administrative services, other; computer/information technology administration and management; computer systems networking and telecommunications; educational/instructional media design; entrepreneurship; general teacher education; health and medical administrative services; human resources management; international business; marketing management and research; marketing operations/marketing and distribution, other; public administration; teacher education, specific academic and vocational programs.

See full description on page 612.

UNIVERSITY OF MASSACHUSETTS AMHERST

Amherst, Massachusetts
Division of Continuing Education
http://www.umassulearn.net

University of Massachusetts Amherst was founded in 1863. It is accredited by New England Association of Schools and Colleges. It first offered distance learning courses in 1974. In fall 2003, there were 750 students enrolled in distance learning courses. Institutionally administered financial aid is available to distance learners.

Services Distance learners have accessibility to bookstore, campus computer network, e-mail services.
Contact Linda Lowry, Director, Division of Continuing Education, University of Massachusetts Amherst, Continuing Education Building, 358 North Pleasant Street, Amherst, MA 01003-9296. *Telephone:* 413-545-2111. *Fax:* 413-545-3351. *E-mail:* llowry@contined.umass.edu.

DEGREES AND AWARDS

BBA Business Administration
BS Hospitality and Tourism Management; Nursing–RN to BS
Certificate Arts Management; Business Studies; Criminal Justices Studies; Exercise Science and Nutrition
MBA Business Administration
MEd Science Teachers
MPH Public Health Practice
MS Electrical and Computer Engineering; Engineering Management; Nursing
MS/MPH Nursing/Public Health–MS in Nursing and MS in Public Health
PhD Electrical and Computer Engineering

COURSE SUBJECT AREAS OFFERED OUTSIDE OF DEGREE PROGRAMS

Undergraduate—accounting; business administration and management; community health services; conservation and renewable natural resources, other; criminal justice and corrections; education, other; English language and literature, general; foods and nutrition studies; hospitality services management; journalism and mass communications; marketing management and research; natural resources conservation; philosophy; psychology; sociology; wildlife and wildlands management.
Graduate—accounting; chemical engineering; education administration and supervision; education, other; engineering/industrial management; mechanical engineering; nursing; public health.
Non-credit—accounting; business administration and management; chemical engineering; criminal justice and corrections; engineering/industrial management; financial management and services; marketing operations/marketing and distribution, other; mechanical engineering; public relations and organizational communications.

See full description on page 614.

UNIVERSITY OF MASSACHUSETTS BOSTON

Boston, Massachusetts
Corporate, Continuing and Distance Education
http://www.ccde.umb.edu

University of Massachusetts Boston was founded in 1964. It is accredited by New England Association of Schools and Colleges. It first offered distance learning courses in 2001. In fall 2003, there were 753 students enrolled in distance learning courses. Institutionally administered financial aid is available to distance learners.

Services Distance learners have accessibility to academic advising, bookstore, e-mail services, library services.
Contact Ms. Katharine Grant Galaitsis, Director of Online Education, University of Massachusetts Boston, Corporate, Continuing and Distance Education, 100 Morrissey Boulevard, Boston, MA 02125-3393. *Telephone:* 617-287-7918. *Fax:* 617-287-7297. *E-mail:* kitty.galaitsis@umb.edu.

DEGREES AND AWARDS

BS Nursing–RN to BS
Certificate Community, Media, and Technology; Fundamentals of Information Technology
Graduate Certificate Adapting Curriculum Frameworks for All Learners; Instructional Technology Design
MEd Counseling–Mental Health Counseling Track; Counseling–School Guidance Track; Instructional Design
PMC Nursing–Gerontological/Adult and Family Nurse Practitioner

COURSE SUBJECT AREAS OFFERED OUTSIDE OF DEGREE PROGRAMS

Undergraduate—anthropology; archaeology; biology, general; business administration and management; chemistry; communications, general; community organization, resources and services; computer and information sciences, general; computer/information technology administration and management; computer science; economics; environmental/environmental health engineering; fine arts and art studies; foreign languages and literatures; history; international relations and affairs; mathematical statistics; music; nursing; political science and government; psychology; sociology; technology education/industrial arts.
Graduate—biological and physical sciences; counseling psychology; educational/instructional media design; gerontology; international relations and affairs; mathematical statistics; nursing; school psychology; sociology; special education; student counseling and personnel services; teaching English as a second language/foreign language; technology education/industrial arts.

UNIVERSITY OF MASSACHUSETTS LOWELL

Lowell, Massachusetts
Continuing Studies and Corporate Education
http://continuinged.uml.edu/online

University of Massachusetts Lowell was founded in 1894. It is accredited by New England Association of Schools and Colleges. It first offered distance learning courses in 1995. In fall 2003, there were 2,400 students enrolled in distance learning courses. Institutionally administered financial aid is available to distance learners.

Services Distance learners have accessibility to academic advising, bookstore, campus computer network, e-mail services, library services.
Contact Catherine A. Kendrick, Director of Corporate and Distance Market Development, University of Massachusetts Lowell, One University Avenue, Lowell, MA 01854-2881. *Telephone:* 800-480-3190. *Fax:* 978-934-4064. *E-mail:* onlinelearning@uml.edu.

DEGREES AND AWARDS

AS Information Technology
BA Liberal Arts (BLA)
BS Information Technology with Business Minor; Information Technology
Certificate Contemporary Communications; Data/Telecommunications; Fundamentals of Information Technology; Intranet Development; Multimedia Applications; Paralegal Studies; Security Management and Homeland Security; UNIX
Graduate Certificate Clinical Pathology; Foundations of Business
MA Criminal Justice
MEd Educational Administration; Reading and Language
DPT Physical Therapy (Transitional Doctorate)

COURSE SUBJECT AREAS OFFERED OUTSIDE OF DEGREE PROGRAMS

Undergraduate—accounting; adult/continuing education; business; business communications; communications, general; computer and

University of Massachusetts Lowell (continued)

information sciences, general; computer programming; cultural studies; English composition; information sciences and systems; liberal arts and sciences, general studies and humanities; mathematics and computer science; philosophy; social sciences and history, other; sociology; telecommunications.
Graduate—education administration and supervision; education, general; electrical and electronic engineering-related technology; health professions and related sciences, other; medical laboratory technology.
Non-credit—educational/instructional media design; education, other.

UNIVERSITY OF MEDICINE AND DENTISTRY OF NEW JERSEY

Newark, New Jersey
http://www.umdnj.edu/

University of Medicine and Dentistry of New Jersey was founded in 1954. It is accredited by Middle States Association of Colleges and Schools. It first offered distance learning courses in 1998. In fall 2003, there were 300 students enrolled in distance learning courses. Institutionally administered financial aid is available to distance learners.

Services Distance learners have accessibility to academic advising, campus computer network, e-mail services, library services.
Contact Mr. Brian Lewis, Assistant Dean of Enrollment Services, University of Medicine and Dentistry of New Jersey, 65 Bergen Street, Room 149, Newark, NJ 07107. *Telephone:* 973-972-8575. *Fax:* 973-972-7463. *E-mail:* lewisbj@umdnj.edu.

DEGREES AND AWARDS

BS Health Sciences
MHS Health Sciences
MS Clinical Nutrition; Health Systems; Psychiatric Rehabilitation
DH Sc Clinical Nutrition (DCN)
PhD Health Sciences

COURSE SUBJECT AREAS OFFERED OUTSIDE OF DEGREE PROGRAMS

Undergraduate—health professions and related sciences, other.
Graduate—health professions and related sciences, other.

UNIVERSITY OF MICHIGAN

Ann Arbor, Michigan
Media Union
http://cpd.engin.umich.edu

University of Michigan was founded in 1817. It is accredited by North Central Association of Colleges and Schools. It first offered distance learning courses in 1969. In fall 2003, there were 316 students enrolled in distance learning courses. Institutionally administered financial aid is available to distance learners.

Services Distance learners have accessibility to academic advising, bookstore, campus computer network, e-mail services, library services.
Contact Kathy Friedrichs, Manager of Off-Campus Education Programs, University of Michigan, Center for Professional Development, College of Engineering, 273 Chrysler Center, 2121 Bonisteel Boulevard, Ann Arbor, MI 48109-2092. *Telephone:* 734-647-7173. *Fax:* 734-647-2243. *E-mail:* kamf@umich.edu.

DEGREES AND AWARDS

ME Manufacturing Engineering
MEngr Automotive Engineering; Integrated Microsystems

COURSE SUBJECT AREAS OFFERED OUTSIDE OF DEGREE PROGRAMS

Graduate—engineering, other; engineering science; industrial/manufacturing engineering.
Non-credit—aerospace, aeronautical and astronautical engineering; atmospheric sciences and meteorology; business quantitative methods and management science; engineering design; engineering, general; engineering/industrial management; engineering, other; engineering-related technologies, other; engineering science; industrial/manufacturing engineering; materials engineering; materials science; mechanical engineering; mechanical engineering-related technologies; miscellaneous engineering-related technologies; ocean engineering; systems engineering.

UNIVERSITY OF MICHIGAN–DEARBORN

Dearborn, Michigan
http://dln.engin.umd.umich.edu

University of Michigan–Dearborn was founded in 1959. It is accredited by North Central Association of Colleges and Schools. It first offered distance learning courses in 2003. In fall 2003, there were 62 students enrolled in distance learning courses. Institutionally administered financial aid is available to distance learners.

Services Distance learners have accessibility to academic advising, bookstore, campus computer network, e-mail services, library services.
Contact Susan Guinn, Program Coordinator, University of Michigan–Dearborn, College of Engineering and Computer Science, 4901 Evergreen Road, 2040 PEC, Dearborn, MI 48128-1491. *Telephone:* 313-593-4000. *Fax:* 313-593-4070. *E-mail:* sguinn@umich.edu.

DEGREES AND AWARDS

MS Software Engineering
MSE Automotive Systems Engineering

COURSE SUBJECT AREAS OFFERED OUTSIDE OF DEGREE PROGRAMS

Graduate—engineering, general; engineering science.

UNIVERSITY OF MINNESOTA, MORRIS

Morris, Minnesota
College of Continuing Education-GenEdWeb Program
http://genedweb.mrs.umn.edu

University of Minnesota, Morris was founded in 1959. It is accredited by North Central Association of Colleges and Schools. It first offered distance learning courses in 1997. In fall 2003, there were 78 students enrolled in distance learning courses. Institutionally administered financial aid is available to distance learners.

Services Distance learners have accessibility to academic advising, bookstore, campus computer network, e-mail services, library services, tutoring.

Contact Ms. Karen M. Johnson, Program Associate, University of Minnesota, Morris, 225 Community Services Building, 600 East 4th Street, Morris, MN 56267. *Telephone:* 800-842-0030. *Fax:* 320-589-1661. *E-mail:* johnsokm@mrs.umn.edu.

DEGREES AND AWARDS

Programs offered do not lead to a degree or other formal award.

COURSE SUBJECT AREAS OFFERED OUTSIDE OF DEGREE PROGRAMS

Undergraduate—economics; education, general; English composition; history; mathematical statistics; mathematics; multi/interdisciplinary studies, other; political science and government; psychology; teacher education, specific academic and vocational programs.

UNIVERSITY OF MINNESOTA, TWIN CITIES CAMPUS

Minneapolis, Minnesota
Independent and Distance Learning
http://www.cce.umn.edu/petersons

University of Minnesota, Twin Cities Campus was founded in 1851. It is accredited by North Central Association of Colleges and Schools. It first offered distance learning courses in 1941. In fall 2003, there were 2,000 students enrolled in distance learning courses. Institutionally administered financial aid is available to distance learners.

Services Distance learners have accessibility to bookstore, campus computer network, e-mail services, library services.

Contact Receptionist, University of Minnesota, Twin Cities Campus, Continuing Education Information Center, 101 Wesbrook Hall, 77 Pleasant Street, SE, Minneapolis, MN 55455. *Telephone:* 800-234-6564. *Fax:* 612-625-1511. *E-mail:* info@cce.umn.edu.

DEGREES AND AWARDS

Programs offered do not lead to a degree or other formal award.

COURSE SUBJECT AREAS OFFERED OUTSIDE OF DEGREE PROGRAMS

Undergraduate—accounting; agriculture/agricultural sciences; agriculture/agricultural sciences, other; American history; anthropology; art history; biochemistry and biophysics; biology; business administration and management; business marketing and marketing management; cell and molecular biology; classical and ancient Near Eastern languages and literatures; communications, general; computer systems networking and telecommunications; creative writing; developmental/child psychology; ecology; economics; educational psychology; English composition; English language and literature, general; English language and literature/letters, other; family/consumer resource management; finance; foods and nutrition studies; foreign languages and literatures; forest production and processing; French; geological and related sciences; Germanic languages and literatures; health and medical administrative services; history; journalism; Latin (ancient and medieval); mathematics; mechanical engineering; music; nursing; occupational therapy; philosophy; physics; psychology; public health; Romance languages and literatures; Russian; social work; Spanish; speech and rhetorical studies; women's studies.

Graduate—communications, general; forest production and processing; public health; social work.

See full description on page 616.

UNIVERSITY OF MISSISSIPPI

Oxford, Mississippi
Office of Independent Study
http://www.outreach.olemiss.edu/

University of Mississippi was founded in 1844. It is accredited by Southern Association of Colleges and Schools. It first offered distance learning courses in 1995. In fall 2003, there were 2,000 students enrolled in distance learning courses. Institutionally administered financial aid is available to distance learners.

Services Distance learners have accessibility to academic advising, bookstore, campus computer network, e-mail services, library services.

Contact Kathy Palan, Admissions Specialist, University of Mississippi, Department of Independent Study and Ole Miss Online, PO Box 729, Martindale Student Services Center, Suite M, Room 371, University, MS 38677-0729. *Telephone:* 877-915-7313. *Fax:* 662-915-1221. *E-mail:* indstudy@olemiss.edu.

DEGREES AND AWARDS

Programs offered do not lead to a degree or other formal award.

COURSE SUBJECT AREAS OFFERED OUTSIDE OF DEGREE PROGRAMS

Undergraduate—accounting; American literature (United States); biology, general; business; business/managerial economics; business marketing and marketing management; chemistry; criminology; dramatic/theater arts and stagecraft; economics; educational/instructional media design; educational psychology; education, general; English creative writing; English literature (British and Commonwealth); finance; fine arts and art studies; foreign languages and literatures; history; liberal arts and sciences, general studies and humanities; mathematics, other; miscellaneous health aides; parks, recreation and leisure facilities management; philosophy; philosophy and religion; real estate.

Graduate—education administration and supervision; educational/instructional media design; education, general; education, other.

Non-credit—computer software and media applications.

UNIVERSITY OF MISSOURI–COLUMBIA

Columbia, Missouri
Center for Distance and Independent Study
http://cdis.missouri.edu

University of Missouri–Columbia was founded in 1839. It is accredited by North Central Association of Colleges and Schools. It first offered distance learning courses in 1941. In fall 2003, there were 14,774 students enrolled in distance learning courses. Institutionally administered financial aid is available to distance learners.

Services Distance learners have accessibility to bookstore, library services.

University of Missouri–Columbia (continued)

Contact Ms. Terrie Nagel, Student Services Advisor, University of Missouri–Columbia, 136 Clark Hall, Columbia, MO 65211-4200. *Telephone:* 800-609-3727. *Fax:* 573-882-6808. *E-mail:* cdis@missouri.edu.

DEGREES AND AWARDS

BGS General Studies

COURSE SUBJECT AREAS OFFERED OUTSIDE OF DEGREE PROGRAMS

Undergraduate—accounting; African-American studies; agricultural engineering; American literature (United States); animal sciences; anthropology; area, ethnic and cultural studies, other; astronomy; atmospheric sciences and meteorology; bible/biblical studies; biology, general; business; business administration and management; business/managerial economics; business marketing and marketing management; child care and guidance workers and managers; classical and ancient Near Eastern languages and literatures; communications, other; computer programming; computer science; consumer and homemaking education; creative writing; cultural studies; curriculum and instruction; developmental/child psychology; economics; educational evaluation, research and statistics; educational psychology; education, general; education, other; engineering mechanics; English composition; English creative writing; English language and literature, general; English language and literature/letters, other; English literature (British and Commonwealth); English technical and business writing; entomology; family and community studies; family/consumer resource management; fine arts and art studies; foreign languages and literatures, other; French; geography; geological and related sciences; Germanic languages and literatures; health and medical administrative services; health and physical education/fitness; health services administration; history; human resources management; human services; individual and family development studies; international business; international relations and affairs; law and legal studies related; liberal arts and sciences, general studies and humanities; marketing management and research; mathematical statistics; mathematics; mathematics related; peace and conflict studies; philosophy; physics; political science and government; psychology; psychology, other; public administration; religion/religious studies; Romance languages and literatures; Russian; social psychology; social work; sociology; Spanish; special education; women's studies.

Graduate—animal sciences; business; counseling psychology; curriculum and instruction; economics; education administration and supervision; educational evaluation, research and statistics; educational psychology; education, general; education, other; English language and literature, general; family and community studies; history; human resources management; human services; international business; organizational behavior; philosophy; political science and government; special education.

Non-credit—city/urban, community and regional planning; fire protection; Romance languages and literatures.

UNIVERSITY OF MISSOURI–COLUMBIA

Columbia, Missouri
MU Direct: Continuing and Distance Education
http://MUdirect.missouri.edu/mu/pg3.htm

University of Missouri–Columbia was founded in 1839. It is accredited by North Central Association of Colleges and Schools. It first offered distance learning courses in 1990. In fall 2003, there were 1,938 students enrolled in distance learning courses. Institutionally administered financial aid is available to distance learners.

Services Distance learners have accessibility to academic advising, bookstore, campus computer network, e-mail services, library services, tutoring.

Contact Juanita Smarr, Administrative Assistant, University of Missouri–Columbia, 105 Whitten Hall, Columbia, MO 65211-6300. *Telephone:* 800-545-2604. *Fax:* 573-882-5071. *E-mail:* mudirect@missouri.edu.

DEGREES AND AWARDS

BHS Radiologic Sciences Bachelors Completion Program–Radiography; Respiratory Therapy Bachelors Completion Program
BSN Nursing Bachelor's Completion Program
Advanced Graduate Diploma Educational Specialist–Mental Health Practices in Schools; Educational Specialist–Technology in Schools
MA Journalism–Media Management; Journalism–Strategic Communications; Library and Information Science
MEd Educational Leadership Focus; Gifted Education Focus; Journalism Education Focus; Literacy Focus; Mental Health Practices in Schools; Network Learning Systems; Social Studies Focus; Technology in Schools; Training Design and Development
MHSA Executive Program in Health Services Management
MS Executive Program in Health Informatics; Nursing–Mental Health Nurse Practitioner; Nursing–Pediatric Nurse Practitioner; Nursing–Public Health or School Health
PhD Architectural Studies

COURSE SUBJECT AREAS OFFERED OUTSIDE OF DEGREE PROGRAMS

Undergraduate—agricultural and food products processing; agricultural business and management; foods and nutrition studies; food sciences and technology; health professions and related sciences, other; miscellaneous health professions; nuclear engineering; nursing; plant sciences; real estate.

Graduate—advertising; agricultural and food products processing; agricultural business and management; economics; education administration and supervision; educational/instructional media design; educational psychology; education, general; education, other; foods and nutrition studies; food sciences and technology; health and medical administrative services; information sciences and systems; journalism and mass communications; library science/librarianship; library science, other; mental health services; nuclear engineering; nursing; radio and television broadcasting; real estate; school psychology; teacher education, specific academic and vocational programs; technology education/industrial arts.

Non-credit—agricultural business and management; business and personal services marketing operations; business management and administrative services, other; consumer and homemaking education; health and medical diagnostic and treatment services; health professions and related sciences, other; personal and miscellaneous services, other; real estate.

THE UNIVERSITY OF MONTANA–MISSOULA

Missoula, Montana
Continuing Education
http://www.umt.edu/ce/deo/external

The University of Montana–Missoula was founded in 1893. It is accredited by Northwest Commission on Colleges and Universities. It first offered distance learning courses in 1989. In fall 2003, there were 1,000 students enrolled in distance learning courses. Institutionally administered financial aid is available to distance learners.

Services Distance learners have accessibility to academic advising, bookstore, campus computer network, career placement assistance, e-mail services, library services.

Contact Division of Educational Outreach, The University of Montana–Missoula, Continuing Education, Missoula, MT 59812. *Telephone:* 406-243-6431. *E-mail:* edp@mso.umt.edu.

DEGREES AND AWARDS

AAS Surgical Technology
Endorsement Library Media
MA School Counseling (weekend cohort program)
MBA Business Administration (Off Campus MBA)
MEd Curriculum Studies (Butte, Bitterroot Valley); Curriculum Studies; Educational Leadership
MPA Public Administration
EdD Educational Leadership (weekend cohort program)
PharmD External Doctor of Pharmacy

COURSE SUBJECT AREAS OFFERED OUTSIDE OF DEGREE PROGRAMS

Undergraduate—accounting; anthropology; biology, general; business; communications, general; computer science; curriculum and instruction; English composition; journalism and mass communications; library science, other; mathematics; miscellaneous health professions; pharmacy; psychology; social work; sociology; speech and rhetorical studies.

Graduate—business administration and management; curriculum and instruction; education administration and supervision; education, general; information sciences and systems; library science, other; mathematics; pharmacy; philosophy; political science and government.

See full description on page 618.

UNIVERSITY OF NEBRASKA AT KEARNEY

Kearney, Nebraska
Division of Continuing Education
http://learn.unk.edu

University of Nebraska at Kearney was founded in 1903. It is accredited by North Central Association of Colleges and Schools. It first offered distance learning courses in 1986. In fall 2003, there were 400 students enrolled in distance learning courses. Institutionally administered financial aid is available to distance learners.

Services Distance learners have accessibility to academic advising, bookstore, campus computer network, career placement assistance, e-mail services, library services, tutoring.

Contact Gloria Vavricka, Director of Off-Campus, University of Nebraska at Kearney, Communications Center, Kearney, NE 68849-4220. *Telephone:* 308-865-8390. *Fax:* 308-865-8090. *E-mail:* vavrickag@unk.edu.

DEGREES AND AWARDS

Endorsement Educational Media Graduate Endorsement; Gifted Graduate Endorsement; Vocational Diversified Occupations Endorsement
Advanced Graduate Diploma Educational Administration Specialists
MS Biology
MSE Instructional Technology

UNIVERSITY OF NEBRASKA AT OMAHA

Omaha, Nebraska
http://www.unomaha.edu/

University of Nebraska at Omaha was founded in 1908. It is accredited by North Central Association of Colleges and Schools. It first offered distance learning courses in 1996. In fall 2003, there were 650 students enrolled in distance learning courses. Institutionally administered financial aid is available to distance learners.

Services Distance learners have accessibility to academic advising, bookstore, campus computer network, e-mail services, library services.

Contact Shelley Schafer, Manager of Distance Education, University of Nebraska at Omaha, Eppley Administration Building, #110-H, 6001 Dodge Street, Omaha, NE 68123. *Telephone:* 402-554-4831. *Fax:* 402-554-3475. *E-mail:* sschafer@mail.unomaha.edu.

DEGREES AND AWARDS

BGS Aviation Studies
MPA Public Administration

COURSE SUBJECT AREAS OFFERED OUTSIDE OF DEGREE PROGRAMS

Undergraduate—astronomy; computer and information sciences, general; history; information sciences and systems; marketing management and research; psychology; sociology; telecommunications.

Graduate—public administration; special education; teacher education, specific academic and vocational programs; telecommunications.

UNIVERSITY OF NEBRASKA-LINCOLN

Lincoln, Nebraska
Extended Education and Outreach
http://extended.unl.edu

University of Nebraska–Lincoln was founded in 1869. It is accredited by North Central Association of Colleges and Schools. It first offered distance learning courses in 1941. In fall 2003, there were 4,000 students enrolled in distance learning courses. Institutionally administered financial aid is available to distance learners.

Services Distance learners have accessibility to academic advising, bookstore, campus computer network, career placement assistance, e-mail services, library services, tutoring.

Contact Dr. Robert E. Mathiasen, Distance Services Coordinator/Adviser, University of Nebraska–Lincoln, Extended Education and Outreach, 900 North 21st Street, Room 202, Lincoln, NE 68588-8802. *Telephone:* 402-472-0400. *Fax:* 402-472-4345. *E-mail:* rmathiasen1@unl.edu.

University of Nebraska–Lincoln (continued)

DEGREES AND AWARDS

Endorsement Educational Administration; Special Education; Teaching, Learning and Teacher Education
Graduate Certificate Educational Technology; Family Financial Planning; NCA CASI School Improvement Specialist; Youth Development
MA Educational Administration; Journalism and Mass Communications; Textiles, Clothing and Design
MAg Agriculture
MBA Business Administration
MEd Educational Administration; Special Education; Teaching, Learning and Teacher Education
MEngr Engineering Management
MS Architecture; Entomology; Family and Consumer Sciences
EdD Educational Administration; Educational Studies
PhD Educational Studies

COURSE SUBJECT AREAS OFFERED OUTSIDE OF DEGREE PROGRAMS

Undergraduate—accounting; agricultural economics; American history; American studies; art history; Asian studies; biology; business marketing and marketing management; curriculum and instruction; developmental/child psychology; ecology; economics; engineering/industrial management; English composition; English language and literature, general; European history; family and community studies; finance; fine arts and art studies; geography; health and physical education/fitness; history; horticulture science; insurance/risk management; international business; journalism and mass communications; Latin American studies; mathematical statistics; mathematics; mathematics related; medieval/Renaissance studies; nursing; organizational behavior; philosophy; physics; political science and government; psychology; radio/television broadcasting; real estate; sociology.
Graduate—accounting; advertising; agricultural business and management; curriculum and instruction; educational psychology; electrical engineering; engineering/industrial management; industrial engineering; international business; journalism and mass communications; marketing management and research; mathematical statistics; political science and government.
Non-credit—business; English composition; mathematics related.

UNIVERSITY OF NEVADA, LAS VEGAS

Las Vegas, Nevada
Distance Education
http://Distance_Ed.unlv.edu

University of Nevada, Las Vegas was founded in 1957. It is accredited by Northwest Commission on Colleges and Universities. It first offered distance learning courses in 1986. In fall 2003, there were 4,500 students enrolled in distance learning courses. Institutionally administered financial aid is available to distance learners.

Services Distance learners have accessibility to academic advising, bookstore, campus computer network, e-mail services, library services.

Contact Pauline Saunders, Program Manager of Distance Education, University of Nevada, Las Vegas, 4505 Maryland Parkway, Box 451038, Las Vegas, NV 89154. *Telephone:* 702-895-0745. *Fax:* 702-895-3647. *E-mail:* psaunders@ccmail.nevada.edu.

DEGREES AND AWARDS

BA Social Science Studies
Graduate Certificate Instructional Technology

Special Message

The University of Nevada, Las Vegas (UNLV), offers a baccalaureate degree in social science studies. This degree completion program is intended primarily for students who have completed, or nearly completed, the equivalent of the first 2 years of college. Students earning this baccalaureate degree obtain a broad, interdisciplinary understanding of many issues addressed by research in the social sciences. In addition, UNLV offers a broad range of liberal arts and education classes, as well as courses in areas of interest to the hospitality industry: casino management, hotel administration, conventions, and tourism. These classes are available completely online and may be taken by any adult anywhere. While all of the courses count in the undergraduate program at UNLV, they may also be useful for individuals in the hospitality industry who want to acquire competency in particular areas without enrolling in a degree program. UNLV also offers an executive master's degree in hotel administration and a master's degree in special education (assistive technology). Additional degree programs are under development. A complete listing of distance education courses is available on the University Web site (http://distance_ed.unlv.edu/) or students may contact Distance Education, University of Nevada, Las Vegas (telephone: 702-895-0334; e-mail: distanceed@ccmail.nevada.edu).

UNIVERSITY OF NEVADA, RENO

Reno, Nevada
Independent Study and Division of Continuing Education
http://istudy.unr.edu

University of Nevada, Reno was founded in 1874. It is accredited by Northwest Commission on Colleges and Universities. It first offered distance learning courses in 1944. In fall 2003, there were 2,500 students enrolled in distance learning courses. Institutionally administered financial aid is available to distance learners.

Services Distance learners have accessibility to bookstore, library services.

Contact Carley Ries, Associate Director, University of Nevada, Reno, Independent Learning, Mail Stop 050, Reno, NV 89557. *Telephone:* 775-784-4652. *Fax:* 775-784-1280. *E-mail:* istudy@unr.edu.

DEGREES AND AWARDS

Programs offered do not lead to a degree or other formal award.

COURSE SUBJECT AREAS OFFERED OUTSIDE OF DEGREE PROGRAMS

Undergraduate—accounting; American history; American literature (United States); American studies; anthropology; area, ethnic and cultural studies, other; business; business/managerial economics; business marketing and marketing management; computer and information sciences, general; criminal justice and corrections; curriculum and instruction; developmental/child psychology; earth sciences; economics; educational psychology; English composition; English creative writing; English language and literature, general; European

history; fine arts and art studies; foods and nutrition studies; foreign languages and literatures; French; geography; Germanic languages and literatures; history; hospitality services management; Italian; library science/librarianship; mathematical statistics; mathematics; music; psychology; sociology; Spanish; teaching English as a second language/foreign language.
Graduate—curriculum and instruction; education, general; library science/librarianship; psychology, other.

See full description on page 620.

UNIVERSITY OF NEW ENGLAND

Biddeford, Maine
Certificate of Advanced Graduate Study in Educational Leadership Program
http://www.uneonline.org

University of New England was founded in 1831. It is accredited by New England Association of Schools and Colleges. Institutionally administered financial aid is available to distance learners.

Services Distance learners have accessibility to academic advising, bookstore, campus computer network, career placement assistance, e-mail services, library services.
Contact Certificate of Advanced Graduate Study in Educational Leadership Program, University of New England, 11 Hills Beach Road, Biddeford, ME 04005. *Telephone:* 207-283-0171 Ext. 2692. *Fax:* 207-294-5942. *E-mail:* cags@mailbox.une.edu.

DEGREES AND AWARDS

CAGS Educational Leadership

COURSE SUBJECT AREAS OFFERED OUTSIDE OF DEGREE PROGRAMS

Graduate—education administration and supervision; education, other.

See full description on page 622.

UNIVERSITY OF NEW HAMPSHIRE

Durham, New Hampshire
Interactive Instructional Television Center
http://e-learn.unh.edu

University of New Hampshire was founded in 1866. It is accredited by New England Association of Schools and Colleges. It first offered distance learning courses in 1980. In fall 2003, there were 70 students enrolled in distance learning courses. Institutionally administered financial aid is available to distance learners.

Services Distance learners have accessibility to academic advising, bookstore, campus computer network, career placement assistance, e-mail services, library services.
Contact Dr. Kent Chamberlin, Faculty Fellow for Distributed and Distance Education, University of New Hampshire, Department of Electrical and Computer Engineering, Kingsbury Hall, Durham, NH 03824. *Telephone:* 603-862-3766. *Fax:* 603-862-1832. *E-mail:* kent.chamberlin@unh.edu.

DEGREES AND AWARDS

Programs offered do not lead to a degree or other formal award.

COURSE SUBJECT AREAS OFFERED OUTSIDE OF DEGREE PROGRAMS

Graduate—computer science; electrical, electronics and communications engineering; health professions and related sciences, other; mathematical statistics; mechanical engineering.

UNIVERSITY OF NEW ORLEANS

New Orleans, Louisiana
UNO Metropolitan College
http://alt.uno.edu

University of New Orleans was founded in 1958. It is accredited by Southern Association of Colleges and Schools. It first offered distance learning courses in 1980. In fall 2003, there were 1,350 students enrolled in distance learning courses. Institutionally administered financial aid is available to distance learners.

Services Distance learners have accessibility to academic advising, bookstore, campus computer network, e-mail services, library services, tutoring.
Contact Mr. Darrin Pruitt, Coordinator, Distance Education, University of New Orleans, Lakefront Campus, Education 122, New Orleans, LA 70148. *Telephone:* 504-280-7100. *Fax:* 504-280-7317. *E-mail:* alt@uno.edu.

DEGREES AND AWARDS

Programs offered do not lead to a degree or other formal award.

COURSE SUBJECT AREAS OFFERED OUTSIDE OF DEGREE PROGRAMS

Undergraduate—business administration and management; city/urban, community and regional planning; English creative writing; English language and literature, general; financial management and services; geological and related sciences; health professions and related sciences, other; history; liberal arts and sciences, general studies and humanities; mathematics; philosophy; physical sciences, general; political science and government; psychology; public administration.
Graduate—business administration and management; dramatic/theater arts and stagecraft; education administration and supervision; educational evaluation, research and statistics; educational/instructional media design; engineering, general; English creative writing; English language and literature, general.

THE UNIVERSITY OF NORTH CAROLINA AT CHAPEL HILL

Chapel Hill, North Carolina
The William and Ida Friday Center for Continuing Education
http://fridaycenter.unc.edu

The University of North Carolina at Chapel Hill was founded in 1789. It is accredited by Southern Association of Colleges and Schools. It first offered distance learning courses in 1941. In fall 2003, there were 3,800 students enrolled in distance learning courses.

The University of North Carolina at Chapel Hill (continued)

Services Distance learners have accessibility to academic advising, bookstore, career placement assistance, library services.

Contact Carol McDonnell, Student Services Manager, The University of North Carolina at Chapel Hill, CB# 1020, Chapel Hill, NC 27599-1020. *Telephone:* 800-862-5669. *Fax:* 919-962-5549. *E-mail:* carol_mcdonnell@unc.edu.

DEGREES AND AWARDS

Programs offered do not lead to a degree or other formal award.

COURSE SUBJECT AREAS OFFERED OUTSIDE OF DEGREE PROGRAMS

Undergraduate—accounting; African-American studies; American history; American studies; anthropology; art history; astronomy; biology; business administration and management; business communications; chemistry; communications, general; computer and information sciences, general; creative writing; criminal justice and corrections; economics; English as a second language; English composition; environmental science; European history; foods and nutrition studies; foreign languages and literatures, other; French; geography; geological and related sciences; history; hospitality services management; Italian; journalism and mass communications; Latin (ancient and medieval); mathematical statistics; mathematics related; music; parks, recreation and leisure studies; philosophy; physics; political science and government; psychology; religion/religious studies; Russian; sociology; Spanish; theater arts/drama.

Non-credit—foreign languages and literatures; nursing.

See full description on page 624.

THE UNIVERSITY OF NORTH CAROLINA AT CHARLOTTE

Charlotte, North Carolina

Continuing Education, Extension and Summer Programs

http://www.DistanceEd.uncc.edu

The University of North Carolina at Charlotte was founded in 1946. It is accredited by Southern Association of Colleges and Schools. It first offered distance learning courses in 1985. In fall 2003, there were 575 students enrolled in distance learning courses. Institutionally administered financial aid is available to distance learners.

Services Distance learners have accessibility to academic advising, bookstore, campus computer network, career placement assistance, e-mail services, library services, tutoring.

Contact Mary Faye Englebert, Associate Director, The University of North Carolina at Charlotte, 9201 University City Boulevard, Charlotte, NC 28223. *Telephone:* 704-687-4594. *Fax:* 704-687-4305. *E-mail:* mfengleb@email.uncc.edu.

DEGREES AND AWARDS

BA Elementary Education
BSET Electrical Engineering Technology; Fire Science
BSN Nursing–RN-BSN Completion
License Middle and Secondary Education (Teacher Licensure); Special Education–Adapted Curriculum; Special Education–General Curriculum (Teacher Licensure)
Graduate Certificate Academically and Intellectually Gifted; Child and Family Development–Early Intervention; Information Systems and Information Security; Nursing Education
MEd Curriculum and Supervision; Middle Grades; School Administration (MSA)
MSN Nursing–Community Health

COURSE SUBJECT AREAS OFFERED OUTSIDE OF DEGREE PROGRAMS

Undergraduate—education, general; engineering, general; nursing.

Graduate—education, general; information sciences and systems; nursing.

Non-credit—accounting; architecture; business administration and management; counseling psychology; engineering, general; film/video and photographic arts; financial management and services; hospitality services management; human resources management; legal studies; nursing; public administration and services, other; taxation.

THE UNIVERSITY OF NORTH CAROLINA AT GREENSBORO

Greensboro, North Carolina

Division of Continual Learning and Summer Session

http://www.calldcl.com

The University of North Carolina at Greensboro was founded in 1891. It is accredited by Southern Association of Colleges and Schools. It first offered distance learning courses in 1972. In fall 2003, there were 987 students enrolled in distance learning courses. Institutionally administered financial aid is available to distance learners.

Services Distance learners have accessibility to academic advising, bookstore, campus computer network, career placement assistance, e-mail services, library services.

Contact William H. Taylor, Director of Distance Learning and Program Analysis, The University of North Carolina at Greensboro, 1100 West Market Street, 3rd Floor, PO Box 26170, Greensboro, NC 27402-6170. *Telephone:* 336-334-5414. *Fax:* 336-334-5628. *E-mail:* whtaylor@uncg.edu.

DEGREES AND AWARDS

BA Liberal Studies (Humanities Concentration)
BS Birth-Kindergarten Teacher Licensure
BSN Nursing
Certificate Nonprofit Management (Post-Baccalaureate)
MA Liberal Studies
MEd Curriculum and Instruction; School Administration; Special Education (Cross-Categorical Emphasis)
MLIS Library and Information Studies
MSN Nursing
PMC Advanced School Counseling

COURSE SUBJECT AREAS OFFERED OUTSIDE OF DEGREE PROGRAMS

Undergraduate—American history; classical and ancient Near Eastern languages and literatures; family and community studies; fine arts and art studies; geological and related sciences; history; liberal arts and sciences, general studies and humanities; philosophy; psychology; public health; religion/religious studies; sociology.

Graduate—curriculum and instruction; education, other; fine arts and art studies; French; historic preservation, conservation and architectural history; liberal arts and sciences, general studies and humanities; library science, other; music; special education; teaching English as a second language/foreign language.

Non-credit—health and medical administrative services.

See full description on page 626.

THE UNIVERSITY OF NORTH CAROLINA AT PEMBROKE

Pembroke, North Carolina
Office of Continuing and Distance Education
http://www.uncp.edu

The University of North Carolina at Pembroke was founded in 1887. It is accredited by Southern Association of Colleges and Schools. It first offered distance learning courses in 1996. In fall 2003, there were 892 students enrolled in distance learning courses. Institutionally administered financial aid is available to distance learners.

Services Distance learners have accessibility to academic advising, bookstore, campus computer network, career placement assistance, e-mail services, library services.
Contact Director, Continuing and Distance Education, The University of North Carolina at Pembroke, One University Drive, Pembroke, NC 28372. *Telephone:* 910-521-6367. *Fax:* 910-521-6762.

DEGREES AND AWARDS

BA Business Administration
BS Business Administration
BSBA Business Administration
MPA Public Administration

COURSE SUBJECT AREAS OFFERED OUTSIDE OF DEGREE PROGRAMS

Undergraduate—accounting; area, ethnic and cultural studies, other; biology, general; business; business administration and management; chemistry; education, general; sociology.
Graduate—business; business administration and management; public administration.

See full description on page 628.

UNIVERSITY OF NORTH DAKOTA

Grand Forks, North Dakota
Division of Continuing Education
http://www.conted.und.edu

University of North Dakota was founded in 1883. It is accredited by North Central Association of Colleges and Schools. It first offered distance learning courses in 1970. In fall 2003, there were 6,500 students enrolled in distance learning courses. Institutionally administered financial aid is available to distance learners.

Services Distance learners have accessibility to academic advising, bookstore, campus computer network, career placement assistance, e-mail services, library services, tutoring.
Contact Heidi Flaten, Coordinator, University of North Dakota, Distance Degree Programs, Box 9021, Grand Forks, ND 58202-9021. *Telephone:* 877-450-1842. *Fax:* 701-777-4282. *E-mail:* heidi.flaten@mail.und.nodak.edu.

DEGREES AND AWARDS

BA Social Science
BBA Information Systems
BGS General Studies
BS Chemical Engineering; Civil Engineering; Electrical Engineering; Mechanical Engineering; Nursing
Endorsement English as a Second Language
Graduate Certificate Autistic Spectrum Disorders
MBA Business Administration
MEd Education Leadership; Special Education
MPA Public Administration
MS Elementary Education; General Studies (Secondary Education); Space Studies
MSN Nursing–Education Specialization
MSW Social Work
PhD Higher Education

COURSE SUBJECT AREAS OFFERED OUTSIDE OF DEGREE PROGRAMS

Undergraduate—accounting; anthropology; business administration and management; chemical engineering; chemistry; civil engineering; communications, general; economics; electrical engineering; English composition; foreign languages and literatures; general teacher education; geography; history; mathematics; mechanical engineering; nursing; organizational psychology; physical sciences, general; physics; psychology; religion/religious studies; social work; sociology; teacher education, specific academic and vocational programs.
Graduate—business administration and management; public administration; social work; teacher education, specific academic and vocational programs; teaching English as a second language/foreign language; technology education/industrial arts.
Non-credit—health and medical administrative services; health professions and related sciences, other; human resources management; mathematics; real estate.

UNIVERSITY OF NORTHERN COLORADO

Greeley, Colorado
Center for Professional Development
http://www.unco.edu/center/es/main

University of Northern Colorado was founded in 1890. It is accredited by North Central Association of Colleges and Schools. It first offered distance learning courses in 1941. In fall 2003, there were 300 students enrolled in distance learning courses. Institutionally administered financial aid is available to distance learners.

Services Distance learners have accessibility to academic advising, bookstore, campus computer network, career placement assistance, e-mail services, library services.
Contact Receptionist, University of Northern Colorado, Michener Library, Southwest Lower Level, Campus Box 21, Greeley, CO 80639. *Telephone:* 800-232-1749. *Fax:* 970-351-2519. *E-mail:* front.desk@unco.edu.

DEGREES AND AWARDS

BA Dietetics (degree completion/didactic program in dietetics)
BS Nursing–RN to BS
Internship Certificate Dietetics
Graduate Certificate Nursing Education
MA Communication Disorders, Speech-Language Pathology; Educational Technology; Special Education, Early Childhood Special Education Emphasis; Special Education, Profound Needs Emphasis; Special Education, Severe Needs Hearing Emphasis; Special Education, Severe Needs Vision Emphasis

University of Northern Colorado (continued)

PhD Nursing Education Emphasis

COURSE SUBJECT AREAS OFFERED OUTSIDE OF DEGREE PROGRAMS

Undergraduate—biology; chemistry; community health services; economics; English creative writing; foods and nutrition studies; geography; geological and related sciences; gerontology; health and medical administrative services; health professions and related sciences, other; human services; mathematics; nursing; political science and government; psychology; rehabilitation/therapeutic services; special education.

Graduate—chemistry; communication disorders sciences and services; education, other; gerontology; health and physical education/fitness; legal studies; marketing management and research; special education.

UNIVERSITY OF NORTHERN IOWA

Cedar Falls, Iowa
Division of Continuing Education
http://www.uni.edu/contined/cp/distance.shtml

University of Northern Iowa was founded in 1876. It is accredited by North Central Association of Colleges and Schools. In fall 2003, there were 1,200 students enrolled in distance learning courses. Institutionally administered financial aid is available to distance learners.

Services Distance learners have accessibility to academic advising, bookstore, career placement assistance, library services.

Contact Kent Johnson, Associate Director of Continuing Education Credit Programs, University of Northern Iowa, Continuing Education Credit Programs, Cedar Falls, IA 50614-0223. *Telephone:* 319-273-5970. *Fax:* 319-273-2872. *E-mail:* kent.johnson@uni.edu.

DEGREES AND AWARDS

BLS Liberal Studies

COURSE SUBJECT AREAS OFFERED OUTSIDE OF DEGREE PROGRAMS

Undergraduate—accounting; area studies; astronomy; business marketing and marketing management; communications, general; criminology; educational psychology; education, general; English language and literature, general; family/consumer resource management; geography; health and physical education/fitness; history; mathematics; music; psychology; religion/religious studies; social work; sociology.

Graduate—criminology; educational psychology; geography; history; religion/religious studies; social work; sociology.

UNIVERSITY OF NORTH FLORIDA

Jacksonville, Florida
http://www.unf.edu/

University of North Florida was founded in 1965. It is accredited by Southern Association of Colleges and Schools. It first offered distance learning courses in 1997. In fall 2003, there were 246 students enrolled in distance learning courses. Institutionally administered financial aid is available to distance learners.

Services Distance learners have accessibility to academic advising, campus computer network, career placement assistance, e-mail services, library services, tutoring.

Contact Dr. Jace Hargis, Director of Faculty Enhancement, University of North Florida, 4567 St. Johns Bluff Road South, Jacksonville, FL 32224-2465. *Telephone:* 904-620-1446. *E-mail:* jhargis@unf.edu.

DEGREES AND AWARDS

Programs offered do not lead to a degree or other formal award.

COURSE SUBJECT AREAS OFFERED OUTSIDE OF DEGREE PROGRAMS

Undergraduate—computer and information sciences, general; curriculum and instruction; health professions and related sciences, other; nursing; sociology.

Graduate—curriculum and instruction; health professions and related sciences, other; human services; special education.

UNIVERSITY OF NORTHWESTERN OHIO

Lima, Ohio
Division of Distance Learning
http://www.unoh.edu

University of Northwestern Ohio was founded in 1920. It is accredited by North Central Association of Colleges and Schools. It first offered distance learning courses in 1993. In fall 2003, there were 400 students enrolled in distance learning courses. Institutionally administered financial aid is available to distance learners.

Services Distance learners have accessibility to academic advising, bookstore, campus computer network, career placement assistance, e-mail services, library services, tutoring.

Contact Mr. Rick Morrison, Director of Admissions, University of Northwestern Ohio, 1441 North Cable Road, Lima, OH 45805. *Telephone:* 419-998-3120. *Fax:* 419-229-6926. *E-mail:* rmorris@unoh.edu.

DEGREES AND AWARDS

AAS Agribusiness; Automotive Management; Information Systems Technology; Legal Assisting; Marketing; Marketing, Management, and Technology; Medical Assistant Technology; Secretarial (Administrative, Legal, Medical); Travel Management; Word Processing–Administrative Support

BS Accounting; Business Administration; Health Care Administration

COURSE SUBJECT AREAS OFFERED OUTSIDE OF DEGREE PROGRAMS

Undergraduate—accounting; administrative and secretarial services; agricultural business and management; business administration and management; computer and information sciences, general; electrical and power transmission installers; health and medical assistants.

UNIVERSITY OF NOTRE DAME

Notre Dame, Indiana
Executive Education
http://executive.nd.edu

University of Notre Dame was founded in 1842. It is accredited by North Central Association of Colleges and Schools. It first offered distance learning courses in 1995. In fall 2003, there were 200 students enrolled in distance learning courses. Institutionally administered financial aid is available to distance learners.

Services Distance learners have accessibility to academic advising, bookstore, campus computer network, career placement assistance, e-mail services, library services, tutoring.
Contact Bill Brewster, Director, International Programs, University of Notre Dame, 126 Mendoza College of Business, Notre Dame, IN 46556. *Telephone:* 800-631-3622. *Fax:* 574-631-6783. *E-mail:* brewster.1@nd.edu.

DEGREES AND AWARDS

Certificate Executive Management
MBA Executive MBA

COURSE SUBJECT AREAS OFFERED OUTSIDE OF DEGREE PROGRAMS

Graduate—accounting; business; business administration and management; business communications; business management and administrative services, other; business quantitative methods and management science; economics; entrepreneurship; financial management and services; marketing operations/marketing and distribution, other; mathematical statistics; taxation.
Non-credit—accounting; business; business administration and management; business communications; business management and administrative services, other; business quantitative methods and management science; economics; entrepreneurship; financial management and services; marketing management and research; marketing operations/marketing and distribution, other; mathematical statistics; taxation.

UNIVERSITY OF OKLAHOMA

Norman, Oklahoma
College of Continuing Education
http://www.occe.ou.edu

University of Oklahoma was founded in 1890. It is accredited by North Central Association of Colleges and Schools. It first offered distance learning courses in 1941. Institutionally administered financial aid is available to distance learners.

Services Distance learners have accessibility to academic advising, bookstore, campus computer network, career placement assistance, e-mail services, library services.
Contact Larry D. Hayes, Information Assistant for Office of the Vice President for University Outreach and College of Continuing Education, University of Oklahoma, 1700 Asp Avenue, Norman, OK 73072. *Telephone:* 800-522-0772 Ext. 4414. *Fax:* 405-325-7196. *E-mail:* lhayes@ou.edu.

DEGREES AND AWARDS

MA Advanced Programs
PhD Advanced Programs

COURSE SUBJECT AREAS OFFERED OUTSIDE OF DEGREE PROGRAMS

Undergraduate—anthropology; astronomy; business administration and management; business communications; chemistry; communications, general; dramatic/theater arts and stagecraft; economics; education, general; engineering, general; English composition; financial management and services; geography; geological and related sciences; health and physical education/fitness; history; journalism and mass communications; library science, other; marketing management and research; mathematics; philosophy; political science and government; sociology.
Graduate—communications, general; economics; education administration and supervision; educational psychology; education, other; human resources management; public administration; social work.

See full description on page 630.

UNIVERSITY OF OREGON

Eugene, Oregon
Distance Education
http://de.uoregon.edu

University of Oregon was founded in 1872. It is accredited by Northwest Commission on Colleges and Universities. It first offered distance learning courses in 1996. In fall 2003, there were 500 students enrolled in distance learning courses. Institutionally administered financial aid is available to distance learners.

Services Distance learners have accessibility to academic advising, bookstore, campus computer network, e-mail services, library services.
Contact Zachary Biggs, Program Assistant Coordinator, University of Oregon, 1277 University of Oregon, Eugene, OR 97403-1277. *Telephone:* 541-346-4231. *Fax:* 541-346-3545. *E-mail:* dasst@continue.uoregon.edu.

DEGREES AND AWARDS

MS Applied Information Management

COURSE SUBJECT AREAS OFFERED OUTSIDE OF DEGREE PROGRAMS

Undergraduate—astronomy; economics; English language and literature, general; geography; geological and related sciences; oceanography; physics; political science and government; visual and performing arts, other.
Graduate—information sciences and systems; management information systems/business data processing.

See full description on page 632.

UNIVERSITY OF PHOENIX ONLINE CAMPUS

Phoenix, Arizona
http://www.uoponline.com

University of Phoenix Online Campus was founded in 1989. It is accredited by North Central Association of Colleges and Schools. It first offered distance learning courses in 1989. In fall 2003, there were 71,052 students enrolled in distance learning courses. Institutionally administered financial aid is available to distance learners.

Services Distance learners have accessibility to academic advising, bookstore, campus computer network, library services, tutoring.
Contact Mr. Larry Etherington, Director of Marketing, University of Phoenix Online Campus, Mail Stop CF-A101, 3157 East Elwood Street, Phoenix, AZ 85034-7209. *Telephone:* 800-366-9699. *Fax:* 602-735-9546. *E-mail:* larry.etherington@apollogrp.edu.

University of Phoenix Online Campus (continued)

DEGREES AND AWARDS

AA General Studies
BS Business Accounting; Business Administration; Business Management; Business Marketing; Business/Finance; Criminal Justice Administration; E-Business; Health Administration; Human Services/Management; Information Technology; Management; Nursing
MA Adult Education and Distance Learning; Education–Administration and Supervision Specialization; Education–Curriculum and Instruction; Education–Curriculum and Technology; Education–Early Childhood Education Specialization; Education–Elementary or Secondary Teacher Education; Education–Special Education Specialization; Organizational Management
MBA Accounting; Business Administration; Business Administration/Marketing; E-Business; Global Management; Health Care Management; Human Resource Management; Technology Management
MM Human Resource Management; International Management; Management
MS Computer Information Systems; Nursing
DBA Business Administration
DH Sc Health Administration–Doctor of Health Administration (DHA)
DM Organizational Management
EdD Educational Leadership

COURSE SUBJECT AREAS OFFERED OUTSIDE OF DEGREE PROGRAMS

Undergraduate—business administration and management; technology education/industrial arts.
Graduate—special education.
Non-credit—education, general.

See full description on page 634.

UNIVERSITY OF PITTSBURGH AT BRADFORD

Bradford, Pennsylvania
http://www.upb.pitt.edu/

University of Pittsburgh at Bradford was founded in 1963. It is accredited by Middle States Association of Colleges and Schools. It first offered distance learning courses in 1995. In fall 2003, there were 18 students enrolled in distance learning courses. Institutionally administered financial aid is available to distance learners.

Services Distance learners have accessibility to campus computer network, e-mail services, library services.
Contact Bob Dilks, Director of Adult Continuing Education, University of Pittsburgh at Bradford, 300 Campus Drive, Bradford, PA 16701-2898. *Telephone:* 814-362-5078. *Fax:* 814-362-0914. *E-mail:* dilks@pitt.edu.

DEGREES AND AWARDS

Programs offered do not lead to a degree or other formal award.

COURSE SUBJECT AREAS OFFERED OUTSIDE OF DEGREE PROGRAMS

Undergraduate—business; business information and data processing services; chemistry; criminal justice and corrections; economics; English creative writing.

UNIVERSITY OF ST. AUGUSTINE FOR HEALTH SCIENCES

St. Augustine, Florida
Division of Distance Education
http://www.usa.edu

University of St. Augustine for Health Sciences was founded in 1978. It is accredited by Distance Education and Training Council. It first offered distance learning courses in 1979. In fall 2003, there were 392 students enrolled in distance learning courses. Institutionally administered financial aid is available to distance learners.

Services Distance learners have accessibility to academic advising, bookstore, e-mail services, library services, tutoring.
Contact Dr. Richard Jensen, Dean of Division of Advanced Studies, University of St. Augustine for Health Sciences, 1 University Boulevard, St. Augustine, FL 32086. *Telephone:* 904-826-0084 Ext. 262. *Fax:* 904-826-0085. *E-mail:* info@usa.edu.

DEGREES AND AWARDS

MS Health Science–Master of Health Science (MHSc)
DH Sc Health Science
DPT Transitional Doctor of Physical Therapy
OTD Occupational Therapy

COURSE SUBJECT AREAS OFFERED OUTSIDE OF DEGREE PROGRAMS

Graduate—occupational therapy; physical therapy.
Non-credit—health professions and related sciences, other.

UNIVERSITY OF ST. FRANCIS

Joliet, Illinois
http://www.stfrancis.edu/

University of St. Francis was founded in 1920. It is accredited by North Central Association of Colleges and Schools. It first offered distance learning courses in 1997. In fall 2003, there were 1,210 students enrolled in distance learning courses. Institutionally administered financial aid is available to distance learners.

Services Distance learners have accessibility to academic advising, bookstore, career placement assistance, e-mail services, library services, tutoring.
Contact Mr. Ron Clement, Director of Admissions, University of St. Francis, 500 Wilcox Street, Joliet, IL 60435. *Telephone:* 800-735-7500. *Fax:* 815-740-5032. *E-mail:* rclement@stfrancis.edu.

DEGREES AND AWARDS

BS Health Arts
BSN Nursing Fast Track
MBA Business Administration
MS Health Services Administration; Training and Development
MSM Management
MSN Nurse Practitioner

COURSE SUBJECT AREAS OFFERED OUTSIDE OF DEGREE PROGRAMS

Undergraduate—business administration and management; cultural studies; English language and literature, general; health professions and related sciences, other; history; nursing; philosophy and religion.

Graduate—business administration and management; educational evaluation, research and statistics; health services administration; marketing management and research; nursing.

See full description on page 636.

UNIVERSITY OF SAINT FRANCIS

Fort Wayne, Indiana

http://www.sf.edu/

University of Saint Francis was founded in 1890. It is accredited by North Central Association of Colleges and Schools. It first offered distance learning courses in 1994. In fall 2003, there were 96 students enrolled in distance learning courses. Institutionally administered financial aid is available to distance learners.

Services Distance learners have accessibility to academic advising, bookstore, career placement assistance, library services, tutoring.
Contact Dr. Carla L. Mueller, Director of Educational Innovation, University of Saint Francis, 2701 Spring Street, Fort Wayne, IN 46763. *Telephone:* 260-434-3257. *Fax:* 260-434-7601. *E-mail:* cmueller@sf.edu.

DEGREES AND AWARDS

BSN Nursing–RN-BSN Completion
MSN Nursing

COURSE SUBJECT AREAS OFFERED OUTSIDE OF DEGREE PROGRAMS

Undergraduate—business communications; economics; English composition; English literature (British and Commonwealth); nursing; religion/religious studies; sociology.
Graduate—nursing; professional studies.

UNIVERSITY OF SASKATCHEWAN

Saskatoon, Saskatchewan, Canada

Extension Credit Studies

http://www.extension.usask.ca

University of Saskatchewan was founded in 1907. It is provincially chartered. It first offered distance learning courses in 1941. In fall 2003, there were 1,500 students enrolled in distance learning courses. Institutionally administered financial aid is available to distance learners.

Services Distance learners have accessibility to academic advising, bookstore, campus computer network, e-mail services, library services, tutoring.
Contact Ms. Grace Milashenko, Independent Studies Coordinator, University of Saskatchewan, 117 Science Place, Kirk Hall, Room 330, Saskatoon, SK S7N 5C8, Canada. *Telephone:* 306-966-5562. *Fax:* 306-966-5590. *E-mail:* grace.milashenko@usask.ca.

DEGREES AND AWARDS

Programs offered do not lead to a degree or other formal award.

COURSE SUBJECT AREAS OFFERED OUTSIDE OF DEGREE PROGRAMS

Undergraduate—adult/continuing education; agricultural business and production, other; agriculture/agricultural sciences; anthropology; archaeology; computer science; curriculum and instruction; economics; English language and literature, general; English literature (British and Commonwealth); geography; geological and related sciences; history; mathematics; music; nursing; philosophy; psychology; religion/religious studies; sociology; teaching English as a second language/foreign language.
Graduate—educational psychology; education, other.
Non-credit—agricultural business and management; agricultural business and production, other; botany; educational/instructional media design; education, other; English as a second language; horticulture services operations and management; landscape architecture; soil sciences; teacher education, specific academic and vocational programs; teaching English as a second language/foreign language.

UNIVERSITY OF SCIENCE AND ARTS OF OKLAHOMA

Chickasha, Oklahoma

http://www.usao.edu/

University of Science and Arts of Oklahoma was founded in 1908. It is accredited by North Central Association of Colleges and Schools. It first offered distance learning courses in 1997. Institutionally administered financial aid is available to distance learners.

Services Distance learners have accessibility to e-mail services.
Contact Dr. Alan Todd, Director of Instructional Technology, University of Science and Arts of Oklahoma, 1727 West Alabama Avenue, Chickasha, OK 73018-5322. *Telephone:* 405-574-1277. *Fax:* 405-574-1396. *E-mail:* atodd@usao.edu.

DEGREES AND AWARDS

Programs offered do not lead to a degree or other formal award.

UNIVERSITY OF SIOUX FALLS

Sioux Falls, South Dakota

http://www.usiouxfalls.edu/

University of Sioux Falls was founded in 1883. It is accredited by North Central Association of Colleges and Schools. It first offered distance learning courses in 2000. In fall 2003, there were 80 students enrolled in distance learning courses. Institutionally administered financial aid is available to distance learners.

Services Distance learners have accessibility to academic advising, bookstore, career placement assistance, e-mail services, library services.
Contact Megan Larsen, Registration Clerk, University of Sioux Falls, 1101 West 22nd Street, Jorden Hall, Sioux Falls, SD 57105. *Telephone:* 605-331-6732. *Fax:* 605-331-6615. *E-mail:* megan.larsen@usiouxfalls.edu.

DEGREES AND AWARDS

Programs offered do not lead to a degree or other formal award.

COURSE SUBJECT AREAS OFFERED OUTSIDE OF DEGREE PROGRAMS

Undergraduate—English language and literature, general; fine arts and art studies; geography; health and physical education/fitness; history; sociology.
Graduate—education administration and supervision; educational evaluation, research and statistics; education, general.

UNIVERSITY OF SOUTH CAROLINA

Columbia, South Carolina
Department of Distance Education and Instructional Support
http://www.sc.edu/deis

University of South Carolina was founded in 1801. It is accredited by Southern Association of Colleges and Schools. It first offered distance learning courses in 1969. In fall 2003, there were 3,628 students enrolled in distance learning courses. Institutionally administered financial aid is available to distance learners.

Services Distance learners have accessibility to academic advising, bookstore, campus computer network, career placement assistance, e-mail services, library services, tutoring.

Contact Robin D. Phillips, Independent Learning Coordinator, University of South Carolina, Independent Learning Program, 915 Gregg Street, Columbia, SC 29208. *Telephone:* 803-777-6285. *Fax:* 803-777-6264. *E-mail:* rdandrid@gwm.sc.edu.

DEGREES AND AWARDS

MBA Business Administration
ME Chemical Engineering; Civil and Environmental Engineering; Electrical Engineering; Mechanical Engineering
MLIS Library and Information Sciences
MS Chemical Engineering; Civil and Environmental Engineering; Electrical Engineering; Mechanical Engineering
PhD Civil and Environmental Engineering; Electrical Engineering; Mechanical Engineering

COURSE SUBJECT AREAS OFFERED OUTSIDE OF DEGREE PROGRAMS

Undergraduate—accounting; astronomy; business administration and management; economics; English language and literature, general; English technical and business writing; financial management and services; foreign languages and literatures; geography; health professions and related sciences, other; history; marketing operations/marketing and distribution, other; mathematics; music; philosophy; political science and government; psychology; social work.

UNIVERSITY OF SOUTH CAROLINA SPARTANBURG

Spartanburg, South Carolina
http://www.uscs.edu/

University of South Carolina Spartanburg was founded in 1967. It is accredited by Southern Association of Colleges and Schools. It first offered distance learning courses in 1996. In fall 2003, there were 275 students enrolled in distance learning courses. Institutionally administered financial aid is available to distance learners.

Services Distance learners have accessibility to academic advising, bookstore, campus computer network, career placement assistance, e-mail services, library services.

Contact Andrew Tate Crosland, Associate Vice Chancellor, University of South Carolina Spartanburg, 800 University Way, Spartanburg, SC 29303-4999. *Telephone:* 864-503-5285. *Fax:* 864-503-5262. *E-mail:* acrosland@gw.uscs.edu.

DEGREES AND AWARDS

BSN Nursing Baccalaureate Program; Nursing

COURSE SUBJECT AREAS OFFERED OUTSIDE OF DEGREE PROGRAMS

Undergraduate—business; education, general; English language and literature, general; geography; nursing; political science and government.
Graduate—education, general.

UNIVERSITY OF SOUTH CAROLINA SUMTER

Sumter, South Carolina
http://www.uscsumter.edu/

University of South Carolina Sumter was founded in 1966. It is accredited by Southern Association of Colleges and Schools. It first offered distance learning courses in 1993. In fall 2003, there were 41 students enrolled in distance learning courses. Institutionally administered financial aid is available to distance learners.

Services Distance learners have accessibility to bookstore, campus computer network, e-mail services, library services.

Contact Dr. Robert Ferrell, Director of Admissions, University of South Carolina Sumter, 200 Miller Road, Sumter, SC 29150. *Telephone:* 803-938-3762. *Fax:* 803-775-2180. *E-mail:* bobf@uscsumter.edu.

DEGREES AND AWARDS

Programs offered do not lead to a degree or other formal award.

COURSE SUBJECT AREAS OFFERED OUTSIDE OF DEGREE PROGRAMS

Undergraduate—American literature (United States); community health services; education administration and supervision; educational evaluation, research and statistics; education, general; engineering, general; history; public administration; public health; social and philosophical foundations of education; social psychology; social sciences, general.
Graduate—business administration and management; education administration and supervision; education, other; nursing; social work; sociology.

THE UNIVERSITY OF SOUTH DAKOTA

Vermillion, South Dakota
State-Wide Educational Services
http://www.usd.edu/swes

The University of South Dakota was founded in 1862. It is accredited by North Central Association of Colleges and Schools. It first offered distance learning courses in 1967. In fall 2003, there were 2,500 students enrolled in distance learning courses. Institutionally administered financial aid is available to distance learners.

Services Distance learners have accessibility to academic advising, bookstore, campus computer network, career placement assistance, e-mail services, library services.

Contact Statewide Educational Services, The University of South Dakota, 414 East Clark Street, Vermillion, SD 57069. *Telephone:* 800-233-7937. *Fax:* 605-677-6118. *E-mail:* swes@usd.edu.

DEGREES AND AWARDS

AA General Studies
MBA Business Administration
MSE Educational Administration; Technology for Education and Training–Master of Science in Technology for Education and Training

COURSE SUBJECT AREAS OFFERED OUTSIDE OF DEGREE PROGRAMS

Undergraduate—accounting; art history; biology; communications, general; comparative literature; criminal justice and corrections; educational/instructional media design; English composition; film studies; geography; history; journalism and mass communication related; mathematical statistics; mathematics related; nursing; political science and government; sociology; theater arts/drama.
Graduate—education administration and supervision; education, other; technology education/industrial arts.
Non-credit—real estate.

UNIVERSITY OF SOUTHERN INDIANA

Evansville, Indiana
Distance Education Programming
http://www.usi.edu/distance

University of Southern Indiana was founded in 1965. It is accredited by North Central Association of Colleges and Schools. It first offered distance learning courses in 1994. In fall 2003, there were 2,450 students enrolled in distance learning courses. Institutionally administered financial aid is available to distance learners.

Services Distance learners have accessibility to academic advising, bookstore, campus computer network, e-mail services, library services.

Contact Dr. Saxon Reasons, Programming Manager for Instructional Technology Services, University of Southern Indiana, 8600 University Boulevard, Evansville, IN 47712. *Telephone:* 800-813-4238. *Fax:* 812-465-7131. *E-mail:* saxrea@usi.edu.

DEGREES AND AWARDS

BS Health Professions and Related Sciences; Radiologic and Imaging Sciences
BSN Nursing
MHA Health Administration
MSN Nursing
MSOT Occupational Therapy

COURSE SUBJECT AREAS OFFERED OUTSIDE OF DEGREE PROGRAMS

Undergraduate—advertising; biology, general; communications, general; computer/information technology administration and management; dental services; economics; educational psychology; education, general; English composition; English language and literature, general; English literature (British and Commonwealth); environmental science; fine arts and art studies; foreign languages and literatures; foreign languages and literatures, other; general teacher education; gerontology; health and medical administrative services; history; journalism; journalism and mass communication related; journalism and mass communications; nursing; political science and government; psychology; public relations and organizational communications; radio and television broadcasting; radio/television broadcasting; speech and rhetorical studies; visual and performing arts.
Graduate—economics; education, general; health professions and related sciences, other; marketing management and research; nursing; social work; teacher education, specific academic and vocational programs.

UNIVERSITY OF SOUTHERN MISSISSIPPI

Hattiesburg, Mississippi
Department of Continuing Education
http://www.usm.edu/cice/ce/index.html

University of Southern Mississippi was founded in 1910. It is accredited by Southern Association of Colleges and Schools. It first offered distance learning courses in 1941. In fall 2003, there were 3,600 students enrolled in distance learning courses. Institutionally administered financial aid is available to distance learners.

Services Distance learners have accessibility to academic advising, bookstore, campus computer network, e-mail services, library services.

Contact Ms. Sue Pace, Director, University of Southern Mississippi, Box 5055, Hattiesburg, MS 39406-5055. *Telephone:* 601-266-4210. *Fax:* 601-266-5839. *E-mail:* sue.pace@usm.edu.

DEGREES AND AWARDS

MEd Music Education–Master of Music Education
MLIS Library Information Science

COURSE SUBJECT AREAS OFFERED OUTSIDE OF DEGREE PROGRAMS

Undergraduate—accounting; anthropology; bible/biblical studies; biology; business information and data processing services; business marketing and marketing management; chemistry; community health services; community organization, resources and services; comparative literature; creative writing; criminology; education administration and supervision; educational evaluation, research and statistics; education, other; electrical engineering; engineering-related technologies, other; English composition; English language and literature, general; English technical and business writing; family and community studies; foods and nutrition studies; foreign languages and literatures; gaming/sports officiating; geography; health and physical education/fitness; health professions and related sciences, other; liberal arts and sciences, general studies and humanities; library science, other; management information systems/business data processing; mathematics related; medical genetics; microbiology/bacteriology; music; nursing; philosophy and religion; social work; sociology; special education.
Graduate—biochemistry and biophysics; biology, general; city/urban, community and regional planning; cognitive psychology and psycholinguistics; communications, general; community health services; construction/building technology; consumer and homemaking education; criminal justice and corrections; curriculum and instruction; demography/population studies; economics; education administration and supervision; educational evaluation, research and statistics; family and community studies; foreign languages and literatures; geography; health and physical education/fitness; individual and family development studies; mathematical statistics; nursing; parks, recreation, leisure and fitness studies, other; public health; social and philosophical foundations of education; social work; special education.
Non-credit—communications, general; health and medical administrative services; health and medical assistants; health and medical preparatory programs; tourism/travel marketing.

UNIVERSITY OF SOUTH FLORIDA

Tampa, Florida
College of Engineering
http://feeds.eng.usf.edu/

University of South Florida was founded in 1956. It is accredited by Southern Association of Colleges and Schools. It first offered distance learning courses in 1984. In fall 2003, there were 300 students enrolled in distance learning courses. Institutionally administered financial aid is available to distance learners.

Services Distance learners have accessibility to academic advising, bookstore, campus computer network, career placement assistance, e-mail services, library services, tutoring.

Contact Jim Manning, Student Service and Materials Coordinator, University of South Florida, College of Engineering, FEEDS Department, 4202 East Fowler Avenue, ENB 118, Tampa, FL 33620. *Telephone:* 813-974-3783. *Fax:* 813-974-8010. *E-mail:* feeds@eng.usf.edu.

DEGREES AND AWARDS

Graduate Certificate Total Quality Management; Wireless Engineering
MSE Engineering Management
MSEE Electrical Engineering

COURSE SUBJECT AREAS OFFERED OUTSIDE OF DEGREE PROGRAMS

Undergraduate—engineering, general.
Graduate—engineering, general.
Non-credit—engineering, general.

THE UNIVERSITY OF TENNESSEE

Knoxville, Tennessee
Department of Distance Education and Independent Study
http://www.anywhere.tennessee.edu

The University of Tennessee was founded in 1794. It is accredited by Southern Association of Colleges and Schools. It first offered distance learning courses in 1941. In fall 2003, there were 1,010 students enrolled in distance learning courses. Institutionally administered financial aid is available to distance learners.

Services Distance learners have accessibility to academic advising, bookstore, campus computer network, e-mail services, library services.

Contact Dr. Fadia Alvic, Assistant Director, Distance Education and Independent Study, The University of Tennessee, 1534 White Avenue, Knoxville, TN 37996-1525. *Telephone:* 800-670-8657. *Fax:* 865-974-4684. *E-mail:* falvic@utk.edu.

DEGREES AND AWARDS

Graduate Certificate Applied Statistical Strategies; Maintenance and Reliability Engineering; Nuclear Criticality Safety
MBA Aerospace; Physician Executive; Professional (weekend) Program; Senior Executive
MCE Public Works Option
MS Engineering Management; Environmental Engineering; Information Systems; Nuclear Engineering

COURSE SUBJECT AREAS OFFERED OUTSIDE OF DEGREE PROGRAMS

Undergraduate—accounting; agricultural business and management; American literature (United States); anthropology; applied mathematics; astronomy; business administration and management; chemistry; curriculum and instruction; economics; education, general; English composition; English creative writing; English language and literature, general; English language and literature/letters, other; English literature (British and Commonwealth); English technical and business writing; fishing and fisheries sciences and management; foreign languages and literatures; geography; Germanic languages and literatures; history; liberal arts and sciences, general studies and humanities; mathematics; physics; political science and government; psychology; religion/religious studies; Romance languages and literatures; sociology.
Non-credit—English creative writing; mathematics.

See full description on page 638.

THE UNIVERSITY OF TENNESSEE AT MARTIN

Martin, Tennessee
Office of Extended Campus and Continuing Education
http://www.utm.edu/~ecce

The University of Tennessee at Martin was founded in 1900. It is accredited by Southern Association of Colleges and Schools. It first offered distance learning courses in 1992. In fall 2003, there were 650 students enrolled in distance learning courses. Institutionally administered financial aid is available to distance learners.

Services Distance learners have accessibility to academic advising, bookstore, campus computer network, career placement assistance, e-mail services, library services.

Contact Katy Crapo, Coordinator, The University of Tennessee at Martin, 110 Gooch Hall, Martin, TN 38238-5050. *Telephone:* 731-587-7080. *Fax:* 731-587-7984. *E-mail:* kcrapo@utm.edu.

DEGREES AND AWARDS

BUS University Studies
MBA Business Administration
MS Agricultural Operations Management
MSE Education

COURSE SUBJECT AREAS OFFERED OUTSIDE OF DEGREE PROGRAMS

Undergraduate—accounting; business administration and management; computer science; economics; English composition; English literature (British and Commonwealth); fine arts and art studies; foreign languages and literatures; geological and related sciences; health and physical education/fitness; history; sociology; special education; visual and performing arts.
Graduate—accounting; business; business administration and management; education administration and supervision; special education; teacher education, specific academic and vocational programs.
Non-credit—accounting; business administration and management; child care and guidance workers and managers; computer and information sciences, general; crafts, folk art and artisanry; criminal justice and corrections; dance; education, general; general teacher education; industrial/manufacturing engineering.

THE UNIVERSITY OF TEXAS AT ARLINGTON

Arlington, Texas
Center for Distance Education
http://distance.uta.edu

The University of Texas at Arlington was founded in 1895. It is accredited by Southern Association of Colleges and Schools. It first offered distance learning courses in 1973. In fall 2003, there were 2,500 students enrolled in distance learning courses. Institutionally administered financial aid is available to distance learners.

Services Distance learners have accessibility to academic advising, bookstore, campus computer network, e-mail services, library services, tutoring.

Contact Dr. Pete Smith, Assistant Vice President of Academic Affairs, The University of Texas at Arlington, Box 19027, Arlington, TX 76019. *Telephone:* 817-272-5727. *Fax:* 817-272-5728. *E-mail:* info@distance.uta.edu.

DEGREES AND AWARDS

BA Criminology and Criminal Justice/Completion Degree
MBA Management, general
ME Aerospace Engineering; Computer Science and Engineering; Mechanical Engineering
MEd Curriculum and Instruction/Reading
MPA Public Administration
MS Industrial Engineering
MSCE Civil Engineering
MSEE Electrical Engineering

COURSE SUBJECT AREAS OFFERED OUTSIDE OF DEGREE PROGRAMS

Undergraduate—biology; criminology; economics; English composition; political science and government; sociology.

Graduate—aerospace engineering; curriculum and instruction; electrical engineering; engineering mechanics; environmental engineering; finance; industrial engineering; mechanical engineering; urban affairs/studies.

Special Message

The University of Texas at Arlington (UTA) is a Carnegie Doctoral I institution with a nationwide reputation for the design and delivery of Web-based classes. High-quality courses and programs and first-rate student support services result in high levels of satisfaction among UTA's distance learners.

UTA provides both certificate and degree programs through the University of Texas System TeleCampus. Programs include the award-winning MBA Online, Master's of Public Administration, and a bachelor's completion degree in criminology and criminal justice.

For educators, UTA offers the unique opportunity to complete graduate course work in reading, which leads to the English as a Second Language (ESL) Endorsement granted through the state of Texas. This endorsement prepares teachers to teach children from all cultural and language backgrounds and is required for those in the state of Texas who are working with students in grades K–12 whose first language is not English.

UTA also offers an online Master's of Education in Curriculum and Instruction in which the course work has the added benefit of preparatory work for certificates granted through the state of Texas, including the Reading Specialist Certificate, the Master Reading Teacher Certificate, and the ESL Endorsement. Transition to Teaching is another special online program offered to graduates seeking teacher certification for secondary education in Texas.

For further information, students should visit UTA's Web site at http://distance.uta.edu or call the Center for Distance Education at 888-UTA-DIST (toll-free).

THE UNIVERSITY OF TEXAS AT AUSTIN

Austin, Texas
Continuing and Extended Education
http://www.utexas.edu/cee/dec/

The University of Texas at Austin was founded in 1883. It is accredited by Southern Association of Colleges and Schools. It first offered distance learning courses in 1941. In fall 2003, there were 5,000 students enrolled in distance learning courses. Institutionally administered financial aid is available to distance learners.

Services Distance learners have accessibility to academic advising, bookstore.

Contact Olga Garza, Manager of Student Services, The University of Texas at Austin, PO Box 7700, Austin, TX 78713-7700. *Telephone:* 888-232-4723. *Fax:* 512-475-7933. *E-mail:* dec@utexas.edu.

DEGREES AND AWARDS

Programs offered do not lead to a degree or other formal award.

COURSE SUBJECT AREAS OFFERED OUTSIDE OF DEGREE PROGRAMS

Undergraduate—American literature (United States); anthropology; area, ethnic and cultural studies, other; astronomy; biology, general; curriculum and instruction; economics; education, general; English creative writing; English language and literature, general; English literature (British and Commonwealth); foreign languages and literatures; geography; history; mathematics; nursing; philosophy; physics; psychology; social psychology; social sciences, general; social work; sociology.

THE UNIVERSITY OF TEXAS AT DALLAS

Richardson, Texas
School of Management
http://som.utdallas.edu/globalmba

The University of Texas at Dallas was founded in 1969. It is accredited by Southern Association of Colleges and Schools. It first offered distance learning courses in 1999. In fall 2003, there were 543 students enrolled in distance learning courses. Institutionally administered financial aid is available to distance learners.

Services Distance learners have accessibility to academic advising, bookstore, campus computer network, career placement assistance, e-mail services, library services.

Contact Mr. George E. Barnes, Director of Global MBA Online, The University of Texas at Dallas, PO Box 830688, SM 27, Richardson, TX 75080-0688. *Telephone:* 972-883-2783. *Fax:* 972-883-2799. *E-mail:* gbarnes@utdallas.edu.

The University of Texas at Dallas (continued)

DEGREES AND AWARDS

MBA Global MBA Online

COURSE SUBJECT AREAS OFFERED OUTSIDE OF DEGREE PROGRAMS

Graduate—accounting; business; business administration and management; business/managerial economics; business quantitative methods and management science; financial management and services; information sciences and systems; international business; Internet and World Wide Web; marketing management and research; taxation.

THE UNIVERSITY OF TEXAS AT TYLER

Tyler, Texas
Interactive Television
http://www.uttyler.edu

The University of Texas at Tyler was founded in 1971. It is accredited by Southern Association of Colleges and Schools. It first offered distance learning courses in 1991. In fall 2003, there were 670 students enrolled in distance learning courses. Institutionally administered financial aid is available to distance learners.

Services Distance learners have accessibility to academic advising, bookstore, e-mail services, library services.

Contact Kelli R. Hannis, Admissions Assistant, The University of Texas at Tyler, Enrollment Management, 3900 University Boulevard, Tyler, TX 75799. *Telephone:* 903-566-7202. *Fax:* 903-566-7068. *E-mail:* khannis@mail.uttyl.edu.

DEGREES AND AWARDS

BSN Nursing
MBA Business Administration
MS Kinesiology; Technology–Human Resource Development

COURSE SUBJECT AREAS OFFERED OUTSIDE OF DEGREE PROGRAMS

Undergraduate—accounting; anthropology; archaeology; biology; business; business and personal services marketing operations; business communications; community health services; computer science; criminal justice and corrections; criminology; curriculum and instruction; financial management and services; fire protection; general teacher education; geography; health and physical education/fitness; health professions and related sciences, other; history; human resources management; industrial production technologies; marketing management and research; mathematical statistics; mathematics; nursing; political science and government; psychology; sociology; special education; technology education/industrial arts.

Graduate—business administration and management; business quantitative methods and management science; computer science; health professions and related sciences, other; human resources management; nursing; public administration; quality control and safety technologies; special education.

THE UNIVERSITY OF TEXAS MEDICAL BRANCH

Galveston, Texas
http://www.utmb.edu/

The University of Texas Medical Branch was founded in 1891. It is accredited by Southern Association of Colleges and Schools. It first offered distance learning courses in 1989. In fall 2003, there were 321 students enrolled in distance learning courses. Institutionally administered financial aid is available to distance learners.

Services Distance learners have accessibility to academic advising, bookstore, campus computer network, e-mail services, library services, tutoring.

Contact Dr. Poldi Tschirch, Director of Distance Education, The University of Texas Medical Branch, UTMB Telehealth Center, Office of Community, 301 University Boulevard, Galveston, TX 77555-1042. *Telephone:* 409-747-6243. *Fax:* 409-747-6299. *E-mail:* ptschirc@utmb.edu.

DEGREES AND AWARDS

BS Clinical Science
BSN Nursing

COURSE SUBJECT AREAS OFFERED OUTSIDE OF DEGREE PROGRAMS

Undergraduate—health professions and related sciences, other; medical laboratory technology; nursing.

Graduate—health and medical diagnostic and treatment services; medical clinical sciences (M.S., Ph.D.); nursing.

THE UNIVERSITY OF TEXAS OF THE PERMIAN BASIN

Odessa, Texas
REACH Program Center
http://www.utpb.edu/reach/

The University of Texas of the Permian Basin was founded in 1969. It is accredited by Southern Association of Colleges and Schools. It first offered distance learning courses in 1996. In fall 2003, there were 1,000 students enrolled in distance learning courses. Institutionally administered financial aid is available to distance learners.

Services Distance learners have accessibility to academic advising, bookstore, e-mail services, library services, tutoring.

Contact MaryAnn Rangel, Administrative Secretary, The University of Texas of the Permian Basin, 4901 East University Drive, Odessa, TX 79762-0001. *Telephone:* 432-552-2870. *Fax:* 432-522-2871. *E-mail:* rangel_a@utpb.edu.

DEGREES AND AWARDS

BA Criminal Justice
MBA Business Administration
MS Kinesiology

COURSE SUBJECT AREAS OFFERED OUTSIDE OF DEGREE PROGRAMS

Undergraduate—accounting; American literature (United States); art history; computer and information sciences, general; criminology; curriculum and instruction; education, other; English as a second language; English composition; geography; health and physical education/fitness; history; industrial and organizational psychology; journalism and mass communications; mathematics; philosophy and religion related; psychology; sociology; special education; teacher education, specific academic and vocational programs; theater arts/drama.

Graduate—criminal justice and corrections; criminology; curriculum and instruction; education administration and supervision; educational psychology; English as a second language; general teacher education; health and physical education/fitness; mathematical statistics; teacher education, specific academic and vocational programs.

THE UNIVERSITY OF TEXAS–PAN AMERICAN

Edinburg, Texas
Center for Distance Learning and Teaching Excellence
http://www.cdl.panam.edu

The University of Texas–Pan American was founded in 1927. It is accredited by Southern Association of Colleges and Schools. It first offered distance learning courses in 1985. In fall 2003, there were 5,075 students enrolled in distance learning courses. Institutionally administered financial aid is available to distance learners.

Services Distance learners have accessibility to campus computer network, career placement assistance, e-mail services, library services.
Contact Douglas Young, Director of Center for Distance Learning, The University of Texas–Pan American, 1201 West University Drive, ABS 2.124, Edinburg, TX 78541. *Telephone:* 956-381-2979. *Fax:* 956-318-5276. *E-mail:* dayoung@panam.edu.

DEGREES AND AWARDS

Programs offered do not lead to a degree or other formal award.

COURSE SUBJECT AREAS OFFERED OUTSIDE OF DEGREE PROGRAMS

Undergraduate—accounting; American history; business administration and management; business communications; business quantitative methods and management science; chemistry; computer science; education, general; mathematics related; music; rehabilitation/therapeutic services.
Graduate—business administration and management; business communications; educational psychology; English as a second language.
Non-credit—computer/information technology administration and management; computer systems networking and telecommunications.

THE UNIVERSITY OF TEXAS SOUTHWESTERN MEDICAL CENTER AT DALLAS

Dallas, Texas
http://www.utsouthwestern.edu/

The University of Texas Southwestern Medical Center at Dallas was founded in 1943. It is accredited by Southern Association of Colleges and Schools. It first offered distance learning courses in 2002. In fall 2003, there were 1 students enrolled in distance learning courses. Institutionally administered financial aid is available to distance learners.

Contact Mr. Charles L. Kettlewell, Registrar and Director of Student Financial Aid, The University of Texas Southwestern Medical Center at Dallas, Office of the Registrar, 5323 Harry Hines Boulevard, Dallas, TX 75390-9096. *Telephone:* 214-648-3606. *Fax:* 214-648-3289. *E-mail:* charles.kettlewell@utsouthwestern.edu.

DEGREES AND AWARDS

Programs offered do not lead to a degree or other formal award.

COURSE SUBJECT AREAS OFFERED OUTSIDE OF DEGREE PROGRAMS

Undergraduate—health professions and related sciences, other.

THE UNIVERSITY OF TEXAS SYSTEM

Austin, Texas
UT TeleCampus
http://www.telecampus.utsystem.edu

The University of Texas System is accredited by Southern Association of Colleges and Schools. It first offered distance learning courses in 1999. In fall 2003, there were 3,328 students enrolled in distance learning courses. Institutionally administered financial aid is available to distance learners.

Services Distance learners have accessibility to academic advising, bookstore, campus computer network, library services, tutoring.
Contact Mrs. Lori McNabb, Student Services Coordinator, The University of Texas System, 702 Colorado, Suite 4.100, Austin, TX 78701. *Telephone:* 888-TEXAS-16. *Fax:* 512-499-4715. *E-mail:* telecampus@utsystem.edu.

DEGREES AND AWARDS

BS Criminal Justice (Completion Degree)
BSN Nursing–RN to BSN
Certificate Chess in Education Online; Paralegal; Reading Specialist
Certification Alternative Teacher; Master Reading Teacher; Trade & Industrial (T&I)
Endorsement English as a Second Language (ESL)
Graduate Certificate Nursing Education
MBA Business Administration and Management
MEd Curriculum and Instruction; Educational Technology; Kinesiology
MPA Public Administration
MS Kinesiology; Technology with the Human Resource Development Option
Post-Master's Certificate Superintendent Certificate

COURSE SUBJECT AREAS OFFERED OUTSIDE OF DEGREE PROGRAMS

Undergraduate—accounting; biology, general; computer and information sciences, general; computer and information sciences, other; curriculum and instruction; developmental and child psychology; economics; educational/instructional media design; education, general; education, other; English as a second language; English composition; English creative writing; English language and literature, general; English language and literature/letters, other; fine arts and art studies; foreign languages and literatures; geological and related sciences; health professions and related sciences, other; history; information sciences and systems; liberal arts and sciences, general studies and humanities; mathematical statistics; mathematics; mathematics, other; medical laboratory technology; music; physical sciences, general; physical sciences, other; political science and government; psychology; social and philosophical foundations of education; social sciences and history, other; social sciences, general; sociology; teacher education, specific academic and vocational programs; telecommunications.

The University of Texas System (continued)

Graduate—computer and information sciences, general; educational/instructional media design; educational psychology; education, general; education, other; health and medical assistants; health professions and related sciences, other; nursing; social and philosophical foundations of education; teacher assistant/aide; teacher education, specific academic and vocational programs; teaching English as a second language/foreign language.

See full description on page 640.

UNIVERSITY OF THE INCARNATE WORD

San Antonio, Texas
Universe Online
http://www.uiw.edu/online

University of the Incarnate Word was founded in 1881. It is accredited by Southern Association of Colleges and Schools. It first offered distance learning courses in 2000. In fall 2003, there were 750 students enrolled in distance learning courses. Institutionally administered financial aid is available to distance learners.

Services Distance learners have accessibility to academic advising, bookstore, career placement assistance, library services, tutoring.

Contact Dr. Cyndi Wilson Porter, Dean, Virtual University and Director, Universe Online, University of the Incarnate Word, CPO #324, 4301 Broadway, San Antonio, TX 78209. *Telephone:* 877-827-2702. *Fax:* 210-829-2756. *E-mail:* virtual@universe.uiwtx.edu.

DEGREES AND AWARDS

AA Business; Communications; Information Systems; Liberal Studies
BA Psychology of Organizations and Development
BBA Business Administration
MA Administration–Communication Arts; Applied Administration; Instructional Technology; Organizational Development; Urban Administration
MBA General Program; International

COURSE SUBJECT AREAS OFFERED OUTSIDE OF DEGREE PROGRAMS

Undergraduate—accounting; advertising; American literature (United States); anthropology; applied mathematics; area, ethnic and cultural studies, other; area studies; bible/biblical studies; biblical and other theological languages and literatures; biology, general; business; business administration and management; business and personal services marketing operations; business communications; business information and data processing services; business management and administrative services, other; business/managerial economics; business quantitative methods and management science; communications, general; communications technologies; computer and information sciences, general; computer and information sciences, other; computer/information technology administration and management; computer programming; computer software and media applications; computer systems analysis; computer systems networking and telecommunications; economics; English composition; English creative writing; enterprise management and operation; entrepreneurship; financial services marketing operations; fine arts and art studies; foreign languages and literatures; general retailing/wholesaling; history; home/office products marketing; information sciences and systems; Internet and World Wide Web; legal studies; liberal arts and sciences, general studies and humanities; marketing management and research; marketing operations/marketing and distribution, other; mathematical statistics; mathematics; philosophy; philosophy and religion; professional studies; psychology; religion/religious studies; sociology; telecommunications.

Graduate—accounting; business; business administration and management; business communications; business information and data processing services; business management and administrative services, other; business/managerial economics; business quantitative methods and management science; communications, general; communications technologies; economics; legal studies; psychology.

See full description on page 642.

UNIVERSITY OF TOLEDO

Toledo, Ohio
Division of Distance Learning
http://www.dl.utoledo.edu

University of Toledo was founded in 1872. It is accredited by North Central Association of Colleges and Schools. It first offered distance learning courses in 1995. In fall 2003, there were 8,096 students enrolled in distance learning courses. Institutionally administered financial aid is available to distance learners.

Services Distance learners have accessibility to academic advising, bookstore, campus computer network, career placement assistance, e-mail services, library services.

Contact Janet Green, Assistant Director for Marketing and Enrollment Management, University of Toledo, Seagate Campus, 401 Jefferson Avenue, Toledo, OH 43604-1005. *Telephone:* 419-321-5130. *Fax:* 419-321-5147. *E-mail:* utdl@utoledo.edu.

DEGREES AND AWARDS

AAB Accounting Technology; Business Management Technology; Marketing and Sales Technology
AIS Interdisciplinary Program in Technical Studies
AS Computer Science and Engineering Technology
BA Adult Liberal Studies
BS Computer Science and Engineering Technology; Health Information Management
Certificate Accounting Technology; Business Management Technology; Diversity Management; Marketing and Sales Technology
MLS Liberal Studies
MSE Engineering

COURSE SUBJECT AREAS OFFERED OUTSIDE OF DEGREE PROGRAMS

Undergraduate—communications, general; computer/information technology administration and management; developmental/child psychology; education, general; education, other; engineering-related technologies, other; English language and literature, general; journalism and mass communication related; journalism and mass communications; liberal arts and sciences, general studies and humanities; mathematical statistics; mathematics; philosophy; philosophy and religion related; psychology; religion/religious studies; sociology; women's studies.

Graduate—counseling psychology; curriculum and instruction; educational evaluation, research and statistics; education, general; education, other; liberal arts and sciences, general studies and humanities; philosophy; political science and government; special education.

See full description on page 644.

UNIVERSITY OF TORONTO

Toronto, Ontario, Canada
School of Continuing Studies
http://learn.utoronto.ca

University of Toronto was founded in 1827. It is provincially chartered. It first offered distance learning courses in 1944. In fall 2003, there were 4,400 students enrolled in distance learning courses. Institutionally administered financial aid is available to distance learners.

Services Distance learners have accessibility to academic advising, e-mail services.

Contact Anne-Marie Brinsmead, Senior Academic Coordinator, University of Toronto, Toronto, ON M5S 1A1, Canada. *E-mail:* a.brinsmead@utoronto.ca.

DEGREES AND AWARDS

Programs offered do not lead to a degree or other formal award.

COURSE SUBJECT AREAS OFFERED OUTSIDE OF DEGREE PROGRAMS

Undergraduate—accounting; business; business administration and management; business communications; business/managerial economics; business quantitative methods and management science; computer/information technology administration and management; computer software and media applications; financial management and services; human resources management; information sciences and systems; marketing management and research; transportation and materials moving workers, other.

Non-credit—accounting; advertising; business administration and management; business communications; business/managerial economics; business marketing and marketing management; business quantitative methods and management science; Chinese; communications, general; computer/information technology administration and management; East and Southeast Asian languages and literatures; finance; foreign languages and literatures; foreign languages and literatures, other; French; Germanic languages and literatures; human resources management; insurance/risk management; Italian; law and legal studies related; organizational behavior; Romance languages and literatures; South Asian languages and literatures; Spanish.

UNIVERSITY OF TULSA

Tulsa, Oklahoma
College of Business Administration
http://www.imba.utulsa.edu

University of Tulsa was founded in 1894. It is accredited by North Central Association of Colleges and Schools. It first offered distance learning courses in 2000. In fall 2003, there were 40 students enrolled in distance learning courses. Institutionally administered financial aid is available to distance learners.

Services Distance learners have accessibility to academic advising, bookstore, campus computer network, career placement assistance, e-mail services, library services, tutoring.

Contact Mr. Kelly S. Sudduth, iMBA Enrollment Coordinator, University of Tulsa, 600 South College, BAH 217, Tulsa, OK 74104-3189. *Telephone:* 918-631-3211. *Fax:* 918-631-2142. *E-mail:* kelly-sudduth@utulsa.edu.

DEGREES AND AWARDS

BN Nursing–RN to BSN
M Tax Taxation
MBA Business Administration Online

COURSE SUBJECT AREAS OFFERED OUTSIDE OF DEGREE PROGRAMS

Undergraduate—nursing.

Graduate—accounting; business; business administration and management; business information and data processing services; business management and administrative services, other; business/managerial economics; business quantitative methods and management science; computer and information sciences, general; computer/information technology administration and management; computer systems networking and telecommunications; economics; enterprise management and operation; entrepreneurship; financial management and services; human resources management; information sciences and systems; international business; Internet and World Wide Web; legal studies; marketing management and research; marketing operations/marketing and distribution, other; taxation; telecommunications.

See full description on page 646.

UNIVERSITY OF UTAH

Salt Lake City, Utah
Distance Education
http://continue.utah.edu/distance

University of Utah was founded in 1850. It is accredited by Northwest Commission on Colleges and Universities. It first offered distance learning courses in 1941. In fall 2003, there were 2,000 students enrolled in distance learning courses. Institutionally administered financial aid is available to distance learners.

Services Distance learners have accessibility to bookstore, library services.

Contact Roberta Lopez, Interim Director, University of Utah, Distance Education, 1901 East South Campus Drive, Room 1215, Salt Lake City, UT 84112-9359. *Telephone:* 801-585-1906. *Fax:* 801-581-6267. *E-mail:* rlopez@aoce.utah.edu.

DEGREES AND AWARDS

Programs offered do not lead to a degree or other formal award.

COURSE SUBJECT AREAS OFFERED OUTSIDE OF DEGREE PROGRAMS

Undergraduate—anthropology; area, ethnic and cultural studies, other; art history; atmospheric sciences and meteorology; biology; chemistry; communications, general; creative writing; developmental/child psychology; economics; educational psychology; English literature (British and Commonwealth); financial management and services; foods and nutrition studies; geography; gerontology; history; mathematical statistics; mathematics; mathematics related; music; organic chemistry; physics; physiology; political science and government; psychology; sign language interpretation; social psychology; social sciences, general; special education; teacher education, specific academic and vocational programs.

Non-credit—real estate.

UNIVERSITY OF VERMONT

Burlington, Vermont
Distance Learning Network
http://learn.uvm.edu

University of Vermont was founded in 1791. It is accredited by New England Association of Schools and Colleges. It first offered distance learning courses in 1995. In fall 2003, there were 920 students enrolled in distance learning courses. Institutionally administered financial aid is available to distance learners.

Services Distance learners have accessibility to academic advising, bookstore, campus computer network, career placement assistance, e-mail services, library services, tutoring.

Contact Carol Vallett, Director of Continuing Education, University of Vermont, Continuing Education, 322 South Prospect Street, Burlington, VT 05401. *Telephone:* 800-639-3210. *Fax:* 802-656-0266. *E-mail:* carol.vallett@uvm.edu.

DEGREES AND AWARDS

Programs offered do not lead to a degree or other formal award.

COURSE SUBJECT AREAS OFFERED OUTSIDE OF DEGREE PROGRAMS

Undergraduate—anthropology; community organization, resources and services; computer science; English language and literature, general; gerontology; international relations and affairs; library science/librarianship; mathematical statistics; nursing; psychology, other; public administration; religion/religious studies; social work.

Graduate—communication disorders sciences and services; library science/librarianship; nursing; public administration; religion/religious studies; social work; speech and rhetorical studies.

Non-credit—accounting; business; business administration and management; business and personal services marketing operations; business communications; business/managerial economics; computer/information technology administration and management; computer programming; computer science; computer software and media applications; computer systems analysis; English composition; English language and literature, general.

THE UNIVERSITY OF VIRGINIA'S COLLEGE AT WISE

Wise, Virginia
http://www.uvawise.edu

The University of Virginia's College at Wise was founded in 1954. It is accredited by Southern Association of Colleges and Schools. It first offered distance learning courses in 1995. In fall 2003, there were 21 students enrolled in distance learning courses. Institutionally administered financial aid is available to distance learners.

Services Distance learners have accessibility to academic advising, bookstore, campus computer network, career placement assistance, e-mail services, library services, tutoring.

Contact Mr. Mitchell R Williams, Director, The University of Virginia's College at Wise, PO Box 1987, Abingdon, VA 24210. *Telephone:* 276-619-4312. *Fax:* 276-619-4309. *E-mail:* mrw4g@uvawise.edu.

DEGREES AND AWARDS

Programs offered do not lead to a degree or other formal award.

COURSE SUBJECT AREAS OFFERED OUTSIDE OF DEGREE PROGRAMS

Undergraduate—accounting; business administration and management; computer science; education, general; nursing; psychology.

UNIVERSITY OF WASHINGTON

Seattle, Washington
Extension
http://onlinelearning.washington.edu/ol/

University of Washington was founded in 1861. It is accredited by Northwest Commission on Colleges and Universities. In fall 2003, there were 9,700 students enrolled in distance learning courses. Institutionally administered financial aid is available to distance learners.

Services Distance learners have accessibility to academic advising, bookstore, campus computer network, e-mail services, library services.

Contact UW Educational Outreach, University of Washington, 4311 11th Avenue, NE, Seattle, WA 98105-4608. *Telephone:* 800-543-2320. *Fax:* 206-685-9359. *E-mail:* distance@u.washington.edu.

DEGREES AND AWARDS

Certificate Brain Research in Education; Business Foundations; C Programming; C++ Programming; Construction Management; Curriculum Integration in Action; Data Resource Management; Database Management; Distance Learning Design and Development; E-Commerce Management; Embedded and Real-Time Systems Programming; Facility Management; Fiction Writing; Gerontology; Heavy Construction Project Management; Infrastructure Construction; Internet Programming; Java 2 Programming; Object-Oriented Analysis and Design Using UML; Project Management; Quantitative Construction Management; School Library Media Specialist; Site Planning; Web Administration; Web Consultant for Small Business; Web Technology Essentials

MAE Aerospace Engineering

MEE Electrical Engineering

MLIS Library and Information Science

MS Aeronautics and Astronautics; Construction Engineering; Strategic Planning for Critical Infrastructure

MSE Manufacturing Engineering; Materials Science and Engineering

MSME Mechanical Engineering

COURSE SUBJECT AREAS OFFERED OUTSIDE OF DEGREE PROGRAMS

Undergraduate—accounting; American literature (United States); anthropology; applied mathematics; archaeology; astronomy; atmospheric sciences and meteorology; business communications; chemistry; cognitive psychology and psycholinguistics; communications, general; computer engineering; computer programming; computer science; construction/building technology; construction management; criminology; cultural studies; curriculum and instruction; developmental and child psychology; East European languages and literatures; economics; educational psychology; education, general; English as a second language; English composition; English creative writing; English language and literature, general; English technical and business writing; geography; geological and related sciences; gerontology; Greek languages and literatures (modern); history; international business; journalism and mass communications; library science/librarianship; marketing management and research; materials engineering; mathematical statistics; mathematics; mathematics, other;

mechanical engineering; pharmacy; philosophy; political science and government; psychology; religion/religious studies; social psychology; sociology; speech and rhetorical studies; urban affairs/studies.
Graduate—city/urban, community and regional planning; civil engineering; computer science; construction/building technology; construction management; electrical and electronic engineering-related technology; engineering, other; gerontology; industrial/manufacturing engineering; library science/librarianship; library science, other; materials engineering; materials science; mechanical engineering; urban affairs/studies.
Non-credit—business administration and management; city/urban, community and regional planning; computer and information sciences, general; computer and information sciences, other; computer/information technology administration and management; computer programming; computer systems analysis; creative writing; English as a second language; English creative writing; English language and literature, general; information sciences and systems; Internet and World Wide Web.

See full description on page 648.

UNIVERSITY OF WATERLOO

Waterloo, Ontario, Canada
Distance and Continuing Education
http://dce.uwaterloo.ca

University of Waterloo was founded in 1957. It is provincially chartered. It first offered distance learning courses in 1968. In fall 2003, there were 4,000 students enrolled in distance learning courses. Institutionally administered financial aid is available to distance learners.

Services Distance learners have accessibility to academic advising, bookstore, campus computer network, e-mail services, library services, tutoring.
Contact Information and Student Services, University of Waterloo, Distance and Continuing Education Office, Waterloo, ON N2L 3G1, Canada. *Telephone:* 519-888-4050. *Fax:* 519-746-4607. *E-mail:* distance@uwaterloo.ca.

DEGREES AND AWARDS

BA Economics; English; French; General Studies, Non-Major; Humanities; Philosophy; Psychology; Religious Studies; Social Development Studies; Social Sciences
BS Science, general for the Non-Major
MS Management Science/Technology Management–Master of Applied Science Management Science, Technology Management

COURSE SUBJECT AREAS OFFERED OUTSIDE OF DEGREE PROGRAMS

Undergraduate—accounting; American history; American literature (United States); anthropology; applied mathematics; area, ethnic and cultural studies, other; astronomy; bible/biblical studies; biblical and other theological languages and literatures; biochemistry; biological and physical sciences; biological sciences/life sciences, other; biology; biology, general; business/managerial economics; Canadian studies; cell and molecular biology; chemistry; city/urban, community and regional planning; community organization, resources and services; computer and information sciences, general; computer science; criminology; cultural studies; dance; developmental and child psychology; earth sciences; East European languages and literatures; ecology; economics; educational psychology; English composition; English literature (British and Commonwealth); entrepreneurship; environmental science; European history; family and community studies; foreign languages and literatures; foreign languages and literatures, other; French; geography; geological and related sciences; Germanic languages and literatures; gerontology; Greek languages and literatures (modern); Hebrew; history; insurance/risk management; investments and securities; Judaic studies; Latin (ancient and medieval); liberal arts and sciences, general studies and humanities; mathematical statistics; mathematics; mathematics, other; medical genetics; medieval/Renaissance studies; microbiology/bacteriology; miscellaneous physical sciences; multi/interdisciplinary studies, other; organic chemistry; organizational behavior; peace and conflict studies; philosophy; philosophy and religion; physical sciences, general; physical/theoretical chemistry; physics; physiology; psychology; psychology, other; religion/religious studies; Russian; social psychology; social sciences and history, other; social sciences, general; social work; sociology; Spanish; women's studies.
Graduate—engineering/industrial management; industrial engineering; management information systems/business data processing.
Non-credit—chemistry; English composition; mathematics related; physics.

UNIVERSITY OF WEST FLORIDA

Pensacola, Florida
Online Campus/Academic Technology Center
http://onlinecampus.uwf.edu

University of West Florida was founded in 1963. It is accredited by Southern Association of Colleges and Schools. It first offered distance learning courses in 1988. In fall 2003, there were 700 students enrolled in distance learning courses. Institutionally administered financial aid is available to distance learners.

Services Distance learners have accessibility to academic advising, bookstore, campus computer network, e-mail services, library services.
Contact Mrs. Sharon Cobb, Program Coordinator, Academic Technology Center, University of West Florida, 11000 University Parkway, Building 77, Room 138A, Pensacola, FL 32514. *Telephone:* 850-473-7468. *Fax:* 850-474-2807. *E-mail:* scobb@uwf.edu.

DEGREES AND AWARDS

BA Maritime Studies
BS Engineering Technology Instructional Support; Oceanography
MEd Comprehensive Masters in Education; Education and Training Management Subspecialty/Human Performance Technology; Education and Training Management Subspecialty/Instructional Technology; Instructional Technology
MS Criminal Justice Administration (MSA); Education Leadership (MSA); Health Care Administration (MSA); Human Performance Technology (MSA); Public Administration (MSA)

COURSE SUBJECT AREAS OFFERED OUTSIDE OF DEGREE PROGRAMS

Undergraduate—advertising; anthropology; archaeology; biological sciences/life sciences, other; biology, general; business communications; communications, general; communications technologies; computer programming; computer science; computer software and media applications; computer systems networking and telecommunications; data entry/microcomputer applications; economics; engineering-related technologies, other; English composition; English language and literature, general; English technical and business writing; fine arts and art studies; history; Internet and World Wide Web; liberal arts

University of West Florida (continued)

and sciences, general studies and humanities; mathematical statistics; mathematics; mathematics related; miscellaneous biological specializations; miscellaneous physical sciences; philosophy; physical sciences, general; physical sciences, other; political science and government; religion/religious studies; telecommunications.
Graduate—educational/instructional media design; professional studies.
Non-credit—business management and administrative services, other; communications technologies; computer engineering; education, other; human resources management; teacher education, specific academic and vocational programs; technology education/industrial arts.

UNIVERSITY OF WISCONSIN COLLEGES

Madison, Wisconsin
UWC On-line
http://www.online.uwc.edu

University of Wisconsin Colleges is accredited by North Central Association of Colleges and Schools. It first offered distance learning courses in 1998. In fall 2003, there were 900 students enrolled in distance learning courses. Institutionally administered financial aid is available to distance learners.

Services Distance learners have accessibility to academic advising, bookstore, campus computer network, e-mail services, library services, tutoring.
Contact Ms. Leanne Johnson, DE Coordinator, University of Wisconsin Colleges, 780 Regent Street, PO Box 8680, Madison, WI 53708-8680. *Telephone:* 608-263-9553. *Fax:* 608-262-7872. *E-mail:* ljohnson@uwc.edu.

DEGREES AND AWARDS

AAS Liberal Arts

COURSE SUBJECT AREAS OFFERED OUTSIDE OF DEGREE PROGRAMS

Undergraduate—anthropology; biological and physical sciences; biology, general; business; chemistry; communications, other; English composition; English language and literature, general; fine arts and art studies; geography; history; journalism and mass communications; mathematical statistics; mathematics; mathematics and computer science; music; philosophy; political science and government; psychology; sociology.

UNIVERSITY OF WISCONSIN–EAU CLAIRE

Eau Claire, Wisconsin
http://www.uwec.edu/

University of Wisconsin–Eau Claire was founded in 1916. It is accredited by North Central Association of Colleges and Schools. It first offered distance learning courses in 1995. In fall 2003, there were 700 students enrolled in distance learning courses. Institutionally administered financial aid is available to distance learners.

Services Distance learners have accessibility to academic advising, bookstore, campus computer network, career placement assistance, e-mail services, library services.
Contact Sue E. Moore, Registrar, University of Wisconsin–Eau Claire, 130 Schofield, Eau Claire, WI 54702. *Telephone:* 715-836-3887. *Fax:* 715-836-3846. *E-mail:* sheltose@uwec.edu.

DEGREES AND AWARDS

BSN Nursing Degree Completion Program
License School Library Media
MBA Business Administration

COURSE SUBJECT AREAS OFFERED OUTSIDE OF DEGREE PROGRAMS

Undergraduate—library science, other; nursing.
Graduate—business administration and management.
Non-credit—accounting; economics; financial management and services; information sciences and systems; marketing management and research; nursing.

UNIVERSITY OF WISCONSIN–LA CROSSE

La Crosse, Wisconsin
http://www.uwlax.edu/

University of Wisconsin–La Crosse was founded in 1909. It is accredited by North Central Association of Colleges and Schools. It first offered distance learning courses in 1995. In fall 2003, there were 55 students enrolled in distance learning courses. Institutionally administered financial aid is available to distance learners.

Services Distance learners have accessibility to academic advising, bookstore, campus computer network, career placement assistance, e-mail services, library services.
Contact Terry Wirkus, DE Site Support Coordiantor, University of Wisconsin–La Crosse, 1725 State Street, La Crosse, WI 54601. *Telephone:* 608-785-8049. *Fax:* 608-785-8825. *E-mail:* wirkus.terr@uwlax.edu.

DEGREES AND AWARDS

Programs offered do not lead to a degree or other formal award.

COURSE SUBJECT AREAS OFFERED OUTSIDE OF DEGREE PROGRAMS

Undergraduate—foreign languages and literatures; health professions and related sciences, other.
Graduate—accounting; business administration and management; economics; educational psychology; finance; marketing operations/marketing and distribution, other; microbiology/bacteriology; parks, recreation and leisure facilities management.
Non-credit—history.

UNIVERSITY OF WISCONSIN–MADISON

Madison, Wisconsin
http://www.wisc.edu/

University of Wisconsin–Madison was founded in 1848. It is accredited by North Central Association of Colleges and Schools. It first offered distance learning courses in 1991. In fall 2003, there were 8,000 students enrolled in distance learning courses.

Services Distance learners have accessibility to academic advising, campus computer network, e-mail services, library services.
Contact University of Wisconsin–Madison. *E-mail:* @ ..

DEGREES AND AWARDS

BS Nursing
Certificate of Completion Distance Education
MEngr Professional Practice; Technical Japanese
MS Computer Engineering; Electrical Engineering; Mechanical Engineering
PharmD Pharmacy

COURSE SUBJECT AREAS OFFERED OUTSIDE OF DEGREE PROGRAMS

Undergraduate—architecture and related programs, other; chemical engineering; civil engineering; computer science; electrical and electronic engineering-related technology; family and community studies; food sciences and technology; foreign languages and literatures; geological and related sciences; human resources management; mechanical engineering; nursing.
Graduate—business; chemical engineering; civil engineering; education administration and supervision; electrical engineering; engineering, general; family and community studies; geography; human resources management; marketing management and research; mechanical engineering; nursing; pharmacy; political science and government; social work.

UNIVERSITY OF WISCONSIN–MILWAUKEE

Milwaukee, Wisconsin
Distance Learning and Instructional Support
http://cfprod01.imt.uwm.edu/sce/elearning.cfm

University of Wisconsin–Milwaukee was founded in 1956. It is accredited by North Central Association of Colleges and Schools. It first offered distance learning courses in 1972. In fall 2003, there were 1,116 students enrolled in distance learning courses. Institutionally administered financial aid is available to distance learners.

Services Distance learners have accessibility to academic advising, bookstore, campus computer network, career placement assistance, e-mail services, library services, tutoring.
Contact Betty Menacher, Distance Learning Manager, University of Wisconsin–Milwaukee, 161 West Wisconsin Avenue, #6000, Milwaukee, WI 53203. *Telephone:* 414-227-3223. *Fax:* 414-227-3330. *E-mail:* bettym@uwm.edu.

DEGREES AND AWARDS

Certificate Internet Technologies; State and Local Taxation; Wisconsin Credential Program for Child Care Administrators
MLIS Library and Information Science
PhD Nursing

COURSE SUBJECT AREAS OFFERED OUTSIDE OF DEGREE PROGRAMS

Undergraduate—accounting; computer and information sciences, general; counseling psychology; finance; information sciences and systems.
Graduate—accounting; child care and guidance workers and managers; computer and information sciences, general; computer and information sciences, other; counseling psychology; education administration and supervision; education, general; education, other; library science/librarianship; library science, other; taxation.
Non-credit—computer and information sciences, other; computer software and media applications; computer systems networking and telecommunications; counseling psychology; liberal arts and sciences, general studies and humanities; transportation and materials moving workers, other.

UNIVERSITY OF WISCONSIN–PARKSIDE

Kenosha, Wisconsin
http://www.uwp.edu/

University of Wisconsin–Parkside was founded in 1968. It is accredited by North Central Association of Colleges and Schools. It first offered distance learning courses in 1996. In fall 2003, there were 27 students enrolled in distance learning courses. Institutionally administered financial aid is available to distance learners.

Services Distance learners have accessibility to academic advising, bookstore, campus computer network, career placement assistance, e-mail services, library services, tutoring.
Contact Bradley R. Piazza, MBA Program Coordinator and Assistant Dean, University of Wisconsin–Parkside, 900 Wood Road, PO Box 2000, Kenosha, WI 53141-2000. *Telephone:* 262-595-2046. *Fax:* 262-595-2680. *E-mail:* bradley.piazza@uwp.edu.

DEGREES AND AWARDS

Programs offered do not lead to a degree or other formal award.

COURSE SUBJECT AREAS OFFERED OUTSIDE OF DEGREE PROGRAMS

Undergraduate—foreign languages and literatures.
Graduate—accounting; business administration and management; business information and data processing services; business/managerial economics; business quantitative methods and management science; economics; financial management and services; marketing operations/marketing and distribution, other; mathematical statistics.
Non-credit—gerontology; legal studies.

UNIVERSITY OF WISCONSIN–PLATTEVILLE

Platteville, Wisconsin
Distance Learning Center
http://www.uwplatt.edu/~disted

University of Wisconsin–Platteville was founded in 1866. It is accredited by North Central Association of Colleges and Schools. It first offered distance learning courses in 1978. In fall 2003, there were 1,000 students enrolled in distance learning courses. Institutionally administered financial aid is available to distance learners.

Services Distance learners have accessibility to academic advising, bookstore, campus computer network, career placement assistance, library services.
Contact Distance Learning Center, University of Wisconsin–Platteville, B12 Karrmann Library, One University Plaza, Platteville, WI 53818. *Telephone:* 800-362-5460. *Fax:* 608-342-1071. *E-mail:* disted@uwplatt.edu.

University of Wisconsin–Platteville (continued)

DEGREES AND AWARDS

BS Business Administration
Certificate Engineering Management; Food Marketing; Human Resource Management; International Business; Leadership and Human Performance; Project Management
Advanced Graduate Diploma Criminal Justice
MEngr Engineering
MS Criminal Justice; Project Management

COURSE SUBJECT AREAS OFFERED OUTSIDE OF DEGREE PROGRAMS

Undergraduate—accounting; business administration and management; business marketing and marketing management; communications, general; economics; finance; food products retailing and wholesaling operations; geography; human resources management; mathematics; music; speech and rhetorical studies.
Graduate—adult/continuing education; business; civil engineering; communications, general; criminal justice and corrections; industrial/manufacturing engineering; management science; mathematics; mechanical engineering; psychology.

UNIVERSITY OF WISCONSIN–PLATTEVILLE

Platteville, Wisconsin
Online Program in Criminal Justice
http://www.uwplatt.edu/~disted/

University of Wisconsin–Platteville was founded in 1866. It is accredited by North Central Association of Colleges and Schools. It first offered distance learning courses in 1978. In fall 2003, there were 1,000 students enrolled in distance learning courses. Institutionally administered financial aid is available to distance learners.

Services Distance learners have accessibility to academic advising, bookstore, campus computer network, career placement assistance, library services.
Contact Dr. Cheryl Banachowski-Fuller, Program Coordinator of Criminal Justice Distance Education Program, University of Wisconsin–Platteville, 1 University Plaza, Platteville, WI 53818. *Telephone:* 608-342-1652. *Fax:* 608-342-1986. *E-mail:* criminaljstc@uwplatt.edu.

DEGREES AND AWARDS

Advanced Graduate Diploma Criminal Justice
MS Criminal Justice

COURSE SUBJECT AREAS OFFERED OUTSIDE OF DEGREE PROGRAMS

Graduate—business; business administration and management; criminal justice and corrections; criminology; political science and government; psychology; sociology.

UNIVERSITY OF WISCONSIN–PLATTEVILLE

Platteville, Wisconsin
Online Program in Project Management
http://www.uwplatt.edu/~disted/

University of Wisconsin–Platteville was founded in 1866. It is accredited by North Central Association of Colleges and Schools. It first offered distance learning courses in 1978. In fall 2003, there were 1,000 students enrolled in distance learning courses. Institutionally administered financial aid is available to distance learners.

Services Distance learners have accessibility to academic advising, bookstore, campus computer network, career placement assistance, library services.
Contact Bill Haskins, Program Coordinator of Project Management Program, University of Wisconsin–Platteville, 1 University Plaza, Platteville, WI 53818. *Telephone:* 608-342-1961. *Fax:* 608-342-1466. *E-mail:* projectmgmt@uwplatt.edu.

DEGREES AND AWARDS

Certificate Project Management
MS Project Management

COURSE SUBJECT AREAS OFFERED OUTSIDE OF DEGREE PROGRAMS

Graduate—accounting; business; business administration and management; business communications; mathematics.

UNIVERSITY OF WISCONSIN–PLATTEVILLE

Platteville, Wisconsin
Online Program in Engineering
http://www.uwplatt.edu/~disted/

University of Wisconsin–Platteville was founded in 1866. It is accredited by North Central Association of Colleges and Schools. It first offered distance learning courses in 1978. In fall 2003, there were 1,000 students enrolled in distance learning courses. Institutionally administered financial aid is available to distance learners.

Services Distance learners have accessibility to academic advising, bookstore, campus computer network, career placement assistance, library services.
Contact Dr. Lisa Riedle, Program Coordinator of Engineering Distance Education Program, University of Wisconsin–Platteville, 1 University Plaza, Platteville, WI 53818. *Telephone:* 608-342-1686. *Fax:* 608-342-1566. *E-mail:* engineering@uwplatt.edu.

DEGREES AND AWARDS

ME Engineering

COURSE SUBJECT AREAS OFFERED OUTSIDE OF DEGREE PROGRAMS

Graduate—business; business administration and management; business communications; computer engineering; engineering design; engineering, general; engineering/industrial management; engineering mechanics; engineering, other; industrial/manufacturing engineering; mathematical statistics; mathematics.

UNIVERSITY OF WISCONSIN–PLATTEVILLE

Platteville, Wisconsin
Bachelor of Science in Business Administration
http://www.uwplatt.edu/~disted/

University of Wisconsin–Platteville was founded in 1866. It is accredited by North Central Association of Colleges and Schools. It first offered distance learning courses in 1978. In fall 2003, there were 1,000 students enrolled in distance learning courses. Institutionally administered financial aid is available to distance learners.

Services Distance learners have accessibility to academic advising, bookstore, campus computer network, career placement assistance, library services.

Contact Marge Karsten, Chair of Business and Accounting Department, University of Wisconsin–Platteville, 1 University Plaza, Platteville, WI 53818. *Telephone:* 608-342-1749. *Fax:* 608-342-1466. *E-mail:* businessadmn@uwplatt.edu.

DEGREES AND AWARDS

BSBA Business Administration
Certificate Human Resource Management; International Business; Leadership and Human Performance

COURSE SUBJECT AREAS OFFERED OUTSIDE OF DEGREE PROGRAMS

Undergraduate—accounting; advertising; business; business administration and management; business communications; communications, general; data entry/microcomputer applications; economics; financial management and services; geography; human resources management; international business; marketing management and research; mathematics.
Graduate—business administration and management; business communications.

UNIVERSITY OF WISCONSIN–RIVER FALLS

River Falls, Wisconsin
Outreach Office
http://www.uwrf.edu/ogs

University of Wisconsin–River Falls was founded in 1874. It is accredited by North Central Association of Colleges and Schools. It first offered distance learning courses in 1982. In fall 2003, there were 200 students enrolled in distance learning courses. Institutionally administered financial aid is available to distance learners.

Services Distance learners have accessibility to academic advising, bookstore, career placement assistance, e-mail services, library services.

Contact Katrina Larsen, Assistant to the Dean of Outreach and Graduate Studies, University of Wisconsin–River Falls, 410 South 3rd Street, River Falls, WI 54022. *Telephone:* 715-425-3256. *Fax:* 715-425-0624. *E-mail:* katrina.larsen@uwrf.edu.

DEGREES AND AWARDS

Programs offered do not lead to a degree or other formal award.

COURSE SUBJECT AREAS OFFERED OUTSIDE OF DEGREE PROGRAMS

Undergraduate—agriculture/agricultural sciences; astronomy; biological and physical sciences; business; business administration and management; communications, general; computer and information sciences, general; computer programming; computer science; geological and related sciences; history; liberal arts and sciences, general studies and humanities; political science and government; psychology; sociology; speech and rhetorical studies; teacher education, specific academic and vocational programs; theater arts/drama.
Graduate—biological sciences/life sciences, other; community organization, resources and services; conservation and renewable natural resources, other; counseling psychology; economics; education, general; food sciences and technology; general teacher education; history; natural resources management and protective services; parks, recreation and leisure facilities management; teacher education, specific academic and vocational programs; tourism/travel marketing; wildlife and wildlands management.

UNIVERSITY OF WISCONSIN–SUPERIOR

Superior, Wisconsin
http://dlc.uwsuper.edu/

University of Wisconsin–Superior was founded in 1893. It is accredited by North Central Association of Colleges and Schools. It first offered distance learning courses in 1978. In fall 2003, there were 256 students enrolled in distance learning courses. Institutionally administered financial aid is available to distance learners.

Services Distance learners have accessibility to academic advising, bookstore, campus computer network, career placement assistance, e-mail services, library services, tutoring.

Contact Barbara Doherty, Student Resources, University of Wisconsin–Superior, Distance Learning Center, PO Box 2000, Belknap and Catlin, Superior, WI 54880. *Telephone:* 715-394-8494. *Fax:* 715-394-8139. *E-mail:* bdoherty@uwsuper.edu.

DEGREES AND AWARDS

BS Individualized Major

COURSE SUBJECT AREAS OFFERED OUTSIDE OF DEGREE PROGRAMS

Undergraduate—accounting; area, ethnic and cultural studies, other; biology, general; business administration and management; communications, general; education, general; English language and literature, general; fine arts and art studies; mathematics and computer science; physical sciences, general; social sciences, general.
Graduate—education administration and supervision; education, general.

UNIVERSITY OF WYOMING

Laramie, Wyoming
Outreach School
http://outreach.uwyo.edu/occ

University of Wyoming was founded in 1886. It is accredited by North Central Association of Colleges and Schools. In fall 2003, there were 3,000 students enrolled in distance learning courses. Institutionally administered financial aid is available to distance learners.

Services Distance learners have accessibility to academic advising, bookstore, campus computer network, career placement assistance, e-mail services, library services, tutoring.

Contact Ms. Judith E. Atencio, Program Manager, Outreach Credit Programs, University of Wyoming, Department 3274, 1000 East University Avenue, Laramie, WY 82071. *Telephone:* 800-448-7801. *Fax:* 307-766-3445. *E-mail:* occ@uwyo.edu.

DEGREES AND AWARDS

BA Criminal Justice; Social Sciences

University of Wyoming (continued)

BS Business Administration; Family and Consumer Sciences (Professional Child Development Option); Psychology; Social Sciences
BSN Nursing–RN to BSN
Certificate Family and Consumer Sciences (Early Childhood Program Director's Certificate); Land Surveying
Certification Real Estate
MA Education–Adult and Post-Secondary Education; Education–Special Education; Education–Teaching and Learning
MBA Business Administration
MPA Public Administration
MS Education–Instructional Technology; Kinesiology and Health; Nursing–Nurse Educator Option; Speech-Language Pathology
MSW Social Work

COURSE SUBJECT AREAS OFFERED OUTSIDE OF DEGREE PROGRAMS

Undergraduate—African-American studies; agriculture/agricultural sciences; American literature (United States); astronomy; biological sciences/life sciences, other; botany; business; chemistry; communications, general; criminal justice and corrections; cultural studies; education, general; English composition; English literature (British and Commonwealth); family/consumer resource management; foods and nutrition studies; geography; history; labor/personnel relations; liberal arts and sciences, general studies and humanities; mathematical statistics; mathematics; music; nursing; physics; real estate; social psychology; women's studies.
Graduate—business administration and management; educational/instructional media design; educational psychology; education, general; health professions and related sciences, other; labor/personnel relations; nursing; public administration; social work.

See full description on page 650.

UPPER IOWA UNIVERSITY

Fayette, Iowa
External Degree
http://www.uiu.edu

Upper Iowa University was founded in 1857. It is accredited by North Central Association of Colleges and Schools. It first offered distance learning courses in 1973. In fall 2003, there were 1,250 students enrolled in distance learning courses. Institutionally administered financial aid is available to distance learners.

Services Distance learners have accessibility to academic advising, bookstore, career placement assistance, library services.
Contact Barbara J. Schultz, Director of External Degree, Upper Iowa University, PO Box 1861, Fayette, IA 52142. *Telephone:* 888-877-3742. *Fax:* 563-425-5353. *E-mail:* extdegree@uiu.edu.

DEGREES AND AWARDS

AA Business; Liberal Arts
BS Accounting; Business Administration; Criminal Justice; Human Resources Management; Human Services; Management; Marketing; Psychology; Public Administration (General); Public Administration (Law Enforcement/Fire Science); Social Sciences; Technology and Information Management
Certificate Human Resources Management; Marketing; Organizational Communications; Organizational Leadership

COURSE SUBJECT AREAS OFFERED OUTSIDE OF DEGREE PROGRAMS

Undergraduate—accounting; advertising; American history; astronomy; biology; business administration and management; business marketing and marketing management; communications, general; criminal justice and corrections; English composition; history; human resources management; human services; industrial and organizational psychology; international business; labor/personnel relations; law and legal studies related; liberal arts and sciences, general studies and humanities; management information systems/business data processing; marketing management and research; mathematical statistics; mathematics; organizational psychology; philosophy and religion; political science and government; psychology; psychology, other; public administration; public administration and services, other; social psychology; sociology.
Non-credit—accounting; American history; biology; business marketing and marketing management; communications, general; English composition; international business; labor/personnel relations; law and legal studies related; management information systems/business data processing; mathematical statistics; organizational psychology; political science and government; psychology; public administration; sociology.

See full description on page 652.

UTAH STATE UNIVERSITY

Logan, Utah
Independent and Time Enhanced Learning
http://extension.usu.edu

Utah State University was founded in 1888. It is accredited by Northwest Commission on Colleges and Universities. It first offered distance learning courses in 1983. Institutionally administered financial aid is available to distance learners.

Services Distance learners have accessibility to academic advising, bookstore, campus computer network, e-mail services, library services.
Contact Independent and Time Enhanced Learning, Utah State University, 3080 Old Main Hill, Logan, UT 84322-3080. *Telephone:* 800-233-2137. *Fax:* 435-797-1399. *E-mail:* enroll@ext.usu.edu.

DEGREES AND AWARDS

AS General Studies
BS Business Administration; Business Information Systems; Computer Science; Psychology; Special Education
MEd Elementary or Secondary Education; Instructional Technology–Educational Technology Emphasis; Special Education
MS Business Information Systems; Computer Science; English/Technical Writing Specialization Online; FCSEE or AST Specialization; Family and Human Development–Master of Family and Human Development; Human Resource Management; Psychology–School Counseling Specialization; Special Education
MSS Public Administration Specialization
EdD Education

COURSE SUBJECT AREAS OFFERED OUTSIDE OF DEGREE PROGRAMS

Undergraduate—accounting; agriculture/agricultural sciences; anthropology; biology, general; business administration and management; business information and data processing services; chemistry; com-

puter science; economics; education administration and supervision; education, general; English literature (British and Commonwealth); English technical and business writing; family/consumer resource management; foods and nutrition studies; geography; history; human resources management.
Graduate—agriculture/agricultural sciences, other; computer science; curriculum and instruction; economics; education administration and supervision; educational psychology; education, general; general teacher education; health and physical education/fitness; human resources management; political science and government; public administration; school psychology; special education.

See full description on page 654.

UTAH VALLEY STATE COLLEGE

Orem, Utah
School of Continuing Education–Center for Distance Learning
http://www.uvsc.edu/disted

Utah Valley State College was founded in 1941. It is accredited by Northwest Commission on Colleges and Universities. It first offered distance learning courses in 1988. In fall 2003, there were 9,000 students enrolled in distance learning courses. Institutionally administered financial aid is available to distance learners.

Services Distance learners have accessibility to academic advising, bookstore, campus computer network, career placement assistance, e-mail services, library services, tutoring.
Contact Karen Merrick, Support Center Coordinator, Utah Valley State College, 800 West University Parkway, MS 149, Orem, UT 84058. *Telephone:* 801-863-HELP. *Fax:* 801-863-7298. *E-mail:* dehelp@uvsc.edu.

DEGREES AND AWARDS

AS Criminal Justice; General Studies
BS Aviation Science

COURSE SUBJECT AREAS OFFERED OUTSIDE OF DEGREE PROGRAMS

Undergraduate—accounting; advertising; American literature (United States); astronomy; biological and physical sciences; biology; business administration and management; communications, general; computer and information sciences, general; electrical and electronics equipment installers and repairers; English composition; English language and literature, general; fire protection; history; legal studies; philosophy; psychology; social sciences, general; sociology.
Non-credit—computer and information sciences, general; computer software and media applications.

UTAH VALLEY STATE COLLEGE

Orem, Utah
Global Aviation Degree Center
http://www.aviationuniversity.com

Utah Valley State College was founded in 1941. It is accredited by Northwest Commission on Colleges and Universities. It first offered distance learning courses in 2000. In fall 2003, there were 1,200 students enrolled in distance learning courses. Institutionally administered financial aid is available to distance learners.

Services Distance learners have accessibility to academic advising, e-mail services.
Contact Claire Downing, Coordinator of Global Aviation, Utah Valley State College, 800 West University Parkway, Orem, UT 84058-5999. *Telephone:* 888-901-7192 Ext. 7816. *Fax:* 801-764-7815. *E-mail:* downincl@uvsc.edu.

DEGREES AND AWARDS

AAS Aviation Job Ready Degree
AS Aviation (Baccalaureate Degree Transfer)
BS Aviation Professional Pilot

COURSE SUBJECT AREAS OFFERED OUTSIDE OF DEGREE PROGRAMS

Undergraduate—aerospace, aeronautical and astronautical engineering; biology, general; English composition; English language and literature/letters, other; fine arts and art studies; health and physical education/fitness; history; mathematics; philosophy; physical sciences, general; social sciences and history, other; social sciences, general.
Graduate—aerospace, aeronautical and astronautical engineering.

VALLEY CITY STATE UNIVERSITY

Valley City, North Dakota
North Dakota Interactive Video Network
http://distancelearning.vcsu.edu

Valley City State University was founded in 1890. It is accredited by North Central Association of Colleges and Schools. It first offered distance learning courses in 2000. In fall 2003, there were 75 students enrolled in distance learning courses. Institutionally administered financial aid is available to distance learners.

Services Distance learners have accessibility to academic advising, campus computer network, e-mail services.
Contact Monte Johnson, Registrar, Valley City State University, 101 College Street, SW, Valley City, ND 58072. *Telephone:* 701-845-7295 Ext. 7297. *Fax:* 701-845-7299. *E-mail:* monte.johnson@vcsu.edu.

DEGREES AND AWARDS

Programs offered do not lead to a degree or other formal award.

COURSE SUBJECT AREAS OFFERED OUTSIDE OF DEGREE PROGRAMS

Undergraduate—communications, other; English composition; library science/librarianship; mathematics; sociology; technology education/industrial arts.

VALPARAISO UNIVERSITY

Valparaiso, Indiana
http://www.valpo.edu/

Valparaiso University was founded in 1859. It is accredited by North Central Association of Colleges and Schools. It first offered distance learning courses in 2002. In fall 2003, there were 1,000 students enrolled in distance learning courses.

Services Distance learners have accessibility to bookstore, campus computer network, library services.

Valparaiso University (continued)

Contact Janice Pedersen, Coordinator of Academic and Student Services, Valparaiso University, Kretzmann Hall #116, 1700 Chapel Drive, Valparaiso, IN 46383. *Telephone:* 800-821-7685. *Fax:* 219-464-5381. *E-mail:* graduate.studies@valpo.edu.

DEGREES AND AWARDS

Programs offered do not lead to a degree or other formal award.

COURSE SUBJECT AREAS OFFERED OUTSIDE OF DEGREE PROGRAMS

Undergraduate—business administration and management; communications, general; computer science; dramatic/theater arts and stagecraft; economics; education, general; financial management and services; mathematics, other; nursing; psychology; sociology; theological studies and religious vocations, other.

Graduate—business administration and management; communications, general; psychology; sociology; theological studies and religious vocations, other.

VANCE-GRANVILLE COMMUNITY COLLEGE

Henderson, North Carolina

http://www.vgcc.edu

Vance-Granville Community College was founded in 1969. It is accredited by Southern Association of Colleges and Schools. It first offered distance learning courses in 1998. In fall 2003, there were 575 students enrolled in distance learning courses. Institutionally administered financial aid is available to distance learners.

Services Distance learners have accessibility to academic advising, bookstore, library services.

Contact Jennifer Meeks, Coordinator of Distance Education, Vance-Granville Community College, PO Box 917, Henderson, NC 27536. *Telephone:* 252-492-2061. *Fax:* 252-738-3372. *E-mail:* meeks@vgcc.edu.

DEGREES AND AWARDS

Programs offered do not lead to a degree or other formal award.

COURSE SUBJECT AREAS OFFERED OUTSIDE OF DEGREE PROGRAMS

Undergraduate—accounting; administrative and secretarial services; American history; American literature (United States); biology; business administration and management; business marketing and marketing management; child care and guidance workers and managers; computer/information technology administration and management; computer programming; computer systems networking and telecommunications; criminal justice and corrections; criminology; economics; English composition; European history; history; human services; information sciences and systems; liberal arts and sciences, general studies and humanities; mathematical statistics; political science and government; psychology; sociology; teacher assistant/aide.

Non-credit—accounting; business; business and personal services marketing operations; business communications; computer and information sciences, general; computer programming; computer software and media applications; computer systems networking and telecommunications; construction management; data entry/microcomputer applications; English technical and business writing; entrepreneurship; Internet and World Wide Web; personal and miscellaneous services, other.

VANGUARD UNIVERSITY OF SOUTHERN CALIFORNIA

Costa Mesa, California

http://www.vanguard.edu/eec

Vanguard University of Southern California was founded in 1920. It is accredited by Western Association of Schools and Colleges. It first offered distance learning courses in 2002. In fall 2003, there were 125 students enrolled in distance learning courses. Institutionally administered financial aid is available to distance learners.

Services Distance learners have accessibility to academic advising, bookstore, e-mail services, library services, tutoring.

Contact Ms. Bren Martin, Associate Director Early Education Certificates, Vanguard University of Southern California, 55 Fair Drive, Costa Mesa, CA 92626. *Telephone:* 714-668-6196 Ext. 472. *Fax:* 714-966-5460. *E-mail:* eecadmissions@vanguard.edu.

DEGREES AND AWARDS

Programs offered do not lead to a degree or other formal award.

COURSE SUBJECT AREAS OFFERED OUTSIDE OF DEGREE PROGRAMS

Undergraduate—education administration and supervision; education, other.

VILLANOVA UNIVERSITY

Villanova, Pennsylvania

Division of Part-time Studies/Summer Sessions

http://engineering.villanova.edu/distanceed/

Villanova University was founded in 1842. It is accredited by Middle States Association of Colleges and Schools. It first offered distance learning courses in 1997. In fall 2003, there were 45 students enrolled in distance learning courses. Institutionally administered financial aid is available to distance learners.

Services Distance learners have accessibility to academic advising, bookstore, campus computer network, career placement assistance, e-mail services, library services.

Contact Mr. James R. Johnson, Director of Part-Time Studies, Villanova University, Villanova, PA 19008. *E-mail:* james.johnson@villanova.edu.

DEGREES AND AWARDS

Graduate Certificate Urban Water Resources Design
MCE Civil Engineering
MSWREE Water Resources and Environmental Engineering

COURSE SUBJECT AREAS OFFERED OUTSIDE OF DEGREE PROGRAMS

Undergraduate—engineering, other.

Graduate—electrical, electronics and communications engineering; mechanical engineering-related technologies.

Non-credit—engineering, general.

VIRGINIA COLLEGE AT BIRMINGHAM

Birmingham, Alabama

http://www.vc.edu

Virginia College at Birmingham was founded in 1989. It is accredited by Accrediting Council for Independent Colleges and Schools. It first offered distance learning courses in 2002. In fall 2003, there were 1,000 students enrolled in distance learning courses. Institutionally administered financial aid is available to distance learners.

Services Distance learners have accessibility to academic advising, bookstore, career placement assistance.

Contact Mr. Kevin Lingerfelt, Admissions, VC Online, Virginia College at Birmingham, 65 Bagby Drive, Birmingham, AL 35209. *Telephone:* 205-802-1200 Ext. 2553. *Fax:* 205-271-8276. *E-mail:* klingerfelt@vc.edu.

DEGREES AND AWARDS

BA Business Management; Business Studies, general
BS Criminal Justice; Management Information Systems
MBA Business Administration
MS Homeland Security

VIRGINIA POLYTECHNIC INSTITUTE AND STATE UNIVERSITY

Blacksburg, Virginia

Institute for Distance and Distributed Learning

http://iddl.vt.edu

Virginia Polytechnic Institute and State University was founded in 1872. It is accredited by Southern Association of Colleges and Schools. It first offered distance learning courses in 1983. In fall 2003, there were 4,322 students enrolled in distance learning courses. Institutionally administered financial aid is available to distance learners.

Services Distance learners have accessibility to academic advising, bookstore, campus computer network, career placement assistance, e-mail services, library services, tutoring.

Contact Ms. Angie Starr, Online Enrollment Specialist, Virginia Polytechnic Institute and State University, Institute for Distance and Distributed Learning, Blacksburg, VA 24061. *Telephone:* 540-231-1264. *Fax:* 540-231-5922. *E-mail:* vto@vt.edu.

DEGREES AND AWARDS

License Career and Technical Education
Graduate Certificate Computer Engineering; IT Business Information Systems; IT Communication; IT Decision Support Systems; IT Networking; Natural Resources; Software Development
MA Instructional Technology–Curriculum and Instruction Emphasis
MBA Business Administration
MIT Information Technology
MS Career and Technical Education; Civil Infrastructure Engineering; Civil and Environmental Engineering; Computer Engineering; Curriculum and Instruction–Health Promotion Emphasis; Electrical and Computer Engineering; Engineering Administration; Ocean Engineering; Political Science; Systems Engineering

COURSE SUBJECT AREAS OFFERED OUTSIDE OF DEGREE PROGRAMS

Undergraduate—agricultural business and production, other; agriculture/agricultural sciences; civil engineering; clothing, apparel and textile workers and managers; communications, general; computer engineering; computer science; electrical and electronic engineering-related technology; engineering, general; English composition; fishing and fisheries sciences and management; foreign languages and literatures; general teacher education; geography; history; horticulture services operations and management; hospitality services management; human resources management; marketing management and research; mathematics; music; philosophy; physics; political science and government; religion/religious studies; science technologies, other; sociology; Spanish; teacher education, specific academic and vocational programs; women's studies.

Graduate—accounting; aerospace engineering; agriculture/agricultural sciences, other; business information and data processing services; computer engineering; computer science; curriculum and instruction; education administration and supervision; education, other; electrical engineering; English language and literature, general; forestry and related sciences; geography; horticulture services operations and management; management information systems/business data processing; marketing management and research; mathematics; mechanical engineering; natural resources management and protective services; political science and government; public administration; science technologies, other; teacher education, specific academic and vocational programs; urban affairs/studies; veterinary clinical sciences (M.S., Ph.D.); veterinary medicine (DVM); women's studies.

Non-credit—architecture; business; computer software and media applications; education, general; engineering, general; engineering-related technologies, other; history; horticulture services operations and management; music; natural resources conservation; public health.

See full description on page 656.

WAKE TECHNICAL COMMUNITY COLLEGE

Raleigh, North Carolina

http://www.waketech.edu

Wake Technical Community College was founded in 1958. It is accredited by Southern Association of Colleges and Schools. It first offered distance learning courses in 1986. In fall 2003, there were 1,505 students enrolled in distance learning courses. Institutionally administered financial aid is available to distance learners.

Services Distance learners have accessibility to academic advising, bookstore, career placement assistance, library services, tutoring.

Contact Diana Osborne, Department Head, Distance Education Support, Wake Technical Community College, 9101 Fayetteville Road, Raleigh, NC 27603-5696. *Telephone:* 919-773-4741. *Fax:* 919-779-3360. *E-mail:* dgosborn@waketech.edu.

DEGREES AND AWARDS

Programs offered do not lead to a degree or other formal award.

COURSE SUBJECT AREAS OFFERED OUTSIDE OF DEGREE PROGRAMS

Undergraduate—administrative and secretarial services; biological and physical sciences; business/managerial economics; child care and guidance workers and managers; computer and information sciences,

Wake Technical Community College (continued)

other; engineering-related technologies, other; English language and literature, general; Internet and World Wide Web; social sciences and history, other.

Non-credit—accounting; business administration and management; child care and guidance workers and managers; computer software and media applications; English creative writing; enterprise management and operation; financial management and services; foreign languages and literatures; Internet and World Wide Web; legal studies; teacher education, specific academic and vocational programs.

WALDEN UNIVERSITY

Minneapolis, Minnesota

http://www.waldenu.edu/

Walden University was founded in 1970. It is accredited by North Central Association of Colleges and Schools. It first offered distance learning courses in 1970. In fall 2003, there were 8,400 students enrolled in distance learning courses. Institutionally administered financial aid is available to distance learners.

Services Distance learners have accessibility to academic advising, bookstore, campus computer network, career placement assistance, e-mail services, library services.

Contact Enrollment Advisor, Walden University, 1001 Fleet Street, Baltimore, MD 21202. *Telephone:* 866-492-5336. *E-mail:* info@waldenu.edu.

DEGREES AND AWARDS

BS Information Systems–Information Technology; Information Systems, general

BSBA Finance; Human Resource Management; Management; Marketing

MBA Business Administration, general; CPCU Accelerated Program; E-Business; Finance; Global Business; Health Services; Human Resource Management; Knowledge and Learning Management; Management of Technology; Marketing; Nonprofit Management; Risk Management/Insurance

MPA E-Government; Health Services; Knowledge Management; Nonprofit Management and Leadership; Public Management and Leadership; Public Policy

MPH Community Health

MS Education–Curriculum, Instruction, and Assessment; Education–Educational Leadership; Education–Elementary Reading and Literacy; Education–Integrating Technology in the Classroom; Education–Literacy and Learning in the Content Areas; Education–Mathematics; Education–Middle Level Education; Education–Science; Nursing Administration; Psychology–Industrial/Organizational Psychology; Psychology, general; Public Health–Community Health

EdD Teacher Leadership

PhD Applied Management and Decision Sciences–Engineering Management; Applied Management and Decision Sciences–Finance; Applied Management and Decision Sciences–Information Systems Management; Applied Management and Decision Sciences–Knowledge Management; Applied Management and Decision Sciences–Leadership and Organizational Change; Applied Management and Decision Sciences–Learning Management; Applied Management and Decision Sciences–Operations Research; Applied Management and Decision Sciences–Self-Designed; Applied Management and Decision Sciences, general; Education–Adult Education Leadership; Education–Community College Leadership; Education–Early Childhood Education; Education–Educational Technology; Education–Higher Education; Education–K-12 Educational Leadership; Education–Knowledge Management; Education–Learning Management; Education–Self-Designed; Education–Special Education; Education, general; Health Services–Community Health; Health Services–Health Management and Policy; Health Services–Health Promotion and Education; Health Services–Health and Human Behavior; Health Services, general; Human Services–Clinical Social Work; Human Services–Counseling; Human Services–Criminal Justice; Human Services–Family Studies and Intervention Strategies; Human Services–Human Services Administration; Human Services–Self-Designed; Human Services–Social Policy Analysis and Planning; Human Services, general; Psychology–Academic Psychology; Psychology–Clinical Psychology (Licensure); Psychology–Counseling (Licensure); Psychology–Health Psychology; Psychology–Organizational Psychology; Psychology–School Psychology (Licensure); Public Health–Community Health; Public Policy and Administration–E-Government; Public Policy and Administration–Health Services; Public Policy and Administration–Knowledge Management; Public Policy and Administration–Nonprofit Management and Leadership; Public Policy and Administration–Public Management and Leadership; Public Policy and Administration–Public Policy

COURSE SUBJECT AREAS OFFERED OUTSIDE OF DEGREE PROGRAMS

Graduate—psychology.

See full description on page 658.

WALSH COLLEGE OF ACCOUNTANCY AND BUSINESS ADMINISTRATION

Troy, Michigan

http://www.walshcollege.edu/

Walsh College of Accountancy and Business Administration was founded in 1922. It is accredited by North Central Association of Colleges and Schools. It first offered distance learning courses in 1998. In fall 2003, there were 1,100 students enrolled in distance learning courses. Institutionally administered financial aid is available to distance learners.

Services Distance learners have accessibility to academic advising, bookstore, campus computer network, career placement assistance, e-mail services, library services, tutoring.

Contact Ms. A'lynne Robinson, Director of Admissions and Advising, Walsh College of Accountancy and Business Administration, PO Box 7006, 3838 Livernois, Troy, MI 48007-7006. *Telephone:* 248-823-1235. *Fax:* 248-689-0938. *E-mail:* arobinso@walshcollege.edu.

DEGREES AND AWARDS

BBA Business Administration

Certificate Interactive Marketing

MBA Business

MSM Management

COURSE SUBJECT AREAS OFFERED OUTSIDE OF DEGREE PROGRAMS

Undergraduate—accounting; business marketing and marketing management; information sciences and systems.

Graduate—accounting; business administration and management; business information and data processing services; business marketing

and marketing management; business quantitative methods and management science; computer and information sciences, general; marketing operations/marketing and distribution, other.
Non-credit—business administration and management; business marketing and marketing management.

WALTERS STATE COMMUNITY COLLEGE

Morristown, Tennessee
Evening and Distance Education Office
http://www.ws.edu

Walters State Community College was founded in 1970. It is accredited by Southern Association of Colleges and Schools. It first offered distance learning courses in 1998. In fall 2003, there were 1,500 students enrolled in distance learning courses. Institutionally administered financial aid is available to distance learners.

Services Distance learners have accessibility to academic advising, bookstore, campus computer network, career placement assistance, e-mail services, library services.
Contact Dr. David Roberts, Dean, Walters State Community College, 500 South Davy Crockett Parkway, Morristown, TN 37813-6899. *Telephone:* 423-585-6938. *Fax:* 423-585-6853. *E-mail:* dave.roberts@ws.edu.

DEGREES AND AWARDS

Programs offered do not lead to a degree or other formal award.

COURSE SUBJECT AREAS OFFERED OUTSIDE OF DEGREE PROGRAMS

Undergraduate—agriculture/agricultural sciences, other; American literature (United States); biology, general; business; business marketing and marketing management; chemistry; computer science; creative writing; criminal justice and corrections; culinary arts and related services; English composition; English language and literature/letters, other; health and physical education/fitness; history; human resources management; mathematics; music; nursing; physical therapy; psychology; real estate; sociology; Spanish.

WASHINGTON STATE UNIVERSITY

Pullman, Washington
Distance Degree Programs
http://www.distance.wsu.edu

Washington State University was founded in 1890. It is accredited by Northwest Commission on Colleges and Universities. It first offered distance learning courses in 1991. In fall 2003, there were 2,700 students enrolled in distance learning courses. Institutionally administered financial aid is available to distance learners.

Services Distance learners have accessibility to academic advising, bookstore, campus computer network, career placement assistance, e-mail services, library services, tutoring.
Contact Student Services, Washington State University, 104 Van Doren Hall, PO Box 645220, Pullman, WA 99164-5220. *Telephone:* 800-222-4978. *Fax:* 509-335-4850. *E-mail:* distance@wsu.edu.

DEGREES AND AWARDS

BA Business Administration; Human Development; Humanities; Social Sciences
BSN Nursing–RN to BS
Certificate Professional Writing
MS Agriculture

COURSE SUBJECT AREAS OFFERED OUTSIDE OF DEGREE PROGRAMS

Undergraduate—accounting; agriculture/agricultural sciences; American history; American studies; anthropology; Asian studies; biology; business administration and management; business marketing and marketing management; creative writing; developmental/child psychology; English composition; European history; finance; history; international business; investments and securities; law and legal studies related; mathematics; philosophy; political science and government; psychology; real estate; social psychology; sociology; soil sciences; Spanish; women's studies; zoology.
Graduate—agricultural and food products processing; agricultural business and management; agricultural business and production, other; agricultural engineering; agricultural supplies and related services; agriculture/agricultural sciences.

See full description on page 660.

WASHTENAW COMMUNITY COLLEGE

Ann Arbor, Michigan
Office of Distance Learning
http://www.wccnet.edu

Washtenaw Community College was founded in 1965. It is accredited by North Central Association of Colleges and Schools. It first offered distance learning courses in 1982. In fall 2003, there were 1,100 students enrolled in distance learning courses. Institutionally administered financial aid is available to distance learners.

Services Distance learners have accessibility to academic advising, bookstore, campus computer network, e-mail services, library services, tutoring.
Contact Mrs. Irene Brock, Distance Learning Technical Assistant, Washtenaw Community College, 4800 East Huron River Drive, Ann Arbor, MI 48106. *Telephone:* 734-477-8713. *Fax:* 734-677-2220. *E-mail:* ibrock@wccnet.edu.

DEGREES AND AWARDS

Programs offered do not lead to a degree or other formal award.

COURSE SUBJECT AREAS OFFERED OUTSIDE OF DEGREE PROGRAMS

Undergraduate—administrative and secretarial services; business administration and management; communications, general; computer and information sciences, general; computer programming; construction management; dental services; English composition; health professions and related sciences, other; Internet and World Wide Web; law and legal studies related; nursing; psychology; sociology.

WAUBONSEE COMMUNITY COLLEGE

Sugar Grove, Illinois
Center for Distance Learning
http://www.waubonsee.edu/

Waubonsee Community College was founded in 1966. It is accredited by North Central Association of Colleges and Schools. It first offered distance learning courses in 1988. In fall 2003, there were 2,200 students enrolled in distance learning courses. Institutionally administered financial aid is available to distance learners.

Services Distance learners have accessibility to academic advising, bookstore, career placement assistance, e-mail services, library services, tutoring.

Contact Ms. Andrea Mary Ahlsen, Manager of Distance Learning, Waubonsee Community College, Route 47 at Waubonsee Drive, COL226, Sugar Grove, IL 60554-9799. *Telephone:* 630-466-7900 Ext. 5758. *Fax:* 630-466-9691. *E-mail:* aahlsen@waubonsee.edu.

DEGREES AND AWARDS

AA General Program
AGS General Studies
AS General Program
Certificate of Achievement Beginning Web Page; General Studies
Certificate of Completion Travel and Tourism
Certificate Midmanagement

COURSE SUBJECT AREAS OFFERED OUTSIDE OF DEGREE PROGRAMS

Undergraduate—accounting; American literature (United States); biology; business administration and management; business information and data processing services; communications, general; computer and information sciences, general; computer programming; creative writing; criminal justice and corrections; criminology; developmental/child psychology; economics; English as a second language; English composition; health and physical education/fitness; history; human resources management; human services; legal studies; liberal arts and sciences, general studies and humanities; mathematical statistics; mathematics; nursing; physical sciences, general; psychology; sign language interpretation; social psychology; social work; sociology; speech and rhetorical studies.

WAYCROSS COLLEGE

Waycross, Georgia
http://www.waycross.edu

Waycross College was founded in 1976. It is accredited by Southern Association of Colleges and Schools. It first offered distance learning courses in 2001. In fall 2003, there were 30 students enrolled in distance learning courses. Institutionally administered financial aid is available to distance learners.

Services Distance learners have accessibility to academic advising, bookstore, campus computer network, career placement assistance, e-mail services, library services, tutoring.

Contact Dr. Tonya Strickland, Associate Professor, Waycross College, 2001 South Georgia Parkway, Waycross, GA 31503. *E-mail:* tstrick@waycross.edu.

DEGREES AND AWARDS

Programs offered do not lead to a degree or other formal award.

COURSE SUBJECT AREAS OFFERED OUTSIDE OF DEGREE PROGRAMS

Undergraduate—criminal justice and corrections; English language and literature, general; general teacher education; mathematics.

WAYLAND BAPTIST UNIVERSITY

Plainview, Texas
http://www.wbu.edu/

Wayland Baptist University was founded in 1908. It is accredited by Southern Association of Colleges and Schools. It first offered distance learning courses in 1998. In fall 2003, there were 684 students enrolled in distance learning courses. Institutionally administered financial aid is available to distance learners.

Services Distance learners have accessibility to library services.

Contact Mr. Stan DeMerritt, Registrar, Wayland Baptist University, 1900 West 7th Street, CMB 735, Plainview, TX 79072. *Telephone:* 806-291-3470. *Fax:* 806-291-1960. *E-mail:* registrar@wbu.edu.

DEGREES AND AWARDS

Programs offered do not lead to a degree or other formal award.

COURSE SUBJECT AREAS OFFERED OUTSIDE OF DEGREE PROGRAMS

Undergraduate—accounting; business administration and management; economics; education, other; history; management information systems/business data processing; music; religious education.

Graduate—accounting; business administration and management; economics; management information systems/business data processing; religious education.

WAYNESBURG COLLEGE

Waynesburg, Pennsylvania
http://www.waynesburg.edu/

Waynesburg College was founded in 1849. It is accredited by Middle States Association of Colleges and Schools. It first offered distance learning courses in 1998. Institutionally administered financial aid is available to distance learners.

Services Distance learners have accessibility to e-mail services, library services.

Contact Richard Noftzger, Vice President for Institutional Planning, Research and Educational Services, Waynesburg College, 51 West College Street, Waynesburg, PA 15370. *Telephone:* 724-852-3271. *Fax:* 724-627-6416. *E-mail:* noftzger@waynesburg.edu.

DEGREES AND AWARDS

Programs offered do not lead to a degree or other formal award.

COURSE SUBJECT AREAS OFFERED OUTSIDE OF DEGREE PROGRAMS

Undergraduate—social sciences and history, other.

Graduate—business administration and management.

WAYNE STATE COLLEGE

Wayne, Nebraska
Regional Education and Distance Learning
http://www.wsc.edu

Wayne State College was founded in 1910. It is accredited by North Central Association of Colleges and Schools. It first offered distance learning courses in 1997. In fall 2003, there were 400 students enrolled in distance learning courses. Institutionally administered financial aid is available to distance learners.

Services Distance learners have accessibility to academic advising, bookstore, campus computer network, career placement assistance, e-mail services, library services.

Contact Mr. Roger Feuerbacher, Director of Continuing Education, Wayne State College, 1111 Main Street, Wayne, NE 68787. *Telephone:* 402-375-7217. *Fax:* 402-375-7204. *E-mail:* rofeuer1@wsc.edu.

DEGREES AND AWARDS

Programs offered do not lead to a degree or other formal award.

COURSE SUBJECT AREAS OFFERED OUTSIDE OF DEGREE PROGRAMS

Undergraduate—accounting; business; business administration and management; child care and guidance workers and managers; computer and information sciences, general; economics; education, general; education, other; foreign languages and literatures; health and physical education/fitness; human resources management; industrial/manufacturing engineering; Internet and World Wide Web; multi/interdisciplinary studies, other; philosophy; physical sciences, general; physics; special education; teacher education, specific academic and vocational programs.

Graduate—accounting; business administration and management; computer and information sciences, general; counseling psychology; economics; education administration and supervision; educational evaluation, research and statistics; educational/instructional media design; education, general; education, other; human resources management; industrial/manufacturing engineering; Internet and World Wide Web; mathematics; multi/interdisciplinary studies, other; special education; teacher education, specific academic and vocational programs.

WEBER STATE UNIVERSITY

Ogden, Utah
Distance Learning and Independent Study
http://departments.weber.edu/ce/dl

Weber State University was founded in 1889. It is accredited by Northwest Commission on Colleges and Universities. It first offered distance learning courses in 1990. In fall 2003, there were 7,000 students enrolled in distance learning courses. Institutionally administered financial aid is available to distance learners.

Services Distance learners have accessibility to academic advising, bookstore, campus computer network, career placement assistance, e-mail services, library services, tutoring.

Contact Susan Smith, Office of Distance Learning, Weber State University, 4005 University Circle, Ogden, UT 84408-4005. *Telephone:* 801-626-6600. *Fax:* 801-626-8035. *E-mail:* dist-learn@weber.edu.

DEGREES AND AWARDS

AAS Clinical Laboratory Technician; Respiratory Therapy
AS Criminal Justice; General Studies; Respiratory Therapy
BS Advanced Respiratory Therapy; Clinical Laboratory Sciences; Health Administrative Services; Health Promotion; Radiological Sciences
Certificate Health Care Coding and Classification; Radiological Sciences

COURSE SUBJECT AREAS OFFERED OUTSIDE OF DEGREE PROGRAMS

Undergraduate—accounting; anthropology; business administration and management; chemistry; communications, general; computer and information sciences, general; construction management; English composition; English language and literature, general; English technical and business writing; family and community studies; foreign languages and literatures; geography; geological and related sciences; gerontology; health and medical administrative services; history; mathematics; microbiology/bacteriology; music; philosophy; physics; political science and government; psychology; zoology.

See full description on page 662.

WEBSTER UNIVERSITY

St. Louis, Missouri
Academic Distance Learning Center
http://www.webster.edu/worldclassroom

Webster University was founded in 1915. It is accredited by North Central Association of Colleges and Schools. It first offered distance learning courses in 1998. In fall 2003, there were 850 students enrolled in distance learning courses. Institutionally administered financial aid is available to distance learners.

Services Distance learners have accessibility to academic advising, bookstore, career placement assistance, e-mail services, library services, tutoring.

Contact Matt Nolan, Director, Graduate and Evening Student Admissions, Webster University, 470 East Lockwood Avenue, St. Louis, MO 63119. *Telephone:* 314-968-7089. *Fax:* 314-968-7462. *E-mail:* nolan@webster.edu.

DEGREES AND AWARDS

Certificate Web Site Development
Graduate Certificate Decision Support Systems
MA Business and Organizational Security Management; Media Communication, Communication Management Emphasis; Procurement and Acquisitions Management
MAT Educational Technology and Multidisciplinary Studies
MBA Business Administration

COURSE SUBJECT AREAS OFFERED OUTSIDE OF DEGREE PROGRAMS

Undergraduate—liberal arts and sciences, general studies and humanities; philosophy.

WESTCHESTER COMMUNITY COLLEGE

Valhalla, New York
http://www.sunywcc.edu/

Westchester Community College was founded in 1946. It is accredited by Middle States Association of Colleges and Schools. It first

Westchester Community College (continued)

offered distance learning courses in 1997. In fall 2003, there were 550 students enrolled in distance learning courses. Institutionally administered financial aid is available to distance learners.

Services Distance learners have accessibility to academic advising, bookstore, library services.

Contact Carol Klein, Acting Distance Learning Coordinator, Westchester Community College, 75 Grasslands Road, Valhalla, NY 10595. *Telephone:* 914-785-6827. *Fax:* 914-785-8550. *E-mail:* carol.klein@sunywcc.edu.

DEGREES AND AWARDS

Programs offered do not lead to a degree or other formal award.

COURSE SUBJECT AREAS OFFERED OUTSIDE OF DEGREE PROGRAMS

Undergraduate—accounting; anthropology; apparel and accessories marketing operations; biological and physical sciences; biology, general; business; business information and data processing services; communications, general; computer and information sciences, general; computer programming; computer science; computer systems networking and telecommunications; data processing technology; economics; English as a second language; English composition; English language and literature, general; English technical and business writing; geography; health and physical education/fitness; history; mathematics; mathematics and computer science; philosophy; psychology; sociology.

WEST CHESTER UNIVERSITY OF PENNSYLVANIA

West Chester, Pennsylvania
The Virtual University
http://wcupa.edu

West Chester University of Pennsylvania was founded in 1871. It is accredited by Middle States Association of Colleges and Schools. It first offered distance learning courses in 1996. In fall 2003, there were 103 students enrolled in distance learning courses. Institutionally administered financial aid is available to distance learners.

Services Distance learners have accessibility to bookstore, career placement assistance, e-mail services.

Contact Mr. Adele Barimani, Executive Director, Academic Computing, West Chester University of Pennsylvania, West Chester, PA 19383. *Telephone:* 610-436-3476. *Fax:* 610-436-3240. *E-mail:* abarimani@wcupa.edu.

DEGREES AND AWARDS

Programs offered do not lead to a degree or other formal award.

WESTERN BAPTIST COLLEGE

Salem, Oregon
Management and Communication Online Program/ Family Studies Online Program
http://www.wbc.edu

Western Baptist College was founded in 1935. It first offered distance learning courses in 1994. In fall 2003, there were 130 students enrolled in distance learning courses. Institutionally administered financial aid is available to distance learners.

Services Distance learners have accessibility to academic advising, bookstore, campus computer network, e-mail services, library services, tutoring.

Contact Ms. Nancy L. Martyn, Director of Adult Studies, Western Baptist College, Adult Studies, 5000 Deer Park Drive, SE, Salem, OR 97301. *Telephone:* 503-375-7590. *Fax:* 503-375-7583. *E-mail:* nmartyn@wbc.edu.

DEGREES AND AWARDS

BS Business, Management and Communication; Psychology/Family Studies

COURSE SUBJECT AREAS OFFERED OUTSIDE OF DEGREE PROGRAMS

Undergraduate—bible/biblical studies; business administration and management; counseling psychology; individual and family development studies; physical sciences, general; psychology, other; religion/religious studies.

See full description on page 664.

WESTERN CAROLINA UNIVERSITY

Cullowhee, North Carolina
Continuing Education and Summer School
http://edoutreach.wcu.edu

Western Carolina University was founded in 1889. It is accredited by Southern Association of Colleges and Schools. It first offered distance learning courses in 1997. In fall 2003, there were 750 students enrolled in distance learning courses. Institutionally administered financial aid is available to distance learners.

Services Distance learners have accessibility to academic advising, bookstore, career placement assistance, e-mail services, library services.

Contact Bronwen Sheffield, Director of Off-Campus Services, Western Carolina University, 138 Outreach Center, Cullowhee, NC 28723. *Telephone:* 828-227-3074. *Fax:* 828-227-7115. *E-mail:* bsheffie@email.wcu.edu.

DEGREES AND AWARDS

BBA Entrepreneurship
BEd Birth-Kindergarten; Elementary Education
BS Criminal Justice
MPM Project Management

COURSE SUBJECT AREAS OFFERED OUTSIDE OF DEGREE PROGRAMS

Undergraduate—communication disorders sciences and services; gerontology; human resources management; special education.
Graduate—communication disorders sciences and services; gerontology; human resources management.

WESTERN KENTUCKY UNIVERSITY

Bowling Green, Kentucky
Distance Learning
http://www.wku.edu/reachu

Western Kentucky University was founded in 1906. It is accredited by Southern Association of Colleges and Schools. It first offered distance learning courses in 1999. In fall 2003, there were 2,061 students enrolled in distance learning courses. Institutionally administered financial aid is available to distance learners.

Services Distance learners have accessibility to academic advising, bookstore, career placement assistance, e-mail services, library services.

Contact Ms. Beth Laves, Assistant Director of Distance Education, Western Kentucky University, Distance Education, 1 Big Red Way, Bowling Green, KY 42101. *Telephone:* 270-745-5308. *Fax:* 270-745-3623. *E-mail:* reachu@wku.edu.

DEGREES AND AWARDS

AAS Paramedicine Completion
AS Interdisciplinary Early Childhood Education
BA Psychology
Certificate Canadian Studies
Endorsement Gifted and Talented Graduate Teaching Endorsement
Graduate Certificate Women's Studies
MA English; Exceptional Education
MS Communication Disorders; Library Media Education

WESTERN MICHIGAN UNIVERSITY

Kalamazoo, Michigan
Department of Distance Education
http://dde.wmich.edu

Western Michigan University was founded in 1903. It is accredited by North Central Association of Colleges and Schools. It first offered distance learning courses in 1996. In fall 2003, there were 1,080 students enrolled in distance learning courses. Institutionally administered financial aid is available to distance learners.

Services Distance learners have accessibility to academic advising, bookstore, career placement assistance, e-mail services, library services.

Contact Rosemary Nichols, Office Manager, Western Michigan University, Ellsworth B-103, Kalamazoo, MI 49008-5161. *Telephone:* 269-387-4129. *Fax:* 269-387-4226. *E-mail:* rosemary.nicholas@wmich.edu.

DEGREES AND AWARDS

MAE Educational Technology

COURSE SUBJECT AREAS OFFERED OUTSIDE OF DEGREE PROGRAMS

Undergraduate—African-American studies; air transportation workers; anthropology; apparel and accessories marketing operations; clothing/apparel and textile studies; computer software and media applications; economics; educational/instructional media design; engineering/industrial management; English composition; family/consumer resource management; geography; occupational therapy; social work; sociology.

Graduate—computer engineering; computer science; counseling psychology; developmental and child psychology; economics; educational/instructional media design; engineering/industrial management; family/consumer resource management; film/video and photographic arts; history; human resources management.

WESTERN NEW ENGLAND COLLEGE

Springfield, Massachusetts
http://www.wnec.edu/CE

Western New England College was founded in 1919. It is accredited by New England Association of Schools and Colleges. It first offered distance learning courses in 1998. In fall 2003, there were 165 students enrolled in distance learning courses. Institutionally administered financial aid is available to distance learners.

Services Distance learners have accessibility to academic advising, bookstore, campus computer network, career placement assistance, e-mail services, library services.

Contact Ms. Judy Cadden, Assistant Director of Student Services, Western New England College, Continuing Education, 1215 Wilbraham Road, Springfield, MA 01119-2684. *Telephone:* 413-782-1249. *Fax:* 441-782-1779. *E-mail:* ce@wnec.edu.

DEGREES AND AWARDS

BBA Business
MBA Business

COURSE SUBJECT AREAS OFFERED OUTSIDE OF DEGREE PROGRAMS

Undergraduate—business; business administration and management; business communications; computer and information sciences, general; criminal justice and corrections; cultural studies; developmental and child psychology; English language and literature, general; psychology; social psychology; social work; sociology.

Graduate—accounting; business; business administration and management; computer/information technology administration and management; financial management and services; marketing management and research.

WESTERN SEMINARY

Portland, Oregon
Center for Lifelong Learning
http://www.westernseminary.edu

Western Seminary was founded in 1927. It is accredited by Association of Theological Schools in the United States and Canada. It first offered distance learning courses in 1981. In fall 2003, there were 120 students enrolled in distance learning courses. Institutionally administered financial aid is available to distance learners.

Services Distance learners have accessibility to academic advising, bookstore, career placement assistance, e-mail services, library services.

Contact Jon Raibley, Assistant Director of Center for Lifelong Learning, Western Seminary, 5511 Southeast Hawthorne Boulevard, Portland, OR 97215. *Telephone:* 800-547-4546. *Fax:* 503-517-1801. *E-mail:* jlraible@westernseminary.edu.

DEGREES AND AWARDS

Programs offered do not lead to a degree or other formal award.

COURSE SUBJECT AREAS OFFERED OUTSIDE OF DEGREE PROGRAMS

Graduate—anthropology; bible/biblical studies; biblical and other theological languages and literatures; religion/religious studies; religious education; theological and ministerial studies; theological studies and religious vocations, other.

Western Seminary (continued)

Non-credit—bible/biblical studies; biblical and other theological languages and literatures; religion/religious studies; religious education; theological and ministerial studies; theological studies and religious vocations, other.

WESTERN WASHINGTON UNIVERSITY

Bellingham, Washington

Extended Education and Summer Programs

http://www.ExtendedEd.wwu.edu

Western Washington University was founded in 1893. It is accredited by Northwest Commission on Colleges and Universities. It first offered distance learning courses in 1941. In fall 2003, there were 2,000 students enrolled in distance learning courses. Institutionally administered financial aid is available to distance learners.

Services Distance learners have accessibility to bookstore, campus computer network, career placement assistance, e-mail services, library services.

Contact Barbara (Bunny) Starbuck, Distance Learning Assistant, Western Washington University, MS 5293, 516 High Street, Bellingham, WA 98225-5996. *Telephone:* 360-650-3650. *Fax:* 360-650-6858. *E-mail:* eesp.distedpeters@wwu.edu.

DEGREES AND AWARDS

BA Human Services

Certificate Birth to Five Care; Emergency Management/Homeland Security

COURSE SUBJECT AREAS OFFERED OUTSIDE OF DEGREE PROGRAMS

Undergraduate—American history; American literature (United States); anthropology; Asian studies; biblical and other theological languages and literatures; business quantitative methods and management science; Canadian studies; child care and guidance workers and managers; communications, other; community health services; creative writing; curriculum and instruction; developmental/child psychology; East and Southeast Asian languages and literatures; economics; education administration and supervision; engineering-related technologies, other; English as a second language; English language and literature, general; environmental science; European history; French; general teacher education; Greek languages and literatures (modern); history; human services; library science, other; mathematics; medieval and Renaissance studies; music; parks, recreation, leisure and fitness studies, other; psychology; social work; sociology; special education; teacher education, specific academic and vocational programs; teaching English as a second language/foreign language; women's studies.

See full description on page 666.

WESTERN WYOMING COMMUNITY COLLEGE

Rock Springs, Wyoming

Extended Education

http://www.wwcc.cc.wy.us/dist.htm

Western Wyoming Community College was founded in 1959. It is accredited by North Central Association of Colleges and Schools. It first offered distance learning courses in 1996. In fall 2003, there were 1,250 students enrolled in distance learning courses. Institutionally administered financial aid is available to distance learners.

Services Distance learners have accessibility to academic advising, bookstore, campus computer network, career placement assistance, e-mail services, library services, tutoring.

Contact Ms. Christine Lustik, Director of Distance Education, Western Wyoming Community College, 2500 College Drive, PO Box 428, Rock Springs, WY 82902. *Telephone:* 307-382-1757 Ext. 1757. *Fax:* 307-382-1812 Ext. 1812. *E-mail:* clustik@wwcc.cc.wy.us.

DEGREES AND AWARDS

AA General Program

COURSE SUBJECT AREAS OFFERED OUTSIDE OF DEGREE PROGRAMS

Undergraduate—accounting; administrative and secretarial services; anthropology; applied mathematics; biological and physical sciences; business; business administration and management; computer science; computer software and media applications; cultural studies; economics; English composition; general teacher education; health and medical assistants; industrial equipment maintenance and repairers; philosophy.

Special Message

Western Wyoming Community College is located on the high desert plains of southwestern Wyoming and has a service area of 25,000 square miles. Because of the distance and small populations in some of the local communities, it was essential for the College to enter the distance learning field.

Western's goal is to provide high-quality instruction to students who might not otherwise be able to continue their education. The College offers videotaped courses, compressed video instruction, and Internet courses that are part of an associate degree program. Standards are the same as they are for traditional instruction, and students are able to complete degree requirements from their home. Western is interested in drawing students from around the country and the world to their classes because they believe it enriches the learning experience for all concerned. Some Wyoming people rarely venture outside the state, and they welcome the chance to interact with students from other cultures and backgrounds.

Because Western is a state-supported institution, tuition and fees are very low, so students on a tight budget find the College to be very attractive. On average, 77% of students receive some type of financial assistance to attend the College. Western offers both need- and academic-based aid.

Western is accredited by the Higher Learning Commission of the North Central Association of Colleges and Schools, so transfer of courses taken is not a problem. Students who plan carefully are able to complete the first 2 years of their bachelor's degree and transfer with junior status. Occupational students find that they are well prepared for jobs in their field.

Students should visit the Web site at http://www.wwcc.cc.wy.us.

WEST LOS ANGELES COLLEGE

Culver City, California
Distance Learning Center
http://www.wlac.edu/online

West Los Angeles College was founded in 1969. It is accredited by Western Association of Schools and Colleges. It first offered distance learning courses in 1999. In fall 2003, there were 1,000 students enrolled in distance learning courses. Institutionally administered financial aid is available to distance learners.

Services Distance learners have accessibility to campus computer network, e-mail services, library services.

Contact Mr. Eric Jean Ichon, Distance Learning Coordinator, West Los Angeles College, 9000 Overland Avenue, Culver City, CA 90230. *Telephone:* 310-287-4305. *Fax:* 310-841-0396. *E-mail:* ichone@wlac.edu.

DEGREES AND AWARDS

Programs offered do not lead to a degree or other formal award.

COURSE SUBJECT AREAS OFFERED OUTSIDE OF DEGREE PROGRAMS

Undergraduate—American literature (United States); computer/information technology administration and management; computer science; criminal justice and corrections; dental clinical sciences/graduate dentistry (M.S., Ph.D.); design and applied arts; dramatic/theater arts and stagecraft; economics; English as a second language; English composition; English creative writing; English language and literature, general; English language and literature/letters, other; English technical and business writing; health and medical preparatory programs; health and physical education/fitness; history; international relations and affairs; library science/librarianship; mathematics; political science and government; psychology; speech and rhetorical studies; tourism/travel marketing.

WEST VALLEY COLLEGE

Saratoga, California
Distance Learning
http://www.westvalley.edu/wvc/dl/dl.html

West Valley College was founded in 1963. It is accredited by Western Association of Schools and Colleges. It first offered distance learning courses in 1985. In fall 2003, there were 2,176 students enrolled in distance learning courses. Institutionally administered financial aid is available to distance learners.

Services Distance learners have accessibility to campus computer network, e-mail services, library services.

Contact Steve Peltz, Instructional Technology and Distance Learning Coordinator, West Valley College, 14000 Fruitvale Avenue, Saratoga, CA 95070. *Telephone:* 408-741-2065. *Fax:* 408-741-2134. *E-mail:* steve_peltz@westvalley.edu.

DEGREES AND AWARDS

AA General Programs

COURSE SUBJECT AREAS OFFERED OUTSIDE OF DEGREE PROGRAMS

Undergraduate—American history; anthropology; art history; business; business administration and management; business marketing and marketing management; computer and information sciences, general; computer science; computer software and media applications; creative writing; developmental/child psychology; economics; English composition; film studies; French; information sciences and systems; law and legal studies related; library science, other; mathematics; oceanography; philosophy; photography; political science and government; psychology; sociology; Spanish.

WEST VIRGINIA UNIVERSITY

Morgantown, West Virginia
Extended Learning
http://www.e-learn.wvu.edu

West Virginia University was founded in 1867. It is accredited by North Central Association of Colleges and Schools. It first offered distance learning courses in 1987. In fall 2003, there were 2,041 students enrolled in distance learning courses. Institutionally administered financial aid is available to distance learners.

Services Distance learners have accessibility to academic advising, bookstore, campus computer network, career placement assistance, e-mail services, library services, tutoring.

Contact Ms. Cindy K. Hart, Coordinator of Distance Learning, West Virginia University, One Waterfront Place, Room 1009, PO Box 6808, Morgantown, WV 26506-6808. *Telephone:* 304-293-3852. *Fax:* 304-293-3853. *E-mail:* lkhart@mail.wvu.edu.

DEGREES AND AWARDS

BA Regents Bachelor of Arts
BSN Nursing–RN to BSN
Certificate Integrated Marketing Communications
EMBA Business Administration
MA Special Education
MS Athletic Coaching; Integrated Marketing Communications; Rehabilitation Counseling; Software Engineering
MSE Physical Education Teacher Education
MSN Nursing
MSOT Occupational Therapy

COURSE SUBJECT AREAS OFFERED OUTSIDE OF DEGREE PROGRAMS

Non-credit—engineering, other; financial management and services; Internet and World Wide Web; music.

See full description on page 668.

WEST VIRGINIA UNIVERSITY AT PARKERSBURG

Parkersburg, West Virginia
http://www.wvup.edu

West Virginia University at Parkersburg was founded in 1961. It is accredited by North Central Association of Colleges and Schools. It first offered distance learning courses in 1999. In fall 2003, there were 1,140 students enrolled in distance learning courses. Institutionally administered financial aid is available to distance learners.

Services Distance learners have accessibility to bookstore, campus computer network, e-mail services, library services.

West Virginia University at Parkersburg (continued)

Contact Dr. Joseph L. Badgley, Dean of Academic Affairs, West Virginia University at Parkersburg, 30 Campus Drive, Parkersburg, WV 26104. *Telephone:* 304-424-8244. *Fax:* 304-424-8315. *E-mail:* joe.badgley@mail.wvu.edu.

DEGREES AND AWARDS

Programs offered do not lead to a degree or other formal award.

COURSE SUBJECT AREAS OFFERED OUTSIDE OF DEGREE PROGRAMS

Undergraduate—accounting; administrative and secretarial services; biological and physical sciences; biology, general; business; business administration and management; business communications; business information and data processing services; computer and information sciences, general; computer/information technology administration and management; criminal justice and corrections; dramatic/theater arts and stagecraft; English composition; English language and literature/letters, other; history; marketing management and research; psychology; technology education/industrial arts.

Non-credit—legal studies.

WESTWOOD ONLINE

Denver, Colorado

http://www.westwood.edu

Westwood Online is accredited by Accrediting Commission of Career Schools and Colleges of Technology. It first offered distance learning courses in 2002. In fall 2003, there were 350 students enrolled in distance learning courses. Institutionally administered financial aid is available to distance learners.

Services Distance learners have accessibility to academic advising, bookstore, campus computer network, career placement assistance, e-mail services, library services, tutoring.

Contact David Eby, Director of Admissions, Westwood Online, 7350 North Broadway, Denver, CO 80221. *Telephone:* 877-817-9525. *Fax:* 303-410.7996. *E-mail:* deby@westwood.edu.

DEGREES AND AWARDS

AAS Computer Network Engineering; Graphic Design and Multimedia; Software Engineering

BS Animation; Business Administration–Accounting Concentration; Business Administration–Marketing and Sales Concentration; Computer Network Management; Criminal Justice; E-Business Management; Game Art and Design; Game Software Development; Information Systems Security; Visual Communications; Web Design and Multimedia

COURSE SUBJECT AREAS OFFERED OUTSIDE OF DEGREE PROGRAMS

Undergraduate—accounting; business administration and management; computer programming; computer software and media applications; computer systems networking and telecommunications; criminal justice and corrections; design and applied arts; Internet and World Wide Web.

See full description on page 670.

WHATCOM COMMUNITY COLLEGE

Bellingham, Washington

http://www.whatcom.ctc.edu/

Whatcom Community College was founded in 1970. It is accredited by Northwest Commission on Colleges and Universities. It first offered distance learning courses in 1991. In fall 2003, there were 500 students enrolled in distance learning courses. Institutionally administered financial aid is available to distance learners.

Services Distance learners have accessibility to academic advising, bookstore, campus computer network, library services, tutoring.

Contact Gillian McLeod, Distance Learning Coordinator, Whatcom Community College, 237 West Kellogg Road, Bellingham, WA 98226. *Telephone:* 360-676-2170 Ext. 3446. *Fax:* 360-676-2171. *E-mail:* gmcleod@whatcom.ctc.edu.

DEGREES AND AWARDS

Programs offered do not lead to a degree or other formal award.

COURSE SUBJECT AREAS OFFERED OUTSIDE OF DEGREE PROGRAMS

Undergraduate—anthropology; astronomy; biology; business; chemistry; economics; education, general; education, other; English composition; English language and literature, general; geography; history; mathematics; music; philosophy; psychology; sociology.

WICHITA STATE UNIVERSITY

Wichita, Kansas

Media Resources Center

http://www.mrc.twsu.edu/mrc/telecourse

Wichita State University was founded in 1895. It is accredited by North Central Association of Colleges and Schools. It first offered distance learning courses in 1982. In fall 2003, there were 879 students enrolled in distance learning courses.

Services Distance learners have accessibility to bookstore, library services.

Contact Mary Morriss, Telecourse Coordinator, Wichita State University, 1845 Fairmount, Wichita, KS 67260-0057. *Telephone:* 316-978-7766. *Fax:* 316-978-3560. *E-mail:* morriss@mrc.twsu.edu.

DEGREES AND AWARDS

Programs offered do not lead to a degree or other formal award.

COURSE SUBJECT AREAS OFFERED OUTSIDE OF DEGREE PROGRAMS

Undergraduate—accounting; anthropology; astronomy; biology; business administration and management; communications, general; comparative literature; family/consumer resource management; geography; gerontology; history; music; psychology; sociology; speech and rhetorical studies.

Graduate—economics.

WILFRID LAURIER UNIVERSITY

Waterloo, Ontario, Canada
Office of Part-Time Studies and Continuing Education
http://www.wlu.ca/pts

Wilfrid Laurier University was founded in 1911. It is provincially chartered. It first offered distance learning courses in 1978. In fall 2003, there were 1,430 students enrolled in distance learning courses. Institutionally administered financial aid is available to distance learners.

Services Distance learners have accessibility to academic advising, bookstore, campus computer network, career placement assistance, e-mail services, library services.
Contact Jeanette McDonald, Manager Distance Education and Instructional Development, Wilfrid Laurier University, 75 University Avenue West, Waterloo, ON N2L 3C5, Canada. *Telephone:* 519-884-0710 Ext. 3211. *Fax:* 519-884-6063. *E-mail:* jmcdonal@wlu.ca.

DEGREES AND AWARDS

BA Psychology; Sociology
Diploma Business Administration

COURSE SUBJECT AREAS OFFERED OUTSIDE OF DEGREE PROGRAMS

Undergraduate—accounting; anthropology; biology; biology, general; business; communications, general; developmental/child psychology; economics; English language and literature, general; environmental science; fine arts and art studies; French; geography; Germanic languages and literatures; history; investments and securities; medical genetics; philosophy; political science and government; psychology; religion/religious studies; social work; sociology; visual and performing arts.

WILKES COMMUNITY COLLEGE

Wilkesboro, North Carolina
Individualized Studies Department
http://www.wilkes.cc.nc.us

Wilkes Community College was founded in 1965. It is accredited by Southern Association of Colleges and Schools. It first offered distance learning courses in 1984. In fall 2003, there were 2,273 students enrolled in distance learning courses. Institutionally administered financial aid is available to distance learners.

Services Distance learners have accessibility to academic advising, bookstore, campus computer network, career placement assistance, e-mail services, library services, tutoring.
Contact Bud Mayes, Distance Learning Coordinator, Wilkes Community College, PO Box 120, Wilkesboro, NC 28697. *Telephone:* 336-838-6236. *Fax:* 336-838-6277. *E-mail:* bud.mayes@wilkescc.edu.

DEGREES AND AWARDS

AAS Business Administration

COURSE SUBJECT AREAS OFFERED OUTSIDE OF DEGREE PROGRAMS

Undergraduate—accounting; advertising; American literature (United States); biology; business; business administration and management; business and personal services marketing operations; business communications; business information and data processing services; business management and administrative services, other; business/managerial economics; child care and guidance workers and managers; communications, general; communications technologies; computer and information sciences, general; computer and information sciences, other; computer/information technology administration and management; computer programming; computer science; criminal justice and corrections; cultural studies; data processing technology; dramatic/theater arts and stagecraft; English composition; English creative writing; English language and literature, general; English language and literature/letters, other; English literature (British and Commonwealth); English technical and business writing; fine arts and art studies; history; marketing management and research; mathematics; philosophy and religion; psychology; religion/religious studies; sociology.

WILLIAM AND CATHERINE BOOTH COLLEGE

Winnipeg, Manitoba, Canada
http://www.boothcollege.ca/extended/

William and Catherine Booth College is provincially chartered. In fall 2003, there were 40 students enrolled in distance learning courses. Institutionally administered financial aid is available to distance learners.

Services Distance learners have accessibility to academic advising, campus computer network, e-mail services, library services.
Contact Vandana Ingle, Extended Learning Admissions Counsellor, William and Catherine Booth College, 447 Webb Place, Winnipeg, MB R3B2P2, Canada. *Telephone:* 204-924-4870. *Fax:* 204-942-3856. *E-mail:* vingle@boothcollege.ca.

DEGREES AND AWARDS

Programs offered do not lead to a degree or other formal award.

COURSE SUBJECT AREAS OFFERED OUTSIDE OF DEGREE PROGRAMS

Undergraduate—bible/biblical studies; English composition; pastoral counseling and specialized ministries; psychology; social work; sociology; theological and ministerial studies.

WILLIAM PATERSON UNIVERSITY OF NEW JERSEY

Wayne, New Jersey
The Center for Continuing Education and Distance Learning (CEDL)
http://www.wpunj.edu/dl

William Paterson University of New Jersey was founded in 1855. It is accredited by Middle States Association of Colleges and Schools. It first offered distance learning courses in 1997. In fall 2003, there were 1,200 students enrolled in distance learning courses. Institutionally administered financial aid is available to distance learners.

Services Distance learners have accessibility to academic advising, bookstore, campus computer network, career placement assistance, e-mail services, library services, tutoring.

William Paterson University of New Jersey (continued)

Contact Mr. Ron Chalmers, Director of Distance Learning, William Paterson University of New Jersey, Center for Continuing Education and Distance Learning, 1600 Valley Road, PO Box 920, Wayne, NJ 07474-0920. *Telephone:* 973-720-3024. *Fax:* 973-720-2298. *E-mail:* chalmersr@wpunj.edu.

DEGREES AND AWARDS

Programs offered do not lead to a degree or other formal award.

COURSE SUBJECT AREAS OFFERED OUTSIDE OF DEGREE PROGRAMS

Undergraduate—accounting; American literature (United States); anthropology; applied mathematics; archaeology; area, ethnic and cultural studies, other; area studies; biological and physical sciences; biological sciences/life sciences, other; biology, general; botany; business; business administration and management; business information and data processing services; business management and administrative services, other; business quantitative methods and management science; communications, other; computer and information sciences, general; conservation and renewable natural resources, other; counseling psychology; criminal justice and corrections; criminology; curriculum and instruction; dramatic/theater arts and stagecraft; East and Southeast Asian languages and literatures; education administration and supervision; educational/instructional media design; education, general; English composition; English creative writing; English language and literature, general; English language and literature/letters, other; enterprise management and operation; foods and nutrition studies; geography; gerontology; health professions and related sciences, other; history; legal studies; liberal arts and sciences, general studies and humanities; marketing management and research; marketing operations/marketing and distribution, other; mathematics; music; nursing; ocean engineering; philosophy; philosophy and religion; political science and government; public health; social sciences and history, other; social sciences, general; social work; special education; speech and rhetorical studies; teacher education, specific academic and vocational programs.

Graduate—business administration and management; business communications; counseling psychology; education administration and supervision; educational/instructional media design; English creative writing; English technical and business writing; history; mathematical statistics; nursing; social work; sociology.

Non-credit—business communications; business management and administrative services, other; computer software and media applications; enterprise management and operation; entrepreneurship; health and medical administrative services; health and medical assistants; health professions and related sciences, other; Internet and World Wide Web; marketing management and research; music.

WILLIAM RAINEY HARPER COLLEGE

Palatine, Illinois
Learning Resource Center
http://www.harpercollege.edu/doit

William Rainey Harper College was founded in 1965. It is accredited by North Central Association of Colleges and Schools. It first offered distance learning courses in 1984. In fall 2003, there were 1,000 students enrolled in distance learning courses. Institutionally administered financial aid is available to distance learners.

Services Distance learners have accessibility to academic advising, bookstore, campus computer network, e-mail services, library services, tutoring.

Contact Fran Hendrickson, Program Assistant, William Rainey Harper College, 1200 West Algonquin Road, Palatine, IL 60067-7398. *Telephone:* 847-925-6586. *Fax:* 847-925-6037. *E-mail:* fhendric@harpercollege.edu.

DEGREES AND AWARDS

Programs offered do not lead to a degree or other formal award.

COURSE SUBJECT AREAS OFFERED OUTSIDE OF DEGREE PROGRAMS

Undergraduate—accounting; administrative and secretarial services; apparel and accessories marketing operations; astronomy; business; business communications; business management and administrative services, other; computer and information sciences, general; computer and information sciences, other; computer/information technology administration and management; computer programming; computer science; computer software and media applications; computer systems networking and telecommunications; criminal justice and corrections; developmental/child psychology; economics; education, general; English as a second language; English composition; English creative writing; English language and literature, general; English language and literature/letters, other; English technical and business writing; film/video and photographic arts; financial management and services; financial services marketing operations; foreign languages and literatures; geography; health and medical assistants; health and medical diagnostic and treatment services; health professions and related sciences, other; history; information sciences and systems; international business; Internet and World Wide Web; liberal arts and sciences, general studies and humanities; marketing operations/marketing and distribution, other; nursing; physical/theoretical chemistry; psychology; real estate; social psychology; sociology.

WILLIAM TYNDALE COLLEGE

Farmington Hills, Michigan
http://www.williamtyndale.edu

William Tyndale College was founded in 1945. It is accredited by North Central Association of Colleges and Schools. It first offered distance learning courses in 2001. In fall 2003, there were 50 students enrolled in distance learning courses. Institutionally administered financial aid is available to distance learners.

Services Distance learners have accessibility to academic advising, bookstore, campus computer network, e-mail services, library services.

Contact Jan Crain, Coordinator of Recruitment Operations, William Tyndale College, 35700 West 12 Mile Road, Farmington Hills, MI 48331. *Telephone:* 248-553-7200 Ext. 306. *Fax:* 248-553-5963. *E-mail:* jcrain@williamtyndale.edu.

DEGREES AND AWARDS

AS Discipleship; General Studies
BBA Business Administration; Product Management

COURSE SUBJECT AREAS OFFERED OUTSIDE OF DEGREE PROGRAMS

Undergraduate—accounting; business; business administration and management; business information and data processing services; English composition; English creative writing; religion/religious studies; religious education.

WINONA STATE UNIVERSITY

Winona, Minnesota

http://www.winona.edu/

Winona State University was founded in 1858. It is accredited by North Central Association of Colleges and Schools. It first offered distance learning courses in 2001. In fall 2003, there were 200 students enrolled in distance learning courses. Institutionally administered financial aid is available to distance learners.

Services Distance learners have accessibility to academic advising, bookstore, campus computer network, career placement assistance, e-mail services, library services, tutoring.

Contact Dr. Ken Graetz, Director of e-Learning, Winona State University, e-Learning Center, Box 5838, Winona, MN 55987. *Telephone:* 507-457-2339. *E-mail:* kgraetz@winona.edu.

DEGREES AND AWARDS

Programs offered do not lead to a degree or other formal award.

COURSE SUBJECT AREAS OFFERED OUTSIDE OF DEGREE PROGRAMS

Undergraduate—accounting; business administration and management; business/managerial economics.

Graduate—education administration and supervision.

WINSTON-SALEM STATE UNIVERSITY

Winston-Salem, North Carolina

http://www.wssu.edu/dl

Winston-Salem State University was founded in 1892. It is accredited by Southern Association of Colleges and Schools. It first offered distance learning courses in 1996. In fall 2003, there were 195 students enrolled in distance learning courses. Institutionally administered financial aid is available to distance learners.

Services Distance learners have accessibility to academic advising, bookstore, campus computer network, career placement assistance, e-mail services, library services, tutoring.

Contact Ms. Avis Ray, Coordinator of Student Services, Winston-Salem State University, Office of Distance Learning, PO Box 19260, Winston-Salem, NC 27110. *Telephone:* 336-750-2634. *Fax:* 336-750-3413. *E-mail:* raya@wssu.edu.

DEGREES AND AWARDS

BS Birth to Kindergarten Education (lateral entry/certification); Business Administration Management Concentration; Clinical Laboratory Science (lateral entry); Physical Education, Teaching Option (lateral entry)

BSN Nursing–RN to BSN (lateral entry)

Certificate Computer Programming (Post-Baccalaureate); Social Work Paraprofessional

COURSE SUBJECT AREAS OFFERED OUTSIDE OF DEGREE PROGRAMS

Undergraduate—business; business administration and management; computer programming; curriculum and instruction; developmental and child psychology; general teacher education; history; liberal arts and sciences, general studies and humanities; microbiology/bacteriology; music; social and philosophical foundations of education; social work; sociology.

WISCONSIN INDIANHEAD TECHNICAL COLLEGE

Shell Lake, Wisconsin

http://www.witc.edu

Wisconsin Indianhead Technical College was founded in 1912. It is accredited by North Central Association of Colleges and Schools. It first offered distance learning courses in 1991. In fall 2003, there were 580 students enrolled in distance learning courses. Institutionally administered financial aid is available to distance learners.

Services Distance learners have accessibility to bookstore, career placement assistance, e-mail services, library services, tutoring.

Contact Ms. Mimi Crandall, Dean of Student Services and Marketing, Wisconsin Indianhead Technical College, 505 Pine Ridge Drive, Shell Lake, WI 54871. *Telephone:* 715-468-2815 Ext. 2280. *Fax:* 715-468-2819. *E-mail:* mcrandal@witc.edu.

DEGREES AND AWARDS

AD Computer Information Systems–Web Analyst Web Programmer

COURSE SUBJECT AREAS OFFERED OUTSIDE OF DEGREE PROGRAMS

Undergraduate—accounting; administrative and secretarial services; advertising; agricultural and food products processing; agricultural business and management; agriculture/agricultural sciences; apparel and accessories marketing operations; applied mathematics; business; business administration and management; child care and guidance workers and managers; communications, general; computer and information sciences, general; computer programming; foods and nutrition studies; nursing.

Non-credit—accounting; administrative and secretarial services; advertising; agricultural and food products processing; agricultural business and management; agriculture/agricultural sciences; apparel and accessories marketing operations; applied mathematics; business; business administration and management; child care and guidance workers and managers; communications, general; computer and information sciences, general; computer programming; foods and nutrition studies; nursing.

WORCESTER POLYTECHNIC INSTITUTE

Worcester, Massachusetts

Advanced Distance Learning Network

http://www.wpi.edu/+ADLN

Worcester Polytechnic Institute was founded in 1865. It is accredited by New England Association of Schools and Colleges. It first offered distance learning courses in 1979. In fall 2003, there were 250 students enrolled in distance learning courses. Institutionally administered financial aid is available to distance learners.

Services Distance learners have accessibility to academic advising, bookstore, campus computer network, career placement assistance, e-mail services, library services.

Contact Pamela S. Shelley, Assistant Director of Advanced Distance Learning Network, Worcester Polytechnic Institute, 100 Institute Road, Worcester, MA 01609-2280. *Telephone:* 508-831-5220. *Fax:* 508-831-5881. *E-mail:* adln@wpi.edu.

Worcester Polytechnic Institute (continued)

DEGREES AND AWARDS

CAGS Environmental Engineering; Fire Protection Engineering
CGMS Management
Graduate Certificate Environmental Engineering; Fire Protection Engineering
MBA Management
MS Civil Engineering; Environmental Engineering; Fire Protection Engineering

COURSE SUBJECT AREAS OFFERED OUTSIDE OF DEGREE PROGRAMS

Graduate—business administration and management; business marketing and marketing management; computer systems networking and telecommunications; engineering/industrial management; environmental engineering; fire science; international business; marketing operations/marketing and distribution, other.

See full description on page 672.

WORCESTER STATE COLLEGE

Worcester, Massachusetts
http://www.worcester.edu/

Worcester State College was founded in 1874. It is accredited by New England Association of Schools and Colleges. It first offered distance learning courses in 2000. In fall 2003, there were 405 students enrolled in distance learning courses. Institutionally administered financial aid is available to distance learners.

Services Distance learners have accessibility to academic advising, bookstore, campus computer network, e-mail services, library services.

Contact Dr. William White, Dean of Graduate and Continuing Education, Worcester State College, Office of Graduate and Continuing Education, 486 Chandler Street, Worcester, MA 01602-2597. *Telephone:* 508-929-8811. *Fax:* 508-929-8100. *E-mail:* wwhite@worcester.edu.

DEGREES AND AWARDS

Programs offered do not lead to a degree or other formal award.

COURSE SUBJECT AREAS OFFERED OUTSIDE OF DEGREE PROGRAMS

Undergraduate—biology, general; business administration and management; communications, general; computer and information sciences, general; economics; English language and literature, general; mathematical statistics; mathematics; philosophy; physical sciences, general; psychology.
Graduate—education, general; English language and literature, general; health professions and related sciences, other; history.
Non-credit—business administration and management; communications, general; computer and information sciences, general; computer science; entrepreneurship; film/video and photographic arts; human resources management; human services; legal studies; public relations and organizational communications.

WRIGHT STATE UNIVERSITY

Dayton, Ohio
Center for Teaching and Learning
http://www.wright.edu/dl

Wright State University was founded in 1964. It is accredited by North Central Association of Colleges and Schools. It first offered distance learning courses in 1995. In fall 2003, there were 8,044 students enrolled in distance learning courses. Institutionally administered financial aid is available to distance learners.

Services Distance learners have accessibility to academic advising, bookstore, e-mail services, library services.

Contact Terri Klaus, Associate Director of Center for Teaching and Learning and Distance Learning, Wright State University, 023 Library, 3640 Colonel Glenn Highway, Dayton, OH 45435. *Telephone:* 937-775-4965. *Fax:* 937-775-3152. *E-mail:* terri.klaus@wright.edu.

DEGREES AND AWARDS

BS Nursing
MS Human Factors Engineering; Rehabilitation Counseling

COURSE SUBJECT AREAS OFFERED OUTSIDE OF DEGREE PROGRAMS

Undergraduate—biological sciences/life sciences, other; biology, general; communications, general; economics; education, general; English composition; English language and literature, general; English technical and business writing; foreign languages and literatures; general teacher education; history; liberal arts and sciences, general studies and humanities; mathematics; music; nursing.
Graduate—communications, general; economics; educational/instructional media design; education, other; English technical and business writing; geological and related sciences; nursing.
Non-credit—economics.

YORK TECHNICAL COLLEGE

Rock Hill, South Carolina
Distance Learning Department
http://www.yorktech.com

York Technical College was founded in 1961. It is accredited by Southern Association of Colleges and Schools. It first offered distance learning courses in 1995. In fall 2003, there were 2,100 students enrolled in distance learning courses. Institutionally administered financial aid is available to distance learners.

Services Distance learners have accessibility to academic advising, bookstore, campus computer network, career placement assistance, e-mail services, library services, tutoring.

Contact Anita McBride, Department Manager, York Technical College, 452 South Anderson Road, Rock Hill, SC 29730. *Telephone:* 803-981-7044. *Fax:* 803-981-7193. *E-mail:* mcbride@yorktech.com.

DEGREES AND AWARDS

Programs offered do not lead to a degree or other formal award.

COURSE SUBJECT AREAS OFFERED OUTSIDE OF DEGREE PROGRAMS

Undergraduate—accounting; biological and physical sciences; business; business administration and management; computer science; developmental/child psychology; economics; electrical engineering; English composition; English language and literature, general; environmental/environmental health engineering; history; industrial engineering; mathematics; nursing; philosophy; psychology; sociology.
Non-credit—computer and information sciences, other.

YORK UNIVERSITY

Toronto, Ontario, Canada

http://www.yorku.ca/

York University was founded in 1959. It is provincially chartered. It first offered distance learning courses in 1994. In fall 2003, there were 10,000 students enrolled in distance learning courses. Institutionally administered financial aid is available to distance learners.

Services Distance learners have accessibility to academic advising, bookstore, campus computer network, e-mail services, library services, tutoring.

Contact Ms. Amalia Syligardakis, Supervisor of Centre for Distance Education, York University, Centre for Distance Education, 4700 Keele Street, Room 2120, TEL Building, Toronto, ON M3J 1P3, Canada. *Telephone:* 416-736-2100 Ext. 30705. *Fax:* 416-736-5637. *E-mail:* amalias@yorku.ca.

DEGREES AND AWARDS

BA Public Service Studies
BBA Administrative Studies

COURSE SUBJECT AREAS OFFERED OUTSIDE OF DEGREE PROGRAMS

Undergraduate—accounting; business administration and management; business communications; business/managerial economics; business quantitative methods and management science; communications, general; economics; fine arts and art studies; history; human resources management; liberal arts and sciences, general studies and humanities; marketing management and research; mathematics; nursing; philosophy; political science and government; psychology, other; public administration and services, other; religion/religious studies; social sciences, general; social work; sociology.

Non-credit—accounting; air transportation workers; business administration and management; computer software and media applications; mathematics, other; social work.

YOUNGSTOWN STATE UNIVERSITY

Youngstown, Ohio

http://www.ysu.edu/metro

Youngstown State University was founded in 1908. It is accredited by North Central Association of Colleges and Schools. It first offered distance learning courses in 1998. In fall 2003, there were 350 students enrolled in distance learning courses. Institutionally administered financial aid is available to distance learners.

Services Distance learners have accessibility to academic advising, bookstore, campus computer network, e-mail services, library services, tutoring.

Contact Dr. Gordon E. Mapley, Executive Director, Metro College, Youngstown State University, Metro College, 100 DeBartolo Place, Youngstown, OH 44512. *Telephone:* 330-965-3607. *Fax:* 330-965-5811. *E-mail:* gmapley@ysu.edu.

DEGREES AND AWARDS

BS Health Professions
MPH Public Health

COURSE SUBJECT AREAS OFFERED OUTSIDE OF DEGREE PROGRAMS

Undergraduate—communications, general; computer science; criminal justice and corrections; foods and nutrition studies; geological and related sciences; health and physical education/fitness; health professions and related sciences, other; mathematics; nursing; philosophy; physics.

Graduate—education administration and supervision; educational/instructional media design; health professions and related sciences, other; public administration; public health; social work.

Non-credit—accounting; administrative and secretarial services; advertising; American literature (United States); business administration and management; business and personal services marketing operations; business management and administrative services, other; business/managerial economics; computer and information sciences, general; computer software and media applications; computer systems networking and telecommunications; English creative writing; English language and literature/letters, other; English technical and business writing; entrepreneurship; health and medical administrative services; health and medical assistants; legal studies.

YUBA COLLEGE

Marysville, California

Learning Resource Center

http://www.yubaonline.edu

Yuba College was founded in 1927. It is accredited by Western Association of Schools and Colleges. It first offered distance learning courses in 1975. In fall 2003, there were 949 students enrolled in distance learning courses. Institutionally administered financial aid is available to distance learners.

Services Distance learners have accessibility to academic advising, bookstore, campus computer network, career placement assistance, e-mail services, library services.

Contact Miss Jeanette O'Bryan, Distributive Education Support Specialist, Yuba College, 2088 North Beale Road, Marysville, CA 95901. *Telephone:* 530-741-6754. *Fax:* 530-741-6824. *E-mail:* jobryan@yccd.edu.

DEGREES AND AWARDS

AAS General Studies

COURSE SUBJECT AREAS OFFERED OUTSIDE OF DEGREE PROGRAMS

Undergraduate—American literature (United States); anthropology; design and applied arts; education, other; English composition; family and community studies; foreign languages and literatures, other; history; human resources management; journalism and mass communications; mathematical statistics; mathematics; nursing; psychology, other; sociology; Spanish; veterinary medicine (DVM).

IN-DEPTH DESCRIPTIONS OF DISTANCE LEARNING PROGRAMS

ADAMS STATE COLLEGE
COLORADO
Great Stories Begin Here
EXTENDED STUDIES

Adams State College

Extended Studies

Alamosa, Colorado

Adams State College (ASC), founded in 1921, is located in the San Luis Valley in south-central Colorado in the city of Alamosa. Alamosa, at an elevation of 7,500 feet above sea level, is surrounded by mountain ranges with peaks rising up to 14,000 feet above sea level. The student body is composed of approximately 2,500 individuals from various ethnic and racial backgrounds. Adams State College is accredited by the Higher Learning Commission of the North Central Association of Colleges and Schools. The School of Education is currently accepted as a candidate in TEAC (Teacher Education Accreditation Council).

DISTANCE LEARNING PROGRAM

Adams State College has been providing programs to off-campus students for more than 25 years. In the past year, more than 18,000 students took advantage of one of the options offered through Extended Studies.

The Distance Degree Completion Program offers a Bachelor of Arts (B.A.) degree in business administration, interdisciplinary studies, and sociology; a Bachelor of Science (B.S.) degree in business administration; and the Associate of Arts (A.A.) and Associate of Science (A.S.) degrees.

Certificate programs are available in alternative dispute resolution (mediation), legal investigation, legal nurse consultant training, legal secretary, management information systems, paralegal studies, and victim advocacy. Students not interested in degree completion can enroll in more than 140 independent study/correspondence courses in accounting, business, business finance, business management, business strategy, criminology, economics, education, English, geography, geology, history, management, marketing, math, psychology, social theory, social welfare, and sociology.

DELIVERY MEDIA

A variety of delivery options are available to students for all the accounting, business administration, criminology, economics, education, English, geography, geology, history, management, sociology, and general education courses and include online delivery, print materials, and face-to-face instruction at various sites. Students enrolling in an online or independent study (correspondence) course are provided with a syllabus explaining course requirements. In many cases the student is able to print the syllabus from the ASC Web site. Students send completed course work directly to the instructor. Some courses require proctored examinations, while others have online examinations. Online and traditional tools are available for courses, such as e-mail, textbooks, and videotapes. All ASC instructors are available by telephone, fax, e-mail, and surface mail.

PROGRAMS OF STUDY

The B.A. and B.S. degrees in business administration require 120 semester credit hours for graduation; 45 must be junior- or senior-level credits, and a minimum of 30 credits must be completed with ASC. B.A./B.S. degree requirements include 40 semester credits in general education and approximately 40 in electives and 40 in the major field (specific requirements subject to the academic major). A maximum of 90 semester credits can be transferred to ASC, of which a maximum of 60 may be from junior/community colleges. Admitted students must maintain active status by enrolling in at least one ASC course per semester.

A.A. and A.S. degree completion program requirements include 43 semester credits in general education and 17 in electives. Students must complete general education course work to satisfy requirements from the following eight areas: oral and written communication, human behavior and institutions, history and culture, and arts and literature (6 credits each); quantitative thinking (3 credits), and speech fundamentals (3 credits; speech is required for A.A. and A.S. degrees only); science foundations and issues (8 credits); and health and fitness (2 credits). For specific course titles that meet these requirements, students should visit the ASC Web site at http://exstudies.adams.edu/degree.html.

Transfer credit is accepted from accredited institutions recommended by the American Association of Collegiate Registrars and Admissions Officers. Credits from a nonaccredited institution may be petitioned for transfer after the student has completed at least 24 semester hours at ASC with a C (2.0 GPA) average or better. Students may petition the appropriate academic dean for approval of courses that are not accepted during the normal admission and transfer process.

SPECIAL PROGRAMS

Courses that have attracted the interests of many students include the popular certificate programs in paralegal studies, alternative dispute resolution (mediation), legal investigation, legal nurse consultant training, legal secretary, and victim advocacy.

More than 200 six-week, noncredit, online interactive courses are available to the student not interested in a standard academic program, but seeking a short-term solution to a current need. These courses are designed to provide the student with new skills and knowledge or to improve current skills. The catagories of courses include business management, computer and software applications, entrepreneur, health, Internet, personal enrichment, small business, and Web page design. For a complete listing, students should visit http://www.ed2go.com/adams/.

ASC offers a wide range of online and independent study graduate courses developed for teachers. Many schools and school districts allow these courses to be used for in-service training or recertification purposes. Customized graduate certificate programs are designed to meet the professional development needs of educators.

STUDENT SERVICES

Free unofficial transfer evaluations are offered to students interested in the degree program. The ASC adviser provides students with a free, preliminary, unofficial credit evaluation upon request. Students must provide copies of transcripts or grade reports showing previous college work. These "unofficial" documents are reviewed by the program adviser, entered on a degree-completion advisement form, and returned to the student. Students have the opportunity to see how their previous college work might meet the ASC requirements. The unofficial evaluation is subject to change based on the outcome of the official admission evaluation and acceptance of transfer credits by the Admissions Office.

Degree-seeking students have access to ASC faculty members via mail, e-mail, or fax or by calling the Extended Studies Office toll-free at 800-548-6679. Books may be purchased from the ASC bookstore via telephone, mail, or fax. All pertinent forms are located on the Extended Studies Web site.

CREDIT OPTIONS

For the bachelor's degrees, students may transfer in a maximum of 90 semester credits to ASC. The remaining 30 semester credits must be completed with ASC. Only 60 credits from community colleges will be applied to the degree. For the associate degree, students may transfer in a maximum of 45 semester credits with the remaining 15 credits completed at ASC.

ASC participates in the College-Level Examination Program (CLEP) (general or subject exams). Students who have performed satisfactorily in college-level courses before college entrance and have demonstrated a requisite achievement (minimum scores of 50th percentile) on tests of the College Board College-Level Examination Program may submit the results to ASC for consideration of college credit. The Records Office records the college credit based on determinations made by the appropriate school's department chair. The maximum credit on the general exams is 18 semester hours (in the areas of humanities, natural science, and social science). The semester hours of credit for each subject exam, as well as credit by examination in total, is determined by the appropriate school's dean.

Military and civilian training is also considered for credit. The chair of the academic department in which the degree is earned evaluates any military and civilian training and make the decision as to how credit will be awarded. ASC uses the American Council on Education Guides for credit recommendations. Military service credit is processed when official documents or transcripts are received at ASC. Courses found in the American Council on Education Guide or on transcripts (CCAF, AARTS, SMART) can be evaluated. Locally conducted (base- or post-level) courses are generally not acceptable due to their unstructured and changing content.

FACULTY

Approximately 65 percent of the faculty members in the External Degree Program have a Ph.D. and are full-time professors on campus at ASC. All professors have experience working with distance learners.

ADMISSION

Transfer students with at least 12 transferable college credits are not required to submit ACT/SAT scores or their high school transcript, but must submit the admission application, application fee, and official transcripts from all colleges previously attended. First-time freshman students must submit the program application fee, the application for admission, and high school transcripts with ACT or SAT scores. The External Degree Completion Program application fee is $75.

TUITION AND FEES

Independent study course tuition for undergraduate credit is $95 per semester hour; for graduate credit, $100 per semester hour. Tuition must be submitted with the registration for the course. Some courses may have additional fees for materials. For course details, applicants should see the specific course description at http://extudies.adams.edu/ind_study/independ.html. The External Degree Completion Program application fee is $75. For admission and application information and details, students should visit http://exstudies.adams.edu/degree.html.

FINANCIAL AID

Currently, students admitted to the External Degree Program are eligible to apply for financial aid. Also, company-sponsored tuition and military tuition assistance programs may be used for ASC courses. Eligible military personnel should process DANTES applications through their education office.

APPLYING

Students can find course and degree application information, application and registration forms, and more answers to their questions by linking to the Extended Studies Web site listed below.

CONTACT

External Degree Programs
Extended Studies
Adams State College
208 Edgemont Boulevard
Alamosa, Colorado 81102
Telephone: 800-548-6679 (toll-free)
Fax: 719-587-7974
E-mail: ascexdeg@adams.edu
WWW:
http://exstudies.adams.edu

The American College of Computer and Information Sciences

Distance Learning Programs

Birmingham, Alabama

The American College of Computer and Information Sciences (ACCIS) is a privately owned independent college, originally founded in 1988 as the American Institute for Computer Sciences. The board of directors adopted the College's new name in January 2001 in order to better represent the credentials the College awards: bachelor's and master's degrees in computer science, information systems, and business and management. ACCIS students typically are adult professionals who wish to study via a self-paced format. ACCIS is accredited by the Accrediting Commission of the Distance Education and Training Council (DETC).

DISTANCE LEARNING PROGRAM

ACCIS offers Bachelor of Science (B.S.) and Master of Science (M.S.) degrees in computer science, information systems, and business and management. All courses follow a flexible, self-paced format, with online chats and full-time faculty assistance offered during the week by phone, fax, and e-mail. There is no on-campus residence; students may enroll at any time and begin classes immediately. ACCIS currently instructs approximately 4,000 students located in more than 120 countries. ACCIS provides students the ultimate in flexibility and academic support. Students not only learn the course content, but also how to study independently using ACCIS' customized academic tools.

DELIVERY MEDIA

ACCIS uses a mixture of texts and technology in all degree programs. Online labs present additional reference material and tutorials written by faculty members. Faculty-student interaction is achieved by small groups meeting weekly for online chats or through electronic mailing lists for each course. Course assignments, progress tests, and final examinations are required in all courses and are generally submitted online or electronically. Students are required to have Internet access, e-mail, word processing software, a printer, and an IBM PC–compatible computer with Microsoft Windows 95/98 or NT.

PROGRAMS OF STUDY

All B.S. programs require the completion of 121 semester credit hours, with 61 hours in the core curriculum and 60 hours in the major. All M.S. programs require the completion of 37 semester credit hours. The B.S. in computer science uses C++ as the core language, as well as offering Java, Visual Basic, and Visual C++. It prepares students for real-world object-oriented programming. Fundamental programming concepts taught include data structures, software engineering, computer architecture, and operating systems. The master's in computer science focuses on in-depth treatment of theoretical foundations and methodologies in computer science. Topics include algorithm design, communication networks, database systems, software engineering, compiler design, and parallel processing. The B.S. in information systems is designed for students seeking a broad-based knowledge of computer information systems as they are used in modern business and organizational settings. Required courses include foundation subjects, such as programming basics, database administration, networking, and IT management. The M.S. in information systems equips managers and information specialists with the advanced skills organizations seek in upper-level IT management. The aim of the M.S.I.S. program is to produce graduates who are capable of leadership in information systems through the formulation and implementation of IT systems to address organizational needs. ACCIS offers two B.S. degrees focused on business and management. The B.S. in management information systems is designed for students seeking to acquire fundamental knowledge of business concepts and information systems applications to create solutions for contemporary business problems. Students use modern learning tools to gain solid technical skills and broad-based knowledge of business management in preparation for entry into the growing field of IT managers. Students looking for a more traditional business path enroll in the B.S. in business administration. Students gain core business competencies in finance, accounting, organization management, economics, marketing, and human resources that are required for success in entry-level management positions in all areas of business. The program uses an integrated approach to tie these competencies to a larger management philosophy to prepare students for real-life management decision making. Building on the undergraduate degrees in business and management, ACCIS' M.B.A. focuses on real-world scenarios managers use on the job. Advanced core topics in marketing, finance, management, and organization are addressed, and key elements of good management, including leadership, decision making, and communication, are stressed throughout the curriculum.

STUDENT SERVICES

ACCIS offers an array of services to assist students in becoming involved participants in online learning as they prepare for careers in technology and management. Students can access a number of services through ACCIS Online, including chat rooms, bulletin boards, course e-mail lists, and ACCIS' online library. Online labs for each course include links to textbook Web sites, practice exercises and self-tests, answers to frequently asked questions, and multimedia tutorials designed to ensure comprehension of complex concepts. Through MY ACCIS, students can check their grades, update their information, and complete other administrative tasks. ACCIS communicates with students weekly through broadcast e-mails about current events and changes. ACCIS also sponsors a number of organizations and events of interest to students. The Mentor Program matches academically strong ACCIS students and graduates with individuals who need additional assistance to improve their academic performance. ACCIS' student chapter of the ACM is the only purely distance learning chapter of this well-known professional organization. Annually, ACCIS inducts outstanding students into Delta Epsilon Tau Honor Society. Social chats, pep rallies, and other events, such as an online graduation ceremony, create a sense of community for ACCIS students and graduates.

CREDIT OPTIONS

Undergraduate students may receive up to a total of 90 hours of credit through a combination of credits transferred from other universities and credit awarded for life and work experience. The total 90 hours can be transfer credit, of which 30 hours may be applied to the student's major. Students may receive up to 30 hours of credit for life and work experience and have it applied to core curriculum courses. Graduate students in computer science may transfer 12 semester hours (three courses) from previous graduate work. Graduate students in the M.B.A. or information systems programs may transfer 9 semester hours (three courses) from previous graduate work. Life and work experience credit is not awarded in the M.S. programs.

FACULTY

ACCIS has 30 full- and part-time faculty members. Seventy percent of all ACCIS faculty members have earned their terminal or M.B.A. degrees. All full-time faculty members have extensive experience in distance education, as well as traditional classroom experience.

ADMISSION

Graduation from high school or satisfactory completion of the GED is required for admission into the B.S. programs. A bachelor's degree from an institution accredited by an agency recognized by the U.S. Department of Education is required for acceptance into the M.B.A. program. Students applying for the M.S. in computer science program must have a bachelor's degree in computer science, information systems, or a related discipline. Students entering the M.S. in information systems program must have a bachelor's degree in information systems, management, or a related field. All M.S. programs at ACCIS require that a student completed the undergraduate degree with a minimum GPA of 2.67 on a 4.0 scale.

TUITION AND FEES

Tuition for the B.S. programs is $145 per semester credit hour. Tuition for the M.S. programs is $195 per semester credit hour and $220 per semester credit hour for the M.B.A. Individual courses may be taken for $695 (undergraduate) or $895 or $995 (graduate). Students purchase all textbooks and other course materials online through ACCIS' educational partner, Specialty Books.

FINANCIAL AID

More than half of all ACCIS students receive financial assistance. ACCIS offers both interest-free and low-cost tuition finance plans. Students may also gain financing through Wells Fargo and corporate reimbursement plans. Military benefits through Tuition Assistance, DANTES, and the VA are available to those who qualify.

APPLYING

ACCIS offers open enrollment; students may begin their program at any time. Both printed and online applications are available. An ACCIS admissions adviser is assigned to each applicant to guide the enrollment process, which can be as short as one week. Following enrollment, each student completes an online orientation course that covers all ACCIS policies and procedures and introduces services and course materials.

CONTACT

American College of Computer and Information Sciences
2101 Magnolia Avenue, Suite 200
Birmingham, Alabama 35205
Telephone: 205-323-6191
800-729-2427 (toll-free in the U.S.)
E-mail: admiss@accis.edu
Web site: http://www.accis.edu

AIU Online—American InterContinental University

IT, Business, Education, and Digital Design Degrees

Hoffman Estates, Illinois

American Intercontinental University (AIU) Online is one of the premier online universities in the United States. With a tradition of educating students for more than thirty years, AIU has created an online education environment that combines the most sophisticated in Internet technology with the tradition of excellent higher education.

AIU is accredited by the Commission on Colleges of the Southern Association of Colleges and Schools (1866 Southern Lane, Decatur, Georgia 30033-4097) to award associate, bachelor's and master's degrees. AIU has also been selected by the Department of Education to participate in the Distance Education Demonstration Program.

DISTANCE LEARNING PROGRAM

AIU Online's virtual campus provides a rich, interactive, world-class education. AIU Online offers degrees with classrooms as close as any Internet-connected computer so students have access to a complete campus experience, 24 hours a day, seven days a week

Best of all, an education from AIU Online provides students with an opportunity to continue their education and advance their careers without disrupting their current lifestyles and schedules. Considering such demands, an education from AIU Online makes the most sense.

DELIVERY MEDIA

The Web-based degree programs delivered from AIU Online are specifically designed for the student who accesses the course from a standard home or work personal computer. Recommended PC specifications are provided to students at the time of enrollment.

PROGRAMS OF STUDY

All AIU Online programs are accelerated, so students can make their move upward sooner. The bachelor's degree programs can be completed in thirteen months, if an associate degree or equivalent course work has been earned. A master's degree or M.B.A. can be completed in ten months.

Business: Today's increasingly complicated business environments demand that existing and future business professionals have a comprehensive knowledge of the economic climate in the modern workforce, and AIU Online's accelerated business administration online degree programs ensure that a student is prepared to meet the challenge in months—not years.

The Business Administration program includes the most sought after concentrations that students can choose from to tailor their business degree to a specific career interest. Business concentrations include accounting and finance, health-care management, human resource management, management, and marketing.

The bachelor's degree in business administration helps provide a solid foundation for any business professional. The curriculum provides an in-depth study in business, management, and marketing and gives students a strong foundation for continued studies, should they wish to advance their business education in the future.

AIU Online's accelerated M.B.A. program ensures that a student is professionally up-to-date and prepared to meet the challenges of today's increasingly complicated business environments. An online education from AIU Online gives students the knowledge and understanding of the economic climate in the modern workplace.

Information Technology (IT): As the modern business world becomes increasingly dependent upon computers, the demand for IT professionals may exceed the number of qualified professionals. AIU Online's online degree programs in information technology offer a real-world education and can qualify a student to meet the demands.

Bachelor's degree students in IT choose one of three concentrations: computer systems, network administration, or programming.

The AIU Online master's degree in information technology with a concentration in Internet security was designed for career-minded students who have the desire to quickly reach the peaks of their professions. The master's degree program combines the technology and Internet security portions of the course work with key information management courses to ensure success in the job market.

Visual Communications: AIU Online is one of the first universities to offer a Bachelor of Fine Arts (B.F.A.) degree in visual communication, with a concentration in digital design—completely online. This program is designed to educate and develop artistic and imaginative students who are interested in such careers as flash animators, Web designers, or computer-based training developers.

The accelerated Bachelor of Fine Arts in visual communication online degree program can be completed in just thirteen months. All required graphics software is included in the cost of course materials, providing students with training in the latest design software necessary to pursue a chosen career upon completion of the degree program.

Criminal Justice: The growing emphasis on homeland security has created an unprecedented demand for criminal justice and security professionals, and AIU Online's accelerated degree program can help students put their fingerprint on this growing employment trend. This accelerated program can be completed in just thirteen months and can help students prepare for such vital, in-demand careers as FBI officers, correction officers, security analysts, U.S. customs agents, directors of airport security, and others.

Education: For students who have a passion for learning and inspiring others, AIU Online offers a master's degree in education. AIU Online's master's degree in education can provide the spark for an individual to start a career as a teacher, corporate instructor, or military trainer. With a concentration in instructional technology, the master's degree in education brings students to the forefront of modern education.

STUDENT SERVICES

To ensure an overall high-quality educational experience and academic success, several student support services are provided to via AIU Online's Virtual Campus, e-mail, and toll-free number, including admissions, academics, financial aid, career placement assistance, and technical support, which are all accessible through a secured Web site. Students also have access to their account information, degree plan, and personal information 24 hours a day through this secured Web site.

CREDIT OPTIONS

In addition to college credit earned at accredited postsecondary institutions, the following can be evaluated for academic advanced standing: CLEP Examination, Advanced Placement (AP) tests, Computer Competency Examination, Extrainstitutional Credit/Experiential Learning, and DANTES/Military Credit.

FACULTY

AIU Online provides experienced faculty members with advanced degrees who bring their real-world experience and expertise to their students. All faculty members teaching online receive training and guidance in online delivery methods and pedagogy. Through this, AIU Online students are ensured that the University places training of the online faculty as a first concern in offering online courses and degree programs.

ADMISSION

To be considered for admission to AIU Online, applicants must submit an application, a $50 application fee, and fulfill all admission requirements for the program. Selection of students for admission into degree programs of study is based on an individual assessment of each applicant. Each applicant must submit proof of high school graduation or the equivalent and participate in an admissions interview arranged by admissions personnel. If the applicant's first language is not English or the applicant graduated from a non-English-speaking university, a TOEFL score of 500 (undergraduate) or 550 (graduate), or other acceptable proof of English proficiency, must be submitted.

TUITION AND FEES

Tuition and fee schedules for programs of study are reviewed with students at the time of entrance. Fees are charged for applications for admission and graduation.

FINANCIAL AID

AIU Online's Financial Aid Department is committed to providing financial aid to those who qualify. AIU Online participates in various federal, state, and private student financial assistance programs. These financial aid programs are designed to provide assistance to students who are currently enrolled or accepted for enrollment but whose financial resources are unable to meet the full cost of their education. In addition, alternative financing options are available to those who qualify.

APPLYING

To apply for admission, a prospective student should submit an online application located at the Web address listed below along with a $50 application fee and complete a personal telephone interview.

CONTACT

Steve Fireng
Vice President of Admissions and Marketing
American InterContinental University Online
5550 Prairie Stone Parkway
Suite 400
Hoffman Estates, Illinois 60192
Telephone: 877-701-3800 (toll-free)
E-mail: info@aiuonline.edu
Web site: http://www.aiuonline.edu

American Military University American Public University System

Distance Learning Programs

Charles Town, West Virginia

American Military University (AMU) is part of the American Public University System, and is a private institution of higher learning licensed by the West Virginia Higher Education Policy Commission. AMU is accredited by the Distance Education and Training Council (DETC) and is a member of the Servicemembers Opportunity Colleges (SOC). The University focuses on the educational needs of the military community, including spouses, and has developed a flexible distance learning model uniquely suited to the military student's lifestyle. Founded in 1993, the University System serves more than 11,000 students studying in 108 countries around the world. The University has continuously broadened its curricula, expanding to include management, business administration, national security, criminal justice, psychology, and space studies in addition to its core military studies and history programs. The University's administrative offices are located in Charles Town, West Virginia.

DISTANCE LEARNING PROGRAM

AMU is exclusively a distance learning institution. All courses are Web based and accessible around the clock through the Electronic Campus from wherever students have Internet access. Students are led through the eight-week or fifteen-week courses with a Student Course Guide that lists weekly study requirements and assignments.

DELIVERY MEDIA

AMU delivers and supports its courses through its Electronic Campus, with classrooms served by Educator® courseware by Ucompass. Through these electronic classrooms, students communicate with professors and each other using LISTSERV, discussion groups, bulletin boards, chat rooms, and e-mail and submit assignments, receive feedback, and take examinations. Electronic communications are supplemented by phone consultations during professors' office hours, with classes restricted to 25 students to ensure adequate student-professor interaction.

PROGRAMS OF STUDY

AMU offers more than fifty graduate and undergraduate degree programs and certificate programs.

Graduate nonthesis programs, consisting of 36 semester hours/twelve courses and a comprehensive final examination, are offered in criminal justice, homeland security, intelligence, management (including public, logistics, and crisis), military studies (including air warfare and special operations), national security studies, political science, public administration, space studies, and transportation management. There are cooperative graduate degree programs in transportation management and marine engineering with the Global Maritime and Transportation School of the U.S. Merchant Marine Academy and in peacekeeping operations with the United Nations Institute for Training and Research (UNITAR).

Certificate programs, consisting of 15 semester hours/five courses, are offered in more than thirty-five specialties within the curriculum and in area studies, period studies, and both historical and contemporary study areas.

Undergraduate programs include the Associate of Arts in general studies, a 63-semester-hour program with 30 semester hours of specified general education courses and electives, and the Bachelor of Arts, a 120-semester-hour program that mirrors the associate degree's lower-division requirements and includes upper-division major requirements of 39 semester hours, with 18 hours of electives. The bachelor's degree is offered in American studies, child development, criminal justice (with an internship for law enforcement professionals), English, family development, history, intelligence studies, interdisciplinary studies, management (with a concentration for military career counselors), marketing (with an internship for military recruiters), military history (with American and world concentrations), military management, philosophy, political science, psychology, religious studies, sociology, and women's studies. Certificate programs are offered in five specialties.

SPECIAL PROGRAMS

AMU offers several unique academic "internship" programs, which consist of a series of courses in a particular degree path that have been modified, allowing students to earn credit for on-the-job learning. These programs are available to students who are working as military recruiters (marketing), to students who are practicing law enforcement professionals (criminal justice), to students working in the security management field, and to any students interested in civic responsibility. Directed reading courses using texts from the military services' recommended reading lists may be taken to satisfy general education requirements or requirements for special military undergraduate certificates. AMU offers military commands the opportunity to set up a Unit Learning Program, a customized curriculum based on a unit's mission or other needs, so students may study together and enhance the unit's performance while the individual progresses along his or her chosen degree path. Other special programs include graduate challenge exams for certain military professional schools, graduate credit programs for certain military schools, and an academic internship program in Special Operations/Low Intensity Conflict.

STUDENT SERVICES

The Student Services department is staffed with counselors available to assist students as needed. These counselors are available by e-mail, phone, and even via online chatrooms. All students experience AMU's online orientation program that prepares them for distance learning, including navigating the electronic campus, using the classroom functions, and understanding student rights and responsibilities, transfer credit, and tuition and financial aid options. Many Student Services' functions are available online and it is easy for students to submit changes and check their status.

CREDIT OPTIONS

Credits may be earned through AMU by traditional courses, challenge examinations, internships, and independent study. Courses may be audited without credit. AMU accepts transfer credit from accredited institutions, training and experience credit recommended by the American Council on Education, and credit by examinations (CLEP, DANTES, etc.).

Credit acceptance by programs is associate degree, up to 45 semester hours; bachelor's degree, up to 90 semester hours; and graduate degree, up to 15 semester hours.

FACULTY

AMU's faculty brings real-world experience and world-class credentials to the online learning experience. More than 300 adjunct faculty members, along with 50 full-time faculty members, work together to ensure AMU students achieve appropriate learning outcomes. All faculty members meet traditional accreditation standards with regard to degrees and professional preparedness.

ADMISSION

Graduate students must possess an accredited baccalaureate degree and a minimum 2.7 GPA in their final 60 undergraduate semester hours. Undergraduate students must have a high school diploma or GED certificate. No examinations are required for admission.

TUITION AND FEES

Tuition is $250 per semester hour for both graduate and undergraduate programs. There is no admission fee. All undergraduate students receive AMU's book grant, covering 100 percent of the costs of all textbooks. Transfer credit evaluations are subject to a one-time fee of $75, and all students who have attended other institutions of higher learning are required to submit a transfer evaluation by the end of their first semester at AMU. A graduation fee of $100 is assessed, which includes a framed and matted degree.

FINANCIAL AID

AMU accepts military tuition assistance, GI Bill and VA educational benefits, and corporate tuition assistance. Undergraduate students may be eligible for the needs-based University Scholarship, which covers up to 25 percent of tuition for students who have no other source of financial aid available. All students are eligible for Sallie Mae education loans, and AMU has an installment payment plan as well. AMU is committed to providing the military community with a quality, low-cost education, and assists military spouses in achieving their educational goals as well, offering a special scholarship program for undergraduate students who are spouses of military personnel.

APPLYING

The application process is easy and is completed online. There is no cost to apply for admission and applicants are conditionally admitted upon submission of the online application form. A Student ID is issued and applicants receive a password via e-mail, allowing them to log in to the electronic campus, complete their online orientation, and register for courses.

CONTACT

Admissions
American Military University
American Public University System
111 West Congress Street
Charles Town, West Virginia 25414
Telephone: 877-468-6268, menu option 2 (toll-free)
E-mail: info@apus.edu
Web site: http://www.apus.edu/amu

The Art Institute of Pittsburgh

The Art Institute Online

Pittsburgh, Pennsylvania

The Art Institute Online, a division of The Art Institute of Pittsburgh, is one of The Art Institutes, with 31 education institutions located throughout North America, providing an important source of design, media arts, fashion and culinary professionals. The parent company of The Art Institutes, Education Management Corporation, is among the largest providers of private postsecondary education in North America, based on student enrollment and revenue. Student enrollment exceeded 58,000 as of fall 2003. The Art Institute of Pittsburgh is accredited by the Accrediting Council for Independent Colleges and Schools (ACICS).

DISTANCE LEARNING PROGRAM

The Art Institute Online began enrolling students in 2000 and is backed by the eighty-year tradition of exceptional academic standards of The Art Institute of Pittsburgh. There is no difference in the outcomes or competencies gained in the courses students take online as compared to those that are taught at The Art Institute of Pittsburgh. The difference is the learning process itself. Available degree programs offered through The Art Institute Online include Advertising, Graphic Design, Game Art & Design, Interactive Media Design, Interior Design, and a bachelor's degree completion program in Culinary Management.

DELIVERY MEDIA

Courses delivered by The Art Institute Online are accessed on a computer using an Internet connection. The Art Institute Online classes are asynchronous, which means that students don't have to attend classes at a specific time of day. Students must log in and participate in class five out of seven days each week, but they can log in at a time of day or night most convenient for them. Asynchronous learning adds a level of convenience for students, but it also means that students must have the discipline and motivation to meet assignment deadlines and attendance requirements. Full-time online students are encouraged to take a maximum of two courses during each 5½-week session, or four courses every quarter.

PROGRAMS OF STUDY

The Art Institute Online is currently offering five bachelor's degree programs, one bachelor's degree completion program, two associate degree programs, and three diploma programs. The bachelor's degree programs consist of 180 credits, the associate degree programs consist of 105 credits, and the diploma programs consist of 36 credits. The Bachelor of Science degree is offered in Advertising, Graphic Design, Game Art & Design, Interactive Media Design, and Interior Design; the Culinary Management bachelor's degree completion program is also offered. The Associate of Science degree is offered in Graphic Design and Interactive Media Design. In addition, diploma programs are offered in Digital Design, Residential Planning, and Web Design.

STUDENT SERVICES

There are several student-support services provided to students of The Art Institute Online. These include a virtual library of full-text and graphic databases that includes 60,000 digitized works of art and full-text articles from 8,000 magazines, online tutorials that help students develop specific skills needed in their program of study, and admission to the Talk-on! forum where students can meet and share ideas outside of class. Through hardware, software, and bookstore partners' online stores, students can purchase the textbooks and supplies they need at special student pricing. In addition, Career Services advisers offer a range of services to support students as they prepare to enter their intended profession.

CREDIT OPTIONS

There are five ways to gain advanced academic credit at The Art Institute Online. These include Advanced Placement exams, CLEP testing, transfer of credit for postsecondary courses, credit for life/work experience, and the Computer Literacy Test-Out Exam. More information about how to utilize these options can be found at The Art Institute Online Web site or through an Admissions representative.

FACULTY

Courses at The Art Institute Online are led by trained, experienced instructors, who aid the learning process by addressing student needs, interjecting real-world industry experience, and providing direction to create a unique learning experience for each student. Instead of using lecture as the primary method of teaching, instructors guide discussion among students and ensure that core course material is covered. Typically, the average class size is 15–20 students, which allows the instructors to provide individualized attention to students.

ADMISSION

A prospective student seeking admission to the Advertising, Graphic Design, Interactive Media Design, or Interior Design program at The Art Institute Online must be a high school graduate with a high school GPA of 2.0, hold a General Educational Development (GED) certificate, or have a bachelor's degree or higher.

A prospective student for the Game Art & Design program seeking admission must be a high school graduate with a high school GPA of 2.5, hold a General Educational Development certificate with a score of 257 or higher, or have a bachelor's degree or higher.

A prospective student for the Culinary Management bachelor's degree completion program must have an associate degree in culinary arts.

TUITION AND FEES

As of June 1, 2004, the standard tuition fee is $373 per credit hour, plus an additional $100 online lab fee per course. Books, software, and other supply costs vary with each program. More information about these costs can be found at The Art Institute Online Web site or through The Art Institute Online Admissions Department.

FINANCIAL AID

Many students receive some form of financial aid to assist them in financing their education. The Art Institute of Pittsburgh participates in federal, some state, and other financial aid programs. The Art Institute of Pittsburgh also offers financial planning to its students, providing payment plans that allow students to budget for the entire program. The goal is to make a student's monthly payments as affordable as possible. After the application forms have been completed, a Student Financial Aid Officer reviews them using a federally required calculation to determine a student's eligibility for financial aid. The Financial Aid Officer works with the student and the student's family to devise a Student Financial Plan to help cover educational expenses, based on the student's financial aid eligibility and family circumstances.

APPLYING

An application for admission must be completed, signed by the applicant, and submitted to The Art Institute Online with a $50 application fee. A prospective student is advised individually about the specific requirements of online programs. In addition, a personal telephone interview and a student's proof of high school graduation are required for acceptance. Applicants must submit a completed enrollment agreement and a $100 enrollment fee within ten days of application. Applicants not accepted for admission receive a full refund of all fees paid.

CONTACT

Admissions Department
The Art Institute Online
420 Boulevard of the Allies
Pittsburgh, Pennsylvania 15219
Telephone: 877-872-8869 (toll-free)
E-mail: aioadm@aii.edu
Web site: http://www.aionline.edu

Athabasca University

Distance Learning

Athabasca, Alberta, Canada

Athabasca University (AU) was created as a publicly funded and fully accredited university under the statutes of the Province of Alberta, Canada. Athabasca University specializes in the delivery of distance education courses and programs.

Athabasca University's mission statement reflects a commitment to innovation, flexibility, excellence in teaching, research, and scholarship. Emphasis has also been placed on international development.

Athabasca University is a full member of the Association of Universities and Colleges of Canada, the Association of Commonwealth Universities, the International Council for Open and Distance Education, the Canadian Association for Distance Education, Canadian Association for Graduate Studies, Canadian Virtual University, Circumpolar Universities Association, Global University Alliance, Inter-American Distance Education Consortium, Smart Education Society, and Western Governor's University (participant). AU has been awarded candidacy status for U.S. accreditation by the Commission on Higher Education of the Middle States Association of Colleges and Schools. Details are available at http://www.athabascau.ca/main/accredit.html.

Athabasca University's Executive M.B.A. (EMBA) has been included on the prestigious list of the world's top seventy-five EMBA programs by the Financial Times *of London, England. Launched as the world's first online M.B.A. in 1994, the AU program is the only fully online Executive M.B.A. to be included in this year's list.*

DISTANCE LEARNING PROGRAM

Athabasca University, Canada's largest online and distance education university, delivers courses and programs at both the undergraduate and graduate levels. The flexibility of online and distance learning allows students to complete courses and full credential programs on a full-time or part-time basis. Students may also complete Athabasca University courses to satisfy the graduation requirements at other universities and colleges. AU courses are accessed by more than 30,000 individuals annually.

DELIVERY MEDIA

Athabasca University uses a variety of learning methods, including multimedia online activities, print materials, e-mail, the Internet, CD-ROMs, computer software, audioconferencing, videoconferencing, audiotapes, videotapes, TV, and radio. Any particular course might use a combination of these methods. Students have support from professors, tutors, advisers, and service departments through contact by e-mail and telephone (toll-free in Canada and the U.S.).

PROGRAMS OF STUDY

Graduate degree and diploma programs offered are the Master of Arts–Integrated Studies, Master of Business Administration (with majors in information technology management and program management), Master of Counselling (collaborative), Master of Distance Education, Master of Health Studies, Master of Nursing, Master of Science–Information Systems, Advanced Graduate Diploma in Advanced Nursing Practice, Advanced Graduate Diploma in Distance Education (Technology), and Advanced Graduate Diploma in Management.

Undergraduate degrees offered are the Bachelor of Administration (concentrations in health administration, industrial relations and human resources, management, organization, and public administration); Bachelor of Arts (three and four year) with concentrations or majors in anthropology, English, French, history, humanities, information systems, labour studies, political economy, psychology, sociology, women's studies, or Canadian studies; Bachelor of Commerce; Bachelor of Commerce: e-commerce major; Bachelor of General Studies with designation in arts and science or applied studies; Bachelor of Health Administration and Bachelor of Health Administration Post-Diploma; Bachelor of Human Resources and Labour Relations; Bachelor of Management (three and four year and post-diploma); Bachelor of Nursing (post-RN); Bachelor of Nursing (post-LPN); Bachelor of Professional Arts (B.P.A.): governance, law, and management major; B.P.A.: criminal justice major; B.P.A.: communications major; B.P.A.: human services major; Bachelor of Science; Bachelor of Science in human science (major or post-diploma); Bachelor of Science in computing and information systems; and Bachelor of Science in computing and information systems (post-diploma).

University certificate programs are offered in accounting, administration, advanced accounting, career development, computers and management information systems, computing and information systems, counseling women, English language studies, French language proficiency, health development administration, home health nursing, industrial relations and human resources, labour studies, and public administration.

University diploma programs in arts and inclusive education are also offered.

SPECIAL PROGRAMS

Canadian Virtual University (CVU) is an innovative partnership of Canada's leading English and French universities. Students can select from among 2,000 courses in the CVU catalogue and apply them to programs at any partner university. There are also fee savings for students who take courses from more than one partner university. For easy searching of courses and complete programs, students should visit CVU's Web site (http://www.cvu-uvc.ca). Athabasca University is a founding partner in CVU.

AU's many partnerships with various institutions and organizations provide a multitude of learning options for students. Approximately twenty of these alliances are international (Japan, China, England, Jamaica, Mexico, Malaysia, Trinidad, South Africa, and Taiwan). For a current list, students should visit http://www.athabascau.ca/html/collab/collab.htm.

STUDENT SERVICES

AU takes pride in providing exceptional service to students. Service departments, including the Information Centre, Academic Centres, Learning Centres, Office of the Registrar, Course Materials, Computing Services, and Library Services offer service, information, and advice. The first point of contact for questions is the Information Centre at 800-788-9041 (toll-free in Canada and the U.S.) or 780-675-6100 (international). Students can also visit the new IntelliResponse system (http://www.askau.ca) for a quick answer to most general questions.

CREDIT OPTIONS

Athabasca University grants credit for approved courses completed at other recognized postsecondary institutions, and its credits are eligible for transfer to programs at other universities worldwide. Some students can apply for a Prior Learning Assessment, which evaluates nonformal university-level learning for credit toward a credential. Athabasca University courses are generally either 3 credits or 6 credits. Typically, a three-year degree program requires 90 credits and four-year degree programs require 120 credits.

FACULTY

Athabasca University employs 247 faculty members and 249 tutors. Academic staff members and tutors contribute to Athabasca University's high student satisfaction rating.

ADMISSION

Undergraduate admission is year-round, and anyone 16 years of age or older is eligible for admission, regardless of previous educational experience, with or without a high school diploma. (A few programs and courses may have academic or geographic restrictions). The admission requirements for graduate programs is typically a baccalaureate degree from a recognized postsecondary institution. Additional requirements vary between programs. Students should consult the calendar or Web site for information.

TUITION AND FEES

It is important to note that textbooks, course materials, and fees are included in the tuition fee. The cost for undergraduate 3-credit registration is Can$541 (in province), Can$596 (out of province), and Can$791 (international); for 6-credit registration, Can$930 (provincial), Can$985 (out of province), and Can$1180 (international). Graduate program fees vary by program, so students should consult the calendar or visit the Web site for graduate fee information.

FINANCIAL AID

Financial assistance is available to full- and part-time students from Alberta Students Finance or the financial aid agency where a student resides. The amount varies according to need. In-province students obtain a financial aid package from Athabasca University. Out-of-province students should contact the financial aid agency in their locale. All students are automatically considered for academic awards and scholarships without application unless specified otherwise. Award recipients are announced twice per year at Convocation.

APPLYING

Admission to undergraduate programs is year-round. Applicants should consider postal and processing times when a particular starting time is desired. To apply, students should complete a General Application Form and Course Registration Form and submit them with applicable fees. Forms are available in the calendar, by fax, or on the Web. Graduate programs have application deadlines, which can be found on the calendar or the Web site listed below.

CONTACT

Athabasca University Information Centre
1 University Drive
Athabasca, Alberta T9S 3A3
Canada
Telephone: 780-675-6100
800-788-9041 (toll-free in Canada and the U.S.)
Fax: 780-675-6437
E-mail: inquire@athabascau.ca
Web site:
http://www.athabascau.ca

Auburn University

Graduate Outreach Program

Auburn, Alabama

Auburn University was chartered in 1856 as the East Alabama Male College. In 1872, Auburn became a state institution—the first land-grant university in the South to be separate from a state university. Auburn University is Alabama's premier engineering and business institution. U.S. News & World Report*'s "America's Best Colleges" ranks both Auburn's College of Business and its College of Engineering among the nation's top forty programs at public institutions. Auburn is dedicated to serving the state and the nation through instruction, research, and extension. Auburn University is accredited by the Commission on Colleges of the Southern Association of Colleges and Schools.*

The campus consists of more than 1,800 acres, with a student body of approximately 22,000. Auburn University, the largest school in the state of Alabama, is located in east-central Alabama. The city of Auburn has a population of about 35,000. Auburn is known for its small-town, friendly atmosphere and is often referred to as "the loveliest village on the Plain."

DISTANCE LEARNING PROGRAM

In response to industry's request, Auburn's College of Engineering began offering courses to off-campus students through the Graduate Outreach Program in 1984. The College of Business made Master of Business Administration (M.B.A.) courses available in 1990. The Graduate Outreach Program allows professionals the opportunity to continue their education while maintaining full-time employment. The program serves more than 400 students in forty states. The M.B.A. program is accredited by AACSB International–The Association to Advance Collegiate Schools of Business.

Note for international inquirers: Due to material distribution methods, the current distance learning program service area is limited to the U.S. and Canada and to U.S. military personnel with APO or FPO mailing addresses.

DELIVERY MEDIA

The Graduate Outreach Program makes every effort to ensure that the off-campus students receive the same high-quality education as on-campus students. Live classes are videotaped daily and distributed in standard VHS or DVD format. Professors establish telephone office hours and/or e-mail communication so that off-campus students may receive answers to any questions they may have. E-mail accounts are established for the Graduate Outreach Program students. Most faculty members also utilize the Internet to post handouts and class materials.

PROGRAMS OF STUDY

The Graduate Outreach Program offers the Master of Management Information Systems, the Master of Accounting, and the Master of Business Administration degrees as well as master's degrees in eight different disciplines in engineering. The Master of Aerospace Engineering, Chemical Engineering, Civil Engineering, Computer Science and Engineering, Electrical and Computer Engineering, Industrial and Systems Engineering, Materials Engineering, and Mechanical Engineering are all nonthesis programs without residency requirements. Each candidate must pass an on-campus, comprehensive, oral examination covering the program of study to graduate. The examination covers the major and minor subjects, including any research or special projects involved. The Master of Science degree, offered in eight disciplines, requires a formal written thesis and at least one quarter of full-time residence.

In the Master of Business Administration program, students may earn a concentration in either finance, health-care administration, human resource management, management information systems, management of technology, marketing, or operations management. The program consists of 36 to 42 semester hours of course work, including eight core courses and four electives. Applicants are required to complete a course in calculus and statistics prior to entering the program. Students with nonbusiness undergraduate degrees may be required to pass foundations exams in economics, finance, marketing, management, and accounting. Incoming students are also advised to have a working knowledge of word processing and spreadsheet software and an elementary understanding of database applications. M.B.A. students must visit the campus for five days during their final fall semester prior to graduating for on-campus presentations.

Nondegree professional development courses are available for those who need to meet job requirements or professional certification.

SPECIAL PROGRAMS

Career and job placement assistance is available through Auburn University's Career and Student Development Services. Accessibility to the R. B. Draughon Library is also available. A valid Auburn University student identification card is required to check out resources. The Division of University Computing provides University-wide computing and networking services to students. Computer accounts are free of charge to currently enrolled students.

CREDIT OPTIONS

Graduate credit taken in residence at another approved graduate school may be transferred to Auburn University but is not accepted until the student has completed at least 9 hours of work in the Graduate School at Auburn University. No prior commitment is made concerning whether transfer credit can be accepted. A student must earn at least 21 semester hours or half of the total hours required for a master's degree (whichever is greater) at Auburn University. No transfer credit is approved without two official transcripts. No course in which a grade lower than B was earned may be transferred.

FACULTY

The Auburn University faculty consists of more than 1,200 members. Eighty percent of the faculty members hold a doctoral degree, and 88 percent hold a terminal degree in their field.

ADMISSION

An applicant to the Graduate School must hold a bachelor's degree or its equivalent from an accredited college or university. The Graduate Record Examinations (GRE) is required for admission to the College of Engineering, and the Graduate Management Admission Test (GMAT) is required for admission to the M.B.A. program. Students whose native language is not English must submit scores of the Test of English as a Foreign Language (TOEFL) for admission to the M.B.A. program. Admission is based on the grade point average of university-level courses, GRE or GMAT scores, and recommendation letters from instructors and supervisors. Students can be informed by the Graduate Outreach Program on how they can enroll as off-campus students once they are accepted by the Graduate School.

TUITION AND FEES

The Graduate Outreach Program fees are $500 per credit hour for engineering and $510 for business. Registration schedules and fee bills are mailed to the student prior to the beginning of each quarter.

FINANCIAL AID

Military personnel who have been accepted into the Graduate School may apply for tuition aid through DANTES at their local education office. Many of the Graduate Outreach Program students receive tuition assistance through their employer's tuition reimbursement plan. The Auburn University Office of Student Financial Aid assists in the awarding of grants, loans, and scholarships for qualified full-time students.

APPLYING

To apply for admission, a prospective student must return a Graduate School application, an M.B.A. application (if applicable), a nonrefundable application fee of $25 for U.S. citizens or $50 for non-U.S. citizens, three letters of recommendation, GRE or GMAT scores, and two official transcripts of all undergraduate and subsequent course work from the respective institutions. Graduate School applicants may apply online at http://www.grad.auburn.edu. This ensures a quicker response in most cases.

CONTACT

Wanda Lambert
Graduate Outreach Program
217 Ramsay Hall
Auburn University
Auburn, Alabama 36849-5331
Telephone: 888-844-5300 (toll-free)
Fax: 334-844-2502
E-mail: lambewf@eng.auburn.edu
Web site: http://www.eng.auburn.edu/gop/

Baker College

Baker Online

Flint, Michigan

Baker College, founded in the true American tradition as a small business college in 1888, is a private, nonprofit, accredited, coeducational institution. The College has more than a dozen campuses and branch locations in the Midwest and has a total enrollment of more than 25,000 students. The College is uniquely designed for one purpose: to provide high-quality higher education that enables graduates to be successful throughout their challenging and rewarding careers. The College offers diploma; certificate; and associate, bachelor's, and master's degree programs in the fields of business, technical, and health service fields. Total commitment to the students' employment success in uniquely evident in all aspects of the College's operations.

Baker College is accredited by the Commission on Institutions of Higher Education of the North Central Association of Colleges and Schools. Baker College is an equal opportunity/affirmative action institution.

DISTANCE LEARNING PROGRAM

Baker Online offers the convenience of classroom accessibility 24 hours a day, seven days a week, from virtually anywhere in the world. It is not a self-paced program. Courses begin and end on specific dates and classwork is assigned deadlines, but as long as students have Internet access, they have access to their courses.

DELIVERY MEDIA

Students are required to have a computer with the following minimum requirements: a Pentium III or higher system, Windows XP Professional or higher, a 56K (minimum) modem, Internet Explorer 5.5 or Netscape 4.7 or higher (AOL is not compatible), and Microsoft Office XP Professional. A CD-ROM and an Internet service provider are required. The virtual classroom is the common meeting area for all students taking classes on line. Communication is accomplished by sending messages back and forth from the student's computer to the classroom computer. Each classroom has a unique name, and only students taking that class have access to the virtual classroom. This ensures privacy for all students.

PROGRAMS OF STUDY

Baker Online offers the delivery of high-quality, respected courses and programs that enable a student to earn an associate, bachelor's, or master's degree at home, on the road, or anywhere in the world.

The Associate of Business Administration degree has been designed specifically for the online college environment, where students have a variety of choices in filling out the degree plan. The curriculum gives students a good background of business facts and knowledge upon which to build or enhance a career in business.

The Bachelor of Business Administration degree is a program designed for the working professional that combines core course work with independent research and experiential credit to provide a contemporary business degree for today's business environment. Each core course contains focused study in the content area accompanied by independent research.

The Master of Business Administration degree program seeks to combine the best of conventional academic training with the best of field-based learning. Most typical business disciplines are represented in the curriculum because the College believes that a successful manager must be conversant with different aspects of running any of today's organizations or companies. Students may also elect to focus their studies in one of the following areas: computer information systems, health-care management, human resource management, industrial management, integrated health care, international business, leadership studies, or marketing.

SPECIAL PROGRAMS

Baker Online offers undergraduate courses at all levels to support all of the campuses and their program offerings as a convenience for students who may have trouble commuting to a campus. Baker Online publishes a listing each quarter showing which classes will be offered.

STUDENT SERVICES

Every Baker College student is assigned an e-mail account on the BakerNet system. Through this system, students can communicate with each other and their instructors and with members of the graduate school staff. Students may also use their accounts to access the World Wide Web. They also have access to the Baker College Library System and FALCON, a consortium of libraries that supports an online catalog database of more than 500,000 holdings. Students also have access to InfoTrac periodical indexing databases, the UMI/ProQuest General Periodicals On-Disc full-article imaging station, Books-in-Print with Reviews, and all available Internet and World Wide Web resources.

Baker College offers a renowned Lifetime Employment Service, with access to thousands of career opportunities and employment databases, to all students. This service can be used for the rest of one's life.

CREDIT OPTIONS

Baker College recognizes the expediency of understandable and universally accepted standards related to transfer of academic credit. The College follows the Michigan Association of Collegiate Registrars and Admissions Officers Official Policies and recognizes the College-Level Examination Program (CLEP) or other standardized tests.

FACULTY

The focus of Baker's faculty is somewhat different from that of traditional universities. Instead of placing an emphasis on empirical research, Baker values practitioner-oriented education. Faculty members remain continually active in their professions by consulting, conducting seminars, running their own businesses, writing, volunteering in their communities, and working with other organizations. The faculty-student ratio in distance education is 1:12.

ADMISSION

Graduate program candidates must have a bachelor's degree from an accredited institution and a 2.5 or better GPA in their undergraduate work, be able to display appropriate communication skills, submit three letters of reference, submit a current resume, and have completed no less than three years of full-time work. Undergraduates must have graduated from high school, completed a GED, or passed an Ability to Benefit assessment before entering.

TUITION AND FEES

Undergraduate tuition for the 2003–04 school year was $170 per credit hour. Graduate tuition was $265 per credit hour. The cost of books ranged from $150 to $200 per quarter.

FINANCIAL AID

Students who are accepted into Baker College may be considered for several forms of state, federal, and institutional financial aid. Students are requested to complete the Free Application for Federal Student Aid (FAFSA) and return it directly to the College.

APPLYING

Baker College uses a rolling admission process, so there are no deadlines for applications. Students are allowed to begin in any quarter. Once the Admissions Committee receives an application, applicants usually receive a decision in approximately four weeks. Once accepted, students participate in a three-week online orientation. They are not required to visit a campus at any time.

CONTACT

Chuck J. Gurden
Vice President for Admissions
Center for Graduate Studies
Baker Online
1116 West Bristol Road
Flint, Michigan 48507-9843
Telephone: 810-766-4390
800-469-3165 (toll-free)
Fax: 810-766-4399
E-mail: cgurde01@baker.edu
Web site: http://online.baker.edu

Bellevue University

Online Programs

Bellevue, Nebraska

Bellevue University is one of Nebraska's largest fully accredited independent colleges. It is accredited by the Higher Learning Commission and a member of the North Central Association of Colleges and Schools' Commission on Institutions of Higher Education (NCA-CIHE), 30 North LaSalle Street, Suite 2400, Chicago, Illinois 60602-2504; telephone: 800-621-7440 (toll-free). Programs serve the needs of more than 4,000 students annually and cater to working adult students as well as traditional undergraduate students. Benefits include accelerated degree completion programs, online programs, an online library, and cooperative credit transfer agreements. Associate degrees are accepted in full, and credit is given for corporate and military training.

DISTANCE LEARNING PROGRAM

Bellevue University is an information-age institution of higher learning with progressive options for online graduate and undergraduate degrees. Graduate and undergraduate programs, online, on campus, and in centers throughout the region, prepare students for an ever-changing environment.

DELIVERY MEDIA

Online education is about taking classes and earning a degree entirely through the Internet. With Internet access, students go online to take classes, participate in discussions with professors and fellow students, conduct research at the online library, and interact with their online adviser. Online classes are small to give the cyberactive learning advantage that characterizes Bellevue University.

PROGRAMS OF STUDY

Undergraduate programs are offered in an accelerated, cohort-based format. The program in business administration of technical studies emphasizes techniques, procedures, and methods for managing the technical functions of business. The business information systems program prepares students who do not have computer technology degrees or course work for management within information technology (IT) and positions with technical applications. The program in criminal justice administration focuses on management and opportunities in the criminal justice system. The program is designed for individuals working in, or closely associated with, the criminal justice system. The e-business program covers the interchange and processing of information using electronic techniques for conducting business within a framework of generally accepted standards and practices. The program in global business management provides the knowledge, skills, and abilities to evaluate and manage international businesses. The health-care administration program provides a systems perspective for those interested in pursuing management opportunities in health care. The program in Internet systems and software technology provides a comprehensive study of the information technology industry. Topics are included in an integrated format built around a common project management theme. The leadership program provides students the theoretical and practical preparation they need to assume positions of leadership in the professional ranks of organizations. The management program gives students a comprehensive background in the skills, methods, and theories that undergird all effective management. The management of human resources program covers methods and practices of the human resource management professional. The management information systems program emphasizes business knowledge and management skills for individuals working in the management information systems field. The marketing management program emphasizes the techniques and methods of managing and planning in marketing. The focus is on proven practices and application of theory.

The Master of Business Administration (M.B.A.) program covers the tools and methods required to run a business. The program requires 36 credit hours of course work. The schedule of course offerings permits an individual working full-time to complete all the requirements for the M.B.A. degree in eighteen months (two classes per term). Students who do not have an undergraduate degree in business generally take the Foundation (12 credits) and the Core (24 credits) to complete the degree. M.B.A. concentrations are offered in accounting, finance, international management, management information systems, and marketing. The Master of Science in computer information systems program has strong elements of both business and computer/telecommunication subjects. Students with business or computer undergraduate preparation typically finish the program with 36 credits of graduate work. For students without a computer background, there are 9 additional prerequisite credits. The Master of Science in health-care administration program provides clinical health-care providers with an opportunity to pursue in depth the various areas of planning, organizing, leading, and controlling as they provide administrative guidance to others within their health-related organization. Students in the Master of Arts in Management program develop a working knowledge of the application of quantitative techniques, marketing analysis, human resource management, financial analysis, influencing behavior in organizations, and sensitivity to the legal environment in which operations occur. The Master of Arts in Leadership program encourages individual thought, synthesis of group contribution, and assimilation of practical and theoretical teachings. Its mission is to combine leadership philosophy, derived from great leaders and their writings, with concepts and theoretical models of organizational leadership. The Master of Arts and the Master of Science in communication studies programs address competencies in the areas of critical thinking, research, professional and social skills, diversity and intercultural communication, applied theory, leadership, and emotional intelligence. The programs are designed to produce graduates who can bridge the modern workplace communication gap, meet internal training and development needs, and identify and utilize effective skills to address important communication issues inherent in all work environments.

CREDIT OPTIONS

Bellevue University grants credit for college-level learning that a student has obtained through sources other than college classes. Students may be granted credit for college-level learning acquired outside of a regionally accredited college setting. Procedures are in place to assess student learning from non–regionally accredited institutions, American Council on Education recommendations, corporate training or programs, CLEP/DANTES tests, and the Experiential Learning Assessment.

FACULTY

The Bellevue University full-time and adjunct faculty consists of 132 men and 58 women teaching students from freshman to graduate level. The student-faculty ratio is 20:1. For most classes and programs, Bellevue University employs adjunct faculty members who are professionals in their respective fields. Faculty members are screened to ensure each is current on issues and technology.

ADMISSION

Online degree completion programs are offered in an accelerated format. To qualify for undergraduate programs, students must have at least 60 credit hours from an accredited institution or an associate degree. To qualify for graduate programs, students must have a baccalaureate degree from an accredited institution, a minimum 2.5 GPA over the course of the last two years of undergraduate work, two letters of recommendation, and a completed essay.

TUITION AND FEES

Online undergraduate tuition for a 36-hour major program is $9360; for the 9-hour Signature Series, it is $1665. Undergraduate fees include the nonrefundable application/assessment fee, $25; student fees, $150; and graduation fees, $75. The estimated total cost for an online undergraduate program is $11,275. This figure excludes the cost of books.

Tuition for the graduate online programs is as follows: the Master of Business Administration and the Master of Science in computer information systems, $295 per credit hour; the Master of Arts in Leadership and the Master of Arts in Management, $10,620 or $295 per credit hour (excluding books); and Master of Science in health-care administration, $2295 for Term I (Comprehensive Learning Modules) and $9375 for Terms II–IV. The application fee is $50 and graduation fee $75 for all online graduate programs. The general college fee is $45 per semester for the M.B.A. and the M.S. in computer information systems programs and $150 for the M.A. in Management, the M.A. in Leadership, and the M.S. in health-care administration. Additional costs for the M.S. in health-care administration program include an assessment fee of $360 and an estimated cost for instructional materials of $1000. Instructional materials include the cost of books and any additional materials, such as software, required to complete the program. Ordering and purchasing these materials is the responsibility of the student.

FINANCIAL AID

Financial aid assists students with the costs of attending college. This assistance comes from the federal and state government, the institution, and private sources. Financial aid includes grants, scholarships, work-study programs, and student loans. Grants and scholarships do not have to be repaid.

APPLYING

Individuals interested in applying should transmit the application online or by mail, pay fees, and submit transcripts for evaluation. Admissions counselors work with students to complete the official admissions process. An educational degree plan is completed for each student, defining the requirements needed to achieve each student's degree goal.

CONTACT

Bellevue University
1000 Galvin Road South
Bellevue, Nebraska 68005
Telephone: 402-293-2000
800-756-7920 (toll-free)
E-mail: info@bellevue.edu
Web site:
http://www.bellevue.edu

Berkeley College

Berkeley College

Berkeley College Online

Paramus, West Paterson, and Woodbridge, New Jersey; White Plains and New York, New York

Since its inception in 1931, Berkeley College has evolved and expanded, and it is recognized as a premier educator in the New York metropolitan area. The College prepares people of all generations for successful careers in business. All of our five urban and suburban campuses are accredited by the Middle States Commission on Higher Education. The New York and New Jersey campuses are authorized to confer bachelor's and associate degrees.

DISTANCE LEARNING PROGRAM

Through the power of the Internet, Berkeley brings its classrooms to students online with the same high standards of its on-site classes. Students receive the same proven curriculum, faculty support, high standards, and ultimate job placement as the on-site programs and learn directly from faculty members with successful records in business and excellent teaching credentials. Small, stimulating classes emphasize the development of creative and analytical skills. Students can log on to Berkeley anytime, anywhere—and earn a Bachelor of Science (B.S.) degree in business administration or a Bachelor of Business Administration (B.B.A.) degree in general business in as little as three years.

DELIVERY MEDIA

Berkeley supports each one of its online students with an instructor, classmates, and an academic adviser, all of whom are just an e-mail away.

Berkeley has always taught courses to all generations. With the understanding that many students may need to balance work, family, and social responsibilities with their course work, a Berkeley student may log on to a course from anywhere in the world, anytime he or she wants.

PROGRAMS OF STUDY

Berkeley is a college committed to excellence in business education and strongly aligned with the business community. The online program delivers an exceptional distance learning education for working adults. Berkeley students receive all of the personal attention and benefits of the traditional educational experience—without ever having to leave home or office.

The following is a sample of distance learning courses offered via the Internet: business organization and management, mathematics for business, entertainment studies, business law II, spreadsheets and database management applications, graphical business presentations and integration, English composition (I–III), international trade, international marketing, world literature, philosophy, contemporary American history, humanities in the media, environmental science, health and heredity, psychology, microeconomics, sociology, the changing family: a multicultural perspective, culture and crisis, principles of management, human resource management, small business management, and consumer behavior.

STUDENT SERVICES

Online learners may use all of Berkeley's services, from libraries to academic advisers. More than 20 Berkeley career service professionals are on the staff to help with students' resumes and interviewing skills. With many connections to professionals in the business world, career service professionals also arrange interviews for students with many of the finest corporations in the New York area.

The Berkeley balance of conceptual and practical education results in 94 percent of their graduates gaining employment in positions related to their course work.

CREDIT OPTIONS

Transfer counselors help students transfer their previously earned credits to Berkeley. Prior learning experiences (including alternatives to classroom instruction) may help students earn credits and complete their programs ahead of schedule.

FACULTY

Berkeley's faculty members are practicing professionals who are as accessible as they are accomplished. Faculty members combine academic credentials and business success in the fields they teach, ensuring that students acquire the most current knowledge and skills.

ADMISSION

Basic requirements for admission to Berkeley College include graduation from an accredited high school or equivalent and entrance exam or SAT/ACT scores. A personal interview is strongly recommended. The following credentials must be submitted as part of the application process: a completed application form, a nonrefundable $40 application fee, and an unofficial transcript for currently enrolled high school students or a high school diploma or its equivalent for high school graduates. Students who graduated from an accredited high school or its equivalent and attended a college or university are considered transfer students. To be considered for admission, transfer students must submit an application for admission and the nonrefundable $40 application fee, a transcript from each college or university attended, and a high school transcript or GED. For all students, applications are accepted after credentials are received.

To be admitted directly to the upper division, students must have completed either a relevant associate degree or at least 60 semester/90 quarter credits in appropriate course work (with a grade of C or better) at Berkeley or another regionally accredited institution.

TUITION AND FEES

In 2004–05, full-time students pay $15,900 in tuition and fees. Berkeley offers protection from tuition increase to students who maintain continuous, full-time enrollment.

FINANCIAL AID

Berkeley is committed to helping students find the financing options that make their education possible. Financial assistance programs are available from federal and state sources and through Berkeley in the forms of scholarships, grants, loans and other awards. Berkeley College awards more than $12 million each year in scholarships and institutional aid based on academic achievement and financial need. Financial advisers are available to meet with students and their families to develop a plan best suited to individual goals and circumstances.

APPLYING

Applications are accepted on an ongoing basis. Current students who wish to apply for online learning must obtain approval from an Academic Dean. Prospective students who wish to apply as online learning students should submit an online application on the Web site listed in the Contact section. Applicants must successfully complete a short introductory course to familiarize themselves with online learning prior to course registration.

CONTACT

Berkeley College
Telephone: 800-446-5400, Ext. G30 (toll-free)
E-mail: info@berkeleycollege.edu
Web site: http://www.berkeleycollege.edu

West Paterson Campus
Berkeley College
44 Rifle Camp Road
West Paterson, New Jersey 07424

Paramus Campus
Berkeley College
64 East Midland Avenue
Paramus, New Jersey 07652

Woodbridge Campus
Berkeley College
430 Rahway Avenue
Woodbridge, New Jersey 07095

New York City Campus
Berkeley College
3 East 43rd Street
New York, New York 10017

White Plains Campus
Berkeley College
99 Church Street
White Plains, New York 10601

Brenau University

Online College

Gainesville, Georgia

Brenau University, founded in 1878, is a historic, private, comprehensive university in Gainesville, Georgia. The University's three colleges—the coeducational Online College and Evening and Weekend College (EWC), and the Women's College—have complementary missions.

The Online College serves a population of students who are unable or unwilling to attend campus-based classes. Degree and certificate programs are offered entirely online, with a focus on collaborative learning. The EWC serves a growing population of working adult men and women by offering degree and certificate programs and other classes in five locations across the state (Atlanta, Augusta, Gainesville, Kings Bay, and Waleska). The Women's College, located on the picturesque main campus in Gainesville, has provided a single-gender liberal arts education since its founding in 1878.

Brenau University is accredited by the Southern Association of Colleges and Schools.

DISTANCE LEARNING PROGRAM

The Online College provides high-quality educational experiences through the delivery of graduate and undergraduate programs utilizing the latest distance learning technology. Programs delivered in the online format are designed for working adult students, providing maximum flexibility without compromising learning outcomes or academic rigor.

DELIVERY MEDIA

Online classes are delivered via the Internet. Common software programs are used to enhance the delivery of course materials. Dialogue among students, using an asynchronous bulletin board system, is central to the collaborative learning goal. Online students bring with them varied life and work experiences that, when shared with classmates, provide relevant applications of theory to real-world situations.

PROGRAMS OF STUDY

Brenau University currently offers fully online degree programs with no residency requirements in business, conflict resolution, education, and nursing.

Brenau's RN to B.S.N. bridge program provides registered nurses the opportunity for career advancement by earning a bachelor's degree. An experienced and academically qualified faculty of registered nurses offers this 120-hour program. The clinical portion of this program may be completed in the student's local community, supervised by a Brenau nursing faculty member.

The Bachelor of Business Administration in Management is a 63-credit hour degree program designed to build on an associate's degree or a student's satisfactory completion of two years of general education course work. This undergraduate degree–completion program, which includes courses in ethics and international management, can be finished in approximately two years.

The Bachelor of Science/Bachelor of Arts degree in public administration (criminal justice emphasis) is a 63-credit hour program, which offers an opportunity to students who have completed two years of general education course work. This undergraduate degree-completion program features courses in ethics, judicial process, law, management, and public administration/policy and can be finished in two years entirely online.

M.B.A. degrees in accounting, advanced management studies, health-care management, and leadership development are available in the Department of Business Administration, which has a long history of offering M.B.A. programs. Students can reach their professional goals easily with Brenau's accelerated ten-course, 30-hour M.B.A. in leadership development, the thirteen-course, 39-hour M.B.A. in advanced management studies, the eleven-course, 33-hour M.B.A. in health-care management, or the twelve course, 36-hour M.B.A. in accounting. Many states have adopted the 150-hour educational requirement to sit for the CPA exam. Brenau students meet this requirement by earning their M.B.A. degrees.

The M.Ed. in early childhood education, a long-standing degree offering at Brenau, is also available online. This program is an eleven-course, 33- or 36-hour program, depending on the student's choice of a capstone activity (comprehensive exam or research project). The M.Ed. in middle grades education prepares professionals to teach children in grades four through eight. Students develop a variety of appropriate teaching methods and strategies that are specifically geared to the middle-grade learner. This program is also an eleven-course, 33- or 36-hour degree program, depending on the student's choice of a capstone activity (comprehensive exam or research project).

Students may earn a graduate certificate in conflict resolution online. This program, composed of six sequential graduate-level courses, is an extension of Brenau's successful undergraduate degree program.

SPECIAL PROGRAMS

Brenau University's accelerated M.B.A. program in leadership development is designed so that students may complete it in five semesters. Classes are small and offer students asynchronous discussion and work-related collaborative projects. These activities are designed to guarantee participation in online classes.

BA 500, the Business Administration Department's intensive business foundations course that covers all undergraduate basics in the field of quantitative methods, management, accounting, and marketing, was designed for nonbusiness majors seeking to earn an M.B.A. in leadership development or health-care management. Experienced faculty members from each of these fields collaborate to teach this unique 6-semester-hour course.

STUDENT SERVICES

In addition to online application, advising, registration, and tuition payment, other student services include career services (job search and career selection), mental health counseling, and disability support services through the campus Learning Center. The Brenau Trustee Library catalog is available online using the popular Voyager software. Supplemental materials are offered via document delivery and interlibrary loan.

CREDIT OPTIONS

Brenau University may accept up to 6 semester hours of transfer credit from other regionally accredited institutions as part of a planned graduate program of study upon approval of the respective department chair.

Alternative credit options toward a Brenau University degree (credit earned from advanced placement exams, international baccalaureate programs, CLEP, military credit, experiential credit, or challenge exams) are limited to a total of 27 semester hours.

FACULTY

Classes are taught by professors trained and certified in online course delivery. Professors teaching in graduate programs have doctorates in their fields and corporate and/or practical experience.

ADMISSION

Prospective students should submit a completed application, a $30 application fee, and transcripts from all institutions previously attended. Standardized test scores (GMAT, GRE, MAT, TOEFL) must be sent from testing services for graduate program applicants.

TUITION AND FEES

Online tuition is $383 per semester credit hour ($50 technology fee per semester). Tuition rates are addressed prior to each academic year. Tuition is payable by check, money order, or credit card (Visa, MasterCard, and Discover).

FINANCIAL AID

Online students who qualify are eligible for all need-based financial aid programs, including Pell Grants, other federal grants and loan programs, state-direct loans for students in nursing, and institutional grants. Program-specific funds are also available. The FAFSA financial aid application is available online.

A total of 1,603 (65 percent) of Brenau University students received some type of financial aid this past academic year. The Office of Scholarship and Financial Assistance receives student loan applications (telephone: 800-252-5119, Ext. 6152).

APPLYING

The completed application, a $30 application fee, and official transcripts and test scores should be sent directly to the Admissions Office, One Centennial Circle, Gainesville, Georgia 30501. Online College representatives are available by telephone at 800-252-5119 (toll-free) and e-mail at the address provided in the Contact section of this description.

CONTACT

Heather S. Gibbons, Ph.D.
Director of the Online College
Brenau University
One Centennial Circle
Gainesville, Georgia 30501
Telephone: 770-718-5328
Fax: 770-718-5329
E-mail: online@lib.brenau.edu
Web site: http://online.brenau.edu

Caldwell College

External Degree Program

Caldwell, New Jersey

Caldwell College is a Catholic, coeducational, four-year liberal arts institution committed to intellectual rigor, individual attention, and the ethical values of the Judeo-Christian academic tradition. Founded in 1939 by the Sisters of St. Dominic, the College is accredited by the Middle States Association of Colleges and Universities, chartered by the State of New Jersey, and registered with the Regents of the University of the State of New York. Located on a 70-acre wooded campus in a quiet suburban community 20 miles from New York City, Caldwell provides a serene and secure environment conducive to study and learning.

Caldwell College offers a 13:1 student-faculty ratio, small classes, and individual attention. Professors know their students by name, challenge them to strive for excellence, and provide the support needed to achieve it. This close relationship between faculty members and students also leads to a spirit of friendship throughout the campus community. Approximately half of the 2,200 men and women enrolled at the College are adults pursuing degrees both full-time and part-time or obtaining new skills to compete in the changing marketplace. Through the College's Center for Continuing Education, these adults seek personal growth, professional enrichment, and career advancement. All students find the staff ready to provide the personalized academic planning that can help them succeed in their studies and careers.

DISTANCE LEARNING PROGRAM

Caldwell College pioneered the external degree concept in 1979, becoming the first higher education institution in the state of New Jersey to offer students the option of completing their degrees without attending on-campus classes. Caldwell designed the program especially for busy adults whose work or family commitments make it difficult to follow a weekly on-campus academic schedule. Traditional course work is presented in a flexible and convenient format. External Degree students are required to be on campus only for External Degree Saturday at the beginning of each semester. Students pursuing their bachelor's degrees through the External Degree Program use the same textbooks and complete the same course work as their on-campus counterparts.

DELIVERY MEDIA

Students learn with the guidance of an academic mentor and through interaction with the faculty via phone, personal conferences, e-mail, mailing or faxing of assignments, audiocassette, videocassette, and computer technologies.

PROGRAM OF STUDY

The External Degree Program offers twenty-eight majors. Bachelor of Science degrees are offered in accounting, business administration, computer information systems, international business, marketing, and management. Bachelor of Arts degrees are offered in art (some on-campus work is required for art majors), communication arts, criminal justice, English, history, political science, psychology, religious studies, sociology, social studies, and eleven majors in multidisciplinary studies.

Eligibility for a degree requires completion of 120 credits and a GPA of at least 2.0 (C). This includes completing 57 liberal arts and science core curriculum credits, requirements specific to the student's major, and open electives. Students must also complete major courses with a minimum grade of C and satisfy all other departmental requirements. Overall, a minimum of 45 credits must be taken at Caldwell College, with the last 30 credits of the 120-credit requirement completed at the College before a degree is awarded. Transfer students must complete at least half the total number of credits for a given major at Caldwell College.

Students enrolled in undergraduate or graduate distance education programs at other institutions are permitted to enroll as visiting (nonmatriculated) students in the Caldwell College External Degree Program. Course registration opens three weeks prior to the beginning of each semester. Permission to enroll as a visiting student is granted by the Associate Dean through the Center for Continuing Education. Visiting students are required to attend new-student orientation and mandatory meetings with instructors on External Degree Saturday to receive course materials. In order to participate in this program, students must submit a completed External Degree Visiting Student Application form with a $10 processing fee to the Center for Continuing Education. Visiting students may register for two courses per semester (four courses per year) and have access to the Caldwell College Library. Tuition costs are the same as those for all other External Degree Program students and are payable at the time of registration.

SPECIAL PROGRAMS

Students majoring in business administration, English, or psychology who have earned at least 60 prior college credits in courses applicable to their major may apply for Accelerated Degree Completion through the External Degree Program. Students admitted to the Accelerated Degree Completion Program can complete their degrees within two years by taking approximately 27 credits per year (9 credits per term) or an equivalent combination of course credits and College Level Examination Program, Prior Learning Assessment, internships, and/or cooperative education credits. Each student is expected to work closely with an academic adviser in developing and following a specific course of study.

STUDENT SERVICES

All of the following services are available to External Degree students. The Jennings Library and the Academic Computing Center are open on evenings and weekends. Students have the ability to access the library's vast database from their home computers. The library's home page also provides links to the Internet and other databases and informational resources. The Career Development Center, Campus Minister, Counseling Office, and Academic Support Center are also available during the evening by appointment. The college bookstore is open evenings and during External Degree Saturday. The Academic Support Center assists students in academic skill development for all majors through tutoring.

CREDIT OPTIONS

Credit is given for courses completed at an accredited college or university with a grade of C or above, provided it is appropriate to the curriculum chosen at Caldwell College. Students may transfer no more than 75 credits from a baccalaureate institution or 60 credits from a junior college. Students may earn credits by examination through standardized testing (CLEP, DANTES, OHIO, and TECEP). Credit is also awarded for noncollegiate military or corporate training courses accredited by the American Council on Education. Credits may be earned through the Prior Learning Assessment portfolio development process.

ADMISSION

Students who are 23 years of age or older and who possess a high school diploma or a GED certificate may matriculate as an External Degree student upon acceptance to the College. Those students with fewer than 12 college credits must complete the following courses to be eligible for the External Degree Program: EN/101 Basic Composition, EN/111 Literary Types and Themes, PS/111 Re-entry Seminar for Adults, and one liberal arts core course.

TUITION AND FEES

Tuition for all students is $408 per credit. The additional cost for books is the responsibility of the student.

FINANCIAL AID

External Degree students are eligible for several of the federal financial aid programs available to full-time students, including Pell Grants and various loans. Approximately 10 percent of External Degree students receive Pell Grants, 70 percent Stafford Loans, 10 percent Caldwell College Grants, and 2 percent Federal Supplemental Educational Opportunity Grants. Tuition Aid Grants are available for full-time External Degree students. Academic advisers of the Center for Continuing Education and the staff of the Financial Aid Office also inform students of special privately funded scholarship opportunities for which they may qualify.

APPLYING

Students wishing to pursue a degree through the External Degree Program must submit the following to the Office of Corporate Education and Adult Undergraduate Admissions: a completed application for adult undergraduate admission; a nonrefundable application fee of $40 made payable to Caldwell College (the student's Social Security number should be included on the memo line); official transcripts from high schools, career schools, or colleges previously attended (GED certification may be submitted in place of a high school transcript); and a photocopy of the student's Social Security card. There is no testing for adults. All application material must be received by the Office of Adult Undergraduate Admissions by the deadline date of each semester, approximately one month prior to the beginning of classes.

Students in the External Degree Program may enroll for a minimum of one and a maximum of five courses per semester, depending on their personal schedules and abilities. The program offers three semesters: fall, spring, and summer. Students are required to be on campus only for the External Degree Saturday at the beginning of each semester. New students attend an orientation program and participate in workshops designed to enhance their college experience. On External Degree Saturday, students meet with their faculty mentor and receive an overview of the course material, faculty evaluation criteria, and dates that assignments are due. Students also attend department meetings and learn about recent developments and career options in their chosen fields of study. Prior to each semester, students consult with their academic advisers for guidance in selecting courses. Academic counseling is available through the semester as a supportive, ongoing service.

CONTACT

Jack Albalah, Director
Corporate and Adult Undergraduate Admissions
Caldwell College
9 Ryerson Avenue
Caldwell, New Jersey 07006
Telephone: 973-618-3285
888-864-9518
(toll-free)
Fax: 973-618-3660
E-mail: jalbalah@caldwell.edu
Web site: http://www.caldwell.edu/adult-admissions/

California Institute of Integral Studies

Online Degree Programs

San Francisco, California

California Institute of Integral Studies (CIIS) in San Francisco is a fully accredited university offering an online M.A. in transformative leadership and a Ph.D. in transformative learning and change in a unique learning community, in addition to residential Ph.D., Psy.D., M.A., and bachelor's completion degrees in psychology and the humanities. The Institute's commitment to the study and practice of multiple cultural and spiritual traditions and to their expression throughout the activities of the community promotes a stimulating learning environment with rigorous scholarship and supportive community—including the online programs.

DISTANCE LEARNING PROGRAM

The master's degree program in transformative leadership attracts those who want to bring deep change to their communities, organizations, or businesses. This program helps learners develop capacities to engage the increasing complexity that faces formal and informal leaders in human systems. In this program, learners grow their awareness of self, other, and organization, and they cultivate effective facilitation processes through reflection, practice, and scholarship. Throughout the program, learners develop their own transformative change projects that they implement and assess as their culminating work.

The doctorate in humanities, with an emphasis on transformative learning and change, is for those who wish to do inquiry about dimensions of transformative learning and its effect on deep change. Though a research degree, the program fosters an experiential pedagogy that engages the would-be researchers in the practice of transformative learning. In addition, learners approach experience and theory through an integral epistemology that involves mind, body, and spirit. Through this program, learners are engaged in fostering capacities to develop original, rigorous, and insightful scholarship.

DELIVERY MEDIA

The online curricula are offered in two formats: distance online and weekend residential. In both formats, students form learning communities and use the online, Web-based virtual campus, in which students and faculty and staff members interact.

In both formats, students also participate in weeklong intensives in a San Francisco Bay Area retreat setting. Intensives are held at the beginning of each semester. Distance online students otherwise take all their courses exclusively on the virtual campus. In contrast, weekend residential students meet face-to-face one weekend a month and may meet in face-to-face study groups and also take some courses via the virtual campus.

PROGRAMS OF STUDY

In the M.A. in transformative leadership program, learners are engaged with the field of leadership and organizational development in the context of transformative learning and change. Three courses on leadership allow learners to study the leadership field, inquire about self and transformative leadership, and, through a capstone project, apply their capacity to evoke change. Other courses develop proficiencies in action and inquiry, collaborative participation, and issues of diversity and difference. Learners are also organized to engage with peers, thus becoming their own human system, one that supports individual leadership projects. Electives allow learners to focus attention on topics appropriate to their development as transformative leaders and significant to their particular work context.

The Ph.D. program, with its emphasis on transformative learning, theory building, and research, engages learners in an array of literatures that illuminate the complexity of learning and change. Studies in transformative learning, paradigms of inquiry, systems, and participatory research methods are foundational to the program. In addition, the program's pedagogical commitment to learning in community allows learners to critically assess deep assumptions of the self and other while developing capacities to engage and research complexity, difference, and conflict.

STUDENT SERVICES

Current information about the program and courses is available on the CIIS Web site, by telephone, or in person at CIIS in San Francisco.

FACULTY

CIIS programs attract scholars who wish to act from a spiritual foundation while helping to improve the effectiveness and well-being of individuals, communities, and organizations. The online degree faculty members bring practical experience and hold doctoral degrees relevant to transformation and change as well as online learning.

ADMISSION

Applicants must meet the general admissions requirements of the Institute. In addition, applicants must submit two letters of recommendation—one from someone familiar with the applicant's ability to do advanced academic work and one from a supervisor in a recent professional or volunteer setting. Applicants are also asked to provide a critical writing essay and an autobiography. The autobiographical statement should describe major steps in the applicant's life that have led to the decision to pursue admission to this program. A resume of relevant experiences and a general statement of the proposed area of interest are also required.

TUITION AND FEES

As of the fall semester 2004, full-time tuition for an M.A. program for a 9-unit semester is $6255 per semester ($12,510 per year). For a Ph.D. program, 9-unit semester, tuition is $7515 per semester ($15,030 per year). For a 10- to 12-unit semester for an M.A. program, tuition is $7155 per semester ($14,310 per year). For a Ph.D. program, 10- to 12-unit semester, tuition is $8585 per semester ($17,170 per year). For less than 11 or more than 12 units per semester, the tuition rate per unit is $695 for an M.A. program and $835 for a Ph.D. program. Rates are subject to change.

FINANCIAL AID

Financial assistance in scholarships, loans, and grants is awarded on the basis of merit and/or need. A serious attempt is made to extend a personalized concerned approach to student financial needs while complying with governmental and donor regulations. General financial aid programs include Federal Pell Grants, Federal Supplemental Educational Opportunity Grants (FSEOG), Institute scholarships, diversity scholarships, international scholarships, Veterans Administration Educational Benefits, Federal Family Education Loan Programs (FFELP), Federal Stafford Student Loans, and other loan and scholarship opportunities based on merit or need.

APPLYING

Individuals who wish to deepen their understanding and effectiveness as transformative change agents are welcome to apply. Typically, candidates have professional experience and are seeking to enhance their abilities through study, action, reflection, and scholarship.

Both master's and doctoral programs are also attractive to mature adults who wish to make a career transition or who are looking to approach change differently in their current site of practice. The ideal candidate also is seeking a program that uses an integral pedagogy, one that honors body, mind, and spirit. And finally, those who require a program that caters to the working professionals find the virtual campus a convenient venue.

Complete admission information and applications are available through the CIIS Web site or through the Admissions Office.

CONTACT

Admissions Counselor
California Institute of Integral Studies
1453 Mission Street
San Francisco, California 94103
Telephone: 415-575-6150
Fax: 415-575-1264
E-mail: admissions@ciis.edu
Web site: http://www.ciis.edu

California State University, Dominguez Hills

Division of Extended Education

Carson, California

California State University, Dominguez Hills (CSUDH), is a national leader in distance learning, named by Forbes *magazine as one of the top cyber universities. The campus is located in the South Bay Area of Los Angeles. Founded in 1960, the University is one of twenty-three California State University (CSU) campuses and has the largest distance learning program in the CSU system. The University offered its first distance learning degree in 1974, and in 1995 offered the first online master's degree program ever approved by the Western Association of Schools and Colleges.*

CSU Dominguez Hills continues to be in the forefront of distance learning technology and academic excellence, garnering numerous awards, including the Best Distance Learning Teacher from the U.S. Distance Learning Association, an Omni Intermedia Award, an Aegis Award, two Telly Awards, and a Top 100 Video Producer Award.

The CSU Dominguez Hills campus is located in the South Bay area of Los Angeles and is accredited by the Western Association of Schools and Colleges.

DISTANCE LEARNING PROGRAM

The distance learning unit is part of the Division of Extended Education, whose mission is to extend the resources of the University to better serve the educational needs of its communities. The University has more than 4,000 students enrolled in distance learning programs in all fifty states and more than sixty countries.

DELIVERY MEDIA

All distance learning courses have a Web site, and participants can interact with faculty and staff members via e-mail, telephone, and correspondence. Courses are conducted via live Internet, where students participate in a live, interactive educational environment, including video transmission of the lecture; via asynchronous Internet, where participants log in at their convenience to complete class assignments and engage in discussion groups with their peers; via television, where CSUDH broadcasts 24 hours a day on cable systems throughout southern California; and via correspondence.

PROGRAMS OF STUDY

CSU Dominguez Hills currently offers eight degree and nine certificate programs via distance learning. There are no on-campus requirements for any CSUDH distance learning program. Programs include the following:

Master of Arts in Behavioral Science: Negotiation and Conflict Management. Taught via live Internet, the program teaches participants valuable skills and knowledge that may be applied directly to police work, counseling, human resources management, labor relations, supervision, administration, alternative dispute resolution, arbitration, public policy, social work, teaching, intercultural and community conflicts, corporate contracts, and purchasing (telephone: 310-243-2162; e-mail: negotiation@csudh.edu; Web site: http://www.csudh.edu/negcon).

Master of Arts in the Humanities. Taught via correspondence, the degree offers an interdisciplinary approach to the disciplines of the humanities—history, literature, philosophy, music, and art—with emphasis on their interrelating effects and influences (telephone: 310-243-3190; e-mail: huxonline@csudh.edu; Web site: http://www.csudh.edu/hux).

Master of Business Administration. Taught via asynchronous Internet, the M.B.A. at CSUDH provides a solid qualification in business management with courses that are wide-ranging in content, covering the essential areas of knowledge and skills required in today's competitive business environment (telephone: 310-243-2714; e-mail: cnicholson@soma.csudh.edu; Web site: http://mbaonline.csudh.edu).

Master of Public Administration. Taught via asynchronous Internet, the program is designed to provide a high-quality graduate professional education for individuals entering or currently employed in public service and non-profit professions (telephone: 310-243-2395; e-mail: mpaonline@soma.csudh.edu; Web site: http://mpaonline.csudh.edu).

Master of Science in Nursing and Bachelor of Science in Nursing. Taught by asynchronous Internet, the bachelor's completion program prepares graduates to function as leaders, managers, and resource people in a variety of health-care settings. The graduate program prepares professional nurses for advanced and specialized practice. Role emphasis options include clinical nurse specialist in gerontological nursing and nursing education (telephone: 310-243-3741; e-mail: pputz@csudh.edu; Web site: http://www.csudh.edu/msn or http://www.csudh.edu/bsn).

Master of Science in Quality Assurance and Bachelor of Science in Quality Assurance. Taught via asynchronous Internet, the bachelor's program provides the academic environment and the requisite course of study to blend the basic sciences, technologies, management principles, quality concepts, and statistical tools needed to prepare professionals for careers in quality assurance and to serve working professionals seeking career enhancement. Master's degree students receive education in both the technical and administrative foundations of quality assurance, an interdisciplinary profession used in management in manufacturing, service, government, and healthcare organizations (telephone: 310-243-3880; e-mail: msqa@csudh.edu; Web site: http://www.csudh.edu/msqa or http://www.csudh.edu/bsqa).

Quality Management Certificate of Completion, Quality Engineering Certificate of Completion, Quality Auditing Certificate of Completion, Reliability Engineering Certificate of Completion, and Software Quality Engineering Certificate of Completion. Taught via asynchronous Internet, the programs allow professionals to gain certification in specialized areas of quality and prepare for American Society for Quality exams. Students who successfully complete three master's degree–level courses and the associated capstone course can earn a certificate of completion (telephone: 310-243-3880; e-mail: msqa@csudh.edu; Web site: http://www.csudh.edu/msqa).

Assistive Technology Certificate. Taught by asynchronous Internet, the program prepares individuals to comply with state and federal laws that require that school personnel be prepared to offer a full range of assistive technology services to disabled people. The program is useful to educational administrators, teachers, special education teachers, occupational and physical therapists, speech and language specialists, rehabilitation specialists, program specialists, resource specialists, and psychologists (telephone: 310-243-3741; e-mail: eeprograms@csudh.edu; Web site: http://www.csudh.edu/at).

Community College Teaching Certificate. Taught via asynchronous Internet, the program is designed to enhance the skills and the employability of potential community college instructors (telephone: 310-243-2781; e-mail: eeprograms@csudh.edu; Web site: http://www.csudh.edu/ccteaching).

Production and Inventory Control Certificate. Taught via asynchronous Internet, the program provides a broad education in the principles of production and inventory control. It is taught by professionals currently employed in the field who are certified in production and inventory management (telephone: 310-243-3741; e-mail: learn@csudh.edu; Web site: http://www.csudh.edu/lapicsonline).

Purchasing Certificate. Taught via asynchronous Internet, the program provides a broad education in the principles of procurement management and also helps students prepare for the Certified Purchasing Manager exam (telephone: 310-243-3741; e-mail: learn@csudh.edu; Web site: http://www.csudh.edu/purchasingonline).

SPECIAL PROGRAMS

The Center for Training and Development at CSUDH works closely with the business community to develop custom-designed training programs to help meet the demands of the fast-paced workplace of the new millennium. Programs are delivered via distance learning, on-site, and on the CSUDH campus.

STUDENT SERVICES

Faculty members are available to students via e-mail, telephone, and mail. Student services available at a distance include academic advising, technical support, online tutoring, and access to the library and bookstore.

CREDIT OPTIONS

Depending on the specific program, students may transfer credit earned at other accredited colleges and universities. For more information, students should visit the Web site (http://www.csudh.edu/dominguezonline).

FACULTY

CSU Dominguez Hills has more than 100 faculty members teaching distance learning courses. Most of these faculty members have doctoral degrees in their chosen fields.

ADMISSION

Admission requirements vary for each program. Students should consult the CSUDH distance learning Web site listed below for specific program requirements.

TUITION AND FEES

Tuition and fees vary for each program. For specific cost information, students should consult the CSUDH distance learning Web site listed below.

FINANCIAL AID

More than $30 million in financial aid is disbursed to CSUDH students each year. Approximately 68 percent of CSUDH students receive some form of financial assistance, and most financial aid programs are available to qualified distance learning students. For further information, students should visit the financial aid Web site (http://www.csudh.edu/fin_aid/default.htm).

APPLYING

Application processes vary for each program, and campus visits are not required for any program. Students should consult the CSUDH distance learning Web site listed below for specific application information.

CONTACT

Extended Education Registration Office
California State University, Dominguez Hills
1000 East Victoria Street
Carson, California 90747
Telephone: 310-243-3741
877-GO-HILLS (toll-free)
Fax: 310-516-3971
E-mail: eereg@csudh.edu
Web site: http://dominguezonline.csudh.edu

Central Michigan University

Distance/Distributed Learning

Mount Pleasant, Michigan

Since its founding in 1892, Central Michigan University (CMU) has grown from a small teachers' college into a world-class Midwestern university offering more than 150 programs at the bachelor's level and nearly sixty programs at the master's, specialist's, and doctoral level. CMU is accredited by the North Central Association of Colleges and Schools. This accreditation includes all on- and off-campus programs. The College of Extended Learning is an institutional member of the Council for Adult and Experiential Learning; the Adult Education Association; the Alliance: An Association of Alternative Degree Programs for Adults; and the National Association of Institutions in Military Education.

DISTANCE LEARNING PROGRAM

Distance/Distributed Learning is a division of CMU, which serves off-campus students. Programs are offered in a compressed format to help balance the demands of work, school, family and other obligations. Compressed format does not mean easier courses. Distance learning courses are held to the same academic standards that on-campus courses must meet. To help insure success in the compressed format, procedures and support services are fast and accessible.

DELIVERY MEDIA

Students have a choice of delivery formats, print-based learning packages, or online courses. Courses that require monitored exams must be administered in a proctored setting.

Learning packages are print-based courses that use textbooks and study guides but may also include audio and videocassettes as well as the use of e-mail and Internet chat rooms to enrich the content.

Online courses use Web technology to involve the student in interactive learning. Students can interact with instructors and others through e-mail, chat sessions, and message forums. Student lecture materials and assignments are all online. Textbooks are still required.

PROGRAMS OF STUDY

Distance/Distributed Learning offers undergraduate-, graduate-, and doctorate-level degree programs.

Bachelor's degrees available are the Bachelor of Science with an option in community development, Bachelor of Science with a major in administration, and a Bachelor of Applied Arts with a major in administration. All undergraduate degrees are based on 124 semester hours of credit.

The Master of Science in Administration (M.S.A.) degree is a 36-semester-hour program, approaching administration and management from a broader perspective than other graduate degrees. The M.S.A. features eight concentrations; however, the general administration and the information resource management concentrations are the only two concentrations available via distance learning.

SPECIAL PROGRAMS

Available entirely through distance learning is the Doctor of Audiology (Au.D.) created exclusively for professional audiologists. It is based on a minimum 36 to 40 semester-hour sequence and a comprehensive exam. There is a 12-hour capstone experience in lieu of a formal thesis.

The Doctor of Health Administration (D.H.A.) is a 63 semester-hour program designed for professionals in upper leadership levels from a variety of health disciplines and organizations. Students work with other senior-level managers who represent the entire spectrum of health delivery modalities. The use of online delivery, combined with occasional face-to-face seminars, provides an effective yet flexible way to complete a doctoral program.

STUDENT SERVICES

Many services are available online, such as admission, registration, textbook purchases, academic advising, and library services. Many of these services are also available via a toll-free phone call or by fax. The service ranked highest by CMU's current students and graduates is the nationally recognized Off-Campus Library Services. Document delivery provides students with books, copies of journal articles, and other materials free of charge.

CREDIT OPTIONS

Credits earned through distance learning are recorded on Central Michigan University's transcripts in the same manner as credits earned in on-campus courses. These courses are part of the regular offerings of Central Michigan University. Relevant transfer credit and prior learning credits are also an option.

FACULTY

Faculty members are selected from the main campus in Mount Pleasant, from other universities, and from the executive ranks of government, business, and industry. They enjoy the challenge of working with adult students, and respect the knowledge and skills the students bring to the classroom. Approval of all faculty members is done by department chairpersons on the basis of their academic and professional qualifications.

ADMISSION

Students must be admitted to CMU in order to take distance learning courses. The minimum requirement for admission to CMU undergraduate programs is a high school diploma or GED certificate. Graduate applicants must have a baccalaureate or equivalent degree from an institution that has received regional accreditation or recognized standing at the time the student attended. Graduate applicants must have an overall grade point average of at least 2.7 (or 3.0 for the final 60 hours) in their bachelor's studies. Applications whose GPA is between 2.0 and 2.7 may be considered for conditional admission. GMAT or GRE scores are not required.

Audiology applicants must have a graduate degree in audiology with a minimum GPA of 3.0 in graduate work, and either the ASHA Certificate of Clinical Competence in Audiology or a valid state license to practice audiology. Five years of professional audiological experience beyond the master's degree is also required.

D.H.A. applicants must have a master's degree from a U.S. regionally accredited university of at least 27 semester hours or have earned a professional doctorate (such as M.D., D.O., J.D., or Pharm.D.).

TUITION AND FEES

Tuition for the 2004–05 academic year is as follows: undergraduate, $230 per credit hour; graduate, $300 per credit hour; Au.D. (government rate), $300 per credit hour; Au.D. (non-government rate), $428 per credit hour; and D.H.A., $798 per credit hour.

Additional fees include a $50 admission fee, $50 graduation fee, $65 prior learning application fee, and a $40 prior learning assessment fee (per credit hour).

FINANCIAL AID

Financial aid is available to those students who qualify. Students interested in financial aid are encouraged to contact CMU for more information.

APPLYING

Students interested in taking classes through Distance/Distributed Learning are encouraged to apply for admission to Central Michigan University. Admission applications can be downloaded from the Web site listed below.

CONTACT

Central Michigan University
Distance/Distributed Learning
Mount Pleasant, Michigan 48859
Telephone: 800-688-4268 (toll-free)
Fax: 989-774-1822
E-mail: help-ddl@cmich.edu
Web site: http://www.ddl.cmich.edu

Central Missouri State University

Office of Extended Campus–Distance Learning Department of Nursing

Warrensburg, Missouri

Founded in 1871, Central Missouri State University is a state university offering approximately 150 areas of study to 11,100 undergraduate and graduate students. In 1996, Central Missouri State University was designated Missouri's lead institution for professional technology, an area long recognized as one of the University's greatest strengths. The new mission has expanded this commitment and means that Central will continue to integrate the latest technologies into every level of its comprehensive liberal arts curriculum. Central is committed to acquiring, disseminating, and utilizing technology to enhance the University's comprehensive educational mission. Central is accredited by the North Central Association of Colleges and Schools.

DISTANCE LEARNING PROGRAM

Central's main distance learning program provides undergraduate- and graduate-level courses through two-way interactive television and Web-based courses. The program currently includes one doctoral degree, two master's degrees, and numerous graduate and undergraduate courses. From fall 1994 through spring 2004, Central provided instruction to more than 13,000 graduate, undergraduate, and high school students in a distance learning environment.

Institutional and financial information about Central Missouri State University may be accessed via the Web at http://www.cmsu.edu/rsearch/ir/toc.htm.

DELIVERY MEDIA

Central uses a variety of technologies to deliver its distance learning courses. These include two-way, interactive television; broadcast television; and Internet technologies, including video and audio streaming. Central links to the Missouri Research and Educational Network (MOREnet) statewide backbone, which connects all of Missouri's public higher education institutions and several K–12 schools, to provide Internet-based and interactive television programming. Central's complement of six 2-way videoconferencing facilities, which are capable of ISDN, H.323, T.120, and audioconferencing, allow Central to provide distance learning content anywhere in the world.

PROGRAMS OF STUDY

There are two degrees offered by the Department of Nursing primarily through distance learning technologies. The Bachelor of Science in Nursing is delivered through a combination of online courses, independent study, and one course on campus; a test-out option is available for the on-campus course. The Master of Science in Nursing degree is also delivered mostly online.

The Bachelor of Science in Nursing degree is designed for the registered nurse who wants to upgrade to a bachelor's degree. The bachelor's degree provides more flexibility and leads to more career opportunities in nursing than an RN license. Employment opportunities increase as the level of education increases. A baccalaureate degree provides many more options in the areas of public health, home health, nursing management, program planning, and health teaching. Registered nurses face increasingly complex demands that require a broad-based bachelor's degree preparation. Central's Bachelor of Science in Nursing includes general arts and science courses and an introduction to other disciplines in addition to the focus on nursing. The program enhances a nurse's ability to think critically, teaches more effective communication skills, and provides a deeper understanding of professional nursing.

The program features flexible scheduling that allows students to start any semester and set their own pace for completion. Full-time students can complete the course work in one year; part-time students can take up to four years to complete the program. The program allows the transfer of up to 64 credit hours of university studies and nursing prerequisites from other institutions. Students receive credit for courses completed within another accredited nursing program and for professional experience. Nursing faculty members understand the needs of working professionals who are students. The program is accredited by the Commission on Collegiate Nursing Education (CCNE). More information is available online in the undergraduate catalog at http://www.cmsu.edu/catalogs/.

The Master of Science in Nursing online degree program is designed for nurses with a baccalaureate degree who seek advanced practice as a specialist. Central, with more than forty years of experience providing high-quality nursing education, uses state-of-the-art technology to deliver the program. Students specialize in one of three professional tracks: family nurse practitioner, nurse informaticist, and nurse education.

There are many benefits for students earning a Master of Science in Nursing degree at Central. All professional tracks offer flexibility at an affordable cost. The online classes provide "anytime, anywhere" access, and the online format eliminates travel time and expense. Online classes expand the student's technical skills, increasing valuable workplace skills. Classes are student centered and user friendly, providing individual attention from the instructors. Earning this degree provides students with the foundation for advanced practice, specialty practice, and advanced study at the doctoral level. More information can be found in the graduate catalog online at http://www.cmsu.edu/catalogs/.

SPECIAL PROGRAMS

Central's Distance Learning Program builds upon the existing curriculum offerings at Central as well as offerings that address special distance learning needs. Central's distance learning students are eligible to participate in the same opportunities as on-campus students. These include study tours and internships in many disciplines. The Office of Career Services reports a 96 percent placement rate for Central graduates within six months of graduation.

STUDENT SERVICES

The toll-free University number allows access to offices involved with student services: extended campus–distance learning, admissions, academic advising, registrar, financial aid, revenue, accounts receivable, University housing, and the Graduate School. All students enrolled at Central are issued a mainframe Internet account. The help desk is available to Central students needing technical computer assistance. Distance learning students receive individualized course information prior to the start of each semester as well as information about University resources available to them. Online library resources are available for distance learning and off-campus students. An online writing lab (OWL) provides writing assistance to distance learning students. A toll-free number provides ordering and delivery service for textbooks from the University Bookstore.

CREDIT OPTIONS

For entering graduate students, Central accepts up to 8 hours of transfer credits in graduate work.

FACULTY

Faculty members at Central exemplify the goals of the institution as they balance personal attention with expertise in their respective fields. Approximately 71 percent of the 446 full-time faculty members hold doctoral degrees. The student-faculty ratio is 17:1.

ADMISSION

Students interested in pursuing an online degree through Central Missouri State University's Department of Nursing should contact the University at the address below. Applicants must be admitted to the University before enrolling in a nursing program. If this is a student's first enrollment at Central, a $25 nonrefundable application fee (international students, $50) must accompany the application and official transcripts of all undergraduate and graduate course work. Admission to the University or Graduate School is not equivalent to admission for a particular program or degree.

TUITION AND FEES

For 2003–04, tuition for distance learning graduate courses was $230 per credit hour. For distance learning undergraduate courses, tuition was $189 per credit hour. Prospective students should note that tuition rates may be changed at any time by action of the Board of Governors.

FINANCIAL AID

Central recognizes a student's continuing need for financial assistance. Federal grant and loan funds are available for eligible students who have been accepted for regular degree programs at Central. Application eligibility information may be obtained by contacting the Office of Financial Aid at 660-543-4040 or at 800-SAY-CMSU (toll-free). Students who are veterans may also be considered for VA educational benefits to help with tuition costs. The University participates in all federal student financial aid grant, loan, and employment programs.

APPLYING

Students should contact the University at 660-543-4621 or at 800-SAY-CMSU (toll-free).

CONTACT

Dr. Michael Penrod
Outreach Coordinator for Distance Learning
Office of Extended Campus
Humphreys 410
Central Missouri State University
Warrensburg, Missouri 64093
Telephone: 660-543-4984
800-SAY-CMSU
Ext. 22 (toll-free)
Fax: 660-543-8333
E-mail: penrod@cmsu1.cmsu.edu
Web site:
http://www.cmsu.edu/extcamp

Central Missouri State University

Office of Extended Campus–Distance Learning Library Science and Information Services

Warrensburg, Missouri

Founded in 1871, Central Missouri State University is a state university offering approximately 150 areas of study to 11,100 undergraduate and graduate students. In 1996, Central Missouri State University was designated Missouri's lead institution for professional technology, an area long recognized as one of the University's greatest strengths. The new mission has expanded this commitment and means that Central will continue to integrate the latest technologies into every level of its comprehensive liberal arts curriculum. Central is committed to acquiring, disseminating, and utilizing technology to enhance the University's comprehensive educational mission. Central is accredited by the North Central Association of Colleges and Schools.

DISTANCE LEARNING PROGRAM

Central's main Distance Learning Program provides undergraduate- and graduate-level courses through two-way interactive television and Web-based courses. The program currently includes one doctoral degree, two master's degrees, and numerous graduate and undergraduate courses. From fall 1994 through spring 2004, Central provided instruction to more than 13,000 graduate, undergraduate, and high school students in a distance learning environment.

Institutional and financial information about Central Missouri State University may be accessed via the Web at http://www.cmsu.edu/rsearch/ir/toc.htm.

DELIVERY MEDIA

Central uses a variety of technologies to deliver its distance learning courses. These include two-way, interactive television; broadcast television; and Internet technologies, including video and audio streaming. Central links to the Missouri Research and Educational Network (MOREnet) statewide backbone, which connects all of Missouri's public higher education institutions and several K–12 schools, to provide Internet-based and interactive television programming. Finally, Central's complement of six 2-way videoconferencing facilities, which are capable of ISDN, H.323, T.120, and audioconferencing, allow Central to provide distance learning content to anywhere in the world.

PROGRAMS OF STUDY

There are two graduate degrees delivered by Library Science and Information Services through a combination of distance learning technologies: the Master of Science in Library Science and Information Services and the Education Specialist in Learning Resources. The graduate uses the knowledge and skills obtained to proactively assess the needs of the information agency's constituents in order to provide customized information resources; design, implement, and evaluate customized systems, services, and information packages; teach information literacy skills to facilitate effective learning; become a leader in cross-disciplinary collaboration; identify and analyze the problems inherent in his or her information communities; become an effective communicator and leader in technology implementation in his or her organization; promote access to the greatest possible diversity of information; and understand the information search process, the interactions between information seekers and information sources, and the role of libraries and other information centers in this process.

The Master of Science in Library Science and Information Services is designed to prepare classroom teachers for positions as school library media specialists. It is the only graduate program in Missouri that exclusively targets education for school librarians. The degree is accredited by the American Library Association/American Association of School Librarians through the National Council for the Accreditation of Teacher Education. The 35-hour graduate degree is delivered in a blended format of weekend, interactive television, and online classes.

The Education Specialist in Learning Resources is designed for students who already hold a master's degree in library science or education and wish to obtain school library media certification or prepare for supervisory positions dealing with information technology. Degree candidates with a Master of Science in Education may design their program to gain the school library media specialist certification, and candidates with a Master of Science in Library Science attain information technology–related competencies. Course work is offered utilizing different formats—summer sessions, weekend, interactive television, and online.

SPECIAL PROGRAMS

Central's Distance Learning Program builds upon the existing curriculum offerings at Central as well as offerings that address special distance learning needs. Central's distance learning students are eligible to participate in the same opportunities as on-campus students. These include study tours and internships in many disciplines. The Office of Career Services reports a 96 percent placement rate for Central students within six months of graduation.

STUDENT SERVICES

A toll-free University number, 800-SAY-CMSU, allows access to offices involved with student services: extended campus–distance learning, admissions, academic advising, registrar, financial aid, revenue, accounts receivable, University housing, and the Graduate School. All students enrolled at Central are issued a mainframe Internet account. The HELP Desk is available to Central students needing technical computer assistance. Distance learning students receive individualized course information prior to the start of each semester as well as information regarding University resources available to them. Online library resources are available for distance learning and off-campus students. An online writing lab (OWL) provides writing assistance to distance learning students. A toll-free number provides ordering and delivery service for textbooks from the University Bookstore.

CREDIT OPTIONS

For entering graduate students, Central will accept up to 8 hours of transfer credits in graduate work.

FACULTY

Faculty members at Central exemplify the goals of the institution as they balance personal attention with expertise in their respective fields. Approximately 71 percent of the 446 full-time faculty members hold doctoral degrees. The student-faculty ratio is 17:1.

ADMISSION

Individuals interested in pursuing a graduate degree at Central Missouri State University should use the form in the graduate catalog, contact the Graduate School for application information at 800-SAY-CMSU (toll-free), or visit the Web site at http://www.cmsu.edu/graduate. The Graduate School should receive all application materials at least three weeks prior to the beginning of the semester in which the student wishes to register.

All degree-seeking student applicants must submit a formal application for admission to the Graduate School and official transcripts of all undergraduate/graduate course work. If this is a student's first enrollment at Central, a $25 nonrefundable application fee is required (international students must remit $50). Admission to the Graduate School, which permits enrollment in classes, is not equivalent to admission for a particular program or degree.

TUITION AND FEES

For 2003–04, graduate tuition for Internet-based courses was $230 per credit hour. Prospective students should note that tuition rates may be changed at any time by action of the Board of Governors.

FINANCIAL AID

Central recognizes a student's continuing need for financial assistance. Federal grant and loan funds are available for eligible students who have been accepted for regular degree programs at Central. Application eligibility information may be obtained by contacting the Office of Financial Aid at 660-543-4040 or 800-SAY-CMSU (toll-free). Students who are veterans may also be considered for VA educational benefits to help with tuition costs. The University participates in all federal student financial aid grant, loan, and employment programs. Visiting and non-degree-seeking students are not eligible to receive federal financial aid.

APPLYING

Graduate students should contact the Graduate School at 660-543-4621 or toll-free at 800-SAY-CMSU.

CONTACT

Dr. Patricia Antrim
Program Coordinator
Central Missouri State University
Warrensburg, Missouri 64093
Telephone: 660-543-8633
E-mail: antrim@cmsu1.cmsu.edu
Web site: http://library.cmsu.edu/lisdept/WebSite/index.html

To enroll:
Dr. Michael Penrod
Outreach Coordinator for Distance Learning
Office of Extended Campus
Humphreys 410
Central Missouri State University
Warrensburg, Missouri 64093
Telephone: 660-543-4984
800-SAY-CMSU Ext. 22 (toll-free)
Fax: 660-543-8333
E-mail: penrod@cmsu1.cmsu.edu
Web site: http://www.cmsu.edu/extcamp

Central Missouri State University

Office of Extended Campus–Distance Learning Master of Science in Criminal Justice

Warrensburg, Missouri

Founded in 1871, Central Missouri State University is a state university offering approximately 150 areas of study to 11,100 undergraduate and graduate students. In 1996, Central Missouri State University was designated Missouri's lead institution for professional technology, an area long recognized as one of the University's greatest strengths. The new mission has expanded this commitment and means that Central will continue to integrate the latest technologies into every level of its comprehensive liberal arts curriculum. Central is committed to acquiring, disseminating, and utilizing technology to enhance the University's comprehensive educational mission. Central is accredited by the North Central Association of Colleges and Schools.

DISTANCE LEARNING PROGRAM

Central's main Distance Learning Program provides undergraduate- and graduate-level courses through two-way interactive television and Web-based courses. The program currently includes one doctoral degree, two master's degrees, and numerous graduate and undergraduate courses. From fall 1994 through spring 2004, Central provided instruction to more than 13,000 graduate, undergraduate, and high school students in a distance learning environment.

Institutional and financial information about Central Missouri State University may be accessed via the Web at http://www.cmsu.edu/rsearch/ir/toc.htm.

DELIVERY MEDIA

Central uses a variety of technologies to deliver its distance learning courses. These include two-way, interactive television; broadcast television; and Internet technologies, including video and audio streaming. Central links to the Missouri Research and Educational Network (MOREnet) statewide backbone, which connects all of Missouri's public higher education institutions and several K–12 schools, to provide Internet-based and interactive television programming. Finally, Central's complement of six 2-way videoconferencing facilities, which are capable of ISDN, H.323, T.120, and audioconferencing, allow Central to provide distance learning content to anywhere in the world.

PROGRAMS OF STUDY

The Master of Science in Criminal Justice program is designed to provide the requisite knowledge, skills, and abilities for those students who intend to enter and/or advance in the criminal justice fields of law enforcement, corrections, and juvenile justice or who seek leadership, professional specialization, research, or teaching positions in criminal justice. Course work emphasizes leading justice system issues, including legal aspects; organization, administration, management, and leadership; and information acquisition, analysis, and interpretation. Distance delivery of the Master of Science in Criminal Justice includes interactive television within the state of Missouri and complete online delivery of the degree program. Site-based programs are also held at various locations in Missouri.

The graduate with a Master of Science in Criminal Justice can use the knowledge and skills obtained in the program to articulate knowledge of the major issues facing the criminal justice system in the nation and world; conduct and present an independent research project; communicate and interact professionally in scholarly, academic settings; and delineate the ethical principles of human subject protection in social science research.

First offered in 1962, the program is one of the most respected criminal justice programs in the world. Among Central's criminal justice alumni are members of numerous police and corrections agencies, judges, attorneys, professors, and approximately 400 chief administrators in all parts of the world.

To be accepted into the program of study for the Master of Criminal Justice, a student must have an undergraduate degree in criminal justice or a related field and have earned a minimum grade point average of 2.75 on all undergraduate course work and 3.0 on all graduate course work. A student without a criminal justice degree may be required to complete up to 15 hours of background courses in criminal justice prior to taking graduate-level courses. The requirement to take background courses may be waived by the department's graduate coordinator based on previous courses taken and/or relevant professional experience. Students not meeting program admission requirements may request that the department's graduate committee admit them provisionally to the program. GRE scores are not required.

The 36-hour Master of Science in Criminal Justice program allows for 6 semester hours of departmentally approved electives under the thesis option and 12 hours under the nonthesis option.

SPECIAL PROGRAMS

Central's Distance Learning Program builds upon the existing curriculum offerings at Central as well as offerings that address special distance learning needs.

Central's distance learning students are eligible to participate in the same opportunities as on-campus students. These include study tours and internships in many disciplines.

The Office of Career Services reports a 96 percent placement rate for Central graduates within six months of graduation.

STUDENT SERVICES

A toll-free University number, 800-SAY-CMSU, allows access to offices involved with student services: extended campus–distance learning, admissions, academic advising, registrar, financial aid, revenue, accounts receivable, University housing, and the Graduate School. All students enrolled at Central are issued a mainframe Internet account. The HELP Desk is available to Central students needing technical computer assistance. Distance learning students receive individualized course information prior to the start of each semester as well as information regarding University resources available to them. Online library resources are available for distance learning and off-campus students. An online writing lab (OWL) provides writing assistance to distance learning students. A toll-free number provides ordering and delivery service for textbooks from the University Bookstore.

CREDIT OPTIONS

For entering graduate students, Central will accept up to 8 hours of transfer credits in graduate work.

FACULTY

Faculty members at Central exemplify the goals of the institution as they balance personal attention with expertise in their respective fields. Approximately 71 percent of the 446 full-time faculty members hold doctoral degrees. The student-faculty ratio is 17:1.

The criminal justice faculty has a unique blend of academic credentials and field experience, with all members holding terminal degrees. In addition, 90 percent of the faculty members had significant experience with a criminal justice agency prior to joining the faculty of Central Missouri State University.

ADMISSION

Individuals interested in pursuing a graduate degree at Central Missouri State University should use the form in the graduate catalog, contact the Graduate School for application information at 800-SAY-CMSU (toll-free) or visit the Web site at http://www.cmsu.edu/graduate. The Graduate School should receive all application materials at least three weeks prior to the beginning of the semester in which the student wishes to register.

All degree-seeking student applicants must submit a formal application for admission to the Graduate School and official transcripts of all undergraduate/graduate course work. If this is a student's first enrollment at Central, a $25 nonrefundable application fee is required (international students must remit $50). Admission to the Graduate School, which permits enrollment in classes, is not equivalent to admission for a particular program or degree.

TUITION AND FEES

For 2003–04, graduate tuition was $230 per credit hour for Internet-based courses. Prospective students should note that tuition rates may be changed at any time by action of the Board of Governors.

FINANCIAL AID

Central recognizes a student's continuing need for financial assistance. Federal grant and loan funds are available for eligible students who have been accepted for regular degree programs at Central. Application eligibility information may be obtained by contacting the Office of Financial Aid at 660-543-4040 or 800-SAY-CMSU (toll-free). Students who are veterans may also be considered for VA educational benefits to help with tuition costs.

The University participates in all federal student financial aid grant, loan, and employment programs. Visiting and non-degree-seeking students are not eligible to receive federal financial aid.

APPLYING

Graduate students should contact the Graduate School at 660-543-4621 or toll-free at 800-SAY-CMSU.

CONTACT

Dr. Joseph Vaughn
Faculty Graduate Coordinator
Central Missouri State University
Warrensburg, Missouri 64093
Telephone: 660-543-4188
E-mail: vaughn@cmsu1.cmsu.edu
Web site: http://www.cmsu.edu/cj/index.html

To enroll:
Dr. Michael Penrod
Outreach Coordinator for Distance Learning
Humphreys 410
Central Missouri State University
Warrensburg, Missouri 64093
Telephone: 660-543-4984
800-SAY-CMSU Ext. 22 (toll-free)
Fax: 660-543-8333
E-mail: penrod@cmsu1.cmsu.edu
Web site: http://www.cmsu.edu/extcamp

Central Missouri State University

Office of Extended Campus–Distance Learning
Master of Science in Industrial Management

Warrensburg, Missouri

Founded in 1871, Central Missouri State University is a state university offering approximately 150 areas of study to 11,100 undergraduate and graduate students. In 1996, Central Missouri State University was designated Missouri's lead institution for professional applied science and technology programs, an area long recognized as one of the University's greatest strengths. The new mission has expanded this commitment and means that Central will continue to integrate the latest technologies into every level of its comprehensive liberal arts curriculum. Central is committed to acquiring, disseminating, and utilizing technology to enhance the University's comprehensive educational mission. Central is accredited by the North Central Association of Colleges and Schools.

DISTANCE LEARNING PROGRAM

Central's main Distance Learning Program provides undergraduate- and graduate-level courses through two-way interactive television and Web-based courses. The program currently includes one doctoral degree, two master's degrees, and numerous graduate and undergraduate courses. From fall 1994 through spring 2004, Central provided instruction to more than 13,000 graduate, undergraduate, and high school students in a distance learning environment.

Institutional and financial information about Central Missouri State University may be accessed via the Web at http://www.cmsu.edu/rsearch/ir/toc.htm.

DELIVERY MEDIA

Central uses a variety of technologies to deliver its distance learning courses. These include two-way, interactive television; broadcast television; and Internet technologies, including video and audio streaming. Central links to the Missouri Research and Educational Network (MOREnet) statewide backbone, which connects all of Missouri's public higher education institutions and several K–12 schools, to provide Internet-based and interactive television programming. Finally, Central's complement of six 2-way videoconferencing facilities, which are capable of ISDN, H.323, T.120, and audioconferencing, allow Central to provide distance learning content to anywhere in the world.

PROGRAMS OF STUDY

The Master of Science in Industrial Management is designed for students who are preparing for upward mobility in supervisory or management positions in business and industry, manufacturing, quality control or quality systems management, or related positions.

In a recent survey of graduates from this degree, the average response age was 40 years old, with a mean salary of $65,000 per year. Some occupational titles include vice president of operations, production manager, shift supervisor, quality systems manager, and plant manager.

Participants in the Master of Science in Industrial Management degree develop skills useful to business and industry. The program provides a balanced curriculum focusing on the human element of the workplace as well as a variety of industrial systems. Specific skills are developed in the fields of leadership, problem solving, and decision making.

The graduate with a Master of Science in Industrial Management degree can use the knowledge and skills obtained in the program to apply management skills and concepts to specific situations, plan and implement a project, analyze and develop a human relations strategy, demonstrate the ability to communicate effectively, explain and apply the basic concepts of an industrial economy, introduce and adapt technical expertise to a given process or product, and perform, interpret, and explain research.

The Master of Science in Industrial Management is a 33-credit-hour degree program. Complete online delivery of the program began in fall 2002. Students may enter the course cycle at the beginning of any semester. Courses are scheduled with the capability of completing the degree program in two calendar years, including one summer session. Degree information is available on the Web at http://www.cmsu/edu/mfgcont/indmnew.htm.

A strength of this program is the flexibility built into the cognate course work and culminating experience. The program allows several curricular paths leading to graduation and facilitates articulation to a cooperative doctoral program in technology management.

To be accepted into this program, a student shall have a minimum GPA of 2.6 in the undergraduate major. A student not meeting this requirement may petition the department for admittance on a conditional basis. GRE or GMAT scores are not required.

SPECIAL PROGRAMS

Central's Distance Learning Program builds upon the existing curriculum offerings at Central as well as offerings that address special distance learning needs.

Central's distance learning students are eligible to participate in the same opportunities as on-campus students. These include study tours and internships in many disciplines.

The Office of Career Services reports a 96 percent placement rate for Central graduates within six months of graduation.

STUDENT SERVICES

A toll-free University number, 800-SAY-CMSU, allows access to offices involved with student services: extended campus–distance learning, admissions, academic advising, registrar, financial aid, revenue, accounts receivable, University housing, and the Graduate School. All students enrolled at Central are issued a mainframe Internet account. The HELP Desk is available to Central students needing technical computer assistance. Distance learning students receive individualized course information prior to the start of each semester as well as information regarding University resources available to them. Online library resources are available for distance learning and off-campus students. An online writing lab (OWL) provides writing assistance to distance learning students. A toll-free number provides ordering and delivery service for textbooks from the University Bookstore.

CREDIT OPTIONS

For entering graduate students, Central will accept up to 8 hours of transfer credits in graduate work.

FACULTY

Faculty members at Central exemplify the goals of the institution as they balance personal attention with expertise in their respective fields. Approximately 71 percent of the 446 full-time faculty members hold doctoral degrees. The student-faculty ratio is 17:1.

ADMISSION

Individuals interested in pursuing a graduate degree at Central Missouri State University should use the form in the graduate catalog, contact the Graduate School for application information at 800-SAY-CMSU (toll-free), or visit the Web site at http://www.cmsu.edu/graduate. The Graduate School should receive all application materials at least three weeks prior to the beginning of the semester in which the student wishes to register.

All degree-seeking student applicants must submit a formal application for admission to the Graduate School and official transcripts of all undergraduate/graduate course work. If this is a student's first enrollment at Central, a $25 nonrefundable application fee is required (international students must remit $50). Admission to the Graduate School, which permits enrollment in classes, is not equivalent to admission for a particular program or degree.

TUITION AND FEES

For 2003–04, graduate tuition was $230 per credit hour for Internet-based courses. Prospective students should note that tuition rates may be changed at any time by action of the Board of Governors.

FINANCIAL AID

Central recognizes a student's continuing need for financial assistance. Federal grant and loan funds are available for eligible students who have been accepted for regular degree programs at Central. Application eligibility information may be obtained by contacting the Office of Financial Aid at 660-543-4040 or 800-SAY-CMSU (toll-free). Students who are veterans may also be considered for VA educational benefits to help with tuition costs.

The University participates in all federal student financial aid grant, loan, and employment programs. Visiting and non-degree-seeking students are not eligible to receive federal financial aid.

APPLYING

Graduate students should contact the Graduate School at 660-543-4621 or toll-free at 800-SAY-CMSU.

CONTACT

Dr. Ronald Woolsey
Faculty Coordinator
Central Missouri State University
Warrensburg, Missouri 64093
Telephone: 660-543-4439
E-mail: woolsey@cmsu1.cmsu.edu
Web site: http://www.cmsu.edu/mfgcont

To enroll:
Dr. Michael Penrod
Outreach Coordinator for Distance Learning
Humphreys 410
Central Missouri State University
Warrensburg, Missouri 64093
Telephone: 660-543-4984
800-SAY-CMSU Ext. 22 (toll-free)
Fax: 660-540-8333
E-mail: penrod@cmsu1.cmsu.edu
Web site: http://www.cmsu.edu/extcamp

Champlain College

Online Distance Learning Program
The Center for Online and Continuing Education

Burlington, Vermont

Since 1878, Champlain College has been dedicated to providing education that reflects the realities and needs of the contemporary workplace. It offers professional certificates, two- and four-year degree programs, and a master's program designed to provide sound professional training or updating for careers in today's complex world, as well as to provide broadening education in the humanities and general education. Champlain College is recognized as one of the leading career-building colleges in northern New England, and it has earned the respect of business, technical, and human services professions for its outstanding career-oriented education.

DISTANCE LEARNING PROGRAM

Champlain College is a pioneer in the use of computer technologies in distance learning applications. Champlain College OnLine serves hundreds of students in the United States and internationally. Champlain offers complete degree and professional certificate programs that may be accessed online at any time of day.

Champlain College is an independent, nonprofit four- and two-year college. It is accredited by the New England Association of Schools and Colleges. It first offered distance learning courses in 1993, with more than eighty courses offered in 2004–05.

DELIVERY MEDIA

Those who have access to a computer and the World Wide Web can access Champlain College OnLine. Once connected, students find messages posted from the instructor and classmates either in the course forum or in private e-mail. All communication occurs online and includes discussion comments from classmates, lectures, instructional material, and assignments. The material covered in Champlain College's online classes is the same as in traditional courses.

PROGRAMS OF STUDY

Champlain College offers an extensive array of traditionally delivered, career-oriented four- and two-year degrees and professional certificates. Through its distance learning program, the College offers Associate in Science (A.S.) degrees in accounting, business, computer and digital forensics, e-business management, global networks and telecommunications, international business, management, software development, and Web site development and management. Bachelor in Science (B.S.) degrees are offered in business, computer and digital forensics, e-business management, professional studies, software engineering, and Web site development and management, all of which are designed to complement associate degrees in career areas. Professional certificates are offered online in all of these career areas. A Master of Science (M.S.) degree is offered in managing innovation and information technology.

Professional certificates require successful completion of 12 to 24 credits. Associate degrees require completion of 60 credits, half of which must be taken through Champlain College. The bachelor's degree requires completion of 120 credits, at least 45 of which must be taken through Champlain. The master's degree consists of 36 credits. Students can also take individual undergraduate courses on a nonmatriculated basis.

SPECIAL PROGRAMS

The College has several expanding international programs that offer degree programs to students in India and the United Arab Emirates. These programs incorporate distance learning into the curriculum.

Corporate partnerships are also available for businesses that are interested in training employees. Since classes are available at any time, from anywhere the Internet can be accessed, distance learning allows businesses to offer high-quality training programs to employees—even when different shifts, different locations, and even different time zones are involved.

STUDENT SERVICES

Champlain College provides a number of services to adult learners. Distance learners receive academic advising from the Advising and Registration Center and the Career Planning Office, a full range of online library services, tutoring, and access to the computer Help Desk and an online bookstore.

CREDIT OPTIONS

Students may transfer credits earned through other accredited postsecondary institutions. Depending on the program selected, students may also transfer credit for life/work experience or credits from approved testing programs. Champlain accepts credit through approved portfolio assessment programs, CLEP, DANTES, and PONSI.

FACULTY

Champlain's strength lies in its faculty. More than 120 full-time and part-time faculty members focus their primary energies on teaching. Faculty members have completed programs of advanced study, and many have doctoral or terminal degrees.

ADMISSION

Admission requirements for degree programs include graduation from a recognized secondary school or possession of a high school equivalency certificate and submission of SAT I or ACT scores. Students who have been out of high school for several years, who may not have taken all of the course work that is required for acceptance to a particular major, or who have not taken SAT or ACT tests, should speak with an admission counselor or academic adviser about how to apply. Admission to the certificate program requires submission of a high school transcript (or GED) and a current resume. Given the method of instructional delivery, online students should be self-motivated and possess effective reading and writing skills as well as basic computer skills. Master's degree candidates must possess a bachelor's degree and have at least two years of professional experience.

TUITION AND FEES

In 2004–05, tuition for undergraduate programs is $400 per credit; most courses are 3 credits. The application fee is $40.

The tuition for the master's degree program is $440 per credit. The application fee is $50.

Textbooks may be purchased online through the bookstore. There are no additional fees.

FINANCIAL AID

Payment and financial aid options depend on personal circumstances and whether students attend full- or part-time. The College participates in several federal financial aid programs, including Federal Pell Grant and Federal Stafford Student Loan, and state loan and grant programs.

APPLYING

Students may enroll for online undergraduate courses as nonmatriculating students by registering online or by mail, fax, or telephone. The College reviews applications for degree programs when they are received. A short, online orientation is required for all online students prior to gaining access to their courses.

CONTACT

R. J. Sweeney, Continuing Education Counselor
Champlain College
Center for Online and Continuing Education
163 South Willard Street
Burlington, Vermont 05402
Telephone: 802-865-6449
888-545-3459 (toll-free)
Fax: 802-865-6447
E-mail: coce@champlain.edu
Web site: http://www.champlain.edu

Charter Oak State College

New Britain, Connecticut

Charter Oak State College was established in 1973 by the Connecticut Legislature to provide an alternate way for adults to earn a college degree. Recognized as the College that offers degrees without boundaries, Charter Oak awards associate and bachelor's degrees. Charter Oak is regionally accredited by the New England Association of Schools and Colleges and is a Servicemembers Opportunity College.

Charter Oak's degree program was designed to be especially appealing to people who work full-time and have family and financial responsibilities as well. The program is designed for independent adult learners who have the capacity and motivation to pursue a degree program that provides flexibility in how, where, and when they can earn credits. The Charter Oak program assumes that its students possess a basic understanding of the elements of a degree program and that they will seek guidance as often as necessary to progress satisfactorily with their studies.

Students earn credits from regionally accredited colleges and universities, including Charter Oak, and from noncollegiate sponsored instruction, standardized tests, special assessment, contract learning, and portfolio assessment.

One of the hallmarks of Charter Oak State College is its individualized professional advisement services. Each student is assigned to an academic counselor, who is a specialist in the student's chosen field of study. That counselor is accessible via telephone, fax, or e-mail and works closely with the student to develop a plan of study for completion of the degree program.

DISTANCE LEARNING PROGRAM

Charter Oak State College offers an external degree program and so, by definition, is a distance learning institution. Students earn their credits "externally" and transfer them into the College, or they can enroll in distance learning courses offered by Charter Oak.

DELIVERY MEDIA

The College offers a selection of distance learning courses; however, students are not required to take Charter Oak courses to earn a degree from the College. Some of the courses use videotapes and texts and some are online courses. The courses are facilitated by faculty mentors who are accessible by e-mail, telephone, and U.S. mail. Students purchase texts at a distance from a designated bookstore and rent videotapes from a mail-order service. A catalog of offerings is available each semester.

PROGRAMS OF STUDY

Charter Oak State College offers four degrees in general studies: Associate in Arts, Associate in Science, Bachelor of Arts, and Bachelor of Science. To earn an associate degree, a student must complete at least 60 credits; a bachelor's degree requires at least 120 credits.

A Charter Oak degree is more than an accumulation of the required number of credits. At least one half of the credits toward a degree must be earned in subjects traditionally included among the liberal arts and sciences: humanities, mathematics, natural sciences, and social sciences. Achievement in these areas demonstrates breadth of learning. In addition, students pursuing a baccalaureate degree must complete a concentration, consisting of at least 36 credits, that demonstrates depth of learning.

A concentration plan, in conjunction with an essay, must be submitted to the faculty for approval. Concentrations may be constructed in many areas, including applied arts, art history, the behavioral sciences, business, child study, communication, computer science, engineering studies, fire service administration, public safety administration, organizational management and leadership, human services, individualized studies, languages, liberal studies, literature, music history, the natural sciences, religious studies, the social sciences, and technology studies.

SPECIAL PROGRAMS

The College has evaluated a number of noncollegiate courses and programs for which it awards credit toward Charter Oak degree programs. Many health-care specialties from hospital-based programs are included, such as medical laboratory technician, nurse practitioner, physician assistant, radiologic technologist, registered nurse, and respiratory therapist or technician. Other evaluations include the Child Development Associate (CDA) credential; the FAA Airman Certificate; Famous Artists School in Westport, Connecticut; Institute of Children's Literature in West Redding, Connecticut; the National Opticianry Competency Examination; the Contact Lens Registry Examination; and several fire certifications, including Fire Marshal,

Deputy Fire Marshal, Fire Inspector, Fire Fighter III, Fire Officer I or II, and Fire Service Instructor I or II.

CREDIT OPTIONS

Students can transfer credits from other regionally accredited colleges and universities; age of credits is not a factor in their transferability. There is no limit to the number of credits that can be earned using standardized examinations, prior learning, including ACE-evaluated military credits, ACE and PONSI-evaluated noncollegiate learning, and portfolio assessment.

FACULTY

Full-time faculty members from public and independent institutions of higher education in Connecticut are appointed to serve as consulting examiners at Charter Oak.

ADMISSION

Admission is open to any person 16 years or older, regardless of level of formal education, who is able to demonstrate college-level achievement. To be admitted, a student must have earned 9 college-level credits from acceptable sources of credit.

TUITION AND FEES

All students pay a $50 application fee. Connecticut residents pay a first-year student services fee of $635 for an associate degree or $925 for a bachelor's degree. Nonresidents pay a first-year matriculation fee of $895 for an associate degree or $1190 for a bachelor's degree. Active-duty service members and their spouses pay in-state resident's rates for all Charter Oak fees and services. All students pay a graduation fee of $165. Tuition for video-based courses is $145 per credit for Connecticut residents and $205 per credit for nonresidents; tuition for online courses is $145 per credit for Connecticut residents and $205 per credit for nonresidents. There is a $24 registration fee for all students.

FINANCIAL AID

Financial aid is available to Charter Oak students from several sources, including federal, state, and institutional grants and loans. All students who wish to apply for aid must complete the Free Application for Federal Student Aid (FAFSA) and Charter Oak State College's Application for Financial Aid. The FAFSA may be completed online and can be accessed at http://www.fafsa.ed.gov. Charter Oak's forms can be accessed online at http://www.charteroak.edu/sfa. The Charter Oak State College school code is 032343.

APPLYING

Charter Oak reviews applications on a rolling basis; students may matriculate anytime during the year.

CONTACT

Admissions Office
Charter Oak State College
55 Paul Manafort Drive
New Britain, Connecticut 06053-1250
Telephone: 860-832-3800
Fax: 860-832-3999
Web site:
http://www.charteroak.edu

City University

Distance Learning Option

Bellevue, Washington

City University is the largest private institution of higher learning in the Northwest, with more than 37,000 graduates and locations throughout the Pacific Northwest, Europe, and Asia. Students are drawn to the school's flexible programs, schedules, and distance learning options. City University offers more than seventy-five programs, including associate, bachelor's, and master's degrees, as well as undergraduate and graduate certificate courses. A not-for-profit institution, City University has been a respected member of the Northwest's academic community since 1973 and is accredited by the Northwest Commission on Colleges and Universities.

City University's programs cover a variety of academic fields, ranging from business management and technology to psychology, counseling, and education. The majority of faculty members actively work in the fields they teach. The combination of innovative program design and outstanding instruction makes City University an exceptional institution of higher learning.

DISTANCE LEARNING PROGRAM

In keeping with its mission of providing convenient, accessible education, City University offers most degree programs through distance learning (DL). The DL option makes degree programs available electronically through the World Wide Web. City University serves approximately 4,000 students worldwide annually through DL.

DELIVERY MEDIA

Online Distance Learning students receive their course content via the World Wide Web utilizing the Blackboard™ course management system. Merging the best of the traditional classroom experience and distance learning, faculty members and students communicate and collaborate using threaded discussions, real-time chats, course e-mail, and online file exchanges. Online students are required to have an e-mail address, a computer with a minimum 56K modem, Internet access, and CD-ROM capacity.

PROGRAMS OF STUDY

City University's undergraduate programs prepare students to compete in today's marketplace. Students may complete an Associate of Science (A.S.), a Bachelor of Science (B.S.), or a Bachelor of Arts (B.A.) degree. Within these degrees, students may pursue one of several areas of study, including accounting, applied psychology, business administration, computer systems, e-commerce, human resource management, information technology, marketing, mass communications and journalism, or project management. Most undergraduate-level courses are 5 credits each; 90 credits are required for completion of an A.S. degree, and 180 credits are required for completion of a B.S. or B.A. degree.

City University's graduate business and public administration programs prepare management professionals for leadership roles at local, national, and international levels. Students may pursue a graduate certificate or a Master of Business Administration (M.B.A.) with an array of specialties, a Master of Public Administration (M.P.A.) degree with an array of specialties, a Master of Arts (M.A.) in management with an array of specialties, or a Master of Science in either project management or computer systems. Most graduate-level courses are 3 credits; total required credits for a degree range from 45 to 60.

SPECIAL PROGRAMS

City University has an open-door admissions policy for most programs. Students may begin a distance learning course at the beginning of any month, and there is no application deadline. City University has partnerships with several institutions and organizations worldwide. Through these affiliations, the University offers in-house programs and evaluates prior training for college-level credit.

All of City University's programs are geared toward adult students. From its student body to its faculty and staff members, City University is a community of professionals. All who are associated with the University understand the needs of adult learners who are seeking high-quality education that applies to their individual lifestyle.

STUDENT SERVICES

Academic advising and assistance is available by phone, fax, or e-mail. Registration is available by contacting an Academic Advisor. Students have full access to the library, including an online search service, a reference librarian (via a toll-free phone number), and a mailing service for circulation of books and articles.

CREDIT OPTIONS

Undergraduate students may transfer up to 90 approved lower-division and

45 approved upper-division credits from approved institutions for baccalaureate programs. The Prior Learning Assessment Program lets students earn credits through documented experiential learning. Students may receive credit for the CLEP or other standardized tests. Graduate students may transfer up to 12 credits from approved programs.

FACULTY

There are more than 250 faculty members included in the distance learning program, 26 of whom are full-time. More than 25 percent of the full-time faculty members have terminal degrees.

ADMISSION

Undergraduate programs are generally open to applicants over 18 years of age who hold a high school diploma or GED certificate. Admission to graduate programs requires that students hold a baccalaureate degree from an accredited or otherwise recognized institution. Additional requirements apply to education and human services programs. International students whose first language is not English are required to submit a TOEFL score of at least 540 for admission to undergraduate programs and 565 for graduate programs.

TUITION AND FEES

Tuition for the 2004–05 academic year is $220 per undergraduate credit and $375 per graduate credit. Other fees may apply depending on the specific course of study. A registration fee of $30 for undergraduates and $38 for graduate students occurs once per quarter.

FINANCIAL AID

For information regarding financial aid options at City University, students should contact the Student Financial Services Department at 800-426-5596 (toll-free).

APPLYING

DL students may enroll on a rolling admissions basis. Students must speak with an Academic Advisor to complete the initial enrollment. Students should then submit the application form, nonrefundable application fee ($80), and admission documents to the Office of Admissions and Student Services. Official transcripts should be sent to the Office of the Registrar.

CONTACT

Admissions and Student Services
City University
11900 NE First Street
Bellevue, Washington 98005
Telephone: 425-737-1010
800-42-CITYU (toll-free)
425-450-4660 (TTY/TDD)
Fax: 425-709-5361
E-mail: info@cityu.edu
Web site: http://www.cityu.edu

Colorado State University

College of Business

Fort Collins, Colorado

The College of Business strives to provide a diverse set of students with the knowledge, skills, and functional competencies they need to become effective decision makers and leaders in a business environment that is becoming more global, more competitive, and increasingly dynamic. Students gain knowledge and resources that are useful to the business community, fellow scholars, and other constituencies seeking expertise.

The Master of Business Administration (M.B.A.) degree program is fully accredited by AACSB International–The Association to Advance Collegiate Schools of Business and ranks in the top 25 percent of business programs in the United States. The M.B.A. from Colorado State University (CSU) is one of the only AACSB-accredited programs available completely via distance education.

DISTANCE LEARNING PROGRAM

The distance learning M.B.A. program delivers a high-quality education while providing students with the flexibility needed to earn their degrees. Content is cross-functional and has a strong emphasis on information technology, global issues, and teamwork. More than 800 professionals have earned their M.B.A.'s through the CSU distance learning program.

Most distance learners are working professionals, with an average of more than thirteen years of work experience. They are drawn from forty-seven states and several Canadian provinces. A number of U.S. military personnel stationed abroad are completing the program. The average age of the distance students is 33; their average GMAT score is 620.

DELIVERY MEDIA

Each student in the program must have access to a computer, the Internet, and a DVD player to watch course recordings. The College of Business's software standard is Microsoft Office XP Professional.

To facilitate communication in the distance education program, all M.B.A. students use an electronic communications software product called EM.B.A.net, which allows greater communication capability among faculty and staff members and students, posting of class materials, group work, and real-time chats.

PROGRAM OF STUDY

The degree program is designed to serve the needs of working professionals who need flexibility in schedule and location. There is no on-campus requirement; course work is completed entirely at a distance. This 36-credit program takes two to four years to complete and includes some summer classes. There is no thesis requirement.

Each class is recorded onto DVD on campus in a specially designed, state-of-the-art multimedia classroom. Through the DVDs, distance learners view classes exactly as they progressed on campus, benefiting from questions asked by on-campus students. The sixteen-week semester is broken into two 8-week terms, with 2 credits earned every eight weeks. Courses follow the on-campus class schedule and must be completed by the end of the term during which they are offered. Each student is required to designate an examination proctor, to whom exams and guidelines to follow in administering the exams are sent.

STUDENT SERVICES

The M.B.A. adviser gives program information to prospective and current students. The CSU library provides to distance learners services comparable to those for the on-campus community, including remote access to databases and the library catalog, document delivery, reference help, and instruction sessions. Students can also request, via the distance users' Web site, books and paper articles to be sent to them.

CREDIT OPTIONS

Transfer credits are not accepted. The M.B.A. courses are sequential, and because of the program's integrative nature, it is not possible to transfer or substitute external courses.

FACULTY

What differentiates CSU's programs from others is the high quality of the faculty members, who integrate real-world experiences into their courses. The professors who teach in the M.B.A. program are full-time faculty members with Ph.D.'s in their disciplines. Many also continue to work as consultants in their industries.

ADMISSION

A primary goal of the program is to select a richly diverse set of students with various undergraduate degrees and professional experiences. The decision to admit an applicant is based on an evaluation of the candidate's potential for successfully completing the graduate business program, the ability of the candidate to add to the perspective of the class, and the school's ability to accommodate a limited number of students. Previous academic performance, GMAT scores, work experience, and recommendations are some of the factors considered. Additional requirements include a minimum of four years' postundergraduate professional work experience. Applicants with all types of undergraduate backgrounds are encouraged to apply.

TUITION AND FEES

For the 2003–04 academic year, the tuition for the distance M.B.A. courses was $448 per credit. This includes the costs of taping, shipping, and EM.B.A.net. There are no additional fees; however, students are responsible for books and materials.

FINANCIAL AID

Financial aid is available to accepted students who take at least 5 credits per semester in the distance M.B.A. program. More information can be obtained by contacting the Financial Aid Office at 800-491-4622 Ext. 6 (toll-free).

APPLYING

The application deadlines for the distance learning M.B.A. program are June 1 and October 1 for the fall and spring semesters, respectively. Because there are a limited number of openings each year, students should apply as early as possible. Applicants must submit a resume, a cover letter that reflects carefully considered reasons for pursuing a business degree at the master's level, GMAT scores, TOEFL scores (for international students), the data sheet, three completed recommendation forms in sealed envelopes, two copies of official transcripts in sealed envelopes, a completed application, and the $50 application fee. If the applicant's grade point average is below 3.0, a separate letter must be included that explains the circumstances.

CONTACT

Kathy Thornhill
College of Business
Colorado State University
Fort Collins, Colorado 80523-1270
Telephone: 800-491-4MBA (toll-free)
Fax: 970-491-2348
E-mail: bizdist@lamar.colostate.edu
World Wide Web: http://www.csumba.com

Colorado State University

Continuing Education

Fort Collins, Colorado

Colorado State University has served the people of Colorado as the state's land-grant university since 1870. Today, the campus in Fort Collins is home to 24,000 students pursuing degrees at all levels in a wide range of subjects in the liberal arts, engineering, business, natural resources, agriculture, and the sciences. The University's instructional outreach activities go far beyond the campus and the state of Colorado.

DISTANCE LEARNING PROGRAM

Colorado State University's distance education courses are designed to begin or to finish a degree, to explore new topics, to enrich life, and to give students an opportunity to develop a level of proficiency in professional development. Approximately 2,500 individuals from all over the country and overseas are enrolled in distance education courses from Colorado State University.

DELIVERY MEDIA

Colorado State offers courses in online, print, and video formats. All courses are supported by Colorado State University faculty members. Students may contact course faculty members via telephone, fax, e-mail, or regular mail. Students should call Educational Outreach or check the Web site listed at the end of this description for contact information for an instructor.

PROGRAMS OF STUDY

Colorado State University's Network for Learning (CSUN) links learners to all of Colorado State's distance options—correspondence courses, telecourses, distance degree programs, online courses, face-to-face programs at satellite locations, and those offering a mix of media.

As an institution, Colorado State has been involved in distance education since 1967 and was one of the first schools to utilize technology in distance education.

Independent Study: Correspondence Study, Telecourses, and Online Courses removes the traditional boundaries of time and location for the distance learner. Through the use of a study guide, textbooks, videotapes, the Internet, and applicable reference materials, students have the opportunity to participate in an individualized mode of instruction offering a high degree of flexibility. Students interested in correspondence courses and telecourses may enroll at any time, set their own pace, and choose the most convenient time and place to study. Online courses are taught according to the regular University semester schedule.

Distance degrees offer working professionals the opportunity to earn credit from Colorado State without coming to campus. These are semester-based courses that use videotape, online, and mixed-media formats. Whether students are working on their degree or taking courses to stay current in their field, distance degrees offer the flexibility to pursue educational objectives as work schedules permit.

Courses are available in several disciplines, including agriculture, business, communication/public affairs, computer science, engineering, fire service, human resource development, statistics, and telecommunications. Distance degree students are located throughout the United States and Canada and at U.S. military APO and FPO addresses. At this time, only correspondence courses and online courses and degrees are available to overseas students. More than 1,200 motivated people have earned their degrees, and countless others have taken individual courses to enhance their skill base or keep current with the latest technology.

SPECIAL PROGRAMS

Colorado State also provides other distance education opportunities. These courses are open-entry/open-exit, meaning students may register at any time and take six months to complete the course. Many of the courses can be used for specific programs, such as Child Care Administration Certification or Seed Analyst Training.

The state of Colorado requires certification of all child-care center directors and substitute directors by the State Department of Human Services. Certification requires both experience working with young children and specific education. Colorado State University is proud to offer courses through distance education that may satisfy some of the educational requirements. Other states may have individual specific educational requirements. Students should contact the appropriate agency in their area for further information.

For instructors wanting to enhance their teaching, Colorado State offers a Postsecondary Teaching Certificate Program, consisting of three 3-credit courses: Models of Teaching, Communication and Classrooms, and Educators, Systems, and Change. In this program, new instructors acquire a practical overview of a range of effective teaching models, ideas for engaging students while addressing measurable learning objectives, and approaches to promote critical and creative thinking. Experienced instructors update and energize their teaching repertoires, connecting personal knowledge with established research on effective classroom practices. Students in the program can earn graduate credit for advanced course work in postsecondary education and apply the 9 credits toward a master's or doctoral degree.

An innovative Seed Analyst Training Program consisting of four distance learning (correspondence) courses has been developed by the National Seed Storage Laboratory and Colorado State University. The courses were prepared over a two-year period by University professors and other experts with the support of the Colorado seed industry. The four courses cover the basics of seed analyst training: 1) Seed Anatomy and Identification, 2) Seed Development and Metabolism, 3) Seed Purity Analysis, and 4) Seed Germination and Viability.

Advising through the University HELP/Success Center is offered to all those interested in continuing their learning. There is no fee for academic advising services. Students may schedule an appointment with an academic adviser by calling 970-491-7095. The Extended University Programs librarian is available to assist students with identifying and accessing library materials. Students should call 970-491-6952 to speak with the librarian.

CREDIT OPTIONS

All credits earned through distance education are recorded on a Colorado State University transcript. Distance education courses are the same as on-campus courses and are accredited by the same organizations as the University. A student currently enrolled in a degree program elsewhere is responsible for checking with the appropriate official at the degree-granting institution to make certain the course will apply.

FACULTY

Distance education faculty members must meet the same high standards any Colorado State University faculty member must meet. Most of the distance faculty members are faculty members within the department granting the course credit. Faculty members are available to answer questions and give feedback via telephone, fax, e-mail, or regular mail.

ADMISSION

Anyone who has the interest, desire, background, and ability may register for distance learning courses. However, if prerequisites are listed for a course, they must be met. Registration in distance learning courses does not constitute admission to Colorado State University.

TUITION AND FEES

Tuition for distance degrees for the 2003–04 academic year was $448 per credit (business courses), $436 per credit (weekly videotaped courses), or $360 per credit (online courses). Tuition for other distance education courses for the 2003–04 academic year was $160 per credit for undergraduate courses and $180 per credit for graduate courses. For current tuition information, students should visit the Web site listed at the end of this description.

FINANCIAL AID

Colorado State University courses are approved for the DANTES program. Eligible military personnel should process DANTES applications through their education office. For information regarding veterans' benefits, students should contact the VA office at Colorado State University. With the exception of distance degrees, distance learning is not a degree-granting program and is therefore not eligible for federal grants. Students are encouraged to seek scholarship aid from organizations and local civic groups that may sponsor such study.

APPLYING

To complete a distance degree, admittance to the University is required. There is no application for distance education. Students should simply register for the course(s) of interest by mail or fax or online and pay the tuition. For more information about these and other distance courses from Colorado State University, or for registration information, students should contact the University.

CONTACT

Telephone: 970-491-5288
877-491-4336 (toll-free)
Fax: 970-491-7885
E-mail: info@learn.colostate.edu
Web site: http://www.learn.colostate.edu

Colorado Technical University

Colorado Technical University Online

Colorado Springs, Colorado

Since 1965, Colorado Technical University (CTU) has helped thousands of students achieve success in business, management, and technology careers. Academic programs are continually evaluated and updated for relevance and currency. Faculty members work closely with industry advisory boards made up of respected professionals who are behind the innovations that drive global business. CTU is accredited by the Higher Learning Commission and a member of the North Central Association of Colleges and Schools.

DISTANCE LEARNING PROGRAM

Colorado Technical University Online provides students with a high-quality education relevant to the needs and demands of the ever-evolving business and technical job markets. CTU Online offers innovative, career-relevant degree programs completely online, so students can learn anywhere, any time, on any computer with Internet-access. Each program's content is continually updated and instantly applicable.

DELIVERY MEDIA

CTU Online offers one of the best e-learning platforms available. Students experience the latest in course delivery systems. Classes are taught in multimedia format, which provides a rich, dynamic, interactive classroom experience. The programs offer many opportunities for students to adapt their learning experiences to their own personal styles. Students who prefer to have a hard copy of notes can print the presentation. Each student is in control of the pace of a professor's presentation. For students who like to ask questions, there is a glossary of terms section available for each course. Students can also participate in discussions with the instructors and other students. Since the participants are employed in a variety of interesting professions, students gain insightful knowledge and learn from each other's experiences.

PROGRAMS OF STUDY

CTU Online offers bachelor's degrees in criminal justice and in business administration with concentrations in human resource management, information technology, management, and marketing; an Executive M.B.A. degree; and Master of Management (M.S.M.) degrees in business management, information systems security, information technology management, and project management. In addition, CTU Online degree programs incorporate multiple professional certificates that students earn as they progress through their degree programs, without added courses or additional cost. This unique aspect of the program enables participants to progressively add certificate credentials to their resumes. Students with no previous college or military training can complete the bachelor's degree programs in about 2½ years. The master's programs take fifteen months to complete online.

The B.S.B.A. in information technology gives students the technical skills and strong management skills they need to position themselves for career advancement in this growing industry. Participants earn seven Professional Certificates as they work toward the completion of their degree program.

The M.S.M. in information systems security prepares technical leaders in systems security management, including methods to combat threats to corporate technical resources. This program provides a strong foundation for students to advance their technical skills in order to plan, manage, certify, and accredit an organization's security plan. The program includes four Professional Certificates: information systems security, information systems security management, project management, and security certifications and accreditation.

The M.S.M. in IT management degree program prepares students to assume positions of leadership with the practical skills and knowledge to get the job done on time and within budget. This program is designed as a broad-based IT management curriculum applicable to private industry, government organizations, and nonprofit organizations. Students gain an understanding of computer architecture, networking and telecommunication, database management, business and financial management strategies, and more. Students also earn four Professional Certificates: database management, networking and telecommunications, systems analysis and integration, and project management.

The B.S.B.A. degree program emphasizes practical competencies, creative leadership approaches, and the development of critical-thinking skills. Students select a concentration in management, information technology, human resource management, or marketing. This degree program incorporates a number of Professional Certificates, including basics of accounting and finance, business fundamentals, business in the global environment, human resource development, management essentials, organizational systems improvement, project planning, and sales and marketing.

The M.S.M. in business management program is designed to provide immediate management applications along with the knowledge and understanding of the critical skills necessary to analyze and solve various business problems. The program equips students with an understanding of the fundamental issues related to technology's role today and in the future. Students develop both technical expertise and business savvy and learn to create new technology-based business paradigms to achieve organizational goals. Three Professional Certificates are earned during the course of this degree program: project management, IT/business transformation, and change management.

Successful management careers demand creative leadership and vision from professionals who are able to solve problems effectively and efficiently. The M.S.M. in project management focuses on the importance of leadership as it pertains to the complete spectrum of management responsibilities. Program content covers such key areas as time and conflict management, HR management, risk analysis and management, and scheduling techniques. The program includes three Professional Certificates: project management, change management, and business management.

The Colorado Tech Online Executive M.B.A. delivers immediate management applications along with the knowledge and understanding of the critical skills necessary to analyze and solve various business problems. The emphasis is on real-world skills and knowledge that managers need to succeed in today's business world. Unlike most other Executive M.B.A. programs, it also incorporates information technology management and project management competencies. Students earn three Professional Certificates in this program: business administration, business management, and change management.

The B.S.B.A. in marketing provides students with the knowledge they need to succeed in an industry that features some of the highest wage and salary growth rates in the entire employment field. The program gives graduates an understanding of the intricate relationships between organizations and their customers. Course content has been developed to emphasize current marketing trends and opportunities for success. Nine Professional Certificates are earned during the course of this program: basics of accounting and finance, business fundamentals, business in the global environment, human resource development, management essentials, organizational systems improvement, project planning, sales and marketing, and marketing research.

Students in the Bachelor of Science in Criminal Justice Program gain a solid knowledge base in the areas of the courts, corrections, and law enforcement in addition to the management skills needed for career advancement. The program is unique in that it offers students a component of forensic study not usually available at the undergraduate level. This program includes four Professional Certificates: corrections technician, crime scene investigation, law enforcement skills, and legal studies and court process.

STUDENT SERVICES

CTU Online has a 24/7 Help Desk to provide technical support to students for the duration of their studies. A toll-free number connects students to trained technical support professionals dedicated to providing assistance whenever they need it.

For research and curriculum support, CTU Online students have access to a full academic library completely online. The texts, journals, and articles and thousands of other resources are accessible whenever a student needs them.

The Career Services Department is staffed by skilled professionals who assist students with their career planning process. The department's full range of services includes career development strategy, individual student consultations, job search strategies, interviewing tips, and resume and cover letter assistance.

CREDIT OPTIONS

Students with college credit or military experience may be eligible for the baccalaureate degree completion program. This can reduce the time required to complete a degree program.

FACULTY

CTU Online's faculty members have advanced degrees and are also established professionals in their fields, giving students valuable opportunities to derive insights and real-world perspectives from experts. They bring situation-specific relevance to every course so that students receive an education that they can apply in the real world. CTU Online also limits the number of students enrolled in each class in order to encourage interaction with and personal attention from professors.

ADMISSION

To apply for admission, students must submit an online application. There is a $50 application fee. CTU Online then contacts applicants to arrange for a personal telephone interview and for the necessary school transcripts to be submitted. TOEFL scores are required from nonnative speakers of English. The entire admission process can take as little as four to seven days.

TUITION AND FEES

Tuition amounts vary. Students should call an admissions representative for more information.

FINANCIAL AID

Financial aid is available for those who qualify.

CONTACT

CTU Online
Suite E
4435 North Chestnut Street
Colorado Springs, Colorado 80907
Telephone: 800-416-8904 (toll-free)
Web site: http://www.ctuonline.edu

Connecticut State University System

OnlineCSU

Hartford, Connecticut

The Connecticut State University System is the largest public university system in Connecticut, with more than 35,000 students and 150,000 alumni. OnlineCSU is the virtual classroom of the four Connecticut State Universities—Central Connecticut State University, Eastern Connecticut State University, Southern Connecticut State University and Western Connecticut State University.

OnlineCSU supports CSU's mission to provide affordable and high-quality active learning opportunities that are geographically and technologically accessible. The collaborative efforts of the four Universities provide a strong educational resource for students in Connecticut and around the world.

CSU institutions are fully accredited by the New England Association of Schools and College and all credits are generally transferable.

DISTANCE LEARNING PROGRAM

More than 15,000 students have taken OnlineCSU's undergraduate and graduate courses and participated in its academic programs. OnlineCSU is not a university; degrees are conferred and credits are awarded by Central, Eastern, Southern or Western Connecticut State University. Courses may be completed entirely online and do not require classroom attendance.

DELIVERY MEDIA

Because OnlineCSU is an asynchronous learning environment, students and teachers do not need to log in to the virtual classroom at the same time. The classroom is available 24 hours a day, seven days a week. Faculty and students share documents and interact regularly through the WebCT learning platform, which utilizes chat rooms, threaded discussions, e-mail and other tools to achieve learning objectives. Students taking online classes must have a computer running a Web browser, preferably Internet Explorer version 5.0 or higher, a connection to the Internet, and an e-mail account.

Off-campus courses are offered in a variety of formats, including face-to-face instruction, online courses, video conferencing, CD-ROM, or through combinations of delivery systems.

PROGRAMS OF STUDY

Three graduate degrees and two certificate programs are available via OnlineCSU. They include a Master of Library Science (M.L.S.) offered by Southern Connecticut State University, a Master of Science (M.S.) in educational technology offered by Eastern Connecticut State University and a Master of Science (M.S.) in data mining offered by Central Connecticut State University. A certificate in data mining is also available from Central, as is a sixth-year certificate in educational foundations from Southern. Additional programs are being added; students should check the Web site for details.

The M.L.S. degree is available from Southern's School of Communication, Information, and Library Science. The program integrates library science, information science, and instructional technology. It offers preparation for careers in various types of libraries, including academic, public, special, and school libraries, and a range of alternative information science occupations. The 36-credit degree program is accredited by the American Library Association. The school media specialist concentration is also approved by the Connecticut Board of Education and offers Connecticut-certified teachers the opportunity to obtain cross-endorsement as a school media specialist.

The M.S. degree in educational technology from Eastern Connecticut State University is a 36-credit program designed to provide practical educational technology skills. To prepare students for success in a highly technological and rapidly changing world, the program integrates educational technology applications with the expertise of professional educators and teachers of grades PreK-12. The program empowers graduates to meet and exceed outcomes standards in Connecticut and throughout the nation. The program is also unique because its curriculum is aligned with standards set by the International Society for Technology in Education.

The M.S. degree in data mining from Central Connecticut State University focuses on statistical methodology, machine learning, and business intelligence. Educated professionals with these skills are sought by industries seeking to improve products, marketing, sales, and customer service. Students gain hands-on experience with the Clementiner data mining software suite from SPSS, Inc., and other state-of-the-art programs to provide actionable results to real-world business problems. A certificate is also available; students should visit the Web site for further information.

The sixth year certificate in educational foundations program explores the framework of education. This versatile 30-credit program examines the world in which today's educator must function, from multicultural, American societal, legal, and moral perspectives.

STUDENT SERVICES

OnlineCSU offers a complete set of support services to its distance learners. This includes a 24-hour, seven-days-a-week, toll-free helpdesk to address technical issues and other questions. All OnlineCSU students are allowed full access to online library resources, a bookstore, tutoring and more through MyOnlineCSU, the program's distance education portal. In addition, on-campus services such as advising, career counseling, and financial aid are available to OnlineCSU students.

CREDIT OPTIONS

Students should refer to the offering university for information about transferring credit, work or life experience evaluations, or admission test waivers. Classes generally are three credits each. Graduate programs require a minimum of 36 credits.

FACULTY

All faculty members have extensive academic experience with advanced degrees and practical experience in their disciplines. Before teaching online, faculty members receive pedagogical and tools training to prepare them for the online education experience. In addition, CSU faculty members do not use "canned" content, having generally personally developed the course they teach.

ADMISSION

Admission information and applications are available online. Students seeking information about the M.L.S. and sixth year degree can contact Southern at 888-500-SCSU (toll-free). For information about admittance to the educational technology program, students can call 860-465-5292. For information about data mining, students can call 860-832-2862.

TUITION AND FEES

Effective with the summer 2004 semester, fees for Connecticut residents who are part-time students are $290 per credit hour for undergraduate courses and $365 per credit hour for graduate courses. Fees for out of-state residents who are part-time students are $362 per credit hour for undergraduate courses and $457 per credit hour for graduate courses. Each registration also requires a $50 online registration fee.

During the regular academic terms of fall and spring, full-time Connecticut State University students must pay only the $50 online fee, as credits are billed as part of the student's full-time tuition. Full-time students taking classes during winter and summer semesters are billed as part-time students, as is the case with on-campus classes.

FINANCIAL AID

Students who receive financial aid may be able to apply all or part of this aid to OnlineCSU courses. Students who would like to apply for financial aid need to do so through their home university. Students at CSU institutions should refer to the corresponding university's Web site for specific information on financial aid policies and procedures.

APPLYING

Generally, students may take up to three courses without formally matriculating at one of the Connecticut State University institutions. To apply to one of the universities, students should visit that university's Web site via http://www.ctstateu.edu. To enroll in an online course, students can create a new student account and register via the site listed below.

CONTACT

OnlineCSU Student Services
Connecticut State University System Office
39 Woodland Street
Hartford, Connecticut 06105-2337
Telephone: 860-493-0001 or 860-493-0081
Fax: 860-493-0120
E-mail: onlinecsu@so.ct.edu
Web site: http://www.OnlineCSU.net

Dallas Baptist University

Online Education Program

Dallas, Texas

The purpose of Dallas Baptist University (DBU) is to provide Christ-centered, high-quality higher education in the arts, sciences, and professional studies at both the undergraduate and graduate levels to traditional age and adult students in order to produce servant leaders who have the ability to integrate faith and learning through their respective callings. Dallas Baptist University celebrated its 100th anniversary in 1998. In fall 2003, DBU reached a record enrollment of 4,538 students from forty states and forty-five countries.

The adult degree-completion program received national recognition by the Commission for the Nation of Lifelong Learners, which recognized DBU's College of Adult Education as one of the most successful adult learning programs in the country. The Master of Business Administration is one of the few programs available online that is both regionally and nationally accreditated.

DBU is accredited by the Commission on Colleges of the Southern Association of Colleges and Schools, 1866 Southern Lane, Decatur, Georgia 30033-4097 (telephone: 404-679-4501) to award associate, bachelor's, and master's degrees. The teacher education programs are accredited by the Texas Education Agency (TEA). The College of Business' Bachelor of Business Administration (B.B.A.) and Master of Business Administration (M.B.A.) degrees are accredited by the Association of Collegiate Business Schools and Programs (ACBSP).

DISTANCE LEARNING PROGRAM

The DBU Online Education Program features asynchronous learning, and students receive the same student services support that local students receive on the main campus. No on-campus component is required for any online course offered through DBU Online. In spring 2004, 911 students were served through DBU's Online Education Program. As DBU seeks to provide students with Christ-centered, high-quality higher education, DBU Online extends the University's reach past traditional geographical boundaries.

DELIVERY MEDIA

Utilizing the Blackboard.com delivery system, DBU Online courses are professor-led and offer a variety of ways, including e-mail, chat rooms, and threaded discussion, for students and the professor to interact. In addition, professors may post online office hours and include telephone and fax information. To participate in online courses, students must have access to appropriate computer hardware and software and to the Internet through an Internet Service Provider (ISP). Information about technical requirements can be accessed at http://www.dbu.edu/online/PC_requirement.asp.

PROGRAMS OF STUDY

The Bachelor of Arts (B.A.) degree, with a major in Biblical studies, is offered through the Mary C. Crowley College of Christian Faith and is designed to prepare students for further seminary or university studies or for a lifetime of study and service without further formal training.

The Bachelor of Arts and Sciences (B.A.S.) degree, with majors in Christian ministries and psychology, and the Bachelor of Business Studies (B.B.S.) degree, with majors in business administration, management, and management information systems, are offered through the College of Adult Education. Adult students may earn up to 30 college credit hours through prior learning assessment, based on the recommendations of academic portfolio evaluators.

The Bachelor of Business Administration (B.B.A.) degree, with majors in management and management information systems, is offered through the College of Business and provides students with an exceptional educational experience to equip them for the global business environment.

The Master of Business Administration (M.B.A.) degree, with concentrations in eBusiness, finance, management, and management information systems, consists of a 24-credit-hour core plus 12 credit hours in a concentration. Applicants without undergraduate degrees in business may need 3–18 additional credit hours of foundational courses. The M.B.A. is offered through the College of Business.

The Master of Arts in Organizational Management (M.A.O.M.) degree, also offered through the College of Business, includes concentrations in general management and human resources management and is a 36-credit-hour program designed to equip students with the communication, leadership, and management skills necessary in today's business organizations. Special attention is given to adapting to organizational change and becoming a change agent.

The exclusively online, 12-hour eBusiness Certificate, offered through the College of Business, consists of four courses exploring such topics as technologies, design and development, entrepreneurship, and marketing at the master level.

The College of Education's Master of Education (M.Ed.) degree, with a concentration in educational organization and administration, assists students in the development of leadership skills for application in both public and private schools. The School of Leadership and Christian Education's M.Ed. degree, with a concentration in higher education, is designed for individuals interested in higher education administration, student personnel work, university development/advancement, or teaching at the college level.

Central to the educational experience at DBU is the integration of Christian faith and values in each of these academic programs.

SPECIAL PROGRAMS

Through the College of Adult Education, adult students with at least four years of full-time work experience may earn up to 30 hours of college credit through prior learning assessment.

STUDENT SERVICES

DBU Online students receive the same high-quality programs, administrative support, library and technology access, bookstore services, academic advising, and University Writing Center access as on-campus students. Orientation for DBU Online is delivered via the Internet and is accessible to registered online students at least two weeks prior to the start of the semester. DBU Online provides a technical support HelpDesk with telephone and online support available 24 hours a day, seven days a week through Collegis, Inc.

CREDIT OPTIONS

For the B.A., B.A.S., B.B.A., and B.B.S. degrees, students may transfer up to 66 semester hours from accredited two-year colleges and an unlimited number of semester hours from accredited four-year institutions. Credit given on other regionally accredited school's transcripts for ACE, CLEP, AP, or departmental exams is transferable provided that the institution's testing standards are comparable to those of DBU. For the M.B.A., M.A.O.M., and M.Ed. degrees, students may transfer up to 12 credit hours of graduate-level courses from other regionally accredited institutions. Students may supplement their online education program by taking courses in DBU's various semesters and terms.

FACULTY

To assure high-quality learning, the faculty members who teach on-campus courses also teach online courses. Of the 120 faculty members who have taught in DBU Online, 49 are full-time and 69 percent hold a doctorate or another earned advanced degree. Graduate students do not teach at DBU.

ADMISSION

Prior to enrolling in an online program or course at DBU, students must be admitted to the University. Information regarding online admission is available at http://www.dbu.edu/admissions. Students must also successfully complete the Online Skills Assessment, which may be accessed at http://www.dbu.edu/online/assess.asp, and receive approval from the Online Student Coordinator.

To enroll in MATH 1301, Math for Liberal Arts, or ACCT 2301, Principles of Financial Accounting, the student must receive a satisfactory score on the Math Advising Tool (MAT). Information about the MAT is available from the Online Student Coordinator.

TUITION AND FEES

Tuition is the same for in-state and out-of-state students. Tuition for online undergraduate courses, as of June 2004, is $427 per credit hour ($437 per credit hour for graduate courses). Fees per semester range from approximately $35 to $300. Tuition and fees are subject to change. Students should visit http://www.dbu.edu/schedule/default.asp for the most up-to-date tuition and fee information.

FINANCIAL AID

A variety of federal, state, and private funds may be available for students who meet specific requirements. Campuswide, in the last academic year, more than $32 million in aid was disbursed, with 69 percent of the students receiving aid. For institutional scholarships, students must be in good standing and satisfactorily progressing toward their educational goals. Other eligibility requirements may exist for specific awards. For federal or state financial assistance, students must meet guidelines established by the U.S. Department of Education and the State of Texas. Students interested in financial assistance should contact the Financial Aid Office at 214-333-5363 or visit http://www.dbu.edu/financialaid/.

APPLYING

Students may apply online at www.dbu.edu/admissions/html, request an undergraduate admission packet by telephoning 214-333-5360 or 800-460-1DBU (toll-free), or request a graduate admission packet by telephoning 214-333-5242 or 800-460-1DBU (toll-free).

All undergraduate applicants must submit a fully completed admissions application form, a nonrefundable $25 application fee, and a 250-word essay relating why the applicant would like to attend DBU.

Traditional freshman applicants must also submit an official high school transcript, bearing the official seal of the school and showing final class rank and official scores of either the ACT or SAT I. Official TOEFL scores are required for applicants who did not graduate from an American high school.

Transfer and adult student applicants must also submit official transcripts of all previous college and high school work or official GED scores and the results of either the ACT or SAT I examination (for applicants with less than 30 hours of acceptable credit only; ACT or SAT I scores are not required of applicants who will be 25 years of age or older on the first day of classes).

Graduate applicants must submit a formal Application for Admission to pursue a specified graduate degree program; a nonrefundable $25 application fee; official transcripts for each institution attended as an undergraduate, postgraduate, or graduate student; an official GRE/GMAT score report, if applicable; and a completed Statement of Purpose Form. M.B.A. and M.A.O.M. applicants must also submit two letters of recommendation and a current resume.

CONTACT

Amy Walker, Online Student Coordinator
Online Education Program
Dallas Baptist University
3000 Mountain Creek Parkway
Dallas, Texas 75211-9299
Telephone: 214-333-6893
800-460-8188
E-mail: online@dbu.edu
Web site: http://online.dbu.edu/

Dallas County Community Colleges

DALLAS

Dallas TeleCollege

Dallas, Texas

Dallas County Community College District (DCCCD) is celebrating more than thirty years of distance education delivery. More than 20,000 students enroll yearly in distance courses that lead to an associate degree or certificate. Many students take core courses that transfer to other institutions. Distance learning is a collaborative effort of all seven colleges in the district, each accredited by the Commission on Colleges of the Southern Association of Colleges and Schools. The Dallas TeleCollege draws its strength from the full-time faculty members of these colleges and from years of experience in the development and implementation of distance learning courses.

Over the years, these programs have evolved to embrace emerging technologies and have expanded to meet a growing student population. The principal mission of the Dallas TeleCollege is to make distance learning options convenient and accessible. The Dallas County Community College District understands that in a rapidly changing world community, learning can take place "anyplace, anytime".

DISTANCE LEARNING PROGRAM

The Dallas TeleCollege, the online campus of the Dallas County Community Colleges, provides greater access to education opportunities for students throughout Dallas, Texas; the U.S.; and the world through the delivery of flexible affordable courses. Courses are offered through a variety of technologies and lead to the Associate of Arts (A.A.) and the Associate of Science (A.S.) degrees. The Dallas TeleCollege also provides opportunities for skill development or enhancement through a variety of noncredit courses.

Dallas TeleCollege offers college-credit programs and courses via distance learning by coupling instruction with an array of student services accessible to students online anyplace, anytime. In addition to individual course transferability, the complete Associate of Arts and Associate of Science degrees as well as various certificate programs are available at a distance through the virtual campus.

DELIVERY MEDIA

Distance learning courses are offered in a number of formats. Each format may utilize a variety of learning technologies, such as video and CD-ROM, that are designed to enhance the learning experience. Course formats are offered either completely at a distance or require on-campus visits.

Completely-at-a-distance online courses are delivered using only computers and computer peripherals. Students are required to have reliable Internet access and the latest version of Internet browser software. The online classroom delivers instruction and facilitates interactions between faculty members and students.

The Telecourse Plus incorporates the use of video and the online classroom. The course includes a preproduced video series with print materials. Students are required to have access to local cable for viewing or a VHS format videocassette player. Students are also required to have reliable Internet access and the latest version of Internet browser software. The online classroom is used to deliver instruction, facilitate interactions between faculty members and students, and more.

The Telecourse allows the student to work and learn independently, with campus-based requirements, including orientations, testing, and review sessions. The course includes a preproduced video series with print materials. Class interaction is offered through telephone, fax, and mail. Students are required to have access to local cable for viewing or a VHS-format videocassette player.

Campus-based distance learning courses may include any of the above formats along with on-campus requirements. This means that students must visit the campus for a portion of their class. Most student services are also delivered on campus and not at a distance.

Individualized Distance Learning Course (IDL) courses are individual study courses that use print materials and required activities related to course topics. This self-paced course requires a faculty-to-student agreement contract for specific work assignments and/or projects. Additional requirements include a study-faculty orientation, written assignments, and tests.

Course formats may include one or more of the following technologies:

The Internet: Courses utilizing the Internet require students have Internet access and the latest version of a browser (Netscape or Internet Explorer).

Video Series: Several course formats utilize preproduced video series that can be viewed by local cable TV through many local cable channels at scheduled times; through videotapes leased from the online bookstore and viewed on a video cassette player or on campus in the media center; through video streaming, which allows students to view video lesson programs from their home or office computer and which requires broadband connectivity such as DSL, cable modems, or wireless connections and payment of a fee; and CD-ROM/DVD.

The CD-ROM format is a student-centered instructional design using fully integrated multimedia course delivery along with supported print materials. This format brings video programs, interactive computer-based activities, and Internet resources to the student's desktop. Materials include a preproduced video series along with print materials.

PROGRAMS OF STUDY

The Associate of Arts and the Associate of Science degrees require the completion of 61 credit hours, including 48 core credit hours and 13 credit hours of electives. The A.A. and A.S. degrees may be earned in their entirety through Dallas TeleCollege. Students may also complete the following certificate programs through distance education: office technology/administrative assistant, veterinary technician, and child development.

Approximately 200 different courses are available in a variety of subjects, including business, communications, computer programming, electronics, health, humanities and arts, literature, mathematics, office technology and software, science, and social sciences.

SPECIAL PROGRAMS

Dallas TeleCollege partners in the open-enrollment Navy College PACE program that reaches ships, submarines, and remote sites of the U.S. Navy. More than 10,000 military personnel have enrolled in courses through Dallas since 1992. Dallas is also a participant in the Southern Regional Electronic Campus (SREC) and the Virtual College of Texas (VCT), which offers distance courses to students in the United States and abroad. In addition, DCCCD is an articulation partner with many four-year institutions to provide students with transferable credit hours to other colleges and institutions. Dallas County Community Colleges also deliver credit and non-credit courses to employees of major corporations based in Texas and other states.

STUDENT SERVICES

Distance learners have access to online advising and admissions and enrollment processes as well as library services, including an online search feature, writing labs, and study skills assistance. These services are available on the Web site.

CREDIT OPTIONS

DCCCD transfers many passing-grade credits from other colleges accredited through one of the U.S. regional associations. The DCCCD registrar completes course evaluations as needed for degree planning. Credits earned through credit-by-examination, military experience, and the U.S. Armed Forces Institute are reviewed by the registrar. Credit may be granted if applicable. The DCCCD requires that at least 25 percent of the credit hours required for graduation be taken by instruction rather than these methods.

FACULTY

Courses in the Distance Learning Program are taught by full-time and adjunct faculty members who also teach on-campus classes. Each of the more than 200 faculty members holds credentials approved by the Colleges' accrediting agency. To ensure high-quality instruction, the number of students assigned to a faculty member in a distance learning course is limited.

ADMISSION

Students must have a high school diploma or its equivalent, be at least 18 years of age, or receive special approval for admission as outlined in the DCCCD catalog. Texas students must also fulfill testing requirements as mandated by state law. International students must take the TOEFL.

TUITION AND FEES

Tuition and fees vary with the student's residence and the number of credit hours. This may range from approximately $30 per credit hour for a local Dallas resident to $200 per credit hour for an out-of-state student. Other expenses may include tape leasing, study guides, textbooks, and course-related software.

FINANCIAL AID

Students accepted for enrollment may be considered for several forms of institutional and federal financial aid. Veterans and financial aid recipients should consult an adviser before enrolling in distance learning courses.

APPLYING

Applicants should submit an official application along with appropriate documentation, such as an official high school transcript, GED scores, or official transcripts from previous colleges, and should complete any required assessment procedures.

CONTACT

Dallas TeleCollege
9596 Walnut Street
Dallas, Texas 75243
Telephone: 972-669-6414
888-468-4268 (toll-free)
Fax: 972-669-6409
E-mail: dtcweba@dcccd.edu
dtcadvisor@dcccd.edu (academic advising)
military_programs@dcccd.edu (military programs)
Web site:
http://www.telecollege.dcccd.edu

Daniel Webster College

Graduate, Continuing, and Distance Education

Nashua, New Hampshire

Daniel Webster College (DWC) was founded in 1965. The classic New England campus rests on approximately 54 wooded acres in Nashua, one of New Hampshire's largest cities. With 1,100 students, of whom typically 50 percent are in-residence, day school undergraduates and 50 percent are adults, the College focuses on providing all students with an educational experience that is rich in theory and practice. Long distinguished as one of the nation's leaders in aviation education, the College has also earned recognition for its leadership in computer science, business, and management programs.

Daniel Webster College educates men and women for professional entry, advancement, and advanced studies in the fields of aviation, computer science, management, engineering, and social sciences. Students prepare through residential, continuing, and distance education programs that emphasize the integration of theory and practice through interactive teaching and learning in professional and liberal studies.

DISTANCE LEARNING PROGRAM

The Daniel Webster College distance education program has been designed specifically to support the needs of adults who cannot attend a site-based program but still want a high-quality education from a respected institution. Courses are typically offered in eight-week terms and are transferable to other accredited institutions, or they can lead to certificates, associate, or bachelor's degrees in information systems, social science, business management, accounting, marketing, and much more.

DELIVERY MEDIA

All distance education courses are delivered using Blackboard Learning System software. Students interact with faculty members and other students in this online version of a site-based classroom.

PROGRAMS OF STUDY

Daniel Webster College offers certificates and Associate of Science (A..S.) and Bachelor of Science (B.S.) degrees. The M.B.A. is not currently offered online. Certificates may be earned in .NET, PC networking, MS Windows programming, client-server application development, UNIX systems administration, C/UNIX programming, Webmaster technology, Web design, marketing, and accounting. The A.S. may be earned in business management or general studies. Students may also earn a B.S. in information systems, social science, or business management with concentrations in marketing, management, or information technology.

Certificate programs vary in length, but all A.S. degrees require the successful completion of 60 credit hours, and B.S. degrees require the successful completion of 120 credit hours. DWC courses are based on a credit-hour system, with a typical course awarding 3 credit hours.

The B.S. in business management prepares students for a successful career in management. Students achieve competence in the three essential functions of a business (finance, marketing, and operations) and learn to execute the four functions of a manager (planning, organizing, leading, and controlling). As part of this process, students develop the leadership and management skills necessary to be able to get results when working with and through others.

The B.S. in management, information systems, and technology provides intensive knowledge of the development and application of communication technology, databases, computer networks and their management, computer programming, systems thinking and analysis, and the management of various computer-based applications. This intensive knowledge is appropriate to positions where information technology (IT) is widely used as a management tool as well as where IT is integral to a firm's operations.

The A.S. in business management is designed to meet the needs of those students who wish to seek immediate employment after graduation from high school as well as those who wish to continue on to a bachelor's degree program. The two-year associate degree in general studies offers students a flexible program of study that allows them to take basic courses in mathematics, English, social science, humanities, and computer studies—the traditional general education foundation required in most four-year colleges and universities.

STUDENT SERVICES

DWC is dedicated to providing distance education (DE) students with a full suite of facilities and support programs and services to ensure a fruitful educational experience. DE students have online access to student services, academic advising, instructional support, technical support, library services, online payment, online registration, and textbook ordering.

DWC has also implemented the Student Online Access to Records (SOAR) program. Using this program, students have direct access to all courses they have taken, the grade earned in each course, their semester and cumulative GPA, current class schedule, and their student account, including all charges, credits, and pending or verified financial aid.

CREDIT OPTIONS

Academic advisers complete a free transfer credit evaluation for all incoming students to ensure maximum college credit as it applies to their chosen academic major. Credit may be awarded in many ways. These include transfer credits and certificates from other regionally accredited institutions, College Level Examination Program (CLEP) tests, DANTES, Credit by Examination (CBE), portfolio/credit for prior learning, military experience (SMART transcript/DD214), high school advanced placement credits, and pilot's license (private or commercial). Daniel Webster College is a Serviceman's Opportunity College (SOC, SOC-AD, SOC-NAV) and accepts American Council on Education (ACE) recommended credits.

FACULTY

DWC has 35 full-time faculty members and, in addition, uses adjunct faculty members as necessary. Adjunct faculty members have proven competence in their discipline and have a minimum of a master's degree; many have a Ph.D., Ed.D., D.B.A., or other doctoral degree or advanced education beyond the master's level.

ADMISSION

Daniel Webster College supports an open and rolling admissions approach. Students are accepted throughout the year.

TUITION AND FEES

The tuition rate for all distance education courses is $233 per credit hour ($699 for a typical 3-credit hour course). As a no-fee college, DWC does not charge students for transfer credit evaluations, and there are no registration or matriculation fees. Students pay for tuition and books only.

FINANCIAL AID

All forms of government tuition assistance, loans, grants, scholarships, GI Bill, VA benefits, and corporate reimbursement are accepted. If needed, a federal financial aid application form (FAFSA) is available online at http://www.fafsa.ed.gov, or students may contact the college financial aid office by phone at 603-577-6590 or via e-mail at finaid@dwc.edu.

APPLYING

Students may apply online. There is no application fee. Students may take up to 12 credit hours prior to acceptance. Students are accepted upon completion of the application process, including submission of proof of high school graduation (or equivalency).

CONTACT

Jan Donahue, Academic Advisor for Distance Education
Daniel Webster College
20 University Drive
Nashua, New Hampshire 03063
Telephone: 800-392-9011 (toll-free)
Fax: 603-577-6503
E-mail: donahue@dwc.edu
Web site: http://www.dwc.edu/gcde

Davenport University

Davenport University Online

Grand Rapids, Michigan

Davenport University has offered specialized, career-focused business education for more than 135 years. In addition, since early 1999, Davenport University has been accredited to offer master's, bachelor's, and associate degrees completely online—with no on-campus residency requirement. However, if students wish to use on-campus services or take a combination of online and on-campus courses, Davenport has more than twenty locations throughout Michigan and northern Indiana. Accredited by the Higher Learning Commission and a member of the North Central Association of Colleges and Schools (NCA), Davenport's online courses are developed by its own faculty members, all of whom are certified to instruct in the online environment. This ensures that the online degree programs and courses are of consistently high quality and that Davenport University can accomplish its mission of preparing individuals and organizations to excel in the knowledge-driven environment of the twenty-first century.

DISTANCE LEARNING PROGRAM

Davenport Online offers the convenience of classroom accessibility 24 hours a day, seven days a week from virtually anywhere in the world. Online courses are truly interactive. Through group assignments, online research projects, and case study analyses, students collaborate with peers and immediately apply textbook theory to real business situations. The computer is simply a tool through which to communicate. Courses begin and end on specific dates, and class work has assigned deadlines.

DELIVERY MEDIA

All online courses are delivered through the Internet using the Blackboard learning platform. It is recommended that the student's computer meet certain minimum specifications. For the most current technology requirements, students may visit http://www.davenport.edu/oasis and then choose *Technology* and *Technology Requirements*.

PROGRAMS OF STUDY

Complete online degree programs include an M.B.A. in strategic management, entrepreneurial management, accounting, human resources management, and health-care management; postbaccalaureate certificates in forensic accounting and computer security; bachelor's degrees in accounting, applied business, business professional studies, entrepreneurship, marketing, management, e-business, computer security, and nursing completion; and associate degrees in accounting, entrepreneurship, management, marketing, administrative office technology, systems application development, computer security, and Web development. Davenport Online also offers diploma programs in accounting, management, desktop applications, medical billing, medical coding and Web applications, and more.

FACULTY

All faculty members who teach for Davenport Online have at least a master's degree in the area of study and practical work experience. Their combined knowledge of theory and practice enhances the learning environment. All faculty members must complete an instructional design training program to become certified as an online instructor.

ADMISSION

Online course work relies heavily on written communication and problem-solving skills. Students are eligible to enroll in Davenport Online courses where assessment indicates their readiness for the first college-level writing courses (nondevelopmental) and the first college-level math course (nondevelopmental) required for their degree. In addition, students who do not have credit for English Composition must enroll in that course during their first online session. This may be done concurrently with another course.

TUITION AND FEES

Davenport University Online undergraduate tuition is $1047 per course; tuition for the master's program is $1125 per course. A $35 technology fee is assessed each semester.

FINANCIAL AID

Financial aid, such as grants, loans, and scholarships, is available to all qualified students. Students must first fill out a Free Application for Federal Student Aid (FAFSA) to begin the process. Many students receive tuition assistance through their employer's tuition reimbursement plan.

APPLYING

Students must apply and be admitted to Davenport University. Students can complete an online application at the school's Web site. There is a $25 application fee for admission into the undergraduate school and a $50 application fee for admission into the M.B.A. program. Once students have been admitted, they receive detailed information about how to schedule and activate their courses and how to purchase their books online through MBS Direct.

CONTACT

Jeff Wiggerman
Online Recruiter
Davenport University Online
415 East Fulton Street
Grand Rapids, Michigan 49503
Telephone: 800-203-5323 (toll-free)
Fax: 800-811-2658 (toll-free)
E-mail: DUOnline@davenport.edu
Web site: http://www.davenport.edu

DePaul University

School for New Learning
Center for Distance Education

Chicago, Illinois

Founded more than a century ago, DePaul University is one of the largest universities in the United States and the fastest growing of its size and type, serving more than 20,000 students. DePaul attracts students from all fifty U.S. states and sixty-five other countries, ensuring multiple perspectives.

The School for New Learning (SNL) was established thirty years ago as one of the eight schools and colleges of DePaul. SNL is a national leader in the design and delivery of competency-based learning for adults. In 1999, SNL was ranked by CAEL (the Council for Adult and Experiential Learning) as one of the six best institutions for serving adult learners in higher education. Choosing from among colleges and universities all across North America, CAEL called SNL a "cutting edge pioneer" and "truly innovative in the understanding of the need to improve education." DePaul University and the School for New Learning are fully accredited, which means that the degree earned is honored throughout the world.

DISTANCE LEARNING PROGRAM

SNL's Distance Education Program allows adult students, 24 years or older, to earn a Bachelor of Arts degree from DePaul University without ever visiting a campus. SNL provides excellent learning opportunities and individualized service to adult students.

The Bachelor of Arts degree consists of fifty requirements allocated across three areas: focus area, lifelong learning skills, and liberal arts. Students meet the requirements through DePaul courses, transfer courses, proficiency examinations, demonstration of prior learning, and independent study. Unique to SNL is its emphasis on experience. The fifty degree requirements are competency-based, and all offerings honor adult experience and provide opportunities to extend learning through additional experience.

DELIVERY MEDIA

The Distance Education Program uses various platforms, such as the World Wide Web, CD-ROMs, and e-mail, for course work and for connecting students, faculty members, advisers, professional experts, and classmates.

PROGRAMS OF STUDY

Students receive a Bachelor of Arts degree from DePaul University. Unique to this program is that students individualize their study by designing a focus area relevant to their life and work goals. Approximately 60 percent of current SNL students graduate with a focus related to business, and other students study any area they choose.

In order to ensure both academic quality and focus area expertise, students work in a personalized committee format during their academic program. A committee consists of the student, faculty mentor, and a professional adviser. The faculty mentor is a DePaul faculty member who works directly with the student throughout his or her program. The professional adviser is an expert in the field in which the student would like to focus. The student selects the professional adviser, with the help of the faculty mentor, to act as a guide to the student, particularly in the focus area.

STUDENT SERVICES

DePaul University offers students the following resources and services: admission, registration, identification cards, access to the library, career counseling, writing and math assistance, financial aid, academic advising, the bookstore, and more.

Students have continuing academic and administrative support throughout their academic programs. Advisers and counselors are available to serve students efficiently and effectively.

CREDIT OPTIONS

There is no maximum to the number of transfer credits accepted in the Distance Education Program, although certain courses will not transfer. Courses with a grade of C- or better from accredited institutions are accepted for credit. Students may also transfer college-level learning from life and work experience into the program.

FACULTY

The faculty members within the SNL community are dedicated to individualized, student-centered education in a collaborative environment. All have graduate degrees and experience in the fields in which they teach. The faculty members teach about what they know best.

ADMISSION

Students must be 24 years or older, be proficient in use of the English language, and have completed secondary education.

Students' computers must meet the following technical requirements in order for them to participate: Windows 98 or higher, at least 32 MB of RAM, 56K baud modem, sound card, speakers, CD-ROM drive, monitor 800 x 600, and Internet access. Macintosh systems should meet equivalent requirements.

TUITION AND FEES

Tuition and fees for the 2003–04 academic year were $348 per credit hour. The cost of textbooks varies from class to class.

FINANCIAL AID

Financial aid opportunities are available to DePaul's SNL students. For more information, students should visit DePaul's financial aid Web site at www.depaul.edu/~saccount/.

APPLYING

Applications for admission are accepted year-round. Students should visit SNL's Web site, listed below, to request that an interactive CD containing information about the program and an application for admission be sent to them (this request can also be made by e-mail or telephone).

CONTACT

School for New Learning
Center for Distance Education
DePaul University
25 East Jackson Boulevard
Chicago, Illinois 60604
Telephone: 312-362-8821
866-SNL-FORU (toll-free)
Fax: 312-362-5053
E-mail: support@snlonline.net
Web site: http://www.snlonline.net

DePaul University

School of Computer Science, Telecommunications, and Information Systems

Chicago, Illinois

Founded more than a century ago, DePaul University is one of the largest universities in the United States and the fastest growing of its size and type, serving more than 20,000 students. DePaul attracts students from all fifty states and sixty-five other countries, ensuring multiple perspectives.

The mission of the School of Computer Science, Telecommunications, and Information Systems (CTI) is to instill in its students an enthusiasm for their discipline, the knowledge necessary for its practice, an appreciation for the liberal arts, the values of a DePaul education, and a passion for lifelong learning.

DISTANCE LEARNING PROGRAM

The School of Computer Science, Telecommunications and Information Systems—commonly known as DePaul CTI—takes an innovative approach to distance learning by offering distance learning courses in conjunction with courses that take place on campus. Using CTI's Course OnLine system, students view lectures online at their own convenience. The ability to convert the vital components of any live class into a course available on the Web allows CTI to offer nearly ninety online courses each quarter and nine entire degree programs online. Requirements are the same for distance learning and on-campus courses and degrees, so students are able to take whatever combination of online and on-campus courses that fits their needs.

DELIVERY MEDIA

DePaul CTI's Course Online (COL) system allows registered students to view classroom lectures online. The COL system captures all of the important events in a class session: what the instructor says, points to, writes on the board, or displays on the projector. The parts are synchronized after class and posted to the Web for the remainder of the quarter. Distance learning students follow the assignment and exam schedule for the on-campus section of the course, but have the flexibility of viewing the weekly lectures at a time that works best for them.

Course OnLine lectures are integrated into CTI's course management system, which contains other important information like assignments, grades, course documents, announcements, instructor information, and links to external Web sites. In addition, courses take advantage of asynchronous communication tools, such as threaded discussion groups and e-mail, and the live interaction of online chat sessions. Distance learning students interact with other distance learning students as well as on-campus students.

PROGRAMS OF STUDY

CTI graduate programs generally follow a three-phase sequence, with each phase preparing the student for the subsequent phase. The prerequisite phase is intended to ensure that all students enter graduate courses with an equivalent background. In the core knowledge phase, students follow a sequence of courses to acquire an understanding of the technological and theoretical foundations for the particular degree. In the advanced phase of the program, students study advanced topics within their chosen degree.

CTI offers the following nine degrees through distance learning: the M.A. in information technology; the M.S. in computer, information, and network security; the M.S. in computer science; the M.S. in distributed systems; the M.S. in e-commerce technology; the M.S. in information systems; the M.S. in instructional technology systems; the M.S. in software engineering; and the M.S. in telecommunication systems.

More information about each degree program is available on CTI's Web site at http://www.dlweb.cti.depaul.edu.

STUDENT SERVICES

DePaul University works hard to make services accessible to all of its students. Distance learning students can remotely access a number of vital University services, including online course registration, account payment, course grades and history, the help desk, degree planning, academic advising, course evaluations, faculty evaluation history, online exam scheduling, the library, career services, and the Graduate Student Association.

CREDIT OPTIONS

Generally, students who have experience with a subject that is required in the prerequisite phase may be able to avoid taking some of these courses. Students review their experience and education with a faculty adviser and may be given a course waiver or be able to take an equivalency exam.

FACULTY

All distance learning courses are taught by the same distinguished CTI professors who teach on-campus courses. The School currently has 82 full-time and 140 part-time faculty members.

ADMISSION

Applicants must possess a bachelor's degree from a regionally accredited institution or be in the final stage of completing the undergraduate degree. The primary criterion in determining eligibility is previous academic achievement. A prospective graduate student is expected to present a superior overall academic record, or at least a superior record in the last two years of undergraduate work. Other factors, such as work experience and career progression, are also considered. There are no additional requirements for admission of distance learning students, and the intention to complete the program via distance learning is not considered in the admissions decision.

TUITION AND FEES

The current costs are $348 per quarter hour or $1392 per 4-credit course for courses numbered 399 and below. Courses numbered 400 and above are $535 per quarter hour or $2140 per 4-credit course. Costs are subject to change. All graduate CTI students are subject to the CTI graduate tuition rate for all graduate level courses regardless of the courses taken. The average course is 4 credit hours. Additional fees may apply. There are no special costs for distance learning. However, distance learning students are responsible for any fees associated with taking exams at another college or university.

FINANCIAL AID

Although CTI does not offer financial aid specifically for distance learning students, all graduate students may apply for financial aid through DePaul's Financial Aid Office Web site or in person at one of two full-service offices in Chicago.

APPLYING

A $25 nonrefundable application fee is required and can be paid online by credit card after the application process. For more information and an online application, students should visit the Web site listed below.

CONTACT

Marueen Garvey, Director of Admissions
School of CTI
DePaul University
243 South Wabash Avenue
Chicago, Illinois 60604
Telephone: 312-362-8714
Fax: 312-362-6166
E-mail: distancelearning@cti.depaul.edu
Web site: http://www.cti.depaul.edu.admissions

DeVry University

Online Center

Oakbrook Terrace, Illinois

The mission of DeVry University is to foster student learning through high-quality, career-oriented undergraduate and graduate programs in technology, business, and management. The University delivers its programs at campuses, centers, and online to meet the needs of a diverse and a geographically dispersed student population.

More than 52,000 students in eighteen states and two Canadian provinces are enrolled at DeVry University's twenty-six undergraduate campuses and thirty-seven adult learning centers, including DeVry's Online Education Center. DeVry University's Keller Graduate School of Management is one of the largest part-time graduate schools in the U.S. Approximately 8,000 students are enrolled annually in the School's practitioner-oriented master's degree programs.

DeVry University is accredited by the Higher Learning Commission and a member of the North Central Association of Colleges and Schools, 30 North LaSalle Street, Chicago, Illinois 60602 (312-263-0456).

DISTANCE LEARNING PROGRAM

Distance learning, delivered through DeVry University's Online Center, integrates today's high-tech capabilities with the University's proven educational methodologies. The result is solid education enhanced by interactive information that enables students to send and receive feedback from instructors as well as to participate in various group and team activities with fellow online students. The Online Center serves approximately 1,600 participants per term.

DELIVERY MEDIA

Typical distance learning technologies include the online graduate site (http://www.online.keller.edu) and undergraduate site (http://www.devry.edu), which are accessible 24 hours a day and offer course syllabi and assignments, a virtual library, and other Web-based resources; text and course materials, available through the online bookstore; CD-ROM companion disks; and study notes on instructor lectures.

PROGRAMS OF STUDY

DeVry University Online currently offers undergraduate degree programs in business administration, computer information systems, information technology, and technical management and master's degree programs in business administration, accounting and financial management, human resource management, information systems management, public administration, project management, and telecommunications management. Graduate certificates are also available for students who wish to develop their expertise in these program areas without completing a degree or who wish to specialize in one of these areas within their graduate degree program.

Undergraduate students must achieve a cumulative grade point average of at least 2.0 (on a 4.0 scale) and satisfactorily complete all curriculum requirements to graduate. Graduate students must achieve a cumulative grade point average of at least 2.7, as well as fulfill the graduation requirements for their specific programs.

STUDENT SERVICES

In addition to offering high-quality education via distance learning, DeVry University is committed to providing online students with electronic access to the same full range of support services available to students attending courses on site. Through the online site, students can access admission and registration information, career services information, academic advising, and financial aid information. DeVry University also maintains an online library, which provides access to resources such as full-text periodical databases and online short courses for self-instruction. These resources are available 24 hours a day, seven days a week, to students and faculty and staff members.

FACULTY

To ensure uniformity of content and rigor in course work delivered via the Online Center, the University taps the expertise of seasoned faculty members who have undergone specialized training designed to prepare and present courses online and then supplement course delivery with a variety of online instructional activities, all of which focus on course objectives.

ADMISSION

DeVry University's admission process is streamlined, so students learn quickly whether they have been accepted. Applicants must complete a personal interview with an admissions representative and complete a written application. Applicants should visit the University's Web sites for further details.

For admission to undergraduate programs, specific requirements must be met regarding age, prior education, demonstrated proficiency in the basic and prerequisite skills needed for college-level work in the chosen field of study, and computer literacy. Each undergraduate applicant pays a $50 application fee.

For regular graduate admission, applicants must hold a baccalaureate degree from a U.S. institution accredited by, or in candidacy status with, a regional accrediting agency recognized by the U.S. Department of Education (international applicants must hold a degree equivalent to a U.S. baccalaureate degree); ensure that the registrar receives an official transcript; and demonstrate quantitative and verbal skills proficiency. Applicants who meet baccalaureate degree requirements and whose undergraduate cumulative grade point average is 2.7 or higher are eligible for admission.

TUITION AND FEES

For undergraduate students, online tuition is $435 per credit hour ($395 per credit hour for information technology program students). For graduate students, online tuition per course is $1795. After acceptance into the graduate school, new students pay a $100 deposit, which is credited toward the first term's tuition. Tuition is payable in full at registration. An installment option is also available (with a small handling fee). Books and materials average $175 per course.

FINANCIAL AID

Federal Stafford Student Loan money is available to graduate students through the Federal Family Education Loan Program (FFELP). Undergraduate students who qualify can take advantage of the five major federal financial aid programs in which DeVry is eligible to participate.

CONTACT

DeVry University
One Tower Lane
Oakbrook Terrace, Illinois 60181
Telephone: 800-839-9009
Web sites: http://www.online.keller.edu
http://www.online.devry.edu

DUKE THE FUQUA SCHOOL OF BUSINESS

Duke University

The Fuqua School of Business

Durham, North Carolina

Duke University is one of the world's preeminent research and teaching universities. Duke consistently ranks among the top schools in the annual survey of "America's Best Colleges" by U.S. News & World Report.

Duke University's Fuqua School of Business is an established world leader among M.B.A. and executive education programs. Founded in 1969 as the Duke Graduate School of Business Administration, the School was renamed in 1980 in honor of entrepreneur and philanthropist J. B. Fuqua.

Fuqua is widely recognized as a worldwide leader in the development of innovative and unique Executive M.B.A. degree programs and nondegree executive education. The School was a pioneer of the "place and space" model of delivering a top M.B.A. in distance learning.

Fuqua's Executive M.B.A. programs were recently ranked fourth in the world by Business Week, *third worldwide by the* Financial Times, *and fourth in the U.S. by* U.S. News & World Report.

DISTANCE LEARNING PROGRAM

Cross Continent: In 2000, the Fuqua School of Business launched its newest M.B.A. format, the Duke M.B.A.–Cross Continent. This twenty-month program targets high-potential professionals who average six years of work experience. Flexibility is maximized through a dynamic format that blends the best aspects of traditional classroom teaching in North Carolina, Europe, and Asia with Internet-enabled distance learning. Students continue their careers while studying from anywhere in the world.

Global Executive: The Duke M.B.A. Global Executive program is geared toward corporate executives with an average of fourteen years' business experience. This pioneering, nineteen-month program combines unique residential sessions in Asia, South America, Europe, and the United States with Internet-enabled distance learning, allowing students to live and work anywhere in the world while participating in the program.

DELIVERY MEDIA

Cross Continent: Beginning in late July, students complete eleven core courses, four electives courses, and one integrative capstone course over a twenty-month period. Students attend nine weeks of residential sessions (8 one-week sessions plus one week of orientation). A typical term includes one week of preclass reading, one week of residential classes, a one-week break, six weeks of Internet-enabled distance learning, and another one-week break.

Of the eight residential sessions, six residencies take place on Duke's main campus in Durham, North Carolina; one is in Europe; and another is in Asia.

Global Executive: The program consists of fifteen courses grouped into five terms over a nineteen-month period beginning each May. Each term includes a three-week reading period, a two-week residential classroom session, a one-week break, ten to twelve weeks of Internet-enabled course work, and a one-week break. As the class travels around the globe, students take the curriculum together in the same sequence. The residential classroom sessions of terms 1 and 5 take place on the Duke campus, while the other three sessions take place in Europe, Asia, and South America.

PROGRAMS OF STUDY

Cross Continent: In the Duke M.B.A.–Cross Continent program, all students take the same courses together in the same sequence, with a heavy emphasis on teamwork. Four of the sixteen courses offered are electives. The courses are designed to build from fundamental business knowledge to functional and strategy courses.

Global Executive: The Duke M.B.A.–Global Executive curriculum, delivered by Duke's world-class faculty, offers a rigorous general management education, with a focus on global management. Global Executive is also a lockstep program, and courses are designed to build from fundamental business courses to functional and strategy courses.

STUDENT SERVICES

Both the Cross Continent and Global Executive programs offer library services online 24 hours a day, seven days a week. The programs offer extensive technical and operational support.

CREDIT OPTIONS

All credits must be earned in either the Cross Continent (48 credit hours) or the Global Executive (45 credit hours) programs. No transferred credits are accepted.

FACULTY

Duke's Fuqua School of Business has one faculty body that teaches across all of its M.B.A. degree programs and executive education program. There are ninety-nine full-time, tenured professors. In 2002, *Business Week* ranked Duke faculty fourth in intellectual capital.

ADMISSION

Cross Continent: Applicants to the Duke M.B.A.–Cross Continent should have three to nine years of professional work experience, a bachelor's degree or the equivalent, company sponsorship, GMAT scores, and TOEFL scores (if applicable). An interview is required.

Global Executive: Applicants to the Duke M.B.A.–Global Executive program should have a minimum of ten years of professional experience, an undergraduate degree from an accredited four-year college or university or the equivalent, strong quantitative skills, proficient written and verbal English skills, company sponsorship, and TOEFL scores (if applicable). An interview is required.

TUITION AND FEES

Cross Continent: The Duke M.B.A.–Cross Continent program tuition for the class that started July 2004 was $82,500. This included all room and board during residential learning sessions and all books and materials. It did not include travel to and from residencies, laptop computers, and Internet service providers.

Global Executive: The Duke M.B.A.–Global Executive program tuition for the class that started May 2004 is $107,000. This included all room and board during residential learning sessions, a laptop computer, and all books and materials. It did not include travel to and from residencies and Internet service providers.

FINANCIAL AID

Financial assistance is available to eligible students in the form of International Student Loans, Federal Stafford Loans, or private loans.

APPLYING

Applicants should request application materials at the address below or by visiting the Web site at http://www.fuqua.duke.edu/executive.

CONTACT

Kelli Kilpatrick, Director of Recruiting and Admissions
Executive M.B.A. Programs
The Fuqua School of Business
1 Towerview Drive
Durham, North Carolina 27708
Telephone: 919-660-7804
Fax: 919-660-2940
E-mail: executive-mba-info@fuqua.duke.edu
Web site: http://www.fuqua.duke.edu/info/pt

Duke University

Nicholas School of the Environment and Earth Sciences
Duke Environmental Leadership Program

Durham, North Carolina

Located in Durham, North Carolina, Duke University is at the heart of a world-renowned center of excellence in medicine, research, high technology, and education, incorporating a sophisticated and unique blend of history, culture, and ethnic diversity. Noted for its magnificent Gothic architecture and its academic excellence, Duke is among the smallest of the nation's leading universities, having a total enrollment of about 12,000. Its spacious campus is bounded on the east by residential sections of Durham and on the west by the Duke Forest.

The Nicholas School of the Environment and Earth Sciences is one of the world's premier graduate and professional schools for the interdisciplinary study of the environment, combining resources from the biological, physical, and social sciences. Located in the heart of the Duke campus, the School functions as an environmental forum, an intellectual hub drawing input from all disciplines at Duke—law, business, medicine, science, and engineering. The goal is to develop critical and creative leaders who will shape tomorrow's Earth. No other university—and no other environmental school—takes such a broad approach to environmental science and policy.

DISTANCE LEARNING PROGRAM

Through the Duke Environmental Leadership (DEL) Program, the Nicholas School of the Environment and Earth Sciences offers a rigorous online and on-campus Master of Environmental Management (M.E.M.) degree program designed specifically for midcareer environmental professionals and business executives. The DEL M.E.M. is an innovative, two-year program made up of courses taught through a combination of written and electronic formats, case studies, and weeklong, intensive place-based sessions. Driven by a broad perspective of interdisciplinary and global themes, strategic approaches to environmental management, communication, and effective leadership, the DEL M.E.M. offers an alternative to traditional full-semester courses, allowing students to update their education while maintaining a commitment to their jobs and families.

DELIVERY MEDIA

The DEL M.E.M. uses advanced interactive technologies to complement the face-to-face sessions on campus. Students use the Blackboard platform as their learning portal to complete individual and group course work and to participate in chat sessions and online meetings. In addition, DEL-sponsored bulletin boards, videoconferences, and conference calls reinforce the curriculum, and Duke e-mail accounts are available through Duke's Office of Information Technology.

Students must arrange network access with a local Internet service provider and are strongly encouraged to have broadband access to the Internet via a cable modem, DSL, or satellite connection.

PROGRAM OF STUDY

The DEL M.E.M. is a two-year, 30-credit program. Requirements include the orientation course at the Duke campus (1 credit); core modules, including ecosystems science and management, economics of environmental management, environmental policy and law, and program management for environmental professionals (12 credits); focused modules developed around more specialized themes (12 credits); an environmental leadership module, which involves prominent leaders from the private, public, and not-for-profit sectors in Washington, D.C. (1 credit); and a master's project directly related to the student's current employment (4 credits).

Through the DEL Program, students can also enroll in 1-credit intensive short courses and 10-credit certificate programs. More information on the short-course program and a list of upcoming courses can be found online.

STUDENT SERVICES

DEL M.E.M. students receive complete student services at a distance and while on campus during place-based sessions. These include registration, academic advising, library resources, and access to the bookstore. Technical support is available online or, for personal support, via e-mail and telephone during business hours, with limited hours during weekends and evenings. The IT orientation during the first place-based session introduces students to the programs and packages preinstalled on the DEL-leased laptop computers. Much of the curriculum during the first session aims to help students gain familiarity with online education and master new learning techniques.

CREDIT OPTIONS

Credit from other institutions may be considered on a case-by-case basis;

however, due to the nature of the DEL M.E.M. program, acceptance of transfer credits is unlikely.

FACULTY

The Nicholas School is known for the strength of its faculty members, as measured by their scholarly achievement, commitment to high-quality education, and impact on the most important environmental and natural resource challenges. More than 50 faculty members hold primary or joint appointments in the School, and a large number have secondary or adjunct status with other units or institutions.

ADMISSION

The admissions committee seeks the following in the selection process: five years of relevant work experience, evidence of leadership potential and an established background in fields directly related to the environment, self-motivation and commitment to learn at a distance, a working knowledge of personal computers for word processing and data analysis, an undergraduate degree from an accredited four-year college or university, written sponsorship from the applicant's employer, and proficiency in English.

TUITION AND FEES

In summer 2004, tuition was $46,600 for four semesters. Tuition includes books, other class materials, and various Duke student fees, including a required technology fee that provides a leased laptop computer and technology support. Tuition does not cover travel to and from the campus, lodging, or meals during the place-based sessions.

FINANCIAL AID

At this time, the DEL Program does not award scholarships or grants to students. However, financial aid is available to U.S. citizens and permanent residents through various student loan programs.

APPLYING

Candidates are requested to apply online by March 1, but applications may be accepted after the final deadline on a space-available basis. A complete application includes an application form; official GRE scores; three letters of recommendation; a sponsor letter written on company letterhead stating that the employer endorses the applicant's participation in the program and grants the necessary time off to attend classes; completed essay questions; official, confidential transcripts from all colleges and universities previously attended, including official English translations if the original is not in English; official TOEFL scores for applicants whose first language is not English; and a nonrefundable application fee of $65 if the application is submitted prior to March 1 or $75 after March 1. Submitting a resume is optional.

CONTACT

Duke Environmental Leadership Program Office
Nicholas School of the Environment and Earth Sciences
Levine Science Research Center, Room A106
Duke University, Box 90328
Durham, North Carolina 27708-0328
Telephone: 919-613-8082
Fax: 919-613-9002
E-mail: del@env.duke.edu
Web site: http://www.nicholas.duke.edu/del

East Carolina University

EAST CAROLINA UNIVERSITY

Division of Continuing Studies

Greenville, North Carolina

Founded in 1907, East Carolina University (ECU) is the third-largest of the sixteen institutions in the University of North Carolina system and offers baccalaureate, master's, specialist, and doctoral degrees in the liberal arts and sciences and professional fields, including medicine. Fully accredited by the Southern Association of Colleges and Schools, the University's goal is to provide students with a rich and distinctive educational experience. ECU's commitment to providing outstanding off-campus educational opportunities is long-standing; the University offered its first distance education course in 1947. The Division of Continuing Studies provides a portal at http://www.options.ecu.edu to the resources of the University as well as assistance that allows adult learners to choose programs that fit their schedules and academic goals. East Carolina University is constantly evaluating and updating its distance learning programs to take advantage of the latest technology and is committed to meeting the evolving needs of the lifelong learner.

DISTANCE LEARNING PROGRAM

East Carolina University's academic community has developed a diverse offering of distance learning programs in direct response to the needs of students. A number of fully online programs are currently available, with additional programs under development. ECU is committed to providing programs designed to meet the professional needs and demanding schedules of busy, working adults. For more information on the latest offerings, students should visit the Web site for the Division of Continuing Studies, which is listed in the Contact section of this description.

DELIVERY MEDIA

East Carolina University's Web-based courses are faculty-member created Web sites that contain course materials and interactive tools. Many use the Blackboard Course Management System. Faculty members may employ a variety of communication tools within their courses, including threaded discussion groups, small-group work, asynchronous Web-based chats, and instant messaging. In addition, faculty members may elect to deliver essential components of their courses via audio and video streaming, by distribution of CDs, or by using desktop videoconferencing technologies.

PROGRAMS OF STUDY

The Master of Arts (M.A.) is offered in English/technical and professional communications and in psychology*. The Master of Arts in Education (M.A.Ed.) is offered in art education, health education, instructional technology, science education, and special education. The Master of Business Administration (M.B.A.) is offered. The Master of Science (M.S.) is offered in criminal justice, instructional technology*, nutrition and dietetics, speech-language pathology*, and vocational education/information technologies. The Master of Science in Industrial Technology (M.S.I.T.) is offered in computer networking management, digital communication technology, distribution and logistics, information security, and manufacturing. The Master of Science in Nursing (M.S.N.) is offered in family nurse practitioner*, nurse midwifery*, and nursing education*. The Master of Library Science (M.L.S.), Master of Music (M.M.) in music education, and Master of Science in Occupational Safety (M.S.O.S.) are also available. The * denotes those programs that require some on-campus attendance.

ECU also offers undergraduate degree completion programs leading to the Bachelor of Science in Business Education (B.S.B.E.) in information technologies, the Bachelor of Science in Industrial Technology (B.S.I.T.), and the Registered Nurse/Bachelor of Science in Nursing (RN/B.S.N.). The Bachelor of Science (B.S.) degree is offered in birth through kindergarten education, communications, health information management, health services management, and information and computer technology.

ECU offers graduate certificate programs in assistive technology, computer network professional studies, professional communication, telelearning, virtual reality in education and training, and Web site development. The assistive technology program requires some on-campus attendance.

ECU offers add-on licensure programs in driver's education and preschool. The preschool program requires some on-campus attendance.

Additional online programs currently under development include the M.A. degree in health education; the M.A.Ed. degree in business education; the Education Specialist (Ed.S.) degree in educational leadership; the B.S. degree in hospitality management; and a certificate in community college teaching.

STUDENT SERVICES

Distance learners at East Carolina University have access to library services, the campus network, e-mail accounts, the bookstore, registration, and academic advising at a distance. Academic advisers are available by phone, e-mail, fax, and in person to assist students with course selection.

CREDIT OPTIONS

Transfer credit is granted on academic course work within degree-specific limits, and no credit is granted on the basis of professional experience. CLEP course credit may also be available.

FACULTY

ECU's approximately 1,300 full-time faculty members, the majority of whom hold terminal degrees, teach both the on-campus and distance-learning courses.

ADMISSION

Before registering for a course, students must first apply and be admitted to ECU. Students may be admitted as degree-seeking or as nondegree/visiting students. Admission for students seeking a degree is based on their previous academic record and standardized test scores. A performance-based admission policy is available for adult students. In addition, graduate students are required to submit letters of recommendation.

TUITION AND FEES

Undergraduate tuition and technology fees are $77 per semester hour for in-state residents, $315 per semester hour for out-of-state students, and $420 per semester hour for in-state nonresidents. Graduate tuition and technology fees are $110 per semester hour for in-state residents, $379 per semester hour for out-of-state students, and $612 per semester hour for in-state nonresidents. Graduate students taking undergraduate courses are charged graduate tuition. Rates are projected and subject to change without prior written notice.

FINANCIAL AID

Distance learning students are eligible to apply for financial aid and are encouraged to contact the Office of Financial Aid at 252-328-6610, faques@mail.ecu.edu, or via the Web at http://www.ecu.edu/financial/ for more information.

APPLYING

Prospective students must submit an application, accompanied by a fee of $50, for admission. Applications can also be obtained online from the Division of Continuing Studies at the Web site listed in the Contact section. While most programs accept students year-round, students are urged to apply early. No on-campus orientation is required for distance learning students.

CONTACT

Carolyn Dunn
Division of Continuing Studies
215 Erwin Building
East Carolina University
Greenville, North Carolina 27858-4353
Telephone: 252-328-2657
800-398-9275 (toll-free)
Fax: 252-328-1600
E-mail: options@mail.ecu.edu
Web site: http://www.options.ecu.edu

Eastern Michigan University

EMU-Online and Independent Learning

Ypsilanti, Michigan

Eastern Michigan University (EMU) is a public, comprehensive, metropolitan university that offers programs in the arts, sciences, and professions. Founded in 1849, the University comprises more than 24,000 students, who are served by 680 full-time faculty members as well as 1,200 staff members—on campus, off campus, and electronically. EMU offers undergraduate, graduate, specialist, doctoral, and certificate programs in its Colleges of Arts and Sciences, Business, Education, Health and Human Services, and Technology.

Eastern Michigan University continues to be the largest producer of educational personnel in the United States, including the largest producer of special education personnel, mathematics teachers, and science teachers, and is among the top ten producers of educational administrators. The University is fully accredited by the North Central Association of Colleges and Schools.

Eastern Michigan University's Continuing Education Office offers programs and courses online, at off-campus locations throughout the state, on weekends, in the evenings during the week, and in accelerated formats.

DISTANCE LEARNING PROGRAM

EMU's Distance Education program offers students three convenient distance learning options. First, EMU's online courses allow students to attend class when it's convenient for their busy schedule—early in the morning, during the weekend, or even at 2 a.m. Whether students live just 5 or 500 miles from EMU's campus, they are able to learn conveniently, using a computer from their home, office, hotel room, military base, or "virtually" any other location in the world. Second, Independent Learning courses allow students to enroll anytime, learn at their own pace, avoid commuting and parking inconveniences, satisfy general education requirements, and submit course work via Internet, fax, or U.S. mail. The third option is Interactive Television courses, which allow students to enroll in a single course that may be offered at multiple locations.

DELIVERY MEDIA

Courses are delivered via World Wide Web, videotapes and DVDs, print, and ITV. Students may meet in person or interact via e-mail, World Wide Web, mail, telephone, fax, or interactive television.

PROGRAMS OF STUDY

EMU-Online offers the Master of Science in engineering management; Master of Science in quality; Bachelor of Science in human nutrition through the Coordinated Program in Dietetics (CPD); Master of Science in human nutrition (CPD); Bachelor of Science in technology management (degree-completion program); Master of Arts in educational media and technology; graduate certificate in legal administration; and graduate certificate in educational media and technology.

SPECIAL PROGRAMS

Prior Learning and Portfolio Development is offered to students seeking credit for prior learning through portfolio assessment. A free workshop helps students identify competencies and document experience to create a portfolio to present for assessment by faculty members in appropriate departments.

STUDENT SERVICES

Distance learners can complete their online education entirely via the Internet. Registration, book buying, discussions, homework assignments, and exams are all available at the click of a computer mouse.

CREDIT OPTIONS

Students may transfer credits from another institution or may earn credits through examinations, portfolio assessment, military training, or business training.

FACULTY

More than 100 faculty members from EMU's academic departments currently teach online, Independent Learning, and Interactive Television courses at EMU.

ADMISSION

Students may register by World Wide Web, mail, fax, and e-mail and in person.

TUITION AND FEES

Out-of-state and international students can take EMU-Online courses at in-state tuition rates. In 2003–04, per-credit-hour rates for Michigan and Ohio residents were $153.15 for all levels (100–400) of undergraduate courses, $270.25 for lower-level (500–

600) graduate courses, and $311.50 for upper-level (700–999) graduate courses.

Rates per credit hour for nonresidents in 2003–04 were $467.10 for all levels of undergraduate courses, $548.10 for lower-level graduate courses, and $618 for upper-level graduate courses.

A registration fee of $40 per semester and a general fee of $21 per credit hour are also assessed. Other fees include $50 for late registration, $10 per credit hour for technology, $30 for installment payment (for fall/winter only), $25 per month for late payments, and $20 for returned checks and declined charge cards. Program support fees also apply and range from $12.50 to $52.50 per credit hour. In addition to tuition and other applicable fees, online students are assessed an additional $40-per-credit-hour program fee. For specific continuing education program fees, candidates should visit http://www.ce.emich.edu.

All tuition and fees are subject to change by action of the EMU Board of Regents without prior notice and at any time.

FINANCIAL AID

For financial aid information, students should visit http://www.emich.edu/finaid/ or call 734-487-0455.

APPLYING

Undergraduate admission requirements include a completed application; a $30 application fee; transcripts from all high schools, colleges, or universities previously attended; and ACT or SAT I scores for persons with fewer than 12 college credits who are under 21 (no ACT or SAT I test scores are required for individuals over the age of 21). Individuals with 12 or more transferable credits apply as transfer students and usually do not need to send high school transcripts.

Graduate admission requirements include a completed application, a $35 application fee, and all transcripts from any colleges or universities the student has attended. In addition, each graduate program has its own requirements, which may include any or all of the following: proof of a GRE or GMAT score, a personal statement, one or more letters of recommendation, and a teaching certificate, for students planning to study education. (Students should contact the graduate coordinator in their department of interest to determine which of these are required). For more information, students may call 800-GO-TO-EMU (toll-free).

CONTACT

EMU-Online and Independent Learning
Continuing Education
Eastern Michigan University
101 Boone Hall
Ypsilanti, Michigan 48197
Telephone: 800-777-3521 (toll-free)
E-mail: distance.education@emich.edu
Web site: http://www.emuonline.edu
http://www.ce.emich.edu

Education Direct

Center for Degree Studies

Scranton, Pennsylvania

Education Direct is one of the oldest and largest distance-learning institutions in the world, providing programs and services designed to meet the lifelong education needs of the adult learner. Programs of study lead to specialized associate degrees and career-specific diplomas. The mission of Education Direct is to empower adult learners to advance or change their careers, learn a new skill, or gain personal satisfaction. The school strives to fulfill this mission by providing breadth and depth of courseware, applicable technology, and a wide array of flexible services. Programs not only teach current marketplace skills but also present liberal arts offerings and develop critical thinking, writing, and mathematical abilities. Education Direct is accredited by the Accrediting Commission of the Distance Education and Training Council (DETC), which is listed by the U.S. Department of Education as a nationally recognized accrediting agency. Education Direct and the Center for Degree Studies are licensed by the Pennsylvania State Board of Private Licensed Schools.

DISTANCE LEARNING PROGRAM

Achieving success means having in-demand skills, and Education Direct's at-home education is the fastest, most convenient way to acquire them. Programs allow busy adults to train for better careers without quitting their current jobs or rearranging their schedules. The Education Direct commitment to education is reflected in every part of its training method, from the ease of enrollment to toll-free instructor support.

First, students choose the program that most interests them, reading online about the projected salary and growth figures and the description of career possibilities. Students should begin their lessons as soon as they receive the learning materials. Each Education Direct program has been written by experts in the field and features the latest techniques and information. All exams are open book and are submitted either online; via Tel-Test, a telephone-based testing system; or by mail. Once students pass an exam, they can proceed to the next lesson.

Students have up to two years to complete a career diploma program and up to eighteen months to complete each semester of a Center for Degree Studies (CDS) degree program. Upon graduation, students receive an official CDS degree or career diploma from Education Direct.

DELIVERY MEDIA

Students can learn online or through the mail, whichever they prefer. They can also choose to take open-book exams by mail, telephone, or online.

PROGRAMS OF STUDY

Education Direct offers a variety of programs. The Associate in Specialized Business (A.S.B.) degree helps students master the business skills and management techniques the modern executive needs to succeed. Degrees are offered in accounting; applied computer science; business management; business management, with an option in finance; business management, with an option in marketing; early childhood education; hospitality management; and paralegal studies.

The Associate in Specialized Technology (A.S.T.) degree is available in civil engineering technology; electrical engineering technology; electronics technology; industrial engineering technology; Internet technology, with an option in e-commerce administration; Internet technology, with an option in multimedia and design; Internet technology, with an option in Web programming; mechanical engineering technology, and veterinary technician studies.

Education Direct offers career diplomas in more than sixty accredited training programs, which can be completed in less than a year, but students may take up to two years. Career diplomas are offered in specializations within the following categories: administrative, building trades, computers, creative/design, education, electrical/electronics engineering, legal/medical management, mechanical, security, and travel and hospitality.

An overall program average of 70 percent or above is required to graduate and earn a career diploma. An overall QPA of 2.0 or above is required to graduate and earn a Center for Degree Studies A.S.B. or A.S.T. degree.

The Thomson High School Program is designed to do more than help students earn their diplomas—it can provide the special job skills needed to achieve success. More information can be found online at Education Direct's Web site.

STUDENT SERVICES

Each program is designed so that students can learn at home, with little or no guidance. Should any questions arise, however, Education Direct has a toll-free instructional-support hotline. Staff members are on duty to answer questions from 8 a.m. to 9 p.m., Eastern Standard Time, Monday through Friday. After 9 p.m., and on weekends and holidays, students can leave a message, which is answered the next business day. Instructors can also be contacted by mail or e-mail.

ADMISSION

Most Education Direct programs are designed so that even beginners with no experience can get off to a fast start to an exciting new career. As long as applicants can read and write—and have at least average intelligence—they should be able to complete the training without any difficulty. Some career diploma programs and all Center for Degree Studies degree programs require that applicants have a high school diploma to enroll. This prerequisite is noted in the individual program descriptions, where applicable.

TUITION AND FEES

The cost of study for one semester of most A.S.B. and A.S.T. degree programs was $808 in 2004, which included $573 for tuition, a $150 registration fee, a $25 credit application fee, a $35 technology fee, and a $25 shipping and handling charge. The total first-semester price of the A.S.B. in paralegal studies degree was $1008 and the A.S.T. in veterinary technician studies program was $908. Books, equipment, and learning aids were included.

FINANCIAL AID

Although Education Direct offers no financial aid, the cost of study is minimal. Unlike many schools, Education Direct offers its programs through easy, monthly payments for the same price as if paid in full. "Zero percent financing" means never paying a penny in interest or finance charges. A variety of payment methods, including the full, automatic, and standard payment plans, ensure that students can easily afford their education.

APPLYING

Students can start immediately. Once an applicant's down payment and enrollment are received and processed, the first shipment of learning materials is sent immediately to the student.

CONTACT

Education Direct
P.O. Box 1900
Scranton, Pennsylvania 18501
Telephone: 800-275-4410 (toll free)
E-mail: info@educationdirect.com
World Wide Web: http://www.educationdirect.com/

Embry-Riddle Aeronautical University

Extended Campus

Daytona Beach, Florida

Embry-Riddle Aeronautical University is an independent, nonsectarian, non-profit coeducational university with a history dating back to the early days of aviation. Embry-Riddle is accredited by the Commission on Colleges of the Southern Association of Colleges and Schools (1866 Southern Lane, Decatur, Georgia 30033-4097; Telephone: 404-679-4501) to award degrees at the associate, bachelor's, and master's levels. Residential campuses in Daytona Beach, Florida, and Prescott, Arizona, provide education in a traditional setting. The Extended Campus network of education centers throughout the United States and Europe and the distance learning program serve civilian and military working adults around the world. Embry-Riddle has served the public and private sectors of aviation through education for more than seventy years and is the only accredited not-for-profit university in the world totally oriented to aviation/aerospace. Alumni are employed in all facets of civilian and military aviation.

DISTANCE LEARNING PROGRAM

Since 1970, Embry-Riddle has provided educational opportunities for professionals working in civilian and military aviation and aerospace careers. To meet the varied needs of the adult working student, Embry-Riddle established the Extended Campus, which includes the College of Career Education's classroom and distance learning operations. The Extended Campus maintains a comprehensive system of academic quality control, sustaining the requirements and elements of courses as delivered on the residential campuses. The curricula, academic standards, and academic policies are the same throughout the University and are modified only to accommodate certain requirements resulting from different delivery methods. The College of Career Education provides working adults with the opportunity to earn undergraduate and graduate degrees through a network of teaching centers spread across the United States and Europe and through distance learning. The College operates more than 130 resident centers and teaching sites in thirty-seven states and five European nations. Resident centers and teaching sites are found at or near major aviation industry installations, both civilian and military. When students are not located near a center or a teaching site, they can enroll in many of the same programs through distance learning. All teaching centers and the distance learning programs are approved for veterans' educational benefits. Students receive personalized academic advisement whether they take their classes in the classroom or by distance learning. Classroom instruction is conducted during hours convenient for working students, and distance learning students can work on their studies at any time and at any place that is convenient for them. Degree requirements are completed through a combination of course work, transfer credit, and prior learning assessment or by achieving the University's required scores in standardized national testing programs, such as CLEP or DANTES.

DELIVERY MEDIA

The distance learning associate, bachelor's, and master's degree courses are delivered via the Internet. Each class is hosted on a private Embry-Riddle Web site, where students and professors interact by way of a bulletin board–type discussion forum. As a result, students are not required to log on to the Web site at specific times, but they may access their course work at a time of day that is most convenient to them. To participate in a distance learning class, students need access to a personal computer and the World Wide Web. Students who do not have access to the Web from home can usually gain access through their local library, military base education center, Embry-Riddle resident center, or another public facility.

PROGRAMS OF STUDY

At the graduate level, Embry-Riddle offers the Master of Aeronautical Science (M.A.S.) degree and the Master of Science in Management (M.S.M.) degree. The M.A.S. degree, with specializations in aeronautics operations, management, human factors, safety, education, space studies, or space operations management requires 36–39 semester hours of course work. The M.A.S. program enables aviation/aerospace professionals to master the application of concepts, methods, and tools used in the development, manufacture, and operation of aircraft and spacecraft, as well as the public and business infrastructure that support them. The degree gives air traffic control personnel, aviation educators, flight crew members, flight operations specialists, and industry technical representatives an unequaled opportunity to enhance their knowledge and pursue additional opportunities. The special intricacies of aviation are woven into a strong, traditional management foundation and examined in greater detail through a wide variety of electives. M.A.S. core topics include air transportation, aircraft and space craft development, human factors in aviation/aerospace, and research methods and statistics. Specialization courses provide a strong knowledge base of subject material. The courses provide the student with skills needed in the professional arena. Electives and a graduate research project provide students with the ability to tailor their degrees, adding greater breadth and depth in aviation/aerospace–related intellectual pursuits.

The M.S.M. degree program is targeted for those students (or those organizations sponsoring students) who need and desire a focused management degree but are looking for a degree with a greater operational approach than a traditional M.B.A. The degree is a 36-semester-hour degree program, which comprises a strong management core of 24 semester hours and the opportunity for several different areas of concentration or specialization.

Undergraduate degree offerings include Associate of Science and Bachelor of Science degree programs in professional aeronautics, Associate of Science and Bachelor of Science degree programs in technical management, the Bachelor of Science degree in technical management–logistics, the Bachelor of Science degree in aviation maintenance management, and an Associate of Science degree in aircraft maintenance. The professional aeronautics degree program is designed specifically for students who work, have worked, or desire to work in aviation-related careers. For students with existing aviation-related knowledge and skills, the program recognizes those skills through award of advanced standing prior-learning credit. The curriculum then builds upon those skills. The program also provides a path for those students new to aviation to acquire these skills through aviation-related courses. The Bachelor of Science in professional aeronautics requires 120 semester hours, and the Associate of Science in professional aeronautics requires 60 semester hours.

The Bachelor of Science degree in technical management is 120 semester hours, and the Associate of Science in technical management is 60 semester hours. In the technical management degree program, students learn how to apply specific management skills to their technical specialty. The degree program prepares students for supervisory and management positions in various segments of civilian and military aviation.

The Bachelor of Science degree in aviation maintenance management is 126 semester hours. In this degree program, students gain the management skills needed to effectively manage aviation maintenance. Students who already have their Airframe and Powerplant Maintenance Certificate gain a comprehensive business foundation that complements the FAA certification. Although the program is geared toward aviation and aerospace, its curriculum prepares graduates for success with companies in any industry.

The Associate of Science degree in aircraft maintenance offers special aircraft maintenance technology courses to students who are experienced, but unlicensed, aircraft specialists. These courses deal largely with the problems, considerations, and practices involved in maintaining aircraft in airworthy condition based on the body of knowledge required of experienced aircraft maintenance specialists under Federal Aviation Regulations, Part 65.

CREDIT OPTIONS

Master's degree applicants may transfer up to 12 semester hours of credit into the University. Credit must be from a regionally accredited institution with a grade of B or better and awarded within seven years of application to Embry-Riddle. Courses must be applicable to the selected degree program. Undergraduate applicants may transfer credit from regionally accredited institutions with a letter grade of C or better. Advanced standing credit may be awarded for prior learning achieved through postsecondary education, testing, and work or training experience.

FACULTY

The faculty is a blend of traditionally prepared academicians and leaders with significant industry track records. Nearly all faculty members have doctoral or terminal degrees.

ADMISSION

Admission to the master's degree program requires a bachelor's degree from a regionally accredited institution. Admission to the undergraduate programs is unique to each degree.

TUITION AND FEES

Tuition for master's degree courses is $368 per credit hour for the 2004–05 academic year. Undergraduate tuition is $169 per credit hour. Textbook and shipping fees vary by course. Tuition is scheduled to increase slightly in October 2004.

FINANCIAL AID

Students accepted for admission may be considered for several forms of federal financial aid. There are three different federal programs available. Additional information is provided at time of application. All Embry-Riddle degree programs have been approved by the U.S. Department of Veterans' Affairs (DVA) for enrollment of persons eligible to receive benefits from DVA.

APPLYING

Applications for admission are accepted continuously. There are six graduate distance learning terms a year and eleven undergraduate distance learning terms a year.

CONTACT

Linda Dammer, Director
Ronald Brownie, Assistant Director
Distance Learning Enrollment Office
Embry-Riddle Aeronautical University
600 South Clyde Morris Boulevard
Daytona Beach, Florida 32114-3900
Telephone: 800-359-3728 (toll-free)
Fax: 386-226-7627
E-mail: Marsha.Lewis@erau.edu
Web site: http://www.erau.edu

Excelsior College

Learning Services

Albany, New York

As a private institution with no residency requirement, Excelsior College—a recognized leader in distance education—has devoted itself to making college degrees more accessible to busy, working adults. In line with its founding philosophy, "What you know is more important than where or how you learned it,®" the College accepts credits from a broad array of approved sources. As a result, many students find that most or all of their prior college-level credits transfer into their Excelsior College degree program.

Since 1977—six years after its founding—Excelsior College has been accredited by the Commission on Higher Education of the Middle States Associations of Colleges and Schools, 3624 Market Street, Philadelphia, Pennsylvania 19104; telephone: 215-662-5606. All of the College's academic programs are approved by the New York State Education Department, and its examinations are recognized by the American Council on Education, Center for Adult Learning and Educational Credentials, for the award of college-level credit.

The associate, baccalaureate, and master's degree programs in nursing are accredited by the National League for Nursing Accrediting Commission (NLNAC), 61 Broadway, New York, New York 10006; telephone 800-669-1656 (toll-free). The NLNAC is a specialized accrediting agency recognized by the U.S. Secretary of Education. The baccalaureate degree programs in electronics engineering technology and nuclear engineering technology are accredited by the Technology Accreditation Commission (TAC) of the Accreditation Board for Engineering and Technology (ABET) 111 Market Place, Baltimore, Maryland 21202; telephone: 410-347-7700. The TAC of ABET is a specialized accrediting agency recognized by the U.S. Secretary of Education.

DISTANCE LEARNING PROGRAM

Excelsior College offers degrees in business and technology, liberal arts, and nursing. With more than 100,000 graduates, the College's associate, baccalaureate, and master's degree programs are accessible worldwide.

Currently, the College has more than 27,000 students enrolled in its associate, baccalaureate, and master's degree programs.

PROGRAMS OF STUDY

Excelsior College offers thirty-three degree programs through distinct schools in three major areas.

In the School of Business and Technology, twelve business programs (associate and baccalaureate) lead to degrees in such fields as accounting, finance, global business, management information systems, management of human resources, marketing, operations management, and risk management and insurance. Similarly, a dozen technology degree programs (also associate and baccalaureate) educate students in fields such as computer information systems, computer technology, electronics engineering technology, electronics technology, nuclear engineering technology, and nuclear technology.

Students in the School of Liberal Arts can earn associate or baccalaureate degrees in majors that include biology, chemistry, communication, criminal justice, economics, geography, geology, history, literature, mathematics, music, philosophy, physics, political science, psychology, sociology, or world language and literature. In addition, a liberal studies option provides flexibility for students to pursue a range of interests while focusing on a particular discipline. The School offers two associate and two baccalaureate degrees as well as a Master of Arts in liberal studies that can be earned entirely online.

The School of Nursing is one of the largest distance education nursing programs in the world. The associate and bachelor's degree programs are made up of guided independent study and nationally recognized Excelsior College Examinations. Excelsior College online offers a Master of Science degree in nursing with a major in clinical systems management, an RN-M.S. in nursing program, and a program leading to an online graduate-level certificate in health-care informatics.

SPECIAL PROGRAMS

Through its Office of Military Education, Excelsior College has addressed educational needs of the members of the U.S. armed forces. The College awards credit for military training recognized for college credit by the American Council on Education (ACE). Four programs, including associate degrees in aviation, technical studies, and administrative/management studies, are specially designed to meet the needs of military personnel. Excelsior College examinations are free to all in active duty military, National Guard, and Reserve Component personnel. Special partnerships allow active duty personnel to take Excelsior College distance courses that are 100 percent covered by military tuition assistance. A college military deployment policy holds the status of deployed students without extension or penalty fees until their return.

STUDENT SERVICES

Excelsior College students draw on a team of experienced academic advisers who develop individualized degree completion plans, recommend and approve sources of credit, and recommend relevant courses.

Students can use Excelsior College DistanceLearn®, a searchable database of distance courses and examinations, to find credit opportunities across the U.S. and abroad. DistanceLearn is the most comprehensive database of such offerings available today.

For research, the Excelsior College Virtual Library gives students online access to millions of the world's most current and authoritative resources. The Electronic Peer Network (EPN) provides a Web-based community where students can join online study groups and buy and sell textbooks, among other things. For those who seek help as they study for Excelsior College exams, the Online Writing and Online Tutoring Services connect students to experienced tutors.

CREDIT OPTIONS

Excelsior College programs are designed to help busy adults pursue their degree at a distance through whatever combination of courses, exams, and training fits their situation. To advance that mission, the College accepts credits from classroom and distance courses at regionally accredited colleges and universities; college-level proficiency examinations, such as Excelsior College Examinations and CLEP; and military and corporate training recognized for college credit by the American Council on Education (ACE), Center for Adult Learning and Educational Credentials, National Program on Noncollegiate Sponsored Instruction (PONSI), or training evaluated for college credit by Excelsior College.

TUITION AND FEES

Excelsior College charges an $825 (associate programs) or $975 (baccalaureate programs) fee at enrollment, which covers a student's initial evaluation, academic advisement and program planning services for one year; a $410 (associate) or $455 (baccalaureate) annual fee for each year after, which covers the ongoing evaluation of academic records submitted by a student; and a $475 (associate) or $490 (baccalaureate) fee for a final evaluation and verification of all academic records prior to program completion and graduation. (Different fees and fee structures apply to military students, to students in the RN-M.S. in nursing, and graduate programs, and to students who choose to pay their Excelsior College enrollment and annual service expenses through a Payment Plan.)

FINANCIAL AID

Excelsior College offers more than fifteen options for financing a degree, including ten scholarship and five private loan programs. Veterans Affairs educational benefits and New York State financial aid programs are also available.

APPLYING

For the liberal arts and business and technology programs, students may submit an undergraduate application of admission. An Excelsior College admissions counselor then advises them how many prior credits can transfer and how many they still have to earn. Then they can enroll in the program with support from admissions counselors if necessary.

Nursing students must first apply to the Excelsior College School of Nursing and, once accepted, can enroll in Excelsior College. The School of Nursing is open primarily to individuals with clinical experience, such as licensed practical nurses and registered nurses.

CONTACT

Admissions Office
Excelsior College
7 Columbia Circle
Albany, New York 12212
Telephone: 518-464-8500 (press 2-7 at the prompt)
888-647-2388 (toll-free)
E-mail: leads@excelsior.edu
Web site: http://www.excelsior.edu

Florida Gulf Coast University

Distance Learning Programs

Fort Myers, Florida

Florida Gulf Coast University (FGCU) opened its doors to students in August 1997 and is housed on a state-of-the-art campus located on the southwest coast of Florida in Fort Myers. Its primary mission is to provide a broad range of undergraduate and graduate programs in arts and sciences, business, technology, environmental science, education, allied health, and social services. FGCU was founded as a dual-mode institution to provide a full range of on-campus degree programs and selected degree programs for distance learners. The University now serves regional, state, national, and international audiences with these programs. FGCU is fully accredited by the Southern Association of Colleges and Schools (SACS). Additional information about the University and its programs may be found on the World Wide Web at http://www.fgcu.edu.

DISTANCE LEARNING PROGRAM

Distance learning at FGCU is an instructional strategy that is central to the University's mission. FGCU is committed to the development of innovative distance learning course designs that utilize a technology-rich learning environment. FGCU's distance-learning students receive personalized attention from faculty members strategically selected to accomplish high-quality instruction and exceptional service.

DELIVERY MEDIA

FGCU supports five methods of distance learning delivery: the Internet, videotape, two-way interactive video, broadcast video, and e-mail. Each course uses one or more of these methods, depending on the intended learning outcomes. All distance-learning courses currently being offered include extensive Web site and e-mail communication. The use of video is incorporated into many, but not all, courses.

PROGRAMS OF STUDY

There are currently three master's and two bachelor's degree programs offered by FGCU via distance learning. Brief descriptions of these programs appear below. For full details, students should visit the Web site (http://itech.fgcu.edu/distance) and select Programs and Courses to see course offerings in the current semester.

The Master of Business Administration (M.B.A.) provides a challenging curriculum designed to prepare students for leadership positions in organizations. Leadership, teamwork, information technology, entrepreneurial vision, and global awareness are integrated throughout the program. All courses for this program are available at a distance. For more information, students should visit the Web site at http://www.fgcu.edu/cob/mba.

The interdisciplinary Master of Science in Health Science program offers a choice of four concentrations: health professions education, practice, health services administration, and gerontology. The education and practice concentrations are limited to those qualified in a health profession. All courses for this program are available at a distance. For more information, students should visit the Web site at http://www.fgcu.edu/chp/hs.

The Master of Public Administration (M.P.A.) is an applied degree program that prepares students for successful administrative careers in the public sector. It is designed for students who have significant in-service experience and for students who have little prior work experience in public agencies. All courses for this program are available at a distance. For more information, students should visit the Web site at http://cps.fgcu.edu.

The Bachelor of Science in criminal justice degree program prepares students for careers in criminal justice professions and/or graduate education. The curriculum provides students the opportunity to acquire knowledge of the roles and challenges faced by police, courts, and corrections and their interrelationship within the justice system. All upper-division undergraduate courses for this program are available at a distance to those students who have completed at least 60 hours of undergraduate course work. For more information, students should visit the Web site at http://cps.fgcu.edu.

The interdisciplinary Bachelor of Science in Health Science program is designed to provide career advancement opportunities for entry-level health profession practitioners and individuals who seek careers in health care, such as physical therapy. All of the upper-division undergraduate courses for this program are available at a distance to those students who have completed at least 60 hours of undergraduate course work. For more information, students should visit the Web site at http://www.fgcu.edu/chp/hs.

SPECIAL PROGRAMS

Florida Gulf Coast University offers a diverse array of certificate programs. To learn more, students should visit the Web at http://www.fgcu.edu/info/certificate.asp.

Florida Gulf Coast University is part of a consortium of forty-six universities that participate in the National Technological University (NTU) Satellite Network, serving the needs of engineers, technical professionals, and managers using advanced telecommunications technology. Degrees and certificates are awarded at the master's level to candidates sponsored by corporations or organizations affiliated with NTU. Students who wish to participate need to confirm NTU sponsorship with employers.

Florida Gulf Coast University is also a member of the Southern Regional Education Board Electronic Campus (SREC). Additional information may be found on the Web at http://www.electroniccampus.org.

STUDENT SERVICES

Many of the services for students on campus are also available to students at a distance. A spirit of cooperation within Student Services fosters a learning environment that promotes the academic success and personal and career development of students, with an emphasis on leadership skills, community services, and an appreciation for diversity. For more information, students should visit the Web site at http://Studentservices.fgcu.edu/supportservices.

CREDIT OPTIONS

Credits earned through distance education are recorded on a Florida Gulf Coast University transcript in the same manner as credits earned in on-campus courses. Individuals may enroll as non-degree-seeking or degree-seeking students, but there are limits on the amount of credit awarded to non-degree-seeking students that may be transferred to a degree-seeking program. Students should contact the Office of Undergraduate Admission at admissions@fgcu.edu or 888-889-1095 (toll-free) for additional details and assistance.

FACULTY

Distance education faculty members meet all of the standards set forth by the Southern Association of Colleges and Schools and the State of Florida. They are available to answer questions and provide feedback via telephone, fax, e-mail, or regular mail.

ADMISSION

Admission decisions are based on standards set by the Florida Board of Education for the State University System of Florida. Criteria for admission depend on applicant status: degree-seeking or non-degree-seeking and graduate or undergraduate. For more information, students should visit the Web site at http://www.fgcu.edu/prospective.

TUITION AND FEES

Current tuition and fees are published on the Web site at http://www.fgcu.edu/info/fees.asp. For the 2004–05 academic year, per-credit-hour costs are $101.85 for undergraduate Florida residents, $219.54 for graduate residents, $505.07 for undergraduate nonresidents, and $840.65 for graduate nonresidents.

FINANCIAL AID

The University offers a comprehensive program of financial assistance for traditional and nontraditional students pursuing undergraduate or graduate degrees. The Financial Aid and Scholarships Office is responsible for helping students secure the necessary funds to pursue education. The office is proactive in offering information to enrolled and prospective students about the availability of financial assistance. Students should contact the Financial Aid and Scholarships Office at FASO@fgcu.edu or 239-590-7920 or visit the Web site at http://enrollment.fgcu.edu/financialaid.

APPLYING

Students may apply for undergraduate admission as a degree-seeking or non-degree-seeking student via the Web site by completing the University's Application for Undergraduate Admission at http://enrollment.fgcu.edu/admissions/applyonline.htm. To complete the application, students must include a $30 application fee with their completed and signed residency statement.

Applicants seeking graduate admission as degree or nondegree status can obtain either application via the Web at http://www.fgcu.edu/graduate.

CONTACT

Florida Gulf Coast University
10501 FGCU Boulevard South
Fort Myers, Florida 33965-6565
Telephone: 239-590-7878
888-889-1095 (toll-free)
239-590-7886 (TTY)
E-mail: admissions@fgcu.edu
graduate@fgcu.edu
Web site: http://www.fgcu.edu

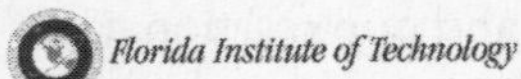

Florida Institute of Technology

The Extended Campus

Melbourne, Florida

Florida Institute of Technology is an accredited, coeducational, independently controlled and supported university that is committed to the pursuit of excellence in teaching and research. Undergraduate programs are offered in science and engineering, aviation, business, humanities, psychology, and communications. Doctoral degrees are offered in science, engineering, and psychology while master's degrees are offered in aeronautics, business, communication, and more.

Founded in 1958, Florida Tech is rich in history, with links to the nation's space program. Originally founded to offer continuing education opportunities to scientists, engineers, and technicians at what is now NASA's Kennedy Space Center, the University's growth has paralleled the area's rapid development.

Florida Tech is located in Melbourne on Florida's Space Coast, home to space shuttle launches and landings, marine science research projects, and alternative energy development projects.

DISTANCE LEARNING PROGRAM

The Extended Campus has reached out to career professionals since 1972 and has awarded more than 9,000 master's degrees in management, engineering, and science. Since 1995, it has also offered online distance learning programs. Graduates include corporate and government leaders, top-rank military officers, and five astronauts.

Ten graduate programs and eleven graduate certificate programs are available completely online. Online enrollments exceed 700 per semester.

DELIVERY MEDIA

Using Blackboard as the learning management system, courses are offered via the Internet. Text information is supported by audio and video clips. Interaction between instructors and students and among students is provided through e-mail, synchronous chats, and asynchronous threaded discussions.

PROGRAMS OF STUDY

Programs currently being offered include a 36-hour professional Master of Business Administration (M.B.A.) with concentrations available in contract and acquisition management, information systems, human resource management, and e-business; a 36-hour Master of Public Administration (M.P.A.); a 33-hour M.S. in acquisition and contract management; a 33-hour M.S. in human resources management; a 33-hour M.S. in logistics management; a 33-hour M.S. in management, with concentrations available in acquisition and contract management, human resources management, information systems, logistics management, transportation management, and e-business; a 33-hour M.S. in materiel acquisition management; a 33-hour M.S. in systems management, with concentrations available in information systems and operations research; a 33-hour M.S. in project management, with concentrations available in information systems and operations research; and a 33-hour M.S. in operations research. All programs require a set of core requirements and a set of electives. Some programs require the completion of specific prerequisites prior to enrollment. Some courses in the programs require prerequisites. All courses are 3 semester hours. Details on each program of study may be found at http://segs.fit.edu/academics/. Course prerequisites may be found at http://www.fit.edu/catalog/.

Graduate certificate programs may be obtained in the following management areas: business, contract, e-business, logistics, human resources, information systems, program, systems, quality, transportation, and materiel acquisition. Each certificate program requires the completion of five 3-semester-hour courses. The curriculum consists of one required course and four electives chosen from a specified list.

Programs being developed in 2004–05 to be delivered online include the M.S. in space systems, the M.S. in space systems management, and the M.S. in computer information systems. Details on these new programs will be available at http://segs.fit.edu/academics.

STUDENT SERVICES

Library service is provided via remote access to all internal holdings and to several electronic databases through http://www.lib.fit.edu. Access is provided to currently registered students via a personal identification number and password for certain restricted databases.

Recommendations for the purchase of computers and related equipment are available at http://ec.fit.edu/cdl/dlfaq.html.

Academic advising is provided through e-mail, fax, and telephone contact on a request basis.

Distance learning students are eligible to use the University's career placement services.

CREDIT OPTIONS

Graduate students may transfer a maximum of 12 graduate credit hours to a Florida Tech master's degree program. To be eligible for transfer, the courses must have been taken for graduate credit at a regionally accredited university within the past six years and have been completed with a grade of A or B. A limited number of military schools have been evaluated by the American Council on Education and the school's faculty and are recommended for some transfer credit award.

FACULTY

There are 14 full-time and 20 to 30 part-time faculty members in the distance learning program. More than 95 percent possess a doctorate in their teaching discipline or in a field closely related to it.

ADMISSION

Applicants must have a minimum cumulative GPA of 3.0 for regular admission to graduate studies. Students with a cumulative GPA lower than 3.0 may be granted provisional admission with additional supporting materials. Applicants not initially qualifying may enroll as continuing education students and take up to four graduate courses for academic credit. Special rules apply to students admitted as continuing education students.

TUITION AND FEES

As of 2003–04, the per-credit-hour tuition rate was $375. The application fee was $50.

FINANCIAL AID

As a general rule, a graduate student must be enrolled half-time (at least 5 credit hours per term) as a regular student in a degree program and must be a U.S. citizen or an eligible non-U.S. citizen to qualify for federal and/or state financial aid. Specific information is available through the University's Office of Student Financial Assistance. Graduate students should file prior to March 20 to ensure timely processing and must reapply for financial aid each year. Students must maintain satisfactory academic progress as defined by the Office of Student Financial Assistance to continue receiving financial assistance.

APPLYING

Application is available online through http://segs.fit.edu/admissions/apply.html. Applicants must sign and mail an affidavit attesting to the accuracy of the application to the University's Graduate Admission Office. Official transcripts are required from all colleges/universities attended. Students may be provisionally authorized to attend one academic term while their admission documents are being collected and submitted for evaluation.

CONTACT

Extended Campus for Distance Learning
School of Extended Graduate Studies
Florida Institute of Technology
150 West University Boulevard
Melbourne, Florida 32901
Telephone: 912-634-6336
888-225-2239 (toll-free in the U.S.)
Fax: 912-634-7783
E-mail: vgc@fit.edu
Web site: http://segs.fit.edu

Florida State University

Office for Distributed and Distance Learning

Tallahassee, Florida

Since its founding more than 150 years ago, Florida State University (FSU) has been guided by its mission to meet the higher education needs of the people of Florida and the U.S. The University remains rooted in its tradition of encouraging critical inquiry, promoting lifelong learning, and responding to radical transformations within professions and society. University faculty members guide students in acquiring the knowledge and skills to learn efficiently and adapt quickly to new settings and challenges, long after earning their degree.

DISTANCE LEARNING PROGRAM

Students learning from a distance receive the same high-quality education and degrees as those students who complete on-campus programs. No distinction is made on transcripts. Using computers and online classrooms, students and instructors exchange ideas and course work via the Internet. Students ask questions via e-mail, collaborate on group projects using a range of communication tools, and post to online class discussions at any time of the day or night.

Most students currently enrolled in FSU's distance-degree programs maintain full-time careers. They attend to their online courses during non-work hours and without relocating. Students may take proctored exams at an institution in their area.

DELIVERY MEDIA

To provide distance students a comprehensive and easy-to-use online learning environment, FSU has partnered with an educational software corporation to create the leading product of its kind. Students "attend" class through course Web sites that deliver communication tools (including discussion boards, live chat, and e-mail) and course materials that are compatible with all computer platforms. FSU's online environment includes nearly every component of a face-to-face class, and some that are only possible via technology. Distance learning at FSU is accessible from anywhere an Internet connection is available.

PROGRAMS OF STUDY

Bachelor's programs are available in computer science, interdisciplinary social science, nursing, and software engineering. Master's programs are available in adult education/human resource development, business administration, communication disorders, criminology/criminal justice, educational leadership, information studies, instructional systems/distance learning, mathematics education, nursing, risk management/insurance, and social work. Students pursuing these degrees online typically take one or two courses per semester.

SPECIAL PROGRAMS

Online certificate programs are available in human resource development and in online instructional development.

STUDENT SERVICES

Florida State University has developed a team exclusively focused on supporting students in its distance-learning programs. Team members include lead faculty members, who are responsible for assuring course quality, mentors or graduate assistants, and distance-learning support staff. Mentors/graduate assistants are selected by FSU faculty members for their background and knowledge of the particular discipline as well as for their ability to guide and encourage a cohort of students. Mentors and graduate assistants are trained to provide each student with individualized tutorial guidance and attention in every course.

CREDIT OPTIONS

Bachelor's degree programs are open to students who have earned an Associate in Arts degree from a Florida public institution or completed at least 60 semester hours of transferable credit. Master's degree programs are open to students who have earned a bachelor's degree and meet University graduate entrance and specific departmental requirements. Florida State University generally awards credit for classes that are offered at a comparable level and taken at regionally accredited community colleges, colleges, and universities in the U.S., and from fully recognized international institutions. After a student is admitted to the University, the Office of Admissions examines the student's transcripts to determine what credit can be transferred toward a degree from FSU.

FACULTY

Approximately 88 percent of the teaching faculty members hold doctorates or other terminal degrees. FSU has had five Nobel laureates on its faculty. The faculty currently includes five National Academy of Sciences elected members and two American Academy of Arts and Sciences fellows.

ADMISSION

All applicants must submit official transcripts from each institution previously attended. Applicants for bachelor's degree programs with 60 or more transferable semester hours must have a 2.5 (out of 4.0) minimum GPA, unless they have earned an Associate in Arts degree from a Florida public institution and completed the University foreign language requirement. Individual departments may have additional requirements.

Master's degree program admission involves gaining acceptance by the department or school in which the applicant expects to study. While there are minimum University admission requirements, the departments can, and frequently do, set admission standards significantly higher than these minimums. Applicants should first determine departmental requirements.

TUITION AND FEES

Tuition rates differ depending on whether a student is a Florida resident or an out-of-state resident, and an undergraduate or graduate student. Partial tuition waivers are available for online graduate students who reside outside of Florida, reducing their tuition to an amount comparable to the University's affordable in-state tuition fee. Complete information is available through the Web site listed in the Contact section.

FINANCIAL AID

Distance students may have access to many of the same types of financial aid as residential students. To qualify, students need to be enrolled for at least six hours per semester. Qualifying for financial aid is sometimes a lengthy process, and should be started at least two semesters in advance of the term for which financial aid is expected. FSU's Office of Financial Aid provides assistance in determining eligibility for financial aid. The academic coordinator for each distance-degree program can also answer questions about obtaining financial aid.

APPLYING

Applications may be submitted online and are accepted one year in advance of the start semester. Notification typically takes four to six weeks from the time all necessary credentials are received. An initial orientation is required and available online. Students may register for courses online or by phone.

CONTACT

Florida State University
Office for Distributed and Distance Learning
3500-C University Center
Tallahassee, Florida 32306-2550
Phone: 877-357-8283 (toll-free)
Fax: 850-644-5803
E-mail: inquiries@oddl.fsu.edu
Website: http://online.fsu.edu

Franklin University

The Virtu@l Campus

Columbus, Ohio

Franklin University's chief objective is to provide services and programs for students who work full- or part-time. Franklin is focused on providing students with a supportive environment that allows achievement of goals and a practical education that increases options. Students learn from professionals who practice what they teach, are accessible, have a wealth of experience, and exhibit a true commitment to teaching and learning. Franklin University is an independent, nonprofit institution that celebrated its 100th anniversary in 2002. It has offered online courses since 1996 and currently has 115 course offerings through its Virtu@l Campus. In 1998, the University unveiled the Community College Alliance (CCA) program, which encourages community college graduates to obtain a bachelor's degree via Franklin University's Virtu@l Campus in coordination with their local community college. Franklin also participates in the eArmyU learning consortium, which addresses learning needs for soldier-students.

DISTANCE LEARNING PROGRAM

Franklin University has a distance education enrollment of 3,689, an Online M.B.A. enrollment of 201, and an eArmyU enrollment of 449.

DELIVERY MEDIA

Students in Franklin's Virtu@l Campus access their educational needs via the Internet. All courses are designed to take advantage of electronic communication tools such as chat rooms, bulletin boards, whiteboards, e-mail, and a grade book.

The Balanced Learning Format (BLF) course design and delivery format provides students with a wide range of offerings to meet their learning needs and busy schedules. With three-, six-, twelve-, and fifteen-week course lengths, new classes start every few weeks. The BLF allows students to anticipate consistent time commitments from week to week and from class to class. Franklin University uses a team of instructional designers, faculty members, and developers to create courses. This guarantees students consistent course outcomes, experiential learning, and consistent grading criteria.

PROGRAMS OF STUDY

Franklin University offers one online graduate degree program, the Master of Business Administration (M.B.A.), which offers the ultimate in convenience. The M.B.A. program, which includes eight focus areas, is a seventeen-month program consisting of six-week courses and two 3-day, high-intensity learning residencies. Admitted students can enter the M.B.A. program at multiple points along the academic calendar. The online graduate program enables students to continue their careers, balance family and social commitments, and still reach their educational goals.

Bachelor's degree completion majors are offered in accounting, applied management, business administration, computer science, digital communication, health-care management, information technology, management information sciences (MIS), and public safety management.

Franklin University continually updates its course offerings and schedule. It offers 115 courses online through the Virtu@l Campus. Franklin serves degree-seeking candidates, students who want to continue their education, or those who are interested in experiencing online learning.

STUDENT SERVICES

Through Franklin University's student-centered approach, each student is matched with a Student Services Associate (SSA), who, along with the course faculty members, becomes an important contact at the University. SSAs serve as both an initial and long-term resource for the student and work with the student until their academic goals are achieved.

The Community College Alliance (CCA) program is an educational alliance with more than 210 two-year colleges in thirty-one states. The CCA enables community college graduates, or those with equivalent credit, to earn a bachelor's degree from Franklin without leaving their community. Students complete their degrees through a combination of onsite courses at the community college and online courses through Franklin. For more information, students may visit the program's Web site at http://www.alliance.franklin.edu.

CREDIT OPTIONS

Franklin University has a credit transfer policy that is more student-friendly than most other institutions. More than 75 percent of Franklin students have transferred credit from other colleges and universities. Students also can earn credit outside the classroom through the College-Level Examination Program (CLEP), Franklin University Proficiency Exams (FUPE), and Prior Learning Portfolios.

TUITION AND FEES

For the 2004–05 academic year, tuition for undergraduate online courses from Franklin University is $233 per credit hour for standard courses and $292 per credit hour for computer science, MIS, and information technology courses. For online M.B.A. courses, tuition is $386 per credit hour.

FACULTY

Franklin faculty members enrich the virtual classroom with special talents and abilities drawn from successful careers in business, industry, government, and social service. Franklin University faculty members are working professionals who provide both excellence in teaching and real-world experience.

FINANCIAL AID

Franklin offers a variety of financial aid options, including a deferred-payment plan for students whose employers offer a tuition reimbursement program. More than 75 percent of Franklin students receive some type of financial assistance through grants, scholarships, loans, employer tuition reimbursement, and student employment. Franklin University awards approximately 250 scholarships every year to new and current students.

APPLYING

Anyone who is a graduate of an accredited high school or has passed the GED test is eligible for admission as a degree-seeking undergraduate student. Those seeking a bachelor's degree must complete an admission application and forward an official high school transcript or an official GED test score report to Franklin.

ADMISSION

Admission to the Franklin M.B.A. program is based on the following selection criteria: a baccalaureate degree from a regionally accredited college or university, a minimum of four years of full-time work experience, a minimum cumulative undergraduate GPA of 2.75 on a 4.0 scale (GMAT scores are considered if the GPA is below 2.75), and a score of 550 (paper-based) or 213 (computer-based) or better on the Test of English as a Foreign Language (TOEFL).

To apply transfer credits from another institution, all official transcripts should be forwarded to Franklin University directly from the previous institution(s); however, a student can begin a distance learning course before the transcripts have been received.

CONTACT

Franklin University Virtu@l Campus
201 South Grant Avenue
Columbus, Ohio 43215
Telephone: 877-341-6300 (toll-free)
E-mail: info@franklin.edu
Web site: http://www.franklin.edu

Georgia Institute of Technology

Center for Distance Learning

Atlanta, Georgia

Founded in 1885, the Georgia Institute of Technology is the Southeast's largest technological institution. Georgia Tech is located on a 330-acre campus near downtown Atlanta—the financial, communications, and cultural hub of the Southeast. The Institute's mission is to be a leader among those few technological universities whose alumni, faculty, students, and staff define, expand, and communicate the frontiers of knowledge and innovation.

U.S. News & World Report *consistently lists Georgia Tech among the fifty best universities in the nation. Georgia Tech also makes their list of the top graduate engineering programs in the country. Seven of the engineering options were ranked in the top ten, with several in the top five.*

In addition to its high-quality undergraduate and graduate instructional programs, Tech has a world-class research program, with $279 million in new grants and contracts awarded during the 2002 fiscal year. This ranks Tech as the South's number one public institution in engineering research.

DISTANCE LEARNING PROGRAM

Georgia Tech's Center for Distance Learning serves more than 450 distance learning students and is housed within a unit that reports directly to the provost. Georgia Tech is accredited by the Southern Association of Colleges and Schools. Engineering disciplines are accredited by the Accrediting Board for Engineering and Technology, Inc.

DELIVERY MEDIA

Video cameras record instructor presentations and student-instructor interaction during regular Georgia Tech graduate classes. The videotapes and supporting materials are sent to off-campus students, who take courses without having to come to the campus. Selected courses are available at some locations via videoconferencing, satellite, and the Internet. Students enrolled in the program communicate with their Georgia Tech professor by telephone, fax, and/or e-mail. Students have access to the Georgia Tech Electronic Library and the computer system via a business or home computer and a modem. Access is also provided over the Internet. Every student is expected to high-quality computer with a printer and Internet access. (High-speed connection is highly recommended.)

PROGRAMS OF STUDY

The Georgia Tech video-based distance delivery program provides high-quality graduate-level courses that can be applied to several master's degree programs. The School of Aerospace Engineering offers two master's degrees, the Master of Science in Aerospace Engineering (M.S.A.E.) and the Master of Science (M.S.). The M.S.A.E is generally referred to as a designated degree, while the M.S. is referred to as an undesignated degree. The difference between the two degree programs is that the designated degree program includes the completion of all academic course work required for a Bachelor of Science in Aerospace Engineering degree. The Master of Science in Electrical and Computer Engineering is offered with options in computer engineering, digital signal processing, power, and telecommunications; all options require 30 hours of course work. The M.S. and the Master of Science in Environmental Engineering (M.S.Env.E.) degrees are offered with concentrations in water quality, surface and subsurface systems, hazardous and solid waste, and air quality; all programs require 30 hours of course work or the equivalent. The Master of Science in Industrial Engineering is offered with specializations in automation, production and logistics systems, and statistical process control and quality assurance; it requires 30 hours of course work and students must hold an undergraduate degree from an ABET-accredited engineering curriculum. The Master of Science in Mechanical Engineering is offered with specializations in thermal science and mechanical systems; it requires 30 hours of course work. The Master of Science in Medical Physics (M.S.M.P.) degree program is intended to prepare students with a bachelor's degree in science or engineering for productive careers as medical physicists. Students have the choice of a thesis or a nonthesis option in the medical physics curriculum. Both options include seven required courses (21 credit hours) and a clinical rotation (3 credit hours). The thesis option includes an additional 6 credit hours for the preparation of a thesis and the elective for a total of 33 credit hours.

Specific information on admission and degree requirements can be obtained by calling the academic coordinators for each area. Students should call the contact name for additional information.

SPECIAL PROGRAMS

Georgia Tech offers a series of graduate-level credit courses in mechanical engineering (ME) that enable qualified students around the world to earn a Georgia Tech master's degree in ME completely online. Georgia Tech also offers online graduate courses in electrical engineering that can be applied toward master's degrees in this discipline.

All Georgia Tech online graduate courses use state-of-the-art streaming audio and video technologies synchronized with slides, simulations, and other multimedia and make maximum use of the pedagogical advantages offered by Web-based courseware and instruction. Further information about these new online degree programs is available at the Georgia Tech Center for Distance Learning Web site at the address listed below.

A Certificate in Manufacturing provides students with the fundamentals in support of education and research in manufacturing. Each student pursuing the certificate develops knowledge and skills in a particular discipline coupled with a general knowledge of the entire manufacturing enterprise and an ability to work well as a member of a team. The certificate emphasizes the philosophy that it is not possible to educate engineers, managers, or scientists in all aspects of manufacturing. Accordingly, the program is structured to broaden and enhance the education of students who are enrolled in traditional academic disciplines. The program encourages students to develop knowledge in multiple disciplines from class work and experiences in multidisciplinary team activities. Thus, the program balances technical depth with a broad exposure and comprehension of the problems (and potential solutions) facing industry in the manufacturing arena. The Certificate in Manufacturing is obtained as part of a graduate degree program (M.S. or Ph.D.) from the Georgia Institute of Technology. Students must complete a graduate degree to obtain the certificate. The certificate program consists of a set of key courses that are fundamental to manufacturing, from the which the students select 12 semester hours or 18 quarter hours. Students are also required to attend seminars.

CREDIT OPTIONS

Students earn credit toward their degree by registering for and completing courses delivered by videotape. Requirements for each course are the same as for on-campus students enrolled in the course. A student may receive transfer credit of up to 6 hours for graduate-level courses (approved by the academic adviser) taken at an accredited institution in the United States or Canada and not used for credit toward another degree.

FACULTY

There are 746 full-time faculty members at Georgia Tech. Of these, 93 percent hold doctoral degrees. Sixteen percent, or 120 faculty members, teach in the Distance Learning Program.

ADMISSION

Admission requirements vary among the academic disciplines. To apply, individuals should contact the academic adviser or admissions office in the School to which he or she is applying.

TUITION AND FEES

Video enrollment fees for in-state and out-of-state students for the 2004–05 academic year are $706 per credit hour. Fees are subject to change each year. There are no supplemental fees; however, students must purchase their own textbooks.

FINANCIAL AID

There are financial aid programs available through Georgia Tech for distance learning students. Most employers have programs that will help students pay the course fees. The Department of Veterans Affairs has approved the Georgia Tech Video Program as independent study. Georgia Tech has a memorandum of understanding with DANTES and with the Air Force.

APPLYING

Application materials can be obtained from the School to which the student is applying. Applicants must submit an Application for Admission, three letters of recommendation, a biographical sketch, two official transcripts of all previous college work, and scores from the Graduate Record Examinations (GRE). Decisions are made by the individual Schools.

CONTACT

Student Support Services Manager
Center for Distance Learning
Georgia Institute of Technology
Atlanta, Georgia 30308-1031
Telephone: 404-894-3378
Fax: 404-894-8924
Web site: http://www.cdl.gatech.edu/

Grantham University

The College of Engineering and Computer Sciences
The School of Business Administration
The College of Arts and Sciences

Slidell, Louisiana

Information technology has transformed the country's economy and created an enormous demand for expertise in business administration, computer science, and engineering technology. For more than fifty years, Grantham has designed degree programs to meet the needs of working adults and the employers that hire them. Grantham University's courses and degree programs are shaped to ensure that students learn the latest technologies and their underlying fundamental principles. Thousands of students throughout the world have discovered the benefits of the Grantham distance education delivery model.

Established in 1951, Grantham University has earned the distinction of being one of the oldest fully accredited colleges offering distance education in the United States. Recognized as a leading institution of higher learning by graduate schools, global employers, and the United States military, Grantham has matriculated thousands of technology and engineering students from around the world for more than 50 years.

Grantham University is located in Slidell, Louisiana, across Lake Pontchartrain from the old city of New Orleans. Once an area of summer homes and fishing camps, Slidell is now a bustling community that resides near high technology firms like the Stennis Space Center, the new high-tech Naval Support Center, and a local office for the National Weather Service.

Grantham University has always been on the forefront of engineering and computer science academic programs and delivers high quality educational programs. The University is accredited by the Accrediting Commission of the Distance Education and Training Council (DETC), a national accrediting agency recognized by the U.S. Department of Education.

DISTANCE LEARNING PROGRAM

Grantham University's degree programs are offered through distance education, or e-learning, formats. None of the programs require on-campus or in-classroom attendance. Grantham students are not required to log on to the Internet on specific days or at specific times. Grantham students enjoy self-paced, self-directed methods of study and course completion. This unique method of learning is advantageous for those students with full-time jobs or who have family or other commitments that do not allow them to participate in a regular classroom environment. Other students who are attracted to the Grantham model are those who travel extensively or find that the nearest college or university may be hundreds of miles away. Grantham University also attracts thousands of military students who appreciate the benefit of being able to complete classes from anywhere in the world. These military students never have to worry about frequent deployments or transfers because they can take their course work with them and complete it anywhere at anytime.

DELIVERY MEDIA

Grantham utilizes the latest technologies to deliver courses electronically to students in more than twenty-six countries. Students have a special section of Grantham's Internet Web site to access course materials, announcements, e-mails, and grades or to request proctor notices, contact the faculty members and school administration, and more. Online testing and grading provides students with immediate test results to ensure that students can work at their own pace. New students take DE-100, a course designed to help them understand the Grantham distance education/e-learning method of course completion and to inform them of the wide array of services offered by Grantham.

PROGRAMS OF STUDY

Associate and bachelor's degree programs are offered in business administration, computer engineering technology, computer science, electronics engineering technology, engineering management, information systems, and software engineering technology. Master of Business Administration and Master of Science degree programs are offered in information management technology, information management–project management, and information technology.

Each degree program is designed around a semester method of completion. A typical Grantham semester consists of four courses (12 credit hour minimum), and students have eight weeks to complete each course. Students may opt to accelerate the courses and semester using the self-paced, self-directed methods of study.

Students must complete 60 credit hours for an associate degree, of which 15 credit hours must be completed with Grantham. The bachelor's programs require 120–125 credit hours, of which 30 credit hours must be completed with Grantham. The master's degree programs require 36 credit hours of which 27 credit hours must be completed with Grantham.

CREDIT OPTIONS

Grantham accepts transfer of credits from other accredited institutions and military transcripts using the American Council on Education's guidelines. More information about this important benefit is available online at Grantham's Web site listed below.

FACULTY

Grantham's faculty comprises distinguished educators, many of whom have affiliations with renowned schools such as Harvard, MIT, the Wharton School of the University of Pennsylvania, and Stanford University. Grantham's faculty, administration, and board of advisers include prominent scholars and leading business executives who remain active in their professions by consulting, conducting seminars, writing, and operating their own businesses.

ADMISSION

Students wishing to apply to Grantham must have earned a high school diploma or GED equivalent. Foreign students must report their TOEFL score or take the TOEFL test prior to admittance.

TUITION AND FEES

Grantham University's tuition and fees are affordable and competitive. Interested students should contact the Admissions Department or visit Grantham's Web site (listed below) for current tuition rates and fees.

FINANCIAL AID

Grantham University does not offer any government-subsidized financial aid. Grantham-approved institutional lenders include the SLM Financial Corporation, a Sallie Mae company, Key Bank, and Education One, a Bank One company. Prospective students who require financing for tuition and fees may contact Grantham's Admissions Department at the e-mail address listed below for more information about applying for these student loans.

APPLYING

Students may apply to Grantham at any time. Grantham University offers continuous enrollment. Students may apply 24 hours a day, 365 days a year using the school's online enrollment services.

CONTACT

Bill Wells
Director of Admissions
Grantham University
34641 Grantham College Road
Slidell, Louisiana 70460-6815
Telephone: 800-955-2527 (toll-free)
Fax: 985-649-1812 or 4183
E-mail: admissions@grantham.edu
Web site: http://www.grantham.edu

Hibbing Community College

Distance Learning

Hibbing, Minnesota

Hibbing Community College (HCC), a technical and community college, provides excellence in lifelong educational and career opportunities in a responsive learning environment.

Hibbing Community College offers associate degrees that transfer and can be applied as the first two years of a baccalaureate degree, career programs, continuing education classes, and workshops and certificates for updating job skills.

HCC is accredited by the North Central Association of Colleges and is part of the Minnesota State Colleges and Universities System (MnSCU).

Hibbing was one of the first towns in the nation to expand educational opportunities by opening a two-year college in 1916. Thus, Hibbing Community College is one of the oldest two-year colleges in Minnesota and the nation.

Today, HCC serves more than 1,800 students each semester, including more than 500 online students.

DISTANCE LEARNING PROGRAM

Hibbing Community College offers A.A., A.S., and A.A.S. degrees online. Many students take HCC online courses to fulfill the requirements of the Minnesota Transfer Curriculum for the first two years of a baccalaureate degree program. HCC is accredited by the Higher Learning Commission of the North Central Association of Colleges and Schools for both on-site and online degrees. HCC is working hard to meet the needs of students who need to learn anywhere, any time.

DELIVERY MEDIA

HCC's online courses use Desire2Learn software. Students have access through HCC's Web pages and interact with the instructor and other students via e-mail and the Message Center (bulletin board discussion). Some courses require online or other testing at proctored test sites. Student support is exceptional, with staff members on hand for technical help, advisement, or other student services.

PROGRAMS OF STUDY

Students may obtain an associate degree or complete the Minnesota Transfer Curriculum requirements entirely online. A selection of courses within ten Minnesota Transfer Curriculum categories allows students to continue the pursuit of a baccalaureate degree with any of the four-year institutions within the Minnesota State Colleges and Universities system. The Medical Laboratory Technician Program is online; it includes some face-to-face time, but some students have managed to participate from outside the state or even outside the country. The Dental Assisting Program is also delivered online. Other degree programs are expected to follow. Some of the courses include Drawing 1, Introduction to Art, Computer Applications, C++ Programming, UNIX/Linux, Web Authoring, Freshman Composition, Advanced Freshman Composition, Environmental Literature, Ethics, U.S. History to 1877, Native American History, Medical Terminology, Psychology of Adjustment, General Psychology, Fitness Walking, Industrial Safety, Principles of Math, History of the Atomic Bomb, Astronomy, and Sociology. Many new general education and technical courses continue to be added.

SPECIAL PROGRAMS

Hibbing Community College offers customized training to business and corporate clients in many areas. Computer, safety and health, and business courses are the most popular.

STUDENT SERVICES

HCC offers a full range of student services for its online students. All students have access to a free online orientation and are able to use the library services (WebPALS). Interlibrary loan service allows students to obtain any materials available throughout the Minnesota State Colleges and Universities' libraries. Students simply request these materials online by entering their account number.

Registration is entirely online. Application forms are downloadable from the College's Web site. Transcripts are required from other institutions and need to be requested for forwarding to HCC.

Computer services provides support for online students. One e-mail and phone number is used for one-stop assistance with any technical matters.

Financial aid application and support is available online. HCC has a toll-free number for students who may need help with anything that develops. Online students receive the same attention as the residential students.

CREDIT OPTIONS

Credits earned at accredited colleges, technical schools, or universities may be transferred to Hibbing Community College, depending upon the applicability of the credit earned to the student's program. Articulation agreements within Minnesota facilitate smooth transition to HCC programs. Students may transfer all HCC credits to Capella University through a partnership HCC has with that virtual university. HCC also partners with Metro State University, offering two-year and four-year online degrees in business administration. Similar agreements with other institutions are pending.

FACULTY

Hibbing Community College has 65 full-time and 35 part-time faculty members. HCC has state-of-the-art technology and faculty members who are well trained in its use. All online faculty members have received extensive training in online course development and delivery. In addition, HCC has an instructional technology department that provides a high degree of support for faculty members at all times, including during online course delivery. If faculty members cannot answer students' questions about online issues, instructional support is available to solve any problems that arise.

ADMISSION

Hibbing Community College is committed to open admissions. The basic requirement of an applicant is a high school diploma or GED certificate. A person who has neither a high school diploma nor a GED certificate may be admitted if, at the discretion of the College, that person demonstrates potential for being a successful college student. Admission to HCC does not guarantee admission to college-level courses.

Students may contact the direct number for admissions. All online students may contact Counselor Kathy Nucech directly, by telephone at 218-262-6752 or by e-mail at kathleennucech@hcc.mnscu.edu.

For technical support or other information, students may contact Jim Antilla, Director of Instructional Technology (e-mail: jamesantilla@hcc.mnscu.edu), or Shelly McCauley, Instructional Technology Assistant (e-mail: shellymccauley@hcc.mnscu.edu). They may be reached by telephone at 218-263-2970 or 800-224-4422 (toll-free).

TUITION AND FEES

Tuition is $110 per credit for on-site courses and $130 per credit for online courses for 2004–05. Students should check the Web site for updated tuition information. Rates are the same for residents and nonresidents for all online courses.

FINANCIAL AID

Most of the students attending Hibbing Community College, a technical and community college, are eligible for some form of financial aid. While a part of the responsibility for financing a college education will be assumed by the students and/or their parents, HCC helps students explore options to receive aid. Complete information is available on the HCC Web site.

APPLYING

Applications are available online at the HCC Web site. Transcripts are required from previous schools attended. Fees are also due before courses begin. More information is available via the Web site and e-mail.

CONTACT

Admissions
Hibbing Community College
1515 East 25th Street
Hibbing, Minnesota 55746
Telephone: 800-224-4422 (toll-free)
Fax: 218-262-6717
E-mail: admissions@hcc.mnscu.edu
Web site: http://www.hcc.mnscu.edu

Indiana State University

Distance Education Program

Terre Haute, Indiana

Indiana State University is a medium-sized, comprehensive university accredited by the North Central Association of Colleges and Schools. Founded in 1865, the University has grown to serve a student population that includes 12,000 students from all fifty states and eighty-two countries. International students comprise 4 percent of the student population.

Attention to and concern for the individual is reflected in the institution's offerings. Flexible and responsive programs are designed to facilitate student attainment of academic, vocational, and personal goals. Classes are designed to meet the needs of full-time and part-time students. Nondegree study is also available for those seeking personal growth, transferable credit, and enrichment through lifelong learning.

In addition to offering distance programs and courses, the University offers undergraduate and graduate programs in more than 120 areas of study on the Indiana State University campus in Terre Haute, Indiana.

DISTANCE LEARNING PROGRAM

Indiana State University (ISU) has offered distance programs since 1969. Many programs can be completed entirely via distance education; others require minimal campus visits. Selected distance programs and numerous courses can be completed by out-of-state and international students. More than 1,000 students enroll in ISU distance learning courses each semester.

DELIVERY MEDIA

Courses are offered via the Internet, videotapes, correspondence, and live television accessible at sites in Indiana. Television courses offer live, two-way interaction among students and the instructor. Students enrolled in correspondence courses work independently, interacting with their instructor via written communications. Students in Internet courses and some videotape courses interact via e-mail and Internet chat rooms. Equipment requirements depend on course format and may include an Internet-connected computer, VCR, and audio cassette player.

PROGRAMS OF STUDY

Students may complete individual undergraduate or graduate courses; each semester, approximately 200 ISU courses are offered via distance education. In addition, eligible students may complete numerous undergraduate and graduate degrees and professional development programs.

Undergraduate degree programs include an Associate of Science in general aviation flight technology and bachelor degree completion programs in business administration, career and technical education, community health, criminology, electronics technology, industrial technology, human resource development, industrial supervision, insurance, mechanical design technology, and nursing. Undergraduate nondegree programs include basic and advanced certificate programs in corrections, law enforcement, and private security; an endorsement in driver education; and a certification program in library media services.

Graduate degree programs include a doctoral program in technology management and master's programs in criminology, electronics and computer technology, health and safety, human resource development, nursing, and student affairs and higher education. Graduate nondegree programs include an endorsement program in driver education, a licensure program in school administration, and certification programs in public administration and library media services.

SPECIAL PROGRAMS

DegreeLink is a bachelor's degree completion program that enables individuals to transfer previously earned credit to ISU and complete selected bachelor's degrees via distance education. Students may transfer credit earned from Ivy Tech State College, Vincennes University, or another accredited institution.

The Library Media Services Certification Program consists of 27 hours of library and media courses leading to an undergraduate minor and certification or graduate certification in library media services.

The Master of Science in electronics and computer technology program is a minimum of 32 semester hours. The program includes a focus or concentration in instrumentation, systems, and automation.

The Ph.D. in technology management is offered through the School of Technology in cooperation with a consortium of eight other universities. Course work includes a general technology core, a technical specialization, cognate studies, an internship, and a research core and dissertation.

STUDENT SERVICES

Indiana State University offers distance learners a comprehensive package of services, including online registration, academic advisement, a virtual bookstore, library services, technical support, and career counseling. The Office of Distance Support Services offers one-stop assistance to individuals interested in pursuing undergraduate and graduate courses and programs via distance learning.

CREDIT OPTIONS

Students earn credit by registering for and completing semester-based courses offered on campus or via distance learning. In addition, undergraduate students may opt to earn credit via year-based study. Selected programs enable undergraduates to earn credit for prior work experience, by examination, and through portfolios. Graduate students are eligible to transfer selected credit; each department determines the number of hours transferable.

FACULTY

Distance courses are developed and taught by ISU's full-time faculty members. Working with instructional designers and media specialists, faculty members transform on-campus courses to distance formats.

ADMISSION

Admission requirements vary by program of study. For information, prospective students should contact the Office of Distance Support Services.

TUITION AND FEES

Distance learners are eligible for fee waivers that equate to in-state fees. For details, students should visit the Web site at http://indstate.edu/distance.

APPLYING

Individuals may obtain undergraduate and graduate applications, information, and assistance by contacting the Office of Distance Support Services.

CONTACT

Melissa Hughes, Director
Office of Distance Support Education
Indiana State University
Erickson Hall, Room 211
Terre Haute, Indiana 47809
Telephone: 888-237-8080 (toll-free)
Fax: 812-237-8540
E-mail: studentservices@indstate.edu
Web site: http://indstate.edu/distance

Indiana University

School of Continuing Studies

Bloomington, Indiana

Indiana University (IU) was established in 1820 in Bloomington, Indiana. There are now eight IU campuses located throughout the state of Indiana. Indiana University has 116 academic programs ranked in the nation's top twenty. For fall semester 2002, the all-campus enrollment was 98,710 students (graduate and undergraduate).

Indiana University has offered University distance education courses since 1912 and high school distance education courses since 1925. It is accredited by the North Central Association.

DISTANCE LEARNING PROGRAM

The IU Independent Study Program (ISP) is one of the world's largest. It offers more than 195 undergraduate courses by correspondence, more than 100 high school courses by correspondence, and a growing inventory of undergraduate and high school online courses. Each year, it enrolls more than 14,500 students from all fifty states and from twenty-five other countries. The Independent Study Program has won fifty-three course awards from the University Continuing Education Association, more than any other program of its kind.

DELIVERY MEDIA

The IU Independent Study Program courses use such technologies as the World Wide Web, e-mail, electronic learning guides, CD-ROMs, computer software, and audio cassettes and videotapes. Students may interact with their instructors by toll-free phone, e-mail, and the World Wide Web.

PROGRAMS OF STUDY

Through the IU Independent Study Program, students can take individual courses, earn an Indiana University high school diploma, or complete all degree requirements leading to an IU Associate of Arts in general studies (60 credit hours) or an IU Bachelor of General Studies (120 credit hours). Students may now earn both degrees online.

ISP courses are open to all students. In fact, many students at other educational institutions use ISP courses to fulfill degree or diploma requirements at their home institution.

STUDENT SERVICES

Students should visit the IU School of Continuing Studies Web site to find course information and enrollment forms. Students can contact the School from 9 a.m. to 9 p.m EST, Monday through Friday. They can enjoy a one-on-one relationship with their instructors either by phone or e-mail. Students enrolling in Independent Study Program courses receive a free IU e-mail account. Through the IU Bloomington Libraries Distance Education Services, students can obtain a library borrower's card; order books, articles, and other library materials to be delivered by mail; get reference help; and learn how to search library databases.

CREDIT OPTIONS

Students can use a variety of options for earning credit toward their Associate of Arts in general studies and their Bachelor of General Studies. Students who started their college education elsewhere may be able to transfer a considerable number of credits to Indiana University. Other options include credit by examination, credit for self-acquired competency, and military service credit.

Students pursuing the Associate of Arts in general studies must successfully complete at least 15 of the 60 required credit hours at Indiana University or through the IU Independent Study Program. Students pursuing the Bachelor of General Studies degree must successfully complete at least 30 of the 120 required credit hours at Indiana University or through the IU Independent Study Program.

FACULTY

The 2003–04 ISP teaching faculty included 43 high school instructors and 135 University instructors.

ADMISSION

Admission to Indiana University is not required for taking ISP courses. Students need only fill out an enrollment form for the desired courses.

Students wanting to earn an Associate of Arts in general studies or a Bachelor of General Studies must submit an admission application to the General Studies Degree Program office. For more information, students should contact the General Studies Degree Program as listed below.

TUITION AND FEES

Fees are the same for all students, regardless of where they live. The 2003–04 fee for University ISP courses was $120.60 per credit hour. The 2003–04 fee for high school ISP courses was $120 per 1-credit course and $60 per half-credit course. Students seeking admission to the General Studies Degree Program pay a $35 application fee ($55 for international students). Fees are subject to change.

FINANCIAL AID

At this time, Indiana University is unable to administer federal or state financial aid for students pursuing degrees entirely through distance education, including those students enrolled in ISP courses.

APPLYING

There are no residency requirements for enrolling in Independent Study Program courses or applying to the General Studies Degree Program, and no on-campus meetings are required; these programs are open to students worldwide.

CONTACT

Independent Study Program
School of Continuing Studies
Owen Hall 001
Indiana University
790 E. Kirkwood Avenue
Bloomington, Indiana 47405-7101
Telephone: 812-855-2292
800-334-1011 (toll-free)
E-mail: scs@indiana.edu
Web site: http://scs.indiana.edu/guest/peterson s_indepth.html

IWUOnline **Indiana Wesleyan University**

Online Degree Programs—IWUOnline

Marion, Indiana

Founded in 1920, Indiana Wesleyan University (IWU) has become one of the fastest-growing evangelical Christian universities in America. More than 7,000 students are enrolled in seventy locations and in online programs leading to undergraduate and graduate degrees. For more than fifteen years, Indiana Wesleyan University has served the educational needs of working adults through innovative degree programs.

Affiliated with the Wesleyan Church, IWU is a "Christ-centered academic community committed to changing the world by developing students in character, scholarship, and leadership." Indiana Wesleyan University is accredited by the Higher Learning Commission of the North Central Association of Colleges and Schools. Indiana Wesleyan University's Master of Education program is accredited by the National Council for Accreditation of Teacher Education (NCATE). This accreditation covers initial teacher preparation programs and advanced educator preparation programs.

IWUOnline offers degree programs to working adult professionals who must overcome time and geographic barriers in order to obtain a degree. Students can get online any time, day or night, from home, the office, or while traveling.

DISTANCE LEARNING PROGRAM

The curriculum for the online degree programs is built upon IWU's successful site-based programs, which are held in traditional classroom settings. IWU's Christ-centered focus in education integrates proven principles with cutting-edge technology to develop creative and compelling leaders.

Indiana Wesleyan University's online degree programs are convenient. Books and materials are shipped directly to students. There are no campus visits or residencies required. In addition, IWU uses learning teams or cohort groups to keep students motivated and give the support needed to finish the program. Students start the program together as a group and complete the program taking one course at a time in sequence.

DELIVERY MEDIA

IWUOnline offers students a virtual classroom forum to interact with faculty members and fellow working professionals on a broad range of relevant issues. Each workshop within the course has deadlines assigned for classroom activities. IWUOnline students are expected to participate in the online classroom on a regular basis. This includes participation, discussion, submission of regular assignments, and participation in team projects and activities.

IWUOnline utilizes the asynchronous type of learning. This means that online classroom participation is neither time nor place dependent. In other words, students can go online to do assignments and participate in online discussions at times that fit their schedule.

PROGRAMS OF STUDY

IWUOnline offers the following online degree programs: Associate of Science in Business (A.S.B.), Bachelor of Science in Management (B.S.M.), Bachelor of Science in Business Information Systems (B.S.B.I.S.), RN-to-Bachelor of Science in Nursing (RN-B.S.), Master of Business Administration (M.B.A.), Master of Science in Management (M.S.M.), and Master of Education (M.Ed.) as well as special education licensure and undergraduate certificates in religious studies, human services, criminal justice, and communications.

Each online degree program is taught in cohort groups of approximately 14–18 students in a lock-step sequence. Students complete one course at a time in an accelerated format. No campus visits or residencies are required with any of the online degree programs.

The online A.S.B. program consists of 62 credit hours and is completed in approximately twenty-eight months. The online B.S.B.I.S. core program consists of 43 credit hours and is completed in approximately twenty-four months. The online B.S.M. core program consists of 40 credit hours and is completed in approximately twenty months.

The online M.B.A. program consists of 41 credit hours and is competed in approximately twenty-four months. The online M.S.M. program consists of 36 credit hours and is completed in approximately eighteen months. The online M.Ed. core program consists of 30 credit hours and is completed in approximately eighteen months.

The online special education licensure entails 24 credit hours plus field application, meeting the requirements for State of Indiana teaching licensure for exceptional needs–mild intervention. The online certificate programs are 15 credit hours in length and may be taken in conjunction with an associate or bachelor's degree program, or it may stand alone.

STUDENT SERVICES

Since the online degree programs are designed for working adult professionals, IWUOnline strives to make the learning experience as convenient as possible. All textbooks and other study materials are mailed to students prior to each class. IWUOnline also offers off-campus library services to all students completing online degree programs. Students may request copies of articles and other items by e-mail or a toll-free number. Academic advising is provided as well.

CREDIT OPTIONS

Students applying for the bachelor's degree completion programs may transfer at least 60 credits earned from a regionally accredited institution. IWU also awards credit for prior learning and accepts credit earned through CLEP and DANTES tests.

FACULTY

Experienced, well-trained faculty members provide guidance for students as they master the knowledge base and seek to apply what they are learning in their vocational settings. Because of the practitioner focus of the programs, many of the faculty members are full-time professionals who facilitate learning on a part-time basis. All faculty members hold advanced degrees.

ADMISSION

Students who wish to be admitted to the online A.S.B. program must provide proof of high school graduation (or GED certificate) and a minimum of two years of significant full-time work experience beyond high school.

Students who wish to be admitted to one of the bachelor's degree completion programs must have completed at least 60 credit hours of transferable credit obtained at an accredited college or university with a minimum overall grade point average of 2.0. In addition, a minimum of two years of significant full-time work experience beyond high school is required.

Students who wish to be admitted to the online M.B.A. or M.S.M. program must have completed a baccalaureate degree from a regionally accredited college or university with a grade point average of 2.5 and have a minimum of two years of significant full-time work experience. M.B.A. candidates must have prior course work in math, economics, finance, and accounting. For the convenience of those students who have not had prior course work in economics, finance, and accounting, IWUOnline has built prerequisite courses in these areas into the program.

Students who wish to be admitted to the online M.Ed. program must have a baccalaureate degree in education (with some exceptions) from a regionally accredited college or university with a minimum overall grade point average of 2.75, at least one year of full-time teaching experience, and a valid (not necessarily current) teaching license. This program is designed for K–12 teachers who wish to pursue an advanced degree. All degree-seeking candidates in this program need to be actively teaching in a K–12 classroom.

TUITION AND FEES

The total cost of the online degree programs includes all of the following: tuition for the core program, books, and fees. The Associate of Science in Business costs $14,878; the Bachelor of Science in Business Information Systems, $14,926; the Bachelor of Science in Management, $13,791; the Master of Business Administration, $19,908; the Master of Science in Management, $16,088; and the Master of Education, $11,185. The total cost is slightly higher for internationalstudents and those residing in Hawaii and Alaska.

FINANCIAL AID

Indiana Wesleyan University offers a variety of assistance to those students who require financial aid. Through IWU's Financial Aid Office, students receive help in exploring alternatives to financing their education, including installment tuition payment plans, employer reimbursement programs, and student loan programs. In addition to the federal loan programs, undergraduate students may also be eligible for Pell Grants.

APPLYING

Prospective students are asked to complete an application data form and a brief narrative statement. Two recommendation forms are also required. For complete application instructions, students should visit the IWUOnline Web site. Applicants are advised to start the application and financial aid process at least one month prior to the scheduled cohort group start date.

CONTACT

Adult Enrollment Services
College of Adult and Professional Studies
Indiana Wesleyan University
4301 South Washington Street
Marion, Indiana 46953-5279
Telephone: 800-895-0036 (toll-free)
800-234-5327 (toll-free, in Indiana)
Fax: 765-677-2601
E-mail: info@IWUOnline.com
Web site: http://IWUOnline.com
http://www.indwes.edu

Jones College

Distance Learning

Jacksonville, Florida

Founded in Jacksonville in 1918 by Annie Harper Jones, Jones College has been expanded and enriched to meet the needs of a student body pursuing relevant professional education. In 1947 the College was chartered by the State of Florida as a non-profit degree-granting institution. Under this charter, a Board of Trustees governs the College, and all income in excess of operating expenses is devoted to providing better equipment and educational facilities.

Jones College is a senior college accredited by the Accrediting Council for Independent Colleges and Schools (ACICS) to award Associate in Science and Bachelor of Science degrees. ACICS is listed as a nationally recognized accrediting agency by the United States Department of Education. Jones College is also recognized by the Council for Higher Education Accreditation. In addition, Jones College participates in Florida's statewide course numbering system, and all professors teaching in that system hold at least a master's degree.

The Arlington campus of Jones College is centrally located minutes away from downtown Jacksonville, suburban areas, and ocean beaches. The West campus is conveniently located on Edgewood Avenue South at Roosevelt Boulevard. In addition, Jones College maintains a Miami campus in Kendall.

DISTANCE LEARNING PROGRAM

Jones College has an extensive distance learning program through which complete bachelor's and associate degrees may be earned in business administration or computer information systems. Details of all programs are contained in the Jones College catalog that is available at the College Web site.

Jones College distance learning class, which are limited to a maximum of 20 students, are more self-paced than most on-campus classes. For each online class, students should set aside 11 hours per week for such aspects of learning as reading the text and online lessons, completing assignments, participating in chat sessions and threaded discussions, testing, and study and research.

Online classes are virtual classrooms that use Web sites and the Internet. Online classes require more work than on-campus classes, but students can work at the times that are most convenient to them.

The diploma earned in distance learning programs is identical to the diploma earned by students on campus. On a transcript, online classes are identical to on-campus classes.

DELIVERY MEDIA

Jones College students can participate in online courses from almost anywhere on the globe. Online courses access course materials, announcements, and other information, plus a range of online activities that facilitate frequent student-teacher and student-student interaction. Faculty members and students interact via real-time electronic classrooms, online forums using threaded bulletin boards, real-time chat rooms, e-mail, and the Electronic Library. Students submit their assignments online in multimedia formats for review by faculty members. Students can find specific hardware the software requirements at http://www.jones.edu/dl/requirements.htm.

PROGRAMS OF STUDY

The Associate in Science degree program with a business administration major is designed to provide a student with the basic business knowledge necessary to operate a small business; to assume an entry-level managerial, manager trainee, or marketing position; or to provide the student with the knowledge necessary to become promotable into an entry-level managerial position in an already established career field.

The Bachelor of Science degree program with a business administration major is designed to provide the student with the skills necessary to obtain an entry-level position in business administration or to provide a student with the knowledge necessary to become promotable into a managerial position in an already established career field. A core of essential business and general education courses supplements a broadly based sequence of business administration courses and an elective component that permits the student to effectuate an educational program which is consistent with the student's objective.

The Associate in Science degree program with a computer information systems major is designed to provide a student with the basic skills necessary to obtain entry-level employment as a junior programmer, programmer trainee, or other position in the computer information systems industry. The basic sequence of computer information systems courses is supplemented with general education and business offerings that help to ensure the student's productivity and mobility in the business environment.

The Bachelor of Science degree program with a computer information system major provides the combination of business administration course work coupled with computer information systems course work and is designed to provide the student with the skills necessary to obtain an entry level position as a computer programmer, systems analyst, or other position in computer information systems. A core of essential business and general education courses, and an elective component that permits the student to effectuate an educational program that is consistent with the student's objective supplements a comprehensive series of data processing courses.

The specific course requirements for the Associate in Science and Bachelor of Science degree programs can be found at the degree programs tab of the Jones College Web site.

CREDIT OPTIONS

A student must be actively enrolled in Jones College to be eligible to apply for credits through non-traditional means, and all such credits must be awarded prior to the beginning of the student's last semester in school. These non-traditional means include Credit by Examination (maximum of 15 hours), College Level Examination Program (CLEP) (25% of the credit hours for the degree program maximum), Advanced Placement, and non-collegiate training or experience, including military, industrial, or professional training or experience (21 credit hours maximum).

FACULTY

Online classes are moderated by instructors who have the same qualifications as the on-campus instructors. In addition to having the approval of their department head and dean, all of them have master's degrees, with at least 18 master's credits in the field that they teach. To become certified to teach distance learning courses, they also take and pass a distance learning course consisting of six online lessons, complete with assignments, tests, and a grade.

ADMISSION

Graduation from high school with a standard diploma or its equivalent is a prerequisite for admission to Jones College. All applicants must have a preadmission interview conducted in person or by telephone.

TUITION AND FEES

The tuition for all courses is $250 per semester hour, and there is a laboratory fee of $25 for each distance learning course taken.

FINANCIAL AID

Financial assistance in the form of loans and grants is available to qualified students. Any qualified student may apply to attend Jones College regardless of personal financial circumstances. The college makes every possible effort to aid those students who need financial assistance. Students should apply for financial assistance at the same time they apply for admission to Jones College.

APPLYING

Students may apply on the Jones College Web site. They are notified of acceptance immediately after all application and financial aid requirements have been submitted. An online orientation is provided for all distance learning students.

CONTACT

For admissions information, students should contact:
LeAnne C. Osburne, Director of Admissions
Telephone: 800-331-0176, Ext 315 (toll-free)
E-mail: losburne@jones.edu.

For distance learning information, students should contact:
Thomas Clift, Director of Distance Learning
Telephone: 800-331-0176, Ext 134 (toll-free)
E-mail: tclift@jones.edu.

Correspondence should be sent to:
Jones College
5353 Arlington Expressway
Jacksonville, Florida 32211
Telephone: 904-743-122
800-331-0176 (toll-free)
Fax: 904-743-4446
E-mail: info@jones.edu
Web site: http:\\www.jones.edu

Jones International University

Englewood, Colorado

Jones International University (JIU) offers degree programs, certificate programs, and individual courses entirely online. JIU is for students who are serious about receiving a real-world education and don't want to put their lives on hold to obtain it. All programs are based on a widely accepted principle: Students learn best when they gain knowledge that is relevant and applicable to the demands of their careers. That's why the Jones International University programs are skill-based, so students take what they learn in the classroom and put it to use on the job immediately. JIU courses are developed specifically for online delivery by highly respected faculty members from leading universities around the world. The programs offer an exciting option for individuals who are committed to making an investment in their future, enabling their professional success, and tackling the challenges of working in today's rapidly changing business environment.

DISTANCE LEARNING PROGRAM

Jones International University offers all degree programs, certificate programs, and individual courses entirely online. As such, JIU is "the world's university," an international institution that brings together a diverse and rich faculty and student population from more than 70 countries around the globe, creating a community of highly motivated students, business executives, and instructors. This collection of perspectives, cultures, and experiences offers an unprecedented education and global perspective like no other university, from the convenience and comfort of the student's own home.

DELIVERY MEDIA

JIU's courses are conducted entirely online. They take full advantage of the Internet, streaming audio, video, and other emerging technologies to foster communication and skill acquisition. Even the Jones *e*-global Library®, Inc. is entirely online. Students work collaboratively with instructors and classmates using e-mail and asynchronous forums. This international community of learners offers a highly interactive exchange of ideas and experiences for a truly innovative learning experience. Using the Internet, students may learn at home, at work, or even while traveling.

PROGRAMS OF STUDY

JIU's M.B.A. students work both independently and collaboratively with classmates to analyze and resolve real business problems. Students translate business theory into action steps for professional success. JIU offers eight high-demand M.B.A. programs: global enterprise management, health-care management, entrepreneurship, finance, information technology management, negotiation and conflict management, and project management.

Keeping up to speed with emerging e-learning techniques and technologies has never been more challenging. JIU offers three skill-packed e-learning M.Ed. programs: corporate training and knowledge management, technology and design, and generalist studies. Three K–12 education programs are also available: educational leadership and administration; elementary curriculum, assessment, and instruction; and secondary curriculum, assessment, and instruction.

Students in the Master of Arts in business communications degree program master the valuable skills of human communication, emerging communication technologies, and oral and written communication skills. Through this course of study, students learn the tools and expert knowledge that lead to improved workplace performance, creativity, and leadership.

JIU's Bachelor of Arts in business communication degree completion program blends theory and practice for the effective management of communication. This program teaches students the skills that are necessary for creative thinking, innovation, entrepreneurship, and leadership.

Jones International University also offers a Bachelor of Business Administration program, which helps students to acquire a keen understanding of the methods and strategies used by businesses in today's marketplace as they implement technology to meet their goals.

SPECIAL PROGRAMS

JIU offers more than fifty Certificate programs, ranging from corporate financial management to team strategy. These focused programs are ideal for students who want to explore a new area of interest or sharply hone their skills for increased success in a targeted area of business. Students receive an outstanding education while taking advantage of the convenience, quality, and cost efficiency of online learning. Credits earned in these programs can be transferred toward the completion of a JIU degree program. Students can get the education they need to maintain their edge in today's rapidly changing marketplace in diverse programs such as entrepreneurship, information technology management, project management, using the Internet in public relations, financial management in the digital age, managing the global enterprise, health-care administration, cyber marketing, and facilitating online learning.

STUDENT SERVICES

Students purchase textbooks through JIU's online bookstore and use the Jones *e*-global Library®, a Web-based library, to access reference resources and other support materials online. Student advisers provide academic guidance to students, including establishing academic and career goals. JIU offers technical assistance for issues relating to the JIU Web site and courses 24 hours a day, seven days a week.

CREDIT OPTIONS

Students in the bachelor's programs may transfer up to 90 credits that they have earned through other regionally accredited institutions toward their JIU degree. Students in JIU's master's programs may transfer up to 9 credits earned through regionally accredited institutions toward their degree. JIU also awards credit for prior learning and accepts credit earned through AP, CLEP, and DANTES tests.

FACULTY

JIU has 6 full-time faculty members and approximately 100 part-time faculty members. Eighty-seven percent of the faculty members hold doctorates.

ADMISSION

Students seeking admission to JIU's degree programs must submit a completed application package, including a nonrefundable $50 application fee, a resume, official transcripts from all colleges previously attended, and an application form.

TUITION AND FEES

Tuition for 3-credit courses at the bachelor's level is $960. Tuition for 3-credit courses in Master of Education program is $1250, and $1500 for a 3-credit course in the M.B.A. or Master of Arts in business communication programs. An application fee and a per-course technology fee may also apply.

FINANCIAL AID

JIU makes every effort to make education an achievable goal for its students. As a result, the University has aligned itself with organizations and agencies in order to make various financial aid options available.

JIU offers its students access to federal student aid. These loan and grant programs allow qualified students to take advantage of need- and non-need-based funds to help them finance their educations. Other options for financing include SLM Financial Loans and P.L.A.T.O. Loans, which are available to U.S. citizens and U.S. national or permanent residents who have demonstrated creditworthiness; corporate tuition assistance; VA benefits; JUI's special program for military personnel; and scholarships.

APPLYING

Admission applications are accepted on a continual basis throughout the year. Courses start every month, and students may begin courses before their applications are complete. Course orientation is available at all times, entirely online.

CONTACT

Jones International University
9697 East Mineral Avenue
Englewood, Colorado 80112
Telephone: 303-784-8904
800-811-5663 (toll-free, U.S. and Canada)
Fax: 303-799-0966
E-mail: info@international.edu
Web site: http://www.jonesinternational.edu

Kansas State University

Division of Continuing Education Distance Education

Manhattan, Kansas

Kansas State University (K-State) was founded on February 16, 1863, as a land-grant institution under the Morrill Act. Originally located on the grounds of the old Bluemont Central College, which was chartered in 1858, the University was moved to its present site in 1875.

The 664-acre campus is in Manhattan, 125 miles west of Kansas City, via Interstate 70, in the rolling Flint Hills of northeast Kansas. The Salina campus, 70 miles west of Manhattan, was established through a merger of the former Kansas College of Technology with the University. This was made possible by an enactment of the 1991 Kansas Legislature.

K-State is accredited by the North Central Association of Colleges and Schools (NCA). One of the six universities governed by the Kansas Board of Regents, Kansas State University continues to fulfill its historic educational mission in teaching, research, and public service.

DISTANCE LEARNING PROGRAM

Kansas State University innovatively offers high-quality courses and degree programs to students who are not geographically located near the Manhattan campus. K-State utilizes cutting-edge technologies that enhance the learning environment and extend it far beyond the University's physical boundaries.

Adults across the country want to complete their education, advance their careers, or change their professions. Success requires dedication, self-direction, and perseverance on the part of the student. Distance education offered by K-State provides people with an opportunity to pursue these goals without leaving a current job or family. K-State offers bachelor's degrees, master's degrees, and certificate programs at a distance.

DELIVERY MEDIA

K-State offers courses through a variety of delivery methods. Most courses follow regular K-State semester dates. Some courses require minimum computer system requirements. Kansas State University offers more than 250 courses per year through distance education. Courses are offered in a variety of subject areas, and students can take many of these without enrolling in a degree program.

Delivery methods include use of videotapes and audiotapes, the Web, listservs, e-mail, discussion rooms, guided study, desktop video, community-based outreach courses, independent study, correspondence course work with other institutions, military training credit evaluations (based on American Council for Education Guidelines), portfolio/experiential credit assessments, standardized test taking, credit by examination and competency assessments, and petitions for special exams.

PROGRAMS OF STUDY

K-State has been offering degree completion programs through distance education for more than thirty years. The goal of the Distance Education Degree Completion Programs is to help students complete the last two years of a Bachelor of Science degree. K-State staff is available to help students get started, stay directed, and earn a Bachelor of Science degree.

A student's requirements include a minimum of 30 K-State hours, with 20 of the last 30 hours earned from K-State. Students may transfer a maximum of 60 credit hours to K-State from other institutions. The average student completes a bachelor's degree in two to six years; the pace is up to the student.

Bachelor's degree completion programs are offered in animal sciences and industry, general business, food science and industry, interdisciplinary social science, early childhood education (limited to Kansas), and dietetics.

Master's degree programs offered include agribusiness, industrial/organizational psychology, personal financial planning, electrical engineering, civil engineering, chemical engineering, software engineering, engineering management, and food science.

SPECIAL PROGRAMS

Certificate/endorsement programs are also offered. These programs include a food science certificate program, a personal financial planning certificate program, an occupational health certificate program, and an early childhood education credential.

K-State is a member of Service Members Opportunity College for the SOCAD-2 flexible-degree network. This network guarantees worldwide transfer of credit for military personnel who take courses from participating colleges and universities.

STUDENT SERVICES

Students in degree programs receive advising from the college offering the degree. The Division of Continuing

Education also has Program Coordinators for each college, who can provide assistance.

Library services are available to students enrolled in degree completion programs. A K-State library services facilitator helps students access materials in the K-State library.

Financial aid is available for students seeking degrees. Scholarships are also available.

The technical support help desk can provide a variety of technical support services once a student is enrolled in a distance education course and has paid the media fee.

For information about all the student services, students should visit the Student Services Web site at http://www.dce.ksu.edu/studentservices.

FACULTY

Kansas State University is an accredited institution offering credit courses through distance education. Distance education courses are taught by faculty members who teach K-State on-campus courses.

ADMISSION

Each distance education degree program has specific admission requirements and procedures. Bachelor's degree completion programs require an application fee of $60. Admission information is available for each program at the Web address listed below.

TUITION AND FEES

Distance education tuition at K-State is the same for both in-state and out-of-state students. Tuition is the cost for an academic course and includes a per-credit-hour charge. It may also include additional tuition components. Tuition components include student services, TELENET 2 media fee, engineering equipment and maintenance, licensing, tape/Web media, and distance education support.

FINANCIAL AID

Students may be eligible for financial aid for distance education courses if federal requirements are met, they are admitted and enrolled in a degree program in Kansas State University, and they are enrolled in a minimum of 6 credit hours of Kansas State University course work. Each student is assigned a financial aid adviser.

Scholarships are also available to students enrolled in degree programs.

APPLYING

The application process for each program varies. For complete information on a specific program, students can access the Web site listed below or contact the Division of Continuing Education at 785-532-5687 or at the toll-free number listed below, or by e-mail at the address listed below.

CONTACT

Division of Continuing Education
Kansas State University
13 College Court Building
Manhattan, Kansas 66506-6002
Telephone: 785-532-5575
800-622-2KSU (toll-free)
Fax: 785-532-5637
E-mail: degrees@dce.ksu.edu
Web site: http://www.dce.ksu.edu/distance

Keiser College

Keiser College eCampus

Fort Lauderdale, Florida

For more than twenty-five years, Keiser College has provided high-quality career education and now offers degree programs online to prepare students for high-demand professions. Associate and bachelor's degrees are offered with a student-centered approach and curriculum that is in pace with technology and workforce demand trends.

Keiser College is accredited by the Commission on Colleges of the Southern Association of Colleges and Schools (1866 Southern Lane, Decatur, Georgia 30033-4097; telephone 404-679-4501) to award the associate and bachelor's degrees.

Keiser College eCampus offers degrees in fields that are in high demand and provides job placement assistance to all its students and alumni. The College researches trends for growing fields and tailors its curriculum to prepare students for entry into rewarding careers.

DISTANCE LEARNING PROGRAM

Online learning is not impersonal at Keiser College eCampus. From admissions to faculty, Keiser College eCampus staff members are dedicated to superior student care accomplished through accessible staff and faculty members who foster a student-centered learning community, state-of-the-practice online classroom technology and user-friendly format to enhance learning, a one-class-at-a-time approach that allows busy students to focus on their education and develop the skills to excel, and extensive online resources that include information and access to all student services.

DELIVERY MEDIA

Technical requirements are listed on the Web site at http://keisercollege.org/D1index.real?area=66.

PROGRAMS OF STUDY

Keiser College eCampus is a fully online education campus. Students interact with their instructors and each other using advanced technology, from anywhere at anytime.

Bachelor's degrees online are offered in business administration (B.A.) and in management information systems (MIS; B.S.). Associate degrees online are offered in accounting, business administration, computer networking and security management, criminal justice, health services administration, medical assistant studies, and paralegal studies.

All online students must log in at least three times a week and actively participate in class. Each student must maintain satisfactory progress. Students must maintain at least a C average or better during each grading period.

STUDENT SERVICES

Keiser College online programs are Web-based courses, designed by qualified faculty and staff members to create an interesting and interactive learning environment. Keiser's virtual classroom is comfortable, and courses can be taken easily by anyone with access to the World Wide Web. Lesson plans, assignments, and class schedules are posted online, while student-teacher interaction and student-student interaction also occur over the Internet. Scheduled discussions, e-mail messages, live chats, and real-time group discussions are a few of the opportunities for interacting during an online course.

Online students have access to all Keiser College resources, from the bookstore to on-campus libraries. In addition, online access to information and services includes application, enrollment and registration procedures, financial aid information, tuition and fee information, course schedules and outlines, course demonstrations, faculty information, and an e-mail directory. Online students also have access to online academic advising and technical support through e-mail or telephone.

CREDIT OPTIONS

Credit for courses or degrees completed at another institution by students enrolling at Keiser College are subject to approval by the Dean of Academic Affairs. These courses or degrees must be similar in content and duration to those offered in the program for which the student has applied. The Dean of Academic Affairs considers only official transcripts mailed directly to Keiser College. Students are responsible for having official transcripts sent to Keiser College from their transfer institutions. Keiser College requires that, as a minimum, the student must complete the last 25 percent of credits in a program of study at the College. All transfer students are informed in writing of any credits accepted as transferable. Preliminary notification is presented, in most cases, prior to enrollment, but in no case, later than the end of the transfer student's first semester.

FACULTY

Keiser College has 70 online instructors, 17 of whom are full-time. Fifteen faculty members have doctoral degrees.

ADMISSION

In order to be considered for enrollment at Keiser College, all applicants must supply verification of high school graduation (such as a transcript or diploma), verification of GED completion (GED scores or GED diploma), or proof of graduation from an international institution comparable to a U.S. secondary school.

Home schooled applicants who have a high school diploma are also considered for admission. Home schooled applicants should present their SAT or ACT scores with their application.

Students should make arrangements to take Keiser College's entrance examination (administered at the College) or provide results of their SAT or ACT exam. The College requirements for admission are a combined score of 800 on the SAT and a composite score of 17 on the ACT. In addition, students in Keiser College's medical programs must sign a Statement of Good Health prior to entrance into the program.

Keiser College is proud of the international character of its student body and welcomes students from other nations. All international students must be fluent in English before they enroll. Applicants must furnish proof that they can read, write, and speak English fluently. Keiser College has been approved by the United States Department of Immigration for students to pursue their studies at any of the College's nine campuses. The College can accept only F-1 visas based upon the student's program of study. International student applicants must meet the following requirements for admission to Keiser College: successful completion of a secondary school program that is equivalent to high school in the U.S., certification of financial ability to meet tuition and other necessary expenses or ability to qualify for financial aid as an eligible noncitizen, and the required minimum TOEFL score of 500 on the paper-based test or 225 on the computer-based test if the primary language is not English.

Applications for international students can be obtained through the Admissions Office. Students should apply at least two months prior to the start of the program.

TUITION AND FEES

Costs for 2003–04 were $1265 per course, plus educational fees of $100 per month and approximately $150 per course for books.

FINANCIAL AID

Keiser College offers a number of financial aid programs to its students, including Federal Pell Grants, Federal Supplemental Educational Opportunity Grants (FSEOG), Keiser College Academic Scholarships, Federal Stafford Student Loans, Federal PLUS Loans, and Federal Perkins Loans.

APPLYING

Applications are accepted on an ongoing basis and can be accessed online at the College Web site.

CONTACT

Susan Ziegelhofer
Vice President of Admissions
Keiser College eCampus
1500 Northwest 49th Street
Fort Lauderdale, Florida 33309
Telephone: 954-351-4040
866-KEISER-1 (toll-free)
E-mail: admissions@keisercollege.edu
Web site: http://online.keisercollege.edu

Kent State University

Department of Political Science
Master of Public Administration Program

Kent, Ohio

Kent State University is Ohio's second-largest university, with more than 34,000 students located on eight campuses. The University is one of ninety colleges and universities in the country to earn the Carnegie Foundation's designation of Doctoral/Research University–Extensive. Kent State is also a national leader in the use of educational technology, ranking among Yahoo's Most Wired Colleges five years in a row (thirty-first in 2001). The University is accredited by the Higher Learning Commission and is a member of the North Central Association. The Master of Public Administration (M.P.A.) degree is fully accredited by the National Association of Schools of Public Affairs and Administration, and is one of only a handful of programs with such accreditation to offer an online degree.

DISTANCE LEARNING PROGRAM

The M.P.A. program provides an advanced online degree for students pursuing management careers in the public or nonprofit sectors. Current students include individuals already working in the field who are seeking professional advancement, and those who wish to establish themselves in such a career. The Web-based program follows the same requirements as the traditional degree program but is designed to be more convenient and accessible for students who are balancing multiple responsibilities or are beyond commuting distance from the campus. Kent State also welcomes individuals with physical disabilities, and has expertise in the use of a variety of adaptive technologies for making Web courses accessible. The small size of the program (about 50 students) permits personal attention in terms of advising and student-instructor interaction. The program is housed in the Department of Political Science, which also has an M.A./Ph.D. program in public policy.

DELIVERY MEDIA

The Kent M.P.A. online degree program incorporates the latest state-of-the-art methods of delivery. In addition to the asynchronous methods used in most online programs (such as lectures posted on the Web site), the Kent M.P.A. program has synchronous features that allow students to participate in live sessions from their homes, with real-time audio-conferencing, an electronic blackboard, document sharing, and a Web browser that students and instructor can use and view simultaneously. Streaming video is also available, and live sessions are recorded for later use.

The Kent M.P.A. online degree program is distinctive because it is specifically designed to comply with federal ADA/Section 508 requirements to accommodate persons with various physical disabilities. Assistive technology is available throughout the program for students with disabilities who live in northeast Ohio. Prospective students should contact the M.P.A. coordinator for further information.

PROGRAM OF STUDY

All core courses for the M.P.A. program are available online and a number of electives are also available on the Web. The required 45 credit hours for the degree consist of ten core courses (30 hours), three electives (9 hours), and an internship or final project (6 hours). For those who choose electives not available online, some or all of the electives may be transferred from other accredited institutions, subject to approval by the department and the University.

Core courses include administrative theory and leadership, budgeting, critical issues, management information systems, methods, program evaluation, public finance, public management concepts, public personnel management, and strategic planning.

Elective courses may be individually chosen with the approval of an adviser, or may be taken from designated courses in one of five areas of concentration: budgeting and finance, municipal management, nonprofit management, nursing management, and public safety. Students can also customize their electives by selecting courses across or outside these areas of concentration.

The internship or final project requires students to use the skills they have learned in course work. Students who are already working in the field develop a project and write a final paper in consultation with an adviser and their present employer. Those who are currently not working in a public or nonprofit sector job are placed in an internship and required to write a related paper, unless alternative arrangements are made for completion of the final project.

SPECIAL PROGRAMS

The Kent M.P.A. program is a contractor with the state of Ohio Department of Human Services (ODHS). Current ODHS employees are eligible for tuition reimbursement through the TOPS program.

A joint Master of Science of Nursing/Master of Public Administration is also available online, and more information about this program is available from the M.P.A. coordinator.

STUDENT SERVICES

A University help desk is available to provide technical assistance via telephone and the Internet.

Course materials are available online through the library's electronic reserves system.

All students have library privileges for Kent's eight campuses and Ohiolink, a statewide consortium of university libraries. Kentlink and Ohiolink feature a number of research databases and electronic journals. For more information on the library and Ohiolink, students may visit the Web at http://library.kent.edu. Reference librarians are available online and via telephone seven days a week and during extended hours.

Web for Students provides real-time access to admission, financial aid, and tuition-payment transactions.

Academic advising and career placement are available to all students, although job placement information and internships are most plentiful for northeast Ohio.

CREDIT OPTIONS

Students may transfer up to 12 graduate credit hours from other accredited institutions, upon approval from the department and the University. Credits must be no more than six years old at the time the M.P.A. degree is conferred, and a grade of B or better is required.

Nondegree options are available for students who wish to take a few graduate courses. If nondegree students decide to enter the M.P.A. program later, they may request that up to 12 hours of credit be applied toward the degree.

FACULTY

Five full-time and 4 part-time faculty members teach courses in the online M.P.A. program. Five of the online instructors have doctorates, 1 is a Juris Doctor, and the remaining 3 have other graduate degrees. Both full-time and part-time faculty members have experience working in public and nonprofit sector agencies.

ADMISSION

Kent's M.P.A. program requires a minimum GPA of 2.75 and scores of 450 or better on all sections of the GRE. Conditional admission is considered under some circumstances. The admission decision is based on an overall view of the applicant's experience, goals, motivation, skills, academic record, and test scores. For students from non-English speaking countries, a TOEFL score of at least 525 on the paper-based exam is required (197 on the computer-based exam).

TUITION AND FEES

Current tuition is $334 per graduate credit hour for Ohio residents, and $627 per graduate credit hour for nonresidents. Because tuition is subject to change, applicants should consult the University's Web site at http://www.kent.edu for the latest information.

FINANCIAL AID

A limited number of graduate assistantships are available in the M.P.A. program, and are awarded competitively. Distance learning students are eligible if they can attend as full-time students and work 20 hours a week on campus. Students may be eligible for other financial aid, including grants and loans. For more information, applicants should consult the University's financial aid Web site at http://www.sfa.kent.edu. Installment payment plans are also available through the bursar's office.

APPLYING

Applicants are required to submit an application (available online at the Web site listed in the Contact section; click on the Application and Admission selection) along with a $30 fee. Admission decisions are based on the applicant's transcripts, GRE scores, letters of recommendation, writing sample, and letter of intent (including the student's goals and background). Information about admission for international students can be found on the Web at http://www.admissions.kent.edu. The University requires that applications be submitted at least six weeks prior to the beginning of the semester, but students are strongly encouraged to submit applications earlier.

At the beginning of each semester, the department provides an on-campus orientation for new M.P.A. students, so that they become familiar with available services and expectations for graduate study. The orientation includes an introduction to the technology and Web site used in the online program. Alternative arrangements can be made for those who are unable to make it to the orientation, although students are strongly urged to attend.

Students who would like more information about whether online courses are appropriate for them can consult the questionnaire on the Web at http://dl.kent.edu/students/eval. For further information on admissions, curriculum, and other topics, prospective students should contact the M.P.A. coordinator or visit the M.P.A. program home page at the Web site listed below.

CONTACT

Karen Mossberger, Ph.D.
M.P.A. Coordinator
Department of Political Science
302 Bowman Hall
Kent State University
Kent, Ohio 44242
Telephone: 330-672-8942 or 2060
Fax: 330-672-3362
E-mail: kmossber@kent.edu
Web site: http://dept.kent.edu/mpa

Kettering University

Graduate Studies Department

Flint, Michigan

In 1919, the Industrial Fellowship League of Flint sponsored a night school for employees of Flint-area industries. General Motors Corporation agreed to underwrite the school in 1926, and General Motors Institute was born. In 1982, GMI became independent of General Motors when the private corporation "GMI Engineering and Management Institute" was established. In January 1998, GMI changed its name to Kettering University. Kettering continues to maintain a close affiliation with industry, as it has throughout its history.

In fall 1982, Kettering began a video-based distance learning graduate program leading to a Master of Science in Manufacturing Management degree. In 1990, the Master of Science in Engineering degree was initiated.

Kettering's mission is to serve society by preparing leaders to meet the technical and managerial needs of business and industry in both the public and private sectors. World renowned as America's Co-op College, Kettering focuses on practice rather than theory. Continuing the University's long and continuous association with industry and the working student, the Master of Science degrees have a strong orientation toward manufacturing. Kettering is accredited by the Commission on Institutions of Higher Education of the North Central Association of Colleges and Schools.

DISTANCE LEARNING PROGRAM

Offering flexibility and convenience, these programs were developed to fit the needs of working professionals. The educational process consists of the on-campus presentation, off-campus communication of the courses via videotape, CD-ROM, videostreamed lectures over the Internet, Web-enabled courses, and other methods. Students can reach professors by e-mail, fax, and/or telephone.

The video-based program is offered at host companies where the number of prospective students is sufficient, or on an individual basis. The video-based distance learning program serves more than 1,300 students at host companies throughout the United States, Canada, Mexico, and Europe. The program, however, is not a correspondence course. It is a rigorous, bona fide accredited graduate program.

DELIVERY MEDIA

Kettering's distance learning programs are offered through videotape, CD-ROM, or Internet video streaming. Students have telephone, facsimile, and e-mail access to the professors. A regular schedule of telephone communication is established in the first session of each course. For some courses, students may need access to a personal computer for homework.

PROGRAMS OF STUDY

Kettering offers a Master of Science in Manufacturing Management (M.S.M.M.) degree and a Master of Science in Operations Management (M.S.O.M.) degree. Each of these degree programs require 40 credit hours. Also, Kettering offers a Master of Science in Manufacturing Operations (M.S.M.O.) degree program that requires 40 credit hours. In addition, the Master of Science in Engineering (M.S.Eng.) programs require 40 credit hours, with concentrations in engineering management, manufacturing engineering, mechanical design, or mechanical-CAE simulation. The newest degree program is the Master of Science in Information Technology (M.S.I.T.) degree. This degree program is also 40 credit hours in length.

The University designed the Master of Science programs to be terminal professional degrees for engineers and managers. The programs are particularly attractive to working professionals who want to extend and broaden their related skills. Although designed as terminal degrees, they also provide preparation for study at the doctoral level.

The degrees can be completed in as few as fifteen months. However, students have up to six years to complete the degree requirements.

The M.S.M.M. program focuses on areas of study such as finance and economics; quantitative skills and computer applications; management and administration; and manufacturing engineering. The M.S.O.M. combines the core areas of business administration with systems and process engineering skills from the engineering disciplines. The M.S.M.O. degree takes a technical approach to the operational manager's role in a manufacturing environment. The M.S.I.T. program teaches the skills necessary to succeed in the rapidly changing technological age.

CREDIT OPTIONS

Credits are earned by completing courses; however, students may transfer up to 8 credit hours. Credit may be transferred for grades of B or better upon the recommendation of the candidate's adviser and is granted only for completed graduate study. Credit is not given for experience.

Anyone interested in transfer credit should obtain an application for transfer credit from the Graduate Office.

FACULTY

There are 41 full- and part-time professors teaching in the Graduate Studies program. Ninety-seven percent of the faculty members have doctoral or other terminal academic degrees.

ADMISSION

No one is accepted into the program without a bachelor's degree. A bachelor's degree in engineering from an ABET-accredited institution is required for the Master of Science in Engineering degree program. Requirements include a minimum 3.0 grade point average in undergraduate work and two supervisor recommendations. The same requirements apply to on-campus and distance learning students.

TUITION AND FEES

In 2004–05, graduate tuition is $562 per credit hour. There are no application or registration fees for U.S. applicants. There is a $50 application fee for international applicants.

APPLYING

Application deadlines are as follows: for fall 2004, September 3; for winter 2005, November 26; and for spring 2005, March 4.

CONTACT

Office of Graduate Studies
Kettering University
1700 West Third Avenue
Flint, Michigan 48504-4898
Telephone: 866-KU GRADS (866-584-7237) (toll-free)
Fax: 810-762-9935
E-mail: gradoff@kettering.edu
Web site: http://www.kettering.edu/graduate

Lakeland College

Lakeland College Online

Sheboygan, Wisconsin

Lakeland College, an independent four-year liberal arts institution in Sheboygan, Wisconsin, was founded in 1862 to provide higher education opportunities for Wisconsin's new frontiersmen. Lakeland became an early adopter of the distance learning concept when, in 1978, it established its first lifelong learning satellite campus. This program has since grown to include ten locations throughout Wisconsin. In 1997, continuing its innovation in education, Lakeland became a world leader in online education and one of the few fully accredited colleges and universities nationwide that offer full bachelor's degrees totally online.

Located about 50 miles north of Milwaukee, Lakeland has an enrollment of more than 4,000 students in its on-campus undergraduate and graduate, lifelong learning, international, and electronically delivered online programs. All Lakeland courses and programs are fully accredited by the North Central Association of Colleges and Schools.

DISTANCE LEARNING PROGRAM

Lakeland offers complete bachelor's degrees in five majors. Courses are conducted online from start to finish, including all prerequisites, and are delivered entirely at each student's convenience. The same fully accredited courses and degrees as those offered on-site are available. More than 1,000 students from across the country and overseas register annually. Master's degrees are also available online. Students should contact one of Lakeland's counselors for more information.

DELIVERY MEDIA

Through national online educational services provider and leader eCollege.com, Lakeland College Online uses a Web-based platform that allows students to participate in an online system orientation and to communicate at their convenience with the College, faculty members, and fellow students. Minimum hardware requirements are an IBM or 100 percent–compatible computer with a Pentium processor and 32 mb RAM, a 150-meg hard drive, and a 56k modem. Recommended specifications are a Pentium II–class computer (200 MHz or higher) with 128 mb RAM; Windows 95, 98, or NT; and a 10-gig hard drive. As the course delivery software is Web-based and requires students to spend significant amounts of time online, a dedicated modem or high-speed (DSL or cable modem) Internet access are recommended.

PROGRAM OF STUDY

Each online course is 4 credits, and each program of study requires students to complete a minimum of 128 credits. Lakeland accepts many transfer credits from other schools. The business administration major encompasses the coordination, implementation, promotion, supervision, and direction of activities of organizations and individuals. Students who wish to be generalists in business find that this program meets their needs. The accounting program prepares students for positions in business and industry. Graduates who have completed the accounting major and a few additional courses are qualified to sit for the CPA and CMA examinations. The computer science program offers a sound basis for careers in information technology, business applications programming, and systems analysis. The marketing major explores consumers' needs and desires for products and services and their willingness to pay for them. Students are prepared for a wide variety of tasks in diverse areas. The specialized administration major is available to students who wish to complete a bachelor's degree after having completed an associate degree in certain technical fields.

SPECIAL PROGRAMS

Lakeland is accredited to offer an online bachelor's degree in specialized administration that is available only to students with associate degrees in a technical field.

STUDENT SERVICES

Lakeland College Online students can do all of the following online: apply for admission, register for classes, participate in chat groups, work with a personal admission counselor for academic advising, and access the Lakeland bookstore and library. Ordering textbooks online is encouraged.

CREDIT OPTIONS

Online courses are 4 credits each. Online students may enroll in three courses without being accepted for admission. Students seeking a degree must be accepted for admission. Degree programs have a minimum requirement of 128 credits.

Lakeland accepts credits transferred from most other regionally accredited schools. Credits earned in the online program can be combined with credits earned on campus to complete a degree.

FACULTY

Lakeland College Online courses are taught by both on-campus instructors and adjunct faculty members. Of the current online faculty members, 85 percent hold advanced academic degrees in their chosen discipline.

ADMISSION

Students must have a high school diploma or its equivalent. They can take three courses before applying for admission. International students must apply for admission before taking classes. Nonnative speakers of English must have a minimum TOEFL score of 500.

TUITION AND FEES

All students pay a $35 application fee. Tuition for all online courses is $850 per 4-credit undergraduate course. Books and other materials (computer course software or other required resources) are additional. Graduate program tuition varies by program.

FINANCIAL AID

Financial aid and/or military benefits are available to any qualifying student who is enrolled part-time (taking at least two courses) or full-time if they have already been accepted to Lakeland.

APPLYING

Applications are available by visiting the College's Web site at http://www.lakeland.edu or calling toll-free at 800-569-2166. Students are asked to submit their application, nonrefundable application fee, and high school and postsecondary school transcripts. Students are notified of acceptance by the Registrar's Office. System orientation is offered completely online.

CONTACT

Carol Butzen
Online Academic Counselor
Lakeland College Online
P.O. Box 359
Sheboygan, Wisconsin 53082-0359
Telephone: 800-569-2166 Ext. 1259 (toll-free)
Fax: 920-565-1341
E-mail: butzencl@lakeland.edu
Web site: http://www.lakeland.edu/online

Kris Eggebeen
Online Academic Counselor
Lakeland College Online
P.O. Box 359
Sheboygan, Wisconsin 53082-0359
Telephone: 800-569-2166 Ext. 1586 (toll-free)
Fax: 920-565-1341
E-mail: eggebeenkl@lakeland.edu
Web site: http://www.lakeland.edu/online

Liberty University

Distance Learning Program

Lynchburg, Virginia

Liberty University (LU) was founded in 1971 as a private, independent, Christian, comprehensive institution. Since then, Liberty has grown to an enrollment of almost 15,000 students through its various undergraduate and graduate divisions, the Liberty Baptist Theological Seminary, the Distance Learning Program, and the Liberty Bible Institute. Liberty University is accredited by the Commission on Colleges of the Southern Association of Colleges and Schools to award associate, baccalaureate, master's, and doctoral degrees.

DISTANCE LEARNING PROGRAM

Liberty University offers students the opportunity to pursue an accredited college degree at a distance on the associate, baccalaureate, master's, and doctoral levels. The University assists students who are pursuing a degree with such services as transcript evaluation, academic advising, and degree planning. Flexible semesters allow course work to begin at the most convenient times for students. Courses start every three weeks, and students have 120 days to complete each course.

DELIVERY MEDIA

Course lectures are presented online; through prerecorded VHS videocassettes that students purchase along with the required print materials, such as books, workbooks, and study notes (all class materials are required to complete each class); and in on-campus intensives. Testing is monitored by a University-approved proctor. Students in need of class assistance may contact the assigned academic adviser, a faculty member, and library services via phone, fax, e-mail, or regular mail. No residency is required for associate or baccalaureate degree programs. Graduate programs have minimal residency requirements offered in flexible formats.

PROGRAMS OF STUDY

Liberty University's Distance Learning Program offers associate degrees in general studies and religion. Baccalaureate degrees are offered in business (accounting, finance, and management), multidisciplinary studies, psychology, and religion. Students may pursue a master's degree in professional counseling. A 30-credit-hour human relations track, a 48-credit-hour certification track, and a 60-credit-hour certification track are available. Other master's degrees include the Master of Arts in religion, the Master of Divinity, the Master of Business Administration, and the Master of Education (M.Ed.). The M.Ed. programs are approved by the Virginia Department of Education for the licensure of school personnel. The LU School of Education also offers the Education Specialist (Ed.S.) and Doctor of Education (Ed.D.), with an emphasis in educational leadership.

SPECIAL PROGRAMS

Distance learners have access to library services, the campus computer network, e-mail services, academic advising, tutoring, and career placement assistance.

CREDIT OPTIONS

Credit is given for courses completed at an accredited institution, provided the credit is appropriate to the curriculum chosen at Liberty University. Undergraduate students may also earn credit through standardized testing (CLEP, PEP, DANTES, and ICE), advanced placement, portfolio assessment, military training (ACE), and business training.

FACULTY

There are 181 full-time and 113 part-time faculty members at Liberty University. Of the 181 full-time faculty members, 63 work specifically for the Distance Learning Program in either a full-time or part-time capacity. Faculty members who work with the Distance Learning Program hold a master's, doctorate, or other terminal degree in their field of specialty and are specially trained in order to ensure the best-quality education possible for students.

ADMISSION

An application with a $35 nonrefundable fee must be submitted prior to admittance. All official transcripts must be sent to the Office of Distance Learning Admissions to determine acceptance to a degree program and the evaluation of credit.

TUITION AND FEES

For the 2004–05 academic year, tuition for the undergraduate programs is $190 per semester hour. Graduate tuition is as follows: $300 per semester hour for the M.A. in counseling; $300 per semester hour for the M.Ed., Ed.S., and Ed.D.; $330 per semester hour for the M.B.A.; and $165 per semester hour for the Master of Arts in religion and Master of Divinity programs. There is a $100 technology fee each semester of enrollment. Course materials are a separate charge and must be purchased by the student through the University's supplier, MBS Direct (telephone: 800-325-3252, toll-free).

FINANCIAL AID

Liberty offers a full range of state (Virginia Tuition Assistance Grant), federal (Pell Grant), and school-sponsored financial assistance programs for those enrolled as matriculated students. Forms for state and federal aid can be obtained through the University's Web site (address below) or by calling the Office of Distance Learning Admissions. All students who apply for a Federal Stafford Student Loan must submit a Free Application for Federal Student Aid (FAFSA).

APPLYING

Distance learning students can apply for admission at any time of the year. Correspondence between the student and the University is conducted through the Office of Distance Learning Admissions. Applications are accepted by mail, fax, or online.

CONTACT

Office of Distance Learning Admissions
Liberty University
1971 University Boulevard
Lynchburg, Virginia 24502
Telephone: 800-424-9595 (toll-free)
Fax: 800-628-7977 (toll-free)
E-mail: edpadmissions@liberty.edu
Web site: http://www.liberty.edu

Lynn University

Institute for Distance Learning

Boca Raton, Florida

Founded in 1962 and located in Boca Raton, Florida, Lynn University is a private coeducational institution whose primary purposes are education; the preservation, discovery, dissemination, and creative application of knowledge; and the preparation of its graduates with the academic foundation for lifelong learning. Service, scholarly activity that includes research, and ongoing professional development allow the faculty, in conjunction with the entire University community, to fulfill its purposes: facilitating student-centered learning and fostering the intellectual life of the University.

DISTANCE LEARNING PROGRAM

Lynn University offers undergraduate, graduate, and doctoral degree programs to students who are unable to participate in a traditional classroom-based environment at the main campus. The aim of the University is to be a global institution for the twenty-first century, where learners can access higher learning opportunities, independent of time schedules and geographical limitations.

The Institute for Distance Learning (IDL) is designed for mature, self-directed learners, using technology and flexible delivery methods. IDL's design and delivery of all programs places a high value on the prior skills and knowledge that mature learners bring to their educational experience. Lynn University's Institute for Distance Learning offers both credit and noncredit courses.

DELIVERY MEDIA

Internet technology allows interactions between faculty members and students, students and other students, and students and resources (books, journals, electronic library services, and the Internet). In addition, videoconferencing facilities deliver interactive courses from the main campus to remote sites. Distance learning courses are delivered in an accelerated format, with six 8-week class terms per academic year. Undergraduate students may begin their studies during any of the terms, while graduate students may start their degree program during the Fall I, Winter I, or Summer I term.

PROGRAMS OF STUDY

The Southern Association of Colleges and Schools (SACS) has approved Lynn University to offer complete distance learning degree programs via the Web. The Ph.D. in global leadership online degree program offers specializations in corporate leadership or educational leadership. At the master's degree level, Lynn University's Institute for Distance Learning offers the M.B.A., with specializations in aviation management, international business, managerial electronic business, marketing, health-care administration, and hospitality management; the Master of Science (M.S.) degree, with majors in criminal justice or emergency planning and administration; and the Master of Education (M.Ed.) degree in educational leadership, with specializations in school administration and higher education administration.

Several bachelor's degrees, designed for adult learners, are available entirely via course work over the Internet. The majors available are behavioral science, business, and criminal justice administration. In addition, numerous undergraduate, graduate, and doctoral courses as well as noncredit courses are available via the Web. Students can find the course schedule on the Institute for Distance Learning's Web site at http://www.lynn.edu/distancelearning.

SPECIAL PROGRAMS

IDL also facilitates a variety of noncredit accelerated courses that can be tailored to address corporate needs. Customized courses on selected topics in business and technology can be delivered via videoconferencing or over the Web.

CREDIT OPTIONS

Most online courses are 3 credits each. Courses with labs are 4 credits. Courses offered with less than 3 credits are identified in the catalog. Lynn University accepts transfer credits from most other regionally accredited schools. Specific information about transfer credits may be found in the Academic Catalog on the University's Web site. Credits earned in the online program can be combined with credits earned on campus to complete a degree.

FACULTY

The faculty and staff members of the Institute of Distance Learning at Lynn University are highly qualified and committed to providing high-quality instruction and learning opportunities for self-directed learners. Along with excellent academic credentials, the faculty members are primarily practitioners in their fields of expertise, thus providing the theoretical context for the practical applications of the subject matter.

ADMISSION

To enroll in an undergraduate degree program, students must have earned a high school diploma or GED. International students whose first language is not English must submit a TOEFL score of at least 500. A student's credit hours are earned through instruction (distance learning or traditional classroom), transfer credits from an accredited college or university, military service course credits (DANTES), Florida Department of Law Enforcement (FDLE) or a similar state training facility, professional training or certification as recognized by the American Council on Education (ACE) or the College Level Examination Program (CLEP), and/or a student's professional experience or experiential learning.

Attendees of foreign schools are required to submit an International Transcript Evaluation and course equivalency report.

Graduate students must have earned a college diploma from a regionally accredited or internationally listed college or university. Applicants whose undergraduate grade point average (GPA) was less than 3.0 must also submit the appropriate entrance examination score from the GRE, GMAT, or MAT. Two recommendation letters, a resume, and a statement of professional goals are also required. Other admission requirements vary by degree program. International graduate students whose native language is not English must submit a TOEFL score at least 550 (213 on the computer-based test).

Ph.D. students have a required course enrollment residency. The enrollment residency requirement in the doctoral program consists of two consecutive terms with enrollment in 6 credits of required course work each term. This excludes course work for RES 897, RES 900, RES 901, or RES 902. Students who are unable to meet this enrollment requirement may develop an alternative plan with the respective program coordinator.

In addition, there is a required campus residency for online students enrolled in the Ph.D. program. There are four required on-campus immersions consisting of three to five days each and a fifth for the defense of the dissertation. These immersions are associated with a program orientation and the RESEARCH core: RES 700Q, RES 702Q, RES 704Q, RES 900Q, and RES 902 (dissertation defense).

TUITION AND FEES

All new students pay a one-time nonrefundable $50 application fee. The tuition fees and registration fees follow the pricing established for the respective colleges and noncredit programs. For the 2004–05 academic year, the fees are as follows: undergraduate (adult evening division), $252 per credit hour; graduate, $483 per credit hour; doctoral, $667 per credit hour; noncredit tuition varies with the individual courses. Students should check the Web site for further details. There is a registration fee of $30 at the beginning of each term enrolled; lab fees of $30 to $60, depending on the specific course; and a portfolio administration fee of $75 per credit placed on the transcript. More information and specific details regarding fees are available in the Academic Catalog on the University's Web site.

FINANCIAL AID

Financial aid is available to any qualified Lynn student. For specific information, students should contact the financial aid office at 561-237-7941.

APPLYING

Students may apply by calling the Admissions Office at 1-800-888-LYNN(5966) from anywhere in the United States or 561-237-7900 from outside the U.S. Applications may also be obtained on the Admissions department's Web site at http://www.lynn.edu/admissions or by phone, fax, or e-mail.

CONTACT

Mary L. Tebes, Ph.D.
Director, Institute for Distance Learning
Lynn University
3601 North Military Trail
Boca Raton, Florida 33431
Telephone: 561-237-7902
Fax: 561-237-7899
E-mail: mtebes@lynn.edu
Web site: http://www.lynn.edu

Marist College

School of Management

Poughkeepsie, New York

Marist College is an independent, coeducational liberal arts and sciences institution located in Poughkeepsie, New York. Marist began offering graduate programs in 1972 and currently serves some 750 graduate students from all over the world. Marist has been listed among the finest colleges and universities in America by both the Barron's Guide *and* U.S. News & World Report.

Marist is registered by the New York State Education Department, Office of Higher Education and the Professions, and is accredited by the Middle States Association of Colleges and Schools. Its business programs are accredited by AACSB International–The Association to Advance Collegiate Schools of Business.

DISTANCE LEARNING PROGRAM

Marist College was among the nation's front-runners in distance learning, offering working adults the unique opportunity to complete challenging graduate programs in business administration or public administration entirely on the Web. Professionals from as far away as Europe, India, and China currently count themselves as members of the Marist College family.

Marist's undergraduate and graduate degree programs in business are fully accredited by AACSB International–The Association to Advance Collegiate Schools of Business. AACSB International is the premier accrediting agency for baccalaureate, master's, and doctoral degree programs in business administration and accounting. It is devoted to the promotion and improvement of higher education in business administration and management. This accreditation places Marist among the top 30 percent of business programs in the country. Marist is proud to be among the 411 colleges, universities, and institutions of higher education worldwide accredited by AACSB International.

Marist's M.B.A. and M.P.A. programs provide an outstanding mix of quality, convenience, and flexibility. Students for whom regularly scheduled on-site classes are difficult may pursue equally challenging graduate course work at their convenience from anywhere in the world.

DELIVERY MEDIA

Cutting-edge instructional technology enables students to interact extensively with their instructors and classmates. Communication is ongoing via e-mail, bulletin boards, group conference rooms, or private chat rooms.

A personal computer with a Pentium 166 processor, 32 megabytes of RAM, a 28.8 modem (56K recommended), and access to the World Wide Web via MS Explorer, Netscape 4.0, or America Online browser version 4.0 are required for the program. In addition, to ensure compatibility in reading attached files and sharing work with other classmates, Microsoft Office 97 is essential throughout the program.

PROGRAMS OF STUDY

Marist's online graduate programs in business administration and public administration are available to students worldwide. Candidates for either program must meet the admissions criteria required by that program and must have completed a baccalaureate degree from an accredited institution. International applicants must submit official TOEFL and TWE scores for admission.

Marist's M.B.A. is designed to cultivate managers who are capable of effective decision-making in today's complex business environment. Emphasis is placed on the management process and the behavioral influences that significantly affect the success of modern organizations. Graduates of the program possess the strategic perspective necessary to identify opportunities and risks in a rapidly changing economic environment. Course requirements consist of a combination of foundation, core, and elective courses designed to develop the professional analytical, communication, and leadership skills needed to keep pace with the competitive demands of a global economy.

Marist's M.P.A. is designed to provide students with the knowledge and skills necessary for effective public-sector and not-for-profit program management.

The curriculum stresses the ethical, legal, and social context of administration. Graduates are proficient in understanding and developing positive organizational behavior and effectively utilizing a full range of management and administrative techniques to solve problems, address issues, and lead important programs.

CREDIT OPTIONS

The M.B.A. program requires a minimum of 30 credit hours, with a maximum of 51 credit hours, for the degree. Up to 21 credits of foundation courses may be waived, based on prior graduate or undergraduate study. Transfer credits are not applicable to foundation course work. Instead, particular foundation requirements are waived on the basis of prior study.

Transfer of credits into the M.B.A. or M.P.A. program requires the prior approval of the program director. Up to 6 graduate credits may be transferred from an AACSB International–accredited graduate program to satisfy graduate core and/or elective requirements. Criteria considered in awarding transfer credit include the grade received (must be B– or higher), the level of the course in the program at which it was taken, and the course content. Transfer credit is awarded for core courses only if the course is substantially equivalent to the Marist course requirement.

FACULTY

The Marist College faculty comprises highly experienced credentialed educators, many of whom are skilled professionals with practical hands-on experience in corporate, government, not-for-profit, and community settings. Faculty members regularly take part in research, publishing, and consulting and are frequently called upon by various organizations and institutions for their expertise in their given academic areas.

ADMISSION

The M.B.A. and M.P.A. programs are concerned with the interest, aptitude, and capacity of a prospective student as indicated in the applicant's previous academic record, achievement on the Graduate Management Admission Test (GMAT) or Graduate Record Examinations (GRE), and past professional achievement and growth. Each applicant's credentials are evaluated on an individual basis. Specific requirements for admission and completion vary by program. All applicants must submit the graduate application, application fee, official transcripts, and current resume. A personal statement is required of M.P.A. candidates. The GMAT/GRE is waived for applicants who already hold a master's degree.

TUITION AND FEES

Tuition for the 2003–04 academic year was $530 per credit, plus a $30 registration fee per semester and a one-time matriculation fee of $30. A $30 nonrefundable application fee is required at application.

FINANCIAL AID

Marist College offers merit-based and need-based financial programs to assist students in meeting the cost of their graduate education. To be eligible, a student must be matriculated in a graduate program and maintain satisfactory academic progress each semester. Awards are made without reference to racial or ethnic origin, sex, age, religion, marital status, or disability. The process of applying for aid should begin in early summer for fall admittance and mid-fall for spring admittance.

APPLYING

Student wishing to pursue their M.B.A. or M.P.A. on line should follow the same procedures as campus-based graduate students. All admissions documents should be sent directly to the Office of Graduate Admissions.

CONTACT

Graduate Admissions
School of Graduate and Continuing Education
Marist College
North Road
Poughkeepsie, New York 12601
Telephone: 845-575-3800
888-877-7900 (toll-free)
Fax: 845-575-3166
E-mail: graduate@marist.edu
Web site: http://www.Marist.edu/management

Montana State University–Billings

MONTANA STATE UNIVERSITY BILLINGS

MSU–B Online Program

Billings, Montana

Established in 1927, Montana State University–Billings provides excellent instructional and learning opportunities in the arts and sciences as well as in its professional programs in business, technology, human services, rehabilitation, and education. MSU–Billings is accredited by the Northwest Association of Schools and Colleges, and its various degree programs, including teacher education, are accredited by other individual organizations. The University offers a wide variety of preprofessional and certification programs and awards degrees at the associate's, bachelor's, and master's levels to more than 4,000 students annually. For more information on Montana State University–Billings, prospective students should visit the University Web site.

DISTANCE LEARNING PROGRAM

Through the Montana State University–Billings (MSU–B) Online University, established in fall 1998, MSU–Billings is pleased to offer students an opportunity to take college courses via the Internet as a way of overcoming barriers of time and place. The program ensures that students can achieve their personal, professional, and academic goals while not having to sacrifice the other things that are important in their lives. The program currently offers more than 130 individual online courses, including eight fully online degree programs, with more than 6,000 annual student enrollments.

DELIVERY MEDIA

All MSU–B online classes are delivered entirely via the Internet using the sophisticated eCollege.com online course delivery system. This system provides for complete course content hosting whereby all readings, assignments, multimedia tutorials, audio and video streaming media, and instructional documents are provided online. In addition to hosting course content, the delivery system provides access to a variety of cutting-edge online interaction tools, including centralized e-mail, Internet and course search tools, chat rooms, and threaded discussions, in addition to an online journal, calendar, Webliography, document sharing, exam manager, and gradebook features. Minimal hardware, software, and Internet connectivity requirements exist for all online classes.

PROGRAMS OF STUDY

The MSU–Billings Online University currently offers eight fully online degree programs. Students may attain the Associate in Applied Science (A.A.S.) degree in accounting technology or customize their own fully online Associate of Arts (A.A.) degree. Bachelor's degrees offered include the Bachelor of Science in Liberal Studies (B.S.L.S.) degree with a concentration in management and communication; a Bachelor of Arts (B.A.) degree in Communication with major options in organizational communication and mass communication; a Bachelor of Science in public relations; the B.S.L.S. degree completion program; and a Bachelor of Science in Health Administration. MSU–Billings also offers a Master of Science in Public Relations and a Master of Health Administration degree online.

The B.S.L.S. degree completion program uses the same curriculum as the full four-year B.S.L.S. degree, but allows students to transfer or substitute prior academic course work into the program while completing the thematic concentration. To complete the B.S.L.S. degree or the B.S.L.S. degree completion program, individuals must earn a minimum of 120 credits with a cumulative grade point average of 2.0 or better. In addition, all students must satisfy the general education requirements at MSU–Billings. MSU–Billings accepts transfer students with completed A.A. or A.S. degrees from other institutions as having fulfilled their MSU–Billings general education requirements. Students must complete a minimum of 30 credits through MSU–Billings.

The B.A. in communication degree program shares much of the same requirements as the B.S.L.S. degree program described above, but allows students to complete a major core of courses in either organizational communication, mass communication, or public relations. The degree is designed to educate students entering the fields of business and social service as managers, public relations personnel, trainers, human resource officers, and corporate communication staff members. The degree also provides students with an excellent preparation for graduate study in communication or law.

For more information on any of the online courses and degree programs, prospective students should visit the MSU–B Online University Web site at http://www.msubonline.org.

SPECIAL PROGRAMS

Through the MSU–B Online University, students can complete the B.S.L.S. degree completion program described above, which offers a number of thematic concentrations. In addition, students can complete a variety of courses in general education requirements typically required of undergraduate students.

STUDENT SERVICES

The MSU–B Online University provides online students with access to all student services offered to MSU–Billings on-site students, including admissions, degree planning and advising, financial aid, ordering books and supplies, fee payment, library, 24-hour HelpDesk technical support, and a number of other student support services. In addition, all students enrolling in an online class receive access to an online orientation course that is designed to help students learn how to use the course delivery system and to maximize their success and satisfaction in online learning.

FACULTY

Most of the 70 faculty members who teach classes online for the MSU–B Online University are also full-time faculty members of Montana State University–Billings. In addition to teaching their online classes, these faculty members teach equivalent courses in traditional on-site classes. Eighty-six percent of the University's faculty members hold the highest degrees in their fields.

ADMISSION

The requirements for admission to MSU–B are the same as those for individuals taking classes on-site. Online students should apply for admission and register for online courses through the MSU–B Online University Web site at http://www.msubonline.org.

TUITION AND FEES

Tuition and fees for online classes are the same as for taking classes on-site with an additional $40 per credit nonrefundable fee that is assessed for all Internet courses. The exact rate of tuition and fees depends upon the number of credits taken and whether the student is a resident or nonresident of Montana. For a current schedule of tuition and fees, prospective students should visit the MSU–B Online University Web site at http://www.msubonline.org.

FINANCIAL AID

Financial aid is awarded to more than 60 percent of the University population—including students taking courses online—in the form of grants, scholarships, tuition waivers, employment, and loans. For more information or to apply for financial aid, prospective students should visit the MSU–B Online University Web site at http://www.msubonline.org.

APPLYING

All students wishing to enroll in MSU–B Online courses or degree programs should do so by submitting an online application and registration form accessible from the MSU–B Online University Web site at http://www.msubonline.org.

CONTACT

Marlow Ockfen
Coordinator, MSU-Billings Online University
College of Professional Studies and Lifelong Learning
Apsaruke Hall 126
Montana State University-Billings
1500 North 30th Street
Billings, Montana 59101
Telephone: 406-657-2030
800-708-0068 Ext. 2030 (toll-free)
Fax: 406-657-2254
E-mail: inquiry@msubonline.org
Web sites: http://www.msubonline.org
http://www.msubillings.edu

National University

Distance Learning Program

La Jolla, California

Since its founding in 1971, National University has been dedicated to making lifelong learning opportunities accessible, challenging, and relevant to a diverse population of adult learners. A pioneer in the nontraditional learning format and in distance learning, National is the second-largest private, accredited, nonprofit university in California, with nearly 17,000 students and 109,000 alumni. National University holds accreditations by the Western Association of Schools and Colleges and by the International Assembly for Collegiate Business Education, and is approved by the California Commission on Teacher Credentialing.

National University offers an alternative to the traditional, four-year college with a unique, flexible, one- to two-course-per-month format that allows students to obtain a quality education in a shortened time frame, so they can enter the workforce faster. National University ranks first in California in granting master's and bachelor's degrees to Hispanics and African Americans, and it ranks fourth in the U.S. in awarding master's degrees to Hispanics.

DISTANCE LEARNING PROGRAM

National University was one of the first institutions to offer a variety of degree programs via the Internet. National University's online courses give students the ease and convenience of earning their degree at home or in their office. Whether students study most efficiently in the morning or at night, National's online classes give students the added flexibility of completing their course work as it suits their schedule, needs, and learning style.

More than thirty online degree programs include graduate and undergraduate programs as well as teaching credential and certificate programs. Growth in online enrollment has increased 493 percent over the past three years. Today, approximately 3,500 students take online classes at National every month. As the demand has grown for new online offerings, National has continually expanded its programs to meet the changing needs of students and the growing demands of the workforce.

DELIVERY MEDIA

National's online classes include the same essential components as its onsite courses, such as lectures, reading assignments, slide presentations, evaluations, quizzes, and exams. National University's online courses are able to move beyond the limits of the classroom by utilizing resources and communication tools that add tremendous value to the learning environment, including a digital dropbox, online collaboration, discussion boards, announcements, e-mail class feature, assignment manager, and multimedia.

Through group projects and threaded discussions and/or chat rooms, students develop an online community with their classmates that develops and strengthens their communication and collaborative skills. Thus, unlike conventional classroom settings, online courses provide ongoing communication with the instructor and with fellow classmates.

PROGRAMS OF STUDY

The National University format allows students to work full-time while attending small, online classes. Courses are one to two months in length, and new courses begin each month. This format enables students to complete as many as 54 quarter units (twelve courses) in a year instead of the traditional 40.5 quarter units (nine courses), allowing students to complete an undergraduate degree in just over three years and a graduate degree in a little more than one year.

Undergraduate degrees available online include Associate of Arts (A.A.); Bachelor of Arts (B.A.) in English, global studies, or psychology; Bachelor of Business Administration (B.B.A.); Bachelor of Science in Nursing (B.S.N.); and Bachelor of Science (B.S.) in accountancy, criminal justice administration, construction engineering, information systems, information technology, and organizational behavior.

Graduate degrees available online include Executive Master of Business Administration (E.M.B.A.); Master of Arts in Teaching (M.A.T.); Master of Arts (M.A.) in English, human behavior, and human resource management and organizational development; Master of Arts in Management (M.A.M.); Master of Fine Arts (M.F.A.) in film art studies and in creative writing; Master of Education (M.Ed.) in cross-cultural teaching; Master of Forensic Sciences (M.F.S.); Master of Public Administration (M.P.A.); Master of Science in Computer Science (M.S.C.S.); Master of Science in Information Systems (M.S.I.S.); Master of Science in Organizational Leadership (M.S.O.L.); Master of Science in Technology Management (M.S.T.M.); and Master of Science (M.S.) in educational administration, educational technology, electronic business, instructional technology, and special education.

STUDENT SERVICES

Each student is assigned to an admissions adviser who assists with enrollment and scheduling. The University offers personalized student services to online students, with access to assistance 24 hours a day, seven days a week. Additionally, class sizes are small, with a high level of faculty member involvement.

National University students throughout the world also have continuous access to one of the largest e-book collections in the U.S., with more than 60,000 e-books and reference works, over 900 e-journals, 60 electronic databases, and more than 8,000 full-text journals and reference sources.

Students can benefit from the online career assistance offered by the Career Assessment Center, including resume writing, job searching, interviewing and negotiating skills, and employment opportunities.

CREDIT OPTIONS

National University awards credit in quarter units. Under the current policy, 4.5 units of credit are awarded for most courses. National University accepts collegiate credits from regionally accredited institutions if the courses were completed satisfactorily. Additionally, the University accepts noncollegiate learning experiences. These credits are granted on a case-by-case basis and can come from such sources as CLEP, DANTES, ACT PEP, University departmental examinations, and military experience.

FACULTY

National's faculty members are experienced in innovative online instruction, and many work in the fields that they teach, ensuring real-world knowledge. Ninety-four percent of the faculty members have a terminal degree.

ADMISSION

National University considers every student for entrance and admission is based on evidence of a student's ability to benefit from its educational program. Such evidence can include the following: the student's academic record in other institutions, test scores, interviews, professional experience, motivation, and educational objectives. A year-round streamlined admissions process helps students start their programs right away, with classes that begin every month and no waiting to enroll.

TUITION AND FEES

Undergraduate courses cost $950 each; graduate courses cost $1070 each. There is an application fee of $60 and a graduation processing fee of $100.

FINANCIAL AID

There are many types of financial aid available to assist students who qualify. These include federal, state, and institution aid programs in the form of grants, loans, and scholarships. At National University, the purpose of financial aid is to bridge the gap between the educational cost and a student's resources. In order to establish eligibility for aid, students are asked to complete the Free Application for Federal Student Aid (FAFSA). Interested students are encouraged to visit the Web site at http://www.nu.edu/financialaid or call the Financial Aid Office at 800-NAT-UNIV Ext. 8500.

APPLYING

Prospective students can take advantage of National's convenient online application process at http://www.nu.edu/getmoreinfo.

CONTACT

National University
Online Admissions
11255 North Torrey Pines Road
La Jolla, California 92037
Telephone: 1-800-NAT-UNIV (toll-free in the U.S.)
E-mail: ldutton@nu.edu
Website: http://www.nu.edu

New Jersey Institute of Technology

Division of Continuing Professional Education eLearning—Extension Programs

Newark, New Jersey

Founded in 1881, New Jersey Institute of Technology (NJIT) is New Jersey's technological research university. An international leader in scientific and technological education, NJIT educates students to become frontrunners in the global marketplace. The university seeks students who are seriously committed to education and can bring energy, creativity, and a practical outlook to solving today's pressing problems. The degree programs are demanding, rewarding, and highly regarded by employers.

NJIT was designated America's "Tier 2" National Research University by U.S. News & World Report. *With more than 150 undergraduate and graduate courses, threaded discussion groups, lectures via CD-ROM, streaming videos, and more, NJIT course work is made available to students regardless of their geographic location. For the adult professional in particular, NJIT courses provide the flexibility and convenience needed to fit in with work, family, and community responsibilities. NJIT's customer-service orientation allows each student to receive the personal attention that is required for successful completion of a degree program or certificate.*

DISTANCE LEARNING PROGRAM

Via eLearning, NJIT conducts full undergraduate and graduate degree programs, graduate certificates, and individual college courses using today's home electronics to provide the college experience. By virtue of the academic quality, focus, and advanced delivery format, NJIT helps adult men and women cross one bridge to knowledge acquisition leading to gainful employment.

DELIVERY MEDIA

Faculty/student eLearning communities are created on a computer platform (e.g., WebCT) that is then used by the professor to present course material in streaming-video clips, animations, and online quizzes and as a forum for discussions anytime and in real time with and among students. Students may also use CD-ROMs or internally produced, standalone videotapes as sources of additional course content. These discussions occur through NJIT e-mail or the WebCT conferencing system. NJIT eLearning recommends that students own a 486 DX100 personal computer with 16 MB of memory, a VGA monitor, a 500 MB hard disk, and a 56k kpbs modem. NJIT's eLearning programs also use interactive television, satellite video distribution, streaming video, and CD-ROMs.

PROGRAMS OF STUDY

With NJIT eLearning, students can obtain a Bachelor of Arts in Information Systems (B.A.I.S.), a Bachelor of Science in Computer Science (B.S.C.S.), and a Bachelor of Science in Information Technology (B.S.I.T.). The B.A.I.S. is a 129-credit program that enables students to apply computing and information systems principles to real problems in business and industry. B.A.I.S. graduates enter careers in accounting, environmental science, finance, manufacturing science, and marketing. The B.S.C.S. is a 134-credit program that equips students with the theoretical and practical elements of computer science. The core curriculum consists of 51 credits in computer science, while elective credit must be earned in engineering, mathematics, and science. The B.S.I.T. is a 127-credit program. The interdisciplinary field of information technology addresses the integration, design, deployment, and management of computing and telecommunications, as well as the development of technology infrastructures in organizations.

NJIT eLearning also offers Master of Science degrees in Computer Science (M.S.C.S.), Information Systems (M.S.I.S.), Engineering Management (M.S.E.M.), and Professional and Technical Communication (M.S. P.T.C.). Students seeking advanced training in artificial intelligence; graphics and image processing; software engineering; systems analysis, simulation, and modeling; or other subdisciplines may wish to enter the 30-credit M.S.C.S. program. The 36-credit M.S.I.S. allows participants to specialize in information systems analysis and design, software development, and software engineering methodology. Individuals with suitable technical qualifications who intend to assume a managerial role in the public or private sector may consider enrolling in the 30-credit M.S.E.M. program. The 30-credit M.S.P.T.C. program is designed to prepare students for careers in the field of technical communication. Students develop skills in communication theory, proposal writing, editing, graphics, multimedia, hypermedia, online publishing, and scientific writing.

The Institute also offers a Master of Business Administration (M.B.A.) in management of technology.

SPECIAL PROGRAMS

NJIT awards graduate certificates in ten disciplines in their entirety via eLearning: computer networking, enterprise system modeling and design, information systems design, information systems implementation, Internet applications development, Internet systems engineering, practice of technical communications, programming environment tools, project management, business management fundamentals, and telecommunications networking. Each certificate, worth 12 graduate credits, can be used as a springboard to advanced-degree study at NJIT or elsewhere. Consisting of four courses, each certificate is in a topic area considered by today's corporations to be employable "hot tracks" through the year 2006.

CREDIT OPTIONS

Students may be awarded transfer credit at the time of admission for courses that were completed at other institutions and are equivalent to courses offered by NJIT. A minimum grade of C must be earned in a course in order to receive transfer credit.

FACULTY

Ninety-eight percent of NJIT's full-time faculty members hold the terminal degree in their field.

ADMISSION

Admission policies for the NJIT eLearning programs follow the same admission criteria as do traditionally delivered NJIT academic programs. In general, admission on a nonmatriculated basis to an undergraduate course requires possession of a high school diploma or General Educational Development (GED) certificate. Admission as a nonmatriculated student to a graduate course requires possession, at minimum, of an undergraduate degree from an accredited college or university with a grade point average that meets NJIT academic department standards for regular admission as a Master of Science degree candidate. In general, an acceptable grade point average is no lower than 2.8 on a 4.0 scale.

TUITION AND FEES

Undergraduate tuition is $278 per credit for New Jersey residents and $544 per credit for nonresidents. Graduate tuition is $520 per credit for New Jersey residents and $715 per credit for nonresidents. Graduate certificate students pay in-state tuition, regardless of location. The total for one eLearning course including fees is $1205 for an undergraduate course and $1950 for a graduate course. Tuition and fees are subject to change. For current tuition and fees, students should visit http://www.njit.edu/old/Registrar/.

FINANCIAL AID

NJIT's Office of Financial Aid provides counseling and administers loans, scholarships, and grants to qualified students. Federal and state programs and private, industrial, and university resources are utilized to support the university's financial aid programs. For more information, students should visit http://www.njit.edu/old/finaid/page4.php.

APPLYING

Applications procedures vary depending on the program of enrollment and the applicant's status. First-time non-degree-seeking and graduate certificate students use the nonmatriculated application; continuing non-degree-seeking and graduate certificate students need only register for courses. For more information on the nonmatriculated process and application, students should visit http://cpe.njit.edu/GradCert/application.htm. Students may apply on a nonmatriculated basis by mail, by fax, or online.

Degree-seeking students and non-degree-seeking students with more than 9 graduate or 15 undergraduate credits should use the matriculated application. For the matriculated process and application, students should visit http://www.njit.edu/Admissions/. To apply for admission on a matriculated basis, students should contact the Office of Admissions at 973-596-3300 or 800-925-6548 (toll-free) to request a degree application or use the online matriculated application form on the admissions Web site.

CONTACT

Division of Continuing Professional Education
New Jersey Institute of Technology
University Heights, New Jersey 07102-1982
Telephone: 973-596-3061
Fax: 973-596-3203
Web site: http://cpe.njit.edu

New Mexico State University

Office of Distance Education and Weekend College

Las Cruces, New Mexico

New Mexico State University (NMSU), which began in 1888 as an agricultural college and preparatory school, is a comprehensive institution dedicated to teaching, research, and service at the graduate and undergraduate levels. It is the only land-grant institution that is also classified as Hispanic serving by the federal government and ranked by the Carnegie Foundation in the top research category, Doctoral/Research University–Extensive. The University is also home to the state's only NASA Space Grant Program. With extension and research sites in every county, New Mexico State is developing distance education capabilities to extend its reach to all the citizens of the state. It is located in the southern New Mexico city of Las Cruces, which has a population of about 75,000. The region features desert mesas, the farmlands of the Rio Grande Valley, and the Organ Mountains, an extension of the Rocky Mountain chain.

Total enrollment for the NMSU main and branch campuses is 23,578. The main campus enrollment is 16,174, which includes 3,377 graduate students. Minority enrollment at the main campus is more than 48 percent (41.7 percent Hispanic, 2.9 percent Native American, 2.7 percent African American, and 1.3 percent Asian American).

New Mexico State University is accredited by the Higher Learning Commission of the North Central Association of Colleges and Schools (NCA-HLC).

DISTANCE LEARNING PROGRAM

The mission of New Mexico State University's Office of Distance Education is to provide comprehensive distance learning opportunities to meet diverse educational and professional needs anytime, anywhere. As the state's land-grant institution, the University has a long history of outreach and distance education, and the future looks bright.

Eighteen degree, certificate, and licensure programs are now available via distance learning at New Mexico State University and include bachelor's degree completion programs, master's degrees, and doctorates. In addition, individual courses are offered to meet the students' interests and needs. With new programs always in development, NMSU continually brings students greater choice in program selection.

DELIVERY MEDIA

Distance education courses from NMSU are delivered using the most innovative, cutting-edge technology and methods available, including satellite television, interactive television (ITV), the World Wide Web, faculty exchanges, and off-site classes. Courses may use one or more types of learning technologies to promote engaging and effective instruction. As the Internet becomes the telecommunications medium of choice for many distance education students around the world, NMSU offers complete programs and individual courses that use Web-based interactive digital technologies. Prospective students are encouraged to learn more about course delivery and to check out the distance education schedule for more details.

PROGRAMS OF STUDY

Four bachelor's degree completion programs are available through NMSU. The College of Arts and Sciences' degree completion program leads to a Bachelor of Arts (B.A.) in sociology. A Bachelor of Business Administration (B.B.A.) can be completed through the College of Business Administration and Economics. The College of Engineering awards a bachelor's degree in information and communication technology, and students may complete a bachelor's degree in human and community services through the College of Health and Social Services.

Four master's degrees are offered. The Master of Criminal Justice (M.C.J.) is conferred by the College of Arts and Sciences, and the College of Education awards the Master of Arts (M.A.) in education with a learning technologies emphasis. The College of Engineering offers the Master of Science (M.S.) in industrial engineering and in mechanical engineering, each with a minor in manufacturing.

The College of Education offers several doctoral-level degrees. The Doctor of Education (Ed.D.) in educational administration is offered with an emphasis in either community college leadership or educational leadership, while the Doctor of Philosophy (Ph.D.) in curriculum and instruction has an emphasis in learning technologies.

Certificates and licenses offered by the College of Education include the Information Technology Coordinator Endorsement and the Special Education Alternative Licensure. Programs in bilingual endorsement and school counseling are under development.

The College of Engineering offers certificates in finite-element analysis, lean manufacturing, and simulation.

FACULTY

Regular faculty members on the main campus number 665. Eighty-four percent of the full-time faculty hold doctoral degrees. The student-faculty ratio is 19:1.

ADMISSION

Students who wish to enroll in distance education courses must apply for admission to New Mexico Sate University. Former students of NMSU who have been out of school for a regular semester or longer are required to make formal application for readmission.

TUITION AND FEES

Residents of New Mexico pay $152.75 per credit hour for undergraduate instruction and $164 per credit hour for graduate instruction. Nonresidents pay $468.75 per credit hour for undergraduate instruction and $481.25 per credit hour for graduate instruction. Nonresidents may take up to 6 credits at in-state rates each semester. Reciprocal tuition agreements are in place for Texas and Colorado residents. There is an additional $15 per credit hour fee for distance education courses. All students (except international students) enrolling at New Mexico State University for the first time pay a nonrefundable $15 admission application fee. International students are charged $35. A late registration fee of $25 is charged for all registrations during the late registration period, plus $5 per day thereafter.

CONTACT

Office of Distance Education and Weekend College
New Mexico State University
MSC 3WEC
P.O. Box 30001
Las Cruces, New Mexico 88001-8001
Telephone: 505-646-4692
800-821-1574 (toll-free in New Mexico)
E-mail: distance@nmsu.edu
Web site: http://www.nmsu.edu/distance

New School University

Robert J. Milano Graduate School of Management and Urban Policy Distance Learning Program

New York, New York

New School University is an innovative educational institution founded eight decades ago as a bastion of intellectual and artistic freedom. Progressive, current, and socially responsible, the Robert J. Milano Graduate School of Management and Urban Policy in New York City offers high-quality graduate-level programs in a number of fields. It is ranked among the top schools in the United States for nonprofit management, social policy, and city management and urban policy. The New School pioneered the idea of lifelong university-level education for adult students, and today it is a residential university in which 7,000 students are enrolled in graduate and undergraduate degree programs. Celebrated for its social science, humanities, and public-policy initiatives, New School University has grown into one of the largest arts education resources in the nation.

DISTANCE LEARNING PROGRAM

Each semester, the Milano Graduate School offers between six and twenty classes totally or partially online in a variety of programs, concentrations, and content clusters. The courses are offered as options to provide more flexibility for students. The courses are taught by both full-time and adjunct faculty members.

DELIVERY MEDIA

Courses are offered over the New School University Online platform, which features e-mail, discussion boards, chat, whiteboard, file sharing, calendar, and an announcements feature. Instructors typically use asynchronous elements for the majority of their courses to allow a "learning anywhere, anytime" atmosphere to take place. Students and faculty members correspond by telephone, mail, fax, e-mail, and face to face.

PROGRAMS OF STUDY

While Milano does not offer an entire graduate degree online, students can complete a significant portion of the nonprofit management, health services management, or human resources management programs online.

Most online classes engage students in facilitated discussions that sometimes include industry leaders as guests and resources. Instructors offer lectures and discussion questions to which students can respond anytime within a few days. The School encourages students to respond to each other, and the dialogues in online classes are educationally and professionally enriching.

Online courses are typically shorter in length than traditional face-to-face courses, usually eight to ten academic weeks, versus the fifteen-week structure of most traditional courses. Though they are shorter, the online classes are comparable in quality to traditional courses. Typically, online courses contain no more than 15 students per instructor.

Milano siteline courses blend online and face-to-face teaching, so students can get the flexibility of the online environment, yet see fellow class members. Some siteline courses substitute online sessions for face-to-face sessions, which means fewer trips to the campus during the semester.

The School encourages innovative teaching models that provide high levels of interaction and connect theory to practice. To this end, instructors have attracted industry leaders as guest speakers or resources for extended periods of time, provided online space for students to bring topical resources to the class, and engaged students in professional group settings where they can practice their leadership and project-management skills.

Milano has provided more than forty-five classes online since 1996. While not all of these classes are offered online every semester, Milano makes available between eight and twenty classes online per semester. To learn more about these classes, applicants should look at the course descriptions on the program's Web site listed at the end of this description; current Milano students should contact their program or faculty adviser.

Milano offers the following online courses, which are listed by cluster. Management courses are Building Organizational Capacity: Strategic Planning and Management Systems; Communications in Nonprofit Organizations; Cost-Effectiveness Analysis; Employee Relations: A Functional Overview; Functions of Human Resources Management; Fundamentals of Accounting in the Nonprofit Environment; Fund Raising and Development; Grantsmanship: Research, Writing and Relationships; Human Resources Information Systems; Human Resources Strategic Planning; Management and Organizational Behavior; Managed Care Administration for the Group Practice Setting; Management Information Systems II; Management of Health Care Facilities;

Management of Long Term Care; Management Compensation; Project Management; Strategic Management in Health Care; Strategic Planning in the Group Practice Environment; and Systems Analysis and Information Systems Management for the Group Practice.

Courses available in economics/finance are Economic Analysis, Financial Management of Group Practice, Financial Impact of Human Resources Major Strategies, Financial Impact of Human Resources Management Strategies, Health Care Financial Management, Health Care Reimbursement, and Physician Compensation.

Courses in history, theory, and concepts are Biostatistics, Community Development, Issues/Concepts in Gerontology, Management Communications, Theory and Practice of Nonprofit Management, and Urban Economic Development Policy.

Courses in institutions/organizations are Institutional Financial Management, Dynamics of the U.S. Health Care System, and Corporate Philanthropy and Social Responsibility.

Courses in technology are Advanced Microcomputer Applications; Computer-Based Management Information Systems; Information Technology in Health Care (Management Information Systems I); PC Applications for Human Resources Professionals; Principles of Database Management; Strategic Technology: Planning and Management for Nonprofit Organizations; Technology, Strategy, and Management; and Technology Strategies for Human Resources Management.

The course in legal and regulatory issues is Legal Aspects of Health Care.

The course in cross-cultural/international issues is Multicultural Issues in Health Care.

Courses in policy are Home Care: Policy and Administration, Policy Analysis, and Policy Issues in Health Care.

SPECIAL PROGRAMS

The Milano Graduate School is active in the New York region and various professional and academic communities through the Center for New York City Affairs, the Community Development Research Center, the Milano Nonprofit Management Knowledge Hub, and the *Milano Review*.

STUDENT SERVICES

The Milano Student Services Office provides assistance with placement services and career guidance, alumni relations, counseling and academic advisement, grade appeals, advising of international students, the newsletter, special events, diagnostic testing and support services, and tutoring.

CREDIT OPTIONS

Credits earned through distance learning are recorded on the transcript in the same manner as credits earned in on-campus courses.

FACULTY

The full-time faculty includes members who have earned the highest degree in their field. Adjunct faculty members include corporation executives, current and former government officials, and executives of nonprofit enterprises. Most are currently practicing their professions and are able to bring to their teaching first-hand experience and insights that make theory come alive. A complete list of faculty members is available upon request.

ADMISSION

The admissions decision is made after a careful examination of transcripts and letters of recommendation. An interview may be required. There is no formal application deadline, but applicants who request financial aid should apply by April 15. Ph.D. candidates must apply by May 1. Students who wish to apply should contact the Office of Admissions at the address below.

TUITION AND FEES

Tuition in 2004–05 for the Milano Graduate School of Management and Urban Policy is $914 per credit, payable at registration. A list of fees is included in the brochure describing the various programs and is available by contacting the School at the address below.

FINANCIAL AID

The Milano Graduate School participates in all federal financial aid programs. These include the Federal Work-Study Program and the Federal Perkins Loan Program. Fellowships, assistantships, merit scholarships, and need-based tuition remission are also available.

APPLYING

Students who apply for admission must submit the following material: official transcripts of all undergraduate programs attended, with grades and proof of degree; two letters of recommendation; a completed application form; a $30 application fee; an essay describing career goals; and an interview in person or by phone.

CONTACT

Office of Admissions
Robert J. Milano Graduate School
New School University
72 Fifth Avenue
New York, New York 10011
Telephone: 212-229-5150
877-528-3321 (toll-free)
E-mail: univadm@newschool.edu
Web site: http://www.newschool.edu/milano

Northcentral University

Northcentral University Online

Prescott, Arizona

Northcentral University (NCU) Online, a modern, regionally accredited, 100 percent online, degree-granting university, is a worldwide institution from its headquarters in Prescott, Arizona. NCU's mission is to provide adult Learners throughout the world with opportunities to acquire competencies, earn degrees, and apply the new knowledge and skills in order to participate and function effectively in modern society.

NCU offers interesting and challenging degree programs to adult students we consider as "Learners," including bachelor's, master's, and doctoral degrees in business and psychology.

NCU prides itself on making accommodations for different learning needs and styles, so that all learning involves real-world experiences, and there is a concentrated interest in and individualized attention to our Learners. NCU lives by its motto, "We put people first in distance learning."™

NCU is accredited by the Higher Learning Commission and is a member of the North Central Association of Colleges and Schools.

DISTANCE LEARNING PROGRAM

Distance learning at NCU means high-quality learning experiences are brought to the Learners, wherever they are, over the Internet. Learners do not have to travel or attend classes. All courses are completed at the individual's pace (within the semester) with the guidance of NCU's credentialed and experienced faculty members. Learners now have the opportunity to earn a high-quality accredited degree without having to travel to a campus. This is a program that is designed to meet the needs of the busy adult Learner. Today, Learners from all over the United States and countries such as Australia, Canada, China, Japan, Malaysia, and Switzerland, to name a few, are benefiting from this customer-oriented university.

NCU's tuition is one of the lowest among distance learning institutions. NCU was designed to operate entirely by distance learning, so there are no extras that increase the cost, such as sports teams, parking structures, or large campuses.

DELIVERY MEDIA

Northcentral University uses electronic communications. Learners must have e-mail access with the capability to send and receive file attachments and must also have a Java-enabled Web browser.

NCU Learners must have word-processing capabilities. It is required that Learners have the ability to save and receive documents in the standard ASCII format (.txt) or Rich Text format (.rtf). NCU has standardized Rich Text format for the information the University sends out, ensuring the widest compatibility.

Hardware requirements include a Pentium 300-MHz or faster processor, a minimum 32 MB RAM, a minimum 2 GB free hard disk space, a CD-ROM drive, 28.8 Kbps or faster modem, a color monitor, a keyboard, and a mouse. Necessary software applications include Windows 95 or 98, an antivirus checker, Microsoft Outlook Express (e-mail), Microsoft Internet Explorer 5, and Microsoft Word 97 or 2000. Microsoft PowerPoint 97 or 2000 is needed, if doing presentations. Microsoft Excel 97 or 2000 is needed, if doing spreadsheets.

A video camera is required for Ph.D. Learners during the dissertation process in which they "meet" with dissertation committee members. NCU uses Microsoft Netmeeting software for its camera.

PROGRAMS OF STUDY

NCU offers such degree programs as the Bachelor of Business Administration (B.B.A.), the Master of Business Administration (M.B.A.), the Doctor of Philosophy (Ph.D.) in business administration, the Bachelor of Arts in Psychology (B.A.Psy.), the Master of Arts in Psychology (M.A.Psy.), the Ph.D. in psychology, the Master of Education (M.Ed.), the Doctor of Education (Ed.D.), and the Doctor of Philosophy in education.

NCU offers the standard 120-semester-credit bachelor's degrees, the master's degrees for 36 semester credits, and the Ph.D., requiring an additional 45 credits. The programs are delivered to the Learner entirely by distance learning by a first-class university that puts the Learner at the center of the learning process. There are no classes that meet by computer at a set time, no classroom attendance required at NCU, no "canned" courses or "talking heads," and no rigid schedules that interfere with the Learner's other adult responsibilities.

In designing the programs, NCU selected the courses a Learner needs to develop professional competencies with a support team that responds to the Learner's individual learning needs and styles; a professional faculty that "meets" with the Learner one-on-one over the Internet, giving individual attention; and NCU-developed software that makes communicating via the Internet an enjoyable experience.

STUDENT SERVICES

From one's own desk, a Learner can communicate directly with his or her faculty mentors, converse with other Learners from around the world, browse through libraries and retrieve articles of interest, download course outlines and syllabi, complete and submit course work, receive direct evaluation feedback and graded work from faculty members, evaluate faculty members, modify the degree plan, see academic progress, check accounting status, make monthly tuition payments, order books, shop in NCU's online gift shop, and earn a degree. Learners always get the courses they are scheduled for; there are no course cancellations, nor are there any impacted courses.

FACULTY

There are 118 online mentors to provide one-on-one guidance and encouragement to NCU Learners. All hold graduate degrees from prestigious accredited universities; 60 percent have doctoral degrees and 40 percent have master's degrees. They have years of relevant practical experience and are willing to share their knowledge and experience to make studying at NCU meaningful and memorable.

ADMISSION

NCU has simplified the application and admission process. Anyone can apply for a bachelor's degree. No SAT or entrance exams are required, and NCU has no quotas based on race, religion, or gender. NCU welcomes applicants who have a bachelor's degree or higher to its master's or doctoral programs. No GMAT scores or entrance exams are required. There are no enrollment quotas.

TUITION AND FEES

Tuition is $375 per unit for undergraduate courses and $475 per unit for graduate courses. Learners in the doctoral program have an additional fee of $1600 associated with their dissertation.

NCU offers tuition payment options to fit individual needs. The first option is to pay for a semester and only for the course(s) taken. There is no long-term commitment or binding contract. The second option is to pay out the semester tuition by making monthly payments (at no additional handling or interest charges). This option appeals to Learners who prefer to budget themselves.

FINANCIAL AID

NCU participates in Title IV federal financial aid and offers Federal Stafford Student Loans, Federal PLUS loans, and Federal Pell Grants.

APPLYING

All applications are made online at NCU's Web site, listed below.

CONTACT

Northcentral University Online
505 West Whipple Street
Prescott, Arizona 86301
Telephone: 928-541-7777
888-327-2877 (toll-free)
E-mail: info@ncu.edu
Web site: http://www.ncu.edu

Northern Arizona University

Distance Learning

Flagstaff, Arizona

Established in 1899, Northern Arizona University (NAU) has maintained a tradition of excellence over the past century, taking pride in its focus on academic excellence and combining highly respected career-oriented programs, a wide choice of majors, and an emphasis on liberal arts and close faculty-student interaction. With thirty campus locations throughout Arizona and a growing number of distance programs, NAU serves more than 20,000 students from all fifty states and sixty-three countries. The NAU mission is to provide educational opportunities in both residential and nonresidential environments as well as to offer instruction that employs a variety of strategies to support distance learning. NAU continues to lead in the preparation of Arizona teachers, the enrollment of Native American students, and nationally and internationally recognized programs within the health and hospitality professions as well as natural resources conservation and management.

DISTANCE LEARNING PROGRAM

With more than twenty-five years of experience, NAU's distance learning program offers a growing number of online degree and certificate programs. The degree students earn online is the same accredited degree awarded to a campus-based student. Although every degree cannot be offered via distance technology, NAU works to meet the needs of its Web-based learners.

DELIVERY MEDIA

NAU offers distance classes via Web-based and Web-streamed classes. In conjunction with the DISH network, students can participate in satellite broadcast classes. All delivery methods allow the instructors and students to interact via e-mail or online chat rooms. Textbooks and materials are available through the NAU bookstore.

PROGRAMS OF STUDY

Dedicated to providing all NAU students with a high-quality education, a degree received via distance technology is the same accredited degree awarded on the NAU campus, holding students and faculty members to the same standards of excellence. Through distance learning technology, NAU currently offers programs leading to the following: the Bachelor of Arts in Liberal Studies (B.A.L.S.) degree, with emphases in arts and letters, enterprise in society, parks and recreation management, and public agency service; the Bachelor of Applied Science (B.A.S.) degree in computer technology, early childhood, health promotion, and public agency service; the Bachelor of Science (B.S.) degree in health promotion, hotel and restaurant management, and parks and recreation management; the Bachelor of Science in Dental Hygiene (B.S.D.H.) degree-completion program; the Bachelor of Science in Nursing (B.S.N.) degree, an RN to B.S.N. program; the Master of Administration (M.Admin.) degree; the Master of Arts (M.A.) degree in applied communication; the Master of Arts in Teaching (M.A.T.) degree in mathematics; the Master of Education (M.Ed.) degree in career and technical education, educational technology, and elementary education; the Master of Engineering (M.Eng.) degree; endorsements in English as a second language, middle school, and reading; and certificates in educational technology, international tourism management, parks and recreation management, professional writing, public management, and restaurant management. Each of these programs of study was developed based on the needs of distance students.

SPECIAL PROGRAMS

A member of the Arizona Regents University, NAU works in conjunction with Arizona State University and the University of Arizona to offer students access to courses and degrees not offered by NAU. Students select a home campus by which all services, including registration, are provided for the student. Students may earn credit from all three institutions, which transfer to degree programs at any one of the three universities.

Western Governors University (WGU) is an online university offering Web-based classes from a variety of educational institutions in sixteen states, Guam, and Canada. NAU is a provider of classes for WGU. Students enrolled in these classes are considered nondegree seeking for NAU purposes, though they may be earning a degree from WGU. Students pay 1½ times in-state tuition.

STUDENT SERVICES

NAU distance students are provided electronic access to academic records, enrollment, online research through Cline Library, and other online student services. Academic advising is available to distance students either online or through NAU's toll-free number. Students who do not have a computer and live in Arizona can complete their classes at one of the twenty-five NAU statewide computer labs.

CREDIT OPTIONS

To be eligible for financial aid, students must be admitted to a degree or certification program. Classes may be taken for audit or professional development credit; however, space may be limited due to for-credit student demand. Most classes are evaluated with a letter grade, but some classes are offered on a pass-fail only basis. These classes are outlined in the current NAU undergraduate and graduate catalogs.

FACULTY

All distance learning instructors are faculty members, 80 percent of whom hold a doctorate or other terminal degree in their field. All faculty members have continued involvement within their fields of expertise.

ADMISSION

NAU has a rolling admissions policy. There is a $45 graduate application fee and a $50 nonresident undergraduate application fee.

TUITION AND FEES

Nonresident students taking only Web or satellite courses are eligible for a special reduced tuition rate of 1½ times in-state tuition. Some classes may have additional fees attached (students should see the online course catalog for those fees).

FINANCIAL AID

NAU maintains an extensive financial assistance program. The amount of financial aid awarded to students is based upon their need as computed from the Free Application for Federal Student Aid (FAFSA). Scholarships are awarded based on academic excellence as well as need. In the 2001–02 academic year, more than $70 million was available for financial aid programs. About 60 percent of NAU students receive some form of aid. Students requiring financial aid or other benefits must comply with deadlines.

APPLYING

Undergraduate applicants must provide transcripts from high school and all higher education institutions attended. Graduate applicants must hold a baccalaureate degree from an accredited institution and provide transcripts of college course work. Students should refer to the NAU catalog for specific program requirements.

CONTACT

Distance Learning
Northern Arizona University
P.O. Box 4117
Flagstaff, Arizona 86001-4117
Telephone: 800-426-8315 (toll-free)
Fax: 928-523-1169
E-mail: distance.program@nau.edu
Web site: http://www.distance.nau.edu

Northwestern College

Center for Distance Education

St. Paul, Minnesota

Northwestern College, founded in 1902, is an independent, Christian four-year college. It is accredited by the North Central Association of Colleges and Schools. It first offered distance learning courses in 1994. In 2000–01, the College offered twenty-six courses at a distance and had approximately 1000 new distance enrollments.

DISTANCE LEARNING PROGRAM

The Center for Distance Education (CDE) at Northwestern College is at the forefront of delivering high-quality Christ-centered education in a flexible and convenient format. More than a correspondence school, the center utilizes the latest strategies in adult education and user-friendly technology to bring college courses to students. Since 1994, the Center for Distance Education has enrolled more than 3,300 students and delivered more than 8,000 courses to students all over the world. With more than forty-five courses to choose from, students can take courses in Bible, history, math, science, speech, music, and physical fitness.

DELIVERY MEDIA

The Center for Distance Education makes use of the most convenient delivery methods possible. While most of the courses do not require a computer and Internet connection, the purely online courses do. Course media is determined by the content of the course but usually consists of printed study guides, video lectures on DVD, CD-ROMs, and textbooks. The online courses require a computer with Internet access. Course work is submitted via postal mail or through the Internet. All courses host a Blackboard course Web site that is used for interaction between students and instructors, although each course varies in the level of participation.

PROGRAMS OF STUDY

The Center for Distance Education seeks to meet the educational needs of adult learners by offering Christ-centered curriculum. The center currently offers a Certificate of Bible, the INSIGHT program (first year of college), a Bachelor of Arts in Intercultural Ministries, and dual-enrollment options for high school students.

The Certificate of Bible prepares students for Christian ministry through the completion of 30 credits in thirty months. The program provides in-depth training in Bible study and develops credentials for ministry-related endeavors. All credits earned in the certificate program may be applied to a degree program at Northwestern.

The first-year INSIGHT program is designed to provide students with a comprehensive Christian worldview as a foundation for the major they eventually choose. The curriculum consists of four modules to be taken consecutively over the course of one year. Each INSIGHT module follows the unfolding of God's work through human developments, revealing His redemptive plan and consequently His glory. Each module is worth 8 semester credits for a total of 32 lower-division college credits.

The Bachelor of Arts in Intercultural Ministries is designed for students who have previously completed two years of postsecondary course work and are serious about full-time ministry. The major is targeted at those preparing for or currently involved in missions endeavors. However, any Christian, whether at home or abroad, who desires to more fully understand God's evangelistic purposes, benefits from this program.

Degrees currently under development are an Associate of Arts and a Bachelor of Arts in Biblical Studies.

SPECIAL PROGRAMS

The Post Secondary Enrollment Option (PSEO) is a program open to high school juniors and seniors who are public-, private-, or home-schooled and who are residents of the state of Minnesota. This program allows high school students to take courses through the Center for Distance Education and earn credit that applies to both high school and college. Credits earned under this program are applicable to degree programs at Northwestern or other institutions. The state of Minnesota finances the program.

STUDENT SERVICES

The Center for Distance Education helps students achieve their educational goals, without feeling like a number in someone's system. From enrollment through course completion, Student Services staff members provide caring, proactive service. The CDE processes course assignments, helps find mentors and exam proctors, and helps maintain contact with faculty members.

Northwestern College's Bernsten Library aids distance learners with research and resource acquisition for projects and papers. The CDE Web site and Course Management System contain independent study tools and helpful resources to facilitate learning.

CREDIT OPTIONS

Some students may transfer credits from another institution or may earn credits through examinations, portfolio assessment, life experience, or military training.

FACULTY

Distance Education faculty members are credentialed professionals who are highly qualified in their academic disciplines. More than 20 faculty members teach distance education courses. Of this group, 17 have earned doctoral degrees. The faculty members at Northwestern College care about each student's spiritual, intellectual, and emotional development as well as their academic development.

ADMISSION

To qualify for a certificate or degree program, students must meet the admission requirements of Northwestern College. Students should contact the Center for Distance Education for specific requirements. Students not seeking to earn credits toward a degree or a certificate are allowed to take up to 16 credits without formal admission to the College. PSEO applicants must be at least 16 years old, have suitable scores on a state recognized benchmark exam or a letter of recommendation from a high school official, and demonstrate competence in college-level work.

TUITION AND FEES

There is a one-time, nonrefundable $25 fee at the time of registration ($50 for Intercultural Ministries degree). Tuition is $220 per semester credit. There is a required fee of $75 for each course's materials. Students enrolled in the Certificate of Bible and Intercultural Ministries programs receive a 10 percent tuition discount. Other discounts apply to groups, senior citizens, and full- or part-time Christian workers.

FINANCIAL AID

Students who register for at least 6 credit hours in one semester may be eligible for financial aid. Northwestern College cooperates with the U.S. Department of Veterans Affairs when eligible students request VA benefits for distance education courses. The College also works with DANTES (Defense Activity for Non-Traditional Education Support). Students should contact the CDE for more information.

APPLYING

Information can be obtained either at the Distance Education Web site or by contacting the Center of Distance Education. Students may register for distance education by mail, fax, telephone, e-mail, online, or in person. To register, students should complete a registration form either online or by mail, pay the nonrefundable registration fee, and contact the CDE to begin the registration process.

CONTACT

The Center for Distance Education
Northwestern College
3003 Snelling Avenue North
Saint Paul, Minnesota 55113
Telephone: 651-631-5495
800-308-5495 (toll-free)
Fax: 651-631-5133
E-mail: distance@nwc.edu
Web site: http://www.distance.nwc.edu

Northwestern University

Communication Systems Strategy and Management Program

Evanston, Illinois

Northwestern University is an ambitious institution, striving for a level of preeminence achieved by only a handful of institutions in the world. Innovative teaching and pioneering research come together in a highly collaborative environment that transcends traditional academic boundaries.

Founded in 1851, Northwestern University is a private institution located in Evanston, Illinois, on the pristine shores of Lake Michigan, just 12 miles north of Chicago. Northwestern University currently has 11,600 students enrolled in seven schools on its Evanston campus.

The University has 2,250 full-time faculty members, including Nobel and Pulitzer Prize winners, MacArthur Fellowship recipients, and members of numerous honorary and professional societies. Northwestern has graduated more than 160,000 students—alumni who became leaders in business, government, law, science, education, medicine, media, and the performing arts. Northwestern is recognized both nationally and internationally for the quality of its educational programs at all levels.

DISTANCE LEARNING PROGRAM

The School of Communication offers its Communication Systems Strategy and Management Program (M.S. degree in communication) in a blended learning environment to a cohort group of 30 midlevel to senior-level managers. This two-year program provides the advanced skills and expertise to effectively close the technology disconnect that occurs between an organization's technical experts and its nontechnical executive decision makers.

The distributed learning component gives students a real-time classroom experience via videoconferencing, the ability to work and learn in group projects with other students over a distance, and an outstanding environment of collaborative learning as compared to other remote classroom programs.

Students enrolled as distance learners interact with Evanston-based instructors and students in real time. All students, on campus or remote, work together on team assignments that allow them to learn from interactions with students employed in different companies.

DELIVERY MEDIA

Distance learners attend three on-campus instructional meetings during each year. In the first year, students participate in a new-student orientation at the beginning of the fall term and two weekend meetings at the beginning of the winter and spring terms. In the second year, students participate in the fall orientation, a weekend meeting at the beginning of the winter term, and a weekend during the spring term for Final Presentations.

The remainder of the program is delivered synchronously via DSL or cable teleconferencing. Students take two courses at a time, meeting one full day per week on alternating Fridays and Saturdays for thirty weeks per year. Classes meet from 9:30 a.m. to 12:30 p.m. and from 2 to 5 p.m. central time. There is no summer school.

Recorded Webcasts of all lectures are available for student review. The program creates a 24-hour-a-day, seven-day-a-week conference bridge for all participants. This feature permits all learners, regardless of where they reside, to create virtual working groups.

PROGRAM OF STUDY

The Communication Systems Strategy and Management Program focuses on business and management expertise, much like an M.B.A., but with the addition of an effective foundation of study in technology and system principles.

As the most effective organizations optimally align IT strategies with company business objectives, this program addresses the ever-increasing demands placed on the investment, productivity, and performance of these technologies and systems, including the development of products and services in both the traditional economy and the continually evolving Internet economy.

All students take the same courses in a lockstep sequence, with no electives or independent studies.

STUDENT SERVICES

The University offers library services online 24 hours a day, seven days a week.

CREDIT OPTIONS

All credits must be earned in the Communication Systems Strategy and Management Program (equivalent to 48 credit hours). No transfer credits are accepted.

FACULTY

The faculty is made up of world-class Northwestern University professors. They possess extensive hands-on work experience as consultants to business and industry as well as government and private institutions.

As the program is interdisciplinary, it draws on faculty members not only from the nationally renowned School of Communication but also from Northwestern's McCormick School of Engineering and Applied Science, Kellogg School of Management, Medill School of Journalism, and Northwestern University Information Technology department.

ADMISSION

Applicants should have a minimum of four years of professional experience, an undergraduate degree from an accredited college or university, three letters of recommendation, and proficient written and oral English skills. Interviews are strongly recommended. Having an engineering degree or technical background is not required. GRE or GMAT scores are not required.

TUITION AND FEES

The all-inclusive fee for the three-term 2003 academic year is $25,785 ($8595 per term). The fee covers tuition, the orientation session, books, the latest equipment and software for learning via videoconferencing, hotel accommodations, and meals for on-site meetings. Distance learners provide their own laptop computers and transportation to and from on-site meetings.

Students take two 10-week courses or one 10-week course and two 5-week courses per year. Each ten-week course is equivalent to 4 credit hours. Each five-week course is equivalent to 2 credit hours. The equivalent per-credit-hour cost is $1075.

FINANCIAL AID

Financial assistance is available to eligible students in the form of Federal Stafford Student Loans or private loans.

APPLYING

Applicants can download application materials from the Web by visiting http://www.communication.northwestern.edu/mscstrategy or may request materials via the contact methods listed below.

CONTACT

Donna Weirich, Director
Communication Systems Strategy and Management Program
Northwestern University
2240 Campus Drive
Evanston, Illinois 60208
Telephone: 847-491-3848
Fax: 847-467-1096
E-mail: jfinn@northwestern.edu

Norwich University

Online Master's Degree Programs

Northfield, Vermont

Norwich University's online master's degree programs combine the full convenience of an online education with a 183-year-old heritage to provide high-quality yet affordable distance offerings. Norwich University is accredited by the New England Association of Schools and Colleges (NEASC), a regional accrediting agency that represents the highest form of accreditation that a university can receive. The four master's degree programs—business, diplomacy, information security, and justice administration—can be completed in twenty-four months or less. Each program is capped by a one- or two-week trip to Norwich University and the Green Mountains of Vermont. The curriculum is highly customized to the professional needs of the student, utilizing the best of modern learning techniques. The programs' student-retention rates are the best in the industry, owing to small class sizes; innovative curricula; emphasis on meeting student needs; 24-hour-a-day, seven-day-a-week technical help; and the ability to generate a sense of community in the online environment. When students become part of Norwich University, they become part of something very old, very proud, and very deep.

Norwich University was founded in 1819. It is the oldest private engineering college in the country, the oldest private military college in the country, the first Corps of Cadets to enroll women (twenty-five years before any other), the first to allow African Americans to join the Corps, and the first university to offer graduate low-residency programs. The University was founded upon innovative educational techniques and has continued to outpace the academic world in the delivery of education. Norwich University is a learning community, American in character yet global in perspective, engaged in personal and intellectual transformation and dedicated to knowledge, mutual respect, creativity, and community service.

DISTANCE LEARNING PROGRAM

Each of the four Norwich online graduate programs delivers a 36-credit degree in twenty-four months or less, while students in the M.B.A. program can go on to receive a certificate of advanced graduate study in dynamic professional subjects in six additional months. Norwich University's graduate programs provide a high-quality, structured, and rigorous education for today's busy professionals. Students log on to the classroom when it is convenient to download assignments, post assignments, engage in asynchronous discussion with classmates, collaborate on group case-study projects, and read lectures from the professor. Each program is composed of six 6-credit, sequential seminars. The seminars are sequenced so that Seminar 2 builds on Seminar 1. Seminars start in January and September.

DELIVERY MEDIA

Norwich University utilizes an online virtual classroom that is supported 24 hours a day, seven days a week. Internet access and proficiency is a requirement for all students. Minimum configurations are Processor 266, Ram 32MB, modem or cable access, CD-ROM, Windows operating system 95 or higher, Microsoft Office 2000, and Internet Explorer 5.0.

PROGRAMS OF STUDY

Norwich University offers online master's degrees in business, diplomacy, information security, and justice administration.

The core seminar subjects for the Master of Business Administration (M.B.A.) are general and human resource management, finance/accounting, marketing, operations management, e-commerce/security, and strategic management. Special tracks of study are provided for engineering professionals, professional women, military personnel, and architecture professionals. Upon completion of the M.B.A., students may enroll in one or more of the following 12-credit certificate programs: marketing research, e-commerce, engineering firm management, international business, computer and information assurance, and architectural firm management.

The Master of Science in information assurance covers the foundations of information assurance, tools (technical and management), prevention (technical measures and human factors), detection and response, management of information assurance, and current hot topics.

The Master of Arts in diplomacy examines balance of power theories and alternatives, regime theory, law and the international system, international economics, conflict prevention, conflict resolution and containment, and force/military intervention.

The Master of Justice Administration (M.J.A.) examines the history of criminal justice, the criminal justice administration system, the nature of crime, the response to crime, and justice policy.

STUDENT SERVICES

Norwich University offers online support services that allow students to inquire about the program, apply for admission, submit application and deposit fees, access library services, and obtain ongoing academic advising.

CREDIT OPTIONS

On a case-by-case basis, students may transfer up to 6 graduate credits for some programs.

FACULTY

Norwich University Online instructors are professors and top executives from nationally recognized universities and corporations, who are the experts in the areas of study.

ADMISSION

Admissions criteria include a completed application form, an application fee, a letter of intent, a resume, three letters of recommendation, official transcripts, and TOEFL scores (for international students).

TUITION AND FEES

For the 2004–05 academic year, the Norwich University Online graduate tuition is between $526 and $624 per credit, or $3156 to $3744 per seminar. Book, resource, and technology fees range from $350 to $425 per semester. Travel, housing, and food for the residency is included in the tuition.

FINANCIAL AID

Financial aid is available in the form of student loans. For information regarding financial aid options, students should contact the Financial Aid Office by e-mail at nufinaid@norwich.edu.

APPLYING

Applications are accepted for the January and September semesters. Students who need the M.B.A. Prerequisite Seminar begin in March or July. Deadline dates for applying are approximately two months prior to the seminar start dates. Students are notified when their application materials arrive in the office. Students are notified in writing within one week of the Admissions Committee meeting.

CONTACT

Graduate Programs
Norwich University
158 Harmon Drive
Northfield, Vermont 05663
Telephone: 802-485-2567
Fax: 802-485-2042
E-mail: mbainfo@norwich.edu (M.B.A.)
diplomacy@norwich.edu (Diplomacy)
mja@norwich.edu(Justice Administration)
msia@norwich.edu (Information Assurance)
Web site: http://www3.norwich.edu/grad

Nova Southeastern University

Graduate School of Computer and Information Sciences

Fort Lauderdale, Florida

A major force in educational innovation, the Graduate School of Computer and Information Sciences (SCIS) provides educational programs of distinction to prepare students for leadership roles in its disciplines. Its strengths include a distinguished faculty, a cutting-edge curriculum, and flexible online formats for its five M.S. and five Ph.D. programs. It has approximately 2,000 graduate students. All programs enable working professionals to earn the M.S., Ph.D., or Ed.D. without interrupting their careers. Online master's degree programs require no campus attendance and are available to part-time or full-time students worldwide. A unique online doctoral program requires only four weekends or two weeklong campus visits each year. The school has online students living in every state in the United States and in more than twenty-five countries. Ranked by Forbes *magazine as one of the nation's top twenty cyber universities, and listed in the* Princeton Review's *"The Best Distance Learning Graduate Schools," the School currently offers more than 300 online classes annually. The School, a pioneer in online graduate education, began offering online programs in 1983 and created the first electronic classroom in 1985. The School has been awarding graduate degrees since 1983.*

In addition to its regional accreditation by the Commission on Colleges of the Southern Association of Colleges and Schools, the school is a certified member of the Electronic Campus of the Southern Regional Education Board. Its curriculum in information security has been certified by the U.S. National Security Agency (NSA) for compliance with CNSS standards. The school participates in several federal and military programs including the DANTES Distance Learning Program and the U.S. Army's new online initiative, eArmyU. The school has been awarded a chapter of Upsilon Pi Epsilon (UPE), the International Honor Society for the Computing and Information Disciplines, and qualified students are initiated into the society. Its student chapter of the Institute of Electrical and Electronic Engineers (IEEE) is the largest in Florida.

Located on a beautiful 300-acre campus in Fort Lauderdale, Florida, Nova Southeastern University (NSU) has more than 20,000 students and is the largest independent institution of higher education in the southeastern United States. The tenth-largest private university in the United States, NSU awards associates, bachelor's, master's, educational specialist, doctoral, and first-professional degrees in more than 90 disciplines. It has a college of arts and sciences, as well as schools of medicine, dentistry, pharmacy, allied health, optometry, law, computer and information sciences, psychology, education, business and entrepreneurship, oceanography, and humanities and social sciences.

DISTANCE LEARNING PROGRAM

All of the school's graduate programs are offered in distance learning formats. Online master's programs require no on-campus classroom attendance. Students may complete the M.S. degree in twelve to eighteen months. Doctoral programs use one of two formats: cluster or institute. Cluster students attend four cluster meetings per year, held quarterly over an extended weekend (Friday, Saturday, and half-day Sunday) at the University. Cluster terms start in September and March. Cluster weekends take place in September, December, March, and June. Institute students attend a weeklong institute twice a year at the University. Institutes are held in mid-January and mid-July at the start of each five-month term. Clusters and institutes bring together students and faculty members for participation in courses, workshops, and dissertation counseling. Doctoral courses also have an online component. Between meetings, students complete assignments, research papers, and projects and participate in a range of online activities.

DELIVERY MEDIA

Online learning methods involve Web pages to access course materials, announcements, the electronic library, and other information, plus a range of activities that facilitate frequent student-professor and student-student interaction. Faculty members and students interact via online forums using threaded discussion boards, e-mail, chat rooms, electronic classrooms, and online submission of assignments in multimedia formats. Students are provided computer accounts but must obtain their own Internet service providers and use their own computers. New students are provided an orientation on computer and software requirements, online access, online tools and methods, and library resources.

PROGRAMS OF STUDY

The School offers distance programs leading to the M.S. in computer information systems (including a specialization in information security), computer science, computing technology in education, information security, and management information systems (including specializations in information security and e-commerce); the Ph.D. in computer information systems, computer science, computing technology in education, information science, and information systems; and the Ed.D. in computing technology in education. The School's master's degree students may apply for early admission into the doctoral program, which provides the opportunity to earn the Ph.D. or Ed.D. in a shorter time. The M.S. requires 36 credit hours (thesis optional). Terms are twelve weeks long, and there are four terms each year. To earn the M.S. in twelve months, the student must enroll in three courses each term. To complete the M.S. in eighteen months, the student must enroll in two courses each term. Master's terms start in September, January, April, and July. Doctoral programs require 64 credits, including eight 3-credit courses, four 4-credit projects, and the dissertation. They may be completed in three years. The Ph.D. in computer information systems and computer science are offered only in cluster format. Doctoral programs in computing technology in education, information science, and information systems are offered in cluster and institute formats. Students attend clusters or institutes during their first two years of the program while completing course work.

SPECIAL PROGRAMS

All of the School's programs are offered through the Southern Regional Education Board's Electronic Campus and the U.S. Army's eArmyU program.

CREDIT OPTIONS

Master's applicants may request a transfer of up to 6 graduate credits. Courses proposed for transfer must have grades of at least B. Credit is not awarded for life or work experience.

FACULTY

SCIS has 20 full-time and 10 part-time faculty members. All faculty members teaching at the graduate level have doctoral degrees.

ADMISSION

The master's applicant must have an appropriate undergraduate degree with a GPA of at least 2.5 and a GPA of at least 3.0 in an appropriate major. The doctoral applicant must have a master's degree with an appropriate graduate major and a graduate GPA of at least 3.25. Degrees must be from regionally accredited institutions. All applicants must submit a summary of professional experience or score report of the GRE, and three evaluations. English proficiency is a requirement for admission.

TUITION AND FEES

Tuition is $425 per credit for master's students; for doctoral students, tuition is $4750 per five-month term, or $475 per credit hour. The registration fee is $30 per term.

FINANCIAL AID

To qualify for financial assistance, a student must be admitted, must be a U.S. citizen or an eligible permanent resident, and must plan on registering for a minimum of 6 credit hours per term. A prospective student who requires financial assistance should apply for it while still a candidate for admission. For financial assistance information or application forms, students should call 800-522-3243 (toll-free).

APPLYING

Admission decisions are made on a rolling basis. To ensure evaluation for the desired starting term, reviewable applications must be received at least one month prior to the start of that term. The application fee is $50. Late applications that cannot be processed in time for the desired starting term are considered for the next term. Applicants may be granted provisional admission status pending completion of the application process. Admission forms, brochures, and the graduate catalog may be downloaded from the School's Web site. Master's terms start in September, January, April, and July. Doctoral cluster terms start in September and March. Doctoral institute terms start in January and July.

CONTACT

Graduate School of Computer and Information Sciences
Nova Southeastern University
Carl DeSantis Building, Fourth Floor
3301 College Avenue
Fort Lauderdale, Florida 33314-4416
Telephone: 954-262-2000
800-986-2247 (toll-free)
E-mail: scisinfo@scis.nova.edu
Web site: http://www.scis.nova.edu

Ohio University

Lifelong Learning Programs

Athens, Ohio

Ohio University, founded in 1804, was the first institution of higher learning in the Northwest Territory. Today it offers all the resources of a major university—diverse intellectual stimulation and an abundance of social and cultural activities—in a quiet, small-city setting. In addition to the main campus in Athens, the University has six regional centers in the southeast quadrant of Ohio.

Ohio University offers degrees in more than 325 subject areas through its colleges: Arts and Sciences, Business, Communication, Education, Engineering and Technology, Fine Arts, Health and Human Services, Honors Tutorial, Osteopathic Medicine, and University College. The University is accredited by the North Central Association of Colleges and Schools and holds membership in a number of professional organizations; in addition, many academic programs are accredited by their respective associations.

Ohio University has also been a leader in providing learning opportunities for nontraditional students, including eighty years of correspondence education, credit for college-level learning from life experience, and the external-student degree program.

DISTANCE LEARNING PROGRAM

Independent and Distance Learning (IDL) serves students at a distance through correspondence and online courses, course credit by examination, individual learning contracts, and experiential learning credit. Credit earned through one of these options is considered residential credit and may be applied without limit to a degree program at Ohio University or transferred to another institution (subject to any conditions set by the accepting institution). Approximately 250 courses are currently available through Independent and Distance Learning; the program has about 4,000 course enrollments each year.

The External Student Program (ESP) assists students at a distance who are working toward Ohio University degrees with such services as transcript evaluation, academic advising, and degree planning. The College Program for the Incarcerated (CPI) offers the same services to incarcerated individuals, along with comprehensive fees unique to this program and staff experienced in meeting the special needs of this population.

DELIVERY MEDIA

Correspondence between students and instructors, using the postal system or fax, is the primary delivery system for IDL courses. E-mail lesson service and videotape supplements are being incorporated into an increasing number of courses. The number of courses using the Internet and World Wide Web for instructional delivery and communications between students and instructors is growing. Online courses are available as self-paced (IDL) and as term-based (Ohio University Online).

PROGRAMS OF STUDY

To earn an Ohio University degree, students must enroll with the External Student Program. Students are assigned an adviser to assist them in choosing courses and creating the degree proposals.

Three associate degrees are available: Associate in Arts (A.A.), Associate in Science (A.S.), and Associate in Individualized Studies (A.I.S.). All require the completion of 96 quarter hours of credit; at least 30 quarter hours of credit from Ohio University.

Through the Bachelor of Specialized Studies (B.S.S.), students design individualized baccalaureate-degree programs, creating unique majors that combine courses from two or more departments. Students must have sophomore rank and a minimum cumulative grade point average of 2.0 in order to submit a proposal. The proposal specifies the course of study and an area of concentration of at least 45 quarter hours (which cannot duplicate an existing major). At least 45 hours must be earned after admission to the B.S.S. program; at least 80 hours of the 192 hours total for the degree must be at the junior/senior level. Sample tracks for the B.S.S. are available for humanities, liberal studies, behavior management, human development, applied business management, and applied health care management. An adviser assists students through the entire B.S.S. proposal process.

SPECIAL PROGRAMS

The Institutes for Adult Learners are held annually on the Ohio University campus. Institute students earn credit, usually four quarters per course, become acquainted with the campus and faculty members, and participate in a residential experience with other nontraditional students. Courses are taught in intensive, one-week classroom formats supplemented by individual work before and after the Institute.

CREDIT OPTIONS

Students at a distance who are interested in completing an Ohio University degree through the External Student Program can use a combination of credit earned through the Institutes, credit for experiential learning documented through a portfolio process, transfer credit (including military and professional training equivalencies established by the American Council on Education), and Independent and Distance Learning options. Students may apply 24 quarter hours of experiential learning credit toward an associate degree; 48 quarter hours may be applied toward a bachelor's degree.

Regularly enrolled students on any Ohio University campus may use IDL or experiential learning credit toward their degrees with their college's approval.

FACULTY

All IDL courses are taught by permanent Ohio University faculty members; more than 90 percent of the 125 faculty members teaching in the program have a doctorate or other terminal degree.

ADMISSION

Enrollment in IDL courses is open to anyone who can profit from the learning. Enrollment in a course does not constitute formal admission to the University. Students must have a high school diploma to be admitted to the External Student program; transfer students must have a minimum 2.0 cumulative grade point average. Admission to the External Student Program does not guarantee on-campus admission to a specific degree program at Ohio University.

TUITION AND FEES

Fees for IDL courses in 2003–04 were correspondence and online courses, $110 per quarter hour; course credit by examination, $55 per quarter hour; and Independent Learning projects, $125 per quarter hour. Fees for the External Student Program were a $125 application fee and, in subsequent years, an $85 annual matriculation fee. In 2003–04, students seeking credit for experiential learning paid $480 for the required portfolio development course plus $175 per course assessment (paid after completion of the portfolio development course).

FINANCIAL AID

Students may use veterans' benefits and employer reimbursement to pay course and program fees. Some students in the External Student Program may qualify for federal financial aid. Standard tuition and fees paid by on-campus students cannot be applied to IDL courses.

APPLYING

Students may enroll in Independent and Distance Learning courses at any time; enrollment forms are provided in the IDL catalog and at the program's Web site. A separate application process is required for the External Student Program; forms are provided in the IDL catalog or online.

CONTACT

Director, Independent and Distance Learning Programs
Haning Hall 222
Ohio University
Athens, Ohio 45701
Telephone: 740-593-2910
800-444-2910 (toll-free within U.S.)
Fax: 740-593-2901
E-mail: independent.study@ohio.edu (General Information)
external.student@ohio.edu (External Student Program)
cpi@ohio.edu (College Program for the Incarcerated)
WWW: http://www.ohiou.edu/independent/

Old Dominion University

Distance Learning/TELETECHNET

Norfolk, Virginia

Old Dominion University, a state-assisted institution in Norfolk, Virginia, is part of a metropolitan and historic area with a population of approximately 1.5 million. Established in 1930, the University enrolls more than 20,000 students, including 5,000 graduate students, and operates centers in Northern Virginia, Hampton, Portsmouth, and Virginia Beach as well as community college and military base locations throughout the commonwealth of Virginia and several additional states.

Old Dominion University is accredited by the Commission on Colleges of the Southern Association of Colleges and Schools (1866 Southern Lane, Decatur, Georgia 30033-4097; telephone: 404-679-4501) to award baccalaureate, master's, and doctoral degrees and certificates of advanced study. The undergraduate and graduate business programs are fully accredited by AACSB–The Association to Advance Collegiate Schools of Business. The graduate and undergraduate education programs are accredited by the National Council for Accreditation of Teacher Learning Education (NCATE). The engineering technology programs are fully accredited by the Technology Accreditation Commission of the Accreditation Board for Engineering and Technology, Inc. (TAC/ABET). The nursing program is accredited by the Commission on Collegiate Nurse Education.

DISTANCE LEARNING PROGRAM

Old Dominion is recognized as an international leader in telecommunications with the creation of TELETECHNET, a distance learning network in partnership with community colleges, military installations, and corporations. Within TELETECHNET, Old Dominion University offers degrees through courses televised to off-campus sites across the country and has an enrollment of more than 5,000 students. Students earn baccalaureate degrees from Old Dominion by completing the first two years of course work at their local community college or other accredited institutions. Old Dominion provides the remaining course work at the site primarily through telecourses using audio and video technologies. In addition to eighteen baccalaureate degrees, TELETECHNET also offers seven master's degrees.

DELIVERY MEDIA

Old Dominion University courses are delivered primarily by Ku-band digital satellite with one-way video and two-way audio for interaction between faculty members and students. Classes originate in Norfolk and are transmitted to receiving sites in five states, the District of Columbia, and the Bahamas. Several classes and degree programs are also offered in a Web-based or CD-ROM format, providing students greater flexibility in completion of course work. In addition, a number of classes are streamed over the Internet, where students have access to them at home or at work.

PROGRAMS OF STUDY

Old Dominion's TELETECHNET program offers baccalaureate degrees in business administration, communication, computer science, criminal justice, engineering technology, health sciences, human services, interdisciplinary studies (elementary school education, leading to a master's degree, and professional writing), medical technology, nursing (RN to B.S.N.), and occupational and technical studies.

The following master's degrees are offered: Master of Engineering Management, Master of Science in community health, Master of Science in Education (elementary school education, which is tied to the bachelor's program, and special education, which meets certification and endorsement requirements in learning disabilities, mental retardation, and emotional/behavioral disorders), Master of Science in Nursing (family nurse practitioner studies), and Master of Science in occupational and technical studies. Online graduate programs include the Master of Science in Education (elementary and/or secondary education) and the Master of Science in Nursing.

STUDENT SERVICES

The Old Dominion library supports the TELETECHNET students by providing library resources, services, and reference assistance that are required for successful completion of course work, research papers and projects, and independent reading and research. Services are available primarily through the library's Web site (http://www.lib.odu.edu), with telephone, e-mail, and fax requests also provided.

TELETECHNET students have the advantage of checking out videotapes or viewing streamed video archives over the Internet if they miss a class session due to family responsibilities or job conflicts. Computer labs, which are connected to the main campus and have Internet access, are available at each site for the students' use.

CREDIT OPTIONS

Students can transfer credits earned at other accredited postsecondary institutions to Old Dominion University and can receive credit through the College-Level Examination Program (CLEP) for certain courses. Returning adult students may also have the option of applying for academic credit through the Experiential Learning Program. This program evaluates college-level learning gained outside the college classroom. Examples are military and workplace training, independent study, professional certification, portfolios, and examination.

FACULTY

More than 50 percent of Old Dominion University's full-time faculty members have taught on television, and this percentage continues to grow as TELETECHNET expands its degree offerings. Specialized training for this unique teaching environment is provided to ensure high-quality instruction for students.

ADMISSION

Prospective students must submit an application accompanied by a $40 fee for degree-seeking admission and request that official transcripts from all previous colleges be sent to the Office of Distance Learning for evaluation of credits earned (transfer admission generally requires a minimum 2.2 grade point average).

TUITION AND FEES

Old Dominion's TELETECHNET program offers affordable tuition for students. Undergraduate TELETECHNET tuition for the 2003–04 school year was $173 per credit for students enrolled outside Virginia. Graduate tuition was $273 per credit for students enrolled outside Virginia. There is a required general services fee of $9 for each semester. Rates may change upon approval of the Board of Visitors.

FINANCIAL AID

Old Dominion University is a direct lending institution and awards financial aid from federally funded and state-funded programs as well as from privately funded sources. The University requires all students applying for need-based assistance to complete the Free Application for Federal Student Aid (FAFSA). Those applying for merit-based awards must complete the Old Dominion University Scholarship Application.

APPLYING

The deadline for admission for the fall semester for transfer students and graduate students is May 1. The deadline for nursing students is February 1. The deadline for applying for the spring semester is October 1. Summer deadline is March 15. Decisions are made on a rolling basis, and applicants are notified of their admission status within four weeks after receipt of all application materials.

CONTACT

Dr. Jeanie P. Kline
Assistant Vice President for Student and Academic Support
424 Gornto TELETECHNET Center
Old Dominion University
Norfolk, Virginia 23529
Telephone: 800-YOU-2ODU (800-968-2638, toll-free)
Fax: 757-683-5492
E-mail: ttnet@odu.edu
Web site: http://www.dl.odu.edu

OSU Oregon State UNIVERSITY Extended Campus

Oregon State University

Extended Campus

Corvallis, Oregon

Founded in 1868 and accredited by the Commission on Colleges and Universities of the Northwest Association of Schools, Colleges, and Universities, Oregon State University (OSU) is one of a select number of schools nationwide to receive the Carnegie Foundation's highest rating for education and research. A land-grant, sea-grant, and space-grant university, Oregon State serves the state of Oregon, the nation, and the world through its teaching, research, and outreach efforts. Today, OSU is home to nearly 19,000 students who are pursuing their degrees in one of 214 undergraduate and graduate academic degree programs. The American Productivity and Quality Center recently named Oregon State a top university for providing electronic services to students.

DISTANCE LEARNING PROGRAM

During fall term 2003, nearly 1,500 individuals throughout Oregon and the world were enrolled in Oregon State University courses off campus. Each term, through OSU Extended Campus (Ecampus), students have access to more than 150 distance courses in more than thirty-five subjects in areas as diverse as education, fisheries and wildlife, history, math, and psychology. Courses are designed as part of bachelor's completion programs, undergraduate minors, certificate programs, and some graduate-level course work.

DELIVERY MEDIA

Oregon State offers the majority of its distance courses via the Web and videotapes and through independent study with an assigned instructor. Courses often entail a combination of delivery methods, such as a video course with class interaction through an electronic listserv or Web site. Students communicate with instructors and administrative staff members via e-mail, phone, fax, or regular mail. Certain courses and programs are also delivered through face-to-face instruction or interactive television broadcasting (ITV) at statewide locations.

PROGRAMS OF STUDY

Oregon State is one of a handful of universities nationwide pioneering the field of online education. Most of the more than 300 distance courses offered each year include some online component such as e-mail communication with faculty members, and the majority of courses are offered partially or entirely on the Web.

Dual-enrollment programs are available through some Oregon community colleges; however, many students work with the Ecampus Student Services staff members to utilize past college experiences and to plan individual programs. Students can complete their degree from anywhere in the world by taking upper-division course work through OSU Extended Campus. Students may select from a Bachelor of Arts/Bachelor of Science (B.A./B.S.) in liberal studies (a preprofessional elementary education option is available statewide), a B.S. in environmental sciences, a B.S. in general agriculture, and a B.S. in natural resources. Students in bachelor's programs must accumulate a minimum of 180 quarter credit hours to graduate.

Undergraduate minors in natural resources, environmental sciences, and fisheries and wildlife are available worldwide. Minors usually include at least 27 quarter credit hours of study and can be pursued as part of a bachelor's program or added to a transcript after graduation.

OSU Ecampus also offers online graduate degrees in education, nuclear engineering, and radiation health physics.

SPECIAL PROGRAMS

Web-based graduate-level course work in education is available through Ecampus for teachers, trainers, and other professional educators who wish to pursue an advanced degree or simply gain skills in advanced teaching strategies, teaching course work online, or business and technology methods. The School of Education offers an on-site/online program for those seeking to earn their Oregon Continuing Teaching License. The Professional Technical Teacher Education Program is delivered online, with on-site student teaching and practicum, and is aligned with Oregon's educational standards. Students may enroll in Web courses and related practicums at a rate based on their individual needs, tailoring their education to meet both time and financial constraints. Students should visit the program's Web site for specific contact information on these and other graduate-level programs.

OSU's Professional Programs of the Ecampus operates as an outreach to corporations, public agencies, organizations, and professionals seeking to upgrade their skill level and increase their employability and productivity. Professional Programs offers a variety of noncredit programs and individualized contract training in areas such as business, human resources management, and health-care leadership. Professional Programs also offers online short courses that fit the busy adult's lifestyle and pocketbook.

OSU Extended Campus offers OSU K–12 Online, a top-quality high school curriculum, which is available to students seeking courses that may not be available through their district or meet their homeschool needs. These online courses can be taken for elective credit and/or high school graduation completion.

STUDENT SERVICES

Oregon State makes it a priority to provide excellent student services to distance learners via e-mail, a toll-free phone number, and a comprehensive Web site, which includes live chat, online forums, and a searchable knowledge base. Students have access to online library services, a toll-free hotline for computer consulting, online writing support, step-by-step assistance with procedures, and an online schedule of classes. Students can subscribe to *OSU E-News,* a free electronic newsletter that provides timely course and program information, student and faculty member profiles, and technical tips.

CREDIT OPTIONS

All credits earned through distance or online education are recorded on an Oregon State University transcript and do not appear any differently than on-campus courses. Each course falls under the same accreditation ratings of the individual department from which it originates. Transfer students enrolled in academic programs must have previous credits evaluated by an OSU adviser or the Ecampus Enrollment Coordinator to ensure that program requirements are met. Forty-five of the last 75 credit hours for bachelor's completion programs must be from Oregon State University.

FACULTY

Oregon State has more than 2,700 faculty members, with nearly 1,100 in the tenure system. Eighty-five percent of faculty members in professorial ranks have doctoral degrees. OSU distance education faculty members must adhere to the same quality standards as any faculty member teaching on campus.

ADMISSION

Students taking distance or online courses to meet OSU degree requirements must be admitted to the University through the regular admission process and must meet the requirements for admission. Nondegree enrollment requires no formal admission and can be attained by contacting the Office of Admissions. For more information on regular or nondegree admission, students can visit the Office of Admissions's Web site at http://oregonstate.edu/admissions.

TUITION AND FEES

Tuition for undergraduate distance degree courses is $177 per quarter credit hour for most courses. Graduate-level courses are generally $381 per quarter credit, depending upon the program. Additional fees may be assessed for tape rental or other course materials. Students may check the Ecampus Web site.

FINANCIAL AID

Distance learners are eligible for financial aid programs according to the same rules as on-campus students. Generally, to be considered, a student must be taking at least 6 quarter hours. Some scholarships are open to part-time distance learning students. Students can consult specific information on the Web site at http://oregonstate.edu/admin/finaid.

APPLYING

Distance learners seeking an OSU degree should apply through the regular application process. Some of the distance programs at the graduate level are cohort based and require admission prior to fall quarter. The undergraduate distance degree programs accept students year-round. It is recommended that students seek initial advising prior to the application process. Registration for individual courses generally requires no application other than to contact the registrar for admission as a nondegree or part-time student.

CONTACT

OSU Extended Campus
Attention: Student Services Center
4943 The Valley Library
Oregon State University
Corvallis, Oregon 97331-4504
Telephone: 541-737-9204
800-667-1465 (toll-free)
Fax: 541-737-2734
E-mail: ecampus@oregonstate.edu
Web site: http://ecampus.oregonstate.edu

Pace University

Online Pace

New York, Pleasantville, and White Plains, New York

Pace University is a private, nonsectarian, coeducational institution. Originally founded as a school of accounting in 1906, Pace Institute was designated Pace College in 1973. Through growth and success, Pace College was designated a university, as approved by the New York State Board of Regents. Today, Pace offers comprehensive undergraduate, graduate, doctoral, and professional-level programs at several campus locations and via distance learning experiences through six schools and colleges.

Pace University's motto is "Opportunitas." It offers talented and ambitious students the opportunity to discover their potential and realize their dreams. Pace provides a supportive environment and challenging programs to prepare students for a responsible life and successful career. Pace is committed to providing students with a learning experience that is respectful of traditional academic values, entrepreneurial in spirit, and responsive to the demands of diverse learners.

DISTANCE LEARNING PROGRAM

The expansion of computer technology and the Internet enables Pace University to add new meaning to its motto as it offers access in new ways. Online courses and programs are offered for students who wish to pursue higher education but are unable to attend classes on campus or who desire the flexibility of learning online. Online courses and programs are developed with the same commitment as traditional courses, and they provide a range of learning opportunities and support services that ensure successful outcomes and positive experiences for students.

Programs and individual courses are offered through the Lubin School of Business, Dyson College of Arts and Sciences, School of Computer Science and Information Systems, School of Education, Lienhard School of Nursing, and School of Law.

DELIVERY MEDIA

Pace University utilizes Blackboard for course delivery. Blackboard 6 is a comprehensive and flexible e-learning software platform through which students have access to virtual classrooms, communication methods, and course content.

PROGRAMS OF STUDY

Three online baccalaureate-completion programs are available. Programs are developed specifically for adult professionals who have earned at least 60 college credits. Students progress through the program at their own pace and can complete the degree program within twenty-four months.

The Bachelor of Science (B.S.) program in professional technology studies with a concentration in telecommunications was designed for individuals in the telecommunications industry. Most of the students in the telecommunications concentration work in corporations that are in the telecommunications business. They want to complete their bachelor's degree program to gain the credentials and knowledge that will enable them to be promoted within their company and to advance within the industry. Specifically, the concentration strives to provide a strong foundation in the technical and nontechnical aspects of emerging telecommunications technologies; establish an understanding of technology management; develop skills that allow students to work effectively with the Internet and to create multimedia Web pages; refine students' abilities to work on teams to solve problems; teach students to use innovative technology to manage projects and establish cost projections; prepare graduates for development of effective interpersonal relationships in organizations, including superior-subordinate relationships, formal and informal group interactions, interpersonal and intergroup conflict, and motivation and job satisfaction; and help students develop an understanding of the theory and practice of effective communication between individuals from diverse domestic and international cultures.

The B.S. program in professional technology studies with a concentration in Internet for e-commerce provides the tools needed to build and design Web sites, including e-commerce applications, and teaches successful marketing of Web sites and products. Providing a strong foundation in the technical and nontechnical aspects of the Internet and e-commerce, this program teaches students the skills to create multimedia Web pages, understand the marketing principles necessary for effective online retail environments, and practice implementing these principles.

The B.S. program in professional communication studies with a concentration in organizational communication teaches students to analyze print and electronic mass-media trends and provides the tools to master public opinion research and public relations and their application to modern organizations. Students develop skills to understand the process of symbolic interaction in organizations, the practical and theoretical ways to provide organizational communication successfully, contemporary speech models for professional situations, effective presentation reports, the concepts and practice of public opinion research, and the theory and practice of effective communication between diverse cultures.

Two online graduate degrees are offered through Pace University. The Master of Science (M.S.) in Internet technology for e-commerce is designed for people interested in working specifically with e-commerce platforms and technology. Students engage in course work that includes programming, Internet marketing, and advertising and promotion. Students are required to register for various elective courses, ranging from strategic management to database management systems, which are all applicable in the corporate world. The program concludes with a capstone experience.

The e.MBA@PACE is a fully accredited, two-year, online executive M.B.A. program designed specifically for the new generation of business leaders. Combining online learning with brief classroom residencies, this project-based program gives students the tools needed to master qualitative and quantitative analytical skills by working in teams on a series of nine large-scale projects and learning exercises centered on realistic business problems. This outcome-based learning approach has been proven highly effective, and the e.MBA@PACE is one of the few online programs offering it. During the residency periods, student teams present their projects to program faculty members and practitioner experts. Students also demonstrate learning through assessment exercises and attend workshops to acquire managerial skills.

The M.S. in telecommunications is a hybrid program; it has both online and on-campus components. The 36-credit program responds to the need for information to move quickly within, between, and among organizations. The program integrates technical courses with a strong foundation in business management policies and an understanding of regulatory restrictions. The curriculum emphasizes the planning and management of infrastructures for data, voice, and video networks.

A Doctor of Professional Studies (D.P.S.) degree program in computing is offered to provide a unique opportunity for information technology (IT) professionals to pursue a part-time doctoral degree. Throughout the program, students expand their knowledge base across applied computer science, information systems, software engineering, telecommunications, and emerging information technologies. Monthly weekend residencies are required. The program allows students to develop solid, working relationships with other students from a wide range of computer-related backgrounds and to integrate the academic and professional aspects of computing.

Certificate programs are available in business aspects of publishing and Internet technologies. Advanced graduate certificate programs are available in telecommunications and Internet technology.

CREDIT OPTIONS

Pace University offers a wide variety of individual courses online through its six schools and colleges. Students may register for credit-bearing and non-credit-bearing course work.

FACULTY

Pace has an outstanding teaching faculty. Senior members, including department heads, teach freshman and sophomore students as well as upper-division classes. Approximately 82 percent of the full-time faculty members hold a doctoral degree, and many act as professional consultants to other educational institutions, businesses, and government agencies. Many adjunct faculty members pursue professional careers while teaching their specialty.

ADMISSION

Admission varies by school and program. For further program information, prospective students should visit http://enrollment.pace.edu/moreinfo or e-mail online@pace.edu. Applications for admission are available online at http://apply.pace.edu.

TUITION AND FEES

Undergraduate tuition for the 2003–04 academic year was $590 per credit, or $10,270 per semester (12–18 credits). Graduate tuition ranged between $600 and $710 per credit and varied by school.

FINANCIAL AID

Financial aid is available to matriculated students. Students may contact the Office of Student Financial Services at 212-346-1300. Pace supports various financing options and payment plans for nonmatriculated students.

CONTACT

Pace University
One Pace Plaza
New York, New York 10038
Telephone: 212-346-1200
800-874-PACE
(toll-free)
E-mail: online@pace.edu
Web site: http://online.pace.edu

Pace University
861 Bedford Road
Pleasantville, New York 10570
Telephone: 914-773-3200
800-874-PACE
(toll-free)
E-mail: online@pace.edu
Web site: http://online.pace.edu

Pace University
1 Martine Avenue
White Plains, New York 10606
Telephone: 914-422-4000
800-874-PACE
(toll-free)
E-mail: online@pace.edu
Web site: http://online.pace.edu

Park University

College for Distance Learning

Parkville, Missouri

Park University was founded in 1875 and is accredited by the Higher Learning Commission of the North Central Association of Colleges and Schools. Park's College for Distance Learning offers Bachelor of Science (B.S.) and Master of Science (M.S.) degrees. Numerous undergraduate courses and degrees are offered through the Internet. Graduate programs in public affairs, education, and business administration are also offered.

Park University is an entrepreneurial institution of learning that is devoted to providing access to academic excellence to prepare learners to think critically, communicate effectively, and engage in lifelong learning while serving a global community.

DISTANCE LEARNING PROGRAM

Hectic schedules are the biggest reason most adults fail to complete their college degrees. With busy schedules, family responsibilities, and travel obligations, it is often impossible for many adults to attend regularly scheduled classes.

The Online learning environment at Park University allows students to go to class when and where their schedule permits. Commuting time disappears, travel conflicts no longer matter, and childcare issues disappear.

The Online learning programs offered by Park University represent more than thirty years of experience in extended learning—experience honed through operating forty-one satellite "campus centers" on military bases where course work needs to be compact and mobile. As a result of this experience, Park developed, and now offers, accelerated eight-week courses as well as standard sixteen-week offerings. Online courses, first developed in 1996, now number in excess of 140. Virtually all in-person courses that are taught at Park University are also taught Online, along with other unique course offerings that were developed specifically for Online delivery.

Surveys of Online students indicate a higher degree of satisfaction for the general learning experience. In traditional classroom settings, people are often treated according to others' preconceived perceptions of age, gender, race, and even income level. In Park University's Online learning program, students are judged only by the caliber of their thoughts and the quality of their contributions. This learning environment is active and student-centered. In fact, the level of interactivity is actually higher in Park's Online courses, and the majority of Online students actually perform better than they do in traditional, face-to-face classes.

DELIVERY MEDIA

Park University offers more than 140 Online courses at five entry points during each year. Most are accelerated eight-week courses. Some courses follow nine- and sixteen-week formats. All courses require minimum computer-system capabilities.

To ensure the highest degree of success, prospective Online students must have a basic level of computer literacy. They must be able to open and transfer files and have a working knowledge of the use of e-mail. Online students also must have a Windows-capable computer with at least a 56.6 kbps modem; Netscape Navigator, Internet Explorer, or an equivalent, reliable Internet access provider; and a personal e-mail account. Students should not borrow someone else's account, use a public-access account (such as a public library terminal), or use a temporary free account when taking the Online courses.

Courses are offered in a variety of subject areas, and students can take many courses without enrolling in a degree program. Park's Internet methodology includes the use of guided study, lectures, incorporated video, e-mail, and discussion rooms, supplemented occasionally with the use of audiotapes, videotapes, and CDs.

Each course is concluded with a proctored exam.

PROGRAM OF STUDY

Park University has provided degree completion programs via distance learning for more than thirty years. The goal of Park's degree completion program is to provide students with the opportunity and assistance to enable them to complete the last two years of their undergraduate degrees. Current fields of study include the Bachelor of Science degree in computer information systems, criminal justice, human resources, management, marketing, and social psychology.

Graduate Online degree programs include the Master of Business Administration with an emphasis in entrepreneurship, health care/health services management, international business, or management of information services; Master of Public Affairs with an emphasis in government/ business relations, health care, management of information services, nonprofit and community services management, and public management; and Master of Education with an emphasis in arts in teaching, educational administration, and special education.

Online learning is a dynamic, growing program at Park University. New courses continue to be developed on an on-going basis.

SPECIAL PROGRAMS

Online students have access to a bookstore and library and such services as registration, financial aid, and advising.

CREDIT OPTIONS

Park University Online courses are transferable to programs at other regionally accredited institutions. In turn, Park accepts credit from other regionally accredited institutions. Specifically, the University accepts up to 84 hours of course completion with a grade of C or better from two-year schools. Official transcripts from previous colleges or universities; official test reports or transcripts from CLEP, USAFI, or DANTES; and ACT/PEP documentation must accompany an application. Up to 24 hours of credit may be awarded for military service and for Validated Learning Equivalency.

FACULTY

Park University has 120 Internet faculty instructors, all of whom have advanced degrees and have taught previously in classroom settings. All Online instructors have taught each of their Online classes for Park University in a face-to-face academic environment. In addition, each Online instructor has completed an intensive eight-week training program to develop the skills necessary for meeting the challenges of teaching Online. This course, which is taught Online, of course, enables instructors to learn firsthand the challenges of being an Online student.

ADMISSION

Park's Online programs are open to anyone who has completed an associate degree or has 60 transferable college credits, or is 25 years old and has 30 transferable college credits, or is in the military on active duty.

TUITION AND FEES

The tuition for the 2004–05 academic year is $184 per credit hour. The application and evaluation fee is $25. There is a discounted rate of $132 per credit hour for active-duty military students. All Online courses require a $10 per credit hour Internet fee. No other fees apply.

FINANCIAL AID

Financial assistance may be awarded to full-time and part-time students who qualify.

APPLYING

Degree-seeking students must meet all admission standards for Park University and pay a one-time $25 application fee.

For more information, students should contact Park University at the telephone number listed below or visit the Web site at the address listed below.

CONTACT

Office of Admissions
Park University
8700 N.W. River Park Drive
Parkville, Missouri 64152-3795
Telephone: 800-745-7275 (toll-free)
E-mail: admissions@park.edu
Web site: http://www.park.edu

Pennsylvania College of Technology, an Affiliate of The Pennsylvania State University

Distance Learning

Williamsport, Pennsylvania

The mission of distance learning at the Pennsylvania College of Technology (Penn College)—a special mission affiliate of Penn State, committed to applied technology education—is to provide educational opportunities, using a variety of media, as an alternative to traditional classroom-based learning. Distance learning courses are accessible to students both off and on campus and are intended to meet the needs of students who desire an alternative to traditional face-to-face courses due to work schedules, geographical distance from the campus, or other special needs.

DISTANCE LEARNING PROGRAM

The Penn College distance learning program was founded on the central principle of providing excellence in instruction and appropriate educational opportunities to students. Five unique bachelor's degree completion programs in Applied Health Studies, Automotive Technology Management, Dental Hygiene, Residential Construction Technology and Management, and Technology Management give students who have previously earned an associate's degree in a technical or professional area or who have met specified professional standards, the opportunity to complete a bachelor's degree via distance learning.

Penn College offers an average of thirty-two distance courses across a range of academic disciplines and enrolls more than 300 distance learning students per semester.

DELIVERY MEDIA

Penn College operates on the WebCT instructional platform. In addition, supported applications include Adobe Photoshop, Adobe Acrobat, Macromedia Director, Flash, Apple QuickTime, Windows Media Player, and Respondus. Certain discipline-specific software programs also are employed.

PROGRAMS OF STUDY

The Bachelor of Science degree in residential construction technology and management allows students who have earned appropriate applied technology skills in their first two years to move into advanced course work related to residential construction and management. Course work includes basic management and accounting as well as advanced estimating and scheduling, residential building systems, cost control, codes compliance, construction law, purchasing, and energy management.

The Bachelor of Science degree in technology management allows students who enter with an associate degree in a technical/professional area to obtain a baccalaureate degree, with the last two years emphasizing the development of business management skills. Technical/professional associate degrees include those with a concentrated area of study in a technical/professional area.

The Bachelor of Science degree in applied health studies is a 127-credit major for individuals who are certified, licensed, or registered in a health-care profession or for students enrolled in the College's occupational therapy assistant, paramedic, or radiography majors, who wish to earn a bachelor's degree. Students acquire the advanced-level core knowledge that guides all health-care practitioners. This degree allows the student to increase knowledge in management and administrative issues; to assist in planning, problem solving, and evaluating health-care delivery methods and systems; and to establish a more marketable, multiskilled background.

The baccalaureate-level dental hygiene program is designed to prepare licensed dental hygienists to contribute to the improvement of oral health in a rapidly changing health-care environment. This program enables hygienists to build upon their current knowledge base and assume positions of responsibility in a variety of alternate care settings as well as in positions created to meet future health-care needs.

The Bachelor of Science degree in automotive technology management is structured to meet the needs of the automotive service and manufacturing industries. The curriculum provides an in-depth study of technical skills, technical knowledge, and management skills as applied in the automotive industry. It emphasizes supervision and personnel management, financial analysis and accounting principles, sales promotion and marketing plan, problem-solving methods, and organization and planning techniques as well as communications and mathematics, which are essential for a management career.

SPECIAL PROGRAMS

The Office of Distance Learning assists in scheduling and determining each semester's class offerings in concert with the academic deans. Courses are offered on a regular and predictable basis to ensure academic progress and adequate course selection of those learning at a distance.

To accommodate the needs of distance learners, selected enrollments are restricted at the start of each semester scheduling period. Resident students also may enroll in distance courses on a space-available basis.

STUDENT SERVICES

Penn College distance learners have full student standing and are entitled to all the privileges and services of a Penn College student. The Financial Aid Office, Career Services, the Advisement Center, and the College Store all have a Web presence and respond to student inquiries via telephone or e-mail. Distance students may order textbooks via the Web site. The library catalog and other references, periodical abstracts, and full-text databases are available through the Penn College Library Web site. An electronic reserve system is provided for assigned readings and supplemental assignments. A College librarian is assigned to each distance learning course to address distance learning and library instruction needs.

CREDIT OPTIONS

Transfer credits, advanced placement, credit for military experience, professional certifications, and credit by exam may be considered during transcript review. Acceptance of credits varies by major.

FACULTY

Thirty-nine faculty members teach the distance learning courses; 92 percent are full-time faculty members.

ADMISSION

Distance learners are accepted to Penn College and the academic department that houses their major. There is no separate admission process for distance learning students.

TUITION AND FEES

Tuition and fee rates for 2003–04, including computer, lab, and activity fees, were $298 per credit hour for in-state students and $375 per credit hour for out-of-state students.

FINANCIAL AID

As students in full standing, distance learners may be eligible for financial aid, including federal aid programs.

APPLYING

Students should submit an application for admission online at http://www.pct.edu/forms or contact the Office of Admissions at the toll-free number listed in the Contact section of this description.

CONTACT

Paul Neal
Distance Learning Services Assistant
Pennsylvania College of Technology
One College Avenue
Williamsport, Pennsylvania 17701
Telephone: 570-320-8019
800-367-9222 (toll-free)
Fax: 570-321-5559
E-mail: distancelearning@pct.edu
World Wide Web: http://www.pct.edu/disteduc

Prescott College

Distance Learning Program

Prescott, Arizona

Prescott College was founded in 1966 based upon the idea that learning occurs through experience as well as traditional means. It is the mission of Prescott College to educate students of diverse ages and backgrounds to understand, thrive in, and enhance the world community and environment. Prescott College seeks to develop the whole person through a unified educational experience in which the acquisition of knowledge and skills is combined with the individual's search for identity and meaning. The College, which is accredited by the Higher Learning Commission and is a member of the North Central Association of Colleges and Schools, grants bachelor's and master's degrees in several fields.

Prescott is located in central Arizona, surrounded by national forests and high plains, at an elevation of higher than 5,200 feet. With four mild seasons and beautiful surroundings, Prescott offers a variety of outside activities, including rock climbing, hiking, mountain biking, and nearby canoeing, rafting, and snow skiing. The city has a population of more than 35,000, including the 125-member Yavapai Apache Indian Tribe, and the county has a population of more than 150,000. Prescott is an interesting combination of old and new. There are more than 500 buildings in Prescott that are recorded on the National Register of Historic Places. Prescott is about 2 hours north of Phoenix.

DISTANCE LEARNING PROGRAM

Prescott College offers flexible programs for full-time lives. The program is designed to allow students to continue working full-time in their home communities, while juggling families and careers, to complete course work and meet regularly with local mentors. Four enrollment periods each year provide students with the opportunity to launch academic programs at a time that is convenient for them. Approximately 300 students are enrolled in the Adult Degree Program (ADP), which requires a residency of six days per program. Degree-seeking students must attend a three-day New Student Orientation and a subsequent three-day Liberal Arts Seminar in Prescott, Arizona. Prescott College also offers a resident undergraduate program and a limited residency Master of Arts program.

DELIVERY MEDIA

Students meet core faculty members during their New Student Orientation in Prescott and subsequently maintain contact through e-mail, telephone, fax, and mail. E-mail addresses are provided to students upon request to aid in communication. Throughout each course, students typically spend 12 to 18 hours meeting with mentors.

PROGRAM OF STUDY

Prescott College's Adult Degree Program provides a community-based, self-designed, independent study model for completion of the Bachelor of Arts degree and postbaccalaureate teacher certification. Because students design individualized programs, almost any degree is possible. Competencies (majors) may be broad and interdisciplinary in content or more narrowly focused to reflect particular student career goals. Popular study programs include counseling psychology/human services, education (early childhood, elementary, special, or secondary), environmental studies, management, postbaccalaureate teacher certification, and sustainable community development.

Many graduates of the counseling psychology/human services program advance their careers in various community mental health or social welfare organizations. Degree plans can be designed to encompass human services, counseling, psychology, ecopsychology, holistic health, and more.

The education program is one of Prescott's most popular programs. Students are able to design an undergraduate education degree, with the option to include endorsements within each degree program.

In environmental studies, many students design programs to conserve natural resources, heal existing environmental maladies, and preserve endangered habitats. Degree plans can encompass agroecology, environmental stewardship, environmental philosophy, environmental education, environmental planning, and management.

The management curriculum often focuses on studying complex human factors involved in organizational decision making. Degree plans are built to specialize in unique areas, in order to fulfill each individual's career goals.

Students may work toward postbaccalaureate teacher certification independently of any other program, or they may obtain teacher certification concurrently with an undergraduate or graduate degree. Students prepare for state certification in accordance with each state's certification requirements.

Through a plan in the sustainable community development program study area, students are able to enact personal visions of ecologically and socially healthy communities.

Students are expected to direct their own learning using mentors as resources and guides. To facilitate community-based education, students find mentors in their home communities who agree to work with them for up to three courses. Mentors must complete a credential file, be approved and meet ADP criteria, including a minimum of a master's degree and teaching experience, preferably at the college level. Finding mentors provides students with a valuable network of professionals in their field of study. Often, these connections lead to internships, recommendations, and jobs. Mentors are paid a stipend for working with ADP students.

Enrolled students, who have worked in their field for at least five years, may develop and submit a life/work experience portfolio for evaluation of credits based on demonstration of prior college-level learning.

SPECIAL PROGRAMS

Prescott College created the CIBTE (Center for Indian Bilingual Teacher Education) in 1988 as an alternative teacher education program to meet the specific need for certification programs for Native American teachers on Arizona reservations.

Students are encouraged to include internships and practicums as part of their demonstration of competence. Many Prescott College ADP students are involved in community-based programs, such as Teach for America.

STUDENT SERVICES

The Student Services Office serves all students during their time with Prescott College. Career development information is updated regularly. Guided by the Prescott College philosophy and the Association of Colleges and Research Libraries (ACRL), Prescott College provides a high level of library service, with more than 28,000 volumes, 125 microforms, 1,200 audiocassettes and videocassettes, and 408 periodical titles, all of which relate specifically to the College's program offerings. The library is computer networked with all of the regional libraries in the area, including two other college libraries and the public libraries. If students are not able to locate necessary information from any of these sources, the College librarian borrows books through the interlibrary loan system. Because the College places great emphasis on student services, the faculty and staff work diligently to assist each student in finding all information necessary for his or her pursuit of knowledge.

Additional student services include resume preparation assistance, college counseling and crisis consultation, events planned by the on-campus student activities coordinator, and access to the computer labs and tutoring facilities. E-mail addresses are provided for students upon request.

CREDIT OPTIONS

Courses completed above remedial level at other regionally accredited colleges, with a grade of C or better, are transferable. Relevant courses are applied to the competence and breadth areas during initial advising. In some cases, courses from unaccredited colleges may be documented through a conversion portfolio for which Prescott College credit may be awarded. This option is available after admission into the undergraduate program. College Level Examination Program (CLEP) scores may be submitted for evaluation.

FACULTY

Core faculty members at Prescott College are actively involved in each student's degree plan to provide expertise and guidance. Mentors play a large part in each student's education because the program is built on individual mentored study. Mentors must have a minimum of a master's degree in their area of expertise and teaching experience, preferably at the college level.

ADMISSION

The focus of the admissions process is to help ensure that students who are admitted enter a program suited to their individual goals. Prospective students applying to the ADP must submit a completed application form, an educational goals essay, an autobiographical essay, two recent letters of recommendation, official transcripts from previously attended institutions, and a $25 nonrefundable application fee. Prescott College Admissions Counselors are available to assist students during the admissions process. More information is available from the Admissions Office at the address and telephone numbers or on the Web site listed below.

TUITION AND FEES

In 2004–05, full-time tuition per six-month enrollment period (18 to 24 quarter credits) is $4230. Part-time tuition (including less than 18 or more than 24 quarter credits) is $235 per credit hour. Tuition is subject to increase in July each year.

FINANCIAL AID

Prescott College's Financial Aid Office makes every attempt to ensure that all qualified students can attend and assists them in finding financial aid, given individual eligibility. Available financial aid includes Federal Pell Grants, Prescott College grants, Federal Perkins Loans, Arizona State Student Incentive Grants, Federal Supplemental Educational Opportunity Grants, work-study programs, Federal Stafford Student Loans, the Arizona Private Postsecondary Education Student Financial Assistance Program, campus employment, and scholarships.

More than 65 percent of Prescott College students receive financial aid. Prescott College uses the Free Application for Federal Student Aid (FAFSA) to determine financial need. Aid is awarded on a first-come, first-served basis until all available funds are used. FAFSA forms take four to six weeks to process. Students are encouraged to file the FAFSA early and online (http://www.fafsa.ed.gov).

APPLYING

Students are encouraged to submit completed applications by the priority due date for the term in which they plan to enroll. After the priority due date has passed, applications are accepted and reviewed on a rolling basis. There is a $25 nonrefundable application fee. Additional clarification is available from the Admissions Office at the telephone numbers listed below.

CONTACT

Admissions Office, ADP
Prescott College
220 Grove Avenue
Prescott, Arizona 86301
Telephone: 877-350-2100 (toll-free)
888-797-4680 (toll-free, Tucson)
Fax: 928-776-5242
E-mail: admissions@prescott.edu
Web site: http://www.prescott.edu

Purdue University

Krannert Executive Education Programs

West Lafayette, Indiana

Purdue University, a state-supported land-grant university, was founded in 1869. It was named after its chief benefactor, John Purdue, and is known for its academic excellence and affordable education. The West Lafayette campus offers nearly 6,700 courses in the Schools of Agriculture, Management, Consumer and Family Sciences, Pharmacy, Nursing and Health Sciences, Education, Science, Engineering, Technology, Liberal Arts, and Veterinary Medicine. The goals of the University are symbolized in its emblem, the griffin, whose three-part shield represents education, research, and service. Purdue is accredited by the North Central Association of Colleges and Schools.

DISTANCE LEARNING PROGRAM

The Krannert Executive Education Programs (KEEP) began its distance learning programs in 1983. The programs were developed specifically for mid-level managers or managers-to-be who are unable to attend classes on a full-time basis. The programs have unique scheduling that makes it possible for participants to be drawn from a wide geographical area. Six 2-week residencies spread across twenty-two months, from orientation to graduation, allow its participants to meet their educational goals while simultaneously fulfilling their job responsibilities. During the nineteen months the students are off campus, they utilize the Internet and World Wide Web, online discussion forums and chatrooms, and other electronic media to stay in touch with each other, the faculty, and Executive Education support staff. These internationally ranked programs are part of the Krannert Graduate School of Management and admit 55 students in each cohort.

DELIVERY MEDIA

KEEP uses the World Wide Web and CDs to deliver its course materials to students. Current business cases provide a focal point for individual and group assignments in all courses, easily available for download from course Web sites and the provided CD.

Students are expected to provide a modern, Microsoft Windows–based laptop with the current version of Microsoft Office Professional installed, beginning with the Program Orientation. The program provides all required software, including Office.

Students are expected to have access to the Internet via an Internet service provider that allows for the free exchange of Web-based materials. While not required, a broadband connection to the Internet is recommended. Use of Internet-based e-mail, course Web sites and online discussion forums, chat rooms and other Internet-based communication technologies are regular components of the program. These collaboration tools enable students to maintain contact with faculty and staff members when at a distance from one another, and to prepare their individual and group assignments.

PROGRAMS OF STUDY

A Master of Business Administration (M.B.A.) is offered through two unique programs: the Executive Master of Business Administration (EMB) Program and the International Master in Management (IMM) Program.

The EMB Program begins each July with an orientation session where the participants are introduced to the course work, the instructors, and the KEEP information technology system. The courses have an applied policymaking orientation and make extensive use of case studies and other experiential material. The third module has an emphasis on international business, and the last residency in the third module is spent at an international location. Upon completion of the program, the M.B.A. degree is awarded by Purdue University.

The IMM Program is taught in conjunction with Tias Business School, Tilburg University, in the Netherlands; the CEU School of Business in Budapest, Hungary; and GISMA, the German International Graduate School of Management and Administration. It is structured like the EMB Program, but the residencies alternate among the campuses of the four collaborating institutions. Orientation initiates the program each February. Graduation yields two master's degrees: an M.B.A. degree from Purdue and an M.B.A. from Tias or CEU.

The EMB and IMM Programs are intensive and demanding, which is consistent with a graduate professional program in management. Serious preparation is expected, and academic standards are carefully maintained to ensure integrity of the earned degrees. As a result, however, the educational benefits are substantial, and the degrees earned are significant professional credentials.

SPECIAL PROGRAMS

Both the EMB and IMM Programs are open to executive students worldwide and are accredited by AACSB International–The Association to Advance Collegiate Schools of Business. Both national and international students are attracted to the program.

STUDENT SERVICES

Students may maintain contact with faculty members, support staff, and KEEP administration on a daily basis, if necessary. Other resources include online library services, tutoring, campus computer networks, e-mail services, academic advising, and online discussion forums and chatrooms.

CREDIT OPTIONS

The programs are cohort in nature; that is, all students in each class enter together, take a common set of courses, and graduate together. There are 48 total credits, 16 per module, that participants must complete within two years.

FACULTY

Classes are taught by the senior faculty members of the Krannert School of Management at Purdue, the Tias Business School at Tilburg University, the CEU School of Business in Budapest, and by experienced teachers from other U.S. and international programs. All faculty members have taught extensively in executive programs containing distance learning aspects, have substantial research and publication records, and have experience as consultants to corporations and government agencies.

ADMISSION

Successful applicants are expected to have a GMAT score of 520 or higher, a completed baccalaureate degree with a grade point average of B or better, a minimum of five years of work experience in positions of increasing professional responsibility, a current position of significant responsibility, and three supporting letters of recommendation. Any applicant whose first language is not English must have a minimum TOEFL score of 213 on the computer-based test or 550 on the paper-based test.

TUITION AND FEES

The total cost for each program is $54,000 ($18,000 per each of the three modules). The tuition covers books and course material, instructional costs, lodging, and most meals during the residencies. Tuition is due before the first residency of each program module. The EMB Program features an international trip in its last module, for which there is an additional charge.

FINANCIAL AID

EMBA loans offered through Purdue's financial aid office are available. Applications may be completed at a distance.

APPLYING

Candidates may apply online at any time. As admission to the program is on a rolling basis throughout the year until class capacity is reached, early application is recommended. Upon receipt of all necessary documents, the application will be reviewed by the Program Admissions Committee and, upon approval, submitted to Purdue's Graduate School for the final decision. Typically, a candidate can expect word of his or her application status within two weeks of receipt of all application documentation.

CONTACT

Erika C. Steuterman
Director, Executive M.B.A. Programs
Purdue University
425 West State Street
West Lafayette, Indiana 47907-2056
Telephone: 765-494-7700
Fax: 765-494-0862
E-mail: keepinfo@krannert.purdue.edu
Web site: http://www2.mgmt.purdue.edu/info/degree

Regent University

Online Distance Learning Programs

Virginia Beach, Virginia

Regent University is primarily a graduate institution offering thirty-four bachelor's, master's, and doctoral degree programs from a Judeo-Christian worldview. Regent's graduate schools include the School of Business, School of Communication and the Arts, School of Divinity, School of Education, Robertson School of Government, School of Law, School of Leadership Studies, and School of Psychology and Counseling. Online programs are offered through all schools at Regent, except for the School of Law.

Since classes began in 1978, Regent University has grown to an enrollment of more than 3,200 students. In addition to the main campus in Virginia Beach, Regent also offers programs at its Graduate Center in Alexandria, Virginia. More than twenty degree programs are offered online via the Regent Worldwide Campus. Regent University is accredited by the Commission on Colleges of the Southern Association of Colleges and Schools (1866 Southern Lane, Decatur, Georgia 30033-4097; telephone: 404-679-4501) to award the bachelor's, master's, and doctoral degrees. The School of Law is fully accredited by the American Bar Association. The School of Divinity is accredited by the Association of Theological Schools (ATS). The Council for Accreditation of Counseling and Related Educational Programs (CACREP), a specialized accrediting body recognized by the Council for Higher Education Accreditation (CHEA), has conferred accreditation to the following program areas of community counseling (M.A.) and school counseling (M.A.), which are offered by Regent University's School of Psychology and Counseling. The Committee on Accreditation of the American Psychological Association (750 First Street, NE, Washington, D.C. 20002-4242; telephone: 202-336-5979; fax: 202-336-5978) has conferred accreditation on the Regent University Doctoral Program in Clinical Psychology, which offers the Doctor of Psychology (Psy.D.) degree.

DISTANCE LEARNING PROGRAM

Regent University serves nearly 1,500 students via its online Worldwide Campus through degree programs in business, communication and the arts, divinity, education, government, leadership, and psychology and counseling. Each fully accredited program is taught from a Judeo-Christian perspective, allowing students to apply relevant ethical values to their professional pursuits within a scholarly framework.

DELIVERY MEDIA

Degrees are offered online via the Regent Worldwide Campus. BlackBoard® is Regent University's choice for distance learning via the Internet. With this powerful application, a student is able to access course material, chat with professors and other students, and submit course work and tests from anywhere in the world. Some materials, such as video and cassette tapes and multimedia CDs, may be sent to the student via postal services. Course previews in BlackBoard and detailed requirements can be found at http://www.regent.edu/distance.

PROGRAMS OF STUDY

Online distance learning programs at Regent University include the Executive Master of Business Administration (M.B.A.), Professional M.B.A., M.A. in management, Certificate of Advanced Graduate Studies (C.A.G.S.) in business, M.A. in communication, M.A. in journalism, Ph.D. in communication, M.A. in practical theology, Master of Divinity (M.Div.) (with practical theology), Master of Education (M.Ed.) (Christian school program, cross-categorical special education, educational leadership, individualized degree plan, master teacher/ESL, TESOL, TESOL/initial licensure with optional reading specialist endorsement, reading specialist), TESOL certificate, Doctor of Education (Ed.D.), M.A. in government, Certificate of Graduate Studies (C.G.S.) in public policy, M.A. in organizational leadership, C.G.S. in leadership, Ph.D. in organizational leadership, Doctor of Strategic Leadership (D.S.L.), C.A.G.S. in leadership, M.A. in human services counseling, and Ph.D. in counselor education and supervision. Some programs require on-campus courses and/or residencies. Regent University also offers five undergraduate programs online: the Bachelor of Science (B.S.) in interdisciplinary studies, the B.S. in organizational leadership, the Bachelor of Arts (B.A.) in religious studies, and the B.S. in psychology.

CREDIT OPTIONS

For all online distance programs, students may transfer a maximum of 25 percent of the total credits required for their chosen program except for programs that have articulation agreements with other schools. Articulation agreements may authorize transfer credit for up to 49 percent of the degree to be earned. Credits must have been earned at an approved institution (determined by each Regent school). Credits for courses with grades below B (C for the M.Div. program) are not accepted for transfer.

FACULTY

Regent online distance learning courses are taught by the same full- and part-time faculty members who teach on campus. Regent has a distinguished faculty of approximately 150 men and women of varying religious denominations and ethnic origins.

ADMISSION

Student admission to Regent University graduate programs requires a completed four-year bachelor's degree for master's programs and a completed master's degree for doctoral programs from an institution that is regionally accredited. Institutions are considered on an individual basis.

While each Regent school maintains specific admissions criteria for its graduate programs, the following are considered the norm: a minimum cumulative undergraduate GPA of 3.0 in the desired area of study, submission of test scores (MAT, GMAT, or GRE), maturity in spiritual and/or character qualities, and personal goals that are consistent with the mission and goals of Regent University.

International student admissions requirements also vary among Regent schools. Students should contact the school of their choice for specific information. Students should visit http://www.regent.edu/admissions for more information.

TUITION AND FEES

Tuition varies by program, as do additional fees. The tuition costs for online distance learning programs for the 2003–04 academic year were as follows: Executive M.B.A., $780 per credit hour; Professional M.B.A., M.A. in management, and C.A.G.S. in business, $585 per credit hour; M.A. in communication, M.A. in journalism, and Ph.D. in communication, $800 per credit hour; M.A. in practical theology, and M.Div., $375 per credit hour; M.Ed. TESOL certificate, $420 per credit hour; Ed.D., $540 per credit hour; M.A. in government and C.G.S. in public policy, $550 per credit hour; M.A. in organizational leadership and C.G.S. in leadership, $445 per credit hour; Ph.D. in organizational leadership, D.S.L., and C.A.G.S. in leadership, $595 per credit hour; M.A. in human services counseling, $450 per credit hour; and Ph.D. in counselor education and supervision, $525 per credit hour.

FINANCIAL AID

Students accepted for enrollment may apply for Federal Stafford Student Loans and a variety of school-specific scholarships and grants. Veterans' benefits also apply.

APPLYING

Application deadlines and processes vary among schools. Students should contact the individual school for specific information.

CONTACT

Regent University
1000 Regent University Drive
Virginia Beach, Virginia 23464-9800
Telephone: 800-373-5504 (toll-free)
E-mail: admissions@regent.edu
Web site: http://www.regent.edu

To contact online distance learning programs directly:

School of Business
Telephone: 800-477-3642 (toll-free)
E-mail: bizschool@regent.edu
Web site: http://www.regent.edu/acad/schbus/

School of Communication and the Arts
Telephone: 757-226-4116
E-mail: commcollege@regent.edu
Web site: http://www.regent.edu/acad/schcom/

School of Divinity
Telephone: 800-723-6162 (toll-free)
E-mail: divschool@regent.edu
Web site: http://www.regent.edu/acad/schdiv/

School of Education
Telephone: 888-713-1595 (toll-free)
E-mail: eduschool@regent.edu
Web site: http://www.regent.edu/acad/schedu/

School of Government
Telephone: 888-800-7735 (toll-free)
E-mail: govschool@regent.edu
Web site: http://www.regent.edu/acad/schgov

School of Leadership Studies
Telephone: 757-226-3063
E-mail: leadercenter@regent.edu
Web site: http://www.regent.edu/acad/cls/

School of Psychology and Counseling
Telephone: 757-226-4121
E-mail: counschool@regent.edu
Web site: http://www.regent.edu/acad/schcou/

R·I·T

Rochester Institute of Technology

Online Learning

Rochester, New York

Online Learning at the Rochester Institute of Technology (RIT) offers a broad selection of courses and full-degree programs, all regionally accredited by the Middle States Association of Colleges and Schools. With more than twenty years of experience in distance education, RIT offers one of the largest and most established online learning programs in the U.S.

DISTANCE LEARNING PROGRAM

Rochester Institute of Technology is one of the nation's leaders in online learning education programs. RIT online learning students have access to more than thirty full degree and certificate programs, including ten graduate degrees, four undergraduate degrees, twenty-one certificate programs, and more than 300 courses. The commitment to quality education is an integral part of RIT online learning programs.

DELIVERY MEDIA

Professors deliver course materials through the Internet and a combination of textbooks, videotapes, audiotapes, audio conferences, chats, electronic library resources, and other components that enhance that particular course experience. Students submit most assignments online, but professors may request students to fax or mail assignments. Students may order course materials online and have complete access to a full range of library services and academic advising online.

In order to participate, students must have full access to the Internet and a personal computer. Students must also have basic computer skills and some Internet experience to be successful. In addition, a VCR that is capable of playing NTSC (American standard video) and a telephone are required. For specific computer requirements, students should visit the Web page listed in the Contact section.

PROGRAMS OF STUDY

All programs offered through RIT are available to students worldwide. Applications for all programs are available online. Most students have some college experience before coming to RIT, but admission into the undergraduate certificate and bachelor's-level programs can be accommodated without previous college experience. Master's degree candidates must meet the admissions standards required by that program and must have completed a baccalaureate degree or equivalent from an accredited institution. International applicants must demonstrate English proficiency, usually through the Test of English as a Foreign Language (TOEFL). TOEFL scores vary by program, but most programs require a score of 550 or better.

The B.S. in applied arts and science program presents a flexible opportunity for a student to create a program tailored to meet his or her educational needs. It requires the completion of 180 credit hours. Twelve concentrations are available.

The B.S. in electrical/mechanical engineering technology program requires experiences that must be completed over several weekends at RIT or by taking an alternative course from an approved institution. The undergraduate degree requires 194 credit hours. This program is accredited by ABET-TAC.

The B.S. in telecommunications engineering technology program (the technical option) is currently available to both working professionals and full-time students. The academic emphasis is placed on backbone technologies that transmit, switch, and manage networks and the information they carry. Individuals who have no background or have not completed basic lab work in this field may need to come to RIT for intensive weekend labs. This program is accredited by ABET-TAC.

The B.S. in safety technology program is structured to be at the leading edge of this field, providing high-quality academic preparation and relevant work experience. All students completing RIT's safety technology bachelor's degree program are eligible to take the associate safety professional examination upon graduation. Individuals may enter the upper-division program from an associate degree program or with two years of college, including appropriate courses in math, science, and liberal arts.

The M.S. in print media program is oriented toward educating individuals for production and management positions in the ever-evolving printing and publishing industry. This master's program addresses publishing from the technological/production viewpoint, including its management, and considers interrelationships among e-commerce, cross-media publishing, and the many digital and variable data aspects of printing as well as traditional printing models. The program is open to students with a variety of undergraduate degree backgrounds. While all courses are provided online, students attend a one-week summer technology practicum course on campus after completing the first five required courses. This M.S. degree requires completion of 48 credit hours.

The M.S. in applied statistics program is designed for full-time professionals who want to learn state-of-the art statistical techniques to enhance their careers and their value to their companies. Students must complete 45 credits. Admission to the degree program is granted to qualified holders of a baccalaureate degree from an accredited college or university who have acceptable mathematics credits, including one academic year of calculus.

The M.S. in software development and management program consists of 48 credit hours, comprising the software engineering core foundation, the software engineering project, and electives. A minimal background is required in mathematics (discrete structures, statistics) and computing (programming in a high-level language, data structures, elementary computer architecture, and digital logic).

The M.S. in information technology program consists of 48 credit hours of graduate study in core courses, with a choice of electives and concentrations in application development, electronic commerce, and telecommunications. Entering students are expected to have programming skills at an intermediate level in an appropriate language and understand the fundamentals of computer hardware.

The M.S. in health systems administration program is designed to meet the needs of health professionals who desire a nonclinical degree in management and administration. Students typically enter in cohort groups, which improves the learning environment, and take two courses per quarter until completion of the 57 credit hours.

The M.S. in cross-disciplinary professional studies program consists of 48 credit hours, which comprise two or three concentrations from various areas. These areas are designed to give the student a comprehensive and customized plan of graduate study tailored to meet either career or educational objectives. Students must take a course in interdisciplinary research techniques and finish a capstone project to complete this degree.

The M.S. in environmental health and safety management program requires 48 credit hours drawn from core courses like environmental health and safety management system design and performance measurement, 20 credits from professional electives, and 6 credits from the graduate thesis and graduate project.

The M.S. in imaging science program emphasizes a systems approach to the study of imaging science, and, with a background in science or engineering, this degree prepares the student for positions in research, product development, and management in the imaging industry. The program requires completion of 45 credits.

The M.E. in microelectronics manufacturing engineering program is designed for students with a B.S. degree in electrical or chemical engineering or other related engineering areas. The degree requires the completion of nine 4-credit courses and a 9-credit thesis for a total of 45 credits.

RIT also offers twenty-one certificates for those wanting to improve or obtain skills in specialized areas. Courses in the certificate programs may be applied toward a degree.

CREDIT OPTIONS

Students have a number of options available for credit, including transfer credit, credit by exam, College-Level Examination Program (CLEP), Excelsior College Examinations, credit for educational experiences in the armed forces and noncollegiate organizations, and credit for nontraditional learning. Advisers work with students to evaluate the number of credits that can be transferred, since the number of non-RIT credits accepted varies by program.

FACULTY

RIT's faculty members are world-renowned and teach both on-campus and distance education courses. More than 200 full- and part-time faculty members teach distance learning courses.

ADMISSION

Requirements for admission and completion of degree or certificate programs vary by academic department. Students should refer to Programs of Study descriptions.

TUITION AND FEES

Graduate tuition is $676 per credit hour. Undergraduate tuition is $330 per credit hour.

FINANCIAL AID

RIT offers a full range of traditional financial aid programs as well as a number of innovative financing plans. Scholarships and assistantships are available to matriculated students in most graduate departments.

APPLYING

Online learning students follow the same procedures as all other students attending RIT. Decisions for selection rest within each college. Correspondence between the student and the Institute is conducted through the Offices of Part-time and Graduate Enrollment Services, which reviews applications as they are received.

CONTACT

Offices of Part-time and
Graduate Enrollment Services
Rochester Institute of Technology
58 Lomb Memorial Drive
Rochester, New York 14623-5604
Telephone: 585-475-2229
800-CALL-RIT (oll-free)
Fax: 585-475-7164
E-mail: opes@rit.edu
Web Site:
http://www.rit.edu/online

Roger Williams University

Open College

Bristol and Providence, Rhode Island

At Roger Williams University (RWU), Learning to Bridge the World is more than a slogan. From its scenic waterfront campus, the University educates and enlightens people from down the street, throughout New England, across the country, and around the world. Roger Williams, accredited by the New England Association of Schools and Colleges, is a premier liberal arts university, strengthened by professional schools and Rhode Island's only law school. Its dedicated faculty members teach more than 4,000 undergraduate and graduate students, all of whom share a love of learning, a commitment to service, and a global perspective. In 2002, Roger Williams became the first university in the United States to offer scholarships to women from Afghanistan to help rebuild their society through education.

The University's Open College is a comprehensive external degree program designed for people interested in nontraditional education. Most of the students are working adults who are able to pursue their educational programs with little or no interference with their personal or professional commitments.

DISTANCE LEARNING PROGRAM

Since its inception in 1974, more than 4,000 students have graduated from the Open College at Roger Williams University. In the 2001–02 academic year, eighty courses were offered via distance learning. The average distance learning enrollment is 200 students per semester.

Academic programs are divided into regular semesters of study, including fall, spring, and summer. Campus residency is not required.

DELIVERY MEDIA

The Open College emphasizes an external approach to education, and the instructional methods available to off-campus students include nonclassroom courses, such as external courses, internships, online courses, and independent study courses. Some of the external courses may include guided instruction via videotapes, audiotapes, computer software, computer conferencing, World Wide Web, e-mail, and print. Students and teachers may meet in person or interact via audioconferencing, mail, telephone, fax, e-mail, and World Wide Web. The following equipment may be required: fax machine, computer, Internet access, and e-mail.

PROGRAMS OF STUDY

Distance education through the Open College at Roger Williams University offers baccalaureate degrees in business management, criminal justice, industrial technology, and public administration.

The business management major provides students with "marketplace" skills such as problem solving, information gathering and processing, and project managing. The degree also prepares students to appreciate the overall challenges of a business operation and to function effectively within an integrated business environment.

The criminal justice major is designed for students who are employed, or who are seeking employment, in direct law enforcement professions or public or private criminal justice–related agencies.

The industrial technology major is designed for students with technical and/or managerial backgrounds and interests and who are employed or seeking employment in manufacturing or service industries.

The public administration major prepares students for government service on the federal, state, or local level and for employment in nonprofit organizations and international administration.

To earn a baccalaureate degree, a minimum of 120 credits are required through any combination of learning experiences, including credit for previous college work, military training and experience, CLEP exams, and credit documentation. Students are required to complete a minimum of 30 credits through the Open College at Roger Williams University. Also, a minimum 2.0 grade point average is required in all courses carrying a letter grade and in all required major courses.

Each student is assigned to a faculty adviser who works with the student to develop an education and degree plan. The adviser also assists in registration, credit documentation, and enrollment procedures; identifies appropriate courses and learning experiences; and supervises student work.

SPECIAL PROGRAMS

The Open College at Roger Williams University offers internships, co-ops, and practicums for employment-related learning experiences in all academic degree programs.

STUDENT SERVICES

All college services available to the traditional student are also available to distance learning students, including access to the University's library, computer support, tutoring, advising, and career placement.

CREDIT OPTIONS

Many students are able to enter the Open College with considerable advanced standing. Students may reduce the total time required for completion of studies and degree requirements with up to three years of credit from military service and training, transfer of credits obtained from other colleges, credit documentation that awards credit for life and job-related learning experiences, and College-Level Examination Program (CLEP) or other advanced credit exams.

FACULTY

The Open College at Roger Williams University has a total of 37 faculty members to provide instruction. Fifteen are full-time faculty members at RWU (41 percent), and 22 are part-time (adjunct) faculty members (59 percent). Nineteen faculty members (51 percent) have doctoral or other terminal degrees. All faculty members have at least one graduate degree.

ADMISSION

Students must be able to enter with advanced standing, based on credits already acquired from previous college attendance, military training, employment experiences, and/or CLEP exams. Also, preference is given to students who have access to various educational and learning resources in the event such resources need to be incorporated into their academic programs. Resources may include, but are not limited to, libraries, classroom courses at local colleges, local proctors, potential sites for internship placement, and computers.

TUITION AND FEES

Open College tuition varies by program and ranged from $750 to $1340 per 3-credit course for the 2002–03 academic year. The application fee is $50; no registration fee is required.

FINANCIAL AID

Aside from various forms of military tuition assistance that might be available to service members, Open College students are eligible for all of the traditional forms of financial aid that are normally associated with adult and continuing education students. Approximately 50 percent of distance learning students receive financial assistance (excluding employer reimbursement programs).

APPLYING

Applications must be submitted with appropriate documentation, such as a resume, official high school transcripts, GED scores, or official transcripts from previous colleges or universities. Service members must submit a copy of credit recommendations for all military training and experience from Form DD295, prepared by military education officers, or SMART/AARTS transcripts.

CONTACT

John Stout, Dean
Open College
Roger Williams University
150 Washington Street
Providence, Rhode Island 02903
Telephone: 401-254-3530
800-458-7144 Ext. 3530 (toll-free)
Fax: 401-254-3560
E-mail: jstout@rwu.edu
Web site: http://www.rwu.edu

Roosevelt University

RU Online, Roosevelt's Fully Online Learning Program

Chicago; Schaumburg, Illinois; and Online

Roosevelt University is a private, metropolitan, nonsectarian institution of higher learning committed to the fundamental values and purposes of higher education in the United States. The University was founded in 1945 with the mission to provide equal educational opportunity to students of all backgrounds. One of the distinctive characteristics of Roosevelt University continues to be the heterogeneity of its students in race and ethnic origin, income, educational program, age, and professional development. Based on this founding ideal, Roosevelt both provides access to higher education to a diverse student population and actively seeks out underserved populations.

Roosevelt University has two strategically located campuses—one in the heart of downtown Chicago, and the other in northwest suburban Schaumburg—in addition to online offerings. More than 7,300 students are enrolled at Roosevelt University in a wide array of certificate, bachelor's, master's, and doctoral programs.

Roosevelt University is governed by a Board of Trustees and is accredited by the North Central Association of Colleges and Schools.

DISTANCE LEARNING PROGRAM

The aim of all programming at Roosevelt University is student-centeredness; programs exist for the students they serve. In addition, Roosevelt's mission has always been to extend educational opportunity to all qualified persons. Online education affords Roosevelt University the opportunity to extend its historic and noble mission to populations previously beyond Roosevelt's reach.

The technologies employed in Roosevelt University's online learning program are appropriate to the intended educational objectives, enhance programmatic quality, and unobtrusively help ensure the technological literacy of the University's graduates, better preparing them for the world of work and for graduate or professional education.

RU Online courses are academically rigorous, highly interactive, and scheduled during regular semester terms. Taught by distinguished Roosevelt University faculty members, the courses offer open and ready access to all University services including registration, library, career placement, and participation in student clubs and organizations.

RU Online was launched in August 2001 thanks to a generous grant from the McCormick Tribune Foundation and currently serves more than 300 students. Part of the Evelyn T. Stone University College, RU Online embraces that college's mission of innovation, outreach, and student-centeredness. For more than thirty years, University College has been a leader in adult education; since 1966, it has been home to its flagship program, the Bachelor of General and Professional Studies, a time-shortened degree program for adults.

DELIVERY MEDIA

RU Online courses are available on the Internet at http://www.roosevelt.edu/ruonline.

PROGRAMS OF STUDY

The 36-semester-hour Master of Arts in Training and Development (M.A.T.D.) degree program includes eleven courses and either a thesis, based on formal study and experience, or a project, designing an original unit of training or applied research in a specialized area. Students prepare to enter any of the many facets of the training field by studying areas such as needs assessment, systematic instructional design, curriculum planning, and distance learning.

The design, development, delivery, and evaluation of training programs are critical to the success of today's organizations. Career opportunities abound for those who have the knowledge, skill, and ability to design and deliver high quality learning programs. The Graduate Certificate in Training and Development, delivered fully online at Roosevelt University, provides a strong foundation for professionals seeking to refresh or redirect their career through education and application. The certificate courses earn full graduate credit within the Master of Arts in Training and Development program.

As technological applications expand and requirements for continuous learning increase, professionals with expertise in the design, development, implementation, and evaluation of e-learning are in great demand. Roosevelt University offers an online Graduate Certificate in E-Learning in conjunction with the Master of Arts in Training and Development degree. Certificate courses earn full graduate credit within the Master of Arts in Training and Development program.

One of the most popular areas of the training and organization development industry is instructional design. Individuals equipped with sound instructional design theory and proven practice in this area are highly valuable in the workplace. Roosevelt University offers the online Graduate Certificate in Instructional Design to prepare future instructional designers or to sharpen the skills of existing professionals. Graduate courses in instructional systems design, evaluation research, human performance technology, and more can be credited toward the Master of Arts in Training and Development degree.

The Undergraduate Certificate in Organizational Leadership program is designed for students who want to be on the cutting edge of their organizations. This certificate provides a basic understanding of organizations and how they fit in society, the skills necessary to function within organizations, the communication skills vital to successful organizations, and exposure to new trends in organizational design and function. Through this program, students examine leadership in a changing business environment and their own leadership skills and potential. Adult students can apply this certificate to an academic major in organizational leadership through the time-shortened Bachelor of Professional Studies program.

Students and professionals who are interested in employment and career advancement in the field of meeting planning, convention, and exposition management should consider the Undergraduate Meeting Coordinator Certificate. This certificate program consists of three undergraduate courses, including Introduction to Meeting, Convention, and Exposition Management and Issues and Trends in Meeting and Conference Management.

Students can prepare for graduate study in psychology by taking introductory statistics, research methods, and child psychopathology.

Undergraduate students can prepare for teacher certification and practicing teachers can enhance their professional study through a series of education courses in special education, teacher leadership, and early childhood education.

STUDENT SERVICES

All Roosevelt University services are available online, including advising and registration, the library, and career placement services.

CREDIT OPTIONS

Students can transfer academic credit from accredited institutions of higher education. CLEP credit is accepted in certain areas of study.

FACULTY

Through teaching, research, and professional service, Roosevelt University faculty members contribute to the creation of a more humane and equitable environment while also fulfilling a primary commitment to the individual learner's personal and intellectual growth. Many of Roosevelt's faculty members hold doctorates or terminal degrees. Small class size—no more than 20 in any online course—assures students of personal attention, ready access to faculty members, and a collegial spirit of learning.

TUITION AND FEES

Information on tuition and fees is available on the Web at http://www.roosevelt.edu/financialaid/tuition.htm.

FINANCIAL AID

Information on financial aid options is available on the Web at http://www.roosevelt.edu/financialaid/default.htm.

APPLYING

Online students should submit an application to the Office of Admission. The application can be found on the Web at http://www.roosevelt.edu/admissions/howto.htm, or students can call 312-341-3515.

CONTACT

Roosevelt University
430 South Michigan Avenue
Chicago, Illinois 60605-1394
Telephone: 312-281-3139
E-mail: ruonline@roosevelt.edu
Web site: http://www.roosevelt.edu/ruonline

Roosevelt University
1400 North Roosevelt Boulevard
Schaumburg, Illinois 60173
Telephone: 847-619-8600

Saint Joseph's College

Division of Graduate and Professional Studies

Standish, Maine

Saint Joseph's College was founded in 1912 by the Sisters of Mercy and chartered by the Maine legislature in 1915. The College grants degrees in keeping with the mission of the College and the ministries of the Sisters of Mercy. Saint Joseph's is a liberal arts college that nurtures intellectual, spiritual, and social growth in students of all ages and all faiths within a value-centered environment.

In 1970, Saint Joseph's became a coeducational institution, and in 1976, the Distance Education Program was introduced to serve the needs of the nontraditional adult learner nationwide.

Saint Joseph's is located on the shores of Sebago Lake, 18 miles from Portland. More than 1,000 students attend classes on the 331-acre campus. The beautiful lakefront of the campus faces the White Mountains. The region's natural beauty and the proximity of the College to Maine's popular ski resorts appeal to the outdoor enthusiast in winter. The nearby rocky Atlantic coastline and picturesque New England countryside offer an ideal setting for the summer experience.

DISTANCE LEARNING PROGRAM

Saint Joseph's College offers the adult learner an opportunity to integrate formal education in the liberal arts tradition with professional experience. Saint Joseph's College is accredited by the New England Association of Schools and Colleges. The Graduate and Professional Studies program provides academic options in a variety of disciplines leading to undergraduate and graduate certificates and to associate, baccalaureate, and graduate degrees. Each option is designed to reflect the special nature of Saint Joseph's commitment to its students. The Graduate and Professional Studies program currently enrolls about 4,400 active students, and approximately 7,500 Saint Joseph's alumni earned their degrees through the distance program.

DELIVERY MEDIA

Faculty-directed independent study is a highly flexible, accessible mode of education that allows students to study where they are. Upon enrollment, students receive the texts, materials, and study guides for their courses. Some courses require access to a computer or a VCR. Approximately half of the 200 courses offered through the Division of Graduate and Professional Studies are available online via the Internet. Faculty members assist each student with their studies through a combination of written feedback on assignments, telephone consultations, and e-mail. An academic adviser is assigned to work with each student from the first enrollment through to graduation. Undergraduate and graduate degree programs require one 2-week summer residency at the campus in Maine. Nondegree classes are also offered.

PROGRAMS OF STUDY

The Division of Graduate and Professional Studies offers the following degree programs at the graduate level: a Master of Science in education with an emphasis in teaching and learning (33 credits), which serves two major professional arenas—K–12 school systems and adult education programs; a Master's degree in health services administration (42 credits) for senior management roles in complex health-care organizations, offering specializations in health services administration, international health care, long-term care administration, and practice management; a Master of Arts (33 credits) with specializations in pastoral ministry, pastoral studies, and pastoral theology for those who seek to minister to the evolving needs of church and society; and a Master of Business Administration (42 credits) with specializations in resort management (full-time residential) and quality leadership. Graduate certificates include programs in health services administration (15 credits), international health care (15 credits), long-term care (15 credits), medical practice management (15 credits), and pastoral studies (18 credits).

At the undergraduate level, the Division offers the following degrees: the Bachelor of Science (128 credits), offering majors in business administration with concentrations in banking, through a joint venture with the Center for Financial Training, and in management; criminal justice, with concentrations in law, management, and psychology; general studies (a degree-completion program for adult students transferring a minimum of 30 credits), with concentrations in adult education and training, business administration, human services, information technology management, and psychology; health-care administration; long-term care administration; professional arts (a degree completion program for licensed health-care professionals), with concentrations in adult education and training, health-care administration, human services, information technology management, and psychology; and radiologic science (a post-certification baccalaureate degree for radiologic science professionals). A Bachelor of Arts (128 credits) is also available at the undergraduate level, with majors in liberal studies and adult religious education. The Division also offers eight majors within the Associate of Science degree (66 credits), including adult education and training, business administration, criminal justice, general studies, human services, information technology management, management, and psychology.

Undergraduate certificate programs (18 credits) are available in adult education and training, American studies, business administration, Christian tradition, criminal justice, health-care management and advanced health-care management, information technology management, long-term-care administration and advanced long-term care administration, and professional studies (self-designed). Students who would like to take individual courses at either the graduate or undergraduate level may enroll as continuing education students.

SPECIAL PROGRAMS

The Department of Nursing offers a Master of Science in Nursing with specializations in nursing administration (39 credits), nursing education (39 credits), and parish nursing (42 credits); graduate certificate programs (18 credits) in nursing and health-care education and parish nursing; and a Bachelor of Science in Nursing with an RN to B.S.N. track (129 credits) for students at a distance. The Division of Graduate and Professional Studies offers the noncredit Lay Ministry Foundation Program, a series of five courses created to help meet the needs of churches in an era of increasing lay participation. The Division is a member of the Army University Access Online program (eArmyU) and the Navy College Program for Afloat College Education (NCPACE) and assists other active and nonactive military personnel in their educational pursuits as a member of Servicemembers Opportunity Colleges (SOC).

CREDIT OPTIONS

The Graduate and Professional Studies program acknowledges the value of certain formal learning and career-based experience. For most programs, the College follows the American Council on Education guidelines in granting transfer credit for courses of study from accredited colleges or universities with a grade of C or better; ACE/PONSI-approved credit; ACE-approved military training and experience credits; CEUs earned through professional seminars, workshops, internships, and in-service education classes as elective credit; and CLEP, ACT/PEP, and DANTES exams. A maximum of 30 credits can be accepted by exam.

FACULTY

More than 100 full-time and part-time faculty members serve students in the Graduate and Professional Studies program. Many teach in the traditional program as well as in distance education. All excel in their fields and have experience with nontraditional students.

ADMISSION

Admission requirements vary by program of study. Prospective students should contact the Admissions Office for the Graduate and Professional Studies program at 800-752-4723 (toll-free) with specific questions about admission requirements. Information can also be obtained from the Web site listed below.

TUITION AND FEES

For the 2004–05 academic year, tuition is $220 per credit hour ($660 per 3-credit course) at the undergraduate level. Graduate course tuition is $275 per credit hour ($825 per 3-credit course), except for the M.B.A. resort management specialization courses, which are $550 per credit hour ($1650 per 3-credit course). Application fees are $50 for degree programs and $25 for certificate programs and continuing education. A complete fee schedule is available in the program catalogs and on the College's Web site.

FINANCIAL AID

Students may be eligible for the Federal Pell Grant and/or Federal Stafford Student Loan. Applying for financial aid is an individualized process requiring consultation and evaluation. For more information and assistance, students should call the Financial Aid Office at 800-752-1266 (toll-free).

APPLYING

Students are accepted on a rolling admissions basis and, therefore, can apply and begin their studies at any time during the year. Students can apply online at http://www.sjcme.edu/gps or by contacting the Admissions Office at the number listed below.

CONTACT

Admissions Office
Division of Graduate and Professional Studies
Saint Joseph's College
278 Whites Bridge Road
Standish, Maine 04084-5263
Telephone: 800-752-4723 (toll-free)
Fax: 207-892-7480
E-mail: info@sjcme.edu
Web site:
http://www.sjcme.edu/gps

Saint Mary-of-the-Woods College

Distance Education Program

Saint Mary-of-the-Woods, Indiana

Founded in 1840, Saint Mary-of-the-Woods College (SMWC) is the nation's oldest Catholic liberal arts college for women and is accredited by the North Central Association of Colleges and Schools. The College offers the rich traditions of academic excellence and dedication to educating women personally and professionally for responsible roles in society. The diverse student community of 1,500 includes traditional resident students, commuters, student mothers and children, and distance learners at both the undergraduate and graduate levels. The College also enrolls men in its postbaccalaureate teacher licensure programs and its graduate programs. A hallmark of the College is an emphasis on personalized service.

The general studies curriculum required of all undergraduates is designed to develop the communication and analytical skills needed for success in college and in the professional world.

DISTANCE LEARNING PROGRAM

Since 1973, the Women's External Degree (WED) program has provided the College curriculum to contemporary adult women who juggle multiple responsibilities yet need or want a college degree. Now serving 1,150 women, this structured but flexible independent-study program is based on five-month semesters that begin with in-person appointments with instructors and faculty advisers, leading to a degree in one of more than thirty majors.

DELIVERY MEDIA

Faculty members and students communicate by telephone, voice mail, e-mail, and postal service. All full-time faculty members, some adjuncts, and many students have access to e-mail. Computers with modems are not required—except for accounting, CIS, and digital media communication majors—but access to a computer for word processing and research is required. Some courses use videotapes, audiotapes, or optional computer programs.

PROGRAMS OF STUDY

The College is chartered to grant the Associate in Arts, Associate in Science, Bachelor of Arts, and Bachelor of Science degrees to women and the Master of Arts degree to both women and men.

Undergraduates complete the general studies curriculum, courses required for their chosen major, and additional electives to total 125 semester hours for a baccalaureate degree and 65 semester hours for an associate degree; a minimum of 30 hours must be earned at the College.

Associate majors available through WED are accounting, early childhood education, general business, gerontology, humanities, and paralegal studies. Baccalaureate majors are accounting, accounting information systems, business administration, computer information systems, digital media communications, E-commerce, education (early childhood, elementary, secondary, and special), English, equine business management, gerontology, history/political science, human resource management, human services, humanities, journalism, marketing, mathematics, not-for-profit administration, occupational therapy applications, paralegal studies, professional writing, psychology, social sciences (history concentration), and theology. Teacher licensure is also available for men and women who have already earned a bachelor's degree.

There are no geographical restrictions, except that education majors must reside within 200 miles of campus for faculty supervision of field experience and student teaching.

The Master of Arts in pastoral theology program is designed for persons who are or plan to be engaged in ministry and for those seeking personal enrichment in theological study.

The Master of Arts in earth literacy program is designed for persons who care for and advocate a sustainable and just earth community.

The Master of Arts in art therapy program emphasizes understanding and applying theories to art therapy, counseling, and psychopathology.

The Master of Arts in music therapy program is designed for professional music therapists who seek an advanced understanding of the therapeutic uses of music, especially as applied to psychotherapy and medicine. Master of Arts degrees require 36 to 40 credit hours.

SPECIAL PROGRAMS

SMWC offers several learning formats: traditional campus-based study, distance learning, and a third format that combines independent study with intensive weekend seminars on campus. WED students may combine these formats in any semester of study; about 400 choose to enroll in weekend alternative format courses each year. However, all degrees offered through WED may be completed entirely through distance learning at home, with the exception of several paralegal, digital media communication, and equine courses, which must be taken via alternative format on campus on weekends.

STUDENT SERVICES

Full-time faculty members serve as academic advisers to the WED students in their departments, meeting each semester to monitor progress and plan subsequent semesters. A WED staff of 8 provides additional support, advocacy, registrarial assistance, and information, including a quarterly newsletter for distance learners. One WED staff person provides referral to other campus services, such as career development (available by phone and in person) and library materials by mail.

CREDIT OPTIONS

Students may transfer credit earned at other accredited colleges and universities, although some credits may be too dated to meet the requirements. WED encourages students to earn credit for previous college-level learning through CLEP and DANTES, ACE/CCRS awards, and portfolio applications documenting other prior learning. At least 30 semester hours of course work must be earned under the direct supervision of SMWC faculty members.

FACULTY

Fifty-seven full-time and 55 adjunct faculty members serve as instructors and academic advisers to WED students. Sixty percent of full-time faculty members have doctoral or other terminal degrees.

ADMISSION

Applicants must have earned a high school diploma or GED certificate and demonstrate potential for success in a distance learning program. Academic history, employment and other life experience, writing skills, and stated goals are considered. Applicants for whom English is a second language must submit TOEFL scores. Applications and all documentation should be submitted at least thirty days prior to the planned enrollment date.

TUITION AND FEES

For 2004–05, undergraduate tuition for the WED program is $332 per semester hour. Fees include a $30 application fee, a one-time fee of $80 for the initial on-campus residency (not including housing), an annual $50 general fee, and modest materials fees for laboratory courses.

FINANCIAL AID

Available financial aid includes Federal Pell Grants, student loans, and, for residents only, Indiana Higher Education Grants. In 2000–01, the College processed about $2.7 million from these sources on behalf of WED students. The College awards small WED grants to eligible seniors and offers 10 percent tuition discounts through cooperating employers; this institutional aid totaled $63,000 in 2000–01. Finally, the WED staff maintains a directory of private grants and scholarships and encourages WED students to apply for them. Approximately 65 percent of WED students receive some form of aid.

APPLYING

Applications are reviewed when all materials are received; the evaluation process is usually completed within a month. Two-day orientation residencies are held on campus five times each year and conclude with enrollment in the initial semester.

CONTACT

Admission:
Director of Distance Education Admission
Saint Mary-of-the-Woods College
Saint Mary-of-the-Woods, Indiana 47876
Telephone: 812-535-5106
800-926-SMWC (toll-free)
Fax: 812-535-5010
E-mail: wedadms@smwc.edu
Web site: http://www.smwc.edu

Graduate Programs:
Mary Lou Dolan, C.S.J.
Earth Literacy Director
Telephone: 812-535-5160
Fax: 812-535-5228
E-mail: mldolan@smwc.edu
elm@smwc.edu

Kathy Gotshall
Art Therapy Program
Telephone: 812-535-5151
E-mail: kgotshal@smwc.edu

Virginia Unverzagt
Pastoral Theology Director
Telephone: 812-535-5170
Fax: 812-535-4613
E-mail: vunver@smwc.edu

Tracy Richardson
Music Therapy Program
Telephone: 812-535-5154
E-mail: trichardson@smwc.edu

St. Mary's University of San Antonio

Online Degree Programs

San Antonio, Texas

In 2002, St. Mary's University celebrated 150 years of Marianist education in Texas. As San Antonio's largest and oldest Catholic university, St. Mary's continues to provide a Catholic educational experience that evokes academic excellence while integrating liberal studies, professional preparation, and ethical commitment.

From its origins, St. Mary's University has been a community of faith permeated by the values of the Gospels and the Judeo-Christian tradition. The University invites faculty, administration, staff, and students of various religious backgrounds to be a part of this community, sharing its values while searching together for a meaningful integration of faith and reason.

St Mary's University's distance learning programs confer online Master of Arts degrees in community counseling and international relations. The degrees earned through the programs are exactly like the degrees earned by students attending courses on the campus; there is no distinction between online and on-campus courses on transcripts or diplomas.

St. Mary's University is accredited by the Commission on Colleges of the Southern Association of Colleges and Schools.

DISTANCE LEARNING PROGRAM

Note: This section includes a general description of your distance learning program—its mission, goals, and features; tells how many students are served by the program; and provides an overview of your program, including how it fits within the framework of your institution.

DELIVERY MEDIA

Note: This section provides specific information about your delivery media (including correspondence) and relates how students use the media and how faculty members and students interact.

PROGRAMS OF STUDY

St. Mary's University awards Master's of Arts (M.A.) degrees in community counseling and in international relations.

The graduate program in community counseling prepares students to work in institutions and agencies offering counseling services, including alcohol and drug programs, family counseling and service programs, child and adolescent programs, and social service agencies. Client problems may include, but are not limited to, the effects of socioeconomic status; unemployment; aging; culture; race; ethnicity; chronic illness, including physical and mental illness; developing transitions; and interpersonal, family, and violence issues. Community counselors have the ability to implement educational, preventative, and remedial programs. This 48-semester-hour program includes 24 semester hours of core courses, 12 semester hours of clinical courses, 12 semester hours of specialization courses, and an intensive 600-clock-hour internship experience. Prior to graduating from the community counseling program, students are expected to understand the essential elements of the counseling profession and related human services professions and the distinctive contributions of each in meeting the needs of the various client populations. Graduates meet the academic requirements to sit for the National Counselor Examination and for licensing by the Texas State Board of Examiners of Professional Counselors. The community counseling program is accredited by the Council for Accreditation of Counseling and Related Educational Programs (CACREP).

The 36-semester-hour graduate program in international relations is currently the largest master's program at St. Mary's. The program in international relations offered by St. Mary's focuses on security policy, as opposed to the majority of programs available elsewhere that offer an M.A. in political science with a focus area in international relations. In the post-Cold War era, a one-discipline approach to contextualizing and analyzing international issues is proving to be inadequate. St. Mary's international relations program offers an interdisciplinary examination and analysis of national and international security issues. All courses are taught from the perspectives of economics, history, political science, international business, sociology, and theology. Topics range from nuclear proliferation and conventional arms trade to narcotrafficking, trade imbalances, environmental conflict, and race, ethnic, gender, and religious issues. Before graduation, all students must pass a comprehensive written examination over the course work required for the degree. They must also demonstrate a working knowledge of a foreign language and a strong theoretical foundation for, and basic quantitative and analytical skills in, the study of international relations.

SPECIAL PROGRAMS

Students in the international relations program have taken internships with international organizations (the European Union's Office of Human Rights), the federal public-service sector (Department of Defense, Secret Service, and FAA), state and city governments (San Antonio's International Affairs Office), non-profit organizations (International Red Cross and Alliance for Justice), and the private sector (Southwestern Bell, Bbancomex, and Hispanic Chamber of Commerce). Other graduates have chosen to continue their education.

STUDENT SERVICES

Students enrolled in St. Mary's distance learning courses may use the services of the Blume Library. Distance learning students are encouraged to seek reference help when they are working on research projects. Students can also request materials be sent directly to them via first-class U.S. mail.

FACULTY

St. Mary's University's faculty members are dedicated to a life that is intellectual, critically rational, and ethically responsible. In its work, the faculty demonstrates the freedom enjoyed by each individual to experience the world, to inquire into its meaning, and to respond to it in a manner that befits their personal gifts and talents.

There are 11 full-time and 22 associate faculty members for the community counseling program. The international relations faculty consists of 12 full-time and 13 regular adjunct members.

ADMISSION

Admission to either program is granted only to those with high promise for success in graduate study. Such potential may be demonstrated by experience in increasingly responsible positions, previous schooling, and/or test scores at the time of enrollment.

In addition to having a bachelor's degree or the equivalent from an accredited college or university, graduate students must be proficient in information technology. To be considered proficient, graduate students must know and be able to use the applications, software, and technologies appropriate for the program in which they are enrolled.

Community counseling prerequisites include 9 hours of social sciences and 3 hours of statistics.

The GRE or the MAT is required of all counseling program candidates; if they are otherwise highly qualified, they may take the GRE or the MAT during their first semester of enrollment, with further enrollment contingent upon their test results. A personal interview with the applicant is usually required prior to an admission decision.

Students applying to the internatonal relations degree program must have adquate scores on the GRE. Students may take the GRE during their first semester of enrollment, with further enrollment contingent upon their test results. Prerequisites include 3 hours of microeconomics and 3 hours of macroeconomics course work and an undergraduate GPA of at least 2.75, with 3.0 in their undergraduate major.

TUITION AND FEES

Tuition for all students is $552 per semester hour.

FINANCIAL AID

Payment is due in full at the time of registration and no later than seven days prior to the start of classes. Students may be eligible for financial assistance. Tuition grants are given to active duty military personnel, military retirees, DOD employees, and dependents of these groups. St. Mary's University must be able to confirm the amount of aid eligibility and that all paperwork is completed by the payment deadline date in order to consider financial aid for all or part of the payment due.

APPLYING

Students may apply to St. Mary's University via an online application at the Web site listed below. There is a $30 application fee.

Before enrolling in the online program, students must apply and be admitted to graduate study.

Graduate students who wish to transfer to St. Mary's from other universities must apply to St. Mary's University Graduate School and send a letter of good standing from their current university, or they may send transcripts and two letters of reference.

CONTACT

Graduate School
St. Mary's University
One Camino Santa Maria
San Antonio, Texas 78228-8543
Telephone: 210-436-3101
Fax: 210-431-2220
E-mail: gradsch@Alvin.stmarytx.edu
Web site: http://www.stmarytx.edu

Salve Regina University

Extension Study, eSalve

Newport, Rhode Island

Salve Regina is an independent, coeducational institution of higher learning that confers degrees in the arts and sciences. It teaches in the tradition of the Catholic Church and according to the Mission of the Sisters of Mercy, who continue as its sponsors. Salve Regina's Charter was amended in June 1991 to change its name to Salve Regina University.

The University serves approximately 2,300 men and women from many states and other countries. Alumni number more than 14,000. Its 65-acre oceanfront campus in Newport's Ochre Point historic district includes thirty-nine new and adapted buildings.

The University, through teaching and research, prepares men and women for responsible lives by imparting and expanding knowledge, developing skills, and cultivating enduring values. Through liberal arts and professional programs, students develop their abilities for thinking clearly and creatively, enhance their capacity for sound judgment, and prepare for the challenge of learning throughout their lives.

The graduate programs of Salve Regina University have two broad goals: to help the individual who enrolls to realize his or her own full potential and to prepare this individual for helping others do the same.

DISTANCE LEARNING PROGRAM

Salve Regina University's Office of Graduate Extension Study provides an alternative to traditional classroom learning by acknowledging the needs of students whose personal and professional circumstances make regular on-campus study difficult. Salve Regina University has been providing master's programs by extension for the past twenty years. Salve offers an M.B.A., an M.A. in international relations, an M.S. in management, and an M.A. in humanities, plus several professional certificates completely online. The program of study completed online is the same as that completed by on-campus students.

DELIVERY MEDIA

All courses are accessed through the World Wide Web. Once students register for a course, they are notified of their username and password. Online courses are offered in two formats: self-paced and interactive.

Online self-paced courses are usually available at the time of registration. The student has four months to complete each course. The course assignments are given as modules. At the end of each module, students send their completed assignments via e-mail to the GES office.

Online interactive courses have specific start and end dates. In these courses, students interact with other students and have the ability to participate in discussions with faculty members. Communication is asynchronous; there is no requirement for members of the class to be online at the same time. This interactive environment enriches course content, provides opportunity for discussion, and encourages the exchange of ideas.

PROGRAMS OF STUDY

Four distance learning master's degree programs are offered in business administration, humanities, international relations, and management.

The Master of Business Administration program is designed to prepare graduates to successfully lead and manage organizations in a constantly changing environment. In both the for-profit and not-for-profit environments, today's executive is faced with myriad concerns ranging from ethical and human rights issues to globalization and environmental protection. The Salve Regina University Master of Business Administration curriculum provides the technical knowledge and skills to appreciate and address these and other critical contemporary issues. The program is directed toward developing leaders with a focus on ethics, organizational behavior, finance, economics, accounting, and strategic management. Social purpose and workplace humanization are underlying program values aligned with the University's mission. This degree program is accredited by the International Assembly for Collegiate Business Education (IACBE).

The curriculum and content of the international relations program is a reflection of the University's mission regarding justice and the increasing need to envision international political behavior in its framework. In its own capacity and within the University's mission, the international relations program promotes international and world politics. The program prepares graduates to be constructively critical of their immediate and broader political environment, whether in their place of work (government, education, the private sector, the media, or nongovernmental organizations) or simply as citizens of both their country and the world. The program's objective is to reinforce the vision of its graduates to view fellow human beings not only as representatives of national and social compartments but also as overlapping circles in a world community. In practical terms, this translates into global solidarity and the elimination of injustice everywhere. Graduates are able to produce creative and pragmatic solutions to problems and dilemmas confronting the world. The program accomplishes its objective by exposing the candidates in a systematic and comprehensive way to the realities of the political environment through a core of courses covering political thought, international relations, and comparative politics.

The Master of Arts in Humanities is an interdisciplinary program that seeks to foster a broad understanding of the qualitative aspects of life and culture through a study of disciplines such as history, literature, philosophy, and religion. The course of study is intended for individuals who want to broaden their intellectual and cultural horizons. It also serves as excellent preparation for the Ph.D. degree in the humanities.

The Master of Science program in management offers a solid theoretical and practical management foundation and integrates information systems into the management role.

Salve Regina University is a fully accredited member of the New England Association of Schools and Colleges (NEASC). Inquiries about NEASC accreditation may be directed to the Vice President for Academic Affairs at Salve Regina or to the Commission on Institutions of Higher Education, NEASC, 209 Burlington Road, Bedford, Massachusetts 01730-1433 (telephone: 781-271-0022; e-mail: cihe@neasc.org).

SPECIAL PROGRAMS

The certificate program in management is for students who already have a bachelor's degree and includes 15 hours of graduate credit. It offers opportunities for those who desire a graduate education without formal pursuit of a master's degree.

CREDIT OPTIONS

The master's degree programs are all twelve courses (36 credits). Students have up to five years to complete all of the requirements for the degree; however, at a rate of four courses per year, students are generally able to complete the degree in three years. Normally, only 40 percent of the total program credits are eligible to transfer into the graduate programs at Salve Regina University. The University, however, does recognize the unique situation of military members who are not located in one area long enough to obtain a graduate degree in the traditional manner. Accordingly, the University accepts up to 18 credits earned at military schools, colleges, or universities in accordance with the recommendations made by the American Council of Education (ACE) and with the University transfer policy regarding academic performance.

FACULTY

The faculty members are a valued resource; many teach full-time on campus and others are adjunct faculty members who are successful professionals within their field. They come from leading doctoral, M.B.A., and law programs and represent a wide variety of backgrounds. Their superior teaching skills, academic training and research, and knowledge of practical application bring a wealth of experience to the curriculum.

ADMISSION

Men and women with bachelor's degrees from accredited institutions of higher learning who are considered to have the ability to pursue graduate study and show a desire for personal development are admitted following a careful evaluation of their credentials, without regard to age, race, sex, creed, national or ethnic origin, or handicap.

TUITION AND FEES

Tuition is $340 per credit hour for all Extension Study courses. All courses are 3 credit hours. Fees include application ($50), incomplete/delay of grade ($150), master's degree graduation ($175), and transcript ($5).

FINANCIAL AID

Salve Regina University assists students in applying for loans through the Federal Family Educational Loan Programs, particularly the Federal Stafford Student Loans. These loans are available to all students and may be used to fund education at the University provided the student maintains continuous quantitative and qualitative progress. Benefit plans for veterans and active-duty service persons and employers' tuition-reimbursement plans are welcome.

APPLYING

The following must be submitted to the Graduate Admissions Office: an application form, a nonrefundable application fee, official transcripts from all accredited degree-granting institutions attended, two letters of recommendation, standardized test scores no more than five years old (GRE, MAT, GMAT, or LSAT), a personal statement of intent of study, and a nonrefundable commitment deposit upon acceptance. The TOEFL and official transcript evaluations are required of international students. A graduate extension study catalog with application may be requested from the Graduate Admissions Office.

CONTACT

Charles H. Reed, Director
Extension Study and Continuing Education
Salve Regina University
100 Ochre Point Avenue
Newport, Rhode Island 02840
Telephone: 800-637-0002 (toll-free)
Fax: 401-341-2931
E-mail: graduate_studies@salve.edu
Web site: http://www.salve.edu/programs_esalve/get_index.htm

Savannah College of Art and Design

SCAD E-Learning Program

Savannah, Georgia

The Savannah College of Art and Design (SCAD) is a private, coeducational college that prepares students for careers in the visual and performing arts, design, the building arts, and the history of art and architecture. The Savannah College of Art and Design was the only art college selected as one of the 100 hidden gems in higher education by Jay Mathews, author of Harvard Schmarvard: Getting Beyond the Ivy League to the College That is Best for You. *A balanced fine arts and liberal arts curriculum has attracted students from every state and from more than eighty countries, making SCAD one of the largest art and design colleges in the United States. Current enrollment is nearly 6,000 students.*

DISTANCE LEARNING PROGRAM

The College is accredited by the Commission on Colleges of the Southern Association of Colleges and Schools (1866 Southern Lane, Decatur, Georgia 30033-4097; telephone: 404-679-4500) to award bachelor's and master's degrees. The Master of Architecture (M. Arch.) is accredited by the National Architectural Accrediting Board (NAAB). Among its many distinctions, the College has been cited by the National Trust for Historic Preservation, the American Institute of Architects, and the International Downtown Association for its adaptive reuse of more than fifty historic buildings for creating a unique urban setting.

DELIVERY MEDIA

Through SCAD e-Learning, the Savannah College of Art and Design uses the Internet and the World Wide Web to extend certificate and degree programs to students who are unable to attend regularly scheduled classes on campus. All courses are led by faculty members and are offered for academic credit.

Program formats are designed for students and working professionals who want to continue their education and advance their careers but who require an adaptive option. SCAD e-Learning allows off-campus learners to take part in the same courses as on-campus students while enjoying the flexibility of distance education. SCAD e-learning programs follow the quarter system, with courses offered in the fall, winter, spring, and summer. Most courses run ten weeks and are partially asynchronous.

While courses have definite start and end dates, they are not tied to specific meeting times. Students are expected to move through course work according to a schedule; however, they are able to decide the times and days they devote to the course work. In several courses, students may work at an accelerated pace, completing the requirements ahead of schedule.

PROGRAMS OF STUDY

Through SCAD e-Learning, the Savannah College of Art and Design offers a certificate in digital publishing; graduate certificates in digital publishing management, historic preservation, and interactive design and game development; and Master of Arts degrees in graphic design and historic preservation. Art history, film and television, foundation studies, graphic design, historic preservation, illustration, interactive design, liberal arts, and photography classes are among the courses that may be offered as well.

In the certificate in digital publishing program, students learn publishing and design fundamentals, including layout, graphic imaging, and typography. They are introduced to a variety of industry-standard computer applications that are used in the production and presentation of print and online media. The certificate in digital publishing is a 20-hour, four-course program that allows students to choose a focus on prepress and/or Web publishing. Students may complete both the Production Design and Web Page Design courses for further specialization.

The graduate certificate in digital publishing management features advanced topics in publishing and design, with an emphasis on content management, design and development processes, and creative teams. Students work with a variety of industry-standard computer applications used in the production and presentation of print and online media. The graduate certificate in digital publishing management is a 20-hour, four-course program.

In the graduate certificate in historic preservation program, students are provided with a fundamental understanding of the discipline's broad applications to art, planning, and modern living. Course work is intended to enhance the knowledge base of professionals working directly or tangentially in the field or may also serve to inspire a new career. The graduate certificate in historic preservation is a 20-hour, four-course program.

Students in the certificate in interactive design and game development program develop skills that allow them to create works of interactive art and design to meet a variety of vendor industry standards. These include content and design for open-source as well as for closed, proprietary systems. Students utilize various applications and programming techniques. The certificate in interactive design and game development is a 25-hour, five-course program.

The M.A. in graphic design features carefully sequenced courses that prepare students for professional careers in the industry and encourage the development of individualized design philosophies. Areas of design concentration include advertising promotions, corporate publications, multidimensional design, multimedia, print, social issues, and typography. The M.A. in graphic design is a 45-hour, nine-course program.

Students in the M.A. in historic preservation program learn the regulatory, technical, and philosophical issues involved in historic preservation. They also participate in hands-on projects such as building assessments, meetings of planning bodies, and investigations of the economic impact of historic preservation on communities. Students may elect to do field work in Savannah and, with required approvals, complete a two-week residency under the direction of on-campus faculty members. The M.A. in historic preservation is a 45-hour, nine-course program.

Upon successful application, courses in any of these programs may be credited toward other applicable degree programs.

STUDENT SERVICES

Student services staff and programs are provided to assist students in making a successful adjustment to classes. Staff members guide students in developing independence and self-direction for their professional and personal goals and are available to help students resolve personal and academic problems.

CREDIT OPTIONS

Through SCAD e-Learning, the Savannah College of Art and Design offers students the option of taking courses without enrolling in a degree or certificate program. Depending on their admission status, students may take courses for credit. Students enrolled in degree programs may complete other online courses for elective credit. Courses offered change quarterly; students should consult the SCAD e-Learning Web site for an updated course list.

FACULTY

A large and distinguished international faculty consists of professors with diverse backgrounds, both professionally and educationally. Classes are taught by faculty members who hold terminal degrees or other outstanding credentials in their fields and individual attention is emphasized.

ADMISSION

To apply to the undergraduate certificate program, prospective students must submit an application for admission, a nonrefundable $50 application fee, official transcripts from the highest level of school attended, recommendations, and a résumé, if applicable. The certificate of digital publishing requires industry experience, and applicants to the graphic design program must submit a portfolio to be evaluated by selected faculty members and the admissions review committee. Interviews are encouraged but are not required.

To apply to the graduate certificate and degree programs, prospective students must submit an application for admission, a nonrefundable $50 application fee, official transcripts from each college attended, recommendations, a statement of purpose, and a résumé, if applicable. The Master of Arts programs in graphic design and historic preservation as well as the graduate certificates in interactive design and historic preservation require a previous baccalaureate degree. Applicants in graphic design and interactive design programs must submit a portfolio, and the applicants in historic preservation must submit a portfolio or research paper. These materials are evaluated by selected faculty members and the admissions review committee. Interviews and GRE scores are encouraged but are not required. GRE scores are considered valuable in evaluating candidates, with preference given to students with GRE scores at or above the national average.

Students who enroll in e-learning courses must possess basic computer skills and have regular access to appropriate computer hardware, software, and Internet connectivity in order to fully participate in the course work. Students should consult the SCAD e-learning Web site for more information about technical requirements.

TUITION AND FEES

Undergraduate tuition is $2250 per class, per quarter; graduate tuition is $2300. Degree-seeking students pay a one-time nonrefundable matriculation fee of $500. All SCAD e-Learning students pay a $100 technology fee for each course.

FINANCIAL AID

Federal financial aid is available to degree-seeking students who are enrolled at least half time (two classes). Aid programs offered by the state of Georgia are available to students who are enrolled full-time (three classes). Students are encouraged to check with their states for availability of state aid. Courses leading to a certificate or continuing education credits do not qualify for either federal or state financial aid.

APPLYING

To apply, explore one's e-learning potential, learn more about e-learning, or take the e-learning self-assessment, students should visit http://www.scad.edu/elearning.

CONTACT

SCAD E-Learning
Savannah College of Art and Design
P.O. Box 2072
Savannah, Georgia 31402-2072
Telephone: 912-525-5100
800-869-7223 (toll-free)
E-mail: admission@scad.edu
WWW: http://www.scad.edu

Saybrook Graduate School

Graduate Programs in Psychology, Human Science, and Organizational Systems

San Francisco, California

Since 1971, Saybrook has been educating mid-career professionals in humanistic values relevant to the work place and the community. Saybrook Graduate School and Research Center's graduate education prepares scholar/practitioners to take effective leadership roles, develop the consciousness to realize the immense possibilities of these times, and minimize the potential for social and individual suffering. Saybrook provides a unique learning-centered environment based in an emancipatory humanistic tradition. Advanced studies in psychology, human science, and organizational systems are offered. Programs are designed for professionals seeking an opportunity to engage in serious scholarly work, and who wish to develop the necessary research skills, scope of knowledge, and intervention skills to become more effective in their chosen sphere of work.

Approximately 500 students are currently enrolled at Saybrook, ranging in age from the mid-20s to the 60s and representing more than forty states and many countries. Saybrook is fully accredited by the Western Association of Schools and Colleges (WASC).

DISTANCE LEARNING PROGRAM

For more than thirty years, Saybrook Graduate School's mode of education has been at-a-distance learning. Because of the unique mix of mentorship, on-site residential programs, and online classes, the Saybrook model encourages close contact between faculty members and students and among students. Programs are structured to meet the personal and professional needs of adult learners and persons not able or willing to travel to traditional classrooms.

DELIVERY MEDIA

Learning takes place through one-on-one mentorships with faculty members in small cohort groups, online courses, and seminars at residential conferences. Using learning guides, students complete course work, which is evaluated by faculty members who communicate by phone, letter, fax, or computer or in person at conferences.

PROGRAMS OF STUDY

Saybrook Graduate School offers programs in psychology, human science, and organizational systems. Students may pursue an M.A. or a Ph.D. in any program. Within each program, students select an area of study, which includes humanistic and transpersonal psychology, health studies, consciousness and spirituality, social transformation, and organizational systems.

Saybrook's psychology degree program prepares its graduates to be scholars and researchers in the broad domain of human experience. Saybrook is an institute providing alternative education that conscientiously challenges many of the axioms of mainstream medicalized and industrialized psychology and offers an emancipatory alternative. Saybrook offers the course work necessary to take the licensing exam for both the marriage and family therapy license and the psychologist license in most states.

The human science program provides an opportunity for a humanistic, action-learning approach to group, family, public and private organizations, and community and global spheres of life. The Saybrook approach combines responsible action with scholarly reflection, exploring transformative change that respects human dignity and creative possibilities. The human science program consists of a set of perspectives pertaining to the human condition in historical, contextual, cross-cultural, political, and religious terms. It employs perspectives such as feminism, post-structuralism, critical theory, existential phenomenology, and postmodernism. The human sciences are a collective understanding of the common condition and contribute to the ongoing story of social improvement and consciousness evolution.

The organizational systems program is designed to develop leaders, scholars, and practitioners who are capable of addressing the challenge of building organizations and communities with greater capacity to deal with the increasing turbulence, interconnection, and diverse frameworks of interpretation of the information age/knowledge era. The mission of the organizational systems program is to educate leaders to become adept at changing and designing organizations that reflect the highest human ideals.

STUDENT SERVICES

It is Saybrook's intent to be responsive to student and institutional needs, to provide programs and services in support of the mission, to assist students in achieving academic success, and to enhance the overall learning environment.

FACULTY

Saybrook Graduate School and Research Center is proud to have an internationally recognized faculty of scholars and practitioners, all of whom hold a doctoral or terminal degree in their field. In addition to teaching, faculty members have extensive experience as researchers, practitioners, consultants, authors, business people, and organizational leaders. They are committed to Saybrook's ideals and values and are supportive of students' personal and scholarly growth.

ADMISSION

Saybrook requires that all applicants seeking admission into a master's program must hold a bachelor's degree from a regionally accredited institution. The minimum expected grade point average (GPA) requirement is 3.0 from the last degree-granting institution; however, exceptions may be made with the approval of the Vice President of Academic Affairs. Doctoral degree applicants must have an appropriate master's degree from a regionally accredited institution. Candidates wishing to pursue the doctoral degree but who lack a master's degree should apply to one of Saybrook's M.A. programs and, upon graduation from the master's program, apply for the Ph.D. program and transfer a maximum of 31 Saybrook credits toward Saybrook's Ph.D. degree.

All candidates whose first (native) language is not English must meet an English language proficiency requirement to qualify for admission. This requirement may be met in a number of ways, including the submission of results from a recent TOEFL exam (Saybrook's TOEFL number is 9007). Prospective students should contact the Admissions Office for details or consult the 2004–05 Catalog.

APPLYING

Students are admitted in September and March. For the September start date, all application materials should be received by June 1. For the March start date, all application materials should be received by December 16. Applications completed after this deadline are considered on a space-available basis or, with the applicant's permission, held for the next enrollment period.

Applicants are evaluated on writing ability, past academic record, and professional background. They should be a good match with the distance learning format, research interests, and Saybrook's mission and values. New students attend a four-day Residential Orientation Conference (ROC) held in the San Francisco Bay area.

Saybrook welcomes admissions application materials from international students with degrees from accredited post-secondary colleges and universities (or equivalent schools). Transcripts created in languages other than English must be submitted as literal translations prior to admission and must be sent for evaluation to the American Association of Collegiate Registrars and Admissions Officers (AACRAO) at AACRAO, Office of International Educational Services, Southwest Regional Office, PMB 606, 15029 North Thompson Peak, Suite B111, Scottsdale, Arizona, 85260, U.S.A. Students should visit the Web site at http://www.aacraosw.org/ for more information. AACRAO issues a Basic Statement of Comparability that is sent directly to Saybrook. All other admissions documents should be submitted in English.

TUITION AND FEES

Tuition for the 2004–05 academic year is $15,800. Fees for attending two Residential Conferences (RC) per year are also required. These fees include the cost of registration, meals, conference materials, and meeting space.

FINANCIAL AID

U.S. citizens or eligible permanent residents may borrow up to $18,500 per year through the Federal Stafford Student Loan Program. Saybrook offers limited tuition assistance to qualified students.

CONTACT

Dean of Admissions
Saybrook Graduate School and Research Center
450 Pacific Avenue
San Francisco, California 94133-4640
Telephone: 415-433-9200
800-825-4480 (toll-free)
Fax: 415-433-9271
E-mail: admissions@saybrook.edu
Web site: http://www.saybrook.edu

Schiller International University

M.B.A. Online Programs in International Business, International Hotel and Tourism Management, and Management of Information Technology

Dunedin, Florida

Schiller International University (SIU), a leader in global education, with eight campuses in six countries, was founded in 1964. SIU is an independent, licensed, and accredited institution offering a curriculum of more than 300 courses in sixteen areas of study that leads to associate, bachelor's, and master's degrees. The mission of SIU is to prepare students, personally and professionally, for future leadership roles in an international setting. Schiller students have the unique opportunity of transferring among SIU's campuses without losing any credits, while continuing their chosen program of study. SIU's campuses are in Dunedin, Florida; London, England; Paris, France; Strasbourg, France; Heidelberg, Germany; Engelberg, Switzerland; Leysin, Switzerland; and Madrid, Spain.

Schiller is a university where personal initiative is encouraged and where faculty members know students by name. The close attention paid to each individual student is one of the hallmarks of an SIU education. SIU is accredited by the Accrediting Council for Independent Colleges and Schools (ACICS) and is licensed by the Florida Commission for Independent Education. The accreditation and licensing applies to both traditional and online programs.

DISTANCE LEARNING PROGRAM

Distance learning is a natural extension of the University's high-quality education, both on the undergraduate and graduate levels, for students from all over the world. This program has been developed in response to the needs of the adult learner in the Information Age. The creative use of modern education technology makes selected SIU programs available, anytime, anywhere, through the World Wide Web. Students may complete the entire M.B.A. program online, or online courses may be combined with one or more terms in residence at an SIU campus in the United States or in Europe. Online courses are usually limited to no more than 20 students per class.

DELIVERY MEDIA

Online M.B.A.s in international business, international hotel and tourism management, and management of information technology are available to all students who have access to a Pentium-based computer, a 28.8-speed modem, usual office software, and an Internet connection. All courses are Web-based and are delivered via the Internet, using the eCollege.com platform. Technical support is provided 24 hours a day, seven days a week, by eCollege.com's help desk. The course Web site contains a home page with the most essential information about the course, e-mail links to the instructor and other students taking the course, a discussion forum that allows instructor and students to communicate with the group as a whole, Web links, and glossaries. Each course utilizes a textbook; a study guide on CD-ROM; and the Web-based course materials, which also provide the medium of interaction. Although most interaction is asynchronous, chat rooms are available for student and faculty member use.

PROGRAMS OF STUDY

Completion of an Online M.B.A. requires 45 credit hours. The curriculum for the international business degree concentrates on the more detailed aspects of international marketing, management, finance, and economics. For the concentrations in international hotel and tourism management (IHTM) or management of information technology (MIT), students complete seven core M.B.A. courses, two elective courses, and six concentrated courses in either IHTM or MIT. Students whose undergraduate background does not include preparation in accounting/finance, economics, or statistics are required to take additional preparatory courses, available online. The degree requirements are designed to provide practical knowledge and training for future business executives. SIU M.B.A. programs promote a professional academic environment without borders, in which world-class education is offered in worldwide classrooms online.

In addition to the Online M.B.A., selected courses on the undergraduate level are offered in a distance learning format. More information about all programs can be accessed from SIU's Web site.

SPECIAL PROGRAMS

SIU offers an Executive M.B.A. program, which combines online courses as well as evening, weekend, and accelerated summer courses at selected campuses. During specific semesters, several undergraduate- and graduate-level courses are available online in a variety of subjects, including accounting, business administration and management, business communications, computer/information technology administration and management, economics, English composition, history, hospitality services management, human resources management, international business, international relations and diplomacy, marketing management and research, mathematics, physical sciences, psychology, statistics, tourism and travel services marketing operations, and more.

STUDENT SERVICES

The University has developed a number of methods to assist students in distance learning programs. Each student receives a copy of SIU's publication, *A Guide to Distance Learning*. Specially trained faculty mentors are always available by e-mail for consultation, and the Web-based host for the courses offers technical assistance 24 hours a day. Students in the distance learning programs have access to the full range of support services, including the Library and Information Resource Network (LIRN) and NET Library, that are used by all Schiller students. Each online course has its own library of study aids and resources. Lecture notes, sample quizzes, assignment checks, and hyperlinks to other interesting sites are available for viewing and downloading.

CREDIT OPTIONS

For the master's program, students must earn at least 36 credit hours, and undergraduates must earn at least 33 credits at SIU. Credit may be awarded to students who receive appropriate scores in CLEP subject examinations. Students admitted to the Executive M.B.A. program at the Florida campus may earn up to 6 credits by portfolio.

FACULTY

All virtual courses are taught by instructors with advanced degrees and extensive practical experience in their fields. The faculty members' abilities to teach in both online and ground-based formats ensures consistency across the programs. All courses in the distance learning program are Web-based. An online course has learning objectives identical to those of a ground-delivered course, incorporating both asynchronous and the possibility of synchronous technology to facilitate learning. Each course has a syllabus describing the course content, assignments, and grading policy. The faculty members choose from many course-delivery technologies, including journals and e-mail for assignment submission and correspondence; and discussion forums and chat rooms for ongoing questions and answers. The instructor uses these technologies to enhance the learning experience.

ADMISSION

Admission to the Online M.B.A. program requires completion of a B.B.A. degree or equivalent; a bachelor's degree or equivalent, with a major in business studies or economics, providing that core courses have been completed in economics, statistics, business law, marketing, management, and accounting; or a bachelor's degree or equivalent in a nonbusiness field, provided that course work in the areas listed above has been completed. Nonnative English speakers must provide scores of at least 550 on a TOEFL test (213 for the computerized test) taken within the past two years. Test scores should be sent directly to the University.

A completed application form must be sent to the SIU Office of Admissions together with a $50 application fee, payable by check, credit card, or international money order. Applicants must also request that official transcripts of academic work be sent via airmail to the Office of Admissions. Applicants must submit transcripts of all college courses attended as well as proof of an earned degree. Undergraduate applicants must submit proof of high school graduation as well as TOEFL test scores, if applicable. Original documents or certified copies must be submitted as well as a certified English translation of those documents not in English.

TUITION AND FEES

Distance learning students pay the same tuition as on-campus students. Tuition for the 2004–05 academic year is $430 per graduate credit and $430 per undergraduate credit and is payable by check, credit card, or international money order. Tuition includes all instruction and faculty-produced materials. Students are responsible for the additional cost of textbooks, and information about online booksellers is provided. Room and board fees vary by campus. Students wishing to complete a portion of their degree in residence should contact the individual campus. Additional fees include a $50 application fee, an $80 graduation fee, and a late registration fee of $115, applicable only after classes commence.

FINANCIAL AID

SIU participates in Title IV programs and is eligible to participate in the Veteran's Training Program. Both programs are for U.S. citizens and residents who qualify. Students should contact the Office of Financial Aid at the e-mail address listed below.

APPLYING

Applications for admission are accepted year-round. Classes begin in September, January, and June. Students interested in online courses must complete two surveys, found on the distance learning page of the SIU Web site at the address listed below. Students can visit this site or contact the Office of Admissions for further information.

CONTACT

Schiller International University
Office of Admissions
453 Edgewater Drive
Dunedin, Florida 34698
Telephone: 727-736-5082
800-336-4133 (toll-free in the U.S.)
Fax: 727-734-0359
E-mail: admissions@schiller.edu
financial_aid@schiller.edu
Web site: http://www.schiller.edu

Seton Hall University

SetonWorldWide

South Orange, New Jersey

Seton Hall University has been distinguished by a number of firsts. It is the first diocesan college in the United States, founded in 1856 by James Roosevelt Bayley, the first Bishop of Newark, and named for Elizabeth Ann Seton, the first American-born saint. And, through SetonWorldWide, it was one of the first traditional universities to offer full online degree programs. The University's mission, to provide an educational experience that imparts concrete knowledge and skills in the context of ethical values, is as timely today as in 1856, and as important on the Internet as in the classroom. At Seton Hall, timeless values intersect with technology to offer high-quality online degree programs that serve the educational aspirations and professional needs of students from across the country and around the world. By utilizing the Internet and the latest teaching technologies, students benefit from the flexibility to fulfill course requirements at the time of day when they are at their best and from the place that is most convenient for them. For its ability to empower students with technology, Seton Hall was awarded the prestigious EDUCAUSE Award for excellence in campus networking.

DISTANCE LEARNING PROGRAM

The online degree programs and certificates that are offered through SetonWorldWide (the online campus of Seton Hall University) are designed for professionals who have demonstrated achievement in their respective fields and have the ability, desire, and dedication to accept the rigors of a fast-paced, challenging curriculum.

The SetonWorldWide degree programs have been designed for working professionals who benefit from "anytime, anywhere" education. As learning team members, students and faculty members have extensive interaction, and these relationships provide a rich and dynamic online learning experience.

Three on-campus weekend residencies enable students to meet their classmates and faculty in person. During the third residency, students participate in commencement activities. All degrees are granted by Seton Hall University, an institution fully accredited by the Middle States Association of Colleges and Schools.

DELIVERY MEDIA

SetonWorldWide online degree programs feature electronic seminar discussions, e-mail, Internet-based audio and video, electronic research, and different types of software to enhance learning. Prior to the start of the program, students receive all the course materials, including books, articles, audiotapes, videotapes, and CD-ROMs. Computer requirements include a midrange desktop or laptop computer with Internet access.

PROGRAMS OF STUDY

The Master of Healthcare Administration (39 credits, twenty months) provides a rigorous and thorough understanding of today's challenging health-care environment, addressing real-world strategies and skills that help managers make significant contributions to their organizations.

The Master of Strategic Communication and Leadership (36 credits, twenty months) program provides executives with the essential communication and leadership skills to achieve personal and organizational success, acknowledging the demands brought about by a diverse workplace and the explosion of electronic media technology.

The Master of Arts in Counseling (48 credits, 2½ to 3 years) provides students with a necessary background and preparation in counseling, and a thorough understanding of theory, skills, and models of intervention. Two 10-day residencies are part of the degree requirements.

The Master of Educational Leadership, Management, and Policy (36 credits, twenty-one months) program is designed to enable students to broaden their knowledge and understanding of the process of education, improve their professional techniques, or prepare for leadership positions and careers in education.

The Master of Science in Nursing (nurse practitioner) program (43–46 credits) is designed for nurses who wish to balance graduate education with career, family, and personal responsibilities. Students are able to study the didactic portion of the program in their homes at their own convenience. The clinical practice is provided within the students' local community. Upon admission to the program, students are assigned a mentor to assist them throughout the learning process.

The Bachelor of Science in Nursing (for RNs) program (33 credits, nineteen months) is designed for registered nurses who wish to obtain their Bachelor of Science degree.

STUDENT SERVICES

Students find everything they need online, including admission information, academic assistance, financial aid assistance, career guidance, and other services. The Help Desk's technical support staff, available 24 hours a day, seven days a week, is dedicated to helping students become confident and productive in the online learning environment. They understand that online classes can be challenging at first, but they have the knowledge and experience to help make every student's transition into the virtual classroom a smooth one. All SetonWorldWide participants also have access to Seton Hall University library resources. During orientation, students meet the librarians and technical staff members who provide assistance throughout the program. Students can use the library's ASK ME service to request and receive assistance from a fully qualified librarian.

ADMISSION

SetonWorldWide online degree programs are designed for professionals who demonstrate significant achievement in their respective fields. Specific program admission requirements are found on SetonWorldWide's Web site.

TUITION AND FEES

The all-inclusive tuition includes all fees, except for the application fee, and all expenses, including books and other materials and room and meals for short residencies. Computer equipment, software, Internet access, and travel expenses to the residencies are not covered.

FINANCIAL AID

Financial aid is available in the form of subsidized and unsubsidized government loan programs. Students who want to apply for Federal Direct Loans should visit http://www.fafsa.ed.gov on the Internet. For further information and guidance, students should contact SetonWorldWide at the Web site listed below.

APPLYING

To apply, students should visit the Web site listed below and click on Apply.

CONTACT

SetonWorldWide
Seton Hall University
400 South Orange Avenue
South Orange, New Jersey 07079
Telephone: 888-SETON-WW (toll-free)
E-mail: SetonWorldWide@shu.edu
Web site: http://www.setonworldwide.net

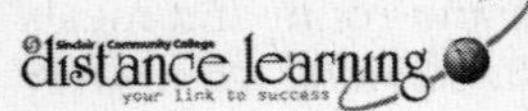

Sinclair Community College

Distance Learning Program

Dayton, Ohio

Sinclair Community College is located on a modern, tree-lined campus in downtown Dayton, Ohio. The College has a rich history in the Dayton community, dating back to 1887. In 1966, Sinclair became a publicly funded community college, enjoying strong community support through ongoing passage of a college levy.

Sinclair offers more than 100 transfer and technical associate degree and certificate programs, as well as continuing education opportunities through a system of diverse resources and delivery alternatives. Sinclair enrolls about 22,000 credit students each quarter.

The College is fully accredited by the Higher Learning Commission and has been authorized by the Ohio Board of Regents to grant associate degrees in arts, sciences, applied science, and individualized and technical study. The College's technical, health, and business programs are fully accredited by national and/or state-approved accrediting organizations.

Sinclair Community College is a proud member of the prestigious League for Innovation in the Community College and has been selected as one of twelve Vanguard Learning Colleges for developing and promoting learner-centered practices and curricula.

DISTANCE LEARNING PROGRAM

Over the past twenty-five years, the Sinclair Distance Learning Program has emerged as a nationally recognized, state-of-the-art entity with in-house video and online course production facilities. The program offers more than 250 distance courses, spanning all six of Sinclair's academic divisions. The program enrolled about 5,000 credit students in fall 2002.

DELIVERY MEDIA

Courses are delivered via the World Wide Web, videotape, videoconferencing, interactive television, CD-ROM, and print. Students and faculty members communicate in person or through a variety of methods, including mail, telephone, fax, e-mail, and videoconference. The following equipment may be required: television, videocassette player, computer, modem, Internet access, e-mail, and CD-ROM.

PROGRAMS OF STUDY

Two associate degree programs are available to students through distance learning. The courses are delivered through a variety of distance learning and independent study methods.

The Associate of Arts degree in liberal arts and sciences is comprised of 94 quarter-credit hours. Twenty-three of the thirty program courses can be taken solely through a distance format. Credit for the remaining courses may be obtained through independent study, by attending on-campus courses, or through transfer credit.

The Associate of Science in business administration is comprised of 98 quarter-credit hours. Twenty-three of the thirty program courses can be taken solely through a distance format. Credit for the remaining courses may be obtained through independent study, by attending on-campus courses, or through transfer credit.

Information about these degree programs can be accessed online by visiting the Sinclair Distance Learning Web site listed in the Contact section.

A short-term, 21-credit hour certificate in Software Applications for the Professional is available online. This certificate provides office workers, managers, professionals, and other interested participants with the opportunity to develop and refine their skills in a variety of current personal computer software applications common in today's work environment. Software applications learned include Microsoft Word, Excel, PowerPoint, Publisher, and Access. Internet capabilities and software integration are also covered in this program. More information is available from the Business Technologies Division counselors at 937-512-3054 or on the Web site at http://www.sinclair.edu/departments/bis/biscert.htm.

There is also a second short-term, 29-credit hour certificate program available online: Medical Office Coding Specialist. Students learn a core set of medical office skills in coding and reimbursement. Specific topics include reading and interpreting medical documentation (diagnoses, conditions, services, and procedures); applying coding systems and regulatory rules in completing billing forms; applying reimbursement methodologies and claims; demonstrating personal behaviors; learning the appropriate attitudes and values that are consistent with a healthcare professional; and demonstrating critical thinking, problem solving, and informational literacy. More information is available from the Allied Health Technologies Division counselors at 937-512-3029. The curriculum for this certificate may be viewed at http://www.sinclair.edu/academics/alh/departments/him/programs/certificate/mocsc/.

SPECIAL PROGRAMS

Through formal partnership with the American Society of Radiologic Technologists (ASRT) and the National Association of Nephrology Technicians/Technologists (NANT), Sinclair Community College provides professionally approved, online, continuing education courses to meet the professional continuing education requirements for the American Registry of Radiologic Technologists, the National Nephrology Certification Organization (NNCO), and the Board of Nephrology Examiners of Nursing and Technology (BONENT). More information is available on these two continuing education programs by visiting http://ce.sinclair.edu or by calling 937-512-2842 and speaking with the Continuing Education Coordinator.

Sinclair has developed partnerships with a number of distance learning programs that enable Sinclair graduates to transfer into bachelor's degree programs at the junior level. Specific transfer requirements vary with each institution. Participating institutions include Capella University, Franklin University, Governors State University, the University of Cincinnati, the University of Phoenix, and the University of Toledo. Information about specific degree programs is available by contacting the Distance Learning office, listed in the Contact section.

STUDENT SERVICES

Services available to Sinclair Community College distance learners include academic advising, support services, and online access to library services. Testing by proctor for placement and course testing is also available.

CREDIT OPTIONS

Sinclair Community College associate degrees range from 91 to 110 quarter-credit hours. Students must take the last 30 hours at Sinclair. Students may transfer credit from regionally accredited institutions for which they received a passing grade or a letter grade of C or higher. Alternative credit assessment options are also available (portfolio, CLEP, PONSI).

FACULTY

Sinclair Community College has more than 400 full-time and 500 part-time faculty members. More than 15 percent of the full-time faculty members hold doctoral degrees or earned advanced degrees. About 100 Sinclair faculty members support the distance learning courses; most of these individuals are experienced, full-time faculty members.

ADMISSION

Sinclair has an open door admission policy. All students are welcome. Students seeking degrees or certificates or who wish to take math and English classes are required to take a placement test. This test and other course testing can be administered by a proctor. To learn more about test proctoring procedures, applicants should visit the distance learning Web site listed below, and click on "Testing Information." Within this section, applicants should select "Proctor Form," print it off, and fax the completed form to the Distance Learning Office prior to the start of the quarter in which they plan to attend.

TUITION AND FEES

Tuition and fees for distance learning students are the same as for other Sinclair Community College students. Students pay a one-time, nonrefundable $10 admission fee. Montgomery County (Ohio) residents pay $40.05 per credit hour, other Ohio residents pay $65.40 per credit hour, and out-of-state residents and international students pay $118 per credit hour.

FINANCIAL AID

The Sinclair Financial Aid and Scholarships Office administers grants and scholarships that do not have to be repaid, low-interest loans, and student employment. A need-based financial aid package may consist of one or more of the following: Federal Pell Grant, Ohio Instructional Grant, Federal Supplemental Educational Opportunity Grant, and Federal Direct Student Loans. Students are required to annually submit a completed FAFSA form six weeks prior to the quarter they plan to attend. Students can complete the FAFSA online at http://www.fafsa.ed.gov. Sinclair's financial aid code is 003119.

Information about financial aid opportunities at Sinclair may be obtained online by visiting the Sinclair College main Web site (http://www.sinclair.edu). Applicants who would like to discuss their specific questions with one of Sinclair's financial aid counselors may e-mail questions to finaid@sinclair.edu.

APPLYING

Students may apply for admission and register for classes online by visiting the Sinclair Distance Learning Web site listed below and accessing the "How Do I Get Started?" selection from the menu and following the subsequent outlined steps. An online orientation is also available to familiarize students with college policies and procedures.

CONTACT

Dodie Munn
Academic Counselor
Distance Learning and
Instructional Support Division
Sinclair Community College
444 West Third Street
Dayton, Ohio 45402
Telephone: 937-512-2990
888-226-2457 (toll-free)
Fax: 937-512-2891
E-mail: distance@sinclair.edu
Web site: http://www.sinclair.edu/distance

Skidmore College

University Without Walls

Saratoga Springs, New York

University Without Walls (UWW) is the external degree program for adults at Skidmore College. UWW was in the vanguard in establishing a program for distance learners. The program began in 1971 as an experiment in nontraditional education jointly funded by the Ford Foundation and the U.S. Department of Education. When the funding for this experiment ended in 1975, Skidmore College took over the program as its own. Over the years, UWW has evolved to serve adult students pursuing baccalaureate degrees in a variety of liberal arts, performing arts, and preprofessional fields.

The UWW program is characterized by its flexibility and the high quality of education students receive. The unique advising system at UWW guarantees that each program meets the student's individual needs and the high standards of Skidmore College.

DISTANCE LEARNING PROGRAM

UWW serves 280 full- and part-time baccalaureate students from as near as the city of Saratoga Springs and as far away as Europe, Africa, and Asia. The UWW program does not require its students to be in residence on campus. Student programs may include on-site UWW seminars, UWW online courses, independent study with Skidmore faculty members, courses at other accredited institutions, internships, and distance learning courses from major universities. Every program includes a final project in the area of the student's focus.

DELIVERY MEDIA

With support from an Alfred P. Sloan Foundation grant, UWW is able to offer students the opportunity to earn a bachelor's degree entirely online. Students also take courses at other accredited institutions. Independent study takes place through telephone, mail, and e-mail communication. Students can work with their advisers to explore an individualized major or, through the Sloan Asynchronous Learning Network, complete their bachelor's degree entirely online in one of the following interdisciplinary concentrations: American History and Culture, Communication and the Arts, and Human Nature and Behavior.

PROGRAMS OF STUDY

UWW offers Bachelor of Arts degrees in most traditional liberal arts fields, including American studies, anthropology, art history, biology, chemistry, classics, computer science, economics, English, French, geology, German, government, history, mathematics, philosophy, physics, political economy, psychology, religion, Russian, sociology, Spanish, and women's studies. Bachelor of Science degrees are available in art, business, dance, exercise science, human services, and theater. Students can also combine fields to create an interdisciplinary program, such as arts management, Asian studies, communications, environmental studies, health studies, human behavior, Latin American studies, management information systems, nonprofit management, organizational behavior, public administration, and religion and culture. Individually designed majors are welcomed.

All degrees are 120-credit programs. Programs are expected to include at least 12 credits in the humanities, 6 credits in history, 12 credits in the social sciences, and 9 credits in math or science, including laboratory experience. Professional programs must include at least 60 credits in the liberal arts. Courses taken prior to entry of UWW may be considered in satisfaction of these requirements.

SPECIAL PROGRAMS

UWW's flexibility allows many students to take advantage of unusual learning opportunities. Recent UWW students have studied abroad in Austria, Canada, Costa Rica, the Czech Republic, Germany, Ireland, Poland, Spain, Switzerland, and Thailand, among other locations. Business students often have the opportunity to include professional management and banking seminars in satisfaction of their degree requirements.

UWW students are often able to participate in programs sponsored by Skidmore College and the Office of Special Programs, including a summer study program in Florence, the New York State Writers Institute, the Skidmore Jazz Institute, the Summer Dance Workshop, and the Siti Summer Theater Workshop. UWW students are eligible for substantial discounts on courses offered by Skidmore Summer Academic Sessions and the Summer Six Art Program.

UWW business students are eligible to apply for 3/2 M.B.A. programs in cooperation with Rensselaer Polytechnic Institute in Troy and Rensselaer–Hartford.

STUDENT SERVICES

UWW is a small, personal program, and the staff members are happy to assist students in any way possible. Typical services include academic advising, registration assistance, financial aid counseling, and book-order assistance. Local students also enjoy library privileges, career counseling, access to recreational facilities, access to computer labs, and an e-mail account. Some summer housing is available for special program participants.

CREDIT OPTIONS

UWW accepts transfer credit for courses completed with a grade of C or better. There is no limit to the number of credits transferred or the age of the work, provided that the course is appropriate to a liberal arts curriculum. Credit is also available for experiential learning. In addition, students may document knowledge through CLEP, ACT-PEP, DANTES, and Regents examinations. Many college-level courses offered through the military are accepted. Credit from international universities is usually accepted.

FACULTY

There are approximately 200 full- and part-time members of the Skidmore faculty. Most participate as advisers and instructors in the UWW program. Ninety-three percent of the Skidmore faculty members have a terminal degree.

ADMISSION

UWW considers any applicant able to succeed at demanding college-level work. However, the program works best for students who have had some college experience. Applicants must have a high school diploma or the equivalent.

TUITION AND FEES

Students pay an initial enrollment fee of $4300; after the first year, an annual enrollment fee of $3600 is charged. Experiential credit review fee is $600. Independent study courses sponsored by Skidmore are $250 per credit hour. The final project fee is $600.

FINANCIAL AID

Students are eligible for Federal Pell Grants, New York State TAP awards, and all federal loan programs. A small amount of scholarship assistance is available.

APPLYING

Application forms are available from UWW or can be downloaded from the UWW Web site. All students are required to attend a personal admissions interview on the Skidmore campus.

CONTACT

Cornel J. Reinhart, Director
University Without Walls
Skidmore College
815 North Broadway
Saratoga Springs, New York 12866
Telephone: 518-580-5450
866-310-6444 (toll-free)
Fax: 518-580-5449
E-mail: uww@skidmore.edu
Web site: http://www.skidmore.edu/uww

Southern Christian University

Distance Learning Programs

SCU

Montgomery, Alabama

Founded in 1967, Southern Christian University (SCU) is an independent, nonsectarian, coeducational institution dedicated to the spirit of its ideals and Christian heritage. All of SCU's programs are taught from a Christian perspective. SCU is the home of one of the nation's leading universities offering distance learning programs and services to adults nationally. Adding to the prestige of this University is its recent designation as a Distance Education Demonstration Program Institution by the U.S. Department of Education. One of fifteen initial participants in the nation, SCU is partnering with the U.S. Department of Education to serve as a national model that will help chart the future of distance learning. Accredited by the Southern Association of Colleges and Schools, SCU grants bachelor's, master's, and doctoral degrees—all available via a distance learning format.

DISTANCE LEARNING PROGRAM

SCU programs are designed with the adult learner in mind. Eighty percent of SCU's students are employed while they are attending SCU. Courses can be taken anywhere there is Internet access and at any time. SCU has enrolled thousands of students in distance learning courses throughout the United States and internationally.

DELIVERY MEDIA

Utilizing state-of-the-art technologies, SCU's distance learning programs are delivered to students over the Internet. Students participate via online discussion groups, testing, e-mail, and telephone. Some courses are streamed live over the Internet and can be viewed as the class is being taught or at the student's convenience. The flexibility of the programs ensures continuity for students in transit, such as military, clergy, or salesmen who must move while still in school.

PROGRAMS OF STUDY

SCU programs are structured with the traditional program in mind. Distance education is approved by the Southern Association of Colleges and Schools and the U.S. Department of Education, ensuring that distance education students receive the same high-quality education as on-campus students. Faculty and student services for online students are available to distance learning students. SCU ensures that students have regular contact with faculty and staff members via e-mail and telephone. Residency is only required in certain programs. No residency is required for undergraduates. Undergraduate degrees are awarded in Bible studies, human development, human resource management, liberal studies, management communication, and public safety and human justice. These degrees promote biblical and Christian ministry skills, human development skills, knowledge in the arts, and management communication skills. Graduate degrees are awarded in counseling/family therapy, organizational leadership, and religious studies. These degrees foster leadership counseling and family therapy skills, knowledge and skills, and biblical and Christian ministry skills. The counseling degrees are designed to help prepare students for licensure. Doctoral degrees include family therapy and ministry. These degrees are advanced professional degrees for community organizations and church-related vocations, with a concentration designed to prepare participants to counsel families and individuals. SCU students are fully matriculated students of Southern Christian University with full student privileges, rights, and responsibilities.

SPECIAL PROGRAMS

Southern Christian University has developed fully accredited programs of study to help working adults obtain their bachelor's degree in a timely manner through the EXCEL program. This program allows undergraduates to receive credit for lifetime learning, enabling students to complete their degree at an accelerated rate. All undergraduate courses are 4 semester hours, rather than 3. A student only has to take three courses (12 semester hours) to be a full-time student and eligible for maximum financial aid benefits. Also, fewer courses are required for degree completion. Undergraduate students who enroll on a full-time basis enjoy a significant savings, receiving 50 percent off the published tuition rate.

SCU is one of only 12 new institutions participating in the expansion of eArmyU colleges and universities. eArmyU is the Army's popular e-learning virtual university, offering more than 30,000 enrolled soldiers the opportunity to earn a college degree during their enlistment. With the flexibility of eArmyU, soldier-students are able to continue their education uninterrupted and complete their degrees in a timely manner while they serve.

STUDENT SERVICES

SCU provides support for all aspects of the distance learning experience. ProQuest Religion Database and First Search library programs give students access to 65 online databases, including the Library of Congress. Students have access to the collections of 150 theological schools online. Personal academic advising is performed via phone or e-mail. Students also receive personal evaluations of their degree program.

CREDIT OPTIONS

Fulfillment of some degree requirements is possible by passing the CLEP/DANTES tests or Regents examinations and through credit for lifetime learning and credit for military experience. Students can register for a course designed to show them how to prepare a portfolio that demonstrates prior learning. Credit is awarded by the Office of Portfolio Development for prior learning that is demonstrated through a documented learning portfolio.

FACULTY

The instructional faculty members total 50. Sixty-seven percent of the full-time faculty members hold doctoral degrees, 100 percent hold master's degrees, and 100 percent hold terminal degrees. Faculty members are specialized in their areas and have training in distance learning delivery.

ADMISSION

There is a rolling admission plan. Admission requirements are verification of high school graduation or GED for undergraduates and demonstrated proficiency in computer literacy. Ninety percent of applicants are accepted.

TUITION AND FEES

Graduate tuition cost per semester hour is $440. Undergraduate tuition per semester hour is $360. Full-time undergraduates receive a 50 percent scholarship. A comprehensive fee of $400 per semester is required of all students.

FINANCIAL AID

Aid from institutionally generated funds is provided on the basis of academic merit, financial need, or other criteria. A limited number of scholarships are available. Priority is given to early applicants. Federal funding available for undergraduates and graduates includes Pell and FSEOG grants for undergraduates, Federal Work-Study, and FFEL subsidized and unsubsidized loans for undergraduates and graduates. Eighty percent of students receive financial aid.

APPLYING

Prospective students must submit a $50 nonrefundable fee along with the completed application for admission. During the first semester, graduate students must submit letters of recommendation, transcripts, and test scores.

CONTACT

Rick Johnson
Southern Christian University
1200 Taylor Road
Montgomery, Alabama 36117
Telephone: 800-351-4040 Ext. 213 (toll-free)
E-mail: rickjohnson@southernchristian.edu
Web site: http://www.southernchristian.edu

Southern Methodist University

School of Engineering

Dallas, Texas

Founded in 1911, SMU is a private, comprehensive university. SMU comprises six degree-granting schools: the School of Engineering, Dedman College of Humanities and Sciences, Meadows School of the Arts, the Edwin L. Cox School of Business, the Dedman School of Law, and Perkins School of Theology. Southern Methodist University is accredited by the Commission on Colleges of the Southern Association of Colleges and Schools.

For more than thirty years, the School of Engineering has been a national pioneer in offering distance education courses for graduate study. In 1964, the School of Engineering established one of the first two regional closed-circuit TV distance learning networks in the nation. In 1978, it instituted its own for-credit videotape program for students living outside the Dallas–Fort Worth area. Today, the program is delivered via DVD and students are enrolled nationally from coast to coast.

DISTANCE LEARNING PROGRAM

The School of Engineering's distance learning program serves more than 600 graduate students. Master of Science degree programs are offered nationally via DVD. No campus attendance is required to complete the degree programs.

DELIVERY MEDIA

Distance learning students are enrolled in classes that are given on the SMU campus. The lectures are recorded on DVD and sent once a week to the distance learning student. Distance learning students interact with their professors via phone, fax, e-mail, or the Internet. Many professors make course materials available to the student via the School of Engineering's Web site.

PROGRAMS OF STUDY

Engineering schools have an obligation to be responsive to challenges and opportunities in a technological society. As a private university, SMU can respond quickly to engineering needs with high-quality academic programs.

The School of Engineering offers the following Master of Science degree programs via distance learning: civil engineering, computer engineering, computer science, electrical engineering, engineering management, environmental engineering, environmental science, environmental science (major in environmental systems management), environmental science (major in hazardous and waste materials management), facilities management, information engineering and management, manufacturing systems management, mechanical engineering, operations research, packaging of electronic and optical devices, software engineering, systems engineering, and telecommunications.

The Master of Science degree requires 30–36 (depending on the program) semester credit hours for completion, with a minimum 3.0 grade point average on a 4.0 scale. Distance learning students may meet the credit requirement entirely by course work or have the option of preparing a thesis for 6 semester hours of credit.

SPECIAL PROGRAMS

The School of Engineering offers a certificate program in telecommunications. This program is designed for students who have extensive experience but do not hold a bachelor's degree or who do not wish to pursue a master's degree. Admission to the telecommunications certificate program requires 60 semester credit hours of college study with a minimum GPA of 2.0 on a 4.0 scale, three years of related work experience, and three letters of recommendation. Certificate students must complete six courses with a minimum grade of 70 percent in each course. All courses are available to the distance learning student via DVD.

CREDIT OPTIONS

Generally, up to 6 semester hours of graduate courses may be transferred from an institution approved by the School of Engineering's Graduate Division, provided that such course work was completed in the five years prior to matriculation, that the transferred courses carried graduate credit, that those courses were not used to meet the requirements of an undergraduate degree, and that grades of B– or higher were received in the courses to be transferred.

FACULTY

Of the 485 full-time faculty members, 88 percent hold the doctorate or terminal professional degree in their fields. In addition, in the professional degree programs, the School of Engineering utilizes outstanding adjunct faculty members to bring into the classroom valuable experience from industry and government.

ADMISSION

Admission to a Master of Science degree program requires the bachelor's degree appropriate to the program to which the student is applying, as well as a minimum grade point average of 3.0 (on a 4.0 scale) in previous undergraduate and graduate study. Scores on the Graduate Record Examinations (GRE) are required for the M.S. programs in civil engineering, computer engineering, computer science, electrical engineering, environmental engineering, environmental science, and mechanical engineering.

TUITION AND FEES

Tuition for distance learning students is $882 per credit hour or $2646 for a 3-credit-hour course.

FINANCIAL AID

Financial aid opportunities are available to distance learning students, including Federal Stafford Student Loans. SMU's distance learning programs are approved for Veterans Administration educational benefits.

APPLYING

Distance learning students must complete an application for admission to the Graduate Division of the School of Engineering and submit transcripts of all previous undergraduate and graduate work. Application deadline dates are as follows: for the fall semester, July 1; for the spring semester, November 15; and for the summer semester, April 15.

CONTACT

Stephanie Dye
Associate Director, Distance Education
School of Engineering
Southern Methodist University
P.O. Box 750335
Dallas, Texas 75275-0335
Telephone: 214-768-3232
800-601-4040 (toll-free)
Fax: 214-768-4482
E-mail: sdye@engr.smu.edu
Web site: http://www.engr.smu.edu

Southern New Hampshire University

Distance Education Program

Manchester, New Hampshire

Southern New Hampshire University (SNHU), founded in 1932, is a private, regional institution that is recognized for its solid academic programs and dedication to teaching. SNHU offers certificate and degree programs in business, community economic development, culinary arts, education, hospitality, and liberal arts, with degrees at the associate level through the doctoral level. SNHU is regionally and nationally accredited by the New England Association of Schools and Colleges, the Association of Collegiate Business Schools and Programs, the New England Postsecondary Education Commission, the New Hampshire State Department of Education for Teacher Certification, the American Culinary Federation Education Institute and the North American Society for Sport Management.

Southern New Hampshire University's Distance Education (DE) program was established in 1996 and is one of New England's largest and fastest-growing programs. SNHU is a recognized leader in fully online learning and offers more than thirty undergraduate and graduate degree and certificate programs. The Distance Education program reports more than 10,000 enrollments annually from all states, several countries, and all time zones.

Southern New Hampshire University is also approved for the education of veterans and the children of veterans and for the rehabilitation training of handicapped students. The program is listed in the Department of Education's Education Directory, Part 3, Higher Education®. *Staff and faculty members are dedicated to delivering high-quality academic and administrative support. Students have access to online applications, registration, academic advising, technical support, course work, the bookstore, and the library.*

DISTANCE LEARNING PROGRAM

SNHU is a recognized leader in fully online learning and Web-based education. Total distance education enrollments exceeded 10,000 for the 2003–04 academic year. The six undergraduate terms are each eight weeks in length while the four graduate terms are twelve weeks in length. The undergraduate residency requirement, which may be satisfied by taking Distance Education courses, is 30 semester hours (ten classes) through SNHU, including 12 semester hours from the major for the bachelor's degree or 9 semester hours from the major for the associate degree. Each student's final 24 semester hours must be taken through SNHU. The final hours requirement is automatically waived for active military duty. The graduate program limits transfer credits to 6 semester hours, which must have been completed from an accredited institution within the last five years. In addition, the grade(s) earned must be a B or better.

DELIVERY MEDIA

The DE Program offers many advantages to students and faculty members. The classes are limited to 18 students, providing a significant measure of faculty-student interaction not found in site-based class environments. Blackboard Learning System™ is the learning management system for all online courses. Students must have a computer with access to the Internet to participate in SNHU's Distance Education courses. The program is not a self-paced, open entrance/open exit or a correspondence study program. Prospective students should refer to the SNHU Distance Education Web site for recommended technical specifications and personal characteristics that would contribute to becoming a successful online student.

PROGRAMS OF STUDY

SNHU DE program provides students with a solid educational foundation through programs in the School of Business, School of Liberal Arts, and School of Hospitality. Degree and certificate programs available online within the School of Business include accounting, accounting/finance, business administration, business studies, information technology, economics/finance, international business, management advisory services, marketing, and technical management. Graduate degree and certificate programs available online include the M.B.A.; the Master of Science (M.S.) degree in business education, international business, and organizational leadership; and a graduate certificate in international business. Online degree and certificate programs offered through the School of Liberal Arts include English language and literature, psychology, and social science. The School of Hospitality, Tourism, and Culinary Management offers the M.S. in hospitality administration online.

SNHU's online classes carry the same accreditation and provide the same semester hours toward a degree as classes taken through the day school or through any one of the university's Continuing Education centers. For an overview of degree requirements, prospective students should visit the SNHU Web site and click on Distance Education.

CREDIT OPTIONS

Students can transfer undergraduate credits earned at other accredited postsecondary institutions to SNHU and can receive undergraduate credit by taking the CLEP, DANTES, Regents College Examinations, institutional exams, military service training programs, ACE-certified career-related workshops and seminars, or other standardized tests. SNHU is designated as a Servicemembers Opportunity Colleges (SOC, SOCNAV, and SOCCOAST)–approved and cooperating institution. As an SOC institution, SHHU awards credit for service-related education and for completion of an associate degree through the Community College of the Air Force.

A maximum of 90 semester hours may be transferred toward a bachelor's degree, and 30 semester hours may be applied to an associate degree. Academic advisers are available to conduct free transfer-credit evaluations. Prospective students can e-mail SNHU's advisers at deadvising@snhu.edu and fax transcripts to 603-645-9706.

FACULTY

SNHU Distance Education program provides an extremely flexible learning environment that allows students to interact with highly qualified and specially trained instructors throughout the world who bring extensive work and life experiences to their classes.

ADMISSION

Applicants for undergraduate degree programs must have graduated from high school or passed the GED. Applicants for graduate programs require a bachelor's degree from an accredited institution. Official transcripts are required for admission.

International undergraduate applicants must have completed the equivalent of a U.S. secondary school. Students who have attended a recognized postsecondary institution may be eligible to receive transfer credits or exemptions. All applicants must submit a completed application and official or attested copies of academic records translated into English, including proof of graduation or completion of a program and proof of English proficiency. A minimum TOEFL score of 530 is required for undergraduate students. International graduate applicants must have completed the equivalent of a U.S. bachelor's degree and have a minimum TOEFL score of 550.

TUITION AND FEES

The tuition for each Distance Education undergraduate course is $720 (3 credits) and $1398 per graduate course (3 credits). Tuition rates are subject to change. Some courses may require the purchase of specific software.

FINANCIAL AID

SNHU accepts employer tuition reimbursement, federal and private loans, grants, VA Programs/Montgomery GI Bill, Navy College Fund (as part of the GI Bill), and scholarships. A federal financial aid application form is available online at http://www.fafsa.gov. Applicants may contact the University's financial aid office at 603-645-9645 or finaid@snhu.edu to explore financial aid options.

APPLYING

Students may enroll in undergraduate classes on a rolling basis. Official acceptance is not necessary to begin undergraduate course work. All applicants (new and transfer students) must submit an application along with an official high school transcript or original copy of GED scores and, if applicable, official college transcripts. Graduate students who indicate they are course work only students are limited to a maximum of two graduate courses (6 semester hours). Applicants may register for course work immediately by visiting the Distance Education Web site and then clicking on Apply and Register.

SNHU does not discriminate on the basis of race, color, national origin, citizenship, religion, marital status, age, sex, sexual orientation, or disability in admission to, access to, treatment in, or employment in its programs and activities.

CONTACT

Distance Education Program
Southern New Hampshire University
2500 North River Road
Manchester, New Hampshire 03106-1045
Telephone: 603-645-9766
866-860-0449 (toll-free)
Fax: 603-645-9706
E-mail: de@snhu.edu
Web site: http://www.snhu.edu/de

State University of New York at Oswego

B.A. in Broadcasting and Mass Communication
B.S. in Vocational Teacher Preparation

Oswego, New York

The State University of New York at Oswego was founded in 1861 as the Oswego Normal School. The institution became Oswego State Teachers College and one of SUNY's charter members in 1948. While maintaining its high standards as a center for teacher education, the college began to broaden its academic perspective in 1962 when it became one of the colleges of arts and science of the State University of New York.

Today, Oswego is one of thirteen university colleges in the SUNY system. About 8,000 students enroll annually. Oswego offers more than 100 academic programs leading to bachelor's degrees, master's degrees, and certificates of advanced study. The college is accredited by the Middle States Association of Colleges and Schools and by the Commission on Higher Education. The School of Education is accredited by the National Council for Accreditation of Teacher Education.

DISTANCE LEARNING PROGRAM

The Bachelor of Arts (B.A.) in broadcasting and mass communication and the Bachelor of Science (B.S.) in vocational teacher preparation are available to students with two-year degrees in appropriate disciplines. Degrees in vocational teacher preparation are offered in the following areas: agriculture subjects education, business/distributive education, family and consumer sciences, health occupations subjects education, technical subjects education, and trade subjects education. All required courses, cognates, and electives as well as courses in other disciplines to fulfill general education requirements are offered online. Students also have the opportunity to complete an economics minor online.

DELIVERY MEDIA

All courses are taught via the World Wide Web in asynchronous mode through the SUNY Learning Network (SLN) (http://sln.suny.edu). Students are required to have reliable access to computers connected to the Internet. Courses use texts/reading materials and involve substantial writing assignments. Students may be required to arrange laboratory experiences with colleges or universities close to home with credits transferred to Oswego.

PROGRAM OF STUDY

Some required courses may be transferred into the program through substitution or through articulation agreements with two-year and four-year colleges. A transfer evaluation of credit assigns previously earned credits to the appropriate program and to general education and college requirements. Students must complete a total of 122 credit hours for broadcasting and 127 credit hours for vocational teacher preparation to graduate, with a minimum of 30 credit hours taken from SUNY Oswego. At least 60 hours must be at the upper-division (300–400) level. General education requirements also apply.

Specific requirements in the broadcasting major and the vocational teacher preparation major, including cognates and electives, are available at the Oswego State Web site. Students can find requirements for broadcasting at http://www.oswego.edu/ODP/ and for vocational teacher preparation at http://www.oswego.edu/vtp/.

SPECIAL PROGRAMS

Some degree program students may benefit from internship opportunities arranged through the Office of Experience-Based Education. Up to 15 hours of internship credit may be applied as electives both in the major and under the general studies curriculum. Past students have performed internships in network television, local and regional media, advertising, media research, and government. Such experiences often lead to job offers and referrals.

STUDENT SERVICES

Some of the campus services and resources that are available online include certain resources in Penfield Library, the Registrar's Office, Student Accounts, the Financial Aid Office, and the Career Services Center. The State University of New York at Oswego Web site is http://www.oswego.edu. Advisement options include e-mail and telephone consultation for all students.

CREDIT OPTIONS

Up to 62 transfer credits from a two-year school may be applied toward the broadcasting degree, and up to 67 transfer credits from a two-year school and 97 transfer credits from a four-year school may be applied toward the vocational teacher preparation degree. The College-Level Examination Program (CLEP) is offered and accepted. Up to 32 credits may be earned through CLEP, which is considered transfer credit.

FACULTY

Approximately 40 full-time and 15 part-time faculty and professional staff members currently teach distance courses at SUNY Oswego. Of these, 70 percent have doctoral degrees. The student/teacher ratio is 20:1.

ADMISSION

Applicants must submit official transcripts indicating that they have graduated with a two-year degree appropriate for their program. Students may enroll full-time or part-time and must become matriculated after completing 22 hours of study at Oswego.

TUITION AND FEES

Part-time undergraduate tuition (in-state) is $181 per credit hour. Part-time undergraduate tuition (out-of-state) is $429 per credit hour. Full-time undergraduate tuition (in-state) is $2175 per semester. Full-time undergraduate tuition (out-of-state) is $5150 per semester.

Part-time fees (in-state and out-of-state) are $25.39 per credit hour.

Tuition and fee amounts are subject to change.

FINANCIAL AID

Students should contact the Office of Financial Aid for information regarding income, credit hours, and other guidelines. In most instances, students must be enrolled in at least 6 credit hours to be eligible for financial aid.

APPLYING

A SUNY application needs to be submitted for both programs. The vocational teacher preparation program has an additional application that may be obtained by contacting that department. Students are notified in writing if and when they are accepted into the program. An orientation session is optional.

CONTACT

For information on broadcasting and mass communication:

Dr. Michael S. Ameigh, Assistant Provost and Coordinator, Online Degree Program
35A Lanigan Hall
State University of New York at Oswego
Oswego, New York 13126
Telephone: 315-312-3500
Fax: 315-312-3195
E-mail: ameigh@oswego.edu
Web site: http://www.oswego.edu/ODP/

For information on vocational teacher preparation:

Dr. Susan S. Camp, Chair, Vocational Teacher Preparation Department
307 Park Hall
State University of New York at Oswego
Oswego, New York 13126
Telephone: 315-312-2480
Fax: 315-312-3062
E-mail: susanc@oswego.edu
Web site: http://www.oswego.edu/vtp/

State University of New York Empire State College

Center for Distance Learning

Saratoga Springs, New York

Empire State College is an internationally recognized innovator in adult education and a pioneer in distance learning. Since 1971, the College has served students who need alternatives to campus-based education because of work, family, or other responsibilities. Providing flexible degree programs at the associate, bachelor's, and master's levels, Empire State College features a number of student-focused study methods, such as one-to-one instruction, intensive mentoring by a faculty adviser, and undergraduate credit for college-level learning gained from life experience.

The College currently enrolls more than 15,000 students per year at thirty-two locations in New York State. Through its Center for Distance Learning (CDL), the College also serves students across the nation and around the world. Empire State College was the first public, nontraditional institution to receive regional accreditation by the Middle States Association of Colleges and Schools.

DISTANCE LEARNING PROGRAM

More than 4,000 students are served annually by the College's Center for Distance Learning (CDL). Established in 1978, CDL offers distance courses in a variety of media, primarily Web and print. As a founding member of the SUNY Learning Network, the College was among the first in the State University of New York to offer online courses. It was also the first within the University to offer an entire degree (in business, management, and economics) online. Today, students may earn online degrees in most areas of study offered by the College. Through the Graduate Studies program, an M.B.A. is offered primarily via the World Wide Web.

DELIVERY MEDIA

The Center for Distance Learning makes use of the latest distance learning technology on the World Wide Web, as well as standard mail and telecommunications. Empire State College's online distance learning courses can be accessed at any time of the day, allowing students and faculty members to share ideas and concepts at times that are convenient to them. In addition, all student services, such as registration, academic advising, career and library services, and peer support, are also available on the Web.

PROGRAMS OF STUDY

The Center for Distance Learning offers both two- and four-year degrees: Associate in Arts, Associate in Science, Bachelor of Arts, Bachelor of Science, and Bachelor of Professional Studies. The College also offers five Master of Arts programs, with concentrations in business and policy studies, labor and policy studies, liberal studies, and social policy, in addition to an M.B.A. with online courses.

One of the strengths of the Empire State College distance learning program is that students are assigned a faculty mentor, who guides them through all phases of their degree program, from academic planning to graduation. With their adviser, undergraduate students design individualized degree programs in any of eleven areas of study: the arts; business, management, and economics; community and human services; cultural studies; educational studies; historical studies; human development; interdisciplinary studies; labor studies; science, mathematics, and technology; and social theory, social structure, and change. Within these degree programs, a number of concentrations can be developed. Some examples of these are fire service administration, criminal justice, and management of health services and information systems.

To earn an associate degree, a student must successfully complete 64 credits, with at least 24 earned through study with Empire State College. A bachelor's degree requires successful completion of 128 credits, with at least 32 being earned through the College.

SPECIAL PROGRAMS

The Center for Distance Learning is one of a select number of institutions of higher learning that offer online degree programs to both the United States Army and the United States Navy. Through eArmyU, soldiers may take part in portable learning that suits the requirements of military life. The College also participates in the Navy College Program Distance Learning Partnership (NCPDLP) and the Navy College Program for Afloat College Education (NCPACE), for sailors who also need maximum flexibility in the ways they study. Many other organizations and corporations work with CDL to sponsor educational options for their employees, including a number of telecommunications companies and unions. A complete list is available at http://www.esc.edu.

In collaboration with nationally recognized online course providers Education To Go and SkillSoft, Inc., Empire State College offers a series of 300 noncredit online courses geared to adult learners in the workplace. The courses are available in two different delivery formats: more than 100 six-week, instructor-supported courses and 150 two- and three-hour independent study courses that are available to students for a three-month usage period.

CREDIT OPTIONS

Students can transfer credits earned at other regionally accredited institutions to Empire State College and can receive credit for college-level learning gained through work and life experience and through the College-Level Examination Program (CLEP), standardized tests, or individualized evaluation. A total of 40 prior learning credits may be granted in the associate degree program; 96 credits may be applied to a bachelor's degree program.

FACULTY

There are 434 full- and part-time mentors at Empire State College. Eighty-five percent of full-time faculty members and nearly half of part-time faculty members have doctoral or other terminal academic degrees. To supplement the academic expertise of its residential faculty, the College makes use of adjunct faculty members.

ADMISSION

There are two principal requirements for admission to Empire State College: possession of a high school diploma or its equivalent and the ability of the College to meet the applicant's educational needs and objectives.

TUITION AND FEES

In 2003–04, undergraduate tuition was $181 per credit. A per-term telecommunications development and support fee of $50 was also charged, which provided access to electronic mail, computer conferencing, the Internet, and other information sources.

FINANCIAL AID

More than $35 million in financial aid was awarded to Empire State College students in 2002–03, with more than 50 percent of the enrolled students receiving some form of financial assistance. General financial aid programs available through Empire State College include the Federal Pell Grant, Federal Supplemental Educational Opportunity Grant, Federal Perkins Loan, and the Federal Work-Study Program. New York State financial aid programs include the Tuition Assistance Program (TAP), Aid for Part-Time Study (APTS), and the SUNY Supplemental Tuition Award. The Empire State College Foundation awards more than $49,000 in scholarships and grants annually.

APPLYING

Empire State College reviews applications in order of date received, and students may apply online. The number of new students accepted depends on available space. There are five deadlines per year posted on the Web site (address listed below). Nonmatriculated students can take up to 16 credits without applying to the College.

CONTACT

Paul Trela
Center for Distance Learning
Empire State College
3 Union Avenue
Saratoga Springs, New York 12866-4391
Telephone: 800-847-3000 Ext. 300 (toll-free)
Fax: 518-587-2660
E-mail: cdl@esc.edu
Web site: http://www.esc.edu

State University of New York Institute of Technology at Utica/Rome

School of Management, M.B.A. in Technology Management

Utica, New York

State University of New York (SUNY) Institute of Technology is the newest and youngest college in the sixty-four-campus SUNY system. It is a leader in technology, innovation, and excellence. The Institute's School of Management is a pioneer in delivering high-quality education over the Internet.

DISTANCE LEARNING PROGRAM

The Master of Business Administration (M.B.A.) in Technology Management program prepares managers for successful careers in a high-tech business world. This program offers both a broad and integrative perspective across business functions and a chance to specialize in a field of the individual's choice. It also responds to the current needs of the business community by combining a rigorous study of management topics with a unique focus on technology and innovations in management. To accommodate working professionals who are unable to travel to campus to participate in the program, all of the courses for the M.B.A. are offered online. This online program offers students a great deal of flexibility—they are able to work on their classes without the time and place constraints imposed by a traditional, on-campus program.

DELIVERY MEDIA

Courses are delivered via an asynchronous learning network (ALN). An ALN is a new approach to teaching and learning that is student centered. ALNs emphasize innovative instruction and learning. The activities of the course are the same as those in a traditional class. Students read course materials, write papers, do research, and communicate with their instructors and fellow students. The learning is both interactive with faculty members and collaborative with other students. Students can work together on case studies, groups projects, and any number of other activities. The students and the faculty members use technology to accomplish these tasks. The course design facilitates these activities through a computer network. Instructors and students can also leverage the wealth of resources available through the Internet to support this instruction.

PROGRAM OF STUDY

The program stresses the use of modern techniques to analyze and develop business solutions to prepare students for upper-level management positions. Course work focuses on the use of quantitative and qualitative analysis in conjunction with financial, accounting, and economic principles to solve current and future business challenges. Students may concentrate their studies in accounting and finance, e-commerce and marketing, human resource management, or health services management or in an individually designed concentration (management).

A total of 48 credit hours are required: 18 in technology management core courses, 12 in business management core courses, and 9 in specialized concentration courses. The technology management core courses are project management; managing new product design and development; business law, ethics, and intellectual property rights; e-commerce and entrepreneurship; cases in technology and innovation management; and strategic planning. Business management core courses are accounting for managers, human resource management, management information systems, marketing survey design and data analysis, multinational economics of technology, financial management problems, and quantitative business analysis. The other three courses in a specialized concentration are as follows. For the accounting and finance concentration, they are investment strategy, financial analysis and reporting, and a seminar in accounting and finance; for e-commerce and marketing, they are marketing research and technology, a seminar in marketing management, and marketing quantitative methods; for human resource management, the concentration courses are compensation, labor relations, and human resource information systems; and for health services management, they are health-care systems, health-care marketing/strategic planning, and financial management for health-care organizations. Students who choose the individually designed concentration select three courses from among the specialized concentration courses.

Students must attain a grade point average of 3.0 for all graduate courses included in their program. No more than three C grades, regardless of overall grade point average, are counted toward graduation. All students must fulfill an on-campus residency requirement. Students come to campus for one weekend for testing, seminars, interviews, and group presentations as part of the capstone course experience.

STUDENT SERVICES

Technical support, online libraries, a virtual bookstore, and a help desk, which provides assistance via phone, e-mail, or Web-page links, are all available. There is an entire online Learning Center, which offers access to numerous Web search engines, reference help and materials, instructional sites and tutorials, and many other services. Transfer and career advisement are also offered to online students.

CREDIT OPTIONS

Up to 12 credit hours may be transferred from another graduate school. Credit is not granted for work experience or for undergraduate course work.

FACULTY

The faculty members have extensive experience and meet the highest standards for quality. All the faculty members who teach in the M.B.A. in Technology Management program have earned a doctorate in their field of expertise.

ADMISSION

GMAT scores are required. Applicants are evaluated using the guideline of a total of 1,000 points based on 200 x the undergraduate GPA + the GMAT score.

TUITION AND FEES

In-state students take advantage of low SUNY tuition rates, making the program very affordable. Graduate tuition rates are $213 per credit hour for students who are New York residents and $351 per credit hour for nonresident students.

FINANCIAL AID

Loans and employer payment plans are available. For more information about loans, students should call the financial aid office at 315-792-7210.

APPLYING

Applications are accepted on a rolling basis. Applications are available online or by contacting the School.

CONTACT

School of Management
P.O. Box 3050
SUNY Institute of Technology at Utica/Rome
Utica, New York 13504-3050
E-mail: scaz@sunyit.edu
Web site: http://www.mba.sunyit.edu

State University of New York Institute of Technology at Utica/Rome

School of Management, M.S. in Accountancy

Utica, New York

State University of New York (SUNY) Institute of Technology is the newest and youngest college in the sixty-four-campus SUNY system. It is a leader in technology, innovation, and excellence. The Institute's School of Management is a pioneer in delivering high-quality education over the Internet.

DISTANCE LEARNING PROGRAM

The School of Management offers a Master of Science (M.S.) in accountancy program online. For students, the advantages of this program are numerous. Graduate accounting students study and take classes at any time from anywhere in the world. No classroom attendance is required. Twenty-first-century technology is employed to create a virtual college on the World Wide Web. The online M.S. in accountancy program eliminates the constraints of time and location that colleges normally place on students as well as the problems of long commutes, child care, conflicting work schedules, handicap accessibility, and absences due to illness. This program combines high-quality education, lifestyle flexibility, and affordable tuition.

Students utilize the Internet for career advancement. The M.S. in Accountancy is an applied program for goal-oriented individuals. Students use the program to prepare for the CPA and CMA exams. The online M.S. in accountancy fully complies with the new AICPA education requirements and is fully accredited. CPAs and CMAs satisfy Continuing Professional Education requirements while earning a graduate degree. It is a convenient and effective way for accountants to continue their education and advance their careers.

DELIVERY MEDIA

Courses are delivered via an asynchronous learning network (ALN). An ALN is a new approach to teaching and learning that is student centered. ALNs emphasize innovative instruction and learning. The activities of the course are the same as those in a traditional class. Students read course materials, write papers, do research, and communicate with their instructors and fellow students. The learning is both interactive with faculty members and collaborative with other students. Students can work together on case studies, groups projects, and any number of other activities. The students and the faculty members use technology to accomplish these tasks. The course design facilitates these activities through a computer network. Instructors and students can also leverage the wealth of resources available through the Internet to support this instruction.

PROGRAM OF STUDY

The degree program requires a total of 33 credit hours. There are ten required courses distributed among courses in financial reporting/analysis, advanced income tax research, fund accounting, advanced auditing theory, advanced financial accounting theory, multinational economics of technology, management information systems, financial management problems, and quantitative business analysis. One elective, which may be chosen from graduate courses offered by the School of Management, completes the requirements of the degree program. These include advanced management accounting, independent study, project management, strategic planning, and quantitative business analysis, among others. Students must attain a grade point average of at least 3.0 for all graduate courses included in their program. No more than three C grades, regardless of overall grade point average, are counted toward graduation.

SPECIAL PROGRAMS

The Master of Science in accountancy program offers an internship program (ACC 595, 3 credit hours). Internship placements provide students with field experience related to their academic preparation, enabling them to apply classroom instruction to the work site. Students are placed with an organization related to their major area of interest to work with experienced professionals. These opportunities cannot be duplicated in the classroom environment and prepare students for the transition into their chosen field.

STUDENT SERVICES

Technical support, online libraries, a virtual bookstore, and a help desk, which provides assistance via phone, e-mail, or Web page links, are all available. There is an entire online Learning Center, which offers access to numerous Web search engines, reference help and materials, instructional sites and tutorials, and many other services. Transfer and career advisement are also offered to online students.

CREDIT OPTIONS

Students from undergraduate accounting programs that are registered as CPA preparation programs typically have no prerequisite foundation course work. Other students are required to complete course work in accounting, business law, finance, statistics, economics, general business, and liberal arts as appropriate to prepare for the accountancy program's course requirements. Students should consult with a graduate adviser to determine appropriate course selection. Prerequisite skills may be fulfilled in a variety of ways, including transfer courses and courses at the Institute of Technology.

FACULTY

The faculty members have extensive experience and meet the highest standards for quality. All the faculty members who teach in the Master of Science in accountancy program have earned a doctorate in their field of expertise.

ADMISSION

To determine admissibility into the program, the Institute combines a student's score from the Graduate Management Admission Test (GMAT) with his or her undergraduate GPA. A total of 1,000 points are available, based on 200 x undergraduate GPA + GMAT score.

TUITION AND FEES

In-state students take advantage of low SUNY tuition rates, making the accountancy program very affordable. Graduate tuition rates are $213 per credit hour for students who are New York residents and $351 per credit hour for nonresident students.

FINANCIAL AID

Scholarships, financial aid, and internships are available.

APPLYING

Applications are available online or by contacting the School.

CONTACT

School of Management
P.O. Box 3050
SUNY Institute of Technology at Utica/Rome
Utica, New York 13504-3050
E-mail: scaz@sunyit.edu
Web site: http://www.sunyit.edu/academics/programs/acc/?select=gprograms

State University of New York Institute of Technology at Utica/Rome

School of Management, M.S. in Health Services Administration

Utica, New York

State University of New York (SUNY) Institute of Technology is the newest and youngest college in the sixty-four-campus SUNY system. It is a leader in technology, innovation, and excellence. The Institute's School of Management is a pioneer in delivering high-quality education over the Internet.

DISTANCE LEARNING PROGRAM

The Health Services Management Program offers a number of courses for the Master of Science in Health Services Administration (M.S.) degree program entirely online in an effort to serve working professionals and other students who are place-bound. The online courses are presented in a Web-based asynchronous learning mode, which allows students to work on their classes with a great deal of flexibility and within the confines of their personal circumstances. All that is required is a computer, an Internet connection, and the desire to pursue a health services degree. Students can complete a substantial number of credit hours online, but at least two campus residencies are required. Residencies last from one to three days and are scheduled in May. The purpose of these residencies is to ensure program integrity and to identify any areas of academic weakness. Students may be advised to repeat some course work or to engage in other academic activities to satisfy any concerns of the reviewing panel. Each 1-credit residency is graded on a pass-fail basis, and the credit does not apply to the degree program. The first residency is scheduled after the completion of 12 credit hours; additional credit hours, but no more than 6, may be permitted before the residency with permission from the student's adviser. The second residency is completed when all course work is finished and/or prior to an internship. During the second residency, a student presentation is required, including the major project completed for the Capstone Course.

The Master of Science in Health Services Administration program is primarily intended for students who have academic preparation in the liberal arts, the applied sciences, or business. However, students without a background in one of these areas may pursue the degree by taking additional courses in prerequisite areas.

DELIVERY MEDIA

Courses are delivered via an asynchronous learning network (ALN). An ALN is a new approach to teaching and learning that is student centered. ALNs emphasize innovative instruction and learning. The activities of the course are the same as those in a traditional class. Students read course materials, write papers, do research, and communicate with their instructors and fellow students. The learning is both interactive with faculty members and collaborative with other students. Students can work together on case studies, groups projects, and any number of other activities. The students and the faculty members use technology to accomplish these tasks. The course design facilitates these activities through a computer network. Instructors and students can also leverage the wealth of resources available through the Internet to support this instruction.

PROGRAM OF STUDY

The Master of Science in Health Services Administration degree program promotes the use of management organization and theory and an understanding of health-care delivery, reimbursement and financing systems, and applied research to formulate, implement, and evaluate managerial decisions in a health-care setting. Areas of focus in the curriculum are management, health policy, legal topics in health care, financial management, health marketing and strategic planning, quantitative methods of data collection and analysis, and research methods.

The program may require up to 45 credit hours of graduate course work depending on the student's prior experience and education. The degree program is flexible in order to accommodate the diverse backgrounds of the targeted student population. Students whose baccalaureate degree programs were in not in areas of business or health care typically need to complete a series of background and prerequisite courses. In addition, students with no previous health-related work experience are required to complete a 6-credit-hour internship, which is determined by the Program Director upon admission. Students who document either previous academic training or occupationally developed expertise may not be required to complete some or all of the prerequisite course work. However, no student may graduate with fewer than 33 credit hours of completed graduate course work.

The core required courses are health-care systems, health policy, health economics, legal issues in health care, organizational management for health-care organizations, financial management problems, financial management of health-care organizations, health-care marketing and strategic planning, quantitative business analysis, quantitative methods for health services administration (research methods), and the integrative Capstone Course in environments and strategies. In addition to the core courses, students are required to complete at least 6 hours of electives. Elective courses that are offered online include advanced management accounting, fund accounting, and management information systems.

At the conclusion of the student's fourth online course, a minimum GPA of 3.0 is required, and no more than two grades of C are permitted, regardless of GPA. A GPA below the minimum results in academic counseling and may require the student to withdraw from the distance learning program.

STUDENT SERVICES

Technical support, online libraries, a virtual bookstore, and a help desk, which provides assistance via phone, e-mail, or Web-page links, are all available. There is an entire online Learning Center, which offers access to numerous Web search engines, reference help and materials, instructional sites and tutorials, and many other services. Transfer and career advisement are also offered to online students.

CREDIT OPTIONS

As noted above, students who document previous academic course work and/or relevant professional experience may have some prerequisite course work waived.

FACULTY

The faculty members have extensive experience in their fields and meet the highest standards for quality.

ADMISSION

Requirements for admission include a baccalaureate degree from an accredited college or university with a minimum GPA of 3.0 and a course in statistics and a course in accounting with a grade of C or better. Students who do not meet these course requirements may be admitted with a deficiency. GMAT or GRE scores are also required. Scores on the GMAT are evaluated using the guideline of a total of 1,000 points based on 200 x the undergraduate GPA + the GMAT score. While prior academic achievement and GMAT or GRE scores are used as the basic guide to determine admissibility, if an applicant has demonstrated through exceptional performance in a management career that his or her undergraduate record is not indicative of academic performance or if a promising candidate does not score well on the GMAT or GRE, conditional admittance may be granted.

TUITION AND FEES

In-state students take advantage of low SUNY tuition rates, making the program very affordable. Graduate tuition rates are $213 per credit hour for students who are New York residents and $351 per credit hour for nonresident students.

FINANCIAL AID

Scholarships, financial aid, and internships are available.

APPLYING

Applications are available online or by contacting the School.

CONTACT

School of Management
P.O. Box 3050
SUNY Institute of Technology at Utica/Rome
Utica, New York 13504-3050
E-mail: scaz@sunyit.edu
Web site: http://www.sunyit.edu/academics/programs/hsm/?select=gprograms

Stevens Institute of Technology

Graduate School Distance Learning Programs

Hoboken, New Jersey

Stevens Institute of Technology, one of the world's premier technical universities, offers an array of Web-based distance learning graduate programs from WebCampus. Stevens ranks first among the top twenty-five most connected campuses. Stevens has won the nation's top award for best "institution-wide online teaching and learning programming." Stevens' online programs include wireless communications, networked information systems, secure network systems design, multimedia technology, systems design and operational effectiveness, pharmaceutical manufacturing practices, financial engineering, cybersecurity, computer science, photonics, atmospheric and environmental science and engineering, and graphics. Management programs are in project management, technology, human resources, telecommunications, and management of wireless networks. Students are instructed by noted faculty members who deliver the same superior courses taught on the main campus. Off-campus courses are conveniently offered at corporate sites in six states. Some classes are delivered using interactive video. Stevens is accredited by the Middle States Commission on Higher Education of the Middle States Association of Colleges and Schools. WebCampus is cosponsored by the Association of Computing Machinery, the Institute of Electrical and Electronics Engineers, ASME International, the Society of Naval Architects and Marine Engineers (SNAME), and the National Exchange Carrier Association (NECA).

DISTANCE LEARNING PROGRAM

Graduate certificates for professionals seeking advanced knowledge in science, engineering, and management are available online through WebCampus. A wide range of off-campus graduate degree programs in engineering, management, computer science, and mathematics, among other disciplines, are taught at corporate sites. Master's degrees in cybersecurity, microelectronics and photonics, network information systems, systems engineering, and telecommunications management are also available online.

DELIVERY MEDIA

Stevens has been at the forefront of distance learning for a number of years, offering courses that exploit the benefits of interactive video, the Internet, and other advanced instructional technologies. WebCampus online graduate students use rich Web features such as threaded discussions, chat, bulletin boards, e-mail, file sharing, whiteboards, and work groups for in-depth online participation. Students also have online library privileges, with instant search and retrieval of important databases.

PROGRAMS OF STUDY

In addition to acquiring a master's degree online in network information systems, graduate students may now take Web-based courses that lead to graduate certificates in atmospheric and environmental science and engineering, cybersecurity, elements of computer science, financial engineering, graphics, multimedia technology, networked information systems, photonics, secure network systems design, system design and operational effectiveness, and wireless communications. Management programs are in human resources, management of wireless networks, telecommunications, project management, and technology.

Graduate certificate programs offer students the opportunity to focus on a specific area of study without having to complete a master's program. Credits earned toward a graduate certificate at Stevens may also be applied to a master's degree should students wish to continue with their studies.

Off campus, at corporate and other sites, graduate students may enroll as part of company-sponsored programs, some of which are delivered using interactive video. Employees at some of the nation's most progressive and prominent companies, including Lucent, Boeing, Verizon, and dozens of others, may take graduate certificate courses and master's degree courses in a number of disciplines at corporate sites. These include computer engineering, computer science, electrical engineering, management, mechanical engineering, project management, technology management, and telecommunications management.

WebCampus also offers professional noncredit short courses in engineering, science, and management. Noncredit courses are open to all. No special background is required.

STUDENT SERVICES

Distance learning graduate students access the entire range of Stevens' student services online, including faculty advising, ordering books and other materials, admissions, registration, and applications for financial aid. Graduate students also have instant online access to the School's digital library. A cyberlibrarian is available via e-mail and telephone to guide students in the use of databases and other research tools and media. Seven days per week, 24-hour technical and other help desk support services are also available online. Stevens' Student Information System allows distance learners to access course schedules, grades, account statements, and other documents entirely online.

CREDIT OPTIONS

All graduate courses are worth 3 credits. Depending upon the program, most graduate certificates are offered after students complete four courses online, on campus, or both. To earn a master's degree in engineering and science, students are required to complete ten courses. Students must complete twelve courses for a master's degree in management.

FACULTY

An impressive graduate faculty teaches courses at Stevens, providing the same superior instruction online and on and off campus. WebCampus faculty members are required to participate in teaching and learning colloquia, which are held periodically during each semester, in order to share their experiences and to demonstrate their online teaching capabilities. Faculty members who teach online are also trained in how to exploit the technological and pedagogical benefits of Web-based courseware applications.

ADMISSION

To be admitted to a distance learning program at Stevens, students are required to satisfy the same qualifications as those who wish to enroll in Stevens' conventional courses. Prospective graduate students need to have completed an undergraduate degree at an accredited institution. Applicants may either apply by mail or complete an application form online at the Internet address listed below. Applications should be accompanied by a nonrefundable check or money order for $50, made payable to Stevens Institute of Technology. The application fee is waived for current Stevens undergraduate students, Stevens alumni, and those entering from selected corporate programs. Two letters of recommendation are required. Applicants must also provide official transcripts in English for each college or university attended. Transcripts translated into English must be prepared by the school attended or by an official translator with a recognized seal. Applicants must provide official confirmation of the degree earned if it was awarded by a non-U.S. institution. The applicant's name, Social Security number, or date of birth must be on all submitted documents. All documents must be in English or have attested English translations.

TUITION AND FEES

Each semester, students are required to pay an $80 enrollment fee. Tuition for management courses is $715 per credit hour. Tuition for engineering and science courses is $825 per credit hour. Other fees may apply for late enrollment and late payment, among other services.

FINANCIAL AID

Stevens has a strong commitment to assisting and investing in talented students. The school offers a number of scholarships, many of which are made available through generous friends and successful alumni. Many graduate students receive tuition reimbursement from their companies. Members of the WebCampus cosponsoring professional societies receive a 10 percent discount upon successful completion of the course.

APPLYING

Before applying to the online or off-campus distance learning programs, it is recommended that students review the Graduate School Web site or Stevens' online learning site, both listed below, in order to obtain information, instructions, and online application forms.

CONTACT

Online programs:
WebCampus.Stevens
Stevens Institute of Technology
Castle Point on Hudson
Hoboken, New Jersey 07030
Telephone: 201-216-5092
800-494-4935 (toll-free)
Fax: 201-216-5011
E-mail: webcampus@stevens-tech.edu
Web site: http://www.webcampus.stevens.edu

Off-campus programs:
Graduate Admissions
Stevens Institute of Technology
Castle Point on Hudson
Hoboken, New Jersey 07030
Telephone: 201-216-5234
Fax: 201-216-5011
E-mail: thegradschool@stevens-tech.edu
Web site: http://www.stevens-tech.edu

Strayer University

Strayer University Online

Newington, Virginia

Strayer University, founded in 1892, has more than 100 years of experience educating working adults. Currently, more than 20,000 students, most of whom work full-time, are enrolled at Strayer University. Undergraduate and graduate degrees are offered in technology and business-oriented programs. Strayer University has twenty-nine campuses located in the District of Columbia, Georgia, Maryland, North Carolina, Pennsylvania, South Carolina, Tennessee, and Virginia and is accredited by the Middle States Commission on Higher Education. Strayer University is a subsidiary of Strayer Education, Inc., a publicly held corporation whose stock is traded on the NASDAQ market (STRA). Each year since 1998, Strayer Education has been recognized by Forbes *magazine as one of the "200 Best Small Companies in America."*

DISTANCE LEARNING PROGRAM

Strayer University Online offers both real-time (synchronous) and time-independent (asynchronous) online courses.

Synchronous courses meet on the same day and time each week. Students and their professor are all online at the same time, engaging in a lively and interactive classroom environment. Students can access these courses from wherever they have access to the Internet but must attend the regularly scheduled class meetings.

Asynchronous courses are not held in real-time. Instead, students and faculty members log in throughout the week, downloading new course materials and uploading assignments and responses while maintaining a high level of interaction with classmates and the professor.

DELIVERY MEDIA

The following is a list of the minimal hardware and software recommended for participation in Strayer University Online classes: a 300-MHz processor (Pentium II equivalent or higher) with Windows '98, Microsoft Office '97 Professional Edition (or more recent version), a 128-KB L2 Cache (laptop) or 512-KB L2 Cache (desktop), 64 MB of memory, a 4-GB hard drive, a 12.1-inch SVGA TFT display (laptop) or larger (desktop), a 1.44-MB floppy drive, 2 MB of video memory, a 24X (laptop) or 40X (desktop) CD-ROM drive, a 56-K PCMCIA modem with fax capability, a 10/100 Ethernet network card (laptop only), and an integrated microphone and speakers.

PROGRAMS OF STUDY

Degree programs available online include the 54-credit Master of Business Administration (M.B.A.), Master of Education (M.Ed.), Master of Health Services Administration (M.H.S.A.), Master of Public Administration (M.P.A.), and Master of Science (M.S.) degrees in communications technology, information systems, management information systems, and professional accounting. Executive graduate certificate programs are offered in business administration, computer information systems, and professional accounting. Bachelor of Science (B.S.) programs (180 credits) in accounting, business administration, computer information systems, computer networking, database technology, economics, international business, and internetworking technology and Associate in Arts (A.A.) programs (90 credits) in accounting, acquisition and contract management, business administration, computer information systems, computer networking, database technology, economics, general studies, internetworking technology, and marketing are available.

There are also diploma programs in accounting, acquisition and contract management, computer information systems, internetworking technology, network security, and Web development. Undergraduate certificate programs are offered in accounting, business administration, and computer information systems.

Courses are taught on the quarter system, and each course provides 4.5 credit hours. Associate in Arts degree programs require twenty courses, or 90 hours, to complete. B.S. degrees require forty courses, or 180 hours. M.S. degrees require twelve courses, or 54 hours, to complete.

Each degree program has a business component and a major component. The undergraduate programs also have liberal arts/general studies and an elective component.

STUDENT SERVICES

Applications for federal financial aid, the Strayer Education Loan (a low-interest loan program), and scholarships are available online. Students may register for classes through the Web site or by telephone. In addition, library resources, other learning resources, and career-development services are available online.

CREDIT OPTIONS

Students who have attended other educational institutions may receive transfer credit or advanced standing in Strayer's degree and diploma programs. College credit may be awarded for CLEP and DANTES tests, certain training received in the military, or prior work/life learning demonstrated through portfolio preparation. The required number of credits taken in residence, online or on campus, is 36 for a master's degree, 54 for a bachelor's degree, 27 for an associate degree, and 31.5 for a diploma.

FACULTY

Strayer University has more than 150 full-time and more than 765 part-time faculty members. Of these, more than 270 teach for Strayer Online.

ADMISSION

Students who apply to undergraduate degree programs must provide certification of high school graduation or the equivalent. For admission to graduate degree programs, students must have graduated from an accredited college or university with a baccalaureate degree.

TUITION AND FEES

For the 2004 academic year, tuition for graduate courses is $324.50 per credit hour. Full-time undergraduate students (13.5 credits or more) pay $243.50 per credit hour, and part-time undergraduate students pay $255.50 per credit hour.

FINANCIAL AID

Students may apply online for financial aid. The Free Application for Federal Student Aid (FAFSA) may be accessed on the Web at http://www.strayer.edu. Students may apply for the following grants, loans, and scholarships: Federal Pell Grant, Federal Supplemental Educational Opportunity Grant, Federal Perkins Loan, Federal Stafford Student Loan, Federal PLUS Loan, Federal Direct Loan Programs, Federal Work-Study Program, Strayer University Education Loan Program, and Strayer University Scholarships.

APPLYING

Applications are accepted on an ongoing basis and can be accessed online at http://www.strayer.edu. There is a $35 application fee.

CONTACT

Strayer University Online
P.O. Box 487
Newington, Virginia 22122
Telephone: 866-344-3286 (toll-free)
Fax: 703-339-1852
E-mail: strayeronline@strayer.edu
Web site: http://petersons.strayer.edu

Suffolk University

Sawyer School of Management
Suffolk MBA Online

Boston, Massachusetts

Listed among U.S. News & World Report*'s Best Accredited Online Programs, the Suffolk MBA Online program was established in 1999.*

Suffolk University is a dynamic, urban university offering undergraduate and graduate degrees in more than seventy areas of study. Suffolk's main campus is strategically located in Boston, a leading world center of finance, high technology, health, biotechnology, law, and government. Suffolk has a current enrollment of 7,500 students, representing more than 100 countries.

Established in 1937, Suffolk's business school, the Sawyer School of Management, serves more than 2,200 undergraduate and graduate students, representing about eighty-five countries. Suffolk's alumni network spans the globe, with active alumni associations worldwide.

Suffolk University is accredited by AACSB International—the trademark of excellence among select business schools; NASPAA—the National Association of Schools of Public Affairs and Administration; and NEASC—the New England Association of Schools and Colleges.

DISTANCE LEARNING PROGRAM

In an increasingly fast-paced and demanding business world, online education is an appealing option for busy professionals. The AACSB-accredited Suffolk MBA Online has no residency requirement; therefore, students can complete the entire degree fully online. Alternatively, students may complement their online courses with four Suffolk MBA campus-based courses in Boston, Franklin, North Andover, or West Barnstable, Massachusetts; or with 6 transfer credits from another AACSB-accredited M.B.A. program.

DELIVERY MEDIA

The Suffolk MBA Online experience includes video clips, PowerPoint slides, two-way audio, threaded ongoing discussions, interactive e-mail, weekly real-time chat rooms, conference calls, and document sharing. Each semester, an online New Student Orientation introduces students to online skills and ensures familiarity with the virtual classroom, faculty members, and classmates prior to class start dates.

Students must have a moderate level of experience working on the Web and access to Microsoft Internet Explorer 5.5 or higher on a PC. To take full advantage of the learning experience, the following minimum system profiles are required: Microsoft Windows—Windows 98, 98Se, Me, NT, 2000, or XP; 64 MB RAM; 56.6 kbps modem (DSL or cable is recommended); SoundCard and speakers. Technical assistance is available 24 hours a day, seven days a week.

PROGRAMS OF STUDY

Suffolk MBA Online is a ten- to eighteen-course program, depending upon a student's previous educational background. The degree can be completed in nine to sixteen months of full-time study. Alternatively, it can be completed in twenty-one to thirty-six months of part-time study, taking two courses per term (fall, spring, and summer). Students have five years to complete the degree. Understanding the importance of the global economy to today's business world, all Suffolk MBA students take the required Managing in the Global Environment course.

Suffolk MBA Online students customize their degree through their choice of electives. Students choose one of four specializations: accounting, finance, information systems, and marketing. A specialization is not required. Instead, students may choose from a wide variety of electives that cross various functional areas.

SPECIAL PROGRAMS

Suffolk MBA Online also offers the Accelerated MBA for Attorneys, the Accelerated MBA for CPAs, and the Accelerated MBA for ASQ (American Society for Quality) members.

CREDIT OPTIONS

Students who have a strong undergraduate preparation in business or management may be able to complete the program in as few as ten courses. Students may waive core courses if they have completed equivalent course work at the undergraduate or graduate level at an accredited school within the past seven years with a grade of B or better. Waiver evaluations are completed at the point of admission to the Suffolk MBA Online program. Alternatively, tentative waiver evaluations can be completed for prospective students upon request.

FACULTY

Suffolk faculty members combine leadership skills with real-world situations and academic theory, providing students with the relevant knowledge they need to excel in today's business environment. Faculty research enhances student learning. Many faculty members are top-notch researchers, known nationally and internationally in their areas of expertise. Many faculty members have had successful full-time business careers or currently work as consultants outside academia.

ADMISSION

Admission criteria include one year of work experience, a completed application form, application fee, current resume, two letters of recommendation, official transcripts of all prior academic work, a statement of professional goals, TOEFL scores (for international students), and official GMAT score.

TUITION AND FEES

For the 2004–05 academic year, the Suffolk MBA Online tuition is $2418 per 3-credit course. Students are also assessed a $120 technology fee per 3-credit course.

FINANCIAL AID

For information regarding financial aid options, students should contact the Financial Aid Office by e-mail at finaid@suffolk.edu.

APPLYING

The Suffolk MBA Online program admits students in the fall, spring, and summer. Suffolk University operates on a rolling admission basis. Applications are available at http://www.suffolk.edu/mbaonline.

CONTACT

Dr. Lillian Hallberg, Assistant Dean, Graduate Programs and Director, MBA Programs
Sawyer School of Management
Suffolk University
8 Ashburton Place
Boston, Massachusetts 02108-2770
Telephone: 617-573-8306
Fax: 617-573-8653
E-mail: mbaonline@suffolk.edu
Web site: http://www.suffolk.edu/mbaonline

Graduate Admissions Office
Suffolk University
8 Ashburton Place
Boston, Massachusetts 02108-2770
Telephone: 617-573-8302
Fax: 617-305-1733
E-mail: grad.admission@suffolk.edu
Web site: http://www.suffolk.edu

Sullivan University

Master of Science in Dispute Resolution

Louisville, Kentucky

Sullivan University's educational mission has remained constant from its founding until the present: "the highest ideals and standards in preparing people for successful careers." Sullivan's commitment to career education has been sustained by the employment record of its graduates: 99.7 percent in 2002, 99.3 percent in 2001, 99.2 percent in 2000, and its lowest percentage, 97.8 percent in 1992.

Sullivan has unusual commitment to all graduates of its official degree, diploma, and certificate programs—graduates are allowed two free lifetime privileges: Graduate Employment Services (GES) and Lifetime Curricular Review (LCR). The GES staff members assist graduates in finding new employment, developing resumes, and participating in job fairs. The LCR allows graduates to reenroll in any class completed in their program to refresh their learning, although no grades are given nor attendance required or recorded.

DISTANCE LEARNING PROGRAM

The methods and skills earned in the Master of Science in Dispute Resolution (M.S.D.R.) degree curriculum are of special usefulness for controlling lost capital due to grievances, complaints, and litigation in the workplace as well as for redirecting human and financial resources toward prevention of disputes, improvement of communication, and development of organizational mission. While the M.S.D.R. provides a strong career building block for students holding undergraduate degrees, it also expands employment applications for students holding professional credentials such as the CPA and the M.B.A., M.P.A., M.P.H., M.P.S.Y., M.S.W., and J.D. degrees. Executives, middle managers, and labor leaders apply knowledge and skills learned in the M.S.D.R. program to maintain and promote healthy workforce environments.

The Program Chair seeks to combine the following goals in all courses: predominance of classical bibliographic mastery in the subject areas—to provide students with long-term, firm theoretical foundations; mainstream workplace applications of theories taught—to enable students to graduate with real-world experiences useful to prospective employers or clients; rigorous academic and professional standards to ensure high-quality learning—to test students' readiness for graduation and employment; superior "best practices" in distance learning instructional design—to maximize the potential of the media and minimize inconvenience or frustration for students or their employment supervisors; and creative yet controlled uses of technology media—to enhance and accommodate learning for the majority of students in the U.S. and around the world, preventing encumbrances created by hardware or software requirements that would pose an unreasonable burden for most students.

Part of the M.S.D.R. program is the Mediation Practicums Module© (MPM). The MPM was created to enable students to transfer online learning into controlled, graduated, real-world dispute resolution experiences in their own workplaces. Certain specific practical interaction and professional skills must be demonstrated, critiqued, and developed in each M.S.D.R. student through professional evaluations in real time or personal observation. Sullivan employs a full-time MPM Director of Mediation Practicums who guides students and their evaluators to ensure the integrity of the student's experiential portfolio. When employers are too busy or unable to participate in the MPM, a network of practitioners in good standing with national dispute resolution organizations are recruited to assist in comediations, mentoring, and other educational experiences, either pro bono or for modest fees. In addition, unemployed students are placed in internships to fulfill the requirements of this portion of the program.

DELIVERY MEDIA

Sullivan uses state-of-the-art technologies that include all standard distance learning methods and systems such as CD assist, videostreaming, and Web conferencing. Connected Learning.Network, a national leader in learning platforms for institutions of higher education, business, and industry, provides a premier media experience for students worldwide. All courses are asynchronous, permitting greater latitude for students in different time zones or continents to study together through common assignments. A 24/7, 365-day helpdesk staff answers questions and resolves problems for students or faculty members.

PROGRAMS OF STUDY

The M.S.D.R. degree is 100 percent online, is asynchronous, and exhibits complete continuity with Sullivan University's career education emphasis as reflected by its pedagogical structure. Five courses are core requirements and build a firm, centrist framework of theoretical understanding: Mediator Diagnostics and Skills© Conflict Theories, Dispute Resolution Methods, Organizational Conflict Management, and Family Conflict Mediation. Four courses are elective and may be drawn from major subject areas, each related to mainstream applications in U.S. and international settings: management, labor, EEO, law, education, health care, construction, legislative/public service, international, and religious. Three additional courses, the MPM courses, are nonelective and move theoretical learning into actual employment or organizational applications.

In addition to the M.S.D.R., Sullivan University also offers a Certificate in Dispute Resolution. The certificate program requires six courses for completion, half of the course load of the M.S.D.R. The certificate program is designed for students with specialized needs whose career applications do not require the broad career base offered by the M.S.D.R.

SPECIAL PROGRAMS

The Chair of the M.S.D.R. degree program actively seeks partnerships, alliances, and collaborations with governmental, public, and private sector organizations. These alliances enhance the quality of Sullivan's educational program and its outreach in the U.S. and world, provide value-added experiences for M.S.D.R. students, and, when possible, provide service to M.S.D.R. students' local employers, organizations, and communities.

Sullivan University is one of six academic partners with the Federal Mediation and Conciliation Service (FMCS) in Washington, D.C. (http://www.fmcs.gov). The FMCS has a revered reputation as a federal agency that functions superbly as a trusted neutral party to resolve major U.S. and international disputes. The M.S.D.R. degree program has been designed in consultation with FMCS staff members to ensure that M.S.D.R. graduates enter the workplace with methods and skills meeting or exceeding employment standards for federal and state agencies.

STUDENT SERVICES

The Sullivan University Library and Resource Center offers 43 searchable databases and portals accessible through the Internet that are available only to registered students. The entire card catalog is online, containing discipline-specific resources and monographs. Staff members are available via telephone at 800-844-1354 Ext. 308 (toll-free) Monday to Thursday 7 a.m. to 9:45 p.m., Friday to Saturday 8 to 4, and Sunday noon to 5, EST, U.S. holidays excepted. The Ask-A-Librarian e-mail reference service provides a 24-hour (or less) turnaround to questions on how to use resources, on the APA style, and on search strategies. Full interlibrary loan services are available to all students.

CREDIT OPTIONS

For information about credit options, students should contact the Financial Planning Office by telephone at 800-844-1354 Ext. 311 (toll-free) or by e-mail at cgeiser@sullivan.edu.

FACULTY

The Chair of the M.S.D.R. degree program has a policy of employing only practitioner-experts as faculty members—those with terminal degrees and years of proven successful experience in the field being taught. Faculty profiles often include an array of publications, presentations at professional societies, training sessions offered around the U.S. and the world, and faculty member-owned corporations or sole proprietorships.

ADMISSION

Students must meet criteria established by the Graduate School of Sullivan University. For current admission criteria, students should visit the Web site at http://www.sullivan.edu/louisville/admissions/index.htm or contact the Graduate Admissions Officer by e-mail at rhinson@sullivan.edu.

TUITION AND FEES

All current tuition and fees information is available from the Graduate Admissions Officer by e-mail at the address listed above and is also listed on the Web site at http://www.sullivan.edu/louisville/admissions/tuition.htm.

FINANCIAL AID

Students in the M.S.D.R. degree program are eligible for two federal loan programs—Stafford Student Loans and Perkins Loans. In 2002–03, Sullivan awarded an estimated $37,048,460 in all forms of financial assistance to about 74 percent of students on all campuses. For more information about financial aid, students should contact the Financial Aid Office at cgeiser@sullivan.edu.

APPLYING

Students may complete an application online at http://www.sullivan.edu/louisville/admissions/application.htm. For further information, students can contact the University by e-mail at rhinson@sullivan.edu.

CONTACT

John D. Willis, Ph.D.
Chair, M.S.D.R. Degree Program
The Graduate School
Sullivan University
3101 Bardstown Road
Louisville, Kentucky 40205
E-mail: jwillis@sullivan.edu
Web site:
http://www.sullivan.edu

Syracuse University

Martin J. Whitman School of Management, Independent Study M.B.A.

Syracuse, New York

Founded in 1870, Syracuse University—a private, nonsectarian liberal arts institution—is one of the largest and most comprehensive independent universities in the nation. The University is one of only sixty American and Canadian universities chosen for membership in the prestigious Association of American Universities. Syracuse University enrolls more than 10,000 undergraduates and 4,800 graduate students for full-time and part-time study. The campus is located in the city of Syracuse, in an area of New York State known as upstate or central New York. Syracuse is less than half a day's drive away from New York City, Boston, Philadelphia, Toronto, and Montreal. The city is served by the Hancock International Airport, a mere 10-minute drive from downtown. Hancock Airport features daily nonstop flights to New York, Boston, Atlanta, Chicago, Philadelphia, Washington, D.C., and other business centers.

The Martin J. Whitman School of Management, in existence since 1919, has offered graduate programs since 1947. The School of Management has been continuously accredited by the premier accrediting body for business schools, AACSB International–The Association to Advance Collegiate Schools of Business, since 1921. The latest reaffirmation of accreditation was achieved by the School in April 2001. The Independent Study M.B.A. has been offered by the School of Management since 1977.

DISTANCE LEARNING PROGRAM

The Independent Study M.B.A., also known as iMBA, is a limited residency distance education program. It allows successful businesspeople, working around the world, to acquire a Master of Business Administration degree on a part-time basis while continuing to advance in their careers. The program enrolls students who reside in many cities within the United States and numerous other countries. The students' employers represent numerous prominent corporations and government agencies.

DELIVERY MEDIA

Students meet on the Syracuse University campus three times each year for a weeklong residency at the beginning of the fall term in August, the spring term in January and the summer term in May. During these intensive weeks, students attend classes that serve to orient the students to the demands and expectations of the curriculum. Students also establish bonds and working relationships with faculty members and fellow students. At the conclusion of each residency, students return to their homes and workplaces with a clear understanding of the course requirements as well as access to the campus resources necessary for the successful completion of their courses. Final exams, if required for the course, are taken on campus at the following residency.

PROGRAM OF STUDY

The iMBA program emphasizes a broad, strategic-management view of business, leading to the Master of Business Administration in general management. The curriculum consists of eighteen courses for a total of 54 credits. There are twelve core courses and six electives in a student's program. Electives are drawn from accounting, entrepreneurship, finance, information systems, marketing, organizational management, and other areas.

SPECIAL PROGRAMS

Optional off-campus residencies are occasionally held in other cities, such as London and Florence. The programs held in these locations are identical in format to the on-campus residencies. Students take courses in the same manner and receive credit in the same manner as if they had attended a residency at Syracuse University.

CREDIT OPTIONS

A student who enters the program with no transfer credits completes 54 credits for the M.B.A. degree. The normal course load is two courses per trimester. Following this model, students typically finish the program within three years. However, the program is flexible, allowing students to skip a residency when necessary for personal or professional reasons.

The School accepts a maximum of 6 transfer credits, with a qualifying grade, if earned from an AACSB International–accredited school of business within five years of enrollment in the program.

FACULTY

The faculty members who teach in the iMBA program include many of the same faculty members who teach in the School's full-time and part-time M.B.A. programs. However, during the residency weeks they are free of teaching obligations in other programs, so that they may concentrate their efforts on their iMBA students.

This creates a strongly cohesive environment and provides a high degree of personal interaction in the program.

ADMISSION

An applicant must have received a bachelor's degree or its equivalent from an accredited college or university to be considered for admission. Admission is competitive. Acceptance is based primarily upon prior academic success and career achievement. Full-time work experience of at least three years is required for this program. A full description of the admissions policy is contained in the application instructions.

TUITION AND FEES

Tuition in 2004–05 is $806 per credit. There is an annual tuition increase beginning with the summer residency. Textbooks average about $40 per credit. Housing and meal costs depend upon the accommodations chosen by the student, usually $70 to $120 per day. There is a $30 program fee for each residency.

FINANCIAL AID

Most iMBA students hold full or partial sponsorship through their employer's tuition assistance program. Government or private loan programs are available for most students who are U.S. citizens or have a U.S. cosigner.

APPLYING

New students may begin the program at any of the three annual residencies. Applications are considered on a continuous year-round basis. The application should be completed at least six weeks prior to the intended first residency. Graduate Management Admission Test (GMAT) scores are required of most applicants. Scores from the Test of English as a Foreign Language (TOEFL) are required of those for whom English is not the first language, unless the undergraduate degree was acquired in a program taught in English. Prospective students may apply online at http://www.theprincetonreview.com.

CONTACT

Paula C. O'Callaghan
Director, iMBA Program
Syracuse University
222 Martin J. Whitman School of Management
Syracuse, New York 13244-2130
Telephone: 315-443-9214
Fax: 315-443-9517
E-mail: paula@som.syr.edu
Web site: http://whitman.syr.edu/imba

Syracuse University

School of Information Studies

Syracuse, New York

Syracuse University is a medium-sized, private, coeducational university with an international reputation. Founded in 1870, it is a comprehensive research university that has eleven degree-granting schools and colleges and several interdisciplinary and continuing education programs. The University's 640-acre, beautifully landscaped campus is situated among the hills of central New York State.

The School of Information Studies was the first information school in the nation. It is a leading center for innovative programs in information policy, information behavior, information management, information systems, information technology, and information services. The School has professional degree programs at the undergraduate and master's levels and a research degree at the doctoral level. The School's approach stands out from other institutions that offer computer science, management, information science, and related programs in that, as a starting point for integrating information and information technology into organizations, the focus is on users and their information needs.

DISTANCE LEARNING PROGRAM

The distance learning programs offered by the School of Information Studies combine online courses with brief on-campus residencies. Distance learning students begin their first year in July with a six-day required on-campus residency. During the fall and spring semesters, students take online courses. Some of these courses may require an initial two-day on-campus residency. During the fall semester, these residencies are held Labor Day weekend. During the spring semester, they are held Martin Luther King Jr. Day weekend. Library and information science students can expect to return to campus one or two times during their program. During the residencies, students are trained on the technology that allows them to complete their courses over the Internet, and they complete activities that are easier to accomplish face-to-face, e.g., hands-on labs and group activities. During these times, they also meet and bond with their cohort group and network with each other and faculty members.

Students in the distance learning programs come from across the United States and from several other countries. They range in age from their 20s through their 60s. Many are already working in the information field, but some are looking for a career change. The rich backgrounds of the students make each incoming class a dynamic group.

DELIVERY MEDIA

The School of Information Studies uses a Web-based teaching and learning environment called WebCT. Each distance learning course has its own space within WebCT, which typically includes the syllabus, lectures, a forum for class discussions, and a place to submit assignments. Students are not required to be online at a specific time. They can log in and complete their assignments whenever it is convenient for them, as long as they meet course deadlines.

PROGRAMS OF STUDY

Three graduate degrees are offered in the distance learning format: Master of Science in information management, in library and information science, and in telecommunications and network management. Graduate certificates of advanced study in information security management, information systems and telecommunications management, digital libraries, and school media are also offered.

The Master of Science in information management program is interdisciplinary in focus, combining expertise in the strategic management of information resources, organizational psychology, information economics, telecommunications policy, e-business, and information technology as well as data management and retrieval. New information and Internet-based technologies are revolutionizing the structure and operation of organizations to enable integrated business processes. Corporate profitability and effective delivery of public services are at stake. Staying competitive and productive in business and government demands a strategic response to the changes and innovations evolving from the computer, communications, and information processing industries.

The Master of Science in Library and Information Science (LIS) program educates students to be leaders in the ever-evolving library and information profession. The program focuses on twenty-first century librarianship within libraries, information centers, the information industry, and other venues. The LIS program is accredited by the American Library Association and is ranked third in the nation by *U.S. News & World Report*.

The Master of Science in telecommunications and network management (TNM) program combines an understanding of networking technologies with knowledge of their applications in organizations. The TNM degree is a selective 36-credit-hour program that provides students with the skills to design networks, make technology adoption and standards decisions, create cost models for new technology implementations, calculate return on investment, and understand the organizational and user implications of networking systems.

STUDENT SERVICES

All students are provided with free computer accounts and have access to the Syracuse University library and computer facilities. Online students have access to a help desk for technical problems. All distance students at Syracuse have access to a full range of online student services, including academic advising, financial aid, assistance, and registration.

During the summer semester, housing is available in Syracuse University residence halls. Students can stay in single or double rooms equipped with a microwave and refrigerator. Meal plans are not provided during the summer sessions, although dining halls and restaurants are within walking distance of campus. During the fall and spring semesters, discounted rates are available at hotels located within walking distance of the University.

CREDIT OPTIONS

On the graduate level, there is no provision for experiential credit. However, 6 credits may be transferred from other accredited graduate programs, with a grade of C or better.

FACULTY

Members of the School of Information Studies faculty teach in both the online and on-campus formats. The faculty combines expertise in information systems, linguistics, computer science, business management, management information systems, library science, telecommunications, and communication. The faculty members are very active in research topics that reflect their diverse intellectual backgrounds and interests.

ADMISSION

All applicants to graduate programs at Syracuse University must have a bachelor's degree from an accredited college or university. The School of Information Studies recommends that applicants have an undergraduate grade point average of 3.0 or better. However, in reviewing applications, all elements are weighed: references, educational record, test scores, honors, work experience, and the statement on academic plans.

TUITION AND FEES

Distance learning students pay the same tuition rate as on-campus students. In 2003–04, tuition was $742 per credit. Tuition payment options for payment plans, company direct billing, and employer tuition deferrals are available for distance learning students.

Summer housing on campus costs approximately $100 to $150 per week. Housing in local hotels for fall and spring semester residencies costs approximately $60 to $130 per night. Students should also consider textbook, computer, Internet, and travel expenses.

FINANCIAL AID

Students must be U.S. citizens to qualify for need-based financial aid. The Financial Aid Office administers a variety of financial aid programs for distance learning students, including Federal Family Education Loan Programs, University College Grants, and Veterans' Education Benefit Programs. A few merit-based scholarships are available through the School of Information Studies.

APPLYING

Students are encouraged to submit their applications by February 15 for priority admission to the distance learning program. Applications are accepted on a space-available basis through June 1. There are two application methods: online and paper. Use of the online application method is encouraged.

CONTACT

School of Information Studies
Syracuse University
4-206 Center for Science and Technology
Syracuse, New York 13244-4100
Telephone: 315-443-2911
Fax: 315-443-5673
E-mail: ist@syr.edu
Web site: http://www.ist.syr.edu

Syracuse University

Undergraduate and Master of Social Science Degree Programs

Syracuse, New York

Founded in 1870, Syracuse University is a major private research university of 14,400 residential students and an additional 3,700 part-time adult students located in central New York State. Organized into twelve separate schools and colleges, each offering a variety of baccalaureate, master's, and doctoral degrees, Syracuse has excellent research facilities, including sophisticated computer networks and a library containing more than 2.8 million volumes. Syracuse is one of the select group of American and Canadian universities chosen for membership in the prestigious Association of American Universities.

Syracuse has a long-standing commitment to adult education. The University's innovative Independent Study Degree Programs (ISDP) are a form of nontraditional education in which Syracuse was a pioneer. Offered through five of the University's academic units, ISDP is one of the three oldest external degree programs in the United States. The programs have been active since 1966 and reflect the University's response to the demands for creative educational techniques and programs in a constantly changing society.

DISTANCE LEARNING PROGRAM

Syracuse's Independent Study Degree Programs (ISDP) have a limited-residency structure: they combine short periods of intensive on-site instruction with longer periods of home study, during which students and faculty members communicate at a distance by correspondence, telephone, fax, and computer. There are currently about 1,000 adults actively enrolled in twelve different degree programs through ISDP, approximately one sixth of whom are international students or Americans living abroad. Syracuse degrees earned through ISDP are the same as those earned by traditional Syracuse students in comparable campus programs and have the same accreditation.

PROGRAMS OF STUDY

University College offers two undergraduate programs and a master's program by means of the limited-residency, distance learning format. Undergraduate degrees include an Associate of Arts and a Bachelor of Arts in liberal studies. The associate degree is 60 credits. The bachelor's degree is a 120-credit program.

The graduate degree is a 30-credit Master of Social Science (M.S.Sc.) with an international relations emphasis. It offers an interdisciplinary, international, and multicultural approach to complex global issues. An internationally renowned faculty teaches courses for the degree from Syracuse University's Maxwell School of Citizenship and Public Affairs.

The three degrees are state and regionally accredited. Students may initially enroll on a nonmatriculated basis.

SPECIAL PROGRAMS

A number of online credit and noncredit courses are offered each semester. Detailed information on these is available at http://www.suce.syr.edu/online.

STUDENT SERVICES

All distance learning students are provided with free computer accounts and have access to the Syracuse University library and computer facilities. Online students have access to a help desk for technical problems. All distance students at Syracuse have access to a full range of online student services, including academic advising, financial aid, assistance, and registration.

CREDIT OPTIONS

The associate degree program accepts a maximum of 30 credits to be transferred from another postsecondary institution. The baccalaureate program accepts a maximum of 90 transfer credits, which may include 66 credits from a junior college. Transfer credit is granted for most courses in which a grade of C or better has been earned, provided courses are from an accredited college and fit the degree requirements. For credit to be accepted from an international institution of higher learning, the institution must be a recognized third-level institution.

A maximum of 30 credits gained through testing may be applied toward an undergraduate degree program. DANTES, CLEP, and Syracuse advanced credit exams may be used for this purpose. However, credit awarded through testing does not count toward the minimum number of credits that must be taken at Syracuse in order to earn a degree. On the graduate level, there is no provision for experiential credit. However, 6 credits may be taken in transfer from other accredited graduate programs, with a grade of C or better.

FACULTY

Distance courses are taught by full-time Syracuse University faculty members, who participate in the limited-residency programs in addition to their full-time campus responsibilities.

ADMISSION

Candidates for admission to the associate and baccalaureate programs should have a high school diploma or its equivalent. Transfer students must have at least a 2.0 (C) average for the liberal studies program. Graduate applicants whose primary language is a language other than English must also take the TOEFL.

Applicants for all programs must submit official transcripts of prior academic work, three letters of recommendation, and a personal statement that accompanies the application form.

TUITION AND FEES

For 2004–05, the undergraduate tuition rate is $465 per credit, and the graduate rate is $806 per credit. Additional expenses for room and board during the on-site residences vary depending upon the choice of facility, and book charges average $150 per course.

FINANCIAL AID

ISDP students who are U.S. citizens are eligible for all the standard federal grants and loans available to part-time students. Selective institutional aid is available; detailed information is available upon request. Syracuse University awards more than $100,000 to ISDP students each year. International students (non-U.S. citizens) are not eligible for financial aid.

APPLYING

Applicants should request application materials from the address below. The programs admit students on a continuous basis, and students can begin in the fall, spring, or summer terms. In-person interviews are not required, although they can be arranged upon request.

CONTACT

Marketing Communications Department
Syracuse University/University College
700 University Avenue
Syracuse, New York 13244-2530
Telephone: 315-443-3480
800-442-0501 (toll-free, U.S. only)
Fax: 315-443-4174
E-mail: distanceed@uc.syr.edu
Web site: http://www.suce.syr.edu/Distance

Tarleton State University

Center for Instructional Technology and Distributed Education

Stephenville, Texas

Founded in 1899 as John Tarleton College, the institution became a member of the Texas A&M System in 1917 and achieved university status in 1973.

Tarleton offers sixty-seven undergraduate and twenty-three graduate programs as well as a doctoral program in educational administration. Beginning in fall 2004, the College of Business Administration offers an M.B.A. and three other fully online master's degree programs in the areas of human resource management, management and leadership, and management information systems.

DISTANCE LEARNING PROGRAM

Tarleton began offering online courses in the spring of 2000. Since that time, enrollment in online courses has increased exponentially from 91 to 936. The number of online courses offered at Tarleton has increased from 6, in 2000, to 59 in 2004.

The University's Purpose and Role Statement notes that "Tarleton pledges to continue meeting the educational needs of a changing society and an expanding world," which can be read as a pledge to distance learning and an indication that distance learning is consistent with Tarleton's stated purpose.

DELIVERY MEDIA

Tarleton's distributed education programs and courses are currently offered in three formats: online, interactive television, and off-campus face-to-face. Students may complete the programs in a traditional face-to-face course environment, in an online-course format, or in a combination of these formats. The programs and courses are designed to accommodate individuals who are unable to attend on-campus classes, prefer independent learning, or would like to take a course at their convenience.

PROGRAMS OF STUDY

Tarleton provides four graduate degree programs from the College of Business Administration.

The Master of Science (M.S.) in information systems requires 30 semester hours in information systems and 6 hours of electives, for a total of 36 semester hours. The program is designed to meet the needs of three distinct groups: students with a baccalaureate degree in information systems; students with baccalaureate degrees in other areas, who have information systems skills and desire to develop a new career in information systems; and students with baccalaureate degrees in another area, who lack information systems skills but desire to develop new career skills in information systems.

The Master of Business Administration (M.B.A.) enhances the students' general business training and prepares them for executive-level positions. Each student's degree program is designed to enhance decision-making and leadership skills. The program requires completion of at least 36 hours of graduate-level course work.

The M.S. degree program in human resource management is a 36-hour program that provides the students with opportunities to develop critical skills in areas such as research and job analysis, recruitment and selection, training and development, compensation and benefits, organizational effectiveness, and labor relations. Students gain knowledge and skills that are applicable in business and not-for-profit entities, including state and local governments and military organizations.

The M.S. in management and leadership is designed for students who have management experience in public or private organizations and who wish to sharpen their management skills. The program focuses on management and leadership skills that can be applied in any organizational setting, regardless of the functional area in which the leader works. Students gain knowledge and skills that are applicable in business, the military, government organizations, and private not-for-profit organizations.

STUDENT SERVICES

Tarleton's student-centered approach to online services is consistent with the University's philosophy of focusing on its students. A virtual Student Commons area offers many online student support services.

CREDIT OPTIONS

Tarleton may accept as many as 12 hours of graduate work completed at another regionally accredited university. All courses accepted in transfer must have been completed within six years of the time that the student will complete the graduate program. Academic work completed by correspondence is not accepted.

FACULTY

Tarleton faculty members enrich the virtual classroom with special talents and abilities drawn from successful careers in business, industry, government, and social service. Tarleton employs 163 full-time and 290 part-time faculty members. Currently, about 50 faculty members are delivering online courses. All instructors have at least a master's degree with 18 hours in the subject they are teaching. About 85 percent of the distance education faculty have an earned doctorate.

ADMISSION

Admission to any graduate degree program is granted by the Dean of the College of Graduate Studies upon recommendation of the department of proposed study. Full admission is awarded to applicants with a bachelor's degree from an accredited U.S. institution or the equivalent from a foreign institution; a minimum grade point average (based on a 4-point scale) of 3.0 in the last 60 hours of credit completed; and an acceptable score on the General Test of the GRE or, for M.B.A. students, the GMAT.

TUITION AND FEES

For the 2004–05 academic year, tuition and fees for an online graduate course are $375 for 3 semester hours. There is also a $300-per-course program fee for all online courses in graduate programs.

FINANCIAL AID

Graduate students may be eligible for student loans, scholarships, and graduate assistantships. Scholarships are available through the University Financial Aid Office, ROTC, and the College of Graduate Studies.

APPLYING

A formal application with a $25 application fee is required of all persons seeking admission. An applicant must submit official transcripts of all previous academic course work. The transcripts must bear the date of the bachelor's degree conferral and indicate that the applicant was in good standing at the last institution attended.

CONTACT

Center for Instructional Technology and Distributed Education
Box T-0810
Tarleton State University
Stephenville, Texas 76402
Telephone: 254-968-9060
E-mail: cited@tarleton.edu
Web site: http://online.tarleton.edu

College of Graduate Studies
Box T-0350
Tarleton State University
Stephenville, Texas 76402
Telephone: 800-687-4723 (toll-free)
E-mail: gradoffice@tarleton.edu
Web site: http://www.tarleton.edu/~graduate

College of Business Administration
Box T-0200
Tarleton State University
Stephenville, Texas 76402
Telephone: 254-968-9350
E-mail: coba@tarleton.edu
Web site: http://www.tarleton.edu/~coba/online.html

Taylor University

Center for Lifelong Learning

Fort Wayne, Indiana

Taylor University is one of America's oldest evangelical Christian institutions. In 1846, it began as a women's college with the conviction that women as well as men should have an opportunity for higher education. In 1855, it became coeducational and, in 1938, it offered its first distance learning course.

Today, U.S. News & World Report *repeatedly ranks Taylor as one of America's best regional liberal arts colleges. The Templeton Foundation has named it one of the nation's top colleges for building character in students, and* Barron's *has listed it as a "best buy in college education."*

Taylor University's mission is to educate men and women for lifelong learning and for ministering the redemptive love of Jesus Christ. It is accredited by the Higher Learning Commission of the North Central Association of Colleges and Schools.

DISTANCE LEARNING PROGRAM

The Center for Lifelong Learning is the virtual campus of Taylor University; it emphasizes the integration of faith and learning through distance education. The Center offers three Associate of Arts (A.A.) degrees, five certificate programs, and more than 100 online courses from most academic disciplines. Annually, it enrolls more than 1,100 students in more than 1,600 courses.

DELIVERY MEDIA

At the Taylor University Center for Lifelong Learning, the antiquated method of correspondence education has been replaced by the advantages of Internet technology and online learning. Rather than repackaging traditional classroom learning methods or simply creating digital versions of correspondence courses, Taylor has designed each course to ensure that it is learner-oriented and specifically designed for online, distance learning students. The eLearning platform brings together the elements that create the most valuable educational experience for the online distance learner—dynamic interaction and discussion with other students; close, continuous access to the instructor; and the convenience of having it all right at the student's fingertips.

PROGRAMS OF STUDY

The 64-credit-hour A.A. degree in biblical studies is designed for individuals preparing for vocational or lay Christian ministry. The curriculum is designed to give the student a foundational understanding of the Bible, Christian theology, and the knowledge and skills required for serving in a church or parachurch setting. It consists of 43 credit hours of general education course work, 15 hours in the discipline, and 6 elective hours.

The 64-credit-hour A.A. degree in justice administration is designed for individuals currently serving in or seeking to enter criminal justice, courts, corrections, law enforcement, or juvenile justice. It consists of 43 credit hours of general education course work and 21 hours in the discipline. Students select a ministry or public policy concentration. The A.A. with a concentration in ministry is the only degree program in the nation from an accredited institution specifically designed to prepare the student for correctional ministry. The degree is designed for individuals currently serving in or seeking to enter corrections, outreach, or ministry to offenders and at-risk populations.

The 64-credit-hour A.A. degree in the liberal arts is for students who desire a breadth of knowledge. It consists of 43 credit hours of general education course work, 15 hours in the chosen discipline, and 6 elective hours. Students select an interdisciplinary, history, or social science concentration.

The five certificate programs include the 24-credit-hour Biblical Studies Certificate, designed for busy pastors, church workers, and lay people who desire in-depth studies in the Bible; the 18-credit-hour Christian Worker Certification, designed for potential missionaries, pastors, and laypeople who desire a greater knowledge of the Bible and a better understanding of the professional challenges of ministry; the 18-credit-hour Justice and Ministry Certificate, specifically aimed at equipping individuals for correctional ministry; the 18-credit-hour Leadership Development Certificate, designed to equip current or potential leaders with the interpersonal skills and organizational abilities necessary for coping with business or ministry issues; and the 18-credit-hour Certificate in Missions Studies, designed to assist those who desire to work in the mission field either as a full-time missionary or through frequent trips overseas for ministry purposes.

SPECIAL PROGRAMS

All courses through the Taylor University Center for Lifelong Learning are competency-based, which means that students can complete the course as soon as the competencies are attained. The motivated student can progress at his or her own pace to ensure that the subject matter is understood well. Credit for each course is given when the expected learning results are documented and demonstrated.

STUDENT SERVICES

The Taylor University Center for Lifelong Learning staff is committed to providing qualified, efficient, and responsive service in a timely manner. Online registration facilitates course enrollments at any time of the day or night. Once enrolled, students become part of the Center's virtual campus, meeting the needs of today's Internet-savvy students. Within the virtual campus, students enjoy a relational, faith-based learning environment.

CREDIT OPTIONS

Students earn credits with the successful completion of courses. Up to 34 hours of transfer credit may be approved toward the 64-credit-hour A.A. degree programs. Only course work with a grade of C- or better is accepted.

To receive credit for work done at other accredited institutions, students should send their transcripts to the Taylor University Center for Lifelong Learning for review. CLEP, AP, and DANTES credit must meet Taylor's standards to be accepted as transfer credit.

FACULTY

The faculty of the Taylor University Center for Lifelong Learning consists of more than 100 highly credentialed, dedicated Christians. These instructors, many of whom hold doctorates, are among the most qualified academic professionals in the field of Christian higher education.

ADMISSION

Admission is open to all students registering for individual courses or beginning a certificate program. Degree-seeking students must meet certain minimum admission standards and complete an application, which includes a personal reference recommendation.

TUITION AND FEES

All courses are $185 per credit hour. Other expenses may include textbooks, study guides, supplemental materials, and shipping and handling fees. Taylor's most current fee structure is maintained at its online registration center.

FINANCIAL AID

Students who have been accepted into online degree programs and who will be registered for at least 6 credit hours in one term may apply for financial aid available through the University's Title IV agreement with the U.S. Department of Education.

The Department of Veterans Affairs has approved courses offered by the Taylor University Center for Lifelong Learning for those students entitled to receive veteran's educational benefits.

APPLYING

The Taylor University Center for Lifelong Learning offers open enrollment year-round through a secure, online registration process. Students may enroll online at any time in individual courses, certificate programs, or degree programs. Students seeking a degree must apply and be accepted. Secure, online registration is available at http://cll.taylor.edu/catalog. Students may also call toll-free at 800-845-3149. Students may also register and/or apply by fax, e-mail, mail, or in person.

CONTACT

Kevin Mahaffy, M.Min.
Director
Taylor University Center for Lifelong Learning
1025 West Rudisill Boulevard
Fort Wayne, Indiana 46807-2197
Telephone: 260-744-8750
800-845-3149 (toll-free enrollment hotline)
Fax: 260-744-8796
E-mail: cllinfo@tayloru.edu
Web site: http://cll.taylor.edu

Teachers College, Columbia University

The Distance Learning Project

New York, New York

Founded in 1887 to provide training for teachers of poor, immigrant children in New York City, Teachers College to date has educated nearly 100,000 individuals from around the world and is consistently ranked among the top three schools of education in the country. One third of the students are in teacher preparation programs, and the rest are planning careers in administration, policy, research, and teaching across the fields of education, health, and psychology. The College's mission is a dual leadership role: first, to be a major player in policy making, ensuring that schools are reformed to welcome learning for all students regardless of their status, and second, to prepare educators who not only serve students directly but also coordinate the educational, psychological, behavioral, technological, and health initiatives to remove the barriers to learning at all ages.

DISTANCE LEARNING PROGRAM

The Distance Learning Project seeks to increase access to educational opportunities at Teachers College and provide a source of research, evaluation, and innovation in computer-mediated learning. Since 1997, enrollment in online courses has steadily increased and the program currently serves approximately 300 students per semester.

DELIVERY MEDIA

Courses are offered through password-protected Web sites with features such as a threaded discussion area, asynchronous chat, easy ways to upload and share documents, and the capacity for multimedia (audio and video) or hypertext links to supplemental materials. Most courses consist of reading and written assignments or project work with supplementary lecture notes and in-depth communication among students, the instructor, and the teaching assistant using the discussion board and e-mail.

PROGRAMS OF STUDY

At present, Teachers College does not offer any degrees entirely via distance learning, but online courses taken for credit can be applied toward most on-campus degree programs, including the intensive M.A. in technology and education, which only requires a short summer residency. Two 15-credit certificate programs can be earned entirely via online course work and consist of four required courses and an independent study project. The Teaching and Learning with Technology certificate is designed to prepare K–12 teachers, technology coordinators, principals, superintendents, and other educational professionals to integrate technology into the classroom. The Designing Interactive Multimedia Instruction certificate provides skills in designing multimedia applications for teachers, school personnel, curriculum developers, software designers, publishing professionals, media specialists, and other educational professionals. Both programs include a combination of essential hands-on and theoretical work designed to make use of new technologies and can be taken on a credit or noncredit basis. Admission criteria include an essay and evidence of the student's achievement and potential to benefit from the program. Both certificates have been approved by the New York State Board of Education. Students who are not enrolled in a degree or certificate program are eligible to register for any single online course, subject to the College's admissions requirements.

STUDENT SERVICES

Online learners receive a University e-mail address and an ID and password that allow access to electronic resources and server space. The library provides online access to electronic databases, full-text articles, and extensive indexes of education, psychology, and health-related Web sites. Students can order course materials through the Teachers College bookstore, and Distance Learning Project staff members are available to provide technical support.

CREDIT OPTIONS

Most courses can be taken for either credit or no credit, but only courses taken for credit can be applied to a campus-based master's or doctoral degree. Online certificates can be earned by taking courses for no credit, but in that case they are not transferable to a degree program. Credits are only awarded for completion of online courses or independent study requirements as outlined by the instructor.

FACULTY

There are more than 20 instructors who regularly teach online courses, including full-time faculty members, adjunct faculty members, and instructors.

ADMISSION

Students taking courses for credit are subject to the same admissions requirements as the University or the degree program to which they are applying.

TUITION AND FEES

Online courses are charged the same rate as on-campus courses, as determined annually by the trustees. For the 2003–04 academic year, tuition for all courses was $825 per credit. The rate for enrolling in courses for no credit varied from $495 to $795 per course.

FINANCIAL AID

Students enrolled in a degree program at Teachers College are eligible for Federal Stafford Student Loans, grants, and scholarships, which can be applied towards online courses. For those not enrolled in a degree program, the only financial assistance available are personal loans, which are available through the Teachers College financial aid office.

APPLYING

All application and registration materials for individual courses and certificate programs are available online at http://dlp.tc.columbia.edu/courses/course_registration.html. Students currently taking courses at Teachers College can register for online courses through the University registration system.

CONTACT

Distance Learning Project
Teachers College, Columbia University
Telephone: 888-633-6933
Fax: 212-678-3291
E-mail: dlp@columbia.edu.
Web site: http://dlp.tc.columbia.edu

Texas Tech University

Distance Learning

Lubbock, Texas

Texas Tech University (TTU), a state-supported comprehensive university, is accredited by the Commission on Colleges of the Southern Association of Colleges and Schools to award bachelor's, master's, and doctoral degrees. Created by legislative action in 1923, Texas Tech University is a four-year research university composed of nine colleges and two schools (Agricultural Sciences and Natural Resources, Architecture, Arts and Sciences, Business Administration, Education, Engineering, Honors, Human Sciences, Visual and Performing Arts, the Graduate School, and the School of Law).

Committed to teaching and the advancement of knowledge, Texas Tech provides the highest standards of excellence in higher education, fosters intellectual and personal development, and stimulates meaningful research and service.

DISTANCE LEARNING PROGRAM

Offering flexibility and convenience, programs provide high-quality course work comparable to traditional on-campus courses. Texas Tech University now offers ten degree programs at a distance.

DELIVERY MEDIA

Courses are delivered via the World Wide Web by two-way interactive video, on audiotape, videotape, and CD-ROM, and by printed correspondence, depending on the course or degree program. E-mail, threaded discussions, chat rooms, and traditional communicative methods allow students to correspond with instructors and peers.

PROGRAMS OF STUDY

The Bachelor of General Studies (B.G.S.) degree is offered by the College of Arts and Sciences through Extended Studies. A highly flexible program, the B.G.S. degree features three core areas of concentration (in lieu of a "major") tailored to students' interests or professional goals. Each concentration area consists of courses that are consistent with the "minor" in various subject disciplines (e.g., English or psychology.)

In addition to administering the Bachelor of General Studies degree, Extended Studies works with academic departments to offer more than sixty college-credit courses. Students may enroll in these courses at any time during the year. For more information, prospective students should visit Texas Tech University's Distance Learning Web site, listed in the Contact section at the end of this description.

The College of Arts and Sciences offers an online Master of Arts in Technical Communication (M.A.T.C.) degree through the Department of English. A nonthesis program, it parallels the on-site M.A.T.C. in admission and degree requirements. Courses are offered on the semester schedule. Texas Tech University is the only university in Texas to offer degrees in technical communication at the bachelor's, master's, and doctoral levels. For more information, students should visit the Department of English distance education M.A.T.C. Web site (http://English.ttu.edu/tc/DL/).

The College of Engineering offers four different Distance Learning master's degrees: the interdisciplinary Master of Engineering degree (M.En.), which allows students to take courses from a number of engineering fields while specializing in one area; the Master of Science in Systems and Engineering Management (M.S.S.E.M.) through industrial engineering; the Master of Science in Petroleum Engineering (M.S.P.E.); and the Master of Science in Software Engineering (M.S.S.E.) through computer science. For more information, prospective students should visit the College of Engineering Web site (http://aln.coe.ttu.edu/).

The College of Education offers a completely online Master of Education in instructional technology with an emphasis in distance education. This program is designed for K–12 educators and professional trainers who want to become online instructors, instructional designers, and managers of distance education programs. The College of Education also offers a completely online/ITV Master of Education in special education, with areas of emphasis in generic special education, educational diagnostician, autism, orientation and mobility (O & M), and vision. This program is designed for K–12 educators, assessment personnel, and O & M specialists. For more information, students should visit the College of Education distance education Web site (http://www.educ.ttu.edu/Distance).

The College of Human Sciences offers a Master of Science in restaurant/hotel and institutional management (RHIM) through the Department of Education, Nutrition, Restaurant, Hotel and Institutional Management. This M.S. program is designed for industry professionals who work in management-level positions and features the same courses and course content as the traditional graduate program. Courses are offered on the semester schedule and are delivered via the Internet. For more information, prospective students should visit the College of Human Sciences Web site (http://www.hs.ttu.edu/ceo).

The College of Agricultural Sciences and Natural Resources, in conjunction with Texas A&M University, offers a Doctor of Education (Ed.D.) in agricultural education through the Department of Agricultural Education and Communications. Geared for midcareer professionals in agricultural education, the degree is designed to engage a cohort of learners. The program includes 64 semester hours and spans four years. Courses are semester-based and are taught using ITV and the Internet. For more information, students should visit the College of Agricultural Sciences and Natural Resources Web site (http://www.casnr.ttu.edu/).

SPECIAL PROGRAMS

Web-based, noncredit certificate programs are offered through Extended Studies; most of these allow students to earn continuing education credits. For more information, prospective students should contact Extended Studies (listed below).

The College of Education offers four college credit distance learning programs leading to state and national certifications in special education. For more information, students should visit http://www.educ.ttu.edu/Distance.

STUDENT SERVICES

College-assigned advisers provide information about accessing course materials online, register students for course work, disseminate course materials, and monitor students' progress through degree programs.

CREDIT OPTIONS

Distance learning college-credit courses or courses taken for continuing education credit are recorded on Texas Tech University transcripts. Distance learning course credits may be transferable to other institutions.

FACULTY

Courses are taught by Texas Tech University faculty members or instructors approved by the respective college. The majority of faculty members hold terminal degrees.

ADMISSION

Prospective students should contact the Graduate or Undergraduate Admissions Office or visit the University's Web site (http://www.ttu.edu) for detailed information about admission requirements.

TUITION AND FEES

Tuition and fees vary from program to program. Prospective students should contact Extended Studies to obtain more information on tuition and fees.

FINANCIAL AID

Distance learning students may be eligible for a variety of financial aid opportunities. Students should contact the Financial Aid Office at 806-742-3681 for more information.

APPLYING

Some degree programs require applications to be submitted by specific deadlines, but students may submit an application for the Bachelor of General Studies degree at any time. Prospective students should contact Extended Studies to obtain specific application procedures and deadlines for degree programs.

CONTACT

For specific information about degree programs, students should visit the respective Web site noted in the Programs of Study section. For general inquiries, students should contact:

Michele Moskos
Marketing Director
Extended Studies
Texas Tech University
Box 42191
Lubbock, Texas 79409-2191
Telephone: 800-MY-COURSE (800-692-6877) Ext. 276 (toll-free)
E-mail: dldegrees.oes@ttu.edu
Web site: http://www.de.ttu.edu

Thomas Edison State College

Trenton, New Jersey

Thomas Edison State College specializes in providing flexible, high-quality educational opportunities for adults. One of New Jersey's twelve senior public institutions of higher education, the College offers fifteen associate, baccalaureate, and master's degrees in more than 100 areas of study. Students earn degrees through a variety of rigorous academic methods, including documenting college-level knowledge they already have and completing independent study courses. Identified by Forbes *magazine as one of the top twenty colleges and universities in the nation in the use of technology to create learning opportunities for adults, this public college is a national leader in the assessment of adult learning and a pioneer in the use of educational technologies. Founded in 1972, Thomas Edison State College is regionally accredited by the Commission on Higher Education of the Middle States Association of Colleges and Schools.*

DISTANCE LEARNING PROGRAM

Thomas Edison State College offers one of the most highly regarded, comprehensive distance learning programs in the United States. Adults may choose from more than 130 distance learning courses, including online classes. Students also take tests and submit portfolios to demonstrate and earn credit for college-level knowledge they already have and may transfer credits earned at other accredited institutions.

DELIVERY MEDIA

Distance education courses are provided through several options, including Thomas Edison State College courses offered through the mail, e-mail, and online. Also available are *e*-Pack courses, which offer online credit-by-examination and allow students to prepare for a comprehensive final examination by taking a series of chapter quizzes delivered via the World Wide Web.

PROGRAMS OF STUDY

Thomas Edison State College offers fifteen associate, baccalaureate, and master's degrees in more than 100 areas of study. Undergraduate degrees offered include the Associate in Applied Science; Associate in Science in Management; Associate in Science in Applied Science and Technology; Associate in Arts; Associate in Science in Natural Science and Mathematics; Associate in Science in Public and Social Services; Bachelor of Arts; Bachelor of Science in Applied Science and Technology; Bachelor of Science in Business Administration; Bachelor of Science in Health Sciences, a joint-degree program with the University of Medicine and Dentistry of New Jersey (UMDNJ) School of Health Related Professions (SHRP); Bachelor of Science in Human Services; and Bachelor of Science in Nursing.

Each undergraduate degree requires work in general education, the area of study, and elective subjects. Students are encouraged to work in conjunction with one of the College's program advisers to develop an individual program plan.

In addition, the College offers three master's programs. The Master of Science in Human Resources Management (M.S.H.R.M.) degree serves human resources professionals who wish to become strategic partners in their organizations. This online program uses a cohort model and is designed to position human resources professionals as leaders within their organizations. The 36-semester-hour program provides practitioners with technical human resources skills in staffing, providing professional development, managing organizational culture, and measuring and rewarding performance. The online Master of Science in Management (M.S.M.) degree program serves employed adults with professional experience in management. It integrates the theory and practice of management as it applies to diverse organizations. The College's online Master of Arts in Professional Studies (M.A.P.S.) degree program provides working professionals an opportunity to study the liberal arts from an applied perspective.

SPECIAL PROGRAMS

Thomas Edison State College's Military Degree Completion Program (MDCP) serves military personnel worldwide and was developed to accommodate the special needs of military personnel whose location, relocation, and time constraints make traditional college attendance difficult, if not impossible. The program allows students to engage in a degree program wherever they may be stationed and receive maximum credit for military training and education. Thomas Edison State College is a partner college for the U.S. Navy's Navy College Program Distance Learning Partnership and is a participant in the U.S. Army's eArmyU program.

The College's unique Degree Pathways Program allows community college students and graduates to complete a baccalaureate degree at home, in the workplace, or at their local two-year college. The Degree Pathways Program lets community college students and graduates make a smooth transition directly into a Thomas Edison State College baccalaureate program by transferring up to 80 credits toward the 120 credits needed for a baccalaureate degree. The program provides coordinated support in admissions, academic programming, advisement, registration, and the sharing of technologies. Students who have earned an associate degree within the past five years or are six months from completing an associate degree are eligible for the Degree Pathways Program. Students may continue to take classes and use technologies that are available at their community or county college as they move closer to the 80-credit limit of the 120 credits required for a baccalaureate degree.

Thomas Edison State College has also developed an 18-credit certificate in fitness and wellness services.

STUDENT SERVICES

Academic advisement is provided to enrolled students by the College's Advisement Center, which assists students in integrating their learning style, background, and educational goals with the credit-earning methods and programs available. Students may access advisement through in-person appointments or through the Advisement Phone Center. They also have 24-hour access through fax and e-mail.

CREDIT OPTIONS

Students have the opportunity to earn degrees through traditional and nontraditional methods and use several convenient methods of meeting degree requirements, depending upon their individual learning styles and preferences. Once a student is enrolled in a specific degree program, an evaluator determines the number of credits the student has already earned and fits those into the degree program requirement.

Credit-earning options for nondegree students benefit individuals who would like to earn credit through examinations, prior learning assessment, and Thomas Edison State College courses. Students may do so by paying the appropriate fee for these programs. An application to the College is not required to take advantage of these nondegree, credit-earning options.

Credit Banking is for students who wish to document college-level learning and consolidate college-level work into a Thomas Edison State College transcript. Credits transcribed under the Credit Banking program may or may not apply to a degree program at Thomas Edison State College.

The College grants credit for current professional licenses or certificates that have been approved for credit by the College's Academic Council. Students must submit notarized copies of their license or certificate and current renewal card, if appropriate, to receive credit. A list of licenses and certificates approved for credit may be found in the College's Undergraduate Prospectus.

FACULTY

There are more than 300 mentors at Thomas Edison State College. Drawn from other highly regarded colleges and universities, mentors provide many services, including assessment of prior knowledge and advisement.

ADMISSION

Adults 21 years of age or older who are seeking an associate, baccalaureate, or master's degree and are high school graduates are eligible to become Thomas Edison State College students. Because Thomas Edison State College delivers high-quality education directly to students wherever they live or work, students may complete degree requirements at their convenience. There are two brief residency requirements for the Master of Science in Management degree. A computer is required to complete graduate degrees and to take undergraduate online courses.

TUITION AND FEES

Tuition is payment for all costs directly associated with the academic delivery of a Thomas Edison State College education. Fees are designated as payment for administrative services and for materials used by students for courses and other activities. Thomas Edison State College offers one annual tuition plan, the Comprehensive Tuition Plan, for students who want access to all components of the tuition package. For those students who have determined that their particular situation is one where only components of the Comprehensive Tuition Plan are required, the College offers the Enrolled Options Plan. A complete listing of tuition and fees is included in the College's information packet and is available by calling the Office of Admissions or by visiting the College Web site (phone number and Web address are listed below).

FINANCIAL AID

Thomas Edison State College participates in a number of federal and state aid programs. Eligible students may receive Federal Pell Grants or federal education loans such as the Federal Stafford Student Loan (subsidized and unsubsidized). Eligible New Jersey residents may also tap a variety of state grant and loan programs. Students may use state aid to meet all or part of their college costs, provided they are taking at least 12 credits per semester. Detailed information about the financial aid process may be found in the financial aid packet, which is available from the Office of Financial Aid & Veterans' Affairs or on the College Web site. To receive this information, students may contact the office (telephone: 609-633-9658; e-mail: finaid@tesc.edu).

APPLYING

Students may apply to Thomas Edison State College by mail or fax or through the College Web site. The Office of Admissions assists potential applicants in determining whether Thomas Edison State College suits their particular academic goals.

CONTACT

Office of Admissions
Thomas Edison State College
101 West State Street
Trenton, New Jersey 08608-1176
Telephone: 888-442-8372 (toll-free)
Fax: 609-984-8447
E-mail: info@tesc.edu
Web site: http://www.tesc.edu

Touro University International

Distance Learning Program

Cypress, California

Touro University International (TUI), located in southern California, is a branch campus of Touro College, New York, which is accredited by the Commission on Higher Education of the Middle States Association of Colleges and Schools.

TUI offers affordable degree programs on the Internet, using the latest technology and innovative live interactive delivery methodology.

TUI is committed to sustaining the high quality of its pedagogical model, its faculty, and its support services. A worldwide university operating 24 hours a day, 365 days a year, TUI offers students an excellent learning experience accessed from their own homes, while allowing them to maintain their work and family responsibilities.

DISTANCE LEARNING PROGRAM

TUI offers high-quality education utilizing online Internet instruction as its primary means of delivery. There is no residency requirement. The student-centered teaching model has two major elements: modular case-based learning and the cyber classroom. These essential elements are part of every module of every course.

DELIVERY MEDIA

The cyber classroom approach includes the use of multimedia for academic transactions and interactive collaboration (live exchange with professors and peers). The multimedia approach includes audio and video on demand, Internet links, PowerPoint presentations, and live conferences among students and between professors and students. This allows students to work as a team with fellow students from around the world. Case-based learning provides real-world application to each topic.

PROGRAM OF STUDY

TUI consists of the College of Business Administration, the College of Education, the College of Health Sciences, and the College of Information Systems. The College of Business Administration offers three degree programs: the Bachelor of Science in Business Administration (120 semester credits), with concentrations in financial management, general management, e-commerce, information technology management, health-care management, and degree completion specially designed for students with an A.A. or A.S. degree; the Master of Science in Business Administration (32 semester credits for students with business-related undergraduate degrees), with concentrations in international business, general management, health-care management, information technology management, criminal justice administration, and e-commerce; and the Doctor of Philosophy in business administration (44 semester credits of course work plus a research dissertation). The concentration depends on the candidate's specific research interests.

The College of Education offers two degree programs: the Master of Arts in Education (36 semester credits), with concentrations in teaching and instruction, educational leadership, higher education, and e-learning, and the Doctor of Philosophy in educational leadership (48 semester credits in course work plus a research dissertation), with specializations in K–12 leadership, higher education leadership, and e-learning leadership.

The College of Health Sciences offers three degree programs: the Bachelor of Science in Health Sciences (124 semester credits), with concentrations in health education, health-care management, emergency and disaster management, emergency and disaster management (certificate), and professional degree completion; the Master of Science in Health Sciences (40 semester credits), with concentrations in international health, health-care management, emergency and disaster management, and public health; and the Doctor of Philosophy in health sciences (44 semester credits in course work plus a research dissertation), with specializations in international health and educator/researcher/practitioner studies.

The College of Information Systems offers three degree programs: the Bachelor of Science in Computer Science (120 semester credits), the Bachelor of Science in Information Technology Management (120 semester credits), and the Master of Science in Information Technology Management (36 semester credits).

STUDENT SERVICES

Touro University International maintains five specific student services. Preadmission advisement assists students with enrollment in the best combination of classes and any other student concerns. Preadmission English competency evaluation is provided for students whose first language is not English, who do not meet

TUI's English competency requirements, or who feel that they do not possess adequate English skills. Postadmission advisement assists students with course selection and sequencing, developing study habits, and addressing other student concerns. Information technology assistance provides the necessary assistance to ensure that students have access to all information technology features of TUI courses. The Information Technology department also assists students with installation and configuration. Library resource assistance is provided by TUI staff members via e-mail in the use of all cyber library holdings.

TUI provides financial assistance under three federal programs that are available to citizens and eligible noncitizens of the United States.

FACULTY

All TUI faculty members hold doctoral degrees and have experience in their respective fields in addition to having sound academic teaching, research, and dissertation advisement records. Exceptional full-time faculty members teach nearly all TUI classes. The highest level of faculty expertise in each field is also available through guest lecturers and visiting faculty members via the cyber classroom delivery mode.

ADMISSION

TUI offers four sessions per year, beginning in March, June, September, and December, with each session lasting twelve weeks. All TUI courses are valued at 4 semester credits. A full-time load is two courses per session, whereby students can earn 32 semester credits per year while continuing with family and work responsibilities.

The Office of Admissions assists potential students in determining their compatibility with the program based on past academic performance and educational goals. For specific details about each degree program, students may visit the Web site at the Internet address listed below.

TUITION AND FEES

TUI's tuition is one of the most affordable in the nation. Tuition is $225 per semester credit for B.S.-level courses, $300 per semester credit for M.S.-level courses, and $500 per semester credit for Ph.D.-level courses. Students should contact TUI registration for information about scholarships, graduate assistantships, and financial aid.

Active-duty military, retired military, military dependents, and civilian military employees receive special tuition rates through TUI's DANTES agreement. Students should contact their base or post educational officer or TUI for details.

APPLYING

Applications may be completed online at www.tourou.edu and are accepted year-round. A complete application package must be received by TUI two weeks prior to the start of the first session. TUI will respond within 24 business hours of receiving the complete package of application materials.

CONTACT

College of Business Administration
5665 Plaza Drive, 3rd Floor
Cypress, California 90630
Telephone: 714-816-0366
Fax: 714-816-0367
E-mail: infocba@tourou.edu
Web site: http://www.tourou.edu

College of Education
5665 Plaza Drive, 3rd Floor
Cypress, California 90630
Telephone: 714-226-9840
Fax: 714-226-9844
E-mail: infocoe@tourou.edu
Web site: http://www.tourou.edu

College of Health Sciences
5665 Plaza Drive, 3rd Floor
Cypress, California 90630
Telephone: 714-226-9840
Fax: 714-226-9844
E-mail: infochs@tourou.edu
Web site: http://www.tourou.edu

College of Information Systems
5665 Plaza Drive, 3rd Floor
Cypress, California 90630
Telephone: 714-816-0366
Fax: 714-816-0367
E-mail: infocis@tourou.edu
Web site: http://www.tourou.edu

Troy University

Distance Learning Center

Troy, Alabama

Since its founding in 1887, Troy University (TU) has been recognized for the quality of its academic programs and its focus on the individual student. The University is dedicated to the preparation of students in a variety of fields in the arts and sciences, fine arts, business, communication, applied science, nursing, and allied health sciences, as well as to its historic role in the preparation of teachers. The administrators, faculty and staff members, and students of the University, through a system of shared governance, are committed to excellence in education. A major commitment exists to provide undergraduate and graduate education for the national and international community, especially for mature students, not only by traditional means of delivery but also by technological means. Additional information about the University may be found at its Web site: http://www.troyst.edu.

DISTANCE LEARNING PROGRAM

The distance learning program at Troy University (TU) is an important and growing part of the mission of the University. A variety of courses are offered, including seven complete graduate degrees that may be completed online. Along with personalized attention from faculty members, the TU distance learning program (http://www.tsulearn.net) is supported by the Distance Learning Center at Troy University in Alabama.

DELIVERY MEDIA

Distance Learning Center course offerings are Web interactive and are delivered through the Blackboard Internet-learning platform. Students may complete course work on an anytime/anyplace basis worldwide. Additional distance learning courses at Troy University are also provided using videoconferencing, cable TV, and Web-enhanced and videotape/DVD media.

PROGRAMS OF STUDY

There are currently seven master's degree programs and a variety of individual courses offered by the Distance Learning Center. Complete details can be found by visiting the Center's Web site listed in the Contact section below.

The Master of Science in Business Administration (M.B.A.) program is designed to provide advanced study to students who have already acquired a common body of knowledge in business administration. It also offers students an opportunity to obtain advanced proficiency in decision-making skills as well as business management skills. The program also prepares students to carry out managerial responsibilities in government, business, and industry and develop the problem solving skills required in a dynamic and uncertain business environment.

The Master of Science in Criminal Justice (M.S.C.J.) program is designed to provide qualified students with an interdisciplinary graduate-level education in criminal justice. It provides students with knowledge or enhancement in the criminal justice field or leads to a terminal degree.

The Master of Science in International Relations (M.S.I.R.) program is designed to offer the graduates of diversified undergraduate programs an opportunity to obtain proficiency in international relations. Topics include foreign policy analysis, defense and security policy, comparative politics, regional and state-specific studies, international economics, and specific instruments of international affairs, such as international organizations and international law. The degree program offers a ten-course option and a twelve-course option.

The Master of Public Administration (M.P.A.) degree program offers a twelve course program with nine concentrations. There is no comprehensive examination, but there is a final capstone course. The M.P.A. is designed to offer graduates of various undergraduate programs an opportunity to obtain high levels of proficiency in public management as the basis for an application of technical and managerial skills to enhance public service work.

The Master of Science in Human Resources Management (M.S.H.R.M.) is a professional degree program designed to offer graduates of diversified undergraduate programs an opportunity to obtain a proficiency in human resources management skills. The program emphasizes fundamental problem-solving, technical, and decision-making skills; communication and interpersonal competencies; and knowledge critical for success in today's and tomorrow's entrepreneurial and business organizations.

The Master of Science in Management (M.S.M.) is a professional program designed to offer the graduate of diversified undergraduate programs an opportunity to obtain proficiency in management skills and decision making that enables them to carry out managerial responsibilities in both the private and public sectors. Students complete a five-course core, a three-course concentration, and two elective courses suitable to their individual academic and employment backgrounds and specific career objectives.

The Master of Education degree program is designed to strengthen and enrich current and future educators in the instructional technology area of study. The degree provides graduate study for students, teachers, and administrators whose career goals call for further education, improved abilities to use new instructional technology effectively, and performance of research and policymaking in this field. This is a noncertification program.

SPECIAL PROGRAMS

The Troy Distance Learning Center is a part of University College. The University College component of TU is unique to Alabama universities, as it provides a global focus to TU's routine operations. University College sites span from Korea to Guantanamo Bay, Cuba, giving meaning to the phrase "the sun never sets on TU." Additional information about the University's programs may be found at its Web site listed in the Contact section.

STUDENT SERVICES

TU is committed to providing a wide range of learning opportunities for a diverse student population. Students come to TU with hopes and high expectations. Professors teach courses using the latest course materials and techniques for rich interaction between students and professors. Professors can advise students on course options and degree requirements. The staff members in the Distance Learning Center also provide advice and assistance with admissions, registration, evaluation of transfer credit, changes of program, and processing of Intents to Graduate.

CREDIT OPTIONS

The Distance Learning Center offers credits through distance learning that are recorded on a Troy University transcript in the same manner as credits earned in on-campus courses. Most students enroll as degree-seeking students, but there is opportunity for students to take individual courses that may apply to degrees at other institutions of higher learning. Students should contact the Student Services staff in the Distance Learning Center to learn more about transient authorizations or other credit opportunities.

FACULTY

All distance learning faculty members meet the standards set forth by the Southern Association of Colleges and Schools, the state of Alabama, and the review agencies of the various TU colleges. Faculty members are full-time or adjunct members of the department granting the course credit.

ADMISSION

Admission to the distance learning degree programs at Troy University has the same criteria as admission for any on-campus student. Interested students should access the Distance Learning Web site listed below for more information. There is a $40 admission fee.

TUITION AND FEES

Current tuition and fees are subject to change and are published on the Web site listed below. With the exception of the M.B.A. program, graduate credit for the 2004–05 academic year is $290 per credit hour ($870 per 3-credit hour course), offered only through the main campus in Troy, Alabama. The fees for the M.B.A. program are $400 per credit, or $1200 for each 3-credit hour course. Additional fees include $40 for admissions, $50 for graduation, and $5 for transcripts.

FINANCIAL AID

Troy University offers a comprehensive program of financial assistance for students pursuing a graduate degree. Application for Financial Aid forms may be obtained by e-mailing a request to the e-mail address listed below in the Contact section. The G.I. Bill, Veterans Administration, and tuition assistance (TA) are also means by which students who are qualified for these forms of financial aid may pay for tuition.

APPLYING

Students can submit an Application for Admission as well as register for courses using the Distance Learning Web site listed below. The Web site provides complete details regarding degree programs and application and registration requirements.

CONTACT

Student Services
Distance Learning Center
Troy University
Troy, Alabama 36082
Telephone: 334-670-5876
800-265-9811 (toll-free)
Fax: 334-670-5679
E-mail: tsulearn@troyst.edu
Web site: http://www.tsulearn.net

Troy University–Florida and Western Region

Undergraduate Distance Learning

Fort Walton Beach, Florida

Since its founding in 1887, Troy University (TU) has been recognized for the high quality of its academic programs and its focus on the individual student. The University is dedicated to the preparation of students in a variety of fields in the arts and sciences, fine arts, business, communication, applied science, nursing, and allied health sciences, as well as to its historic role in the preparation of teachers. The administrators, faculty and staff members, and students of the University, through a system of shared governance, are committed to excellence in education. A major commitment exists to provide undergraduate and graduate education for the national and international community, especially for mature students, not only by traditional means of delivery but also by technological means. Additional information about the University may be found at its Web site (http://www.troyst.edu).

DISTANCE LEARNING PROGRAM

The distance learning program at TU is an important and growing part of the mission of the University. A variety of different courses are offered throughout the TU system, including eight complete undergraduate degrees that may be completed online through Troy University–Florida and Western Region (TUF&WR).

TUF&WR's distance learning program is designed to support students both locally and around the globe. Troy University implements emerging technologies coupled with traditional methodology to create an optimal learning environment—the virtual classroom.

Students enjoy the flexibility of distance learning course work, and while distance learning may not be for everyone, it can certainly help students reach their academic goals by lifting the barriers of proximity, geography, and time.

Distance learning students need a steadfast work ethic, independent study skill, good communication habits, and a working knowledge of the Internet. Students must maintain the self-discipline to complete course work within their environmental pressures of work and home. While there is some flexibility in the completion of distance learning requirements, the classes do operate within the same time structure as traditional courses.

Distance learning also mirrors traditional classroom courses in admissions and registration, as well as content and instruction, evaluation, and testing criteria. All valid financial aid and tuition assistance programs accepted by TU are honored for distance learning courses. Along with personalized attention from faculty members, the TUF&WR distance learning program is supported by the distance learning department located at the Florida and Western Regional Office in Fort Walton Beach, Florida.

DELIVERY MEDIA

Distance Learning Center course offerings are Web interactive and are delivered through the Blackboard Internet-learning platform. Students may complete course work on an anytime/anyplace basis worldwide.

PROGRAMS OF STUDY

There are currently eight undergraduate degree programs available in their entirety online through the Florida and Western Region. Complete details can be found by visiting the Web site listed in the Contact section.

Two associate degrees are offered in business administration (A.S.B.A.) and general studies (A.S.G.E., with various concentrations). In order to receive the associate degree, students must complete all course requirements for the degree being taken and declare for the associate degree before declaring for the bachelor's degree. Six bachelor's degrees are offered.

Through the Bachelor of Applied Science in Resources Management (B.A.S.R.M.) program, the University offers a baccalaureate degree especially designed for individuals with skills and understanding obtained from accredited postsecondary technical schools, community colleges, military schools, and nontraditional sources. The academic curricula taught by the University have been developed to supplement, not duplicate, the vocational/technical training or other experiential learning the individual may possess in a manner designed to provide these individuals greater career opportunities.

The Bachelor of Science in Computer Science (B.S.C.S.) program is an academic computer training program that prepares its graduates to be successful, whether they are entering the fast-paced world of commercial computer processing or continuing their academic training by attending graduate school. This goal is accomplished by maximizing student proficiency in both theoretical and practical aspects of computer science. The computer science (CS) program gives students experience with both mainframe systems and microcomputer systems. This blend of theoretical and practical training, as well as mainframe and PC experience, allows graduates to minimize the time it takes them to become valuable contributing employees. Also, the flexibility of the CS program allows students to obtain additional background experience in other areas of interest, such as mathematics or business.

The Bachelor of Science in Criminal Justice (B.S.C.J.) is designed to provide a broad introduction to the social, psychological, administrative, and legal aspects of law enforcement. The criminal justice curriculum provides an understanding of the American justice system and develops the student's ability to critically analyze the problems associated with that system.

The Bachelor of Science in Management (B.S.M.) program prepares individuals for managerial positions and the responsibilities of leadership. It emphasizes setting and accomplishing goals by the efficient and effective utilization of a manager's resources: money, machines, materials, and people.

The Bachelor of Science in Political Science (B.S.P.S.) is a rigorous academic program that provides both a general foundation for the study of politics and focused study in one of three major subfields: American politics, international relations, or public administration.

The Bachelor of Science in Psychology (B.S.Psy.) is designed to provide students with an understanding of human behavior from a psychological point of view. Psychology is the science that is concerned with the understanding of behavior and mental processes. A major in psychology provides preparation that should enable students to pursue graduate study in psychology and related fields. It also may enhance employability in areas where a knowledge of human behavior would be deemed beneficial. The psychology major provides students an opportunity to acquire a thorough grounding in the field of psychology. The 36-hour major provides students an opportunity to select courses that meet their professional and personal objectives.

SPECIAL PROGRAMS

The Troy Distance Learning Center is a part of University College. The University College component of TU is unique, as it provides a global focus to TU's routine operations. University College sites span from Korea to Guantanamo Bay, Cuba, giving meaning to the phrase "the sun never sets on TU." Additional information about the University's programs may be found at its Web site listed in the Contact section.

STUDENT SERVICES

TU is committed to providing a wide range of learning opportunities for a diverse student population. Students come to TU with hopes and high expectations. Professors teach courses using the latest course materials and techniques for rich interaction with students. Professors can advise students on course options and degree requirements. The staff members in the TUF&WR distance learning department also provide advice and assistance with admissions, financial aid processing, registration, evaluation of transfer credit, changes of program, and processing of intents to graduate.

CREDIT OPTIONS

The TUF&WR distance learning department offers credits through distance learning that are recorded on a Troy University transcript in the same manner as credits earned in on-campus courses. Most students enroll as degree-seeking students, but there is opportunity for students to take individual courses that may apply to degrees at other institutions of higher learning. Students should contact the Student Services staff in the TUF&WR distance learning department to learn more about transient authorization or other credit opportunities.

FACULTY

All distance learning faculty members meet the standards set forth by the Southern Association of Colleges and Schools, the state of Alabama, and the review agencies of the various TU colleges. Faculty members are full-time or adjunct members of the department granting the course credit.

ADMISSION

Admission to the distance learning degree programs at Troy University has the same criteria as admission for any on-campus student. Interested students should access the distance learning Web site for more information. There is a $55 admission fee.

TUITION AND FEES

Current tuition and fees are subject to change and are published on the Web site. For the 2004–05 academic year, TUF&WR undergraduate distance learning tuition is $145 per credit hour ($435 for a 3-credit-hour course).

FINANCIAL AID

Troy University offers a comprehensive program of financial assistance for students pursuing a graduate degree. Application for financial aid forms may be obtained by e-mailing a request to the e-mail address listed below in the Contact section. The G.I. Bill, Veterans Administration, and tuition assistance are also means by which students who are qualified for these forms of financial aid may pay for tuition.

APPLYING

Students can submit an application for admission as well as register for courses using the distance learning Web site, which provides complete details regarding degree programs and application and registration requirements.

CONTACT

Student Services
Distance Learning Department
Troy University–Florida and Western Region
326 Green Acres Road
Fort Walton Beach, Florida 32547
Telephone: 866-MY-TSUDL (toll-free)
Fax: 850-863-2702
E-mail: distlearn@troyst.edu
Web site: www.tsufl.edu/distancelearning

Union Institute & University

Center for Distance Learning and Vermont College

Cincinnati, Ohio

A pioneer in innovative higher education, Union Institute & University (UI&U) was founded to accommodate the goals, aspirations, career, and educational needs of adults seeking alternatives to traditional processes. Individualized degree plans include the arts (both visual and creative writing), business, education, government, health professions, holistic studies, leadership and philanthropy, management, and more. UI&U recently acquired Vermont College and its highly acclaimed master's programs, and is now uniquely positioned to offer bachelor's, master's, and doctoral programs both on-site and at a distance (online). On-site residency requirements vary by program and range from no residential attendance requirement, two days to two weeks at the Vermont College campus, or a ten-day doctoral program entry colloquia at sites around the nation. More than 2,500 learners are enrolled from all fifty states and more than twenty countries worldwide, studying independently outside traditional classroom settings, in vibrant online learning communities, or in communities of learners with similar interests. The average age of the undergraduate learners is 37; the average age of the doctoral candidates is 47. Degree programs build on previous learning and employ the creative engagement of knowledge through a wide variety of learning resources under the close guidance and evaluation of the University's highly qualified faculty. Union Institute & University is accredited by the Higher Learning Commission of the North Central Association of Colleges and Schools.

DISTANCE LEARNING PROGRAM

All degrees offered at UI&U can be earned at a distance. All Union Institute & University distance learning programs emphasize individualized learning plans, one-to-one mentoring, flexible scheduling of academic activities, and academic rigor.

DELIVERY MEDIA

UI&U's distance learning activities are supported by instructional technology and learning management systems that provide opportunities for collaborative learning environments to be created anytime, anyplace. Union's programs utilize both asynchronous and synchronous methodologies. Courses, seminars, and individually designed learning activities involve a high degree of learner-faculty interaction supported by computer conferencing. Library and other learner support services are also available to distance learners electronically through the University's Research Engine and Campus Web student information system.

PROGRAMS OF STUDY

Each degree program is carefully designed by the learner and faculty member to meet the needs and goals of the learner. The emphasis is on interdisciplinary studies in the humanities and social sciences through a powerful integration of theory and practical application.

Degrees in the College of Undergraduate Studies (CUS) and Vermont College's Undergraduate Program (VCU) can be completed in eighteen months to four years. They feature a focused area of concentration (major field of study) and general education requirements, which ensure breadth and depth of knowledge across a wide range of disciplines. Learners complete 120–128 semester credit hours to earn their degree. Common concentrations include business and management, communications, criminal justice studies, education, psychology, social sciences, and a variety of arts and humanities, many of which are individually designed.

Since 1969, the graduate division has offered a Master of Arts degree with concentrations in humanities and social sciences that can be completed in a minimum of eighteen months through an individually tailored study plan. Licensure in counseling psychology is offered through the Department of Graduate Psychology and Counseling, based at the Vermont College Brattleboro campus. The Master of Education features areas of study in curriculum and instruction (including a teaching licensure option), educational leadership (including an administrative licensure option), guidance (with a guidance licensure option), and issues in education. The Master of Fine Arts (M.F.A.) in writing offers a two-year terminal degree for adult students and working writers, with concentrations in poetry, fiction, and creative nonfiction. The M.F.A. in writing for children and young adults offers a two-year terminal degree for adult students and working writers, with concentrations in picture book and middle grade. The M.F.A. in visual art is a two-year terminal degree program for working artists. Areas of study include painting, drawing, printmaking, sculpture, photography, craft as fine art, video/film, and nontraditional media.

Lifelong Learning offers online credit (undergraduate and graduate) and noncredit seminars and workshops that draw on the person's experience and are designed to integrate one-to-one and collaborative learning using activity-based learning. Areas of specialty include writing, family history, interdisciplinary arts, and sciences.

UI&U's doctoral program offers the Ph.D., which can be completed in a minimum of three years enrollment and includes an internship and a capstone project demonstrating excellence. Union also provides educational programs that are designed for particular populations of adult learners, including substance abuse counselors and criminal justice professionals.

STUDENT SERVICES

UI&U uses an extensive online Research Engine, accessible through its Web site and the Campus Web feature, which allows learners to customize their Web interfaces. The Research Engine is a global "library without walls," providing unlimited access to electronic databases, links to authoritative resources, and an extensive reference desk. In addition, the Gary Library on Vermont College's Montpelier campus supports research and study. The University has interlibrary loan arrangements with many schools and local libraries, most of which are accessible via personal computer. Financial Aid, Academic Records, Business Office, and learner advising services are accessible electronically.

CREDIT OPTIONS

Union Institute & University's Undergraduate Programs accept academic course credit (grade C or better) earned at regionally accredited postsecondary institutions when appropriate to the learner's degree plan. The programs may also accept credit recommendations from the American Council on Education (ACE) and the College-Level Examination Program (CLEP). Articulation agreement leads to additional transfer credit possibilities. Matriculating learners earn credit toward the remaining degree requirements through new learning or prior learning assessment. Credit and requirements for graduation vary by program at Vermont College. Admissions counselors can assist with specific information.

FACULTY

More than 260 full- and part-time scholars, writers, artists, and experts serve as faculty members, equipped with outstanding academic and professional qualifications as well as in-depth experience working with adults. Learners develop close working relationships with the faculty members, who serve as mentors throughout the process. More than 90 percent of the full-time faculty members and 92 percent of the part-time faculty members have a Ph.D. or terminal degree in their field.

ADMISSION

Admission requirements vary by program but rely on a variety of measures. Applicants should send transcripts from previous education, professional references, and narratives detailing life experiences and education goals.

TUITION AND FEES

Tuition varies by program. Undergraduate tuition for 2004–05 is $322 per semester credit hour. Master's programs tuition ranges from $5590 to $6310 per six-month semester. Doctoral program tuition is approximately $7875 per six-month semester. Applicants should contact the Business Office for more specific information.

FINANCIAL AID

General financial aid programs available include the Federal Pell Grant, Perkins, and Stafford Student Loans, and Federal Work-Study Programs. Learners may also be eligible for state-based financial aid. Veteran's benefits are available to eligible veterans enrolled through the Cincinnati, Vermont College, and California centers. Scholarships are also available. Learners should complete a Free Application for Federal Student Aid (FAFSA) and contact the Office of Financial Aid for more information.

APPLYING

For most programs, Union Institute & University accepts and reviews applications for admission on a rolling basis, and admitted learners may begin the program in any semester. Prospective learners should contact the Admissions Office for application information.

CONTACT

Union Institute & University
440 East McMillan Street
Cincinnati, Ohio 45206
Telephone: 513-861-6400
800-486-3116 (toll-free)
E-mail: admissions@tui.edu
Web site: http://www.tui.edu

United States Sports Academy

Continuing Education and Distance Learning

Daphne, Alabama

The United States Sports Academy (USSA) is a nonprofit, private graduate school designed to serve the nation and the world as a sport education resource, with programs of instruction, research, and service. Since 1972, the Academy has been addressing the need to provide high-quality, sport-specific programs. The Academy is accredited by the Commission on Colleges of the Southern Association of Colleges and Schools to award the Master of Sport Science degree (M.S.S.), Level III, and the Doctor of Sport Management degree (D.S.M.), Level V.

DISTANCE LEARNING PROGRAM

Learning experiences and student requirements in distance learning are similar and equivalent to courses offered in the traditional on-campus setting. Courses are taught by an Academy faculty member, who is responsible for advising and facilitating the learning experience during the structured offering of distance learning. The vast majority of the Academy's students are using the distance learning system for part or all of their degree program.

The flexibility of the Academy's distance learning delivery system offers students the ability to pursue educational interests on their schedule and at their location.

DELIVERY MEDIA

Distance learning students at USSA receive a code for the Web-based course and textbooks. The USSA library and its extensive reference database can be accessed through the USSA Web site. All students are required to have access to a computer and the Internet at the time they start the first course.

PROGRAMS OF STUDY

Distance learning offers the student an opportunity to earn a master's degree or a doctoral degree through a Web-based environment, though there is a residency requirement for the doctoral degree.

The Master of Sport Science degree is offered in the following majors: fitness management, sports coaching, sports management, sports medicine, and sports studies. Each major requires 33 semester hours of course work. The Academy offers a dual major in sports management/sports coaching that is 45 semester hours of course work.

The graduate program in fitness management examines issues in health and physical fitness, such as obesity. The fitness major is versatile in that it offers individuals opportunities to pursue careers in corporate, private, public, and not-for-profit organizations.

The graduate program in sports coaching is designed to prepare a student for leadership in the dynamic career of sports coaching. Program objectives are established to prepare each student for the multiplicity of demands involved in the control and operation of individual and team sports. The graduate curriculum is designed to prepare students for further study in sport at a higher level or develop and build their own concentration.

The graduate curriculum in sports management is designed to prepare each student for the increasing number of career leadership opportunities in the field of sport and recreational management. Program objectives prepare the student for a multiplicity of demand involved in the operation of sport programs at various levels. Sports management students are prepared for careers as sports facility managers, sport information directors, sport front office administrators, or sport community relations directors.

The graduate program in sports medicine is designed to prepare students for prevention, management, and rehabilitation of athletic injuries with the multiplicity of demands involved with the successful operation of sports medicine programs at various levels. Upon graduation, successful students receive the United States Sports Academy's certification in sports medicine.

In the sports studies curriculum, students work with their adviser to select the courses from any major to build their own concentration. The courses are selected in accordance to the student's interest.

The Doctor of Sports Management, like the master's degree, is designed for the working professional. The 60 semester hours required to complete the degree may be earned through a combination of on-campus study and distance learning online, mentorship, and directed individualized study. The doctoral program is designed to prepare students to perform with a high degree of efficiency and proficiency in the sports industry, including sport education. There are three specialization areas: finance, marketing, and human resource management. There is also an emphasis in sports medicine for those already licensed or certified in the area. The curriculum is designed to enable students who are recent master's degree graduates, working professionals, sports enthusiasts, athletic administrators, and sports education instructors to achieve their personal, educational, and professional objectives in a sport-specific environment. The degree normally requires three to five years to complete.

Each course requires the student to complete online quizzes, assignments, a research paper, and a proctored final examination. A course is graded as follows: discussion, 10 percent; quizzes, 0 percent; written assignments, 20 percent; class paper, 35 percent; and the final exam, 35 percent.

All degree-seeking students must pass a written comprehensive examination in order to graduate. This examination is the only residential requirement for distance learning students. Students must have completed and passed all course work before taking this examination. Students at USSA have the option of a thesis and a mentorship.

SPECIAL PROGRAMS

USSA has certification programs in several areas, including fitness instructor, human performance analysis, personal trainer, sport agency, sport coaching, sport management, and strength and conditioning. These programs are available to people of all educational backgrounds. The cost for the continuing education program is $150 per course, which is equivalent to 4 continuing education units (CEUs).

CREDIT OPTIONS

A student may transfer up to 15 semester hours from a regionally accredited graduate school as long as such courses are equivalent to courses offered in the Academy's graduate program, credit was earned in the past four calendar years, the student received a grade of B or better in the course(s), and the academic committee approves the transfer of credit. For more information, students should contact the Office of Student Services.

FACULTY

The Academy has more than 30 faculty members. They are located both on-site and at various locations around the country. All faculty members have terminal degrees. The majority of them are specialized in a sport science.

ADMISSION

For full-standing admission to the master's degree program, an applicant must be a graduate of a four-year regionally accredited undergraduate institution, with a cumulative grade point average of 2.5 or better, and obtain either a GRE score of at least 800, an MAT score of at least 27, or a GMAT score of at least 400. In the case in which the student's reported standardized test score (one of the three above) is below the stipulated score, students may still attain full standing by achieving a minimum 3.0 grade point average in their first 12 credits of course work.

TUITION AND FEES

For online delivery, master's degree courses are $400 per semester hour, and doctoral courses are $500 per semester hour. The cost does not include additional fees, textbooks, or shipping. International shipping is slightly higher. Prices are subject to change without notice, though current pricing can always be found on the Academy's Web site (listed at the end of this description).

FINANCIAL AID

USSA has a wide variety of financial aid programs available to qualified students. Students can obtain more information by visiting http://www.fafsa.gov.

APPLYING

Approval of applications from students currently enrolled in a bachelor's program are conditional based upon the successful completion of that degree prior to their commencement of study at the Academy. A student applying for admission to the master's degree program is required to submit the following to the Office of Student Services: a completed application form accompanied by a $50 application fee (the fee is nonrefundable and constitutes part of the admission credentials); an official copy of all college transcripts; three letters of recommendation; an official score report of the GRE, MAT, or GMAT results taken within the last five years; a written personal statement which describes the personal motivation or reasons for desiring a master's degree; and a resume or vita.

A student applying for admission to the doctoral degree program is required to submit the following to the Office of Student Services: a completed application form accompanied by a $100 application fee; an official copy of all college transcripts; three letters of recommendations; an official score report of the GRE (minimum 950), MAT (minimum 40) or GMAT (minimum 500) results within the last five years; a qualifying essay (not to exceed 3,000 words, in narrative form); and a resume or vita.

For further information, the complete catalogs of the United States Sports Academy can be viewed by visiting the Academy's home Web page (listed at the end of this description).

CONTACT

United States Sports Academy
1 Academy Drive
Daphne, Alabama 36526
Telephone: 251-626-3303
800-223-2668 (toll-free)
Fax: 251-625-1035
E-mail: admissions@ussa.edu
Web site: http://www.ussa.edu

The University of Alabama

College of Continuing Studies
Division of Academic Outreach

Tuscaloosa, Alabama

Founded in 1831, the University of Alabama has been selected repeatedly as one of the top fifty public universities in the country. By using technology and flexible formats, the Division of Academic Outreach provides diverse and convenient academic programs to students pursuing educational and personal development.

DISTANCE LEARNING PROGRAM

The Division of Academic Outreach accommodates distance and adult learners who are limited by time, geography, work schedules, or personal obligations. Degrees and courses are available via the Internet, written correspondence, videotape, and videoconferencing.

DELIVERY MEDIA

Academic Outreach delivers high school and college courses over the Internet directly to the student's computer. Students are instructed through a secure Internet site, and they interact with their professors and complete lessons via e-mail. Courses are offered in both synchronous (semester-based) and asynchronous formats.

Through Independent Study, students may select their hours of study and work at their own pace to complete courses through written correspondence. With certain stipulations, the undergraduate courses may be used to complete a maximum of 25 percent of the work leading to the bachelor's degree. Nine of the last 18 hours required for a degree may be taken by written correspondence, provided that all residence requirements have been met.

Academic Outreach delivers undergraduate and graduate courses via videotape to students who cannot attend classes on campus. Courses are filmed as they occur, and videotapes are mailed to students the same week. Students take proctored exams at convenient locations. Videocourses are semester based, with enrollment typically occurring during August, January, and May.

The Intercampus Interactive Telecommunication System (IITS) is a network of conference rooms connected to Vianet, a statewide videoconferencing network. Approximately 120 sites throughout Alabama are equipped with cameras, monitors, and other devices that allow teachers and students to interact as if they were in the same room. Courses are semester based, with enrollment typically occurring during August, January, and May.

PROGRAMS OF STUDY

The University of Alabama offers the following programs through distance learning: B.A. or B.S. in interdisciplinary studies (requires a three-day, on-campus orientation), B.S. in human environmental sciences (general studies), B.S. in human environmental sciences (restaurant and hospitality management), B.S. in mechanical engineering (available in Dothan, Alabama), Bachelor of Science in Nursing (RN to B.S.N.), M.S. in aerospace engineering, M.A. in health studies (health promotion), M.S. in human environmental sciences (family financial planning and counseling), M.S. in human environmental sciences (food and nutrition), M.S. in human environmental sciences (general studies), M.S. in human environmental sciences (interactive technology), M.S. in nursing case management, M.A. in rehabilitation counseling (in Alabama only), and Master of Law and Taxation.

SPECIAL PROGRAMS

The External Degree Program is an interdisciplinary undergraduate distance learning program. Students may apply previously earned academic credits transferred from regionally accredited colleges or earned through national tests such as the College-Level Examination Program (CLEP), independent study, out-of-class learning contracts, correspondence studies, classroom work, and demonstrated prior learning toward a B.A. or a B.S. in interdisciplinary studies.

Applicants must have high school diplomas or minimum General Educational Development (GED) equivalency scores of 50, be 25 years of age or older, and have educational goals that are attainable through the program. As with most of the University's distance programs, applicants need not be Alabama residents.

CREDIT OPTIONS

Applicability of credit toward an undergraduate degree refers to the prerogative of the respective academic divisions to count specific credit toward a student's degree requirements. A maximum of 64 semester hours of two-year college credit may be applied toward graduation requirements. At the graduate level, a maximum of 12 semester hours of work taken as a nondegree student may be applied to the credit-hour requirements for a degree. Responsibility rests with the student to observe the limitations imposed on credit hours, course work, and transfer of credit. Procedures and forms are furnished upon request.

FACULTY

Approximately 180 full-time and 10 part-time faculty members are involved in these programs. Of this group, 99 percent of the full-time faculty members and 90 percent of the part-time faculty members have doctoral or other terminal degrees.

ADMISSION

Formal admission is not required for undergraduate students to enroll in Independent Study or Internet courses. However, admission to the University is required for students who wish to enroll in undergraduate courses delivered via videotape and videoconferencing and for all graduate-level courses. Undergraduate admission to the University requires acceptable evidence of previous academic performance and scores on a recognized admission test. All graduate students must satisfy the University's Graduate School admission criteria.

The Division of Academic Outreach provides services to assist students with the admission process, registration, advising and schedule building, and financial aid. Students should contact Nina Smith for assistance (telephone: 205-348-0089 or 800-452-5971 (toll-free); e-mail: nsmith@ccs.ua.edu).

TUITION AND FEES

Tuition varies by program and format. Students should contact the Division of Academic Outreach for current tuition rates.

FINANCIAL AID

Loans are administered through the Office of Student Financial Services. Academic Outreach offers several scholarships for adult students each academic year. Applications are generally available in the fall semester, and the deadline is usually in early January.

APPLYING

Students may obtain information or complete registration by contacting the Division of Academic Outreach.

CONTACT

Division of Academic Outreach
College of Continuing Studies
The University of Alabama
Box 870388
Tuscaloosa, Alabama 35487-0388
Telephone: 205-348-9278
800-452-5971 (toll-free)
Fax: 205-348-0249
E-mail: disted@ccs.ua.edu
Web site: http://www.academicoutreach.ua.edu

University of Alaska Fairbanks

Center for Distance Education and Independent Learning

Fairbanks, Alaska

In 1917, just fifteen years after the discovery of gold in the heart of the Alaskan wilderness, the Alaska Agricultural College and School of Mines was created by a special act of the Alaska Territorial Legislature. In 1922, the college opened with 6 faculty members and 6 students. Today, the University of Alaska Fairbanks (UAF), whose name was changed in 1931, continues to grow, both in size and stature. In addition to the main campus in Fairbanks, UAF has branch campuses in Bethel, Dillingham, Kotzebue, Nome, and the Interior/Aleutians. UAF is the state's land-, sea-, and space-grant institution. Its College of Rural Alaska has the primary responsibility for Alaska Native education and study, and UAF remains the only university in Alaska that offers doctoral degrees. UAF's colleges and schools offer more than seventy fields of study and a wide variety of technical and vocational programs. All courses are approved and meet the accreditation standards of the Commission on Colleges and Universities of the Northwest Association of Schools and Colleges.

DISTANCE LEARNING PROGRAM

UAF developed a Correspondence Study Program in the late 1950s, but the current Center for Distance Education and Independent Learning (CDE) was created in 1987. The Independent Learning Program offers more than 120 courses and serves approximately 6,000 students throughout the world each year.

Independent Learning courses are open for enrollment any time of the year. Students have up to one year from the date of enrollment to finish course work. Extensions may be available, depending on the circumstances. Students are encouraged to use e-mail to submit lessons to circumvent delays in the standard mailing process.

CDE also supports close to 400 distance-delivered courses offered on a semester basis for several certificate and degree programs through the master's level within Alaska each academic year. The department is part of the College of Rural Alaska, with branch campuses in Bethel, Dillingham, Interior-Aleutians, Kotzebue, and Nome, as well as participating with extended campuses of the University of Alaska Anchorage and University of Alaska Southeast.

DELIVERY MEDIA

A wide range of media, including basic written materials, audiotapes, videotapes, CD-ROMS, electronic mail, and the World Wide Web, is utilized to deliver instruction. Many courses are available online and more are being developed. Not all modes of delivery are available for every course, and students must have access to the appropriate equipment as specified in individual course descriptions. Most interaction between students and instructors is asynchronous in nature and may be via written communication, e-mail, or by phone interview.

PROGRAMS OF STUDY

Approximately 120 independent learning courses can be used to fulfill degree program requirements within the University of Alaska's statewide system or at any other university that accepts the credits. The Center for Distance Education and Independent Learning is not a degree-granting organization. Future plans include delivery of certificates and degrees online.

For students residing in-state, certificates and degrees available through the College of Rural Alaska include a certificate in rural human services; the A.A. in general studies; the A.A.S. in human service technology; the A.A.S. and a certificate in community health, early childhood, educational paraprofessional, information technology specialist, and tribal management; the B.A. in social work; the B.A. and M.A. in rural development; and the B.A. and M.Ed. in education.

Individual course requirements vary for Independent Learning courses and are detailed in the course description. Many courses list prerequisites and it is up to the student to determine if he or she has fulfilled the requirements.

SPECIAL PROGRAMS

The Center for Distance Education and Independent Learning participates in the Defense Activity for Non-Traditional Education Support (DANTES) programs; information is available from base personnel or education officers. Veterans' educational benefits are also applicable. DANTES students must complete a UAF enrollment form as well as the DANTES forms.

People interested in being certified to teach in Alaska find courses available that fulfill teacher certificate and recertification requirements for the State of Alaska Department of Education. Students may choose among several courses that satisfy the Alaska studies and multicultural requirements.

STUDENT SERVICES

Students have access to the state library system and the UAF Rasmuson Library directly or through the Statewide Library Electronic Doorway (SLED). All students can obtain accounts on the University of Alaska computer network, which also gives access to the wider Internet and the World Wide Web. The UAF Writing Center offers free tutoring for student use. Papers are faxed to the center, and a telephone appointment is made between the tutor and the student. Students may not schedule more than one appointment per day. A toll-free UAF math hotline for problem solving and math help is also available for student use. Available hours may change each semester.

CREDIT OPTIONS

Since the Center for Distance Education and Independent Learning is not a degree-granting organization, there is no transfer of credit or credit for prior learning available.

FACULTY

The Independent Learning Program includes approximately 90 faculty members, about half of whom are also full-time members of the UAF faculty and have terminal academic degrees. Adjunct faculty members and discipline professionals are hired to supplement the University's full-time faculty.

ADMISSION

Students may enroll in individual courses any time during the year and have one year to complete the course. There are no admissions requirements or procedures since the Center for Distance Education and Independent Learning is not a degree-granting organization.

TUITION AND FEES

All students enrolled in UAF Independent Learning courses are charged the same tuition whether they are Alaska residents or not. Tuition for 100- to 200-level courses is $99 per credit, 300- to 400-level courses are $112 per credit, and 600-level courses are $222 per credit. The only other costs for courses are materials fees that vary by course and a $25 service fee per course. Students outside the U.S. must submit payment in U.S. dollars and are charged an extra $30 per course plus any additional shipping charges for the delivery of materials. (Actual costs of delivery are determined upon registration.)

FINANCIAL AID

Alaska students who are full-time (enrolled in at least 12 credits per semester) and are taking independent learning courses on a semester basis are eligible for all the types of financial aid available to other students, including Federal Pell Grants, Federal Supplemental Educational Opportunity Grants, State Educational Incentive grants, Bureau of Indian Affairs grants, Federal Stafford Student Loans, and State of Alaska student loans. Students enrolled in regular yearlong courses are not eligible to receive financial aid.

APPLYING

No application is required of students taking Independent Learning courses. Completion of a UAF enrollment form and payment of fees are all that are required of students to take courses. Verification of enrollment and course materials are mailed to the student, and the student may begin the course work.

CONTACT

Curt Madison, Director
Center for Distance Education and Independent Learning
College of Rural Alaska
P.O. Box 756700
University of Alaska Fairbanks
Fairbanks, Alaska 99775-6700
Telephone: 907-474-5353
800-277-8060 (toll-free)
Fax: 907-474-5402
E-mail: distance@uaf.edu
Web site: http://distance.uaf.edu

University of Central Florida

Center for Distributed Learning

Orlando, Florida

The University of Central Florida (UCF) is a major metropolitan research university whose mission is to deliver a comprehensive program of teaching, research, and service. UCF was established in 1963 and opened in the fall of 1968. Its original name, Florida Technological University, was changed by the Florida Legislature on December 6, 1978.

UCF proudly identifies with its geographic region while striving for national and international excellence in selected programs of teaching and research. The University of Central Florida is accredited by the Commission on Colleges of the Southern Association of Colleges and Schools to award degrees at the associate, baccalaureate, master's, and doctoral levels.

DISTANCE LEARNING PROGRAM

UCF delivers courses and programs over the Internet to meet the diverse needs of a growing student population and to fulfill the general University mission.

UCF provides this delivery for those who would not otherwise be able to attend classes on one of the UCF campuses. In the last full academic year, UCF has served 12,884 individual students with Web-based courses.

The course materials and methods were developed by UCF to maximize the distant learner's achievement of course objectives. All distributed learning courses provide full University credit, and are subject to standard campus tuition charges and UCF policies.

DELIVERY MEDIA

To participate in Web-based courses, students must have access to the UCF campus network or another Internet service provider and, at minimum, either a Pentium III PC running Windows 2000 or a Macintosh G4.

Students viewing video streams need a broadband Internet connection, such as cable or DSL, with a download speed of at least 128 Kb, with 256 Kb or greater preferred. Students also need to have at least Microsoft Windows Media Player 6.4, although Windows Media Player 9 is required to take advantage of some playback features.

PROGRAMS OF STUDY

Distance learning degree programs offered by Florida's public universities are generally limited to upper-division and graduate course work. For more information on UCF's programs, students should visit the Web site listed in the Contact section.

The Web-based bachelor's degree in liberal studies leads to either the Bachelor of Arts or Bachelor of Science in liberal studies degrees. The liberal arts track is an honors-linked program available to students seeking an individualized, nontraditional, interdisciplinary major.

The Web-based RN to bachelor's degree in nursing curriculum is available for Florida RNs seeking a Bachelor of Science in Nursing (B.S.N). Some campus attendance is required. Students may complete course work and clinical practicums in five semesters or eighteen months. The School validates registered nurses' knowledge in the areas of adult health, childbearing and child rearing, and psychiatric–mental health.

UCF offers Web-based programs leading to the Bachelor of Science (B.S.), Master of Arts (M.A.), or Master of Education (M.Ed.) degree in technical education and industry training. These programs are for individuals with occupational course work and/or work experience who wish to teach in middle or secondary schools, correctional institutions, postsecondary technical institutes, community colleges, or to become technical trainers in business or industry. Courses for vocational teacher certification, curriculum development, and career and technical education are included.

The Web-based bachelor's degree in health service administration is an upper division curriculum. The program is designed for registered nurses, respiratory therapists, EMTs, radiographers, medical laboratory technologists, dental hygienists, and others holding A.A./A.S. degrees or licenses that are nationally recognized. Students without a background in the health-care industry can also be accommodated to build a background in health service administration to enter the industry.

The B.S. in health information management is designed to prepare managers who are part of a health-care team. The curriculum is approved by the Commission on Accreditation of Allied Health Education Programs.

The video-based Bachelor of Science in Engineering Technology (B.S.E.T.) degree program is comprised of courses that are offered via video streaming, with Internet enhancement. Special arrangements are made for laboratory courses. This track provides an orientation for professional careers in technical management and operations in the manufacturing, sales, service, and construction industries.

The University offers graduate study via the video-based Florida Engineering Education Delivery System (FEEDS), a product of the cooperative effort of the State University System (SUS) and private sector industries in Florida.

FEEDS offers access to high-quality graduate programs and extended studies through the use of live and recorded television, teleconferencing, and computer-aided communication.

The Master of Science (M.S.) in forensic science provides two tracks for full-time students and practicing professionals, forensic analysis and forensic biochemistry. Approximately 60 percent of the course work can be accessed online and the remainder can be taken on site at UCF or other qualified institutions.

The College of Education offers a master's program in exceptional education that leads to an Master of Education or Master of Arts degree. The M.Ed. degree prepares exceptional education teachers to work in programs serving K–12 students with varying exceptionalities. It is designed for teachers already certified in an area of exceptional education. The M.A. program is for noneducation majors or teachers previously certified in another field.

The Master of Nonprofit Management (M.N.M.) provides opportunities for students to prepare for employment or advance their careers in nonprofit organizations. the program is intended to produce graduates equipped with the management skills and analytical skills needed for successful careers in the nonprofit sector.

The online M.Ed. in instructional technology/media, media track, is designed for individuals who wish to become media specialists and work as leaders of school library media programs in public schools. The M.A. track in this same program is focused on educational technology. It is designed for classroom teachers looking for ways to become highly skilled at successfully integrating technology into the curriculum.

The Master of Science in Nursing program is designed to build upon the student's baccalaureate nursing education and professional experience. The goal of the program is to prepare advanced practice nurses to assume leadership positions in a variety of health-care settings.

UCF also offers Web-based graduate certificates. From the College of Health and Public Affairs, students may earn a graduate certificate in nonprofit management, designed to provide graduate-level education for individuals who are currently working in the nonprofit sector or in organizations that are in partnership with the nonprofit sector. From the College of Education, a graduate certificate for community colleges is offered, designed to prepare academic leaders in community colleges by strengthening their knowledge base with practical content in curriculum and instruction. The graduate certificate in professional writing, offered through the Department of English, is designed for immediate relevance in the workplace. A new graduate certificate in nursing and health professional education is designed to prepare nurses and allied health professionals to teach in nursing and health professional programs, health-care institutions and agencies, and in the community. A graduate certificate in domestic violence, offered through the Department of Sociology and Anthropology, is designed for persons working or planning to work in the domestic violence field or whose occupational responsibilities include contact with the victims or perpetrators of domestic violence.

FACULTY

UCF employs more than 1,150 full-time and 280 (FTE) part-time faculty members in the six distinct colleges that are part of the University. Eighty percent of the full-time faculty members have terminal or doctoral degrees. More than 420 resident faculty members have completed an eight-week, in-house faculty development course for Web-based instruction.

ADMISSION

Students who plan to enroll in Web-based courses must be admitted to the University and use the same admission procedures as other students.

TUITION AND FEES

The nonrefundable application fee is $30. The UCF campus card fee is $10. The 2003–04 semester registration fees for residents were $94.42 per credit hour for undergraduate study and $207 per credit hour for graduate study; nonresident fees were $462.02 for undergraduate study and $776.27 for graduate study.

FINANCIAL AID

Information regarding financial aid is available from UCF's Office of Student Financial Assistance online at http://finaid.ucf.edu.

APPLYING

Undergraduate applicants with more than 60 credit hours or who have earned an A.A. degree from a Florida public community college must submit high school transcripts and transcripts from all colleges attended. Applicants with fewer than 60 credit hours must also submit SAT or ACT scores and must meet the freshmen State University System eligibility requirements. Graduate applicants must submit official GRE (or GMAT scores for selected programs) test scores and official transcripts showing a bachelor's degree earned at a regionally accredited institution. The minimum University requirements for admission into a graduate program are a 3.0 GPA on a 4.0 scale or a score of 1000 on the combined verbal-quantitative portions of the GRE or 450 on the GMAT (for programs that require it). Requirements for specific programs are in addition to or different from the minimum University requirements.

CONTACT

Dr. Steven E. Sorg
Assistant Vice President for Distributed Learning
12424 Research Parkway, Suite 256
Orlando, Florida 32826-3271
Telephone: 407-823-4910
Fax: 407-207-4911
E-mail: online@ucf.edu
Web site: http://online.ucf.edu/

University of Colorado at Denver

CU Online

Denver, Colorado

The University of Colorado at Denver is one of four institutions in the University of Colorado system and the only public university in the Denver metropolitan area. It is an urban, nonresidential campus located in downtown Denver. The University of Colorado at Denver was founded in 1965 and is accredited by the North Central Association of Colleges and Schools.

DISTANCE LEARNING PROGRAM

For the student who wants to work on a degree to get ahead or who wants to take a course but has a difficult work schedule, CU Online provides an opportunity to take a course without having to rearrange schedules, commute across town, find a place to park, or sit in a crowded classroom.

Whether the student wants to start a degree, finish a degree, or just take a course or two, CU Online provides educational opportunities that meet these goals. CU Online is the virtual campus of the University of Colorado at Denver, with a variety of collegiate and professional development programs offering more than 200 courses via the Internet.

DELIVERY MEDIA

Students enjoy a greater scheduling flexibility than in a traditional classroom by logging into class several times each week at the times of their choice. Professors use cutting-edge technology such as streaming audio, video, and multimedia slide shows to present materials. Bulletin boards, live chats, threaded discussions, and other technologies let the student interact with their professor and peers.

PROGRAMS OF STUDY

Students take undergraduate and graduate courses in liberal arts and sciences, arts and media, business, education, engineering, public affairs, and architecture and planning. Complete online degree programs include a Bachelor of Arts in sociology and master's degrees in business administration, engineering (geographic information systems), and public administration, with more programs under development. Students should check the Web site for the latest developments. All of the courses may be applied to a degree program at the University of Colorado at Denver or may be transferred to a student's home institution, pending approval.

SPECIAL PROGRAMS

CU Online offers hybrid courses that meet on campus only half as often as more traditional courses, while the remainder is completed online. Hybrid courses follow the same faculty governance policies as the established on-campus courses.

STUDENT SERVICES

Students benefit from a full range of student services, apply for admission, pay tuition, search the course catalog, register for courses, order textbooks, get academic advising, and apply for financial aid—all online.

CREDIT OPTIONS

Students may take credit, noncredit, and CEU courses through CU Online. The methods of evaluation are letter grades or pass/fail.

FACULTY

Four out of five full-time faculty members hold doctoral degrees, and many are actively engaged in their fields outside the classroom. CU Online faculty members are recognized scholars and researchers in their fields, with many years of teaching experience. Not only do they have real-world experience, but many are consultants, advisers, and partners to the leading organizations that frequently hire CU Online graduates.

ADMISSION

Students living in the state of Colorado must be accepted to the University either as degree-seeking or non–degree-seeking students. Students living outside of the state of Colorado do not need to be admitted to take CU Online courses; however, if students wish to complete their degree through CU Online, formal admission must be made. Students may visit the CU Online Web site for further information regarding admission requirements.

TUITION AND FEES

Tuition rates vary between colleges and depending on residency status.

Most undergraduate courses cost approximately $160–$280 per credit hour for resident students. There is a $100 course fee that is added to each online course, a $5 fee for technology resources, and a $10 fee for the student information system. For specific information regarding tuition for online courses, students should visit the CU Online Web site.

FINANCIAL AID

To be eligible for financial aid, students must be enrolled as degree-seeking students at the University of Colorado at Denver. Students may contact the financial aid office for more information at 303-556-2886 or e-mail: finaid@carbon.cudenver.edu.

APPLYING

Admission requirements vary by college and school. To find specific information about applying to the University of Colorado at Denver, students may visit the CU Online Web site.

CONTACT

For more information about CU Online, students should contact:

University of Colorado at Denver
Campus Box 198
P.O. Box 173364
Denver, Colorado 80217-3364
Telephone: 303-556-6505
Fax: 303-556-6530
E-mail: inquiry@cuonline.edu
Web site: http://www.cuonline.edu/petersons

University of Connecticut

College of Continuing Studies

Storrs, Connecticut

Founded in 1881, the University of Connecticut (UConn) is categorized by the Carnegie Foundation among the Doctoral/Research Universities–Extensive, a distinction shared by fewer than 4 percent of America's higher education institutions that confer the widest number and range of degrees. UConn is the only public institution in New England with its own Schools of Law, Social Work, Medicine, and Dental Medicine. The University is accredited by the New England Association of Schools and Colleges.

The College of Continuing Studies (CCS) offers a bachelor's degree program and two master's degree programs that are available online. The College identifies, develops, and provides high-quality, research-based interdisciplinary, academic, professional, and enrichment programs as well as appropriate support services to diverse communities of learners in a fiscally responsible manner. Working with academic and student support units across the University, the College of Continuing Studies provides a gateway linking the University with individuals as well as with corporate and public service sectors statewide, nationally, and internationally. CCS is dedicated to engaging learners in a lifelong academic partnership with the University of Connecticut.

DISTANCE LEARNING PROGRAM

Based on educational demand and market research, the College of Continuing Studies provides a variety of learning opportunities that utilize the most effective and efficient mode of delivery, given the course/program content and the intended learners. Individuals in CCS programs achieve relevant academic, professional, and technical competence and/or the personal enrichment they seek through a student-centered approach that reflects a high-quality education. Students may take individual courses or enroll in one of the online graduate or undergraduate degree or certificate programs. The asynchronous course format allows students to take courses from anywhere in the world. Faculty members are a key component of the online courses and programs and ensure that online students receive a high-quality education and personalized attention.

DELIVERY MEDIA

All online courses are offered completely through the Internet using WebCT in a paced, asynchronous environment. The asynchronous format allows access to courses seven days a week, 24 hours a day, including holidays. Discussion and interactivity among the students and the instructor are a key component of all of the online courses. Much of this interactivity is accomplished using an asynchronous threaded discussion tool within the course. An e-mail system that is internal to the course is used for private communication. Some assignments have been designed for students working in groups. Online programs offered through the College of Continuing Studies are geared toward working adults who need the flexibility to juggle work, family, and academic responsibilities. Courses are accessible using either a PC or a Macintosh. Prospective students are encouraged to review the list of frequently asked questions located at http://continuingstudies.uconn.edu/onlinecourses/faqs.html.

PROGRAMS OF STUDY

The College of Continuing Studies offers a Master of Professional Studies (M.P.S.) and a Bachelor of General Studies (B.G.S.). The online M.P.S. degree offers two fields of study: human resource management and humanitarian services administration. The M.P.S. degree is specifically designed for individuals and practitioners who are developing marketable skills to meet evolving workforce demands, seeking professional development or expanded promotional opportunities, or interested in changing careers. The M.P.S. requires 36 graduate-level credits, including 30 credits of course work and 6 credits of a capstone project toward the end of the program. The M.P.S. also includes an issues-based two-week on-site residency requirement.

The M.P.S. in human resource management is designed to meet the professional development needs of individuals who are currently working in the field of human resource management or who are interested in pursuing a career in human resource management. Interested individuals who do not have human resource management or supervisory experience are strongly encouraged to participate in an internship, which may be taken for course credit. Students may select a career track in either labor relations or personnel or may select a program combining electives from both tracks, depending upon their career interests.

The M.P.S. in humanitarian services administration is designed to meet the educational needs of individuals involved or interested in humanitarian assistance programs, whether in disaster relief or sustainability programs. Students develop theoretical and professional knowledge to operate and conduct humanitarian response missions with nongovernmental, governmental, and international organizations. Students can choose courses related to disaster relief or sustainability, or they may select courses from both areas, depending on their interests. A graduate certificate program (12 credits) is also available in humanitarian services administration.

The B.G.S. degree can be completed online. Two foci are offered: occupational and environmental safety and health and information technology. The B.G.S. program, established in 1977, is an interdisciplinary major designed for returning adults. A student needs at least 60 college credits or an associate degree from a regionally accredited college to be admitted to the program. B.G.S. students work one on one with the same academic adviser through graduation. The adviser and student work together to develop an academic program that suits the student's educational and career goals through an individualized major or by following a B.G.S. focus. B.G.S. alumnae have been accepted into graduate programs at Yale, Princeton, Columbia, MIT, Berkeley, and William and Mary in such fields as medicine, dentistry, law, ministry, and business.

The B.G.S. degree with a focus in occupational and environmental safety and health has served more than 450 students since its inception in 1995. The courses are designed for practitioners and nonpractitioners and provide students with marketable skills and knowledge that are relevant to a broad spectrum of industries and work environments. Students can also use the courses to prepare for the national Certified Safety Professional (CSP) examination, a prestigious designation in the occupational safety and health field.

The B.G.S. degree with a focus in information technology is geared toward preparing students for the variety of information technologies they will encounter in their career paths. This program provides immediate practical benefits and a solid foundation for corporate IT training programs and advanced study by taking a hands-on approach toward the understanding of IT. Courses generally fall under the areas of Web content development and Web system administration.

Undergraduate certificate programs are available in environmental health and safety, Himalayan studies, occupational safety and health, Web content development, and Web system administration. General education courses are also available online and may be taken individually or as part of an undergraduate degree program.

Students may enroll in a degree or certificate program, or they may take individual courses. Online noncredit programs are offered in health-care information technology and project management.

SPECIAL PROGRAMS

Students can take individual courses as nondegree students, allowing working adults to enroll in University of Connecticut undergraduate and graduate courses and earn academic credit without being formally admitted to a degree program. Nondegree study allows high school graduates of all ages to return to college at their own pace and gain the confidence they need to complete their education. If students later choose to apply for a degree program, it is likely that these credits can be applied toward their degree. Taking a course as a nondegree student at UConn is also a convenient way for students from other colleges and universities to take credit courses at UConn and then transfer the credits to their own university. Students in the online programs can take on-campus courses. If students are degree students, they need permission from their advisers. Nondegree students do not need to see an adviser before registering.

STUDENT SERVICES

All major student services are available to online students, including registration services, advising, bookstore ordering, library, e-mail, and tutoring. Technical support is available to all students in online courses.

CREDIT OPTIONS

Students in the B.G.S. program may transfer up to 90 credits that they have earned through other regionally accredited institutions.

FACULTY

The College of Continuing Studies employs full-time and adjunct faculty members. Faculty members who teach online are approved by the department and also teach on-campus courses. All full-time faculty members and all faculty members teaching in the graduate program have earned doctorates. Adjunct faculty members are accomplished practitioners and have the requisite educational experience to make them effective online instructors.

ADMISSION

Applicants to the M.P.S. program must have completed a baccalaureate degree from a regionally accredited college or university. For further admission information for the M.P.S. program, students should visit http://continuingstudies.uconn.edu/mps/academicinfo.html. Applicants to the B.G.S. degree must have an associate degree from a regionally accredited college or university or must have completed at least 60 college credits from a regionally accredited college or university. For further admission information for the B.G.S. program, students should visit http://continuingstudies.uconn.edu/bgs/admissions.html. Students may register for individual courses without matriculating into a program, provided they meet specific course requirements. For course registration information, students should visit http://web.uconn.edu/ccsde/reg/reg.html.

TUITION AND FEES

Undergraduate course fees are $854 per 3-credit course. Graduate course fees are $1366 per 3-credit course. There is a $37 infrastructure maintenance fee for undergraduate and graduate courses. Course fees are calculated on a per-credit basis; current fees are subject to change. Students who enroll in the College's online courses pay the same fees as in-state students. Students should visit the Web site listed below for current fees.

FINANCIAL AID

Financial aid is available to online students who have matriculated into a degree program. For further information, students should contact the Office of Student Financial Aid Services at 860-486-2819 or visit the Web site at http://www.financialaid.uconn.edu.

APPLYING

Application to the M.P.S. degree program is available online at http://continuingstudies.uconn.edu/mps/academicinfo.html. Application to the B.G.S. degree program is available online at https://secure.uconn.edu/~wwwcce/regforms/admissionsapplication.html.

CONTACT

Dr. Judy Buffolino, Director
Distance Education Office
College of Continuing Studies
University of Connecticut
One Bishop Circle, Unit 4056
Storrs, Connecticut 06269-4056
Telephone: 860-486-1080
Fax: 860-486-0756
E-mail: ccsonline@uconn.edu
Web site:
http://continuingstudies.uconn.edu/onlinecourses

University of Dallas

Graduate School of Management Center for Distance Learning

Irving, Texas

The University of Dallas (UD) was founded in 1956 as in independent Catholic university dedicated to excellence in its educational programs.

The Graduate School of Management (GSM) is the largest Master of Business Administration–granting (M.B.A.) institution in the Southwest. GSM was founded in 1966 with a distinctive mission: to create a professionally sound M.B.A. program accessible to individuals who are already employed in business. More than 75 percent of GSM students work full-time. The student body is made up of Americans and international students representing more than sixty countries. The UD main campus is in Irving, adjacent to the thriving Las Colinas business community and near downtown Dallas and Dallas/Fort Worth International Airport.

The Commission on Colleges of the Southern Association of Colleges and Schools (SACS) accredits UD.

DISTANCE LEARNING PROGRAM

GSM began its Internet-based M.B.A. program (IMBA) in 1997 with three courses and 30 students. Now GSM offers the entire M.B.A. core curriculum and nine specializations online. More than 500 students are taking online courses that represent more than 25 percent of all GSM credit hours. GSM has developed more than fifty courses for the IMBA.

While taking an IMBA class, there is no requirement to come to the campus. However, many students take a blend of on-campus and Internet-based courses. Other students take their entire M.B.A. online. There is no distinction made on the transcript between classroom and IMBA courses.

Students are attracted to the GSM because it offers a comprehensive background in the general business disciplines, as well as industry-specific fields of knowledge, such as corporate finance, e-commerce, health services, information technology, marketing, supply chain management, and telecommunications, all online.

Students indicate that the IMBA allows them to fit classes into their hectic business and personal schedule. Many of them travel extensively and can take courses, using a laptop, from a hotel or airport. Others who have been transferred outside of Dallas are able to complete their degree at their new location. Some find that they can effectively merge their family commitments and school responsibilities by taking online courses. An increasing number of students are enrolling in the GSM from outside of the Dallas area, even from outside of the U.S., in order to take advantage the unique GSM IMBA program.

DELIVERY MEDIA

The virtual campus was created with the understanding that students need the ability to organize their class schedules without being confined to a certain time, campus, or even country. Students access the IMBA using a standard Internet connection and Web browser. The courses use an instructor-led, asynchronous method of teaching, which means that students and their professor do not have to be online at the same time. However, both are expected to be online multiple times during the week.

PROGRAMS OF STUDY

The Master of Business Administration degree is offered online with concentrations in corporate finance, health services management, information assurance, information technology, marketing management, market logistics, sports and entertainment management, supply chain management, and telecommunications management. An interdisciplinary option is also available. The M.B.A. program can be completed in three to four trimesters of full-time study. Part-time students normally take 2½ to 3½ years to complete the M.B.A. degree.

Master of Management degrees (post-M.B.A.) and graduate certificates are also available online in any of the above concentrations.

SPECIAL PROGRAMS

GSM has partnerships with Fortune 500 corporations to provide classes to their employees through the Internet. Inquiries are welcomed from other organizations that may be interested in offering graduate business studies to their employees.

STUDENT SERVICES

The primary support structure is the IMBA professor. Class size is kept moderate, thus permitting professors and students to interact with one another.

At the Graduate School of Management there are 5 talented individuals—all of whom have had personal experience with GSM programs—who provide customer support and service for prospective, current, and past students. Each program director specializes in one of the five groups of specialization concentrations offered: finance, management, marketing, operations, and technology.

These professionals work for the students and are their advocates within the GSM community. Each program director stands ready to answer students' questions, address their unique concerns, and guide them through the application, admissions, and registration process—and beyond. Staff members in the Online Learning Department are available to address questions unique to distance learning. A help desk that operates 24 hours a day handles Web- and PC-based questions.

CREDIT OPTIONS

For the M.B.A. program, a maximum of four courses or 12 hours of transfer credits may be applied. A transfer course must be a 3-semester-hour (5-quarter-hour) graduate-level course from an accredited school. The transfer course must not be more than six years old. A grade of at least a B (3.0) is required. For further information, students can contact the GSM Admissions Office at the address below.

FACULTY

GSM professors have business experience in addition to their academic qualifications. They have held positions ranging from entrepreneurs to senior-level executives in large companies. Full-time faculty members engage in consulting within their field, while adjunct professors hold jobs in their area of teaching, thus keeping the classes current and relevant.

ADMISSION

Admission to the University of Dallas College of Business is competitive. The College seeks highly motivated individuals demonstrating potential for management and leadership responsibility and possessing the intellectual ability, initiative, and creativity to excel in its programs as well as in the globally competitive marketplace.

Success in the Master of Business Administration program offered at the Graduate School of Management by the University of Dallas College of Business depends on a number of factors ranging from motivation to practical knowledge to academic ability. The primary purpose of the School's admission criteria and application process is to determine a prospective student's potential to successfully complete the requirements for the M.B.A. degree.

To apply for admission, applicants must hold a U.S. bachelor's degree from a regionally accredited college or university or the international equivalent. International applicants, including permanent residents living in the U.S., must also provide proof of proficiency in the English language. Some applicants meet the Full Admission requirements prior to starting their course work. Others applicants may be permitted to begin a limited number of courses under specific conditions designed to determine their potential to pursue graduate studies. Students who meet any two of the following requirements (and who possess a bachelor's degree as described above) are granted full admission. Applicants who meet any one of the following conditions may be granted conditional admission. Those conditions are a minimum grade point average (GPA) of 3.0 or better (on a 4.0 scale) in the applicant's last 60 hours, GMAT scores of 500 or above, at least 12 semester hours of graduate work at a regionally accredited U.S. college or university with a GPA or 3.2 or better, and five or more years of relevant managerial, professional, or military experience.

Prospective students may apply for admission to the Graduate School of Management for any fall, fall II, spring, spring II, or summer II trimester, or intermester.

TUITION AND FEES

Graduate tuition was $466 per credit hour in 2003–04 for residents and nonresidents.

FINANCIAL AID

U.S. graduate students may obtain financial assistance through various loan programs. The University of Dallas Financial Aid Office (telephone: 972-721-5266; Web site: http://www.udallas.edu/admiss/gradaid.html) has information and application forms for loans.

APPLYING

Those interested are encouraged to contact GSM at the address below or visit the Web site for additional information. Students can apply online from anywhere in the world.

CONTACT

Graduate School of Management
University of Dallas
1845 East Northgate Drive
Irving, Texas 75062-4736
Telephone: 800-832-5622 (toll-free)
E-mail: info@gsm.udallas.edu
Web site: http://www.thedallasmba.com

University of Delaware

UD Online/Distance Learning

Newark, Delaware

A private university with public support, the University of Delaware is a land-grant, sea-grant, space-grant, and urban-grant institution with a rich 250-year history. Its main campus is located in Newark, Delaware, a suburban community situated between Philadelphia and Baltimore. The University offers more than 100 undergraduate majors and more than seventy graduate degrees. The University has been fully accredited by the Middle States Association of Colleges and Schools since 1921. There are more than 21,000 students enrolled at the University as undergraduate, graduate, or continuing education students.

DISTANCE LEARNING PROGRAM

The University's UD Online/Distance Learning system supports more than 3,700 registrations a year in a variety of undergraduate and graduate courses involving twenty-eight academic departments and six degree programs. UD Online offers a way for busy professionals to continue their education on a schedule tailored to their needs.

DELIVERY MEDIA

More than 140 University of Delaware courses are available in videotape, CD-ROM, or Internet formats. Student-faculty interaction is maintained through e-mail, telephone office hours, and chat rooms.

PROGRAMS OF STUDY

Students can use distance learning to pursue the following degree programs:

Bachelor of Science in Nursing: Baccalaureate for the Registered Nurse major (BRN): Nine of twelve required nursing courses are offered in distance learning format. Students are required to enroll in two 1-credit weekend courses held on the Newark, Delaware, campus. The BRN major requires 120 credits for program completion. For more information, students should visit http://www.udel.edu/DSP/BRN/.

Master of Science in Nursing (M.S.N.) with a concentration in health services administration or Master of Science (M.S.) with a major in health services administration: Delivered entirely on the Internet except for a one-day seminar that takes place on the Newark, Delaware, campus. For students at a great distance, special accommodations may be made. For more information, students can visit http://www.udel.edu/DSP/page4.html.

Master of Science in Nursing for the Registered Nurse (RN to M.S.N.) has been developed to build on basic nursing knowledge, enhancing nursing practice in an increasingly complex society. Recognizing the challenges of combining advanced education with professional and personal responsibilities, this program is structured to permit part-time study utilizing fall and spring semesters plus winter and summer sessions. The RN to M.S.N. program requires a total of 134 credits. For more information, students can visit http://www.udel.edu/DSP/RN-MSN/.

Bachelor of Science in Hotel, Restaurant, and Institutional Management (HRIM): The specialized HRIM core courses, as well as most of the required liberal arts and business courses, are available in distance-learning format, except for a required one-week management institute held on the Newark, Delaware, campus. For more information, students can visit http://www.continuingstudies.udel.edu/udonline/hrim/.

Master of Engineering, Mechanical (M.E.M.): A 30-credit, nonthesis program made up of five required courses and 15 credits of graduate electives. Popular concentration, available in distance format, is in composite materials. For more information, students should visit http://www.engr.udel.edu/outreach/MEM.html.

Master of Science in Electrical Engineering (M.S.E.E.): A nonthesis master's program requiring 30 credits of graduate courses, including 6 credits (2 "foundation" courses) chosen from signal processing, devices and materials, or optics and electromagnetics (other options to be added); 24 credits in advanced technical courses with a maximum of 6 credits outside of the department. For more information, students can visit http://www.engr.udel.edu/outreach/MSEE.html.

SPECIAL PROGRAMS

To pursue a graduate degree, engineering professionals may enroll in courses for professional development or may combine distance learning courses with campus courses. A graduate certificate program in composite materials is designed for engineering and science professionals who already possess a bachelor's degree. Students may access the program Web site at http://www.engr.udel.edu/outreach/composites-program.html. In addition, the Fundamentals of Engineering (FE) review course, providing intensive review of the FE exam topics, as well as a review course for the Professional Engineer (PE) licensing exam in environmental engineering, are available via videotape. The environmental PE review is also available on CD-ROM. Further information can be found online at http://www.engr.udel.edu/outreach/fe-video.html for the FE course and http://www.engr.udel.edu/outreach/PE-review.html for the PE course.

The University's dietetic internship is delivered entirely online with the exception of a one-week professional orientation that takes place on the Newark, Delaware, campus. Students complete internship rotations in their local areas. This program is accredited by the Commission on Accreditation for Dietetic Education of the American Dietetic Association. For more information, students can visit http://www.udel.edu/NTDT/internship/.

CREDIT OPTIONS

In order to be eligible for a University of Delaware degree, students must complete either the first 90 or the last 30 credits of the degree program with the University of Delaware. A credit-by-examination option allows students to demonstrate competence obtained through professional experience. Exam requirements are determined by each University academic department.

FACULTY

Of the 998 full-time University faculty members, 87 percent hold the doctoral or terminal professional degree in their field. Approximately 10 percent of the faculty members participate in distance learning instruction.

ADMISSION

An admissions committee considers all academic credentials, including high school and any previous college work. Students transferring from other schools are normally required to have at least a 2.5 grade point average to be considered for admission.

TUITION AND FEES

Students registering as official UD Online/Distance Learning site participants pay $284 per credit hour (undergraduate) or $729 per credit hour (graduate). Students may also register as individual/nonsite participants and pay resident (undergraduate, $246 per credit hour; graduate, $327 per credit hour) or nonresident (undergraduate, $643 per credit hour; graduate, $857 per credit hour) tuition plus a handling fee of $90 per videotaped course. Tuition and fees are subject to change. For current information on fees and tuition, students should visit the Web site listed below.

FINANCIAL AID

The Financial Aid Office administers grants and scholarships, which do not have to be repaid; low-interest loans; and student employment. A need-based financial aid package may include one or more of the following: Federal Pell Grant, Federal Supplemental Educational Opportunity Grant, Federal Perkins Loan, and a Federal Direct Loan. The Federal Direct Parents Loan Program is also available. Delaware residents may also be eligible for need-based funding through General Fund Scholarships and Delaware Right to Education Scholarships. Students must be matriculated and carry at least 6 credit hours per semester.

APPLYING

A completed application consists of the Distance Learning Application for Admission, application fee, and official college and high school transcripts. Due dates for applications are no later than August 1 for fall admission and no later than December 1 for spring admission. BRN and RN to M.S.N. applicants need to provide a copy of their current nursing license.

CONTACT

Dr. Dayle Thorpe
Director of Academic and Professional Programs
UD Online/Distance Learning
214 John M. Clayton Hall
University of Delaware
Newark, Delaware 19716
Telephone: 800-597-1444 (toll-free)
Fax: 302-831-3292
E-mail: ud-online@udel.edu
Web site: http://www.continuingstudies.udel.edu/udonline/

University of Denver

University College

Denver, Colorado

The University of Denver (DU), the oldest independent university in the Rocky Mountain region, is a premier liberal arts university that was founded in 1864. In addition to its rich history, DU is known for its research and high-quality teaching. To augment the traditional undergraduate and graduate programs, this outstanding institution offers innovative graduate programs through its division for working adult professionals—University College. University College was founded in 1983. With more than forty national awards and many other distinctions from its peers, University College of the University of Denver is recognized as one of the very best providers of adult education in the nation. University College offered its first online master's degree program in 1996. Today, it offers five master's degrees online, twenty-nine Certificates of Advanced Study, and numerous individual courses in a variety of subject areas. University College is accredited by the North Central Association of Colleges and Schools.

DISTANCE LEARNING PROGRAM

The University College distance learning program provides the same premier, internationally recognized University of Denver program quality to students who, because of geographic location, work schedule, or personal commitments, would otherwise not have the opportunity to attend DU. The learning experience for the distance student goes beyond the traditional classroom by capitalizing on the advantages of distance learning technology. University College provides an anytime, anywhere support service as well as consistent high-quality instruction. University College has 250 students actively taking courses online from a wide list of states and countries.

DELIVERY MEDIA

All of the University College distance learning master's degrees and Certificates of Advanced Study can be taken entirely online. A wide array of learning techniques is used to help students develop their knowledge, understanding, and problem-solving skills. University College has an entire team dedicated to utilizing emerging technologies and understanding individualized learning styles to enhance the educational experience. University College uses Blackboard® as its courseware management tool. The system is interactive, allows students to work collaboratively in lively discussion boards and chat rooms, and promotes the exchange of ideas and the development of a learning community. This interaction includes extensive communication with faculty members over the Internet, virtual teams, individual and group assignments, online projects, and online papers and connects students to experts from around the world.

PROGRAMS OF STUDY

University College online programs offer five master's degrees and twenty-nine graduate Certificates of Advanced Study. There are no on-campus requirements for any of the distance learning programs. The master's degrees are 54 quarter credit hours and certificates are 18–24 quarter credit hours. For each of the following programs listed, a bachelor's degree is not required for a certificate, and certificate course credits may be applied toward a master's degree.

The Computer Information Systems program is designed for computer professionals as well as for those planning a new career in the computer industry. This flexible program keeps current with today's changing technology and how it relates to new technologies, existing systems, and customers' needs. The online master's degree requires 54 quarter hours of study in five years or less. Typically, it can be completed in 2½ years. In addition, five online certificate programs of advanced study are offered in computer information systems, database administration, distributed object-oriented analysis and design, information security and network administration, and Web design and development technologies. Certificates typically take twelve to eighteen months to complete.

The Environmental Policy and Management program provides a seamlessly blended graduate education that emphasizes ethical management, science-based environmental policies, and professional applications of technical knowledge. The master's degree requires 54 quarter hours of study to be completed in five years or less. Six certificate programs of advanced study are offered in environmental, health, and safety management; environmental information management; environmental management; environmental policy; environmental project management; and natural resource management. Certificates typically take twelve to eighteen months to complete.

The Geographic Information Systems (GIS) program provides great job opportunities for those interested in managing physical facilities, providing services, analyzing markets, and managing information in public agencies or private organizations. The master's degree, designed in conjunction with DU's Department of Geography, allows students in the University College GIS certificate program to transfer up to 24 quarter hours from their certificate. For more information on the master's degree program, students should call 303-871-2513. The certificate program, also designed in conjunction with the DU's Department of Geography, offers working professionals the opportunity to acquire the background information and hands-on-expertise necessary to capitalize on the emerging technology. Certificates typically take twelve to eighteen months to complete.

The Online Professional Studies program is a flexible management and leadership degree program that incorporates both the analytic and interpersonal skills necessary to be an effective manager in a variety of enterprises. Distance students each choose a specific concentration based on their area of interest and career goals. Examples include computer information systems, electronic commerce, environmental policy and management, geographic information systems, leadership, organizational security, project management, technology management, and telecommunication. The online master's degree is structured around a core of 21-quarter hours of required management and leadership courses, including Principled Leadership, Managerial Decision Making, Integrated Public Relations and Marketing Strategies, Financial Analysis, Leading Organizational Change, Enterprise Management, and Graduate Research and Writing. Two certificate programs of advanced study are offered: civic leadership and development and organizational security. Certificates typically take twelve to eighteen months to complete.

The Technology Management program is designed for those who understand the power of leveraging technology in business to create their own competitive advantage. Career opportunities are limitless for those who can create, manage, and use emerging technology. The master's degree requires 54 quarter hours of study to be completed in five years or less. Typically, it can be completed in 2½ years. Four certificate programs of advanced study are offered in electronic commerce, leadership, project management, and technology management. Certificates typically take twelve to eighteen months to complete.

The Telecommunications program fosters an integration of telecommunications technologies and effective management. In an industry driven by new technology, new applications, and an increasing demand for services, professionals need to maintain a current understanding of fundamental issues surrounding those technologies and the regulations which govern them. The telecommunications offerings at University College are designed to help students keep abreast of changes and take advantage of the opportunities change offers. The master's degree requires 54 quarter hours of study to be completed in five years or less. Typically, it can be completed in 2½ years. Four certificate programs of advanced study are offered in broadband, telecommunications management and policy, telecommunications networks, and telecommunications technology. Certificates typically take twelve to eighteen months to complete.

STUDENT SERVICES

University College is dedicated to providing complete student services online. This includes admissions, registration, student advising, online resources through the library, access to the bookstore, and an individualized career counselor. There is a complete support team for technical issues as well as student support and training for Blackboard.

CREDIT OPTIONS

Students may be able to transfer credit earned at other accredited graduate colleges and universities. The credit hours for the certificates may apply toward the related master's degree.

FACULTY

University College has 300 faculty members, all with advanced degrees, who are practicing professionals in the areas in which they teach. At any given time there are 20 to 30 faculty members teaching online. University College engages in advanced and continual training for its faculty members in the methods and application of distance learning.

ADMISSION

Entrance examinations are not required. Students who are applying for admission to the master's degree programs must have a bachelor's degree from a regionally accredited institution and a minimum 3.0 undergraduate GPA. Applicants must also submit an essay, a career goal statement, and letters of recommendation.

TUITION AND FEES

Tuition is $325 per credit hour, and there is a technology fee of $4 per credit hour. Tuition rates remain the same for programs overseas.

FINANCIAL AID

Some financial aid programs are available to assist University College students. The University of Denver's Office of Student Financial Services handles all financial aid applications (http://www.du.edu/sfs/).

APPLYING

To apply for admission to a master's degree program, students must complete a full application, including a degree plan. Registration is available on the University College Web site at http://www.universitycollege.du.edu/registernow/registerinstructions.asp# online. For more information or an application, students should visit the Web site at the address below.

CONTACT

Distance Learning Programs
University College
University of Denver
2211 South Josephine
Denver, Colorado 80208
Telephone: 303-871-3315
800-347-2042 (toll-free)
Fax: 303-871-3070
E-mail: ucolinfo@du.edu
Web site: http://www.universitycollege.du.edu

University of Houston

Educational Technology and Outreach—Distance Education

Houston, Texas

The University of Houston (UH) is the premier urban teaching and research institution in Texas. Founded in 1927, its activities include a broad range of academic programs encompassing undergraduate, graduate, and professional education; basic and applied research; and public service programs. Its professional schools include architecture, business, education, engineering, hotel, law, optometry, pharmacy, and social work. It is the doctoral degree granting and research-oriented component of the University of Houston System.

Serving more than 34,000 students, University of Houston educational programs include full-time programs for traditional students and part-time and evening programs for employed individuals. Research laboratories and institutes work directly with area corporations and governments, while public service programs contribute to and enhance the cultural and social climate of the community. UH has placed special emphasis on outreach and access for students, both locally and internationally.

DISTANCE LEARNING PROGRAM

Serving more than 16,000 students annually, UH Distance Education offers junior-, senior-, and graduate-level credit courses each semester. UH has the highest number of upper-level and graduate enrollments in distance education courses of any university in the state of Texas. Students may complete degrees through a combination of classes offered online, via television and/or videotape, and through face-to-face or live interactive classes at three off-campus sites in the greater Houston area.

DELIVERY MEDIA

UH Distance Education courses are delivered face-to-face, live interactive (compressed video) at off-campus sites, or asynchronously via tape, cable, public broadcast, or online. Students in asynchronous classes may be required to participate in scheduled, real-time sessions with the instructor and/or other class members. Special arrangements must be made for lab requirements in some degree programs. Proctored exams are arranged as needed. In order to take classes through UH Distance Education, students must have access to the Internet and have a reliable e-mail address.

PROGRAMS OF STUDY

UH Distance Education students may complete degrees in several fields of study. All admissions, degree program requirements, course work, and prerequisites are the same as for on-campus students. Courses generally carry 3 credits. The number of credits needed for degree completion varies by program. Students can obtain more detailed information through the UH Distance Education Web site at the address listed below.

Undergraduate Distance Education program areas include consumer science and merchandising, English, history, hotel and restaurant management, and technology leadership and supervision. Undergraduate courses are available at the junior and senior level. Freshman- and sophomore-level courses may be taken on the UH campus or transferred from other institutions.

Graduate degree program areas available through Distance Education include hospitality management and kinesiology. In the Houston metro area, graduate degrees in computer science, educational leadership, health, industrial engineering and post-baccalaureate teacher certification are available at off-campus teaching centers. Most of these programs are 36-hour, non-thesis options.

Additional credit courses outside of these program areas are available each semester. Students not seeking a degree may enroll in a limited number of selected credit courses.

STUDENT SERVICES

University of Houston's award-winning Distance Education program provides students access to excellent academic support services.

Library support is provided for enrolled students through access to the UH Online Catalog; support includes borrowing privileges, reference services, remote access to electronic databases, guides to research, mail delivery of journal articles on request, and cooperative arrangements with other libraries.

Computer support services that are available to all enrolled students include e-mail and a World Wide Web browser. Documentation, training, and software are also available.

These services for Distance Education students include admissions (online and via mail), registration (online and via telephone), fee payment (online and via telephone and mail), book and videotape ordering (online and by telephone, fax, and mail), remote-site proctored exams, online paper exchange (at the discretion of the instructor), and online advising.

The University of Houston is an equal opportunity institution. Accommodations on the basis of disability are available. For more information, students should contact the Center for Students with Disabilities (telephone: 832-842-7104, TTY: 713-749-1527, Web: http://www.uh.edu/csd/).

CREDIT OPTIONS

Upon application for admission, students must submit transcripts from work completed at all other postsecondary institutions. The amounts and types of credit transferable to the University of Houston depend on the degree program.

FACULTY

The University of Houston has 1,900 full- and part-time faculty members. All UH faculty members teaching Distance Education courses participate in special training programs and ongoing assessment.

ADMISSION

Undergraduate admission is based on graduation from an accredited high school, college transfer, or entrance examination, or through a combination of these criteria. Graduate applicants must have an earned bachelor's degree from an accredited institution. Individual programs have additional specific requirements.

TUITION AND FEES

In 2004–05, tuition and fees for one 3 credit hour undergraduate course are $705.50 for residents and $1479.50 for non-residents; for a graduate course, the cost was $849.50 for residents and $1623.50 for non-residents.

For two courses (6 credit hours), the undergraduate cost is $1150 for residents and $2698 for non-residents; the graduate cost is $1438 for residents and $2986 for non-residents. Rates are subject to change. Additional college fees may apply.

FINANCIAL AID

General financial aid programs through the University of Houston include the Texas Public Education Grant, the Texas Public Educational State Student Incentive Grant, Federal Pell Grant, the Federal Supplemental Educational Opportunity Grant, the Federal Perkins Student Loan, the Hinson-Hazelwood College Student Loan, the Federal Stafford Student Loan, the Federal Parent Loan Program, and other loan and scholarship opportunities based on merit or need. In 1999–2000, approximately 65 percent of all University of Houston students received some form of financial assistance.

APPLYING

To enroll in any UH credit course, students must first be admitted to the University of Houston. Complete admission information is available through the UH Distance Education Web site at the address listed below. The Texas Common application is available on the World Wide Web at http://www.applytexas.org for undergraduate, graduate, and international admissions.

CONTACT

Distance Education Adviser
Educational Technology and University Outreach
Distance Education
University of Houston
111 C.N. Hilton
Houston, Texas 77204-3051
Telephone: 713-743-8627
Fax: 713-743-3300
E-mail: DEadvisor@uh.edu
Web site: http://distance.uh.edu

University of Houston Clear Lake

University of Houston–Clear Lake

Distance Education Program

Houston, Texas

The University of Houston–Clear Lake (UHCL) is located just minutes from downtown Houston, amid the pleasant recreational environment of Clear Lake, Galveston Bay, and the Gulf of Mexico. NASA's Johnson Space Center is nearby, making the campus a hub of technology in a relaxing natural environment. The University of Houston–Clear Lake is the largest upper-level educational institution in the nation, serving a diverse student population from the state, the nation, and abroad by offering programs on and off campus.

The Commission on Colleges of the Southern Association of Colleges and Schools accredits UHCL to award bachelor's and master's degrees. The School of Education's programs are fully accredited by both the National Council for Accreditation of Teacher Education (NCATE) and the State Board for Educator Certification (SBEC).

DISTANCE LEARNING PROGRAM

UHCL offers the Master of Science degree in instructional technology and the Master of Science degree in software engineering completely online. In addition, the School of Education offers certificates, which can be completed entirely online: the Technology Application Certificate for all grade levels, the Online Distance Educator Certificate, and the Master Technology Teacher Certificate. UHCL will be offering the foundation courses for the Master of Business Administration degree program online in 2004. Undergraduate terms are sixteen weeks in length for the fall and spring terms, while summer terms are nine weeks in length.

DELIVERY MEDIA

WebCT is the courseware system used for all UHCL online classes. Most online class sections are limited to 23 registrants. To participate in online degree programs, students must have a computer and access to the Internet. Prospective students should review the requirements listed on UHCL's distance education Web site for required hardware and software, which students need to be successful in online classes.

PROGRAMS OF STUDY

The online degree programs currently available are the Master of Science in software engineering offered by the School of Science and Computer Engineering and the Master of Science in instructional technology offered by the School of Education. The School of Education also offers the following certificates, which can be completed online: the Technology Application Certificate for all grade levels, the Online Distance Educator Certificate, and the Master Technology Teacher Certificate. UHCL's online classes carry the same accreditation and provide the same credit toward a degree as classes taken onsite at the main campus or at one of the University of Houston System Centers. For an overview of degree requirements, prospective students should visit UHCL's distance education Web site listed at the end of this description and click on Academic Programs.

SPECIAL PROGRAMS

Through the University of Houston–Clear Lake's participation in the Electronic Campus program of the Southern Regional Education Board, UHCL students are provided with increased opportunities to pursue certified degree programs via distance learning by removing out-of-state tuition barriers. Participating institutions offer their Electronic Campus programs at the in-state rates to qualified students. For additional information, students should visit the Electronic Campus Web site at http://www.electroniccampus.org.

CREDIT OPTIONS

Master's degree programs require a minimum of 30 semester hours; at least the final 24 hours must be credit hours earned at UHCL. UHCL's Distance Education Academic Advising Coordinator is available by telephone (281-275-3325), e-mail (gabriel@cl.uh.edu), and regularly scheduled chat room office hours to answer students' questions regarding online degree programs. Prospective students should visit UHCL's distance education Web site listed at the end of this description and click on Advising to check on chat room hours and/or e-mail the Distance Education Advisor.

FACULTY

UHCL faculty members must meet stringent educational and background criteria and are considered subject-matter experts in their fields. Faculty members are initially trained in meeting the needs of students at a distance and encouraged to participate in continuing education opportunities to ensure implementation of the latest pedagogical techniques, which positively impact student-learning outcomes.

ADMISSION

All applicants must present documented evidence that they meet the appropriate admissions requirements, including a completed application for admission and the nonrefundable $35 application fee ($70 for international students). Official transcripts and confirmation of degrees or diplomas of any and all academic studies attempted at other colleges/universities must be submitted prior to enrollment. Two sets of official transcripts in the original language and English translation describing all academic studies completed or attempted must be on file before evaluation can proceed. International students must also submit an official TOEFL score report with minimum or higher scores.

TUITION AND FEES

The tuition rate for graduate distance education courses is approximately $1100 ($366.67 per semester hour); this rate is subject to change. The University may change tuition rates, student fees, and other charges without notice when so directed by the Board of Regents. Other general expenses include textbooks (ordered online). Some courses require students to purchase specific software packages.

FINANCIAL AID

Students may seek financial assistance in the form of loans, grants, and scholarships through the Office of Financial Aid and Veterans Affairs. The Free Application for Federal Student Aid (FAFSA) is available online at http://www.fafsa.ed.gov/. Applicants may contact the University's financial aid office by telephone (281-283-2481) or by visiting UHCL's distance education Web site listed below and clicking on Financial Aid to e-mail the financial aid staff.

APPLYING

Students must submit an application for admission by fax or mail or online at the UHCL Web site listed below and clicking on Admission. When all required documentation has been submitted and the file is complete, the student is eligible to register for classes. Students may register for classes by telephone or online by accessing the EASE On-Line Registration System. Students can review registration guidelines on UHCL's Web site at http://www.uhcl.edu/admissions and clicking on Registration. Students may use a credit card to pay tuition fees by telephone or online or via mail by the fee payment deadline.

CONTACT

Kate Finstad, Director
Telephone: 281-283-3032
E-mail: finstad@cl.uh.edu

Lisa Gabriel, Academic Advising Coordinator
Telephone: 281-275-3325
Fax: 281-275-3307
E-mail: gabriel@cl.uh.edu

Distance Education Program
University of Houston–Clear Lake
2700 Bay Area Boulevard
Box 101
Houston, Texas 77058
Telephone: 281-283-3031
Fax: 281-283-2119
E-mail: disted@cl.uh.edu
Web site: http://www.uhcl.edu/disted

University of Idaho

Engineering Outreach and Independent Study in Idaho

Moscow, Idaho

The University of Idaho, established in 1889, is the land-grant institution for the state of Idaho. The University has a student population of more than 13,000 and offers degree programs in the liberal arts, sciences, agriculture, architecture, engineering, natural resources, and law. Extended program delivery and outreach activities are central to the University's mission. The University of Idaho is a member of the National Association of State Universities and Land-Grant Colleges and the National Commission on Accrediting. The University is accredited by the Northwest Commission on Colleges and Universities.

DISTANCE LEARNING PROGRAM

Using innovative technology, the Engineering Outreach (EO) program offers complete distance-delivered graduate degree programs in ten disciplines. The program delivers more than eighty courses per semester to over 350 students in locations around the world. Some undergraduate courses are also available to students who are completing undergraduate degrees or who need to take prerequisite courses before beginning an advanced degree.

The Independent Study in Idaho (ISI) program, a consortium of four Idaho colleges and universities, offers more than 100 undergraduate, graduate, and high school courses. Independent Study in Idaho has been providing courses to students for more than twenty-eight years, currently in over thirty-one academic areas.

DELIVERY MEDIA

Engineering Outreach uses DVD, videotape, Internet, and CD technology in an integrated approach to deliver courses to students at a distance. Courses do not require attendance at the University of Idaho campus. They are professionally produced in studio classrooms and are offered to students on a semester schedule. Students must complete the courses within the semester deadlines.

Independent Study in Idaho's self-paced courses are delivered online or in print format, and some courses are supplemented with videotapes or CDs. Students may register at any time and they have a full year to complete the course. Courses do not require attendance at or admission to any of the consortium institutions.

PROGRAMS OF STUDY

Engineering Outreach courses carry regular University of Idaho credits that may be used toward a degree at the University of Idaho or transferred to other institutions. By taking courses through Engineering Outreach, a student can obtain a graduate degree in biological and agricultural engineering with an emphasis in water and management (M.S. and M.Engr.), civil engineering (M.Engr.), computer engineering (M.S. and M.Engr.), computer science (M.S.), electrical engineering (M.S. and M.Engr.), engineering management (M.Engr.), geological engineering (M.S.), mechanical engineering (M.Engr.), psychology with an emphasis in human factors (M.S.), and teaching mathematics (M.A.T.).

Independent Study in Idaho courses carry credits that may be used toward a degree at the University of Idaho or transferred to other institutions. The courses may also be used to fulfill requirements for a real estate license or for professional advancement. College courses are offered in the areas of accounting, agricultural economics, anthropology, business, child and family studies, dental hygiene, economics, education, English, environmental science, family and consumer science, health-care administration, history, hotel/restaurant management, journalism and mass media, justice studies, library science, mathematics, microbiology, museology, music history, philosophy, physics, political science, psychology, real estate, social science, sociology, Spanish, and special education.

SPECIAL PROGRAMS

Engineering Outreach offers certificates and noncredit short courses in selected areas for students at a distance. Short courses are typically 12 hours in duration and are designed for background study or professional advancement. Admission to the University is not required for short courses. A certificate indicates that a student has successfully completed a series of predetermined credit classes in a specific emphasis area. Certificates are issued by academic departments and are noted on transcripts. With approval, the certificate courses may also be included in a student's graduate degree study plan. For complete details, students should visit the Engineering Outreach Web site, which is listed at the end of this description.

Independent Study in Idaho offers focused courses in the areas of library science and real estate. The library science program consists of fourteen courses, allowing students to fulfill specific state teaching certification requirements, including the Education Media Generalist Endorsement. Independent Study also offers three courses that help meet the education requirements for an Idaho real estate salesperson's license or an Idaho real estate broker's license. The real estate courses are approved by the Idaho Real Estate Commission.

STUDENT SERVICES

Communication with faculty members is facilitated by e-mail and toll-free telephone numbers. Current information about the programs and courses is available on the Internet. Students may register online or by fax, phone, or mail. All Engineering Outreach students have access to the University of Idaho Library's database.

CREDIT OPTIONS

The master's degree programs require a minimum of 30 to 36 credits. A combined total of 12 transfer, correspondence, nondegree, or approved overaged (more than 8 years old) credits may be used toward the degree. With the consent of the student's committee and the College of Graduate Studies, some credits may be transferred to the University of Idaho from other institutions that grant similar graduate degrees.

FACULTY

Up to 80 University of Idaho faculty members teach through Engineering Outreach each semester. More than 90 percent hold doctorates in their fields of expertise. Independent Study in Idaho draws experienced faculty members from the University of Idaho, Boise State University, Idaho State University, and Lewis and Clark State College.

ADMISSION

Requirements for admission to EO programs vary by program and department. Students should check online to see the current admission requirements for each course or degree program. ISI students may register for courses without being admitted to any institutions in the consortium.

TUITION AND FEES

Engineering Outreach fees are currently $457 per credit hour for students enrolled in a graduate program and for all graduate-level courses or $430 per credit hour for non-degree-seeking students in undergraduate courses. There are no additional fees for nonresidents.

Independent Study in Idaho fees are currently $100 per undergraduate credit hour and $115 per graduate credit hour, with a $25 administrative fee per course.

Course fees are subject to change at any time by the Board of Regents of the University of Idaho. Students should visit the Web site listed below for current fees for both programs.

FINANCIAL AID

Engineering Outreach degree-seeking students may be eligible for federal financial aid. Determination for eligibility is made by the Student Financial Aid Services Office. Students enrolled in Independent Study in Idaho courses are not eligible for financial aid.

APPLYING

Applications for both programs may be completed online or with registration forms provided in Engineering Outreach or Independent Study in Idaho catalogs. There is a $55 fee ($60 for international students) for Engineering Outreach students applying for graduate admission. Students should contact the University of Idaho College of Graduate Studies at http://www.grad.uidaho.edu for more information regarding graduate policies.

CONTACT

For information about Engineering Outreach:
Diane Bancke
Engineering Outreach
P.O. Box 441014
Moscow, Idaho 83844-1014
Telephone: 800-824-2889 (toll-free)
Fax: 208-885-9249
E-mail: outreach@uidaho.edu
Web site: http://www.uidaho.edu/eo

For information about Independent Study in Idaho:
Mandy Buck
Independent Study in Idaho
P.O. Box 443225
Moscow, Idaho 83844-3225
Telephone: 877-464-3246 (toll-free)
Fax: 208-885-5738
E-mail: indepst@uidaho.edu
Web site: http://www.uidaho.edu/isi

University of Illinois

University of Illinois Online

Urbana, Illinois

Ever since the first student walked through its doors in 1867, the University of Illinois (U of I) has been a tremendous resource for the State of Illinois. Founded in response to the federal Land Grant Act of 1862, the University immediately met an important need of providing higher education opportunities for working-class people.

For more than 135 years, the University has educated hundreds of thousands of sons and daughters of Illinois, the nation, and the world. The U of I Alumni Association is the second largest in the country, drawing its membership from about 520,000 living alumni.

The University of Illinois continually seeks to expand its critical role in the economic, educational, and technological health of the state. University operations have a direct yearly impact of $4.6 billion on the state's economy, a payback more than seven times greater than the state's annual tax investment. More than 68,000 jobs are directly tied to the University, including nearly 9,000 manufacturing and construction jobs and nearly 20,000 jobs tied to spending by staff, students, and visitors.

University of Illinois Online (U of I Online) is the central source for information regarding the online degree programs, online courses, and public service activities offered by the Chicago, Springfield, and Urbana-Champaign campuses of the University of Illinois.

The three campuses are fully accredited by the North Central Association of Colleges and Schools. Many of the individual programs are additionally accredited by associations specific to their fields of study.

DISTANCE LEARNING PROGRAM

Established in winter of 1997, U of I Online is a university-wide initiative providing coordination and support to the three campuses of the University of Illinois (Chicago, Springfield, and Urbana-Champaign) in the area of online education and public service. Its primary goal is to increase the number of high-quality online education programs available to place-bound and time-restricted students in the U.S. and internationally.

During its brief history, U of I Online has supported the development of more than forty-nine new online programs (including professional degrees, master's degrees, and several baccalaureate-completion programs). Several U of I Online master's programs have already had four or more graduating classes. During the spring 2003 semester, the three campuses reported 8,089 total enrollments with 7,459 of these via the Internet.

U of I Online is administered through the Office of the Vice President for Academic Affairs. An Online Management Committee, with representatives from all three campuses, serves as the core planning group for U of I Online programs and services. In addition, a small administrative staff attends to intercampus coordination, public relations and outreach, program development, support, research, and evaluation.

DELIVERY MEDIA

Online courses can be quite varied in their overall approach to the teaching and learning process, but they often have certain characteristics in common. In most online courses, students use a computer to connect to a course site on the World Wide Web. Standard classroom books and printed materials are typically used in combination with online lectures, assignments, and supplementary course materials. Some courses have formal lectures, similar in length and content to lectures given in face-to-face classes. Online lectures may be entirely text-based or consist of some combination of text, graphics, sound and video. Other courses break the content up into smaller units or abandon the lecture entirely, instead relying on group discussion and other types of learning activities.

Students communicate with their professors and other students via e-mail and electronic submissions. The courses are designed so that students receive course assignments, complete them on their own time, and then return them as electronic documents. Instructors evaluate them and provide feedback. Many courses also use, as an integral part of the course, a threaded discussion forum, which students can use to share information, collaborate, and interact with other members of the class.

Depending on the course design, students may take tests or exams online or go to a testing room on campus or at a local community college. Additionally, some courses and programs may require predetermined trips to campus, which students should plan for before registering.

Students should expect to spend as much time, or perhaps more, for study as they would for a classroom course since they are managing their own learning using the online information and materials. This requires that they be self-disciplined, motivated, and have some skills using a networked computer and a Web browser. The content and rigor of the online courses offered by the University of Illinois is generally equivalent to the on-campus version of the same course. In fact, in some cases, on-campus and off-campus students are combined into the same course section.

PROGRAMS OF STUDY

U of I Online offers programs of study leading to bachelor's, master's, and professional degrees and to certificates.

Bachelor's degrees can be earned in four areas: computer science, English, history, and liberal studies.

Graduate programs lead to the Master of Arts in educational leadership (MTL), the Master of Business Administration Online, the Master of Computer Science, Master of Engineering, Master of Health Professions Education; and the Master of Science in electrical or mechanical engineering.

Other master's degrees offered include agriculture education; community college teaching and learning; curriculum, technology, and education reform; global human resource development; library and information science (LEEP); management information systems; and public health informatics (MPH).

A professional degree can be earned in the Continuation Curriculum Option (CCO) pathway to the Doctor of Pharmacy.

The wide range of certificate programs include business English online; career specialist studies; certified fire fighter II; computer science (information systems, networks and distributed systems, software engineering, systems software); CME online–specialty needs for primary care physicians; e-business e-commerce; electrical and computer engineering (integrated circuits, power and energy systems, telecommunications and signal processing); engineering (material, materials failure); GME core curriculum; health informatics; math teacher link; NetMath; nonprofit management; philosophy; planning commissioner online; renewing public housing; school nursing; specialist in blood bank technology; teaching certificate in nursing education; the culture of U.S. business, and veterinarian education online.

Professional development sequences are available in community college teaching and learning; dairy science; finance engineering and risk management; and translation, French.

SPECIAL PROGRAMS

The University of Illinois offers several Guided Individual Study (GIS) courses and other special programs. Because these offerings change frequently, students should refer to the Office of Continuing Education's Academic Outreach Web site for more information (http://www.continuinged.uiuc.edu/outreach/).

STUDENT SERVICES

The University of Illinois provides a wide variety of support services to online students. Detailed information about these services is available at the following Web sites: http://www.online.uillinois.edu/students/academic-services.asp and http://www.online.uillinois.edu/students/studentsupport.asp.

CREDIT OPTIONS

Credit options vary depending upon the individual program of interest as well as the campus from which it is offered. Students should visit http://www.online.uillinois.edu/admissions/index.asp for detailed information.

FACULTY

Online courses or programs offered by the three campuses of the University of Illinois are taught by many of the same professors who teach in-person. Approximately 95 percent of all online faculty members hold a doctoral degree. Approximately 75 percent of all online faculty members are employed full time.

ADMISSION

Admission requirements and procedures vary depending upon the individual program of interest as well as the campus from which it is offered. Detailed information concerning these requirements and procedures is available at http://www.online.uillinois.edu/admissions/index.asp.

TUITION AND FEES

Tuition and fees for U of I Online courses vary from campus to campus and program to program. In many cases, the costs are similar to those for on-campus classes at the University of Illinois. There are, however, some exceptions. General information about the tuition and fees for courses on each campus is provided at http://www.online.uillinois.edu/admissions/tuition.asp.

FINANCIAL AID

Financial aid varies from campus to campus. For detailed information see http://www.online.uillinois.edu/admissions/financial.asp.

APPLYING

The application process varies from campus to campus. Please contact the individual program of interest regarding the application process and requirements.

CONTACT

University of Illinois Online
176 Henry Administration Building
506 South Wright Street, MC 353
Urbana, Illinois 61801
Telehone: 217-244-6465
866-633-UIOL (8465)
(toll-free)
Fax: 217-333-5040
E-mail: uiol-info@uillinois.edu

University of Illinois at Urbana-Champaign

Curriculum, Technology, and Education Reform Program

Champaign, Illinois

Since its founding in 1867, the University of Illinois at Urbana-Champaign (UIUC) has earned a reputation as a world-class leader in research, teaching, and public engagement. Located in east central Illinois in the twin cities of Urbana and Champaign (combined population 100,000), the University is the state's flagship public university. The rich and varied academic environment of UIUC means that students are exposed to a wide range of intellectual opportunities and substantial resources and support with which to pursue ideas.

DISTANCE LEARNING PROGRAM

The Department of Educational Psychology, which is ranked among the top educational psychology departments in the nation, is located in the College of Education—also one of the best in the nation. Teachers, administrators, and technology coordinators are now offered the option of pursuing a master's degree in the areas of curriculum, technology, and education reform (CTER) in an online format. This program is not solely a professional development program. The courses have been put together to offer hands-on technology training that enables education professionals to integrate technology into their classroom and to enhance students' understanding about new technologies and how they impact society.

DELIVERY MEDIA

Students enrolled in CTER online courses are expected to have basic knowledge of a microcomputer operating system (Windows or Mac) and general knowledge of such software tools as word processors, e-mail software, and Web browsers. CTER instructors use a blend of synchronous and asynchronous technologies to teach their courses. Before starting with the program, admitted students take part in an orientation that prepares them to take classes and interact in the online classroom environment. This orientation also provides training in the technologies that are used in the program.

PROGRAMS OF STUDY

The College of Education offers an online Master of Education (Ed.M.) degree for practicing teachers and administrators with a focus on curriculum, technology, and education reform. This offers an opportunity to earn a coherent, high-quality master's degree online, with most of the interactions through personal computers and Internet connections at home or at local schools. CTER comprises eight online courses (32 credit hours). For CTER online, there are five required and three elective courses, some of which are offered in sequence during six academic semesters. CTER students begin the program with an orientation program that is offered online and in a two-day on-campus visit. In this orientation, students receive a University e-mail account, library card, a CD-ROM with communication tools to be used during the program, and additional training in the tools and applications that are used in the online courses.

The Graduate College permits master's degree candidates five years from the date of the student's first enrollment in Graduate College to complete degree requirements. This enables a student whose professional or personal commitments prohibit the attendance of graduate school on a full-time basis to enjoy considerable flexibility in planning a program. Students are required to notify the department of their intent to graduate. Students unable to complete the degree requirements within this time limit must petition for an extension of time.

STUDENT SERVICES

Upon admission to the Master of Education program, each student is assigned an academic adviser in an area of specialization. The student and adviser plan a program of study to meet the student's individual goals and general degree requirements.

CREDIT OPTIONS

A Master of Education candidate may petition to transfer up to 2.5 units of graduate credit earned at other universities to apply toward the 8-unit requirement. Work involved must be at the graduate level and must have been completed within the last five years with grades of A or B. A petitioner must have completed at least 2 units at the University of Illinois at Urbana-Champaign.

FACULTY

The CTER faculty of approximately 100 members is made up of professors in the College of Education who reflect a wide diversity of experience, culture, and interests. More than half are women, and 30 percent are either African American, Hispanic, or from another underrepresented population.

Whether exploring what qualities are found in the most successful public school administrators or conducting studies on children's cognitive development, the faculty members understand that teachers are charged with finding real solutions for real problems. Faculty research and scholarship lead to better models of professional practice and create a dynamic setting that improves the learning environment for the students. These internationally known faculty members are in high demand as collaborators and partners in research efforts around the world. These partnerships, beyond their role in expanding the impact of their work, also provide a solid financial foundation for continuing excellence. Faculty research initiatives have secured an average of $9 million each year from state, federal, and private sources. This funding is an investment in the future of the educational field, providing new knowledge, supporting graduate students, and supplying resources to classroom teachers in local schools.

ADMISSION

CTER, together with the Department of Educational Psychology, carefully considers all applicants for graduate study. The undergraduate GPA should be at least 3.0 for the last 60 hours of undergraduate work, and the graduate GPA should be at least 3.5. An applicant should have earned at least a 1200 on the verbal and quantitative sections of the GRE. An applicant whose measures fall below the guidelines may be accepted for graduate study when experience, references, or other information strongly suggest that success in a graduate program is highly probable. The program admits 25 students each year.

TUITION AND FEES

For the 2004–05 academic year, tuition and fees per online course are $1468. Students are also responsible for the cost of an Internet provider, textbooks, required hardware and software, and travel and accommodations for any on-campus instruction.

FINANCIAL AID

Students must be enrolled in at least two courses each semester that financial aid is requested. More information is available from the Financial Aid office.

APPLYING

Students must submit the completed admission application; the $40 application fee; original (signed and sealed) copies of all undergraduate and graduate transcripts; three letters of reference, preferably from persons who can speak about the scholarly potential of the applicant; a support letter signed by the applicant's principal or school administrator indicating awareness and support of the student's participation; and Graduate Record Examination (GRE) scores. All students are required to attend a face-to-face weekend orientation meeting. The application deadline for the program, which begins in June, is February 15 every year.

CONTACT

Norma Scagnoli, Program Coordinator
Curriculum, Technology, and Education Reform
Educational Psychology
188P Education Building
University of Illinois at Urbana-Champaign
1310 South 6th Street MC 708
Champaign, Illinios 61820
Telephone: 217-244-3315
E-mail: scagnoli@ uiuc.edu
Web site: http://cter.ed.uiuc.edu/

University of Illinois at Urbana-Champaign

Graduate School of Library and Information Science

Champaign, Illinois

The University of Illinois at Urbana-Champaign is considered one of the finest universities in the world. With a wealth of resources and highly ranked departments, the University has long been recognized for accomplishments in research and graduate education. Illinois boasts the third-largest academic research library in the United States, which includes a separate library and information science (LIS) library.

DISTANCE LEARNING PROGRAM

The University extends its program in library and information science through an online scheduling option called LEEP. Candidates can complete the ALA-accredited Master of Science (M.S.) degree or certificate of advanced study (CAS). The LEEP server provides the Graduate School of Library Information Science (GSLIS) community with a variety of synchronous and asynchronous communication technologies that enable faculty and staff members and students to collaborate across geographic boundaries. Brief periods of on-campus instruction (an initial ten-day session in the summer, followed by a long weekend each semester thereafter) are combined with Web-based instruction. The LEEP scheduling option is unique among schools of library and information science, providing significant advantages in a field that is increasingly involved in organizing and using electronic information. In its most recent ranking of LIS programs, *U.S. News & World Report* ranked GSLIS the top program in the nation.

DELIVERY MEDIA

LEEP's technologies support asynchronous discussions through an electronic bulletin board (class discussions via threaded text messages), live session interactivity (class presentations by faculty members, students, and guest lecturers; group Web browsing; text chatting; and breakout rooms for small-group discussions), archive of live sessions (including all class components: audio, images, and text), and collaborative document creation and editing—students can create, edit, and share documents online without leaving their Web browser. Courses may have up to 2 hours per week of "live" Internet interaction at a regularly scheduled time; additional communication and course work is accomplished at times convenient to the student. In addition to instructor-written Web pages, students use textbooks, course packs, and materials available at libraries near their homes or obtained with assistance from the Academic Outreach library. In many cases, live session lectures are recorded and made available via RealAudio from the LEEP Web pages.

PROGRAMS OF STUDY

The master's degree program requires 40 semester hours of graduate study, 28 of which must be taken in library and information science at the University of Illinois. A master's degree candidate with a full-time load can complete the 40-hour program in two semesters and one summer, although most LEEP students pursue the degree part-time over a longer period of time. Master's degree students must complete all requirements for the degree within five years after registering for graduate work.

The certificate of advanced study in library and information science is open to those who hold a master's degree in library and information science. This 40-hour course of study, which does not lead into the Ph.D. program, is structured to encourage students to design programs that meet specific educational and career goals. A sequence of 32 semester hours is developed by students with their advisers. Up to 16 hours may be taken outside of GSLIS. The final 8 hours are the CAS project, a substantive investigation of a problem in librarianship or information science, which is followed by a final oral examination. Time to complete the program varies widely. Full-time students may finish in two semesters and one summer, but students have five years to complete the program.

STUDENT SERVICES

Two full-time instructional technology staff members and several graduate assistants provide training and technical support to faculty members and LEEP students. Other technical support tasks include troubleshooting when students call or e-mail with technical problems, helping faculty members put material online, setting up and monitoring synchronous sessions, and identifying and evaluating possible new technologies.

CREDIT OPTIONS

Students should wait to transfer credit until they have completed their first semester of course work. Up to 8 semester hours of graduate credit in library and information science from another ALA-accredited library science education program may be transferred. Alternatively, up to 4 hours of graduate credit that is related to but not in library and information science from any accredited institution may be transferred in place of one of the units of LIS credit. Students are not allowed to transfer core courses from other LIS programs.

FACULTY

The faculty's areas of interest are as diverse as the students enrolled. Highly regarded, faculty members pursue their scholarly interests and share discoveries and theories with students and colleagues alike. Current faculty projects include collaborations on campus with the National Center for Supercomputing Applications (NCSA), the Beckman Institute for Advanced Science and Technology, and the University Library and the Center for Children's Books as well as off campus with a variety of libraries, other universities, and corporations.

ADMISSION

LEEP students are expected to be strong academically, able to learn independently, and willing to collaborate with faculty members in refining new ways to deliver instruction. GSLIS basic computer literacy requirements are needed; additional technological knowledge is not required, but may be helpful. Master's degree applicants must have a bachelor's degree from an accredited university. CAS applicants must have completed a master's degree in library and information science or a closely related field, with a minimum GPA of 3.0 on a 4.0 scale.

TUITION AND FEES

LEEP students pay full tuition charges at the in-state or out-of-state rates, depending on where they reside. Tuition for students in the LEEP program is charged per course. For the 2004–05 academic year, tuition and fees are $1352 per 4-hour course for an Illinois resident and $3352 per 4-hour course for a nonresident. Students budget for books and supplies, technology upgrades, transportation for campus trips, housing during campus trips, and Internet access.

FINANCIAL AID

Students are eligible for loans but not for graduate assistantships, which require on-campus residency. Complete information about the tuition and fee assessments is available from the Division of Academic Outreach.

APPLYING

Students must submit part 1 of the Application for Admission to the Graduate College and the application fee ($40 for domestic applicants, $50 for international applicants) to the Office of Admissions and Records, 901 W. Illinois Street, Urbana, Illinois 61801. All remaining items, including transcripts (two copies from all colleges and universities attended; one must be an official transcript), two essays (which replace the personal statement requested in part 2, question 5), three letters of reference in support of the application for admission and financial aid (at least one should be from an employer and one from an instructor), and a resume to the Graduate School of Library and Information Science.

Instead of the two essays, CAS applicants must submit a brief written statement that indicates a commitment to advanced study, the reasons for seeking the CAS, and an outline of a proposed program of study, including possible CAS project areas. Applicants whose native language is not English, including U.S. citizens, must submit TOEFL scores, which should be dated no earlier than two years prior to the application date. Any applicant whose grade point average was below 3.0 (on a 4.0 scale) in the final 60 hours of undergraduate course work must submit official scores from the Graduate Record Examination (GRE) Aptitude Test taken within the last five years.

LEEP students enter the CAS and master's programs in the summer. The application deadline for the M.S. program is March 1 for first consideration. Applications are accepted until the program is full. Applicants to the CAS program should complete their application process nine to twelve months before the intended date of registration.

CONTACT

The Graduate School of Library and Information Science
University of Illinois at Urbana-Champaign
501 East Daniel Street
Champaign, Illinois 61820
Telephone: 217-333-7197
Fax: 217-244-3302
E-mail: gslis@alexia.lis.uiuc.edu
Web Site: http://www.lis.uiuc.edu/gslis/degrees/leep.html

University of Illinois at Urbana-Champaign

Human Resource Education Program

Champaign, Illinois

Since its founding in 1867, the University of Illinois at Urbana-Champaign has earned a reputation as a world-class leader in research, teaching, and public engagement. Located in east central Illinois in the twin cities of Urbana and Champaign (combined population 100,000), the University is the state's flagship public university.

DISTANCE LEARNING PROGRAM

The Department of Human Resource Education (HRE) is recognized as an international leader in the preparation of human resource development and college professionals. HRE Online, established in 1998, is one of the oldest online graduate programs in the world. This cutting-edge degree program—which is 100 percent Web-based—uses a variety of online technologies to provide high-quality learning in a collaborative environment. Based on the results of several research studies, HRE Online is very effective and receives high praise from students.

DELIVERY MEDIA

Three basic formats are used for the online course delivery in the Department of Human Resource Education: the Internet and World Wide Web, synchronous conferencing, and textbook and other printed materials. Content is delivered through Web pages, which are secured by passwords. These include lecture notes, graphic material (audio and visual), links to other resources, homework assignments, and exam study reviews. Conferencing is one of the most important aspects of the online education program. Class discussions, collaborative learning exercises, case study presentations, and discussions between the students and instructor are easily facilitated by the use of streaming audio, WebBoards, and Java chat rooms. Standard textbooks are normally used to support the online materials. Reading packets, e-journals, and online library gateway materials are also employed. Additional communications may also be conducted via e-mail, instant messaging, and audio conferencing.

PROGRAMS OF STUDY

HRE Online provides a variety of learning opportunities within several areas of study. Students can enroll in either the Global Human Resource Development (HRD) master's degree program or the Community College Teaching and Learning (CCTL) master's degree or certificate program. The Global HRD graduate program is designed for individuals currently working in or aspiring to HRD positions in either the private or public sector. This program focuses on employee training and development, organization development, and the use of information and technology to improve individual and organizational performance, with an emphasis on HRD leadership in both domestic and international settings. This program awards a Master of Education (Ed.M.) degree after the completion of nine courses (at 4 credit hours each).

The Community College Teaching and Learning certificate program is designed to increase the teaching effectiveness of community college faculty members and to build instructional leadership capabilities of supervisory personnel. The curriculum emphasizes the effective design of instruction, the application of technologies to instruction, and the use of such innovations as peer-based collaboration and active learning. The sequence of courses collectively provides participants with a foundation of instructional theories, skills, and practices to support existing professional development efforts in community colleges. The CCTL online curriculum is a cost-effective professional development model that is accessible to all faculty members and instructional leaders in community colleges, irrespective of fields of specialization or location. A certificate of professional development is awarded after the completion of the four core courses; a Master of Education (Ed.M.) degree is awarded after the completion of all eight courses (one course equals 4 credit hours).

Students in the HRD program are part of a cohort and enroll in one course per semester. This schedule allows students to complete their degrees within three years. Some students can be given special permission to enroll in more than one course per semester and complete the degree at a faster pace. CCTL students are offered per semester enrollment based on availability.

STUDENT SERVICES

The HRE Online Support Team offers students technical assistance. Students who need help with course content or methodology can contact their instructors by AIM (Free AOL Instant Messenger), e-mail, the toll-free telephone number (during office hours), or fax. The WebBoard also offers students a place to post concerns.

FACULTY

The department's faculty members are scholars with disciplinary backgrounds and expertise in areas such as training and development, instructional technology, organizational development, instructional design, adult education, education policy, industrial/organizational psychology, business and management, entrepreneurship, and cross-cultural studies. Adjunct faculty members and visiting scholars provide additional areas of knowledge and experience. In addition to conducting cutting edge research in HRE, all faculty members have professional experience and remain actively involved in professional practice and leadership at the local, national, and international levels. This combination of scholarly expertise and professional practice in a range of disciplines and application areas provides students with a rich academic and applied body of knowledge and exposure to a wide range of practical experiences and applications in many diverse organizational and institutional settings. Currently, there are 9 full-time faculty members in the HRE department, comprising 4 professors, 2 associate professors, and 3 assistant professors.

ADMISSION

The Department of Human Resource Education considers all applicants based on the quality of undergraduate work, which includes an earned bachelor's degree with a minimum GPA of 3.0 on a 4.0 scale for the last 60 hours of undergraduate course work; the quality of graduate work, including grades; the quality of recommendations contained in the three required letters of reference; and a personal statement, which explains the student's experience and interest in the program.

TUITION AND FEES

In 2004, the cost per course in the Ed.M. program was $1468. The cost for the CCTL program was $1036 per course.

FINANCIAL AID

Since the online students take one (sometimes two) courses per semester, they are generally not eligible for financial aid. Most HRE Online students are only eligible for financial aid in the summer semesters, unless permission has been granted to take more than one course per semester. For the summer semester, students must be enrolled in .75 units (3 hours); for the fall or spring semesters, students must be enrolled in 1.5 units (6 hours). To qualify for financial aid, a student must be accepted into a degree program. More information on obtaining financial aid can be obtained from the UIUC Financial Aid Web site. Students may also contact Academic Outreach at 1-800-252-1360 Ext. 33060. Consistent with University guidelines, veterans' grants and UI employee waivers are accepted. Assistantships for online students are not offered.

APPLYING

A student must submit the completed admission application; three letters of reference from persons familiar with the student's work or past academic achievements; transcripts from all colleges and universities attended, sent directly from the institutions; and a nonrefundable application fee of $40 for domestic students and $50 for international students. Students should visit the Web site at http://www.hre.uiuc.edu/online/admissions.htm for more information.

CONTACT

Department of Human Resource Education
351 Education Building
University of Illinois at Urbana-Champaign
1310 South Sixth Street
Champaign, Illinois 61820
Telephone: 217-333-0807
Fax: 217-244-5632
E-mail: hreonline@uiuc.edu
Web Site: http://www.hre.uiuc.edu/online/

THE UNIVERSITY OF IOWA

The University of Iowa

Center for Credit Programs

Iowa City, Iowa

Established in 1847, the University of Iowa is a major national research university with a solid liberal arts foundation. Iowa was the first U.S. public university to admit men and women on an equal basis. It has won international recognition for its wealth of achievements in the arts, sciences, and humanities. A member of the select Association of American Universities, the University of Iowa maintains a balance between scholarly research and teaching. It places a strong emphasis on undergraduate, international, and interdisciplinary education. The University is accredited by the North Central Association of Colleges and Schools and other accrediting agencies.

DISTANCE LEARNING PROGRAM

In cooperation with University of Iowa academic colleges and departments, the Center for Credit Programs (CCP) of the University of Iowa's Division of Continuing Education delivers University credit courses, both in Iowa City and off campus, to nontraditional and other part-time students who seek a college degree, career advancement, or self-improvement. The CCP supports some 20,000 enrollments annually, including some 3,000 Guided Independent Study (GIS) registrations. Distance education courses may use interactive and broadcast television (available only within Iowa), streaming video, or independent study and Web courses (available worldwide to English-speaking students). Approximately 120 GIS courses are available at both the undergraduate and graduate levels.

DELIVERY MEDIA

University of Iowa distance education courses employ a variety of delivery media. Asynchronous independent study has been available for nine decades. All GIS courses are available on the Web in an eBook format. Printed study guides are available for a fee. Web courses provide students with numerous benefits: assignment submission/return by e-mail, online text ordering, instructional enhancements, access to library resources, and others. Streaming video/audio or CD-ROMs supplement some courses. Students interact with instructors via mail, fax, e-mail, or toll-free telephone. Within Iowa, degree program and other courses are offered via interactive video through the Iowa Communications Network (ICN), an advanced fiber-optic telecommunications network linking educational sites across the state. Semester-based Web courses also support these programs.

PROGRAMS OF STUDY

The Bachelor of Liberal Studies (B.L.S.) external degree program provides an opportunity for students to complete a bachelor's degree from the University of Iowa without attending classes on campus or without ever visiting the campus. The B.L.S. degree has no specific major. Instead, students concentrate course work in three of five distribution areas (humanities, communications and arts, natural science and math, social sciences, or professional fields).

The B.L.S. degree is a flexible program offering convenient, self-paced work; advisers who work with students to create an individual plan of study; the diverse preparation a liberal arts degree provides; the flexibility to match education efforts with career goals; and an undergraduate degree awarded by a nationally recognized institution. More than 700 students have graduated from the program since it was established in 1977 by the Iowa Board of Regents, and hundreds of students are currently active. For more specific information, see the CCP Web site or call the toll-free number below.

SPECIAL PROGRAMS

The LionHawk program represents a formal partnership between Pennsylvania State University and the University of Iowa that allows students to earn both two- and four-year degrees without on-campus study. Students who complete Penn State's Extended Letters, Arts, and Sciences (ELAS) associate degree are ensured admission to the B.L.S. program. Upon admission to the B.L.S. program, all General Education Program requirements are considered satisfied except for the foreign language requirement.

STUDENT SERVICES

Students receive ongoing registration assistance, advising, library access, and other services. The CCP provides extended office hours (Monday–Thursday, 8 a.m. to 6 p.m.; Friday 8 a.m. to 5 p.m., Central Time) to better accommodate nontraditional students.

CREDIT OPTIONS

Credit for B.L.S. degree requirements may be met in several ways, including University of Iowa campus, off-campus, or evening classes (available only in Iowa); transfer credit from other institutions (a minimum number of credits from the University of Iowa are required); and other methods. B.L.S. students primarily take GIS courses, which are available anywhere, are available for enrollment continuously, and allow for self-paced learning. GIS courses provide semester-hour credit. There is no limit on the number of GIS courses that may be applied toward the B.L.S. degree.

FACULTY

All courses and instructors are approved by appropriate departmental and collegiate officers. Courses are taught by regular or adjunct faculty members or advanced graduate students.

ADMISSION

Students applying for admission to the B.L.S. degree program may request an information packet by calling the CCP toll-free number. No special admission requirements are necessary to enroll in GIS courses. Enrollment in GIS courses does not constitute admission to the University of Iowa.

TUITION AND FEES

Tuition for GIS and semester-based distance learning courses is the same as University of Iowa residential tuition. For 2003–04, tuition was $181 per semester hour for undergraduates and $280 per semester hour for graduates. GIS tuition is the same for both in-state and out-of-state students. Students should check with the CCP for new tuition rates after July 1, 2004.

FINANCIAL AID

For information concerning the use of federal financial aid for GIS courses, University of Iowa degree-seeking students should contact the Office of Student Financial Aid (319-335-1450).

APPLYING

Students may enroll in GIS courses at any time. Enrollment forms may be found in the GIS catalog or on the CCP Web site. Students paying by credit card may enroll by phone. For information or enrollment in other CCP courses, students should call the toll-free number.

CONTACT

Center for Credit Programs
116 International Center
The University of Iowa
Iowa City, Iowa 52242-1802
Telephone: 800-272-6430 (toll-free)
Fax: 319-335-2740
E-mail: credit-programs@uiowa.edu
Web site: http://www.continuetolearn.uiowa.edu/bls

University of Maryland, College Park

Online Studies

College Park, Maryland

The University of Maryland is the flagship institution among the University System of Maryland's eleven state public colleges and universities. Founded in 1856 as the original land-grant institution in Maryland, the University is the top public research institution in the mid-Atlantic region and one of the nation's best. Sixty-nine of its programs are ranked in the top twenty-five in the country, with fifty Maryland programs ranked in the top fifteen. The University of Maryland is accredited by the Middle States Association of Colleges and Schools and is a member of the Association of American Universities.

In 2000, the University of Maryland Office of Continuing and Extended Education introduced a University-wide online-learning strategy and launched its first program: Master of Life Sciences. The Web-based Master of Life Sciences is a content-rich, interdisciplinary program, with options in biology and chemistry, that focuses on the most contemporary issues in modern science. Designed to enable practicing teachers to conveniently pursue an advanced degree, the program has attracted students worldwide. In 2003 the University launched an online Master of Engineering in fire protection program for practicing engineers working in fire safety anywhere in the world.

DISTANCE LEARNING PROGRAM

The University of Maryland is dedicated to increasing the visibility and reputation of its high-quality professional and graduate programs, measured not only by advances in research but by innovations in the delivery of programs to a worldwide audience. Online Studies provides the platform by which these programs can be conveniently delivered to students anywhere, at anytime.

DELIVERY MEDIA

Courses are delivered asynchronously through the Internet using a range of technologies including chat rooms, threaded discussions, and links to campus libraries and academic resources. Faculty members are available in person, through e-mail, and by prescribed phone appointments.

PROGRAMS OF STUDY

Online Studies at the University of Maryland offers two completely Web-based graduate programs, a 30-credit Master of Life Sciences and a 30-credit Master of Engineering in fire protection.

The Master of Life Sciences provides in-depth knowledge of current research areas in the chemical, biological, biochemical, and biomedical sciences. Courses cover modern biology, modern molecular genetics, transmission genetics, human physiology, biodiversity and conservation biology, chemical ecology, principles of chemical biology, biochemistry, natural products chemistry, electrochemical cells, evolutionary biology and behavior, and experimental biology. Students may follow concentrations in chemistry or biology.

The Master of Engineering in fire protection is a graduate-level program in applied fire safety science and engineering. The curriculum supports the emerging international movement toward performance-based building approaches to building fire safety analysis and design. It provides students with an understanding of the physics and chemistry of fire necessary for predicting building system performance and analyzing failures. Course work covers fire risk assessment, fire dynamics, advanced fire modeling, smoke detection and management, toxicity evaluation and analysis, and structural fire protection.

STUDENT SERVICES

Through Single Point of Contact (SPOC), listed in the Contact section below, students may inquire, apply for admission, register, pay their bills, and purchase textbooks. Students also have access to equipment and software specifications needed for successful completion of course work, online library resources, and technical support.

FACULTY

The Master of Life Sciences program has 11 full-time University of Maryland faculty members with doctoral degrees. The Master of Engineering in fire protection program is taught by faculty members with outstanding teaching and research credentials.

ADMISSION

The Master of Life Sciences program requires an undergraduate degree in biological science, chemistry, biochemistry, or science education; one year of teaching experience or the equivalent; letters of recommendation from a school principal and a science supervisor; and successful completion of a gateway review class, LFSC510 Concepts of Modern Biology or LFSC520 Concepts of Modern Chemistry, or acceptable performance on an admission exam based on LFSC510 or LFSC520.

The Master of Engineering in fire protection requires an earned bachelor's degree in engineering or a related field from an accredited institution and courses in structural mechanics, differential equations, fluid mechanics, and heat transfer or equivalent. Applicants may be admitted on a provisional basis if they have demonstrated satisfactory performance in another graduate program or salutary work experience.

TUITION AND FEES

The Master of Life Sciences program costs $341 per credit hour, and there is a $60-per-term technology/distance learning fee and an admission exam fee of $20.

The Master of Engineering in fire protection costs $660 per credit hour, and there is a $60-per-term technology/distance learning fee.

All tuition and fees are subject to change. All graduate students pay a one-time $50 application fee.

FINANCIAL AID

For information regarding financial assistance, students should visit http://www.onlinestudies.umd.edu/financialaid.html.

CONTACT

Single Point of Contact (SPOC)
Mitchell Building, First Floor
University of Maryland
College Park, Maryland 20742-5231
Telephone: 301-314-3572
877-989-SPOC (toll-free)
Fax: 301-314-1282
E-mail: onlinestudies@umail.umd.edu
Web site: http://www.onlinestudies.umd.edu

University of Maryland University College

Undergraduate and Graduate Online Programs

Adelphi, Maryland

Founded in 1947, University of Maryland University College (UMUC) is one of eleven degree-granting institutions in the University System of Maryland; its Graduate School was founded in 1978. UMUC's principal mission is to serve part-time students by providing high-quality educational opportunities in Maryland and around the world.

Through its online programs, UMUC offers nineteen bachelor's degree programs, twenty-three undergraduate certificates, seventeen master's degree programs, and thirty-nine graduate certificates.

UMUC is accredited by the Commission on Higher Education of the Middle States Association of Colleges and Schools, 3624 Market Street, Philadelphia, Pennsylvania 19104 (telephone: 215-662-5606) and is certified by the State Council for Higher Education in Virginia.

DISTANCE LEARNING PROGRAM

UMUC's online courses provide the same rigor, requirements, assignments, and tests as are available in a classroom environment. However, students are free to participate at times and from locations that are convenient to them. Online courses are highly structured and require students to log in several times a week and to participate actively in asynchronous, full-class, and small-group discussions and assignments.

DELIVERY MEDIA

UMUC provides undergraduate and graduate degree programs via WebTycho, its proprietary virtual campus interface, completely online. Students taking online classes via WebTycho require a computer running a Web browser, such as Netscape Navigator (version 7 or higher) or Microsoft Internet Explorer (version 6.0 or higher), connection to the Internet, and an e-mail account.

PROGRAMS OF STUDY

The School of Undergraduate Programs offers Bachelor of Arts (B.A.) and Bachelor of Science (B.S.) degree programs, with nineteen majors and twenty-four minors available online. Majors include accounting, business administration, communication studies, computer and information science, computer studies, English, environmental management, finance, fire science, global business and public policy, history, human resource management, humanities, information systems management, legal studies, management studies, marketing, psychology, and social science. In addition, UMUC offers twenty-three undergraduate certificate programs online.

The Graduate School offers seventeen online master's degree programs, including the Master of Business Administration, the Master of International Management, the Master of Software Engineering, the Master of Arts in Teaching, the Master of Education, and the Master of Distance Education. In addition, the Master of Science degree is available in the following areas: accounting and financial management, accounting and information technology, biotechnology studies, computer systems management, e-commerce, environmental management, health-care administration, information technology, management, technology management, and telecommunications management. The Graduate School also offers nine dual-degree programs and thirty-nine certificate programs.

STUDENT SERVICES

UMUC offers a complete range of support services online that allow students to apply for admission, obtain pre-entry advising, register, order books and materials, search for scholarships, apply for financial aid, and obtain ongoing academic advising. Once students have been admitted, they also have access to UMUC's Interactive Student Information System (ISIS), which allows them to check their course schedules and grade reports from past and current semesters, financial aid status, statements of account, and unofficial transcripts; and to update their personal information.

UMUC students have access to a wealth of online library resources, including more than 100 Web databases and 24-hour library assistance. In addition, students who live outside of Maryland (but inside the continental United States) are eligible for home delivery of University System of Maryland library books. Through the University's Career and Cooperative Education Center, students can access online search tools, receive assistance with resume and interview preparation, find a career mentor, and participate in online career development seminars.

CREDIT OPTIONS

UMUC offers undergraduate students a number of innovative options for earning credit, all of which are available at a distance. EXCEL Through Experiential Learning enables students to earn up to 30 credits for one semester's work toward a first undergraduate degree (15 credits toward a second degree) by having learning from previous work or life experience evaluated. Through Cooperative Education (Co-op), undergraduate students can earn academic credit in the workplace for new on-the-job learning.

Graduate students can transfer up to 6 semester hours of graduate credit (3 semester hours for the Master of Business Administration) to UMUC if the credit was earned at a regionally accredited institution and is relevant to the student's area of study, subject to approval by the Graduate School.

FACULTY

Before teaching online, UMUC faculty members must complete a five-week intensive training course and be certified. Of the more than 900 faculty members in the School of Undergraduate Studies, more than 50 percent have taught UMUC courses in distance formats. The undergraduate faculty is composed of full-time and part-time faculty members who work actively in the fields in which they teach. The Graduate School's 60 full-time faculty members have terminal degrees that are relevant to the online degrees. They teach, are responsible for the design of the online curriculum, and provide leadership for the school's approximately 300 adjunct faculty members. More than 85 percent of those adjunct faculty members hold terminal degrees in their disciplines; all have years of practical experience in their fields.

ADMISSION

Students who are applying for undergraduate admission must have graduated from a regionally accredited high school or have completed the General Educational Development (GED) exams with a total score of at least 2250 and no individual score less than 410. (If they completed the GED exam before January 2002, they must have a total score of at least 225 and no individual test score lower than 40.) To be granted regular admission status, students should also have maintained a cumulative grade point average (GPA) of at least 2.0 on all college-level work attempted at other colleges and universities.

Applicants to the Graduate School must have a bachelor's degree from a regionally accredited college or university and an overall undergraduate GPA of at least 3.0 on a 4.0 scale to be accepted as a degree-seeking student. If the applicant's GPA falls slightly below the criterion listed above, admission may be granted on a conditional basis. Individual programs may have additional requirements. Details are provided in the Graduate Catalog and the UMUC Web site. Test scores such as SAT, GMAT, or GRE are not required for any UMUC bachelor's or master's programs.

TUITION AND FEES

Undergraduate tuition per semester hour is $221 for Maryland residents and $407 for nonresidents. Graduate tuition for Maryland residents is $339 per semester hour; it is $553 per semester hour for nonresidents, except for the Master of Business Administration program, which is $582 per semester hour. Books, certain course materials, and some fees are additional. Active-duty military personnel and their spouses are eligible for the in-state tuition for undergraduate and graduate courses. The undergraduate application fee is $30. The graduate application fee is $50. For both undergraduate and graduate students, schedule adjustments (including withdrawals) are $15, and the late registration fee is $30. Tuition and fees are subject to change. Students are advised to consult the UMUC Web site for the most up-to-date information.

FINANCIAL AID

UMUC offers a variety of financial aid programs to suit the needs of both undergraduate and graduate students. Students are eligible to apply for low-interest loans, state scholarship program funds, the Federal Work-Study Program, and UMUC grants and scholarships. Federal Direct Loans are available to students regardless of income. While UMUC handles most of the processes involved in delivering federal, state, and institutional funds, students are responsible for completing the Free Application for Federal Student Aid (FAFSA) and the UMUC Student Data Form and for adhering to deadlines. For more information and deadlines, students may contact UMUC by phone or e-mail (listed below) or visit the Web site at http://www.umuc.edu/financialaid.

APPLYING

Students interested in applying to any of UMUC's online programs can find information from the points of contact or at the school's Web address. UMUC accepts and processes applications throughout the year.

CONTACT

University of Maryland University College
3501 University Boulevard East
Adelphi, Maryland 20783
Telephone: 301-985-7000
800-888-UMUC (toll-free)
E-mail: umucinfo@umuc.edu
Web site: http://www.umuc.edu

University of Massachusetts Amherst

Division of Continuing Education

Amherst, Massachusetts

The University of Massachusetts Amherst (UMass Amherst) was founded in 1863 under the Land-Grant College Act of 1862 and is accredited by the New England Association of Schools and Colleges. The UMass Amherst Division of Continuing Education, founded in 1971, provides access to the academic resources of the University to part-time students, working professionals, local and national business firms, and the general community.

DISTANCE LEARNING PROGRAM

The Division of Continuing Education, in partnership with the University's schools and colleges, began offering distance education courses in 1995. Online courses have the same rigorous academic requirements as on-campus courses.

DELIVERY MEDIA

The UMass Amherst Division of Continuing Education utilizes the Internet to deliver Web-based courses. Students interact with instructors via e-mail, chat rooms, telephone, fax, and mail.

PROGRAMS OF STUDY

In addition to online credit courses in accounting, English, journalism, management, marketing, philosophy, psychology, sociology, and wildlife and fisheries conservation, seven online degree programs are offered.

The Master of Science (M.S.) degree program in nursing prepares advanced-practice nurses as expert clinicians in the care of children, adolescents, and their families in diverse community and school health settings. The School of Nursing is accredited by the National League for Nursing and the Commission on Collegiate Nursing Education.

The Master of Public Health (M.P.H.) degree program offers a broad-based, comprehensive, graduate-level public health curriculum designed for health professionals currently working in the field. Working health professionals may expand their knowledge base in public health, extend and sharpen their professional skills, broaden their perspective of public health problems, and prepare to assume greater professional responsibility.

The Master of Science in Nursing/Master of Public Health dual degree program builds on previous nursing education and clinical experience, and prepares graduates for leadership positions in public health. The 60-credit program includes 30 credits in nursing and 30 credits in public health; it integrates nursing science, public health science, administration, and leadership.

The RN to Bachelor of Science degree program is designed to meet the educational goals of Massachusetts registered nurses. Under faculty guidance, students provide nursing care to clients of all ages and develop skills in critical thinking, leadership, and research utilization.

The Professional M.B.A. program is an accelerated program for professionals who want to continue their education in the management field but cannot attend traditional classes because of full-time career commitments. The program is fully accredited by AACSB International–The Association to Advance Collegiate Schools of Business.

The Bachelor of Business Administration is geared toward individuals who are working full time and need flexibility in completing the degree; the curriculum is delivered in an asynchronous format, allowing courses to be taken anytime and anywhere. The program is offered by the Isenberg School of Management and is accredited by AACSB International.

The Bachelor of Science degree in hospitality and tourism management is for working adults, both international and domestic, who are unable to pursue a residential degree program on the Amherst campus. The program integrates a variety of courses in the humanities and social and physical sciences, with a heavy concentration of business and hospitality/tourism courses.

SPECIAL PROGRAMS

The Certificate of Business Studies is a credit-based program intended for students who want to broaden their academic background with business courses without completing a bachelor's degree program. It is ideal for students who intend to pursue graduate-level work in business or for those who are looking to further their professional goals.

The Certificate of Online Journalism Program equips students with skills in reporting, writing, and online research. The program welcomes students from any discipline who wish to gain an understanding of this exciting new area of journalism. It provides assessments of the current state of online journalism as well as the future of information technology.

The Criminal Justice Studies Certificate Program is designed to provide students with a solid foundation in the field of criminal justice and is intended to attract those planning or developing careers ranging from law enforcement to probation, and from the courts to corrections.

The Basics in Exercise and Nutrition for Health and Human Performance Program is a collaboration between the Departments of Exercise Science and Nutrition and the School of Public Health and Health Services. It is designed to meet the needs of individuals with degrees in such fields as exercise physiology, nutrition, athletic training, and other health-related disciplines.

The Certificate of Individual Study in Arts Management is a valuable professional development opportunity for arts managers as well as people employed by nonprofit organizations or agencies. Courses teach strategic planning, board development, fundraising, marketing, and arts programming and may also be taken for University of Massachusetts undergraduate credit.

STUDENT SERVICES

Academic advisers are available by phone, e-mail, fax, and in person to assist students in course selection and academic matters. Continuing Education has its own registration and business offices, which can provide assistance in registration, transcripts, financial aid, and billings.

CREDIT OPTIONS

Credits earned through distance education are University of Massachusetts Amherst credits, and may be transferable to other colleges and universities.

FACULTY

The distance education courses are taught by UMass Amherst faculty members who hold doctorates or terminal degrees in their respective fields, or by qualified adjunct faculty members or graduate teaching assistants.

ADMISSION

The UMass Amherst Division of Continuing Education allows any person with a high school diploma or its equivalent to register for courses. Some courses require prerequisite college-level work. Enrollment does not imply acceptance into a degree program. For both graduate and undergraduate degree programs, students must apply to the University for admission.

TUITION AND FEES

Fees vary depending on whether the course offered is noncredit or for credit and whether the level of that credit is undergraduate or graduate. Generally, a noncredit course costs from $200 to $350, while an undergraduate course costs from $220 to $400 per credit; graduate-level courses vary in cost from $250 to $600 per credit. All students, regardless of location, pay the same tuition.

FINANCIAL AID

Availability of financial aid varies depending on course status and matriculation. Financial assistance may be available from employers, The Education Resources Institute (TERI) Continuing Education loans, and for eligible military personnel under the G.I. Bill.

APPLYING

Students can find information regarding application and registration procedures for degree programs and individual courses on the UMass Amherst Division of Continuing Education Web site listed in the Contact section.

CONTACT

Director, Division of Continuing Education
University of Massachusetts Amherst
358 North Pleasant Street
Amherst, Massachusetts 01003-9296
Telephone: 413-545-2111
Fax: 413-545-3351
E-mail: info@contined.umass.edu
Web site: http://www.umassulearn.net

University of Minnesota

University of Minnesota, Twin Cities Campus

Independent and Distance Learning, College of Continuing Education

Minneapolis, Minnesota

The University of Minnesota, with its four campuses, is one of the most comprehensive universities in the United States and ranks among the most prestigious. It is both a land-grant university with a strong tradition of education and public service and a major research institution. It was founded as a preparatory school in 1851 and was reorganized as a university in 1869, benefiting from the Morrill (or Land-Grant) Act of 1862.

The University of Minnesota has campuses in the Twin Cities (Minneapolis and St. Paul), Duluth, Morris, and Crookston, Minnesota. The Twin Cities campus, home of the College of Continuing Education, is a classic Big Ten campus with comprehensive academic programs offering unlimited opportunities for students and faculty.

DISTANCE LEARNING PROGRAM

Independent and Distance Learning (IDL) offers outstanding university credit courses using mail and electronic technologies. In a recent year, the department received approximately 6,000 registrations from students throughout the United States and abroad. The 170 courses are fully accredited each year by approximately fifty different academic departments of the University. IDL is part of the College of Continuing Education (CCE), the division of the University of Minnesota that serves adult and part-time learners.

DELIVERY MEDIA

Most courses are self-paced and available by mail for home study and mail lesson exchange with faculty members. Many faculty members provide the option of e-mail for lesson exchange. A growing number of online courses are fully interactive. Many of the online courses take place in fixed semester terms. All students who register for college credit with Independent and Distance Learning receive an e-mail and Internet account.

PROGRAMS OF STUDY

Approximately 170 credit courses are offered in a wide range of academic departments, including such varied subjects as applied business, child psychology, ecology, English literature and writing courses, management, math, and physics. Two science courses come with home lab kits: general biology and elementary physics. Independent and Distance Learning courses are known for their high academic quality and variety of topics. There are no degree programs available. There are two upper-level undergraduate certificates available online: applied business and paper science and engineering.

STUDENT SERVICES

The Continuing Education Information Center helps with finding information about specific courses, how to register, and financial aid.

University of Minnesota libraries fully support distance learners with reference services, research assistance, and home delivery of documents.

If students have a disability, Independent and Distance Learning coordinates efforts to provide accommodations that remove academic and physical barriers to earning credits. Such accommodations may include more time to complete exams or an alternate format for an exam, a separate testing room, audiotaping required materials, and taped rather than written comments from an instructor. Requests for such accommodations should be made well in advance of when they are needed so that necessary documentation may be obtained and accommodations facilitated.

FACULTY

IDL has approximately 90 faculty members. Approximately 40 percent are University of Minnesota professors, 30 percent are graduate student teaching assistants, and 30 percent are adjunct faculty members, lecturers, or others. All professors and many adjunct faculty members hold doctorates or other terminal degrees, and all are approved by the relevant academic departments.

ADMISSION

There are no admission requirements to register for courses through Independent and Distance Learning. Students who want to earn a certificate in applied business or paper science and engineering should visit http://www.cce.umn.edu/certificates.

TUITION AND FEES

Students who are not admitted to University of Minnesota certificate or degree programs qualify for in-state tuition rates, regardless of location. Tuition for 2003–04 was $208.45 per semester credit. A University-wide fee of $30 per credit was assessed. An administrative fee of $75 per IDL course enrollment was assessed. Course study guides are included in the fee. Texts and other materials are purchased separately from the University of Minnesota Book Store.

FINANCIAL AID

Financial aid is limited. Eligibility requirements may vary, but most aid programs place restrictions on some types of IDL enrollment and require admission to a University of Minnesota, Twin Cities, degree program or eligible certificate program. Nonadmitted students who reside in Minnesota may be eligible for College of Continuing Education grants or scholarships, which have more flexible eligibility criteria. Employer assistance may also be an option for some students.

APPLYING

No application is needed to register in individual courses. For information about applying for the online certificate programs in applied business or paper science and engineering, students can visit http://www.cce.umn.edu/certificates.

CONTACT

College of Continuing Education Information Center
101 Wesbrook Hall
University of Minnesota
77 Pleasant Street, SE
Minneapolis, Minnesota 55455
Telephone: 612-624-4000
800-234-6564 (toll-free)
Fax: 612-625-1511
E-mail: info@cce.umn.edu
Web site: http://www.cce.umn.edu/petersons

The University of Montana–Missoula

Continuing Education, Educational Outreach

Missoula, Montana

The University of Montana–Missoula (UM-M), the main campus of the University of Montana System and founded in 1893, is a midsize, state-supported university located in Missoula, Montana, a small city of about 65,000 people located in the Rocky Mountain West. Approximately 10,500 undergraduate and 1,250 graduate students are enrolled, some of whom are taking courses through distance programs. UM-M is a Carnegie doctoral level–intensive university offering a variety of undergraduate and graduate degree programs through centers of excellence in its colleges and professional schools: Arts and Sciences, Business Administration, Education, Fine Arts, Forestry, Journalism, Law, Technology, and Pharmacy and Allied Health Sciences. The University of Montana–Missoula is governed by the Montana University System Board of Regents and accredited by the Northwest Association of Schools and Colleges (professional schools and departments are approved by specialized accrediting organizations). The University of Montana–Missoula ranks seventeenth in the nation and fifth among public universities in producing Rhodes scholars.

DISTANCE LEARNING PROGRAM

For students who live elsewhere in Montana, in the United States, or around the world or for students who are unable to attend class during the traditional school day, academic departments at the University of Montana–Missoula team with Continuing Education to offer programs through External Degree Programs (EDP) and/or individual courses through UMOnline and Extended Studies. The University of Montana–Missoula serves a large, rural state and has a special commitment to the continued development of high-quality, affordable distance learning options.

External Degree Programs delivers programs via a combination of traditional classroom, videoconferencing, and UMOnline/Internet instruction. Classes typically meet during evenings or on weekends, and program courses are offered each semester. Programs are open to qualified, regularly admitted UM-M students, and all aspects of the degrees are equivalent to those earned on campus. Although students are encouraged to pursue programs in their entirety, nondegree students may also register for individual courses with consent of the program's academic coordinator. For information about academic coordinators, logistics, costs, and schedules, students should contact External Degree Programs. Students are also advised to consult the University of Montana–Missoula's catalogs for complete program details and admission requirements.

UMOnline is the University of Montana–Missoula's online teaching and learning environment. Every semester, a growing variety of regularly offered on-campus courses at the undergraduate and graduate levels are also made available online. Online course sections are open to qualified, regularly admitted UM-M students and are equivalent in every respect to those available on campus.

DELIVERY MEDIA

The University of Montana–Missoula delivers courses to distance students online over the Internet, via televised videoconferencing systems, or in person to locations throughout Montana.

PROGRAMS OF STUDY

The Doctor of Education program is an external cohort program in educational leadership that meets on weekends on the Missoula campus.

The Doctor of Pharmacy, External, is offered through UMOnline and is intended for working pharmacists who wish to upgrade a previously earned bachelor's degree in pharmacy to the next level.

The Master of Arts in school counseling is an external cohort program that meets on weekends on the Missoula campus.

The Master of Business Administration is offered via videoconference. This off-campus M.B.A. program is broadcast on a flexible evening schedule to classrooms in nine Montana cities.

The Master of Education in curriculum studies is delivered in partly online through UMOnline and partly in person in Butte and Corvallis, Montana, during evenings throughout the school year and via condensed daytime schedules during the summer. The degree is expected to be available soon delivered entirely through UMOnline.

The Master of Education in educational leadership is delivered throughout the year entirely over the Internet through UMOnline.

The Master of Public Administration is delivered year-round entirely over the Internet through UMOnline.

The Associate of Applied Science in surgical technology is offered through

UMOnline, with clinical experiences in Butte and Billings, Montana. The UM-M College of Technology coordinates with UMOnline, other colleges of technology, and hospitals to bring the complete degree program to students in Butte and Billings.

SPECIAL PROGRAMS

The Library Media Endorsement Program is an online program intended for upper-division and graduate-level students who wish to receive endorsement in this field from the State of Montana Office of Public Instruction. The enhanced program is now offered jointly by UM-M and UM–Western.

The M.B.A. Foundation Program is an online program that prepares students for graduate studies in the UM-M Master of Business Administration degree program. The Foundation Program comprises a series of five courses offered through UMOnline over a one-year period.

STUDENT SERVICES

Distance learning students enjoy access to a wide variety of UM-M student services, including the Mansfield Library's distance education delivery services and UM-M's admission, academic advising, financial aid, registration, and career services. Select campus services are also available.

CREDIT OPTIONS

Courses are offered for undergraduate and graduate academic credit.

FACULTY

Courses are developed and taught by UM-M faculty members.

ADMISSION

EDP and UMOnline courses are available to qualified, regularly admitted UM-M students. Students may enroll in EDP, UMOnline, and on-campus course sections simultaneously or mix delivery modes over successive semesters.

TUITION AND FEES

Depending upon the program, fees may be based on a state-support resident/nonresident model approved by the Montana University System Board of Regents or on a self-support model. The typical cost for a 3-credit UMOnline course is $495 for undergraduate courses or $555 for graduate courses.

FINANCIAL AID

Students receiving any form of financial assistance are advised to check with the UM-M Financial Aid Office to determine coverage. Fee waivers and state fee matrix cost plateaus do not apply for self-supported courses.

CONTACT

Educational Outreach, Continuing Education
The University of Montana–Missoula
Missoula, Montana 59812
Telephone: 406-243-2900
E-mail: edoutreach@mso.umt.edu
Web site: http://www.montanaeducation.com

University of Nevada, Reno

Extended Studies Independent Learning Program

Reno, Nevada

Established in 1864, the University of Nevada first offered classes in Elko, Nevada. In 1885, the campus was moved to Reno with 2 faculty members and 50 students. Today, the University of Nevada, Reno is the oldest of seven institutions in the University and Community College System of Nevada.

A land-grant university with an enrollment of approximately 16,000 students in ten schools and colleges, the University of Nevada, Reno offers a wide range of undergraduate and graduate programs, including selected doctoral and professional studies. The University emphasizes programs and activities that best serve the needs of the state, region, and nation. More than one fourth of the students enrolled are pursuing advanced degrees. The University encourages and supports faculty research and its application to state and national problems and conducts more than $70 million in research grants and contracts each year.

The 255-acre campus is located just north of Interstate 80 near the majestic Sierra Nevada range and Lake Tahoe. The University of Nevada, Reno is an integral part of the thriving Reno-Sparks metropolitan area, home to about 311,000 people. With its blend of ivy-covered buildings, sweeping lawns, and functional, progressive architecture, the University's academic atmosphere is filled with rich surroundings for the cultural and intellectual development of students.

The University of Nevada, Reno is an Equal Opportunity/Affirmative Action, ADA institution. The University of Nevada, Reno is accredited by the Northwest Association of Schools and Colleges Commission on Colleges and is recognized by the Council on Postsecondary Accreditation and the U.S. Department of Education.

DISTANCE LEARNING PROGRAM

The Independent Learning Program at the University of Nevada, Reno offers an individualized method of learning and a flexible way to earn University credit. Students who are unable to attend on-campus courses due to location, scheduling conflicts, work, or other commitments can choose from more than 200 academic credit courses in thirty subject areas as well as high school and noncredit offerings. Students may enroll any day of the year and take up to one year to complete a course.

DELIVERY MEDIA

Instruction is given by means of a course syllabus, textbooks, video and CDs (where appropriate), and additional reference and instructional materials. Lessons are accepted via mail, fax, and e-mail. After review by the course instructor, work is returned to students. A number of online courses are available, both semester-based and open-enrollment. No classroom attendance is necessary for correspondence study courses. All courses have a final examination, which must be taken in a proctored setting; many courses have two or three progress examinations. Students who reside away from campus may take examinations using an approved proctor in their area.

PROGRAM OF STUDY

The University of Nevada, Reno is the sole provider of university credit through independent study in the state of Nevada. Academic credit courses are offered from the University of Nevada, Reno and the University of Nevada, Las Vegas. Courses for high school credit and continuing education units are also available. Undergraduate credit courses are offered in thirty subject areas, which include accounting, anthropology, Basque studies, core humanities, counseling and educational psychology, criminal justice, curriculum and instruction, economics, educational leadership, English, environment, French, geography, German, health ecology, history, hotel administration, human development/family studies, Italian, journalism, managerial sciences, mathematics, nutrition, political science, psychology, sociology, Spanish, speech communication, and women's studies. Graduate credit is available in counseling and educational psychology, educational leadership, human development/family studies, and Basque studies. All credit courses have been approved by the departments and colleges of the University of Nevada, Reno and the University of Nevada, Las Vegas. High School credit courses meet Nevada State Department of Education approval.

SPECIAL PROGRAMS

New online courses are a convenient way to study at home and communicate with instructors via the Internet. Some classes also include a listserv feature, so students can join a mail group, ask questions of fellow online students, and discuss course topics.

STUDENT SERVICES

All textbooks, videotapes, and course materials are mailed directly to students anywhere in the world. Returning lessons for grading uses convenient e-mail or fax services or traditional mail and air mail. Independent Learning students who live in the Reno area can take full advantage of the many student services available on the University of Nevada, Reno campus; these services include tutoring, math centers, academic counseling, and support group information for nontraditional students. Local students can also receive library and computer lab privileges and use the library's video loan service. Upon enrollment, each correspondence study student receives a student handbook containing useful information, study tips, and guidelines. The Independent Learning staff is available to answer questions via phone, fax, or e-mail. Information about courses and programs is also included on the Independent Learning Web site, listed below.

CREDIT OPTIONS

A maximum of 60 credits earned through Independent Learning may be applied toward a University of Nevada, Reno bachelor's degree. The University of Nevada, Las Vegas awards up to a maximum of 15 semester hours of credit through Independent Learning toward a degree. Students interested in transfer credit may contact the University's Transfer Center office (telephone: 775-784-4700) for more information. Grades for all completed credit courses are recorded on a University transcript, which may be ordered from the University.

FACULTY

All instructors for Independent Learning have been approved by the departments and colleges of the University of Nevada, Reno and the University of Nevada, Las Vegas. High school faculty members are certified high school teachers in Nevada high schools or are faculty members at the university or community college level.

ADMISSION

Formal admission to the University of Nevada, Reno or the University of Nevada, Las Vegas is not required before enrolling in Independent Learning courses. Likewise, enrollment in Independent Learning does not constitute admission to either of these universities. Students who wish to apply may contact the University of Nevada, Reno Office of Admissions and Records (telephone: 775-784-4700).

TUITION AND FEES

The standard course fee for all undergraduate Independent Learning courses is $99 per credit. Graduate tuition is $132 per credit. High school courses are $100 per one-half unit course. Textbook costs are not included in the course fee. Additional fees are charged for handling, stationery, syllabus, faxing, and special materials, as well as for air mail, international mail, and Internet courses. All students taking a college course must pay a one-time $60 application fee.

FINANCIAL AID

Some financial aid may be available to certain qualified individuals through the University of Nevada, Reno Financial Aid Office (telephone: 775-784-4666), where students can call for application deadlines and forms. Independent Learning courses at the University of Nevada, Reno are approved for veterans benefits and for military personnel (DANTES) within or outside the United States.

APPLYING

Students can enroll any time and take up to one year to complete each open-enrollment course. Semester-based courses are restricted to the University's general deadlines. Instruction by Independent Learning affords students the convenience of studying when and where they choose. Enrollment is accepted in person, via the Web, or by mail, phone, or fax.

CONTACT

Independent Learning Staff
Extended Studies/050
University of Nevada, Reno
Reno, Nevada 89557
Telephone: 775-784-4652
800-233-8928 Ext. 4652 (toll-free)
Fax: 775-784-1280
E-mail: istudy@unr.edu
Web site: http://www.istudy.unr.edu

University of New England

Certificate of Advanced Graduate Study in Educational Leadership

Biddeford, Maine

The University of New England (UNE) is an independent university whose mission it is to educate men and women to advance the quality of human life and the environment. The University was created in 1978 in Biddeford, Maine, by combining St. Francis College and the New England College of Osteopathic Medicine. In 1996 the University merged with Westbrook College, a small liberal arts college in Portland, Maine, giving UNE two distinctive campuses. The University now recognizes Westbrook College's 1831 charter date as the University of New England's founding date.

The University is accredited by the New England Association of Schools and Colleges. The Certificate of Advanced Graduate Study in Educational Leadership is approved by the Maine Board of Education to be offered in Maine and elsewhere. The University of New England's Certificate of Advanced Graduate Study in Educational Leadership meets or exceeds the national standard set by the Interstate School Leader Licensure Consortium (ISSLC) for post-master's certification and preparation in educational leadership.

DISTANCE LEARNING PROGRAM

Designed and developed for working professionals who aspire to administrative and leadership roles in an educational environment, the Certificate of Advanced Graduate Study (C.A.G.S.) in Educational Leadership provides an innovative and convenient program of study, leading to a post-master's professional credential. The part-time online program offers the self-directed, motivated adult learner the needed flexibility to accommodate a busy lifestyle while pursuing career goals.

Degree candidates in educational leadership join other graduate students at the University continuing their professional education in osteopathic medicine, human services, health and life sciences, management, and education. The online educational leadership program builds on a successful distance learning model—the master's degree in education for experienced teachers has hundreds of students enrolled throughout the country.

DELIVERY MEDIA

Courses in educational leadership are offered online, so study is convenient and accessible. Students may opt to study at home or in their school environment, wherever they have access to the Internet. With technical support from the University's instructional technology partner, eCollege.com, students quickly become adept with the technology, which is simple and easy to use. There are many opportunities for interaction with faculty mentors and other students, using Internet tools developed and adapted specifically for online learners; these include threaded discussions, online class sessions, and an electronic bulletin board designed for communication from a faculty mentor to the students. Highlighting the program is the one-week residential Integration Seminar, which brings together all of the students in the program for an intensive session offered in the summer.

PROGRAM OF STUDY

The University of New England currently offers the Certificate of Advanced Graduate Study in Educational Leadership in an online format. The curriculum consists of fifteen 3-credit online courses and a one-week residential summer seminar. Ten courses, including the seminar, are required; the additional five courses are available as electives. A minimum of ten 3-credit courses must be taken in the University's C.A.G.S. program to be awarded the Advanced Degree. The particular program of study chosen depends upon the existing requirements in the state where students work or seek certification as educational administrators. Students who do not wish to seek the Certificate of Advanced Graduate Study may enroll in an individual course. Up to four courses may be taken as a nonmatriculated student.

The curriculum is designed to apply as broadly as possible to requirements throughout the country; however, it is the responsibility of the candidate to confirm what course content is needed in the state in which certification is sought.

STUDENT SERVICES

As a part of the University of New England's online campus, students are just a mouse click away from the services and support they need. The certificate program staff and faculty members are ready to advise on course work and program procedures. The library staff helps in locating and accessing learning materials. The eCollege.com staff members are available 24 hours a day on a helpline for technology-related assistance.

CREDIT OPTIONS

Upon acceptance to the C.A.G.S. program, students may apply for a transfer of up to two 3-credit post-masters-level courses. For transfer credit to be considered, the graduate-level course work must have been taken following the completion of the master's degree. To request a review of course work for transfer credit, students must provide an official transcript for each course, a course description, a syllabus, and a comprehensive student statement supporting the rationale for the transfer request. Transfer of credit is at the discretion of UNE's Department of Education. The Summer Seminar and Internship cannot be satisfied through transfer credit, and no credit for experiential learning in lieu of Educational Leadership courses is given.

FACULTY

The faculty mentors for the program are University professors as well as practicing professionals. All are certified administrators, and the majority have earned a doctorate. Faculty mentors include talented educators with extensive backgrounds as principals, superintendents, specialists in curriculum development and special services, educational consultants, and guidance supervisors.

ADMISSION

Applications for admission into the Educational Leadership program are considered as received, and a new cohort begins online every term. Applicants are encouraged to prepare application materials carefully and completely in order to ensure timely action by the admissions committee. Admission criteria for advanced-degree candidacy are a master's degree from an accredited institution (an exception is made for nonmatriculated students who can take up to 12 credits prior to having a master's degree); a minimum of three years' teaching experience; current employment in an educational setting or have ready access to one; ability to pursue challenging online graduate study; interest in continuing professional development and a role in educational leadership; and potential to improve practice through application of new knowledge and skills. Experience in a leadership capacity (i.e., committee chair, project supervisor, team leader) is highly desirable.

TUITION AND FEES

Tuition for the 2003–04 academic year was $1140 for a 3-credit course. For further information, prospective students should visit the Web site at the address below.

FINANCIAL AID

There is currently a variety of private loan programs available to educational leadership students. For more information, students should contact the Financial Aid Office (telephone: 207-283-0170 Ext. 2342; fax: 207-282-6379; e-mail: finaid@mailbox.une.edu).

APPLYING

The application process consists of six steps: completing the application forms (available in paper or online) no later than forty-five days prior to the start of a term (i.e., August 15, December 15, and April 15); submitting the nonrefundable application fee of $40; submitting official transcripts of all graduate work; sending in three letters of recommendation (one must be from a supervisor); writing a personal goal statement; and demonstrating evidence of teaching or administrative experience. An abbreviated online application is required for those applying as nonmatriculated students. This admission form enables students to enroll in up to four courses without formal admission into the University of New England.

CONTACT

Certificate of Advanced Graduate Study in Educational Leadership Program
University of New England
11 Hills Beach Road
Biddeford, Maine 04005
Telephone: 207-283-0171
Fax: 207-294-5942
E-mail: cags@mailbox.une.edu
Web site: http://www.uneonline.org
http://www.une.edu

The University of North Carolina at Chapel Hill

The William and Ida Friday Center for Continuing Education

Chapel Hill, North Carolina

As the nation's first state university, the University of North Carolina (UNC) at Chapel Hill was chartered in 1789 and opened to students in 1795. UNC–Chapel Hill was the only public university to award degrees to students in the eighteenth century. Today, there are more than 2,600 faculty members and 25,000 students enrolled at UNC. Carolina's academic offerings span more than 100 fields, including eighty-four bachelor's, 165 master's, and 108 doctoral degrees as well as professional degrees in dentistry, medicine, pharmacy, and law. Distance learning has been available since 1913. The University is accredited by the Southern Association of Colleges and Schools.

DISTANCE LEARNING PROGRAM

The Friday Center for Continuing Education offers a variety of credit and noncredit courses though Carolina Courses Online, Independent Studies, and Self-paced Study Online. These college-level print-based and online courses enable students to earn college credit without having to be admitted to UNC or travel to the campus. The Friday Center administers courses from eight institutions of the University of North Carolina: Appalachian State University, East Carolina University, Elizabeth City State University, North Carolina State University, UNC–Chapel Hill, UNC–Greensboro, Western Carolina University, and Winston-Salem State University. More than 5,000 students enroll in distance education courses through the Friday Center each year.

DELIVERY MEDIA

The Independent Studies program offers traditional self-paced correspondence courses. Students enrolled in an Independent Studies course receive a printed course manual that contains all lessons, assignments, and instructions. They work through the course at their own pace. Each course has an instructor who grades assignments and answers questions. The minimum completion time for an Independent Studies course is twelve weeks, and students have nine months to complete the course. Students may take two courses at a time. More than 100 Independent Studies courses are available, and most courses are offered for credit at the undergraduate college level.

The Carolina Courses Online program follows the UNC calendar. Students enrolled in a Carolina Courses Online course receive information on how to access the Web pages that contain all lessons, assignments, and instructions. They communicate with classmates and their instructor via e-mail and discussion forums and are encouraged to use the vast resources available through the Internet as they complete their course work. Approximately sixty Carolina Courses Online courses are available, and most courses are offered for credit at the undergraduate college level.

The Self-paced Study Online program offers self-paced online courses. Students enrolled in a Self-paced Study Online course receive information on how to access the Web pages that contain all lessons, assignments, and instructions. Each course has an instructor who grades assignments and answers questions. The minimum completion time for a Self-paced Study Online course is twelve weeks, and students have nine months to complete the course. Students may take two courses at a time. More than twenty Self-paced Studies Online courses are available, and most are offered for credit at the undergraduate college level.

PROGRAMS OF STUDY

The Friday Center offers a variety of courses in more than thirty subjects, including accounting, African and Afro-American studies, art, biology, business, chemistry, classics, criminal justice, communication studies, drama, economics, education, English, environmental sciences, French, geography, geology, health administration, history, hospitality management, Italian, journalism, Latin, law, mathematics, music, nursing, nutrition, philosophy, physics, political science, psychology, recreation administration, religious studies, Russian, sociology, Spanish, and statistics. Credit earned in courses offered through the Friday Center can be applied toward degree requirements at UNC–Chapel Hill and other institutions.

SPECIAL PROGRAMS

Credit courses offered by the Friday Center may be used for teacher license renewal at the discretion of the local district. Students should visit the Friday Center Web site listed in the Contact section for more information.

STUDENT SERVICES

Friday Center staff members are available to answer questions, provide academic advising, and process enrollments. Online library services are available through the UNC–Chapel Hill library system.

CREDIT OPTIONS

Most courses are offered for credit at the undergraduate college level. Credit earned in these courses may be applied toward a degree, if the course is applicable to the requirements of the particular degree program.

FACULTY

Faculty members are appointed by the department or school offering the course. Approximately 120 faculty members teach in the program at any given time.

ADMISSION

Carolina Courses Online, Independent Studies, and Self-paced Study Online courses are open to anyone who wishes to enroll; there are no admission requirements.

TUITION AND FEES

Tuition must be paid in full at the time of enrollment. Tuition is $100 per credit hour for North Carolina residents and $205 per credit hour for nonresidents. Most courses are 3 credit hours. Tuition and other charges are subject to change without notice. Textbooks must be purchased separately.

FINANCIAL AID

Financial aid may be available through VA benefits, vocational rehabilitation grants, local education agencies, and Defense Activity for Non-Traditional Education Support (DANTES).

APPLYING

Enrollments in Independent Studies or Self-paced Study Online courses are accepted at any time by mail, fax, or in person. Carolina Courses Online enrollments must be received by specified deadlines. Students should visit the Friday Center Web site for more information.

CONTACT

Student Services Manager
CB #1020
University of North Carolina-Chapel Hill
Chapel Hill, North Carolina 27599-1020
Telephone: 919-962-1134
800-862-5669 (toll-free)
Fax: 919-962-5549
E-mail: ceinfo@unc.edu
Web site: http://fridaycenter.unc.edu

The University of North Carolina at Greensboro

Division of Continual Learning

Greensboro, North Carolina

The University of North Carolina at Greensboro (UNCG) was founded in 1891 and became coeducational in 1963. Accredited by the Southern Association of Colleges and Schools, it first offered distance learning courses in 1972. Today, there are more than 830 faculty members and 14,000 students, including 900 students enrolled in some type of distance learning course. UNCG offers more than one hundred undergraduate, fifty-nine master's programs, and twenty-two doctoral programs.

DISTANCE LEARNING PROGRAM

The Division of Continual Learning offers credit and non-credit courses and several no-credit certificates through the CALL program and UNCG *i*Campus. The Division also runs programs for children and youth. These programs include the All-Arts and Sciences Camp, which introduces youngsters, ages 7–15, to courses in the arts and sciences, and the Fast Forward program, which provides the opportunity for high school students to take distance learning courses during the school day at their high school, earning credit that can be transferred to any college or university that accepts UNCG transfer credits.

In 2004, the division, along with the College of Arts and Sciences, launched UNCG's first undergraduate degree offered completely online. The Bachelor of Arts in Liberal Studies is a degree-completion program in which students who are admitted and can transfer up to 60 credit hours into the school and finish their degree via the Internet.

The Master of Arts in Liberal Studies is also available completely online.

The goal of UNCG's online degree programs is to provide a quality, highly-interactive experience.

DELIVERY MEDIA

UNCG *i*Campus programs are delivered entirely via the Internet. Students receive information on accessing their Web courses upon registration for a course. Students also have access to the *i*Campus site, which incorporates extensive help features on learning styles, writing, time management, and technology, to name a few.

PROGRAMS OF STUDY

UNCG offers three online programs: a Bachelor of Science in liberal studies, a Master of Arts in liberal studies, and a post-master's certificate in advanced school counseling.

The Bachelor of Science (humanities concentration) is an online degree-completion program for adult students who have earned a minimum of 60 hours of transferable credit. The program is designed to provide students with an opportunity to earn their baccalaureate degree in an e-learning environment by gaining a thorough understanding of the humanities, the interconnections among them, and their relevance to individuals and to modern society.

The humanities are defined to include those disciplines that study people—their ideas, history, literature, artifacts, and values. The program investigates individual people in their solitude, life together in societies, and models of and for reality that constitute cultures. Individual courses tackle the big questions that have been the traditional province of the humanities, such as what makes a life worth living.

The Master of Arts in liberal studies (MALS) is an interdisciplinary program designed for unique freedom and flexibility of study. Its course work encourages critical and imaginative thinking on intellectual, social, political, historical, literary, and artistic issues within a broad humanistic perspective.

Seminar-style courses, taught by professors noted for teaching excellence, encourage lively dialogue and debate among the adult participants. Students freely explore study outside rigidly constructed specializations.

The program is open to all college graduates regardless of their undergraduate majors. Students can take all course work completely online or by a mix of campus, off-campus, and Web-based courses.

UNCG also offers off-campus and online courses outside of degree programs in a variety of subject areas.

Undergraduate courses include classical studies, family and community studies, fine arts and art studies, general studies and humanities, geological and related sciences, liberal arts and sciences, philosophy, public health, religion/religious studies, sociology, and U.S. and world history.

Graduate courses comprise curriculum and instruction; education; fine arts and art studies; French language and literature; general studies and humanities; historic preservation, conservation, and architectural history; liberal arts and sciences, library science; music; special education; teaching English as a second language/foreign language.

SPECIAL PROGRAMS

UNCG runs a wintersession term between the fall and spring semesters of each school year, usually offering between six and ten undergraduate and graduate courses delivered via the Internet. Courses are typically five weeks long, with a workload similar to a summer session course. More information is available by accessing the Web site.

STUDENT SERVICES

UNCG's Division of Continual Learning staff members are available to answer advising questions, provide technical support, process enrollments, and find any help that is needed. There is a dedicated person for each of the liberal studies degree programs. Online library services are available through UNCG's Jackson Library. Other student resources are available through the Web site.

CREDIT OPTIONS

Courses are offered for credit at the undergraduate and graduate levels. Credit earned in these courses may be applied toward a degree if the course is applicable to the degree requirements of the particular degree program.

FACULTY

UNCG online courses are taught by the same faculty members that teach the course in the face-to-face environment. Several members of the faculty have won distinguishing awards. For more faculty details, interested students should visit the Web site.

ADMISSION

Students seeking admission to a degree program must follow the usual admissions process. For more information, students should visit the UNCG Web site. Students seeking to take single courses for credit should follow the guidelines for visiting students.

TUITION AND FEES

Tuition must be paid in full at the time of enrollment. Tuition is approximately $69 per undergraduate credit hour and $104 per graduate credit hour for North Carolina residents. Non-resident tuition is higher. Most courses are 3 credit hours. Tuition and other charges are subject to change without notice. Textbooks must be purchased separately.

FINANCIAL AID

Financial aid may be available for degree seeking students through VA benefits, vocational rehabilitation grants, local education agencies, and Defense Activity for Non-Traditional Education Support (DANTES). Students should call the financial aid office for more details (Telephone: 336-334-5000).

APPLYING

Applications for degree-seeking programs and other courses are accepted throughout the year, but vary by program. Most programs have deadlines, although online programs like BLS and MALS online have less restrictive timetables. Students should visit the UNCG *i*Campus Web site for more information.

All offerings require enrollment prior to the first class session. Enrollment forms are available at the Web address or the toll-free number, listed below.

CONTACT

Distance Learning Program Manager
UNCG Division of Continual Learning
University of North Carolina at Greensboro
P.O. Box 26170
1100 West Market Street
Greensboro, North Carolina 27402-6170
Telephone: 336-256-CALL
866-334-CALL (toll-free)
Fax: 336-334-5628
E-mail: info@calldcl.com
Web site: http://www.CALLDCL.com
http://www.UNCGiCampus.com

University of North Carolina at Pembroke

UNCP Online

Pembroke, North Carolina

Founded in 1887 as a normal school to train Native American public school teachers, the University of North Carolina at Pembroke (UNCP) is located just off Interstate 95 in the coastal plains of North Carolina. A regional public university, UNCP offers fifty-five undergraduate majors and fourteen master's degree programs. Enrollment is 5,000 and growing. The University offers one of the most diverse student bodies in the nation according to U.S. News & World Report, *which also ranks UNCP as one of the most affordable universities in the nation. A member of the Peach Belt Athletic Conference, the University competes in fourteen intercollegiate sports in the NCAA Division II. UNC Pembroke is a constituent member of the University of North Carolina system.*

The Commission on Colleges of the Southern Association of Colleges and Schools accredits UNC Pembroke to award bachelor's and master's degrees. In addition, a number of the individual University departments, degree programs, and service functions are accredited by appropriate professional organizations.

DISTANCE LEARNING PROGRAM

UNC Pembroke brings education to the student through a number of off-campus and Internet-based programs and courses. The Office of Continuing and Distance Education provides administrative services to the adult or nontraditional learner and takes great pride in assuring the same level of excellence in teaching for which UNCP is widely known.

DELIVERY MEDIA

UNC Pembroke offers a number of face-to-face instructional sites in partnership with community colleges in southeastern North Carolina as well as interactive video classes to a number of sites. For students outside the region, distance education opportunities are available through the World Wide Web in a quickly expanding online program. Online courses are generally asynchronous but demand interaction with the professor.

PROGRAMS OF STUDY

Currently, the University offers the second two years of the Bachelor of Science in Business Administration with a concentration in management (in conjunction with approved community colleges and other senior institutions) and the Master of Public Administration completely online. Degree programs in education and computer science and a wide variety of general electives from the arts to the sciences are in the planning stages. For a complete list of courses offered each semester, students should visit the UNCP Office of Continuing and Distance Education Web site at http://www.uncp.edu/ced.

The University of North Carolina at Pembroke is committed to providing a variety of continuing education opportunities and special activities that contribute to its mission. Two of the overall purposes of the University are to meet the educational needs of students and to serve the community and society at large by providing cultural and educational leadership. The programs offered through the Office of Continuing Education and Distance Education help carry out the purposes of the University. At UNCP, programs involving continuing education, outreach, and service are coordinated through the Office of Continuing Education and Distance Education.

SPECIAL PROGRAMS

UNC Pembroke's Office of Continuing and Distance Education, in conjunction with the Regional Center for Economic, Community, and Professional Development, offers noncredit continuing education programs in a wide variety of subject areas. Special programs can be designed for business, industry, and professional development.

STUDENT SERVICES

All services available to traditional on-campus students are available to distance education students as well. Counselors are available to assist the student with their needs from course selection to career choices, and the Office of Financial Aid provides access to the full range of available financial aid. Library resources are available and accessible via the Internet, and University Computing and Information Services (UCIS) provides a helpline for online students in need of assistance. The University attempts to make online learning easily accessible for the adult or nontraditional student and to make the educational experience beneficial in every way.

CREDIT OPTIONS

In general, transfer credits from accredited institutions are readily accepted with a grade of C or better. Transfer from North Carolina community colleges is relatively seamless, and the University makes every effort to allow transfer credit for courses outside the state if the courses are deemed equivalent. The A.S. or A.A. transfer student receives up to 64 hours of credit, while the A.A.S. degree student receives up to 60 hours of transfer credit. The University reviews transfer credit individually and notifies the student as quickly as possible as to which credit is deemed acceptable by the registrar and faculty. Additional credit options include DANTES and CLEP testing.

FACULTY

There are approximately 200 full-time faculty members, most of whom hold the doctorate. Faculty members meet rigorous approval processes established by the respective school or college to which they are assigned. UNC Pembroke is a teaching institution; therefore, most classes are taught by full-time faculty members. Online courses are developed and taught by the same faculty members who teach on campus and provide the learner with well-designed educational experiences.

ADMISSION

First-year students are evaluated on the quality of their college-preparatory classes, standardized test results, and classroom and extracurricular activities. Students must have completed 4 units of English, 3 units of mathematics (including algebra I and II and geometry), 2 units of social studies (including U.S. history), and 3 units of science (including 1 biological, 1 physical, and 1 lab course). A recommendation from the high school guidance counselor is helpful, and, in some cases, an interview with an admissions counselor is required.

Transfer students must have a GPA of at least 2.0 on all transferable work. Students who graduated from high school after 1990 may have additional requirements. Transfer applicants who do not meet first-year student admission requirements must complete 6 semester hours in English, mathematics, science, and social science at a community college. Students should call one of the University's admission counselors for details.

TUITION AND FEES

Current tuition and fees for distance learning courses are $51 per undergraduate credit hour for in-state students and $352 per undergraduate credit hour for out-of-state students. Graduate students pay $76 per credit hour in state and $521 per credit hour out of state. Some special programs are billed at special rates. For questions concerning those programs, students should contact the Office of Continuing and Distance Education.

FINANCIAL AID

Distance learning students have full access to any and all financial aid offered by the University. For a complete list of financial aid programs, students should see the Web page for the financial aid office at http://www.uncp.edu/fa/.

APPLYING

UNC Pembroke is on the semester system. Application can be made at any time, and schedules of classes and a direct link to register are available at the UNCP Office of Continuing and Distance Education Web site listed below.

CONTACT

Warren G. McDonald, Ph.D., Director, Continuing and Distance Education
Courtney McMillan, Program Coordinator
University of North Carolina at Pembroke
P.O. Box 1510
Pembroke, North Carolina 28372-1510
Telephone: 910-521-6367
Fax: 910-521-6762.
E-mail: warren.mcdonald@uncp.edu
courtney.mcmillan@uncp.edu
Web site: http://www.uncp.edu/ced

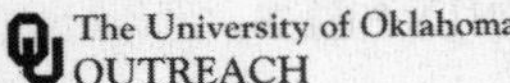

The University of Oklahoma

University Outreach
College of Continuing Education
College of Liberal Studies

Norman, Oklahoma

The University of Oklahoma's (OU) College of Continuing Education (CCE) is a lifelong learning organization dedicated to helping individuals, businesses, groups, and communities transform themselves through knowledge. Formally organized in 1913, CCE is the outreach arm of the University of Oklahoma. Nationally recognized for its pioneering efforts in continuing education, CCE extends the educational resources of the University through more than thirty different program formats, including graduate and undergraduate degree programs, correspondence and other distance programs, on- and off-campus courses, and a wide variety of programs conducted under the auspices of federal and state grants and contracts. On the Norman campus, adult and other learners attend programs at the Oklahoma Center for Continuing Education, one of eleven W. K. Kellogg Foundation–funded, University-based residential conference centers in the world. Annually, CCE offers some 2,000 courses and activities to more than 250,000 nontraditional learners in Oklahoma and in locations all over the world.

The mission of the College of Liberal Studies is to provide nontraditional students with high-quality coherent, interdisciplinary graduate and undergraduate liberal arts programs through innovative formats. By combining independent study with weekend classes or brief seminars on campus or Internet-guided study, adult students can earn a Bachelor of Liberal Studies or Master of Liberal Studies degree. The College of Liberal Studies is a fully accredited, academic division of the University of Oklahoma.

DISTANCE LEARNING PROGRAM

In carrying out its mission to help nontraditional learners transform themselves through knowledge, CCE offers a variety of credit and noncredit distance learning courses and programs within the state of Oklahoma and beyond. Each year, CCE extends the educational resources of the University of Oklahoma through more than thirty different program formats. Annually, CCE offers some 2,000 courses and activities to more than 250,000 nontraditional learners in Oklahoma and worldwide.

DELIVERY MEDIA

Courses are delivered via television, videotapes, videoconferencing, interactive television, audiotapes, audioconferencing, computer software, CD-ROM, computer conferencing, World Wide Web, e-mail, and print. Students and faculty members may meet in person or interact via videoconferencing, audioconferencing, mail, telephone, fax, e-mail, interactive television, or World Wide Web. The following equipment may be required: audiocassette player, fax machine, television, cable television, videocassette player, computer, modem, Internet access, e-mail, and CD-ROM.

PROGRAMS OF STUDY

A variety of programs are available in various distance formats. Independent study courses (credit and noncredit)—some of which are offered online—are available in the following subjects: anthropology, astronomy, business administration, business communication, chemistry, Chinese, classical culture, communication, drama, economics, education, engineering, English, finance, French, geography, geology, German, Greek, health and sport sciences, history, human relations, journalism and mass communication, Latin, library and information studies, management, marketing, mathematics, modern languages, music, philosophy, political science, psychology, Russian, sociology, and Spanish. Master's degree programs in the following areas are presented onsite at military and civilian locations around the world: communication, economics, human relations (including a human resource development emphasis and a community services emphasis), public administration, and social work. In addition, a Ph.D. in organizational leadership is available at some overseas sites. (These programs combine on-site course delivery with online and correspondence study.) In addition, students in Oklahoma have access to telecourses and OneNet courses.

SPECIAL PROGRAMS

CCE offers a number of distance learning special programs. Among these are the DHS/SATTRN (Satellite Training Network) programs held for Oklahoma Department of Human Services and other state employees. CCE's Independent Study Department works closely with the DANTES program and the Navy College PACE program. In addition, this department offers a number of noncredit writing courses and more than seventy-five high school courses, many of them available online.

STUDENT SERVICES

Students enrolled in CCE's Advanced Programs have access to the facilities and resources of OU's Norman-based library. Advanced Programs students order all their textbooks online through Follett, and Independent Study offers students a complete array of bookstore services.

CREDIT OPTIONS

CCE's Independent Study Department provides students various options to earn credit through testing. Among these are the College-Level Examination Program (CLEP), DANTES, and institutionally developed advanced-standing examinations.

FACULTY

The faculty for OU distance programs includes regular University of Oklahoma faculty members, adjunct faculty members, and instructors with special appointments. All are experienced and highly qualified instructional professionals who are knowledgeable about the needs, concerns, and capabilities of distance education students.

ADMISSION

Admission to the University of Oklahoma is necessary for credit courses other than those offered through Independent Study. Independent Study students need not be first admitted to OU. To participate in graduate programs, admission to OU's Graduate College is required. For more information, prospective students should use the contact information below.

TUITION AND FEES

Tuition and fees vary based on the chosen program. Prospective students are encouraged to inquire about the costs associated with the program in which they are interested. Expenses relating to continuing education courses taken to maintain and improve professional skills may be tax deductible (Treas. Reg. 1.162-5, Coughlin v. Commissioner, 203f.2d 307). A tax adviser can make this determination based on the particular facts relating to one's professional situation. All tuition and fees at the University of Oklahoma are subject to changes made by the State Regents for Higher Education.

FINANCIAL AID

Financial aid is available for many of the semester-based programs offered through CCE. Financial aid is not available to Independent Study students. Each program has different eligibility requirements. Interested students are encouraged to use the contact information below. They will then be put in touch with the appropriate CCE department that can fully answer their financial aid questions.

APPLYING

Distance learners interested in credit and noncredit programs may enroll by telephone (800-522-0772 Ext. 2248) or by fax (405-325-7164). Prospective students should use the contact information below to determine the appropriate telephone number.

CONTACT

Larry Hayes
College of Continuing Education
The University of Oklahoma
1700 Asp Avenue
Norman, Oklahoma 73072-6400
Telephone: 405-325-4414
Fax: 405-325-7196
E-mail: lhayes@ou.edu
Web site: http://www.outreach.ou.edu

UNIVERSITY OF OREGON

University of Oregon

Applied Information Management Program

Eugene, Oregon

The interdisciplinary master's degree Applied Information Management (AIM) Program is designed to respond to rapid developments in information technologies and the resulting impact on organizations. Faculty members from both academic and professional settings teach AIM courses. AIM is a fully accredited degree offered by the University of Oregon (UO).

This degree, specifically designed to serve midcareer professionals, was first offered in 1986. The AIM Program is based on the belief that information managers must have more than an understanding of new technologies. They must combine knowledge in management, business, and visual communications with an awareness of high technology and its global context in order to meet the challenges of the future. The AIM Program offers innovative graduate study in management education as an alternative to the traditional Master of Business Administration or a master's degree in information systems.

DISTANCE LEARNING PROGRAM

AIM Online provides the same dynamic curriculum as the AIM Onsite Program through a combination of core (seven-week) and short (four-week) courses. Courses run year-round with periodic short breaks in the schedule. It takes approximately 2½ years to earn the degree.

DELIVERY MEDIA

AIM online offers asynchronous courses over the Web. The Blackboard Internet-learning platform used to deliver AIM courses includes e-mail, chat, threaded discussion, video, audio, and document-sharing functions. Courses are accessible using either a PC or a Mac computer. AIM provides students with an e-mail account to use for course-related messages. Prospective students are encouraged to visit the Web site for specific requirements (http://www.aimdegree.com/tech.html).

PROGRAM OF STUDY

To earn the AIM degree requires 54 credits, 44 from core courses and 10 from short courses.

The required core courses are distributed among four content areas. The information management courses include Virtual Learning and Teams (3 credits), Data Management and Communications (3 credits), Information Systems and Management (3 credits), Project Management (3 credits), Creating Business Solutions (3 credits), and Information and Society (3 credits). The business management courses consist of Management of Organizations (3 credits) and Marketing Management and Planning (3 credits). The information design courses consist of Information Design and Communications (3 credits) and Information Design Trends (3 credits). The applied research courses consist of Writing for Research (2 credits), Electronic Information and Research (2 credits), Research Methods (4 credits), and AIM capstone (6 credits).

The short-course online options include information architecture, conflict resolution, information emergency management, knowledge management, enterprise content management, systems analysis, and tools for systems thinking.

AIM provides an online orientation to students.

SPECIAL PROGRAMS

Students admitted to the online program may take on-site courses with permission. Students in the AIM Onsite Program may take online courses after taking the Virtual Learning and Teams course.

STUDENT SERVICES

Academic advising is available from the AIM Program Coordinator via telephone or e-mail, listed below.

It is the student's responsibility to obtain all equipment and software necessary to access the courses.

Admitted students have access to University of Oregon electronic library resources and may visit any Oregon University System library.

CREDIT OPTIONS

Students earn credit by successfully completing offered courses. AIM offers all 3-credit core courses on a graded basis. Short courses and AIM Capstone are offered on a pass/no-pass basis. Although rarely done, AIM may accept transfer credits with approval of the AIM Academic Director. AIM offers courses for graduate credit only.

FACULTY

AIM primarily employs tenure-track faculty members with doctoral degrees to teach core courses. Tenure-track faculty members, as well as practitioners from the field with at least a master's degree, teach short courses.

ADMISSION

Requirements for admission to the AIM Program include an application form; a $50 application fee; official transcripts; a statement of purpose; an autobiographical essay; a resume; three letters of recommendation; and, if the applicant does not have a degree from an English-speaking institution, results of the Test of English as a Foreign Language (TOEFL).

TUITION AND FEES

The total cost for the AIM online program is $26,000, which includes $24,300 for tuition, a $1500 technology fee, a $50 application fee, and a $150 matriculation fee.

Tuition is $450 per credit (in state or out of state).

Tuition and fees are subject to change at any time.

FINANCIAL AID

Students may receive consideration for financial assistance through Federal Perkins Loans and the Stafford/Ford Loan programs. To be eligible, a student must enroll for at least 5 credits per academic quarter (half-time). Students pursuing the AIM degree may meet this minimum standard. Recipients of financial aid must be U.S. citizens or in the United States for other than temporary purposes.

For more information, prospective students should contact the UO Office of Financial Aid by telephone at 541-346-3221 or 800-760-6953 (toll-free) or via the Web (http://financialaid.uoregon.edu/).

APPLYING

The entire application may be completed online by visiting the Web site, http://www.aimdegree.com/materials.html. There are no set application deadlines. Applications are considered after all materials are received.

CONTACT

AIM Program Coordinator
University of Oregon
722 SW Second Avenue, Suite 230
Portland, Oregon 97204
Telephone: 800-824-2714 (toll-free)
Fax: 503-725-3067
E-mail: aim@continue.uoregon.edu
Web site: http://www.aimdegree.com/

University of Phoenix

Online Campus

Phoenix, Arizona

Founded in 1976, University of Phoenix is now the largest private University in the United States. The University is accredited by the Higher Learning Commission and is a member of the North Central Association. University of Phoenix serves more than 200,000 students per year with more than 17,000 highly qualified instructors at 142 campuses and Internet delivery worldwide.

High academic standards, commitment to quality, and programs designed specifically to address the needs of today's marketplace have earned University of Phoenix a reputation for leadership in both the academic and business communities. A distinguishing blend of proven academic models and innovative instructional delivery systems, combined with a focus on excellent service to students, has pioneered the University's phenomenal growth. The mission of University of Phoenix is to educate working adults to develop the knowledge and skills that will enable them to achieve their professional goals, improve the productivity of their organizations, and provide leadership and service to their communities.

DISTANCE LEARNING PROGRAM

The Online program utilizes computer communications to link faculty members and students from around the world into interactive learning groups. Class size is limited to 15 for maximum interaction. Degrees are completed entirely online for the convenience of working adults who find it difficult or impossible to attend classes at fixed times and places.

Of the more than 99,000 students attending class from all over the world, 20 percent are executives or owners of their own businesses, 30 percent are middle managers in business and industry, and 44 percent are technical or licensed professionals. Roughly 56 percent are women, and the average student is 35 years old.

DELIVERY MEDIA

Once enrolled in an online degree program, students log on at least five days each week to participate in class discussions focused on the topics they are studying. Students go online to send and receive material to and from class groups, while conducting most of their communication and class work off-line. This balance of both online and off-line interaction is referred to as asynchronous communication.

PROGRAMS OF STUDY

The Master of Management program emphasizes the skills and knowledge it takes to manage both people and projects at an advanced level. The Master of Business Administration (M.B.A.) program is designed to enhance the management skills student need to function effectively within an organization. The M.B.A. in health-care management program is designed for professionals seeking management positions in the health-care field. The M.B.A. in global management program is designed to ingrain the abilities to identify business opportunities and threats and to develop effective courses of action within the parameters of the international environment. The M.B.A. in technology management is a highly specialized program that focuses on proven methods and techniques for anticipating, managing, and marketing technology. The M.B.A. in e-business degree program prepares graduates for a leadership role in the rapidly expanding area of e-business. The M.B.A. in accounting is designed to develop or enhance the financial management skills necessary to function effectively within private businesses, nonprofit organizations, and public agencies. The M.B.A. in marketing was created in response to the important role played by marketing managers in any organization, particularly as organizations diversify to capitalize upon Internet opportunities to expand their markets. The M.B.A. in human resources management program prepares the graduate to lead large and medium-sized HR departments from a technical and strategic vantage point. The Master of Science in computer information systems provides the tools not only to understand technology but also to keep current in its many kinds of development. The Master of Arts in Education (M.A.Ed.) program with a specialization in administration and supervision is designed for educators interested in gaining knowledge and expertise in the area of school administration. The M.A.Ed. program with a specialization in early childhood education is a graduate degree for educators seeking knowledge and expertise in the field of early childhood development and teaching. The M.A.Ed. program with a specialization in special education prepares candidates to be cross-categorical special educators. A supervised student-teaching experience is incorporated into the degree. The M.A.Ed. program with an emphasis in adult education and distance learning equips students to develop educational courses and materials for adult learners both in classrooms and at a distance. The M.A.Ed. program with an emphasis in curriculum and instruction provides students with a foundation for understanding and analyzing curriculum and instruction theories and philosophies. The M.A.Ed. program with an emphasis in curriculum and technology covers how to integrate technology into the K–12 curriculum. The M.A.Ed. programs with emphases on elementary or secondary education are programs for candidates who have already earned a bachelor's degree and wish to gain the pedagogical skills and knowledge that will assist them in becoming competent and effective educators. The Master of Science in Nursing program is designed to develop and enhance the knowledge and skills of registered nurses. The Master of Health Administration program prepares leaders who can effectively respond to the dynamic and ever-changing health-care industry.

The Doctor of Management in organizational leadership provides those students with a professional master's degree a means of exploring their personal readiness to become leaders in their professions or their current organizations. The Doctor of Business Administration degree program provides learners with a professional master's degree a means of exploring their personal readiness to become senior leaders in management professions. The Doctor of Education in leadership program prepares learners to become transformational leaders who will strategically manage and lead complex educational organizations. The Doctor of Health Administration program prepares leaders to respond effectively to the dynamic and ever-changing health-care industry.

Each Bachelor of Science (B.S.) in business degree program requires 120 credits. The business administration program is suited ideally for men and women who need to be familiar with every aspect of running a business. The business management program focuses on the skills necessary to manage both people and projects effectively. The business marketing program provides a foundation from which to build creative, analytical, and leadership abilities individually and in a team environment. The accounting program promotes and orientation to the accounting profession and is designed to provide the knowledge, skills, and abilities necessary to pursue a successful accounting career. the business finance program is designed to prepare graduates with the requisite knowledge and skills to effectively apply financial concepts and tools in various organizational scenarios from a generalist perspective. The B.S. in business information systems program is designed graduates with the requisite knowledge, skills, and values to effectively apply various business principles and tools in an organizational setting. The information technology program provides fundamental knowledge and practice in both the information technology function and system development. The e-business program provides fundamental knowledge and practice in business management and information technology. The B.S. in management degree program provides the knowledge and skills needed to successfully manage almost any dynamic and evolving organization. The curriculum is ideal for community college students who have earned an associate degree. The B.S. in health administration program equips students with basic skills needed for the health-care environment. The B.S. in criminal justice administration program provides students interested in law enforcement, criminal law, or corrections with an interdisciplinary study of crime. The B.S. in human services management program prepares graduates for a successful career by giving them practical knowledge and basic skills to manage in the human services industry. The Bachelor of Science in Nursing program is designed to develop the professional knowledge and skills of working registered nurses.

In addition, students may study toward the Associate of Arts degree, a two-year program providing solid academic training, and apply those credits toward the B.S. in business majors.

CREDIT OPTIONS

Graduate students are permitted to waive up to 9 credits by transferring comparable graduate-level course work taken at other accredited institutions.

For undergraduate study, no more than 69 credits of lower-division courses may be applied toward the degree requirement. At least 39 of the 120 total credits must satisfy University of Phoenix's general education requirement. Students can apply for credit by examination and/or portfolio.

FACULTY

University of Phoenix Online has more than 9,000 faculty members. All faculty members have both academic credentials (more than one third hold doctoral degrees) and demonstrated success in the fields they teach. The University recruits only those who are working in their area of expertise, bringing practical, real-world experience to the students who are working professionals. Faculty members undergo extensive training in online instruction, and all participate in periodic evaluation that includes peer review components.

ADMISSION

For graduate applicants, an undergraduate degree from a regionally accredited college or university, with a cumulative GPA of 2.5 or better (3.0 for prior graduate work) is required. Students must also be currently employed; have a minimum of three years of full-time, post–high school work experience providing exposure to organizational systems and management processes; or have access to an organizational environment appropriate for the application of theoretical concepts learned in the classroom.

Undergraduate applicants must have a high school diploma or its equivalent, be at least 21 years old, and currently employed or have access to an organizational environment. Students must complete the University-proctored Comprehensive Cognitive Assessment. For international applicants and those with a primary language other than English, a minimum score of 550 on the TOEFL is required.

TUITION AND FEES

Graduate tuition is $620 per credit for the doctoral programs and $545 per credit for the master's programs. Undergraduate tuition is $440 per credit. Additional costs include an application fee of $110 and a graduate fee of $55. Textbook costs vary by course.

APPLYING

Unless students are relying on foreign transcripts for admission, all that is needed to begin the first course is to complete an application, enrollment agreement, and disclosure form. While students are in their first three classes, academic counselors work with them to complete transcript requests, the Comprehensive Cognitive Assessment, and any other items necessary for formal registration.

CONTACT

Enrollment Department
University of Phoenix Online
3157 East Elwood Street
Phoenix, Arizona 85034
Telephone: 800-833-0287 (toll-free in U.S.)
Fax: 602-387-6440
Web site: http://www.uopx.com/petersons

University of St. Francis

Distance Learning

Joliet, Illinois

The University of St. Francis is a private, Catholic, Franciscan institution offering more than sixty undergraduate areas of study and ten graduate programs. Courses are offered at more than eighty sites throughout the nation and online. The University serves more than 4,200 students nationwide.

DISTANCE LEARNING PROGRAM

The distance education programs at the University of St. Francis (USF) are delivered online and through faculty-directed instruction.

DELIVERY MEDIA

Online courses use computer and information technologies to link faculty members and students from around the world into interactive classes. The online courses are designed for working professionals at both the undergraduate and graduate levels. USF uses the WebCT program to deliver its online courses. Online courses are not "time-bound;" students work on the course at a time and place convenient to their schedule. Like any class, however, students read texts, participate in class discussions, write papers, and take exams through the USF online program. Student interaction is an important component of USF online courses.

For the bachelor's degree completion program in health arts, faculty-directed instruction (FDI) courses are available. FDI courses are home-based correspondence courses that encompass the same course requirements as traditional classes. Course content, syllabi, textbooks, and assignments are the same as for on-site classes. Students are provided with a comprehensive and rigorous course outline that includes a schedule for completion of assignments, "lectures" and comments from the instructor, study guide questions, directions for projects and assignments, and examination materials. Students submit assignments to their instructor via mail, e-mail, and/or fax. Instructors telephone students periodically throughout the course to provide more in-depth interaction.

PROGRAMS OF STUDY

The new world of health care challenges the knowledge and flexibility of today's nurses. USF offers an RN-B.S.N. Fast Track degree in nursing. Registered nursing students prepare for these challenges through course work and clinical experiences developed to meet the individual needs of each RN student. After completion of prerequisites, the nursing course work may be completed in about 1½ years. The entire RN-B.S.N. Fast Track program is available online in eight-week modules, except for clinical experiences, which are set up at health-care agencies in the RN nursing student's locale. Highly qualified and dedicated faculty members in the College of Nursing and Allied Health teach all online course work.

The Bachelor of Science in health arts program is a degree-completion program for licensed health-care professionals. The program gives adult workers access to higher education and allows them to work toward the completion of their bachelor's degree while providing college credit for prior learning experiences.

The Master of Science (M.S.) in health services administration program prepares health-care professionals for management in the dynamic health-care field. This high-quality program of challenging content meets the ever-changing demands of the profession. The program is designed for students who have knowledge and experiences in specific areas of health care and are seeking a broader understanding of the field. While the program is offered in a convenient format, the content is rigorous. The curriculum includes both the theories of management and their practical applications in the health-care field. The graduate program emphasizes administration rather than a concentration with a specialty.

Students in the Master of Business Administration (M.B.A.) program have the convenience of completing their M.B.A. anytime, anyplace, through their laptop, home, or office computers and an Internet connection. This program provides a flexible, viable alternative for professionals with busy personal, work, and travel schedules. Students interact with faculty members who are specially trained to offer a challenging, exciting, and meaningful online course experience.

The Master of Science in management program is appropriate for professionals who want to remain in their specialty field (such as social work, research and development, engineering, or nursing), but who want to step into a managerial role or enhance their managerial role and abilities. The M.S. in management student gains an understanding of the social, managerial, economic, environmental, and organizational concepts that comprise the public and business fields. The program is designed for business professionals looking for a flexible, convenient path toward degree completion.

The Master of Science in training and development program helps meet the growing need for professionals' continuing education and training programs in business and industry, higher education, continuing professional education, governmental and community agencies, community education, religious organizations, gerontology programs, and health-care delivery systems. The curriculum includes areas of adult learning theory, needs analysis, instructional design, evaluation, program planning, management, marketing, and finance. The curriculum includes both theory and application.

STUDENT SERVICES

The goal of the University of St. Francis is to provide its online students with a wide array of academic support services equivalent to those available to on-campus students. A full range of library support services are available to USF distance students, including remote access to the online catalog and online databases, access to online database tutorials and subject guides, toll-free telephone and e-mail access to reference librarians, and assistance locating local libraries, interlibrary loan services, and periodic e-mail updates.

The University offers an Academic Resource Center with evening hours for distance students, providing assistance with all aspects of the writing process, such as paper formatting, source citation, grammar questions, and topic selection. Services are available via toll-free telephone and by e-mail. Career counseling, assistance with creating resumes and cover letters, and job-seeking assistance are provided online through the Career Resource Center. USF also provides an online bookstore, from which students can order books, clothing items, gifts, and other general merchandise items. Through the Student Information Center, students receive general information on financial aid, access the University's online catalog and class schedule, request transcripts, and access their individual accounts.

CREDIT OPTIONS

Credit for graduate work completed at another nationally accredited institution may be accepted toward a graduate degree. Up to a total of 8 semester hours may be transferred with certain provisions. The student must complete a petition for transfer of credit; the course(s) must be appropriate to the student's degree program and not be in conflict with credit limitations; the petition must be approved by the academic adviser and the program administrators; and the student must have earned a grade of B or higher in the course.

Credit is considered for transfer only after the above conditions have been met and the student's official transcript has been sent directly to the Off-Campus Admissions Office by the appropriate institution(s). In addition to the requirements listed, the course work should have been completed within seven years of applying to USF to be considered for credit. Transfer credits are not included in the computation of the student's GPA. Petition for transfer of credit must be processed, approved, and recorded before a student is considered eligible for candidacy and comprehensive examination.

Students applying for the M.B.A. program must also request an official copy of the transcript(s) from all colleges and universities they have attended. The Off-Campus Admissions Office must receive their transcripts before they may take certain courses.

FACULTY

The same high-quality faculty members who teach on-site courses at USF also teach the distance education courses. Besides being experts in the content area of the course, faculty members have experience and training to provide students with an excellent distance learning experience.

ADMISSION

Students may begin the admission process and register for their first class while completing the admission requirements to a specific program and college during the first month of enrollment. However, all admission requirements must be satisfied for eligibility for financial assistance.

TUITION AND FEES

Tuition and fees vary by program. For tuition rates of particular courses or programs of interest, applicants should visit the Web site.

FINANCIAL AID

About 95 percent of USF students receive some form of financial aid, with the average award being more than 80 percent of tuition expenses. Applicants should complete a Free Application for Federal Student Aid (FAFSA).

APPLYING

In order to register for an online class for the first time, students must complete the online permit request form and the class registration. The permit is a questionnaire about the computer and browser the student is planning to use for his or her online class. In order to be successful in an online course, the student's computer must meet or exceed certain hardware and software requirements. The student completes this questionnaire only once, before the first online class. Registration for class includes an e-mail address. New students to the University register with their admissions counselor; continuing students enrolling in an online class for the first time register through their academic program.

CONTACT

University of St. Francis
500 Wilcox Street
Joliet, Illinois 60435
Telephone: 800-735-7500 (toll-free)
E-mail: admissions@stfrancis.edu
Web site:
http://admissions.stfrancis.edu

University of Tennessee

Distance Education and Independent Study

Knoxville, Tennessee

The University of Tennessee (UT) is a state-supported, land-grant university that traces its roots to Blount College, which was founded in 1794. The University of Tennessee is dedicated to excellence in undergraduate and graduate studies, research and creative activities, and public service. UT is accredited by the Southern Association of Colleges and Schools. UT participates in Southern Regional Educational Board's Academic Common Market.

DISTANCE LEARNING PROGRAM

Distance Education and Independent Study (DEIS), in conjunction with academic colleges and departments, coordinates educational opportunities designed primarily for working professionals who are unable to attend classes on campus. From the Executive M.B.A. and the sign language interpreter sequence to the nuclear or civil engineering M.S. degrees and noncredit classes in information technology (IT) fields, hundreds of students each semester find distance education and independent study can help them meet their educational goals.

UT offers Web and correspondence courses to home school, high school, or college students. Courses for high school credit, graduation or entrance requirements, college credit toward a degree, professional development, or personal enhancement are offered in a variety of subjects, including foreign languages, social sciences, natural sciences, engineering, business, communications, math, English, history, and many others. More information about UT Distance Education and Independent Study is available on the Web site listed in the Contact section.

DELIVERY MEDIA

Courses are delivered by a wide variety of technologies. Some courses are offered via the Web and correspondence while others are offered via advanced voice/data interactive "cyberclass" technology over the Internet. Students "meet" using multimedia computers and the Internet. Correspondence courses via postal mail, e-mail, and "click-to-learn" Web delivery methods provide undergraduate credit to individuals anywhere, anytime.

PROGRAMS OF STUDY

UT offers many undergraduate courses, graduate degrees, and certificate programs. The College of Engineering offers the Master of Science in Civil Engineering, public works option; Master of Science in Environmental Engineering, waste management option; Master of Science in Industrial Engineering, engineering management concentration; and the Master of Science in Nuclear Engineering.

The Master of Science in Information Science, accredited by the American Library Association, focuses on electronic and traditional print media. Available via the Internet, the program requires 42 semester graduate course hours. The Master of Science in Nuclear Engineering, available via the Internet, requires 24 semester graduate course hours, plus 6 credit hours of research, and is intended for students interested in nuclear engineering, health physics, or radiological engineering careers.

The three flexibly delivered Executive M.B.A. programs, offered through UT's College of Business Administration, combine Internet-delivered courses with on-campus residence periods.

Online certificate programs include UT's Graduate Certificates in applied statistics, maintenance and reliability engineering, and nuclear criticality safety.

SPECIAL PROGRAMS

The Internet eLearning Institute (IEI) provides certificate programs, professional development courses, and training for information technology professionals interested in updating their skills and for students seeking high-quality Web training to pursue IT careers. Courses in the areas of e-commerce, Web databases, Web mastering, network systems engineering, administrative technology, technical sales, and instructional technology are offered via the Internet. More information on IEI is available on the Web site at http://www.iei.utk.edu.

STUDENT SERVICES

UT's Information Center, available via Web or phone, provides support for inquiries, bookstore, and library services. Access to library services, academic advising, books, materials, and career placement assistance are provided through a central portal, creating a convenient and friendly environment for students.

CREDIT OPTIONS

College credits for distance education graduate programs are recorded on a UT transcript in the same manner as credits earned in on-campus courses. Credits earned in independent study courses are generally transferable to other colleges and universities toward the completion of a degree. Internet eLearning Institute courses qualify for CEU professional credit.

FACULTY

To better ensure quality, all credit courses and their instructors are approved by University of Tennessee academic departments.

ADMISSION

University admission is not required to take undergraduate correspondence or Internet eLearning Institute courses. Application to the UT Graduate School is required for credit or audit of graduate distance education courses.

TUITION AND FEES

Tuition and fees vary. For the most current listing of tuition and fees, students should visit the Web site listed in the Contact section. Fees for Internet eLearning Institute certificate courses vary according to course. As fees and tuition are subject to change, students should visit the Web site or contact the Information Center for current information.

APPLYING

Students should visit the Web site listed below or contact the Information Center for detailed application information. Students may register by mail, fax, telephone, Internet, or in person.

CONTACT

Distance Education and Independent Study
University of Tennessee
1534 White Avenue, Room 018
Knoxville, Tennessee 37996-1525
Telephone: 865-974-5134
800-670-8657 (toll-free)
865-974-5078 (TDD)
Fax: 865-974-4684
E-mail: disteducation@utk.edu
Web site: http://anywhere.tennessee.edu

The University of Texas System

UT TeleCampus (UTTC)–Online Courses and Degrees

Austin, Texas

The University of Texas (UT) System offers several fully online degree programs and courses via the award-winning UT TeleCampus (UTTC). The UT TeleCampus is the central support center for online learning within the UT System's fifteen campuses and research facilities. Students can access virtual classrooms, links to University services and offices, a UT TeleCampus digital library, and many other service features. Launched in May 1998, the UT TeleCampus gives students the assurance of accredited universities, expert faculty members, and quality online education, along with the support services students need to succeed. The UT TeleCampus has received numerous national and regional awards since its development. All UT campuses participating in UT TeleCampus–based degrees are SACS (Southern Association of Colleges and Schools) accredited. To learn more about online degrees or courses, prospective students should go to the TeleCampus Web site or call or e-mail the TeleCampus office via the information at the end of this description.

DISTANCE LEARNING PROGRAM

UT TeleCampus–based programs and courses are comprised of the same rigorous content found on-site at UT's fifteen campuses and research facilities. From application to graduation, students face the same general expectations and receive the same high-quality courses on-site or online. Online courses follow a semester schedule, allowing flexibility during the week for study and participation in Web-based group discussions. An online syllabus identifies when tests and projects are due.

DELIVERY MEDIA

The UT TeleCampus uses Internet technologies for course delivery and student support via the World Wide Web. Courses may also utilize additional distance education tools, including CDs, audiotapes and videotapes, streaming video and audio, e-mail, discussion groups, and chat rooms.

PROGRAMS OF STUDY

The UT TeleCampus offers several fully online master's degrees, two bachelor's degree completion programs, undergraduate curriculum, nursing programs, professional development, and various other courses and certification programs.

The M.B.A. in general management is a 48-hour program that received the 2001 U.S. Distance Learning Association's Excellence in Distance Learning Programming award.

The 36-hour M.Ed. in educational technology is designed for teachers, technology coordinators, administrators, and corporate trainers who want to excel at integrating technology into their curriculum.

The 36-hour M.Ed. in curriculum and instruction with a reading specialization includes a Master Reading Teacher (MRT) certification program and a four-course English as a second language (ESL) endorsement program. The ESL course work can also be taken separately.

A four-course superintendent certification program, UTOPS, prepares candidates for superintendent certification in Texas and includes practicum components to ensure that candidates have a thoroughly developed portfolio upon completion.

Physical educators, athletic directors, wellness trainers, and coaches can earn their master's degree in kinesiology online from their choice of four UT campuses. This 36-hour program received the 2002 U.S. Distance Learning Association's Excellence in Distance Learning Programming award.

The M.S. in technology is offered with a human resource development option. This 36-hour program is ideal for corporate trainers, HR directors, and administrators in education, as well as others with an interest in technology for human resource development.

The Master of Public Administration is a 36-hour nonthesis program designed to provide students with the skills needed for effective public leadership.

Online nursing programs include an RN to BSN program, which offers the five required nursing courses for registered nurse students to complete their B.S. in nursing degree, and a graduate certificate in nursing education, a three-course program designed for registered nurses interested in pursuing the role of a nurse educator.

A bachelor's degree completion program in criminology and criminal justice is available entirely online. The program consists of 66 hours of upper-level course work.

An alternative teacher certification program (ATCP Online) is available to individuals with bachelor's degrees in areas other than education wanting to become fully-certified teachers.

Other areas of academic study include most general undergraduate curriculum required in Texas, an undergraduate track in management information systems, and a Chess in Education Program.

SPECIAL PROGRAMS

A professional development paralegal certificate program is available. This intensive three-course program trains students to become knowledgeable, ethical, and effective assistants to attorneys.

STUDENT SERVICES

The UT TeleCampus was designed with the student in mind. It provides all of the services students need to succeed, including technical support (available 24 hours a day, seven days a week, 365 days each year), an extensive digital library, and free online academic support that provides students with tutorials and writing labs. In addition, several liaisons are available at each campus to aid online students with questions about the library, registration, financial aid, and more. In order to better meet the needs of online students, the UT TeleCampus has automated cross-campus registration, thereby facilitating inter-campus collaborative programs.

CREDIT OPTIONS

Transfer credit toward online courses and programs is generally the same as comparable on-site programs. Students should contact the program advisers listed on the UT TeleCampus Web site for specifics.

FACULTY

The same expert faculty members who teach on-campus courses at the University of Texas campuses teach online academic courses offered through the UT TeleCampus. Courses are designed and developed by these faculty members with production support and faculty development provided by the UT TeleCampus.

ADMISSION

Admission criteria and processes for online offerings are generally the same as on-site courses. It is advisable to start the initial application process at least 90 days prior to the beginning of a semester. Applications may be downloaded from links within the UT TeleCampus. Students may use e-mail, fax, and phone to facilitate the process in most cases.

TUITION AND FEES

The amount of tuition and fees charged by each UT System campus varies and is based on residency status. Students should access the UT TeleCampus Web site for links to campus tuition and fee information.

FINANCIAL AID

Financial aid opportunities are available for students enrolled in UT TeleCampus courses. Links to financial aid offices are found within the UT TeleCampus Web site.

APPLYING

Application processes for online programs are generally the same as for on-site programs, although they can be completed without going to the campus. Calendars can be referenced from within the UT TeleCampus Web site. Registration can also be completed from a distance, and the UT TeleCampus Web site has detailed instructions.

CONTACT

Student Services
UT TeleCampus
The University of Texas System
702 Colorado Street, Suite 4.100
Austin, Texas 78701
Telephone: 888-TEXAS-16 (toll-free)
Fax: 512-499-4715
E-mail: telecampus@utsystem.edu
Web site: http://www.telecampus.utsystem.edu

The University of the Incarnate Word

Universe Online

San Antonio, Texas

The University of the Incarnate Word (UIW) was founded in 1881 as an outgrowth of the original mission of the Sisters of Charity of the Incarnate Word who settled in San Antonio, Texas, in 1869. The school maintains the mission of the founders by providing quality educational opportunities to all students, developing graduates who are concerned and enlightened citizens. UIW is accredited by a variety of regional and national associations, but most notably by the regional accrediting body of the Commission on Colleges of the Southern Association of Colleges and Schools. Through its College of Professional Studies, UIW is nationally accredited by the Association of Collegiate Business Schools and Programs. Universe Online is accredited by the Association of Accredited Online Programs International.

DISTANCE LEARNING PROGRAM

Universe Online is a natural extension of the mission and the entrepreneurial nature of UIW. By utilizing personal computers and asynchronous instruction, the program addresses the changing needs of adult learners. Maintaining the quality for which it is known, UIW allows students to complete a degree program totally online.

DELIVERY MEDIA

Students accepted into the program use computer-conferencing software that allows for asynchronous interaction, in an eight-week-term format. Students interact five out of seven days each week in both private and group discussions. Students are required to have an Internet service provider (ISP) to connect and upload/download assignments.

PROGRAMS OF STUDY

Universe Online offers a variety of undergraduate degree programs and graduate programs.

Associate of Arts degrees are currently available in the fields of business, information systems, communications, and liberal arts.

The Bachelor of Business Administration (B.B.A.) prepares the student for today's changing business climate. The required core and choice of specialization prepare students for positions of leadership in the business world. Areas of specialization include accounting, marketing, management, international business, and information systems.

The Bachelor of Arts in psychology of organizations and development is an interdisciplinary major that combines the findings and methods of psychology with business and specialized human resources courses.

The Bachelor of Arts degrees in applied administration and organizational administration are designed for the person who has an associate's degree in a specialized field or up to 60 credits of concentration area. Both degrees build a degree around the specialized field.

The Master of Business Administration (M.B.A.) degree program seeks to develop in each student a broad understanding of how the elements and processes of business organizations relate to one another and to the external environment. Degree requirements are designed to develop students' proficiency and confidence in all of the functional areas of business. Students can elect the general or international focus.

The Master of Arts in Administration (M.A.A.) degree program provides participants with the knowledge and skills required for managers, administrators, and supervisors to function more effectively in all types of organizations, plus the specialized managerial expertise needed for management positions within or related to the organizational development profession. Concentrations are communication arts, organizational development, and urban administration.

Students must complete both the course work in their major field of study and the University's general studies core as required in all courses. A minimum of 128 credits of course work is required to graduate in all undergraduate programs. All classes, including graduate classes, are 3 credits (semester hours). Students must complete 36 semester hours to graduate from the graduate programs.

STUDENT SERVICES

All students at UIW, including Universe Online students, have a wide variety of student service options. Online students have access to academic and financial aid advising, library and bookstore services, and online admission application and registration. In addition, students have access to career planning services.

CREDIT OPTIONS

Universe Online welcomes transfer students. UIW accepts a maximum of

66 transferable hours from accredited two-year schools. These courses are used to fulfill only lower-level division requirements. UIW accepts a total of 92 semester hours from senior colleges (or a combination of colleges).

Upon acceptance as a degree-seeking student at the University, a student must obtain prior written approval to transfer any additional credits from other institutions.

FACULTY

Given the stringent requirements of national/regional accreditation, faculty members must meet a very exacting set of requirements; this has led to a high-quality educational program delivered by highly credentialed and dedicated faculty members.

ADMISSION

Undergraduate students must possess a high school diploma or its equivalent. Students having previous college work must have a 2.5 GPA or better. Students must have worked for three years prior to application, in or outside of the home. Students who have not completed English composition I and II and college algebra must take these courses and may be tested for level.

Nonnative speakers of English must have a minimum score of 560 on the TOEFL. International student transcripts and course descriptions must be translated.

TUITION AND FEES

Undergraduate tuition is $340 per credit and graduate tuition is $495 per credit. There is an application fee of $20 and a one-time transcript fee of $30.

FINANCIAL AID

Financial aid and payment plans are available for all qualified students. Military benefits, as well as employer reimbursement benefits, may be used for online courses.

APPLYING

To apply for admission, students can fill out an application for admission through the Web site listed below. In order to be considered for admission, students must fill out an application, remit a $20 nonrefundable application fee, and submit official high school or postsecondary school transcripts from all institutions attended. Students are notified of application decisions via e-mail and U.S. mail.

CONTACT

Universe Online
University of the Incarnate Word
CPO #324
4301 Broadway
San Antonio, Texas 78209
Telephone: 877-827-2702 (toll-free)
Fax: 210-829-2756
E-mail: virtual@universe.uiwtx.edu
Web site: http://www.uiw.edu/online

University of Toledo

Division of Distance Learning

Toledo, Ohio

Established in 1872, the University of Toledo (UT) has a diverse enrollment of more than 20,000 students representing nearly ninety countries. Located in the heart of Toledo in northwest Ohio, the University plays an important role in the region. Faculty members participate in research, are involved in the community, and are committed to teaching. Eight colleges—Arts and Sciences, Business, Education, Engineering, Health and Human Services, Pharmacy, Law, and University College—offer a variety of certificate, associate, bachelor's, master's, and doctoral degree programs. UT is regionally accredited by the North Central Association of Colleges and Schools and is recognized as a leader among Ohio's public colleges and universities.

Campus features include beautiful grounds, new residence halls, a nationally recognized Student Recreation Center, and the Glass Bowl Stadium, home of the Rockets. Yahoo! Internet Life *magazine ranks UT as one of the Top 100 Most Wired Colleges in the country.*

DISTANCE LEARNING PROGRAM

The Division of Distance Learning was established in June 1995 to meet UT's distance learning mission. The Division provides greater access to educational opportunities for learners in Ohio and worldwide.

DELIVERY MEDIA

Student-faculty interaction is accomplished through e-mail, chat room discussions, bulletin board postings, CD-ROM, and telephone. The majority of courses are offered via the Internet in an asynchronous environment.

PROGRAMS OF STUDY

Academic success in a flexible, anytime, anywhere course is the Division of Distance Learning's goal. The Division works with colleges throughout the University to provide a variety of courses and degree programs taught by leading UT faculty members. The Division of Distance Learning has programs and courses to fit students' busy lifestyles. Courses are offered in business, communications, education, English, humanities, natural science, and social science. Among the programs that are currently in development is the Certificate in Business Management Technology, which is designed to cover all areas of management, including human resources, economics, marketing, and workplace diversity. The 24-credit program consists of eight courses: business principles, workplace communication and presentation, organizational behavior, workplace management, human resource development, managing in a global economy, managing diversity in the workplace, and marketing principles. Participants can finish the program in one year. Upon its completion, students are eligible to apply to the associate degree program.

The associate degree in business management technology program provides students with the foundation skills required for managing or owning a business. The 65-credit curriculum explores aspects of human resources, computer technology, marketing, accounting, and workplace diversity. Participants can obtain their associate degree within two years.

The associate degree in marketing and sales technology program allows students to develop the business skills necessary to recognize changes in the marketplace and in technology. This program gives students the ability to specialize in the process of bringing raw materials from the producer to the customer. Credits can be applied to a bachelor's degree.

The Bachelor of Science degree in health information management (HIM) is a degree completion program. Students with an associate degree in health information technology or a related field may apply those credits to the bachelor's degree program. The program has been approved by the Ohio Board of Regents. After review by the AHIMA Council on Accreditation, a recommendation is forwarded to the Commission on Accreditation of Allied Health Education Programs. Upon approval of the HIM program by AHIMA, graduates are able to sit for the national certification examination to become registered health information administrators (RHIA). The development of the online courses for the health information management program is made possible through a grant from the Ohio Learning Network.

The Diversity Management Certificate provides participants with the necessary skills to understand and manage diversity in the workplace as it relates to cultural knowledge; cultural sensitivity; cultural communications; hiring, training, and promotion tactics; equal employment opportunity; and inclusivity. Participants learn how to create a bias-free workplace, develop diversity training for all types of organizations as well as learn to set up mentoring programs and diversity councils. Upon completion of the Diversity Management Certificate, students may choose to apply the completed courses to an associate degree.

The Adult Liberal Studies Program is intended for students aged 25 and older. Students complete topical seminars in humanities, natural sciences, and social sciences along with an individualized component of traditional courses. Students may qualify for experiential credit via portfolio or credit through CLEP testing.

The computer science and engineering technology program provides the last two years of a B.S. degree in computer science and engineering technology. The curriculum focuses on aspects of computer networking and Web-based programming. Applicants must have an associate degree in electrical engineering technology or a closely related program. UT partners with several community colleges throughout Ohio in providing the first two years of the curriculum.

The Master of Liberal Studies is a flexible customized graduate program offered by the College of Arts and Sciences. It provides students the option of taking courses from a variety of areas. Students are required to complete seminars in the humanities, social sciences, natural science, and visual arts, as well as a master's thesis. Admission to the program is open year-round. A minimum undergraduate GPA of 2.7 is required. Applicants with a lower GPA can enroll provisionally and must take the GRE.

The Master of Science in Engineering (M.S.E.) program consists of 36 credits, 30 for course work and 6 in a work-related project. The 9-credit engineering core has courses in management of projects and technical innovation, advanced computational methods, and applied probability and statistics in engineering and management science. The 9-credit business core has courses in financial and managerial accounting, analysis of manufacturing and service systems, and business, government, and society. The work-related project is completed in coordination with the student's employer. It is meant to study and solve a challenge the organization faces. To qualify for the M.S.E. program, students must have a related bachelor's degree and significant work experience. Applicants with an undergraduate GPA under 2.7 must take the GRE.

STUDENT SERVICES

The University of Toledo's Division of Distance Learning offers a wide range of services to assist students in becoming involved participants in the online learning process. Students have access to a number of services through the Division of Distance Learning's Web site, including online applications, applications for financial aid, registration, academic advising, information on software to purchase, and access to the UT Bookstore, Career Services, and UT's online library (Ohio Link). Technical support is available to all online students. To view technical support hours, students may visit http://www.dl.utoledo.edu. The University of Toledo's Division of Distance Learning makes it a priority to provide excellent student services to distance learners.

CREDIT OPTIONS

College credits earned through distance learning courses are recorded on a University of Toledo transcript in the same manner as credits earned in on-campus courses. Students who have attended a regionally accredited college or university may be able to transfer credits. Students should contact the Division of Distance Learning at 866-886-5336 (toll-free) or utdl@utoledo.edu. NCA accreditation for online programs is in process.

ADMISSION

All distance learners must be admitted to the University of Toledo. Distance learners must meet the same requirements as traditional college students and must meet the minimum computer requirements for Internet and CD-ROM courses. Special-status admission is available for nondegree students.

TUITION AND FEES

Tuition for online courses is the same as that for on-campus courses. Tuition rates vary depending on residency status. An admissions fee of $40 and a matriculation fee of $25 are charged upon submission of an application. Tuition and fees are subject to change.

APPLYING

Prospective students should submit an official application along with necessary documentation, an official high school transcript, GED scores, or official transcripts from a previous college or university and should complete any assessment procedures. Applications are available online or through the mail.

CONTACT

Janet Green, Assistant Director of Marketing and Enrollment
Distance Learning
University of Toledo
401 Jefferson Avenue
Toledo, Ohio 43604-1005
Telephone: 866-886-5336 (toll-free)
Fax: 419-321-5147
E-mail: utdl@utoledo.edu
Web site: http://www.dl.utoledo.edu

University of Tulsa

Internet-mediated MBA (iMBA)
Internet-mediated Master of Taxation (MTAX)

Tulsa, Oklahoma

The University of Tulsa is a private institution that was founded in 1894 in Indian Territory. The College of Business Administration was established in 1935 and is fully accredited by AACSB International–The Association to Advance Collegiate Schools of Business at both the graduate and undergraduate levels. As faculty members in the College of Business have sought to provide programs that are on the leading edge of technology, they have acted on the need to address new ways of delivering advanced education. The Internet-mediated MBA (iMBA) and an online Master of Taxation (MTAX) are their response to professionals whose schedules do not permit regular classroom attendance. Interaction between student and professor is emphasized and encouraged in the iMBA and MTAX. Graduates of the iMBA program receive the fully accredited University of Tulsa M.B.A. degree. Graduates of the MTAX program receive the fully accredited Master of Taxation degree. The MTAX program prepares students to become successful, integral members of the business team, and the iMBA program prepares graduates to be the effective leaders businesses have come to expect from the University of Tulsa.

DISTANCE LEARNING PROGRAM

The iMBA and MTAX program make graduate business education accessible to the motivated professional who wishes to earn an M.B.A. or graduate tax degree but whose schedule does not permit regular classroom attendance. Students in classes of no more than 50 people enjoy more options for interaction with their professors and classmates than ever before.

DELIVERY MEDIA

The technology-based online programs require students to have a computer with Internet access; Win98 SE, Win2K, or WinXP; Office 2K or Office XP; Netscape or Internet Explorer; speakers; and a sound card. All courses have been developed utilizing WebCT. Students are able to access chat rooms, e-mail, online forums, and bulletin boards. To access a sample course, visitors may visit the iMBA Web site at http://www.imba.utulsa.edu or the MTAX Web site at http://bus.cba.utulsa.edu/mtax.

PROGRAMS OF STUDY

The University of Tulsa has designed a successful M.B.A. curriculum that can be delivered online. This program, known as the iMBA, encompasses a solid M.B.A. curriculum with an added emphasis on information technology. It consists of two courses per term, three terms per year, and requires two years for completion. This is a part-time, 48-hour program in which 12 hours may be waived, depending on the student's undergraduate degree and grades. Those applying for this program must have at least two years of working experience following completion of their baccalaureate degree. Students earn a high-quality M.B.A. from the University of Tulsa, which is internationally recognized and accredited by AACSB International.

Interactivity is a key component of the iMBA. Chat rooms, e-mail, electronic bulletin boards, and online forums provide a powerful arena for discussion, analysis, and collaboration. Students also have access to an online library. Students come to the campus for two 2-day sessions during the course of the program to meet with their professors and classmates, receive orientation materials, and participate in various workshops and seminars.

Building on the successes of the iMBA, the University of Tulsa now offers a two-year Internet-based Master of Taxation program. This 30-hour specialized program consists of two courses per term, three terms per year, with no on-campus requirement. The program offers high-potential professional employees currently holding a bachelor's degree the opportunity to earn a Master of Taxation in as little as two years from an institution that is accredited by AACSB International while continuing to meet the demands of the workplace. Because the specifics of tax code vary from year to year, the curriculum focus is on big-picture issues with enduring applicability.

Interactivity is also a key component of the MTAX program. The virtual classroom includes application-sharing software, CD-ROM multimedia courseware, audio/video, electronic bulletin boards, e-mail, an online library, and lecture resources with direct links to other course materials. The entire program is taught online; no campus time is required.

Students are able to complete a high-quality degree in an extremely flexible format without the need to miss work in order to attend regular classes. Course materials are available anytime and anywhere. Course work can be completed at home, at work, or while away on business or personal travel.

STUDENT SERVICES

All students in the online programs receive training in the use of WebCT, the software in which all of the distance education courses reside. Students have an e-mail address within WebCT for communicating directly with classmates and faculty members. In addition, all students enrolled at the University of Tulsa are assigned a universal e-mail account. With the establishment of a University e-mail account, students may access McFarlin Library electronically. Both part-time and full-time students and alumni of the University of Tulsa may utilize Career Services.

CREDIT OPTIONS

University policy allows for transfer of up to 6 credit hours at the master's level. Any such graduate credit must have been earned at an accredited graduate school and have been completed within the last six years. The graduate program director is responsible for determining the applicability of transfer work to the student's program, subject to final approval by the Dean of Research and Graduate Studies.

FACULTY

All faculty members who teach in the iMBA program have obtained a Ph.D. and/or a J.D. All faculty members who teach in the M.Tax. have advanced degrees and extensive professional experience.

ADMISSION

Enrollment in the iMBA is limited to the fall term. However, iMBA foundation courses are offered year-round. Students must have a baccalaureate degree, two years of work experience, preferably a 3.0 or better GPA, an acceptable GMAT score, and three letters of reference.

Enrollment in the MTAX program is offered for the fall, spring, and summer terms. Students must have a baccalaureate degree (from any field—a business degree is not required), preferably a 3.0 or better GPA, an acceptable GMAT or LSAT score, and three letters of reference.

TUITION AND FEES

The iMBA costs $22,680 for the entire six terms of advanced curriculum courses, billed on a per-semester basis. Foundation work for the iMBA and all M.Tax. program courses cost $630 per credit hour. There is a one-time fee of $100 for international students.

FINANCIAL AID

Students are eligible to apply for Federal Stafford Student Loans (subsidized and unsubsidized) as well as other funded loans. Graduate students can normally apply year-round for these loans. Students who are residents of the state of Oklahoma may apply for an Oklahoma Tuition Aid Grant. The annual deadline for these grants is March 1. Students receiving reimbursement from their employers may arrange to defer tuition to match their employer's reimbursement policy. For more information on available financial aid, students should visit http://www.utulsa.edu/financialaid.

APPLYING

For more detailed information on the iMBA or to apply online, students should visit http://www.imba.utulsa.edu. For more detailed information on the MTAX program or to apply online, students should visit http://bus.cba.utulsa.edu/mtax.

CONTACT

Graduate Business Programs, BAH 217
University of Tulsa
600 South College Avenue
Tulsa, Oklahoma 74104-3189
Telephone: 918-631-2242
Fax: 918-631-2142
E-mail: graduate-business@utulsa.edu
Web site: http://www.imba.utulsa.edu/info

University of Washington

UW Extension

Seattle, Washington

Founded in 1861, the University of Washington (UW) is one of the oldest state-supported institutions of higher education on the Pacific coast. The University comprises three campuses: the Seattle campus, made up of seventeen schools and colleges offering educational opportunities to students ranging from first-year undergraduates through doctoral-level candidates; the Bothell campus; and the Tacoma campus.

The primary mission of the University of Washington is the preservation, advancement, and dissemination of knowledge. UW advances new knowledge through many forms of research, inquiry, and discussion. Accreditation is by the Northwest Association of Schools and Colleges.

DISTANCE LEARNING PROGRAM

The University of Washington offers twelve degree programs, twenty-five certificate programs, and hundreds of courses via distance learning, making it one of the leading public institutions in the online field. The UW online program has been rated among the top ten distance learning education offerings available through U.S. universities. Distance learning courses at UW are developed by a team of distance learning designers working with UW faculty members and academic departments. They create courses that are academically rigorous, suitable for a distance format, and convenient. Several courses have won the prestigious Helen Williams Award for Excellence in Collegiate Independent Study from the well-respected American Association for Collegiate Independent Study (AACIS) as well as awards from the University Continuing Education Association (UCEA). The distance learning program at UW has 4,074 students enrolled.

DELIVERY MEDIA

Most programs rely on the Internet and e-mail to access instruction and to communicate with teachers and fellow students. Some classes start and finish at set times; others enable students to start according to their own schedule. Students can contact their instructors at any time with questions about the courses. Many courses use online discussion, and some courses incorporate chats into their curriculum.

PROGRAMS OF STUDY

UW offers a Master in Strategic Planning for Critical Infrastructures degree program that was developed in partnership with the Washington National Guard for leaders who are responsible for ensuring the reliability and security of critical infrastructures and emergency services. This program was developed for officials in public and private infrastructure, emergency management, and homeland security.

Masters' degrees in engineering are available through UW's Education at a Distance for Growth and Excellence (UW/EDGE), with five areas of specialization: aeronautics and astronautics, aerospace engineering, manufacturing engineering, materials science and engineering, and mechanical engineering.

The master's in construction engineering is designed for professionals in the heavy construction industry, combining courses in construction management and civil engineering.

The Master of Library and Information Science degree was established to meet the high demand for library and information professionals. Delivery of instruction is primarily Internet-based, with on-campus three-day residencies at the beginning of each quarter.

Twenty-five certificate programs are offered, with each requiring three to nine intensive courses. Certificate programs include Brain Research in Education, Business Foundations, C++ Programming, Construction Management, Curriculum Integration in Action, Data Resource Management, Distance Learning Design and Development, Facility Management, Gerontology, Heavy Construction Project Management, Infrastructure Construction, Internet Programming, Java 2 Programming, Object-Oriented Analysis and Design Using UML, Project Management, Quantitative Construction Management, School Library Media Specialist, Site Planning, Web Administration, Web Consultant for Small Business, Web Technology Essentials, Writers' Program: Literary Fiction Writing and Nonfiction Writing.

More than 200 courses are available in architecture and urban planning, arts and sciences, business and management, computing, engineering and technology, education, health sciences, languages, and library and information science. The OpenUW program at the UW offers twelve free noncredit classes.

STUDENT SERVICES

Academic advising is available by e-mail, telephone, and for those who are able to come to the campus, in person. Advisers can answer questions about prerequisite requirements and course content. Students enrolled in online learning courses receive student numbers and have library checkout privileges at UW libraries. Distance learning students living outside the Seattle area may request specific library materials by mail. Technical support for courses is provided. Textbooks may be ordered online.

CREDIT OPTIONS

Credit earned by taking a distance learning course can be applied to an undergraduate degree or can help students prepare for UW admission. Distance learning credits are not considered residence credits. It is not possible to earn an undergraduate degree from the University of Washington through online learning alone. However, nine master's degrees may be completed solely through distance learning.

FACULTY

Most UW online learning courses are designed and taught by faculty members who teach the same courses on the UW campus. The instructors are familiar with student questions and needs. With the help of instructional designers, they have developed the appropriate methods and materials, interactive strategies, and online activities to help students achieve the course objectives in a distance-learning format.

ADMISSION

It is not necessary to be admitted to the University of Washington before taking distance learning courses. (There are prerequisites for some courses, and TOEFL scores are required for international students.) Certificate and graduate degree programs have an application process.

TUITION AND FEES

All registrants pay a nonrefundable $30 registration fee. Fees for credit courses through distance learning are $151 per credit for undergraduate students and $306 per credit for Tier 1 graduate and graduate courses. Prices for graduate instruction vary by degree program.

FINANCIAL AID

UW distance learning students are ineligible for the University's financial aid programs in most cases. For information about alternative funding, students should visit http://www.outreach.washington.edu/extinfo/loan_sources.asp.

APPLYING

Prospective students can register online for courses. Application forms for certificates and degree programs can be downloaded.

CONTACT

University of Washington Online Learning
4311 11th Avenue, NE
Seattle, Washington 98105-4608
Telephone: 206-897-8936
800-506-1338 (toll-free)
E-mail: uwonline@ese.washington.edu
Web site: http://www.onlinelearning.washington.edu

UNIVERSITY OF WYOMING
New Thinking

The University of Wyoming

Outreach School

Laramie, Wyoming

The University of Wyoming (UW), a land-grant university founded in 1886, is accredited by the Higher Learning Commission and is a member of the North Central Association of Colleges and Schools. The University of Wyoming was the first university west of the Missouri River to offer correspondence courses. In its outreach mission, the University of Wyoming is guided by the following vision: the state of Wyoming is the campus of the University of Wyoming. The University has one faculty and staff, one student body, and one set of academic programs. Teaching, research, and service are the missions of the University, regardless of location. The University recognizes that its "one student body" is composed of a wide variety of students whose needs differ.

DISTANCE LEARNING PROGRAM

The UW Outreach School delivers the University's distance learning programs. The mission of the Outreach School is to extend the University of Wyoming's educational programs and services to people in the state of Wyoming and beyond. The School delivers more than 300 courses and complete degree and certificate programs to approximately 3,000 students per semester.

DELIVERY MEDIA

The Outreach School launched Online UW, the University of Wyoming's virtual campus, in the spring of 1999 in cooperation with eCollege. In addition, the School delivers programs via correspondence study, audio-teleconference, and compressed video. For more information, students can access the Online UW Web site at http://online.uwyo.edu. For a list of audio, compressed video, and correspondence study courses, students should visit the Web site listed at the end of this description. All correspondence study courses, a limited number of audio-teleconference courses, and all Online UW courses are available to students outside the state of Wyoming.

PROGRAMS OF STUDY

Degrees and certificates are available to students outside Wyoming. Certificate programs include land surveying (offered nationwide through audio-teleconference with videotaped lectures), real estate (available online), and family and consumer sciences/early childhood program director's certificate (available online). Graduate programs include an M.S. in speech-language pathology (available nationwide through audio-teleconference with videotaped lectures) and an M.S. in education, with a specialization in instructional technology (available online). Other available distance degrees are bachelor's degrees in business administration (online), criminal justice, psychology, and social science (statewide, some courses nationwide); an RN/B.S.N. completion program (online); an M.S. in nursing, with an advanced practice in rural health/nurse educator option (online); an M.B.A. (available statewide via compressed video); an M.S. in kinesiology and health (statewide, some courses nationwide); an M.S.W. in social work (statewide); an M.P.A. (available through audio-teleconference and compressed video statewide); and master's degrees in education, with specialization options in special education, adult and postsecondary education, and teaching and learning (statewide, some courses nationwide).

SPECIAL PROGRAMS

The University of Wyoming's Internet campus, Online UW, currently offers more than eighty courses and seven degrees completely online. Courses are available worldwide via http://online.uwyo.edu. Online courses are available in the areas of adult learning, astronomy, biochemistry, business administration, child development, directing preschool and daycare programs, economics, education, engineering, family and consumer sciences, human resources management, instructional technology, nutrition, physics, psychology, real estate, religion, and statistics.

STUDENT SERVICES

All student services (such as admission, enrollment, tuition payment, grade reporting, financial aid, bookstore, and library outreach) are available through the UW Outreach School. The library outreach service is available at http://www.lib.uwyo.edu. Students can purchase textbooks and course packets online at the University Bookstore at http://www.uwyobookstore.com.

CREDIT OPTIONS

Students may transfer courses from accredited institutions of higher education to the University of Wyoming. Credit is also available through AP, CLEP, portfolio assessment, and departmental examinations. Degrees require a minimum of 48 hours of upper-division credit, with a minimum of 30 credits from the University of

Wyoming. Most degree programs require 120–124 credits for graduation.

FACULTY

The majority of those who teach at the Outreach School are full-time faculty members at the University of Wyoming. A limited number of adjunct faculty members, who are approved by the academic departments, offer distance learning courses. In any given semester, approximately 75 regular full-time faculty members and 15 part-time adjunct faculty members teach distance learning courses for the Outreach School. The programs offered via distance learning are the same as the programs offered on the main University campus in Laramie, Wyoming.

ADMISSION

Students not seeking University of Wyoming degrees may enroll in distance learning courses without being admitted to the University. Students can apply a maximum of 12 credit hours toward the requirements for a UW undergraduate degree prior to admission to the University. Degree-seeking students should apply at the admissions office. Undergraduate admission generally requires completion of at least 13 high school units in a precollege curriculum, a cumulative high school grade point average of at least 2.75, and an ACT score of at least 20 or an SAT score of at least 960. Conditional admission is available for adult learners who do not meet these criteria. Graduate programs require a Graduate Record Examinations (GRE) combined verbal and quantitative score of at least 900. The University offers GRE testing through the University of Wyoming Testing Center. For more information, students can visit the Web site at http://www.uwyo.edu/ucc/utc/.

TUITION AND FEES

All outreach students are charged tuition at an in-state rate. Undergraduate tuition for outreach courses is $84 per credit hour, with a $10-per-credit-hour delivery fee or a $40-per-credit-hour delivery fee for Online UW courses. Graduate tuition for outreach courses is $142 per credit hour, with a $10-per-credit-hour delivery fee or a $40-per-credit-hour delivery fee for Online UW courses. Tuition for the M.B.A. program is $207 per credit hour, and tuition for the land surveying program is $175 per credit hour.

FINANCIAL AID

All forms of federal financial aid and other scholarship aid are available to Outreach students. The Outreach School also has a number of scholarships available to Outreach students. Information describing available aid and award criteria is available from the Office of Student Financial Aid, Department 3335, University of Wyoming, 1000 East University Avenue, Laramie, Wyoming 82071.

APPLYING

Non-degree-seeking students may apply through the Division of Outreach Credit Programs. Degree-seeking students should apply through the admissions office (telephone: 800-DIAL-WYO (toll-free) or 307-766-2287; Web site: http://www.uwyo.edu) or Graduate Admissions (telephone: 307-766-2287; Web site: http://www.uwyo.edu/uwgrad).

CONTACT

Outreach School
Division of Outreach Credit Programs
Department 3274
University of Wyoming
1000 East University Avenue
Laramie, Wyoming 82071
Telephone: 307-766-4300
800-448-7801 (toll-free)
Fax: 307-766-3445
E-mail: occ@uwyo.edu
Web site: http://outreach.uwyo.edu/occ

Upper Iowa University

Extended University

Fayette, Iowa

Upper Iowa University (UIU) was established in 1857 and has since become the largest private university in the state of Iowa. Unlike some of the newer schools offering distance learning programs, UIU has a beautiful residential campus on 90 acres with seven academic buildings and three residence halls. Upper Iowa also has seventeen sports teams, known as the Peacocks, who compete in the NCAA Division II. As a nonprofit, rapidly growing, four-year liberal arts institution of higher learning, UIU offers a wide range of high-quality degree programs to more than 5,000 students worldwide. UIU provides educational opportunities to the global community, focusing on the future while preserving the traditions of the past. Upper Iowa University is accredited by the Higher Learning Commission and is a member of the North Central Association of Colleges and Schools (Web: http://www.ncahigherlearningcommission.org; telephone: 312-263-0456.

DISTANCE LEARNING PROGRAM

The Extended University's distance learning programs are offered through two primary modes of delivery. Its External Degree program offers Associate of Arts and Bachelor of Science degree programs with ten majors through independent study/correspondence, and its Online program currently offers a Bachelor of Science (B.S.) with six business majors, criminal justice, public administration, and a Master of Business Administration (M.B.A.). Courses offered through both External Degree and Online formats meet the same standards as courses offered through the residential University in Fayette, Iowa. The External Degree program, which began in 1972, has been successfully delivered to more than 10,000 learners. Upper Iowa's External Degree program was one of the first and most successful in the United States. Both the External Degree and Online programs continue to be vital components in serving both civilian and military learners worldwide.

DELIVERY MEDIA

In the External Degree program, students communicate with instructors via e-mail, fax, and regular mail. Classes are self-paced with no minimum completion time. Upper Iowa's Online program is noted for its e-mail–like feel. Online students log on (via the Internet) just long enough to send and receive materials, anytime, anywhere, day or night. Most work is accomplished off-line, or through asynchronous communication. Online students may also communicate with their instructors through course software, e-mail, fax, or phone.

PROGRAMS OF STUDY

Upper Iowa University has a long history of offering high-quality degree programs through distance learning. In the External Degree program, associate and bachelor's degree programs are available in a wide range of academic areas including accounting, business, criminal justice, human resources management, human services, management, marketing, psychology, public administration (general, law enforcement, or fire science), social science, and technology and information management. Upper Iowa's Online program offers a Bachelor of Science degree with eight majors to choose from: accounting, criminal justice, finance, human resources management, management, marketing, public administration, and technology and information management. The M.B.A. offers five areas of emphasis: accounting, global business, human resources management, organizational development, and quality. The course work focuses on the theories and skills that are the foundation for tomorrow's organizations, including organizational design, total quality management, self-managed teams, employee empowerment, change management, facilitation skills, high-performance work systems, and more.

SPECIAL PROGRAMS

Each summer, the External Degree program sponsors the Institute for Experiential Learning (IEXL) for undergraduate students. During an intensive weeklong session held on the Fayette campus, students have the opportunity to earn 3 semester hours of undergraduate credit while visiting the residential campus and networking with other learners from around the world.

STUDENT SERVICES

External Degree and Online students are provided with one-on-one academic advising via U.S. mail, e-mail, telephone, fax communication, and through use of a special software/courseware package (for Online program students). In addition to local university libraries, undergraduate and graduate students and faculty members have access to the Henderson Wilder Library holdings through Upper Iowa University's Web site (listed below).

CREDIT OPTIONS

Full credit is given for college-level courses completed at regionally accredited colleges and universities. Students can transfer a maximum of 45 semester hours for an associate degree, 90 semester hours for a bachelor's degree, and 12 semester hours for a master's degree. Other sources of credit include the American Council on Education (ACE), the College-Level Examination Program (CLEP), Defense Activity for Nontraditional Education support (DANTES) subject exams, and experiential learning.

FACULTY

Upper Iowa University has more than 100 adjunct faculty members, many of whom have doctoral or terminal degrees. Faculty members are experienced in the areas in which they teach.

ADMISSION

Admission criteria for undergraduate degrees include graduation from an accredited public or private high school or completion of the GED test or its equivalent. For the graduate program, prospective students must hold an undergraduate degree from a regionally accredited college or university. More information regarding grade point requirements, TOEFL scores for international students, and transfer credit is available upon request or on the UIU Web site (listed below).

TUITION AND FEES

Associate- and baccalaureate-level tuition for courses taken through External Degree (independent study/correspondence) or at off-campus learning centers (classroom) for 2003–04 was $537 per 3-semester-credit course. Undergraduate and graduate online (Internet-based) courses were $735 and $933, respectively, per 3-semester-credit course.

FINANCIAL AID

Financial aid in the form of Federal Stafford Student Loans, Federal Pell Grants, Iowa Tuition Grants (Iowa residents only), Veterans Assistance, and Military Tuition Assistance is available. Recently, a total of $273,420 in financial aid was disbursed to 21 percent of Upper Iowa University's distance learning students.

APPLYING

Students may enroll in UIU distance learning programs at any time. In the External Degree program, students may start courses at any time. In the Online program, eight-week terms begin six times a year. Students should send official transcripts (including CLEP, DANTES, or DD-214), GRE/GMAT score reports (if required), and a completed Application for Admission form (available online or by contacting the school via telephone or e-mail) directly to Upper Iowa University at the address below.

CONTACT

Extended University
Upper Iowa University
605 Washington Street
P.O. Box 1857
Fayette, Iowa 52142-1857
Telephone: 877-366-0581 (toll-free)
Fax: 563-425-5771
E-mail: moreinfo@uiu.edu
Web site: http://www.uiu.edu

Utah State University

Time Enhanced Learning

Logan, Utah

Utah State University (USU) was founded in 1888 as part of the public educational system of Utah and operates under the constitution and laws of the state. It belongs to the family of institutions known as land-grant universities, which had their origin in 1862. USU is governed by the State Board of Regents and accredited by Northwest Association of Accredited Schools.

USU integrates teaching, research, extension, and service to meet its unique role as Utah's land-grant university.

DISTANCE LEARNING PROGRAM

USU Extension Services is an integral part of USU's outreach mission. Extension's Time Enhanced Learning (TEL) division provides educational opportunities for time- and place-bound students who are not able to come to the campus to attend classes.

Time Enhanced Learning offers off-campus classes at education centers, several bachelor's and master's degree programs over the digital satellite system, and a master's degree over the Internet. Many other Internet-based classes, independent study CD-ROM courses, and educational conferences are offered.

Enrollments through Time Enhanced Learning average 3,000 each semester, and USU is one of the leading institutions in the United States for its off-campus programs.

Since 1989, nearly 4,500 students have received degrees through the University's distance education component.

DELIVERY MEDIA

Time Enhanced Learning is made up of three main program delivery units: distance education (satellite), online education, and independent study (CD-ROM) course delivery.

Distance education degree programs offered over the digital satellite system are only available to Utah students who live near a USU Extension Center. Online courses are designed for access any time of the day or night. Online students submit assignments electronically and interact with their instructors and classmates via e-mail and online discussions.

Students who register for independent study CD-ROM courses receive a CD-ROM or printed course outline at registration. Independent study students mail in assignments, take proctored examinations, and may contact their instructors by phone or e-mail.

PROGRAMS OF STUDY

USU Time Enhanced Learning offers an online Master of Science in English degree with a specialization in technical writing.

The graduate technical writing degree program is designed mainly to help practicing professional writers advance their careers, and most students in the program are employed full-time as writers in nonacademic workplaces. Some students in the program may be considering careers that involve both practicing and teaching technical writing, but the program is oriented toward educating the practicing specialist and does not focus on pedagogical issues.

The Master of Science in human environments places emphasis on teaching and curriculum/program development and/or extension. It prepares students for community professions in secondary teaching, urban and rural extension, social sciences, and business.

STUDENT SERVICES

Student services available to distance learners include access to the University bookstore, Library Support System for Distance Learners, Online Book Exchange, Academic Resource Center, and writing and researching resources. For more information on student services available to distance learners, prospective students should visit the Web site http://online.usu.edu/student_resources/.

CREDIT OPTIONS

Credit earned through USU Time Enhanced Learning is measured in semester units and is transferable to most colleges and universities in the U.S. Students who plan to transfer credit should make arrangements with the transfer institution prior to registration.

FACULTY

Ninety percent of Time Enhanced Learning instructors are USU faculty members; many are leading researchers in their field. Time Enhanced Learning faculty members recognize that the needs of individuals are of major importance; programs have been established to give students optimal individual attention.

ADMISSION

Admission requirements are program specific and may be obtained by contacting the Admissions Office at 435-797-1079. Prospective students may complete an application for admission online at http://www.usu.edu/admissions. Applicants to the graduate technical writing degree program must be admitted to the program prior to registering for online courses in technical writing.

TUITION AND FEES

Tuition for classes in the graduate technical writing degree program is $200 per credit.

FINANCIAL AID

Financial aid is available for distance education students. Utah State University participates in the following financial aid programs: Federal Pell Grants, Federal Supplemental Educational Opportunity Grants (FSEOG), LEAAP Grants, Federal Perkins Loans, Federal Work-Study, Federal Stafford Loans, Plus Loans, scholarships, and emergency loans. For more information, prospective students should contact the financial aid office at 435-797-0173 or visit the Web site at http://www.usu.edu/finaid/.

APPLYING

Students working toward any of the degree programs offered through Time Enhanced Learning must be admitted to the University. Prospective students may complete an application for admission online at http://www.usu.edu/admissions or request a printed application by contacting the Admissions Office at 435-797-1079.

CONTACT

Time Enhanced Learning
3080 Old Main Hill
Utah State University
Logan, Utah 84322-3080
Telephone: 800-233-2137 (toll-free)
Fax: 435-797-1399
E-mail: enroll@ext.usu.edu
Web sites: http://extension.usu.edu
http://online.usu.edu/

Virginia Polytechnic Institute and State University

Institute for Distance and Distributed Learning

Blacksburg, Virginia

Virginia Polytechnic Institute and State University is a public land-grant university serving the Commonwealth of Virginia, the nation, and the world community. The discovery and dissemination of new knowledge are central to its mission. Through its focus on teaching and learning, research, and outreach, the University creates, conveys, and applies knowledge to expand personal growth and opportunity, advance social and community development, foster economic competitiveness, and improve the quality of life. Founded in 1872, Virginia Tech currently ranks in the nation's top 50 research universities, offering 170 degree programs to Virginia's largest full-time student population (28,027 total enrollments).

The University's growing reputation for excellence includes national recognition as a leader in distance and distributed learning. Virginia Tech is helping to meet the changing needs of undergraduate and graduate students with online and distance-delivered master's degree programs, certificates, and licensures as well as noncredit offerings for personal and professional growth. Innovative use of technology is transforming the educational process, while making it more accessible and learner-centered. Virginia Tech is fully accredited by the Commission on Colleges of the Southern Association of Colleges and Schools.

DISTANCE LEARNING PROGRAM

As part of the Office of the University Provost and Vice President for Academic Affairs, Virginia Tech's Institute for Distance and Distributed Learning (IDDL) provides leadership, coordination, management, and support to the growing distance learning activities of Virginia Tech. Through these activities, Virginia Tech extends its campus to communities throughout the world and provides an open campus environment that allows individuals to engage in learning at anytime and from anywhere. In addition, Virginia Tech shares the practical application of the University's knowledge and expertise in support of economic development, increases the University's access to the world and the world's access to the University, and researches new teaching and learning environments through the application of technology.

Approximately 12,000 enrollments are accounted for in 486 courses and twenty-one master's degree programs, certificates, and licensures. Virginia Tech actively participates in the Electronic Campus of Virginia and collaboratively delivers courses and degree programs at a distance with other Virginia colleges and universities through the Commonwealth Graduate Engineering Program and Virginia Consortium of Engineering and Science Universities. Virginia Tech also participates in the Southern Region Electronic Campus and the Natural Resources Distance Learning Consortium.

PROGRAMS OF STUDY

Virginia Tech offers certificate programs in business information systems, communications, computer engineering, decision support systems, natural resources, networking, and software development.

Licensure is available in career and technical education.

Programs leading to a Master of Arts degree are available in instructional technology and political science.

The Master of Science can be earned in career and technical education, civil and environmental engineering, civil infrastructure engineering, computer engineering, electrical and computer engineering, engineering administration, health promotion, ocean engineering, and systems engineering.

The Master of Business Administration (M.B.A.) and the Master of Information Technology (M.I.T.) are also awarded.

A wide variety of credit and noncredit courses is also offered through distance learning in the areas of accounting, architecture, art, biology, black studies, building construction, business, communications, computer science, economics, education, engineering, English, entomology, finance, geography, history, hotel management, horticulture, information science, landscape architecture, management, marketing, math, music, philosophy, physics, psychology, science and technology, sociology, Spanish, statistics, women's studies, and more.

STUDENT SERVICES

Recognizing the diverse needs of distance learners, Virginia Tech employs a holistic approach to distance learning in which the student's total educational experience is considered. This approach provides learners with accessible learning resources, support services, and interactive technologies in addition to renowned faculty members who create and teach the wide array of distance and distributed learning courses. Through cross-University collaboration, Virginia Tech works to create accessible online support services that include academic program information, the admissions process, preadmissions advising, enrollment services, an orientation to distance learning, a distance learning compatibility self-test, course delivery format descriptions, technical requirements, degree requirements, program of study descriptions, library resources and services, bookstore services, academic advising, tutoring, writing center, study skills, an online wellness resource center, services for students with disabilities, career services, technical help, and FAQ.

CREDIT OPTIONS

Distance learners can transfer credits earned at other accredited postsecondary institutions to Virginia Tech following the established University policies. Students admitted to the University who have been certified by the Virginia Community College System or Richard Bland College as completing the transfer module are deemed to have completed the University core curriculum components and receive 35 total credits for the module.

FACULTY

The faculty is the foundation of Virginia Tech's distance learning programs and assures its academic excellence. The same faculty members, including some of the most highly honored faculty at the University, who teach traditional classroom-based campus courses also teach distance learning courses. Currently, 85 percent of Virginia Tech's academic teaching departments are involved in teaching distance learning courses.

ADMISSION

To become undergraduate or graduate degree candidates at Virginia Tech, students must apply formally for admission. Students' records at Virginia Tech and all other colleges and universities attended are reviewed within the context of current admission policies. Virginia Tech allows qualified students at other Virginia universities and colleges to enroll in its courses as non-degree-seeking or Commonwealth Campus students. For more information on undergraduate admission, students should visit the IDDL Web site listed below; those interested in graduate programs should visit http://www.grads.vt.edu.

TUITION AND FEES

For the latest information, students should visit http://www.bursar.vt.edu

FINANCIAL AID

Virginia Tech is a direct lending institution and awards financial aid from federally funded and state-funded programs as well as privately funded sources. Financial aid sources include the Federal Direct Stafford Loan, Federal Perkins Loan, Federal Direct PLUS Loan, Federal Pell Grant, Federal Work-Study, Virginia Guaranteed Assistance program, Commonwealth Award, and the College Scholarship Assistance Program.

APPLYING

Students applying for undergraduate admission can access current information at http://www.admiss.vt.edu. Students applying for graduate admission can access current information at http://www.grads.vt.edu. Students can register for Internet-based courses at http://www.vto.vt.edu.

There is a nonrefundable fee ($40 undergraduate, $45 graduate) for non-Virginia Tech, non-program-bound undergraduate students.

CONTACT

Angie Starr
Learning Support Specialist
Institute for Distance and Distributed Learning
Virginia Tech (0445)
Blacksburg, Virginia 24061
Telephone: 540-231-1264
Fax: 540-231-2079
E-mail: vto@vt.edu
Web site: http://www.iddl.vt.edu
http://www.vto.vt.edu
(online catalog)

Walden University

Walden University

Graduate Distance Education

Minneapolis, Minnesota

Academic programs at Walden University combine high-quality curricula and innovative distance delivery models. The result is a collection of highly applied, rigorous programs that are flexible. These programs are ideally suited for adult learners who want to pursue an advanced degree without the professional and personal sacrifices associated with traditional, campus-based programs.

Four schools make up Walden University: the School of Management, the School of Education, the School of Health and Human Services, and the School of Psychology. Walden students complete much of their work online. Both doctoral and master's degrees are offered.

A pioneer in distance delivery, Walden has been serving the needs of adult learners since the University's founding in 1970. Walden University is accredited by the Higher Learning Commission and is a member of the North Central Association of Colleges and Schools.

DISTANCE LEARNING PROGRAM

Walden University enrolls nearly 8,500 students from all fifty states and thirty countries. More than half of the University's students are women and members of minority groups. The University offers programs that allow busy adults to complete a master's or Ph.D. degree from home or work on their own schedules.

DELIVERY MEDIA

Depending on the program in which they are enrolled, Walden students complete many of their degree requirements through online interaction, instruction, and submission of work. Individual mentoring, online courses, and progress based on demonstrations of knowledge are among the ingredients found in Walden's delivery system. Students who enroll in a Walden program should be comfortable using a personal computer, a word processor, and e-mail.

PROGRAMS OF STUDY

Ph.D. programs are offered in applied management and decision sciences, education, health services, human services, psychology, public health, and public policy and administration. A Doctor of Education (Ed.D.) program is offered with a specialization in teacher leadership. Master's degrees are offered in business administration, education, psychology, public administration, and public health.

The Ph.D. in applied management and decision sciences program comprises 128 quarter credit hours. Students may elect a broad program or a self-designed specialization or specialize in engineering management, finance, information systems management, knowledge management, leadership and organizational change, learning management, or operations research.

The Ph.D. in education program comprises 128 quarter credit hours. Enrollment options include a general program and specializations in adult education leadership, community college leadership, early childhood education, educational technology, higher education, K–12 educational leadership, knowledge management, learning management, special education, and a self-designed specialization.

The Ph.D. in health services program comprises 128 quarter credit hours. General study is available, as are a self-designed specialization and specializations in community health, health administration, health and human behavior, health promotion and education, and a self-designed specialization.

The Ph.D. in human services program comprises 128 quarter credit hours. Students may design a specialization or specialize in clinical social work, counseling, criminal justice, family studies and intervention strategies, human services administration, social policy analysis and planning, and a self-designed specialization.

The Ph.D. in public health comprises 120 quarter credits, with a specialization in community health.

The Ph.D. in psychology program comprises 127 quarter credit hours. Specializations offered include academic psychology, clinical psychology, counseling psychology, health psychology, organizational psychology, and school psychology.

The Ph.D. in public policy and administration program comprises 128 quarter credit hours. Specializations include democratic institutions (nonprofit management and leadership), e-government, health services, knowledge management, public management and leadership, public policy, emergency response policy and coordination, and public safety management.

The Doctor of Education (Ed.D.) comprises 69 semester credits, with a specialization in teacher leadership.

The Master of Business Administration (M.B.A.) program is a dynamic program of 40 to 68 quarter credit hours (depending on the student's background). Students may elect from several specializations: Chartered Property Casualty Underwriter (CPCU) accelerated, e-business, finance, finance/risk management/insurance, global business, health services, human resource management, knowledge management, learning management, management of technology, marketing, and nonprofit management.

The Master of Public Administration (M.P.A.) program comprises 56 quarter credit hours with specializations in democratic institutions (nonprofit management and leadership), e-government, health services, knowledge management, public management and leadership, public policy, emergency response policy and coordination and public safety management.

The course-based, online M.S. in psychology program comprises 45 quarter credit hours and includes a specialization in industrial/organizational psychology.

The M.S. in education program comprises 30 to 36 semester credit hours and has specializations in curriculum, instruction, and assessment; educational leadership; elementary reading and literacy; integrating technology in the classroom; literacy and learning in the content areas; mathematics; and middle-level education.

The Master of Public Health (M.S.) program comprises 50 quarter credit hours and has a focus on community health.

The M.S. in nursing program comprises 41 semester credit hours, and has specializations in education, and leadership and management.

SPECIAL PROGRAMS

Walden University offers a limited number of National Service Fellowships to enrolled doctoral students who have dedicated their careers to public service. National Service Fellowships are competitive among enrolled students who have completed at least one full academic quarter. Each fellowship includes an annual (twelve-month) remission of tuition and fees of $1500 per academic year, renewable up to three years.

STUDENT SERVICES

Student services include academic advising, course management, financial aid services, an information technology help desk, orientation programming, and dissertation editing. Walden University's partnership with the Indiana University Bloomington library provides reference, search, catalog, and distribution services.

CREDIT OPTIONS

Transfer of credit from other institutions is encouraged and is available in all Walden University degree programs. Applicants may request an informal transfer of credit evaluation prior to admission. Official notification of credits that have been accepted for transfer to a program may be issued at the time an offer of admission is made or during the first quarter or semester of enrollment. Credits evaluated for transfer from other educational institutions must have been earned and recorded on an official transcript at a school that was accredited by one of the regional accrediting agencies. Walden will also consider transferring credits from an institution accredited by an accrediting body recognized by the Council for Higher Education Accreditation.

FACULTY

Walden attracts esteemed scholars, researchers, and distinguished professionals as faculty members. The distance delivery model allows students to fully benefit from the diverse talents and experiences of the finest faculty members, regardless of where they reside. Some are deans or faculty members at major universities, while others are corporate executives, educators, clinicians, or military leaders. Their specializations range from entrepreneurship and strategic planning to change theory and individual coherence theory. All faculty members are credible subject experts who demonstrate vast experience and a profound commitment to adult learners.

ADMISSION

For admission, a bachelor's or master's degree from a regionally accredited institution is required. Professional experience may be required, depending on the program of study.

TUITION AND FEES

Doctoral program tuition is $3850 per quarter. Master's degree tuition ranges from $265 to $395 per quarter or semester credit hour.

FINANCIAL AID

Walden offers prospective students a variety of options to assist in funding their educational expenses. Approximately 70 percent of Walden students receive some form of financial assistance. Many receive 100 percent assistance in the payment of tuition and fees. Options available include federal financial assistance programs, veterans' education benefits, and institutional fellowships. Discounts are also available for group/spousal enrollment. Walden can also assist students in securing private scholarships, employer tuition benefits, and loans from private lenders.

APPLYING

Submission of a completed and signed application, a $50 application fee, and a personal/professional statement of purpose is required. Applicants must also send a resume, official transcripts from the institution that conferred the bachelor's or master's degree, and, in health and human services, two required recommendation forms. Students can also apply online.

CONTACT

Walden University
155 Fifth Avenue South
Minneapolis, Minnesota 55401
Telephone: 866-492-5336 (toll-free)
E-mail: info@waldenu.edu
Web site: http://www.waldenu.edu

Washington State University

Distance Degree Programs

Pullman, Washington

Washington State University (WSU), the state's land-grant institution, is dedicated to the preparation of students for productive lives and professional careers, to basic and applied research, and to the dissemination of knowledge. Founded in 1890, the University is a statewide institution with a main campus in Pullman, three branch campuses, ten community learning centers, and numerous Cooperative Extension and research facilities throughout the state. WSU is accredited by the Northwest Association of Schools and Colleges. In addition, the University is an acknowledged leader in developing and delivering distance education programs. Since 1992, WSU's Office of Distance Degree Programs (DDP) has been serving students in Washington and across the nation. The University's undergraduate core curriculum, including world civilization courses and expanded writing requirements, is nationally recognized. Money *magazine has called WSU a "public ivy" and rated the honors program as one of the nation's best, and in 1998,* Yahoo! Internet Life *magazine rated WSU as the Most Wired College in the nation.*

DISTANCE LEARNING PROGRAM

WSU's Office of Distance Degree Programs offers degree-completion programs leading to a Bachelor of Arts (B.A.) in business administration (with majors in management information systems (MIS) or general business), human development, humanities, or social sciences; a Bachelor of Science in Nursing (B.S.N.); and a Master of Science (M.S.) in agriculture. These programs are designed primarily for students who have completed the equivalent of the first two years of college. They are delivered directly to students' homes through a variety of distance learning technologies, primarily the Internet. They are the same degrees offered on three WSU campuses; requirements are the same, but students can complete their degrees without attending WSU in person.

DELIVERY MEDIA

Courses are delivered primarily by the Internet, videotape (for rent), and print materials. Most courses have Web and e-mail requirements.

PROGRAMS OF STUDY

WSU's B.A. in social sciences is a liberal arts degree that offers students multiple options and emphases in the social sciences and provides a broad background applicable to a variety of careers. It emphasizes an interdisciplinary approach with possible major and/or minor concentrations in anthropology, criminal justice, history, human development, political science, psychology, sociology, and women's studies. A formal minor in business administration is also available.

A B.A. in human development is also available with an asynchronous distance format from WSU. The human development degree is especially effective for individuals who work in child- or elder-care programs or in direct service roles with a variety of special-needs clients. The degree program includes an internship component supervised by a WSU faculty member.

The B.A. in business administration with a major in general business is designed to provide a broad foundation for employment in the world of business, either at a large corporation or in a small private company. A set curriculum, fully accredited by AACSB International–The Association to Advance Collegiate Schools of Business, leads students through courses in finance, management, information systems, marketing, international business, business law, and economics.

Within the B.A. in business administration, WSU now offers an MIS major. This major, available entirely in an online, asynchronous format, is designed to enable graduates to enter the working world as systems analysts, systems project managers, or Web masters. The set curriculum, also fully accredited by AACSB International–The Association to Advance Collegiate Schools of Business, takes students through computer hardware issues, software applications, and networking protocol. Graduates are employed with the nation's top corporations and consulting firms, as well as in numerous international settings.

The B.A. in humanities is a broad-based, interdisciplinary liberal arts degree program. It is configured in the same manner as the social sciences program. There is not a set list of required courses for students to take. Working with an academic adviser, each student develops a program of study that best meets his or her educational goals. The focus of the program is on developing skills in communication, writing, problem solving, and critical thinking, with a focus on the humanities.

A Bachelor of Science in Nursing degree program is available for registered nurses. The Intercollegiate College of Nursing/WSU College of Nursing offer ten theory courses using Web-based software. In some circumstances, clinical courses may be taken close to home. Out-of-state students may be required to complete two clinical courses in Washington, which are scheduled based on negotiations between the student and faculty. RNs work with B.S.N.-prepared preceptors; nursing faculty members supervise the course. RN students must meet specific criteria prior to application to this program.

Emphasis of the M.S. in agriculture program is on the agricultural professional, practitioner, and educator. The program is designed for students, at a distance and on campus, who wish to prepare for or further their careers in agriculture without having to relocate or interfere with their current employment. A maximum number of electives is permitted to enable the student to concentrate in one or two fields, or otherwise tailor the curriculum to fit their particular needs. Students may choose between a thesis or nonthesis program. If it is a nonthesis program, the student is required to complete 6 credits of practicums instead of a thesis. The practicums must be approved by the student's graduate committee at least one semester prior to registering for the course.

To earn a bachelor's degree, WSU generally requires the completion of at least 120 semester credits, 40 at the upper-division level. At least 30 of the 120 credits must be taken through WSU. The 120 credits must include courses that meet WSU General Education Requirements.

Nearly 200 courses are available to the students. Courses are also available from the National Universities Degree Consortium (NUDC), a group of nine land-grant and state universities formed to address the needs of adult and part-time learners.

STUDENT SERVICES

Academic advising is available to all prospective and currently enrolled degree-seeking students through toll-free telephone or e-mail. The WSU Office of Admissions prepares an official evaluation of a student's transcript when he or she is admitted to the University. A DDP adviser assists DDP students in developing a study plan based on the program options and University requirements. A student services coordinator is available to help students with logistical details.

Students register online or with support from DDP staff members. Videotapes, lab kits, and other supplementary materials are available through the DDP office. Students may order textbooks and course guides from the WSU Students Book Corporation online or via toll-free telephone.

All DDP students have access to the WSU libraries. The DDP librarian is available via toll-free telephone to assist students with database searches, checking out materials, and copying.

The ASWSU-DDP Career Counselor is available to WSU DDP students to discuss career-related concerns. These may range from developing a school-to-career identity to providing assistance and resources to find satisfying work or a graduate school program.

CREDIT OPTIONS

Students may transfer to WSU a maximum of 60 semester credits of lower-division credit and up to 30 credits from other four-year institutions. The exact number of transfer credits accepted by WSU may vary depending upon an individual's choice of degree.

WSU recognizes there are alternative ways students may gain knowledge and credit. The University has developed a method of accepting credit by examination, including Advanced Placement (AP), College-Level Examination Program (CLEP), DANTES, and American Council on Education (ACE). Interested students should check with their advisers for details.

FACULTY

There are 1,082 full-time and 186 part-time instructional faculty members in the Washington State University system. Eighty-two percent have terminal academic degrees.

ADMISSION

Admission to Distance Degree Programs requires at least 27 semester or 40 quarter credits of transferable college course work from an accredited community or four-year college, with at least a 2.0 cumulative GPA.

TUITION AND FEES

In 2003–04, undergraduate tuition (semester-based) was $242 per semester credit for Washington residents and $353 per semester credit for nonresidents. Videotape rental averages $60 per course. Correspondence (flexible enrollment) course tuition is $177 per credit. Payment options for full-time students are available as well.

FINANCIAL AID

A financial aid adviser is available to all DDP students. WSU students receive aid from all federal programs, such as the Federal Pell Grants and Federal Supplemental Educational Opportunity Grants (FSEOG) and the Federal Perkins, Federal Stafford Student, and Federal PLUS Loans. Washington residents are eligible for institutional and state need grants. In 2003–04, WSU awarded approximately $157 million in financial aid. Approximately 67 percent of all WSU students and 63 percent of distance degree students receive financial aid.

APPLYING

WSU degree-seeking students must be admitted to the University. Admission requires that a student submit an admissions form, have official copies of his or her transcript(s) sent directly from the postsecondary institution(s) attended to WSU's Office of Admissions, and pay the $36 application fee.

CONTACT

Student Services
Distance Degree Programs
Van Doren 104
Washington State University
P.O. Box 645220
Pullman, Washington 99164-5220
Telephone: 509-335-3557
800-222-4978 (toll-free)
Fax: 509-335-4850
E-mail: distance@wsu.edu
Web site:
http://www.distance.wsu.edu

Weber State University

Distance Learning

Ogden, Utah

Weber State University (WSU) provides lifelong opportunities for diverse learners on and off campus. It offers degrees through seven colleges and forty departments via distance learning. Students may receive specialized training in health professions, criminal justice, and manufacturing. WSU's academic programs prepare students for immediate employment or further study and equip them with liberal education concepts and skills to support their lifelong learning.

WSU serves as Utah's premier public undergraduate university. The institution was founded in 1889, became a state junior college in 1933, and added upper-division courses and began bachelor's degree programs in 1959. On January 1, 1991, Weber State further expanded its offerings and was granted university status.

Weber State University is accredited by the Northwest Association of Schools and Colleges. In addition, professional agencies such as the Commission on Accreditation for Allied Health Education Programs and the Association of University Programs in Health Administration accredit specific disciplines.

DISTANCE LEARNING PROGRAM

The WSU Distance Learning Program serves students who cannot attend college classes in person. During the 2003–04 academic year, more than 12,000 students enrolled in print- and Internet-based courses. Students use distance learning to earn general education credits, as well as degrees and professional credentials in manufacturing, criminal justice, and health science areas.

DELIVERY MEDIA

Students follow study guides, read textbooks, view videotapes, hear cassettes, and/or participate in online courses. They interact with other students, instructors, and advisers by using mail, telephone, e-mail, and online discussion groups. Exams are delivered online or through the mail and are administered by approved proctors. Access to a videocassette player, audiocassette player, word processor, or a computer with browser software and an Internet service provider may be required.

PROGRAMS OF STUDY

The WSU Distance Learning degree program evolved from a commitment to providing education for health-care professionals and other working adults regardless of location. Combining independent study with Internet courses, a bachelor's degree requires 120 semester hours (40 upper-division, 30 through WSU) with a minimum GPA of at least a 2.0 (or C).

Bachelor's degrees are available in clinical laboratory science, health services administration, health information management, health promotion, radiologic science (emphases in computed tomography, magnetic resonance imaging, cardiovascular-interventional technology, advanced radiography, mammography, quality management), nuclear medicine, radiation therapy, diagnostic medical sonography (medical-vascular), respiratory therapy, computer engineering technology, and electronics engineering technology.

Associate of Science degrees are available in clinical laboratory science, health information technology, and respiratory therapy. An Associate of Applied Science degree is also available in respiratory therapy.

The associate degree in general studies serves the needs of students who want to individualize the first two years of their academic programs, students who want to obtain a broad liberal education, and students who want to lay broad foundations for continued higher education.

The Weber State University Distance Learning Associate of Science degree program in criminal justice and the professional certificate programs in production and inventory management are designed for professionals whose work and travel schedules and far-flung locations make it difficult for them to participate in campus classwork.

Law enforcement and security professionals register online with Weber State University or one of its six collaborating institutions and take their training on their home or work computers.

Weber State University works in partnership with APICS, the 70,000-member Educational Society for Resource Management, to offer its certification program through WSU Online for people who work in production and resource management.

WSU certificate programs include health information technology, health-care coding and classification, and radiologic sciences. Radiologic sciences classes can be used toward continuing education units (CEU).

SPECIAL PROGRAMS

WSU Online, the award-winning extension of the University on the Internet, allows students to take online courses, use online support services, and participate in online discussions and activities with faculty and staff members and other students. WSU

Online makes it possible for students with busy schedules and/or long commutes to take advantage of the convenience of online courses with support services and interpersonal experiences that are essential to their success. For current course listings and additional information, students can visit the WSU Web site at http://wsuonline.weber.edu.

Courses from a wide range of academic disciplines are available through Weber State University's independent study program, allowing students to complete their course work at their convenience. Each year, more than 2,000 students enroll in these print-based courses and take advantage of this self-paced, individualized mode of study.

STUDENT SERVICES

WSU recognizes that most of its students have work, family, and other responsibilities that limit their participation in traditional classroom college courses; therefore, convenience is a major factor in the design of the Distance Learning Program.

Students receive guidance from distance learning staff and faculty members. Degree-seeking students are assigned academic advisers who review transcripts and past learning experiences. This information is used to design individualized programs of study.

Students may access Stewart Library's catalog, interlibrary loan, reference help, document delivery, and other services electronically at http://library.weber.edu. Textbooks can be purchased directly from the WSU bookstore, by telephone (800-848-7770 Ext. 6352), or online (http://bookstore.weber.edu) for a small handling charge.

CREDIT OPTIONS

WSU may grant credit for active military, National Guard, or reserve experience; 38 or more credits to registered radiographers; a maximum of 45 credits to diploma nursing school graduates; and varying credits to registered respiratory therapy technicians and graduates of accredited therapy/specialty programs. Official transcripts should be sent directly from universities and colleges attended. WSU also recognizes College-Level Examination Program (CLEP) credits.

FACULTY

WSU Distance Learning currently employs 111 full-time university faculty members and 14 adjunct faculty members. Nearly all faculty members hold terminal degrees in their respective fields.

ADMISSION

Degree-seeking Distance Learning applicants must meet WSU admission requirements. The programs in health professions require separate applications and information specific to their academic areas. Students not seeking to complete a degree at WSU may be eligible for simplified, nonmatriculated admission.

TUITION AND FEES

Distance Learning tuition averages $125 per semester hour. Additional materials may include course study guides ($3–$40) and audiotape or videotape deposits of $60, with a $40 refund upon their return.

Tuition fees for online courses are $163 per semester hour for non-Utah residents. All fees are subject to change. Students can consult the current catalog or visit the Web site at http://www.weber.edu/ce/dl/ for more information.

FINANCIAL AID

Eligible students may apply for federal financial aid such as Pell Grants, Supplemental Educational Opportunity Grants (SEOG), Perkins Loans, and Stafford Student Loans. Students can contact the office of financial aid toll-free at 800-848-7770 Ext. 7569.

Veterans may also be considered for VA educational benefits (office of Veteran Affairs telephone: 800-848-7770 Ext. 6039, toll-free). Health professions degree programs are approved by DANTES.

APPLYING

Students should send an admissions application; an individual program application, if required; official transcripts from previous colleges; and an application fee of $30 to the contact address. Students may also apply online at http://weber.edu/admissions/. Distance Learning students need not attend an orientation.

CONTACT

Office of Distance Learning
Weber State University
4005 University Circle
Ogden, Utah 84408-4005
Telephone: 801-626-6600
800-848-7770 Ext. 6600 (toll-free)
Fax: 801-626-8035
E-mail: ceservices@weber.edu
Web site: http://wsuonline.weber.edu
http://weber.edu/ce/dl/

Western Baptist College

Adult Studies Online Programs

Salem, Oregon

Western Baptist College is an independent, Christian liberal arts college and is accredited by the Northwest Association of Schools and Colleges. Its core purpose is to educate Christians who will make a difference in the world for Jesus Christ.

The College offered its first distance learning program in 1994, which developed into a uniquely online format in 1997. It now offers two online degree completion programs for Christian students in the areas of management and communication and family studies.

DISTANCE LEARNING PROGRAM

Western's online degree completion programs are specifically and conveniently formatted for the Christian student who has two years of college credit and desires a Christian college education but is unable to attend on-campus classes. With only a three-day residency orientation, the entirety of the sixteen-month program is completed from home via computer.

DELIVERY MEDIA

Online course work requires an IBM-compatible computer system, Internet access, and completion of an initial orientation held on campus. Complete precourse training is provided for all students via self-paced tutorials, hands-on workshops, and follow-up technical support. Course instruction is accomplished by utilizing facilitated discussion forums, live chat conferences, and collaborative project reports, which are supported by Internet course-management software, audio-video and keyboard conferencing programs, e-mail, and telephone.

PROGRAMS OF STUDY

Western Baptist offers two degree completion programs entirely online. Individual online courses are also offered to assist students in completing general education requirements. The online degree completion programs lead to a B.S. or B.A. degree. Students enrolling in the degree completion program must have completed 60 semester hours of transferable credit. A total of 128 semester hours is required for the bachelor's degree.

Both online degree completion programs in management and communication and family studies are excellent preparation for graduate study. The Management and Communication online degree completion program is 37 semester hours. The curriculum is structured to develop leadership, analytical, and problem-solving skills with a Christian perspective. Course work provides expertise in management, organization development, and communication—three of the most important aspects of business and public administration. The Family Studies online degree completion program is 44 semester hours. It is an applied interdisciplinary approach, focusing on the study of family dynamics and the relationships between families and the society at large. The curriculum is integrated with biblical principles and is taught by Christian professionals. Students completing the program are eligible for certification as family life educators through the National Council on Family Relations.

SPECIAL PROGRAMS

Students are given the opportunity to earn college credit for prior learning through the Prior Learning Assessment program. Students learn how to identify, document, and describe appropriate prior learning experiences. Weekend classes are offered both online as well as on-campus and are designed to meet general education requirements. The course offerings vary in length. Internships and research projects are required in the online degree completion programs. They are generally completed within the workplace or in a related local business or agency.

STUDENT SERVICES

Online students enjoy complete access to the same College services as campus students via Web-based communication, fax, or telephone. In addition to academic advising and project mentoring, financial aid, registrar's office, technical support, campus bookstore, and library services are available. Online library resources include EBSCOhost, ERIC, Academic Universe, ProQuest Direct, and other comprehensive databases.

CREDIT OPTIONS

Qualifying college credit may be transferred subject to the approval of the College registrar. Students may earn a maximum of 32 semester hours of credit through college-level exams (CLEP, DANTES) and 30 semester hours of credit through the Prior Learning Assessment program.

ADMISSION

Enrollment in the online degree completion program requires applicants to have a minimum of 60 semester hours of transferable college credit as well as profession of a personal faith in Jesus Christ.

TUITION AND FEES

The 2001 tuition for the online degree completion program is $12,300. Tuition includes all textbooks and graduation fees.

FINANCIAL AID

Financial aid is available through federal and state financial aid programs. For further information, students should contact the financial aid office at 800-845-3005 (toll-free) or via e-mail at aid@wbc.edu.

APPLYING

Applicants for online degree completion programs must complete an application and submit transcripts, two references, an acceptable writing sample, and a profession of faith in Jesus Christ.

CONTACT

Adult Studies Online Program
Western Baptist College
5000 Deer Park Drive, SE
Salem, Oregon 97301
Telephone: 800-764-1383 (toll-free)
Fax: 503-375-7583
E-mail: asd@wbc.edu
Web site: http://www.wbc.edu

Western Washington University

Extended Education and Summer Programs

Bellingham, Washington

Since its founding in 1899, Western Washington University (WWU) has provided high-quality educational opportunities to the community, the region, the nation, and beyond. Western's distance education program began in 1912 and continues to grow and evolve in response to the times. WWU faculty members and administrators, many of them affiliated with distance learning, have recently garnered several important national awards. Among them are Columbia University's Bancroft Prize; the Presidential Award for Excellence in Science, Mathematics and Engineering; North American Leader status from the American Association of Higher Education and Carnegie Foundation for the Advancement of Teaching; and a Coastal and Ocean Resource Management Excellence Award from the National Oceanic and Atmospheric Administration (NOAA). U.S. News & World Report *rates WWU as one of the top ten public master's-granting universities in the country. WWU is accredited by the Northwest Association of Schools, Colleges and Universities. The University holds membership in the Council of Graduate Schools in the United States.*

DISTANCE LEARNING PROGRAM

As part of Western Washington University's outreach mission, Extended Education offers a degree-completion program, credit and noncredit certificates, and stand-alone courses through print or online distance learning. Several sites in the Puget Sound region provide classroom-based certificate and degree programs.

Students come from all age groups and may use courses and programs to earn a degree or to bolster their careers. Many are employed full-time or have family obligations that require flexible course scheduling.

All courses and programs undergo careful scrutiny prior to being offered. Credit courses are equally as rigorous as those offered on campus.

DELIVERY MEDIA

A variety of media are employed to meet the needs of distant learners. Several courses are offered fully online using Blackboard course management software; many more are print-based. Some courses are supplemented with videotapes, audiocassettes, CDs, or interactive diskettes. Language courses that use the Cyrillic alphabet are enhanced by workbooks illustrating letter formation and pronunciation.

Students communicate with faculty members via e-mail, telephone, voice mail, surface mail or, when possible, in person.

PROGRAMS OF STUDY

The final two years of a Bachelor of Arts in human services can be earned entirely online. Students may start any quarter and can graduate as soon as eighteen months, depending on credit load and starting quarter. Formal admission to the University is required. More information is available online at http://www.wce.wwu.edu/depts/hs/sites/cyber.shtml.

A certificate program in emergency management/homeland security is available online. The credit certificate may be used by students entering the field or increasing their level of skill. Dr. Wayne Blanchard, the Federal Emergency Management Agency's (FEMA's) Higher Education Project Manager, gave approval to the instructors and curriculum. For more information, students should visit http://www.extendeded.wwu.edu/emergencymgmt.

The certificate in birth-to-five care requires completion of four credit-bearing courses. This program provides training for Early Head Start and the Early Childhood Education and Assistance Program (ECEAP) workers, among others. For more information, students should visit http://www.extendeded.wwu.edu/birthto5.

More than 130 stand-alone credit courses, in thirty-five subjects, are available to all learners. Classes are offered at lower division, upper division, and graduate levels. Course lists can be found online at http://www.extendeded.wwu.edu/ilearn .

Educators, human services professionals, and others can use any of several online and print-based courses aimed at job enhancement or promotion. These professional development classes follow the quarter system, including a summer quarter. For a complete list and in-depth information, students should visit http://www.extendeded.wwu.edu/cil.

SPECIAL PROGRAMS

WWU offers a minor in East Asian studies that can be completed wholly at a distance. Courses are primarily print-based and carry a nine-month completion deadline. To receive official recognition of the minor from WWU, students must be formally admitted to the University.

Several unique language courses are available through distance learning. Students may complete three quarters of Mongolian, taught by a former lawyer from Mongolia. One quarter each of elementary Greek and Latin are also offered. Specially designed supplements—audiotapes and workbooks—are used in some language courses.

STUDENT SERVICES

Students have access to thousands of databases and interlibrary loan through the WWU library, one-on-one advising on course and program selection, and access to an information technology help desk. For those considering online study, a sample course is available to demonstrate Blackboard. Students may check grades and transcripts online during the academic quarter of enrollment.

Extended Education staff members provide personalized assistance to current and future students from 8 to 5 (Pacific Time), Monday–Friday, by phone, e-mail, or in person.

CREDIT OPTIONS

College credits earned through distance learning courses are recorded on a WWU transcript and carry the same weight as those gained through traditional classroom study. Up to 90 quarter hours of distance learning credits can be applied to a WWU bachelor's degree.

FACULTY

All faculty members are approved by the appropriate department prior to developing a course. Most teach the same courses on campus and nearly all have a terminal degree, usually a doctorate, in their subject area. Many have won local or national awards for teaching excellence or professional achievement. The majority of faculty members are available for student interaction through e-mail, phone, or voice mail.

ADMISSION

Formal admission to WWU is required for the human services online degree program. General University application materials must be submitted to the WWU Office of Admissions concurrently with application to the WWU Woodring College of Education Human Services Department. For details, prospective students should visit http://www.wce.wwu.edu/depts/hs/admission/appprocess.shtml .

TUITION AND FEES

Course tuition varies among programs and is subject to change upon action by the Board of Trustees. At the time of publication, tuition for independent learning (print-based correspondence) courses was $93 per credit; tuition for online courses was $163 per credit for undergraduate courses, $183 for graduate-level courses. Fees for certificate modules vary. Other fees may apply for admission, registration, and materials.

FINANCIAL AID

Financial aid is available only for programs that require formal admission to the University. Matriculated Western Washington University students who are taking distance learning courses in addition to classroom courses are sometimes eligible for financial aid.

APPLYING

Print-based courses are available to anyone for enrollment at any time. Many online courses are also open to anyone but follow the academic calendar. Interested students may review course descriptions on the Web site or call or e-mail for a printed catalog. Students may register by phone, confidential fax, or surface mail. People interested in the human services B.A. completion program should see the Admission section above.

CONTACT

Extended Education and Summer Programs
MS 5293
Western Washington University
516 High Street
Bellingham, Washington 98225-5996
Telephone: 360-650-3308
Fax: 360-650-3486
E-mail: eesp.distedpeters@wwu.edu
Web site: http://www.extendeded.wwu.edu

West Virginia University

Extended Learning Program

Morgantown, West Virginia

West Virginia University (WVU) is a student-centered learning community meeting the changing needs of West Virginia and the nation through teaching, research, service, and technology. Among the University's core values are focus, teamwork, intensive communication, and character building. The University fosters a high-quality, holistic education on all of its campuses, and its graduate teaching programs and research efforts focus on excellence, impact, and reputation.

DISTANCE LEARNING PROGRAM

Extended Learning offers West Virginia University courses around the state and around the globe through off-campus programming and distance technology. Both undergraduate and graduate programs are offered online. Most students are adult learners, but many high school students have their first taste of college through WVU classes offered in their high schools. WVU has expanded into the noncredit field in its quest to meet the needs of all lifelong learners.

The Extended Learning Program's vision is to facilitate West Virginia University programming to state, regional, and global audiences. Extended Learning promotes a positive image of the University through public service activities, effective programming, and delivery of student services. The Extended Learning mission is to provide seamless access to academic courses, lifelong learning opportunities, student services, and library materials through a personalized yet convenient process. This service includes online registration and payment as well as online, multimedia, and/or technology-enhanced courses.

Extended Learning seeks to identify and satisfy the academic needs of adult learners by working with WVU's colleges and academic departments to offer courses at convenient times and locations as well as through accessible formats.

DELIVERY MEDIA

West Virginia University employs a variety of technologies to deliver high-quality degree programs. Classes may be taught via the Internet, IViN (a two-way interactive video system), and public television. Faculty members who teach these classes are committed to offering off-campus students the same high-quality experience that on-campus students receive. Courses are offered in high schools, colleges, and local business operations that are conveniently located around the state.

PROGRAMS OF STUDY

West Virginia University offers an expanding array of courses every semester. Undergraduate courses are especially popular with students in the Regents Bachelor of Arts program or those who have to be away from campus during the academic year.

Graduate degrees delivered via distance technology include the Master of Science (M.S.) in athletic coaching education, which allows students to complete most of their work online and spend only two weeks in the summer in Morgantown; the Executive M.B.A., which requires the completion of 48 credit hours; the M.S. in integrated marketing communications, which is taught exclusively online and provides students with the first-hand knowledge of industry experts; the Master of Science in Nursing (M.S.N.), a 44-credit program that can be completed in four semesters; the Master of Occupational Therapy (M.O.T.), which is offered online with on-site participation; the M.S. in physical education teacher education, a 36-credit program with both on-site and distance education components; the M.S. in rehabilitation counseling, designed for completion in two years; the Master of Science in Software Engineering (M.S.S.E.), which provides graduate-level software engineering expertise to individuals currently working in the computer and information technology industry or who have certain academic credentials; and the M.A. in special education, which prepares master-clinical teachers of children and adults with special needs.

Professional certificate programs include health-care administration, integrated marketing communications, and software engineering. An undergraduate degree via distance technology is the RN to B.S.N., which offers all courses online and is designed for completion in three semesters of full-time study.

SPECIAL PROGRAMS

Distance technology enables off-campus students to design much of their own degrees through the Regents Bachelor of Arts (R.B.A.) program, a flexible degree for adults. R.B.A. students can earn credit though many online classes, with upper-division credits available in two online areas of emphasis. Students can design their own programs of study in the R.B.A. program.

High school students have the opportunity to take West Virginia University courses and earn college credit through the ACCESS program. Credit for course work taken is recorded on an official WVU transcript, which applies to a student's academic progress at WVU or may be transferred to other institutions of higher education.

STUDENT SERVICES

The WVU Career Services Center assists students in identifying meaningful career options and preparing them for the world of work. The center offers a variety of services for students at all levels of career development. The Office of Information Technology Support Services provides the OIT Help Desk, a support team that serves WVU students as well as faculty and staff members at all WVU campuses. Help Desk staff members are available to answer calls during normal WVU office hours and extended hours during evenings and weekends.

FACULTY

WVU professors are leaders in their fields who always have time to talk with their students—both on- and off-campus.

ADMISSION

Admission to West Virginia University is necessary to enroll in credit courses, including those offered through Extended Learning. An applicant may enroll as a graduate, a professional development student, an undergraduate, a high school student in the ACCESS program, or as a guest. To be considered for freshman admission, a student must successfully complete 4 units of English (including grammar, composition, and literature), 3 units of social studies (including U.S. history), 3 units of college preparatory mathematics (algebra I and II and plane geometry), and 3 units of science (2 of which must be laboratory science). More information about program-specific application requirements can be found online at the Extended Learning Program's Web site.

TUITION AND FEES

Tuition and fees vary depending on the college or program in which the student is enrolled as well as whether the student is a West Virginia resident. In the 2003–04 academic year, graduate tuition and fees for in-state residents ranged from $1782 to $3924 for 9 credit hours. Out-of-state graduate students paid between $5384 and $8531 for 9 credit hours. In-state undergraduate tuition and fees ranged between $1703 and $2081 for 12 credit hours, while out-of-state students paid between $5313 and $6465 for the same number of credit hours.

FINANCIAL AID

WVU students receive more than $164 million a year in grants, loans, work-study opportunities, fee waivers, and scholarships. Awards are based on financial need and academic ability. Determination of eligibility for financial aid is complex, but financial aid counselors are available to help students. Interested students should contact the WVU Financial Aid Office, toll free at 800-344-WVU1 or online at http://www.wvu.edu/~finaid/.

APPLYING

WVU has a rolling admissions policy, which means that applicants receive an admission decision within a few weeks after receipt of all required application materials. The Office of Admissions and Records begins the process of formally reviewing applications on September 15. The graduate degrees offered through Extended Learning require that students first be accepted into one of WVU's graduate programs. Students who have earned a baccalaureate degree may enroll in professional development courses by completing a registration form through Extended Learning and by paying an application fee. Professional development status is valid for only one semester. Criteria for undergraduate admission varies according to academic program. Advanced high school students may register for WVU courses through the ACCESS program. Prospective students may submit a guest application/registration form for enrollment in WVU Extended Learning undergraduate courses for one term of course work. Specific application procedures can be found online.

CONTACT

Extended Learning Program
West Virginia University
P.O. Box 6800
Morgantown, West Virginia 26506-6800
Telephone: 304-293-2834
800-2LEARN2 (toll-free)
E-mail: exlearn@mail.wvu.edu
Web Site: http://elearn.wvu.edu/

Westwood College–Denver North Online Programs

Westwood College Online

Denver, Colorado

Westwood College has been providing accelerated career-focused education since 1953. In addition to online degree programs, Westwood College currently operates fourteen Technology campuses and three Aviation Technology campuses with locations in California, Colorado, Georgia, Illinois, and Texas.

Westwood's accelerated programs enable a student to complete an associate degree in as little as seventeen months, or a bachelor's degree in thirty-four months, allowing that student to enter or advance in a chosen field in less time.

Online degree programs are offered through Westwood College–Denver North Online Programs and are accredited by the Accrediting Commission of Career Schools and Colleges of Technology (ACCSCT).

DISTANCE LEARNING PROGRAM

Westwood College started offering online degree programs in May 2002. Westwood College Online is an excellent option for students who are outside of the metro areas served by Westwood campuses or students whose work or family obligations do not allow time to attend scheduled classes on campus.

DELIVERY MEDIA

The online courses are instructor-led, not self-paced. Assignments are due weekly. The online courses may include the use of threaded discussions simulating in-class discussion and interaction; group projects; student-to-student, student-to-instructor, and instructor-to-student e-mails, chat rooms, short online audio and video lectures, and graphical demonstrations of concepts.

PROGRAMS OF STUDY

Currently, Westwood offers ten bachelor's degree programs and three associate degree programs though distance learning. Students should check the Web site for up-to-date listings.

The Bachelor of Science (B.S.) in animation (183 quarter credit hours) equips students with the skills necessary to enter the field of animation. This program covers topics such as the laws of human motion, physics, and psychology as applied to 2-D and 3-D characters, life drawing and rendering techniques, and the application of audio and video to an animation project.

The Bachelor of Science in Business Administration with a concentration in accounting (180 quarter credit hours) equips students with the business and financial skills necessary to advance in the field of accounting. In addition, the combination of management and general education courses in the program helps students apply skills in general management, critical thinking, logic, communication, and problem solving to workplace challenges. This program also includes critical courses that cover such topics as cost accounting, financial accounting, auditing, and financial reporting.

The Bachelor of Science in Business Administration with a concentration in marketing and sales (180 quarter credit hours) equips students with the business skills necesary to advance in the field of marketing and sales. In addition, the combination of management and general education courses in the program helps students apply skills in general management, critical thinking, logic, communication, and problem solving to workplace challenges. This program also includes critical marketing and sales courses that cover such topics as consumer behavior, marketing research, professional selling, and Internet marketing and sales.

The Bachelor of Science in computer network management program (180 quarter credit hours) is designed to provide students with the advanced networking skills required to design, install, configure, and maintain enterprise-wide networks.

The Bachelor of Science in criminal justice (183 quarter credit hours) equips students academically and professionally by developing a knowledge base, social awareness, and technological skills for an entry-level position in today's criminal justice environment.

The Bachelor of Science in e-business management program (181.5 quarter credit hours) is designed to integrate technology, business, and employability skills to prepare students for entry-level jobs in the burgeoning field of e-business.

The Bachelor of Science in visual communications program (183 quarter credit hours) is designed to prepare students with the design, marketing, and technical skills necessary to advance in the field of visual communications.

The Bachelor of Science in Web design and multimedia (183 quarter credit hours) equips students with Web design, e-commerce, scripting, and authoring skills necessary to advance in the field of Web design.

The Game Software Development Bacheolor Program (193.5 quarter credit hours) is designed to provide students with the ability to apply core knowledge of software engineering to employment settings through a curriculum that emphasizes game and interactive software development. In addition, general education courses assist students in applying critical thinking, logic, communication, and problem-solving skills in managing challenges that occur in a game development environment.

The Information Systems Security Bachelor Program (180 quarter credit hours) is designed to provide students with the advanced security skills required to implement e-business security solutions and policies, identify security threats and develop countermeasures using firewall systems and attack recognition technologies, and manage the deployment of security solutions.

The Associate of Applied Science (A.A.S.) in computer network engineering program (108 quarter credit hours) is designed to provide students with the skills required to design, install, configure, and maintain enterprise-wide networks.

The Associate of Applied Science in graphic design and multimedia program (90 quarter credit hours) prepares students for entry-level jobs in the graphic design and multimedia industry. Students learn to create effective designs that communicate visually in both print and multimedia environments.

The Associate of Applied Science in software engineering program (91.5 quarter credit hours) provides students with the skills required to design and implement computer software.

SPECIAL PROGRAMS

Alumni retraining is a special program at Westwood. All Westwood alumni are entitled to tuition-free graduate retraining in the program they completed at Westwood. Graduates are able to audit classes to update their skills as curriculum changes in their field of study. Charges for books and student fees may apply.

STUDENT SERVICES

Westwood distance learning students receive online access to the same student services that are provided to on-campus students. With its academic advising, Westwood is dedicated to helping students remove obstacles to success. There are several programs that provide students with the opportunity to solve problems, share ideas, and set goals with members of the college staff. Westwood has a free tutoring program that provides online help. There is a full research library that is available online to students 24 hours a day, seven days a week. Distance learning students also have access to technical assistance 24 hours a day, 7 days a week.

The primary objective of the Career Development Services Office is to help students achieve their career goals. At Westwood, successful job-placement assistance begins long before graduation. In fact, Westwood's unique approach to career planning and job-placement assistance begins at registration and continues beyond graduation.

CREDIT OPTIONS

There are four ways to achieve advanced academic standing at Westwood College: with transfer credits from accredited colleges or universities, through articulation agreements with selected high schools and colleges, through Westwood College Proficiency Exams, and through Advanced Placement (AP) exams, College Level Examination Program (CLEP) exams, or nationally recognized certification exams.

FACULTY

Westwood Online's faculty is composed of full-time and part-time instructors from Westwood's fourteen technology campuses, plus additional experts in the individual field of study.

ADMISSION

Each applicant must demonstrate proficiency in basic college-level skills as evidenced by attaining passing scores on any of the following examinations: For the ACT, the applicant must have a composite score of at least 17 on both the English and the Mathematics sections of the exam. For the SAT, the applicant must have a score of at least 460 on both the Mathematics and Verbal sections of the exam. For the Accuplacer Computerized Placement Tests, applicants must have passing scores on at least three of the following four exams: Reading Comprehension, Sentence Skills, Arithmetic, and Elementary Algebra.

TUITION AND FEES

The standard tuition fee is $3729 per term plus a $30 online fee per credit hour. Lab charges, tool kits, and books are additional and vary with the program of study.

FINANCIAL AID

Tuition assistance is available for those who qualify. In order to help guide applicants through the tuition assistance application process, Westwood provides a step-by-step guide as well as links to all of the forms that can be filled out online.

APPLYING

To qualify for admission, students must submit an application fee of $25 and a registration fee of $75, provide proof of a high school diploma or GED completion, and provide passing test scores from college-level exams outlined in the Admission section.

CONTACT

Westwood College Online
Westwood College–Denver North–Online Programs
7350 North Broadway
Denver, Colorado 80221
Telephone: 888-996-6546 (toll-free)
Fax: 303-426-1832
E-mail: wolinternet@westwood.edu
Web site: http://www.westwoodonline.edu

Worcester Polytechnic Institute

Advanced Distance Learning Network

Worcester, Massachusetts

Founded in 1865, Worcester Polytechnic Institute (WPI) has long been a pioneer in technological higher education. Three decades after it was created, the university's distinctive outcomes-oriented approach to education is being viewed as a model for reform at the national level, and WPI is recognized as the leader in global technological education. WPI is fully accredited by the New England Association of Schools and Colleges.

WPI awarded its first advanced degree in 1893. Today, most of its academic departments offer master's and doctoral programs and support leading-edge research in a broad range of fields. Through the years, WPI has earned a reputation for its academic excellence, its responsiveness to the needs of the marketplace, and for its faculty of renowned academicians and industry experts who are practitioners in their fields.

DISTANCE LEARNING PROGRAM

In 1979, WPI's commitment to active, lifelong learning prompted the creation of the Advanced Distance Learning Network (ADLN), a partnership between several academic departments and WPI's Instructional Media Center. ADLN programs empower working professionals to continue to grow within their chosen field without having to take classes on campus. There is no residency requirement.

DELIVERY MEDIA

ADLN delivers the same courses, content, and material as the on-campus programs but through a different delivery system. On-campus courses are taught by a faculty member in a face-to-face classroom environment. The delivery system for ADLN, taught by the same WPI faculty, is through a combination of technologies, including via the Web, videotape, and videoconferencing, thereby utilizing the best delivery method for the specific course content. Materials such as books, handouts, and supplemental readings are sent by express mail, fax, or e-mail or are posted on the Internet. An e-mail account and access to the Internet are required for participation in an ADLN course.

PROGRAMS OF STUDY

ADLN offers a Master of Business Administration (M.B.A.) in technology organizations, a Master of Science (M.S.) in fire protection engineering, and a Master of Science (M.S.) in civil and environmental engineering. In addition to these degree options, WPI's ADLN also offers numerous graduate certificate programs in these areas.

The M.B.A. program focuses on the management of technology and features a highly integrative curriculum that emphasizes leadership, ethics, communication, and a global perspective. Concentration areas include electronic commerce, information technology, and management of technology. This 49-credit M.B.A. program may be reduced to as few as 31 credits with an appropriate academic background. A customized 14-credit graduate certificate program in management is also available.

The Fire Protection Engineering (FPE) program is oriented toward developing a well-rounded professional who can be successful in a competitive career environment. The curriculum is designed to teach students current standards of practice and expose them to state-of-the-art research literature that will support future practices. In addition to the ten-course (30-credit) M.S. option, professionals with a B.S. degree in an engineering, engineering technology, or science field who complete four thematically related FPE courses can receive a graduate certificate in FPE. Master's degree holders may instead opt to complete five thematically related courses for an advanced certificate in FPE.

The Environmental Engineering program is arranged to meet the interests and objectives of individual students and their employers. The curriculum focuses on today's environmental issues in water quality systems and water remediation systems and their relationship to engineering, business, and law. The 33-credit Master of Science degree is a professional practice–oriented degree designed to meet the continuing challenges faced by practicing environmental engineers. A four-course graduate certificate is also available through ADLN.

Credits earned in any WPI certificate program can later be applied toward an advanced degree, contingent upon formal admission to graduate study. A maximum of two courses taken at WPI as a non-degree-seeking student may be applied for credit to the M.B.A. program; a maximum of four courses taken at WPI as a non-degree-seeking student may be applied for credit to an M.S. in fire protection engineering or an M.S. in environmental engineering.

SPECIAL PROGRAMS

ADLN and appropriate academic personnel are always willing to consider the addition of new programs for which there is sufficient interest.

STUDENT SERVICES

Academic advisers are assigned upon admission. Online library services are free, and reference services are available by phone or e-mail. Dial-up UNIX accounts (for e-mail, etc.) and career placement and counseling are available for matriculated students. Books can be ordered toll-free from the WPI bookstore (888-WPI-BOOKS) and are typically delivered one to three days after ordering.

CREDIT OPTIONS

The M.B.A. program allows 18 foundation-level credits to be waived for those with appropriate academic backgrounds via waiver exams. The M.B.A. program, the M.S. in fire protection engineering, and the M.S. in environmental engineering allow students to transfer up to 9 credits from graduate-level course work at other schools. Graduate and Advanced Certificate programs require all credits to come from WPI.

FACULTY

Management has 29 faculty members (21 full-time members and 8 part-time members), 26 of whom have Ph.D. degrees. Fire protection engineering has 6 full-time faculty members, all with Ph.D. degrees, and 2 part-time professors. Environmental engineering has 13 full-time faculty members, all with Ph.D. degrees, and 8 part-time professors.

ADMISSION

To be considered for admission to the M.B.A. program or a graduate certificate in management, an applicant must hold a B.S. degree and possess the analytic aptitude necessary to complete a technology-oriented program. Admission to WPI's M.S. programs or graduate certificate options in fire protection engineering or environmental engineering require an applicant to hold a B.S. degree in an appropriate field of engineering, engineering technology, or science and meet department-specific admission standards. Conditional admission is available if all requirements are not met at the time of application.

Non-degree-seeking students wishing to take management courses must demonstrate that they hold a bachelor's degree with an overall 3.0 (or equivalent) undergraduate grade point average or a completed graduate degree from an accredited university prior to being permitted to register for the courses. This requirement must be met with an official transcript submitted to the Office of Graduate Management Programs prior to registering for the first course. In addition, students must provide a personal statement explaining the motivation for their interest in WPI's graduate management program.

TUITION AND FEES

Tuition is $897 per credit for all programs in the 2004–05 academic year. Students wishing to earn Continuing Education Units (CEU) instead of graduate credit may opt to audit courses at half tuition.

FINANCIAL AID

Loan-based aid is available only through special arrangements. Students must be registered on at least a half-time basis (two courses per semester).

APPLYING

All departments require standard forms, official transcripts, and a $70 application fee. Management degree programs also require three letters of recommendation and GMAT scores. All international applicants must submit TOEFL scores. GRE scores are not required but may be substituted for the GMAT scores when applying for a graduate certificate in management.

CONTACT

Pamela Shelley, Assistant Director
Advanced Distance Learning Network
Worcester Polytechnic Institute
100 Institute Road
Worcester, Massachusetts 01609-2280
Telephone: 508-831-5220
Fax: 508-831-5881
E-mail: adln@wpi.edu
Web site: http://www.wpi.edu/+ADLN

IN-DEPTH DESCRIPTIONS OF DISTANCE LEARNING CONSORTIA

Florida Distance Learning Consortium

Florida's Online Presence for K–20 Education

Tallahassee, Florida

The Florida Distance Learning Consortium (FDLC) was established by the State Board of Community Colleges in 1996. In 2003, it completed a merger with the Florida Virtual Campus to provide coordination among Florida's colleges and universities in the development, delivery, marketing, and acquisition of distance learning instruction and its infrastructure.

FDLC provides an online catalog of distance learning courses and degree programs at http://www.distancelearn.org. The catalog lists thousands of courses and more than 200 degree and certificate programs in many disciplines offered by Florida's eleven state universities, twenty-eight community colleges, and some of Florida's private colleges and universities. Each institution is fully accredited by the Southern Association of Colleges and Schools. More than 160,000 students are currently taking courses or earning a degree at a distance from participating institutions at the associate, baccalaureate, and graduate levels.

DISTANCE LEARNING PROGRAM

FDLC provides information about distance learning opportunities at Florida institutions. The programs and courses listed on the Consortium's Web site meet the same academic standards of those found on-site at participating institutions. Students can generally study, take classes, and complete entire degree programs at any time and from any place.

The electronic catalog provides information about distance learning programs offered and lists thousands of distance learning courses in several different subject areas. Students can search the database by institution, term/semester, delivery method, subject/discipline, keywords, or course prefix and/or number. Once a student has located a course of interest, clicking on the college offering the course links the student to that institution and allows them to enroll. Each institution enters its own course information; therefore, the catalog reflects only those courses currently entered by each institution.

DELIVERY MEDIA

Participating institutions select the delivery methods and have their own distance learning policies and procedures. Courses and programs are taught in a variety of delivery formats including the Internet, real-time two-way television conference, audio tapes or audio conferencing, printed materials through a correspondence or independent-study program, videos that can be viewed on a local TV channel or checked out of the library, or through a combination of these technologies.

The predominant delivery method is via the Internet, and courses are offered in real time or asynchronously. Internet courses require students to have access to a computer, a modem with an Internet connection, a World Wide Web browser, and e-mail. Two-way television courses include live audio and visual communication between multiple parties and locations using video and computer technology and satellite transmission. Audio courses are presented via audiotapes or through audio conferencing. Print courses use instructor-student print-based communication and are exchanged by postal service. Telecourses take advantage of public educational broadcast channels for distribution. Videotape courses can be checked out from the library and viewed by attaching a VCR to a television. Multimode courses incorporate a variety of technologies, such as the Internet, CD-ROM, video, TV, and print materials.

PROGRAMS OF STUDY

The individual colleges and universities grant the degrees offered through FDLC. Students need to work with their home campus to ensure that they fulfill the requirements of the degree program. Each institution is fully accredited by the Southern Association of Colleges and Schools. Appropriate national organizations accredit the academic programs. Currently, more than 140 associate, bachelor's, master's, and a few doctoral degrees are offered. In addition, more than sixty special or certificate programs are listed in the online catalog. Participating institutions regularly add degree programs.

STUDENT SERVICES

To better assist students in searching the catalog, the Consortium's Web site has a "personal assistant" function that allows students to save course searches as well as searches for the specific classes of interest to them; it also enbles students to receive information from a selected college or university as a way to help them get started. Each institution provides its own student support services. The distancelearn.org Web site provides links to student support services, such as admissions, financial aid, registration, and academic advising for each institution.

CREDIT OPTIONS

Credits can be earned as a combination of on-campus and distance learning courses or, for many programs, credit can be completed entirely at a distance. Each institution determines the number of credits required to complete the degree programs offered. Credits are typically transferable, but students should check with their home institution before taking a course.

FACULTY

The same faculty members who teach on-campus courses at the institutions often design and teach the distance learning courses as well. Participating institutions determine who teaches each course and provide ongoing training and support to both the face-to-face and distance learning faculty members. The percentage of faculty members who have doctoral or advanced degrees varies among the participating institutions.

ADMISSION

Participating institutions have their own admission requirements and make admission decisions to accept students into a program. Admission criteria are the same as those for on-campus courses. Students may be able to complete the entire application for admission online for many of the participating institutions.

TUITION AND FEES

Each college or university determines tuition and fees for the courses and programs it offers. Some institutions also charge supplemental fees for particular classes or, in some cases, there is an additional fee to take a course at a distance.

FINANCIAL AID

Financial aid opportunities are available for students enrolled in distance learning courses. Students should apply for financial aid via the college or university offering the courses.

APPLYING

Application procedures for distance learning offerings are the same as those for on-campus courses. Application requirements vary among the participating institutions. FDLC's Web site provides links to each institution's academic calendar, which includes application deadlines and other important dates for students to note during the application process. Students can often complete the application for admission online.

CONTACT

Florida Distance Learning Consortium
1753 West Paul Dirac Drive
Tallahassee, Florida 32310-3708
Telephone: 850-922-3359
Fax: 850-922-3109
E-mail: info@distancelearn.org
Web site: http://www.distancelearn.org

SREB's Electronic Campus

Atlanta, Georgia

In February 2004, the Southern Regional Education Board (SREB) launched a more robust Electronic Campus, establishing a regional "learning network for the South." The Electronic Campus now provides a set of regional-level information and online services and connectivity across the sixteen SREB states, colleges, and universities and builds on and adds significant levels of functionality to the original Electronic Campus. The "learning network" is targeted at the unique needs of adult and e-learners and is designed to help them get the education they need for the demands of this century's workforce. The Electronic Campus now helps adults and e-learners find courses and degrees, secure career information and guidance, locate financial aid, and complete the admission process online.

The Electronic Campus is a comprehensive source for information about higher education opportunities in the South, whether traditional campus study or e-learning. With the focus on adult and e-learners, it provides a simpler, friendlier one-stop place for adults to learn about and understand educational opportunities, to select campuses and/or e-learning opportunities that best match their needs, and to apply online and enroll in courses or programs.

SREB's original Electronic Campus functioned as an "electronic marketplace" of courses and programs from hundreds of participating colleges and universities from the sixteen member states. Established in January 1998, the Electronic Campus has grown from 104 courses to more than 9,000 courses and over 450 degree programs from colleges and universities throughout the South. New courses and programs are added continually.

The Southern Regional Education Board, the nation's first interstate compact for education, was created in 1948 at the request of Southern business, education, and governmental leaders. It was designed to help leaders in government and education work together to advance education and to improve the region's social and economic life. The SREB member states are Alabama, Arkansas, Delaware, Florida, Georgia, Kentucky, Louisiana, Maryland, Mississippi, North Carolina, Oklahoma, South Carolina, Tennessee, Texas, Virginia, and West Virginia.

DISTANCE LEARNING PROGRAM

The Electronic Campus provides detailed and common information about distance learning courses and programs offered by participating colleges and universities. The goal is to provide enhanced educational opportunities for adult e-learners as well as traditional and nontraditional students in a method that removes many of the barriers that have long hindered access to higher education.

DELIVERY MEDIA

Courses and programs are available in a variety of delivery formats. The predominant delivery method is the World Wide Web. Courses and programs are available via the Web in both synchronous and asynchronous modes. Other delivery formats are videotapes, satellite, CD-ROMs, compressed video, and open broadcast. Information on the delivery formats for each course and program is available on the Electronic Campus Web site at the address listed in the Contact section.

PROGRAMS OF STUDY

The Electronic Campus provides access to more than 450 regionally accredited academic programs in higher education. Programs are available in a variety of disciplines and majors at the associate, bachelor's, master's, and doctoral levels. Certificate programs at various levels are also available. More than 9,000 credit courses at the undergraduate and graduate levels, all offered electronically, are available and fully searchable on the site.

All courses and programs available at the Electronic Campus meet SREB's Principles of Good Practice and undergo a review at the institutional, state, and regional levels. The Principles are the quality cornerstone of the Electronic Campus. Courses and programs must meet a variety of requirements: the course or program must provide appropriate interaction between faculty members and students and among students, quality faculty members must provide appropriate supervision of the program or course that is offered electronically, and academic standards for all programs or courses offered electronically must be the same as those for other courses or programs delivered at the institution from which they originate.

SPECIAL PROGRAMS

The Teacher Center is a "subportal" of the Electronic Campus. It is designed to address the needs of educators, both new and experienced, in meeting career goals. The Teacher Center is a "one-stop shop" of online resources designed to help educators find information relevant to the teaching profession and to aid them in meeting the continuing education requirements of their state or district.

The Teacher Center includes: online courses and programs, professional development services, financial aid and scholarship information, state licensure and certification information, alternative routes to teaching, highly qualified teacher information, testing information and services, and job search services.

The Academic Common Market/ Electronic Campus program enables a student in the SREB states to get a waiver of out-of-state tuition if certain conditions are met. Those conditions include: no public college or university in a student's home state (state of residence) offers a degree program in the chosen field of study; the program is available in another SREB state participating in the Academic Common Market; the program is available through distance learning; the home state adopts/accepts the program for its residents; the student meets admissions requirements; and the student can be certified as a resident in their home state to participate. Several degree programs are now available through the Academic Common Market/ Electronic Campus.

FACULTY

Many of the SREB region's most respected professors have courses and programs on the Electronic Campus. The faculty members respond to students' questions and often list times that they can be reached by telephone in their campus offices. Students often say communication with online professors is as effective as or even more effective than in a classroom setting.

ADMISSION

The offering college or university handles admission to the degree programs. Students can access this information from the Electronic Campus Web site. Many institutions allow potential students to complete the application for admission online, which can be completed by clicking on a few links from the Electronic Campus Web site. Students who wish to enroll in a course may be able to do so without formal application and admission. The enrollment procedure and requirements are outlined for all colleges and universities participating in the Electronic Campus and are available on the Web site.

TUITION AND FEES

The college or university offering the courses and programs sets tuition and fees. Tuition and fee charges are available at the Electronic Campus Web site.

A growing number of colleges and universities in the Electronic Campus are offering courses at a single or "electronic or e-rate." These rates apply to students enrolling in e-rate courses irrespective of their residence. These courses are clearly marked when searching at the Electronic Campus site and help more students to access and afford these learning opportunities.

FINANCIAL AID

Participating colleges and universities coordinate financial aid. Specific information on financial aid is available from colleges and universities; general information is available on the Electronic Campus Web site.

APPLYING

Anyone with Internet access may search courses and programs available through the Electronic Campus. There is no charge for accessing or using the services available at the site. A simple registration can be completed when visiting the site, which also provides access to more than thirty-five Mentor™ systems across the country. Creating an account (registration) allows users to use (and re-use) data in completing online applications, save searches, establish e-mail and personal calendars, and other services described at the Electronic Campus site.

CONTACT

Mary Agnes Larson
Associate Director, Electronic Campus
Southern Regional Education Board
592 10th Street, NW
Atlanta, Georgia 30318-5790
Telephone: 404-875-9211
Fax: 404-872-1477
E-mail: electroniccampus@sreb.org
Web site: http://www.electroniccampus.org

SUNY Learning Network

Distance Learning Program

Albany, New York

The SUNY Learning Network (SLN) is a growing consortium, currently with more than fifty campuses in the State University of New York System that have joined together to offer graduate and undergraduate online courses. Many of the SUNY campuses now offer complete online degree programs through the SUNY Learning Network. Online degree programs are available in many disciplines at the associate, baccalaureate, and graduate levels.

State University of New York campuses participating in the SUNY Learning Network are fully accredited by the Middle States Association of Colleges and Schools.

The SUNY Learning Network is a constituent organization within the Office of Advanced Learning and Information Services and the Office of the Provost and Vice Chancellor for Academic Affairs.

DISTANCE LEARNING PROGRAM

Students can study, take classes, and complete entire degree programs at any time and from any place. For those who find it difficult to adjust their schedule or commute to a campus, the SUNY Learning Network offers a new approach to teaching and learning that eliminates the constraints of time and location that higher education normally places on students.

The SUNY Learning Network now offers more than 3,000 online courses with more than 50,000 statewide, national, and international student enrollments. The online courses are designed and taught by State University of New York faculty members at the fifty-three participating SUNY institutions located around the state. Online courses are available to degree-seeking students or to students who simply want to take courses for personal or professional development (nonmatriculating students). In addition to online courses, there are more than forty-five online degree programs now available entirely through the World Wide Web. The consortium, which began in fall 1995 with just four courses, continues to evolve and expand each academic year.

DELIVERY MEDIA

In an online college course through the SUNY Learning Network, the instructor and the students are connected to each other through the Internet. Using the Internet, students can at any time receive instruction, compose and submit assignments, ask questions of the instructor and other students, discuss issues, and actively participate in the class—all from their home, office, or the nearest campus computer lab. Depending on the faculty member and the discipline, courses may also incorporate other Web-based materials, textbooks, application software, simulations, and even learning activities outside of the Internet, such as experiments, observations, or other projects. Students are welcome to see a sample SLN course located on the SLN Web site listed below.

To participate in an SLN course, students need access to a computer having the minimum of a Pentium processor; 64 MB of RAM; a 56K baud modem; a PPP/SLIP Internet connection to the World Wide Web; a Web browser that supports file attachments; an Internet e-mail account that accepts re-directed mail and does not block Internet mail messages; and access to a word processor with the capability to save files in the Microsoft Word 6.0 (or higher) file format. Macintosh users must have System 8 or higher.

PROGRAMS OF STUDY

Many of the SUNY campuses participating in SLN offer complete degree programs through the SUNY Learning Network. Online degree programs are available in many disciplines at the associate, baccalaureate, and graduate levels. The SUNY Learning Network is not a separate degree-granting institution. Students need to matriculate at one of the SUNY campuses and work with their adviser on their home campus to make sure they fulfill the requirements of the degree program. For more information on the more than thirty-five online degree programs offered through SLN, students should visit the SLN Web site.

Students can also earn credits by combining traditional on-campus courses and distance learning studies from the colleges participating in the SUNY Learning Network.

SPECIAL PROGRAMS

The State University of New York General Education Requirement requires baccalaureate degree candidates to complete no fewer than 30 credit hours in ten core subject areas. Each campus creates its own set of core courses using guidelines established by the Provost's Task Force on General Education. Many courses that satisfy the General Education requirements are available through the SUNY Learning Network.

STUDENT SERVICES

The SUNY Learning Network Helpdesk is available seven days a week to answer students' technical questions and to assist students throughout the semester as they complete their courses.

CREDIT OPTIONS

While students should always check with their adviser, credits earned in the SLN program are typically transferable. Students can also earn credits by combining traditional on-campus courses and distance learning studies from the colleges participating in the SUNY Learning Network.

FACULTY

Online courses offered through SLN are designed and taught by State University of New York faculty members on staff at the participating SUNY institutions located around the state of New York.

ADMISSION

Admission into degree programs offered through the SUNY Learning Network is handled directly by the individual SUNY campus that offers the degree program. Campus contact information is available on the SLN Web site.

TUITION AND FEES

Tuition costs vary depending on campus, course level, and residency status. For detailed information on tuition costs for the campuses participating in SLN, students should visit the SLN Web site.

FINANCIAL AID

Students should contact the financial aid office on their home campus regarding information on financial aid before registering for an SLN course.

APPLYING

For complete instructions on how to apply and register for courses offered through the SUNY Learning Network, students should visit the SLN Web site.

CONTACT

Students should visit the SUNY Learning Network Web site at http://SLN.suny.edu for the most up-to-date information on hundreds of courses, online degree programs, semester dates, tuition, and books and materials and to view a sample SUNY Learning Network course.

For additional questions, students may also call the SLN office at 518-443-5331 or 800-875-6269 (toll-free).

APPENDIX

GLOSSARY

accreditation—in the United States, the process by which private, nongovernmental educational agencies with regional or national scope certify that colleges and universities provide educational programs at basic levels of quality

ACT Assessment—a standardized undergraduate admissions test that is based on the typical high school curriculum

associate degree—a degree awarded upon the successful completion of a prebaccalaureate-level program, usually consisting of two years of full-time study at the college level

asynchronous—not simultaneous or concurrent; for example, discussion groups in online courses are asynchronous because students can log on and post messages at any time

audioconferencing—electronic meeting in which participants in remote locations can communicate with one another using phones

bachelor's degree—a degree awarded upon the successful completion of about four years of full-time study at the college level

bandwidth—the width of frequencies required to transmit a communications signal without too much distortion; video, animation, and sound require more bandwidth than text

broadband—a high-speed, high-capacity transmission channel carried on coaxial or fiber-optic cable; it has a higher *bandwidth* than telephone lines and so can transmit more data more quickly than telephone lines

broadcast radio and television—radio and television programs sent out over the airwaves; one of the earliest distance learning technologies still used today

browser—a computer program used to view, download, upload, or otherwise access documents (sites) on the World Wide Web

bulletin board—a site on the Internet where people can post messages

cable television—television programming transmitted over optical fiber, coaxial, or twisted pair (telephone) cables

CD-ROM—compact disc, read-only memory; an optical storage technology that allows you to store and play back data

certificate—an educational credential awarded upon completion of a structured curriculum, typically including several courses but lasting for a period of time less than that required for a degree

certification—the awarding of a credential, usually by a professional or industry group, usually after a course of study and the passing of an exam

chat room—a site on the Internet in which people can communicate synchronously by typing messages to one another

CLEP—the College Level Examination Program, administered by the College Board, that tests students' subject knowledge in order to award college-level credit for noncollegiate learning

common application form—a standardized basic admissions application form, available online, that is used by many colleges

consortium—a group of colleges and universities that pool resources to enable students to take courses as needed from all participating institutions

continuing education unit—10 contact hours of participation in an organized continuing education program; a nationwide, standardized measure of continuing education courses

correspondence course—individual or self-guided study by mail from a college or university for which credit is typically granted through written assignments and proctored examinations; also referred to as *independent study*

correspondence school—a school whose primary means of delivering instruction is via *correspondence courses*

cost of attendance—the total cost, including tuition, fees, living expenses, books, supplies, and miscellaneous expenses, of attending a particular school for an academic year

DANTES Subject Standardized Tests—a series of equivalency examinations used primarily by the U.S. Department of Defense but available to civilians as well

distance learning—the delivery of educational programs to students who are off site; also called *distance education*

doctoral degree—the highest degree awarded upon demonstrated mastery of a subject, including the ability to do scholarly research

DVD—digital video disc; an optical storage technology that allows you to store and retrieve audio and video data

e-learning—distance learning via the Internet; sometimes called *online learning*

e-mail—text or other messages sent over the Internet

enrollment status—whether a student is enrolled full-time, three-quarter-time, half-time, or less than half-time in a degree or certificate program

equivalency examination—an examination similar to the final exam of a college-level course; if you pass, you may be awarded college-level credit; for example, the CLEP and DANTES exams

Excelsior College Examinations—a series of equivalency examinations administered by Excelsior College; formerly the Regents College Examinations

Expected Family Contribution (EFC)—the amount a student and his or her family are expected to contribute to the cost of the student's education per academic year

FAFSA—the Free Application for Federal Student Aid; needed to apply for federal aid programs

fax machine—a telecopying device that transmits written or graphic material over telephone lines to produce a hard copy at a remote location

Federal Supplemental Educational Opportunity Grant (FSEOG)—a federal grant awarded to students that demonstrate the greatest financial need

Federal Work-Study Program—provides part-time jobs in public and private nonprofit organizations to both undergraduate and graduate students who demonstrate financial need; the government pays up to 75 percent of the student's wages, and the employer pays the balance

fellowship—monies to be used for a student's education that does not have to be repaid; also called a *grant* or *scholarship*

financial need—the amount of money a student needs to be given or loaned or earn through work-study, in order to attend school for one year, calculated by subtracting Expected Family Contribution (EFC) from cost of attendance

first-professional degree—a degree awarded upon the successful completion of a program of study (for which a bachelor's degree is normally the prerequisite) that prepares a student for a specific profession

GMAT—the Graduate Management Admissions Test, a standardized test used by many graduate programs in business

graduate degree—a degree awarded upon the successful completion of a program of study at the postbaccalaureate level; usually a master's or doctoral degree

grant—monies to be used for a student's education that do not have to be repaid; also called a *scholarship* or *fellowship*

GRE General Test—the Graduate Record Examinations General Test, which tests verbal, quantitative, and analytical skills; usually taken by prospective graduate students

GRE Subject Area Tests—examinations that assess knowledge usually acquired in college-level courses

instructional design—the way course content is organized for the learner; it varies from one distance technology to another

Internet—the global computer network of networks that allows for the transmission of words, images, and sound to anyone with an Internet connection; one of the major instructional delivery systems for distance learning

Internet service provider (ISP)—a company such as AOL or Earthlink that serves as a gateway to the Internet; by subscribing to its service, an individual can connect to the Internet

life experience—a basis for earning college credit, usually demonstrated by means of a portfolio

LSAT—the Law School Admissions Test, taken by law school applicants

master's degree—a degree awarded upon the successful completion of a program of study beyond the baccalaureate level that typically requires one or two years of full-time study

MAT—the Miller Analogies Test, a standardized admissions test used by some graduate programs

MCAT—the Medical College Admissions Test, taken by medical school applicants

merit-based aid—funding awarded on the basis of academic merit, regardless of financial need

modem—MOdulator DEModulator; a device that allows a computer to connect with other computers (and therefore the Internet) over telephone lines; the faster the modem speed, the faster data is transmitted

need-based aid—financial aid awarded on the basis of financial need; it may take the form of grants, loans, or work-study

online course—a course offered primarily over the Internet

online learning—distance learning via the Internet; sometimes called *e-learning*

Pell Grant—a federal grant that is awarded to students on the basis of financial need

Perkins Loan—a loan offered by the federal government to students with exceptional financial need

PowerPoint—a software program that enables the user to prepare slides with text, graphics, and sound; often used by instructors in their class presentations

PROFILE®—the financial aid application service of the College Board is a standardized financial aid application form used by many colleges and universities

SAT I—a standardized undergraduate admissions test

SAT II—subject area tests that assess high school–level knowledge; used by some schools for undergraduate admissions

satellite television—programming beamed to an orbiting satellite, then retrieved by one or more ground-based satellite dishes

scholarship—monies to be used for a student's education that do not have to be repaid; also called a *grant* or *fellowship*

Stafford Loan—a subsidized or unsubsidized loan that is offered by the federal government

streaming video—high *bandwidth* video data transmission

synchronous—occurring simultaneously, in real time

Title IV funds—federal money disbursed to eligible students through eligible, accredited institutions of higher learning or directly from the government

TOEFL—the Test of English as a Foreign Language, taken by students who are not native speakers of English

two-way interactive video—two-way communication of video and audio signals so that people in remote locations can see and hear one another

videoconferencing—one-way video and two-way audio transmission, or two-way video transmission conducted via satellite; instructors and students can communicate between remote locations

videotaped lecture—recording of an on-campus lecture or class session; usually mailed to distance learners enrolled in the course

virtual university—a college or university that offers most or all of its instruction exclusively via technology and usually for a profit

whiteboard—a program that allows multiple users at their own computers to draw and write comments on the same document

work-study award—an amount a student earns through part-time work as part of the Federal Work-Study Program

INDEXES

INSTITUTIONS OFFERING DEGREE AND CERTIFICATE PROGRAMS

2+2 Transfer to Central Michigan University
Lansing Community College (A)

6-12 Alternative Certification
Marquette University (UC)

A+ Certificate
Hopkinsville Community College (UC)

Academic Advising
Kansas State University (GC)

Academically and Intellectually Gifted
The University of North Carolina at Charlotte (GC)

Accelerated Degree Completion
Tiffin University (B)

Accelerated MBA for Attorneys
Suffolk University (M)

Accelerated MBA for CPAs
Suffolk University (M)

Accountancy
Auburn University (M)
National University (B, UC)
State University of New York Institute of Technology (M)
State University of New York Institute of Technology (M)

Accountant
Lake Superior College (A)

Accounting
Alaska Pacific University (A, B)
Ashworth College (A)
Athabasca University (UC)
Brenau University (M)
Caldwell College (B)
Champlain College (A, UC)
City University (B, UC)
Darton College (A)
Davenport University Online (A)
Excelsior College (B)
Florida Atlantic University (M)
Florida Metropolitan University-Brandon Campus (A, B)
Florida Metropolitan University-Tampa Campus (A)
Franklin University (A, B)
Golden Gate University (M, GC)
Indiana Institute of Technology (A, B)
Ivy Tech State College-Bloomington (A)
Ivy Tech State College-Central Indiana (A)
Ivy Tech State College-Columbus (A)
Ivy Tech State College-Eastcentral (A)
Ivy Tech State College-Kokomo (A)
Ivy Tech State College-Lafayette (A)
Ivy Tech State College-North Central (A)
Ivy Tech State College-Northeast (A)
Ivy Tech State College-Northwest (A)
Ivy Tech State College-Southcentral (A)
Ivy Tech State College-Southeast (A)
Ivy Tech State College-Southwest (A)
Ivy Tech State College-Wabash Valley (A, UC)
Ivy Tech State College-Whitewater (A)
Keiser College (A)
Lakeland College (B)
Madison Area Technical College (A)
New Jersey City University (M)
Northampton County Area Community College (A)
Northwest Missouri State University (B)
Randolph Community College (A)
Saint Leo University (B)
Saint Mary-of-the-Woods College (A, B)
Shoreline Community College (UC)
Southern New Hampshire University (A, B, UC)
Strayer University (GC, A, B, UC)
Thomas Edison State College (A, B)
University of Maryland University College (B)
University of Northwestern Ohio (B)
University of Phoenix Online Campus (M)
Upper Iowa University (B)

Accounting and Business Administration
Indiana Institute of Technology (B)

Accounting and Finance Concentration (10-month program)
American InterContinental University Online (M)

Accounting and Finance Concentration (13-month program)
American InterContinental University Online (B)

Accounting and Financial Management
DeVry University Online (M)
University of Maryland University College (M)

Accounting and Information Systems
Cardean University (M)
New York Institute of Technology (M)

Accounting Applications
Seminole Community College (UC)

Accounting ASB
Education Direct Center for Degree Studies (A)

Accounting Assistant
Davenport University Online (UC)

Accounting Clerk
Shoreline Community College (UC)

Accounting Emphasis
City University (M)

GC–Graduate Certificate; D–Doctorate; M–Master's; A–Associate; B–Bachelor's; UC–Undergraduate Certificate

Accounting Information Management-Management Accounting Specialty
Davenport University Online (B)

Accounting Information Management-Public Accounting Specialty
Davenport University Online (B)

Accounting Information Systems
Saint Mary-of-the-Woods College (B)

Accounting Specialty
Davenport University Online (M)

Accounting Technician
Minot State University-Bottineau Campus (A)

Accounting Technology
University of Toledo (A, UC)

Accounting Transfer Option
Hopkinsville Community College (A)

Accounting/Finance
Southern New Hampshire University (B)

Accounts Receivable/Payable Clerk
Shoreline Community College (UC)

Acquisition and Contract Management
Florida Institute of Technology (M)
Strayer University (A, UC)

Acquisition Management-Master of Acquisition Management
American Graduate University (M)

Action for a Viable Future
Sonoma State University (M)

Adapting Curriculum Frameworks for All Learners
University of Massachusetts Boston (GC)

Addiction Counseling Certification Program
Bethany College of the Assemblies of God (UC)

Addiction Studies
Bethany College of the Assemblies of God (B)
University of Cincinnati (B)

Addictions Studies
The Pennsylvania State University University Park Campus (GC)

Administration
Athabasca University (UC)
Central Michigan University (B)

Administration of Criminal Justice
Mountain State University (B)

Administration of Justice
Maui Community College (A)
Thomas Edison State College (A, B)
University of Louisville (B)

Administration of Justice-Master of Science in the Administration of Justice
University of Louisville (M)

Administration-Bachelor of Administration (with Concentration)
Athabasca University (B)

Administration-Bachelor of Administration Post-Diploma (with Concentration)
Athabasca University (B)

Administration-Communication Arts
University of the Incarnate Word (M)

Administration, general
Central Michigan University (M)

Administrative Assistant
Madison Area Technical College (A)
Minot State University-Bottineau Campus (A)

Administrative Office Management
Thomas Edison State College (A, B)

Administrative Office Technology-Executive Office Administration Specialty
Davenport University Online (A)

Administrative Principal Program
California University of Pennsylvania (M)

Administrative Studies
Southwest Missouri State University (M)
Thomas Edison State College (A)
York University (B)

Administrative Support
Rappahannock Community College (UC)

Administrative/Management Studies
Excelsior College (A)

Adult Development and Aging Services
The Pennsylvania State University University Park Campus (UC)

Adult Education
Brock University (B, UC)
Buffalo State College, State University of New York (GC, M)
Indiana University System (M)
Northwestern State University of Louisiana (M)
The Pennsylvania State University University Park Campus (M)

Adult Education and Distance Learning
University of Phoenix Online Campus (M)

Adult Education and Training
Colorado State University (M)
Saint Joseph's College of Maine (A, UC)

Adult Education-Human Resource Development Major
Florida State University (M)

Adult Learning
University of Calgary (UC)

Adult Learning and Development
Cleveland State University (GC, M)

Adult Liberal Studies
University of Toledo (B)

Adult Religious Education
Saint Joseph's College of Maine (B)

Advanced Accounting
Athabasca University (UC)

Advanced Business Management
The Pennsylvania State University University Park Campus (UC)

Advanced Catechist Certificate
The Catholic Distance University (UC)

Advanced Electronics
Illinois Institute of Technology (GC)

Advanced Health Care Management
Saint Joseph's College of Maine (UC)

Advanced Long-Term Care Administration
Saint Joseph's College of Maine (UC)

Advanced Management Studies
Brenau University (M)

GC–Graduate Certificate; D–Doctorate; M–Master's; A–Associate; B–Bachelor's; UC–Undergraduate Certificate

Advanced Material Design
University of Idaho (UC)

Advanced Medical Transcription
Minot State University-Bottineau Campus (UC)

Advanced Programs
University of Oklahoma (D, M)

Advanced Respiratory Therapy
Weber State University (B)

Advanced School Counseling
The University of North Carolina at Greensboro (GC)

Advanced Software Systems
Stanford University (GC)

Advanced Studies in Teaching and Learning
Middle Tennessee State University (M)

Advanced Technical Communications
Rochester Institute of Technology (UC)

Advanced Technological Education
Bowling Green State University (B)

Advanced Turfgrass Management
The Pennsylvania State University University Park Campus (UC)

Advanced Web Design
Northeastern University (UC)

Adventure Education
Prescott College (M, B)

Advertising
The Art Institute Online (B)

Advertising Design
Syracuse University (M)

Advertising Management
Thomas Edison State College (B)

Aeronautical Science
Embry-Riddle Aeronautical University, Extended Campus (M)

Aeronautics and Astronautics
Stanford University (M)
University of Washington (M)

Aerospace
The University of Tennessee (M)

Aerospace Engineering
Auburn University (M)
Georgia Institute of Technology (M)
North Carolina State University (M)
The University of Alabama (M)
University of Colorado at Boulder (M)
The University of Texas at Arlington (M)
University of Washington (M)

Aerospace Studies
American Public University System (B)

African American Ministry Leadership
Defiance College (UC)

African and African American Studies
American Public University System (B)

Agribusiness
Kansas State University (M)
University of Northwestern Ohio (A)

Agribusiness Sales and Marketing
University of Guelph (UC)

Agricultural Development, Fisheries, Plant Science, Poultry Science, Natural Resource Development, or Wildlife
Texas A&M University (M)

Agricultural Education
Oklahoma State University (M)
Texas Tech University (D)
University of Florida (M)
University of Illinois (M)

Agricultural Operations Management
The University of Tennessee at Martin (M)

Agricultural Sciences
Colorado State University (M)

Agriculture
Iowa State University of Science and Technology (M)
University of Nebraska-Lincoln (M)
Washington State University (M)

Agriculture, general
Oregon State University (B)

Agronomy
Iowa State University of Science and Technology (M)

Air Traffic Control
Thomas Edison State College (A, B)

Aircraft Maintenance
Embry-Riddle Aeronautical University, Extended Campus (A)

Alternative Education
Lock Haven University of Pennsylvania (M)

Alternative Teacher
The University of Texas System (UC)

American Studies
American Public University System (B)
Saint Joseph's College of Maine (B, UC)

Analytical Method Development
Illinois Institute of Technology (GC)

Analytical Spectroscopy
Illinois Institute of Technology (GC)

Animal Science and Industry
Kansas State University (B)

Animation
Westwood Online (B)

Anthropology
Darton College (A)
Thomas Edison State College (B)

Anthropology (4 year)
Athabasca University (B)

Anthropology Concentration (3 year)
Athabasca University (B)

Antithrombosis Management Service
University of Illinois at Chicago (UC)

Antithrombosis Therapy Management
University of Illinois (GC)

Apostolic Catechetical Diploma
The Catholic Distance University (UC)

Apparel and Merchandising
Colorado State University (UC)

Applied Administration
University of the Incarnate Word (M)

Applied Arts and Science
Rochester Institute of Technology (B)

Applied Business
Davenport University Online (B)

Applied Communication
Northern Arizona University (M)
Royal Roads University (B)

Applied Communications
Royal Roads University (M)

Applied Computer Science
Columbus State University (M)

Applied Computer Science ASB
Education Direct Center for Degree Studies (A)

Applied Computer Studies
Thomas Edison State College (A)

Applied Electronic Studies
Thomas Edison State College (A)

Applied Geotechnics
University of Idaho (UC)

Applied Gerontology
Shippensburg University of Pennsylvania (M)

Applied Health Studies
Pennsylvania College of Technology (B)
Thomas Edison State College (A)

Applied Information Management
University of Oregon (M)

Applied Management
Everglades University (B)
Franklin University (B)

Applied Management and Decision Sciences
Walden University (D)

Applied Management and Decision Sciences-Engineering Management
Walden University (D)

Applied Management and Decision Sciences-Finance
Walden University (D)

Applied Management and Decision Sciences-Information Systems Management
Walden University (D)

Applied Management and Decision Sciences-Knowledge Management
Walden University (D)

Applied Management and Decision Sciences-Leadership and Organizational Change
Walden University (D)

Applied Management and Decision Sciences-Learning Management
Walden University (D)

Applied Management and Decision Sciences-Operations Research
Walden University (D)

Applied Management and Decision Sciences-Self-Designed
Walden University (D)

Applied Management and Decision Sciences, general
Walden University (D)

Applied Mathematics
Columbia University (UC)

Applied Professional Studies
Bethany College of the Assemblies of God (B)

Applied Psychology
City University (B)
St. Cloud State University (M)

Applied Science
Central Texas College (A)
Florida Community College at Jacksonville (A)

Applied Science in Technology (BAST)
Dickinson State University (B)

Applied Social Sciences
Maui Community College (B)

Applied Statistical Strategies
The University of Tennessee (GC)

Applied Statistics
Rochester Institute of Technology (M)

Applied Statistics and Data Analysis
Colorado State University (UC)

Applied Technology
Central Texas College (A)

Architectural Design
Thomas Edison State College (A, B)

Architectural Drafting and Estimating Technology
North Dakota State College of Science (A)

Architectural Lighting Design
The Pennsylvania State University University Park Campus (UC)

Architectural Studies
University of Missouri-Columbia (D)

Architecture
University of Nebraska-Lincoln (M)

Art
Darton College (A)
Thomas Edison State College (B)

Art Education
East Carolina University (M)
Mansfield University of Pennsylvania (M)

Art History
Mansfield University of Pennsylvania (B)

Art Therapy
Saint Mary-of-the-Woods College (M)

Artificial Intelligence
Stanford University (GC)

Arts
Athabasca University (UC)
Bethany College of the Assemblies of God (M)

Arts and Humanities
Ohio University (A)

Arts and Sciences
Clarion University of Pennsylvania (A)
Florida Community College at Jacksonville (A)
Northeastern University (A)

Arts and Sciences for Transfer
John Tyler Community College (A)

Arts Management
University of Massachusetts Amherst (UC)

Asian Studies
American Public University System (B)

Asset Management
The American College (GC)

Assistive Technology
California State University, Dominguez Hills (UC)
East Carolina University (GC)

GC–Graduate Certificate; D–Doctorate; M–Master's; A–Associate; B–Bachelor's; UC–Undergraduate Certificate

Athletic Coaching
West Virginia University (M)

Atmospheric and Environmental Science and Engineering
Stevens Institute of Technology (GC)

Audiology
Central Michigan University (GC)
University of Florida (M)

Autism
University of Louisville (M)

Autistic Spectrum Disorders
University of North Dakota (GC)

Automotive Engineering
University of Michigan (M)

Automotive Management
University of Northwestern Ohio (A)

Automotive Systems Engineering
University of Michigan-Dearborn (M)

Automotive Technology Management
Pennsylvania College of Technology (B)

Aviation (Baccalaureate Degree Transfer)
Utah Valley State College (A)

Aviation Flight Technology
Thomas Edison State College (A, B)

Aviation Flight Technology, general
Indiana State University (A)

Aviation Job Ready Degree
Utah Valley State College (A)

Aviation Maintenance Management
Embry-Riddle Aeronautical University, Extended Campus (B)

Aviation Maintenance Technology
Thomas Edison State College (A, B)

Aviation Management
Mountain State University (B)

Aviation Professional Pilot
Utah Valley State College (B)

Aviation Science
Utah Valley State College (B)

Aviation Studies
Excelsior College (A)
University of Nebraska at Omaha (B)

Aviation Technology
Mountain State University (A, UC)

BAILS Arts and Letters
Northern Arizona University (B)

BAILS Criminal Justice
Northern Arizona University (B)

BAILS Enterprise in Society
Northern Arizona University (B)

BAILS Environmental Sciences
Northern Arizona University (B)

BAILS Learning and Pedagogy
Northern Arizona University (B)

BAILS Mathematics/Statistics
Northern Arizona University (B)

BAILS Organizational Communication
Northern Arizona University (B)

BAILS Parks and Recreation Management
Northern Arizona University (B)

BAILS Psychology
Northern Arizona University (B)

BAILS Sociology
Northern Arizona University (B)

Banking
Mercy College (M)
Thomas Edison State College (A, B)

Banking and Finance
Mountain State University (A)

Basic Accounting Certification
Pitt Community College (UC)

Basic Grounds Worker Skills
Minot State University-Bottineau Campus (UC)

Basic Office Technology Skills
Pitt Community College (UC)

Basic Quality Management
Rochester Institute of Technology (UC)

Basic Technical Communications
Rochester Institute of Technology (UC)

Basic Web Page Development
Bristol Community College (UC)

Beginning Web Page
Waubonsee Community College (UC)

Behavioral Interventions for ADHD
Alliant International University (UC)

Behavioral Science
Lynn University (B)

Bible
Briercrest Distance Learning (UC)
North Central University (UC)
Northwestern College (UC)
Prairie Bible College (UC)
Southwestern Assemblies of God University (A)

Bible and Theology
Global University of the Assemblies of God (A, B)

Bible, Theology, Ministry
Prairie Bible College (B)

Bible/Pastoral Ministries
Global University of the Assemblies of God (B)

Biblical and Theological Studies
Bethany College of the Assemblies of God (B)

Biblical Studies
The Baptist College of Florida (B)
Dallas Baptist University (B)
Global University of the Assemblies of God (M)
Hope International University (A, UC)
Life Pacific College (A)
Moody Bible Institute (A, B, UC)
Northwestern College (A, B)
Southern Christian University (M, B)
Taylor University (A, UC)
Taylor University (A, UC)

Bilingual Education Endorsement
Northern Arizona University (UC)

Bilingual Endorsement-College of Education
New Mexico State University (UC)

Bilingual/Multicultural Education
Northern Arizona University (M)

Bioethics
Cleveland State University (GC)

Bioinformatics
Stanford University (GC)

Biological and Agricultural Engineering
University of Idaho (M)

Biological Science
Darton College (A)

Biology
Illinois Institute of Technology (M)
Thomas Edison State College (A, B)
University of Nebraska at Kearney (M)

Biomedical Electronics
Thomas Edison State College (A, B)

BioMedical Informatics
Stanford University (M)

Bioscience Management
George Mason University (M)

Biotechnology Studies
University of Maryland University College (M)

Birth to Five Care
Western Washington University (UC)

Birth to Kindergarten Education (lateral entry/certification)
Winston-Salem State University (B)

Birth-Kindergarten
Western Carolina University (B)

Birth-Kindergarten Education
East Carolina University (B)

Birth-Kindergarten Teacher Licensure
The University of North Carolina at Greensboro (B)

Blood Bank Specialist
University of Illinois at Chicago (UC)

Blood Bank Technology Specialist
University of Illinois (GC)

Bookkeeping/Accounting
Rappahannock Community College (UC)

Brain Research in Education
University of Washington (UC)

Broadband
University of Denver (GC)

Building a Sustainable World
Saybrook Graduate School and Research Center (GC)

Business
Alaska Pacific University (A)
Andrew Jackson University (A, B)
Brevard Community College (A)
Buena Vista University (B)
Caldwell College (B)
Capella University (B)
Champlain College (A, B, UC)
Columbia Southern University (A)
Dallas County Community College District (A)
Drexel University (M)
Excelsior College (A)
Fort Hays State University (A, B)
Judson College (B)
Keiser College (A)
Lansing Community College (A)
Liberty University (B)
Lynn University (B)
Maui Community College (UC)
Missouri Southern State University (B)
New York Institute of Technology (M)
St. John's University (A)
Salve Regina University (B)
Southwestern Assemblies of God University (B)
University of Houston-Victoria (M, B)
University of the Incarnate Word (A)
Upper Iowa University (A)
Walsh College of Accountancy and Business Administration (M)
Western New England College (M, B)

Business (ABus)
Coconino Community College (A)

Business (ASB)
Indiana Wesleyan University (A)

Business (various)
Regent University (GC)

Business Accounting
University of Phoenix Online Campus (B)

Business Administration
Acadia University (UC)
Adams State College (B)
Adirondack Community College (A)
American College of Computer & Information Sciences (M, B)
American Public University System (M, B)
Anne Arundel Community College (A)
Ashworth College (M)
Aspen University (M)
Athabasca University (M)
Auburn University (M)
Baker College of Flint (M, A, B)
Baker College of Jackson (B)
Ball State University (M)
Bellevue University (M)
Berkeley College (A, B)
Brookdale Community College (A)
Bucks County Community College (A)
California National University for Advanced Studies (M, B)
Capella University (M)
Capitol College (M)
Carl Albert State College (A)
Cayuga County Community College (A)
Chadron State College (M)
Clinton Community College (A)
College of The Albemarle (A)
Colorado Christian University (M)
Colorado State University (M)
Colorado Technical University (M)
Columbia College (A, B)
Columbia Southern University (M, B)
Columbia Union College (B)
The Community College of Baltimore County (A)
Community College of Denver (A, UC)
Concordia University Wisconsin (M)
Dallas Baptist University (B)
Daniel Webster College (A)
Darton College (A)
Des Moines Area Community College (A)
DeVry University Online (M, B)
East Carolina University (M)
Eastern Oregon University (B)
Edmonds Community College (A)
Endicott College (M)
Everglades University (M, B)
Florida Gulf Coast University (M)
Florida International University (M)
Florida Metropolitan University-Brandon Campus (M, A, B)
Franklin University (A, B)
Frederick Community College (A)
Georgia Southern University (M, B)
Golden Gate University (M, B)
Grantham University (M, A, B)
Harford Community College (A)
Indiana Institute of Technology (A, B)
Indiana State University (B)

GC–Graduate Certificate; D–Doctorate; M–Master's; A–Associate; B–Bachelor's; UC–Undergraduate Certificate

Indiana Wesleyan University (M)
Ivy Tech State College-Bloomington (A)
Ivy Tech State College-Central Indiana (A)
Ivy Tech State College-Columbus (A)
Ivy Tech State College-Eastcentral (A)
Ivy Tech State College-Kokomo (A)
Ivy Tech State College-Lafayette (A)
Ivy Tech State College-North Central (A)
Ivy Tech State College-Northeast (A)
Ivy Tech State College-Northwest (A)
Ivy Tech State College-Southcentral (A)
Ivy Tech State College-Southeast (A)
Ivy Tech State College-Southwest (A)
Ivy Tech State College-Wabash Valley (A, UC)
Ivy Tech State College-Whitewater (A)
Jefferson Community College (A)
Jones College (A, B)
Jones International University (M, B)
Keiser College (B)
Lakeland College (M, B)
Lake Superior College (A)
Lehigh University (M)
Liberty University (M)
Limestone College (A, B)
Lynn University (M)
Maharishi University of Management (M)
Marist College (M)
Marylhurst University (M)
Maui Community College (M, B)
Memorial University of Newfoundland (B, UC)
Mercy College (M, B)
Metropolitan State University (B)
Midstate College (B)
Mississippi State University (M)
Monroe Community College (A)
Montgomery County Community College (A)
Mountain Empire Community College (A)
Mount Saint Vincent University (B, UC)
Mount Wachusett Community College (A)
National University (M, B)
New Mexico State University (B)
New York Institute of Technology (B)
Northampton County Area Community College (A)
Northcentral University (D, M, B)
Northeastern University (A, UC)
Northern Virginia Community College (A)
The Ohio State University (M)
Oklahoma State University (M)
Old Dominion University (B)
Oral Roberts University (B)
Park University (M)
The Pennsylvania State University University Park Campus (A)
Pitt Community College (A)
Randolph Community College (A)
Rappahannock Community College (A)
Raritan Valley Community College (A)
Regent University (M)
Regis University (M, B)
Saint Joseph's College of Maine (A, B, UC)
Saint Leo University (B)
Saint Mary-of-the-Woods College (B)
Salve Regina University (M)
Shippensburg University of Pennsylvania (M)
Sinclair Community College (A)
Southeast Community College, Beatrice Campus (A)
Southeast Community College, Lincoln Campus (A)
Southeastern Community College (A)
Southern New Hampshire University (M, A, B)
Southwestern Assemblies of God University (A)
Southwestern College (B)
Southwest Missouri State University (M)
State University of New York Empire State College (M)
State University of New York Institute of Technology (GC)
Stephens College (B)
Strayer University (GC, M, A, B)
Suffolk University (M)
Syracuse University (M)
Syracuse University (M)
Tarleton State University (M)
Teikyo Post University (B)
Texas Woman's University (M)
Tiffin University (M)
Touro University International (D, M, B)
Troy University-Florida Region (A)
Troy University Montgomery (A, B)
University of Alaska Southeast (M, B)
University of Baltimore (M, B)
University of Colorado at Colorado Springs (M)
University of Colorado at Denver (M)
The University of Findlay (M)
University of Florida (M)
University of Great Falls (B)
University of Hawaii-West Oahu (B)
University of Illinois (M)
University of La Verne (M)
The University of Maine at Augusta (A)
University of Management and Technology (A)
University of Maryland University College (M, B)
University of Massachusetts Amherst (M, B)
University of Nebraska-Lincoln (M)
The University of North Carolina at Pembroke (B)
University of North Dakota (M)
University of Northwestern Ohio (B)
University of Phoenix Online Campus (D, M, B)
University of St. Francis (M)
University of South Carolina (M)
The University of South Dakota (M)
The University of Tennessee at Martin (M)
The University of Texas at Tyler (M)
The University of Texas of the Permian Basin (M)
University of the Incarnate Word (B)
University of Wisconsin-Eau Claire (M)
University of Wisconsin-Platteville (B)
University of Wisconsin-Platteville (B)
University of Wyoming (M, B)
Upper Iowa University (B)
Utah State University (B)
Virginia College at Birmingham (M)
Virginia Polytechnic Institute and State University (M)
Walsh College of Accountancy and Business Administration (B)
Washington State University (B)
Webster University (M)
West Virginia University (M)
Wilfrid Laurier University (UC)
Wilkes Community College (A)
William Tyndale College (B)

Business Administration (10-month program)

American InterContinental University Online (M)

Business Administration (13-month program)

American InterContinental University Online (B)

Business Administration (Bachelor of Applied Science)

Mayville State University (B)

Business Administration (BS)

University of Florida (UC)

Business Administration (E-Commerce Emphasis)

City University (B)

Business Administration (Europe)

City University (B)

Business Administration (General Management Emphasis)
City University (B)

Business Administration (Human Resource Emphasis)
City University (B)

Business Administration (Information Systems/Technology Emphasis)
City University (B)

Business Administration (Marketing Emphasis)
City University (B)

Business Administration (Off Campus MBA)
The University of Montana-Missoula (M)

Business Administration (Project Management Emphasis)
City University (B)

Business Administration and Leadership
AIB College of Business (A)

Business Administration and Management
Hope International University (B)
Madonna University (B)
The University of Texas System (M)

Business Administration Career
Middlesex Community College (A)

Business Administration in Aviation
Embry-Riddle Aeronautical University (M)

Business Administration Management Concentration
Winston-Salem State University (B)

Business Administration of Technical Studies
Bellevue University (B)

Business Administration Online
University of Tulsa (M)

Business Administration Transfer
Middlesex Community College (A)

Business Administration with Business Law Concentration
Peirce College (A, B)

Business Administration with Management Concentration
Peirce College (A, B)

Business Administration with Marketing Concentration
Peirce College (A, B)

Business Administration with Real Estate Management Concentration
Peirce College (B)

Business Administration-Accounting
Mountain State University (A, B)

Business Administration-Accounting Concentration
Westwood Online (B)

Business Administration-Applied Management
Tompkins Cortland Community College (A)

Business Administration-Bachelor of Science in Business Administration
Aspen University (B)

Business Administration-Business Concentration (13-month program)
American InterContinental University Online (A)

Business Administration-Business Law
Mountain State University (A, B)
Peirce College (UC)

Business Administration-E-Commerce Emphasis (Bulgaria)
City University (B)

Business Administration-General Business
Mountain State University (A, B)

Business Administration-General Management Emphasis (Bulgaria)
City University (B)

Business Administration-Human Resources Management
Pitt Community College (UC)

Business Administration-Individualized Study Emphasis
City University (B)

Business Administration-Information Systems Concentration (13-month program)
American InterContinental University Online (A)

Business Administration-Information Systems/Technology Emphasis (Bulgaria)
City University (B)

Business Administration-Management
Berkeley College-New York City Campus (B)
Mountain State University (A, B)
Peirce College (UC)

Business Administration-Marketing and Sales Concentration
Westwood Online (B)

Business Administration-Office Management
Mountain State University (A, B)

Business Administration, Entrepreneurship
Community College of Denver (UC)

Business Administration, general
Walden University (M)

Business Administration, International Business
Community College of Denver (UC)

Business Administration, Management Emphasis
Community College of Denver (A)

Business Administration/Marketing
University of Phoenix Online Campus (M)

Business Administration; Liberal Arts and Sciences
DePaul University (B)

Business and Economics
Eastern Oregon University (B)

Business and Management
Daniel Webster College (B)

Business and Organizational Security Management
Webster University (M)

GC–Graduate Certificate; D–Doctorate; M–Master's; A–Associate; B–Bachelor's; UC–Undergraduate Certificate

Business and Technology
Columbia University (UC)
Lake Superior College (A)

Business Aspects of Publishing
Pace University (GC)

Business Communication
Jones International University (M, B)

Business Completion Program, general
Southwest Missouri State University (B)

Business Computer Specialist Option
Darton College (A)

Business Education
Darton College (A)
Edmonds Community College (A)
Southern New Hampshire University (M)

Business English
Northeastern University (UC)
University of Illinois (GC)

Business English Online
University of Illinois at Chicago (UC)

Business Foundations
University of Washington (UC)

Business Fundamentals
New Jersey Institute of Technology (UC)

Business Generalist Emphasis
Community College of Denver (A)

Business Information Systems
Bellevue University (B)
Utah State University (M, B)

Business Information Systems-Bachelor Completion Program
Indiana Wesleyan University (B)

Business Information Technology
Edmonds Community College (A)

Business Management
Anne Arundel Community College (A)
Burlington County College (A)
Central Texas College (A)
Columbus State Community College (A)
Davenport University Online (UC)
Dawson Community College (A)
Edmonds Community College (A)
Northampton County Area Community College (A)
Northern Virginia Community College (A)
Northwest Missouri State University (B)
The Pennsylvania State University University Park Campus (UC)
Rappahannock Community College (A)
The University of Findlay (B)
University of Phoenix Online Campus (B)
Virginia College at Birmingham (B)

Business Management ASB
Education Direct Center for Degree Studies (A)

Business Management Concentration
Colorado Technical University (M)

Business Management Technology
University of Toledo (A, UC)

Business Management with Finance Option ASB
Education Direct Center for Degree Studies (A)

Business Management with Marketing Option ASB
Education Direct Center for Degree Studies (A)

Business Management, Public Management Specialization
Northern Virginia Community College (A)

Business Marketing
University of Phoenix Online Campus (B)

Business Marketing and Marketing Management Transfer Framework
Hopkinsville Community College (A)

Business Microcomputing
Minnesota State College-Southeast Technical (UC)

Business Online
Bryant and Stratton Online (A)

Business Professional Studies
Davenport University Online (B)

Business Quality Management
Southwestern College (B)

Business Software Specialist-Business Technology Systems
Bellevue Community College (UC)

Business Strategy
Northwestern University (M)

Business Studies
Southern New Hampshire University (B)
University of Massachusetts Amherst (UC)

Business Studies, general
Virginia College at Birmingham (B)

Business Succession Planning
The American College (GC)

Business Technology
Chemeketa Community College (UC)

Business Technology Management-Master of Science in Business Technology Management
Coleman College (M)

Business Transfer Framework
Hopkinsville Community College (A)

Business-Bachelor of Science in Business
Murray State University (B)

Business, Accelerated Degree
Florida Community College at Jacksonville (A)

Business, general
Excelsior College (B)
Kansas State University (B)
Mott Community College (A)
Saint Mary-of-the-Woods College (A)
Southwestern Assemblies of God University (A)

Business, History, Political Science, Psychology, Social Science, and Child Care
Troy University Montgomery (A)

Business, Humanities, Social Sciences
Columbia Basin College (A)

Business, Management and Communication
Western Baptist College (B)

Business, Management and Economics
State University of New York Empire State College (A, B)

Business/Finance
University of Phoenix Online Campus (B)

Business/Management
Andrew Jackson University (M)

C Programming
University of Washington (UC)

C++ Client-Server Programming
Minnesota State College-Southeast Technical (UC)

C++ Programming
City University (GC)
University of Washington (UC)

C++ Windows Programming
Minnesota State College-Southeast Technical (UC)

C++/Unix Programming
Northeastern University (UC)

C/UNIX Programming
Daniel Webster College (UC)

Canadian Studies
Western Kentucky University (UC)

Canadian Studies (4 year)
Athabasca University (B)

Career and Technical Education
Ball State University (M)
Indiana State University (B)
Northern Arizona University (M)
Virginia Polytechnic Institute and State University (M, UC)

Career and Technical Education (BS Ed.)
Northern Arizona University (B)

Career Development
Athabasca University (UC)
Memorial University of Newfoundland (UC)

Career Master of Public Health Program
Emory University (M)

Career Specialist Studies
University of Illinois (GC)

Career Studies-Allied Health
Patrick Henry Community College (UC)

Career Studies-Management Assistant
Patrick Henry Community College (UC)

Career Studies-Medical Transcriptionist
Patrick Henry Community College (UC)

Career Studies-Office Assisting
Patrick Henry Community College (UC)

Career Studies-Wellness
Patrick Henry Community College (UC)

Catholic School Leadership
Marymount University (M)

Certificate of Advanced Graduate Study
Norwich University (M)

Certified Fire Fighter II
University of Illinois (GC)

CFP(r) Certification Curriculum
The American College (UC)

Characterization of Organic and Inorganic Materials
Illinois Institute of Technology (GC)

Charitable Planning
The American College (GC)

Chartered Advisor for Senior Living (CASL) Designation
The American College (UC)

Chartered Advisor in Philanthropy(r)(CAP) Designation
The American College (GC)

Chartered Financial Consultant (ChFC(r)) Designation
The American College (UC)

Chartered Leadership Fellow(r) (CLF(r)) Designation
The American College (UC)

Chartered Life Underwriter (CLU(r)) Designation
The American College (UC)

Chemical Dependency Studies Counseling
Tompkins Cortland Community College (A)

Chemical Engineering
Auburn University (M)
Illinois Institute of Technology (M)
Kansas State University (M)
Lehigh University (M)
Mississippi State University (M)
University of North Dakota (B)
University of South Carolina (M)

Chemistry
Lehigh University (M)

Chess in Education Online
The University of Texas System (UC)

Child and Family Development-Early Intervention
The University of North Carolina at Charlotte (GC)

Child Care Basics
Minnesota State College-Southeast Technical (UC)

Child Development
Concordia University, St. Paul (B)

Child Development Services
Thomas Edison State College (A, B)

Children, Youth and Family Services
The Pennsylvania State University University Park Campus (UC)

Christian Care and Counseling
Oral Roberts University (B)

Christian Education
Union Theological Seminary and Presbyterian School of Christian Education (M)

Christian Ministries
Crown College (A)
Dallas Baptist University (B)

Christian Ministries-Associate of Christian Ministries
The King's College and Seminary (A)

Christian Ministry
Crown College (B)
Hope International University (A, B, UC)
Southern Christian University (D)

Christian Ministry Certificate-Pastoral Leadership
Master's College and Seminary (UC)

Christian School Administration
Oral Roberts University (M)

Christian School Administration (PK-12)
Oral Roberts University (D)

Christian School Curriculum
Oral Roberts University (M)

GC–Graduate Certificate; D–Doctorate; M–Master's; A–Associate; B–Bachelor's; UC–Undergraduate Certificate

Christian School Postsecondary Administration
Oral Roberts University (M)

Christian School Program
Regent University (M)

Christian Studies
Briercrest Distance Learning (A, B)

Christian Tradition
Saint Joseph's College of Maine (B, UC)

Christian Worker
Taylor University (UC)
Taylor University (UC)

Chromatography
Illinois Institute of Technology (GC)

Church Education
Defiance College (UC)

Church Leadership
Bethany College of the Assemblies of God (B)

Church Ministries
Bethany College of the Assemblies of God (A)
North Central University (B, UC)
Oral Roberts University (B)
Southwestern Assemblies of God University (B)

Cisco Certified Network Associate Preparation, Accelerated
Fort Hays State University (UC)

Cisco Certified Network Associate Preparation, Military
Fort Hays State University (UC)

Civil and Construction Engineering Technology
Thomas Edison State College (A)

Civil and Environmental Engineering
University of South Carolina (D, M)
Virginia Polytechnic Institute and State University (M)

Civil Engineering
Auburn University (M)
Colorado State University (M)
Columbia University (UC)
Georgia Institute of Technology (M)
Kansas State University (M)
Mississippi State University (M)
North Carolina State University (M)
Norwich University (M)
Southern Methodist University (M)
University of Idaho (M)
University of North Dakota (B)
The University of Texas at Arlington (M)
Villanova University (M)
Worcester Polytechnic Institute (M)

Civil Engineering Technology
Education Direct Center for Degree Studies (A)
Old Dominion University (B)
Thomas Edison State College (B)

Civil Engineering-Construction Engineering and Management
Columbia University (M)

Civil Infrastructure Engineering
Virginia Polytechnic Institute and State University (M)

CLAD Multiple or Single Subject Certificate
National University (UC)

Clerical Studies
Patrick Henry Community College (UC)

Client-Server Application Development
Daniel Webster College (UC)

Clinical Information Systems Management
Stephens College (M)

Clinical Investigation
Boston University (GC)
Boston University (GC)
MGH Institute of Health Professions (GC)

Clinical Investigations
MGH Institute of Health Professions (M)

Clinical Lab Science
Thomas Edison State College (A, B)

Clinical Laboratory Science
University of Cincinnati (B)
University of Cincinnati (B)

Clinical Laboratory Science (lateral entry)
Winston-Salem State University (B)

Clinical Laboratory Sciences
Weber State University (B)

Clinical Laboratory Technician
Weber State University (A)

Clinical Nutrition
University of Medicine and Dentistry of New Jersey (M)

Clinical Nutrition (DCN)
University of Medicine and Dentistry of New Jersey (D)

Clinical Nutrition/Nutrition Education
Rosalind Franklin University of Medicine and Science (M)

Clinical Pathology
University of Massachusetts Lowell (GC)

Clinical Psychology
Fielding Graduate Institute (D)

Clinical Psychopharmacology (Post-Doctoral)
Alliant International University (M)

Clinical Science
The University of Texas Medical Branch (B)

Collaborative Educational Leadership
Fielding Graduate Institute (M)

Collaborative Teacher and Early Childhood Education
Auburn University (M)

College Transfer
Caldwell Community College and Technical Institute (A)
Randolph Community College (A)
Southeastern Community College (A)

Commerce (4 year)
Athabasca University (B)

Commerce (General)
Memorial University of Newfoundland (B)

Commonwealth Master of Public Health
George Mason University (M)

Communication
Andrew Jackson University (A)
Regent University (D, M)
University of Louisville (B)

Communication Arts
Caldwell College (B)

Communication Disorders
Western Kentucky University (M)

Communication Disorders and Sciences
California State University, Northridge (M)

Communication Disorders, Speech-Language Pathology
University of Northern Colorado (M)

Communication Studies
Athabasca University (B)
University of Maryland University College (B)

Communication Systems
University of Idaho (UC)

Communication/Organizational Communications/Mass Communication/Public Relations
Montana State University-Billings (B)

Communication/Public Relations/Journalism Concentration
East Carolina University (B)

Communications
Andrew Jackson University (B)
State University of New York at Oswego (B)
Thomas Edison State College (B)
University of the Incarnate Word (A)

Communications Management
Syracuse University (M)

Communications Studies
The Pennsylvania State University University Park Campus (UC)

Communications Technology
Strayer University (M)

Communications Transfer Framework
Hopkinsville Community College (A)

Community and Economic Development
The Pennsylvania State University University Park Campus (GC)

Community and Human Services
State University of New York Empire State College (A, B)

Community College Education
University of Central Florida (GC)

Community College Leadership
Mississippi State University (D, M)

Community College Teaching
California State University, Dominguez Hills (UC)

Community College Teaching and Learning (CCTL)
University of Illinois at Urbana-Champaign (M)

Community College Teaching and Learning (CCTL) Certificate of Professional Development
University of Illinois at Urbana-Champaign (GC)

Community College Teaching and Learning (Ed.M)
University of Illinois (M)

Community Counseling
St. Mary's University of San Antonio (M)

Community Development
Central Michigan University (B)

Community Education
Concordia University, St. Paul (M)

Community Employment Services
Auburn University (UC)

Community Health
Indiana State University (B)
Walden University (M)

Community Health and Development
Saybrook Graduate School and Research Center (GC)

Community Mental Health
New York Institute of Technology (B)

Community Rehabilitation
University of Calgary (B)

Community Services
Thomas Edison State College (A, B)

Community Studies
University College of Cape Breton (B)

Community Supports for People with Disabilities
South Central Technical College (A)

Community, Media, and Technology
University of Massachusetts Boston (UC)

Comprehensive Masters in Education
University of West Florida (M)

Computational Engineering
Mississippi State University (M)

Computational Fluid Dynamics (Aeronautics and Astronautics/Mechanical Engineering)
Stanford University (GC)

Computational Genomics
Stanford University (GC)

Computer and Information Science
University of Maryland University College (B)

Computer and Information Science-Computer Science or Software Engineering Majors
Florida State University (B)

Computer and Information Systems
Strayer University (UC)

Computer and Network Security Technologies
Illinois Institute of Technology (GC)

Computer Architecture
Stanford University (GC)

Computer Assisted Drafting (CAD)
Chemeketa Community College (UC)

Computer Engineering
Florida International University (M)
Illinois Institute of Technology (GC, M)
Iowa State University of Science and Technology (M)
Southern Methodist University (M)
University of Florida (M)
University of Idaho (M)
University of Wisconsin-Madison (M)
Virginia Polytechnic Institute and State University (GC, M)

Computer Engineering Technology
Grantham University (A, B)

Computer Game Development
Edmonds Community College (UC)

GC–Graduate Certificate; D–Doctorate; M–Master's; A–Associate; B–Bachelor's; UC–Undergraduate Certificate

Computer Graphics
Stevens Institute of Technology (GC)

Computer Hardware and VLSI Design
Stanford University (GC)

Computer Information Management
Ashworth College (A)

Computer Information Skills
Teikyo Post University (UC)

Computer Information Systems
Bellevue University (M)
Bossier Parish Community College (A)
Caldwell College (B)
Champlain College (B)
Darton College (A)
DeVry University Online (B)
Excelsior College (B)
Golden Gate University (B)
Ivy Tech State College-Bloomington (A)
Ivy Tech State College-Central Indiana (A)
Ivy Tech State College-Columbus (A)
Ivy Tech State College-Eastcentral (A)
Ivy Tech State College-Kokomo (A)
Ivy Tech State College-Lafayette (A)
Ivy Tech State College-North Central (A)
Ivy Tech State College-Northeast (A)
Ivy Tech State College-Northwest (A)
Ivy Tech State College-Southcentral (A)
Ivy Tech State College-Southeast (A)
Ivy Tech State College-Southwest (A)
Ivy Tech State College-Wabash Valley (A)
Ivy Tech State College-Whitewater (A)
Jamestown Community College (A)
Jones College (A, B)
Moberly Area Community College (A)
Mount Wachusett Community College (A)
Nova Southeastern University (D, M)
Regis University (B)
Saint Leo University (B)
Saint Mary-of-the-Woods College (B)
Southwest Missouri State University (M)
Strayer University (GC, A, B, UC)
Teikyo Post University (B)
Thomas Edison State College (A, B)
University of Phoenix Online Campus (M)

Computer Information Systems (Bachelor of Applied Science)
Mayville State University (B)

Computer Information Systems Specialization
University of Denver (M)

Computer Information Systems-Master of Science in Computer Information Systems
Boston University (M)

Computer Information Systems-MIS option
Brevard Community College (A)

Computer Information Systems-Web Analyst Web Programmer
Wisconsin Indianhead Technical College (A)

Computer Information Systems-Web Design
North Dakota State College of Science (UC)

Computer Information Systems/ Computer Programming
Bristol Community College (A)

Computer Information Systems/ Multimedia and Internet
Bristol Community College (A)

Computer Information Technology
Mountain State University (A)
Regis University (M)
Seminole Community College (A)

Computer Languages and Operating Systems
Stanford University (GC)

Computer Network Engineering
Westwood Online (A)

Computer Network Management
Westwood Online (B)

Computer Network Professional
East Carolina University (GC)

Computer Networking
George Mason University (GC)
Mountain State University (B)
Regis University (B, UC)
Strayer University (A, B)

Computer Networking Technology
Mountain State University (A)

Computer Programming
Bristol Community College (UC)
North Carolina State University (UC)
Northeastern University (UC)
Pitt Community College (A)

Computer Programming (Post-Baccalaureate)
Winston-Salem State University (UC)

Computer Programming and Analysis
Seminole Community College (A)

Computer Programming and Analysis (C++ Programming Specialization)
Seminole Community College (A)

Computer Programming Technology
Southwestern College (B)

Computer Programming, Web Applications Emphasis
Minnesota State College-Southeast Technical (A)

Computer Related Crime Investigations
St. Petersburg College (UC)

Computer Science
Acadia University (UC)
American College of Computer & Information Sciences (M, B)
Boston University (M)
California National University for Advanced Studies (B)
California State University, Chico (M, B)
Capitol College (M)
Colorado State University (M)
Columbia University (GC, M)
DePaul University (M)
Franklin University (A, B)
Grantham University (A, B)
Illinois Institute of Technology (M)
Jamestown Community College (A)
Lakeland College (B)
Maui Community College (B)
Mercy College (B)
Mississippi State University (M)
Mott Community College (UC)
National University (M)
New Jersey Institute of Technology (B)
North Carolina State University (M)
Northwest Missouri State University (B)
Nova Southeastern University (D, M)
Oklahoma State University (M)
Old Dominion University (B)
Regis University (B)
Southern Methodist University (M)
Stanford University (M)
Thomas Edison State College (A, B)
Touro University International (B)
Troy University-Florida Region (B)
University of Colorado at Boulder (M)
University of Idaho (M)

University of Illinois (M, B)
University of Illinois at Springfield (B)
University of Management and Technology (M)
Utah State University (M, B)

Computer Science and Engineering
Auburn University (M)
The University of Texas at Arlington (M)

Computer Science and Engineering Technology
University of Toledo (A, B)

Computer Science and Technology
Keiser College (A)

Computer Science Internet Management
Limestone College (A, B)

Computer Science Management Information Systems
Limestone College (A, B)

Computer Science Programming
Limestone College (A, B)

Computer Science Technology
Thomas Edison State College (A, B)

Computer Science with CyberSecurity Concentration
Stevens Institute of Technology (M)

Computer Science-Information Technology
Central Texas College (A)

Computer Science/Telecom Management w/ Consentration in Security
Stevens Institute of Technology (M)

Computer Software
Excelsior College (A, B)

Computer Software Applications
Pitt Community College (UC)

Computer Studies
University of Maryland University College (B)

Computer Systems (Networking/ Telecommunications Emphasis)
City University (B)

Computer Systems (Programming in C++ Emphasis)
City University (B)

Computer Systems (Web Design Emphasis)
City University (B)

Computer Systems Management
University of Maryland University College (M)

Computer Systems-C++ Programming Emphasis
City University (M)

Computer Systems-Database Technology Emphasis
City University (B)

Computer Systems-Individualized Study Emphasis
City University (M, B)

Computer Systems-Information Technology Security Emphasis
City University (B)

Computer Systems-Technology Management Emphasis
City University (M)

Computer Systems-Web Development Emphasis
City University (M)

Computer Systems-Web Languages Emphasis
City University (B)

Computer Systems-Web Programming in E-Commerce Emphasis
City University (M)

Computer Technology
Excelsior College (B)

Computer Technology (BAS)
Northern Arizona University (B)

Computer, Information, and Network Security
DePaul University (M)

Computer/Technology
Cleveland State University (UC)

Computers and Management Information Systems
Athabasca University (UC)

Computing and Information Systems
Athabasca University (UC)

Computing and Information Systems (4 year)
Athabasca University (B)

Computing and Information Systems-Post-Diploma
Athabasca University (B)

Computing Technology in Education
Nova Southeastern University (D, M)

Computing-Doctor of Professional Studies in Computing
Pace University (UC)

Conflict Analysis and Management
Royal Roads University (M)

Conflict Resolution
Brenau University (GC)

Congregational Leadership
Concordia University, St. Paul (M)

Construction
Thomas Edison State College (B)

Construction Engineering
University of Washington (M)

Construction Management
Florida International University (M)
University of Washington (UC)

Construction Science and Management
Clemson University (M)

Contemplative Education
Naropa University (M)

Contemporary Communications
University of Massachusetts Lowell (UC)

Continuing Education
University of Calgary (M)

Continuing Medical Education-Specialty Needs for PCPs
University of Illinois at Chicago (UC)

GC–Graduate Certificate; D–Doctorate; M–Master's; A–Associate; B–Bachelor's; UC–Undergraduate Certificate

Contract Management-Master of Contract Management
American Graduate University (M)

Control and System Engineering
Stanford University (GC)

Control Systems
Illinois Institute of Technology (GC)

Control Systems Engineering
Oklahoma State University (M)

Convergent Technologies
Arapahoe Community College (A)

Corporate Communication
Austin Peay State University (M)

Corporate Finance
University of Dallas (GC, M)

Correctional Administration and Management
Bellevue University (B)

Corrections
Indiana State University (UC)

Corrections Management
American Public University System (B)

Corrections Pre-Certification
Tunxis Community College (UC)

Counseling
Liberty University (D)
Mercy College (M)
Northern Arizona University (M)
Seton Hall University (M)

Counseling and Guidance, Rehabilitation Counseling
Maui Community College (M)

Counseling and Psychology
Prescott College (M)

Counseling Psychology (Canada)
City University (M)

Counseling Psychology (US)
City University (M)

Counseling Psychology/Human Services
Prescott College (B)

Counseling Women
Athabasca University (UC)

Counseling-Mental Health Counseling Track
University of Massachusetts Boston (M)

Counseling-School Guidance Track
University of Massachusetts Boston (M)

Counseling, Human Relations Track
Liberty University (M)

Counseling, Marriage and Family Therapy Track
Liberty University (M)

Counseling/Human Relations
Northern Arizona University (M)

Counseling/School Counseling
Northern Arizona University (M)

Counselling (Collaborative)
Athabasca University (M)

Counselor Education and Supervision
Regent University (D)

Court Reporting and Captioning
Lenoir Community College (A)

CPCU Accelerated Program
Walden University (M)

Creative Studies
Buffalo State College, State University of New York (M)

Creative Writing
Naropa University (M)
National University (M)

Creativity Studies
Saybrook Graduate School and Research Center (GC)

Creativity, Change Leadership, and Creative Problem Solving
Buffalo State College, State University of New York (GC)

Crime Scene Technology
St. Petersburg College (A, UC)

Criminal Justice
American Public University System (M, B)
Andrew Jackson University (M, A, B)
Ashworth College (M, A)
Athabasca University (B)
Bemidji State University (A, B)
Bismarck State College (A)
Bossier Parish Community College (A)
Boston University (M)
Boston University (M)
Caldwell College (B)
Central Missouri State University (M)
Central Missouri State University (M)
Central Texas College (A)
Clovis Community College (A)
College of The Albemarle (A)
College of the Southwest (B)
Columbia College (A, B)
Concordia University, St. Paul (B)
Darton College (A)
East Carolina University (M)
Excelsior College (B)
Florida Gulf Coast University (B)
Florida Metropolitan University-Brandon Campus (M, A, B)
Grantham University (A, B)
Jefferson Community College (A)
Judson College (B)
Lynn University (B)
Missouri Southern State University (B)
Monroe Community College (A)
Mountain State University (A, B)
New Mexico State University (M)
New York Institute of Technology (B)
Northern Arizona University (B)
Northwestern State University of Louisiana (A)
Old Dominion University (B)
The Paralegal Institute, Inc. (A)
Randolph Community College (A)
Roger Williams University (B)
St. John's University (A)
Saint Joseph's College of Maine (A, B, UC)
Saint Leo University (B)
Southwestern College (B)
Stanly Community College (A)
Teikyo Post University (B)
Tiffin University (M)
Troy University (M)
Troy University-Florida Region (B)
Tunxis Community College (A)
University of Arkansas at Little Rock (B)
University of Central Florida (M)
University of Cincinnati (M)
University of Great Falls (B)
University of Massachusetts Lowell (M)
The University of Texas of the Permian Basin (B)
University of Wisconsin-Platteville (GC, M)
University of Wisconsin-Platteville (GC, M)
University of Wyoming (B)
Upper Iowa University (B)
Utah Valley State College (A)
Virginia College at Birmingham (B)
Weber State University (A)

Western Carolina University (B)
Westwood Online (B)

Criminal Justice (13-month program)
American InterContinental University Online (B)

Criminal Justice (BSCJ)
Colorado Technical University (B)

Criminal Justice (Completion Degree)
The University of Texas System (B)

Criminal Justice (Police Science)
Adirondack Community College (A)

Criminal Justice Administration
Bellevue University (B)
Columbia Southern University (B)
Lynn University (M)
National University (B)
Park University (B)
Taft College (A)
The University of Findlay (B)
University of Phoenix Online Campus (B)

Criminal Justice Administration (MSA)
University of West Florida (M)

Criminal Justice ASB
Education Direct Center for Degree Studies (A)

Criminal Justice Professional Certificate
National University (UC)

Criminal Justice Technology
Gaston College (A)

Criminal Justice-Computer Science
Grantham University (A, B)

Criminal Justice-Homeland Security
Grantham University (A, B)

Criminal Justice, Law Enforcement
Hopkinsville Community College (A)
Lansing Community College (A)

Criminal Justices Studies
University of Massachusetts Amherst (UC)

Criminology
Danville Area Community College (A)
Indiana State University (M, B)
Memorial University of Newfoundland (UC)

Criminology and Criminal Justice/ Completion Degree
The University of Texas at Arlington (B)

Criminology-Criminal Justice Studies Major
Florida State University (M)

Critical Care (Advanced Technical Certification)
St. Petersburg College (UC)

Cross Cultural Education with Credential Options
National University (M)

Cross Disciplinary Professional Studies
Rochester Institute of Technology (M)

Culinary Management Degree Completion Program
The Art Institute Online (B)

Cultural Studies
State University of New York Empire State College (A, B)

Culture of U.S. Business
University of Illinois at Chicago (UC)

Current Energy Issues
Illinois Institute of Technology (GC)

Curriculum and Instruction
Black Hills State University (GC)
The College of St. Scholastica (M)
Concordia University Wisconsin (M)
Florida Gulf Coast University (M)
The Pennsylvania State University University Park Campus (M)
The University of North Carolina at Greensboro (M)
The University of Texas System (M)

Curriculum and Instruction Specialized Study
City University (M)

Curriculum and Instruction with a Learning Technologies Emphasis
New Mexico State University (D)

Curriculum and Instruction-Educational Leadership
University of Colorado at Colorado Springs (M)

Curriculum and Instruction-Health Promotion Emphasis
Virginia Polytechnic Institute and State University (M)

Curriculum and Instruction-Instructional Technology
La Sierra University (M)

Curriculum and Instruction-Online
Seattle Pacific University (M)

Curriculum and Instruction/Reading
The University of Texas at Arlington (M)

Curriculum and Supervision
The University of North Carolina at Charlotte (M)

Curriculum Integration in Action
University of Washington (UC)

Curriculum Studies
The University of Montana-Missoula (M)

Curriculum Studies (Butte, Bitterroot Valley)
The University of Montana-Missoula (M)

Curriculum Studies in Learning and Technology
Acadia University (M)

Curriculum, Technology, and Education Reform
University of Illinois (M)

Curriculum, Technology, and Education Reform (CTER)
University of Illinois at Urbana-Champaign (M)

Curriculum, Technology, and Instruction (Canada)
City University (M)

Cyber Security
Keiser College (A)
Stevens Institute of Technology (GC)

Cytotechnology
Thomas Edison State College (B)

Data Mining
Connecticut State University System (M)

GC–Graduate Certificate; D–Doctorate; M–Master's; A–Associate; B–Bachelor's; UC–Undergraduate Certificate

Data Mining and Applications (Statistics)
Stanford University (GC)

Data Resource Management
University of Washington (UC)

Data/Telecommunications
University of Massachusetts Lowell (UC)

Database Design and Administration
Northeastern University (UC)

Database Management
University of Washington (UC)

Database Systems
Stevens Institute of Technology (GC)

Database Technologies (MSCIT)
Regis University (GC)

Databases
Stanford University (GC)

Deaf Education
Texas Woman's University (M)

Decision Support Systems
Webster University (GC)

Degree Completion
Duquesne University (B)

Dental Assisting
Monroe Community College (UC)

Dental Hygiene
Pennsylvania College of Technology (B)
St. Petersburg College (B)
Thomas Edison State College (B)

Dental Hygiene Completion Program
Northern Arizona University (B)

Dental Hygiene Online (degree completion program)
University of Bridgeport (B)

Dental Hygiene-Degree Completion in Dental Hygiene
Oregon Institute of Technology (B)

Design
Ivy Tech State College-Wabash Valley (UC)

Design for Customer Value and Market Success
Stanford University (GC)

Design Technology
Ivy Tech State College-Bloomington (A)
Ivy Tech State College-Central Indiana (A)
Ivy Tech State College-Columbus (A)
Ivy Tech State College-Eastcentral (A)
Ivy Tech State College-Kokomo (A)
Ivy Tech State College-Lafayette (A)
Ivy Tech State College-North Central (A)
Ivy Tech State College-Northeast (A)
Ivy Tech State College-Northwest (A)
Ivy Tech State College-Southcentral (A)
Ivy Tech State College-Southeast (A)
Ivy Tech State College-Southwest (A)
Ivy Tech State College-Wabash Valley (A)
Ivy Tech State College-Whitewater (A)

Designing and Implementing Web-based Learning Environments
University of Colorado at Denver (UC)

Desktop Applications
Davenport University Online (UC)

Desktop Publishing Technology
Bristol Community College (UC)

Dietary Management
Auburn University (UC)

Dietary Manager
The Pennsylvania State University University Park Campus (UC)
Southwest Wisconsin Technical College (UC)

Dietetic Food Systems Management
The Pennsylvania State University University Park Campus (A)

Dietetic Technician
Baltimore City Community College (A)

Dietetics
Eastern Michigan University (B)
Gaston College (A)
Kansas State University (B)
University of Northern Colorado (UC)

Dietetics (degree completion/didactic program in dietetics)
University of Northern Colorado (B)

Dietetics and Aging
The Pennsylvania State University University Park Campus (UC)

Differentiated Learning
Concordia University, St. Paul (M)

Digital Communication
Franklin University (B)
Stanford University (GC)

Digital Design
The Art Institute Online (UC)

Digital Libraries
Syracuse University (GC)

Digital Media Communication
Saint Mary-of-the-Woods College (B)

Digital Publishing
Savannah College of Art and Design (GC, UC)

Digital Signal Processing
Stevens Institute of Technology (GC)

Digital Technologies Management
Royal Roads University (M)

Diplomacy
Norwich University (M)

Direct Marketing
Mercy College (M)

Direct Transfer
Everett Community College (A)

Disaster and Emergency Management
Rochester Institute of Technology (UC)

Discipleship
William Tyndale College (A)

Discovery Teacher Training
Mississippi State University (UC)

Dispute Resolution
Sullivan University (UC)

Dispute Resolution, Conflict Management
Sullivan University (M)

Distance Education
Athabasca University (M)
Indiana University System (UC)
The Pennsylvania State University University Park Campus (GC)
University of Wisconsin-Madison (UC)

Distance Education Technology
Athabasca University (GC)

Distance Learning
University of Maryland, Baltimore County (GC)

Distance Learning Design and Development
University of Washington (UC)

Distance MBA
Colorado State University (M)

Distributed Learning
Royal Roads University (M)

Distributed Systems
DePaul University (M)

Diversity Management
University of Toledo (UC)

Divinity
The Baptist College of Florida (A)
Global University of the Assemblies of God (M)
The King's College and Seminary (M)
Liberty University (M)
Oral Roberts University (M)
Regent University (M)

Doctoral Completion Program
Saybrook Graduate School and Research Center (D)

Drama Therapy
Kansas State University (UC)

Driver Education
Indiana State University (UC)

Duke Environmental Leadership Program
Duke University (M)

E-Business
Bellevue University (B)
Dallas Baptist University (M, UC)
Lansing Community College (A, UC)
National University (UC)
University of Phoenix Online Campus (M, B)
Walden University (M)

E-Business and Commerce
Champlain College (UC)

E-Business Management
The Community College of Baltimore County (A)
University of Dallas (GC, M)
Westwood Online (B)

E-Business Strategy
University of Illinois (GC)
University of Illinois at Chicago (UC)

E-Business Technology
The Community College of Baltimore County (A)

E-Business Web Developer
North Harris Montgomery Community College District (A)

E-Business-Web Development Specialty
Davenport University Online (B)

E-Commerce
Athabasca University (B)
City University (GC)
Columbus State Community College (GC)
New York Institute of Technology (M)
Rappahannock Community College (UC)
Texas State Technical College-Waco (UC)
University of Maryland University College (M)

E-Commerce Engineering (MSCIT)
Regis University (GC)

E-Commerce Management
University of Washington (UC)

E-Commerce Specialization
University of Denver (M)

E-Commerce Technology
DePaul University (M)

E-Government
Walden University (M)

E-Learning
Jones International University (M)
Roosevelt University (GC)
University of Calgary (UC)

e.MBA
Pace University (M)

Early Child Development
Bethany College of the Assemblies of God (A, B)

Early Childhood
Concordia University, St. Paul (M)

Early Childhood (BAS)
Northern Arizona University (B)

Early Childhood Administration
Teikyo Post University (UC)

Early Childhood Education
Ashworth College (A)
Brenau University (M)
Clarion University of Pennsylvania (A)
Ivy Tech State College-Bloomington (A, UC)
Ivy Tech State College-Central Indiana (A, UC)
Ivy Tech State College-Columbus (A, UC)
Ivy Tech State College-Eastcentral (A, UC)
Ivy Tech State College-Kokomo (A, UC)
Ivy Tech State College-Lafayette (A, UC)
Ivy Tech State College-North Central (A, UC)
Ivy Tech State College-Northeast (A, UC)
Ivy Tech State College-Northwest (A)
Ivy Tech State College-Southcentral (A, UC)
Ivy Tech State College-Southeast (A, UC)
Ivy Tech State College-Southwest (A, UC)
Ivy Tech State College-Wabash Valley (A, UC)
Ivy Tech State College-Whitewater (A, UC)
Mayville State University (B)
Northampton County Area Community College (A)
Northern Arizona University (M)
Oral Roberts University (M)
Southwestern Assemblies of God University (A)
Taft College (A)
Teikyo Post University (A, UC)
University of Alaska Southeast (M, UC)
University of Cincinnati (A)

Early Childhood Education Administration Credential
Kansas State University (UC)

Early Childhood Education ASB
Education Direct Center for Degree Studies (A)

Early Childhood Education, Group/Leader/Child Development Associate-Infant/Toddler
Community College of Denver (UC)

Early Childhood Education, Group/Leader/Child Development Associate-Preschool
Community College of Denver (UC)

GC–Graduate Certificate; D–Doctorate; M–Master's; A–Associate; B–Bachelor's; UC–Undergraduate Certificate

Early Childhood Intervention
Auburn University (UC)

Early Childhood/Child Development
Saint Mary-of-the-Woods College (A)

Earth Literacy
Saint Mary-of-the-Woods College (M)

Ecommerce
Cardean University (M)

Economics
Darton College (A)
Strayer University (A, B)
Thomas Edison State College (B)
University of Waterloo (B)

Economics Emphasis
Community College of Denver (A)

Economics/Finance
Southern New Hampshire University (B)

Education
Aspen University (M)
Bemidji State University (M)
California State University, Hayward (M, UC)
Capella University (D, M)
Concordia University (M)
Cumberland University (M)
Indiana Wesleyan University (M)
Judson College (B)
Lakeland College (M)
Liberty University (D, M)
Montana State University-Bozeman (M)
Mountain Empire Community College (A)
Mount Saint Vincent University (M)
Prescott College (M, B)
Regent University (GC, D)
Regis University (M)
Saint Joseph's College of Maine (M)
Southwestern Assemblies of God University (M, A, B)
Strayer University (M)
Touro University International (M)
University of Maryland University College (M)
The University of Tennessee at Martin (M)
Utah State University (D)

Education (10-month program)
American InterContinental University Online (M)

Education (K-8)
Alaska Pacific University (A, B, UC)

Education Administration
Concordia University Wisconsin (M)

Education and Training Management Subspecialty/Human Performance Technology
University of West Florida (M)

Education and Training Management Subspecialty/Instructional Technology
University of West Florida (M)

Education Counseling
Concordia University Wisconsin (M)
University College of Cape Breton (M)

Education Curriculum
University College of Cape Breton (M)

Education Leadership
University of North Dakota (M)

Education Leadership (MSA)
University of West Florida (M)

Education Leadership and Principal Certification
City University (M)

Education Leadership-Master of Arts in Education Leadership
University of Illinois (M)

Education Specialist
Liberty University
Northwestern State University of Louisiana (GC)

Education Technology
University College of Cape Breton (M)

Education-Administration and Supervision Specialization
University of Phoenix Online Campus (M)

Education-Adult and Post-Secondary Education
University of Wyoming (M)

Education-Adult Education Leadership
Walden University (D)

Education-Community College Leadership
Walden University (D)

Education-Curriculum and Instruction
University of Phoenix Online Campus (M)

Education-Curriculum and Technology
University of Phoenix Online Campus (M)

Education-Curriculum, Instruction, and Assessment
Walden University (M)

Education-Early Childhood Education
Walden University (D)

Education-Early Childhood Education Specialization
University of Phoenix Online Campus (M)

Education-Educational Leadership
Walden University (M)

Education-Educational Technology
Walden University (D)

Education-Elementary Education
City University (B)

Education-Elementary or Secondary Teacher Education
University of Phoenix Online Campus (M)

Education-Elementary Reading and Literacy
Walden University (M)

Education-Higher Education
Walden University (D)

Education-Instructional Leadership
Marquette University (M)

Education-Instructional Technology
University of Wyoming (M)

Education-Integrating Technology in the Classroom
Walden University (M)

Education-K-12 Educational Leadership
Walden University (D)

Education-Knowledge Management
Walden University (D)

Education-Learning Management
Walden University (D)

Education-Learning Technologies
New Mexico State University (M)

Education-Literacy and Learning in the Content Areas
Walden University (M)

Education-Master of Education at a Distance
University of Calgary (M)

Education-Mathematics
Walden University (M)

Education-Middle Level Education
Walden University (M)

Education-Pre-K Through 6
Old Dominion University (M)

Education-Science
Walden University (M)

Education-Self-Designed
Walden University (D)

Education-Special Education
City University (B)
University of Wyoming (M)
Walden University (D)

Education-Special Education Specialization
University of Phoenix Online Campus (M)

Education-Teacher Preparation
Old Dominion University (B)

Education-Teaching and Learning
University of Wyoming (M)

Education, general
Gadsden State Community College (A)
Gaston College (A)
Southeastern Community College, North Campus (A)
Troy University-Florida Region (A)
Walden University (D)

Educational Administration
Marygrove College (M)
Maui Community College (M)
National University (M)
St. Cloud State University (M)
St. John's University (GC, M)
Texas A&M University (M)
University of Cincinnati (M)
University of Cincinnati (M)
University of Massachusetts Lowell (M)
University of Nebraska-Lincoln (D, M, UC)
The University of South Dakota (M)

Educational Administration and Counseling
College of the Southwest (M)

Educational Administration and Leadership
Buena Vista University (M)

Educational Administration and Supervision
Ball State University (M)
Seton Hall University (M)

Educational Administration Specialists
University of Nebraska at Kearney (GC)

Educational Administration-Community College Leadership Emphasis
New Mexico State University (D)

Educational Diagnostician
College of the Southwest (M)
Texas Tech University (UC)

Educational Foundations
Maui Community College (M)

Educational Human Resource Development
Texas A&M University (M)

Educational Leadership
City University (M)
Clemson University (D)
Northern Arizona University (D, M)
Touro University International (D)
The University of Montana-Missoula (M)
University of New England (GC)
University of Phoenix Online Campus (D)

Educational Leadership (Alberta, Canada)
City University (M)

Educational Leadership (British Columbia, Canada)
City University (M)

Educational Leadership (weekend cohort program)
The University of Montana-Missoula (D)

Educational Leadership and Change
Fielding Graduate Institute (D)

Educational Leadership and Principal Certification
City University (GC)

Educational Leadership Focus
University of Missouri-Columbia (M)

Educational Media
University of Central Florida (GC, M)

Educational Media and Technology
The College of St. Scholastica (M)
Eastern Michigan University (GC, M)

Educational Media Graduate Endorsement
University of Nebraska at Kearney (UC)

Educational Organization and Administration
Dallas Baptist University (M)

Educational Psychology with Bilingual Education Emphasis
Texas A&M University (M)

Educational Specialist-Mental Health Practices in Schools
University of Missouri-Columbia (GC)

Educational Specialist-Technology in Schools
University of Missouri-Columbia (GC)

Educational Studies
State University of New York Empire State College (A, B)
University of Nebraska-Lincoln (D)

Educational Technology
Azusa Pacific University (M)
Boise State University (M)
Cleveland State University (M)
Connecticut State University System (M)
Dakota State University (M)
National University (M, UC)
Northern Arizona University (M, UC)
Northwestern State University of Louisiana (M)
Texas A&M University (M)
University of Alaska Southeast (M, UC)
University of Nebraska-Lincoln (GC)
University of Northern Colorado (M)
The University of Texas System (M)
Western Michigan University (M)

Educational Technology and Multidisciplinary Studies
Webster University (M)

Educational Technology Emphasis
Boise State University (M)

GC–Graduate Certificate; D–Doctorate; M–Master's; A–Associate; B–Bachelor's; UC–Undergraduate Certificate

Educational Technology Integration
The Pennsylvania State University University Park Campus (GC)

Educational Technology-Master of Educational Technology
The University of British Columbia (M)

Electric Machines and Drives
University of Idaho (UC)

Electric Power Technology
Bismarck State College (A)
Bismarck State College (A, UC)

Electric Transmission System Technology
Bismarck State College (A, UC)

Electrical and Computer Engineering
Colorado State University (M)
Illinois Institute of Technology (M)
Mississippi State University (M)
Northeastern University (M)
Oklahoma State University (M)
University of Colorado at Boulder (M)
University of Massachusetts Amherst (D, M)
Virginia Polytechnic Institute and State University (M)

Electrical Engineering
Bradley University (M)
California State University, Fullerton (M)
Capitol College (M)
Clemson University (M)
Colorado State University (D)
Columbia University (GC, M)
Fairleigh Dickinson University, Metropolitan Campus (M)
Florida International University (M)
Georgia Institute of Technology (M)
Illinois Institute of Technology (M)
Iowa State University of Science and Technology (M)
Kansas State University (M)
Michigan Technological University (D, M)
Southern Illinois University Carbondale (B)
Southern Methodist University (M)
Stanford University (M)
University of Delaware (M)
University of Idaho (M)
University of North Dakota (B)
University of South Carolina (D, M)
University of South Florida (M)
The University of Texas at Arlington (M)
University of Washington (M)
University of Wisconsin-Madison (M)

Electrical Engineering Technology
Old Dominion University (B)
The University of North Carolina at Charlotte (B)

Electrical Engineering Technology AST
Education Direct Center for Degree Studies (A)

Electrical Technology
Thomas Edison State College (A, B)

Electrical/Mechanical Engineering Technology
Rochester Institute of Technology (B)

Electricity Markets
Illinois Institute of Technology (GC, M)

Electromagnetics Technology
University of Illinois (GC)
University of Illinois at Chicago (UC)

Electronic Business
National University (M)

Electronic Circuits
Stanford University (GC)

Electronic Commerce
Southeastern Community College (A)
University of Denver (GC)

Electronic Devices and Technology
Stanford University (GC)

Electronic Engineering Technology
Thomas Edison State College (A, B)

Electronic Publishing
Northeastern University (UC)

Electronics and Computer Technology
Indiana State University (M)

Electronics Engineering Technology
Grantham University (A, B)

Electronics Technology
Excelsior College (A, B)
Indiana State University (B)

Electronics Technology AST
Education Direct Center for Degree Studies (A)

Elementary Education
Ball State University (M)
Bemidji State University (B)
Buena Vista University (B)
Coconino Community College (A)
Community College of Denver (A)
Maui Community College (B)
Mississippi State University (M, B)
Northern Arizona University (M)
Southwest Missouri State University (M, B)
University of Alaska Southeast (M)
The University of North Carolina at Charlotte (B)
University of North Dakota (M)
Western Carolina University (B)

Elementary Education (BS Ed.)
Northern Arizona University (B)

Elementary Education (Post-Baccalaureate Certification)
Stephen F. Austin State University (UC)

Elementary Education Postdegree
Northern Arizona University (UC)

Elementary Education with Certification
Oral Roberts University (B)

Elementary Education/Special Education
Maui Community College (B)

Elementary or Secondary Education
Utah State University (M)

Elementary Teacher Preparation
Mountain State University (A)

Elementary, Middle Grades, and Special Education
Southeastern Community College (A)

Elements of Computer Science
Stevens Institute of Technology (GC)

Embedded and Real-Time Systems Programming
University of Washington (UC)

Emergency Administration and Management
St. Petersburg College (A, UC)

Emergency and Disaster Management
American Public University System (B)

Emergency Disaster Management
Thomas Edison State College (A, B)

Emergency Health Services
University of Maryland, Baltimore County (M)

Emergency Management
Jacksonville State University (M)

Emergency Management (Public Safety Communications minor)
Jacksonville State University (B)

Emergency Management/Homeland Security
Western Washington University (UC)

Emergency Medical Services
Mountain State University (A)

Emergency Preparedness Technology
Caldwell Community College and Technical Institute (A)

Energy Management
New York Institute of Technology (M)

Engineering
California National University for Advanced Studies (M, B)
Eastern Michigan University (M)
Kettering University (M)
Michigan Technological University (B)
Northern Arizona University (M)
Texas Tech University (M)
The University of Arizona (M)
University of Illinois (M)
University of Illinois at Chicago (M)
University of Toledo (M)
University of Wisconsin-Platteville (M)
University of Wisconsin-Platteville (M)

Engineering Administration
Virginia Polytechnic Institute and State University (M)

Engineering and Management Systems
Columbia University (M)

Engineering Design
Michigan Technological University (UC)

Engineering Graphics
Thomas Edison State College (A, B)

Engineering Law and Management
University of Illinois (GC)
University of Illinois at Chicago (UC)

Engineering Management
California State University, Northridge (M)
Colorado State University (M)
Grantham University (A, B)
Kansas State University (M)
New Jersey Institute of Technology (M)
Old Dominion University (M)
Southern Methodist University (M)
The University of Alabama in Huntsville (M)
University of Colorado at Boulder (GC, M)
University of Idaho (M)
University of Massachusetts Amherst (M)
University of Nebraska-Lincoln (M)
University of South Florida (M)
The University of Tennessee (M)
University of Wisconsin-Platteville (UC)

Engineering Online
North Carolina State University (M)

Engineering Systems Management
Texas A&M University (M)

Engineering Technology
Michigan Technological University (A)
University of Central Florida (B)

Engineering Technology Instructional Support
University of West Florida (B)

Engineering Technology Management
Oklahoma State University (M)

English
American Public University System (B)
Buena Vista University (B)
Caldwell College (B)
Darton College (A)
Judson College (B)
Maui Community College (B)
Mercy College (M)
National University (M, B)
Northern Arizona University (M)
Saint Mary-of-the-Woods College (B)
Southwestern Assemblies of God University (A, B)
Stephens College (B)
Thomas Edison State College (B)
Troy University Montgomery (B)
University of Illinois (B)
University of Illinois at Springfield (B)
University of Maryland University College (B)
University of Waterloo (B)
Western Kentucky University (M)

English (4 year)
Athabasca University (B)

English as a Second Language
Fairleigh Dickinson University, Metropolitan Campus (UC)
Murray State University (UC)
Northern Arizona University (UC)
University of North Dakota (UC)

English as a Second Language (ESL)
The University of Texas System (UC)

English Bible Concentration
Regent University (M)

English Concentration (3 year)
Athabasca University (B)

English for Nurses
Northeastern University (UC)

English Language and Literature
Southern New Hampshire University (B)

English Language Studies
Athabasca University (UC)

English-Professional and Technical Communication Concentration
East Carolina University (M)

English/Literature Emphasis
Community College of Denver (A)

English/Technical Writing Specialization Online
Utah State University (M)

Enterprise Systems Management
Golden Gate University (M)

Entomology
University of Nebraska-Lincoln (M)

Entrepreneurial Management
Royal Roads University (B)

Entrepreneurial Specialty
Davenport University Online (M)

Entrepreneurial Studies
Stephens College (M)

Entrepreneurship
Bucks County Community College (UC)
Davenport University Online (A, B)
Western Carolina University (B)

Environment and Management
Royal Roads University (M)

GC–Graduate Certificate; D–Doctorate; M–Master's; A–Associate; B–Bachelor's; UC–Undergraduate Certificate

Environmental Management
University of Maryland University College (M)

Environmental Education and Communication
Royal Roads University (M)

Environmental Engineering
Georgia Institute of Technology (M)
Illinois Institute of Technology (M)
Southern Methodist University (M)
The University of Tennessee (M)
Worcester Polytechnic Institute (GC, M)

Environmental Health
University College of Cape Breton (B)

Environmental Health and Safety
University of Connecticut (UC)

Environmental Health and Safety Management
Rochester Institute of Technology (M)
University of Denver (GC)

Environmental Information Management
University of Denver (GC)

Environmental Management
Columbia Southern University (B)
Duquesne University (M)
Royal Roads University (B)
University of Calgary (UC)
University of Denver (GC)
The University of Findlay (M, B)
University of Maryland University College (B)

Environmental Management and Technology
Rochester Institute of Technology (UC)

Environmental Policy
University of Denver (GC)

Environmental Policy and Management
University of Denver (GC, M)

Environmental Policy and Management Specialization
University of Denver (M)

Environmental Project Management
University of Denver (GC)

Environmental Science
Southern Methodist University (M)
University College of Cape Breton (B)
University of Florida (M)
University of Guelph (UC)

Environmental Science (Environmental Systems Management Major)
Southern Methodist University (M)

Environmental Science (Hazardous and Waste Materials Management Major)
Southern Methodist University (M)

Environmental Science/Management
Oklahoma State University (M)

Environmental Sciences
Northern Arizona University (B)
Oregon State University (B)
Thomas Edison State College (A, B)

Environmental Studies
Mountain State University (A)
Prescott College (M, B)
Thomas Edison State College (B)

Equine Business Management
Saint Mary-of-the-Woods College (B)

ESR Access
Earlham School of Religion (M)

Estate Planning
Golden Gate University (GC)

Estate Planning and Taxation
The American College (GC)

Exceptional Education
University of Central Florida (M)
Western Kentucky University (M)

Exceptional Needs with Mild Interventions (licensure)
Indiana Wesleyan University (UC)

Executive Bachelor's Degree Completion Program
Boston University (B)

Executive International Management (MSM)
Regis University (GC)

Executive Leadership (MSM)
Regis University (GC)

Executive Management
Royal Roads University (M)
University of Notre Dame (UC)

Executive Master of Business Administration
Purdue University (M)

Executive Master of Taxation
Florida Atlantic University (M)

Executive MBA
University of Notre Dame (M)

Executive Program in Health Informatics
University of Missouri-Columbia (M)

Executive Program in Health Services Management
University of Missouri-Columbia (M)

Executive Project Management (MSM)
Regis University (GC)

Executive Undergraduate Degree Completion
Boston University (B)

Exercise Science and Health Promotion-Performance Enhancement and Injury Prevention
California University of Pennsylvania (M)

Exercise Science and Nutrition
University of Massachusetts Amherst (UC)

Expressive Arts for Healing and Social Change
Saybrook Graduate School and Research Center (GC)

External Doctor of Pharmacy
The University of Montana-Missoula (D)

Facilities Management
Southern Methodist University (M)

Facility Management
University of Washington (UC)

Family and Consumer Sciences
University of Nebraska-Lincoln (M)

Family and Consumer Sciences (Early Childhood Program Director's Certificate)
University of Wyoming (UC)

Family and Consumer Sciences (Professional Child Development Option)
University of Wyoming (B)

Family and Financial Planning
Montana State University-Bozeman (M)

Family and Human Development-Master of Family and Human Development
Utah State University (M)

Family Child Care
Northampton County Area Community College (UC)

Family Financial Planning
North Dakota State University (M)
University of Nebraska-Lincoln (GC)

Family Life Education
Concordia University, St. Paul (B)

Family Literacy
The Pennsylvania State University University Park Campus (GC, UC)

Family Studies
Texas Woman's University (M)

Family Support Studies/Human Development
Edmonds Community College (A)

Family Therapy
Southern Christian University (D)

FCSEE or AST Specialization
Utah State University (M)

Fiber Optics
Three Rivers Community College (GC)

Fiction Writing
University of Washington (UC)

Finance
Cardean University (M)
Colorado State University (UC)
Dallas Baptist University (M)
Excelsior College (B)
Golden Gate University (GC, M, B, UC)
National University (UC)
New York Institute of Technology (M, B)
Regis University (B)
Thomas Edison State College (A, B)
Walden University (M, B)

Financial Engineering
Columbia University (UC)
Stevens Institute of Technology (GC)

Financial Management
City University (GC)

Financial Management Emphasis
City University (M)

Financial Planning
Golden Gate University (GC, M)

Financial Services
The American College (M)
Nipissing University (B)

Financial Services and Risk Management
Stephens College (M)

Finite Element Method/Computational Fluid Dynamics
Columbia University (UC)

Fire and Emergency Management Administration
Oklahoma State University (M)

Fire and Emergency Services (BS)
University of Florida (UC)

Fire Inspector I
St. Petersburg College (UC)

Fire Inspector II
St. Petersburg College (UC)

Fire Investigator I
St. Petersburg College (UC)

Fire Investigator II
St. Petersburg College (UC)

Fire Officer I
St. Petersburg College (UC)

Fire Officer II
St. Petersburg College (UC)

Fire Protection
Middlesex Community College (A)

Fire Protection Engineering
Worcester Polytechnic Institute (GC, M)

Fire Protection Science
Thomas Edison State College (A, B)

Fire Protection Technology-Fire Prevention
Chemeketa Community College (A)

Fire Protection Technology-Fire Suppression
Chemeketa Community College (A)

Fire Science
University of Maryland University College (B)
The University of North Carolina at Charlotte (B)

Fire Science Administration
Columbia College (A)
University of Cincinnati (B)

Fire Science Management
American Public University System (B)

Fire Services Administration
Eastern Oregon University (B)

Fitness and Wellness Services
Thomas Edison State College (A)

Fitness Management
United States Sports Academy (M)

Fitness Specialist
United States Sports Academy (UC)

Fluids (Aeronautics and Astronautics/Mechanical Engineering)
Stanford University (GC)

Food Marketing
University of Wisconsin-Platteville (UC)

Food Science
Kansas State University (GC, M, UC)
University of Guelph (UC)

Food Science and Industry
Kansas State University (B)

Food Service Supervision
The Pennsylvania State University University Park Campus (UC)

Food Service Training Program
Southeast Community College, Beatrice Campus (UC)

Foreign Language
Auburn University (M)
Caldwell College (B)
Darton College (A)

GC–Graduate Certificate; D–Doctorate; M–Master's; A–Associate; B–Bachelor's; UC–Undergraduate Certificate

Thomas Edison State College (B)

Forensic Accounting
Davenport University Online (UC)

Forensic Science
Florida International University (M)
University of Central Florida (M)

Forensic Sciences-Master of Forensic Sciences
National University (M)

Forensic Toxicology
University of Florida (GC)

Forestry
Thomas Edison State College (A, B)

Foundations in Computer Science
Stanford University (GC)

Foundations of Business
University of Massachusetts Lowell (GC)

French
Mount Saint Vincent University (UC)
University of Waterloo (B)

French (4 year)
Athabasca University (B)

French Concentration (3 year)
Athabasca University (B)

French Language Proficiency
Athabasca University (UC)

Fund Development
University of Illinois (GC)

Fundamentals of Information Technology
University of Massachusetts Boston (UC)
University of Massachusetts Lowell (UC)

Funeral Services
St. Petersburg College (A)

Game Art and Design
The Art Institute Online (B)
Westwood Online (B)

Game Software Development
Westwood Online (B)

Gas Engineering
Illinois Institute of Technology (M)

General 3 year Program
Athabasca University (B)

General 4 year Program
Athabasca University (B)

General Business
Missouri Southern State University (A)
Mountain State University (UC)
The Pennsylvania State University University Park Campus (UC)
Taft College (A)

General Education
Ashland Community and Technical College (A)
Edison Community College (A)
Montana State University-Great Falls College of Technology (A)
Park University (M)
Troy University Montgomery (A)

General Education Requirements
Adams State College (A)

General Education Transfer
Northwestern Michigan College (A)

General Information Technology
The Community College of Baltimore County (A)

General Management
City University (GC)
New York Institute of Technology (B)

General Management Emphasis
City University (M)

General Ministries
Bethany College of the Assemblies of God (B)

General Post-Diploma
Athabasca University (B)

General Program
Ball State University (A)
Cardean University (M)
Concordia University, St. Paul (A)
Copiah-Lincoln Community College-Natchez Campus (A)
Dickinson State University (A)
Howard Community College (A)
Metropolitan Community College (A)
Mississippi Delta Community College (A)
New York Institute of Technology (M)
North Idaho College (A)
NorthWest Arkansas Community College (A)
Peninsula College (A)
Pulaski Technical College (A)
Rowan Technical College (A)
St. Louis Community College System (A)
Saint Mary-of-the-Woods College (A, B)
St. Petersburg College (A)
Seattle Central Community College (A)
Snead State Community College (A)
University of the Incarnate Word (M)
Waubonsee Community College (A)
Western Wyoming Community College (A)

General Programs
Kirkwood Community College (A)
Spoon River College (A)
West Valley College (A)

General Studies
American Public University System (A)
Andrew Jackson University (A)
Anne Arundel Community College (A)
Bellevue Community College (A)
Bethany College of the Assemblies of God (A)
Bossier Parish Community College (A)
Brevard Community College (A)
Butler County Community College (A)
Central Texas College (A)
Charter Oak State College (A, B, UC)
Chemeketa Community College (A)
City University (B)
College for Lifelong Learning (A)
Columbia College (A, B)
Columbia Union College (A, B)
Columbus State Community College (A)
The Community College of Baltimore County (A)
Cossatot Community College of the University of Arkansas (A)
Dallas County Community College District (A)
Daniel Webster College (A)
Darton College (A)
Delaware County Community College (A)
Delta College (A)
Eastern Illinois University (B)
Everett Community College (A)
Franklin Pierce College (A, B)
Frederick Community College (A)
Gadsden State Community College (A)
Harford Community College (A)
Howard Community College (A)
Indiana University System (A, B, UC)
Johnson County Community College (A)
Lansing Community College (A)

Liberty University (A)
Los Angeles Trade-Technical College (A)
Marshall University (A)
Missouri Southern State University (A, B)
Montgomery County Community College (A)
Mountain Empire Community College (A)
Mountain State University (A)
Mount Wachusett Community College (A)
Northampton County Area Community College (A)
Northern Virginia Community College (A)
North Harris Montgomery Community College District (A)
Northwestern State University of Louisiana (A)
Palm Beach Community College (A)
Pratt Community College (A)
Quinebaug Valley Community College (A)
Rappahannock Community College (A)
Saint Joseph's College of Maine (A, B)
Southwestern Assemblies of God University (A)
Southwest Virginia Community College (A)
Strayer University (A)
Tarrant County College District (A)
Texas Tech University (B)
Texas Woman's University (B)
University of Missouri-Columbia (B)
University of North Dakota (B)
University of Phoenix Online Campus (A)
The University of South Dakota (A)
Utah State University (A)
Utah Valley State College (A)
Waubonsee Community College (A, UC)
Weber State University (A)
William Tyndale College (A)
Yuba College (A)

General Studies (for transferring)
Mott Community College (A)

General Studies (Secondary Education)
University of North Dakota (M)

General Studies Emphasis
City University (A)

General Studies with Designation (Arts/Science or Applied Studies)
Athabasca University (B)

General Studies-Transfer
Arapahoe Community College (A)

General Studies, Non-Major
University of Waterloo (B)

General Studies/Liberal Arts
Tunxis Community College (A)

Generalist
Community College of Denver (A)

Genomic Engineering
Columbia University (UC)

Geographic Information Science
Northwest Missouri State University (M)

Geographic Information Systems
Columbus State Community College (GC)
North Carolina State University (GC)
The Pennsylvania State University University Park Campus (UC)

Geographic Information Systems (GIS)
University of Colorado at Denver (M)
University of Denver (GC)

Geographic Information Systems Specialization
University of Denver (M)

Geological Engineering
University of Idaho (M)

Geriatric Rehabilitation and Wellness
Sacred Heart University (M)

Gerontology
Florida Atlantic University (UC)
Florida International University (UC)
Fort Hays State University (B)
Kansas State University (M)
Mount Saint Vincent University (UC)
North Dakota State University (M)
Saint Mary-of-the-Woods College (A, B, UC)
Thomas Edison State College (A, B)
University of Washington (UC)

Gifted and Talented
Murray State University (UC)

Gifted and Talented Graduate Teaching Endorsement
Western Kentucky University (UC)

Gifted Education
Northern Arizona University (UC)

Gifted Education Focus
University of Missouri-Columbia (M)

Gifted Graduate Endorsement
University of Nebraska at Kearney (UC)

Global Affairs
University of Denver (GC)

Global Business
Walden University (M)

Global Business Management
Bellevue University (B)

Global Human Resource Development
University of Illinois (M)

Global Human Resource Development (HRD)
University of Illinois at Urbana-Champaign (M)

Global Logistics
Lenoir Community College (A)

Global Management
Cardean University (M)
New York Institute of Technology (M)
University of Phoenix Online Campus (M)

Global Master of Business Administration for Latin American Managers
Thunderbird, The Garvin School of International Management (M)

Global MBA Online
The University of Texas at Dallas (M)

Global Networks and Telecommunications
Champlain College (A, UC)

Global Studies
National University (B)

GME Core Curriculum
University of Illinois (GC)

Golf Fitness Instructor
United States Sports Academy (UC)

Governance, Law, and Management
Athabasca University (B)

Government
Regent University (M)

Government-Business Relations
Park University (M)

GC–Graduate Certificate; D–Doctorate; M–Master's; A–Associate; B–Bachelor's; UC–Undergraduate Certificate

Governmental Services
Darton College (A)

Graduate Financial Planning Track
The American College (GC)

Graduate Medical Education Core Curriculum
University of Illinois (UC)
University of Illinois at Chicago (UC)

Graduate Teacher Education
Newman University (M)

Graphic Design
The Art Institute Online (A, B)
Savannah College of Art and Design (M)

Graphic Design and Multimedia
Westwood Online (A)

Graphics and Animation-2-D Web Animation Specialty
Bellevue Community College (A)

Group Fitness Instructor
United States Sports Academy (UC)

Guidance and Control (Aeronautics and Astronautics)
Stanford University (GC)

Guidance and Counseling
City University (M)

HACCP/Food Safety Managers
North Carolina State University (UC)

Hawaiian Studies
Maui Community College (B)

Hazardous Waste Engineering
Illinois Institute of Technology (GC)

Hazardous Waste Risk and Remediation
University of Illinois (GC)

Health Administration
Central Michigan University (B)
Montana State University-Billings (M)
University of Phoenix Online Campus (B)
University of Southern Indiana (M)

Health Administration-DHA
Central Michigan University (GC)

Health Administration-Doctor of Health Administration (DHA)
University of Phoenix Online Campus (D)

Health Administrative Services
Weber State University (B)

Health and Human Performance
Northwestern State University of Louisiana (M)

Health and Nutrition Counseling
Thomas Edison State College (B)

Health and Physical Ed-Teacher Ed Option
Darton College (A)

Health and Safety
Indiana State University (M)

Health Arts
University of St. Francis (B)

Health Care Administration
Bellevue University (M, B)
Cardean University (M)
Columbia Southern University (B)
Lynn University (B)
New York Institute of Technology (M)
Oklahoma State University (M)
Saint Joseph's College of Maine (B)
University of Maryland University College (M)
University of Northwestern Ohio (B)

Health Care Administration (MSA)
University of West Florida (M)

Health Care and Second Area
Stephens College (B)

Health Care Business Leadership
Clarkson College (M)

Health Care Business Management
Clarkson College (B)

Health Care Coding and Classification
Weber State University (UC)

Health Care Management
Davenport University Online (M)
Franklin University (B)
Saint Joseph's College of Maine (UC)
University of Phoenix Online Campus (M)

Health Care Management-Health Care Administration
Mountain State University (B)

Health Care Management-Health Care Informatics
Mountain State University (B)

Health Care/Health Services Management
Park University (M)

Health Development Administration
Athabasca University (UC)

Health Informatics
The College of St. Scholastica (UC)
University of Illinois (GC)
University of Illinois at Chicago (UC)

Health Information Administration
Stephens College (B, UC)

Health Information Administration Degree Completion Program
Dakota State University (B)

Health Information Coding Specialist
Montana State University-Great Falls College of Technology (UC)

Health Information Management
Ashworth College (A)
Clarkson College (A, UC)
The College of St. Scholastica (M)
East Carolina University (B)
University of Central Florida (B)
University of Toledo (B)

Health Information Management Degree Completion
The College of St. Scholastica (B)

Health Information Management Technology
Quinebaug Valley Community College (UC)

Health Information Technician
North Dakota State College of Science (A)

Health Information Technology
Davenport University Online (A)
Montana State University-Great Falls College of Technology (A)
Passaic County Community College (A)
Pitt Community College (A)

Health Management
Northeastern University (B)

Health Physics
Illinois Institute of Technology (M)

Health Professions
Youngstown State University (B)

Health Professions and Related Sciences
University of Southern Indiana (B)

Health Professions Education
Florida Gulf Coast University (M)
University of Illinois at Chicago (M)

Health Professions Education-Master of Health Professions Education
University of Illinois (M)

Health Promotion
Florida International University (UC)
Northern Arizona University (B)
Weber State University (B)

Health Promotion (BAS)
Northern Arizona University (B)

Health Science
Cleveland State University (M)
University of St. Augustine for Health Sciences (D)

Health Science and Second Area
Stephens College (B)

Health Science-Master of Health Science (MHSc)
University of St. Augustine for Health Sciences (M)

Health Sciences
Mercy College (M)
Old Dominion University (B)
Touro University International (D, M, B)
University of Medicine and Dentistry of New Jersey (D, M, B)

Health Service Administration
Keiser College (A)

Health Services
Thomas Edison State College (B)
Walden University (M)

Health Services Administration
Davenport University Online (B)
Florida Gulf Coast University (M, B)
Saint Joseph's College of Maine (GC, M)
State University of New York Institute of Technology (M)
State University of New York Institute of Technology (M)
Strayer University (M)
Thomas Edison State College (B)
University of Central Florida (B)
University of Delaware (M)
University of Florida (M)
University of St. Francis (M)

Health Services Administration and Nursing Dual Degree
Saint Joseph's College of Maine (M)

Health Services Education
Thomas Edison State College (B)

Health Services Management
East Carolina University (B)
University of Dallas (GC, M)

Health Services-Community Health
Walden University (D)

Health Services-Health and Human Behavior
Walden University (D)

Health Services-Health Management and Policy
Walden University (D)

Health Services-Health Promotion and Education
Walden University (D)

Health Services, general
Walden University (D)

Health Studies
Texas Woman's University (B)

Health Studies-Health Promotion
The University of Alabama (M)

Health Studies-Master of Health Studies
Athabasca University (M)

Health Studies-Sports Medicine Health Care
The University of Alabama (M)

Health Systems
University of Medicine and Dentistry of New Jersey (M)

Health Systems Administration
Rochester Institute of Technology (M, UC)

Health Systems Finance
Rochester Institute of Technology (GC)

Health/Teacher Education
East Carolina University (M)

Healthcare Accounting
Pitt Community College (UC)

Healthcare Accounting and Financial Management
Indiana University System (UC)

Healthcare Administration
Seton Hall University (M)

Healthcare Leadership and Management
Pitt Community College (UC)

Healthcare Management
Brenau University (M)
Pitt Community College (UC)
Rosalind Franklin University of Medicine and Science (M)

Healthcare Management Concentration (10-month program)
American InterContinental University Online (M)

Healthcare Management Concentration (13-month program)
American InterContinental University Online (B)

Healthcare Management Technology
Pitt Community College (A)

Hearing Healthcare
Arkansas State University-Mountain Home (A)

Heating, Ventilation, and Air Conditioning (HVAC) Systems
University of Idaho (UC)

Heavy Construction Project Management
University of Washington (UC)

Higher Education
Dallas Baptist University (M)
University of Louisville (M)
University of North Dakota (D)

Himalayan Studies
University of Connecticut (UC)

GC–Graduate Certificate; D–Doctorate; M–Master's; A–Associate; B–Bachelor's; UC–Undergraduate Certificate

Hispanic Studies
Texas A&M University (D)

Histologic Technology
Darton College (A)

Historic Preservation
Savannah College of Art and Design (GC, M)

Historical Studies
State University of New York Empire State College (A, B)

History
American Public University System (B)
Buena Vista University (B)
Caldwell College (B)
Darton College (A)
Fort Hays State University (A, B)
Judson College (B)
Southwestern Assemblies of God University (B)
Thomas Edison State College (B)
Troy University Montgomery (A, B)
University of Illinois (B)
University of Illinois at Springfield (B)
University of Maryland University College (B)

History (4 year)
Athabasca University (B)

History and Political Studies
Saint Mary-of-the-Woods College (B)

History Concentration (3 year)
Athabasca University (B)

History Emphasis
Community College of Denver (A)

Home-based Early Childhood Education
Northampton County Area Community College (UC)

Homeland Security
American Public University System (B)
Virginia College at Birmingham (M)

Horticulture
Thomas Edison State College (A, B)

Hospital Health Care Administration
Thomas Edison State College (A, B)

Hospitality Administration
Southern New Hampshire University (M)

Hospitality and Tourism
University of Guelph (M)

Hospitality and Tourism Management
Chemeketa Community College (A)
University of Massachusetts Amherst (B)

Hospitality Management
Central Texas College (A)
Florida International University (M)
New York Institute of Technology (B)
The Pennsylvania State University University Park Campus (UC)

Hospitality Management ASB
Education Direct Center for Degree Studies (A)

Hospitality Studies
University of Guelph (UC)

Hotel and Restaurant Management
Auburn University (M)
Northern Arizona University (B)
Tompkins Cortland Community College (A)

Hotel, Restaurant, and Institutional Management
The Pennsylvania State University University Park Campus (A)
University of Delaware (B)

Hotel/Motel/Restaurant Management
Thomas Edison State College (A, B)

Human and Community Services-Bachelor of Human and Community Services
New Mexico State University (B)

Human and Organizational Development
Fielding Graduate Institute (D)

Human Development
Hope International University (B)
Pacific Oaks College (M, B)
Southern Christian University (B)
State University of New York Empire State College (A, B)
Washington State University (B)

Human Development and Family Studies
The Pennsylvania State University University Park Campus (A)

Human Environmental Sciences-Food and Nutrition
The University of Alabama (M)

Human Environmental Sciences-General Studies Option
The University of Alabama (B)

Human Environmental Sciences-Interactive Technology
The University of Alabama (M)

Human Environmental Sciences-Restaurant and Hospitality Management
The University of Alabama (B)

Human Factors Engineering
Wright State University (M)

Human Nutrition
Eastern Michigan University (M)
University of Bridgeport (M)

Human Performance Coach
United States Sports Academy (UC)

Human Performance Technology (MSA)
University of West Florida (M)

Human Relations and Business
Amberton University (M)

Human Resource Development
Buffalo State College, State University of New York (GC)
Clemson University (M)
Indiana State University (M, B)
Limestone College (B)
Southwestern College (B)

Human Resource Education
University of Louisville (M)

Human Resource Leadership
Southern Christian University (B)

Human Resource Management
Ashworth College (A)
Boston University (M)
Dallas Baptist University (M)
DeVry University Online (M)
Golden Gate University (M)
Saint Mary-of-the-Woods College (B)
Tarleton State University (M)
Thomas Edison State College (A)
Troy University (M)
University of Calgary (UC)

University of Connecticut (M)
University of Maryland University College (B)
University of Phoenix Online Campus (M)
University of Wisconsin-Platteville (UC)
University of Wisconsin-Platteville (UC)
Utah State University (M)
Walden University (M, B)

Human Resource Management and Organizational Development
National University (M)

Human Resource Management Concentration
Colorado Technical University (B)

Human Resource Management Emphasis
City University (M)

Human Resource Management Practice
California National University for Advanced Studies (UC)

Human Resource Management Specialty
Davenport University Online (M)

Human Resources
California National University for Advanced Studies (M)
Indiana Institute of Technology (B)
The Pennsylvania State University University Park Campus (UC)
Saint Paul College-A Community & Technical College (UC)

Human Resources and Labour Relations
Athabasca University (B)

Human Resources Concentration (10-month program)
American InterContinental University Online (M)

Human Resources Concentration (13-month program)
American InterContinental University Online (B)

Human Resources Management
Cardean University (M)
Florida Institute of Technology (M)
New York Institute of Technology (M, B)
Royal Roads University (M)
Southern New Hampshire University (UC)
Stevens Institute of Technology (GC)
Thomas Edison State College (M, B)
Upper Iowa University (B, UC)

Human Science
Athabasca University (B)
Saybrook Graduate School and Research Center (D, M)

Human Science-Post-Diploma
Athabasca University (B)

Human Security and Peacebuilding
Royal Roads University (M)

Human Services
Alaska Pacific University (A, B)
Athabasca University (B)
Bismarck State College (A)
Capella University (D, M)
Dawson Community College (A)
Fort Hays State University (A, B)
Ivy Tech State College-Bloomington (A)
Ivy Tech State College-Central Indiana (A)
Ivy Tech State College-Columbus (A)
Ivy Tech State College-Eastcentral (A)
Ivy Tech State College-Kokomo (A)
Ivy Tech State College-Lafayette (A)
Ivy Tech State College-North Central (A)
Ivy Tech State College-Northeast (A)
Ivy Tech State College-Northwest (A)
Ivy Tech State College-Southcentral (A)
Ivy Tech State College-Southeast (A)
Ivy Tech State College-Southwest (A)
Ivy Tech State College-Wabash Valley (A)
Ivy Tech State College-Whitewater (A)
Mount Wachusett Community College (A)
Saint Joseph's College of Maine (A)
Saint Mary-of-the-Woods College (B)
Upper Iowa University (B)
Western Washington University (B)

Human Services Counseling
Old Dominion University (B)
Regent University (M)
Southwestern Assemblies of God University (M)

Human Services Criminal Justice for Juvenile Justice Practitioners
Concordia University, St. Paul (M)

Human Services-Clinical Social Work
Walden University (D)

Human Services-Counseling
Walden University (D)

Human Services-Criminal Justice
Concordia University, St. Paul (M)
Walden University (D)

Human Services-Family Life Education
Concordia University, St. Paul (M)

Human Services-Family Studies and Intervention Strategies
Walden University (D)

Human Services-Human Services Administration
Walden University (D)

Human Services-Self-Designed
Walden University (D)

Human Services-Social Policy Analysis and Planning
Walden University (D)

Human Services, general
Walden University (D)

Human Services/Management
University of Phoenix Online Campus (B)

Humane and Environmental Studies (MNM)
Regis University (GC)

Humanitarian Services Administration
University of Connecticut (GC, M)

Humanities
California State University, Dominguez Hills (M)
Maysville Community College (A)
Prescott College (M, B)
Saint Mary-of-the-Woods College (A, B)
Thomas Edison State College (B)
University of Maryland University College (B)
University of Waterloo (B)
Washington State University (B)

Humanities (4 year)
Athabasca University (B)

Humanities Concentration (3 year)
Athabasca University (B)

GC–Graduate Certificate; D–Doctorate; M–Master's; A–Associate; B–Bachelor's; UC–Undergraduate Certificate

Humanities-Transformative Learning and Change
California Institute of Integral Studies (D)

Humanities/Philosophy Emphasis
Community College of Denver (A)

Illustration
Syracuse University (M)

Imaging Science
Rochester Institute of Technology (M)

iMBA
The Pennsylvania State University University Park Campus (M)

Inclusive Education
Athabasca University (UC)

Independent Studies-Bachelor of Independent Studies/General Studies
Murray State University (B)

Individual Studies
Jefferson Community College (A)

Individualized
Metropolitan State University (B)

Individualized Degree Plan
Regent University (M)

Individualized Major
University of Wisconsin-Superior (B)

Individualized Studies
Ohio University (A)
Skidmore College (B)

Individualized Transfer Studies
Northampton County Area Community College (A)

Individualized/Interdisciplinary Major
Madonna University (B)

Individually Designed Focus Area
DePaul University (B)

Indoor Air Quality
Illinois Institute of Technology (GC)

Industrial and Systems Engineering
Auburn University (M)
Georgia Institute of Technology (M)
The University of Alabama in Huntsville (D)

Industrial Distribution Technology
Darton College (A)

Industrial Engineering
Colorado State University (D, M)
Columbia University (UC)
Mississippi State University (M)
The University of Alabama in Huntsville (M)
The University of Texas at Arlington (M)

Industrial Engineering Technology AST
Education Direct Center for Degree Studies (A)

Industrial Environmental Management
Rochester Institute of Technology (UC)

Industrial Hygiene
Montana Tech of The University of Montana (M)

Industrial Management
Central Missouri State University (M)
Central Missouri State University (M)

Industrial Supervision
Indiana State University (B)

Industrial Technology
Bemidji State University (M)
East Carolina University (B)
Indiana State University (B)
Roger Williams University (B)

Industrial Technology and Operations
Illinois Institute of Technology (M)

Industrial Technology-Bachelor of Applied Science in Industrial Technology (Two-Year Completion)
Southwest Missouri State University (B)

Industrial Technology-Computer Networking Management
East Carolina University (M)

Industrial Technology-Digital Communication Technology
East Carolina University (M)

Industrial Technology-Distribution and Logistics
East Carolina University (M)

Industrial Technology-Information Security
East Carolina University (M)

Industrial Technology-Manufacturing
East Carolina University (M)

Industrial Technology-Performance Improvement
East Carolina University (M)

Industrial/Organizational Psychology
Kansas State University (M)

Information and Computer Sciences
Maui Community College (M, B)

Information and Computer Security
Davenport University Online (A, B, UC)

Information and Telecommunication Systems Management
Capitol College (M)

Information Architecture
Capitol College (M)

Information Assurance
Iowa State University of Science and Technology (UC)
Norwich University (M)
University of Dallas (M, GC, M)

Information Engineering and Management
Southern Methodist University (M)

Information Management
Aspen University (M)
Buena Vista University (B)
Grantham University (M)
Syracuse University (M)
Syracuse University (M)

Information Management Technology
Grantham University (M)

Information Management-Project Management
Grantham University (M)

Information Networking and Telecommunications
Fort Hays State University (A, B)

Information Networks Professional
Northeastern University (UC)

Information Processing Specialist
Bismarck State College (UC)

Information Resource Management
Central Michigan University (M)

Information Science and Technology
Colorado State University (UC)

The Pennsylvania State University University Park Campus (UC)

Information Sciences
Nova Southeastern University (D)
Tarleton State University (M)

Information Security
James Madison University (M)
Nova Southeastern University (M)

Information Security Management
Syracuse University (GC)

Information Studies
Florida State University (M)

Information Systems
American College of Computer & Information Sciences (M, B)
Aspen University (M)
Athabasca University (M)
City University (GC)
Columbia Union College (B)
Columbia University (UC)
Dakota State University (M)
DePaul University (M)
Fairleigh Dickinson University, Metropolitan Campus (UC)
Grantham University (A, B)
National University (M, B)
New Jersey Institute of Technology (B)
Northeastern University (M)
Nova Southeastern University (D)
Randolph Community College (A)
Shippensburg University of Pennsylvania (M)
Strayer University (M)
University of Great Falls (M)
University of Illinois (GC)
University of Maryland, Baltimore County (M)
University of North Dakota (B)
The University of Tennessee (M)
University of the Incarnate Word (A)

Information Systems (4 year)
Athabasca University (B)

Information Systems and Information Security
The University of North Carolina at Charlotte (GC)

Information Systems and Telecommunications Management
Syracuse University (GC)

Information Systems Concentration (3 year)
Athabasca University (B)

Information Systems Design
New Jersey Institute of Technology (UC)

Information Systems Emphasis
City University (M)

Information Systems Generalist
Pitt Community College (A)

Information Systems Implementation
New Jersey Institute of Technology (UC)

Information Systems Management
DeVry University Online (M)
University of Maryland University College (B)

Information Systems Security
Westwood Online (B)

Information Systems Security Concentration
Colorado Technical University (M)

Information Systems Technology
Northern Virginia Community College (UC)
Patrick Henry Community College (A)
Pitt Community College (UC)
University of Central Florida (B)
University of Northwestern Ohio (A)

Information Systems-Information Technology
Walden University (B)

Information Systems, general
Walden University (B)

Information Technologies
East Carolina University (B)

Information Technology
Capella University (M, B)
College for Lifelong Learning (B)
Columbia Southern University (B)
DePaul University (M)
DeVry University Online (B)
Everglades University (B)
Franklin University (A, B)
Golden Gate University (M, B)
Grantham University (M)
Jones International University (B)
Kettering University (M)
Memorial University of Newfoundland (M)
National University (B)
Rochester Institute of Technology (M)
Southern New Hampshire University (A, B)
University of Dallas (GC, M)
University of Maryland University College (M)
University of Massachusetts Lowell (A, B)
University of Phoenix Online Campus (B)
Virginia Polytechnic Institute and State University (M)

Information Technology (10-month program)
American InterContinental University Online (M)

Information Technology Basics
Lansing Community College (UC)

Information Technology Concentration
Colorado Technical University (B)

Information Technology Fluency
Bristol Community College (UC)

Information Technology Focus
University of Connecticut (B)

Information Technology Management
Athabasca University (M)
Illinois Institute of Technology (M)
Mount Saint Vincent University (UC)
Saint Joseph's College of Maine (A, UC)
Touro University International (M, B)
University of Management and Technology (B)

Information Technology Management Concentration
Colorado Technical University (M)

Information Technology Management for Law Enforcement
Franklin Pierce College (M)

Information Technology Networking Option
Hopkinsville Community College (A)

Information Technology Online
Bryant and Stratton Online (A)

Information Technology with Business Information Systems Concentration
Peirce College (A)

GC–Graduate Certificate; D–Doctorate; M–Master's; A–Associate; B–Bachelor's; UC–Undergraduate Certificate

Information Technology with Business Minor
University of Massachusetts Lowell (B)

Information Technology with Networking Concentration
Peirce College (A, B)

Information Technology with Technology Management Concentration
Peirce College (A, B)

Information Technology-Bachelor of Science in Information Technology (BSIT)
New Jersey Institute of Technology (B)

Information Technology-BIT (13-month program)
American InterContinental University Online (B)

Information Technology-Help Desk Technician
Peirce College (UC)

Information Technology-Web Content Development
University of Connecticut (UC)

Information Technology-Web Systems Administration
University of Connecticut (UC)

Information Technology-Windows Networking Operating Systems
Peirce College (UC)

Infrastructure Construction
University of Washington (UC)

Instructional and Performance Technology
Boise State University (M)
Boise State University (M)

Instructional Design
Roosevelt University (GC)
University of Massachusetts Boston (M)

Instructional Design and Technology
California State University, Fullerton (M)

Instructional Systems Development
University of Maryland, Baltimore County (GC)

Instructional Systems Development-Training Systems
University of Maryland, Baltimore County (M)

Instructional Systems-Distance Learning Major
Florida State University (M)

Instructional Technology
Boston University (GC)
Boston University (GC)
East Carolina University (M)
National University (M)
New York Institute of Technology (M)
Troy University (M)
University of Houston-Clear Lake (M)
University of Nebraska at Kearney (M)
University of Nevada, Las Vegas (GC)
University of the Incarnate Word (M)
University of West Florida (M)

Instructional Technology Design
University of Massachusetts Boston (GC)

Instructional Technology Education Specialist
Bloomsburg University of Pennsylvania (M)

Instructional Technology Specialist
Southwest Missouri State University (GC)

Instructional Technology Systems
DePaul University (M)

Instructional Technology-Curriculum and Instruction Emphasis
Virginia Polytechnic Institute and State University (M)

Instructional Technology-Distance Education Emphasis
Texas Tech University (M)

Instructional Technology-Educational Technology Emphasis
Utah State University (M)

Instructional/Educational Technology
University of Central Florida (GC, M)

Insurance
Indiana State University (B)
Thomas Edison State College (A, B)

Insurance Management-Master of Science in Insurance Management
Boston University (M)

Integrated Circuits
University of Illinois (GC)

Integrated Health Systems
Rochester Institute of Technology (GC)

Integrated Marketing Communications
Golden Gate University (M)
West Virginia University (M, UC)

Integrated Microsystems
University of Michigan (M)

Integrated Studies
Athabasca University (M)
Endicott College (M)

Integrated Technology and Learning
City University (M)

Integrating Arts and Performance Learning
City University (M)

Integrative Professional Studies
Davenport University Online (B)

Intelligent Information Systems
Illinois Institute of Technology (GC)

Intelligent Systems
Columbia University (UC)

Interactive Design
Savannah College of Art and Design (GC)

Interactive Marketing
Walsh College of Accountancy and Business Administration (UC)

Interactive Media Design
The Art Institute Online (A, B)

Intercultural Ministries Degree Completion
Northwestern College (B)

Intercultural Studies
Crown College (M)

Interdepartmental Studies-Judaic Studies
The Jewish Theological Seminary (M)

Interdisciplinary
Union Institute & University (M)

Interdisciplinary Early Childhood Education
Western Kentucky University (A)

Interdisciplinary Program in Technical Studies
University of Toledo (A)

Interdisciplinary Social Sciences
Kansas State University (B)

Interdisciplinary Studies
Adams State College (B)
American Public University System (B)
Columbia College (B)
Marylhurst University (B)
Mississippi State University (B)
New York Institute of Technology (B)
North Central University (B)
State University of New York Empire State College (A, B)
Union Institute & University (D)
The University of Alabama (B)

Interdisciplinary Studies-Biology
Mountain State University (B)

Interdisciplinary Studies-Environmental Studies
Mountain State University (B)

Interdisciplinary Studies-Health Services Management
Mountain State University (B)

Interdisciplinary Studies-Natural Sciences
Mountain State University (B)

Interdisciplinary Studies-Pre-Medicine
Mountain State University (B)

Interdisciplinary Studies-Psychology
Mountain State University (B)

Interdisciplinary Studies-Social and Behavioral Sciences
Mountain State University (B)

Interdisciplinary Studies, Human Relations in Organizations
Maui Community College (B)

Interdisciplinary Studies, Information Resource Management
Maui Community College (B)

Interdisciplinary Studies/Behavioral Sciences
New York Institute of Technology (B)

Interdisciplinary Studies/Business
New York Institute of Technology (B)

Interdisciplinary Studies/Communication Arts
New York Institute of Technology (B)

Interdisciplinary Studies/Computer Science
New York Institute of Technology (B)

Interdisciplinary Studies/English
New York Institute of Technology (B)

Interdisciplinary Studies/Hospitality Management
New York Institute of Technology (B)

Interdisciplinary Studies/Humanities
New York Institute of Technology (B)

Interdisciplinary Studies/Labor Relations
New York Institute of Technology (B)

Interdisciplinary Studies/Math-Physics
New York Institute of Technology (B)

Interdisciplinary Studies/Social Sciences
New York Institute of Technology (B)

Interdisciplinary Studies/Technical Writing
New York Institute of Technology (B)

Interdisciplinary Studies/Technology
New York Institute of Technology (B)

Interdisciplinary Studies/Telecommunications Management
New York Institute of Technology (B)

Interior Design
The Art Institute Online (B)
Northern Arizona University (B)

International
University of the Incarnate Word (M)

International Affairs
Tufts University (M)

International Business
Caldwell College (B)
Champlain College (UC)
Excelsior College (B)
Florida International University (B)
Golden Gate University (M)
Lansing Community College (A)
National University (UC)
New York Institute of Technology (B)
Park University (M)
Southern New Hampshire University (GC, M, B)
Strayer University (B)
Thomas Edison State College (A, B)
University of Wisconsin-Platteville (UC)
University of Wisconsin-Platteville (UC)

International Business Administration
Teikyo Post University (B, UC)

International Business and Management of Information Technology
Schiller International University (M)

International Business Emphasis
Community College of Denver (A)

International Construction Management
University of Florida (M)

International Development
Hope International University (M)

International Health Care
Saint Joseph's College of Maine (GC)

International Management
University of Management and Technology (B)
University of Phoenix Online Campus (M)

International Masters in Management Program (IMM)
Purdue University (M)

International Peace and Conflict Resolution
American Public University System (M, B)

International Regulatory Affairs
Northeastern University (GC)

International Relations
American Public University System (B)
St. Mary's University of San Antonio (M)
Salve Regina University (M)
Troy University (M)

International Security
Stanford University (GC)

GC–Graduate Certificate; D–Doctorate; M–Master's; A–Associate; B–Bachelor's; UC–Undergraduate Certificate

International Sport Diploma
United States Sports Academy (UC)

International Studies
Montgomery County Community College (UC)

International Taxation
Golden Gate University (GC)

International Tourism Management
Northern Arizona University (UC)

Internet
Illinois Institute of Technology (GC)

Internet and E-Commerce
Mountain State University (B)

Internet Applications Development
New Jersey Institute of Technology (UC)

Internet Business Systems
Mercy College (M)

Internet for Business
Lansing Community College (UC)

Internet Programming
University of Washington (UC)

Internet SQL
Texas State Technical College-Waco (UC)

Internet Systems and Software Technology
Bellevue University (B)

Internet Technologies
Northeastern University (UC)
Pace University (GC)
University of Wisconsin-Milwaukee (UC)

Internet Technology
Pace University (GC)

Internet Technology for E-Commerce
Pace University (M)

Internet Technology Multimedia and Design AST
Education Direct Center for Degree Studies (A)

Internet Technology Web Programming AST
Education Direct Center for Degree Studies (A)

Internet Technology-E-Commerce Administration AST
Education Direct Center for Degree Studies (A)

Internetworking
Fort Hays State University (UC)

Intranet Development
University of Massachusetts Lowell (UC)

Introduction to Programming
Rochester Institute of Technology (UC)

Irish Studies
Regis University (UC)

IT Business Information Systems
Virginia Polytechnic Institute and State University (GC)

IT Communication
Virginia Polytechnic Institute and State University (GC)

IT Decision Support Systems
Virginia Polytechnic Institute and State University (GC)

IT Networking
Virginia Polytechnic Institute and State University (GC)

Java 2 Programming
University of Washington (UC)

Java Programming
Regis University (UC)

Jewish Education
The Jewish Theological Seminary (M)

Jewish Education-Master of Science in Jewish Education (MSJE)
Spertus Institute of Jewish Studies (M)

Jewish Studies
California State University, Chico (B)
Hebrew College (M)
Spertus Institute of Jewish Studies (D, M)

Journalism
Regent University (M)
Saint Mary-of-the-Woods College (B)
Thomas Edison State College (B)

Journalism and Mass Communication
Darton College (A)

Journalism and Mass Communications
University of Nebraska-Lincoln (M)

Journalism Education Focus
University of Missouri-Columbia (M)

Journalism-Media Management
University of Missouri-Columbia (M)

Journalism-Strategic Communications
University of Missouri-Columbia (M)

Justice Administration
Norwich University (M)
Taylor University (A)

Justice Administration-Ministry Concentration
Taylor University (A)

Justice Administration-Public Policy Concentration
Taylor University (A)

Justice and Ministry
Taylor University (UC)
Taylor University (UC)

Justice Studies
Fort Hays State University (B)
Royal Roads University (B)

Justice Studies Information Networking
Fort Hays State University (UC)

Justice Systems and Policy Planning (BAS)
Northern Arizona University (B)

K-12 Educators and Administration
Jones International University (M)

Kindergarten-Elementary Education
Saint Mary-of-the-Woods College (B)

Kinesiology
The University of Texas at Tyler (M)
The University of Texas of the Permian Basin (M)
The University of Texas System (M)

Kinesiology and Health
University of Wyoming (M)

Knowledge and Learning Management
Walden University (M)

Knowledge Management
Northeastern University (GC)
Walden University (M)

Labor Studies
State University of New York Empire State College (A, B)
Thomas Edison State College (B)

Labor Studies and Industrial Relations
The Pennsylvania State University University Park Campus (UC)

Laboratory Animal Science
Thomas Edison State College (A, B)

Labour Studies
Athabasca University (UC)

Labour Studies (4 year)
Athabasca University (B)

Labour Studies Concentration (3 year)
Athabasca University (B)

Land Surveying
University of Wyoming (UC)

Latin
University of Florida (M)

Law Enforcement
Baltimore City Community College (A)
Indiana State University (UC)
Metropolitan State University (GC)
Missouri Southern State University (A)

Leadership
Bellevue University (M, B)
Cardean University (M)
Franklin Pierce College (M)
New York Institute of Technology (M)
Pitt Community College (UC)
University of Denver (GC)
University of Guelph (M)

Leadership (Graduate Studies Certificate)
Regent University (GC)

Leadership (MNM)
Regis University (GC)

Leadership and Business Ethics
Duquesne University (M)

Leadership and Human Performance
University of Wisconsin-Platteville (UC)
University of Wisconsin-Platteville (UC)

Leadership and Liberal Studies
Duquesne University (M)

Leadership and Organizational Transformation (Weekend Program)
Saybrook Graduate School and Research Center (M)

Leadership and Training
Royal Roads University (M)

Leadership Development
Brenau University (M)
Taylor University (UC)
Taylor University (UC)

Leadership in Organizations
Rappahannock Community College (UC)

Leadership Specialization
University of Denver (M)

Leadership Studies
Madonna University (M)
Memorial University of Newfoundland (M)

Leadership Studies-Healthcare
Madonna University (M)

Leading Organizational Transformation
Saybrook Graduate School and Research Center (GC)

Learning, Design and Technology
Stanford University (M)

LEEP-Library and Information Science
University of Illinois (M)

Legal Assistant/Paralegal
Florida Metropolitan University-Brandon Campus (A)

Legal Assisting
University of Northwestern Ohio (A)

Legal Office
North Harris Montgomery Community College District (A)

Legal Services
Thomas Edison State College (A, B)

Legal Studies
Brevard Community College (A)
Teikyo Post University (A, B, UC)
University of Maryland University College (B)

Legal Studies-Law and Public Policy
California University of Pennsylvania (M)

Letters, Arts, and Sciences
The Pennsylvania State University University Park Campus (A, B)

Liberal Arts
Bethany College of the Assemblies of God (B)
Brookdale Community College (A)
Bucks County Community College (A)
Citrus College (A)
Excelsior College (A, B)
Greenville Technical College (A)
Kirkwood Community College (A)
Lake Region State College (A)
Maui Community College (A)
Metropolitan Community College (A)
Minot State University-Bottineau Campus (A)
Monroe Community College (A)
Mountain Empire Community College (A)
Northern Virginia Community College (A)
St. Cloud State University (A)
St. John's University (A)
San Bernardino Valley College (A)
Schoolcraft College (A)
Seattle Central Community College (A)
Southern New Hampshire University (A)
Syracuse University (A)
Taft College (A)
Taylor University (A)
University of Alaska Southeast (B)
University of Arkansas at Little Rock (B)
The University of Maine at Augusta (A)
University of Wisconsin Colleges (A)
Upper Iowa University (A)

Liberal Arts (BLA)
University of Massachusetts Lowell (B)

Liberal Arts and General Studies
Dallas County Community College District (A)
Mount Saint Vincent University (B)

Liberal Arts and Humanities
Cayuga County Community College (A)

GC–Graduate Certificate; D–Doctorate; M–Master's; A–Associate; B–Bachelor's; UC–Undergraduate Certificate

Liberal Arts and Sciences
Burlington County College (A)
Mercy College (A)
Middlesex Community College (A)
Rockland Community College (A)
Sinclair Community College (A)
Union Institute & University (B)

Liberal Arts and Sciences/Mathematics and Sciences
Cayuga County Community College (A)

Liberal Arts and Studies
Iowa Western Community College (A)

Liberal Arts with Business Minor
Northeastern University (B)

Liberal Arts-History Concentration
Taylor University (A)

Liberal Arts-Humanities and Social Science
Jefferson Community College (A)

Liberal Arts-Interdisciplinary Concentration
Taylor University (A)

Liberal Arts-Master of Liberal Arts
Texas Christian University (GC)

Liberal Arts-Social Science
Colorado State University (B)

Liberal Arts-Social Science Concentration
Taylor University (A)

Liberal Arts, General Studies, Humanities
Andrews University (A, B)

Liberal Arts/General Studies
Thomas Edison State College (A)

Liberal Arts/Humanities and Social Science
Clinton Community College (A)

Liberal Education
Lake Superior College (A)

Liberal Studies
Alaska Pacific University (A, B)
California State University, Chico (B)
Eastern Oregon University (B)
Excelsior College (M, B)
Fort Hays State University (M)
Limestone College (A, B)
Maui Community College (B)
Middlesex Community College (A)
Middle Tennessee State University (B)
Montgomery County Community College (A)
Oral Roberts University (B)
Oregon State University (B)
Salve Regina University (B)
Sonoma State University (B)
Southern Christian University (B)
State University of New York Empire State College (M)
Stony Brook University, State University of New York (M)
Syracuse University (B)
Thomas Edison State College (B)
University of Central Florida (B)
University of Illinois (B)
University of Illinois at Springfield (B)
The University of Iowa (B)
The University of Maine at Augusta (A)
The University of North Carolina at Greensboro (M)
University of Northern Iowa (B)
University of the Incarnate Word (A)
University of Toledo (M)

Liberal Studies (Humanities Concentration)
The University of North Carolina at Greensboro (B)

Liberal Studies Degree Completion
California State University, Monterey Bay (B)

Liberal Studies-Management and Communication Concentration
Montana State University-Billings (B)

Library and Information Science
Maui Community College (M)
Syracuse University (M)
Syracuse University (M)
University of Illinois at Urbana-Champaign (GC, M)
University of Missouri-Columbia (M)
University of Washington (M)
University of Wisconsin-Milwaukee (M)

Library and Information Sciences
University of South Carolina (M)

Library and Information Services
The University of Maine at Augusta (A, B)

Library and Information Studies
The University of North Carolina at Greensboro (M)

Library Information Science
University of Southern Mississippi (M)

Library Information Technology
Central Missouri State University (M)
Central Missouri State University (M)

Library Media
The University of Montana-Missoula (UC)

Library Media Education
Western Kentucky University (M)

Library Media Services
Indiana State University (GC, UC)

Library Media Teaching
Azusa Pacific University (UC)

Library Science
Clarion University of Pennsylvania (M)
Connecticut State University System (M)
East Carolina University (M)
Texas Woman's University (M)

Library Science and Information Services
Central Missouri State University (M)
Central Missouri State University (M)

Library Studies
Memorial University of Newfoundland (UC)

Library Technical Services
Northampton County Area Community College (UC)

Life Sciences
University of Maryland, College Park (UC)

Literacy Focus
University of Missouri-Columbia (M)

Logistics
Thomas Edison State College (B)

Logistics and Supply Chain Management
The Pennsylvania State University University Park Campus (GC)

Logistics Management
Florida Institute of Technology (M)

Long-Term Care
Saint Joseph's College of Maine (GC)

Long-Term Care Administration
Saint Joseph's College of Maine (B, UC)

Loss Prevention and Safety
Eastern Kentucky University (M)

Low Vision Rehabilitation
Pennsylvania College of Optometry (M, UC)

LUTC Fellow Designation
The American College (UC)

Maine Studies
University of Maine (UC)

Maintenance and Reliability Engineering
The University of Tennessee (GC)

Management
Amberton University (M, B)
American Public University System (M, B)
Ashworth College (A)
Athabasca University (GC)
Bellevue University (M, B)
Brenau University (B)
Bucks County Community College (A, UC)
Caldwell College (B)
Champlain College (A, UC)
Dallas Baptist University (M, B)
Darton College (A)
Davenport University Online (A)
Embry-Riddle Aeronautical University, Extended Campus (M)
Florida Atlantic University (M)
Florida Institute of Technology (M)
Franklin Pierce College (A, B)
Franklin University (B)
Golden Gate University (M, B)
Hope International University (M)
Indiana Institute of Technology (A, B)
Indiana Wesleyan University (M)
Marylhurst University (B)
Metropolitan State University (B)
National University (M)
North Harris Montgomery Community College District (A)
Park University (B)
Prescott College (B)
Regent University (M)
Regis University (M)
Saint Joseph's College of Maine (A)
Salve Regina University (M, UC)
Stephens College (M)
Teikyo Post University (A, B)
Thomas Edison State College (M)
Troy University (M)
Troy University-Florida Region (B)
University of Houston-Victoria (B)
University of Management and Technology (M, B)
University of Maryland University College (M)
University of Phoenix Online Campus (M, B)
University of St. Francis (M)
Upper Iowa University (B)
Walden University (B)
Walsh College of Accountancy and Business Administration (M)
Worcester Polytechnic Institute (GC, M)

Management (3 year)
Athabasca University (B)

Management (4 year)
Athabasca University (B)

Management (BSBA)
Northern Arizona University (B)

Management Advisory Services
Southern New Hampshire University (B)

Management and Correctional Administration
Salve Regina University (UC)

Management and Forensics
Stevens Institute of Technology (M)

Management and Leadership
Judson College (B)

Management Application and Principles
Pitt Community College (UC)

Management Communication
Southern Christian University (B)

Management Concentration
Colorado Technical University (B)

Management Concentration (13-month program)
American InterContinental University Online (B)

Management Development
University of Louisville (UC)

Management Emphasis, General Management
Community College of Denver (A)

Management Essentials
New Jersey Institute of Technology (M)

Management Information Sciences
Franklin University (B)

Management Information Systems
American College of Computer & Information Sciences (B)
Auburn University (M)
Bellevue University (B)
Dallas Baptist University (M, B)
Excelsior College (B)
Northeastern University (A)
Nova Southeastern University (M)
Raritan Valley Community College (A)
Regis University (UC)
Stevens Institute of Technology (GC)
Strayer University (M)
University of Illinois (M)
University of Illinois at Springfield (M)
University of Management and Technology (M)
Virginia College at Birmingham (B)

Management of Human Resources
Bellevue University (B)
Excelsior College (B)

Management of Information Systems
Cardean University (M)
Keiser College (B)
New York Institute of Technology (M, B)

Management of Information Technology
Schiller International University (M)

Management of Technology
Cardean University (M)
New Jersey Institute of Technology (M)
New York Institute of Technology (M)
Walden University (M)

Management of Technology (MSCIT)
Regis University (GC)

Management Post-Diploma (3 year)
Athabasca University (B)

Management Post-Diploma (4 year)
Athabasca University (B)

GC–Graduate Certificate; D–Doctorate; M–Master's; A–Associate; B–Bachelor's; UC–Undergraduate Certificate

Management Science and Engineering
Stanford University (GC, M)

Management Science/Technology Management-Master of Applied Science Management Science, Technology Management
University of Waterloo (M)

Management Studies
University of Maryland University College (B)

Management-Bachelor Completion Program
Indiana Wesleyan University (B)

Management-Financial Administration Specialty
Davenport University Online (B)

Management-General Management Emphasis
City University (M)

Management-Human Resource Management Emphasis
City University (M)

Management-Human Resource Management Specialty
Davenport University Online (B)

Management-Individualized Study Emphasis
City University (M)

Management-Manufacturing Management Specialty
Davenport University Online (B)

Management, general
Dallas Baptist University (M)
Thomas Edison State College (A, B)
University of Calgary (UC)
University of Dallas (GC, M)
University of Management and Technology (M)
The University of Texas at Arlington (M)

Management/Computer Information Systems
Park University (B)

Management/Human Resources
Park University (B)

Management/Marketing
Park University (B)

Managerial Accounting
New York Institute of Technology (B)

Managerial Leadership Emphasis
City University (M)

Managerial/Small Business Accounting
Pitt Community College (UC)

Managing Innovation and Information Technology
Champlain College (M)

Manufacturing
University College of Cape Breton (B)

Manufacturing Engineering
Columbia University (UC)
Illinois Institute of Technology (M)
University of Michigan (M)
University of Washington (M)

Manufacturing Engineering Technology
Thomas Edison State College (A, B)

Manufacturing Management
Kettering University (M)

Manufacturing Systems Engineering
Lehigh University (M)

Manufacturing Systems Management
Southern Methodist University (M)

Marine Engineering Technology
Thomas Edison State College (A, B)

Marine Science
Maui Community College (B)

Maritime Studies
University of West Florida (B)

Maritime Studies-Bachelor of Maritime Studies (BMS)
Memorial University of Newfoundland (B)

Marketing
Adirondack Community College (A)
American Public University System (B)
Bucks County Community College (A)
Caldwell College (B)
Cardean University (M)
City University (GC, UC)
Columbus State Community College (A)
Davenport University Online (A)
Excelsior College (B)
Franklin Pierce College (A, B)
Golden Gate University (GC, M)
Indiana Institute of Technology (B)
Lakeland College (B)
Metropolitan State University (B)
Mountain State University (A, B)
National University (UC)
New York Institute of Technology (M, B)
Pitt Community College (UC)
Regis University (B)
St. Cloud State University (M)
Saint Mary-of-the-Woods College (B)
Southern New Hampshire University (A, B)
Strayer University (A)
Teikyo Post University (A, B)
Thomas Edison State College (A, B)
University of Houston-Victoria (B)
University of Maryland University College (B)
University of Northwestern Ohio (A)
Upper Iowa University (B, UC)
Walden University (M, B)

Marketing and Sales Technology
University of Toledo (A, UC)

Marketing Concentration
Colorado Technical University (B)

Marketing Concentration (10-month program)
American InterContinental University Online (M)

Marketing Concentration (13-month program)
American InterContinental University Online (B)

Marketing Emphasis
City University (M)
Community College of Denver (A)

Marketing Management
Bellevue University (B)
Concordia University, St. Paul (B)
The Pennsylvania State University University Park Campus (UC)
University of Dallas (GC, M)
University of Management and Technology (B)

Marketing Strategy in the Digital Age
University of Illinois (GC)
University of Illinois at Chicago (UC)

Marketing-Advertising/Promotion Specialty
Davenport University Online (B)

Marketing-Business to Business Specialty
Davenport University Online (B)

Marketing-E-Business Specialty
Davenport University Online (B)

Marketing-Marketing Management Specialty
Davenport University Online (B)

Marketing, Management, and Technology
University of Northwestern Ohio (A)

Marriage and Family Therapy
Saybrook Graduate School and Research Center (M)
Southern Christian University (M)

Marriage Education (for credit)
University of Bridgeport (UC)

Marriage Education (non-credit)
University of Bridgeport (UC)

Mass Communication and Journalism
City University (B)

Master Apostolic Catechetical Diploma
The Catholic Distance University (GC)

Master Reading Teacher
The University of Texas System (UC)

Material Acquisition Management
Florida Institute of Technology (M)

Materials
University of Illinois (GC)

Materials and Science Engineering
Illinois Institute of Technology (M)

Materials Engineering
Auburn University (M)

Materials Failure
University of Illinois (GC)

Materials Science and Engineering
Columbia University (M, UC)
University of Florida (M)
University of Washington (M)

Math
Chadron State College (M)

Math Teacher Link
University of Illinois (GC)

Mathematics
Middle Tennessee State University (M)
Montana State University-Bozeman (M)
Northern Arizona University (M)
Ohio University (A)
Saint Mary-of-the-Woods College (B)
Thomas Edison State College (A, B)
University of Illinois (B)

Mathematics Education
Florida State University (M)

Mathematics-Teaching Track
Texas A&M University (M)

Maîtrise en éducation-enseignement du FLS
Universite Sainte-Anne (M)

Mechanical and Aerospace Engineering
Illinois Institute of Technology (M)
University of Florida (M)

Mechanical Design Technology
Indiana State University (B)

Mechanical Engineering
Auburn University (M)
Bradley University (M)
Colorado State University (D, M)
Columbia University (GC, M)
Georgia Institute of Technology (M)
Iowa State University of Science and Technology (M)
Kansas State University (M)
Michigan Technological University (D, M)
Mississippi State University (M)
North Carolina State University (M)
Oklahoma State University (M)
Southern Methodist University (M)
Stanford University (M)
The University of Alabama (B)
University of Delaware (M)
University of Idaho (M)
University of Illinois (M)
University of North Dakota (B)
University of South Carolina (D, M)
The University of Texas at Arlington (M)
University of Washington (M)
University of Wisconsin-Madison (M)

Mechanical Engineering Technology
Old Dominion University (B)
Thomas Edison State College (A, B)

Mechanical Engineering Technology AST
Education Direct Center for Degree Studies (A)

Mechanics and Maintenance
Thomas Edison State College (A)

Med-Assistive Technology
University of Louisville (M)

Media
Southwestern Assemblies of God University (A)

Media Communication, Communication Management Emphasis
Webster University (M)

Media Psychology
Fielding Graduate Institute (D)

Medical Assistant Technology
University of Northwestern Ohio (A)

Medical Administrative Secretary
Minnesota State College-Southeast Technical (A)

Medical and Dental Practice Administration
Madonna University (M)

Medical Assistant
Minot State University-Bottineau Campus (A, UC)

Medical Assisting
Mountain State University (A)

Medical Assisting (ASMA)
Keiser College (A)

Medical Billing
Davenport University Online (UC)

Medical Billing Specialist
Montana State University-Great Falls College of Technology (UC)

Medical Coding
Davenport University Online (UC)

GC–Graduate Certificate; D–Doctorate; M–Master's; A–Associate; B–Bachelor's; UC–Undergraduate Certificate

Medical Coding and Insurance Specialist
Minot State University-Bottineau Campus (UC)

Medical Coding Specialist
Southwest Wisconsin Technical College (UC)

Medical Imaging
Clarkson College (B)
Thomas Edison State College (A, B)

Medical Lab Tech
Hibbing Community College (A)

Medical Laboratory Technician
South Central Technical College (A)

Medical Laboratory Technology
Central Virginia Community College (A)
Darton College (A)
St. Petersburg College (A)

Medical Office Assistant
Edison State Community College (A)

Medical Office Coding Specialist
Sinclair Community College (UC)

Medical Office Technology
Arapahoe Community College (A)

Medical Office Technology, Health Information Specialist–Medical Records Emphasis
Community College of Denver (UC)

Medical Physics
Georgia Institute of Technology (M)

Medical Secretary
Minnesota State College-Southeast Technical (UC)
Minot State University-Bottineau Campus (A)

Medical Secretary Transcriptionist
Minnesota State College-Southeast Technical (UC)

Medical Transcription
Montana State University-Great Falls College of Technology (UC)
North Dakota State College of Science (UC)
Southwest Wisconsin Technical College (UC)

Mental Health and Human Services
The University of Maine at Augusta (B)

Mental Health and Rehabilitation Services
Thomas Edison State College (B)

Mental Health Practices in Schools
University of Missouri-Columbia (M)

Microcomputer Applications Career Studies
Rappahannock Community College (UC)

Microcomputer Database Specialist
Lansing Community College (UC)

Microcomputer Office Specialist
Lake Superior College (UC)

Microcomputer Support Specialist
Minnesota State College-Southeast Technical (A)

Microcomputers
Des Moines Area Community College (UC)

Microelectronics and Photonics
Stevens Institute of Technology (M)

Microelectronics Manufacturing Engineering
Rochester Institute of Technology (M)

Microsoft Certified Systems Administrator
Seminole Community College (UC)

Microsoft Certified Systems Engineer
Seminole Community College (UC)

Microsoft Office
Bucks County Community College (UC)

Microsoft Office Certificate
Minnesota State College-Southeast Technical (UC)

Mid-range Computing
North Harris Montgomery Community College District (A)

Middle and Secondary Education (Teacher Licensure)
The University of North Carolina at Charlotte (UC)

Middle Grades
The University of North Carolina at Charlotte (M)

Middle Grades Education
Brenau University (M)

Middle School Education
Buena Vista University (UC)
Northern Arizona University (UC)

Middle School/High School Special Education
Saint Mary-of-the-Woods College (B)

Midmanagement
Waubonsee Community College (UC)

Midwifery
Philadelphia University (M)

Military History, Military Management, Intelligence Studies
American Public University System (M, B)

Military Specialties
Fort Hays State University (B)

Military Studies
American Public University System (M)

Ministerial Leadership
Southern Christian University (M)

Ministerial Studies
Global University of the Assemblies of God (M, A)

Ministry
Global University of the Assemblies of God (UC)
The King's College and Seminary (D)
Oral Roberts University (D)

Ministry Leadership
Crown College (M)

Ministry Studies
Judson College (B)

Ministry Training
Bethany Theological Seminary (M)

Ministry-Ministerial Leadership and Youth Ministry Concentrations
Indiana Wesleyan University (M)

Ministry/Bible
Southern Christian University (B)

Missions
Global University of the Assemblies of God (B)

Missions Studies
Taylor University (UC)
Taylor University (UC)

Moderate/Severe Disabilities
University of Louisville (M)

Molecular Biology
Lehigh University (M)

Montana University System General Core
Montana State University-Great Falls College of Technology (A)

Mortuary Science
Arapahoe Community College (A)

MS Windows Programming
Daniel Webster College (UC)

Multi-Cultural Education
Park University (M)

Multidisciplinary Studies
Liberty University (B)

Multidisciplinary Studies/ Social Science/ Fire Science
Caldwell College (B)

Multidisciplinary Studies/Humanities
Caldwell College (B)

Multidisciplinary Studies/Social Sciences
Caldwell College (B)

Multidisciplinary Study
Johnson County Community College (A)

Multimedia Applications
University of Massachusetts Lowell (UC)

Multimedia Communications
Bristol Community College (UC)

Multimedia Networking
Columbia University (UC)

Multimedia Technology
Stevens Institute of Technology (GC)
University of Management and Technology (M)

Municipal Administration
Memorial University of Newfoundland (UC)

Music
Auburn University (M)
Darton College (A)
Judson College (B)
Thomas Edison State College (B)

Music Education
East Carolina University (M)
Stephen F. Austin State University (M)

Music Education-Master of Music Education
University of Southern Mississippi (M)

Music Education-Masters in Music Education
Duquesne University (M)

Music Therapy
Saint Mary-of-the-Woods College (M)

National Coaching Certification
United States Sports Academy (UC)

National Security Studies
American Public University System (M)

Natural Resources
Oregon State University (B)
Virginia Polytechnic Institute and State University (GC)

Natural Resources and the Environment
Colorado State University (UC)

Natural Resources Management
University of Denver (GC)

Natural Science
Ohio University (A)

Natural Sciences/Mathematics
Thomas Edison State College (B)

NCA CASI School Improvement Specialist
University of Nebraska-Lincoln (GC)

Negotiation and Conflict Management
California State University, Dominguez Hills (M)

NetMath
University of Illinois (GC)

Network and Internet Administration
Southwest Virginia Community College (UC)

Network Learning Systems
University of Missouri-Columbia (M)

Network Security
Capitol College (M)

Networked Information Systems
Stevens Institute of Technology (GC, M)

Networking (Electrical Engineering)
Stanford University (GC)

Networking and Systems
Columbia University (UC)

Networking and Telecommunications
Illinois Institute of Technology (GC)

Networking Technologies (MSCIT)
Regis University (GC)

Networking/Telecommunications
City University (UC)

Networks and Distributed Systems
University of Illinois (GC)

Neuropsychology
Fielding Graduate Institute (UC)

New Church Development
Calvin Theological Seminary (M)

New Media Engineering
Columbia University (UC)

New Testament
Johnson Bible College (M)

New York State Coaching Certification
Monroe Community College (UC)

Newfoundland Studies
Memorial University of Newfoundland (UC)

Noise Control Engineering
The Pennsylvania State University University Park Campus (GC)

Nondestructive Testing Technology
Thomas Edison State College (A, B)

Nonprofit and Community Services Management
Park University (M)

GC–Graduate Certificate; D–Doctorate; M–Master's; A–Associate; B–Bachelor's; UC–Undergraduate Certificate

Nonprofit Management
George Mason University (GC)
Hope International University (M)
Northeastern University (GC)
Oral Roberts University (M, UC)
Regis University (M)
University of Central Florida (GC, M)
University of Illinois (GC)
University of Illinois at Chicago (UC)
Walden University (M)

Nonprofit Management (Post-Baccalaureate)
The University of North Carolina at Greensboro (UC)

Nonprofit Management and Leadership
Walden University (M)

NonTraditional PharmD
The Ohio State University (D)

Not-for-Profit Child Care Administration
Saint Mary-of-the-Woods College (B)

Not-for-Profit Financial Administration
Saint Mary-of-the-Woods College (B)

Not-for-Profit Human Services
Saint Mary-of-the-Woods College (B)

Not-for-Profit Public Relations
Saint Mary-of-the-Woods College (B)

Nuclear Criticality Safety
The University of Tennessee (GC)

Nuclear Engineering
The University of Tennessee (M)

Nuclear Engineering Technology
Thomas Edison State College (A, B)

Nuclear Medicine Technology
Thomas Edison State College (A, B)

Nuclear Power Technology
Bismarck State College (A)

Nuclear Technology
Excelsior College (A, B)

Nurse Educator Track
Florida State University (M)

Nurse Midwifery
East Carolina University (M)

Nurse Practitioner
Seton Hall University (M)
University of St. Francis (M)

Nurse Practitioner Advancement
Northern Kentucky University (GC)

Nurse Practitioner and Clinical Specialist
University of Colorado at Colorado Springs (M)

Nursing
Alcorn State University (M)
Ball State University (M, B)
California State University, Chico (B)
California State University, Dominguez Hills (M)
California State University, Dominguez Hills (M, B)
California State University, Fullerton (B)
Central Missouri State University (B)
Central Missouri State University (B)
Clemson University (M, B)
Concordia University Wisconsin (M)
Darton College (A)
Duquesne University (D, M)
Excelsior College (M, A, B)
Florida State University (B)
Gonzaga University (M, B)
Illinois State University (B)
Indiana State University (M, B)
Lock Haven University of Pennsylvania (A)
Maui Community College (M, B)
Memorial University of Newfoundland (M)
Middle Tennessee State University (M, B)
Mississippi University for Women (B)
Montana State University-Bozeman (M)
National University (B)
Northern Arizona University (M, B)
Northern Kentucky University (M)
Northwestern Michigan College (A)
Northwestern State University of Louisiana (B)
Old Dominion University (B)
Pennsylvania College of Technology (B)
Sacred Heart University (B)
Saint Joseph's College of Maine (M, B)
Saint Louis University (M, GC, D, M)
Samuel Merritt College (M)
Slippery Rock University of Pennsylvania (B)
Southern Illinois University Edwardsville (B)
Southwest Missouri State University (B)
Texas A&M University-Corpus Christi (B)
Texas Christian University (M)
Texas Woman's University (D)
Thomas Edison State College (B)
The University of Alabama (B)
University of Calgary (B)
University of Central Florida (B)
University of Delaware (B)
University of Massachusetts Amherst (M)
The University of North Carolina at Greensboro (M, B)
University of North Dakota (B)
University of Phoenix Online Campus (M, B)
University of Saint Francis (M)
University of South Carolina Spartanburg (B)
University of Southern Indiana (M, B)
The University of Texas at Tyler (B)
The University of Texas Medical Branch (B)
University of Wisconsin-Madison (B)
University of Wisconsin-Milwaukee (D)
West Virginia University (M)
Wright State University (B)

Nursing Administration
Madonna University (M)
Texas A&M University-Corpus Christi (M)
Walden University (M)

Nursing Administration and Leadership
Saint Joseph's College of Maine (GC)

Nursing Administration Track
Fort Hays State University (M)

Nursing and Health Professional Education
University of Central Florida (GC)

Nursing and Healthcare Education
Saint Joseph's College of Maine (GC)

Nursing Baccalaureate Program
University of South Carolina Spartanburg (B)

Nursing Bachelor's Completion Program
University of Missouri-Columbia (B)

Nursing Case Management
The University of Alabama (M)

Nursing Completion Program
California State University, Dominguez Hills (B)
Davenport University Online (B)

Nursing Degree Completion Program
University of Wisconsin-Eau Claire (B)

Nursing Education
East Carolina University (M)
Mansfield University of Pennsylvania (M)
The University of North Carolina at Charlotte (GC)
University of Northern Colorado (GC)
The University of Texas System (GC)

Nursing Education Emphasis
University of Northern Colorado (D)

Nursing Education Teaching Certificate
University of Illinois at Chicago (UC)

Nursing Education Track
Fort Hays State University (M)

Nursing Fast Track
University of St. Francis (B)

Nursing Home Administration
Southeast Community College, Beatrice Campus (UC)

Nursing Leadership and Management
University of Central Florida (M)

Nursing – Accelerated Option
Northern Arizona University (B)

Nursing – Accelerated RN-BSN
Holy Names University (B)

Nursing – Administration
Clarkson College (M)

Nursing – Advanced Nursing Practice
Athabasca University (GC)

Nursing – BSN/MSN
Gonzaga University (M)

Nursing – Community Health
The University of North Carolina at Charlotte (M)

Nursing – Education
Clarkson College (M)

Nursing – Education Emphasis
Nebraska Methodist College (M)

Nursing – Education Specialization
University of North Dakota (M)

Nursing – Family Nurse Practitioner
Clarion University of Pennsylvania (M)
The College of St. Scholastica (M)
East Carolina University (M)

Nursing – Family Nurse Practitioner Graduate Program
Slippery Rock University of Pennsylvania (M)

Nursing – Family Nurse Practitioning Major
Clarkson College (M)

Nursing – Gerontological/Adult and Family Nurse Practitioner
University of Massachusetts Boston (GC)

Nursing – Health Care Systems Management
Loyola University New Orleans (M)

Nursing – Health Services Administration
University of Delaware (M)

Nursing – Home Health Nursing
Athabasca University (UC)

Nursing – Master of Science in Nursing Family Nurse Practitioner
Clarkson College (UC)

Nursing – Mental Health Nurse Practitioner
University of Missouri-Columbia (M)

Nursing – Nurse Educator Option
University of Wyoming (M)

Nursing – Nurse Leader and Nurse Educator Options
Old Dominion University (M)

Nursing – Parish Nursing
Saint Joseph's College of Maine (GC, UC)

Nursing – Patient Care Services Administration-Family Nurse Practitioner
Sacred Heart University (M)

Nursing – Pediatric Nurse Practitioner
University of Missouri-Columbia (M)

Nursing – Perioperative Nursing
St. Petersburg College (UC)

Nursing – Post-Basic RN
Memorial University of Newfoundland (B)

Nursing – Post-BSN
Duquesne University (UC)

Nursing – Post-LPN
Athabasca University (B)

Nursing – Post-Master's
Duquesne University (GC)

Nursing – Post-Master's Certification
Northern Kentucky University (UC)

Nursing – Post-Master's Family Nurse Practitioner
California State University, Dominguez Hills (GC)

Nursing – Post-RN
Athabasca University (B)

Nursing – Practical Nursing
North Dakota State College of Science (A)

Nursing – Public Health or School Health
University of Missouri-Columbia (M)

Nursing – RN to BS
University of Massachusetts Amherst (B)
University of Massachusetts Boston (B)
University of Northern Colorado (B)
Washington State University (B)

Nursing – RN to BSN
East Carolina University (B)
Fort Hays State University (B)
Liberty University (B)
Mansfield University of Pennsylvania (B)
Mountain State University (B)
Northern Arizona University (B)
Regis University (B)
Seton Hall University (B)
University of Maryland (B)
The University of Texas System (B)
University of Tulsa (B)
University of Wyoming (B)
West Virginia University (B)

Nursing – RN to BSN (lateral entry)
Winston-Salem State University (B)

Nursing – RN to BSN Degree Completion
Madonna University (B)

Nursing – RN to MSN
University of Delaware (M)

Nursing – RN-BS
Florida Hospital College of Health Sciences (B)

GC–Graduate Certificate; D–Doctorate; M–Master's; A–Associate; B–Bachelor's; UC–Undergraduate Certificate

Nursing – RN-BSN
Loyola University New Orleans (B)

Nursing – RN-BSN Bridge Degree
Brenau University (B)

Nursing – RN-BSN Completion
Northern Kentucky University (B)
The University of North Carolina at Charlotte (B)
University of Saint Francis (B)

Nursing – RN-BSN/MSN
Duquesne University (B)

Nursing – RN/BSN
Clarkson College (B)

Nursing – RNBS Adult Completion Program
Indiana Wesleyan University (B)

Nursing – Rural Family Nursing
Central Missouri State University (M)
Central Missouri State University (M)

Nursing – School Nurse
University of Illinois (GC)

Nursing – School Nursing
University of Illinois at Chicago (UC)

Nursing – Teaching Certificate in Nursing Education
University of Illinois (GC)

Nursing/Public Health-MS in Nursing and MS in Public Health
University of Massachusetts Amherst (M)

Nutrition
American Academy of Nutrition, College of Nutrition (A)

Nutrition and Dietetics
East Carolina University (M)

Object Oriented Programming
Pitt Community College (UC)

Object-Oriented Analysis and Design Using UML
University of Washington (UC)

Object-Oriented Technologies (MSCIT)
Regis University (GC)

Occupational and Environmental Safety and Health Focus
University of Connecticut (B)

Occupational and Technical Studies
Old Dominion University (M, B)

Occupational Health
Kansas State University (UC)

Occupational Medicine
Medical College of Wisconsin (M)

Occupational Safety
East Carolina University (M)

Occupational Safety and Health
Columbia Southern University (M, B)
Montana Tech of The University of Montana (B)
University of Connecticut (UC)

Occupational Safety and Health Technology
Odessa College (A)

Occupational Studies
Thomas Edison State College (A)

Occupational Therapy
Florida International University (M)
Texas Woman's University (M)
University of Florida (M)
University of St. Augustine for Health Sciences (D)
University of Southern Indiana (M)
West Virginia University (M)

Occupational Therapy Applications
Saint Mary-of-the-Woods College (B)

Occupational Training and Development
University of Louisville (B)

Occupational/Technical Studies, general
Hopkinsville Community College (A)

Ocean Engineering
Virginia Polytechnic Institute and State University (M)

Oceanography
University of West Florida (B)

Office Administration
Albuquerque Technical Vocational Institute (A)
Darton College (A)
Delaware Technical & Community College, Jack F. Owens Campus (A)
Delaware Technical & Community College, Stanton/Wilmington Campus (A)

Office Support
Seminole Community College (UC)

Office Systems Technology
Randolph Community College (A)

Office Technology-Secretarial Skills
Mountain State University (UC)

Office Technology-Word Processing
Mountain State University (UC)

Oil and Natural Gas Engineering Management
The Pennsylvania State University University Park Campus (M)

OMNIBUS
Schoolcraft College (A)

One Year Bible Certificate
Eugene Bible College (UC)

Online MBA
Franklin University (M)

Online Secondary Math
University of Illinois (GC)

Operations and Supply Chain Management
Golden Gate University (M)

Operations Management
Excelsior College (B)
Kettering University (M)
Thomas Edison State College (A, B)

Operations Research
Columbia University (UC)
Florida Institute of Technology (M)
Southern Methodist University (M)

Operations Technology
Northeastern University (B)

Optical Sciences
The University of Arizona (GC, M)

Opticianry
Arkansas State University-Mountain Home (A)
Hillsborough Community College (A)

Optics, Imaging and Communications
Stanford University (GC)

Optometric Technician
Madison Area Technical College (UC)

Oregon Transfer
Central Oregon Community College (A)
Chemeketa Community College (A)

Organization and Management
Capella University (D, M)

Organization Development and Organizational Management
Fielding Graduate Institute (UC)

Organizational Communication and Leadership
Marist College (M)

Organizational Communications
Marylhurst University (B)
Upper Iowa University (UC)

Organizational Consulting
Saybrook Graduate School and Research Center (GC)

Organizational Development
University of the Incarnate Word (M)

Organizational Leadership
Austin Peay State University (B)
Fort Hays State University (A, B)
Gonzaga University (M)
Mercy College (M)
National University (M)
Northern Kentucky University (B)
The Pennsylvania State University University Park Campus (B)
Regent University (GC, D, M)
Roosevelt University (UC)
Southern Christian University (M)
Southern New Hampshire University (M)
Upper Iowa University (UC)

Organizational Management
Endicott College (M)
Spring Arbor University (M)
University of La Verne (B)
University of Phoenix Online Campus (D, M)

Organizational Management and Communications
Concordia University, St. Paul (B)

Organizational Management with a Nonprofit Emphasis
Alaska Pacific University (B)

Organizational Management with an emphasis in Healthcare Administration
Alaska Pacific University (B)

Organizational Management; Organizational Development
Fielding Graduate Institute (M)

Organizational Security
University of Denver (GC)

Organizational Security Specialization
University of Denver (M)

Organizational Studies
Saybrook Graduate School and Research Center (D)

Organizational Systems
Saybrook Graduate School and Research Center (M)

Orientation and Mobility
Pennsylvania College of Optometry (M, UC)
Texas Tech University (UC)
University of Louisville (M)

Packaging of Electronic and Optical Devices
Southern Methodist University (M)

Paraeducation
Minot State University-Bottineau Campus (A)

Paralegal
Ashworth College (A)
Ivy Tech State College-Bloomington (A)
Ivy Tech State College-Central Indiana (A)
Ivy Tech State College-Columbus (A)
Ivy Tech State College-Eastcentral (A)
Ivy Tech State College-Kokomo (A)
Ivy Tech State College-Lafayette (A)
Ivy Tech State College-North Central (A)
Ivy Tech State College-Northeast (A)
Ivy Tech State College-Northwest (A)
Ivy Tech State College-Southcentral (A)
Ivy Tech State College-Southeast (A)
Ivy Tech State College-Southwest (A)
Ivy Tech State College-Wabash Valley (A)
Ivy Tech State College-Whitewater (A)
The Paralegal Institute, Inc. (A)
The University of Texas System (UC)

Paralegal Studies
Colorado State University-Pueblo (UC)
Education Direct Center for Degree Studies (A)
Ivy Tech State College-Northwest (A)
Keiser College (A)
Mount Wachusett Community College (A)
Peirce College (A, B, UC)
Saint Mary-of-the-Woods College (A, B, UC)
Tompkins Cortland Community College (A)
University of Great Falls (B)
University of Massachusetts Lowell (UC)

Paramedicine Completion
Western Kentucky University (A)

Park and Resource Management
Slippery Rock University of Pennsylvania (M)

Parks and Recreation Management
Northern Arizona University (B, UC)

Particle Processing
Illinois Institute of Technology (GC)

Pastoral Counseling
Southern Christian University (M)

Pastoral Ministry
Newman University (B)
Saint Joseph's College of Maine (M)

Pastoral Studies
Saint Joseph's College of Maine (GC, M)
Southwestern College (B)

Pastoral Theology
Saint Joseph's College of Maine (M)
Saint Mary-of-the-Woods College (M)

Payroll Clerk
Shoreline Community College (UC)

PC Networking
Daniel Webster College (UC)

Peace and Conflict Resolution (International Focus)
Saybrook Graduate School and Research Center (GC)

Pensions and Executive Compensation
The American College (UC)

Perfusion Technology
Thomas Edison State College (B)

GC–Graduate Certificate; D–Doctorate; M–Master's; A–Associate; B–Bachelor's; UC–Undergraduate Certificate

Personal Financial Planning
City University (GC, M)
Kansas State University (M, UC)

Personal Financial Planning and Counseling
The University of Alabama (UC)

Personal Fitness Trainer
United States Sports Academy (UC)

Petroleum Engineering
Texas A&M University (M)
Texas Tech University (M)

Pharmaceutical Chemistry
Lehigh University (M)

Pharmaceutical Manufacturing Practices
Stevens Institute of Technology (GC)

Pharmaceutical Marketing
Saint Joseph's University (M)

Pharmaceutical Processing
Illinois Institute of Technology (GC)

Pharmacogenetics Essentials
Northeastern University (GC)

Pharmacy
Auburn University (D)
Creighton University (D)
Ohio Northern University (D)
University of Cincinnati (D)
University of Florida (D)
University of Wisconsin-Madison (D)

Pharmacy Concentration in Forensic Drug Chemistry
University of Florida (M)

Pharmacy-Forensic DNA and Serology Concentration
University of Florida (M)

Pharmacy-Nontraditional Doctor of Pharmacy
Duquesne University (D)

Philosophy
American Public University System (B)
Holy Apostles College and Seminary (M)
Thomas Edison State College (B)
University of Waterloo (B)

Philosophy, Politics and Economics
Eastern Oregon University (B)

Physical Education Studies
Monroe Community College (A)

Physical Education Teacher Education
West Virginia University (M)

Physical Education-Coaching Specialization
Ball State University (M)

Physical Education-Health Education/ Health Promotion Emphasis
Mississippi State University (M)

Physical Education, Health, and Leisure Studies
Central Washington University (M)

Physical Education, Teaching Option (lateral entry)
Winston-Salem State University (B)

Physical Education/Health
Eastern Oregon University (B)

Physical Therapy
Boston University (D)
Creighton University (D)

Physical Therapy (Transitional Doctorate)
University of Massachusetts Lowell (D)

Physical Therapy Assistant
Darton College (A)

Physician Assistant
East Carolina University (M)
Lock Haven University of Pennsylvania (M)

Physician Executive
The University of Tennessee (M)

Physicians Executive MBA
Auburn University (M)

Physics (WINPC)
Indiana University of Pennsylvania (UC)

Planning Commissioner
University of Illinois (GC)

Planning Commissioner Online
University of Illinois at Chicago (UC)

Police and Public Safety Psychology (CopDoc)
Saybrook Graduate School and Research Center (D)

Police Science and Administration
Austin Peay State University (A)

Policy Studies
State University of New York Empire State College (M)

Political Economy (4 year)
Athabasca University (B)

Political Economy Concentration (3 year)
Athabasca University (B)

Political Science
American Public University System (M, B)
Caldwell College (B)
Darton College (A)
Thomas Edison State College (B)
Troy University-Florida Region (B)
Troy University Montgomery (A, B)
Virginia Polytechnic Institute and State University (M)

Political Science-Criminal Justice
Buena Vista University (B)

Polymer Science and Engineering
Lehigh University (M)

Post-Secondary Studies
Memorial University of Newfoundland (M)

Post-Secondary Teaching
Colorado State University (GC)

Postsecondary School Administration
Oral Roberts University (D)

Postsecondary Teaching
Colorado State University (UC)

Power and Energy Systems
University of Illinois (GC)

Power Electronics
University of Colorado at Boulder (GC)

Power Engineering
Illinois Institute of Technology (GC)

Power Plant Technology
Bismarck State College (A, UC)

Power System Protection and Relaying
University of Idaho (UC)

Power Systems Engineering
Iowa State University of Science and Technology (UC)

Practical Theology
Oral Roberts University (M)
Regent University (M)
Southern Christian University (M)

Practical Theology-Master of Practical Theology
The King's College and Seminary (M)

Practice Management
Saint Joseph's College of Maine (GC)

Practice of Technical Communications
New Jersey Institute of Technology (UC)

Pre-Dentistry
Darton College (A)

Pre-Law
Darton College (A)

Pre-MBA Certificate of Completion
Alliant International University (UC)

Pre-Optometry
Darton College (A)

Preliminary Level 1 Education Specialist-Mild/Moderate with Concurrent CLD/BCLAD
National University (UC)

Preliminary Level I Education Specialist Credential: Mild/Mod
National University (UC)

Preliminary Level I Education Specialist Credential: Mod/Severe
National University (UC)

Preliminary Multiple Subject Teaching Credential with TED or BCLAD Emphasis
National University (UC)

Preliminary Single Subject Teaching Credential with TED or BCLAD Emphasis
National University (UC)

Preschool-Grade 3 Education/Mild Intervention
Saint Mary-of-the-Woods College (B)

Preventive Medicine, general
Medical College of Wisconsin (M)

Principalship
Northern Arizona University (UC)

Print Media
Rochester Institute of Technology (M)

Private Security and Loss Prevention
Indiana State University (UC)

Process Operations Management
Illinois Institute of Technology (GC)

Process Plant Technology
Bismarck State College (A, UC)

Procurement
Thomas Edison State College (A, B)

Procurement and Acquisitions Management
Webster University (M)

Product Creation and Innovative Manufacturing
Stanford University (GC)

Product Management
William Tyndale College (B)

Production and Inventory Control
California State University, Dominguez Hills (UC)

Professional (weekend) Program
The University of Tennessee (M)

Professional Accounting
Cardean University (M)
New York Institute of Technology (M, B)
Strayer University (M)

Professional Aeronautics
Embry-Riddle Aeronautical University, Extended Campus (A, B)

Professional and Technical Communications
New Jersey Institute of Technology (M)

Professional Arts
Saint Joseph's College of Maine (B)

Professional Bookkeeper
Lake Superior College (UC)

Professional Certification for Teachers
City University (GC)

Professional Communication
East Carolina University (GC)

Professional Communication Studies
Pace University (B)

Professional Communications
Stevens Institute of Technology (GC)

Professional Counseling
Liberty University (M)
Southern Christian University (M)

Professional Development
Amberton University (M, B)

Professional Development Sequence in Community College Teaching and Learning
University of Illinois (GC)

Professional Development Sequence in Dairy Science
University of Illinois (GC)

Professional Development Sequence in Financial Engineering and Risk Management
University of Illinois (GC)

Professional Development Sequence in Translation, French
University of Illinois (GC)

Professional Level II Education Specialist Credential: Mild/Mod
National University (UC)

Professional Level II Education Specialist Credential: Mod/Severe
National University (UC)

Professional Master of Business Administration
Florida Institute of Technology (M)
Florida State University (M)
Regent University (M)

Professional Master of Engineering in Fire Protection
University of Maryland, College Park (M)

Professional Nanny/Family Child Care
Minnesota State College-Southeast Technical (A)

Professional Practice
University of Wisconsin-Madison (M)

GC–Graduate Certificate; D–Doctorate; M–Master's; A–Associate; B–Bachelor's; UC–Undergraduate Certificate

Professional Studies
Champlain College (B)
Metropolitan Community College (A)
Saint Joseph's College of Maine (UC)
Southwestern Assemblies of God University (B)
Thomas Edison State College (M)

Professional Studies, Concentration in Information Technology
Middle Tennessee State University (B)

Professional Studies, Concentration in Organizational Leadership
Middle Tennessee State University (B)

Professional Technology Studies
Pace University (B)

Professional Tier I Administrative Services
National University (UC)

Professional Tier II Administrative Services Credential
National University (UC)

Professional Writing
Northern Arizona University (UC)
Saint Mary-of-the-Woods College (B)
University of Central Florida (GC)
Washington State University (UC)

Program Management (MNM)
Regis University (GC)

Programming in C++
City University (UC)

Programming Specialist
North Harris Montgomery Community College District (A)

Project Engineering and Management
Montana Tech of The University of Montana (M)

Project Management
Athabasca University (M)
Cardean University (M)
City University (GC, M, UC)
DeVry University Online (M)
Florida Institute of Technology (M)
Grantham University (M)
New Jersey Institute of Technology (UC)
New York Institute of Technology (M)
Southwest Missouri State University (GC)
Stevens Institute of Technology (GC, M)
University of Colorado at Boulder (GC)
University of Denver (GC)
University of Illinois at Chicago (UC)
University of Management and Technology (GC, M, UC)
University of Washington (UC)
University of Wisconsin-Platteville (M, UC)
University of Wisconsin-Platteville (M, UC)
Western Carolina University (M)

Project Management Concentration
Colorado Technical University (M)

Project Management Emphasis
City University (M)

Project Management Online
University of Illinois (GC)

Project Management Specialization
University of Denver (M)

Project Management-Master of Project Management
American Graduate University (M)

Psychiatric Rehabilitation
University of Medicine and Dentistry of New Jersey (M)

Psychology
American Public University System (B)
Ashworth College (A)
Bethany College of the Assemblies of God (B)
Caldwell College (B)
Capella University (D, M)
Columbia College (B)
Columbia Union College (B)
Dallas Baptist University (B)
Darton College (A)
Eastern Oregon University (B)
Judson College (B)
Liberty University (B)
Limestone College (B)
Maui Community College (B)
Mercy College (B)
New York Institute of Technology (B)
Northcentral University (D, M, B)
Northern Arizona University (B)
Pacific Graduate School of Psychology (M)
Saint Joseph's College of Maine (A)
Saint Mary-of-the-Woods College (B)
Saybrook Graduate School and Research Center (D, M)
Southern New Hampshire University (B)
Southwestern Assemblies of God University (A)
Stephens College (B)
Thomas Edison State College (B)
Troy University-Florida Region (B)
Troy University Montgomery (A, B)
University of Great Falls (B)
University of Idaho (M)
University of Maryland University College (B)
University of Waterloo (B)
University of Wyoming (B)
Upper Iowa University (B)
Utah State University (B)
Western Kentucky University (B)
Wilfrid Laurier University (B)

Psychology (4 year)
Athabasca University (B)

Psychology Concentration (3 year)
Athabasca University (B)

Psychology Emphasis
Community College of Denver (A)

Psychology of Organizations and Development
University of the Incarnate Word (B)

Psychology – Academic Psychology
Walden University (D)

Psychology – Clinical Psychology (Licensure)
Walden University (D)

Psychology – Counseling (Licensure)
Walden University (D)

Psychology – Health Psychology
Walden University (D)

Psychology – Industrial/Organizational Psychology
Walden University (M)

Psychology – Organizational Psychology
Walden University (D)

Psychology – School Counseling Specialization
Utah State University (M)

Psychology – School Psychology (Licensure)
Walden University (D)

Psychology, general
East Carolina University (M)
Walden University (M)

Psychology/Family Studies
Western Baptist College (B)

Psychology/Sociology
Carl Albert State College (A)

Psychopharmacology
Fairleigh Dickinson University, Metropolitan Campus (UC)

Public Administration
American Public University System (M)
Andrew Jackson University (M)
Athabasca University (UC)
DeVry University Online (M)
Florida Gulf Coast University (M)
Florida Institute of Technology (M)
Georgia Southern University (M)
Indiana State University (GC)
Kent State University (M)
Marist College (M)
Memorial University of Newfoundland (UC)
National University (M)
Regis University (B, UC)
Roger Williams University (B)
Strayer University (M)
Thomas Edison State College (A, B)
Troy University (M)
University College of Cape Breton (UC)
University of Alaska Southeast (M)
University of Baltimore (M)
University of Colorado at Denver (M)
University of La Verne (B)
University of Management and Technology (M)
The University of Montana-Missoula (M)
University of Nebraska at Omaha (M)
The University of North Carolina at Pembroke (M)
University of North Dakota (M)
The University of Texas at Arlington (M)
The University of Texas System (M)
University of Wyoming (M)

Public Administration (Criminal Justice)
Brenau University (B)

Public Administration (General)
Upper Iowa University (B)

Public Administration (Law Enforcement/Fire Science)
Upper Iowa University (B)

Public Administration (MSA)
University of West Florida (M)

Public Administration Specialization
Utah State University (M)

Public Agency Services (BAS)
Northern Arizona University (B)

Public Health
Florida International University (M)
Youngstown State University (M)

Public Health Informatics
University of Illinois (M)
University of Illinois at Chicago (M, UC)

Public Health Nurse
California State University, Dominguez Hills (GC)

Public Health Practice
University of Massachusetts Amherst (M)

Public Health Preparedness
University of Illinois at Chicago (UC)

Public Health-Community Health
Walden University (D, M)

Public Management
Northern Arizona University (GC)
Park University (M)

Public Management and Leadership
Walden University (M)

Public Policy
Regent University (GC)
Walden University (M)

Public Policy Administration
Mississippi State University (M)

Public Policy and Administration-E-Government
Walden University (D)

Public Policy and Administration-Health Services
Walden University (D)

Public Policy and Administration-Knowledge Management
Walden University (D)

Public Policy and Administration-Nonprofit Management and Leadership
Walden University (D)

Public Policy and Administration-Public Management and Leadership
Walden University (D)

Public Policy and Administration-Public Policy
Walden University (D)

Public Relations
Montana State University-Billings (M)

Public Relations and Communication Management
Royal Roads University (M)

Public Relations-Professional Writing
Rochester Institute of Technology (UC)

Public Safety and Human Justice
Southern Christian University (B)

Public Safety Management
Franklin University (B)

Public School Administration
Oral Roberts University (D, M)

Public Service Studies
York University (B)

Public Works Option
The University of Tennessee (M)

Publishing
Pace University (M)

Pupil Personnel Services-School Counseling Specialization
National University (UC)

Purchasing
California State University, Dominguez Hills (UC)

Purchasing and Materials Management
Thomas Edison State College (A, B)

Purchasing and Supply Chain Professional
University of Louisville (UC)

Purchasing Management
Shoreline Community College (UC)

Quality
Eastern Michigan University (M)

GC–Graduate Certificate; D–Doctorate; M–Master's; A–Associate; B–Bachelor's; UC–Undergraduate Certificate

Quality Assurance
California State University, Dominguez Hills (M, B, UC)
Mott Community College (UC)

Quality Assurance and Software Testing
St. Petersburg College (UC)

Quality Assurance Science
California National University for Advanced Studies (B)

Quality Engineering
Lehigh University (M)

Quality Implementation
Rochester Institute of Technology (UC)

Quality Improvement and Outcomes Management
George Mason University (GC)

Quality Improvement for Nursing
California State University, Dominguez Hills (GC)

Quality Leadership
Saint Joseph's College of Maine (M)

Quality Management
Madison Area Technical College (UC)

Quantitative Construction Management
University of Washington (UC)

Quantitative Methods in Finance and Risk Management (Statistics)
Stanford University (GC)

Quantitative Software Engineering
Stevens Institute of Technology (GC, M)

Radiation Protection
Thomas Edison State College (A, B)

Radiation Therapy
Thomas Edison State College (A, B)

Radiologic and Imaging Sciences
University of Southern Indiana (B)

Radiologic Sciences
Florida Hospital College of Health Sciences (B)

Radiologic Sciences Bachelors Completion Program-Radiography
University of Missouri-Columbia (B)

Radiologic Technology
Northwestern State University of Louisiana (B)

Radiologic Technology Continuing Education Units (CEUs)
Sinclair Community College (UC)

Radiologic Technology Program
Southeast Community College, Beatrice Campus (A)

Radiological Science-Degree Completion in Radiological Science
Oregon Institute of Technology (B)

Radiological Sciences
Saint Joseph's College of Maine (B)
Weber State University (B, UC)

Radiological Technology
Southeast Community College, Lincoln Campus (A)

Rangeland Ecosystem Science
Colorado State University (M)

Reading
Concordia University Wisconsin (M)
Northern Arizona University (UC)
University of Alaska Southeast (M, UC)

Reading and Language
University of Massachusetts Lowell (M)

Reading and Literacy
City University (M)

Reading Specialist
The University of Texas System (UC)

Real Estate
Marylhurst University (B)
Thomas Edison State College (A, B)
University of Wyoming (UC)

Reception Services
Minot State University-Bottineau Campus (UC)

Recreation Services
Thomas Edison State College (A, B)

Regents Bachelor of Arts
West Virginia University (B)

Regents Online Degree Program
Austin Peay State University (B)

Registered Employee Benefits Consultant(r) (REBC(r)) Designation
The American College (UC)

Registered Health Underwriter(r) (RHU(r)) Designation
The American College (UC)

Rehabilitation Counseling
Auburn University (M)
The University of Alabama (M)
University of Arkansas at Little Rock (M)
West Virginia University (M)
Wright State University (M)

Rehabilitation Sciences
The University of British Columbia (GC)

Rehabilitation Teaching
Pennsylvania College of Optometry (M, UC)

Rehabilitative Science
Clarion University of Pennsylvania (M)

Reliability and Quality Engineering
The University of Arizona (GC)

Reliability Maintenance
Rochester Institute of Technology (UC)

Religion
American Public University System (B)
Columbia Union College (B)
Liberty University (M, A, B)
Thomas Edison State College (B)

Religious Education
Defiance College (A, B)
Global University of the Assemblies of God (B)
Newman Theological College (GC)

Religious Education-Bachelor of Religious Education
Master's College and Seminary (A)

Religious Studies
The Catholic Distance University (M)
Global University of the Assemblies of God (A)
Judson College (B)
Prairie Bible College (A)
University of Waterloo (B)

Religious Studies-Catholic Theology (MRS)
The Catholic Distance University (M)

Renewing Public Housing
University of Illinois (GC)
University of Illinois at Chicago (UC)

Residential Construction Technology and Management
Pennsylvania College of Technology (B)

Residential Planning
The Art Institute Online (UC)

Resort Management
Saint Joseph's College of Maine (M)

Resource Development (MNM)
Regis University (GC)

Resources Management (BAS)
Troy University-Florida Region (B)

Resources Management (Business), English, History, Political Science, Psychology, and Social Science
Troy University Montgomery (B)

Respiratory Care
Oregon Institute of Technology (B)
Southeast Community College, Beatrice Campus (A)
Southeast Community College, Lincoln Campus (A)
Thomas Edison State College (A, B)

Respiratory Therapy
Darton College (A)
Weber State University (A)

Respiratory Therapy Bachelors Completion Program
University of Missouri-Columbia (B)

Restaurant Management
Northern Arizona University (UC)

Restaurant, Hotel, and Institutional Management
Texas Tech University (M)

Retail Management
The Pennsylvania State University University Park Campus (UC)

Retail Management I
The Pennsylvania State University University Park Campus (UC)

Retail Management II
The Pennsylvania State University University Park Campus (UC)

Retailing
Bucks County Community College (UC)

Retailing Management
Thomas Edison State College (A, B)

Risk Analysis (Management Science and Engineering)
Stanford University (GC)

Risk Management
Cardean University (M)
Excelsior College (B)
New York Institute of Technology (M)

Risk Management/Insurance
Florida State University (M)
Walden University (M)

Safety and Health Technology
Rochester Institute of Technology (UC)

Safety Sciences
Indiana University of Pennsylvania (GC)

Safety Technology
Rochester Institute of Technology (B)

School Administration
Indiana State University (UC)
The University of North Carolina at Greensboro (M)

School Administration (MSA)
The University of North Carolina at Charlotte (M)

School Age Child Care
Northampton County Area Community College (UC)

School Age Child Development
Concordia University, St. Paul (M)

School Aged Child Development
Concordia University, St. Paul (B)

School Counseling (weekend cohort program)
The University of Montana-Missoula (M)

School Guidance and Counseling
Buena Vista University (M)

School Law
Park University (M)

School Librarianship
Azusa Pacific University (M)

School Library and Information Technologies
Mansfield University of Pennsylvania (M)

School Library Media
University of Wisconsin-Eau Claire (UC)

School Library Media Specialist
University of Washington (UC)

School Media
Syracuse University (GC)

School Media Specialist
Northwestern State University of Louisiana (UC)

Science
Bucks County Community College (A)

Science Education
Florida State University (M)
Montana State University-Bozeman (M)

Science in Information Technology
Aspen University (M)

Science Teacher Education
East Carolina University (M)

Science Teachers
University of Massachusetts Amherst (M)

Science, general for the Non-Major
University of Waterloo (B)

Science, Math and Technology
State University of New York Empire State College (A, B)

Secondary Education
Buena Vista University (UC)
Judson College (B)
Northern Arizona University (M)

Secondary Education (BS Ed.)
Northern Arizona University (B)

Secondary Education Postdegree
Northern Arizona University (UC)

GC–Graduate Certificate; D–Doctorate; M–Master's; A–Associate; B–Bachelor's; UC–Undergraduate Certificate

Secondary Education with Certification Emphasis
Northern Arizona University (M)

Secondary Education-English
Saint Mary-of-the-Woods College (B)

Secondary Education-Mathematics
Saint Mary-of-the-Woods College (B)

Secondary Education-Social Studies
Saint Mary-of-the-Woods College (B)

Secondary Teacher Preparation
Mountain State University (A)

Secretarial (Administrative, Legal, Medical)
University of Northwestern Ohio (A)

Secretarial Science Transfer Framework
Hopkinsville Community College (A)

Secretarial Science-Administrative
Mountain State University (A)

Secretarial Science-Legal
Mountain State University (A)

Secretarial Science-Medical
Mountain State University (A)

Secure and Dependable Computing Systems
University of Idaho (UC)

Secure Network Systems Design
Stevens Institute of Technology (GC)

Security Management
American Public University System (B)
Southwestern College (B)
University of Calgary (UC)

Security Management and Homeland Security
University of Massachusetts Lowell (UC)

Security Studies
East Carolina University (GC)

Self Designed
St. Cloud State University (B)

Self Designed Studies
St. Cloud State University (M)

Senior Executive
The University of Tennessee (M)

Signal Processing
Illinois Institute of Technology (GC)
Stanford University (GC)

Site Planning
University of Washington (UC)

Sixth Year in Educational Foundations
Connecticut State University System (UC)

Small Business and Entrepreneurship
New York Institute of Technology (B)

Small Business Management
Middlesex Community College (UC)
The Pennsylvania State University University Park Campus (UC)

Small Business Management/Entrepreneurship
Thomas Edison State College (A, B)

Social Development Studies
University of Waterloo (B)

Social Psychology
Park University (B)

Social Science
Montgomery County Community College (A)
Southern New Hampshire University (B)
University of Maryland University College (B)
University of North Dakota (B)

Social Science Studies
University of Nevada, Las Vegas (B)

Social Science-Interdisciplinary Social Science
Florida State University (B)

Social Science/History
Saint Mary-of-the-Woods College (B)

Social Sciences
Brookdale Community College (A)
Buena Vista University (B)
California State University, Chico (B)
Carl Albert State College (A)
Colorado State University-Pueblo (B)
Daniel Webster College (B)
Edmonds Community College (A)
Ohio University (A)
Syracuse University (M)
Troy University Montgomery (A, B)
University of Waterloo (B)
University of Wyoming (B)
Upper Iowa University (B)
Washington State University (B)

Social Sciences-Applied Track
University of Hawaii-West Oahu (B)

Social Sciences/History
Thomas Edison State College (B)

Social Services
Thomas Edison State College (A, B)
The University of Maine at Augusta (A)

Social Services Administration
Thomas Edison State College (B)

Social Services for Special Populations
Thomas Edison State College (A, B)

Social Studies
Southwestern Assemblies of God University (A)

Social Studies Focus
University of Missouri-Columbia (M)

Social Theory, Social Structure and Change
State University of New York Empire State College (A, B)

Social Work
Cleveland State University (M)
Darton College (A)
Florida State University (M)
Kellogg Community College (A)
Madonna University (B)
Maui Community College (M)
Northampton County Area Community College (A)
Northern Arizona University (B)
Southwest Missouri State University (M)
University of North Dakota (M)
University of Wyoming (M)

Social Work Paraprofessional
Winston-Salem State University (UC)

Socially Engaged Spirituality
Saybrook Graduate School and Research Center (GC)

Sociology
Adams State College (B)
American Public University System (B)
Caldwell College (B)
Colorado State University-Pueblo (B)
Darton College (A)
Fort Hays State University (A, B)

New Mexico State University (B)
New York Institute of Technology (B)
Thomas Edison State College (B)
University of Colorado at Denver (B)
Wilfrid Laurier University (B)

Sociology (4 year)
Athabasca University (B)

Sociology Concentration (3 year)
Athabasca University (B)

Sociology Emphasis
Community College of Denver (A)

Sociology/Criminology
Colorado State University-Pueblo (B)

Software Applications for the Professional
Sinclair Community College (UC)

Software Development
Champlain College (A, UC)
Southern New Hampshire University (UC)
Virginia Polytechnic Institute and State University (GC)

Software Development and Management
Rochester Institute of Technology (M)

Software Engineering
California State University, Fullerton (M)
Champlain College (B)
DePaul University (M)
Illinois Institute of Technology (GC)
Kansas State University (M)
Southern Methodist University (M)
Texas Tech University (M)
University of Colorado at Boulder (GC)
University of Houston-Clear Lake (M)
University of Illinois (GC)
University of Management and Technology (M)
University of Maryland University College (M)
University of Michigan-Dearborn (M)
West Virginia University (M)
Westwood Online (A)

Software Engineering Technology
Grantham University (A, B)

Software Quality Assurance
Northeastern University (UC)

Software Support Specialist/Help Desk
Saint Paul College-A Community & Technical College (UC)

Software Systems
Stanford University (GC)

Space Studies
American Public University System (M)
University of Colorado at Colorado Springs (M)
University of North Dakota (M)

Spacecraft Design and Operation Proficiency
Stanford University (GC)

Spanish
Northern Arizona University (B)

Spatial Analysis and Management Concentration
Jacksonville State University (M)

Special and Elementary Education (BS Ed.)
Northern Arizona University (B)

Special Education
Ball State University (M)
East Carolina University (M)
Northern Arizona University (M)
Northwest Missouri State University (M)
Old Dominion University (M)
Texas Tech University (M)
University of Alaska Southeast (UC)
University of Nebraska-Lincoln (M, UC)
University of North Dakota (M)
Utah State University (M, B)
West Virginia University (M)

Special Education (Cross-Categorical Emphasis)
The University of North Carolina at Greensboro (M)

Special Education Postdegree
Northern Arizona University (UC)

Special Education with Credential Options
National University (M)

Special Education-Adapted Curriculum
The University of North Carolina at Charlotte (UC)

Special Education-General Curriculum (Teacher Licensure)
The University of North Carolina at Charlotte (UC)

Special Education-Instructional Specialist I
Buena Vista University (UC)

Special Education-Master of Special Education
University of Louisville (M)

Special Education, Early Childhood Special Education Emphasis
University of Northern Colorado (M)

Special Education, generic
Texas Tech University (UC)

Special Education, Profound Needs Emphasis
University of Northern Colorado (M)

Special Education, Severe Needs Hearing Emphasis
University of Northern Colorado (M)

Special Education, Severe Needs Vision Emphasis
University of Northern Colorado (M)

Specialized Studies
Ohio University (B)

Specialty Needs for Primary Care Physicians (CME Online)
University of Illinois (GC)

Speech Communication
St. Cloud State University (M)

Speech Language and Auditory Pathology
East Carolina University (M)

Speech Pathology
California State University, Northridge (M)

Speech-Language Pathology
Texas Woman's University (M)
University of Wyoming (M)

Sports Agency
United States Sports Academy (UC)

Sports Coaching
United States Sports Academy (M, UC)

GC–Graduate Certificate; D–Doctorate; M–Master's; A–Associate; B–Bachelor's; UC–Undergraduate Certificate

Sports Coaching (International Certification)
United States Sports Academy (UC)

Sports Management
National University (UC)
United States Sports Academy (D, M, UC)

Sports Management (International Certification)
United States Sports Academy (UC)

Sports Management-Sports Medicine Emphasis
United States Sports Academy (D)

Sports Medicine
United States Sports Academy (M, UC)

Sports Studies
United States Sports Academy (M)

Starting Your Own Business
Pitt Community College (UC)

State and Local Taxation
University of Wisconsin-Milwaukee (UC)

Statistical Methods for Product and Process Improvement
Rochester Institute of Technology (GC)

Statistical Quality
Rochester Institute of Technology (GC)

Statistical Theory and Methods
Colorado State University (UC)

Statistics
Colorado State University (M)
Iowa State University of Science and Technology (M)

Strategic Business Management (MSM)
Regis University (GC)

Strategic Communication and Leadership
Seton Hall University (M)

Strategic Intelligence
American Public University System (M)

Strategic Leadership
Regent University (D)

Strategic Management Specialty
Davenport University Online (M)

Strategic Planning for Critical Infrastructure
University of Washington (M)

Strategic Technology
University of Illinois (GC)

Strategy and Economics
Cardean University (M)
New York Institute of Technology (M)

Strength and Conditioning
United States Sports Academy (UC)

Structural Design
Rochester Institute of Technology (UC)

Structural Engineering
University of Idaho (UC)

Student Affairs and Higher Education
Indiana State University (M)

Substance Abuse
East Carolina University (GC)
Maui Community College (UC)

Superintendency
Northern Arizona University (UC)

Superintendent Certificate
The University of Texas System

Supervision
Bucks County Community College (UC)

Supervisory
Northern Arizona University (UC)

Supervisory Leadership
The Pennsylvania State University University Park Campus (UC)

Supervisory Management
Mid-State Technical College (A)

Supervisory Management/Leadership Development
Madison Area Technical College (A)

Supply Chain Management
Lehigh University (UC)
Northeastern University (A, UC)

Supply Chain Management/Market Logistics
University of Dallas (GC, M)

Surgical Technology
Southeast Community College, Beatrice Campus (A)
Southeast Community College, Lincoln Campus (A)
The University of Montana-Missoula (A)

Surveying
Michigan Technological University (B)
Thomas Edison State College (A, B)

Sustainable Community Development
Prescott College (B)

Synthesis and Characterization of Inorganic Material
Illinois Institute of Technology (GC)

Synthesis and Characterization of Organic Materials
Illinois Institute of Technology (GC)

Systems and Engineering Management
Texas Tech University (M)

Systems and Network Management
Golden Gate University (M)

Systems Application Development
Davenport University Online (A)

Systems Engineering
Colorado State University (D)
Iowa State University of Science and Technology (M)
Southern Methodist University (M)
Stevens Institute of Technology (M)
The University of Alabama in Huntsville (M)
Virginia Polytechnic Institute and State University (M)

Systems Engineering (Professional Graduate Certificate)
The University of Arizona (GC)

Systems Management
Florida Institute of Technology (M)

Systems Software
University of Illinois (GC)

Taxation
Golden Gate University (GC, M)
University of Tulsa (M)

Teacher Assistant
University of Calgary (UC)

Teacher Certification
Prescott College (UC)

Teacher Certification-Master of Teaching
City University (M)

Teacher Education
Marygrove College (M)
Newman University (B)

Teacher Education-Early Childhood
Darton College (A)

Teacher Education-Middle Grades
Darton College (A)

Teacher Education-Secondary
Darton College (A)

Teacher Education-Special Education
Darton College (A)

Teacher Education, Paraeducator
Community College of Denver (UC)

Teacher Leadership
Walden University (D)

Teacher of Children who are Blind or Visually Impaired
Pennsylvania College of Optometry (M, UC)

Teachers Using Technology
National University (UC)

Teaching
La Sierra University (M)
Texas Woman's University (M)

Teaching and Learning
Lock Haven University of Pennsylvania (M)
Memorial University of Newfoundland (M)

Teaching At-Risk Students
Park University (M)

Teaching Emphasis
Alliant International University (M)

Teaching English as a Second Language
Northern Arizona University (M)

Teaching English as a Second Language (TESL)
Oral Roberts University (M)

Teaching Leadership-Master in Teaching Leadership Degree Concentration
University of Illinois at Springfield (M)

Teaching Mathematics
University of Idaho (M)

Teaching with Certification
Oral Roberts University (M)

Teaching, Learning and Teacher Education
University of Nebraska-Lincoln (M, UC)

Teaching/Education with Credential Options
National University (M)

Technical Communication
Texas Tech University (M)

Technical Communications
Northeastern University (B)

Technical Education and Industry Training
University of Central Florida (B)

Technical Engineering Management
The University of Arizona (UC)

Technical Information Design
Rochester Institute of Technology (GC)

Technical Japanese
University of Wisconsin-Madison (M)

Technical Management
DeVry University Online (B)
Embry-Riddle Aeronautical University, Extended Campus (A, B)
Southern New Hampshire University (B)

Technical Sales
Bellingham Technical College (A)

Technical Studies
Excelsior College (A)

Technical Writing
Northeastern University (UC)

Technology
Alliant International University (UC)
Excelsior College (A, B)

Technology and Information Management
Upper Iowa University (B)

Technology Education
Ball State University (M)

Technology for Education and Training-Master of Science in Technology for Education and Training
The University of South Dakota (M)

Technology for Educators
Pitt Community College (UC)

Technology in Education
Lesley University (M)

Technology in Schools
University of Missouri-Columbia (M)

Technology Leadership
Fort Hays State University (B)

Technology Management
Bowling Green State University (D)
Central Missouri State University (D)
Central Missouri State University (D)
City University (GC)
Indiana State University (D)
National University (M)
Pennsylvania College of Technology (B)
St. Petersburg College (B)
State University of New York Institute of Technology (M)
State University of New York Institute of Technology (M)
Stevens Institute of Technology (GC)
University of Denver (GC, M)
University of Maryland University College (M)
University of Phoenix Online Campus (M)

Technology Management (Degree Completion)
Eastern Michigan University (B)

Technology Management Specialization
University of Denver (M)

Technology Studies
Austin Peay State University (B)

Technology with the Human Resource Development Option
The University of Texas System (M)

GC–Graduate Certificate; D–Doctorate; M–Master's; A–Associate; B–Bachelor's; UC–Undergraduate Certificate

Technology-Bachelor of Technology (BTech)
Memorial University of Newfoundland (B)

Technology-Human Resource Development
The University of Texas at Tyler (M)

Technology-Based Distributed Learning
The University of British Columbia (GC)

Technology-Based Learning for Schools
The University of British Columbia (GC)

Tele-Learning
East Carolina University (GC)

Telecommunication and Information Resource Management
Maui Community College (GC)

Telecommunication Management
Stevens Institute of Technology (M)

Telecommunication Systems
DePaul University (M)

Telecommunications
Colorado State University (UC)
Columbia University (UC)
Pace University (GC)
Southern Methodist University (M)
Stanford University (GC)
University of Colorado at Boulder (M)
University of Denver (GC, M)

Telecommunications and Network Management
Syracuse University (M)
Syracuse University (M)

Telecommunications and Signal Processing
University of Illinois (GC)

Telecommunications and Software Engineering
Illinois Institute of Technology (M)

Telecommunications Engineering Technology
Rochester Institute of Technology (M)

Telecommunications Management
DeVry University Online (M)
Golden Gate University (B)
Oklahoma State University (M)
Stevens Institute of Technology (GC)
University of Dallas (GC, M)
University of Management and Technology (M)
University of Maryland University College (M)

Telecommunications Management and Policy
University of Denver (GC)

Telecommunications Networking
New Jersey Institute of Technology (UC)

Telecommunications Networks
University of Denver (GC)

Telecommunications Specialization
University of Denver (M)

Telecommunications Systems Management
Murray State University (B)

Telecommunications Technology
Rochester Institute of Technology (B)
University of Denver (GC)

Telecommunications-Data Communications
Rochester Institute of Technology (UC)

Telecommunications-Network Management
Rochester Institute of Technology (UC)

Telecommunications-Voice Communications
Rochester Institute of Technology (UC)

Tennis Fitness Instructor
United States Sports Academy (UC)

TESOL
Regent University (M, UC)

Textile and Apparel Marketing
Philadelphia University (M)

Textile Off-Campus Televised Education (TOTE)
North Carolina State University (M)

Textiles, Clothing and Design
University of Nebraska-Lincoln (M)

the Arts
National University (UC)
State University of New York Empire State College (A, B)

The Continuation Curriculum Option (CCO) Pathway to the Doctor of Pharmacy
University of Illinois (GC)

The Duke MBA-Cross Continent
Duke University (M)

The Duke MBA-Global Executive
Duke University (M)

Theater Arts
Thomas Edison State College (B)

Theological Studies
Andrews University (B)
Newman Theological College (UC)
Prairie Bible College (GC)
Southwestern Assemblies of God University (M)

Theological Studies (Graduate)
Prairie Bible College (UC)

Theological Studies-Bachelor of Theological Studies
The King's College and Seminary

Theology
Caldwell College (B)
Columbia Union College (B)
Covenant Theological Seminary (GC, M)
Franciscan University of Steubenville (M)
Global University of the Assemblies of God (UC)
Holy Apostles College and Seminary (M)
Lakeland College (M)
Master's College and Seminary
Newman Theological College
North Central University (A)
Saint Mary-of-the-Woods College (B, UC)
St. Mary's University of San Antonio (M)

Thin Films and Nanomaterials
Stanford University (GC)

Total Quality Management
University of South Florida (GC)

Tourism and Hospitality Management
Mount Saint Vincent University (B)

Trade & Industrial (T&I)
The University of Texas System (UC)

Trade and Industrial Education
Darton College (A)

Training and Development
North Carolina State University (GC, M)
Roosevelt University (GC, M)
University of St. Francis (M)

Training Design and Development
University of Missouri-Columbia (M)

Transfer Degree
Bellevue Community College (A)

Transfer Degree for Business Students
Bellevue Community College (A)

Transfer Studies, general
St. Louis Community College System (A)

Transfer to Walsh College
Lansing Community College (A)

Transfer, general
Mott Community College (A)

Transformative Leadership
California Institute of Integral Studies (M)

Transition Doctor of Physical Therapy
Rosalind Franklin University of Medicine and Science (D)

Transitional Doctor of Physical Therapy
MGH Institute of Health Professions (D)
University of St. Augustine for Health Sciences (D)

Transpersonal Psychology
Naropa University (M)

Transpersonal Psychology with Ecopsychology Concentration
Naropa University (M)

Transpersonal Studies
Atlantic University (M)

Transportation Management
American Public University System (M)

Transportation Policy, Operations, and Logistics
George Mason University (M)

Transportation/Distribution Management
Thomas Edison State College (A, B)

Travel
Mountain State University (A)

Travel and Tourism
Mountain State University (UC)
Waubonsee Community College (UC)

Travel Industry Management
Maui Community College (GC)

Travel Management
University of Northwestern Ohio (A)

Turfgrass Management
The Pennsylvania State University University Park Campus (UC)

Ultrasound-Degree Completion in Ultrasound with Option in Echocardiography
Oregon Institute of Technology (B)

Ultrasound-Degree Completion in Ultrasound with Option in Vascular Technology
Oregon Institute of Technology (B)

Universal Degree
Lorain County Community College (A)

University Studies
Dickinson State University (B)
University of Maine (B)
The University of Tennessee at Martin (B)

University Transfer
Cossatot Community College of the University of Arkansas (A)

UNIX
University of Massachusetts Lowell (UC)

UNIX (Solaris)
Regis University (UC)

Unix and Linux for Business
Northeastern University (UC)

UNIX Systems Administration
Daniel Webster College (UC)

Urban Administration
University of the Incarnate Word (M)

Urban Water Resources Design
Villanova University (GC)

Vaccines: Technologies, Trends, and Bioterrorism
Northeastern University (GC)

Veterinary Education Online
University of Illinois (GC)

Veterinary Hospital Management
St. Petersburg College (UC)

Veterinary Hospital Manager
St. Petersburg College (UC)

Veterinary Professionals
Colorado State University (UC)

Veterinary Technician AST
Education Direct Center for Degree Studies (A)

Veterinary Technology
St. Petersburg College (A)

Violence Prevention and Response
Saybrook Graduate School and Research Center (GC)

Virtual Fine Arts
Florida Atlantic University (M)

Virtual Reality in Education and Training
East Carolina University (GC)

Visual Communication-Digital Design (13-month program)
American InterContinental University Online (B)

Visual Communications
Westwood Online (B)

Visual Impairment
University of Louisville (M)

Visual Impairment and Blindness
Illinois State University (UC)

Visually Handicapped
Texas Tech University (UC)

Vocational Diversified Occupations Endorsement
University of Nebraska at Kearney (UC)

Vocational Education-Information Technologies
East Carolina University (M)

Vocational Teacher Licensure
Mississippi State University (UC)

GC–Graduate Certificate; D–Doctorate; M–Master's; A–Associate; B–Bachelor's; UC–Undergraduate Certificate

Vocational Teacher Preparation
State University of New York at Oswego (B)

Water and Wastewater Treatment
Illinois Institute of Technology (GC)

Water Resources and Environmental Engineering
Villanova University (M)

Water Resources Engineering
University of Idaho (UC)

Water/Wastewater Specialization
Mountain Empire Community College (A)

Web Administration
University of Washington (UC)

Web Applications
Davenport University Online (UC)

Web Applications Programming
Minnesota State College-Southeast Technical (UC)

Web Consultant for Small Business
University of Washington (UC)

Web Design
The Art Institute Online (UC)
City University (UC)

Web Design and Development
Minnesota State College-Southeast Technical (A)

Web Design and Multimedia
Westwood Online (B)

Web Designer
Bucks County Community College (UC)

Web Development
City University (GC)

Web Languages
City University (UC)

Web Programming in E-Commerce
City University (GC)

Web Publishing
Middlesex Community College (UC)

Web Site Development
Webster University (UC)

Web Site Development and Management
Champlain College (A, UC)

Web Technology Essentials
University of Washington (UC)

Web/Multimedia Authoring
Bellevue Community College (A, UC)

Webmaster
Texas State Technical College-Waco (A, UC)

Webmaster Technology
Daniel Webster College (UC)

Website Developer
East Carolina University (GC)

Wireless and Mobile Communications
Columbia University (UC)

Wireless Communication Technology
University of Illinois (GC)
University of Illinois at Chicago (UC)

Wireless Communications
Illinois Institute of Technology (GC)
Stevens Institute of Technology (GC)

Wireless Engineering
University of South Florida (GC)

Wireless Personal Communication
Stanford University (GC)

Wisconsin Credential Program for Child Care Administrators
University of Wisconsin-Milwaukee (UC)

Women's Studies
American Public University System (B)
Western Kentucky University (GC)

Women's Studies (4 year)
Athabasca University (B)

Women's Studies Concentration (3 year)
Athabasca University (B)

Wood and Paper Science
North Carolina State University (M)

Word Processing-Administrative Support
University of Northwestern Ohio (A)

Workforce Education Leadership
Mississippi State University (M)

Working Professional Doctor of Pharmacy Program
University of Florida (D)

World History for Educators
University of Colorado at Denver (UC)

Writing Social Commentary
The Pennsylvania State University University Park Campus (UC)

Youth Development
Concordia University, St. Paul (M, B)
Kansas State University (M)
University of Nebraska-Lincoln (GC)

Youth Development Alternative Education
Concordia University, St. Paul (M)

Youth Ministry Leadership
Defiance College (UC)

NON-DEGREE-RELATED COURSE SUBJECT AREAS

Accounting

Acadia University (U)
Adams State College (N, U)
Adirondack Community College (U)
AIB College of Business (U)
Albuquerque Technical Vocational Institute (U)
Allan Hancock College (U)
Alliant International University (U)
American College of Computer & Information Sciences (U, G)
American Graduate University (G)
Anne Arundel Community College (U)
Arapahoe Community College (U)
Arkansas State University–Beebe (U)
Asheville-Buncombe Technical Community College (U)
Ashworth College (N)
Aspen University (G)
Athabasca University (N, U, G)
Athens Technical College (U)
Bainbridge College (U)
Baltimore City Community College (N, U)
Beaufort County Community College (N, U)
Bellevue Community College (U)
Bellingham Technical College (N, U)
Berkeley College (U)
Berkeley College-New York City Campus (U)
Berkeley College-Westchester Campus (U)
Bishop State Community College (U)
Blackhawk Technical College (U)
Black Hills State University (U)
Blue Mountain Community College (U)
Boise State University (U)
Brazosport College (U)
Brenau University (U, G)
Brevard Community College (U)
Bridgewater State College (N)
Brigham Young University (U)
Bristol Community College (N, U)
Brookdale Community College (U)
Broome Community College (N, U)
Broward Community College (U)
Bryant and Stratton Online (U)
Bucks County Community College (U)
Butler County Community College (U)
Butler County Community College (U)
Caldwell College (U)
Caldwell Community College and Technical Institute (N, U)
California National University for Advanced Studies (N, U, G)
California State University, Chico (U)
California State University, Dominguez Hills (N)
California State University, Fullerton (G)
California State University, Sacramento (U)
Campbell University (U)
Cape Fear Community College (U)
Cardean University (G)
Carl Albert State College (U)
Carleton University (U)
Cascadia Community College (U)
Casper College (U)
Cayuga County Community College (U)
Central Missouri State University (N)
Central Missouri State University (N)
Central Missouri State University (N)
Central Missouri State University (N)
Central Missouri State University (N)
Central Texas College (U)
Central Virginia Community College (U)
Central Washington University (U, G)
Central Wyoming College (U)
Century College (N)
Chadron State College (U, G)
Chaminade University of Honolulu (U)
Champlain College (U)
Chattanooga State Technical Community College (U)
Chemeketa Community College (U)
Chesapeake College (U)
Cincinnati State Technical and Community College (U)
Clackamas Community College (U)
Clatsop Community College (U)
Cleveland State University (N)
Clinton Community College (U)
Coleman College (U)
College of DuPage (U)
College of Menominee Nation (U)
College of San Mateo (U)
College of The Albemarle (N, U)
College of the Siskiyous (U)
College of the Southwest (U)
Collin County Community College District (U)
Colorado Mountain College District System (U)
Colorado State University (N)
Columbia Basin College (U)
Columbia College (U)
Columbia Union College (U)
Columbus State Community College (U)
The Community College of Baltimore County (U)
Community College of Denver (U)
Concordia University Wisconsin (U)
Connecticut State University System (U, G)
Copiah-Lincoln Community College–Natchez Campus (U)
Corning Community College (U)
Cossatot Community College of the University of Arkansas (N, U)
Dakota State University (U)
Dallas Baptist University (U, G)
Dallas County Community College District (U)
Daniel Webster College (U)
Danville Area Community College (U)
Danville Community College (U)
Darton College (U)
Davenport University Online (U, G)
Delaware County Community College (U)
Delaware Technical & Community College, Jack F. Owens Campus (U)
Delaware Technical & Community College, Stanton/Wilmington Campus (U)

N–Noncredit; U–Undergraduate; G–Graduate

Des Moines Area Community College (U)
DeVry University Online (U, G)
Dickinson State University (U)
Drake University (U)
Drexel University (U, G)
Duke University (G)
East Carolina University (G)
Eastern Illinois University (G)
Eastern Michigan University (N)
Eastern Oregon University (U)
Eastern Washington University (U)
Eastern Wyoming College (U)
East Los Angeles College (U)
Edgecombe Community College (N, U)
Edison State Community College (N, U)
Edmonds Community College (U)
Education Direct Center for Degree Studies (N)
Elgin Community College (U)
Elizabeth City State University (U)
Elizabethtown College (U)
Everett Community College (U)
Fairleigh Dickinson University, Metropolitan Campus (N, G)
Fashion Institute of Technology (N)
Feather River Community College District (N)
Florida Atlantic University (U, G)
Florida Community College at Jacksonville (U)
Florida Gulf Coast University (U)
Florida Institute of Technology (G)
Florida Metropolitan University–Brandon Campus (U)
Florida National College (U)
Forrest Junior College (U)
Fort Hays State University (U)
Franklin Pierce College (U)
Franklin University (U)
Frederick Community College (N, U)
Fulton-Montgomery Community College (N, U)
Gaston College (U)
George C. Wallace Community College (U)
Georgia Southern University (U, G)
Glenville State College (U)
Gogebic Community College (U)
Golden Gate University (U, G)
Golden West College (U)
Grantham University (U)
Greenville Technical College (U)
Grossmont College (U)
Halifax Community College (U)
Harrisburg Area Community College (U)
Heartland Community College (U)
Hibbing Community College (N, U)
Hopkinsville Community College (U)
Horry-Georgetown Technical College (U)
Houston Community College System (U)
Howard College (U)
Howard Community College (U)
Hudson County Community College (N, U)
Illinois Eastern Community Colleges, Olney Central College (U)
Illinois Eastern Community Colleges, Wabash Valley College (U)
Immaculata University (U)
Indiana Institute of Technology (U)
Indiana State University (U)
Indiana University of Pennsylvania (U)
Indiana University–Purdue University Fort Wayne (U)
Iowa Western Community College (U)
Irvine Valley College (U)
Ivy Tech State College–Bloomington (U)
Ivy Tech State College–Central Indiana (U)
Ivy Tech State College–Columbus (U)
Ivy Tech State College–Kokomo (U)
Ivy Tech State College–North Central (U)
Ivy Tech State College–Northwest (U)
Ivy Tech State College–Southcentral (U)
Ivy Tech State College–Southwest (U)
Ivy Tech State College–Wabash Valley (U)
Ivy Tech State College–Whitewater (U)
Jacksonville State University (U, G)
James Madison University (U)
Jamestown Community College (N)
Jefferson Davis Community College (U)
John A. Logan College (U)
Johnson County Community College (U)
John Tyler Community College (U)
John Wood Community College (U)
Jones College (U)
Kansas City Kansas Community College (U)
Kansas State University (U)
Keiser College (U)
Kellogg Community College (U)
Kentucky State University (U)
Kirkwood Community College (U)
Lakeland College (U)
Lakeland Community College (N, U)
Lake Region State College (U)
Lake Superior College (U)
Lansing Community College (U)
Lawson State Community College (U)
Liberty University (U)
Limestone College (U)
Long Beach City College (U)
Lorain County Community College (U)
Lord Fairfax Community College (U)
Los Angeles Harbor College (U)
Los Angeles Pierce College (U)
Louisiana State University and Agricultural and Mechanical College (N, U)
Maharishi University of Management (N, U, G)
Manatee Community College (U)
Manchester Community College (N)
Mansfield University of Pennsylvania (U)
Marist College (G)
Marshall University (U, G)
Martin Community College (U)
Maryville University of Saint Louis (N)
Massasoit Community College (U)
Maui Community College (U)
Maysville Community College (U)
Mayville State University (U)
Mercy College (U)
Mesalands Community College (U)
Metropolitan Community College (U)
Metropolitan State University (U)
Miami Dade College (U)
Middlesex Community College (U)
Middle Tennessee State University (U)
Midstate College (U)
Minnesota School of Business–Brooklyn Center (U)
Minnesota School of Business-Richfield (U)
Minnesota State College–Southeast Technical (N)
MiraCosta College (N, U)
Mississippi Delta Community College (U)
Mississippi State University (U)
Missouri Southern State University (U)
Moberly Area Community College (U)
Modesto Junior College (U)
Monroe Community College (U)
Montana State University–Billings (U)
Montgomery County Community College (U)
Motlow State Community College (U)
Mott Community College (U)
Mountain Empire Community College (U)
Mountain State University (U)
Mt. Hood Community College (U)
Mount Saint Mary College (U)
Mount Saint Vincent University (U)
Mt. San Antonio College (U)
Nassau Community College (U)
National University (U, G)
Naugatuck Valley Community College (N, U)
New Hampshire Community Technical College System (U)
New Jersey City University (U, G)
New York Institute of Technology (U, G)
New York Institute of Technology (U, G)
Nipissing University (U)
Normandale Community College (U)

N–Noncredit; U–Undergraduate; G–Graduate

Northampton County Area Community College (U)
North Carolina State University (U)
North Dakota State College of Science (U)
Northeastern Oklahoma Agricultural and Mechanical College (N, U)
Northeast State Technical Community College (U)
Northern New Mexico Community College (U)
Northern Virginia Community College (U)
North Harris Montgomery Community College District (U)
North Hennepin Community College (U)
North Idaho College (U)
NorthWest Arkansas Community College (U)
Northwestern Michigan College (U)
Northwestern Oklahoma State University (U)
Northwestern State University of Louisiana (U)
Ocean County College (U)
Odessa College (U)
Ohio University (U)
Okaloosa-Walton College (U)
Oklahoma State University (U)
Old Dominion University (U, G)
Orange Coast College (U)
Oregon Institute of Technology (U)
Owensboro Community and Technical College (U)
Oxnard College (U)
Pace University (U)
Palm Beach Community College (U)
Palomar College (U)
Park University (U)
Patrick Henry Community College (U)
Paul D. Camp Community College (U)
Peninsula College (U)
Pennsylvania College of Technology (U)
The Pennsylvania State University University Park Campus (U)
Pitt Community College (U)
Prairie State College (U)
Pratt Community College (U)
Quinnipiac University (U, G)
Randolph Community College (N, U)
Rappahannock Community College (U)
Reading Area Community College (U)
Regis University (U, G)
Rend Lake College (N)
Richland Community College (U)
Rio Hondo College (U)
Riverland Community College (U)
Riverside Community College (U)
Roosevelt University (U)
Rowan Technical College (U)
Ryerson University (U)
Sacred Heart University (G)
Saddleback College (U)
St. Cloud Technical College (N)
St. Edward's University (U, G)
Saint Joseph's College of Maine (U, G)
Saint Leo University (U)
Saint Mary-of-the-Woods College (U)
Saint Mary-of-the-Woods College (U)
St. Petersburg College (U)
Sam Houston State University (U)
San Bernardino Valley College (U)
San Jacinto College District (U)
Santa Fe Community College (N)
Santa Rosa Junior College (U)
Santiago Canyon College (U)
Sauk Valley Community College (U)
Schenectady County Community College (U)
Schiller International University (U, G)
Schoolcraft College (U)
Seattle Central Community College (U)
Seminole Community College (U)
Seton Hill University (G)
Seward County Community College (U)
Shawnee State University (U)
Shippensburg University of Pennsylvania (G)
Shoreline Community College (U)
Simpson College (U)
Sinclair Community College (U)
Skidmore College (U)
Slippery Rock University of Pennsylvania (U)
Snead State Community College (U)
South Central Technical College (U)
Southeast Community College, Beatrice Campus (U)
Southeast Community College, Lincoln Campus (U)
Southeastern Community College (U)
South Piedmont Community College (U)
Southwestern Assemblies of God University (U)
Southwestern Oregon Community College (U)
Southwest Missouri State University (U, G)
Southwest Wisconsin Technical College (U)
Spartanburg Technical College (U)
Stanly Community College (U)
State University of New York at Oswego (G)
State University of New York College at Potsdam (N)
State University of New York Empire State College (U)
State University of New York Institute of Technology (U, G)
State University of New York Institute of Technology (U, G)
State University of New York Institute of Technology (U, G)
State University of New York Institute of Technology (U, G)
Stephen F. Austin State University (U)
Stephens College (U, G)
Strayer University (U, G)
Suffolk University (G)
Sullivan University (G)
Syracuse University (G)
Tacoma Community College (U)
Taft College (U)
Tarleton State University (N, U)
Tarrant County College District (U)
Taylor University (N)
Teikyo Post University (U)
Texas A&M University–Commerce (G)
Texas A&M University–Corpus Christi (G)
Texas A&M University–Texarkana (G)
Texas Tech University (U)
Three Rivers Community College (U)
Thunderbird, The Garvin School of International Management (G)
Tompkins Cortland Community College (U)
Touro University International (U, G)
Tri-State University (U)
Triton College (U)
Troy University Montgomery (U)
Tulane University (U)
Umpqua Community College (U)
University College of Cape Breton (U)
The University of Akron (U, G)
The University of Alabama (U, G)
The University of Alabama in Huntsville (G)
University of Arkansas at Little Rock (U)
University of Arkansas at Pine Bluff (U)
University of Central Arkansas (U)
University of Cincinnati (U)
University of Colorado at Denver (U, G)
University of Dallas (G)
The University of Findlay (U, G)
University of Georgia (U)
University of Great Falls (U)
University of Hawaii–West Oahu (U)
University of Houston–Downtown (U)
University of Houston–Victoria (U, G)
University of Idaho (U)
University of Illinois at Springfield (U)
University of Maine (U)
The University of Maine at Augusta (U)
University of Maryland University College (U, G)
University of Massachusetts Amherst (N, U, G)
University of Massachusetts Lowell (U)
University of Minnesota, Twin Cities Campus (U)
University of Mississippi (U)

Non-Degree-Related Course Subject Areas

Accounting

University of Missouri–Columbia (U)
The University of Montana–Missoula (U)
University of Nebraska–Lincoln (U, G)
University of Nevada, Reno (U)
The University of North Carolina at Chapel Hill (U)
The University of North Carolina at Charlotte (N)
The University of North Carolina at Pembroke (U)
University of North Dakota (U)
University of Northern Iowa (U)
University of Northwestern Ohio (U)
University of Notre Dame (N, G)
University of South Carolina (U)
The University of South Dakota (U)
University of Southern Mississippi (U)
The University of Tennessee (U)
The University of Tennessee at Martin (N, U, G)
The University of Texas at Dallas (G)
The University of Texas at Tyler (U)
The University of Texas of the Permian Basin (U)
The University of Texas–Pan American (U)
The University of Texas System (U)
University of the Incarnate Word (U, G)
University of Toronto (N, U)
University of Tulsa (G)
University of Vermont (N)
The University of Virginia's College at Wise (U)
University of Washington (U)
University of Waterloo (U)
University of Wisconsin–Eau Claire (N)
University of Wisconsin–La Crosse (G)
University of Wisconsin–Milwaukee (U, G)
University of Wisconsin–Parkside (G)
University of Wisconsin–Platteville (U)
University of Wisconsin–Platteville (G)
University of Wisconsin–Platteville (U)
University of Wisconsin–Superior (U)
Upper Iowa University (N, U)
Utah State University (U)
Utah Valley State College (U)
Vance-Granville Community College (N, U)
Virginia Polytechnic Institute and State University (G)
Wake Technical Community College (N)
Walsh College of Accountancy and Business Administration (U, G)
Washington State University (U)
Waubonsee Community College (U)
Wayland Baptist University (U, G)
Wayne State College (U, G)
Weber State University (U)
Westchester Community College (U)
Western New England College (G)
Western Wyoming Community College (U)
West Virginia University at Parkersburg (U)
Westwood Online (U)
Wichita State University (U)
Wilfrid Laurier University (U)
Wilkes Community College (U)
William Paterson University of New Jersey (U)
William Rainey Harper College (U)
William Tyndale College (U)
Winona State University (U)
Wisconsin Indianhead Technical College (N, U)
York Technical College (U)
York University (N, U)
Youngstown State University (N)

Administrative and secretarial services

AIB College of Business (U)
Albuquerque Technical Vocational Institute (U)
Alvin Community College (N, U)
Athabasca University (N)
Auburn University Montgomery (N)
Augusta Technical College (N)
Bainbridge College (U)
Blackhawk Technical College (N, U)
Blue Mountain Community College (U)
Brevard Community College (U)
Bridgewater State College (N)
Bristol Community College (N)
Brunswick Community College (U)
Caldwell Community College and Technical Institute (N, U)
Carl Albert State College (U)
Carroll Community College (N)
Central Texas College (U)
Central Virginia Community College (U)
Cerritos College (U)
Chemeketa Community College (U)
Cincinnati State Technical and Community College (U)
Clackamas Community College (U)
Clemson University (N)
College of The Albemarle (N)
College of the Canyons (U)
Colorado State University-Pueblo (N)
Columbia Basin College (U)
The Community College of Baltimore County (U)
Copiah-Lincoln Community College–Natchez Campus (U)
Corning Community College (U)
Cossatot Community College of the University of Arkansas (N)
Dallas County Community College District (U)
Danville Community College (U)
Davenport University Online (U)
Delaware County Community College (U)
Des Moines Area Community College (U)
East Carolina University (U)
East Los Angeles College (U)
Edgecombe Community College (N)
Edison State Community College (N, U)
Education Direct Center for Degree Studies (N)
Elgin Community College (U)
Feather River Community College District (U)
Florida National College (U)
Forrest Junior College (U)
Fort Hays State University (U)
Hopkinsville Community College (U)
Horry-Georgetown Technical College (U)
Hudson County Community College (N, U)
Indiana University–Purdue University Fort Wayne (N)
Irvine Valley College (U)
Ivy Tech State College–Bloomington (U)
Ivy Tech State College–Central Indiana (U)
Ivy Tech State College–Columbus (U)
Ivy Tech State College–Eastcentral (U)
Ivy Tech State College–Kokomo (U)
Ivy Tech State College–North Central (U)
Ivy Tech State College–Northeast (U)
Ivy Tech State College–Northwest (U)
Ivy Tech State College–Southcentral (U)
Ivy Tech State College–Southeast (U)
Ivy Tech State College–Wabash Valley (U)
Ivy Tech State College–Whitewater (U)
Jamestown Community College (N)
John Tyler Community College (U)
Kansas City Kansas Community College (U)
Kirkwood Community College (U)
Lakeland Community College (N)
Lake Superior College (U)
Lamar State College–Port Arthur (N)
Lewis-Clark State College (U)
Long Island University, C.W. Post Campus (N)
Louisiana State University at Eunice (U)
Madison Area Technical College (U)
Marion Technical College (U)
Minnesota School of Business–Brooklyn Center (U)
Minot State University–Bottineau Campus (U)
Mitchell Technical Institute (N)
Montgomery Community College (U)
Mt. Hood Community College (U)

N–Noncredit; U–Undergraduate; G–Graduate

Naugatuck Valley Community College (U)
North Central Texas College (U)
North Dakota State University (N)
Northeastern Oklahoma Agricultural and Mechanical College (N)
Northern Kentucky University (U)
North Harris Montgomery Community College District (U)
Northwestern Technical College (U)
Odessa College (U)
Ohio University (U)
Orange Coast College (U)
Oxnard College (U)
Randolph Community College (N)
Rend Lake College (N)
Riverland Community College (U)
St. Cloud Technical College (N)
Saint Paul College–A Community & Technical College (U)
Santa Fe Community College (N)
Santa Rosa Junior College (U)
Sauk Valley Community College (U)
Seminole Community College (U)
Sinclair Community College (U)
Sullivan University (U)
Tarleton State University (N)
Taylor University (N)
Temple College (U)
Tompkins Cortland Community College (N)
The University of Akron (U)
University of Arkansas at Pine Bluff (N)
University of Northwestern Ohio (U)
Vance-Granville Community College (U)
Wake Technical Community College (U)
Washtenaw Community College (U)
Western Wyoming Community College (U)
West Virginia University at Parkersburg (U)
William Rainey Harper College (U)
Wisconsin Indianhead Technical College (N, U)
Youngstown State University (N)

Adult/continuing education

Bellevue Community College (U)
California Institute of Integral Studies (N, G)
Clackamas Community College (U)
Cleveland State University (G)
College for Lifelong Learning (U)
Connecticut State University System (U, G)
Cumberland County College (U)
James Madison University (U)
Louisiana State University and Agricultural and Mechanical College (U)
Mount Saint Vincent University (G)
Oregon State University (G)
Pitt Community College (N)
Regis University (G)
Southeast Community College, Lincoln Campus (U)
University of Calgary (N)
University of Massachusetts Lowell (U)
University of Saskatchewan (U)
University of Wisconsin–Platteville (G)

Advertising

AIB College of Business (U)
The Art Institute Online (U)
Athabasca University (U)
Berkeley College (U)
Berkeley College-New York City Campus (U)
Berkeley College-Westchester Campus (U)
Brevard Community College (U)
California State University, Fullerton (G)
Champlain College (U)
College of the Southwest (U)
Dakota County Technical College (U)
Daniel Webster College (U)
Davenport University Online (U)
Delaware County Community College (U)
Drake University (U, G)
Eastern Shore Community College (U)
Edison State Community College (U)
Fashion Institute of Technology (U)
Immaculata University (U)
Iowa Western Community College (U)
Judson College (U)
Kellogg Community College (U)
Lakeland Community College (N)
Lamar State College–Port Arthur (N)
Linn-Benton Community College (U)
Madonna University (U)
Maryville University of Saint Louis (N)
Middlesex Community College (U)
Minnesota School of Business–Brooklyn Center (U)
Monroe Community College (U)
Mountain State University (U)
Mount Saint Vincent University (U)
Mount Wachusett Community College (U)
North Country Community College (U)
Northern Virginia Community College (U)
Northwestern Oklahoma State University (U)
Okaloosa-Walton College (U)
Oxnard College (U)
Paul D. Camp Community College (U)
Pitt Community College (U)
St. Cloud Technical College (N)
San Jacinto College District (U)
Santa Fe Community College (N)
Schoolcraft College (U)
Seward County Community College (U)
Southern Illinois University Carbondale (U)
State University of New York at New Paltz (U)
Taylor University (N)
The University of Alabama (U, G)
University of Alaska Fairbanks (U)
University of Florida (U)
University of Missouri–Columbia (G)
University of Nebraska–Lincoln (G)
University of Southern Indiana (U)
University of the Incarnate Word (U)
University of Toronto (N)
University of West Florida (U)
University of Wisconsin–Platteville (U)
Upper Iowa University (U)
Utah Valley State College (U)
Wilkes Community College (U)
Wisconsin Indianhead Technical College (N, U)
Youngstown State University (N)

Aerospace engineering

Georgia Institute of Technology (N, G)
Illinois Institute of Technology (G)
Old Dominion University (G)
The University of Alabama (G)
The University of Arizona (G)
The University of Texas at Arlington (G)
Virginia Polytechnic Institute and State University (G)

Aerospace, aeronautical and astronautical engineering

Embry-Riddle Aeronautical University (U)
Everglades University (U, G)
Indiana State University (U)
Middle Tennessee State University (U, G)
North Dakota State University (N)
St. Cloud State University (U)
University of Colorado at Boulder (N, G)
University of Colorado at Colorado Springs (G)
University of Michigan (N)
Utah Valley State College (U, G)

African-American studies

Eastern Michigan University (U, G)
Eastern Washington University (U)
The University of Iowa (U)
University of Missouri–Columbia (U)
The University of North Carolina at Chapel Hill (U)
University of Wyoming (U)
Western Michigan University (U)

Agricultural and food products processing

North Carolina State University (U, G)
NorthWest Arkansas Community College (U)

Non-Degree-Related Course Subject Areas

Agricultural and food products processing

University of Missouri–Columbia (U, G)
Washington State University (G)
Wisconsin Indianhead Technical College (N, U)

Agricultural business and management

Arkansas Tech University (U)
Athabasca University (G)
Cossatot Community College of the University of Arkansas (U)
Dawson Community College (U)
Delaware Technical & Community College, Jack F. Owens Campus (U)
Delaware Technical & Community College, Stanton/Wilmington Campus (U)
Eastern Oregon University (U)
Glenville State College (U)
Iowa Western Community College (U)
Kansas State University (U, G)
Mesalands Community College (U)
Middle Tennessee State University (U)
Murray State University (U)
Northeastern Oklahoma Agricultural and Mechanical College (U)
Santa Fe Community College (N)
Southeast Community College, Lincoln Campus (N)
Southern Illinois University Carbondale (U)
University of Arkansas at Pine Bluff (U)
University of Georgia (U)
University of Guelph (N, U)
University of Idaho (U)
University of Missouri–Columbia (N, U, G)
University of Nebraska–Lincoln (G)
University of Northwestern Ohio (U)
University of Saskatchewan (N)
The University of Tennessee (U)
Washington State University (G)
Wisconsin Indianhead Technical College (N, U)

Agricultural business and production, other

Brunswick Community College (U)
Delaware Technical & Community College, Jack F. Owens Campus (U)
Delaware Technical & Community College, Stanton/Wilmington Campus (U)
Kansas State University (U)
Murray State University (U)
North Carolina State University (G)
University of Georgia (U)
University of Saskatchewan (N, U)
Virginia Polytechnic Institute and State University (U)
Washington State University (G)

Agricultural economics

Iowa State University of Science and Technology (G)
Murray State University (U)
Nova Scotia Agricultural College (U)
Oklahoma State University (U)
Oregon State University (U)
Texas Tech University (N, U)
The University of British Columbia (U)
University of Nebraska–Lincoln (U)

Agricultural engineering

Glenville State College (U)
University of Idaho (U, G)
University of Missouri–Columbia (U)
Washington State University (G)

Agricultural mechanization

Southern Illinois University Carbondale (U)

Agricultural supplies and related services

Washington State University (G)

Agriculture/agricultural sciences

Allen County Community College (U)
Auburn University (U)
Colorado State University (U)
Dawson Community College (U)
Delaware Technical & Community College, Jack F. Owens Campus (U)
Delaware Technical & Community College, Stanton/Wilmington Campus (U)
Glenville State College (U)
Hopkinsville Community College (U)
Horry-Georgetown Technical College (U)
Iowa State University of Science and Technology (U, G)
Kansas State University (U)
Maui Community College (U)
Mississippi State University (G)
Murray State University (U)
North Carolina State University (G)
NorthWest Arkansas Community College (U)
Nova Scotia Agricultural College (N, U)
Oregon State University (U, G)
Seward County Community College (U)
Stephen F. Austin State University (U)
Texas A&M University (G)
Texas Tech University (U, G)
University of Arkansas at Pine Bluff (U)
The University of British Columbia (U)
University of Georgia (N, U)
University of Illinois (G)
University of Minnesota, Twin Cities Campus (U)
University of Saskatchewan (U)
University of Wisconsin–River Falls (U)
University of Wyoming (U)
Utah State University (U)
Virginia Polytechnic Institute and State University (U)
Washington State University (U, G)
Wisconsin Indianhead Technical College (N, U)

Agriculture/agricultural sciences, other

Danville Area Community College (U)
Glenville State College (U)
Kansas State University (U)
Oklahoma State University (U)
Oregon State University (U)
Tarleton State University (U)
University of California, Riverside (N)
University of Minnesota, Twin Cities Campus (U)
Utah State University (G)
Virginia Polytechnic Institute and State University (G)
Walters State Community College (U)

Air Force R.O.T.C.

Glenville State College (U)
Southwestern Assemblies of God University (U)
University of Arkansas at Pine Bluff (N)

Air transportation workers

Embry-Riddle Aeronautical University (N)
Embry-Riddle Aeronautical University, Extended Campus (N, G)
Western Michigan University (U)
York University (N)

Alcohol/drug abuse counseling

Central Texas College (U)
Madonna University (U)
The Pennsylvania State University University Park Campus (G)
Pitt Community College (U)
Southwest Missouri State University (N)
Tompkins Cortland Community College (U)

American history

Anne Arundel Community College (U)
Bossier Parish Community College (U)
Brigham Young University (U)
Broward Community College (U)
Bucks County Community College (U)
Burlington County College (U)
Central Texas College (U)
Cerritos College (U)
Clackamas Community College (U)
Clovis Community College (U)
College of DuPage (U)

N–Noncredit; U–Undergraduate; G–Graduate

Concordia University at Austin (N, U)
Delta College (U)
Eastern Kentucky University (U)
Eastern Michigan University (U)
Eastern Washington University (U)
Floyd College (U)
Hopkinsville Community College (U)
Houston Community College System (U)
Jefferson College (U)
Johnson County Community College (U)
John Wood Community College (U)
Kansas State University (U)
Kellogg Community College (U)
Louisiana State University and Agricultural and Mechanical College (U)
Manatee Community College (U)
Manchester Community College (U)
Marylhurst University (U)
Maysville Community College (U)
Mercy College (U)
Mountain Empire Community College (U)
Mountain State University (U)
Mount Allison University (U)
Mount Wachusett Community College (U)
Murray State University (U)
Northern Virginia Community College (U)
Northwestern Michigan College (U)
Northwest Missouri State University (U)
Oklahoma State University (U)
Oregon State University (U)
Park University (U)
Patrick Henry Community College (U)
The Pennsylvania State University University Park Campus (U)
Riverland Community College (U)
Saddleback College (U)
Sam Houston State University (U)
Sauk Valley Community College (U)
Seattle Pacific University (G)
Southeast Community College, Lincoln Campus (U)
Southwest Missouri State University (U)
Southwest Virginia Community College (U)
State University of New York Empire State College (U)
Texas Christian University (U)
Texas Tech University (U)
Triton College (U)
University of Colorado at Denver (U)
University of Delaware (U)
University of Minnesota, Twin Cities Campus (U)
University of Nebraska–Lincoln (U)
University of Nevada, Reno (U)
The University of North Carolina at Chapel Hill (U)
The University of North Carolina at Greensboro (U)
The University of Texas–Pan American (U)
University of Waterloo (U)
Upper Iowa University (N, U)
Vance-Granville Community College (U)
Washington State University (U)
Western Washington University (U)
West Valley College (U)

American literature (United States)

Alvin Community College (U)
Ashland Community and Technical College (U)
Bellevue Community College (U)
Black Hills State University (U)
Blue Mountain Community College (U)
Bowling Green State University (U, G)
Brigham Young University (U)
Brookdale Community College (U)
Campbell University (U)
Cape Fear Community College (U)
Chemeketa Community College (U)
Columbia College (U)
Columbus State Community College (U)
Copiah-Lincoln Community College–Natchez Campus (U)
Darton College (U)
Dawson Community College (U)
Delaware County Community College (U)
Delta College (U)
Elizabethtown College (U)
Florida Metropolitan University–Brandon Campus (U)
Gaston College (U)
Harrisburg Area Community College (U)
Heartland Community College (U)
Hillsborough Community College (U)
Horry-Georgetown Technical College (U)
Houston Community College System (U)
Howard Community College (U)
Iowa Western Community College (U)
Irvine Valley College (U)
Jacksonville State University (U)
James Madison University (N)
Kansas City Kansas Community College (U)
Limestone College (U)
Linn-Benton Community College (U)
Louisiana State University at Eunice (U)
Manatee Community College (U)
Marylhurst University (U)
Mercy College (G)
Miami Dade College (U)
Middle Tennessee State University (U)
Minneapolis College of Art and Design (U)
Minnesota School of Business–Brooklyn Center (U)
Monroe Community College (U)
Montgomery Community College (U)
Mt. Hood Community College (U)
Naropa University (U)
North Carolina State University (U)
North Idaho College (U)
Ohio University (U)
Oklahoma State University (U)
Oregon State University (U)
Oxnard College (U)
Park University (U)
Peninsula College (U)
Pierce College (U)
Pulaski Technical College (U)
Rappahannock Community College (U)
Raritan Valley Community College (U)
Riverland Community College (U)
St. Cloud State University (U)
St. Petersburg College (U)
San Jacinto College District (U)
Schoolcraft College (U)
Seward County Community College (U)
Skidmore College (U)
Snead State Community College (U)
State University of New York at New Paltz (U)
Tarleton State University (U)
Taylor University (U)
Taylor University (U)
Texas Tech University (U)
Umpqua Community College (U)
The University of Alabama (U)
University of Alaska Fairbanks (U)
University of Arkansas at Pine Bluff (U)
University of Central Arkansas (U)
University of Colorado at Colorado Springs (U)
University of Colorado at Denver (U)
University of Georgia (U)
University of Great Falls (U)
The University of Maine at Augusta (U)
University of Mississippi (U)
University of Missouri–Columbia (U)
University of Nevada, Reno (U)
University of South Carolina Sumter (U)
The University of Tennessee (U)
The University of Texas at Austin (U)
The University of Texas of the Permian Basin (U)
University of the Incarnate Word (U)
University of Washington (U)
University of Waterloo (U)
University of Wyoming (U)
Utah Valley State College (U)
Vance-Granville Community College (U)
Walters State Community College (U)
Waubonsee Community College (U)
Western Washington University (U)
West Los Angeles College (U)
Wilkes Community College (U)

Non-Degree-Related Course Subject Areas

American literature (United States)

William Paterson University of New Jersey (U)
Youngstown State University (N)
Yuba College (U)

American studies

Andrews University (U)
Bellevue Community College (U)
Seattle Central Community College (U)
The University of Iowa (U)
University of Nebraska–Lincoln (U)
University of Nevada, Reno (U)
The University of North Carolina at Chapel Hill (U)
Washington State University (U)

Analytical chemistry

Illinois Institute of Technology (G)

Anatomy

American Academy of Nutrition, College of Nutrition (U)
Century College (N)
Floyd College (U)
John Wood Community College (U)
Louisiana State University and Agricultural and Mechanical College (U)
Mountain State University (U)

Animal sciences

Ashworth College (N)
Brevard Community College (U)
Colorado State University (U)
Kansas State University (U)
Mesalands Community College (U)
Murray State University (U)
Nova Scotia Agricultural College (N, U)
Oklahoma State University (U)
The Pennsylvania State University University Park Campus (U)
Texas Tech University (G)
University of Arkansas at Pine Bluff (U)
The University of British Columbia (U)
University of Delaware (U)
University of Guelph (N)
University of Maine (G)
University of Missouri–Columbia (U, G)

Anthropology

Athabasca University (N, U)
Bellevue Community College (U)
Bemidji State University (U)
Bethany College of the Assemblies of God (U)
Blue Mountain Community College (U)
Boise State University (U)
Bridgewater State College (U)
Brigham Young University (U)
Bristol Community College (U)
Brookdale Community College (U)
Broward Community College (U)
Burlington County College (U)
California Institute of Integral Studies (N, G)
California State University, Chico (U)
California State University, Sacramento (U)
Carleton University (U)
Casper College (U)
Cayuga County Community College (U)
Cedarville University (U)
Central Texas College (U)
Central Wyoming College (U)
Cerritos College (U)
Chaminade University of Honolulu (U)
Charter Oak State College (U)
Chemeketa Community College (U)
Citrus College (U)
Clackamas Community College (U)
Clatsop Community College (U)
College of DuPage (U)
College of San Mateo (U)
College of the Canyons (U)
Colorado Mountain College District System (U)
Colorado State University-Pueblo (U)
Columbia Basin College (U)
Columbus State Community College (U)
Community College of Denver (U)
Connecticut State University System (U, G)
Cumberland County College (U)
Cuyamaca College (U)
Dallas County Community College District (U)
Danville Area Community College (U)
Dawson Community College (U)
Delaware County Community College (U)
Eastern Kentucky University (U)
Eastern Oregon University (U)
Eastern Shore Community College (U)
Edison State Community College (U)
El Camino College (U)
Elgin Community College (U)
Emmanuel Bible College (U)
Everett Community College (U)
Evergreen Valley College (U)
Fairleigh Dickinson University, Metropolitan Campus (U)
Florida Community College at Jacksonville (U)
Golden West College (U)
Greenfield Community College (U)
Harrisburg Area Community College (U)
Henry Ford Community College (U)
Honolulu Community College (U)
Houston Community College System (U)
Indiana Wesleyan University (U)
Iowa Western Community College (U)
Jacksonville State University (U)
Johnson County Community College (U)
John Wood Community College (U)
Kansas City Kansas Community College (U)
Kellogg Community College (U)
Lake Superior College (U)
Long Beach City College (U)
Louisiana State University and Agricultural and Mechanical College (U)
Manatee Community College (U)
Massasoit Community College (U)
Memorial University of Newfoundland (U)
Metropolitan Community College (U)
Metropolitan State University (U)
Modesto Junior College (U)
Montgomery County Community College (U)
Mt. San Antonio College (U)
Murray State University (U)
Naropa University (U, G)
Nassau Community College (U)
New York Institute of Technology (U)
Northampton County Area Community College (U)
North Carolina State University (U)
North Country Community College (U)
North Idaho College (U)
Northwestern Michigan College (U)
Ohio University (U)
Oklahoma State University (U)
Orange Coast College (U)
Oregon Institute of Technology (U)
Oregon State University (U)
Oxnard College (U)
Pace University (U)
Palm Beach Community College (U)
Palomar College (U)
Peninsula College (U)
The Pennsylvania State University University Park Campus (U)
Pierce College (U)
Prairie Bible College (U, G)
Raritan Valley Community College (U)
Reading Area Community College (U)
Regis University (G)
Rend Lake College (U)
The Richard Stockton College of New Jersey (U)
Rio Hondo College (U)
Riverside Community College (U)
Rockland Community College (U)
Sacramento City College (U)
Saddleback College (U)
St. Cloud State University (U)
St. Edward's University (U)

N–Noncredit; U–Undergraduate; G–Graduate

St. Petersburg College (U)
Sam Houston State University (U)
San Bernardino Valley College (U)
Santa Rosa Junior College (U)
Schoolcraft College (U)
Seattle Central Community College (U)
Seminole Community College (U)
Shawnee State University (U)
Sinclair Community College (U)
Skidmore College (U)
Southeast Arkansas College (U)
Southeast Community College, Lincoln Campus (U)
Southwestern College (U)
Southwestern Oregon Community College (U)
Southwest Missouri State University (U)
State University of New York at New Paltz (U)
State University of New York at Oswego (U)
State University of New York at Plattsburgh (U)
Syracuse University (U, G)
Tacoma Community College (U)
Texas Tech University (U)
Trinity Western University (U)
Triton College (U)
Tunxis Community College (U)
University of Alaska Fairbanks (U)
University of Arkansas at Little Rock (U)
University of Colorado at Denver (U)
University of Connecticut (U)
University of Florida (U)
University of Georgia (U)
University of Guelph (U)
University of Hawaii–West Oahu (U)
University of Houston (U)
University of Idaho (U)
University of La Verne (N, U)
University of Maine (G)
The University of Maine at Augusta (U)
University of Maryland University College (U)
University of Massachusetts Boston (U)
University of Minnesota, Twin Cities Campus (U)
University of Missouri–Columbia (U)
The University of Montana–Missoula (U)
University of Nevada, Reno (U)
The University of North Carolina at Chapel Hill (U)
University of North Dakota (U)
University of Oklahoma (U)
University of Saskatchewan (U)
University of Southern Mississippi (U)
The University of Tennessee (U)
The University of Texas at Austin (U)
The University of Texas at Tyler (U)
University of the Incarnate Word (U)
University of Utah (U)
University of Vermont (U)
University of Washington (U)
University of Waterloo (U)
University of West Florida (U)
University of Wisconsin Colleges (U)
Utah State University (U)
Washington State University (U)
Weber State University (U)
Westchester Community College (U)
Western Michigan University (U)
Western Seminary (G)
Western Washington University (U)
Western Wyoming Community College (U)
West Valley College (U)
Whatcom Community College (U)
Wichita State University (U)
Wilfrid Laurier University (U)
William Paterson University of New Jersey (U)
Yuba College (U)

Apparel and accessories marketing operations

Berkeley College (U)
Eastern Michigan University (U)
Hudson County Community College (U)
Immaculata University (U)
Stephen F. Austin State University (U)
University of Georgia (U)
University of Houston (U)
Westchester Community College (U)
Western Michigan University (U)
William Rainey Harper College (U)
Wisconsin Indianhead Technical College (N, U)

Applied mathematics

AIB College of Business (U)
Alvin Community College (U)
American College of Computer & Information Sciences (U, G)
Anne Arundel Community College (U)
Asheville-Buncombe Technical Community College (U)
Bainbridge College (U)
Bethany College of the Assemblies of God (U)
Bishop State Community College (U)
Bismarck State College (U)
Blue Mountain Community College (U)
Bossier Parish Community College (U)
Bowling Green State University (U)
Brevard Community College (U)
Butler County Community College (U)
Butler County Community College (U)
California National University for Advanced Studies (N)
Central Texas College (U)
Central Virginia Community College (U)
Century College (N)
Chemeketa Community College (U)
Clinton Community College (U)
Columbia University (N, G)
The Community College of Baltimore County (U)
County College of Morris (U)
Daniel Webster College (U)
Danville Area Community College (U)
Darton College (U)
Delaware Technical & Community College, Jack F. Owens Campus (U)
Delaware Technical & Community College, Stanton/Wilmington Campus (U)
Eastern Michigan University (U)
Embry-Riddle Aeronautical University, Extended Campus (U)
Eugene Bible College (U)
Everett Community College (U)
Harrisburg Area Community College (U)
Heart of Georgia Technical College (U)
Hibbing Community College (U)
Hillsborough Community College (U)
Howard Community College (U)
Illinois Institute of Technology (U)
Immaculata University (U)
Iowa Western Community College (U)
Irvine Valley College (U)
Jacksonville State University (U)
James Madison University (N)
John Tyler Community College (U)
Lakeland Community College (U)
Linn-Benton Community College (U)
Lock Haven University of Pennsylvania (U)
Lord Fairfax Community College (U)
Manatee Community College (U)
Minnesota School of Business–Brooklyn Center (U)
North Dakota State University (U)
NorthWest Arkansas Community College (U)
Northwestern Technical College (U)
Oxnard College (U)
Peninsula College (U)
Pierce College (U)
Raritan Valley Community College (U)
The Richard Stockton College of New Jersey (U)
St. Cloud Technical College (N)
San Jacinto College District (U)
Santa Fe Community College (U)
Seminole Community College (U)
Southeast Arkansas College (U)

Non-Degree-Related Course Subject Areas

Applied mathematics

Southeast Community College, Lincoln Campus (U)
Southwest Wisconsin Technical College (U)
Spartanburg Technical College (U)
Stanly Community College (U)
Tacoma Community College (U)
Taft College (U)
Tarleton State University (U)
Taylor University (N)
The University of Akron (G)
University of Alaska Fairbanks (U)
University of Florida (U)
The University of Maine at Augusta (U)
The University of Tennessee (U)
University of the Incarnate Word (U)
University of Washington (U)
University of Waterloo (U)
Western Wyoming Community College (U)
William Paterson University of New Jersey (U)
Wisconsin Indianhead Technical College (N, U)

Archaeology

Bellevue Community College (U)
Bethany College of the Assemblies of God (U)
Blue Mountain Community College (U)
Brigham Young University (U)
Chemeketa Community College (U)
Colorado Mountain College District System (U)
Everett Community College (U)
James Madison University (N)
The Jewish Theological Seminary (N, U, G)
Kansas City Kansas Community College (U)
Northwestern College (U)
St. Petersburg College (U)
Santa Fe Community College (U)
Skidmore College (U)
Umpqua Community College (U)
The University of Akron (U)
University of California, Los Angeles (G)
University of Massachusetts Boston (U)
University of Saskatchewan (U)
The University of Texas at Tyler (U)
University of Washington (U)
University of West Florida (U)
William Paterson University of New Jersey (U)

Architectural engineering technology

Honolulu Community College (U)
John Tyler Community College (U)
Sinclair Community College (U)

Architectural engineering

University of Arkansas at Pine Bluff (U)

Architectural environmental design

Auburn University (N)
Madison Area Technical College (U)
The Pennsylvania State University University Park Campus (N, G)

Architectural urban design and planning

Auburn University (N)

Architecture and related programs, other

Arapahoe Community College (U)
Minneapolis College of Art and Design (U)
University of Wisconsin–Madison (U)

Architecture

Auburn University (N)
Dakota County Technical College (U)
James Madison University (N)
Lansing Community College (U)
Louisiana Tech University (U)
Orange Coast College (U)
Pennsylvania College of Technology (U)
Texas Tech University (N, G)
Triton College (U)
University of Colorado at Denver (G)
The University of North Carolina at Charlotte (N)
Virginia Polytechnic Institute and State University (N)

Area studies

American Public University System (U)
Delaware County Community College (U)
Goddard College (U)
Naropa University (N)
Oxnard College (U)
St. Petersburg College (U)
Taylor University (U)
University of Maryland University College (U)
University of Northern Iowa (U)
University of the Incarnate Word (U)
William Paterson University of New Jersey (U)

Area, ethnic and cultural studies, other

Berkeley College-New York City Campus (U)
Berkeley College-Westchester Campus (U)
Bethany College of the Assemblies of God (U)
California State University, Chico (U)
Central Texas College (U)
Central Wyoming College (U)
Chemeketa Community College (U)
Cleveland State University (G)
Delaware County Community College (U)
DeVry University Online (U)
Edgecombe Community College (N)
Elizabethtown College (U)
Fort Hays State University (U)
Goddard College (U)
Hibbing Community College (U)
Immaculata University (U)
John F. Kennedy University (U, G)
Mercy College (U)
Middlesex Community College (U)
Middle Tennessee State University (N, U)
Minnesota School of Business–Brooklyn Center (U)
Naropa University (N, U, G)
North Idaho College (U)
Oregon State University (U)
Oxnard College (U)
Palomar College (U)
Park University (U)
Prescott College (G)
Raritan Valley Community College (U)
Seminole Community College (U)
Shoreline Community College (U)
Skidmore College (U)
State University of New York at Plattsburgh (U)
Strayer University (U)
Tunxis Community College (U)
The University of Akron (N)
University of Bridgeport (U)
University of Colorado at Colorado Springs (U)
University of Connecticut (U)
University of Georgia (U)
University of Missouri–Columbia (U)
University of Nevada, Reno (U)
The University of North Carolina at Pembroke (U)
The University of Texas at Austin (U)
University of the Incarnate Word (U)
University of Utah (U)
University of Waterloo (U)
University of Wisconsin–Superior (U)
William Paterson University of New Jersey (U)

Army R.O.T.C.

Eastern Michigan University (U)
John Wood Community College (U)
North Georgia College & State University (U)

N–Noncredit; U–Undergraduate; G–Graduate

Art history

Acadia University (U)
Atlantic University (N, G)
Bossier Parish Community College (U)
Brigham Young University (U)
Bucks County Community College (U)
Burlington County College (U)
Charter Oak State College (U)
Clovis Community College (U)
College of The Albemarle (U)
Colorado Mountain College District System (U)
Columbia Basin College (U)
Community College of Denver (U)
Duquesne University (U)
Eastern Kentucky University (U)
Edison State Community College (U)
Greenville Technical College (U)
Houston Community College System (U)
John Wood Community College (U)
Lakeland Community College (U)
Lenoir Community College (U)
Manatee Community College (U)
Mercy College (U)
Minneapolis College of Art and Design (U)
Montana State University–Billings (U)
Mountain Empire Community College (U)
Mountain State University (U)
North Country Community College (U)
Northern Arizona University (U)
Northern Virginia Community College (U)
Patrick Henry Community College (U)
Pennsylvania College of Technology (U)
The Pennsylvania State University University Park Campus (U)
Richland Community College (U)
Sinclair Community College (U)
Texas Christian University (U)
Texas State University-San Marcos (U)
Triton College (U)
University of Alaska Fairbanks (U)
University of Minnesota, Twin Cities Campus (U)
University of Nebraska–Lincoln (U)
The University of North Carolina at Chapel Hill (U)
The University of South Dakota (U)
The University of Texas of the Permian Basin (U)
University of Utah (U)
West Valley College (U)

Asian studies

California Institute of Integral Studies (N, G)
Connecticut State University System (U, G)
Seattle Central Community College (U)
University of Maine (U)
University of Nebraska–Lincoln (U)
Washington State University (U)
Western Washington University (U)

Astronomy

Andrews University (U)
Athabasca University (N, U)
Austin Peay State University (U)
Bellevue Community College (U)
Brevard Community College (U)
Brigham Young University (U)
Broome Community College (U)
Bucks County Community College (U)
Butler County Community College (U)
Carleton University (U)
Carroll Community College (U)
Cascadia Community College (U)
Casper College (U)
Cecil Community College (U)
Central Virginia Community College (U)
Charter Oak State College (U)
Chemeketa Community College (U)
Clemson University (U)
Coastal Bend College (U)
College of San Mateo (U)
College of the Canyons (U)
Colorado Mountain College District System (U)
The Community College of Baltimore County (U)
Community College of Denver (U)
Culver-Stockton College (U)
Cuyamaca College (U)
Dallas County Community College District (U)
Danville Area Community College (U)
Delaware County Community College (U)
Edison Community College (U)
El Camino College (U)
Evergreen Valley College (U)
Frederick Community College (U)
Grossmont College (U)
Harrisburg Area Community College (U)
Henry Ford Community College (U)
Hillsborough Community College (U)
Honolulu Community College (U)
Hopkinsville Community College (U)
Horry-Georgetown Technical College (U)
Houston Community College System (U)
Howard Community College (U)
Illinois Eastern Community Colleges, Lincoln Trail College (U)
Independence Community College (U)
Iowa Western Community College (U)
James Madison University (N)
John Wood Community College (U)
Judson College (U)
Lake Superior College (U)
Lamar State College–Port Arthur (U)
Lansing Community College (U)
Long Beach City College (U)
Maui Community College (U)
Mesalands Community College (U)
Middle Tennessee State University (U)
Mississippi Delta Community College (U)
Mountain Empire Community College (U)
Mountain State University (U)
Mt. Hood Community College (U)
Nassau Community College (U)
Northampton County Area Community College (U)
Northeast State Technical Community College (U)
Northwestern College (U)
Oxnard College (U)
Palm Beach Community College (U)
Peninsula College (U)
Pierce College (U)
Quinebaug Valley Community College (U)
Raritan Valley Community College (U)
Rend Lake College (U)
Riverside Community College (U)
St. Clair County Community College (U)
St. Petersburg College (U)
San Bernardino Valley College (U)
Santa Fe Community College (U)
Santa Rosa Junior College (U)
Schenectady County Community College (U)
Schoolcraft College (U)
Seattle Pacific University (G)
Seminole Community College (U)
Sinclair Community College (U)
Southwestern College (U)
Southwest Missouri State University (U)
State University of New York at New Paltz (U)
Stephen F. Austin State University (U)
Temple College (U)
Triton College (U)
The University of Akron (U)
The University of Alabama (U)
University of Arkansas at Little Rock (U)
University of Florida (U)
University of Georgia (U)
University of La Verne (N)
University of Missouri–Columbia (U)
University of Nebraska at Omaha (U)
The University of North Carolina at Chapel Hill (U)
University of Northern Iowa (U)
University of Oklahoma (U)
University of Oregon (U)
University of South Carolina (U)
The University of Tennessee (U)
The University of Texas at Austin (U)

Non-Degree-Related Course Subject Areas
Astronomy

University of Washington (U)
University of Waterloo (U)
University of Wisconsin–River Falls (U)
University of Wyoming (U)
Upper Iowa University (U)
Utah Valley State College (U)
Whatcom Community College (U)
Wichita State University (U)
William Rainey Harper College (U)

Astrophysics

James Madison University (N)

Atmospheric sciences and meteorology

Bellevue Community College (U)
Dallas Baptist University (U)
Delaware County Community College (U)
Howard Community College (U)
Iowa State University of Science and Technology (U, G)
Jacksonville State University (U)
Miami Dade College (U)
Millersville University of Pennsylvania (U)
Mountain Empire Community College (U)
Nassau Community College (U)
Oregon State University (U)
Santa Rosa Junior College (U)
Seminole Community College (U)
Snead State Community College (U)
University of California, Riverside (N)
University of La Verne (N)
University of Michigan (N)
University of Missouri–Columbia (U)
University of Utah (U)
University of Washington (U)

Bible/biblical studies

Abilene Christian University (U, G)
Alliance University College (U, G)
Andrews University (U)
Arlington Baptist College (N, U)
Assemblies of God Theological Seminary (G)
Atlantic School of Theology (N, G)
Atlantic University (N, G)
Baptist Bible College of Pennsylvania (G)
The Baptist College of Florida (U)
Baptist Theological Seminary at Richmond (N, G)
Barclay College (U)
Bethany College of the Assemblies of God (U)
Bethune-Cookman College (U)
Boise Bible College (U)
Briercrest Distance Learning (N, U, G)
Calvin Theological Seminary (G)
Campbell University (U)
Central Baptist Theological Seminary (N, G)
Central Bible College (N, U)
Central Texas College (U)
Clovis Community College (U)
Columbia Union College (U)
Community College of Denver (U)
Concordia College (U)
Covenant Theological Seminary (N, G)
Crown College (G)
Dallas Baptist University (U)
Defiance College (U)
Denver Seminary (G)
Earlham School of Religion (G)
Eastern Mennonite University (G)
Emmanuel Bible College (U)
Eugene Bible College (U)
Feather River Community College District (N)
Gannon University (U)
Global University of the Assemblies of God (N)
Hebrew College (N, U, G)
Hope International University (N, U, G)
Immaculata University (U)
Indiana Wesleyan University (U)
Institute for Christian Studies (G)
The Jewish Theological Seminary (N, U, G)
Johnson Bible College (G)
Judson College (U)
Judson College (U)
The King's College and Seminary (N, U, G)
LeTourneau University (U)
Liberty University (U, G)
Life Pacific College (N, U)
Limestone College (U)
Lipscomb University (U, G)
Lutheran Theological Seminary at Gettysburg (G)
Martin Luther College (U)
Master's College and Seminary (U)
Miami Dade College (U)
Mid-America Christian University (N, U)
Montgomery Community College (N)
Moody Bible Institute (N, U, G)
North Central University (N, U)
Northwest Christian College (U)
Northwestern College (U)
Northwest Graduate School of the Ministry (G)
Oral Roberts University (N)
Park University (U)
Patrick Henry College (U)
Prairie Bible College (U, G)
Saint Joseph's College of Maine (N, U, G)
St. Petersburg College (U)
Shasta Bible College (N)
Snead State Community College (U)
Southeastern College of the Assemblies of God (U)
Southwestern Assemblies of God University (U, G)
Southwestern Baptist Theological Seminary (U, G)
Summit Pacific College (N, U)
Taylor University (N, U)
Taylor University (U)
Trinity Bible College (U)
The University of Findlay (U)
University of Missouri–Columbia (U)
University of Southern Mississippi (U)
University of the Incarnate Word (U)
University of Waterloo (U)
Western Baptist College (U)
Western Seminary (N, G)
William and Catherine Booth College (U)

Biblical and other theological languages and literatures

Alliance University College (U, G)
Assemblies of God Theological Seminary (G)
Baptist Theological Seminary at Richmond (N, G)
Bethany College of the Assemblies of God (U)
Black Hills State University (U)
Briercrest Distance Learning (G)
Calvin Theological Seminary (G)
Central Baptist Theological Seminary (N, G)
Central Bible College (N)
Colorado Christian University (U)
Columbia Union College (U)
Earlham School of Religion (G)
Eugene Bible College (U)
Global University of the Assemblies of God (N)
Hebrew College (N, U, G)
Immaculata University (U)
Indiana Wesleyan University (U)
The Jewish Theological Seminary (N, U, G)
The King's College and Seminary (N, U, G)
Lamar State College–Port Arthur (U)
Life Pacific College (N)
Lutheran Theological Seminary at Gettysburg (G)
Master's College and Seminary (U)
Moody Bible Institute (U)
Prairie Bible College (U)
Southwestern Baptist Theological Seminary (G)
Taylor University (N, U)
Taylor University (U)
University of the Incarnate Word (U)
University of Waterloo (U)
Western Seminary (N, G)

N–Noncredit; U–Undergraduate; G–Graduate

Western Washington University (U)

Bilingual/bicultural education

Baltimore City Community College (U)
Bethany College of the Assemblies of God (U)
California State University, Fullerton (N)
Hamline University (G)
Kansas City Kansas Community College (U)
Middle Tennessee State University (N)
Murray State University (G)
Northern Arizona University (G)
Oxnard College (U)
Pace University (G)
Seattle Pacific University (G)
Texas A&M University–Kingsville (G)
Texas Woman's University (U, G)
University of Arkansas at Pine Bluff (N, U)

Biochemistry and biophysics

Drake University (U)
Illinois Institute of Technology (U, G)
Iowa State University of Science and Technology (U, G)
The University of Akron (U)
University of Bridgeport (G)
University of Colorado at Denver (U)
University of Minnesota, Twin Cities Campus (U)
University of Southern Mississippi (G)

Biochemistry

Kansas State University (U)
Mountain State University (U)
Pitt Community College (U)
University of Waterloo (U)

Bioengineering and biomedical engineering

Columbia University (N, G)
Georgia Institute of Technology (G)
Illinois Institute of Technology (G)
Louisiana Tech University (G)
Madison Area Technical College (U)
Stanford University (N)
University of Colorado at Boulder (N, G)

Biological and physical sciences

American Academy of Nutrition, College of Nutrition (U)
Anne Arundel Community College (U)
Arkansas State University–Beebe (U)
Athabasca University (U)
Baltimore City Community College (U)
Bethany College of the Assemblies of God (U)
Boise State University (U)
Bossier Parish Community College (U)
Brevard Community College (U)
Caldwell Community College and Technical Institute (U)
Cascadia Community College (U)
Casper College (U)
Central Oregon Community College (U)
Chadron State College (U)
Chemeketa Community College (U)
Citrus College (U)
Clinton Community College (U)
College of the Canyons (U)
Delaware County Community College (U)
Des Moines Area Community College (U)
Eastern Illinois University (U)
Eugene Bible College (U)
Flathead Valley Community College (U)
Florida Community College at Jacksonville (U)
Fontbonne University (U)
George C. Wallace Community College (U)
Gogebic Community College (U)
Harrisburg Area Community College (U)
Hibbing Community College (U)
Hopkinsville Community College (U)
Horry-Georgetown Technical College (U)
Illinois Institute of Technology (U, G)
Immaculata University (U)
Independence Community College (U)
Jacksonville State University (U)
James Madison University (N)
Jefferson College (U)
John A. Logan College (U)
Judson College (U)
Kansas City Kansas Community College (U)
Kellogg Community College (U)
Kentucky State University (U, G)
Lake Superior College (U)
Lehigh University (G)
Massasoit Community College (U)
Miami Dade College (U)
Minnesota School of Business–Brooklyn Center (U)
Mississippi Delta Community College (U)
Mississippi State University (U)
Montana State University–Bozeman (G)
Mount Saint Vincent University (U)
National University (U)
North Carolina State University (U)
Northeast State Technical Community College (U)
Northwestern State University of Louisiana (U)
Ohio University (U)
Okaloosa-Walton College (U)
Palm Beach Community College (U)
Patrick Henry Community College (U)
The Pennsylvania State University University Park Campus (U)
Quinnipiac University (U)
Riverland Community College (U)
Sacred Heart University (U)
St. Joseph's College, Suffolk Campus (U)
St. Petersburg College (U)
Seminole Community College (U)
Snead State Community College (U)
Taft College (U)
Taylor University (U)
Taylor University (U)
The University of Akron (U)
The University of Alabama (U)
University of Arkansas at Pine Bluff (U)
University of Great Falls (U)
University of Houston–Downtown (U)
University of Illinois at Springfield (U)
University of La Verne (N)
University of Massachusetts Boston (G)
University of Waterloo (U)
University of Wisconsin Colleges (U)
University of Wisconsin–River Falls (U)
Utah Valley State College (U)
Wake Technical Community College (U)
Westchester Community College (U)
Western Wyoming Community College (U)
West Virginia University at Parkersburg (U)
William Paterson University of New Jersey (U)
York Technical College (U)

Biological sciences/life sciences, other

Arkansas Tech University (U)
Athabasca University (U)
Bethany College of the Assemblies of God (U)
Bossier Parish Community College (U)
Brevard Community College (U)
Brigham Young University (U)
Bucks County Community College (U)
Caldwell Community College and Technical Institute (U)
Casper College (U)
Chemeketa Community College (U)
Cleveland State University (U)
Colorado State University-Pueblo (U)
Columbia College (U)
Columbus State Community College (U)
County College of Morris (U)
Dakota County Technical College (U)
Danville Area Community College (U)
Danville Community College (U)
Darton College (U)
DeVry University Online (U)
Eastern Illinois University (U)
Eastern Shore Community College (U)
El Camino College (U)
Feather River Community College District (U)

Florida Hospital College of Health Sciences (U)
Gaston College (U)
George Mason University (G)
Hopkinsville Community College (U)
Illinois Institute of Technology (G)
Immaculata University (U)
Inter American University of Puerto Rico, San Germán Campus (U)
Iowa Western Community College (U)
Jacksonville State University (U)
James Madison University (N)
John F. Kennedy University (G)
Lake Region State College (U)
Lipscomb University (U)
Louisiana Tech University (U)
Marylhurst University (U)
Miami Dade College (U)
Middlesex Community College (U)
Minot State University–Bottineau Campus (U)
MiraCosta College (U)
Mississippi Delta Community College (U)
Northampton County Area Community College (U)
North Central Texas College (U)
Northern Kentucky University (U)
Northwestern Technical College (U)
Oxnard College (U)
Pennsylvania College of Technology (U)
Quinnipiac University (U)
Reading Area Community College (U)
Riverland Community College (U)
Rosalind Franklin University of Medicine and Science (N, G)
Saint Leo University (U)
Schoolcraft College (U)
Shelton State Community College (U)
Shoreline Community College (U)
Snead State Community College (U)
Southeast Community College, Beatrice Campus (U)
Southeastern College of the Assemblies of God (U)
Southern Illinois University Carbondale (U)
Stanford University (N)
State University of New York College at Fredonia (U)
Texas State University-San Marcos (U)
University of Colorado at Colorado Springs (U)
University of La Verne (N)
University of Waterloo (U)
University of West Florida (U)
University of Wisconsin–River Falls (G)
University of Wyoming (U)
William Paterson University of New Jersey (U)
Wright State University (U)

Biological technology

Delta College (U)
Frederick Community College (U)
James Madison University (U)
Stanford University (N)
University of Houston–Downtown (U)

Biology

Alvin Community College (U)
American Academy of Nutrition, College of Nutrition (U)
American River College (U)
Bellevue Community College (U)
Brigham Young University (U)
Brookdale Community College (U)
Broward Community College (U)
Bucks County Community College (U)
Burlington County College (U)
Carleton University (U)
Cedarville University (U)
Central Virginia Community College (U)
Central Wyoming College (U)
Charter Oak State College (U)
Clackamas Community College (U)
Clovis Community College (U)
College of DuPage (U)
College of Mount St. Joseph (U)
College of the Southwest (U)
Colorado Mountain College District System (U)
Community College of Denver (U)
Concordia University at Austin (N, U)
Dallas County Community College District (U)
Dawson Community College (U)
Delta College (U)
Eastern Kentucky University (U)
Edison State Community College (U)
Fairleigh Dickinson University, Metropolitan Campus (U)
Greenville Technical College (U)
Iowa State University of Science and Technology (U)
Johnson County Community College (U)
Lakeland Community College (U)
Lawson State Community College (U)
Louisiana State University and Agricultural and Mechanical College (U)
Manatee Community College (U)
Marylhurst University (U)
Maui Community College (U)
Memorial University of Newfoundland (U)
Mercy College (U)
Montana State University–Billings (U)
Montana State University–Bozeman (G)
Montgomery County Community College (U)
Mountain Empire Community College (U)
Mountain State University (U)
Mount Wachusett Community College (U)
Northern Virginia Community College (U)
North Harris Montgomery Community College District (U)
Northwestern Michigan College (U)
Odessa College (U)
Ohio University (U)
Palomar College (U)
Park University (U)
Pennsylvania College of Technology (U)
The Pennsylvania State University University Park Campus (U)
Pierce College (U)
Pitt Community College (U)
St. Cloud State University (U)
Sauk Valley Community College (U)
Skidmore College (U)
Southwestern Assemblies of God University (U)
Spoon River College (U)
State University of New York Empire State College (U)
Tarrant County College District (U)
Texas Christian University (U)
Texas State University-San Marcos (U)
Triton College (U)
University of Alaska Fairbanks (U)
University of Colorado at Denver (U)
University of Delaware (U)
University of Florida (U)
University of Guelph (U)
University of Idaho (U)
University of Maine (U)
University of Minnesota, Twin Cities Campus (U)
University of Nebraska–Lincoln (U)
The University of North Carolina at Chapel Hill (U)
University of Northern Colorado (U)
The University of South Dakota (U)
University of Southern Mississippi (U)
The University of Texas at Arlington (U)
The University of Texas at Tyler (U)
University of Utah (U)
University of Waterloo (U)
Upper Iowa University (N, U)
Utah Valley State College (U)
Vance-Granville Community College (U)
Washington State University (U)
Waubonsee Community College (U)
Whatcom Community College (U)

N–Noncredit; U–Undergraduate; G–Graduate

Wichita State University (U)
Wilfrid Laurier University (U)
Wilkes Community College (U)

Biology, general

Acadia University (U)
Adams State College (G)
Albuquerque Technical Vocational Institute (U)
Alvin Community College (U)
American College of Computer & Information Sciences (U)
Arkansas State University–Beebe (U)
Arkansas Tech University (U)
Asheville-Buncombe Technical Community College (U)
Athabasca University (N, U)
Baltimore City Community College (U)
Bethany College of the Assemblies of God (U)
Bismarck State College (U)
Blue Mountain Community College (U)
Brigham Young University (U)
Bucks County Community College (U)
Butler County Community College (U)
Caldwell College (U)
Caldwell Community College and Technical Institute (U)
Carroll Community College (U)
Casper College (U)
Cayuga County Community College (U)
Chattanooga State Technical Community College (U)
Chemeketa Community College (U)
Cleveland Community College (U)
The College of St. Scholastica (U)
College of The Albemarle (U)
Columbia Union College (U)
The Community College of Baltimore County (U)
Community College of Denver (U)
Copiah-Lincoln Community College–Natchez Campus (U)
Cossatot Community College of the University of Arkansas (U)
County College of Morris (U)
Culver-Stockton College (U)
Dakota County Technical College (U)
Dallas Baptist University (U)
Davenport University Online (U)
Delaware County Community College (U)
Des Moines Area Community College (U)
Drake University (U)
East Carolina University (U)
East Central College (U)
Eastern Illinois University (U)
Eastern Michigan University (U)
Eastern Oregon University (U)
Eastern Wyoming College (U)
Eugene Bible College (U)
Fairleigh Dickinson University, Metropolitan Campus (G)
Frederick Community College (U)
George C. Wallace Community College (U)
Glenville State College (U)
Golden West College (U)
Houston Community College System (U)
Immaculata University (U)
Indiana University–Purdue University Fort Wayne (U)
Iowa Western Community College (U)
Ivy Tech State College–Columbus (U)
Ivy Tech State College–North Central (U)
Ivy Tech State College–Wabash Valley (U)
Ivy Tech State College–Whitewater (U)
Jacksonville State University (U)
Jefferson College (U)
John Tyler Community College (U)
Kansas City Kansas Community College (U)
Lake Region State College (U)
Lansing Community College (U)
Lenoir Community College (U)
LeTourneau University (U)
Liberty University (U)
Limestone College (U)
Long Beach City College (U)
Lord Fairfax Community College (U)
Louisiana State University and Agricultural and Mechanical College (N)
Manatee Community College (U)
Maysville Community College (U)
Mayville State University (U)
Mesa Community College (U)
Metropolitan Community College (U)
Miami Dade College (U)
Middlesex Community College (U)
Minnesota School of Business–Brooklyn Center (U)
Minnesota School of Business-Richfield (U)
Mississippi Delta Community College (U)
Mississippi State University (U)
Missouri Southern State University (U)
Moberly Area Community College (U)
Monroe Community College (U)
Mountain Empire Community College (U)
Mountain State University (U)
Mount Saint Vincent University (U)
Mt. San Antonio College (U)
Nassau Community College (U)
New Hampshire Community Technical College System (U)
New York Institute of Technology (U)
Northampton County Area Community College (U)
Northern Arizona University (U)
North Hennepin Community College (U)
North Idaho College (U)
NorthWest Arkansas Community College (U)
Northwestern Michigan College (U)
Northwestern Technical College (U)
Okaloosa-Walton College (U)
Orange Coast College (U)
Oxnard College (U)
Pace University (U)
Pasco-Hernando Community College (U)
Patrick Henry College (U)
Paul D. Camp Community College (U)
Pratt Community College (U)
Pulaski Technical College (U)
Rend Lake College (U)
Rockland Community College (U)
St. Joseph's College, Suffolk Campus (U)
St. Petersburg College (U)
San Bernardino Valley College (U)
Seminole Community College (U)
Seward County Community College (U)
Shawnee State University (U)
Snead State Community College (U)
Southeastern Community College (U)
Southern Illinois University Carbondale (U)
South Piedmont Community College (U)
Spoon River College (U)
Stanly Community College (U)
Sul Ross State University (U)
Tacoma Community College (U)
Taylor University (U)
Teikyo Post University (U)
Temple College (U)
Texas A&M University–Commerce (U)
Treasure Valley Community College (U)
The University of Akron (U)
The University of Alabama (U)
University of Alaska Fairbanks (U)
University of Arkansas at Pine Bluff (U)
University of Houston–Victoria (U)
University of Idaho (U)
University of Illinois at Springfield (U)
University of La Verne (U)
University of Maryland University College (U)
University of Massachusetts Boston (U)
University of Mississippi (U)
University of Missouri–Columbia (U)
The University of Montana–Missoula (U)
The University of North Carolina at Pembroke (U)
University of Southern Indiana (U)
University of Southern Mississippi (G)
The University of Texas at Austin (U)
The University of Texas System (U)
University of the Incarnate Word (U)
University of Waterloo (U)
University of West Florida (U)

Non-Degree-Related Course Subject Areas
Biology, general

University of Wisconsin Colleges (U)
University of Wisconsin–Superior (U)
Utah State University (U)
Utah Valley State College (U)
Walters State Community College (U)
Westchester Community College (U)
West Virginia University at Parkersburg (U)
Wilfrid Laurier University (U)
William Paterson University of New Jersey (U)
Worcester State College (U)
Wright State University (U)

Biopsychology

Feather River Community College District (N)
State University of New York at Plattsburgh (U)

Botany

Bellevue Community College (U)
Brigham Young University (U)
Cossatot Community College of the University of Arkansas (U)
Eastern Oregon University (U)
Feather River Community College District (N)
Mississippi Delta Community College (U)
Mountain State University (U)
Oregon State University (U)
Oxnard College (U)
Palomar College (U)
Santa Fe Community College (N)
The University of Akron (U)
University of Bridgeport (G)
University of Illinois at Springfield (U)
University of Saskatchewan (N)
University of Wyoming (U)
William Paterson University of New Jersey (U)

Business administration and management

Adirondack Community College (U)
AIB College of Business (U)
Albuquerque Technical Vocational Institute (U)
Alliant International University (U)
Alvin Community College (U)
The American College (U, G)
American College of Computer & Information Sciences (U, G)
American Graduate University (G)
American Public University System (U)
American River College (U)
Andrew Jackson University (G)
Anne Arundel Community College (U)
Arapahoe Community College (U)
Arkansas Tech University (U)
Asheville-Buncombe Technical Community College (N, U)
Ashworth College (N)
Aspen University (G)
Athabasca University (N, U, G)
Auburn University Montgomery (N)
Augusta Technical College (N)
Bainbridge College (N)
Baker College of Flint (U)
Baltimore City Community College (N, U)
Beaufort County Community College (U)
Bellevue University (U, G)
Bellingham Technical College (U)
Bemidji State University (U)
Berkeley College (U)
Berkeley College-New York City Campus (U)
Berkeley College-Westchester Campus (U)
Bishop State Community College (U)
Bloomfield College (U)
Brenau University (U, G)
Brevard Community College (U)
Bridgewater State College (N)
Briercrest Distance Learning (U)
Brigham Young University (U)
Bristol Community College (N)
Brookdale Community College (U)
Broome Community College (N)
Brunswick Community College (U)
Bryant and Stratton Online (U)
Bucks County Community College (U)
Butler County Community College (U)
Caldwell College (U)
Caldwell Community College and Technical Institute (N, U)
California National University for Advanced Studies (N, U, G)
California State University, Monterey Bay (U)
Campbell University (U)
Cape Cod Community College (U)
Cape Fear Community College (U)
Capella University (N, G)
Carl Albert State College (U)
Carroll Community College (N, U)
Casper College (U)
Central Oregon Community College (U)
Central Texas College (U)
Century College (N)
Chadron State College (U, G)
Chaminade University of Honolulu (U, G)
Champlain College (U)
Chattanooga State Technical Community College (U)
Chemeketa Community College (U)
Chesapeake College (U)
Cincinnati State Technical and Community College (U)
Clackamas Community College (U)
Clark College (U)
Clemson University (G)
Cleveland State University (N)
Clinton Community College (U)
Clovis Community College (U)
Coastal Bend College (U)
Coleman College (U, G)
College for Lifelong Learning (U)
College of DuPage (U)
College of Mount St. Joseph (U)
College of The Albemarle (N, U)
College of the Southwest (U)
Colorado Christian University (U, G)
Colorado State University-Pueblo (N)
Columbia Basin College (U)
Columbia College (U)
Columbia Union College (U)
Columbus State Community College (U)
The Community College of Baltimore County (U)
Community College of Denver (U)
Concordia University Wisconsin (G)
Corning Community College (U)
Cossatot Community College of the University of Arkansas (N)
Cumberland County College (U)
Dakota County Technical College (U)
Dallas Baptist University (U, G)
Daniel Webster College (U)
Danville Area Community College (U)
Danville Community College (U)
Darton College (N, U)
Davenport University Online (U, G)
Dawson Community College (U)
Delaware County Community College (U)
Delaware Technical & Community College, Jack F. Owens Campus (U)
Delaware Technical & Community College, Stanton/Wilmington Campus (U)
DePaul University (U)
Des Moines Area Community College (U)
Dickinson State University (U)
Drake University (U, G)
Drexel University (U, G)
East Carolina University (G)
Eastern Illinois University (G)
Eastern Michigan University (U, G)
Eastern Shore Community College (U)
Eastern Wyoming College (U)
Edgecombe Community College (N, U)
Edison Community College (U)
Edison State Community College (N, U)
Edmonds Community College (U)

N–Noncredit; U–Undergraduate; G–Graduate

Elizabeth City State University (U)
Elizabethtown College (U)
Embry-Riddle Aeronautical University (U, G)
Embry-Riddle Aeronautical University, Extended Campus (G)
Erie Community College (U)
Everglades University (U, G)
Fayetteville State University (G)
Feather River Community College District (N)
Florida Atlantic University (G)
Florida Community College at Jacksonville (U)
Florida Institute of Technology (G)
Florida International University (U)
Florida Metropolitan University–Brandon Campus (G)
Florida National College (U)
Forrest Junior College (U)
Fort Hays State University (U)
Franklin Pierce College (U)
Franklin University (U, G)
Frederick Community College (U)
Fulton-Montgomery Community College (N, U)
George C. Wallace Community College (U)
Georgia Southern University (U)
Grantham University (U)
Halifax Community College (N)
Harrisburg Area Community College (U)
Heart of Georgia Technical College (U)
Hibbing Community College (U)
Hopkinsville Community College (U)
Horry-Georgetown Technical College (U)
Houston Community College System (U)
Howard Community College (U)
Immaculata University (U)
Indiana Institute of Technology (U)
Indiana State University (U)
Indiana University–Purdue University Fort Wayne (G)
Inter American University of Puerto Rico, San Germán Campus (U, G)
Iowa Western Community College (U)
Irvine Valley College (U)
Ivy Tech State College–Columbus (U)
Ivy Tech State College–Eastcentral (U)
Ivy Tech State College–Kokomo (U)
Ivy Tech State College–North Central (U)
Ivy Tech State College–Northwest (U)
Ivy Tech State College–Southcentral (U)
Ivy Tech State College–Southwest (U)
Ivy Tech State College–Wabash Valley (U)
Ivy Tech State College–Whitewater (U)
Jacksonville State University (U, G)
Jamestown Community College (N)
Jefferson Community College (U)
John F. Kennedy University (U, G)
John Tyler Community College (U)
John Wood Community College (U)
Jones College (U)
Jones International University (U)
Judson College (U)
Kansas City Kansas Community College (U)
Kansas State University (U)
Keiser College (U)
Kirkwood Community College (U)
Lakeland College (G)
Lake Region State College (U)
Lamar State College–Port Arthur (N, U)
Lawrence Technological University (U, G)
Lehigh University (N, G)
Lewis-Clark State College (U)
Liberty University (G)
Limestone College (U)
Linn-Benton Community College (U)
Lipscomb University (U, G)
Long Beach City College (U)
Long Island University, C.W. Post Campus (N)
Lord Fairfax Community College (N)
Louisiana State University and Agricultural and Mechanical College (U)
Louisiana State University at Eunice (U)
Louisiana State University in Shreveport (U)
Madison Area Technical College (U)
Manatee Community College (U)
Manchester Community College (N, U)
Mansfield University of Pennsylvania (U)
Marist College (G)
Marist College (G)
Marshall University (U)
Maryville University of Saint Louis (N)
Massasoit Community College (U)
Maui Community College (U)
Maysville Community College (N)
Mayville State University (U)
Memorial University of Newfoundland (U)
Mercy College (U, G)
Mesa Community College (U)
Metropolitan State University (U)
Middlesex Community College (N, U)
Middle Tennessee State University (N, U)
Mid-State Technical College (U)
Millersville University of Pennsylvania (U)
Minnesota School of Business–Brooklyn Center (U)
Minnesota School of Business-Richfield (U)
Minnesota State College–Southeast Technical (N)
MiraCosta College (N)
Mississippi State University (G)
Missouri Baptist University (U)
Moberly Area Community College (U)
Modesto Junior College (U)
Montana State University–Billings (U)
Montgomery Community College (N, U)
Montgomery County Community College (U)
Motlow State Community College (U)
Mountain State University (U)
Mt. Hood Community College (U)
Mount Saint Mary College (G)
Mount Saint Vincent University (U)
Mt. San Antonio College (U)
Mount Wachusett Community College (U)
Murray State University (U)
Nassau Community College (U)
National University (U, G)
Naugatuck Valley Community College (U)
New Hampshire Community Technical College System (N, U)
New Jersey City University (G)
New Jersey Institute of Technology (G)
New Mexico State University (U)
New School University (G)
New York Institute of Technology (U, G)
New York Institute of Technology (U)
Nipissing University (U)
Normandale Community College (N, U)
Northampton County Area Community College (U)
Northcentral University (U, G)
Northeastern Oklahoma Agricultural and Mechanical College (U)
Northeastern University (U, G)
Northeast State Technical Community College (U)
Northern Arizona University (G)
Northern New Mexico Community College (U)
North Harris Montgomery Community College District (U)
North Hennepin Community College (N)
Northwestern Michigan College (U)
Northwestern Oklahoma State University (U)
Northwestern State University of Louisiana (U)
Northwood University (U)
Nova Southeastern University (G)
Ocean County College (U)
Odessa College (N)
The Ohio State University (G)
Okaloosa-Walton College (U)
Oklahoma State University (U)
Oregon Institute of Technology (U)
Owensboro Community and Technical College (U)
Oxnard College (U)
Pace University (U, G)
Park University (U, G)
Pasco-Hernando Community College (U)

Patrick Henry Community College (U)
Paul D. Camp Community College (U)
Peirce College (U)
Peninsula College (U)
The Pennsylvania State University University Park Campus (N, U, G)
Prairie State College (N)
Pratt Community College (U)
Quinnipiac University (U)
Rappahannock Community College (U)
Raritan Valley Community College (U)
Reading Area Community College (U)
Regis University (U)
Rend Lake College (N)
The Richard Stockton College of New Jersey (U)
Riverland Community College (U)
Riverside Community College (N, U)
Roosevelt University (U)
Rosalind Franklin University of Medicine and Science (N, G)
Royal Roads University (U, G)
Ryerson University (U)
Sacred Heart University (U, G)
St. Ambrose University (U, G)
St. Clair County Community College (U)
St. Edward's University (N, U, G)
St. John's University (U)
Saint Joseph's College of Maine (U, G)
St. Joseph's College, Suffolk Campus (U)
Saint Leo University (U, G)
St. Louis Community College System (N, G)
Saint Mary-of-the-Woods College (U)
Saint Mary-of-the-Woods College (U)
Saint Paul College–A Community & Technical College (U)
St. Petersburg College (U)
Salem Community College (U)
Salve Regina University (G)
San Bernardino Valley College (U)
Santa Fe Community College (N)
Santa Rosa Junior College (U)
Santiago Canyon College (U)
Sauk Valley Community College (U)
Schenectady County Community College (U)
Schiller International University (U, G)
Seminole Community College (U)
Shawnee State University (U)
Shippensburg University of Pennsylvania (G)
Shoreline Community College (U)
Sinclair Community College (U)
Skidmore College (U)
Sonoma State University (N)
Southeast Arkansas College (U)
Southeast Community College, Beatrice Campus (U)
Southeast Community College, Lincoln Campus (U)
Southeastern Community College (U)
Southwestern Assemblies of God University (U)
Southwestern College (U)
Spartanburg Technical College (U)
Spring Arbor University (U, G)
Stanford University (N)
Stanly Community College (U)
State University of New York at Oswego (N, G)
State University of New York at Plattsburgh (G)
State University of New York College at Potsdam (N)
State University of New York Institute of Technology (U, G)
State University of New York Institute of Technology (U, G)
State University of New York Institute of Technology (U, G)
State University of New York Institute of Technology (U, G)
Stephen F. Austin State University (U)
Sullivan University (G)
Sullivan University (U, G)
Syracuse University (U)
Syracuse University (G)
Tacoma Community College (N)
Taft College (U)
Taylor University (N, U)
Teikyo Post University (U)
Temple College (U)
Texas A&M University–Commerce (U)
Texas Tech University (N, U)
Three Rivers Community College (U)
Thunderbird, The Garvin School of International Management (G)
Touro University International (U, G)
Trinity Western University (G)
Tri-State University (U)
Tunxis Community College (U)
Umpqua Community College (U)
Université Sainte-Anne (U)
The University of Akron (U, G)
University of Alaska Fairbanks (U)
University of Arkansas at Pine Bluff (U)
University of California, Los Angeles (G)
University of Central Arkansas (N)
University of Cincinnati Raymond Walters College (U)
University of Colorado at Denver (G)
University of Dallas (G)
University of Denver (G)
The University of Findlay (U, G)
University of Georgia (U)
University of Great Falls (U)
University of Guelph (G)
University of Hawaii–West Oahu (U)
University of Houston–Clear Lake (G)
University of Houston–Downtown (U)
University of Illinois (G)
University of Illinois at Springfield (U)
University of La Verne (G)
The University of Maine at Augusta (U)
University of Management and Technology (N, U, G)
University of Maryland, Baltimore County (N)
University of Maryland University College (U, G)
University of Massachusetts Amherst (N, U)
University of Massachusetts Boston (U)
University of Minnesota, Twin Cities Campus (U)
University of Missouri–Columbia (U)
The University of Montana–Missoula (G)
University of New Orleans (U, G)
The University of North Carolina at Chapel Hill (U)
The University of North Carolina at Charlotte (N)
The University of North Carolina at Pembroke (U, G)
University of North Dakota (U, G)
University of Northwestern Ohio (U)
University of Notre Dame (N, G)
University of Oklahoma (U)
University of Phoenix Online Campus (U)
University of St. Francis (U, G)
University of South Carolina (U)
University of South Carolina Sumter (G)
The University of Tennessee (U)
The University of Tennessee at Martin (N, U, G)
The University of Texas at Dallas (G)
The University of Texas at Tyler (G)
The University of Texas–Pan American (U, G)
University of the Incarnate Word (U, G)
University of Toronto (N, U)
University of Tulsa (G)
University of Vermont (N)
The University of Virginia's College at Wise (U)
University of Washington (N)
University of Wisconsin–Eau Claire (G)
University of Wisconsin–La Crosse (G)
University of Wisconsin–Parkside (G)
University of Wisconsin–Platteville (U)
University of Wisconsin–Platteville (G)

N–Noncredit; U–Undergraduate; G–Graduate

University of Wisconsin–Platteville (G)
University of Wisconsin–Platteville (G)
University of Wisconsin–Platteville (U, G)
University of Wisconsin–River Falls (U)
University of Wisconsin–Superior (U)
University of Wyoming (G)
Upper Iowa University (U)
Utah State University (U)
Utah Valley State College (U)
Valparaiso University (U, G)
Vance-Granville Community College (U)
Wake Technical Community College (N)
Walsh College of Accountancy and Business Administration (N, G)
Washington State University (U)
Washtenaw Community College (U)
Waubonsee Community College (U)
Wayland Baptist University (U, G)
Waynesburg College (G)
Wayne State College (U, G)
Weber State University (U)
Western Baptist College (U)
Western New England College (U, G)
Western Wyoming Community College (U)
West Valley College (U)
West Virginia University at Parkersburg (U)
Westwood Online (U)
Wichita State University (U)
Wilkes Community College (U)
William Paterson University of New Jersey (U, G)
William Tyndale College (U)
Winona State University (U)
Winston-Salem State University (U)
Wisconsin Indianhead Technical College (N, U)
Worcester Polytechnic Institute (G)
Worcester State College (N, U)
York Technical College (U)
York University (N, U)
Youngstown State University (N)

Business and personal services marketing operations

Adams State College (N)
Athabasca University (N, G)
Bellevue University (U, G)
Bossier Parish Community College (N)
Brenau University (U, G)
Brevard Community College (U)
Bristol Community College (N)
Caldwell Community College and Technical Institute (N)
California State University, Dominguez Hills (N)
Capella University (G)
Chadron State College (U, G)
Clackamas Community College (U)
Cleveland State University (N)
Cossatot Community College of the University of Arkansas (N)
Darton College (N)
Delaware County Community College (U)
Des Moines Area Community College (U)
Edgecombe Community College (N)
Florida Metropolitan University–Brandon Campus (G)
Forrest Junior College (U)
Glenville State College (U)
Horry-Georgetown Technical College (U)
Jacksonville State University (U, G)
James Madison University (N)
Lakeland Community College (N)
Lake Region State College (U)
Lamar State College–Port Arthur (N)
Lord Fairfax Community College (N)
Manatee Community College (U)
Marist College (G)
Massasoit Community College (N)
Maysville Community College (N)
Mercy College (G)
Middle Tennessee State University (N)
Minnesota State College–Southeast Technical (N)
Modesto Junior College (U)
Mount Saint Vincent University (U)
Mt. San Antonio College (U)
New Hampshire Community Technical College System (N, U)
Ocean County College (U)
Oregon State University (N)
Pasco-Hernando Community College (N)
Santiago Canyon College (U)
Southeast Community College, Beatrice Campus (U)
Taylor University (N)
Thunderbird, The Garvin School of International Management (G)
Tulane University (U)
University of Colorado at Denver (G)
University of Dallas (G)
University of Missouri–Columbia (N)
The University of Texas at Tyler (U)
University of the Incarnate Word (U)
University of Vermont (N)
Vance-Granville Community College (N)
Wilkes Community College (U)
Youngstown State University (N)

Business communications

Adirondack Community College (U)
Alvin Community College (U)
American College of Computer & Information Sciences (U)
American Graduate University (G)
American River College (U)
Arkansas State University–Beebe (U)
Asheville-Buncombe Technical Community College (N)
Athabasca University (N, U, G)
Beaufort County Community College (N)
Bellevue University (G)
Bellingham Technical College (U)
Bismarck State College (U)
Brenau University (U, G)
Brevard Community College (U)
Bridgewater State College (U)
Brigham Young University (U)
Bristol Community College (N)
Bryant and Stratton Online (U)
Bucks County Community College (U)
Caldwell Community College and Technical Institute (N, U)
California National University for Advanced Studies (N, U)
California State University, Dominguez Hills (N)
California State University, Sacramento (U)
Campbell University (U)
Capella University (N, G)
Cardean University (G)
Cedarville University (U)
Central Texas College (U)
Chadron State College (U)
Champlain College (U)
Chemeketa Community College (U)
Clackamas Community College (U)
Cleveland State University (N)
Clinton Community College (U)
Coleman College (G)
College of San Mateo (U)
College of The Albemarle (N, U)
College of the Canyons (U)
College of the Siskiyous (U)
Colorado Mountain College District System (U)
Columbus State Community College (U)
The Community College of Baltimore County (U)
Community College of Denver (U)
Concordia College (U)
Cossatot Community College of the University of Arkansas (N, U)
Darton College (N)
Delaware County Community College (U)
Delta College (U)
Des Moines Area Community College (U)
Dickinson State University (U)
Drexel University (U)
East Carolina University (U)
Eastern Michigan University (U, G)
Edgecombe Community College (N, U)
Edison State Community College (U)
Elizabeth City State University (U)

Non-Degree-Related Course Subject Areas
Business communications

Elizabethtown College (U)
Fairmont State University (U)
Feather River Community College District (N)
Florida Metropolitan University–Brandon Campus (U)
Forrest Junior College (U)
Fort Hays State University (U)
Frederick Community College (N, U)
Gannon University (U)
Gaston College (U)
Horry-Georgetown Technical College (U)
Howard Community College (U)
Hudson County Community College (N)
Immaculata University (U)
Indiana University–Purdue University Fort Wayne (N)
Iowa Western Community College (U)
Jacksonville State University (G)
James Madison University (N)
Jamestown Community College (N)
Jones College (U)
Jones International University (U, G)
Kellogg Community College (U)
Lakeland Community College (N)
Lake Superior College (U)
Lehigh University (N)
Limestone College (U)
Lord Fairfax Community College (N)
Manatee Community College (U)
Manchester Community College (U)
Marylhurst University (U)
Massasoit Community College (U)
Maui Community College (U)
Mercy College (G)
Middlesex Community College (U)
Middle Tennessee State University (N, U)
Mid-South Community College (N)
Minnesota School of Business–Brooklyn Center (U)
Montana State University–Billings (U)
Montgomery Community College (N)
Mott Community College (U)
New Hampshire Community Technical College System (N)
Northampton County Area Community College (U)
North Country Community College (U)
Northeastern Oklahoma Agricultural and Mechanical College (U)
NorthWest Arkansas Community College (U)
Northwestern Michigan College (U)
Northwestern Oklahoma State University (U)
Oakland City University (U)
Okaloosa-Walton College (U)
Oklahoma State University (U)
Old Dominion University (U)
Oregon State University (U)
Oxnard College (U)
Park University (U)
Pasco-Hernando Community College (N)
Paul D. Camp Community College (U)
The Pennsylvania State University University Park Campus (N, U)
Pierce College (U)
Prairie State College (U)
Rappahannock Community College (U)
Regis University (G)
Richland Community College (U)
Roosevelt University (U)
Royal Roads University (G)
Ryerson University (U)
St. Clair County Community College (U)
St. Cloud Technical College (N)
St. Edward's University (U, G)
Saint Joseph's College of Maine (G)
St. Joseph's College, Suffolk Campus (U)
Saint Leo University (U)
Saint Paul College–A Community & Technical College (U)
St. Petersburg College (U)
Salem Community College (N)
Santa Fe Community College (N)
Santa Rosa Junior College (U)
Schiller International University (U, G)
Seminole Community College (U)
Shoreline Community College (U)
Snead State Community College (U)
Sonoma State University (N)
South Central Technical College (U)
Southeast Arkansas College (U)
Southeast Community College, Beatrice Campus (U)
Southwest Wisconsin Technical College (U)
Spring Arbor University (G)
Stephen F. Austin State University (U)
Syracuse University (U)
Tarleton State University (N)
Taylor University (N)
Thunderbird, The Garvin School of International Management (G)
Tompkins Cortland Community College (U)
Tulane University (U)
The University of Akron (U)
University of Arkansas at Pine Bluff (U)
University of Colorado at Denver (G)
The University of Findlay (G)
University of Florida (N)
University of Georgia (U)
University of Houston–Downtown (U)
The University of Maine at Augusta (U)
University of Maryland, Baltimore County (N)
University of Massachusetts Lowell (U)
The University of North Carolina at Chapel Hill (U)
University of Notre Dame (N, G)
University of Oklahoma (U)
University of Saint Francis (U)
The University of Texas at Tyler (U)
The University of Texas–Pan American (U, G)
University of the Incarnate Word (U, G)
University of Toronto (N, U)
University of Vermont (N)
University of Washington (U)
University of West Florida (U)
University of Wisconsin–Platteville (G)
University of Wisconsin–Platteville (G)
University of Wisconsin–Platteville (U, G)
Vance-Granville Community College (N)
Western New England College (U)
West Virginia University at Parkersburg (U)
Wilkes Community College (U)
William Paterson University of New Jersey (N, G)
William Rainey Harper College (U)
York University (U)

Business information and data processing services

American College of Computer & Information Sciences (U)
American Public University System (U)
Arapahoe Community College (U)
Athabasca University (N, U, G)
Beaufort County Community College (U)
Bellevue University (U, G)
Brenau University (U, G)
Brevard Community College (U)
Bristol Community College (N, U)
Bucks County Community College (U)
Capella University (G)
Cardean University (G)
Carl Albert State College (U)
Central Texas College (U)
Central Wyoming College (N)
Chadron State College (U, G)
Chemeketa Community College (U)
Cincinnati State Technical and Community College (U)
Clackamas Community College (U)
Cleveland State University (N)
College of The Albemarle (N)
Colorado State University-Pueblo (N)
Cossatot Community College of the University of Arkansas (N)
Danville Area Community College (U)

N–Noncredit; U–Undergraduate; G–Graduate

Davenport University Online (U)
Delaware County Community College (U)
Des Moines Area Community College (U)
Drake University (U)
East Carolina University (U)
East Los Angeles College (U)
Edgecombe Community College (N, U)
Edison State Community College (U)
Everett Community College (N)
Feather River Community College District (N)
Florida Metropolitan University–Brandon Campus (G)
Forrest Junior College (U)
Fort Hays State University (U)
Gaston College (U)
Heart of Georgia Technical College (U)
Howard Community College (U)
Hudson County Community College (N)
Immaculata University (U)
Inter American University of Puerto Rico, San Germán Campus (U, G)
Irvine Valley College (U)
Jacksonville State University (U, G)
Jones College (U)
Kentucky State University (U)
Kirkwood Community College (U)
Lakeland Community College (N)
Lamar State College–Port Arthur (N)
Lewis-Clark State College (U)
Limestone College (U)
Lord Fairfax Community College (N)
Madison Area Technical College (U)
Manatee Community College (U)
Marion Technical College (U)
Maryville University of Saint Louis (N)
Mercy College (G)
Middle Tennessee State University (N)
Motlow State Community College (U)
Mount Wachusett Community College (U)
New Hampshire Community Technical College System (N)
New York Institute of Technology (G)
Normandale Community College (N)
Northwestern Michigan College (U)
Norwalk Community College (U)
Nova Southeastern University (G)
Old Dominion University (U)
Park University (U)
Patrick Henry Community College (U)
Paul D. Camp Community College (U)
Peirce College (U)
Royal Roads University (G)
Ryerson University (U)
Saddleback College (U)
St. Cloud State University (U)
St. Louis Community College System (N)
Saint Paul College–A Community & Technical College (U)
Santa Fe Community College (N)
Santiago Canyon College (U)
Seminole Community College (U)
Seward County Community College (U)
Shawnee State University (U)
Shippensburg University of Pennsylvania (G)
Sinclair Community College (U)
Southwest Missouri State University (N)
Southwest Wisconsin Technical College (U)
Stanly Community College (U)
Syracuse University (G)
Syracuse University (G)
Tacoma Community College (N)
Taylor University (N, U)
Texas A&M International University (U)
Texas A&M University–Texarkana (G)
Thunderbird, The Garvin School of International Management (G)
Troy University–Florida Region (U)
Tunxis Community College (U)
University of Arkansas at Little Rock (U)
University of Colorado at Denver (G)
The University of Findlay (N)
University of Pittsburgh at Bradford (U)
University of Southern Mississippi (U)
University of the Incarnate Word (U, G)
University of Tulsa (G)
University of Wisconsin–Parkside (G)
Utah State University (U)
Virginia Polytechnic Institute and State University (G)
Walsh College of Accountancy and Business Administration (G)
Waubonsee Community College (U)
Westchester Community College (U)
West Virginia University at Parkersburg (U)
Wilkes Community College (U)
William Paterson University of New Jersey (U)
William Tyndale College (U)

Business management and administrative services, other

AIB College of Business (U)
Albuquerque Technical Vocational Institute (U)
Anne Arundel Community College (U)
Arapahoe Community College (U)
Athabasca University (N, U, G)
Bellevue University (U, G)
Berkeley College (U)
Berkeley College-New York City Campus (U)
Berkeley College-Westchester Campus (U)
Black Hills State University (U)
Bloomsburg University of Pennsylvania (U, G)
Blue Mountain Community College (U)
Boise State University (U)
Brenau University (U, G)
Brevard Community College (U)
Bridgewater State College (N)
Brigham Young University (U)
Bristol Community College (N)
Bucks County Community College (U)
Butler County Community College (U)
California National University for Advanced Studies (N)
California State University, Dominguez Hills (N)
California State University, Sacramento (U, G)
Capella University (N, G)
Casper College (U)
Central Texas College (U)
Chadron State College (U, G)
Chemeketa Community College (U)
Clackamas Community College (U)
College of The Albemarle (N)
Community College of Denver (U)
Concordia University Wisconsin (U)
Cossatot Community College of the University of Arkansas (N)
Dakota County Technical College (U)
Darton College (N)
Davenport University Online (U, G)
Delaware County Community College (U)
Des Moines Area Community College (U)
Drexel University (G)
East Carolina University (U, G)
Edgecombe Community College (N, U)
Elizabeth City State University (U)
Everglades University (U)
Florida National College (U)
Forrest Junior College (U)
Fort Hays State University (U)
Gaston College (U)
George Mason University (G)
Georgia Southern University (G)
Glenville State College (U)
Gogebic Community College (U)
Gonzaga University (G)
Grand View College (U)
Harrisburg Area Community College (U)
Howard Community College (U)
Hudson County Community College (U)
Indiana State University (U)
Indiana University of Pennsylvania (U)
Indiana University–Purdue University Fort Wayne (N)
Jacksonville State University (U, G)
James Madison University (N)
Jefferson Community College (U)

John Tyler Community College (U)
Jones International University (G)
Kansas City Kansas Community College (U)
Kansas State University (U)
Lakeland Community College (N)
Lamar State College–Port Arthur (N)
Lewis-Clark State College (N)
Long Island University, C.W. Post Campus (N)
Lord Fairfax Community College (N)
Manatee Community College (U)
Marist College (G)
Marymount University (G)
Mercy College (G)
Middle Tennessee State University (N)
Minot State University–Bottineau Campus (U)
MiraCosta College (N)
Mitchell Technical Institute (N)
Modesto Junior College (U)
Mountain State University (U)
New Hampshire Community Technical College System (N)
New Jersey Institute of Technology (G)
New York Institute of Technology (U)
Northampton County Area Community College (U)
Odessa College (N)
Okaloosa-Walton College (U)
Orange Coast College (U)
Oregon State University (N)
Oxnard College (U)
Park University (U, G)
Paul D. Camp Community College (U)
Peirce College (U)
Quinnipiac University (G)
Raritan Valley Community College (U)
Regis University (G)
Rio Hondo College (U)
Rowan Technical College (U)
Royal Roads University (G)
Saddleback College (U)
St. Cloud Technical College (N)
St. Edward's University (U)
St. John's University (G)
Saint Joseph's College of Maine (G)
St. Louis Community College System (N)
San Bernardino Valley College (U)
Santiago Canyon College (U)
Seminole Community College (U)
Sonoma State University (N)
Southeast Arkansas College (U)
State University of New York College at Fredonia (U)
Sullivan University (G)
Tarleton State University (U)
Taylor University (N)
Thunderbird, The Garvin School of International Management (G)
Tompkins Cortland Community College (N)
University of Bridgeport (U)
University of Colorado at Denver (G)
University of Delaware (N)
The University of Findlay (N)
University of Hawaii–West Oahu (U)
University of Idaho (G)
The University of Maine at Augusta (U)
University of Management and Technology (N)
University of Maryland University College (G)
University of Missouri–Columbia (N)
University of Notre Dame (N, G)
University of the Incarnate Word (U, G)
University of Tulsa (G)
University of West Florida (N)
Wilkes Community College (U)
William Paterson University of New Jersey (N, U)
William Rainey Harper College (U)
Youngstown State University (N)

Business marketing and marketing management

American Academy of Nutrition, College of Nutrition (U)
American River College (U)
Anne Arundel Community College (U)
Brigham Young University (U)
Brookdale Community College (U)
Broward Community College (U)
Bucks County Community College (U)
Burlington County College (U)
California National University for Advanced Studies (U, G)
Central Virginia Community College (U)
College of San Mateo (U)
College of The Albemarle (U)
Colorado Christian University (G)
Colorado Mountain College District System (U)
Colorado State University (G)
Columbus State Community College (U)
Connecticut State University System (U, G)
Dallas County Community College District (U)
Danville Community College (U)
Davenport University Online (U)
Delta College (U)
Duke University (G)
Eastern Kentucky University (U)
Edison State Community College (U)
Embry-Riddle Aeronautical University (U)
Fairleigh Dickinson University, Metropolitan Campus (U)
Fashion Institute of Technology (U)
Golden Gate University (G)
Hillsborough Community College (U)
Houston Community College System (U)
Ivy Tech State College–Northwest (U)
Johnson County Community College (U)
Kansas State University (U)
Kellogg Community College (U)
Lakeland Community College (U)
Liberty University (U)
Lord Fairfax Community College (U)
Louisiana State University and Agricultural and Mechanical College (U)
Madison Area Technical College (U)
Maharishi University of Management (N, G)
Manatee Community College (U)
Marshall University (U)
Marylhurst University (U, G)
Mercy College (U, G)
Metropolitan State University (U, G)
Montana State University–Billings (U)
Mountain Empire Community College (U)
Mountain State University (U)
Mount Wachusett Community College (U)
Nassau Community College (U)
New York Institute of Technology (U, G)
North Country Community College (U)
Northern Arizona University (U)
Northern Virginia Community College (U)
Oklahoma State University (U)
Old Dominion University (U, G)
Park University (U)
Pennsylvania College of Technology (U)
The Pennsylvania State University University Park Campus (U)
Pitt Community College (U)
Randolph Community College (U)
Regis University (U, G)
The Richard Stockton College of New Jersey (U)
Saddleback College (U)
Sam Houston State University (U)
Santa Rosa Junior College (U)
Sinclair Community College (U)
Southwest Missouri State University (U, G)
Spring Arbor University (U, G)
Stanly Community College (U)
Stephens College (G)
Tarleton State University (G)
Texas A&M University–Commerce (G)
Texas Tech University (U)
Tompkins Cortland Community College (U)
Triton College (U)
Troy University Montgomery (U)
University College of Cape Breton (U)

N–Noncredit; U–Undergraduate; G–Graduate

University of Central Arkansas (U)
University of Dallas (G)
University of Delaware (U)
University of Houston–Downtown (U)
University of Minnesota, Twin Cities Campus (U)
University of Mississippi (U)
University of Missouri–Columbia (U)
University of Nebraska–Lincoln (U)
University of Nevada, Reno (U)
University of Northern Iowa (U)
University of Southern Mississippi (U)
University of Toronto (N)
University of Wisconsin–Platteville (U)
Upper Iowa University (N, U)
Vance-Granville Community College (U)
Walsh College of Accountancy and Business Administration (N, U, G)
Walters State Community College (U)
Washington State University (U)
West Valley College (U)
Worcester Polytechnic Institute (G)

Business quantitative methods and management science

American College of Computer & Information Sciences (U, G)
Athabasca University (N, G)
Bellevue University (U, G)
Berkeley College (U)
Berkeley College-New York City Campus (U)
Berkeley College-Westchester Campus (U)
Brenau University (U, G)
Bristol Community College (N)
California National University for Advanced Studies (N)
Capella University (G)
Capitol College (G)
Cardean University (G)
Chadron State College (U, G)
Concordia University Wisconsin (U)
Cossatot Community College of the University of Arkansas (N)
Dallas Baptist University (G)
Davenport University Online (U)
Delaware County Community College (U)
Des Moines Area Community College (U)
Drake University (U)
Drexel University (U, G)
Elizabeth City State University (U)
Embry-Riddle Aeronautical University (U, G)
Florida Gulf Coast University (U)
Florida Institute of Technology (G)
Georgia Southern University (U)
Immaculata University (U)
Jacksonville State University (U, G)
James Madison University (N)
Lakeland Community College (N)
Limestone College (U)
Manchester Community College (U)
Marist College (G)
Mercy College (G)
National University (U)
New Hampshire Community Technical College System (N)
Nipissing University (U)
Northeastern Oklahoma Agricultural and Mechanical College (U)
Old Dominion University (U)
The Pennsylvania State University University Park Campus (G)
Quinnipiac University (G)
Ryerson University (U)
Saint Joseph's College of Maine (G)
Saint Leo University (U)
Southeast Community College, Beatrice Campus (N)
Stanford University (N)
Syracuse University (G)
Tompkins Cortland Community College (U)
University of Colorado at Denver (G)
The University of Findlay (N)
University of Michigan (N)
University of Notre Dame (N, G)
The University of Texas at Dallas (G)
The University of Texas at Tyler (G)
The University of Texas–Pan American (U)
University of the Incarnate Word (U, G)
University of Toronto (N, U)
University of Tulsa (G)
University of Wisconsin–Parkside (G)
Walsh College of Accountancy and Business Administration (G)
Western Washington University (U)
William Paterson University of New Jersey (U)
York University (U)

Business

Acadia University (U)
Adams State College (N, U)
Adirondack Community College (U)
AIB College of Business (U)
Albuquerque Technical Vocational Institute (U)
Allan Hancock College (U)
Allen County Community College (U)
Alliance University College (U)
Alliant International University (U, G)
Alvin Community College (U)
The American College (U, G)
American College of Computer & Information Sciences (U, G)
American Public University System (G)
American River College (U)
Andrew Jackson University (U)
Arkansas State University–Beebe (U)
Athabasca University (N, U)
Athens Technical College (U)
Bainbridge College (U)
Baltimore City Community College (U)
Bellevue Community College (U)
Bellevue University (U, G)
Bellingham Technical College (U)
Berkeley College (U)
Berkeley College-New York City Campus (U)
Berkeley College-Westchester Campus (U)
Bismarck State College (U)
Black Hills State University (U)
Blue Mountain Community College (U)
Brenau University (U, G)
Brevard Community College (U)
Bridgewater State College (N)
Bristol Community College (N, U)
Broome Community College (U)
Broward Community College (U)
Bryant and Stratton Online (U)
Bucks County Community College (U)
Caldwell Community College and Technical Institute (U)
California State University, Dominguez Hills (G)
California State University, Fullerton (N, U)
Cape Fear Community College (N, U)
Capella University (N, U, G)
Cardean University (G)
Carroll Community College (N)
Casper College (U)
Cayuga County Community College (U)
Cecil Community College (U)
Central Washington University (U)
Central Wyoming College (N, U)
Cerritos College (U)
Chadron State College (U)
Champlain College (U)
Charter Oak State College (U)
Chattanooga State Technical Community College (U)
Chemeketa Community College (U)
Chesapeake College (U)
Cincinnati State Technical and Community College (U)
Citrus College (U)
Clackamas Community College (U)
Clatsop Community College (U)
Clemson University (N, U)
Cleveland State University (N)
Coconino Community College (U)
Coleman College (G)
College of Menominee Nation (U)
College of San Mateo (U)

College of The Albemarle (N, U)
College of the Siskiyous (U)
Collin County Community College District (U)
Colorado Mountain College District System (U)
Colorado State University (N)
Colorado State University-Pueblo (U)
Columbia Basin College (N, U)
Columbia Union College (U)
Columbia University (N, G)
The Community College of Baltimore County (U)
Concordia University, St. Paul (N, U, G)
Copiah-Lincoln Community College–Natchez Campus (U)
Cossatot Community College of the University of Arkansas (N, U)
County College of Morris (U)
Cumberland County College (U)
Cuyamaca College (U)
Daemen College (U)
Daniel Webster College (U)
Danville Community College (U)
Darton College (U)
Davenport University Online (U, G)
Delaware County Community College (U)
DePaul University (U)
Des Moines Area Community College (U)
DeVry University Online (U, G)
Dickinson State University (U)
Drake University (U, G)
Drexel University (U)
East Carolina University (U, G)
East Central College (U)
Eastern Michigan University (U)
Eastern Oregon University (U)
Eastern Washington University (U)
Eastern Wyoming College (U)
Edgecombe Community College (N, U)
Edison State Community College (N, U)
Elgin Community College (U)
Elizabeth City State University (U)
Elizabethtown College (U)
Embry-Riddle Aeronautical University, Extended Campus (U, G)
Endicott College (N, U, G)
Everett Community College (U)
Evergreen Valley College (U)
Fairleigh Dickinson University, Metropolitan Campus (N, G)
Fairmont State University (U)
Fashion Institute of Technology (N, U)
Fayetteville State University (U)
Feather River Community College District (N)
Florida Atlantic University (U)
Florida Institute of Technology (G)
Florida International University (U)
Florida Metropolitan University–Brandon Campus (U, G)
Florida National College (U)
Forrest Junior College (U)
Fort Hays State University (U)
Frederick Community College (N)
Fulton-Montgomery Community College (N)
Gannon University (U)
Gaston College (U)
Gateway Community College (U)
George C. Wallace Community College (U)
Glenville State College (U)
Gogebic Community College (U)
Golden West College (U)
Grantham University (U)
Halifax Community College (U)
Harrisburg Area Community College (U)
Heartland Community College (U)
Hillsborough Community College (U)
Hopkinsville Community College (U)
Horry-Georgetown Technical College (U)
Howard College (U)
Howard Community College (U)
Hudson County Community College (U)
Illinois Eastern Community Colleges, Frontier Community College (U)
Illinois Eastern Community Colleges, Lincoln Trail College (U)
Illinois Eastern Community Colleges, Olney Central College (U)
Illinois Eastern Community Colleges, Wabash Valley College (U)
Immaculata University (U)
Indiana Institute of Technology (U)
Indiana State University (U)
Indiana University of Pennsylvania (U)
Indiana University–Purdue University Fort Wayne (U)
Iowa Western Community College (U)
Irvine Valley College (U)
Jacksonville State University (U, G)
James Madison University (N, U)
Jamestown Community College (N)
Jefferson College (U)
John A. Logan College (U)
John F. Kennedy University (U)
John Wood Community College (U)
Jones College (U)
Kansas City Kansas Community College (U)
Kansas State University (U)
Kellogg Community College (U)
Kirkwood Community College (N)
Lakeland College (U)
Lake Superior College (U)
Lamar State College–Port Arthur (N)
Liberty University (U)
Limestone College (U)
Linn-Benton Community College (U)
Lorain County Community College (N)
Lord Fairfax Community College (N, U)
Los Angeles Harbor College (U)
Los Angeles Valley College (U)
Manatee Community College (U)
Manchester Community College (N)
Martin Community College (U)
Marymount University (G)
Massasoit Community College (N, U)
Maui Community College (U)
Maysville Community College (U)
Mercy College (U, G)
Mesalands Community College (U)
Metropolitan Community College (U)
Middlesex Community College (N, U)
Middle Tennessee State University (N)
Minnesota School of Business–Brooklyn Center (U)
Minnesota State College–Southeast Technical (N)
MiraCosta College (U)
Mississippi Delta Community College (U)
Mississippi State University (G)
Modesto Junior College (U)
Monroe Community College (U)
Monroe County Community College (U)
Montana State University–Billings (U)
Montana Tech of The University of Montana (U)
Montgomery Community College (U)
Montgomery County Community College (U)
Mott Community College (U)
Mountain Empire Community College (U)
Mountain State University (U)
Mount Saint Mary College (U)
Mount Saint Vincent University (N, U)
Murray State University (U)
Nassau Community College (U)
National University (U, G)
New Hampshire Community Technical College System (N)
New Jersey City University (U)
New Mexico State University (U)
New York Institute of Technology (U)
Northampton County Area Community College (U)
North Carolina State University (U)
North Dakota State University (N)
Northeastern Oklahoma Agricultural and Mechanical College (U)
Northern Kentucky University (U)
North Hennepin Community College (U)

N–Noncredit; U–Undergraduate; G–Graduate

North Idaho College (U)
Northwestern Oklahoma State University (U)
Northwestern University (G)
Oakland City University (U)
Odessa College (U)
The Ohio State University (U)
Ohio University (U)
Oregon Institute of Technology (U)
Oregon State University (U)
Owensboro Community and Technical College (U)
Oxnard College (U)
Pace University (N, U, G)
Palm Beach Community College (U)
Palomar College (U)
Park University (U)
Pasco-Hernando Community College (U)
Passaic County Community College (U)
Peirce College (U)
Pennsylvania College of Technology (U)
The Pennsylvania State University University Park Campus (U)
Prairie State College (U)
Pulaski Technical College (U)
Quinnipiac University (U)
Reading Area Community College (U)
Rend Lake College (U)
Riverland Community College (U)
Riverside Community College (U)
Rockland Community College (U)
Roosevelt University (U)
Ryerson University (U)
St. Cloud Technical College (N)
St. Joseph's College, Suffolk Campus (U)
St. Louis Community College System (N)
Saint Mary-of-the-Woods College (U)
St. Petersburg College (U)
Salve Regina University (N, G)
San Bernardino Valley College (U)
San Jacinto College District (U)
Santa Fe Community College (U)
Santa Rosa Junior College (U)
Santiago Canyon College (U)
Sauk Valley Community College (U)
Schiller International University (U)
Schoolcraft College (U)
Seton Hill University (U)
Shelton State Community College (U)
Shoreline Community College (U)
Snead State Community College (U)
Southeast Arkansas College (U)
Southeast Community College, Beatrice Campus (U)
Southern Illinois University Carbondale (U)
Southern Illinois University Edwardsville (G)
Southwestern Assemblies of God University (U)
Southwestern College (U)
Southwestern Oregon Community College (U)
Spartanburg Technical College (U)
State University of New York at Plattsburgh (U)
State University of New York College at Potsdam (N)
State University of New York Empire State College (G)
State University of New York Institute of Technology (U, G)
State University of New York Institute of Technology (U, G)
State University of New York Institute of Technology (U, G)
State University of New York Institute of Technology (U, G)
Stephens College (U)
Strayer University (U, G)
Syracuse University (G)
Tacoma Community College (U)
Taft College (U)
Tarleton State University (N, U)
Taylor University (N, U)
Taylor University (U)
Texas A&M University–Texarkana (U)
Texas State University-San Marcos (U)
Texas Woman's University (G)
Thomas College (U, G)
Tompkins Cortland Community College (U)
Touro University International (U, G)
Treasure Valley Community College (U)
Tri-State University (U)
Troy University–Florida Region (U)
Tunxis Community College (N)
The University of Akron (U)
The University of Alabama (U)
University of Alaska Fairbanks (U)
University of Bridgeport (U)
University of California, Los Angeles (G)
University of Cincinnati (N, U)
University of Cincinnati Raymond Walters College (U)
University of Colorado at Colorado Springs (G)
University of Colorado at Denver (G)
The University of Findlay (U, G)
University of Georgia (U)
University of Idaho (U)
University of Illinois (N)
University of Illinois at Chicago (N, G)
University of La Verne (G)
University of Maine (G)
The University of Maine at Augusta (U)
University of Massachusetts Lowell (U)
University of Mississippi (U)
University of Missouri–Columbia (U, G)
The University of Montana–Missoula (U)
University of Nebraska–Lincoln (N)
University of Nevada, Reno (U)
The University of North Carolina at Pembroke (U, G)
University of Notre Dame (N, G)
University of Pittsburgh at Bradford (U)
University of South Carolina Spartanburg (U)
The University of Tennessee at Martin (G)
The University of Texas at Dallas (G)
The University of Texas at Tyler (U)
University of the Incarnate Word (U, G)
University of Toronto (U)
University of Tulsa (G)
University of Vermont (N)
University of Wisconsin Colleges (U)
University of Wisconsin–Madison (G)
University of Wisconsin–Platteville (G)
University of Wisconsin–Platteville (G)
University of Wisconsin–Platteville (G)
University of Wisconsin–Platteville (G)
University of Wisconsin–Platteville (U)
University of Wisconsin–River Falls (U)
University of Wyoming (U)
Vance-Granville Community College (N)
Virginia Polytechnic Institute and State University (N)
Walters State Community College (U)
Wayne State College (U)
Westchester Community College (U)
Western New England College (U, G)
Western Wyoming Community College (U)
West Valley College (U)
West Virginia University at Parkersburg (U)
Whatcom Community College (U)
Wilfrid Laurier University (U)
Wilkes Community College (U)
William Paterson University of New Jersey (U)
William Rainey Harper College (U)
William Tyndale College (U)
Winston-Salem State University (U)
Wisconsin Indianhead Technical College (N, U)
York Technical College (U)

Business/managerial economics

Adams State College (U)
Albuquerque Technical Vocational Institute (U)
Alliant International University (U)
American Graduate University (G)
American River College (U)
Anne Arundel Community College (U)
Aspen University (G)
Athabasca University (N, U, G)
Bellevue University (U, G)

Non-Degree-Related Course Subject Areas
Business/managerial economics

Berkeley College (U)
Berkeley College-New York City Campus (U)
Berkeley College-Westchester Campus (U)
Brenau University (U, G)
Brevard Community College (U)
Bridgewater State College (N, U)
Caldwell Community College and Technical Institute (N)
California National University for Advanced Studies (N, U)
Cardean University (G)
Chadron State College (U, G)
Cleveland Community College (U)
Coastal Bend College (U)
Corning Community College (U)
Cossatot Community College of the University of Arkansas (N, U)
Daniel Webster College (U)
Davenport University Online (U)
Delaware County Community College (U)
Des Moines Area Community College (U)
Drake University (U)
Drexel University (U, G)
East Arkansas Community College (U)
Edgecombe Community College (N)
Elizabeth City State University (U)
Embry-Riddle Aeronautical University (U)
Florida Atlantic University (G)
Florida Institute of Technology (G)
Florida Metropolitan University–Brandon Campus (G)
Florida National College (U)
Forrest Junior College (U)
Franklin Pierce College (U)
Frederick Community College (N)
Grand View College (U)
Grantham University (U)
Harrisburg Area Community College (U)
Jacksonville State University (U, G)
Jones College (U)
Lakeland Community College (N)
Lamar State College–Port Arthur (N)
Linn-Benton Community College (U)
Lord Fairfax Community College (N)
Manatee Community College (U)
Marian College of Fond du Lac (U)
Marist College (G)
Marshall University (U)
Mercy College (G)
Middlesex Community College (U)
Middle Tennessee State University (N)
Mississippi State University (G)
Mount Saint Vincent University (U)
New Hampshire Community Technical College System (N)
New School University (G)
Northampton County Area Community College (U)
Ocean County College (U)
Old Dominion University (U)
Paul D. Camp Community College (U)
The Pennsylvania State University University Park Campus (G)
Quinnipiac University (G)
Regis University (U, G)
Ryerson University (U)
St. Edward's University (U, G)
Saint Joseph's College of Maine (G)
St. Joseph's College, Suffolk Campus (U)
Schiller International University (U, G)
Southeast Arkansas College (U)
Spring Arbor University (G)
Stanford University (N)
State University of New York at Oswego (U)
Sullivan University (U, G)
Syracuse University (G)
Tarleton State University (U)
Taylor University (U)
Tulane University (U)
The University of Akron (U)
University of Colorado at Denver (G)
The University of Findlay (N, U, G)
University of Georgia (U)
University of Great Falls (U)
University of Houston–Downtown (U)
University of Mississippi (U)
University of Missouri–Columbia (U)
University of Nevada, Reno (U)
The University of Texas at Dallas (G)
University of the Incarnate Word (U, G)
University of Toronto (N, U)
University of Tulsa (G)
University of Vermont (N)
University of Waterloo (U)
University of Wisconsin–Parkside (G)
Wake Technical Community College (U)
Wilkes Community College (U)
Winona State University (U)
York University (U)
Youngstown State University (N)

Canadian studies

The University of British Columbia (U)
University of Waterloo (U)
Western Washington University (U)

Carpenters

Ashworth College (N)
Bossier Parish Community College (N)
Cleveland Community College (U)
Education Direct Center for Degree Studies (N)
Maui Community College (U)
University of Arkansas at Pine Bluff (N)

Cell and molecular biology

The Community College of Baltimore County (U)
Illinois Institute of Technology (U, G)
Lehigh University (G)
University of Minnesota, Twin Cities Campus (U)
University of Waterloo (U)

Cell biology

Edison State Community College (U)
University of Colorado at Denver (U)
University of Guelph (U)

Chemical engineering

Brigham Young University (U)
Cleveland State University (G)
Colorado State University (G)
Illinois Institute of Technology (U, G)
Kansas State University (G)
Lehigh University (N, G)
Mississippi State University (G)
North Carolina State University (G)
Oklahoma State University (G)
Texas Tech University (G)
University of Delaware (U, G)
University of Idaho (U, G)
University of Massachusetts Amherst (N, G)
University of North Dakota (U)
University of Wisconsin–Madison (U, G)

Chemistry

Acadia University (U)
American Academy of Nutrition, College of Nutrition (U)
American College of Computer & Information Sciences (U)
Anne Arundel Community College (U)
Arkansas State University–Beebe (U)
Arkansas Tech University (U)
Athabasca University (N, U)
Bellevue Community College (U)
Boise State University (U)
Brazosport College (U)
Brevard Community College (U)
Brigham Young University (U)
Brookdale Community College (U)
Broome Community College (U)
Brunswick Community College (U)
Butler County Community College (U)
Butler County Community College (U)
Caldwell College (U)
Cape Fear Community College (U)
Carleton University (U)
Cascadia Community College (U)
Casper College (U)

N–Noncredit; U–Undergraduate; G–Graduate

Cecil Community College (U)
Central Oregon Community College (U)
Central Virginia Community College (U)
Central Wyoming College (U)
Champlain College (U)
Charter Oak State College (U)
Chemeketa Community College (U)
Clackamas Community College (U)
Cleveland State University (U)
College of DuPage (U)
College of San Mateo (U)
College of the Canyons (U)
Colorado Mountain College District System (U)
Colorado State University-Pueblo (U)
Columbus State Community College (U)
Community College of Denver (U)
Corning Community College (U)
Des Moines Area Community College (U)
East Carolina University (U)
Eastern Michigan University (U)
Eastern Oregon University (U)
Edison State Community College (U)
Fairleigh Dickinson University, Metropolitan Campus (U)
Florida Atlantic University (U)
Florida Community College at Jacksonville (U)
Floyd College (U)
Gaston College (U)
George C. Wallace Community College (U)
Grantham University (U)
Honolulu Community College (U)
Hopkinsville Community College (U)
Houston Community College System (U)
Illinois Eastern Community Colleges, Wabash Valley College (U)
Illinois Institute of Technology (G)
Immaculata University (U)
Iowa Western Community College (U)
Johnson County Community College (U)
John Tyler Community College (U)
Lake Region State College (U)
Lansing Community College (U)
Lehigh University (N, G)
Los Angeles Pierce College (U)
Marshall University (U)
Massasoit Community College (U)
Maui Community College (U)
Maysville Community College (U)
Mayville State University (U)
Mississippi Delta Community College (U)
Montana State University–Bozeman (G)
Mountain State University (U)
Mt. Hood Community College (U)
Mt. San Antonio College (U)
North Carolina State University (U)
North Dakota State College of Science (U)
Northeast State Technical Community College (U)
Northern Arizona University (U)
North Hennepin Community College (U)
North Idaho College (U)
NorthWest Arkansas Community College (U)
Northwestern College (U)
Northwestern Michigan College (U)
Northwestern State University of Louisiana (U)
Norwalk Community College (U)
Ohio University (U)
Okaloosa-Walton College (U)
Oregon State University (U)
Oxnard College (U)
Pacific Union College (U)
Palm Beach Community College (U)
Palomar College (U)
Peninsula College (U)
Pennsylvania College of Technology (U)
The Pennsylvania State University University Park Campus (U)
Portland State University (U)
Pratt Community College (U)
Quinnipiac University (U)
Rockland Community College (U)
Sacred Heart University (U)
St. Clair County Community College (U)
St. Cloud State University (U)
St. Petersburg College (U)
San Bernardino Valley College (U)
Seward County Community College (U)
Shawnee State University (U)
Shelton State Community College (U)
Sinclair Community College (U)
Snead State Community College (U)
South Central Technical College (U)
South Dakota School of Mines and Technology (U)
Southeastern Community College (U)
Southwest Missouri State University (U)
Tacoma Community College (U)
Treasure Valley Community College (U)
Triton College (U)
The University of Akron (U)
University of Arkansas at Pine Bluff (U)
University of Colorado at Colorado Springs (U)
University of Delaware (U)
The University of Findlay (U)
University of Florida (U)
University of Illinois at Springfield (U)
University of La Verne (U)
University of Maryland University College (U)
University of Massachusetts Boston (U)
University of Mississippi (U)
The University of North Carolina at Chapel Hill (U)
The University of North Carolina at Pembroke (U)
University of North Dakota (U)
University of Northern Colorado (U, G)
University of Oklahoma (U)
University of Pittsburgh at Bradford (U)
University of Southern Mississippi (U)
The University of Tennessee (U)
The University of Texas–Pan American (U)
University of Utah (U)
University of Washington (U)
University of Waterloo (N, U)
University of Wisconsin Colleges (U)
University of Wyoming (U)
Utah State University (U)
Walters State Community College (U)
Weber State University (U)
Whatcom Community College (U)

Child care and guidance workers and managers

American Public University System (U)
Asheville-Buncombe Technical Community College (U)
Ashworth College (N)
Athabasca University (N, U, G)
Augusta Technical College (N)
Bethany College of the Assemblies of God (U)
Blackhawk Technical College (N)
Brunswick Community College (U)
Caldwell Community College and Technical Institute (U)
Chesapeake College (U)
Cleveland Community College (U)
College of The Albemarle (U)
Community College of Denver (U)
Cossatot Community College of the University of Arkansas (U)
Dakota County Technical College (U)
Dallas County Community College District (U)
Danville Community College (U)
East Carolina University (U)
Eastern Illinois University (G)
Edgecombe Community College (U)
Edison State Community College (U)
Education Direct Center for Degree Studies (N)
El Camino College (U)
Everett Community College (U)
Feather River Community College District (N)
Gaston College (U)
Grossmont College (U)
Heartland Community College (U)

Houston Community College System (U)
Hudson County Community College (U)
Iowa Western Community College (U)
Ivy Tech State College–Central Indiana (U)
Ivy Tech State College–Eastcentral (U)
Ivy Tech State College–Northeast (U)
Ivy Tech State College–Northwest (U)
Ivy Tech State College–Southwest (U)
Jacksonville State University (U)
John Tyler Community College (U)
Kansas City Kansas Community College (U)
Kansas State University (U)
Lewis-Clark State College (U)
Linn-Benton Community College (U)
Long Beach City College (U)
Los Angeles Valley College (U)
Madison Area Technical College (U)
Martin Community College (U)
Marylhurst University (U)
Massasoit Community College (U)
Mayville State University (U)
Metropolitan Community College (U)
MiraCosta College (N)
Mississippi State University (U)
Moberly Area Community College (U)
Mountain Empire Community College (U)
Mt. Hood Community College (U)
Mount Saint Vincent University (U)
Naugatuck Valley Community College (U)
Northampton County Area Community College (U)
North Dakota State University (N, U)
Northeastern Oklahoma Agricultural and Mechanical College (U)
North Idaho College (U)
Northwestern Technical College (U)
Orange Coast College (U)
Owensboro Community and Technical College (U)
Oxnard College (U)
Paul D. Camp Community College (U)
Peninsula College (U)
Randolph Community College (U)
Ryerson University (U)
St. Cloud Technical College (N, U)
San Jacinto College District (U)
Santa Fe Community College (N)
Santa Rosa Junior College (U)
Schenectady County Community College (U)
Snead State Community College (U)
Southeast Community College, Lincoln Campus (N)
Southwestern College (U)
Southwestern Oregon Community College (U)
Spoon River College (U)
Stanly Community College (U)
Sullivan University (U)
Tacoma Community College (U)
Taft College (U)
Tarleton State University (N)
The University of Maine at Augusta (U)
University of Missouri–Columbia (U)
The University of Tennessee at Martin (N)
University of Wisconsin–Milwaukee (G)
Vance-Granville Community College (U)
Wake Technical Community College (N, U)
Wayne State College (U)
Western Washington University (U)
Wilkes Community College (U)
Wisconsin Indianhead Technical College (N, U)

Chinese

University of Toronto (N)

City/urban, community and regional planning

Athabasca University (N)
Cleveland State University (U, G)
Middle Tennessee State University (N)
New School University (G)
The Pennsylvania State University University Park Campus (G)
University of Missouri–Columbia (N)
University of New Orleans (U)
University of Southern Mississippi (G)
University of Washington (N, G)
University of Waterloo (U)

Civil engineering

Brigham Young University (U)
Columbia University (N, G)
Georgia Institute of Technology (N, G)
Kansas State University (G)
Michigan Technological University (U)
Mississippi State University (G)
North Carolina State University (G)
Southern Methodist University (G)
Stanford University (N)
Texas Tech University (G)
The University of British Columbia (U)
University of Colorado at Boulder (N, G)
University of Colorado at Denver (U)
University of Delaware (U, G)
University of Idaho (U)
University of Maine (G)
University of North Dakota (U)
University of Washington (G)
University of Wisconsin–Madison (U, G)
University of Wisconsin–Platteville (G)
Virginia Polytechnic Institute and State University (U)

Civil engineering/civil technology

Cincinnati State Technical and Community College (U)
Sinclair Community College (U)
Stanford University (N)
University of Maine (U)

Classical and ancient Near Eastern languages and literatures

Alliance University College (U)
Bethany College of the Assemblies of God (U)
Goddard College (U)
The Jewish Theological Seminary (N, U, G)
Moody Bible Institute (U)
University of Georgia (U)
University of Minnesota, Twin Cities Campus (U)
University of Missouri–Columbia (U)
The University of North Carolina at Greensboro (U)

Clinical psychology

Athabasca University (N)
Bethany College of the Assemblies of God (U)
Capella University (N, G)
Delaware County Community College (U)
Immaculata University (G)
John F. Kennedy University (G)
Naropa University (U)
North Dakota State University (N, U, G)
Oxnard College (U)
Santa Fe Community College (U)
Saybrook Graduate School and Research Center (G)

Clothing, apparel and textile workers and managers

Hudson County Community College (U)
Virginia Polytechnic Institute and State University (U)

Clothing/apparel and textile studies

Blackhawk Technical College (N)
Immaculata University (U)
Maui Community College (U)
North Carolina State University (U)
NorthWest Arkansas Community College (U)
Orange Coast College (U)
University of Arkansas at Pine Bluff (U)
Western Michigan University (U)

Cognitive psychology and psycholinguistics

Horry-Georgetown Technical College (U)
Immaculata University (U)

N–Noncredit; U–Undergraduate; G–Graduate

Saybrook Graduate School and Research Center (G)
Tarleton State University (U)
Teachers College Columbia University (N, G)
University of Southern Mississippi (G)
University of Washington (U)

Communication disorders sciences and services

Athabasca University (N, U)
Bridgewater State College (U)
Brigham Young University (U)
California State University, Northridge (N)
East Carolina University (G)
Fontbonne University (G)
Fort Hays State University (U)
Hudson County Community College (N)
James Madison University (N)
Lakeland Community College (N)
MGH Institute of Health Professions (G)
Murray State University (U, G)
Northern Arizona University (U)
Oklahoma State University (U)
University of Cincinnati (U)
University of Georgia (U)
University of Maine (U)
University of Northern Colorado (G)
University of Vermont (G)
Western Carolina University (U, G)

Communications technologies

Arapahoe Community College (U)
Athabasca University (N, U)
Bethany College of the Assemblies of God (U)
California State University, Fullerton (N)
DePaul University (G)
DeVry University Online (G)
Gaston College (U)
Hudson County Community College (N)
Indiana University of Pennsylvania (U)
James Madison University (U)
Jones International University (U)
Lakeland Community College (N)
Lawrence Technological University (U)
Maryville University of Saint Louis (N)
Mercy College (U)
Middlesex Community College (U)
Montana State University–Billings (U)
National University (U)
Northeastern University (N)
North Georgia College & State University (N)
Northwestern University (G)
Quinnipiac University (U)
Roosevelt University (G)
Santa Rosa Junior College (U)
Seton Hill University (G)
Southern Illinois University Carbondale (U)
Stanford University (N)
Syracuse University (G)
Teachers College Columbia University (N, G)
The University of Akron (N)
University of the Incarnate Word (U, G)
University of West Florida (N, U)
Wilkes Community College (U)

Communications, general

Abilene Christian University (U)
Albuquerque Technical Vocational Institute (U)
Andrew Jackson University (U)
Anne Arundel Community College (U)
Arkansas State University–Beebe (U)
Athabasca University (N, U)
Auburn University (U)
Bainbridge College (N)
Bellevue Community College (U)
Bethany College of the Assemblies of God (U)
Bowling Green State University (U)
Bradley University (U)
Brenau University (U)
Brevard Community College (U)
Bridgewater State College (N, U, G)
Brigham Young University (U)
Bristol Community College (N)
Bucks County Community College (U)
Butler County Community College (U)
Caldwell Community College and Technical Institute (U)
California State University, Fullerton (U)
Cape Fear Community College (U)
Central Oregon Community College (U)
Central Texas College (U)
Central Wyoming College (N)
Century College (N)
Champlain College (U)
Chattanooga State Technical Community College (U)
Citrus College (U)
Clarion University of Pennsylvania (U)
Clemson University (N, U)
Clovis Community College (U)
Coconino Community College (U)
College for Lifelong Learning (U)
College of DuPage (U)
College of The Albemarle (N)
Collin County Community College District (U)
Columbia Basin College (U)
Columbia Union College (U)
The Community College of Baltimore County (U)
Concordia University, St. Paul (N)
Connecticut State University System (U)
Cossatot Community College of the University of Arkansas (U)
Dallas Baptist University (U)
Danville Community College (U)
Darton College (U)
Davenport University Online (U)
Dawson Community College (U)
DeVry University Online (U, G)
Drake University (U)
East Carolina University (U)
Eastern Michigan University (U)
Edgecombe Community College (N)
Edison Community College (U)
Elizabethtown College (U)
Fairleigh Dickinson University, Metropolitan Campus (U)
Fontbonne University (U)
Fort Hays State University (U)
Franklin University (U)
Frederick Community College (N, U)
Gaston College (U)
Goddard College (U)
Grossmont College (U)
Halifax Community College (U)
Heartland Community College (U)
Hopkinsville Community College (U)
Howard Community College (U)
Hudson County Community College (U)
Illinois Eastern Community Colleges, Olney Central College (U)
Immaculata University (U)
Indiana University–Purdue University Fort Wayne (U)
Indiana Wesleyan University (U)
Iowa Western Community College (U)
Ivy Tech State College–Central Indiana (U)
Ivy Tech State College–Northwest (U)
Ivy Tech State College–Wabash Valley (U)
Ivy Tech State College–Whitewater (U)
James Madison University (U)
Jamestown Community College (N)
Jones College (U)
Judson College (U)
The King's College and Seminary (N, U)
Lakeland Community College (N)
Lake Superior College (U)
LeTourneau University (U)
Lewis-Clark State College (U)
Lord Fairfax Community College (N)
Louisiana State University and Agricultural and Mechanical College (U)
Manchester Community College (N)
Marian College of Fond du Lac (U)
Marist College (U, G)
Marshall University (U)
Martin Community College (U)

Marylhurst University (N)
Massasoit Community College (N)
Maui Community College (U)
Maysville Community College (U)
McDaniel College (U)
Mesa Community College (U)
Middle Tennessee State University (U)
Millersville University of Pennsylvania (U)
Minnesota School of Business–Brooklyn Center (U)
Minnesota School of Business-Richfield (U)
Minnesota State College–Southeast Technical (N)
MiraCosta College (U)
Mississippi State University (U)
Missouri Southern State University (U)
Monroe Community College (U)
Montana State University–Billings (U, G)
Mountain Empire Community College (U)
Mount Saint Mary College (U)
Mount Saint Vincent University (N)
New York Institute of Technology (U)
New York Institute of Technology (U)
North Carolina State University (U)
North Dakota State University (U, G)
Northern Kentucky University (U)
North Hennepin Community College (U)
North Idaho College (U)
NorthWest Arkansas Community College (U)
Northwestern College (U)
Northwest Missouri State University (U)
Ohio University (U)
Old Dominion University (U)
Oregon State University (N, U)
Owensboro Community and Technical College (U)
Oxnard College (U)
Pace University (U)
Palm Beach Community College (U)
Park University (U)
Passaic County Community College (U)
Patrick Henry Community College (U)
The Pennsylvania State University University Park Campus (U)
Pratt Community College (U)
Prescott College (U, G)
Regis University (U)
Royal Roads University (U, G)
Ryerson University (U)
Sacred Heart University (U)
St. Cloud State University (U)
St. Edward's University (U)
Saint Joseph's College of Maine (U)
St. Petersburg College (U)
Santa Fe Community College (N)
Santa Rosa Junior College (U)
Schoolcraft College (U)
Seward County Community College (U)
Shippensburg University of Pennsylvania (U, G)
Simpson College (U)
Sinclair Community College (U)
Skidmore College (U)
Southeastern College of the Assemblies of God (U)
Southwestern Oregon Community College (U)
Southwest Wisconsin Technical College (U)
State University of New York at New Paltz (U)
State University of New York at Oswego (U)
State University of New York College at Potsdam (N)
State University of New York Institute of Technology (U, G)
State University of New York Institute of Technology (U, G)
State University of New York Institute of Technology (U, G)
State University of New York Institute of Technology (U, G)
Sul Ross State University (U)
Taylor University (N)
Taylor University (U)
Teachers College Columbia University (N)
Teikyo Post University (U)
Tompkins Cortland Community College (U)
Tunxis Community College (U)
The University of Akron (U)
The University of Alabama (U)
University of Arkansas at Little Rock (U)
University of Arkansas at Pine Bluff (U)
University of Colorado at Colorado Springs (U)
University of Colorado at Denver (U)
University of Connecticut (U)
University of Delaware (U)
University of Denver (G)
University of Georgia (U)
University of Houston (U)
University of Houston–Victoria (G)
University of Illinois at Springfield (U, G)
University of La Verne (U)
The University of Maine at Augusta (U)
University of Maryland University College (U)
University of Massachusetts Boston (U)
University of Massachusetts Lowell (U)
University of Minnesota, Twin Cities Campus (U, G)
The University of Montana–Missoula (U)
The University of North Carolina at Chapel Hill (U)
University of North Dakota (U)
University of Northern Iowa (U)
University of Oklahoma (U, G)
The University of South Dakota (U)
University of Southern Indiana (U)
University of Southern Mississippi (N, G)
University of the Incarnate Word (U, G)
University of Toledo (U)
University of Toronto (N)
University of Utah (U)
University of Washington (U)
University of West Florida (U)
University of Wisconsin–Platteville (U, G)
University of Wisconsin–Platteville (U)
University of Wisconsin–River Falls (U)
University of Wisconsin–Superior (U)
University of Wyoming (U)
Upper Iowa University (N, U)
Utah Valley State College (U)
Valparaiso University (U, G)
Virginia Polytechnic Institute and State University (U)
Washtenaw Community College (U)
Waubonsee Community College (U)
Weber State University (U)
Westchester Community College (U)
Wichita State University (U)
Wilfrid Laurier University (U)
Wilkes Community College (U)
Wisconsin Indianhead Technical College (N, U)
Worcester State College (N, U)
Wright State University (U, G)
York University (U)
Youngstown State University (U)

Communications, other

American College of Computer & Information Sciences (U)
Athabasca University (U)
Austin Peay State University (G)
Brevard Community College (U)
Bristol Community College (N)
Caldwell College (U)
Cascadia Community College (U)
Champlain College (U)
Clackamas Community College (U)
Collin County Community College District (U)
Danville Area Community College (U)
Drake University (U)
East Carolina University (U)
Eastern Michigan University (U)
Elizabethtown College (U)
Fort Hays State University (U)
Goddard College (U)
Horry-Georgetown Technical College (U)

N–Noncredit; U–Undergraduate; G–Graduate

James Madison University (N)
Jones International University (G)
Lakeland Community College (N)
Lord Fairfax Community College (N)
Marshall University (U)
Metropolitan State University (U)
Nassau Community College (U)
New Jersey Institute of Technology (G)
Normandale Community College (U)
Northern Arizona University (U)
North Hennepin Community College (N)
Oklahoma State University (N)
Park University (U)
The Pennsylvania State University University Park Campus (G)
Royal Roads University (G)
St. Clair County Community College (U)
St. John's University (U)
San Bernardino Valley College (U)
Santa Rosa Junior College (U)
Seton Hill University (U)
Southwest Missouri State University (U)
Southwest Wisconsin Technical College (U)
Taylor University (N)
Teachers College Columbia University (G)
Texas A&M International University (U)
The University of Akron (U)
University of Arkansas at Little Rock (U)
The University of Findlay (U)
University of Missouri–Columbia (U)
University of Wisconsin Colleges (U)
Valley City State University (U)
Western Washington University (U)
William Paterson University of New Jersey (U)

Community health services

Athabasca University (N, U, G)
California State University, Chico (U)
Danville Community College (U)
Edgecombe Community College (N)
Feather River Community College District (N)
Fort Hays State University (U)
Houston Community College System (U)
Hudson County Community College (U)
Jacksonville State University (U)
Jefferson College of Health Sciences (U)
John Tyler Community College (U)
Lakeland Community College (N)
Louisiana State University and Agricultural and Mechanical College (U)
Mercy College (G)
New Mexico State University (U)
New School University (G)
Northern Arizona University (G)
Oklahoma State University (N)
Old Dominion University (U)
Rappahannock Community College (U)
Ryerson University (U)
Santa Fe Community College (N)
Schoolcraft College (N)
Tarleton State University (U)
Teachers College Columbia University (N, G)
The University of Akron (U)
University of Bridgeport (U)
The University of Maine at Augusta (U)
University of Massachusetts Amherst (U)
University of Northern Colorado (U)
University of South Carolina Sumter (U)
University of Southern Mississippi (U, G)
The University of Texas at Tyler (U)
Western Washington University (U)

Community organization, resources and services

Athabasca University (N, U, G)
Capella University (G)
Feather River Community College District (N)
Ferris State University (N)
Hudson County Community College (N, U)
Lakeland Community College (N)
Mercy College (U)
New School University (G)
Saybrook Graduate School and Research Center (G)
Sullivan University (G)
The University of Akron (U)
University of Massachusetts Boston (U)
University of Southern Mississippi (U)
University of Vermont (U)
University of Waterloo (U)
University of Wisconsin–River Falls (G)

Community psychology

Athabasca University (N, U, G)
Bethany College of the Assemblies of God (U)
Central Texas College (U)
Delaware County Community College (U)
Jones College (U)
Marylhurst University (G)
Middlesex Community College (U)
Naropa University (U)
Saybrook Graduate School and Research Center (G)

Comparative literature

Athabasca University (U)
Cascadia Community College (U)
Columbus State Community College (U)
Community College of Denver (U)
Delaware County Community College (U)
Des Moines Area Community College (U)
Goddard College (U)
Indiana University–Purdue University Fort Wayne (U)
Limestone College (U)
Lock Haven University of Pennsylvania (U)
Mercy College (U, G)
Naropa University (U)
New Hampshire Community Technical College System (U)
The Pennsylvania State University University Park Campus (U)
Santa Fe Community College (N)
State University of New York at New Paltz (U)
University of Georgia (U)
The University of Maine at Augusta (U)
The University of South Dakota (U)
University of Southern Mississippi (U)
Wichita State University (U)

Computer and information sciences, general

Albuquerque Technical Vocational Institute (U)
Allan Hancock College (U)
Alliant International University (U, G)
Alvin Community College (N, U)
American College of Computer & Information Sciences (U, G)
American River College (U)
Anne Arundel Community College (U)
Arapahoe Community College (U)
Arkansas State University–Beebe (U)
Arkansas Tech University (U)
Asheville-Buncombe Technical Community College (U)
Ashworth College (N)
Athabasca University (N, U, G)
Athens Technical College (U)
Bainbridge College (U)
Beaufort County Community College (N, U)
Bellingham Technical College (N)
Bishop State Community College (U)
Bismarck State College (U)
Bossier Parish Community College (N, U)
Bowling Green State University (U)
Brenau University (U, G)
Brevard Community College (U)
Brigham Young University (N)
Bristol Community College (N, U)
Broome Community College (N)
Bucks County Community College (U)
Caldwell Community College and Technical Institute (U)
California National University for Advanced Studies (N, U, G)

California State University, Dominguez Hills (N)
California State University, Monterey Bay (U)
California State University, Sacramento (U)
Capitol College (G)
Carl Albert State College (U)
Carroll Community College (U)
Casper College (U)
Central Oregon Community College (U)
Central Texas College (U)
Central Virginia Community College (U)
Central Wyoming College (N, U)
Century College (N)
Champlain College (U)
Chattanooga State Technical Community College (U)
Chemeketa Community College (U)
Chesapeake College (U)
Cincinnati State Technical and Community College (U)
Citrus College (U)
Clackamas Community College (U)
Clatsop Community College (U)
Clemson University (N)
Clinton Community College (U)
Clovis Community College (U)
Coconino Community College (U)
Coleman College (U)
College of Mount St. Joseph (U)
College of The Albemarle (N, U)
College of the Canyons (U)
Colorado Christian University (U)
Columbia College (U)
Columbia Union College (U)
The Community College of Baltimore County (N, U)
Cossatot Community College of the University of Arkansas (N, U)
Culver-Stockton College (U)
Dakota State University (N, U)
Dallas Baptist University (U)
Dallas County Community College District (U)
Davenport University Online (U)
Delaware County Community College (N, U)
Delta College (U)
DePaul University (G)
Des Moines Area Community College (U)
DeVry University Online (U, G)
Drake University (U)
East Carolina University (U)
East Central College (U)
Eastern Illinois University (G)
Eastern Wyoming College (U)
East Los Angeles College (U)
Edgecombe Community College (N, U)
Edison State Community College (N, U)
Elgin Community College (U)
Eugene Bible College (U)
Everett Community College (N, U)
Evergreen Valley College (U)
Feather River Community College District (N)
Florida National College (U)
Forrest Junior College (N, U)
Fort Hays State University (U)
Franklin Pierce College (U)
Frederick Community College (N, U)
Gaston College (U)
George C. Wallace Community College (U)
Gogebic Community College (U)
Golden Gate University (U, G)
Grantham University (U)
Harford Community College (N, U)
Henry Ford Community College (U)
Hibbing Community College (N, U)
Hillsborough Community College (U)
Howard Community College (U)
Hudson County Community College (N, U)
Illinois Eastern Community Colleges, Lincoln Trail College (U)
Illinois Eastern Community Colleges, Olney Central College (U)
Illinois Institute of Technology (U)
Immaculata University (U)
Independence Community College (U)
Indiana Institute of Technology (U)
Indiana Wesleyan University (U)
Iowa Western Community College (U)
Irvine Valley College (U)
Ivy Tech State College–Bloomington (U)
Ivy Tech State College–Columbus (U)
Ivy Tech State College–Kokomo (U)
Ivy Tech State College–Lafayette (U)
Ivy Tech State College–North Central (U)
Ivy Tech State College–Southeast (U)
Ivy Tech State College–Southwest (U)
Ivy Tech State College–Wabash Valley (U)
Ivy Tech State College–Whitewater (U)
Jacksonville State University (U, G)
Jamestown Community College (N)
John A. Logan College (U)
John Tyler Community College (U)
John Wood Community College (N, U)
Jones College (U)
Kansas City Kansas Community College (U)
Kansas State University (U)
Kauai Community College (U)
Kellogg Community College (U)
Kentucky State University (U)
The King's College and Seminary (N, U, G)
Kirkwood Community College (N)
Lakeland Community College (N, U)
Lake Superior College (U)
Lamar State College–Port Arthur (N, U)
Lansing Community College (U)
Lawson State Community College (U)
Lewis-Clark State College (U)
Limestone College (U)
Long Beach City College (U)
Lorain County Community College (U)
Lord Fairfax Community College (N)
Los Angeles Harbor College (U)
Los Angeles Pierce College (U)
Los Angeles Valley College (U)
Madison Area Technical College (U)
Manchester Community College (N, U)
Mansfield University of Pennsylvania (U)
Marshall University (U, G)
Martin Community College (U)
Maryville University of Saint Louis (N)
Massasoit Community College (N, U)
Maui Community College (U)
Maysville Community College (U)
Mercy College (G)
Mesalands Community College (U)
Miami Dade College (U)
Middlesex Community College (U)
Middle Tennessee State University (N)
Mid-South Community College (N, U)
Mid-State Technical College (U)
Minnesota School of Business–Brooklyn Center (U)
MiraCosta College (U)
Mitchell Technical Institute (N, U)
Monroe County Community College (U)
Montgomery Community College (N, U)
Montgomery County Community College (U)
Motlow State Community College (U)
Mott Community College (U)
Mountain Empire Community College (U)
Mt. Hood Community College (U)
Mount Saint Mary College (U)
Mount Saint Vincent University (N)
Mt. San Antonio College (U)
Murray State University (U)
National University (G)
Naugatuck Valley Community College (U)
New Hampshire Community Technical College System (N, U)
New Jersey Institute of Technology (U)
New York Institute of Technology (N)
North Country Community College (U)
North Dakota State College of Science (U)
North Dakota State University (N, U)
Northeastern Oklahoma Agricultural and Mechanical College (U)

N–Noncredit; U–Undergraduate; G–Graduate

Northeast State Technical Community College (U)
Northern Arizona University (U)
Northern Kentucky University (N)
North Georgia College & State University (N, U)
North Harris Montgomery Community College District (U)
North Hennepin Community College (U)
NorthWest Arkansas Community College (U)
Northwestern Michigan College (U)
Northwestern State University of Louisiana (U)
Northwestern Technical College (U)
Northwest Missouri State University (U)
Nova Southeastern University (G)
Ocean County College (U)
Odessa College (U)
Okaloosa-Walton College (U)
Old Dominion University (U)
Orange Coast College (U)
Owensboro Community and Technical College (U)
Oxnard College (U)
Pace University (N, G)
Palm Beach Community College (U)
Palomar College (U)
Park University (U, G)
Pasco-Hernando Community College (N)
Passaic County Community College (U)
Peninsula College (U)
Pennsylvania College of Technology (U)
Pierce College (U)
Prairie State College (U)
Pulaski Technical College (U)
Randolph Community College (U)
Raritan Valley Community College (U)
Reading Area Community College (U)
Regis University (G)
Rio Hondo College (U)
Riverside Community College (N, U)
Sacramento City College (U)
Sacred Heart University (U)
St. Ambrose University (U)
St. Clair County Community College (U)
St. Cloud Technical College (N, U)
Saint Leo University (U)
Saint Mary-of-the-Woods College (U)
Saint Mary-of-the-Woods College (U)
San Jacinto College District (U)
Santa Rosa Junior College (U)
Santiago Canyon College (U)
Sauk Valley Community College (N)
Seminole Community College (U)
Seton Hill University (U)
Shawnee State University (U)
Shelton State Community College (U)
Shenandoah University (U)
Shoreline Community College (U)
Sinclair Community College (U)
Snead State Community College (U)
Southeastern Community College (U)
Southern Methodist University (G)
South Piedmont Community College (U)
Southwest Missouri State University (U)
Southwest Wisconsin Technical College (U)
Stanly Community College (U)
State University of New York at Plattsburgh (U)
State University of New York College at Potsdam (N)
Stephens College (U)
Syracuse University (G)
Tacoma Community College (N, U)
Tarleton State University (G)
Taylor University (N, U)
Teikyo Post University (U)
Temple College (U)
Texas Woman's University (G)
Three Rivers Community College (U)
Tompkins Cortland Community College (U)
Triton College (N)
Troy University–Florida Region (N)
Tulane University (U)
Tunxis Community College (N, U)
Umpqua Community College (U)
The University of Akron (N, U, G)
The University of Alabama (U)
University of Alaska Fairbanks (U)
University of Arkansas at Pine Bluff (U)
The University of British Columbia (U)
University of Central Arkansas (N)
University of Cincinnati (N)
University of Dallas (G)
University of Denver (G)
University of Great Falls (U, G)
University of Houston–Clear Lake (G)
University of Houston–Victoria (U)
University of Illinois (U, G)
University of Illinois at Urbana–Champaign (G)
The University of Maine at Augusta (U)
University of Management and Technology (U, G)
University of Maryland University College (U)
University of Massachusetts Boston (U)
University of Massachusetts Lowell (U)
University of Nebraska at Omaha (U)
University of Nevada, Reno (U)
The University of North Carolina at Chapel Hill (U)
University of North Florida (U)
University of Northwestern Ohio (U)
The University of Tennessee at Martin (N)
The University of Texas of the Permian Basin (U)
The University of Texas System (U, G)
University of the Incarnate Word (U)
University of Tulsa (G)
University of Washington (N)
University of Waterloo (U)
University of Wisconsin–Milwaukee (U, G)
University of Wisconsin–River Falls (U)
Utah Valley State College (N, U)
Vance-Granville Community College (N)
Walsh College of Accountancy and Business Administration (G)
Washtenaw Community College (U)
Waubonsee Community College (U)
Wayne State College (U, G)
Weber State University (U)
Westchester Community College (U)
Western New England College (U)
West Valley College (U)
West Virginia University at Parkersburg (U)
Wilkes Community College (U)
William Paterson University of New Jersey (U)
William Rainey Harper College (U)
Wisconsin Indianhead Technical College (N, U)
Worcester State College (N, U)
Youngstown State University (N)

Computer and information sciences, other

Alvin Community College (N, U)
American College of Computer & Information Sciences (G)
Athabasca University (U, G)
Bellingham Technical College (U)
Bossier Parish Community College (U)
Brevard Community College (U)
Bristol Community College (N, U)
Caldwell College (U)
Caldwell Community College and Technical Institute (N)
California State University, Monterey Bay (N)
Capitol College (G)
Central Texas College (U)
Champlain College (U)
Chemeketa Community College (U)
Clackamas Community College (U)
College of the Canyons (U)
Columbia Basin College (U)
The Community College of Baltimore County (N)
Cossatot Community College of the University of Arkansas (N)
Dakota State University (U, G)

Dallas County Community College District (U)
Delaware County Community College (N, U)
DePaul University (G)
Des Moines Area Community College (U)
Edgecombe Community College (N, U)
Forrest Junior College (N, U)
Fort Hays State University (U)
George Mason University (U)
Halifax Community College (U)
Heart of Georgia Technical College (U)
Hudson County Community College (U)
Immaculata University (U)
Jacksonville State University (U, G)
Jamestown Community College (N)
John Tyler Community College (U)
Jones College (U)
Kansas City Kansas Community College (U)
Lakeland Community College (N)
Limestone College (U)
Lord Fairfax Community College (N)
Marshall University (U)
Mercy College (G)
Middlesex Community College (U)
Mid-State Technical College (U)
Nebraska Methodist College (U, G)
New Hampshire Community Technical College System (N, U)
New York Institute of Technology (N)
Northcentral University (G)
Northern Arizona University (U)
NorthWest Arkansas Community College (U)
Northwestern Michigan College (U)
Nova Southeastern University (G)
Pace University (U, G)
Pierce College (U)
Raritan Valley Community College (U)
Regis University (G)
Sacramento City College (U)
Saint Leo University (U)
Santa Rosa Junior College (U)
Seminole Community College (U)
Southern Methodist University (G)
Stanly Community College (U)
State University of New York College at Fredonia (U)
Tarleton State University (G)
Taylor University (N)
Teikyo Post University (U)
Texas Tech University (G)
Treasure Valley Community College (U)
Troy University–Florida Region (N)
The University of Akron (N)
The University of Alabama (G)
University of Central Arkansas (G)
University of Connecticut (U)
University of Dallas (G)
University of Denver (G)
University of Maine (U)
The University of Texas System (U)
University of the Incarnate Word (U)
University of Washington (N)
University of Wisconsin–Milwaukee (N, G)
Wake Technical Community College (U)
Wilkes Community College (U)
William Rainey Harper College (U)
York Technical College (N)

Computer engineering

Bellingham Technical College (N)
Bristol Community College (N)
California National University for Advanced Studies (N, G)
College of The Albemarle (N)
Cossatot Community College of the University of Arkansas (N)
Dallas County Community College District (U)
Delaware County Community College (N, U)
Edison State Community College (U)
Georgia Institute of Technology (N, G)
Grantham University (U)
Illinois Institute of Technology (U, G)
Iowa State University of Science and Technology (G)
Jacksonville State University (G)
Kansas State University (G)
Lakeland Community College (N)
Marshall University (U)
Maui Community College (U)
Minnesota School of Business–Brooklyn Center (U)
Mississippi State University (G)
North Carolina State University (G)
North Dakota State University (U, G)
Oxnard College (U)
Shawnee State University (U)
Shenandoah University (U)
Southern Methodist University (G)
Southwestern Oregon Community College (U)
Troy University–Florida Region (N)
University of Colorado at Boulder (N, G)
University of Idaho (U, G)
University of Washington (U)
University of West Florida (N)
University of Wisconsin–Platteville (G)
Virginia Polytechnic Institute and State University (U, G)
Western Michigan University (G)

Computer programming

Acadia University (U)
Albuquerque Technical Vocational Institute (U)
Alvin Community College (U)
American College of Computer & Information Sciences (U, G)
American River College (U)
Arkansas State University–Beebe (U)
Asheville-Buncombe Technical Community College (N, U)
Ashworth College (N)
Athabasca University (N, U)
Bossier Parish Community College (N)
Brevard Community College (U)
Bristol Community College (N, U)
Broome Community College (N)
Bryant and Stratton Online (U)
Bucks County Community College (U)
Butler County Community College (U)
California National University for Advanced Studies (N)
California State University, Fullerton (N, U)
Capella University (N, G)
Casper College (U)
Central Missouri State University (N)
Central Missouri State University (N)
Central Missouri State University (N)
Central Missouri State University (N)
Central Missouri State University (N)
Central Texas College (U)
Champlain College (U)
Chemeketa Community College (U)
Cleveland Community College (U)
Cleveland State University (U)
Clinton Community College (U)
Coleman College (U)
College of DuPage (U)
College of San Mateo (U)
College of The Albemarle (N)
College of the Canyons (U)
Colorado State University (N)
Columbia Basin College (U)
Columbus State Community College (U)
Columbus State University (G)
The Community College of Baltimore County (N, U)
Corning Community College (U)
Cossatot Community College of the University of Arkansas (N, U)
Dakota State University (N, U)
Dallas County Community College District (U)
Daniel Webster College (U)
Danville Community College (U)
Davenport University Online (U)

N–Noncredit; U–Undergraduate; G–Graduate

Delaware County Community College (N, U)
Delta College (U)
DePaul University (U, G)
Des Moines Area Community College (U)
Edgecombe Community College (N, U)
Edison Community College (U)
Edison State Community College (U)
Edmonds Community College (U)
Education Direct Center for Degree Studies (N)
Fairleigh Dickinson University, Metropolitan Campus (N, G)
Feather River Community College District (N)
Florida National College (U)
Fort Hays State University (U)
Frederick Community College (N)
Gaston College (U)
Grantham University (U)
Hagerstown Community College (N)
Harford Community College (N, U)
Harrisburg Area Community College (U)
Hibbing Community College (U)
Hillsborough Community College (U)
Hudson County Community College (N)
Illinois Institute of Technology (U)
Immaculata University (U)
Irvine Valley College (U)
Ivy Tech State College–Bloomington (U)
Ivy Tech State College–Columbus (U)
Ivy Tech State College–Kokomo (U)
Ivy Tech State College–Lafayette (U)
Ivy Tech State College–North Central (U)
Ivy Tech State College–Northwest (U)
Ivy Tech State College–Southeast (U)
Ivy Tech State College–Southwest (U)
Ivy Tech State College–Wabash Valley (U)
Ivy Tech State College–Whitewater (U)
Jacksonville State University (U, G)
James Madison University (N)
Jones College (U)
Kentucky State University (U)
Lakeland Community College (N)
Lamar State College–Port Arthur (N, U)
Lansing Community College (U)
Limestone College (U)
Lock Haven University of Pennsylvania (U)
Long Beach City College (U)
Long Island University, C.W. Post Campus (N)
Los Angeles Harbor College (U)
Madison Area Technical College (U)
Manchester Community College (N)
Mesa Community College (U)
Metropolitan Community College (U)
Middlesex Community College (U)
Middle Tennessee State University (N)
MiraCosta College (N)
Modesto Junior College (U)
Montgomery County Community College (U)
Mott Community College (U)
Mount Wachusett Community College (U)
Murray State University (U)
New Hampshire Community Technical College System (N, U)
New Jersey Institute of Technology (N)
North Carolina State University (U)
North Dakota State College of Science (U)
North Dakota State University (N)
Northeastern Oklahoma Agricultural and Mechanical College (N)
Northeastern University (N, U)
Northwestern Michigan College (U)
Nova Southeastern University (G)
Oklahoma State University (N)
Orange Coast College (U)
Oxnard College (U)
Pace University (U, G)
Park University (U)
Pasco-Hernando Community College (U)
Paul D. Camp Community College (U)
Raritan Valley Community College (U)
Regis University (U, G)
Rio Hondo College (U)
Riverside Community College (N)
Sacramento City College (U)
St. Cloud Technical College (N)
Saint Leo University (U)
Santa Fe Community College (N)
Santa Rosa Junior College (U)
Sauk Valley Community College (U)
Schoolcraft College (N)
Seminole Community College (U)
Shawnee State University (U)
Sinclair Community College (U)
Southwestern College (U)
Southwest Wisconsin Technical College (U)
State University of New York College at Potsdam (N)
Syracuse University (U)
Tarleton State University (N, U, G)
Taylor University (N)
Texas State Technical College–Waco (N, U)
Tompkins Cortland Community College (U)
Treasure Valley Community College (U)
Troy University–Florida Region (N, U)
Tulane University (U)
Umpqua Community College (U)
University College of Cape Breton (N)
The University of Akron (N)
University of Colorado at Denver (U)
University of Connecticut (U)
University of Florida (N)
University of Houston–Clear Lake (G)
University of Houston–Downtown (U)
University of Idaho (N, U)
University of Illinois (N)
University of Management and Technology (G)
University of Massachusetts Lowell (U)
University of Missouri–Columbia (U)
University of the Incarnate Word (U)
University of Vermont (N)
University of Washington (N, U)
University of West Florida (U)
University of Wisconsin–River Falls (U)
Vance-Granville Community College (N, U)
Washtenaw Community College (U)
Waubonsee Community College (U)
Westchester Community College (U)
Westwood Online (U)
Wilkes Community College (U)
William Rainey Harper College (U)
Winston-Salem State University (U)
Wisconsin Indianhead Technical College (N, U)

Computer science

Acadia University (U)
Allan Hancock College (U)
Alvin Community College (U)
American College of Computer & Information Sciences (U, G)
Anne Arundel Community College (U)
Arkansas State University–Mountain Home (U)
Athabasca University (N, U, G)
Azusa Pacific University (U, G)
Bellingham Technical College (U)
Bismarck State College (U)
Bossier Parish Community College (U)
Bowling Green State University (U)
Bristol Community College (N, U)
Broome Community College (U)
Broward Community College (U)
Butler County Community College (U)
California National University for Advanced Studies (N)
California State University, Chico (G)
Capitol College (G)
Casper College (U)
Cayuga County Community College (U)
Central Missouri State University (U)
Central Missouri State University (U)
Central Missouri State University (U)
Central Missouri State University (U)
Central Missouri State University (U)
Central Texas College (U)
Chattanooga State Technical Community College (U)
Chemeketa Community College (U)
Clackamas Community College (U)

Coastal Bend College (U)
College of The Albemarle (N, U)
College of the Canyons (U)
College of the Siskiyous (U)
College of the Southwest (U)
Colorado Mountain College District System (U)
Colorado State University (U)
Columbia Basin College (U)
Columbia University (N, U, G)
Columbus State University (U)
The Community College of Baltimore County (U)
Connecticut State University System (U)
Cossatot Community College of the University of Arkansas (N)
County College of Morris (U)
Dakota State University (U)
Dallas County Community College District (U)
Danville Community College (U)
Delaware County Community College (N, U)
Delaware Technical & Community College, Jack F. Owens Campus (U)
Delaware Technical & Community College, Stanton/Wilmington Campus (U)
DePaul University (G)
Des Moines Area Community College (U)
East Carolina University (G)
Eastern Kentucky University (G)
Edgecombe Community College (N)
Edison State Community College (U)
Embry-Riddle Aeronautical University, Extended Campus (U)
Fairleigh Dickinson University, Metropolitan Campus (N, U, G)
Florida Atlantic University (U, G)
Florida Community College at Jacksonville (U)
Florida Gulf Coast University (U)
Fort Hays State University (U)
Franklin University (U)
George Mason University (U, G)
Grantham University (U)
Halifax Community College (U)
Harrisburg Area Community College (U)
Hibbing Community College (U)
Hillsborough Community College (U)
Horry-Georgetown Technical College (U)
Houston Community College System (U)
Illinois Institute of Technology (U, G)
Indiana University–Purdue University Fort Wayne (U)
Inter American University of Puerto Rico, San Germán Campus (U)
Ivy Tech State College–Kokomo (U)
Ivy Tech State College–Lafayette (U)
Jacksonville State University (U, G)
James Madison University (N)
Kansas City Kansas Community College (U)
Kansas State University (G)
Lakeland College (U)
Lamar State College–Port Arthur (N, U)
LeTourneau University (U)
Limestone College (U)
Long Beach City College (U)
Long Island University, C.W. Post Campus (N)
Los Angeles Pierce College (U)
Marymount University (G)
Maui Community College (U)
Memorial University of Newfoundland (U)
Mercy College (G)
Mesa Community College (U)
Mesalands Community College (U)
Middlesex Community College (U)
Middle Tennessee State University (N)
Minnesota School of Business-Richfield (U)
Mississippi State University (G)
Moberly Area Community College (U)
Modesto Junior College (U)
Montgomery County Community College (U)
Murray State University (U)
New Hampshire Community Technical College System (N, U)
New Jersey Institute of Technology (U, G)
New York Institute of Technology (U)
Northampton County Area Community College (U)
Northcentral University (U)
North Dakota State University (N)
Northern New Mexico Community College (U)
Northwestern Technical College (U)
Nova Southeastern University (G)
Old Dominion University (U)
Oxnard College (U)
Pace University (U)
Quinnipiac University (U, G)
Regis University (U, G)
Rend Lake College (U)
Rockland Community College (U)
Sacred Heart University (U, G)
Saddleback College (U)
St. Cloud Technical College (N)
St. Petersburg College (U)
Santa Rosa Junior College (U)
Schoolcraft College (U)
Seminole Community College (U)
Simpson College (U)
Snead State Community College (U)
Southeast Arkansas College (U)
Southern Methodist University (G)
Southwestern Oregon Community College (U)
Stanford University (N)
State University of New York at New Paltz (U)
Stevens Institute of Technology (N)
Sullivan University (U)
Tacoma Community College (U)
Taft College (U)
Tarleton State University (G)
Teikyo Post University (U)
Texas A&M University–Commerce (U)
Texas State Technical College–Waco (U)
Texas Tech University (G)
Touro University International (U)
Troy University–Florida Region (N)
The University of Akron (N, U)
The University of Alabama (U)
University of Alaska Fairbanks (U)
University of Arkansas at Pine Bluff (U)
University of Colorado at Boulder (N, G)
University of Great Falls (U)
University of Houston (G)
University of Houston–Clear Lake (G)
University of Houston–Downtown (U)
University of Idaho (U, G)
University of Illinois (G)
University of Illinois at Springfield (U, G)
University of Management and Technology (U)
University of Massachusetts Boston (U)
University of Missouri–Columbia (U)
The University of Montana–Missoula (U)
University of New Hampshire (G)
University of Saskatchewan (U)
The University of Tennessee at Martin (U)
The University of Texas at Tyler (U, G)
The University of Texas–Pan American (U)
University of Vermont (N, U)
The University of Virginia's College at Wise (U)
University of Washington (U, G)
University of Waterloo (U)
University of West Florida (U)
University of Wisconsin–Madison (U)
University of Wisconsin–River Falls (U)
Utah State University (U, G)
Valparaiso University (U)
Virginia Polytechnic Institute and State University (U, G)
Walters State Community College (U)
Westchester Community College (U)
Western Michigan University (G)
Western Wyoming Community College (U)
West Los Angeles College (U)
West Valley College (U)

N–Noncredit; U–Undergraduate; G–Graduate

Wilkes Community College (U)
William Rainey Harper College (U)
Worcester State College (N)
York Technical College (U)
Youngstown State University (U)

Computer software and media applications

Adams State College (N)
Adirondack Community College (U)
AIB College of Business (U)
Allen County Community College (U)
American College of Computer & Information Sciences (G)
American River College (U)
Arapahoe Community College (U)
Athabasca University (N, U)
Auburn University Montgomery (N)
Augusta Technical College (N)
Bainbridge College (N)
Baltimore City Community College (N, U)
Bellingham Technical College (N)
Berkeley College (U)
Berkeley College-New York City Campus (U)
Berkeley College-Westchester Campus (U)
Bismarck State College (U)
Blackhawk Technical College (N)
Boise State University (U, G)
Boise State University (G)
Bossier Parish Community College (N, U)
Bowling Green State University (N)
Brevard Community College (U)
Brigham Young University (N)
Bristol Community College (N, U)
Broome Community College (N)
Brunswick Community College (U)
Bryant and Stratton Online (U)
Bucks County Community College (U)
Caldwell Community College and Technical Institute (N)
California State University, Fullerton (N)
California State University, Hayward (U)
California State University, Monterey Bay (U)
Cape Cod Community College (U)
Carroll Community College (N)
Casper College (U)
Central Missouri State University (N)
Central Missouri State University (N)
Central Missouri State University (N)
Central Missouri State University (N)
Central Missouri State University (N)
Champlain College (U)
Chemeketa Community College (U)
Cincinnati State Technical and Community College (U)
Clackamas Community College (U)
Cleveland State University (N, G)
Coconino Community College (N)
College of DuPage (U)
College of The Albemarle (N)
Colorado Christian University (U)
Colorado Mountain College District System (N, U)
Colorado State University-Pueblo (N)
Columbus State Community College (U)
The Community College of Baltimore County (N)
Community College of Denver (U)
Cossatot Community College of the University of Arkansas (N)
Dakota County Technical College (U)
Dallas County Community College District (U)
Danville Community College (U)
Darton College (U)
Dawson Community College (U)
Delaware County Community College (N, U)
DePaul University (G)
Des Moines Area Community College (N)
Duquesne University (G)
East Central College (U)
Eastern Wyoming College (U)
Edgecombe Community College (N, U)
Edison Community College (U)
Edison State Community College (N, U)
Erie Community College (U)
Everett Community College (N)
Fairleigh Dickinson University, Metropolitan Campus (N)
Feather River Community College District (N)
Flathead Valley Community College (N, U)
Florida Community College at Jacksonville (U)
Florida Metropolitan University–Brandon Campus (U)
Florida National College (U)
Fontbonne University (U, G)
Forrest Junior College (U)
Fort Hays State University (U)
Frederick Community College (N)
Fulton-Montgomery Community College (N, U)
Gaston College (U)
Gateway Community College (N)
Golden West College (U)
Grantham University (U)
Greenville Technical College (U)
Hagerstown Community College (N)
Halifax Community College (N)
Harrisburg Area Community College (U)
Henry Ford Community College (U)
Hibbing Community College (N, U)
Hudson County Community College (U)
Illinois Eastern Community Colleges, Lincoln Trail College (U)
Immaculata University (U)
Indiana University–Purdue University Fort Wayne (N)
Iowa Western Community College (U)
Irvine Valley College (U)
Ivy Tech State College–Columbus (U)
Ivy Tech State College–Kokomo (U)
Ivy Tech State College–Lafayette (U)
Ivy Tech State College–North Central (U)
Ivy Tech State College–Northwest (U)
Ivy Tech State College–Southeast (U)
Ivy Tech State College–Southwest (U)
Ivy Tech State College–Wabash Valley (U)
Ivy Tech State College–Whitewater (U)
Jacksonville State University (U, G)
Jamestown Community College (N)
Jefferson College (U)
Jefferson College of Health Sciences (U)
Jefferson Davis Community College (U)
Johnson County Community College (N, U)
Judson College (U)
Kansas City Kansas Community College (U)
Kansas State University (G)
Kellogg Community College (U)
Kirkwood Community College (N)
Lake Superior College (U)
Lamar State College–Port Arthur (N, U)
Lewis-Clark State College (N)
Limestone College (U)
Long Beach City College (U)
Long Island University, C.W. Post Campus (N)
Lorain County Community College (N)
Lord Fairfax Community College (N, U)
Los Angeles Pierce College (U)
Los Angeles Valley College (U)
Louisiana State University at Eunice (N, U)
Louisiana State University in Shreveport (U)
Madison Area Technical College (U)
Manchester Community College (N)
Maryville University of Saint Louis (N)
Maysville Community College (N)
Mesa Community College (U)
Middlesex Community College (N, U)
Middle Tennessee State University (N)
Midstate College (U)
Minnesota State College–Southeast Technical (N)
MiraCosta College (N, U)
Mitchell Technical Institute (N)
Modesto Junior College (U)
Montana Tech of The University of Montana (U)
Montgomery Community College (N, U)

Montgomery County Community College (U)
Mt. Hood Community College (U)
Mt. San Antonio College (N)
Mount Wachusett Community College (N, U)
National University (U)
New Hampshire Community Technical College System (N, U)
New York Institute of Technology (N)
Normandale Community College (U)
North Georgia College & State University (N)
North Harris Montgomery Community College District (U)
North Hennepin Community College (N)
Northwestern College (U)
Northwestern Michigan College (U)
Northwestern State University of Louisiana (U)
Northwestern Technical College (U)
Nova Southeastern University (G)
Odessa College (N)
Orange Coast College (U)
Oregon State University (N)
Pace University (G)
Palomar College (U)
Pasco-Hernando Community College (N)
Randolph Community College (N, U)
Raritan Valley Community College (U)
Rend Lake College (N)
Sacramento City College (U)
Saint Paul College–A Community & Technical College (U)
San Jacinto College District (U)
Santa Fe Community College (N)
Santa Rosa Junior College (U)
Schenectady County Community College (U)
Schoolcraft College (N)
Seminole Community College (U)
Seward County Community College (U)
Shenandoah University (U)
Sinclair Community College (U)
Snead State Community College (U)
Sonoma State University (N)
South Central Technical College (U)
Southwest Wisconsin Technical College (U)
Spartanburg Technical College (U)
Spoon River College (N)
Spring Arbor University (U)
State University of New York College at Potsdam (N)
Stevens Institute of Technology (G)
Tarleton State University (N, U, G)
Taylor University (N)
Teachers College Columbia University (N, G)
Texas State Technical College–Waco (N, U)
Tompkins Cortland Community College (N, U)
Troy University–Florida Region (N)
University College of Cape Breton (N)
The University of Akron (N, U)
University of Alaska Fairbanks (U)
University of California, Riverside (N)
University of Cincinnati (U)
University of Cincinnati Raymond Walters College (U)
University of Connecticut (U)
University of Houston–Clear Lake (G)
University of Houston–Downtown (U)
The University of Maine at Augusta (U)
University of Management and Technology (G)
University of Mississippi (N)
University of the Incarnate Word (U)
University of Toronto (U)
University of Vermont (N)
University of West Florida (U)
University of Wisconsin–Milwaukee (N)
Utah Valley State College (N)
Vance-Granville Community College (N)
Virginia Polytechnic Institute and State University (N)
Wake Technical Community College (N)
Western Michigan University (U)
Western Wyoming Community College (U)
West Valley College (U)
Westwood Online (U)
William Paterson University of New Jersey (N)
William Rainey Harper College (U)
York University (N)
Youngstown State University (N)

Computer systems analysis

American College of Computer & Information Sciences (U)
Athabasca University (N, U, G)
Bossier Parish Community College (N)
Bridgewater State College (N)
Bristol Community College (N, U)
Central Texas College (U)
Cleveland State University (U)
The Community College of Baltimore County (U)
Dakota State University (U)
Dallas County Community College District (U)
Delaware County Community College (N)
DePaul University (G)
Edgecombe Community College (U)
Edison State Community College (U)
Fort Hays State University (U)
Grantham University (U)
Heart of Georgia Technical College (U)
Immaculata University (U)
Ivy Tech State College–Bloomington (U)
Ivy Tech State College–Columbus (U)
Ivy Tech State College–Kokomo (U)
Ivy Tech State College–Lafayette (U)
Ivy Tech State College–North Central (U)
Ivy Tech State College–Northwest (U)
Ivy Tech State College–Southeast (U)
Ivy Tech State College–Southwest (U)
Ivy Tech State College–Wabash Valley (U)
Ivy Tech State College–Whitewater (U)
Jacksonville State University (U, G)
Jones College (U)
Kirkwood Community College (N)
Lamar State College–Port Arthur (N)
Limestone College (U)
Long Island University, C.W. Post Campus (N)
Lord Fairfax Community College (N)
Maryville University of Saint Louis (N)
Mercy College (G)
Middlesex Community College (N)
New Hampshire Community Technical College System (N)
Northeastern Oklahoma Agricultural and Mechanical College (N)
Nova Southeastern University (G)
Oxnard College (U)
Pace University (G)
Pulaski Technical College (U)
Quinnipiac University (U)
St. Edward's University (N, U, G)
Saint Leo University (U)
Santa Fe Community College (N)
Seminole Community College (U)
Syracuse University (G)
Tarleton State University (G)
Texas State Technical College–Waco (U)
Troy University–Florida Region (N)
The University of Akron (N)
University of Dallas (G)
University of Florida (N)
University of Houston–Downtown (U)
University of the Incarnate Word (U)
University of Vermont (N)
University of Washington (N)

Computer systems networking and telecommunications

Alpena Community College (U)
American College of Computer & Information Sciences (U)
American River College (U)

N–Noncredit; U–Undergraduate; G–Graduate

Arapahoe Community College (U)
Asheville-Buncombe Technical Community College (N)
Athabasca University (U)
Bainbridge College (N)
Bellingham Technical College (U)
Brevard Community College (U)
Bristol Community College (N, U)
Bryant and Stratton Online (U)
California National University for Advanced Studies (N)
California State University, Fullerton (N)
Capella University (U, G)
Capitol College (G)
Carroll Community College (N, U)
Central Missouri State University (N)
Central Missouri State University (N)
Central Missouri State University (N)
Central Missouri State University (N)
Central Missouri State University (N)
Central Texas College (U)
Champlain College (U)
Chemeketa Community College (U)
Cincinnati State Technical and Community College (U)
Clackamas Community College (U)
Cleveland State University (N, G)
College of DuPage (U)
College of The Albemarle (N)
The Community College of Baltimore County (U)
Community College of Denver (U)
Connecticut State University System (G)
Corning Community College (U)
Dakota County Technical College (U)
Dallas County Community College District (U)
Darton College (U)
Davenport University Online (U)
Delaware County Community College (N, U)
DePaul University (G)
East Carolina University (G)
Edgecombe Community College (U)
Edison State Community College (U)
Fairmont State University (N)
Florida National College (U)
Forrest Junior College (N, U)
Fort Hays State University (U)
Frederick Community College (N)
Fulton-Montgomery Community College (N)
Gaston College (U)
George Mason University (G)
Grantham University (U)
Grossmont College (U)
Hagerstown Community College (N)
Halifax Community College (N)
Harford Community College (N, U)
Heart of Georgia Technical College (U)
Hopkinsville Community College (U)
Independence Community College (U)
Indiana University–Purdue University Fort Wayne (N)
Irvine Valley College (U)
Ivy Tech State College–Bloomington (U)
Ivy Tech State College–Columbus (U)
Ivy Tech State College–Kokomo (U)
Ivy Tech State College–Lafayette (U)
Ivy Tech State College–North Central (U)
Ivy Tech State College–Northwest (U)
Ivy Tech State College–Southeast (U)
Ivy Tech State College–Southwest (U)
Ivy Tech State College–Wabash Valley (U)
Ivy Tech State College–Whitewater (U)
Jacksonville State University (U, G)
James Madison University (N)
Jamestown Community College (N)
Johnson County Community College (U)
John Tyler Community College (U)
Kansas City Kansas Community College (U)
Keiser College (U)
Kirkwood Community College (N)
Lamar State College–Port Arthur (N, U)
Limestone College (U)
Long Beach City College (U)
Long Island University, C.W. Post Campus (N)
Lord Fairfax Community College (N, U)
Madison Area Technical College (U)
Manchester Community College (N, U)
Maryville University of Saint Louis (N)
Middle Tennessee State University (N)
Murray State University (U)
New Hampshire Community Technical College System (N, U)
Northeastern University (N)
North Harris Montgomery Community College District (U)
North Hennepin Community College (N)
NorthWest Arkansas Community College (U)
Northwestern Michigan College (U)
Nova Southeastern University (G)
Old Dominion University (U)
Oxnard College (U)
Pace University (G)
Pasco-Hernando Community College (U)
Patrick Henry Community College (U)
Peirce College (U)
Pulaski Technical College (U)
Raritan Valley Community College (U)
Regis University (U, G)
Riverland Community College (U)
Saint Leo University (U)
Salem Community College (U)
Santa Fe Community College (N)
Santa Rosa Junior College (U)
Seminole Community College (U)
Shenandoah University (U)
Sinclair Community College (U)
Sonoma State University (N)
Southwest Wisconsin Technical College (U)
Stanford University (N)
Syracuse University (G)
Tarleton State University (G)
Taylor University (N)
Texas State Technical College–Waco (U)
Tompkins Cortland Community College (N)
Troy University–Florida Region (N)
Tunxis Community College (U)
The University of Akron (N)
University of Denver (G)
University of Florida (N)
University of Houston–Downtown (U)
University of Illinois (G)
University of Management and Technology (G)
University of Maryland University College (G)
University of Minnesota, Twin Cities Campus (U)
The University of Texas–Pan American (N)
University of the Incarnate Word (U)
University of Tulsa (G)
University of West Florida (U)
University of Wisconsin–Milwaukee (N)
Vance-Granville Community College (N, U)
Westchester Community College (U)
Westwood Online (U)
William Rainey Harper College (U)
Worcester Polytechnic Institute (G)
Youngstown State University (N)

Computer/information technology administration and management

Allan Hancock College (U)
Alpena Community College (U)
Alvin Community College (U)
American Public University System (U)
Athabasca University (N, U, G)
Baker College of Flint (U)
Bellingham Technical College (N)
Brevard Community College (U)
Bridgewater State College (U)
Bristol Community College (N, U)
Broome Community College (U)
Bryant and Stratton Online (U)
Caldwell Community College and Technical Institute (N)
California State University, Dominguez Hills (N)
Capella University (N, U, G)

Computer/information technology administration and management

Capitol College (G)
Carroll Community College (U)
Central Washington University (U)
Champlain College (U)
Cincinnati State Technical and Community College (U)
Cleveland Community College (U)
Cleveland State University (G)
Coleman College (U)
College for Lifelong Learning (U)
College of The Albemarle (N)
The Community College of Baltimore County (U)
Community College of Denver (U)
Cossatot Community College of the University of Arkansas (N)
Dallas Baptist University (G)
Dallas County Community College District (U)
Davenport University Online (U)
Delaware County Community College (U)
DePaul University (G)
Drexel University (G)
East Carolina University (G)
Edgecombe Community College (N, U)
Edison State Community College (N, U)
Fairmont State University (N)
Forrest Junior College (N, U)
Fort Hays State University (U)
Franklin Pierce College (U)
Gogebic Community College (U)
Grantham University (U)
Greenfield Community College (U)
Hillsborough Community College (U)
Houston Community College System (U)
Immaculata University (U)
Jacksonville State University (U, G)
John Jay College of Criminal Justice of the City University of New York (U)
John Tyler Community College (U)
Jones International University (U)
Keiser College (U)
Lakeland Community College (N)
Lamar State College–Port Arthur (N)
Limestone College (U)
Long Island University, C.W. Post Campus (N)
Lord Fairfax Community College (N)
Madison Area Technical College (U)
Martin Luther College (U)
Mercy College (G)
Mesa Community College (U)
Middle Tennessee State University (N)
Mount Saint Vincent University (U)
New York Institute of Technology (N)
Normandale Community College (N)
Northeastern University (U)
Nova Southeastern University (G)
Orange Coast College (U)
Oregon Institute of Technology (U)
Oxnard College (U)
Pace University (G)
Patrick Henry Community College (U)
Paul D. Camp Community College (U)
Peirce College (U)
Peninsula College (U)
Raritan Valley Community College (U)
Regis University (U, G)
Riverland Community College (U)
St. Edward's University (N, G)
Saint Joseph's College of Maine (U)
Salem Community College (U)
Santa Fe Community College (N)
Schiller International University (G)
Seminole Community College (U)
Seward County Community College (U)
Sonoma State University (N)
Southeast Arkansas College (U)
Southern Illinois University Carbondale (U)
Southern Methodist University (G)
South Piedmont Community College (U)
Southwestern College (U)
Stanford University (N)
Sullivan University (G)
Syracuse University (G)
Tarleton State University (G)
Taylor University (N, U)
Touro University International (U)
Troy University–Florida Region (N, U)
The University of Akron (N)
University of Arkansas at Pine Bluff (N)
University of Cincinnati Raymond Walters College (U)
University of Connecticut (U)
University of Denver (G)
University of Houston–Downtown (U)
University of Illinois (G)
University of Illinois at Urbana–Champaign (G)
University of Maryland University College (G)
University of Massachusetts Boston (U)
University of Southern Indiana (U)
The University of Texas–Pan American (N)
University of the Incarnate Word (U)
University of Toledo (U)
University of Toronto (N, U)
University of Tulsa (G)
University of Vermont (N)
University of Washington (N)
Vance-Granville Community College (U)
Western New England College (G)
West Los Angeles College (U)
West Virginia University at Parkersburg (U)
Wilkes Community College (U)
William Rainey Harper College (U)

Conservation and renewable natural resources, other

Berkeley College-New York City Campus (U)
Glenville State College (U)
James Madison University (N)
Oregon State University (U)
Prescott College (G)
Saint Mary-of-the-Woods College (G)
University of La Verne (N)
University of Massachusetts Amherst (U)
University of Wisconsin–River Falls (G)
William Paterson University of New Jersey (U)

Construction management

Albuquerque Technical Vocational Institute (U)
Asheville-Buncombe Technical Community College (N)
Athabasca University (N)
Bowling Green State University (G)
Chattanooga State Technical Community College (U)
Clemson University (N)
Eastern Illinois University (G)
James Madison University (N)
National University (U)
Northern Arizona University (U)
Northern Kentucky University (U)
Pennsylvania College of Technology (U)
Santa Fe Community College (N)
Stanford University (N)
Sullivan University (G)
Sullivan University (U)
University of Washington (U, G)
Vance-Granville Community College (N)
Washtenaw Community College (U)
Weber State University (U)

Construction trades, other

Colorado Mountain College District System (U)
Delaware County Community College (U)
James Madison University (N)
Maui Community College (U)

Construction/building technology

Bowling Green State University (G)
Clemson University (N)
Delaware County Community College (U)
Indiana State University (U)
Ivy Tech State College–Northeast (U)
James Madison University (N)
Madison Area Technical College (U)

N–Noncredit; U–Undergraduate; G–Graduate

National University (U)
North Hennepin Community College (U)
Orange Coast College (U)
Stanford University (N)
University of Southern Mississippi (G)
University of Washington (U, G)

Consumer and homemaking education

Blackhawk Technical College (N)
Colorado State University (U)
Eastern Illinois University (U)
Edgecombe Community College (N)
Evergreen Valley College (U)
Hudson County Community College (U)
James Madison University (N)
Lamar State College–Port Arthur (U)
Louisiana Tech University (U)
MiraCosta College (N)
The University of Alabama (G)
University of Idaho (U)
University of Missouri–Columbia (U)
University of Missouri–Columbia (N)
University of Southern Mississippi (G)

Cosmetic services

James Madison University (N)
Madison Area Technical College (U)
Southwest Wisconsin Technical College (U)

Counseling psychology

American River College (U)
Athabasca University (N, U, G)
Baptist Bible College of Pennsylvania (G)
The Baptist College of Florida (U)
Bethany College of the Assemblies of God (U)
Briercrest Distance Learning (U)
Capella University (N, G)
Central Texas College (U)
Chadron State College (G)
College of the Southwest (G)
Columbia Basin College (U)
Delaware County Community College (U)
Eastern Kentucky University (G)
Goddard College (U)
James Madison University (N)
John F. Kennedy University (G)
The King's College and Seminary (N, U, G)
Lander University (U)
Liberty University (G)
Master's College and Seminary (U)
Mississippi State University (U, G)
Moody Bible Institute (U)
Naropa University (U)
National University (U)
Oklahoma State University (U)
Prescott College (U)
St. Cloud State University (U)
St. Edward's University (G)
Santa Rosa Junior College (U)
Saybrook Graduate School and Research Center (G)
Southwestern Assemblies of God University (G)
State University of New York at Oswego (U, G)
Tarleton State University (U, G)
Taylor University (U)
The University of Akron (G)
University of Bridgeport (U)
University of Great Falls (U)
University of Hawaii–West Oahu (U)
University of La Verne (N)
The University of Maine at Augusta (U)
University of Massachusetts Boston (G)
University of Missouri–Columbia (G)
The University of North Carolina at Charlotte (N)
University of Toledo (G)
University of Wisconsin–Milwaukee (N, U, G)
University of Wisconsin–River Falls (G)
Wayne State College (G)
Western Baptist College (U)
Western Michigan University (G)
William Paterson University of New Jersey (U, G)

Crafts, folk art and artisanry

Blackhawk Technical College (N)
Bossier Parish Community College (N)
Feather River Community College District (N)
James Madison University (N)
Maryville University of Saint Louis (N)
Middle Tennessee State University (N)
Naugatuck Valley Community College (N)
Santa Fe Community College (N)
The University of Tennessee at Martin (N)

Creative writing

Atlantic University (N, G)
Brookdale Community College (U)
College of the Southwest (U)
Cumberland County College (U)
Dallas County Community College District (U)
Dawson Community College (U)
Eastern Washington University (U)
Lansing Community College (U)
Lorain County Community College (U)
Marylhurst University (U)
Mt. San Antonio College (U)
Northern Virginia Community College (U)
Northwestern Michigan College (U)
Northwestern State University of Louisiana (U)
Ohio University (U)
Oklahoma State University (U)
Oregon State University (U)
Park University (U)
The Pennsylvania State University University Park Campus (U)
Pitt Community College (N)
Richland Community College (U)
Sam Houston State University (U)
Skidmore College (U)
Southwestern Assemblies of God University (U)
Southwest Virginia Community College (U)
Spring Arbor University (U)
Tarrant County College District (U)
Texas A&M University–Commerce (U)
University College of Cape Breton (U)
University of Arkansas at Little Rock (U)
University of Colorado at Denver (U)
University of Denver (G)
University of Maine (U)
University of Minnesota, Twin Cities Campus (U)
University of Missouri–Columbia (U)
The University of North Carolina at Chapel Hill (U)
University of Southern Mississippi (U)
University of Utah (U)
University of Washington (N)
Walters State Community College (U)
Washington State University (U)
Waubonsee Community College (U)
Western Washington University (U)
West Valley College (U)

Criminal justice and corrections

Adirondack Community College (U)
Albuquerque Technical Vocational Institute (U)
Alpena Community College (U)
American Public University System (U, G)
Andrew Jackson University (U, G)
Arapahoe Community College (U)
Ashland Community and Technical College (U)
Athabasca University (N, U)
Auburn University Montgomery (U, G)
Baltimore City Community College (U)
Bemidji State University (U)
Bismarck State College (U)
Blackhawk Technical College (N)
Bossier Parish Community College (U)
Brenau University (U)
Brunswick Community College (U)
Bucks County Community College (U)
Butler County Community College (U)

Caldwell College (U)
Caldwell Community College and Technical Institute (N)
California State University, Sacramento (U)
California University of Pennsylvania (G)
Capella University (N, G)
Carl Albert State College (U)
Carroll Community College (U)
Central Missouri State University (U, G)
Central Missouri State University (U, G)
Central Missouri State University (U, G)
Central Missouri State University (U, G)
Central Missouri State University (U, G)
Central Oregon Community College (U)
Central Texas College (U)
Central Washington University (U)
Central Wyoming College (U)
Chaminade University of Honolulu (U)
Chemeketa Community College (U)
Clackamas Community College (U)
Clinton Community College (U)
Clovis Community College (U)
Coastal Bend College (U)
Coconino Community College (U)
College for Lifelong Learning (U)
College of DuPage (U)
College of the Southwest (U)
Columbia College (U)
The Community College of Baltimore County (U)
Concordia University at Austin (U)
Connecticut State University System (U)
Dallas Baptist University (U, G)
Danville Area Community College (U)
Danville Community College (U)
Darton College (U)
Dawson Community College (U)
Delaware County Community College (U)
Delaware Technical & Community College, Jack F. Owens Campus (U)
Delaware Technical & Community College, Stanton/Wilmington Campus (U)
Delta College (U)
Des Moines Area Community College (U)
East Carolina University (G)
Eastern Kentucky University (G)
Eastern Shore Community College (U)
Eastern Wyoming College (U)
Edison Community College (U)
Elizabeth City State University (U)
Fairleigh Dickinson University, Metropolitan Campus (U)
Fayetteville State University (U)
Florida Gulf Coast University (U)
Florida Metropolitan University–Brandon Campus (U, G)
Fort Hays State University (U)
Franklin Pierce College (U)
Gannon University (U)
Gaston College (U)
Glenville State College (U)
Golden West College (U)
Grand View College (U)
Grantham University (U)
Grossmont College (U)
Harrisburg Area Community College (U)
Henry Ford Community College (U)
Hopkinsville Community College (U)
Horry-Georgetown Technical College (U)
Indiana State University (U, G)
Indiana Wesleyan University (U)
Iowa Western Community College (U)
Irvine Valley College (U)
Ivy Tech State College–Bloomington (U)
Ivy Tech State College–Eastcentral (U)
Ivy Tech State College–Kokomo (U)
Jacksonville State University (U, G)
James Madison University (N)
John Jay College of Criminal Justice of the City University of New York (U)
John Tyler Community College (U)
John Wood Community College (U)
Judson College (U)
Judson College (U)
Keiser College (U)
Lander University (U)
Limestone College (U)
Linn-Benton Community College (U)
Los Angeles Harbor College (U)
Madison Area Technical College (U)
Madonna University (N)
Mansfield University of Pennsylvania (U)
Marian College of Fond du Lac (U)
Maui Community College (U)
Mesa Community College (U)
Metropolitan Community College (U)
Metropolitan State University (U)
Middlesex Community College (U)
Middle Tennessee State University (U)
Mississippi Delta Community College (U)
Missouri Southern State University (U)
Modesto Junior College (U)
Monroe Community College (U)
Montgomery Community College (U)
Mountain Empire Community College (U)
Mountain State University (U, G)
Mountain State University (U)
Mount Wachusett Community College (U)
National University (U)
Naugatuck Valley Community College (U)
New Jersey City University (U)
New Mexico State University (G)
New York Institute of Technology (U)
Northeastern Oklahoma Agricultural and Mechanical College (U)
Northern Arizona University (U)
NorthWest Arkansas Community College (U)
Northwestern Michigan College (U)
Northwestern State University of Louisiana (U)
Okaloosa-Walton College (U)
Old Dominion University (U)
Oxnard College (U)
Pace University (U)
The Paralegal Institute, Inc. (U)
Park University (U)
Peninsula College (U)
The Pennsylvania State University University Park Campus (U)
Portland State University (U)
Randolph Community College (U)
Rappahannock Community College (U)
Raritan Valley Community College (U)
Roger Williams University (U)
Ryerson University (U)
St. Cloud State University (U)
St. Edward's University (U)
St. John's University (U)
Saint Leo University (U)
Santa Rosa Junior College (U)
Sauk Valley Community College (U)
Seminole Community College (U)
Shippensburg University of Pennsylvania (U, G)
Shoreline Community College (U)
Simpson College (U)
Snead State Community College (U)
Southeast Arkansas College (U)
Southern Illinois University Carbondale (U)
Southwestern College (U)
Southwestern Oregon Community College (U)
Spring Arbor University (U)
Stanly Community College (U)
State University of New York at Oswego (U)
Tacoma Community College (U)
Taft College (U)
Taylor University (U)
Taylor University (U)
Temple College (U)
Texas A&M International University (U, G)
Texas A&M University–Texarkana (U)
Texas State University-San Marcos (U)
Touro University International (U, G)
Tunxis Community College (N, U)
The University of Akron (U)
The University of Alabama (U)
University of Arkansas at Little Rock (U, G)
University of Cincinnati (U)

N–Noncredit; U–Undergraduate; G–Graduate

University of Colorado at Colorado Springs (G)
University of Delaware (U)
The University of Findlay (U)
University of Great Falls (U)
University of Hawaii–West Oahu (U)
University of Houston–Downtown (U, G)
University of Idaho (U)
University of Louisville (N)
University of Louisville (N)
The University of Maine at Augusta (U)
University of Maryland University College (U)
University of Massachusetts Amherst (N, U)
University of Nevada, Reno (U)
The University of North Carolina at Chapel Hill (U)
University of Pittsburgh at Bradford (U)
The University of South Dakota (U)
University of Southern Mississippi (G)
The University of Tennessee at Martin (N)
The University of Texas at Tyler (U)
The University of Texas of the Permian Basin (G)
University of Wisconsin–Platteville (G)
University of Wisconsin–Platteville (G)
University of Wyoming (U)
Upper Iowa University (U)
Vance-Granville Community College (U)
Walters State Community College (U)
Waubonsee Community College (U)
Waycross College (U)
Western New England College (U)
West Los Angeles College (U)
West Virginia University at Parkersburg (U)
Westwood Online (U)
Wilkes Community College (U)
William Paterson University of New Jersey (U)
William Rainey Harper College (U)
Youngstown State University (U)

Criminology

Adirondack Community College (U)
American Public University System (U)
Athabasca University (N, U)
Bemidji State University (U)
Blue Mountain Community College (U)
Brenau University (U)
Brevard Community College (U)
Bridgewater State College (U)
Bucks County Community College (U)
Butler County Community College (U)
Butler County Community College (U)
California State University, Fullerton (N)
Central Texas College (U)
Chadron State College (U)
Chemeketa Community College (U)
Chesapeake College (U)
Clackamas Community College (U)
Clatsop Community College (U)
The Community College of Baltimore County (U)
Danville Community College (U)
Des Moines Area Community College (U)
East Carolina University (G)
Florida Metropolitan University–Brandon Campus (U, G)
Fort Hays State University (U)
Gannon University (U)
Gaston College (U)
Glenville State College (U)
Houston Community College System (U)
Howard Community College (U)
Indiana State University (U, G)
Indiana University of Pennsylvania (U)
Indiana Wesleyan University (U)
Iowa Western Community College (U)
Jacksonville State University (U, G)
John F. Kennedy University (G)
Kirkwood Community College (U)
Lock Haven University of Pennsylvania (U)
Los Angeles Harbor College (U)
Louisiana State University and Agricultural and Mechanical College (U)
Memorial University of Newfoundland (G)
Montgomery County Community College (U)
Mountain Empire Community College (U)
Mountain State University (U)
Mountain State University (U)
Mount Wachusett Community College (U)
National University (G)
Neumann College (U)
New Jersey City University (G)
Ohio University (U)
Pace University (U)
Park University (U)
Pratt Community College (U)
Raritan Valley Community College (U)
Roger Williams University (U)
Saint Joseph's College of Maine (U)
Saint Leo University (U)
San Jacinto College District (U)
Santa Rosa Junior College (U)
Sauk Valley Community College (U)
Seminole Community College (U)
Snead State Community College (U)
Southeast Arkansas College (U)
Southern Illinois University Carbondale (U)
Southwestern Oregon Community College (U)
Texas State University-San Marcos (U)
Tunxis Community College (U)
The University of Akron (U)
The University of Findlay (U)
University of Florida (U)
University of Hawaii–West Oahu (U)
University of La Verne (N, U)
University of Mississippi (U)
University of Northern Iowa (U, G)
University of Southern Mississippi (U)
The University of Texas at Arlington (U)
The University of Texas at Tyler (U)
The University of Texas of the Permian Basin (U, G)
University of Washington (U)
University of Waterloo (U)
University of Wisconsin–Platteville (G)
Vance-Granville Community College (U)
Waubonsee Community College (U)
William Paterson University of New Jersey (U)

Culinary arts and related services

Albuquerque Technical Vocational Institute (U)
The Art Institute Online (U)
Ashworth College (N)
Bossier Parish Community College (N)
Central Texas College (U)
Fairleigh Dickinson University, Metropolitan Campus (U)
Feather River Community College District (N)
James Madison University (N)
Lord Fairfax Community College (N)
Middle Tennessee State University (N)
Mitchell Technical Institute (U)
Naugatuck Valley Community College (U)
New York Institute of Technology (N)
Oxnard College (U)
Santa Rosa Junior College (U)
Schenectady County Community College (U)
Southwest Wisconsin Technical College (U)
State University of New York College at Potsdam (N)
Sullivan University (U)
Walters State Community College (U)

Cultural studies

American Public University System (G)
Athabasca University (N)
Bethany College of the Assemblies of God (U)
Bowling Green State University (U)
Brevard Community College (U)
Bridgewater State College (U)
California State University, Monterey Bay (U)
Central Texas College (U)
Central Wyoming College (N)
Chemeketa Community College (U)

Columbia Basin College (U)
Columbus State Community College (U)
Delaware County Community College (U)
Edgecombe Community College (U)
Feather River Community College District (N)
Fort Hays State University (U)
Hope International University (N, G)
John F. Kennedy University (U, G)
Louisiana State University and Agricultural and Mechanical College (U)
Marylhurst University (N)
Master's College and Seminary (U)
Middlesex Community College (U)
Mount Saint Vincent University (U)
Naropa University (N, U)
Northwestern College (U)
The Pennsylvania State University University Park Campus (U)
Prescott College (U, G)
Randolph Community College (U)
Skidmore College (U)
State University of New York at Plattsburgh (U)
Syracuse University (U, G)
Teachers College Columbia University (N, G)
University of Alaska Fairbanks (U)
University of Colorado at Denver (U)
University of Connecticut (U)
The University of Findlay (U)
University of Massachusetts Lowell (U)
University of Missouri–Columbia (U)
University of St. Francis (U)
University of Washington (U)
University of Waterloo (U)
University of Wyoming (U)
Western New England College (U)
Western Wyoming Community College (U)
Wilkes Community College (U)

Curriculum and instruction

Alcorn State University (U)
Athabasca University (G)
Baltimore City Community College (U)
Bloomsburg University of Pennsylvania (G)
Boise State University (G)
Bossier Parish Community College (U)
Boston University (G)
Bridgewater State College (U)
Brigham Young University (U)
California State University, Chico (U)
California State University, Fullerton (N)
Central Missouri State University (U, G)
Central Missouri State University (U, G)
Central Missouri State University (U, G)
Central Missouri State University (U, G)
Central Missouri State University (U, G)
Cerritos College (U)
Chadron State College (G)
Chemeketa Community College (U)
Cleveland State University (G)
The College of St. Scholastica (G)
College of the Southwest (G)
Columbia College (U)
Concordia University Wisconsin (G)
Connecticut State University System (U, G)
Dallas Baptist University (G)
Duquesne University (G)
East Carolina University (U)
Eastern Kentucky University (U, G)
Ferris State University (N)
Georgia Southern University (G)
Hudson County Community College (N)
Illinois State University (G)
Immaculata University (G)
Indiana State University (U, G)
Jacksonville State University (U, G)
Lesley University (G)
Liberty University (G)
Louisiana State University and Agricultural and Mechanical College (U)
Mississippi State University (U, G)
Mitchell Technical Institute (U)
Montana State University–Billings (U, G)
North Carolina State University (G)
North Dakota State University (G)
Northern Arizona University (U, G)
The Pennsylvania State University University Park Campus (G)
Regis University (G)
Saint Joseph's College of Maine (G)
Seattle Pacific University (G)
Shoreline Community College (N)
Southwestern Assemblies of God University (U)
Southwestern Oregon Community College (U)
Southwest Missouri State University (G)
Southwest Wisconsin Technical College (U)
State University of New York at New Paltz (U)
State University of New York at Oswego (G)
Stephen F. Austin State University (U)
Tarleton State University (U, G)
Texas A&M University–Commerce (G)
Texas Tech University (G)
The University of Akron (N, U)
University of Central Arkansas (G)
University of Illinois (G)
University of Missouri–Columbia (U, G)
The University of Montana–Missoula (U, G)
University of Nebraska–Lincoln (U, G)
University of Nevada, Reno (U, G)
The University of North Carolina at Greensboro (G)
University of North Florida (U, G)
University of Saskatchewan (U)
University of Southern Mississippi (G)
The University of Tennessee (U)
The University of Texas at Arlington (G)
The University of Texas at Austin (U)
The University of Texas at Tyler (U)
The University of Texas of the Permian Basin (U, G)
The University of Texas System (U)
University of Toledo (G)
University of Washington (U)
Utah State University (G)
Virginia Polytechnic Institute and State University (G)
Western Washington University (U)
William Paterson University of New Jersey (U)
Winston-Salem State University (U)

Custodial, housekeeping and home services workers and managers

Bossier Parish Community College (N)
Hudson County Community College (U)
Naugatuck Valley Community College (N)

Dance

Bossier Parish Community College (N)
Brigham Young University (U)
California State University, Chico (U)
Central Wyoming College (N)
Goddard College (U, G)
Hudson County Community College (U)
Maui Community College (U)
Middle Tennessee State University (N)
Naugatuck Valley Community College (N)
Orange Coast College (U)
Skidmore College (U)
Texas State University-San Marcos (U)
University of Houston (U)
The University of Tennessee at Martin (N)
University of Waterloo (U)

Data entry/microcomputer applications

AIB College of Business (U)
Allan Hancock College (U)
Asheville-Buncombe Technical Community College (N, U)
Athabasca University (N)
Bristol Community College (N, U)
Broome Community College (N)
Butler County Community College (U)
Butler County Community College (U)
Carl Albert State College (U)

N–Noncredit; U–Undergraduate; G–Graduate

Central Wyoming College (N)
Century College (N)
Cerritos College (U)
Chemeketa Community College (U)
Cincinnati State Technical and Community College (U)
Clemson University (N)
Cleveland State University (N)
College of The Albemarle (N)
Colorado State University-Pueblo (N)
Dallas County Community College District (U)
Delaware County Community College (U)
Des Moines Area Community College (U)
East Carolina University (U)
Edgecombe Community College (N, U)
Edison Community College (U)
Frederick Community College (N)
George C. Wallace Community College (U)
Grantham University (U)
Halifax Community College (N)
Hibbing Community College (U)
Iowa Western Community College (U)
Irvine Valley College (U)
James Madison University (N)
John Tyler Community College (U)
John Wood Community College (U)
Kansas City Kansas Community College (U)
Kirkwood Community College (N)
Lakeland Community College (N)
Lamar State College–Port Arthur (N, U)
Lewis-Clark State College (N)
Limestone College (U)
Maryville University of Saint Louis (N)
Middlesex Community College (U)
Mitchell Technical Institute (N)
Naugatuck Valley Community College (N)
North Dakota State University (N, U)
Northwestern Technical College (U)
Oxnard College (U)
Paul D. Camp Community College (U)
Santa Fe Community College (N)
Seminole Community College (U)
South Central Technical College (U)
Spartanburg Technical College (U)
State University of New York College at Potsdam (N)
Tacoma Community College (U)
Tarleton State University (N)
Taylor University (N)
Texas State Technical College–Waco (U)
The University of Akron (N)
University of Arkansas at Little Rock (U)
University of West Florida (U)
University of Wisconsin–Platteville (U)
Vance-Granville Community College (N)

Data processing technology

Adams State College (N)
Albuquerque Technical Vocational Institute (U)
Athabasca University (N, U)
Bristol Community College (N, U)
Cincinnati State Technical and Community College (U)
College of The Albemarle (N)
The Community College of Baltimore County (U)
Dallas County Community College District (U)
Danville Area Community College (U)
Delaware County Community College (U)
Des Moines Area Community College (U)
East Carolina University (U, G)
Feather River Community College District (U)
Frederick Community College (N)
Jacksonville State University (U)
Jones College (U)
Kirkwood Community College (N)
Lakeland Community College (N)
Lamar State College–Port Arthur (N)
Limestone College (U)
Lord Fairfax Community College (N)
Martin Community College (U)
Maryville University of Saint Louis (N, U)
Naugatuck Valley Community College (N)
Seminole Community College (U)
Syracuse University (G)
Taylor University (N)
Tompkins Cortland Community College (N)
The University of Akron (N)
Westchester Community College (U)
Wilkes Community College (U)

Demography/population studies

Athabasca University (U)
Bethany College of the Assemblies of God (U)
Delaware County Community College (U)
Prescott College (U)
University of Southern Mississippi (G)

Dental clinical sciences/graduate dentistry (M.S., Ph.D.)

Danville Community College (U)
Oregon Institute of Technology (U)
West Los Angeles College (U)

Dental services

Blackhawk Technical College (U)
Danville Community College (U)
Madison Area Technical College (U)
Martin Community College (U)
Maui Community College (U)
Middlesex Community College (U)
Monroe Community College (U)
Montgomery County Community College (U)
Northern Arizona University (U)
Oxnard College (U)
Pennsylvania College of Technology (U)
Tunxis Community College (U)
University of Bridgeport (U)
The University of British Columbia (U)
University of Idaho (U)
University of Southern Indiana (U)
Washtenaw Community College (U)

Design and applied arts

American River College (U)
The Art Institute Online (U)
Bossier Parish Community College (N)
Brenau University (U)
Central Wyoming College (N)
Colorado State University (U)
Dakota County Technical College (U)
Danville Community College (U)
Edison State Community College (U)
Ivy Tech State College–Southwest (U)
Ivy Tech State College–Wabash Valley (U)
John F. Kennedy University (G)
Lansing Community College (U)
Madison Area Technical College (U)
Minneapolis College of Art and Design (N, U)
Northeastern Oklahoma Agricultural and Mechanical College (N)
Santa Fe Community College (N)
Tacoma Community College (U)
The University of Akron (U)
University of California, Los Angeles (G)
West Los Angeles College (U)
Westwood Online (U)
Yuba College (U)

Developmental and child psychology

Adirondack Community College (U)
Arkansas State University–Beebe (U)
Athabasca University (N, U, G)
Bellevue Community College (U)
Bethany College of the Assemblies of God (U)
Bucks County Community College (U)
Cape Cod Community College (U)
Capella University (G)
Central Oregon Community College (U)
Central Texas College (U)
Chadron State College (U)
Chemeketa Community College (U)
College of the Canyons (U)
Concordia University, St. Paul (U, G)
Cuyamaca College (U)
Delaware County Community College (U)

Edison Community College (U)
Gannon University (U)
Goddard College (U, G)
Golden West College (U)
Halifax Community College (U)
Harrisburg Area Community College (U)
Horry-Georgetown Technical College (U)
Jacksonville State University (U, G)
John F. Kennedy University (G)
John Tyler Community College (U)
The King's College and Seminary (N, U)
Liberty University (U)
Maysville Community College (U)
Middlesex Community College (U)
Mississippi State University (U)
Modesto Junior College (U)
Mount Saint Vincent University (U)
Naropa University (U)
Northampton County Area Community College (U)
North Dakota State University (U)
Oxnard College (U)
Palm Beach Community College (U)
Peninsula College (U)
Reading Area Community College (U)
Saddleback College (U)
Saybrook Graduate School and Research Center (G)
Seminole Community College (U)
Southwestern Oregon Community College (U)
State University of New York at New Paltz (U)
Stephens College (U)
Taylor University (U)
Taylor University (U)
Texas Tech University (U)
Tompkins Cortland Community College (U)
Triton College (U)
Tunxis Community College (U)
University of Arkansas at Little Rock (U)
University of Bridgeport (U)
University of Georgia (U)
University of Great Falls (U)
University of La Verne (U)
The University of Texas System (U)
University of Washington (U)
University of Waterloo (U)
Western Michigan University (G)
Western New England College (U)
Winston-Salem State University (U)

Developmental/child psychology

Adams State College (U)
American Academy of Nutrition, College of Nutrition (U)
Andrews University (U)
Anne Arundel Community College (U)
Black Hills State University (U, G)
Blue Mountain Community College (U)
Bossier Parish Community College (U)
Brevard Community College (U)
Brigham Young University (U)
Brookdale Community College (U)
Broward Community College (U)
Bucks County Community College (U)
Burlington County College (U)
Carleton University (U)
Chadron State College (U)
Chattanooga State Technical Community College (U)
Clovis Community College (U)
College of DuPage (U)
College of the Southwest (U)
Colorado Mountain College District System (U)
Colorado State University (U)
Concordia University at Austin (U)
Cuyamaca College (U)
Dallas County Community College District (U)
Dawson Community College (U)
Delaware County Community College (U)
Delta College (U)
Des Moines Area Community College (U)
Edison Community College (U)
Edmonds Community College (U)
Floyd College (U)
Greenville Technical College (U)
Hillsborough Community College (U)
Houston Community College System (U)
Jacksonville State University (U)
John Wood Community College (U)
Lawson State Community College (U)
Louisiana State University and Agricultural and Mechanical College (U)
Manatee Community College (U)
Marshall University (U)
Maui Community College (U)
Mercy College (U)
Missouri Southern State University (U)
Montgomery County Community College (U)
Mountain Empire Community College (U)
Mountain State University (U)
Nassau Community College (U)
North Country Community College (U)
North Dakota State College of Science (U)
Northern Virginia Community College (U)
Odessa College (U)
Ohio University (U)
Oklahoma State University (U)
Palomar College (U)
Patrick Henry Community College (U)
Pierce College (U)
Richland Community College (U)
Riverland Community College (U)
Saint Joseph's College of Maine (U)
Schoolcraft College (U)
Seattle Central Community College (U)
Sinclair Community College (U)
Skidmore College (U)
Southwestern Assemblies of God University (U)
Southwest Virginia Community College (U)
Stanly Community College (U)
Tarrant County College District (U)
Texas A&M University–Commerce (U)
Triton College (U)
Troy University Montgomery (U)
University College of Cape Breton (U)
University of Guelph (U)
University of Houston–Downtown (U)
University of Maine (U)
The University of Maine at Augusta (U)
University of Minnesota, Twin Cities Campus (U)
University of Missouri–Columbia (U)
University of Nebraska–Lincoln (U)
University of Nevada, Reno (U)
University of Toledo (U)
University of Utah (U)
Washington State University (U)
Waubonsee Community College (U)
Western Washington University (U)
West Valley College (U)
Wilfrid Laurier University (U)
William Rainey Harper College (U)
York Technical College (U)

Drafting

Blackhawk Technical College (N)
Butler County Community College (U)
Chemeketa Community College (U)
Clackamas Community College (U)
Dallas County Community College District (U)
Danville Community College (U)
Hibbing Community College (U)
Ivy Tech State College–Wabash Valley (U)
John Tyler Community College (U)
Kentucky State University (U)
Madison Area Technical College (U)
Maui Community College (U)
North Dakota State College of Science (U)
Orange Coast College (U)
Sinclair Community College (U)
Triton College (U)
Umpqua Community College (U)
University of Alaska Fairbanks (U)

N–Noncredit; U–Undergraduate; G–Graduate

Dramatic/theater arts and stagecraft
Chaminade University of Honolulu (U)
Eastern Oregon University (U)
Goddard College (U, G)
Iowa Western Community College (U)
Limestone College (U)
Middle Tennessee State University (N)
Oxnard College (U)
Santa Fe Community College (N)
Snead State Community College (U)
State University of New York at Oswego (U)
Triton College (U)
University of Alaska Fairbanks (U)
University of Georgia (U)
University of Mississippi (U)
University of New Orleans (G)
University of Oklahoma (U)
Valparaiso University (U)
West Los Angeles College (U)
West Virginia University at Parkersburg (U)
Wilkes Community College (U)
William Paterson University of New Jersey (U)

Earth sciences
Carleton University (U)
College of DuPage (U)
Colorado Mountain College District System (U)
Houston Community College System (U)
Indiana Wesleyan University (U)
Lansing Community College (U)
Montana State University–Bozeman (G)
Mountain State University (U)
North Country Community College (U)
Northwest Missouri State University (U)
The Pennsylvania State University University Park Campus (U)
Pierce College (U)
Southeast Community College, Lincoln Campus (U)
University of Nevada, Reno (U)
University of Waterloo (U)

East and Southeast Asian languages and literatures
Darton College (U)
Feather River Community College District (N)
Naropa University (G)
Southern Illinois University Carbondale (U)
University of Toronto (N)
Western Washington University (U)
William Paterson University of New Jersey (U)

East European languages and literatures
Feather River Community College District (N)
Santa Fe Community College (N)
University of Washington (U)
University of Waterloo (U)

Ecology
Burlington County College (U)
California Institute of Integral Studies (N, G)
Edison State Community College (U)
Gogebic Community College (U)
Mountain State University (U)
Oregon State University (U)
University of Guelph (U)
University of Minnesota, Twin Cities Campus (U)
University of Nebraska–Lincoln (U)
University of Waterloo (U)

Economics
Acadia University (U)
Adirondack Community College (U)
AIB College of Business (U)
Albuquerque Technical Vocational Institute (U)
Allan Hancock College (U)
Allen County Community College (U)
Alliant International University (U)
American College of Computer & Information Sciences (U)
Anne Arundel Community College (U)
Arapahoe Community College (U)
Asheville-Buncombe Technical Community College (U)
Ashland Community and Technical College (U)
Athabasca University (N, U, G)
Athens Technical College (U)
Baltimore City Community College (U)
Bemidji State University (U)
Berkeley College (U)
Berkeley College-New York City Campus (U)
Berkeley College-Westchester Campus (U)
Bishop State Community College (U)
Black Hills State University (U)
Boise State University (U)
Brenau University (U, G)
Brevard Community College (U)
Bridgewater State College (G)
Brigham Young University (U)
Broward Community College (U)
Brunswick Community College (U)
Butler County Community College (U)
Butler County Community College (U)
Caldwell College (U)
California National University for Advanced Studies (U)
California State University, Sacramento (U)
Cape Fear Community College (U)
Carleton University (U, G)
Carroll Community College (U)
Cascadia Community College (U)
Casper College (U)
Cayuga County Community College (U)
Central Texas College (U)
Central Virginia Community College (U)
Central Wyoming College (U)
Chadron State College (U)
Chaminade University of Honolulu (U)
Champlain College (U)
Charter Oak State College (U)
Chattanooga State Technical Community College (U)
Chemeketa Community College (U)
Citrus College (U)
Clarion University of Pennsylvania (U)
Clemson University (U)
Clinton Community College (U)
Clovis Community College (U)
College of DuPage (U)
The College of St. Scholastica (U)
College of The Albemarle (U)
College of the Canyons (U)
College of the Southwest (U)
Collin County Community College District (U)
Colorado Mountain College District System (U)
Colorado State University (N, U)
Colorado State University-Pueblo (U)
Columbia Basin College (U)
Columbia Union College (U)
Columbus State Community College (U)
The Community College of Baltimore County (U)
Community College of Denver (U)
Concordia University Wisconsin (U)
Connecticut State University System (U)
Copiah-Lincoln Community College–Natchez Campus (U)
Cossatot Community College of the University of Arkansas (U)
County College of Morris (U)
Cumberland County College (U)
Cuyamaca College (U)
Dakota County Technical College (U)
Dallas Baptist University (U, G)
Dallas County Community College District (U)
Danville Area Community College (U)
Darton College (U)
Davenport University Online (U, G)
Delaware County Community College (U)
Delaware Technical & Community College, Jack F. Owens Campus (U)

Delaware Technical & Community College, Stanton/Wilmington Campus (U)
Delta College (U)
Des Moines Area Community College (U)
DeVry University Online (U, G)
Drake University (U, G)
East Central College (U)
Eastern Oregon University (U)
Eastern Wyoming College (U)
Edison Community College (U)
Edison State Community College (U)
El Camino College (U)
Embry-Riddle Aeronautical University, Extended Campus (U)
Fairleigh Dickinson University, Metropolitan Campus (U)
Fairmont State University (U)
Florida Community College at Jacksonville (U)
Florida Metropolitan University–Brandon Campus (U, G)
Fontbonne University (U)
Fort Hays State University (U)
Franklin Pierce College (U)
Franklin University (U)
Frederick Community College (U)
Fulton-Montgomery Community College (U)
Gannon University (U)
George C. Wallace Community College (U)
Glenville State College (U)
Grantham University (U)
Halifax Community College (U)
Harrisburg Area Community College (U)
Heartland Community College (U)
Hibbing Community College (U)
Hillsborough Community College (U)
Houston Community College System (U)
Howard College (U)
Illinois Eastern Community Colleges, Olney Central College (U)
Indiana State University (U)
Indiana University–Purdue University Fort Wayne (U)
Iowa State University of Science and Technology (U)
Iowa Western Community College (U)
Ivy Tech State College–North Central (U)
Ivy Tech State College–Northwest (U)
Ivy Tech State College–Southcentral (U)
Ivy Tech State College–Wabash Valley (U)
Ivy Tech State College–Whitewater (U)
Jacksonville State University (U, G)
Jefferson College (U)
Jefferson Community College (U)
Jefferson Davis Community College (U)
John Jay College of Criminal Justice of the City University of New York (U)
Johnson County Community College (U)
John Tyler Community College (U)
John Wood Community College (U)
Jones College (U)
Kansas City Kansas Community College (U)
Kellogg Community College (U)
Kentucky State University (U)
Lakeland Community College (U)
Lake Superior College (U)
Liberty University (U)
Limestone College (U)
Linn-Benton Community College (U)
Lord Fairfax Community College (U)
Los Angeles Harbor College (U)
Los Angeles Pierce College (U)
Louisiana State University and Agricultural and Mechanical College (U)
Louisiana Tech University (U)
Mansfield University of Pennsylvania (U)
Marshall University (U)
Martin Community College (U)
Maui Community College (U)
Maysville Community College (U)
Memorial University of Newfoundland (U)
Mesa Community College (U)
Mesalands Community College (U)
Metropolitan Community College (U)
Metropolitan State University (U)
Miami Dade College (U)
Michigan Technological University (U)
Middlesex Community College (U)
Middle Tennessee State University (U, G)
Millersville University of Pennsylvania (U)
Minnesota School of Business–Brooklyn Center (U)
MiraCosta College (U)
Mississippi Delta Community College (U)
Modesto Junior College (U)
Monroe County Community College (U)
Montana State University–Billings (U)
Montgomery County Community College (U)
Motlow State Community College (U)
Mountain Empire Community College (U)
Mountain State University (U)
Mount Allison University (U)
Mt. Hood Community College (U)
Mt. San Antonio College (U)
Mount Wachusett Community College (U)
Nassau Community College (U)
New Jersey City University (U)
New York Institute of Technology (U)
New York Institute of Technology (G)
Nipissing University (U)
Normandale Community College (U)
Northampton County Area Community College (U)
North Carolina State University (U)
North Country Community College (U)
Northeastern Oklahoma Agricultural and Mechanical College (U)
Northeast State Technical Community College (U)
Northern New Mexico Community College (U)
North Hennepin Community College (U)
NorthWest Arkansas Community College (U)
Ocean County College (U)
Ohio University (U)
Okaloosa-Walton College (U)
Oklahoma State University (U)
Oregon State University (U)
Oxnard College (U)
Palm Beach Community College (U)
Palomar College (U)
Park University (U)
Patrick Henry College (U)
Patrick Henry Community College (U)
Peirce College (U)
Peninsula College (U)
The Pennsylvania State University University Park Campus (U)
Portland State University (U)
Pratt Community College (U)
Quinnipiac University (U, G)
Randolph Community College (U)
Raritan Valley Community College (U)
Reading Area Community College (U)
Rio Hondo College (U)
Riverside Community College (N, U)
Rockland Community College (U)
Ryerson University (U)
Sacred Heart University (G)
St. Cloud State University (U)
St. Edward's University (U)
St. John's University (U, G)
St. Petersburg College (U)
Salem Community College (U)
Sam Houston State University (U)
San Bernardino Valley College (U)
Sauk Valley Community College (U)
Schoolcraft College (U)
Seminole Community College (U)
Seward County Community College (U)
Shippensburg University of Pennsylvania (U)
Sinclair Community College (U)
Snead State Community College (U)
Southeast Arkansas College (U)
Southeast Community College, Beatrice Campus (U)
Southeastern Community College (U)

N–Noncredit; U–Undergraduate; G–Graduate

South Piedmont Community College (U)
Southwestern College (U)
Southwestern College (U)
Southwest Missouri State University (U, G)
Southwest Wisconsin Technical College (U)
State University of New York at New Paltz (U)
State University of New York at Oswego (U, G)
State University of New York at Plattsburgh (U)
Stephen F. Austin State University (U)
Stephens College (U)
Strayer University (U, G)
Tarleton State University (U)
Taylor University (U)
Teikyo Post University (U)
Temple College (U)
Texas A&M University–Commerce (G)
Texas A&M University–Texarkana (G)
Texas Tech University (U)
Touro University International (U)
Tri-State University (U)
Triton College (U)
Troy University–Florida Region (U)
Troy University Montgomery (U)
The University of Akron (U, G)
The University of Alabama (U)
University of Alaska Fairbanks (U)
University of Arkansas at Pine Bluff (U)
University of Bridgeport (U)
University of California, Los Angeles (G)
University of Colorado at Colorado Springs (U)
University of Colorado at Denver (U)
University of Connecticut (U)
University of Delaware (U)
The University of Findlay (U)
University of Florida (U)
University of Georgia (U)
University of Hawaii–West Oahu (U)
University of Houston–Clear Lake (G)
University of Idaho (U)
The University of Iowa (G)
The University of Maine at Augusta (U)
University of Maryland University College (U)
University of Massachusetts Boston (U)
University of Minnesota, Morris (U)
University of Minnesota, Twin Cities Campus (U)
University of Mississippi (U)
University of Missouri–Columbia (U, G)
University of Missouri–Columbia (G)
University of Nebraska–Lincoln (U)
University of Nevada, Reno (U)
The University of North Carolina at Chapel Hill (U)
University of North Dakota (U)
University of Northern Colorado (U)
University of Notre Dame (N, G)
University of Oklahoma (U, G)
University of Oregon (U)
University of Pittsburgh at Bradford (U)
University of Saint Francis (U)
University of Saskatchewan (U)
University of South Carolina (U)
University of Southern Indiana (U, G)
University of Southern Mississippi (G)
The University of Tennessee (U)
The University of Tennessee at Martin (U)
The University of Texas at Arlington (U)
The University of Texas at Austin (U)
The University of Texas System (U)
University of the Incarnate Word (U, G)
University of Tulsa (G)
University of Utah (U)
University of Washington (U)
University of Waterloo (U)
University of West Florida (U)
University of Wisconsin–Eau Claire (N)
University of Wisconsin–La Crosse (G)
University of Wisconsin–Parkside (G)
University of Wisconsin–Platteville (U)
University of Wisconsin–Platteville (U)
University of Wisconsin–River Falls (G)
Utah State University (U, G)
Valparaiso University (U)
Vance-Granville Community College (U)
Waubonsee Community College (U)
Wayland Baptist University (U, G)
Wayne State College (U, G)
Westchester Community College (U)
Western Michigan University (U, G)
Western Washington University (U)
Western Wyoming Community College (U)
West Los Angeles College (U)
West Valley College (U)
Whatcom Community College (U)
Wichita State University (G)
Wilfrid Laurier University (U)
William Rainey Harper College (U)
Worcester State College (U)
Wright State University (N, U, G)
York Technical College (U)
York University (U)

Education administration and supervision

Alliant International University (G)
Athabasca University (N, G)
Auburn University Montgomery (U, G)
Azusa Pacific University (G)
Bowling Green State University (U)
Brenau University (G)
Bridgewater State College (U, G)
Brigham Young University (U)
California State University, Dominguez Hills (U)
California University of Pennsylvania (G)
Capella University (N, G)
Chadron State College (G)
College of The Albemarle (N)
College of the Southwest (G)
Columbus State University (G)
Concordia University at Austin (G)
Concordia University Wisconsin (G)
Dallas Baptist University (G)
Eastern Illinois University (G)
Eastern Kentucky University (G)
Eastern Michigan University (G)
Fairmont State University (G)
Florida Atlantic University (G)
Florida Gulf Coast University (U)
Florida International University (G)
Fort Hays State University (U)
Georgia Southern University (U, G)
Hamline University (N)
Heart of Georgia Technical College (U)
Illinois State University (G)
Indiana State University (G)
Indiana University–Purdue University Fort Wayne (G)
Jacksonville State University (U, G)
Liberty University (G)
Louisiana Tech University (U, G)
Marquette University (N)
Mercy College (U)
Mississippi State University (G)
Missouri Baptist University (U, G)
Murray State University (G)
National University (G)
New Jersey City University (G)
North Carolina State University (G)
North Dakota State University (G)
Northern Arizona University (G)
North Georgia College & State University (G)
Northwestern Oklahoma State University (G)
Northwestern State University of Louisiana (G)
The Ohio State University (G)
Oregon State University (G)
Pace University (G)
Park University (G)
Regis University (G)
Royal Roads University (G)
St. Cloud State University (U)
St. John's University (G)
Saint Joseph's College of Maine (G)
Santa Fe Community College (N)
Shasta Bible College (G)
Shenandoah University (G)

Education administration and supervision

Southern Illinois University Carbondale (U)
South Piedmont Community College (U)
Southwestern Assemblies of God University (U, G)
Southwestern Baptist Theological Seminary (G)
Southwest Missouri State University (G)
State University of New York at Plattsburgh (G)
Stephen F. Austin State University (G)
Sullivan University (G)
Tarleton State University (U, G)
Texas A&M International University (U, G)
Texas A&M University (G)
Texas A&M University–Commerce (G)
Texas A&M University–Kingsville (G)
Texas A&M University–Texarkana (G)
Texas Tech University (G)
The University of Akron (U, G)
University of Alaska Fairbanks (U, G)
University of Calgary (G)
University of Colorado at Colorado Springs (G)
University of Georgia (U)
University of La Verne (G)
University of Massachusetts Amherst (G)
University of Massachusetts Lowell (G)
University of Mississippi (G)
University of Missouri–Columbia (G)
University of Missouri–Columbia (G)
The University of Montana–Missoula (G)
University of New England (G)
University of New Orleans (G)
University of Oklahoma (G)
University of Sioux Falls (G)
University of South Carolina Sumter (U, G)
The University of South Dakota (G)
University of Southern Mississippi (U, G)
The University of Tennessee at Martin (G)
The University of Texas of the Permian Basin (G)
University of Wisconsin–Madison (G)
University of Wisconsin–Milwaukee (G)
University of Wisconsin–Superior (G)
Utah State University (U, G)
Vanguard University of Southern California (U)
Virginia Polytechnic Institute and State University (G)
Wayne State College (G)
Western Washington University (U)
William Paterson University of New Jersey (U, G)
Winona State University (G)
Youngstown State University (G)

Education of the speech impaired

St. Cloud State University (U)

Education related

College of The Albemarle (U)

Education, general

Acadia University (U)
Adams State College (G)
Alliant International University (G)
Arkansas Tech University (G)
Auburn University (N)
Baptist Bible College of Pennsylvania (G)
Bemidji State University (G)
Black Hills State University (G)
Bossier Parish Community College (N, U)
Brazosport College (U)
Brenau University (U, G)
Brevard Community College (U)
Bridgewater State College (U)
Brigham Young University (U)
Brock University (U)
Bucks County Community College (U)
Butler County Community College (U)
Caldwell College (U)
California State University, Chico (U)
California State University, Dominguez Hills (N, U)
California State University, Fullerton (N, U)
California State University, Monterey Bay (U)
Capella University (N, G)
Casper College (U)
Central Bible College (U)
Central Washington University (N)
Chadron State College (U, G)
Chaminade University of Honolulu (U, G)
Chattanooga State Technical Community College (U)
Chemeketa Community College (U)
Clackamas Community College (U)
Clarion University of Pennsylvania (G)
Coconino Community College (U)
College of Menominee Nation (U)
College of Mount St. Joseph (U, G)
College of the Southwest (U)
Colorado State University-Pueblo (U, G)
Columbia College (U)
Columbia Union College (U)
Columbus State University (U)
Concordia University, St. Paul (U, G)
Corning Community College (U)
Cossatot Community College of the University of Arkansas (U)
Cumberland University (G)
Daemen College (U)
Dallas Baptist University (U)
Dallas County Community College District (U)
Darton College (U)
Drake University (U, G)
East Carolina University (U, G)
Eastern Illinois University (U)
Eastern Michigan University (N, G)
Eastern Washington University (U)
Edison Community College (U)
Elizabeth City State University (U)
Endicott College (N, U, G)
Eugene Bible College (U)
Fairleigh Dickinson University, Metropolitan Campus (N, G)
Fairmont State University (U, G)
Fayetteville State University (G)
Feather River Community College District (N)
Florida Atlantic University (U)
Florida Community College at Jacksonville (U)
Florida National College (U)
Fort Hays State University (U, G)
Glenville State College (U)
Goddard College (U, G)
Gonzaga University (U, G)
Goucher College (G)
Greenfield Community College (U)
Hamline University (N, G)
Harrisburg Area Community College (U)
Howard Community College (U)
Immaculata University (N, G)
Indiana State University (U)
Indiana University–Purdue University Fort Wayne (U)
Inter American University of Puerto Rico, San Germán Campus (G)
Iowa Western Community College (U)
Jacksonville State University (U, G)
James Madison University (N)
John F. Kennedy University (U)
John Tyler Community College (U)
Judson College (U)
Lesley University (G)
LeTourneau University (U)
Lewis-Clark State College (U)
Liberty University (U)
Lipscomb University (U, G)
Lock Haven University of Pennsylvania (N, G)
Louisiana State University at Eunice (U)
Marian College of Fond du Lac (G)
Marquette University (N, U, G)
Martin Luther College (G)
Maysville Community College (U)
Mayville State University (U)
Memorial University of Newfoundland (U)
Mesalands Community College (U)
Miami Dade College (U)
Middle Tennessee State University (U)

N–Noncredit; U–Undergraduate; G–Graduate

Millersville University of Pennsylvania (U, G)
Montana State University–Billings (U, G)
Montgomery County Community College (U)
Mount Saint Mary College (U, G)
Murray State University (U)
Naropa University (N, G)
National University (U, G)
Nebraska Methodist College (N)
New Hampshire Community Technical College System (U)
Northampton County Area Community College (U)
North Dakota State University (U, G)
Northeastern Oklahoma Agricultural and Mechanical College (U)
Northeast State Technical Community College (U)
North Hennepin Community College (U)
Northwest Missouri State University (G)
Nova Southeastern University (G)
Oregon State University (U, G)
Oxnard College (U)
Pace University (N, U, G)
Palm Beach Community College (U)
Park University (G)
Pratt Community College (U)
Prescott College (U, G)
Quinnipiac University (U, G)
Roosevelt University (U, G)
Rowan Technical College (U)
Sacred Heart University (G)
St. Edward's University (U)
St. John's University (U, G)
St. Joseph's College, Suffolk Campus (U)
Saint Mary-of-the-Woods College (U)
St. Norbert College (G)
Saint Paul College–A Community & Technical College (U)
St. Petersburg College (U)
Seattle Pacific University (G)
Seminole Community College (U)
Shawnee State University (U)
Shenandoah University (G)
South Central Technical College (U)
Southern Illinois University Edwardsville (G)
Southwestern Assemblies of God University (U, G)
Southwestern College (G)
Southwest Missouri State University (G)
Spoon River College (U)
State University of New York at New Paltz (G)
State University of New York at Oswego (G)
State University of New York at Plattsburgh (U, G)
Stony Brook University, State University of New York (G)
Tarleton State University (U, G)
Taylor University (U)
Taylor University (U)
Texas A&M International University (U)
Texas A&M University–Texarkana (U)
Texas Tech University (G)
Texas Woman's University (U, G)
Touro University International (G)
Troy University–Florida Region (U)
Union University (G)
Université Sainte-Anne (U)
The University of Akron (U, G)
The University of Alabama (U)
University of Arkansas at Pine Bluff (U, G)
University of Bridgeport (U)
The University of British Columbia (U, G)
University of Calgary (G)
University of Colorado at Denver (G)
University of Delaware (U, G)
University of Georgia (U)
University of Houston–Downtown (U)
University of Houston–Victoria (U, G)
University of Illinois (G)
The University of Iowa (U)
University of La Verne (N)
The University of Lethbridge (G)
University of Maine (G)
University of Massachusetts Lowell (G)
University of Minnesota, Morris (U)
University of Mississippi (U, G)
University of Missouri–Columbia (U, G)
University of Missouri–Columbia (G)
The University of Montana–Missoula (G)
University of Nevada, Reno (G)
The University of North Carolina at Charlotte (U, G)
The University of North Carolina at Pembroke (U)
University of Northern Iowa (U)
University of Oklahoma (U)
University of Phoenix Online Campus (N)
University of Sioux Falls (G)
University of South Carolina Spartanburg (U, G)
University of South Carolina Sumter (U)
University of Southern Indiana (U, G)
The University of Tennessee (U)
The University of Tennessee at Martin (N)
The University of Texas at Austin (U)
The University of Texas–Pan American (U)
The University of Texas System (U, G)
University of Toledo (U, G)
The University of Virginia's College at Wise (U)
University of Washington (U)
University of Wisconsin–Milwaukee (G)
University of Wisconsin–River Falls (G)
University of Wisconsin–Superior (U, G)
University of Wyoming (U, G)
Utah State University (U, G)
Valparaiso University (U)
Virginia Polytechnic Institute and State University (N)
Wayne State College (U, G)
Whatcom Community College (U)
William Paterson University of New Jersey (U)
William Rainey Harper College (U)
Worcester State College (G)
Wright State University (U)

Education, other

Acadia University (G)
Alliance University College (U, G)
Arkansas Tech University (U, G)
Ashland Community and Technical College (U)
Athabasca University (N, G)
Atlantic University (N, G)
Auburn University Montgomery (U)
Baptist Theological Seminary at Richmond (G)
Barclay College (U)
Black Hills State University (U, G)
Boise State University (G)
Boise State University (U, G)
Bossier Parish Community College (U)
Brenau University (G)
Brevard Community College (U)
Brigham Young University (U)
Brock University (U)
Broward Community College (U)
Buena Vista University (U, G)
California State University, Dominguez Hills (U)
California State University, Fullerton (N)
California State University, Hayward (G)
Capella University (N, G)
Casper College (U)
Chadron State College (U, G)
Chemeketa Community College (U)
Clarion University of Pennsylvania (U)
Clark College (U)
Cleveland State University (N, G)
Colorado Mountain College District System (U)
Concordia University Wisconsin (G)
Dakota State University (U, G)
Dallas Baptist University (G)
Dallas County Community College District (U)
Darton College (U)
Drake University (U)
Eastern Michigan University (N, G)

Elgin Community College (U)
Fairmont State University (U, G)
Florida Atlantic University (G)
Florida Gulf Coast University (U, G)
Fort Hays State University (U, G)
The Franciscan University (G)
Glenville State College (U)
Goddard College (U, G)
Gonzaga University (G)
Hamline University (N, G)
Heart of Georgia Technical College (U)
Hebrew College (N, U, G)
Hudson County Community College (N)
Illinois State University (U)
Indiana State University (U, G)
Indiana University of Pennsylvania (G)
Indiana University System (G)
Institute for Christian Studies (G)
Jacksonville State University (U, G)
Jones International University (G)
La Sierra University (G)
Lenoir Community College (U)
Liberty University (G)
Manchester Community College (N)
Marquette University (N, U)
McDaniel College (G)
Memorial University of Newfoundland (U, G)
Mississippi State University (U)
Naropa University (N)
New Hampshire Community Technical College System (U)
New Mexico State University (G)
Northampton County Area Community College (N, U)
Northern Arizona University (G)
Northwestern Oklahoma State University (G)
Northwestern State University of Louisiana (U, G)
Nova Southeastern University (G)
The Ohio State University (G)
Oklahoma State University (U)
Old Dominion University (U, G)
Oregon State University (G)
Pace University (G)
Pacific Oaks College (U, G)
Park University (U)
Pennsylvania College of Optometry (G)
Regis University (G)
Rio Hondo College (U)
Rosalind Franklin University of Medicine and Science (N, G)
Saint Mary-of-the-Woods College (U)
Shasta Bible College (U)
Shenandoah University (G)
Southern Illinois University Carbondale (U)
Southwestern Assemblies of God University (U, G)
Southwestern Baptist Theological Seminary (G)
State University of New York at Plattsburgh (U, G)
Stephen F. Austin State University (G)
Tarleton State University (G)
Teachers College Columbia University (N, G)
Texas A&M University–Corpus Christi (G)
Texas A&M University–Texarkana (G)
Texas Tech University (G)
Texas Woman's University (G)
Tunxis Community College (N)
Union Theological Seminary and Presbyterian School of Christian Education (N, G)
Université Sainte-Anne (U, G)
The University of Akron (N, U, G)
University of Alaska Fairbanks (G)
University of Bridgeport (N)
University of California, Riverside (N)
University of Central Arkansas (G)
University of Central Florida (U)
University of Colorado at Denver (G)
University of Idaho (U)
University of Illinois at Chicago (N)
University of Illinois at Springfield (G)
University of La Verne (N)
The University of Lethbridge (U, G)
University of Maryland, Baltimore County (G)
University of Massachusetts Amherst (U, G)
University of Massachusetts Lowell (N)
University of Mississippi (G)
University of Missouri–Columbia (U, G)
University of Missouri–Columbia (G)
University of New England (G)
The University of North Carolina at Greensboro (G)
University of Northern Colorado (G)
University of Oklahoma (G)
University of Saskatchewan (N, G)
University of South Carolina Sumter (G)
The University of South Dakota (G)
University of Southern Mississippi (U)
The University of Texas of the Permian Basin (U)
The University of Texas System (U, G)
University of Toledo (U, G)
University of West Florida (N)
University of Wisconsin–Milwaukee (G)
Vanguard University of Southern California (U)
Virginia Polytechnic Institute and State University (G)
Wayland Baptist University (U)
Wayne State College (U, G)
Whatcom Community College (U)
Wright State University (G)
Yuba College (U)

Educational evaluation, research and statistics

Adams State College (G)
Athabasca University (N, U, G)
Auburn University Montgomery (G)
Azusa Pacific University (G)
Black Hills State University (G)
Boise State University (G)
Brenau University (G)
Bridgewater State College (U)
California State University, Sacramento (G)
Central Missouri State University (U, G)
Central Missouri State University (U, G)
Central Missouri State University (U, G)
Central Missouri State University (U, G)
Central Missouri State University (U, G)
Chadron State College (G)
College of the Southwest (G)
Colorado Christian University (G)
Dallas Baptist University (G)
Eastern Michigan University (G)
Fairmont State University (G)
Ferris State University (N)
Florida Atlantic University (G)
Fort Hays State University (U)
Howard Community College (U)
Immaculata University (G)
Jacksonville State University (U, G)
Marquette University (N)
McDaniel College (G)
Middle Tennessee State University (G)
Mississippi State University (G)
North Dakota State University (G)
Northern Arizona University (G)
North Georgia College & State University (G)
Northwestern State University of Louisiana (G)
Oklahoma State University (U, G)
The Pennsylvania State University University Park Campus (U)
Saint Joseph's College of Maine (U, G)
St. Petersburg College (U)
Southwestern Baptist Theological Seminary (G)
Tarleton State University (G)
Teachers College Columbia University (N, G)
The University of Akron (U, G)
University of Arkansas at Little Rock (G)
University of Calgary (G)

N–Noncredit; U–Undergraduate; G–Graduate

The University of Findlay (G)
The University of Lethbridge (G)
University of Missouri–Columbia (U, G)
University of New Orleans (G)
University of St. Francis (G)
University of Sioux Falls (G)
University of South Carolina Sumter (U)
University of Southern Mississippi (U, G)
University of Toledo (G)
Wayne State College (G)

Educational psychology

American College of Computer & Information Sciences (U)
Athabasca University (N, G)
Brenau University (G)
Brevard Community College (U)
Brigham Young University (U)
Butler County Community College (U)
Caldwell Community College and Technical Institute (U)
Capella University (N, G)
Casper College (U)
Central Missouri State University (U, G)
Central Missouri State University (U, G)
Central Missouri State University (U, G)
Central Missouri State University (U, G)
Central Missouri State University (U, G)
Chadron State College (U, G)
College of DuPage (U)
College of the Southwest (U)
Colorado State University (U)
Concordia University Wisconsin (G)
Delaware County Community College (U)
Des Moines Area Community College (U)
Duquesne University (U)
East Carolina University (U)
Eastern Kentucky University (U)
Eastern Michigan University (G)
Edison Community College (U)
Elizabeth City State University (U)
Eugene Bible College (U)
Fairmont State University (G)
Fort Hays State University (U)
Georgia Southern University (G)
Goddard College (G)
Gonzaga University (U, G)
Harford Community College (U)
Indiana State University (G)
Indiana University of Pennsylvania (G)
Indiana Wesleyan University (G)
Jacksonville State University (U, G)
John Wood Community College (U)
Lawson State Community College (U)
Liberty University (U)
Louisiana State University and Agricultural and Mechanical College (U)
Marquette University (N)
Marshall University (U)
Marylhurst University (U)
Mercy College (U)
Middlesex Community College (U)
Middle Tennessee State University (U)
Mississippi State University (U, G)
Moody Bible Institute (U)
Mount Saint Mary College (U)
Naropa University (N)
Northern Arizona University (G)
Northwestern State University of Louisiana (G)
Ohio University (U)
Okaloosa-Walton College (U)
Oklahoma State University (U)
Rowan Technical College (U)
Saint Joseph's College of Maine (U)
St. Petersburg College (U)
Shenandoah University (G)
Southern Illinois University Carbondale (U)
Southwestern Baptist Theological Seminary (G)
Southwest Virginia Community College (U)
Stephen F. Austin State University (U, G)
Tarleton State University (U, G)
Taylor University (U)
Teachers College Columbia University (N, G)
Texas A&M University–Commerce (U, G)
Texas Tech University (U)
Triton College (U)
The University of Akron (G)
University of Alaska Fairbanks (U, G)
University of Calgary (G)
University of Central Arkansas (U)
University of Houston (G)
University of Maine (U)
University of Minnesota, Twin Cities Campus (U)
University of Mississippi (U)
University of Missouri–Columbia (U, G)
University of Missouri–Columbia (G)
University of Nebraska–Lincoln (G)
University of Nevada, Reno (U)
University of Northern Iowa (U, G)
University of Oklahoma (G)
University of Saskatchewan (G)
University of Southern Indiana (U)
The University of Texas of the Permian Basin (G)
The University of Texas–Pan American (G)
The University of Texas System (G)
University of Utah (U)
University of Washington (U)
University of Waterloo (U)
University of Wisconsin–La Crosse (G)
University of Wyoming (G)
Utah State University (G)

Educational/instructional media design

Acadia University (U, G)
Adams State College (G)
Arkansas Tech University (G)
Athabasca University (N)
Azusa Pacific University (G)
Bemidji State University (G)
Black Hills State University (G)
Bloomsburg University of Pennsylvania (G)
Boise State University (G)
Boise State University (U, G)
Boise State University (G)
Boston University (G)
Brevard Community College (U)
California State University, Fullerton (G)
California State University, Monterey Bay (U)
California State University, Sacramento (G)
Capella University (N, G)
Chadron State College (G)
Connecticut State University System (G)
Dakota State University (G)
Danville Community College (U)
Delaware Technical & Community College, Jack F. Owens Campus (U)
Delaware Technical & Community College, Stanton/Wilmington Campus (U)
DePaul University (G)
Duquesne University (G)
East Carolina University (G)
Eastern Michigan University (G)
Elizabeth City State University (U)
Fairmont State University (G)
Florida Atlantic University (U, G)
Florida State University (G)
Fort Hays State University (U, G)
Georgia Southern University (G)
Grossmont College (U)
Hamline University (N, G)
Henry Ford Community College (U)
Immaculata University (G)
Indiana State University (U, G)
Jacksonville State University (G)
Jones International University (G)
Kent State University (U)
La Sierra University (G)
Lesley University (G)
Lipscomb University (U, G)
Marquette University (N, U)
McDaniel College (G)
Mississippi State University (U, G)
National University (G)
New Jersey City University (G)
New York Institute of Technology (G)
North Dakota State University (G)
Northern Arizona University (G)
North Georgia College & State University (N)

Northwestern State University of Louisiana (U, G)
Nova Southeastern University (G)
Pace University (G)
The Pennsylvania State University University Park Campus (G)
Royal Roads University (G)
St. Petersburg College (U)
Seton Hill University (G)
Slippery Rock University of Pennsylvania (G)
Sonoma State University (U)
Southern Illinois University Carbondale (G)
Southwestern Baptist Theological Seminary (G)
Southwest Wisconsin Technical College (U)
State University of New York at Plattsburgh (G)
State University of New York College at Potsdam (G)
Tarleton State University (U)
Taylor University (U)
Teachers College Columbia University (N, G)
Texas A&M University (G)
Texas A&M University–Commerce (G)
Texas Tech University (G)
The University of Akron (N, U, G)
University of Arkansas at Little Rock (G)
The University of British Columbia (U, G)
University of Calgary (G)
University of Central Florida (G)
The University of Findlay (G)
University of Houston–Clear Lake (G)
University of Illinois at Urbana–Champaign (G)
University of Maryland, Baltimore County (G)
University of Maryland University College (G)
University of Massachusetts Boston (G)
University of Massachusetts Lowell (N)
University of Mississippi (U, G)
University of Missouri–Columbia (G)
University of New Orleans (G)
University of Saskatchewan (N)
The University of South Dakota (U)
The University of Texas System (U, G)
University of West Florida (G)
University of Wyoming (G)
Wayne State College (G)
Western Michigan University (U, G)
William Paterson University of New Jersey (U, G)
Wright State University (G)
Youngstown State University (G)

Electrical and electronic engineering-related technology

Alpena Community College (U)
Arapahoe Community College (U)
Arkansas Tech University (U)
Augusta Technical College (N)
Bishop State Community College (U)
Bismarck State College (U)
Bismarck State College (N)
Bristol Community College (N)
California National University for Advanced Studies (N)
College of The Albemarle (U)
Cossatot Community College of the University of Arkansas (N)
Frederick Community College (N)
Grantham University (U)
Heart of Georgia Technical College (U)
Indiana State University (G)
Iowa Western Community College (U)
Ivy Tech State College–Bloomington (U)
Ivy Tech State College–Wabash Valley (U)
Lord Fairfax Community College (N)
Maui Community College (U)
Maysville Community College (U)
Moberly Area Community College (U)
North Dakota State University (U, G)
Northern Arizona University (G)
Oklahoma State University (U)
Palm Beach Community College (U)
St. Clair County Community College (U)
Seminole Community College (U)
Southern Methodist University (G)
Texas Tech University (G)
University of Colorado at Boulder (N, G)
University of Massachusetts Lowell (G)
University of Washington (G)
University of Wisconsin–Madison (U)
Virginia Polytechnic Institute and State University (U)

Electrical and electronics equipment installers and repairers

Allan Hancock College (U)
Athens Technical College (U)
Bristol Community College (N)
Cossatot Community College of the University of Arkansas (N)
Lord Fairfax Community College (N)
Orange Coast College (U)
Seminole Community College (U)
Utah Valley State College (U)

Electrical and power transmission installers

Bismarck State College (U)
Bristol Community College (N)
Central Wyoming College (N)
Cossatot Community College of the University of Arkansas (N)
University of Northwestern Ohio (U)

Electrical engineering

Bradley University (G)
California National University for Advanced Studies (U, G)
California State University, Fullerton (G)
California State University, Sacramento (U)
Cleveland State University (G)
Colorado State University (G)
Columbia University (N, G)
Fairleigh Dickinson University, Metropolitan Campus (G)
Georgia Institute of Technology (N, G)
Grantham University (U)
Illinois Institute of Technology (U, G)
Iowa State University of Science and Technology (G)
Michigan Technological University (G)
Northeastern University (G)
Oklahoma State University (G)
Old Dominion University (G)
The Pennsylvania State University University Park Campus (G)
Rochester Institute of Technology (U, G)
Sinclair Community College (U)
Southern Methodist University (G)
Stanford University (N)
The University of Arizona (G)
University of Central Florida (U, G)
University of Delaware (N, U, G)
University of Idaho (U, G)
University of Maine (N, U, G)
University of Nebraska–Lincoln (G)
University of North Dakota (U)
University of Southern Mississippi (U)
The University of Texas at Arlington (G)
University of Wisconsin–Madison (G)
Virginia Polytechnic Institute and State University (G)
York Technical College (U)

Electrical, electronics and communications engineering

Bristol Community College (N)
California State University, Sacramento (G)
Cossatot Community College of the University of Arkansas (N)
Danville Area Community College (U)
Florida Atlantic University (U)
Grantham University (U)
Indiana State University (U)
Polytechnic University, Long Island Graduate Center (G)

N–Noncredit; U–Undergraduate; G–Graduate

Stanford University (N)
University of Idaho (N)
University of New Hampshire (G)
Villanova University (G)

Electromechanical instrumentation and maintenance technology

Bismarck State College (U)
Bristol Community College (N)
Cossatot Community College of the University of Arkansas (N)
Orange Coast College (U)
The Pennsylvania State University University Park Campus (G)
Shawnee State University (U)

Engineering design

Edison State Community College (U)
Georgia Institute of Technology (G)
Pierce College (U)
Stanford University (N)
University of Colorado at Denver (G)
University of Michigan (N)
University of Wisconsin–Platteville (G)

Engineering mechanics

Colorado State University (G)
Florida International University (U, G)
Georgia Southern University (U)
Illinois Institute of Technology (U, G)
Kansas State University (G)
Michigan Technological University (N, U)
Mississippi State University (G)
Rochester Institute of Technology (U)
Tarrant County College District (U)
The University of Alabama (G)
The University of Arizona (G)
University of Colorado at Denver (U, G)
University of Delaware (G)
University of Missouri–Columbia (U)
The University of Texas at Arlington (G)
University of Wisconsin–Platteville (G)

Engineering physics

California National University for Advanced Studies (N)
Northampton County Area Community College (U)
Northeastern Oklahoma Agricultural and Mechanical College (U)
Tacoma Community College (U)

Engineering science

Casper College (U)
Eastern Michigan University (G)
Kansas State University (G)
Oklahoma State University (U)
University of Colorado at Denver (U)
University of Delaware (U)
University of Michigan (N, G)
University of Michigan–Dearborn (G)

Engineering, general

Auburn University (N)
California National University for Advanced Studies (N, U, G)
Capitol College (G)
Casper College (U)
Eastern Michigan University (G)
Florida Atlantic University (G)
Florida International University (U, G)
Harrisburg Area Community College (U)
Inter American University of Puerto Rico, San Germán Campus (U)
Jacksonville State University (U)
Kansas State University (G)
Memorial University of Newfoundland (U)
Mississippi State University (G)
Montgomery County Community College (U)
North Carolina State University (G)
Northern Arizona University (U)
North Hennepin Community College (U)
Schoolcraft College (U)
Stevens Institute of Technology (N)
Texas Tech University (G)
The University of Akron (G)
The University of Alabama (U)
University of Colorado at Denver (U, G)
University of Illinois (G)
University of Illinois at Chicago (G)
University of Michigan (N)
University of Michigan–Dearborn (G)
University of New Orleans (G)
The University of North Carolina at Charlotte (N, U)
University of Oklahoma (U)
University of South Carolina Sumter (U)
University of South Florida (N, U, G)
University of Wisconsin–Madison (G)
University of Wisconsin–Platteville (G)
Villanova University (N)
Virginia Polytechnic Institute and State University (N, U)

Engineering, other

California National University for Advanced Studies (N)
Eastern Michigan University (G)
Florida International University (G)
Kansas State University (G)
Lakeland Community College (N)
North Georgia College & State University (U)
The Ohio State University (U, G)
The Pennsylvania State University University Park Campus (N)
Tacoma Community College (U)
Texas Tech University (G)
The University of Akron (U)
University of Colorado at Denver (G)
University of Michigan (N, G)
University of Washington (G)
University of Wisconsin–Platteville (G)
Villanova University (U)
West Virginia University (N)

Engineering-related technologies, other

Arapahoe Community College (U)
Bismarck State College (U)
Bristol Community College (N)
Cincinnati State Technical and Community College (U)
Cleveland State University (U, G)
Dakota County Technical College (U)
Eastern Michigan University (G)
Heart of Georgia Technical College (U)
Indiana University of Pennsylvania (G)
LeTourneau University (N)
Michigan Technological University (N, U)
Mississippi State University (G)
New Jersey Institute of Technology (G)
Northern Kentucky University (G)
Oklahoma State University (U)
Old Dominion University (U)
Texas A&M University (G)
University of Colorado at Denver (G)
University of Michigan (N)
University of Southern Mississippi (U)
University of Toledo (U)
University of West Florida (U)
Virginia Polytechnic Institute and State University (N)
Wake Technical Community College (U)
Western Washington University (U)

Engineering/industrial management

Bristol Community College (N)
Central Missouri State University (U, G)
Central Missouri State University (U, G)
Central Missouri State University (U, G)
Central Missouri State University (U, G)
Central Missouri State University (U, G)
Cleveland State University (U, G)
Colorado State University (G)
Columbia University (N, G)
East Carolina University (U)
Eastern Michigan University (G)
Edison State Community College (U)
Florida Institute of Technology (G)
Florida International University (U)
Georgia Institute of Technology (G)
Indiana University–Purdue University Fort Wayne (U)
Kansas State University (G)

Engineering/industrial management

Lehigh University (N)
Middle Tennessee State University (N)
Montana Tech of The University of Montana (G)
Northcentral University (G)
Northeastern University (G)
Old Dominion University (G)
Oregon Institute of Technology (U)
The Pennsylvania State University University Park Campus (G)
Rochester Institute of Technology (U)
Roger Williams University (U)
Southern Methodist University (G)
Stanford University (N)
Stevens Institute of Technology (U)
Sullivan University (G)
Texas A&M University (G)
Texas A&M University–Commerce (G)
The University of Alabama in Huntsville (G)
The University of Arizona (G)
University of Colorado at Boulder (N, G)
University of Colorado at Denver (G)
University of Dallas (G)
University of Idaho (U, G)
University of Massachusetts Amherst (N, G)
University of Michigan (N)
University of Nebraska–Lincoln (U, G)
University of Waterloo (G)
University of Wisconsin–Platteville (G)
Western Michigan University (U, G)
Worcester Polytechnic Institute (G)

English as a second language

Ashworth College (N)
Athabasca University (N, U)
Blackhawk Technical College (N)
Bossier Parish Community College (N)
Clackamas Community College (U)
College of DuPage (U)
College of the Southwest (U)
Cossatot Community College of the University of Arkansas (U)
Dallas County Community College District (U)
Delaware Technical & Community College, Jack F. Owens Campus (U)
Delaware Technical & Community College, Stanton/Wilmington Campus (U)
Edgecombe Community College (N)
Fairleigh Dickinson University, Metropolitan Campus (U)
Fashion Institute of Technology (U)
Feather River Community College District (N)
Florida Gulf Coast University (U, G)
Gateway Community College (U)
Hamline University (N, G)
Honolulu Community College (U)
Inter American University of Puerto Rico, San Germán Campus (U)
James Madison University (N)
Linn-Benton Community College (N, U)
Long Beach City College (U)
Lorain County Community College (U)
Lord Fairfax Community College (N)
Manchester Community College (N)
Middle Tennessee State University (N)
Minnesota State College–Southeast Technical (N)
MiraCosta College (N, U)
Mt. San Antonio College (U)
Murray State University (G)
Naugatuck Valley Community College (N)
Northwestern University (N)
Oregon State University (N)
Oxnard College (U)
St. Cloud State University (U, G)
St. Petersburg College (U)
Shawnee State University (U)
Sinclair Community College (U)
Southwestern College (N, U)
Tarleton State University (N)
Texas A&M University–Kingsville (G)
Tompkins Cortland Community College (U)
University of Florida (U)
University of Maine (U)
The University of North Carolina at Chapel Hill (U)
University of Saskatchewan (N)
The University of Texas of the Permian Basin (U, G)
The University of Texas–Pan American (G)
The University of Texas System (U)
University of Washington (N, U)
Waubonsee Community College (U)
Westchester Community College (U)
Western Washington University (U)
West Los Angeles College (U)
William Rainey Harper College (U)

English composition

Acadia University (U)
Adams State College (N, U)
Adirondack Community College (U)
AIB College of Business (U)
Albuquerque Technical Vocational Institute (U)
Allan Hancock College (U)
Allen County Community College (U)
Alpena Community College (U)
Alvin Community College (U)
American College of Computer & Information Sciences (U)
American Public University System (U)
American River College (U)
Andrews University (U)
Anne Arundel Community College (U)
Arkansas State University–Beebe (U)
Ashland Community and Technical College (U)
Athabasca University (N, U)
Athens Technical College (U)
Baltimore City Community College (U)
Barclay College (U)
Bellevue Community College (U)
Bemidji State University (U)
Berkeley College (U)
Berkeley College-New York City Campus (U)
Berkeley College-Westchester Campus (U)
Bethany College of the Assemblies of God (U)
Bismarck State College (U)
Black Hills State University (U)
Boise State University (U)
Bossier Parish Community College (U)
Bowling Green State University (U)
Brazosport College (U)
Bridgewater State College (U)
Brigham Young University (U)
Bristol Community College (U)
Brookdale Community College (U)
Broome Community College (U)
Broward Community College (U)
Bucks County Community College (U)
Burlington County College (U)
Butler County Community College (U)
Butler County Community College (U)
Caldwell Community College and Technical Institute (U)
Campbell University (U)
Cape Fear Community College (U)
Carl Albert State College (U)
Carroll Community College (U)
Cascadia Community College (U)
Casper College (U)
Central Texas College (U)
Central Virginia Community College (U)
Central Wyoming College (U)
Century College (N)
Cerritos College (U)
Chadron State College (U)
Chaminade University of Honolulu (U)
Champlain College (U)
Charter Oak State College (U)
Chattanooga State Technical Community College (U)
Chemeketa Community College (U)
Chesapeake College (U)
Citrus College (U)
Clackamas Community College (U)

N–Noncredit; U–Undergraduate; G–Graduate

Clarion University of Pennsylvania (U)
Clark College (U)
Clatsop Community College (U)
Clemson University (N, U)
Clinton Community College (U)
Clovis Community College (U)
Coastal Bend College (U)
Coconino Community College (N, U)
Coleman College (U)
College of DuPage (U)
College of San Mateo (U)
College of The Albemarle (N, U)
College of the Canyons (U)
College of the Siskiyous (U)
College of the Southwest (U)
Collin County Community College District (U)
Colorado Mountain College District System (U)
Colorado State University-Pueblo (U)
Columbia Basin College (U)
Columbia Union College (U)
Columbus State Community College (U)
The Community College of Baltimore County (U)
Community College of Denver (U)
Connecticut State University System (U, G)
Copiah-Lincoln Community College–Natchez Campus (U)
Corning Community College (U)
Cossatot Community College of the University of Arkansas (U)
County College of Morris (U)
Cumberland County College (U)
Daemen College (U)
Dakota County Technical College (U)
Dakota State University (U)
Dallas County Community College District (U)
Daniel Webster College (U)
Danville Area Community College (U)
Danville Community College (U)
Darton College (U)
Davenport University Online (U)
Dawson Community College (U)
Delaware County Community College (U)
Delaware Technical & Community College, Jack F. Owens Campus (U)
Delaware Technical & Community College, Stanton/Wilmington Campus (U)
Delta College (U)
Des Moines Area Community College (U)
DeVry University Online (U)
Drake University (U)
East Arkansas Community College (U)
East Central College (U)
Eastern Kentucky University (U)
Eastern Michigan University (U)
Eastern Wyoming College (U)
East Los Angeles College (U)
Edgecombe Community College (U)
Edison Community College (U)
Edison State Community College (U)
El Camino College (U)
Elgin Community College (U)
Elizabeth City State University (U)
Embry-Riddle Aeronautical University (U)
Erie Community College (U)
Eugene Bible College (U)
Everett Community College (U)
Evergreen Valley College (U)
Fairleigh Dickinson University, Metropolitan Campus (U)
Fairmont State University (U)
Feather River Community College District (N, U)
Flathead Valley Community College (U)
Florida Community College at Jacksonville (U)
Florida Metropolitan University–Brandon Campus (U)
Floyd College (U)
Fontbonne University (U)
Fort Hays State University (U)
Frederick Community College (U)
Fulton-Montgomery Community College (U)
Gannon University (U)
Gaston College (U)
George C. Wallace Community College (U)
George Mason University (U)
Georgia Southern University (U)
Glenville State College (U)
Goddard College (U)
Gogebic Community College (U)
Golden Gate University (U, G)
Golden West College (U)
Grand View College (U)
Grantham University (U)
Greenfield Community College (U)
Greenville Technical College (U)
Grossmont College (U)
Halifax Community College (U)
Harford Community College (U)
Harrisburg Area Community College (U)
Heartland Community College (U)
Henry Ford Community College (U)
Hibbing Community College (U)
Hillsborough Community College (U)
Honolulu Community College (U)
Horry-Georgetown Technical College (U)
Houston Community College System (U)
Howard College (U)
Howard Community College (U)
Illinois Eastern Community Colleges, Lincoln Trail College (U)
Illinois Eastern Community Colleges, Olney Central College (U)
Immaculata University (U)
Independence Community College (U)
Indiana Institute of Technology (U)
Indiana State University (U)
Indiana University–Purdue University Fort Wayne (U)
Indiana Wesleyan University (U)
Iowa Western Community College (U)
Ivy Tech State College–Columbus (U)
Ivy Tech State College–Kokomo (U)
Ivy Tech State College–North Central (U)
Ivy Tech State College–Northwest (U)
Ivy Tech State College–Wabash Valley (U)
Ivy Tech State College–Whitewater (U)
Jacksonville State University (U)
James Madison University (N, U)
Jamestown Community College (N)
Jefferson College (U)
Jefferson College of Health Sciences (U)
Jefferson Community College (U)
Jefferson Davis Community College (U)
John A. Logan College (U)
Johnson County Community College (U)
John Tyler Community College (U)
John Wood Community College (U)
Jones College (U)
Judson College (U)
Judson College (U)
Kansas City Kansas Community College (U)
Kellogg Community College (U)
Kentucky State University (U)
The King's College and Seminary (N, U)
Lake Superior College (U)
Lansing Community College (U)
LeTourneau University (U)
Lewis-Clark State College (U)
Liberty University (U)
Limestone College (U)
Lock Haven University of Pennsylvania (U)
Long Beach City College (U)
Lorain County Community College (U)
Lord Fairfax Community College (U)
Los Angeles Harbor College (U)
Los Angeles Pierce College (U)
Los Angeles Valley College (U)
Louisiana State University and Agricultural and Mechanical College (N, U)
Louisiana State University at Eunice (U)
Loyola University New Orleans (U)
Madison Area Technical College (U)
Madonna University (U)
Manatee Community College (U)
Manchester Community College (U)
Marion Technical College (U)
Marshall University (U)
Marylhurst University (U)

Maui Community College (U)
Maysville Community College (U)
Mayville State University (U)
Mercy College (U)
Mesa Community College (U)
Metropolitan Community College (U)
Metropolitan State University (U)
Miami Dade College (U)
Middlesex Community College (U)
Middle Tennessee State University (U)
Midstate College (U)
Millersville University of Pennsylvania (U)
Minnesota School of Business–Brooklyn Center (U)
MiraCosta College (U)
Mississippi Delta Community College (U)
Modesto Junior College (U)
Monroe Community College (U)
Monroe County Community College (U)
Montana State University–Billings (U)
Montana Tech of The University of Montana (U)
Montgomery Community College (N, U)
Montgomery County Community College (U)
Moody Bible Institute (U)
Mott Community College (U)
Mountain Empire Community College (U)
Mountain State University (U)
Mt. Hood Community College (U)
Mt. San Antonio College (U)
Mount Wachusett Community College (U)
Murray State University (U)
New England Institute of Technology (U)
New Hampshire Community Technical College System (U)
New York Institute of Technology (U)
Normandale Community College (U)
Northampton County Area Community College (U)
North Carolina State University (U)
North Central Texas College (U)
North Country Community College (U)
North Dakota State College of Science (U)
Northeastern Oklahoma Agricultural and Mechanical College (U)
Northeast State Technical Community College (U)
Northern New Mexico Community College (U)
Northern Virginia Community College (U)
North Harris Montgomery Community College District (U)
North Idaho College (U)
NorthWest Arkansas Community College (N, U)
Northwestern Michigan College (U)
Northwestern State University of Louisiana (U)
Norwalk Community College (U)
Oakland City University (U)
Ocean County College (U)
Odessa College (U)
Ohio University (U)
Okaloosa-Walton College (U)
Oklahoma State University (U)
Orange Coast College (U)
Oregon State University (U)
Oxnard College (U)
Palomar College (U)
Park University (U)
Pasco-Hernando Community College (U)
Patrick Henry College (U)
Patrick Henry Community College (U)
Peninsula College (U)
The Pennsylvania State University University Park Campus (U)
Pierce College (U)
Pitt Community College (U)
Portland State University (U)
Prairie Bible College (U)
Pulaski Technical College (U)
Queen's University at Kingston (U)
Randolph Community College (U)
Rappahannock Community College (U)
Raritan Valley Community College (U)
Reading Area Community College (U)
The Richard Stockton College of New Jersey (U)
Richland Community College (U)
Rio Hondo College (U)
Riverland Community College (U)
Rochester Institute of Technology (U)
Rockland Community College (U)
Sacramento City College (U)
Sacred Heart University (U)
St. Clair County Community College (U)
St. Cloud State University (U)
Saint Joseph's College of Maine (U)
Saint Leo University (U)
San Jacinto College District (U)
Santa Rosa Junior College (U)
Sauk Valley Community College (U)
Schenectady County Community College (U)
Schiller International University (U)
Schoolcraft College (U)
Seattle Central Community College (U)
Seminole Community College (U)
Seward County Community College (U)
Shoreline Community College (U)
Sinclair Community College (U)
Skidmore College (U)
Snead State Community College (U)
Southeast Arkansas College (U)
Southeast Community College, Beatrice Campus (U)
Southeast Community College, Lincoln Campus (U)
Southeastern College of the Assemblies of God (U)
Southeastern Community College (U)
South Piedmont Community College (U)
Southwestern Assemblies of God University (U)
Southwestern College (U)
Southwest Virginia Community College (U)
Spartanburg Technical College (U)
Spoon River College (U)
Spring Arbor University (U)
Stanly Community College (U)
State University of New York at New Paltz (U)
State University of New York Empire State College (U)
Strayer University (U)
Sullivan University (U)
Sul Ross State University (U)
Syracuse University (U)
Tacoma Community College (U)
Taft College (U)
Tarleton State University (U)
Tarrant County College District (U)
Taylor University (N, U)
Teikyo Post University (U)
Temple College (U)
Texas A&M University–Commerce (U, G)
Texas A&M University–Corpus Christi (U)
Texas State Technical College–Waco (U)
Texas State University-San Marcos (U)
Texas Tech University (U)
Tompkins Cortland Community College (U)
Triton College (U)
Troy University Montgomery (U)
Tulane University (U)
Tunxis Community College (U)
Umpqua Community College (U)
The University of Akron (U)
The University of Alabama (U)
University of Alaska Fairbanks (U)
The University of British Columbia (N)
University of Central Arkansas (U)
University of Cincinnati Raymond Walters College (U)
University of Colorado at Colorado Springs (U)
University of Colorado at Denver (U)
University of Delaware (U)
University of Florida (U)
University of Georgia (U)
University of Guelph (U)

N–Noncredit; U–Undergraduate; G–Graduate

University of Houston–Victoria (U)
University of Idaho (U)
University of Illinois (N)
University of Illinois at Springfield (U)
University of La Verne (U)
University of Maine (U)
The University of Maine at Augusta (U)
University of Massachusetts Lowell (U)
University of Minnesota, Morris (U)
University of Minnesota, Twin Cities Campus (U)
University of Missouri–Columbia (U)
The University of Montana–Missoula (U)
University of Nebraska–Lincoln (N, U)
University of Nevada, Reno (U)
The University of North Carolina at Chapel Hill (U)
University of North Dakota (U)
University of Oklahoma (U)
University of Saint Francis (U)
The University of South Dakota (U)
University of Southern Indiana (U)
University of Southern Mississippi (U)
The University of Tennessee (U)
The University of Tennessee at Martin (U)
The University of Texas at Arlington (U)
The University of Texas of the Permian Basin (U)
The University of Texas System (U)
University of the Incarnate Word (U)
University of Vermont (N)
University of Washington (U)
University of Waterloo (N, U)
University of West Florida (U)
University of Wisconsin Colleges (U)
University of Wyoming (U)
Upper Iowa University (N, U)
Utah Valley State College (U)
Utah Valley State College (U)
Valley City State University (U)
Vance-Granville Community College (U)
Virginia Polytechnic Institute and State University (U)
Walters State Community College (U)
Washington State University (U)
Washtenaw Community College (U)
Waubonsee Community College (U)
Weber State University (U)
Westchester Community College (U)
Western Michigan University (U)
Western Wyoming Community College (U)
West Los Angeles College (U)
West Valley College (U)
West Virginia University at Parkersburg (U)
Whatcom Community College (U)
Wilkes Community College (U)
William and Catherine Booth College (U)
William Paterson University of New Jersey (U)
William Rainey Harper College (U)
William Tyndale College (U)
Wright State University (U)
York Technical College (U)
Yuba College (U)

English creative writing

Adams State College (N)
Albuquerque Technical Vocational Institute (U)
Alvin Community College (U)
American College of Computer & Information Sciences (U)
Arkansas State University–Beebe (U)
Ashland Community and Technical College (U)
Athabasca University (U)
Bellevue Community College (U)
Blackhawk Technical College (N)
Bossier Parish Community College (N)
Bowling Green State University (U, G)
Brevard Community College (U)
Bridgewater State College (N)
Brigham Young University (N)
Bucks County Community College (U)
Butler County Community College (U)
Caldwell Community College and Technical Institute (N)
California National University for Advanced Studies (N)
California State University, Fullerton (N)
Carroll Community College (N)
Casper College (U)
Chaminade University of Honolulu (U)
Champlain College (U)
Chemeketa Community College (U)
Chesapeake College (U)
Clatsop Community College (U)
Clemson University (N)
Coconino Community College (N)
Coleman College (U)
Columbus State Community College (U)
Community College of Denver (U)
County College of Morris (U)
Dakota County Technical College (U)
Darton College (N)
Delaware County Community College (U)
DeVry University Online (U)
Drake University (U)
Feather River Community College District (N)
Fort Hays State University (U)
Frederick Community College (U)
Gannon University (U)
Goddard College (U, G)
Hillsborough Community College (U)
Howard Community College (U)
Irvine Valley College (U)
James Madison University (N)
Jamestown Community College (N)
John A. Logan College (U)
John Tyler Community College (U)
Lamar State College–Port Arthur (N)
Limestone College (U)
Linn-Benton Community College (U)
Long Beach City College (U)
Maryville University of Saint Louis (N)
Massasoit Community College (N)
Maysville Community College (U)
Mercy College (U)
Mesa Community College (U)
Middlesex Community College (N)
MiraCosta College (N)
Mt. Hood Community College (U)
Mount Saint Vincent University (N)
Mt. San Antonio College (U)
Naropa University (N, U)
National University (G)
New York Institute of Technology (U)
Northampton County Area Community College (U)
North Harris Montgomery Community College District (U)
Odessa College (N)
Oregon State University (U)
Oxnard College (U)
Park University (U)
The Pennsylvania State University University Park Campus (U)
Pierce College (U)
Prescott College (U)
Pulaski Technical College (U)
Queen's University at Kingston (U)
Raritan Valley Community College (U)
Riverland Community College (U)
Riverside Community College (N)
Sacramento City College (U)
St. Clair County Community College (U)
St. Cloud State University (U)
Saint Mary-of-the-Woods College (U)
Saint Mary-of-the-Woods College (U)
Santa Rosa Junior College (N, U)
Seton Hill University (G)
Shippensburg University of Pennsylvania (G)
Sinclair Community College (U)
Snead State Community College (U)
Southwest Missouri State University (U)
State University of New York College at Potsdam (N)
Stephens College (U)
Syracuse University (U)
Taft College (U)
Tarleton State University (N, U)
Taylor University (N)

Teikyo Post University (U)
Temple College (U)
Texas State University-San Marcos (U)
The University of Akron (U)
The University of Alabama (U)
University of Arkansas at Little Rock (U)
University of Central Arkansas (U)
University of Colorado at Denver (U)
University of Illinois (N)
University of Illinois at Springfield (U)
The University of Iowa (U, G)
University of La Verne (U)
The University of Maine at Augusta (U)
University of Mississippi (U)
University of Missouri–Columbia (U)
University of Nevada, Reno (U)
University of New Orleans (U, G)
University of Northern Colorado (U)
University of Pittsburgh at Bradford (U)
The University of Tennessee (N, U)
The University of Texas at Austin (U)
The University of Texas System (U)
University of the Incarnate Word (U)
University of Washington (N, U)
Wake Technical Community College (N)
West Los Angeles College (U)
Wilkes Community College (U)
William Paterson University of New Jersey (U, G)
William Rainey Harper College (U)
William Tyndale College (U)
Youngstown State University (N)

English language and literature, general

Abilene Christian University (U)
Acadia University (U)
Adams State College (N)
Adirondack Community College (U)
AIB College of Business (U)
Albuquerque Technical Vocational Institute (U)
Allan Hancock College (U)
Alvin Community College (U)
American Academy of Nutrition, College of Nutrition (U)
American Public University System (U)
American River College (U)
Arkansas Tech University (U, G)
Athabasca University (N, U)
Barclay College (U)
Beaufort County Community College (U)
Bethany College of the Assemblies of God (U)
Bishop State Community College (U)
Black Hills State University (U)
Bossier Parish Community College (U)
Bowling Green State University (U, G)
Brenau University (U)
Brevard Community College (U)
Briercrest Distance Learning (U)
Brookdale Community College (U)
Bucks County Community College (U)
Caldwell Community College and Technical Institute (U)
Carleton University (U)
Cayuga County Community College (U)
Cedarville University (U)
Central Texas College (U)
Central Virginia Community College (U)
Chadron State College (G)
Chaminade University of Honolulu (U)
Champlain College (U)
Charter Oak State College (U)
Chattanooga State Technical Community College (U)
Clatsop Community College (U)
Cleveland State University (U, G)
Clinton Community College (U)
College of The Albemarle (N)
College of the Canyons (U)
Colorado State University-Pueblo (U)
Columbia Basin College (U)
Columbia Union College (U)
Columbus State Community College (U)
Community College of Denver (U)
Cuyamaca College (U)
Dakota County Technical College (U)
Dakota State University (U)
Dallas Baptist University (U)
Daniel Webster College (U)
Danville Community College (U)
Darton College (U)
Delaware County Community College (U)
Delta College (U)
Des Moines Area Community College (U)
Drake University (U, G)
East Central College (U)
Eastern Michigan University (U)
Eastern Oregon University (U)
Eastern Washington University (U)
Eastern Wyoming College (U)
Edgecombe Community College (N)
Edmonds Community College (U)
Elgin Community College (U)
Elizabethtown College (U)
Embry-Riddle Aeronautical University, Extended Campus (U)
Fairleigh Dickinson University, Metropolitan Campus (U, G)
Flathead Valley Community College (U)
Florida National College (U)
Fort Hays State University (U)
Gaston College (U)
Goddard College (U)
Grand View College (U)
Harford Community College (U)
Harrisburg Area Community College (U)
Heart of Georgia Technical College (U)
Henry Ford Community College (U)
Hillsborough Community College (U)
Honolulu Community College (U)
Hopkinsville Community College (U)
Howard Community College (U)
Illinois State University (U)
Indiana State University (U)
Iowa Western Community College (U)
Irvine Valley College (U)
Jacksonville State University (U)
James Madison University (N)
John Tyler Community College (U)
Jones College (U)
Judson College (U)
Judson College (U)
Kansas City Kansas Community College (U)
Kansas State University (U)
Kentucky State University (U)
Lamar University (U)
Lenoir Community College (U)
LeTourneau University (U)
Limestone College (U)
Los Angeles Harbor College (U)
Los Angeles Pierce College (U)
Louisiana State University and Agricultural and Mechanical College (U)
Louisiana State University in Shreveport (U)
Louisiana Tech University (G)
Manchester Community College (U)
Mansfield University of Pennsylvania (U)
Marian College of Fond du Lac (U)
Maysville Community College (U)
Memorial University of Newfoundland (U)
Mercy College (U, G)
Mesa Community College (U)
Mesalands Community College (U)
Miami Dade College (U)
Middlesex Community College (U)
Middle Tennessee State University (U)
Minnesota School of Business–Brooklyn Center (U)
Mississippi Delta Community College (U)
Moberly Area Community College (U)
Montgomery Community College (N, U)
Mount Allison University (U)
Mount Saint Vincent University (U)
Naropa University (G)
National University (U)
Neumann College (U)
New York Institute of Technology (U)
Normandale Community College (U)
North Carolina State University (U)

N–Noncredit; U–Undergraduate; G–Graduate

Northeast State Technical Community College (U)
Northern Arizona University (U)
Northern Kentucky University (U)
North Harris Montgomery Community College District (U)
North Hennepin Community College (U)
NorthWest Arkansas Community College (U)
Northwestern Oklahoma State University (U)
Northwestern State University of Louisiana (U)
Northwestern Technical College (U)
Norwalk Community College (U)
Oakland City University (U)
Ohio University (U)
Oregon State University (N, U)
Owensboro Community and Technical College (U)
Oxnard College (U)
Pace University (U)
Park University (U)
Passaic County Community College (U)
Paul D. Camp Community College (U)
Peninsula College (U)
Pierce College (U)
Portland State University (U)
Prescott College (U, G)
Raritan Valley Community College (U)
Rio Hondo College (U)
Riverland Community College (U)
Riverside Community College (U)
Rockland Community College (U)
Ryerson University (U)
St. Cloud State University (U)
St. Edward's University (U)
St. John's University (U)
St. Joseph's College, Suffolk Campus (U)
Saint Leo University (U)
San Bernardino Valley College (U)
Santa Fe Community College (U)
Santa Rosa Junior College (U)
Shawnee State University (U)
Shippensburg University of Pennsylvania (U, G)
Simpson College (U)
Snead State Community College (U)
Southeast Community College, Beatrice Campus (U)
Southeastern Community College (U)
Southwestern College (U)
Spartanburg Technical College (U)
Spoon River College (U)
Stephens College (U)
Strayer University (U)
Sul Ross State University (U)
Syracuse University (U)
Taft College (U)
Tarleton State University (U)
Taylor University (U)
Texas A&M University–Commerce (U)
Texas A&M University–Texarkana (U)
Texas State University-San Marcos (U)
Texas Woman's University (U)
Tompkins Cortland Community College (U)
Troy University–Florida Region (U)
Tunxis Community College (U)
Université Sainte-Anne (U)
The University of Alabama (U)
University of Alaska Fairbanks (U)
University of Arkansas at Little Rock (U)
University of Arkansas at Pine Bluff (U)
The University of British Columbia (U)
University of Central Arkansas (N)
University of Colorado at Denver (U)
University of Connecticut (U)
University of Delaware (U)
University of Georgia (U)
University of Great Falls (U)
University of Houston (U)
University of Idaho (U)
University of Illinois (N, U)
The University of Maine at Augusta (U)
University of Massachusetts Amherst (U)
University of Minnesota, Twin Cities Campus (U)
University of Missouri–Columbia (U, G)
University of Nebraska–Lincoln (U)
University of Nevada, Reno (U)
University of New Orleans (U, G)
University of Northern Iowa (U)
University of Oregon (U)
University of St. Francis (U)
University of Saskatchewan (U)
University of Sioux Falls (U)
University of South Carolina (U)
University of South Carolina Spartanburg (U)
University of Southern Indiana (U)
University of Southern Mississippi (U)
The University of Tennessee (U)
The University of Texas at Austin (U)
The University of Texas System (U)
University of Toledo (U)
University of Vermont (N, U)
University of Washington (N, U)
University of West Florida (U)
University of Wisconsin Colleges (U)
University of Wisconsin–Superior (U)
Utah Valley State College (U)
Virginia Polytechnic Institute and State University (G)
Wake Technical Community College (U)
Waycross College (U)
Weber State University (U)
Westchester Community College (U)
Western New England College (U)
Western Washington University (U)
West Los Angeles College (U)
Whatcom Community College (U)
Wilfrid Laurier University (U)
Wilkes Community College (U)
William Paterson University of New Jersey (U)
William Rainey Harper College (U)
Worcester State College (U, G)
Wright State University (U)
York Technical College (U)

English language and literature/letters, other

Acadia University (U)
Alvin Community College (U)
Ashland Community and Technical College (U)
Berkeley College (U)
Berkeley College-New York City Campus (U)
Berkeley College-Westchester Campus (U)
Brigham Young University (N)
College of the Siskiyous (U)
Concordia University at Austin (N, U)
Cossatot Community College of the University of Arkansas (U)
Iowa Western Community College (U)
Jacksonville State University (U)
Jones College (U)
Limestone College (U)
Los Angeles Pierce College (U)
Louisiana State University and Agricultural and Mechanical College (U)
Mercy College (G)
Middlesex Community College (U)
Mountain State University (U)
Nassau Community College (U)
New York Institute of Technology (U)
Northern Arizona University (U)
Pennsylvania College of Technology (U)
Raritan Valley Community College (U)
Riverland Community College (U)
Sacred Heart University (U)
Schoolcraft College (U)
Taft College (U)
Texas State University-San Marcos (U)
The University of Alabama (U)
University of Alaska Fairbanks (U)
University of Arkansas at Little Rock (U)
University of Delaware (U)
University of Houston–Downtown (U)
University of Minnesota, Twin Cities Campus (U)
University of Missouri–Columbia (U)
The University of Tennessee (U)

The University of Texas System (U)
Utah Valley State College (U)
Walters State Community College (U)
West Los Angeles College (U)
West Virginia University at Parkersburg (U)
Wilkes Community College (U)
William Paterson University of New Jersey (U)
William Rainey Harper College (U)
Youngstown State University (N)

English literature (British and Commonwealth)

Bellevue Community College (U)
Bowling Green State University (U, G)
Bristol Community College (U)
Chadron State College (U)
Chattanooga State Technical Community College (U)
Clackamas Community College (U)
College of The Albemarle (U)
College of the Siskiyous (U)
Columbia College (U)
Columbus State Community College (U)
Copiah-Lincoln Community College–Natchez Campus (U)
Danville Community College (U)
Darton College (U)
Eugene Bible College (U)
Gaston College (U)
George C. Wallace Community College (U)
Halifax Community College (U)
Harrisburg Area Community College (U)
Houston Community College System (U)
Howard College (U)
Jacksonville State University (U)
Johnson County Community College (U)
Kauai Community College (U)
Louisiana State University and Agricultural and Mechanical College (U)
Maui Community College (U)
Mercy College (U, G)
Middlesex Community College (U)
Mississippi Delta Community College (U)
Montgomery County Community College (U)
Mount Allison University (U)
Neumann College (U)
Northampton County Area Community College (U)
North Central Texas College (U)
Oklahoma State University (U)
Pasco-Hernando Community College (U)
Patrick Henry Community College (U)
Pulaski Technical College (U)
Queen's University at Kingston (U)
San Jacinto College District (U)
Snead State Community College (U)
Southeastern College of the Assemblies of God (U)
State University of New York at New Paltz (U)
Taylor University (U)
Temple College (U)
Texas State University-San Marcos (U)
Texas Tech University (U)
The University of Alabama (U)
University of Georgia (U)
University of Mississippi (U)
University of Missouri–Columbia (U)
University of Saint Francis (U)
University of Saskatchewan (U)
University of Southern Indiana (U)
The University of Tennessee (U)
The University of Tennessee at Martin (U)
The University of Texas at Austin (U)
University of Utah (U)
University of Waterloo (U)
University of Wyoming (U)
Utah State University (U)
Wilkes Community College (U)

English technical and business writing

Adirondack Community College (U)
AIB College of Business (U)
American River College (U)
Athens Technical College (U)
Baltimore City Community College (U)
Bismarck State College (U)
Black Hills State University (U)
Boise State University (U)
Bowling Green State University (U, G)
Brevard Community College (U)
Bridgewater State College (U)
Bristol Community College (U)
Bucks County Community College (U)
Butler County Community College (U)
Caldwell Community College and Technical Institute (N, U)
Cape Fear Community College (U)
Carroll Community College (N, U)
Central Texas College (U)
Central Virginia Community College (U)
Chadron State College (U)
Chattanooga State Technical Community College (U)
Chemeketa Community College (U)
Chesapeake College (U)
Clackamas Community College (U)
Coleman College (U)
College of The Albemarle (N)
Columbia Basin College (U)
Columbus State Community College (U)
The Community College of Baltimore County (U)
Community College of Denver (U)
Cossatot Community College of the University of Arkansas (U)
Dakota County Technical College (U)
Darton College (N)
Delaware Technical & Community College, Jack F. Owens Campus (U)
Delaware Technical & Community College, Stanton/Wilmington Campus (U)
Delta College (U)
Des Moines Area Community College (U)
DeVry University Online (U)
East Carolina University (G)
Edgecombe Community College (U)
Embry-Riddle Aeronautical University, Extended Campus (U)
Feather River Community College District (N)
Frederick Community College (N)
George Mason University (U)
Grantham University (U)
Harrisburg Area Community College (U)
Heart of Georgia Technical College (U)
Henry Ford Community College (U)
Indiana University of Pennsylvania (U)
James Madison University (U)
Jefferson College of Health Sciences (U)
Jefferson Community College (U)
John Jay College of Criminal Justice of the City University of New York (U)
Johnson County Community College (U)
Jones College (U)
Jones International University (U)
Judson College (U)
Lake Superior College (U)
Lamar State College–Port Arthur (N)
Limestone College (U)
Linn-Benton Community College (U)
Lord Fairfax Community College (N)
Louisiana State University and Agricultural and Mechanical College (U)
Louisiana Tech University (U)
Manchester Community College (N)
Maui Community College (U)
Mesa Community College (U)
Middlesex Community College (N, U)
Minnesota School of Business-Richfield (U)
Monroe County Community College (U)
Montana Tech of The University of Montana (U)
Montgomery Community College (U)
Montgomery County Community College (U)
Mott Community College (U)
Mt. Hood Community College (U)

N–Noncredit; U–Undergraduate; G–Graduate

Neumann College (U)
North Carolina State University (U)
Northeastern University (N, U)
Northern Arizona University (U)
North Harris Montgomery Community College District (U)
North Hennepin Community College (U)
Northwestern Michigan College (U)
Northwestern State University of Louisiana (U)
Northwestern Technical College (U)
Ohio University (U)
Oklahoma State University (N, U)
Oregon State University (U)
Oxnard College (U)
Pasco-Hernando Community College (N)
The Pennsylvania State University University Park Campus (U)
St. Cloud Technical College (U)
Saint Mary-of-the-Woods College (U)
San Jacinto College District (U)
Schenectady County Community College (U)
Seminole Community College (U)
Sinclair Community College (U)
Southeast Community College, Beatrice Campus (U)
Stephen F. Austin State University (U)
Sullivan University (G)
Syracuse University (U)
Tarleton State University (U)
Taylor University (N)
Temple College (U)
Texas Tech University (U, G)
The University of Akron (U)
University of Alaska Fairbanks (U)
University of Arkansas at Little Rock (U)
University of California, Los Angeles (G)
University of Central Florida (G)
University of Colorado at Denver (U)
University of Delaware (U)
University of Georgia (U)
University of Great Falls (U)
University of Illinois (N)
University of Maine (U)
The University of Maine at Augusta (U)
University of Missouri–Columbia (U)
University of South Carolina (U)
University of Southern Mississippi (U)
The University of Tennessee (U)
University of Washington (U)
University of West Florida (U)
Utah State University (U)
Vance-Granville Community College (N)
Weber State University (U)
Westchester Community College (U)
West Los Angeles College (U)
Wilkes Community College (U)
William Paterson University of New Jersey (G)
William Rainey Harper College (U)
Wright State University (U, G)
Youngstown State University (N)

Enterprise management and operation

Central Missouri State University (N)
Central Missouri State University (N)
Central Missouri State University (N)
Central Missouri State University (N)
Central Missouri State University (N)
Colorado State University-Pueblo (N)
Columbia College (U)
Dallas Baptist University (G)
Jamestown Community College (N)
Lakeland Community College (N)
Lamar State College–Port Arthur (N)
Lord Fairfax Community College (N)
Maryville University of Saint Louis (N)
Mitchell Technical Institute (N)
The Pennsylvania State University University Park Campus (U)
Schenectady County Community College (U)
University of Bridgeport (U)
University of the Incarnate Word (U)
University of Tulsa (G)
Wake Technical Community College (N)
William Paterson University of New Jersey (N, U)

Entomology

Iowa State University of Science and Technology (U)
University of Missouri–Columbia (U)

Entrepreneurship

Adams State College (N)
AIB College of Business (U)
Albuquerque Technical Vocational Institute (U)
American River College (U)
Asheville-Buncombe Technical Community College (N)
Ashworth College (N)
Berkeley College (U)
Berkeley College-New York City Campus (U)
Berkeley College-Westchester Campus (U)
Bridgewater State College (U)
Broward Community College (U)
California State University, Monterey Bay (U)
Capella University (N, G)
Central Texas College (U)
Champlain College (U)
Charter Oak State College (U)
Clark College (U)
Cleveland State University (N)
The Community College of Baltimore County (U)
Community College of Denver (U)
Cuyamaca College (U)
Daemen College (U)
Dakota County Technical College (U)
Dallas Baptist University (G)
Daniel Webster College (U)
Davenport University Online (U, G)
Des Moines Area Community College (U)
DeVry University Online (G)
Feather River Community College District (N)
Fulton-Montgomery Community College (N)
Goddard College (G)
Immaculata University (U)
Iowa Western Community College (U)
James Madison University (N)
Jones International University (U, G)
Lakeland Community College (N, U)
Lamar State College–Port Arthur (N)
Maryville University of Saint Louis (N)
Minnesota School of Business-Richfield (U)
MiraCosta College (U)
Mitchell Technical Institute (N)
Nassau Community College (U)
New Hampshire Community Technical College System (U)
New York Institute of Technology (U)
Normandale Community College (N)
Peninsula College (U)
Prairie State College (N)
Rend Lake College (N)
Ryerson University (U)
St. Edward's University (G)
Saint Joseph's College of Maine (G)
St. Petersburg College (U)
Santa Fe Community College (N)
Shippensburg University of Pennsylvania (G)
Sinclair Community College (U)
Southeast Arkansas College (U)
Stanford University (N)
State University of New York at Plattsburgh (U, G)
State University of New York College at Potsdam (N)
Stephens College (G)
Syracuse University (U)
Syracuse University (G)
Taylor University (N)
United States Sports Academy (G)
The University of Akron (N)
University of Bridgeport (U)
University of Maryland University College (G)

University of Notre Dame (N, G)
University of the Incarnate Word (U)
University of Tulsa (G)
University of Waterloo (U)
Vance-Granville Community College (N)
William Paterson University of New Jersey (N)
Worcester State College (N)
Youngstown State University (N)

Environmental control technologies

Athabasca University (N, U)
Bowling Green State University (U)
Immaculata University (U)
Ivy Tech State College–Southeast (U)
Jacksonville State University (U, G)
Judson College (U)
Lakeland Community College (N)
New Jersey Institute of Technology (N)
New York Institute of Technology (U)
Northeastern University (N, U, G)
Odessa College (U)
Oxnard College (U)
The Pennsylvania State University University Park Campus (G)
Shawnee State University (U)
The University of British Columbia (U)
The University of Findlay (G)

Environmental engineering

California National University for Advanced Studies (U, G)
Colorado State University (G)
Columbia University (N, G)
Georgia Institute of Technology (N, G)
Illinois Institute of Technology (G)
Northern Arizona University (U)
Oklahoma State University (G)
Old Dominion University (G)
Southern Methodist University (G)
University College of Cape Breton (U)
The University of Alabama in Huntsville (G)
The University of Texas at Arlington (G)
Worcester Polytechnic Institute (G)

Environmental health

Alcorn State University (G)
American Academy of Nutrition, College of Nutrition (U)
Louisiana State University and Agricultural and Mechanical College (U)
Mountain State University (U)
Skidmore College (U)
University College of Cape Breton (U)
The University of Iowa (U, G)
University of Maine (U)

Environmental science

Adams State College (U)
Bellevue Community College (U)
Bristol Community College (U)
Duquesne University (U, G)
Houston Community College System (U)
Ivy Tech State College–Northwest (U)
Johnson County Community College (U)
Louisiana State University and Agricultural and Mechanical College (U)
Maysville Community College (U)
Mountain Empire Community College (U)
Mountain State University (U)
North Country Community College (U)
Northern Arizona University (U)
Oregon State University (U)
The Pennsylvania State University University Park Campus (U)
Rochester Institute of Technology (U)
St. Cloud State University (U)
Seattle Central Community College (U)
University of Guelph (U)
The University of North Carolina at Chapel Hill (U)
University of Southern Indiana (U)
University of Waterloo (U)
Western Washington University (U)
Wilfrid Laurier University (U)

Environmental/environmental health engineering

Bowling Green State University (U)
Clackamas Community College (U)
Danville Area Community College (U)
East Central College (U)
Florida Gulf Coast University (U)
Glenville State College (U)
Harrisburg Area Community College (U)
Lakeland Community College (N)
New Mexico Institute of Mining and Technology (G)
Odessa College (U)
Oregon State University (G)
Pennsylvania College of Technology (U)
Royal Roads University (U)
St. Cloud State University (U)
Texas A&M University–Kingsville (G)
Texas Tech University (G)
Three Rivers Community College (U)
University of Colorado at Boulder (N, G)
University of Idaho (G)
University of Idaho (U)
University of Massachusetts Boston (U)
York Technical College (U)

European history

Bossier Parish Community College (U)
Brigham Young University (U)
Bristol Community College (U)
Broward Community College (U)
Bucks County Community College (U)
Burlington County College (U)
Clackamas Community College (U)
Floyd College (U)
Houston Community College System (U)
Jefferson College (U)
Louisiana State University and Agricultural and Mechanical College (U)
Maysville Community College (U)
Mercy College (U)
Mountain State University (U)
Mount Allison University (U)
Northwestern Michigan College (U)
Oregon State University (U)
Prairie Bible College (U)
Randolph Community College (U)
Richland Community College (U)
Southeast Community College, Lincoln Campus (U)
Texas Tech University (U)
University of Nebraska–Lincoln (U)
University of Nevada, Reno (U)
The University of North Carolina at Chapel Hill (U)
University of Waterloo (U)
Vance-Granville Community College (U)
Washington State University (U)
Western Washington University (U)

Experimental psychology

Acadia University (U)
Goddard College (G)
Naropa University (U)

Family and community studies

Alliance University College (U)
Athabasca University (N, U, G)
Bethany College of the Assemblies of God (U)
Bowling Green State University (U)
Brigham Young University (N)
Butler County Community College (U)
California State University, Chico (U)
California State University, Sacramento (U)
Central Wyoming College (N)
Chadron State College (U)
Chemeketa Community College (U)
Clackamas Community College (U)
Cleveland State University (N)
College for Lifelong Learning (U)
College of the Canyons (U)
Concordia University, St. Paul (U, G)
Delaware County Community College (U)
Eastern Illinois University (G)
Hillsborough Community College (U)

N–Noncredit; U–Undergraduate; G–Graduate

Jacksonville State University (G)
Lakeland Community College (N)
Louisiana Tech University (G)
Maryville University of Saint Louis (N)
Mississippi Delta Community College (U)
Modesto Junior College (U)
Mount Saint Vincent University (G)
Murray State University (U)
North Dakota State University (G)
Oklahoma State University (U)
Peninsula College (U)
Prescott College (U, G)
Raritan Valley Community College (U)
Reading Area Community College (U)
Ryerson University (U)
San Bernardino Valley College (U)
San Jacinto College District (U)
Santa Fe Community College (N)
Santa Rosa Junior College (U)
Saybrook Graduate School and Research Center (G)
Seminole Community College (U)
South Central Technical College (U)
Southeast Community College, Lincoln Campus (N)
South Piedmont Community College (U)
Southwestern Baptist Theological Seminary (G)
Southwestern Oregon Community College (U)
Taylor University (N)
Troy University–Florida Region (U)
The University of Alabama (U)
University of Alaska Fairbanks (U)
University of Bridgeport (N, U)
University of Georgia (U)
University of Idaho (U)
University of Missouri–Columbia (U, G)
University of Nebraska–Lincoln (U)
The University of North Carolina at Greensboro (U)
University of Southern Mississippi (U, G)
University of Waterloo (U)
University of Wisconsin–Madison (U, G)
Weber State University (U)
Yuba College (U)

Family and marriage counseling

Central Wyoming College (U)
Eastern Kentucky University (U)
Mountain State University (U)
Mount Wachusett Community College (U)

Family/consumer resource management

Asheville-Buncombe Technical Community College (N)
Cleveland State University (N)
College of the Siskiyous (U)
Eastern Illinois University (U, G)
East Los Angeles College (U)
Feather River Community College District (N)
Immaculata University (U)
Iowa State University of Science and Technology (G)
Lakeland Community College (N)
North Dakota State University (G)
The Ohio State University (U)
Oregon State University (N)
Palomar College (U)
Pasco-Hernando Community College (N)
Sam Houston State University (U)
Stephen F. Austin State University (U)
Taylor University (N)
Texas Tech University (G)
Texas Woman's University (U, G)
The University of Alabama (U, G)
University of Idaho (U)
University of Minnesota, Twin Cities Campus (U)
University of Missouri–Columbia (U)
University of Northern Iowa (U)
University of Wyoming (U)
Utah State University (U)
Western Michigan University (U, G)
Wichita State University (U)

Film studies

Brigham Young University (U)
Burlington County College (U)
College of San Mateo (U)
Marylhurst University (U)
Minneapolis College of Art and Design (U)
MiraCosta College (U)
Northern Virginia Community College (U)
Seattle Central Community College (U)
Southwest Missouri State University (U)
University of Alaska Fairbanks (U)
The University of British Columbia (U)
The University of South Dakota (U)
West Valley College (U)

Film/video and photographic arts

Asheville-Buncombe Technical Community College (N)
Auburn University (U)
Blackhawk Technical College (N)
Bossier Parish Community College (N, U)
Brevard Community College (U)
Charter Oak State College (U)
Cleveland State University (N)
College of the Canyons (U)
Delta College (U)
Feather River Community College District (N)
Flathead Valley Community College (U)
James Madison University (N)
Lakeland Community College (N, U)
Long Beach City College (U)
Massasoit Community College (U)
Nassau Community College (U)
North Carolina State University (U)
Northeastern Oklahoma Agricultural and Mechanical College (U)
Oregon State University (N)
Oxnard College (U)
The Richard Stockton College of New Jersey (U)
University of Bridgeport (U)
University of California, Los Angeles (G)
University of Cincinnati Raymond Walters College (U)
University of La Verne (N)
The University of North Carolina at Charlotte (N)
Western Michigan University (G)
William Rainey Harper College (U)
Worcester State College (N)

Finance

Adams State College (U)
The American College (U)
Anne Arundel Community College (U)
California National University for Advanced Studies (U)
Chaminade University of Honolulu (U)
Colorado State University (G)
Columbus State Community College (U)
Duke University (G)
Embry-Riddle Aeronautical University (U)
Florida Community College at Jacksonville (U)
Golden Gate University (U, G)
Hillsborough Community College (U)
Kansas State University (U)
Louisiana State University and Agricultural and Mechanical College (U)
Maharishi University of Management (N, G)
Marylhurst University (U, G)
Maysville Community College (U)
Mountain State University (U)
New York Institute of Technology (U)
Northern Virginia Community College (U)
Oklahoma State University (U)
Old Dominion University (U, G)
Palomar College (U)
Park University (U)
Pennsylvania College of Technology (U)
The Pennsylvania State University University Park Campus (U)
Pitt Community College (N)
Randolph Community College (U)
Regis University (U, G)

Sam Houston State University (U)
Southwest Missouri State University (U, G)
State University of New York Empire State College (U)
Stephens College (G)
Suffolk University (G)
Texas A&M University–Commerce (G)
Troy University Montgomery (U)
University of Dallas (G)
University of Guelph (U)
University of Houston–Downtown (U)
University of Minnesota, Twin Cities Campus (U)
University of Mississippi (U)
University of Nebraska–Lincoln (U)
The University of Texas at Arlington (G)
University of Toronto (N)
University of Wisconsin–La Crosse (G)
University of Wisconsin–Milwaukee (U)
University of Wisconsin–Platteville (U)
Washington State University (U)

Financial management and services

AIB College of Business (U)
Alliant International University (U)
The American College (U, G)
Ashworth College (N)
Athabasca University (N, U)
Black Hills State University (U)
Boston University (N)
Brenau University (G)
Bridgewater State College (N)
Butler County Community College (U)
Caldwell Community College and Technical Institute (N)
California State University, Dominguez Hills (N)
Carroll Community College (N)
Central Wyoming College (N)
Champlain College (U)
Chattanooga State Technical Community College (U)
Clark College (U)
College for Lifelong Learning (U)
Colorado Christian University (G)
Concordia University Wisconsin (U)
Dallas Baptist University (U, G)
Darton College (N, U)
Davenport University Online (U, G)
Delaware County Community College (U)
DeVry University Online (G)
Duke University (N)
Feather River Community College District (N)
Florida Atlantic University (G)
Florida Gulf Coast University (U)
Florida Institute of Technology (N)
Franklin Pierce College (U)
Franklin University (U)
Iowa Western Community College (U)
Jacksonville State University (U, G)
Jamestown Community College (N)
Kansas State University (N, U, G)
Lakeland Community College (N)
Lamar State College–Port Arthur (N)
Limestone College (U)
Louisiana State University in Shreveport (U)
Maharishi University of Management (U)
Manchester Community College (N)
Maysville Community College (N)
Metropolitan Community College (U)
Metropolitan State University (U)
Middlesex Community College (N)
Mount Saint Mary College (N)
New School University (G)
Nipissing University (U)
Northcentral University (G)
Northern Kentucky University (U)
Pace University (U)
Quinnipiac University (G)
Rockland Community College (U)
Rosalind Franklin University of Medicine and Science (N, G)
Sacred Heart University (G)
St. Cloud Technical College (N)
St. Petersburg College (U)
Santa Fe Community College (N)
Saybrook Graduate School and Research Center (N)
Schiller International University (G)
Simpson College (U)
South Piedmont Community College (U)
Spring Arbor University (U, G)
Stanford University (N)
State University of New York College at Potsdam (N)
Stephen F. Austin State University (U)
Strayer University (U)
Sullivan University (G)
Syracuse University (N)
Syracuse University (G)
The University of Akron (U)
The University of Alabama (U, G)
University of Dallas (G)
University of Idaho (U)
University of La Verne (U)
The University of Maine at Augusta (U)
University of Massachusetts Amherst (N)
University of New Orleans (U)
The University of North Carolina at Charlotte (N)
University of Notre Dame (N, G)
University of Oklahoma (U)
University of South Carolina (U)
The University of Texas at Dallas (G)
The University of Texas at Tyler (U)
University of Toronto (U)
University of Tulsa (G)
University of Utah (U)
University of Wisconsin–Eau Claire (N)
University of Wisconsin–Parkside (G)
University of Wisconsin–Platteville (U)
Valparaiso University (U)
Wake Technical Community College (N)
Western New England College (G)
West Virginia University (N)
William Rainey Harper College (U)

Financial services marketing operations

The American College (U)
Athabasca University (N, G)
Feather River Community College District (N)
Jacksonville State University (G)
James Madison University (N)
Lakeland Community College (N)
Lamar State College–Port Arthur (N)
Lord Fairfax Community College (U)
Middle Tennessee State University (N)
Odessa College (N)
St. Edward's University (G)
The University of Alabama (U)
University of the Incarnate Word (U)
William Rainey Harper College (U)

Fine arts and art studies

Adirondack Community College (U)
Allan Hancock College (U)
Alpena Community College (U)
Athabasca University (N, U)
Atlantic University (N, G)
Bethany College of the Assemblies of God (U)
Black Hills State University (U)
Brazosport College (U)
Butler County Community College (U)
Caldwell College (U)
Caldwell Community College and Technical Institute (U)
California State University, Hayward (U)
Campbell University (U)
Cape Cod Community College (U)
Cape Fear Community College (U)
Casper College (U)
Central Texas College (U)
Chemeketa Community College (U)
Clackamas Community College (U)
Concordia University, St. Paul (N)
Cossatot Community College of the University of Arkansas (U)

N–Noncredit; U–Undergraduate; G–Graduate

Dallas Baptist University (U)
Dawson Community College (U)
Delta College (U)
Drake University (U)
East Carolina University (G)
East Central College (U)
Eastern Michigan University (U)
East Los Angeles College (U)
Edison State Community College (U)
Fairleigh Dickinson University, Metropolitan Campus (U)
Fashion Institute of Technology (U)
Florida Atlantic University (G)
George C. Wallace Community College (U)
Glenville State College (U)
Goddard College (U, G)
Halifax Community College (U)
Hibbing Community College (U)
Independence Community College (U)
Indiana State University (U)
Indiana Wesleyan University (U)
Iowa Western Community College (U)
Irvine Valley College (U)
James Madison University (N)
John A. Logan College (U)
John F. Kennedy University (G)
John Tyler Community College (U)
Judson College (U)
Lakeland Community College (N)
Lake Superior College (U)
Lord Fairfax Community College (U)
Los Angeles Pierce College (U)
Louisiana State University and Agricultural and Mechanical College (U)
Maryland Institute College of Art (N, U)
Maysville Community College (U)
Middlesex Community College (N, U)
Middle Tennessee State University (N)
Minneapolis College of Art and Design (N, U)
MiraCosta College (U)
Mississippi State University (U)
Moberly Area Community College (U)
Montgomery County Community College (U)
Naugatuck Valley Community College (U)
Northeastern Oklahoma Agricultural and Mechanical College (U)
Northern New Mexico Community College (U)
North Hennepin Community College (U)
North Idaho College (U)
NorthWest Arkansas Community College (U)
Northwestern State University of Louisiana (U)
Oakland City University (U)
Ocean County College (U)
Oregon State University (N)
Oxnard College (U)
Pace University (U)
Palomar College (U)
The Pennsylvania State University University Park Campus (U)
Rappahannock Community College (U)
Rio Hondo College (U)
Rockland Community College (U)
Sacred Heart University (U)
Saint Leo University (U)
St. Petersburg College (U)
San Bernardino Valley College (U)
San Jacinto College District (U)
Savannah College of Art and Design (U, G)
Schoolcraft College (U)
Shawnee State University (U)
Snead State Community College (U)
Southeastern College of the Assemblies of God (U)
Spoon River College (U)
State University of New York at Plattsburgh (U)
Syracuse University (U)
Tacoma Community College (U)
Taylor University (U)
Tompkins Cortland Community College (U)
Trinity Western University (U)
Tri-State University (U)
University of Colorado at Denver (U)
University of Connecticut (U)
The University of Findlay (U)
University of Georgia (U)
University of Illinois (N)
The University of Iowa (U, G)
University of La Verne (N)
University of Massachusetts Boston (U)
University of Mississippi (U)
University of Missouri–Columbia (U)
University of Nebraska–Lincoln (U)
University of Nevada, Reno (U)
The University of North Carolina at Greensboro (U, G)
University of Sioux Falls (U)
University of Southern Indiana (U)
The University of Tennessee at Martin (U)
The University of Texas System (U)
University of the Incarnate Word (U)
University of West Florida (U)
University of Wisconsin Colleges (U)
University of Wisconsin–Superior (U)
Utah Valley State College (U)
Wilfrid Laurier University (U)
Wilkes Community College (U)
York University (U)

Fire protection

Albuquerque Technical Vocational Institute (U)
Allan Hancock College (U)
Bellevue Community College (U)
Blackhawk Technical College (N)
Bucks County Community College (N, U)
Butler County Community College (U)
Caldwell Community College and Technical Institute (U)
Carleton University (G)
Central Texas College (U)
Chemeketa Community College (U)
Cossatot Community College of the University of Arkansas (U)
Des Moines Area Community College (U)
Houston Community College System (U)
Ivy Tech State College–Northeast (U)
Jacksonville State University (G)
James Madison University (N)
Kansas City Kansas Community College (U)
Madison Area Technical College (U)
Middlesex Community College (U)
Oklahoma State University (N)
Oxnard College (U)
Palomar College (U)
Rio Hondo College (U)
San Jacinto College District (U)
Schenectady County Community College (U)
Southeast Arkansas College (U)
The University of Akron (U)
University of Illinois (N)
University of Maryland University College (U)
University of Missouri–Columbia (N)
The University of Texas at Tyler (U)
Utah Valley State College (U)

Fire science

Bossier Parish Community College (U)
Chattanooga State Technical Community College (U)
Honolulu Community College (U)
Ivy Tech State College–Central Indiana (U)
Ivy Tech State College–Northwest (U)
Louisiana State University and Agricultural and Mechanical College (U)
Louisiana State University at Eunice (U)
Oklahoma State University (U, G)
Worcester Polytechnic Institute (G)

Fire services administration

State University of New York Empire State College (U)

Fishing and fisheries sciences and management

Bossier Parish Community College (N)
Oregon State University (U)
University of Arkansas at Pine Bluff (U, G)

The University of Tennessee (U)
Virginia Polytechnic Institute and State University (U)

Floristry marketing operations

Ashworth College (N)
Blackhawk Technical College (N)
Bossier Parish Community College (N)
Lakeland Community College (N)

Food products retailing and wholesaling operations

Eastern Michigan University (U)
James Madison University (N)
North Georgia College & State University (N)
University of Wisconsin–Platteville (U)

Food sciences and technology

Allan Hancock College (U)
Bossier Parish Community College (U)
Brigham Young University (U)
Delaware County Community College (U)
Eastern Michigan University (U, G)
Illinois Institute of Technology (G)
Iowa State University of Science and Technology (U, G)
Jamestown Community College (N)
Kansas State University (N, U)
Maui Community College (U)
Middle Tennessee State University (U)
North Georgia College & State University (N)
Orange Coast College (U)
Santa Rosa Junior College (U)
Texas Tech University (U)
University of Missouri–Columbia (U, G)
University of Wisconsin–Madison (U)
University of Wisconsin–River Falls (G)

Foods and nutrition studies

Acadia University (U)
Adirondack Community College (U)
American Academy of Nutrition, College of Nutrition (N, U)
Athabasca University (N, U)
Auburn University (N)
Bowling Green State University (U)
Butler County Community College (U)
California State University, Sacramento (U)
Central Missouri State University (U)
Central Missouri State University (U)
Central Missouri State University (U)
Central Missouri State University (U)
Central Missouri State University (U)
Central Oregon Community College (U)
Chemeketa Community College (U)
Clackamas Community College (U)
Cleveland State University (N)
Colorado State University (U)
Columbia Union College (U)
Columbus State Community College (U)
Danville Community College (U)
Davenport University Online (U)
Des Moines Area Community College (U)
East Carolina University (G)
Eastern Michigan University (U, G)
East Los Angeles College (U)
Education Direct Center for Degree Studies (N)
Fairmont State University (U)
Feather River Community College District (N)
Harrisburg Area Community College (U)
Heartland Community College (U)
Hibbing Community College (U)
Hillsborough Community College (U)
Honolulu Community College (U)
Houston Community College System (U)
Howard College (U)
Illinois Eastern Community Colleges, Frontier Community College (U)
Immaculata University (N, U, G)
Indiana University of Pennsylvania (U)
Iowa State University of Science and Technology (G)
Jacksonville State University (U)
James Madison University (N)
Jefferson College of Health Sciences (U)
Kansas State University (U)
Lamar State College–Port Arthur (U)
Long Beach City College (U)
Louisiana Tech University (G)
Mesa Community College (U)
Middlesex Community College (U)
North Dakota State University (U)
North Georgia College & State University (N)
Oklahoma State University (U)
Orange Coast College (U)
Oregon State University (G)
Palomar College (U)
The Pennsylvania State University University Park Campus (U)
Rosalind Franklin University of Medicine and Science (N, G)
Ryerson University (U)
Southwest Wisconsin Technical College (U)
Texas Tech University (U)
The University of Alabama (U)
University of Arkansas at Little Rock (U)
University of Bridgeport (U, G)
The University of British Columbia (U)
University of Cincinnati Raymond Walters College (U, G)
University of Delaware (N, U, G)
University of Florida (N, U)
University of Georgia (U)
University of Massachusetts Amherst (U)
University of Minnesota, Twin Cities Campus (U)
University of Missouri–Columbia (U, G)
University of Nevada, Reno (U)
The University of North Carolina at Chapel Hill (U)
University of Northern Colorado (U)
University of Southern Mississippi (U)
University of Utah (U)
University of Wyoming (U)
Utah State University (U)
William Paterson University of New Jersey (U)
Wisconsin Indianhead Technical College (N, U)
Youngstown State University (U)

Foreign languages and literatures

Acadia University (U)
Adams State College (N)
Asheville-Buncombe Technical Community College (N, U)
Athabasca University (N, U)
Bainbridge College (N)
Baptist Theological Seminary at Richmond (G)
Bethany College of the Assemblies of God (U)
Bethune-Cookman College (U)
Bossier Parish Community College (U)
Brenau University (U)
Bridgewater State College (G)
Caldwell Community College and Technical Institute (N)
California State University, Monterey Bay (U)
Central Wyoming College (N)
Coconino Community College (N)
Columbia Union College (U)
Cumberland County College (U)
Daemen College (U)
Darton College (U)
Fairleigh Dickinson University, Metropolitan Campus (U)
Feather River Community College District (N)
Florida Atlantic University (G)
Goddard College (U)
Golden West College (U)
Harford Community College (U)
Hebrew College (N, U, G)
Illinois State University (U, G)
Immaculata University (U)

N–Noncredit; U–Undergraduate; G–Graduate

Irvine Valley College (U)
James Madison University (N, U)
Jamestown Community College (N)
Kansas City Kansas Community College (U)
Kentucky State University (U)
Lansing Community College (U)
Lenoir Community College (U)
Louisiana State University and Agricultural and Mechanical College (U)
Maui Community College (U)
Maysville Community College (N)
Mesa Community College (U)
Middlesex Community College (U)
Middle Tennessee State University (N)
Millersville University of Pennsylvania (U, G)
Montgomery County Community College (U)
Mountain Empire Community College (U)
North Georgia College & State University (U)
North Hennepin Community College (U)
Northwest Missouri State University (U)
Odessa College (N)
The Ohio State University (U)
Ohio University (U)
Oregon State University (N)
Pace University (U)
The Pennsylvania State University University Park Campus (U)
Riverside Community College (N, U)
Sacramento City College (U)
Sacred Heart University (U)
St. Petersburg College (U)
Santa Fe Community College (N, U)
Snead State Community College (U)
Southwestern Baptist Theological Seminary (G)
Southwestern Oregon Community College (U)
State University of New York College at Potsdam (N)
Strayer University (U)
Tacoma Community College (U)
Tarleton State University (N)
Triton College (U)
Tunxis Community College (U)
The University of Alabama (U)
University of Alaska Fairbanks (U)
University of Colorado at Denver (U)
University of Denver (G)
University of Georgia (U)
University of Idaho (U)
University of Massachusetts Boston (U)
University of Minnesota, Twin Cities Campus (U)
University of Mississippi (U)
University of Nevada, Reno (U)
The University of North Carolina at Chapel Hill (N)
University of North Dakota (U)
University of South Carolina (U)
University of Southern Indiana (U)
University of Southern Mississippi (U, G)
The University of Tennessee (U)
The University of Tennessee at Martin (U)
The University of Texas at Austin (U)
The University of Texas System (U)
University of the Incarnate Word (U)
University of Toronto (N)
University of Waterloo (U)
University of Wisconsin–La Crosse (U)
University of Wisconsin–Madison (U)
University of Wisconsin–Parkside (U)
Virginia Polytechnic Institute and State University (U)
Wake Technical Community College (N)
Wayne State College (U)
Weber State University (U)
William Rainey Harper College (U)
Wright State University (U)

Foreign languages and literatures, other

Blackhawk Technical College (N)
Central Wyoming College (U)
Clarion University of Pennsylvania (U)
Cleveland State University (N)
Darton College (U)
Florida Atlantic University (U)
Hudson County Community College (N)
John Tyler Community College (U)
Middlesex Community College (U)
Oxnard College (U)
Sacred Heart University (U)
Santa Rosa Junior College (U)
Shawnee State University (U)
Tarleton State University (N)
University of California, Los Angeles (G)
University of Maine (U)
University of Missouri–Columbia (U)
The University of North Carolina at Chapel Hill (U)
University of Southern Indiana (U)
University of Toronto (N)
University of Waterloo (U)
Yuba College (U)

Forest production and processing

Mount Wachusett Community College (N)
The University of British Columbia (U)
University of Minnesota, Twin Cities Campus (U, G)

Forestry and related sciences

Glenville State College (U)
James Madison University (N)
Louisiana Tech University (U)
North Carolina State University (U)
Northern Arizona University (U)
Oregon State University (U)
Stephen F. Austin State University (G)
The University of British Columbia (U)
Virginia Polytechnic Institute and State University (G)

Forestry

The Ohio State University (U)
Oregon State University (U)
The University of British Columbia (U)

French

Andrews University (U)
Burlington County College (U)
California State University, Sacramento (U)
College of San Mateo (U)
Louisiana State University and Agricultural and Mechanical College (U)
Mount Saint Vincent University (U)
Nassau Community College (U)
Northern Virginia Community College (U)
Oklahoma State University (U)
The Pennsylvania State University University Park Campus (U)
Pierce College (U)
Skidmore College (U)
The University of British Columbia (U)
University of Guelph (U)
The University of Iowa (U)
University of Minnesota, Twin Cities Campus (U)
University of Missouri–Columbia (U)
University of Nevada, Reno (U)
The University of North Carolina at Chapel Hill (U)
The University of North Carolina at Greensboro (G)
University of Toronto (N)
University of Waterloo (U)
Western Washington University (U)
West Valley College (U)
Wilfrid Laurier University (U)

Funeral services and mortuary science

John Tyler Community College (U)
Mt. Hood Community College (U)
St. Petersburg College (U)

Gaming/sports officiating

Bossier Parish Community College (N)
California State University, Monterey Bay (U)
James Madison University (N)
University of Southern Mississippi (U)

General retailing/wholesaling

Adams State College (N)
Berkeley College (U)
Berkeley College-New York City Campus (U)
Chadron State College (U)
Columbus State Community College (U)
Feather River Community College District (N)
Lakeland Community College (N)
Lamar State College–Port Arthur (N)
Limestone College (U)
Minnesota State College–Southeast Technical (N)
Okaloosa-Walton College (U)
Ryerson University (U)
University of the Incarnate Word (U)

General teacher education

Bemidji State University (U)
Brenau University (U)
Bucks County Community College (U)
Caldwell College (U)
Capella University (G)
Chadron State College (U)
Community College of Denver (U)
Darton College (U)
Eastern Michigan University (G)
Fairmont State University (U)
Fayetteville State University (U)
Feather River Community College District (N)
Fort Hays State University (U)
Glenville State College (U)
Goddard College (U, G)
Halifax Community College (N)
Hamline University (G)
Immaculata University (G)
Inter American University of Puerto Rico, San Germán Campus (U)
Jacksonville State University (U)
James Madison University (N)
John F. Kennedy University (G)
La Sierra University (U, G)
Limestone College (U)
Mississippi State University (U)
Mount Saint Mary College (U)
Mount Saint Vincent University (U)
North Dakota State University (G)
North Georgia College & State University (N, U, G)
Northwest Christian College (U)
Northwestern State University of Louisiana (U)
Oregon State University (G)
Pasco-Hernando Community College (U)
St. Clair County Community College (U)
Saint Mary-of-the-Woods College (U)
Seattle Pacific University (G)
Southwest Missouri State University (G)
Stephen F. Austin State University (G)
Tarleton State University (U, G)
Université Sainte-Anne (U)
The University of Akron (N, U, G)
The University of Alabama (U)
University of Great Falls (G)
University of Houston–Downtown (G)
The University of Iowa (G)
University of Maryland University College (G)
University of North Dakota (U)
University of Southern Indiana (U)
The University of Tennessee at Martin (N)
The University of Texas at Tyler (U)
The University of Texas of the Permian Basin (G)
University of Wisconsin–River Falls (G)
Utah State University (G)
Virginia Polytechnic Institute and State University (U)
Waycross College (U)
Western Washington University (U)
Western Wyoming Community College (U)
Winston-Salem State University (U)
Wright State University (U)

Geography

Alvin Community College (U)
American River College (U)
Andrews University (U)
Anne Arundel Community College (U)
Athabasca University (U)
Auburn University (U)
Bellevue Community College (U)
Bemidji State University (U)
Berkeley College-New York City Campus (U)
Berkeley College-Westchester Campus (U)
Bethany College of the Assemblies of God (U)
Black Hills State University (U)
Bowling Green State University (U)
Bridgewater State College (U)
Brigham Young University (U)
Bristol Community College (U)
Broward Community College (U)
Campbell University (U)
Carleton University (U)
Carroll Community College (U)
Casper College (U)
Central Oregon Community College (U)
Central Wyoming College (U)
Chadron State College (U)
Champlain College (U)
Charter Oak State College (U)
Chattanooga State Technical Community College (U)
Chemeketa Community College (U)
Clatsop Community College (U)
Cleveland State University (U)
Coconino Community College (U)
Collin County Community College District (U)
Colorado Mountain College District System (U)
Colorado State University-Pueblo (U)
Columbia Basin College (U)
Columbia Union College (U)
Columbus State Community College (U)
The Community College of Baltimore County (U)
Community College of Denver (U)
Copiah-Lincoln Community College–Natchez Campus (U)
Danville Area Community College (U)
Delaware County Community College (U)
Des Moines Area Community College (U)
Dickinson State University (U)
Eastern Kentucky University (U)
Eastern Michigan University (U)
Eastern Oregon University (U)
Erie Community College (U)
Fairmont State University (U)
Florida Community College at Jacksonville (U)
Gaston College (U)
George Mason University (U)
Goddard College (U)
Harrisburg Area Community College (U)
Houston Community College System (U)
Indiana State University (U)
Iowa Western Community College (U)
Jacksonville State University (U, G)
James Madison University (N)
Jefferson College (U)
Lakeland Community College (U)
Lake Superior College (U)
Lansing Community College (U)
Limestone College (U)
Long Beach City College (U)
Louisiana State University and Agricultural and Mechanical College (U)
Marshall University (U)
Martin Luther College (U)
Massasoit Community College (U)
Maysville Community College (U)
Memorial University of Newfoundland (U)
Mesalands Community College (U)
Middlesex Community College (U)
Mississippi Delta Community College (U)
Moberly Area Community College (U)

N–Noncredit; U–Undergraduate; G–Graduate

Modesto Junior College (U)
Montana State University–Billings (U)
Montgomery County Community College (U)
Mott Community College (U)
Mountain State University (U)
Mount Saint Mary College (U)
Murray State University (U)
Northampton County Area Community College (U)
North Country Community College (U)
Northeastern Oklahoma Agricultural and Mechanical College (U)
Northern Arizona University (U)
Northern Virginia Community College (U)
Northwest Missouri State University (U, G)
Oakland City University (U)
Ohio University (U)
Oklahoma State University (U)
Park University (U)
The Pennsylvania State University University Park Campus (N)
Pratt Community College (U)
Queen's University at Kingston (U)
Riverland Community College (U)
Riverside Community College (U)
Rockland Community College (U)
Ryerson University (U)
Sacramento City College (U)
St. Clair County Community College (U)
St. Edward's University (U)
St. Petersburg College (U)
Sam Houston State University (U)
San Bernardino Valley College (U)
Seattle Central Community College (U)
Seattle Pacific University (G)
Seminole Community College (U)
Seward County Community College (U)
Shawnee State University (U)
Shelton State Community College (U)
Shippensburg University of Pennsylvania (U)
Skidmore College (U)
Snead State Community College (U)
South Dakota School of Mines and Technology (U)
Southeast Arkansas College (U)
Southeast Community College, Lincoln Campus (U)
Southern Illinois University Carbondale (U)
State University of New York at New Paltz (U)
Sul Ross State University (U)
Syracuse University (U)
Tacoma Community College (U)
Taylor University (U)
Teikyo Post University (U)
Temple College (U)
Texas State University-San Marcos (U, G)
Troy University Montgomery (U)
The University of Akron (U)
The University of Alabama (U)
University of Alaska Fairbanks (U)
University of Arkansas at Little Rock (U)
The University of British Columbia (U)
University of California, Riverside (N)
University of Central Arkansas (G)
University of Cincinnati (U)
University of Colorado at Colorado Springs (U)
University of Colorado at Denver (U)
University of Connecticut (U)
University of Florida (U)
University of Georgia (U)
University of Guelph (U)
University of Idaho (U)
University of Missouri–Columbia (U)
University of Nebraska–Lincoln (U)
University of Nevada, Reno (U)
The University of North Carolina at Chapel Hill (U)
University of North Dakota (U)
University of Northern Colorado (U)
University of Northern Iowa (U, G)
University of Oklahoma (U)
University of Oregon (U)
University of Saskatchewan (U)
University of Sioux Falls (U)
University of South Carolina (U)
University of South Carolina Spartanburg (U)
The University of South Dakota (U)
University of Southern Mississippi (U, G)
The University of Tennessee (U)
The University of Texas at Austin (U)
The University of Texas at Tyler (U)
The University of Texas of the Permian Basin (U)
University of Utah (U)
University of Washington (U)
University of Waterloo (U)
University of Wisconsin Colleges (U)
University of Wisconsin–Madison (G)
University of Wisconsin–Platteville (U)
University of Wisconsin–Platteville (U)
University of Wyoming (U)
Utah State University (U)
Virginia Polytechnic Institute and State University (U, G)
Weber State University (U)
Westchester Community College (U)
Western Michigan University (U)
Whatcom Community College (U)
Wichita State University (U)
Wilfrid Laurier University (U)
William Paterson University of New Jersey (U)
William Rainey Harper College (U)

Geological and related sciences

Acadia University (U)
Athabasca University (N, U)
Bellevue Community College (U)
Bowling Green State University (U)
Brigham Young University (U)
Broome Community College (U)
Broward Community College (U)
California State University, Monterey Bay (U)
California State University, Sacramento (U)
Cascadia Community College (U)
Chemeketa Community College (U)
Cleveland State University (U)
Coastal Bend College (U)
Colorado State University-Pueblo (U)
Community College of Denver (U)
Cuyamaca College (U)
Dallas Baptist University (U)
Eastern Wyoming College (U)
El Camino College (U)
Florida International University (U)
Gaston College (U)
Harrisburg Area Community College (U)
Hillsborough Community College (U)
Honolulu Community College (U)
Howard Community College (U)
Indiana University of Pennsylvania (U)
Jacksonville State University (U, G)
James Madison University (N)
Lake Superior College (U)
Lewis-Clark State College (U)
Louisiana State University and Agricultural and Mechanical College (U)
Mesalands Community College (U)
Middle Tennessee State University (U)
MiraCosta College (U)
Modesto Junior College (U)
Montgomery County Community College (U)
Mountain Empire Community College (U)
Murray State University (U)
Nassau Community College (U)
Northampton County Area Community College (U)
Northern Arizona University (U)
Oklahoma State University (U)
Oregon State University (U)
Oxnard College (U)
Park University (U)
Peninsula College (U)
Pierce College (U)
Portland State University (U)
Rio Hondo College (U)
San Bernardino Valley College (U)
Santa Fe Community College (U)

Seminole Community College (U)
Shoreline Community College (U)
Taft College (U)
Temple College (U)
Tri-State University (U)
University of Arkansas at Little Rock (U)
University of Cincinnati (U)
University of Colorado at Denver (U)
University of Georgia (U)
University of La Verne (N)
University of Minnesota, Twin Cities Campus (U)
University of Missouri–Columbia (U)
University of New Orleans (U)
The University of North Carolina at Chapel Hill (U)
The University of North Carolina at Greensboro (U)
University of Northern Colorado (U)
University of Oklahoma (U)
University of Oregon (U)
University of Saskatchewan (U)
The University of Tennessee at Martin (U)
The University of Texas System (U)
University of Washington (U)
University of Waterloo (U)
University of Wisconsin–Madison (U)
University of Wisconsin–River Falls (U)
Weber State University (U)
Wright State University (G)
Youngstown State University (U)

Germanic languages and literatures

Brigham Young University (U)
Darton College (U)
James Madison University (N)
Jefferson College (U)
Louisiana State University and Agricultural and Mechanical College (U)
Marian College of Fond du Lac (U)
Oklahoma State University (U)
The Pennsylvania State University University Park Campus (U)
Queen's University at Kingston (U)
The University of Akron (U)
University of Central Arkansas (U)
University of Georgia (U)
University of Minnesota, Twin Cities Campus (U)
University of Missouri–Columbia (U)
University of Nevada, Reno (U)
The University of Tennessee (U)
University of Toronto (N)
University of Waterloo (U)
Wilfrid Laurier University (U)

Gerontology

Acadia University (U)
Adams State College (N)
The American College (U)
American River College (U)
Athabasca University (N)
Bowling Green State University (G)
Butler County Community College (U)
California State University, Sacramento (U)
The College of St. Scholastica (U)
College of The Albemarle (N)
Columbus State University (G)
Feather River Community College District (N)
Florida Gulf Coast University (U)
Jefferson College of Health Sciences (U)
Lakeland Community College (N)
Liberty University (U)
Limestone College (U)
Madonna University (N, U)
Massasoit Community College (N)
Middlesex Community College (N)
Mountain State University (U)
Mount Saint Vincent University (N)
Naropa University (U)
North Georgia College & State University (U, G)
The Ohio State University (N)
The Pennsylvania State University University Park Campus (U)
Randolph Community College (N)
The Richard Stockton College of New Jersey (U)
Ryerson University (U)
Sacramento City College (U)
Sacred Heart University (G)
Saint Mary-of-the-Woods College (U)
Saint Mary-of-the-Woods College (U)
Saybrook Graduate School and Research Center (G)
Shippensburg University of Pennsylvania (U, G)
Slippery Rock University of Pennsylvania (U)
State University of New York at Oswego (G)
University of Alaska Fairbanks (U)
The University of Arizona (G)
University of Arkansas at Little Rock (U, G)
University of Colorado at Colorado Springs (U)
The University of Iowa (U, G)
University of La Verne (N)
University of Maryland University College (U)
University of Massachusetts Boston (G)
University of Northern Colorado (U, G)
University of Southern Indiana (U)
University of Utah (U)
University of Vermont (U)
University of Washington (U, G)
University of Waterloo (U)
University of Wisconsin–Parkside (N)
Weber State University (U)
Western Carolina University (U, G)
Wichita State University (U)
William Paterson University of New Jersey (U)

Graphic and printing equipment operators

Danville Community College (U)
Murray State University (U)
Riverside Community College (N, U)
Santa Rosa Junior College (U)

Graphic design/commercial art/illustration

Maryland Institute College of Art (U)

Greek languages and literatures (modern)

Baptist Theological Seminary at Richmond (G)
Bethany College of the Assemblies of God (U)
Eugene Bible College (U)
Northwestern College (U)
University of Washington (U)
University of Waterloo (U)
Western Washington University (U)

Health and medical administrative services

Alpena Community College (U)
American Public University System (U)
Arapahoe Community College (U)
Athabasca University (U)
Auburn University Montgomery (N)
Boise State University (U, G)
Bossier Parish Community College (U)
Bowling Green State University (U)
Brenau University (G)
Bridgewater State College (N)
Broome Community College (U)
Bucks County Community College (U)
California State University, Chico (U)
California State University, Dominguez Hills (N)
Century College (N, U)
Chattanooga State Technical Community College (U)
Cincinnati State Technical and Community College (U)
Cleveland State University (G)

N–Noncredit; U–Undergraduate; G–Graduate

The College of St. Scholastica (U, G)
Colorado State University-Pueblo (N)
Columbus State Community College (U)
Creighton University (G)
Daemen College (U)
Dallas County Community College District (U)
Darton College (U)
Davenport University Online (U, G)
Des Moines Area Community College (U)
Edgecombe Community College (N, U)
Education Direct Center for Degree Studies (N)
Feather River Community College District (N)
Florida Gulf Coast University (U)
Florida National College (U)
Forrest Junior College (U)
Fort Hays State University (U)
Gogebic Community College (U)
Hudson County Community College (U)
Jamestown Community College (N)
Johnson County Community College (N)
Keiser College (U)
Linn-Benton Community College (U)
Louisiana State University in Shreveport (G)
Miami Dade College (U)
Minnesota School of Business-Richfield (U)
Minot State University–Bottineau Campus (U)
Mountain State University (G)
Mt. Hood Community College (U)
New York Institute of Technology (U, G)
North Dakota State College of Science (U)
Northeastern Oklahoma Agricultural and Mechanical College (N)
Northern Arizona University (G)
Orange Coast College (U)
Oregon State University (N, U, G)
Quinebaug Valley Community College (U)
Rio Hondo College (U)
Saint Joseph's College of Maine (U, G)
Salve Regina University (N, G)
Santa Fe Community College (N, U)
Seminole Community College (N, U)
Southeast Community College, Beatrice Campus (U)
State University of New York Institute of Technology (U, G)
State University of New York Institute of Technology (U, G)
State University of New York Institute of Technology (U, G)
State University of New York Institute of Technology (U, G)
Stephens College (U)
Sullivan University (G)
Tacoma Community College (U)
Texas State University-San Marcos (N, U)
The University of Akron (U)
University of Houston–Clear Lake (G)
University of Idaho (U)
University of Illinois at Chicago (N)
University of La Verne (G)
University of Maryland University College (G)
University of Minnesota, Twin Cities Campus (U)
University of Missouri–Columbia (U)
University of Missouri–Columbia (G)
The University of North Carolina at Greensboro (N)
University of North Dakota (N)
University of Northern Colorado (U)
University of Southern Indiana (U)
University of Southern Mississippi (N)
Weber State University (U)
William Paterson University of New Jersey (N)
Youngstown State University (N)

Health and medical assistants

Ashworth College (N)
Bainbridge College (N)
Bossier Parish Community College (U)
Brenau University (U)
Brevard Community College (U)
Bridgewater State College (N)
Butler County Community College (U)
Central Wyoming College (N)
Century College (N)
Chattanooga State Technical Community College (U)
Chemeketa Community College (U)
Cincinnati State Technical and Community College (U)
Darton College (U)
Education Direct Center for Degree Studies (N)
Florida National College (U)
Forrest Junior College (U)
Frederick Community College (U)
Gaston College (U)
Grossmont College (U)
Harrisburg Area Community College (U)
Hudson County Community College (N)
Iowa Western Community College (U)
Jones College (U)
Keiser College (U)
Martin Community College (U)
Maui Community College (U)
Middle Tennessee State University (N)
Minnesota School of Business–Brooklyn Center (U)
Minot State University–Bottineau Campus (U)
Montgomery Community College (N)
North Dakota State University (N)
Northern Arizona University (U)
North Idaho College (U)
Orange Coast College (U)
Randolph Community College (N, U)
Santa Rosa Junior College (U)
Seminole Community College (U)
Shawnee State University (U)
Sinclair Community College (U)
Southwestern Oregon Community College (U)
Southwest Wisconsin Technical College (U)
Tacoma Community College (U)
The University of Akron (N)
University of Northwestern Ohio (U)
University of Southern Mississippi (N)
The University of Texas System (G)
Western Wyoming Community College (U)
William Paterson University of New Jersey (N)
William Rainey Harper College (U)
Youngstown State University (N)

Health and medical diagnostic and treatment services

Brenau University (G)
Central Wyoming College (N)
Eastern Kentucky University (G)
James Madison University (N)
Jefferson College of Health Sciences (N, U)
Manchester Community College (N)
NorthWest Arkansas Community College (U)
Oregon Institute of Technology (U)
Randolph Community College (N)
Tacoma Community College (U)
University of Illinois at Chicago (N)
University of Missouri–Columbia (N)
The University of Texas Medical Branch (G)
William Rainey Harper College (U)

Health and medical preparatory programs

Athabasca University (U, G)
Bellingham Technical College (N)
Brenau University (U)
Caldwell Community College and Technical Institute (N)
Century College (U)
Chattanooga State Technical Community College (U)
Community College of Denver (U)
Daemen College (U)
Darton College (U)
Edgecombe Community College (U)
Florida Metropolitan University–Brandon Campus (U)

Health and medical preparatory programs

Hibbing Community College (U)
James Madison University (N)
Jefferson College of Health Sciences (U)
Johnson County Community College (N)
Kirkwood Community College (U)
Lake Superior College (U)
Mesa Community College (U)
Naugatuck Valley Community College (N)
Northeastern Oklahoma Agricultural and Mechanical College (U)
Northern Arizona University (U)
Rockland Community College (U)
Saddleback College (U)
Seminole Community College (U)
Southern Illinois University Carbondale (U)
Southwestern College (U)
Southwest Wisconsin Technical College (U)
Texas A&M International University (U)
University of Southern Mississippi (N)
West Los Angeles College (U)

Health and physical education/fitness

Adirondack Community College (U)
Allan Hancock College (U)
Allen County Community College (U)
Anne Arundel Community College (U)
Asheville-Buncombe Technical Community College (U)
Austin Peay State University (U, G)
Bemidji State University (U)
Brigham Young University (U)
Broward Community College (U)
Bucks County Community College (U)
Butler County Community College (U)
Butler County Community College (U)
California State University, Sacramento (U)
California University of Pennsylvania (G)
Cape Fear Community College (U)
Carl Albert State College (U)
Cayuga County Community College (U)
Central Texas College (U)
Central Washington University (G)
Central Wyoming College (N, U)
Chemeketa Community College (U)
Clackamas Community College (U)
Clarion University of Pennsylvania (U)
Clark College (U)
Clatsop Community College (U)
Cleveland State University (N)
College of San Mateo (U)
College of The Albemarle (U)
College of the Canyons (U)
College of the Siskiyous (U)
Columbia Basin College (U)
Corning Community College (U)
Cossatot Community College of the University of Arkansas (U)
County College of Morris (U)
Cuyamaca College (U)
Dallas Baptist University (U)
Danville Community College (U)
Darton College (U)
Delta College (U)
Eastern Oregon University (U)
Eastern Wyoming College (U)
East Los Angeles College (U)
El Camino College (U)
Floyd College (U)
Fort Hays State University (U)
Frederick Community College (N, U)
Glenville State College (U)
Howard Community College (U)
Illinois Eastern Community Colleges, Frontier Community College (U)
Indiana State University (G)
Iowa Western Community College (U)
Jacksonville State University (U, G)
James Madison University (N, U)
Jefferson College (U)
Jefferson College of Health Sciences (U)
Jefferson Davis Community College (U)
John Jay College of Criminal Justice of the City University of New York (U)
John Wood Community College (U)
Lakeland Community College (N, U)
Lake Region State College (U)
Linn-Benton Community College (U)
Louisiana State University and Agricultural and Mechanical College (U)
Louisiana State University in Shreveport (U)
Middle Tennessee State University (U)
Millersville University of Pennsylvania (U, G)
Modesto Junior College (U)
Montana State University–Bozeman (G)
Montgomery County Community College (U)
Mountain Empire Community College (U)
Nassau Community College (U)
Naugatuck Valley Community College (N)
Northampton County Area Community College (U)
North Carolina State University (U)
North Dakota State College of Science (U)
NorthWest Arkansas Community College (U)
Northwestern State University of Louisiana (U)
Ocean County College (U)
Oklahoma State University (U)
Pasco-Hernando Community College (U)
Patrick Henry Community College (U)
Paul D. Camp Community College (U)
Peninsula College (U)
The Pennsylvania State University University Park Campus (U)
Rappahannock Community College (U)
Rend Lake College (U)
Rio Hondo College (U)
Shawnee State University (U)
Snead State Community College (U)
Southeast Arkansas College (U)
Southwest Missouri State University (U)
State University of New York at Plattsburgh (U)
Tarleton State University (U, G)
Texas Woman's University (U, G)
Triton College (U)
United States Sports Academy (N, G)
University of Arkansas at Little Rock (U)
University of California, Los Angeles (G)
University of Houston (U)
University of Idaho (U)
University of Missouri–Columbia (U)
University of Nebraska–Lincoln (U)
University of Northern Colorado (G)
University of Northern Iowa (U)
University of Oklahoma (U)
University of Sioux Falls (U)
University of Southern Mississippi (U, G)
The University of Tennessee at Martin (U)
The University of Texas at Tyler (U)
The University of Texas of the Permian Basin (U, G)
Utah State University (G)
Utah Valley State College (U)
Walters State Community College (U)
Waubonsee Community College (U)
Wayne State College (U)
Westchester Community College (U)
West Los Angeles College (U)
Youngstown State University (U)

Health products and services marketing operations

The American College (U)
Charter Oak State College (U)
Lakeland Community College (N)
Saint Joseph's College of Maine (G)
Southwest Missouri State University (G)

Health professions and related sciences, other

American Academy of Nutrition, College of Nutrition (N)
Athabasca University (N, U, G)
Brenau University (U, G)
Brevard Community College (U)
Brunswick Community College (U)
California Institute of Integral Studies (G)
California University of Pennsylvania (G)

N–Noncredit; U–Undergraduate; G–Graduate

Chattanooga State Technical Community College (U)
Chemeketa Community College (U)
Cincinnati State Technical and Community College (U)
Cleveland State University (N, U, G)
Coconino Community College (U)
Colorado Mountain College District System (U)
Columbia Union College (U)
Columbus State Community College (U)
Creighton University (G)
Daemen College (U)
Dallas County Community College District (U)
Danville Area Community College (U)
Darton College (U)
Davenport University Online (U)
DeVry University Online (G)
Drake University (U, G)
East Central College (U)
Eastern Kentucky University (U)
Florida Atlantic University (U, G)
Florida National College (U)
Fontbonne University (U)
Forrest Junior College (N)
Fort Hays State University (U)
Fulton-Montgomery Community College (N)
George Mason University (G)
Heart of Georgia Technical College (U)
Hillsborough Community College (U)
Illinois Eastern Community Colleges, Lincoln Trail College (U)
Illinois State University (U)
Inter American University of Puerto Rico, San Germán Campus (U)
Jacksonville State University (U, G)
James Madison University (U)
Jefferson College of Health Sciences (U)
Lakeland Community College (N)
Lake Superior College (U)
Lamar State College–Port Arthur (U)
Lorain County Community College (N)
Louisiana Tech University (U)
Massasoit Community College (N)
Mesa Community College (U)
MGH Institute of Health Professions (G)
Miami Dade College (N)
MiraCosta College (N)
Mississippi State University (G)
Mitchell Technical Institute (N)
Montana Tech of The University of Montana (U, G)
Naugatuck Valley Community College (U)
Nebraska Methodist College (U, G)
Northeastern Oklahoma Agricultural and Mechanical College (N)
Northeastern University (U)
Northern Arizona University (U)
Northern Kentucky University (U)
North Georgia College & State University (N)
Orange Coast College (U)
Pasco-Hernando Community College (N)
Passaic County Community College (U)
Pennsylvania College of Technology (U)
Pierce College (N)
The Richard Stockton College of New Jersey (U)
Riverside Community College (N)
Rockland Community College (U)
Rosalind Franklin University of Medicine and Science (N, G)
Ryerson University (U)
Sacramento City College (U)
Sacred Heart University (U, G)
St. Joseph's College, Suffolk Campus (U)
San Jacinto College District (U)
Santa Fe Community College (N)
Santa Rosa Junior College (U)
Seminole Community College (U)
Shelton State Community College (U)
Shoreline Community College (U)
Sinclair Community College (N)
Southeast Arkansas College (U)
Southeast Community College, Beatrice Campus (U)
Southeast Community College, Lincoln Campus (N)
South Piedmont Community College (U)
Spoon River College (U)
State University of New York Institute of Technology (U, G)
State University of New York Institute of Technology (U, G)
State University of New York Institute of Technology (U, G)
State University of New York Institute of Technology (U, G)
Tacoma Community College (U)
Teachers College Columbia University (N, G)
Texas Woman's University (U)
Touro University International (U, G)
The University of Akron (G)
The University of Alabama (U, G)
University of Alaska Fairbanks (U)
University of Arkansas at Little Rock (U)
University of Central Arkansas (G)
University of Cincinnati Raymond Walters College (U)
University of Colorado at Colorado Springs (U, G)
University of Connecticut (N, U, G)
University of Delaware (G)
University of Illinois (G)
University of Illinois at Chicago (G)
University of Maryland, Baltimore County (G)
University of Massachusetts Lowell (G)
University of Medicine and Dentistry of New Jersey (U, G)
University of Missouri–Columbia (N, U)
University of New Hampshire (G)
University of New Orleans (U)
University of North Dakota (N)
University of Northern Colorado (U)
University of North Florida (U, G)
University of St. Augustine for Health Sciences (N)
University of St. Francis (U)
University of South Carolina (U)
University of Southern Indiana (G)
University of Southern Mississippi (U)
The University of Texas at Tyler (U, G)
The University of Texas Medical Branch (U)
The University of Texas Southwestern Medical Center at Dallas (U)
The University of Texas System (U, G)
University of Wisconsin–La Crosse (U)
University of Wyoming (G)
Washtenaw Community College (U)
William Paterson University of New Jersey (N, U)
William Rainey Harper College (U)
Worcester State College (G)
Youngstown State University (U, G)

Health services administration

College for Lifelong Learning (U)
Dakota State University (U)
Franklin University (U)
Golden Gate University (G)
Montana State University–Billings (G)
Mountain State University (U)
Park University (U)
The Pennsylvania State University University Park Campus (U)
Texas State University-San Marcos (U)
University of Central Florida (U, G)
University of Dallas (G)
University of Missouri–Columbia (U)
University of St. Francis (G)

Heating, air conditioning and refrigeration mechanics and repairers

Ashworth College (N)
Augusta Technical College (N)
Flathead Valley Community College (U)
Lakeland Community College (N)
Mitchell Technical Institute (N)
Orange Coast College (U)
Oxnard College (U)

Hebrew

Brigham Young University (U)
University of Waterloo (U)

Historic preservation, conservation and architectural history

Bucks County Community College (U)
Feather River Community College District (N)
Lakeland Community College (N)
University of La Verne (N)
The University of North Carolina at Greensboro (G)

History of science and technology

Oregon State University (U)
Pennsylvania College of Technology (U)
Roger Williams University (U)

History

Acadia University (U)
Allan Hancock College (U)
Allen County Community College (U)
Alliance University College (U, G)
Alvin Community College (U)
American College of Computer & Information Sciences (U)
American Public University System (U, G)
American River College (U)
Andrews University (U)
Anne Arundel Community College (U)
Arkansas State University–Beebe (U)
Arkansas Tech University (U)
Asheville-Buncombe Technical Community College (U)
Assemblies of God Theological Seminary (G)
Athabasca University (N, U, G)
Azusa Pacific University (U)
Bellevue Community College (U)
Bemidji State University (U)
Berkeley College (U)
Berkeley College-New York City Campus (U)
Berkeley College-Westchester Campus (U)
Bethany College of the Assemblies of God (U)
Bethune-Cookman College (U)
Bismarck State College (U)
Boise State University (U)
Bossier Parish Community College (U)
Bowling Green State University (U)
Brazosport College (U)
Brenau University (U)
Brevard Community College (U)
Bridgewater State College (U)
Briercrest Distance Learning (N, U, G)
Brigham Young University (N, U)
Bristol Community College (U)
Broome Community College (U)
Bucks County Community College (U)
Butler County Community College (U)
Butler County Community College (U)
Caldwell Community College and Technical Institute (U)
California State University, Chico (U)
California State University, Sacramento (U)
Cape Cod Community College (U)
Cape Fear Community College (U)
Carl Albert State College (U)
Carleton University (U)
Carroll Community College (U)
Cascadia Community College (U)
Cayuga County Community College (U)
Cedarville University (U)
Central Oregon Community College (U)
Central Texas College (U)
Central Virginia Community College (U)
Central Wyoming College (N, U)
Chadron State College (U, G)
Chaminade University of Honolulu (U)
Champlain College (U)
Charter Oak State College (U)
Chattanooga State Technical Community College (U)
Chemeketa Community College (U)
Chesapeake College (U)
Citrus College (U)
Clatsop Community College (U)
Clinton Community College (U)
Coastal Bend College (U)
Coconino Community College (U)
Coleman College (U)
College of DuPage (U)
College of The Albemarle (U)
College of the Canyons (U)
College of the Siskiyous (U)
College of the Southwest (U)
Collin County Community College District (U)
Colorado Christian University (U)
Colorado Mountain College District System (U)
Colorado State University (U)
Colorado State University-Pueblo (U)
Columbia Basin College (U)
Columbia College (U)
Columbia Union College (U)
Columbus State Community College (U)
The Community College of Baltimore County (U)
Community College of Denver (U)
Concordia University Wisconsin (U)
Copiah-Lincoln Community College–Natchez Campus (U)
Corning Community College (U)
Cossatot Community College of the University of Arkansas (U)
County College of Morris (U)
Cumberland County College (U)
Cuyamaca College (U)
Dakota County Technical College (U)
Dallas Baptist University (U)
Dallas County Community College District (U)
Daniel Webster College (U)
Danville Area Community College (U)
Darton College (U)
Davenport University Online (U)
Delaware County Community College (U)
Denver Seminary (G)
Des Moines Area Community College (U)
Dickinson State University (U)
Drake University (U, G)
East Central College (U)
Eastern Michigan University (U)
Eastern Shore Community College (U)
Eastern Washington University (U)
East Los Angeles College (U)
Edgecombe Community College (U)
Elizabeth City State University (U)
Elizabethtown College (U)
Eugene Bible College (U)
Everett Community College (U)
Evergreen Valley College (U)
Fairleigh Dickinson University, Metropolitan Campus (U)
Fairmont State University (U)
Fayetteville State University (U, G)
Feather River Community College District (N, U)
Florida Community College at Jacksonville (U)
Florida Gulf Coast University (U)
Florida Metropolitan University–Brandon Campus (U)
Fort Hays State University (U)
Frederick Community College (U)
Fulton-Montgomery Community College (U)
George C. Wallace Community College (U)
Goddard College (U)
Gogebic Community College (U)
Golden West College (U)
Grand View College (U)
Grantham University (U)
Grossmont College (U)
Hamline University (U)
Harrisburg Area Community College (U)
Heartland Community College (U)
Hibbing Community College (U)
Honolulu Community College (U)

N–Noncredit; U–Undergraduate; G–Graduate

Hope International University (N, U)
Horry-Georgetown Technical College (U)
Houston Community College System (U)
Howard Community College (U)
Illinois Eastern Community Colleges, Wabash Valley College (U)
Illinois State University (U)
Immaculata University (U)
Indiana State University (U)
Indiana University–Purdue University Fort Wayne (U)
Indiana Wesleyan University (U)
Iowa Western Community College (U)
Ivy Tech State College–Kokomo (U)
Ivy Tech State College–Northwest (U)
Ivy Tech State College–Southcentral (U)
Ivy Tech State College–Wabash Valley (U)
Ivy Tech State College–Whitewater (U)
Jacksonville State University (U)
James Madison University (N)
Jefferson Community College (U)
The Jewish Theological Seminary (N, U, G)
John A. Logan College (U)
Judson College (U)
Judson College (U)
Kansas City Kansas Community College (U)
Lakeland Community College (N, U)
Lake Region State College (U)
Lake Superior College (U)
Lamar University (U)
Lansing Community College (U)
Lenoir Community College (U)
LeTourneau University (U)
Limestone College (U)
Lock Haven University of Pennsylvania (U)
Long Beach City College (U)
Lord Fairfax Community College (U)
Louisiana State University and Agricultural and Mechanical College (U)
Louisiana State University in Shreveport (U)
Louisiana Tech University (G)
Madonna University (U)
Manchester Community College (N)
Marshall University (U)
Massasoit Community College (U)
Maui Community College (U)
Maysville Community College (U)
Memorial University of Newfoundland (U)
Mesa Community College (U)
Mesalands Community College (U)
Metropolitan Community College (U)
Middlesex Community College (U)
MiraCosta College (U)
Mississippi Delta Community College (U)
Moberly Area Community College (U)
Modesto Junior College (U)
Montana State University–Billings (U)
Montgomery County Community College (U)
Mott Community College (U)
Mountain Empire Community College (U)
Mountain State University (U)
Mount Allison University (U)
Mount Saint Vincent University (U)
Murray State University (U)
Nassau Community College (U)
New Hampshire Community Technical College System (U)
North Carolina State University (U)
North Central Texas College (U)
Northeastern Oklahoma Agricultural and Mechanical College (U)
Northeast State Technical Community College (U)
Northern Arizona University (U)
Northern New Mexico Community College (U)
North Harris Montgomery Community College District (U)
NorthWest Arkansas Community College (U)
Northwestern College (U)
Northwestern Michigan College (U)
Northwestern State University of Louisiana (U)
Oakland City University (U)
Ocean County College (U)
Ohio University (U)
Oklahoma State University (U)
Oklahoma Wesleyan University (U)
Oregon State University (U)
Owensboro Community and Technical College (U)
Oxnard College (U)
Pace University (U)
Park University (U)
Pasco-Hernando Community College (U)
Patrick Henry College (U)
Paul D. Camp Community College (U)
Peninsula College (U)
The Pennsylvania State University University Park Campus (U)
Pierce College (U)
Portland State University (U)
Pratt Community College (U)
Prescott College (U, G)
Queen's University at Kingston (U)
Quinebaug Valley Community College (U)
Quinnipiac University (U)
Randolph Community College (U)
Rappahannock Community College (U)
Raritan Valley Community College (U)
Regis University (U)
Rend Lake College (U)
Rio Hondo College (U)
Riverland Community College (U)
Riverside Community College (U)
Rockland Community College (U)
Rowan Technical College (U)
Ryerson University (U)
Sacramento City College (U)
Sacred Heart University (U)
St. Clair County Community College (U)
St. Cloud State University (U)
St. Edward's University (U)
St. John's University (U)
St. Joseph's College, Suffolk Campus (U)
Saint Mary-of-the-Woods College (U)
Saint Mary-of-the-Woods College (U)
St. Petersburg College (U)
Salem Community College (U)
Santa Fe Community College (N)
Schenectady County Community College (U)
Schiller International University (U)
Seattle Pacific University (G)
Seminole Community College (U)
Seton Hill University (U)
Seward County Community College (U)
Shawnee State University (U)
Shelton State Community College (U)
Shoreline Community College (U)
Sinclair Community College (U)
Snead State Community College (U)
Southeast Arkansas College (U)
Southeast Community College, Beatrice Campus (U)
Southeastern Community College (U)
Southern Illinois University Carbondale (U)
Southwestern Assemblies of God University (U)
Southwestern College (U)
Southwest Missouri State University (G)
Spring Arbor University (U)
State University of New York at New Paltz (U)
State University of New York at Oswego (U)
Stephens College (U)
Strayer University (U)
Sul Ross State University (U)
Syracuse University (N, U, G)
Taft College (U)
Tarleton State University (U, G)
Taylor University (U)
Taylor University (U)
Teachers College Columbia University (N, G)
Teikyo Post University (U)
Temple College (U)
Texas A&M International University (U)
Texas State University-San Marcos (U)
Texas Tech University (U)
Texas Woman's University (U)

Three Rivers Community College (U)
Tri-State University (U)
Triton College (U)
Troy University Montgomery (U)
Tunxis Community College (U)
Université Sainte-Anne (U)
The University of Alabama (U)
University of Alaska Fairbanks (U, G)
University of Arkansas at Little Rock (U, G)
University of Bridgeport (U)
The University of British Columbia (U)
University of Central Arkansas (U)
University of Cincinnati (U)
University of Colorado at Colorado Springs (U)
University of Colorado at Denver (U, G)
University of Florida (U)
University of Georgia (U)
University of Great Falls (U)
University of Hawaii–West Oahu (U)
University of Houston (U)
University of Houston–Downtown (U)
University of Houston–Victoria (U)
University of Idaho (U)
University of Illinois (U)
The University of Iowa (U, G)
University of La Verne (N, U)
The University of Maine at Augusta (U)
University of Massachusetts Boston (U)
University of Minnesota, Morris (U)
University of Minnesota, Twin Cities Campus (U)
University of Mississippi (U)
University of Missouri–Columbia (U, G)
University of Nebraska at Omaha (U)
University of Nebraska–Lincoln (U)
University of Nevada, Reno (U)
University of New Orleans (U)
The University of North Carolina at Chapel Hill (U)
The University of North Carolina at Greensboro (U)
University of North Dakota (U)
University of Northern Iowa (U, G)
University of Oklahoma (U)
University of St. Francis (U)
University of Saskatchewan (U)
University of Sioux Falls (U)
University of South Carolina (U)
University of South Carolina Sumter (U)
The University of South Dakota (U)
University of Southern Indiana (U)
The University of Tennessee (U)
The University of Tennessee at Martin (U)
The University of Texas at Austin (U)
The University of Texas at Tyler (U)
The University of Texas of the Permian Basin (U)
The University of Texas System (U)
University of the Incarnate Word (U)
University of Utah (U)
University of Washington (U)
University of Waterloo (U)
University of West Florida (U)
University of Wisconsin Colleges (U)
University of Wisconsin–La Crosse (N)
University of Wisconsin–River Falls (U, G)
University of Wyoming (U)
Upper Iowa University (U)
Utah State University (U)
Utah Valley State College (U)
Utah Valley State College (U)
Vance-Granville Community College (U)
Virginia Polytechnic Institute and State University (N, U)
Walters State Community College (U)
Washington State University (U)
Waubonsee Community College (U)
Wayland Baptist University (U)
Weber State University (U)
Westchester Community College (U)
Western Michigan University (G)
Western Washington University (U)
West Los Angeles College (U)
West Virginia University at Parkersburg (U)
Whatcom Community College (U)
Wichita State University (U)
Wilfrid Laurier University (U)
Wilkes Community College (U)
William Paterson University of New Jersey (U, G)
William Rainey Harper College (U)
Winston-Salem State University (U)
Worcester State College (G)
Wright State University (U)
York Technical College (U)
York University (U)
Yuba College (U)

Home economics business services
The University of Alabama (U)

Home economics, general
Chadron State College (U)
Delaware County Community College (U)
Feather River Community College District (N)
Frederick Community College (N)
James Madison University (N)
MiraCosta College (N)
Mississippi Delta Community College (U)
Texas Woman's University (U)
The University of Alabama (U)

Home economics, other
Chadron State College (U)
Mesa Community College (U)
Tarleton State University (U)
The University of Alabama (U)

Home/office products marketing
Asheville-Buncombe Technical Community College (N)
Massasoit Community College (N)
University of the Incarnate Word (U)

Horticulture science
Kansas State University (U, G)
The Ohio State University (U, G)
Rend Lake College (U)
University of Maine (U)
University of Nebraska–Lincoln (U)

Horticulture services operations and management
Cincinnati State Technical and Community College (U)
Clackamas Community College (U)
Colorado State University (U)
County College of Morris (U)
Feather River Community College District (N)
Lakeland Community College (N)
Minot State University–Bottineau Campus (U)
Oklahoma State University (U)
Texas Tech University (U)
University of California, Riverside (N)
University of Georgia (U)
University of Saskatchewan (N)
Virginia Polytechnic Institute and State University (N, U, G)

Hospitality services management
Arkansas Tech University (U)
Ashworth College (N)
Baltimore City Community College (U)
Black Hills State University (G)
Bossier Parish Community College (N)
Central Texas College (U)
Chemeketa Community College (U)
College of the Canyons (U)
Colorado Mountain College District System (U)
Des Moines Area Community College (U)
East Carolina University (U)
Eastern Michigan University (U)
Horry-Georgetown Technical College (U)
Hudson County Community College (N)
Indiana University of Pennsylvania (U)
Ivy Tech State College–Central Indiana (U)
Ivy Tech State College–Northwest (U)

N–Noncredit; U–Undergraduate; G–Graduate

Lakeland Community College (N)
Louisiana State University at Eunice (U)
MiraCosta College (U)
New York Institute of Technology (U)
Normandale Community College (U)
North Dakota State University (U)
Northern Arizona University (U)
Orange Coast College (U)
The Pennsylvania State University University Park Campus (U)
Roosevelt University (U)
Ryerson University (U)
Schenectady County Community College (U)
Schiller International University (G)
Southwest Wisconsin Technical College (U)
Stephen F. Austin State University (U)
Sullivan University (G)
Sullivan University (U)
Tompkins Cortland Community College (U)
The University of Akron (U)
The University of Alabama (U)
University of Delaware (N, U)
University of Houston (U, G)
University of Massachusetts Amherst (U)
University of Nevada, Reno (U)
The University of North Carolina at Chapel Hill (U)
The University of North Carolina at Charlotte (N)
Virginia Polytechnic Institute and State University (U)

Hospitality/recreation marketing

Bossier Parish Community College (N)
California State University, Hayward (U)
Central Texas College (U)
Chemeketa Community College (U)
College of The Albemarle (N)
East Carolina University (U)
James Madison University (N)
Lakeland Community College (N)
Madison Area Technical College (U)
Orange Coast College (U)
Seton Hill University (N)
The University of Akron (U)
The University of Alabama (U)

Housing studies

Chadron State College (U)
Mount Saint Vincent University (N)

Human resources management

AIB College of Business (U)
The American College (U, G)
American College of Computer & Information Sciences (U)
American Public University System (U)
Asheville-Buncombe Technical Community College (N)
Athabasca University (N, U, G)
Berkeley College (U)
Berkeley College-New York City Campus (U)
Berkeley College-Westchester Campus (U)
Black Hills State University (U)
Boise State University (U, G)
Boise State University (G)
Bossier Parish Community College (N)
Brenau University (U)
Bristol Community College (N)
Butler County Community College (U)
California National University for Advanced Studies (N, U, G)
California State University, Dominguez Hills (N)
Capella University (N, U, G)
Central Texas College (U)
Chadron State College (U, G)
Champlain College (U)
Charter Oak State College (U)
Clemson University (G)
Coleman College (U)
Columbus State Community College (U)
The Community College of Baltimore County (U)
Dakota State University (U)
Dallas Baptist University (G)
Dallas County Community College District (U)
Daniel Webster College (U)
Davenport University Online (U, G)
Delaware County Community College (U)
DeVry University Online (G)
Drake University (U, G)
Eastern Michigan University (N, U, G)
Eastern Washington University (U)
Edison State Community College (N, U)
Elizabeth City State University (U)
Elizabethtown College (U)
Feather River Community College District (N)
Florida Institute of Technology (G)
Florida Metropolitan University–Brandon Campus (U)
Florida State University (G)
Forrest Junior College (U)
Franklin University (U)
Gonzaga University (G)
Grantham University (U)
Houston Community College System (U)
Indiana State University (U)
Jacksonville State University (G)
James Madison University (N, U)
Jamestown Community College (N)
Jefferson College of Health Sciences (U)
Jones International University (U)
Kansas State University (G)
Lamar State College–Port Arthur (N)
Lawrence Technological University (G)
Limestone College (U)
Maharishi University of Management (U)
Maryville University of Saint Louis (N)
Massasoit Community College (N)
Mesalands Community College (U)
Metropolitan State University (U)
Middlesex Community College (U)
Middle Tennessee State University (N, U)
Minnesota State College–Southeast Technical (N)
Modesto Junior College (U)
Montgomery Community College (U)
Mount Saint Vincent University (U)
National University (G)
Neumann College (U)
New School University (G)
New York Institute of Technology (U, G)
Nipissing University (U)
Normandale Community College (U)
Northcentral University (G)
North Country Community College (U)
Northern Arizona University (G)
Ohio University (U)
Park University (U)
The Pennsylvania State University University Park Campus (N, U)
Prescott College (U)
Rend Lake College (N)
Rosalind Franklin University of Medicine and Science (N, G)
Royal Roads University (G)
Ryerson University (U)
St. Edward's University (U, G)
Saint Leo University (U)
Saint Mary-of-the-Woods College (U)
Saint Mary-of-the-Woods College (U)
Saint Paul College–A Community & Technical College (U)
Salve Regina University (N)
Schiller International University (U, G)
Seton Hill University (N, U)
Simpson College (U)
Southwestern Assemblies of God University (U)
Southwestern College (U)
Southwest Wisconsin Technical College (U)
Spring Arbor University (U)
State University of New York Institute of Technology (U, G)
State University of New York Institute of Technology (U, G)
State University of New York Institute of Technology (U, G)

State University of New York Institute of Technology (U, G)
Suffolk University (G)
Sullivan University (G)
Tarleton State University (N, G)
Taylor University (N)
Teachers College Columbia University (N, G)
Texas A&M University (G)
The University of Akron (N, U, G)
University of Connecticut (G)
The University of Findlay (U, G)
University of Georgia (N)
University of Hawaii–West Oahu (U)
University of Houston–Clear Lake (G)
University of Illinois (G)
University of Illinois at Springfield (U)
The University of Maine at Augusta (U)
University of Maryland University College (U, G)
University of Missouri–Columbia (U, G)
The University of North Carolina at Charlotte (N)
University of North Dakota (N)
University of Oklahoma (G)
The University of Texas at Tyler (U, G)
University of Toronto (N, U)
University of Tulsa (G)
University of West Florida (N)
University of Wisconsin–Madison (U, G)
University of Wisconsin–Platteville (U)
University of Wisconsin–Platteville (U)
Upper Iowa University (U)
Utah State University (U, G)
Virginia Polytechnic Institute and State University (U)
Walters State Community College (U)
Waubonsee Community College (U)
Wayne State College (U, G)
Western Carolina University (U, G)
Western Michigan University (G)
Worcester State College (N)
York University (U)
Yuba College (U)

Human services

Athabasca University (N, U, G)
Bismarck State College (U)
Broome Community College (U)
Capella University (N, G)
Chadron State College (U)
College of DuPage (U)
College of The Albemarle (N)
Corning Community College (U)
Dawson Community College (U)
Delaware Technical & Community College, Jack F. Owens Campus (U)
Delaware Technical & Community College, Stanton/Wilmington Campus (U)
Florida Gulf Coast University (U)
Fort Hays State University (U)
Frederick Community College (U)
Gonzaga University (G)
Houston Community College System (U)
Ivy Tech State College–Central Indiana (U)
Ivy Tech State College–Columbus (U)
Ivy Tech State College–Eastcentral (U)
Ivy Tech State College–North Central (U)
Ivy Tech State College–Northeast (U)
Ivy Tech State College–Northwest (U)
Ivy Tech State College–Southwest (U)
Ivy Tech State College–Wabash Valley (U)
Ivy Tech State College–Whitewater (U)
James Madison University (N)
Jamestown Community College (N)
Kirkwood Community College (U)
Limestone College (U)
Louisiana State University and Agricultural and Mechanical College (G)
Metropolitan State University (U)
Mount Wachusett Community College (U)
Murray State University (G)
New Mexico State University (U)
Oxnard College (U)
Prescott College (U, G)
St. Edward's University (U, G)
Saint Joseph's College of Maine (U)
Saint Mary-of-the-Woods College (U)
Saint Mary-of-the-Woods College (U)
Santiago Canyon College (U)
Southeast Community College, Beatrice Campus (U)
Southern Christian University (N, U, G)
Southwestern Oregon Community College (U)
Stanly Community College (U)
Sullivan University (G)
Tacoma Community College (U)
Université Sainte-Anne (N)
The University of Akron (G)
University of Bridgeport (U)
University of Connecticut (G)
University of Great Falls (U)
The University of Maine at Augusta (U)
University of Missouri–Columbia (U, G)
University of Northern Colorado (U)
University of North Florida (G)
Upper Iowa University (U)
Vance-Granville Community College (U)
Waubonsee Community College (U)
Western Washington University (U)
Worcester State College (N)

Individual and family development studies

Asheville-Buncombe Technical Community College (N)
Athabasca University (N, U)
Chadron State College (U)
Cleveland State University (N)
Colorado State University (U)
Eastern Illinois University (U)
Horry-Georgetown Technical College (U)
Iowa State University of Science and Technology (U)
Jacksonville State University (G)
The King's College and Seminary (N, U)
Miami Dade College (U)
Mount Saint Vincent University (N)
Naropa University (N)
North Dakota State University (G)
Oklahoma State University (U)
Pacific Oaks College (U, G)
The Pennsylvania State University University Park Campus (U)
Saddleback College (U)
Salem Community College (U)
Saybrook Graduate School and Research Center (G)
The University of Alabama (U)
University of Bridgeport (N)
University of Delaware (U)
University of Missouri–Columbia (U)
University of Southern Mississippi (G)
Western Baptist College (U)

Industrial and organizational psychology

AIB College of Business (U)
Athabasca University (N, U, G)
Berkeley College (U)
Berkeley College-New York City Campus (U)
Berkeley College-Westchester Campus (U)
Capella University (N, G)
Chadron State College (U, G)
Kansas State University (G)
Middle Tennessee State University (N)
Montana State University–Billings (U)
Northcentral University (G)
The Pennsylvania State University University Park Campus (U)
Saybrook Graduate School and Research Center (N, G)
Schiller International University (G)
Tunxis Community College (U)
The University of Texas of the Permian Basin (U)
Upper Iowa University (U)

N–Noncredit; U–Undergraduate; G–Graduate

Industrial engineering

Cleveland State University (G)
Colorado State University (G)
Columbia University (N, G)
Georgia Institute of Technology (N, G)
Illinois Institute of Technology (G)
Kansas State University (G)
New York Institute of Technology (U)
Northeastern University (G)
Oklahoma State University (G)
Stanford University (N)
The University of Alabama in Huntsville (G)
The University of Arizona (G)
University of Central Florida (U, G)
University of Nebraska–Lincoln (G)
The University of Texas at Arlington (G)
University of Waterloo (G)
York Technical College (U)

Industrial equipment maintenance and repairers

Bismarck State College (U)
Bismarck State College (N)
Ivy Tech State College–Whitewater (U)
Lord Fairfax Community College (N)
Madison Area Technical College (U)
Western Wyoming Community College (U)

Industrial production technologies

Bemidji State University (U, G)
Bismarck State College (N)
Delta College (U)
East Carolina University (U, G)
Eastern Illinois University (U)
Edison State Community College (U)
Kent State University (U)
Southwestern College (U)
Southwest Missouri State University (G)
The University of Texas at Tyler (U)

Industrial/manufacturing engineering

Cleveland State University (G)
East Carolina University (U, G)
East Central College (U)
Eastern Illinois University (G)
Edison State Community College (U)
Iowa State University of Science and Technology (G)
Lehigh University (G)
Maysville Community College (U)
Middle Tennessee State University (N)
Moberly Area Community College (U)
New Mexico State University (G)
Roger Williams University (U)
Stanford University (N)
Texas Tech University (G)
University of Michigan (N, G)
The University of Tennessee at Martin (N)
University of Washington (G)
University of Wisconsin–Platteville (G)
University of Wisconsin–Platteville (G)
Wayne State College (U, G)

Information sciences and systems

Albuquerque Technical Vocational Institute (U)
American College of Computer & Information Sciences (U, G)
Arkansas Tech University (G)
Aspen University (G)
Athabasca University (G)
Bismarck State College (U)
Bowling Green State University (U)
Brenau University (U)
Brevard Community College (U)
Bridgewater State College (N)
Brigham Young University (U)
Bristol Community College (N, U)
Caldwell College (U)
Capitol College (G)
Central Oregon Community College (U)
Central Virginia Community College (U)
Chadron State College (U)
Champlain College (G)
Chemeketa Community College (U)
Cincinnati State Technical and Community College (U)
Cleveland State University (U)
College of The Albemarle (N)
Connecticut State University System (U)
Dakota State University (U, G)
Dallas Baptist University (G)
Delaware County Community College (U)
DePaul University (G)
Drake University (U, G)
East Carolina University (U)
Everglades University (U, G)
Fairleigh Dickinson University, Metropolitan Campus (N, G)
Fairmont State University (U)
Florida Atlantic University (G)
Florida Institute of Technology (G)
Fort Hays State University (U)
Franklin University (U)
Gaston College (U)
Grantham University (U)
Harrisburg Area Community College (U)
Hibbing Community College (U)
Indiana University of Pennsylvania (U)
Jacksonville State University (U, G)
James Madison University (N)
Jones College (U)
Juniata College (U)
Kent State University (U)
Lamar State College–Port Arthur (N)
Lawrence Technological University (G)
Limestone College (U)
Louisiana State University at Eunice (U)
Marist College (G)
Marymount University (G)
Maryville University of Saint Louis (N, U)
Maui Community College (U)
Metropolitan State University (U)
National University (U)
New Hampshire Community Technical College System (U)
New Jersey Institute of Technology (N, U, G)
New York Institute of Technology (G)
North Carolina State University (G)
Northeastern Oklahoma Agricultural and Mechanical College (N)
Northeastern University (G)
North Hennepin Community College (N)
Nova Southeastern University (G)
Peirce College (U)
The Pennsylvania State University University Park Campus (U)
Regis University (U)
The Richard Stockton College of New Jersey (G)
Royal Roads University (G)
Shippensburg University of Pennsylvania (G)
Southern Illinois University Carbondale (U)
Southern Methodist University (G)
Southwest Missouri State University (N)
State University of New York at Oswego (U, G)
Strayer University (U, G)
Suffolk University (G)
Syracuse University (G)
Tacoma Community College (U)
Tarleton State University (G)
Taylor University (N, U)
Taylor University (U)
Texas A&M University–Texarkana (U)
Tunxis Community College (N)
The University of Akron (N, G)
University of Maryland (G)
University of Maryland, Baltimore County (G)
University of Maryland University College (U)
University of Massachusetts Lowell (U)
University of Missouri–Columbia (G)
The University of Montana–Missoula (G)
University of Nebraska at Omaha (U)
The University of North Carolina at Charlotte (G)
University of Oregon (G)
The University of Texas at Dallas (G)
The University of Texas System (U)
University of the Incarnate Word (U)
University of Toronto (U)

Non-Degree-Related Course Subject Areas
Information sciences and systems

University of Tulsa (G)
University of Washington (N)
University of Wisconsin–Eau Claire (N)
University of Wisconsin–Milwaukee (U)
Vance-Granville Community College (U)
Walsh College of Accountancy and Business Administration (U)
West Valley College (U)
William Rainey Harper College (U)

Inorganic chemistry

Illinois Institute of Technology (G)
Sam Houston State University (U)

Institutional food workers and administrators

Albuquerque Technical Vocational Institute (U)
Blackhawk Technical College (N)
Central Texas College (U)
College of the Canyons (U)
North Georgia College & State University (N)
The Pennsylvania State University University Park Campus (U)
Southeast Community College, Beatrice Campus (U)

Insurance marketing operations

Blackhawk Technical College (N)
Taylor University (N)

Insurance/risk management

The American College (U, G)
Indiana State University (U)
John Wood Community College (N)
Mountain State University (U)
Sam Houston State University (U)
University of Nebraska–Lincoln (U)
University of Toronto (N)
University of Waterloo (U)

Interior design

New York Institute of Technology (U)

International and comparative education

North Georgia College & State University (U, G)

International business

AIB College of Business (U)
Albuquerque Technical Vocational Institute (U)
American Public University System (U)
Athabasca University (N, G)
Berkeley College (U)
Berkeley College-New York City Campus (U)
Berkeley College-Westchester Campus (U)
Black Hills State University (U)
Brenau University (U, G)
Brevard Community College (U)
Broome Community College (U)
California National University for Advanced Studies (N, U)
California State University, Monterey Bay (U)
Capella University (N, G)
Champlain College (U)
Community College of Denver (U)
Dallas Baptist University (G)
Davenport University Online (U)
Duke University (G)
Ferris State University (U)
Florida Metropolitan University–Brandon Campus (U)
Howard Community College (U)
Immaculata University (U)
James Madison University (N)
Jones College (U)
Jones International University (U, G)
Lawrence Technological University (G)
Limestone College (U)
Long Beach City College (U)
Maharishi University of Management (N, G)
Massasoit Community College (U)
Mercy College (U)
Metropolitan State University (U)
Minnesota School of Business-Richfield (U)
Missouri Southern State University (U)
Mountain State University (U)
New York Institute of Technology (U)
Nipissing University (U)
Northcentral University (G)
Oxnard College (U)
Pace University (U)
Park University (G)
Pennsylvania College of Technology (U)
Pitt Community College (U)
Regis University (G)
Rio Hondo College (U)
Sacred Heart University (U)
Saddleback College (U)
Sauk Valley Community College (U)
Schiller International University (U, G)
Shippensburg University of Pennsylvania (U, G)
Spring Arbor University (G)
State University of New York Empire State College (U)
Strayer University (U)
Suffolk University (G)
Sullivan University (G)
Texas A&M University–Texarkana (U)
Thunderbird, The Garvin School of International Management (G)
Tompkins Cortland Community College (U)
Touro University International (G)
Tufts University (G)
University College of Cape Breton (U)
University of Dallas (G)
The University of Findlay (U)
University of Houston–Downtown (U)
University of Illinois (G)
University of Management and Technology (U)
University of Maryland University College (G)
University of Missouri–Columbia (U, G)
University of Nebraska–Lincoln (U, G)
The University of Texas at Dallas (G)
University of Tulsa (G)
University of Washington (U)
University of Wisconsin–Platteville (U)
Upper Iowa University (N, U)
Washington State University (U)
William Rainey Harper College (U)
Worcester Polytechnic Institute (G)

International relations and affairs

American Public University System (U, G)
Athabasca University (N, U, G)
Brevard Community College (U)
Drake University (U)
Ferris State University (N)
Jones College (U)
Miami Dade College (U)
New Jersey City University (U)
North Georgia College & State University (U)
Salve Regina University (G)
Schiller International University (U)
Syracuse University (U)
Texas A&M University (G)
Tufts University (G)
University of Massachusetts Boston (U, G)
University of Missouri–Columbia (U)
University of Vermont (U)
West Los Angeles College (U)

Internet and world wide web

Alvin Community College (U)
The Art Institute Online (U)
Beaufort County Community College (N)
Bellevue Community College (U)
Bismarck State College (U)
Boise State University (U, G)
Bowling Green State University (U, G)
Brevard Community College (U)
Bristol Community College (N)

N–Noncredit; U–Undergraduate; G–Graduate

Broome Community College (U)
Bryant and Stratton Online (U)
California State University, Monterey Bay (U)
California State University, Sacramento (U)
Cape Fear Community College (U)
Capella University (N, U, G)
Capitol College (G)
Central Missouri State University (N)
Central Missouri State University (N)
Central Missouri State University (N)
Central Missouri State University (N)
Central Missouri State University (N)
Central Texas College (U)
Central Wyoming College (N)
Champlain College (U)
Cincinnati State Technical and Community College (U)
Cleveland State University (N, G)
College of the Canyons (U)
Columbia Basin College (U)
Columbus State Community College (U)
Daniel Webster College (U)
Danville Area Community College (U)
Darton College (N)
East Arkansas Community College (U)
East Carolina University (G)
East Central College (U)
Eastern Michigan University (G)
Edison State Community College (N, U)
Fairmont State University (U)
Florida Metropolitan University–Brandon Campus (U)
Fort Hays State University (U)
Frederick Community College (N)
Gaston College (U)
Gateway Community College (N)
Grantham University (U)
Harrisburg Area Community College (U)
Hibbing Community College (N, U)
Hillsborough Community College (U)
Horry-Georgetown Technical College (U)
Hudson County Community College (N)
Immaculata University (U)
Indiana Wesleyan University (U)
Irvine Valley College (U)
Jamestown Community College (N)
John Wood Community College (U)
Jones College (U)
Jones International University (U, G)
Lamar State College–Port Arthur (N)
Limestone College (U)
Linn-Benton Community College (U)
Long Island University, C.W. Post Campus (N)
Manchester Community College (N, U)
Martin Community College (U)
Maryville University of Saint Louis (N)
Massasoit Community College (N, U)
Maui Community College (U)
Mercy College (G)
Middlesex Community College (N, U)
MiraCosta College (U)
Northampton County Area Community College (U)
North Dakota State University (N)
Northeastern Oklahoma Agricultural and Mechanical College (N)
Northeastern University (N, U)
Northern Kentucky University (N)
North Georgia College & State University (N)
NorthWest Arkansas Community College (U)
Northwestern Michigan College (U)
Nova Southeastern University (G)
Odessa College (N)
Okaloosa-Walton College (U)
Oklahoma Wesleyan University (U)
Oregon State University (N)
Oxnard College (U)
Pace University (U, G)
Pasco-Hernando Community College (N, U)
Peirce College (U)
Richland Community College (U)
Riverland Community College (U)
Riverside Community College (N)
Rosalind Franklin University of Medicine and Science (N, G)
Saint Leo University (U)
San Jacinto College District (U)
Seattle Pacific University (G)
South Central Technical College (U)
State University of New York College at Potsdam (N)
Sullivan University (G)
Syracuse University (G)
Taylor University (N)
Texas State Technical College–Waco (N, U)
Tompkins Cortland Community College (U)
Tulane University (U)
The University of Akron (G)
University of Cincinnati Raymond Walters College (U)
University of Connecticut (U)
University of Great Falls (U)
University of Illinois (N)
University of Illinois at Chicago (N)
University of Illinois at Urbana–Champaign (G)
The University of Lethbridge (U)
The University of Texas at Dallas (G)
University of the Incarnate Word (U)
University of Tulsa (G)
University of Washington (N)
University of West Florida (U)
Vance-Granville Community College (N)
Wake Technical Community College (N, U)
Washtenaw Community College (U)
Wayne State College (U, G)
West Virginia University (N)
Westwood Online (U)
William Paterson University of New Jersey (N)
William Rainey Harper College (U)

Internet

Delta College (U)

Investments and securities

The American College (U, G)
Eastern Michigan University (U)
Maharishi University of Management (N, G)
The Pennsylvania State University University Park Campus (U)
Roger Williams University (U)
University of Waterloo (U)
Washington State University (U)
Wilfrid Laurier University (U)

Italian

College of San Mateo (U)
Nassau Community College (U)
University of Nevada, Reno (U)
The University of North Carolina at Chapel Hill (U)
University of Toronto (N)

Japanese

The University of Akron (U)

Journalism and mass communication related

Charter Oak State College (U)
Concordia University at Austin (N)
Cumberland County College (U)
Eastern Kentucky University (U)
Missouri Southern State University (U)
Nassau Community College (U)
Palomar College (U)
The Richard Stockton College of New Jersey (U)
St. Ambrose University (U)
St. Cloud State University (G)
Seattle Central Community College (U)
The University of South Dakota (U)
University of Southern Indiana (U)
University of Toledo (U)

Journalism and mass communications

Arkansas Tech University (U, G)
Athabasca University (N, U)
Brenau University (U)
Bucks County Community College (U)
California State University, Sacramento (U)

Cedarville University (U)
Citrus College (U)
Cleveland State University (N)
College of DuPage (U)
Collin County Community College District (U)
Dallas County Community College District (U)
Delaware County Community College (U)
Drake University (U, G)
East Carolina University (U)
Education Direct Center for Degree Studies (N)
El Camino College (U)
Everett Community College (U)
Feather River Community College District (N)
Henry Ford Community College (U)
Indiana University–Purdue University Fort Wayne (U)
James Madison University (N)
Jamestown Community College (N)
Kauai Community College (U)
Kirkwood Community College (U)
Linn-Benton Community College (U)
Louisiana Tech University (U)
Marist College (U)
Maryville University of Saint Louis (N)
Massasoit Community College (N)
Middle Tennessee State University (U)
Minnesota State College–Southeast Technical (N)
Murray State University (U)
New York Institute of Technology (U)
Northampton County Area Community College (U)
Northern Kentucky University (U)
Northwestern State University of Louisiana (U)
Ohio University (U)
Oxnard College (U)
The Pennsylvania State University University Park Campus (U)
Pulaski Technical College (U)
Quinnipiac University (U, G)
Sacramento City College (U)
Saint Mary-of-the-Woods College (U)
Saint Mary-of-the-Woods College (U)
Santa Rosa Junior College (U)
Shawnee State University (U)
Simpson College (U)
Southern Illinois University Carbondale (U)
State University of New York at Oswego (U)
Taylor University (U)
Texas Tech University (U)
The University of Akron (U)
The University of Alabama (U, G)
University of Alaska Fairbanks (U)
University of Arkansas at Little Rock (U)
University of Central Arkansas (N)
University of Florida (U)
University of Georgia (U)
University of Idaho (U)
University of Maryland University College (U)
University of Massachusetts Amherst (U)
University of Missouri–Columbia (G)
The University of Montana–Missoula (U)
University of Nebraska–Lincoln (U, G)
The University of North Carolina at Chapel Hill (U)
University of Oklahoma (U)
University of Southern Indiana (U)
The University of Texas of the Permian Basin (U)
University of Toledo (U)
University of Washington (U)
University of Wisconsin Colleges (U)
Yuba College (U)

Journalism

Brevard Community College (U)
Cerritos College (U)
Columbia University (N, G)
Louisiana State University and Agricultural and Mechanical College (U)
Marshall University (U)
Mt. San Antonio College (U)
Murray State University (U)
Northern Virginia Community College (U)
Ohio University (U)
Oklahoma State University (U)
Old Dominion University (U)
The Pennsylvania State University University Park Campus (U)
Seattle Central Community College (U)
Skidmore College (U)
Texas A&M University–Commerce (U)
University of Alaska Fairbanks (U)
The University of Iowa (U, G)
University of Minnesota, Twin Cities Campus (U)
University of Southern Indiana (U)

Judaic studies

California State University, Chico (U)
Hebrew College (N, U, G)
University of Waterloo (U)

Labor/personnel relations

Embry-Riddle Aeronautical University (G)
Kansas State University (U, G)
Louisiana State University and Agricultural and Mechanical College (U)
Mountain State University (U)
Park University (U)
The Pennsylvania State University University Park Campus (U)
State University of New York Empire State College (U)
University of Wyoming (U, G)
Upper Iowa University (N, U)

Landscape architecture

Ashworth College (N)
James Madison University (N)
Maui Community College (U)
Mississippi State University (U)
The University of British Columbia (U)
University of Saskatchewan (N)

Latin (ancient and medieval)

Louisiana State University and Agricultural and Mechanical College (U)
University of Alaska Fairbanks (U)
University of Colorado at Denver (U)
The University of Iowa (U)
University of Minnesota, Twin Cities Campus (U)
The University of North Carolina at Chapel Hill (U)
University of Waterloo (U)

Latin American studies

Triton College (U)
University of Nebraska–Lincoln (U)

Law and legal studies related

Adams State College (U)
Anne Arundel Community College (U)
Broward Community College (U)
Bucks County Community College (U)
Central Texas College (U)
Cerritos College (U)
College of San Mateo (U)
College of The Albemarle (U)
Columbus State Community College (U)
Delaware County Community College (U)
Delta College (U)
Eastern Michigan University (U, G)
Embry-Riddle Aeronautical University (U)
Fashion Institute of Technology (U)
Greenville Technical College (U)
Kellogg Community College (U)
Lansing Community College (U)
Louisiana State University and Agricultural and Mechanical College (U)
Mercy College (U)
Mountain Empire Community College (U)
Mountain State University (U)
Mt. San Antonio College (U)
Murray State University (U)

N–Noncredit; U–Undergraduate; G–Graduate

Nassau Community College (U)
Northern Virginia Community College (U)
Oklahoma State University (U)
Palomar College (U)
Pitt Community College (U)
Randolph Community College (U)
Roger Williams University (U)
Roosevelt University (U)
Sam Houston State University (U)
Sinclair Community College (U)
Southeast Community College, Lincoln Campus (U)
State University of New York Empire State College (U)
Tompkins Cortland Community College (U)
Triton College (U)
Troy University Montgomery (U)
University of Houston–Downtown (U)
University of Missouri–Columbia (U)
University of Toronto (N)
Upper Iowa University (N, U)
Washington State University (U)
Washtenaw Community College (U)
West Valley College (U)

Leatherworking/upholstery

Blackhawk Technical College (N)

Legal studies

Adams State College (N)
Albuquerque Technical Vocational Institute (U)
Asheville-Buncombe Technical Community College (N)
Athabasca University (N, U)
Athens Technical College (U)
Bainbridge College (N)
Berkeley College (U)
Berkeley College-Westchester Campus (U)
Bossier Parish Community College (N)
Brenau University (U)
Brevard Community College (U)
Bristol Community College (N)
Bucks County Community College (U)
California State University, Dominguez Hills (N)
California State University, Monterey Bay (N)
California University of Pennsylvania (G)
Cape Fear Community College (U)
Carleton University (U)
Chadron State College (U)
Cincinnati State Technical and Community College (U)
Colorado State University (N)
The Community College of Baltimore County (U)
Delaware County Community College (U)
DeVry University Online (U)
Eastern Illinois University (N)
Eastern Michigan University (U)
Elgin Community College (U)
Embry-Riddle Aeronautical University, Extended Campus (U)
Feather River Community College District (N)
Florida Hospital College of Health Sciences (U)
Florida International University (N)
Florida Metropolitan University–Brandon Campus (U)
Forrest Junior College (U)
Fulton-Montgomery Community College (N)
Gannon University (U)
Gaston College (U)
Grantham University (U)
Hillsborough Community College (U)
Iowa Western Community College (U)
Ivy Tech State College–Central Indiana (U)
Ivy Tech State College–Eastcentral (U)
Ivy Tech State College–North Central (U)
Jamestown Community College (N)
John F. Kennedy University (G)
John Jay College of Criminal Justice of the City University of New York (U)
Jones College (U)
Keiser College (U)
Limestone College (U)
Lord Fairfax Community College (U)
Marion Technical College (U)
Maysville Community College (N)
Metropolitan Community College (U)
Metropolitan State University (U, G)
Middlesex Community College (U)
Mid-South Community College (N)
Minnesota School of Business–Brooklyn Center (U)
Minnesota School of Business-Richfield (U)
MiraCosta College (N)
Murray State University (U)
New York Institute of Technology (U)
Northeastern Oklahoma Agricultural and Mechanical College (N)
North Hennepin Community College (U)
Northwestern Michigan College (U)
Odessa College (N)
Oxnard College (U)
Pace University (U)
The Paralegal Institute, Inc. (U)
Peirce College (U)
Raritan Valley Community College (U)
Riverland Community College (U)
Roosevelt University (U)
Royal Roads University (U)
Ryerson University (U)
St. John's University (U)
Santa Fe Community College (N)
Schenectady County Community College (U)
Schiller International University (G)
Seminole Community College (U)
Shawnee State University (U)
Shelton State Community College (U)
Shenandoah University (U)
Southwestern College (U)
Southwest Missouri State University (G)
State University of New York College at Potsdam (N)
Strayer University (U, G)
Sullivan University (G)
Sullivan University (U)
Tacoma Community College (U)
Teikyo Post University (U)
Texas Tech University (U)
Tompkins Cortland Community College (U)
Tri-State University (U)
The University of Akron (G)
University of Bridgeport (U)
University of Florida (N)
University of Georgia (U)
University of Great Falls (U)
The University of North Carolina at Charlotte (N)
University of Northern Colorado (G)
University of the Incarnate Word (U, G)
University of Tulsa (G)
University of Wisconsin–Parkside (N)
Utah Valley State College (U)
Wake Technical Community College (N)
Waubonsee Community College (U)
West Virginia University at Parkersburg (N)
William Paterson University of New Jersey (U)
Worcester State College (N)
Youngstown State University (N)

Liberal arts and sciences, general studies and humanities

Alvin Community College (U)
American Public University System (U)
Arkansas Tech University (G)
The Art Institute Online (U)
Athabasca University (N)
Bainbridge College (U)
Beaufort County Community College (U)
Bethany College of the Assemblies of God (U)
Brevard Community College (U)
Brigham Young University (U)
Bucks County Community College (U)
Caldwell Community College and Technical Institute (U)
California State University, Chico (U)

Liberal arts and sciences, general studies and humanities

California State University, Dominguez Hills (G)
Central Oregon Community College (U)
Chadron State College (U)
Champlain College (U)
Chattanooga State Technical Community College (U)
Chemeketa Community College (U)
Citrus College (U)
Clinton Community College (U)
College for Lifelong Learning (U)
College of DuPage (U)
College of the Siskiyous (U)
Colorado State University-Pueblo (U)
Community College of Denver (U)
Dakota County Technical College (U)
Dallas Baptist University (G)
Dallas County Community College District (U)
Darton College (U)
Delaware County Community College (U)
DePaul University (U)
DeVry University Online (U)
Dickinson State University (U)
Drake University (U, G)
East Los Angeles College (U)
Everett Community College (U)
Fairmont State University (U)
Florida Community College at Jacksonville (U)
Florida Hospital College of Health Sciences (U)
Florida National College (U)
Fort Hays State University (U)
Franklin Pierce College (U)
Frederick Community College (U)
Gaston College (U)
Goddard College (U, G)
Gogebic Community College (U)
Gonzaga University (U, G)
Hibbing Community College (U)
Hopkinsville Community College (U)
Howard Community College (U)
Illinois Eastern Community Colleges, Olney Central College (U)
Illinois Eastern Community Colleges, Wabash Valley College (U)
Indiana University of Pennsylvania (U)
Indiana University System (U)
Iowa Western Community College (U)
James Madison University (N)
Jamestown Community College (N)
John A. Logan College (U)
John F. Kennedy University (U)
John Tyler Community College (U)
John Wood Community College (U)
Jones College (U)
Judson College (U)
Kansas City Kansas Community College (U)
The King's College and Seminary (N, U)
Lake Superior College (U)
Lewis-Clark State College (U)
Linn-Benton Community College (U)
Long Beach City College (U)
Lord Fairfax Community College (U)
Madison Area Technical College (U)
Madonna University (N, U)
Marist College (U)
Marylhurst University (U, G)
Miami Dade College (U)
Middlesex Community College (U)
Middle Tennessee State University (U)
Mid-South Community College (U)
Minnesota School of Business-Richfield (U)
Minot State University–Bottineau Campus (U)
Monroe Community College (U)
Montana State University–Billings (U)
Montgomery Community College (U)
Montgomery County Community College (U)
Mountain State University (U)
Mount Saint Mary College (U)
Naropa University (U, G)
Naugatuck Valley Community College (U)
North Central University (N, U)
Northeastern Oklahoma Agricultural and Mechanical College (U)
Northeastern University (U)
Northern Arizona University (U)
Northern Kentucky University (U)
Northern New Mexico Community College (U)
North Hennepin Community College (U)
NorthWest Arkansas Community College (U)
Northwestern College (U)
Northwestern Technical College (U)
Oregon State University (U)
Pace University (N)
Palomar College (U)
Patrick Henry College (U)
Pratt Community College (U)
Prescott College (U, G)
Quinebaug Valley Community College (U)
The Richard Stockton College of New Jersey (U)
Rockland Community College (U)
Roosevelt University (U)
Ryerson University (U)
Sacred Heart University (U)
St. Edward's University (G)
Saint Leo University (U)
Saint Mary-of-the-Woods College (U)
St. Petersburg College (U)
San Bernardino Valley College (U)
Santa Rosa Junior College (U)
Seminole Community College (U)
Simpson College (U)
Sinclair Community College (U)
Skidmore College (G)
Southeast Community College, Beatrice Campus (U)
Southern Christian University (N, U)
Southwestern College (U)
Stony Brook University, State University of New York (G)
Tarrant County College District (U)
Taylor University (U)
Taylor University (U)
Texas Tech University (U)
Tri-State University (U)
Triton College (U)
The University of Akron (U)
The University of Alabama (U)
University of Alaska Fairbanks (U)
University of Arkansas at Little Rock (U)
University of Bridgeport (U)
University of California, Los Angeles (G)
University of Colorado at Denver (U)
University of Connecticut (U)
University of Denver (G)
University of Florida (U)
University of Georgia (U)
University of Great Falls (U)
University of Houston (U)
University of Houston–Downtown (U)
University of Illinois (U)
The University of Iowa (U)
University of La Verne (U)
University of Maine (G)
The University of Maine at Augusta (U)
University of Massachusetts Lowell (U)
University of Mississippi (U)
University of Missouri–Columbia (U)
University of New Orleans (U)
The University of North Carolina at Greensboro (U, G)
University of Southern Mississippi (U)
The University of Tennessee (U)
The University of Texas System (U)
University of the Incarnate Word (U)
University of Toledo (U, G)
University of Waterloo (U)
University of West Florida (U)
University of Wisconsin–Milwaukee (N)
University of Wisconsin–River Falls (U)
University of Wyoming (U)
Upper Iowa University (U)
Vance-Granville Community College (U)
Waubonsee Community College (U)

N–Noncredit; U–Undergraduate; G–Graduate

Webster University (U)
William Paterson University of New Jersey (U)
William Rainey Harper College (U)
Winston-Salem State University (U)
Wright State University (U)
York University (U)

Library assistant

College of DuPage (U)
James Madison University (N)
Northampton County Area Community College (U)
Syracuse University (G)

Library science, other

Black Hills State University (U)
Bowling Green State University (U)
Central Virginia Community College (U)
Chadron State College (U)
The College of St. Scholastica (G)
Colorado Mountain College District System (U)
Des Moines Area Community College (U)
Everett Community College (U)
Evergreen Valley College (U)
Harrisburg Area Community College (U)
Indiana State University (U, G)
Jones International University (G)
Louisiana State University and Agricultural and Mechanical College (U)
Miami Dade College (U)
Modesto Junior College (U)
Northwestern State University of Louisiana (U)
Nova Southeastern University (G)
Oxnard College (U)
Palomar College (U)
Rio Hondo College (U)
Sacramento City College (U)
Saddleback College (U)
Santa Rosa Junior College (U)
Seminole Community College (U)
Shoreline Community College (U)
State University of New York at Plattsburgh (U)
Syracuse University (G)
Tacoma Community College (U)
Texas A&M University–Commerce (G)
The University of British Columbia (U)
University of Central Arkansas (G)
University of Cincinnati (U)
University of Idaho (U, G)
The University of Maine at Augusta (U)
University of Missouri–Columbia (G)
The University of Montana–Missoula (U, G)
The University of North Carolina at Greensboro (G)
University of Oklahoma (U)
University of Southern Mississippi (U)
University of Washington (G)
University of Wisconsin–Eau Claire (U)
University of Wisconsin–Milwaukee (G)
Western Washington University (U)
West Valley College (U)

Library science/librarianship

Central Missouri State University (U, G)
Central Missouri State University (U, G)
Central Missouri State University (U, G)
Central Missouri State University (U, G)
Central Missouri State University (U, G)
Chadron State College (U)
Clarion University of Pennsylvania (U, G)
College of DuPage (U)
East Carolina University (G)
Eastern Kentucky University (G)
Inter American University of Puerto Rico, San Germán Campus (G)
Kent State University (U)
Long Beach City College (U)
Louisiana State University in Shreveport (G)
Mayville State University (U)
Memorial University of Newfoundland (U, G)
Missouri Baptist University (U, G)
Nova Southeastern University (G)
Santa Rosa Junior College (U)
Seattle Pacific University (G)
Seminole Community College (U)
Syracuse University (G)
Tacoma Community College (U)
Texas Woman's University (G)
University of Alaska Fairbanks (U)
The University of Arizona (G)
University of Cincinnati Raymond Walters College (U)
University of Idaho (U, G)
University of Illinois (G)
University of Illinois at Urbana–Champaign (G)
University of Missouri–Columbia (G)
University of Nevada, Reno (U, G)
University of Vermont (U, G)
University of Washington (U, G)
University of Wisconsin–Milwaukee (G)
Valley City State University (U)
West Los Angeles College (U)

Management information systems/ business data processing

Adams State College (U)
Bellevue Community College (U)
California National University for Advanced Studies (U, G)
California State University, Sacramento (U)
Capitol College (G)
Cerritos College (U)
College for Lifelong Learning (U)
Connecticut State University System (U, G)
Embry-Riddle Aeronautical University (G)
Fashion Institute of Technology (U)
Golden Gate University (U, G)
Houston Community College System (U)
Kansas State University (U)
Louisiana State University and Agricultural and Mechanical College (U)
Maharishi University of Management (N, G)
Manatee Community College (U)
Marshall University (U)
Mercy College (U, G)
Metropolitan State University (U, G)
Mountain State University (U)
Northern Virginia Community College (U)
Oklahoma State University (U)
Old Dominion University (U, G)
The Pennsylvania State University University Park Campus (U)
Regis University (G)
State University of New York Empire State College (U)
Stevens Institute of Technology (G)
University of Colorado at Denver (G)
University of Dallas (G)
University of Houston–Downtown (U)
University of Illinois at Springfield (G)
University of Oregon (G)
University of Southern Mississippi (U)
University of Waterloo (G)
Upper Iowa University (N, U)
Virginia Polytechnic Institute and State University (G)
Wayland Baptist University (U, G)

Management science

Regis University (G)
Stevens Institute of Technology (G)
University of Wisconsin–Platteville (G)

Marketing management and research

Acadia University (U)
Adirondack Community College (U)
AIB College of Business (U)
Alliant International University (U)
Asheville-Buncombe Technical Community College (N)
Athabasca University (N, U, G)
Brenau University (U, G)
Bristol Community College (N)
Butler County Community College (U)
Caldwell Community College and Technical Institute (U)
California State University, Monterey Bay (U)

Capella University (N, G)
Carroll Community College (U)
Central Texas College (U)
Central Virginia Community College (U)
Chadron State College (U, G)
Clackamas Community College (U)
Coastal Bend College (U)
Coleman College (U, G)
College of the Southwest (U)
Colorado Christian University (U)
Columbia Union College (U)
The Community College of Baltimore County (U)
Concordia University Wisconsin (U)
Cossatot Community College of the University of Arkansas (N)
Dakota County Technical College (U)
Dallas Baptist University (U, G)
Davenport University Online (U, G)
Delaware County Community College (U)
DeVry University Online (U, G)
Drexel University (U, G)
Duke University (N)
Eastern Illinois University (G)
Eastern Michigan University (U, G)
Fashion Institute of Technology (N)
Florida Atlantic University (U, G)
Florida Gulf Coast University (U)
Florida Institute of Technology (G)
Florida Metropolitan University–Brandon Campus (U)
Fort Hays State University (U)
Franklin University (U)
Frederick Community College (N)
Gannon University (U)
Georgia Southern University (U)
Horry-Georgetown Technical College (U)
Illinois Eastern Community Colleges, Frontier Community College (U)
Indiana University of Pennsylvania (U)
Ivy Tech State College–Southcentral (U)
Ivy Tech State College–Southwest (U)
Ivy Tech State College–Wabash Valley (U)
Ivy Tech State College–Whitewater (U)
Jacksonville State University (U, G)
James Madison University (N)
Jamestown Community College (N)
Lamar State College–Port Arthur (N)
Lawrence Technological University (U, G)
Limestone College (U)
Long Beach City College (U)
Louisiana State University at Eunice (U)
Maharishi University of Management (U)
Marshall University (G)
Martin Community College (U)
Marylhurst University (G)
Maysville Community College (U)
Mercy College (G)
Mesalands Community College (U)
Metropolitan State University (U, G)
Middlesex Community College (U)
Middle Tennessee State University (G)
Minnesota State College–Southeast Technical (N)
Murray State University (G)
Nipissing University (U)
Normandale Community College (U)
Northern Arizona University (U)
North Harris Montgomery Community College District (U)
North Hennepin Community College (U)
Northwestern State University of Louisiana (U)
Ohio University (U)
Oxnard College (U)
Pace University (U, G)
Park University (U)
Peirce College (U)
Pennsylvania College of Technology (U)
Quinnipiac University (U, G)
Raritan Valley Community College (U)
Regis University (U)
Riverside Community College (U)
Rockland Community College (U)
Ryerson University (U)
Sacred Heart University (U, G)
St. Edward's University (G)
St. John's University (U)
Saint Joseph's College of Maine (U, G)
Saint Leo University (U)
St. Louis Community College System (U)
Saint Mary-of-the-Woods College (U)
San Jacinto College District (U)
Schiller International University (U, G)
Shippensburg University of Pennsylvania (U)
Simpson College (U)
Southeast Arkansas College (U)
Southern Illinois University Carbondale (N, U)
State University of New York at Plattsburgh (U)
Stephens College (G)
Suffolk University (G)
Sullivan University (G)
Syracuse University (G)
Tarleton State University (G)
Taylor University (N)
Teikyo Post University (U)
Texas A&M University–Corpus Christi (G)
Tri-State University (U)
United States Sports Academy (G)
University of Central Arkansas (U)
University of Colorado at Denver (G)
University of Dallas (G)
The University of Findlay (U, G)
University of Georgia (U)
University of Great Falls (U)
University of Illinois (N)
University of Illinois at Chicago (N, G)
University of Management and Technology (U)
University of Maryland University College (G)
University of Massachusetts Amherst (U)
University of Missouri–Columbia (U)
University of Nebraska at Omaha (U)
University of Nebraska–Lincoln (G)
University of Northern Colorado (G)
University of Notre Dame (N)
University of Oklahoma (U)
University of St. Francis (G)
University of Southern Indiana (G)
The University of Texas at Dallas (G)
The University of Texas at Tyler (U)
University of the Incarnate Word (U)
University of Toronto (U)
University of Tulsa (G)
University of Washington (U)
University of Wisconsin–Eau Claire (N)
University of Wisconsin–Madison (G)
University of Wisconsin–Platteville (U)
Upper Iowa University (U)
Virginia Polytechnic Institute and State University (U, G)
Western New England College (G)
West Virginia University at Parkersburg (U)
Wilkes Community College (U)
William Paterson University of New Jersey (N, U)
York University (U)

Marketing operations/marketing and distribution, other

Albuquerque Technical Vocational Institute (U)
Athabasca University (N, U, G)
Berkeley College (U)
Berkeley College-New York City Campus (U)
Berkeley College-Westchester Campus (U)
Bismarck State College (U)
Brenau University (G)
Bristol Community College (N)
Broome Community College (U)
California National University for Advanced Studies (N)
California State University, Dominguez Hills (N)
California State University, Monterey Bay (U)
California State University, Sacramento (U)

N–Noncredit; U–Undergraduate; G–Graduate

Cape Fear Community College (U)
Capella University (N, U, G)
Chadron State College (U, G)
Chemeketa Community College (U)
College of DuPage (U)
Columbia College (U)
Columbus State Community College (U)
Community College of Denver (U)
Cossatot Community College of the University of Arkansas (N)
Dallas Baptist University (G)
Davenport University Online (U)
Delaware County Community College (U)
Drexel University (U, G)
East Central College (U)
Eastern Michigan University (U, G)
Elizabeth City State University (U)
Florida Metropolitan University–Brandon Campus (U)
Fort Hays State University (U)
Grantham University (U)
Iowa Western Community College (U)
Irvine Valley College (U)
Ivy Tech State College–Columbus (U)
Ivy Tech State College–North Central (U)
Jacksonville State University (U, G)
James Madison University (N)
Jones College (U)
Kansas City Kansas Community College (U)
Kentucky State University (U)
Lakeland College (U)
Lansing Community College (U)
Lord Fairfax Community College (N)
Madison Area Technical College (U)
Massasoit Community College (N)
Middle Tennessee State University (U)
New York Institute of Technology (U, G)
Oklahoma State University (U)
Oregon State University (U)
Park University (U)
Peirce College (U)
The Pennsylvania State University University Park Campus (U, G)
Quinnipiac University (G)
Raritan Valley Community College (U)
Regis University (U)
Rend Lake College (N)
Saddleback College (U)
St. Edward's University (U, G)
Saint Mary-of-the-Woods College (U)
Santa Fe Community College (N)
South Central Technical College (U)
Southern Illinois University Carbondale (U)
South Piedmont Community College (U)
Spartanburg Technical College (U)
Strayer University (U)
Syracuse University (G)
Taylor University (N)
Texas A&M University–Texarkana (U)
The University of Akron (U)
University of Alaska Fairbanks (U)
University of Bridgeport (U)
University of Colorado at Denver (G)
University of Dallas (G)
The University of Findlay (G)
University of Houston–Downtown (U)
University of Maryland University College (U, G)
University of Massachusetts Amherst (N)
University of Notre Dame (N, G)
University of South Carolina (U)
University of the Incarnate Word (U)
University of Tulsa (G)
University of Wisconsin–La Crosse (G)
University of Wisconsin–Parkside (G)
Walsh College of Accountancy and Business Administration (G)
William Paterson University of New Jersey (U)
William Rainey Harper College (U)
Worcester Polytechnic Institute (G)

Materials engineering

Delta College (U)
Illinois Institute of Technology (G)
Lord Fairfax Community College (U)
University of Illinois (G)
University of Michigan (N)
University of Washington (U, G)

Materials science

Columbia University (N, G)
Delta College (U)
Stanford University (N)
University of Michigan (N)
University of Washington (G)

Mathematical statistics

Adams State College (U)
Anne Arundel Community College (U)
Asheville-Buncombe Technical Community College (U)
Athabasca University (N, U)
Bainbridge College (U)
Bethany College of the Assemblies of God (U)
Brigham Young University (U)
Bristol Community College (U)
Broome Community College (U)
Broward Community College (U)
Bucks County Community College (U)
Burlington County College (U)
California State University, Sacramento (U)
Campbell University (U)
Carroll Community College (U)
Casper College (U)
Central Texas College (U)
Chadron State College (U, G)
Chattanooga State Technical Community College (U)
Chemeketa Community College (U)
Clatsop Community College (U)
Clinton Community College (U)
Coleman College (U)
Colorado Mountain College District System (U)
Columbia Union College (U)
The Community College of Baltimore County (U)
Connecticut State University System (U, G)
Daniel Webster College (U)
Danville Area Community College (U)
Darton College (U)
Davenport University Online (U)
Delaware Technical & Community College, Jack F. Owens Campus (U)
Delaware Technical & Community College, Stanton/Wilmington Campus (U)
Delta College (U)
Duke University (G)
Edison Community College (U)
Edison State Community College (U)
Elizabeth City State University (U)
Embry-Riddle Aeronautical University (U)
Embry-Riddle Aeronautical University, Extended Campus (U)
Franklin University (U)
Harrisburg Area Community College (U)
Howard Community College (U)
Illinois Eastern Community Colleges, Wabash Valley College (U)
Indiana State University (U)
Iowa State University of Science and Technology (G)
Iowa Western Community College (U)
Jacksonville State University (U, G)
James Madison University (U)
Jefferson College of Health Sciences (U)
Jefferson Davis Community College (U)
John Wood Community College (U)
Kansas State University (U)
Lakeland Community College (U)
Limestone College (U)
Louisiana State University and Agricultural and Mechanical College (U)
Loyola University New Orleans (U)
Madison Area Technical College (U)
Manatee Community College (U)
Marshall University (U)
Marylhurst University (U)
Massasoit Community College (U)
Maysville Community College (U)
Memorial University of Newfoundland (U)
Mercy College (U)

Middlesex Community College (U)
Minnesota School of Business–Brooklyn Center (U)
Mississippi State University (U)
Montana State University–Billings (U)
Montana State University–Bozeman (G)
Montgomery County Community College (U)
Mountain State University (U)
Mount Allison University (U)
Mount Wachusett Community College (U)
Nassau Community College (U)
New Hampshire Community Technical College System (U)
New York Institute of Technology (U)
Northern Arizona University (G)
Northern New Mexico Community College (U)
Northern Virginia Community College (U)
Northwestern Michigan College (U)
Oklahoma State University (U)
Oregon State University (U)
Pace University (U)
Park University (U)
Passaic County Community College (U)
Pennsylvania College of Technology (U)
The Pennsylvania State University University Park Campus (U, G)
Portland State University (U)
Queen's University at Kingston (U)
Raritan Valley Community College (U)
Regis University (U)
Riverland Community College (U)
St. Ambrose University (G)
St. Clair County Community College (U)
Schiller International University (U, G)
Seattle Central Community College (U)
Seminole Community College (U)
Seward County Community College (U)
Snead State Community College (U)
Southwest Virginia Community College (U)
Southwest Wisconsin Technical College (U)
Spartanburg Technical College (U)
State University of New York at Plattsburgh (U)
State University of New York Empire State College (U)
Stephens College (G)
Taft College (U)
Teachers College Columbia University (N, G)
Texas A&M University–Corpus Christi (U)
Texas Tech University (G)
Texas Woman's University (G)
Triton College (U)
University College of Cape Breton (U)
The University of Akron (U, G)
The University of Alabama in Huntsville (G)
University of Alaska Fairbanks (U)
University of Central Florida (U, G)
University of Colorado at Denver (U)
The University of Findlay (U)
University of Georgia (U)
University of Guelph (U)
University of Houston–Downtown (U)
University of Idaho (U, G)
University of Illinois at Springfield (U)
The University of Maine at Augusta (U)
University of Massachusetts Boston (U, G)
University of Minnesota, Morris (U)
University of Missouri–Columbia (U)
University of Nebraska–Lincoln (U, G)
University of Nevada, Reno (U)
University of New Hampshire (G)
The University of North Carolina at Chapel Hill (U)
University of Notre Dame (N, G)
The University of South Dakota (U)
University of Southern Mississippi (G)
The University of Texas at Tyler (U)
The University of Texas of the Permian Basin (G)
The University of Texas System (U)
University of the Incarnate Word (U)
University of Toledo (U)
University of Utah (U)
University of Vermont (U)
University of Washington (U)
University of Waterloo (U)
University of West Florida (U)
University of Wisconsin Colleges (U)
University of Wisconsin–Parkside (G)
University of Wisconsin–Platteville (G)
University of Wyoming (U)
Upper Iowa University (N, U)
Vance-Granville Community College (U)
Waubonsee Community College (U)
William Paterson University of New Jersey (G)
Worcester State College (U)
Yuba College (U)

Mathematics and computer science

Alliance University College (U)
Alvin Community College (U)
American College of Computer & Information Sciences (U, G)
Athabasca University (N, U, G)
Austin Peay State University (U)
Brevard Community College (U)
Caldwell College (U)
Campbell University (U)
Chadron State College (U, G)
Champlain College (U)
Chemeketa Community College (U)
Columbia College (U)
Concordia University, St. Paul (N)
Dallas County Community College District (U)
Daniel Webster College (U)
Delaware County Community College (U)
Drake University (U)
Edison State Community College (U)
Franklin University (U)
Grantham University (U)
Harrisburg Area Community College (U)
Jacksonville State University (U, G)
James Madison University (N)
Marshall University (U)
Maui Community College (U)
Middlesex Community College (U)
New Hampshire Community Technical College System (U)
North Hennepin Community College (U)
Snead State Community College (U)
Taylor University (N)
Texas State University-San Marcos (U)
Touro University International (U)
Umpqua Community College (U)
The University of Akron (U, G)
University of Massachusetts Lowell (U)
University of Wisconsin Colleges (U)
University of Wisconsin–Superior (U)
Westchester Community College (U)

Mathematics related

Andrews University (U)
Anne Arundel Community College (U)
Bellevue Community College (U)
Bossier Parish Community College (U)
Brigham Young University (U)
Bristol Community College (U)
Broward Community College (U)
Central Texas College (U)
Clovis Community College (U)
College of The Albemarle (U)
Colorado Mountain College District System (U)
Columbia Basin College (U)
Dallas County Community College District (U)
Delta College (U)
Eastern Kentucky University (U)
Embry-Riddle Aeronautical University (U)
Florida Community College at Jacksonville (U)
Floyd College (U)
Grantham University (U)
Horry-Georgetown Technical College (U)
Houston Community College System (U)

N–Noncredit; U–Undergraduate; G–Graduate

Illinois Eastern Community Colleges, Wabash Valley College (U)
Indiana State University (U)
Jefferson Community College (U)
Kellogg Community College (U)
Lansing Community College (U)
Louisiana State University and Agricultural and Mechanical College (U)
Madison Area Technical College (U)
Manatee Community College (U)
Marylhurst University (U)
Mercy College (U)
Mountain State University (U)
Mount Wachusett Community College (U)
Murray State University (U)
Nassau Community College (U)
Northeastern University (U)
Northern Virginia Community College (U)
Northwestern Michigan College (U)
Oklahoma State University (U)
Oregon State University (U)
The Pennsylvania State University University Park Campus (U)
Portland State University (U)
Sam Houston State University (U)
Sauk Valley Community College (U)
Seattle Central Community College (U)
Southwest Missouri State University (U)
Southwest Virginia Community College (U)
State University of New York Empire State College (U)
University of Alaska Fairbanks (U)
University of Colorado at Denver (U)
University of Delaware (U)
University of Idaho (U, G)
University of Missouri–Columbia (U)
University of Nebraska–Lincoln (N, U)
The University of North Carolina at Chapel Hill (U)
The University of South Dakota (U)
University of Southern Mississippi (U)
The University of Texas–Pan American (U)
University of Utah (U)
University of Waterloo (N)
University of West Florida (U)

Mathematics

Acadia University (N, U)
Adirondack Community College (U)
AIB College of Business (U)
Albuquerque Technical Vocational Institute (U)
Allan Hancock College (U)
Allen County Community College (U)
Alvin Community College (U)
American Academy of Nutrition, College of Nutrition (U)
Arkansas State University–Beebe (U)
Arkansas State University–Mountain Home (U)
Arkansas Tech University (U, G)
Asheville-Buncombe Technical Community College (U)
Athabasca University (N, U)
Athens Technical College (U)
Bismarck State College (U)
Boise State University (U)
Bossier Parish Community College (U)
Bowling Green State University (U)
Brazosport College (U)
Brenau University (U)
Brevard Community College (U)
Bristol Community College (N, U)
Brookdale Community College (U)
Broome Community College (U)
Bucks County Community College (U)
Butler County Community College (U)
Butler County Community College (U)
Caldwell Community College and Technical Institute (U)
California State University, Sacramento (U)
Cape Cod Community College (U)
Cape Fear Community College (U)
Carl Albert State College (U)
Cascadia Community College (U)
Casper College (U)
Cayuga County Community College (U)
Cecil Community College (U)
Central Oregon Community College (U)
Central Texas College (U)
Central Wyoming College (U)
Century College (N)
Chadron State College (U, G)
Chaminade University of Honolulu (U)
Champlain College (U)
Charter Oak State College (U)
Chattanooga State Technical Community College (U)
Chemeketa Community College (U)
Chesapeake College (U)
Citrus College (U)
Clackamas Community College (U)
Clark College (U)
Clatsop Community College (U)
Clovis Community College (U)
Coastal Bend College (U)
Coconino Community College (U)
Coleman College (U)
College of DuPage (U)
College of San Mateo (U)
College of the Siskiyous (U)
Colorado State University-Pueblo (U)
Columbia Basin College (U)
Columbia College (U)
Columbia Union College (U)
Columbus State Community College (U)
The Community College of Baltimore County (U)
Community College of Denver (U)
Concordia University at Austin (N, U)
Copiah-Lincoln Community College–Natchez Campus (U)
Cossatot Community College of the University of Arkansas (U)
County College of Morris (U)
Dakota County Technical College (U)
Dakota State University (U)
Dallas Baptist University (U)
Dallas County Community College District (U)
Daniel Webster College (U)
Danville Area Community College (U)
Danville Community College (U)
Darton College (U)
Davenport University Online (U)
Delaware County Community College (U)
Delaware Technical & Community College, Jack F. Owens Campus (U)
Delaware Technical & Community College, Stanton/Wilmington Campus (U)
Delta College (U)
Des Moines Area Community College (U)
DeVry University Online (U, G)
East Arkansas Community College (U)
Eastern Michigan University (U)
Eastern Washington University (U)
East Los Angeles College (U)
Edison State Community College (U)
Edmonds Community College (U)
Elgin Community College (U)
Eugene Bible College (U)
Everett Community College (U)
Fashion Institute of Technology (N, U)
Feather River Community College District (U)
Ferris State University (U)
Florida Gulf Coast University (U)
Florida Hospital College of Health Sciences (U)
Florida Metropolitan University–Brandon Campus (U)
Fontbonne University (U)
Frederick Community College (U)
Gaston College (U)
George C. Wallace Community College (U)
Georgia Institute of Technology (N, G)
Georgia Southern University (U)
Gogebic Community College (U)
Golden Gate University (U)
Golden West College (U)
Halifax Community College (U)
Hamline University (G)
Harford Community College (U)
Harrisburg Area Community College (U)

Heart of Georgia Technical College (U)
Hibbing Community College (U)
Hopkinsville Community College (U)
Houston Community College System (U)
Howard College (U)
Howard Community College (U)
Illinois Eastern Community Colleges, Lincoln Trail College (U)
Illinois Eastern Community Colleges, Wabash Valley College (U)
Immaculata University (U)
Indiana University of Pennsylvania (U)
Indiana University–Purdue University Fort Wayne (U)
Indiana Wesleyan University (U)
Iowa Western Community College (U)
Irvine Valley College (U)
Ivy Tech State College–Columbus (U)
Ivy Tech State College–Eastcentral (U)
Ivy Tech State College–Northwest (U)
Ivy Tech State College–Southcentral (U)
Ivy Tech State College–Southwest (U)
Ivy Tech State College–Wabash Valley (U)
Ivy Tech State College–Whitewater (U)
Jacksonville State University (U)
Jefferson College (U)
Johnson County Community College (U)
John Wood Community College (U)
Jones College (U)
Judson College (U)
Kansas City Kansas Community College (U)
Lake Region State College (U)
Lake Superior College (U)
Lamar State College–Port Arthur (U)
Lamar University (U)
Lansing Community College (U)
Lewis-Clark State College (U)
Limestone College (U)
Linn-Benton Community College (N, U)
Long Beach City College (U)
Lorain County Community College (U)
Lord Fairfax Community College (U)
Los Angeles Pierce College (U)
Louisiana State University and Agricultural and Mechanical College (N, U)
Louisiana Tech University (U)
Manchester Community College (U)
Mansfield University of Pennsylvania (U)
Marion Technical College (U)
Marshall University (U)
Martin Community College (N, U)
Marylhurst University (N)
Massasoit Community College (U)
Maui Community College (U)
Maysville Community College (U)
Memorial University of Newfoundland (U)
Mesa Community College (U)
Mesalands Community College (U)
Metropolitan Community College (U)
Metropolitan State University (U)
Miami Dade College (U)
Michigan Technological University (N, U)
Middlesex Community College (U)
Middle Tennessee State University (U, G)
Minnesota School of Business-Richfield (U)
MiraCosta College (N, U)
Mississippi Delta Community College (U)
Moberly Area Community College (U)
Modesto Junior College (U)
Monroe Community College (U)
Monroe County Community College (U)
Montana State University–Billings (U)
Montana State University–Bozeman (G)
Montgomery County Community College (U)
Motlow State Community College (U)
Mott Community College (U)
Mountain Empire Community College (U)
Mountain State University (U)
Mount Allison University (U)
Mount Saint Vincent University (N, U)
Mount Wachusett Community College (U)
Nassau Community College (N, U)
Nebraska Methodist College (U)
New England Institute of Technology (U)
New Hampshire Community Technical College System (U)
New Jersey City University (U)
New Mexico Institute of Mining and Technology (G)
New York Institute of Technology (U)
Normandale Community College (U)
Northampton County Area Community College (U)
North Carolina State University (U)
North Central Texas College (U)
North Dakota State College of Science (U)
North Dakota State University (U)
Northeastern Oklahoma Agricultural and Mechanical College (U)
Northeast State Technical Community College (U)
Northern New Mexico Community College (U)
North Georgia College & State University (N)
North Harris Montgomery Community College District (U)
North Idaho College (U)
NorthWest Arkansas Community College (N, U)
Northwestern College (U)
Northwestern State University of Louisiana (U)
Northwestern Technical College (U)
Northwest Missouri State University (U)
Ocean County College (U)
Odessa College (U)
Ohio University (U)
Oxnard College (U)
Pacific Union College (U)
Park University (U)
Patrick Henry Community College (U)
Peirce College (U)
Peninsula College (U)
The Pennsylvania State University University Park Campus (U)
Pierce College (U)
Pratt Community College (U)
Quinnipiac University (N, U)
Rappahannock Community College (U)
Raritan Valley Community College (U)
Reading Area Community College (U)
Rend Lake College (U)
Rio Hondo College (U)
Riverside Community College (U)
Rockland Community College (U)
Sacred Heart University (G)
St. Clair County Community College (U)
St. Cloud State University (U)
St. John's University (U)
Saint Leo University (U)
Saint Mary-of-the-Woods College (U)
Saint Mary-of-the-Woods College (U)
St. Petersburg College (U)
San Jacinto College District (U)
Schenectady County Community College (U)
Schiller International University (U)
Schoolcraft College (U)
Seminole Community College (U)
Seward County Community College (U)
Shawnee State University (U)
Shippensburg University of Pennsylvania (U)
Shoreline Community College (U)
Sinclair Community College (U)
Snead State Community College (U)
Southeast Arkansas College (U)
Southeast Community College, Beatrice Campus (N, U)
Southeastern College of the Assemblies of God (U)
Southeastern Community College (U)
Southern Illinois University Carbondale (U)
Southwest Wisconsin Technical College (U)
Spartanburg Technical College (U)
Stephens College (U)
Stevens Institute of Technology (U)
Strayer University (U, G)
Sul Ross State University (U)
Tacoma Community College (U)

N–Noncredit; U–Undergraduate; G–Graduate

Taft College (U)
Taylor University (N, U)
Taylor University (U)
Teikyo Post University (U)
Temple College (U)
Texas A&M University (G)
Texas State Technical College–Waco (U)
Texas State University-San Marcos (U, G)
Texas Tech University (G)
Three Rivers Community College (U)
Tompkins Cortland Community College (U)
Troy University–Florida Region (U)
Umpqua Community College (U)
The University of Akron (U, G)
The University of Alabama (U)
University of Alaska Fairbanks (U)
University of Arkansas at Little Rock (U)
University of California, Los Angeles (G)
University of Central Arkansas (U)
University of Colorado at Colorado Springs (U)
The University of Findlay (U)
University of Florida (U)
University of Georgia (U)
University of Great Falls (U)
University of Houston (G)
University of Idaho (U)
University of Illinois (U, G)
University of Illinois at Springfield (U)
The University of Iowa (U, G)
The University of Maine at Augusta (U)
University of Maryland University College (U)
University of Minnesota, Morris (U)
University of Minnesota, Twin Cities Campus (U)
University of Missouri–Columbia (U)
The University of Montana–Missoula (U, G)
University of Nebraska–Lincoln (U)
University of Nevada, Reno (U)
University of New Orleans (U)
University of North Dakota (N, U)
University of Northern Colorado (U)
University of Northern Iowa (U)
University of Oklahoma (U)
University of Saskatchewan (U)
University of South Carolina (U)
The University of Tennessee (N, U)
The University of Texas at Austin (U)
The University of Texas at Tyler (U)
The University of Texas of the Permian Basin (U)
The University of Texas System (U)
University of the Incarnate Word (U)
University of Toledo (U)
University of Utah (U)
University of Washington (U)
University of Waterloo (U)
University of West Florida (U)
University of Wisconsin Colleges (U)
University of Wisconsin–Platteville (U, G)
University of Wisconsin–Platteville (G)
University of Wisconsin–Platteville (G)
University of Wisconsin–Platteville (U)
University of Wyoming (U)
Upper Iowa University (U)
Utah Valley State College (U)
Valley City State University (U)
Virginia Polytechnic Institute and State University (U, G)
Walters State Community College (U)
Washington State University (U)
Waubonsee Community College (U)
Waycross College (U)
Wayne State College (G)
Weber State University (U)
Westchester Community College (U)
Western Washington University (U)
West Los Angeles College (U)
West Valley College (U)
Whatcom Community College (U)
Wilkes Community College (U)
William Paterson University of New Jersey (U)
Worcester State College (U)
Wright State University (U)
York Technical College (U)
York University (U)
Youngstown State University (U)
Yuba College (U)

Mathematics, other

Alvin Community College (U)
Berkeley College-New York City Campus (U)
Bristol Community College (U)
Chadron State College (U, G)
Chemeketa Community College (U)
Eastern Illinois University (U)
Glenville State College (N, U)
Iowa Western Community College (U)
Irvine Valley College (U)
Jacksonville State University (U)
Jones College (U)
Lenoir Community College (U)
Los Angeles Pierce College (U)
Marshall University (U)
Middlesex Community College (U)
Neumann College (U)
New Hampshire Community Technical College System (U)
Pace University (U)
Passaic County Community College (U)
Raritan Valley Community College (U)
San Bernardino Valley College (U)
Southeast Arkansas College (U)
Taft College (U)
Tarleton State University (U)
Teikyo Post University (U)
Texas Tech University (U)
Treasure Valley Community College (U)
The University of Akron (G)
University of Arkansas at Little Rock (U)
University of Bridgeport (U)
University of Colorado at Denver (U)
University of Great Falls (U)
University of Mississippi (U)
The University of Texas System (U)
University of Washington (U)
University of Waterloo (U)
Valparaiso University (U)
York University (N)

Mechanical engineering

Bradley University (G)
California National University for Advanced Studies (N, U, G)
Colorado State University (G)
Columbia University (N, G)
Connecticut State University System (U, G)
Florida Atlantic University (G)
Georgia Institute of Technology (N, G)
Illinois Institute of Technology (U, G)
Iowa State University of Science and Technology (G)
Kansas State University (G)
Louisiana State University and Agricultural and Mechanical College (U)
Michigan Technological University (N, U, G)
New Mexico Institute of Mining and Technology (G)
New Mexico State University (G)
New York Institute of Technology (U)
Northeastern University (G)
Northern Virginia Community College (U)
The Ohio State University (G)
Oklahoma State University (G)
Old Dominion University (G)
Rochester Institute of Technology (U)
Southern Methodist University (G)
Stanford University (N)
Tarrant County College District (U)
Texas Tech University (G)
The University of Arizona (G)
University of Central Florida (G)
University of Colorado at Boulder (N, G)
University of Colorado at Colorado Springs (U, G)
University of Colorado at Denver (U)
University of Delaware (N, U, G)
University of Idaho (U, G)
University of Illinois (G)
University of Maine (U, G)

University of Massachusetts Amherst (N, G)
University of Michigan (N)
University of Minnesota, Twin Cities Campus (U)
University of New Hampshire (G)
University of North Dakota (U)
The University of Texas at Arlington (G)
University of Washington (U, G)
University of Wisconsin–Madison (U, G)
University of Wisconsin–Platteville (G)
Virginia Polytechnic Institute and State University (G)

Mechanical engineering-related technologies
Bristol Community College (N)
Cincinnati State Technical and Community College (U)
Columbus State Community College (U)
Southern Methodist University (G)
University of Michigan (N)
Villanova University (G)

Mechanics and repairers, other
Bristol Community College (N)
John Tyler Community College (U)
Oxnard College (U)

Medical basic sciences
Athabasca University (N)
Bellingham Technical College (U)
Colorado State University (N)
Jacksonville State University (U, G)
Lackawanna College (N, U)
Manchester Community College (U)
Maysville Community College (N)
Minot State University–Bottineau Campus (U)
Montgomery Community College (U)
NorthWest Arkansas Community College (U)
The Paralegal Institute, Inc. (U)
Randolph Community College (N)
Rockland Community College (U)
St. Cloud Technical College (N)
The University of Akron (U)

Medical clinical sciences (M.S., Ph.D.)
Daemen College (G)
Memorial University of Newfoundland (U)
University of Illinois at Chicago (G)
The University of Texas Medical Branch (G)

Medical genetics
Eastern Michigan University (U)
Maysville Community College (U)
University of Colorado at Denver (U)
University of Southern Mississippi (U)

University of Waterloo (U)
Wilfrid Laurier University (U)

Medical laboratory technology
Albuquerque Technical Vocational Institute (U)
Arapahoe Community College (U)
California State University, Sacramento (U)
Chesapeake College (U)
Clinton Community College (U)
Darton College (U)
Hibbing Community College (U)
Madison Area Technical College (U)
Marion Technical College (U)
Randolph Community College (N)
Shawnee State University (U)
South Central Technical College (U)
Triton College (U)
University of Illinois (G)
University of Massachusetts Lowell (G)
The University of Texas Medical Branch (U)
The University of Texas System (U)

Medical residency programs
Jacksonville State University (U, G)
University of Illinois at Chicago (N)

Medieval and Renaissance studies
California State University, Sacramento (U)
Elizabethtown College (U)
Seattle Central Community College (U)
Taylor University (U)
The University of British Columbia (U)
University of Georgia (U)
University of Nebraska–Lincoln (U)
University of Waterloo (U)
Western Washington University (U)

Mental health services
Athabasca University (N, U, G)
Central Texas College (U)
Central Wyoming College (N)
College of The Albemarle (N)
The Ohio State University (N)
Pierce College (U)
Sullivan University (G)
The University of Maine at Augusta (U)
University of Missouri–Columbia (G)

Metallurgical engineering
Delta College (U)
Illinois Institute of Technology (G)
The University of British Columbia (U)

Microbiology/bacteriology
Acadia University (U)
Albuquerque Technical Vocational Institute (U)

Arkansas State University–Beebe (U)
Baltimore City Community College (U)
Brigham Young University (U)
Community College of Denver (U)
Delta College (U)
Gateway Community College (U)
Harrisburg Area Community College (U)
Honolulu Community College (U)
Immaculata University (U)
Manatee Community College (U)
Montana State University–Bozeman (G)
Mountain State University (U)
North Dakota State College of Science (U)
Oxnard College (U)
Queen's University at Kingston (U)
Rend Lake College (U)
St. Petersburg College (U)
Skidmore College (U)
Snead State Community College (U)
The University of Akron (U)
University of Guelph (U)
University of Idaho (U)
University of Southern Mississippi (U)
University of Waterloo (U)
University of Wisconsin–La Crosse (G)
Weber State University (U)
Winston-Salem State University (U)

Middle Eastern languages and literatures
Feather River Community College District (N)
Hebrew College (N, U, G)
Henry Ford Community College (U)
The Jewish Theological Seminary (N, U, G)
University of Colorado at Colorado Springs (U)

Military studies
American Public University System (U, G)
Central Texas College (U)
Fort Hays State University (U)
John Wood Community College (U)
Limestone College (U)
North Georgia College & State University (N, U)
Syracuse University (N)
Touro University International (G)
University of Colorado at Colorado Springs (U)

Military technologies
American Public University System (U)
Glenville State College (U)

Military technology
American Public University System (G)

N–Noncredit; U–Undergraduate; G–Graduate

Mining and mineral engineering
New Mexico Institute of Mining and Technology (G)

Miscellaneous biological specializations
James Madison University (N)
University of West Florida (U)

Miscellaneous engineering-related technologies
Bristol Community College (N)
Cleveland State University (G)
Normandale Community College (U)
Stanford University (N)
University of Michigan (N)

Miscellaneous health aides
Bossier Parish Community College (N)
Forrest Junior College (U)
James Madison University (N)
Lamar State College–Port Arthur (N)
Pratt Community College (U)
University of Mississippi (U)

Miscellaneous health professions
Alvin Community College (U)
Athabasca University (N)
Baptist Theological Seminary at Richmond (N)
Brenau University (U, G)
Capella University (G)
Chattanooga State Technical Community College (U)
Cincinnati State Technical and Community College (U)
Cleveland State University (N)
Des Moines Area Community College (U)
Eastern Michigan University (G)
Forrest Junior College (U)
Gogebic Community College (U)
Jacksonville State University (G)
James Madison University (N)
Jefferson College of Health Sciences (U)
Kansas City Kansas Community College (U)
Kirkwood Community College (U)
Lackawanna College (N, U)
Massasoit Community College (N)
Middle Tennessee State University (N)
North Dakota State University (N)
Northeastern Oklahoma Agricultural and Mechanical College (N)
Northern Arizona University (U)
North Georgia College & State University (N)
NorthWest Arkansas Community College (U)
Northwestern Technical College (U)
Oregon Institute of Technology (U)
Santa Fe Community College (N)
Seminole Community College (U)
Sinclair Community College (U)
South Central Technical College (U)
Southeast Community College, Beatrice Campus (U)
United States Sports Academy (N, G)
Université Sainte-Anne (N)
University of Alaska Fairbanks (U)
University of Connecticut (N, U)
University of Missouri–Columbia (U)
The University of Montana–Missoula (U)

Miscellaneous mechanics and repairers
James Madison University (N)
Massasoit Community College (N)
Maui Community College (U)

Miscellaneous physical sciences
Darton College (U)
James Madison University (N)
Lord Fairfax Community College (U)
Snead State Community College (U)
University of La Verne (N)
University of Waterloo (U)
University of West Florida (U)

Missions/missionary studies and missiology
Alliance University College (G)
Assemblies of God Theological Seminary (G)
Baptist Bible College of Pennsylvania (G)
Barclay College (U)
Bethany College of the Assemblies of God (U)
Briercrest Distance Learning (U)
Calvin Theological Seminary (G)
Covenant Theological Seminary (N, G)
Crown College (U, G)
Eugene Bible College (U)
Global University of the Assemblies of God (N)
The King's College and Seminary (N, U, G)
Master's College and Seminary (U)
Northwestern College (U)
Prairie Bible College (U, G)
Southern Christian University (N, U, G)
Southwestern Assemblies of God University (U, G)
Taylor University (U)
Taylor University (U)

Multi/interdisciplinary studies, other
Acadia University (U)
Central Texas College (U)
College for Lifelong Learning (U)
Columbia College (U)
Fairmont State University (U)
Fort Hays State University (U, G)
Hibbing Community College (U)
Jones International University (U, G)
Marylhurst University (G)
Mississippi State University (U)
Mountain State University (G)
Naropa University (U, G)
North Carolina State University (U)
Prescott College (U, G)
Roosevelt University (U)
Saint Joseph's College of Maine (U)
Southwestern Assemblies of God University (U)
Taylor University (U)
University of Arkansas at Little Rock (U)
University of Florida (U)
University of Minnesota, Morris (U)
University of Waterloo (U)
Wayne State College (U, G)

Museology/museum studies
Brenau University (U)
Feather River Community College District (N)
James Madison University (N)
John F. Kennedy University (G)
University of Idaho (U)
University of La Verne (N)

Music
Allan Hancock College (U)
Allen County Community College (U)
Arkansas Tech University (U)
Athabasca University (N, U)
Boise State University (U)
Bowling Green State University (U)
Brevard Community College (U)
Bridgewater State College (U)
Brigham Young University (U)
Bucks County Community College (U)
Butler County Community College (U)
Butler County Community College (U)
Caldwell College (U)
Caldwell Community College and Technical Institute (U)
California State University, Chico (U)
California State University, Dominguez Hills (N)
California State University, Sacramento (U)
Casper College (U)
Central Virginia Community College (U)
Central Wyoming College (N)
Chaminade University of Honolulu (U)
Chattanooga State Technical Community College (U)
Chemeketa Community College (U)
Clackamas Community College (U)
Clarion University of Pennsylvania (U)
Clinton Community College (U)

Coastal Bend College (U)
Coconino Community College (N)
College of DuPage (U)
College of Mount St. Joseph (U)
The College of St. Scholastica (U, G)
College of the Canyons (U)
Collin County Community College District (U)
Colorado State University (N)
Columbia Union College (U)
Dakota State University (U)
Dallas County Community College District (U)
Danville Area Community College (U)
Danville Community College (U)
Darton College (U)
Des Moines Area Community College (U)
Eastern Oregon University (U)
Eastern Shore Community College (U)
El Camino College (U)
Elizabeth City State University (U)
Eugene Bible College (U)
Everett Community College (U)
Evergreen Valley College (U)
Feather River Community College District (N)
Gannon University (U)
Goddard College (U)
Gonzaga University (U)
Howard Community College (U)
Immaculata University (U, G)
Indiana State University (U)
Indiana Wesleyan University (U)
Inter American University of Puerto Rico, San Germán Campus (U)
Irvine Valley College (U)
Jacksonville State University (U)
James Madison University (N)
Jefferson College (U)
John Tyler Community College (U)
John Wood Community College (U)
Judson College (U)
The King's College and Seminary (N, U, G)
Lansing Community College (U)
Limestone College (U)
Long Beach City College (U)
Los Angeles Pierce College (U)
Louisiana State University and Agricultural and Mechanical College (U)
Massasoit Community College (U)
Mesalands Community College (U)
Metropolitan State University (U)
MiraCosta College (U)
Mississippi Delta Community College (U)
Modesto Junior College (U)
Mountain Empire Community College (U)
Mountain State University (U)
Murray State University (U)
Nassau Community College (U)
Naugatuck Valley Community College (U)
Northampton County Area Community College (U)
North Carolina State University (U)
Northeastern Oklahoma Agricultural and Mechanical College (U)
Northeastern University (U)
Northeast State Technical Community College (U)
Northern Arizona University (U)
Northern Kentucky University (U)
North Harris Montgomery Community College District (U)
Northwestern Michigan College (U)
Northwest Missouri State University (U)
Oklahoma State University (U)
Orange Coast College (U)
Oxnard College (U)
Palomar College (U)
Peninsula College (U)
The Pennsylvania State University University Park Campus (U)
Prairie Bible College (U)
Pratt Community College (U)
Randolph Community College (U)
Rend Lake College (U)
Riverside Community College (U)
Sacramento City College (U)
Sacred Heart University (U)
Saddleback College (U)
Saint Mary-of-the-Woods College (G)
St. Petersburg College (U)
San Jacinto College District (U)
Santa Fe Community College (U)
Schenectady County Community College (U)
Schoolcraft College (U)
Seminole Community College (U)
Shawnee State University (U)
Shoreline Community College (U)
Snead State Community College (U)
Southeastern Community College (U)
Southern Illinois University Carbondale (U)
Southwestern Assemblies of God University (U)
Southwest Missouri State University (U)
Spring Arbor University (U)
Stephen F. Austin State University (U, G)
Tacoma Community College (U)
Taylor University (U)
Teikyo Post University (U)
Texas State University-San Marcos (U)
Texas Tech University (U, G)
Treasure Valley Community College (U)
Tunxis Community College (U)
The University of Akron (U)
University of Alaska Fairbanks (U)
University of Arkansas at Little Rock (U)
University of Bridgeport (U)
The University of British Columbia (U)
University of Colorado at Denver (U)
University of Delaware (U)
University of Georgia (U)
University of Idaho (U)
University of La Verne (N, U)
University of Maine (U)
The University of Maine at Augusta (U)
University of Massachusetts Boston (U)
University of Minnesota, Twin Cities Campus (U)
University of Nevada, Reno (U)
The University of North Carolina at Chapel Hill (U)
The University of North Carolina at Greensboro (G)
University of Northern Iowa (U)
University of Saskatchewan (U)
University of South Carolina (U)
University of Southern Mississippi (U)
The University of Texas–Pan American (U)
The University of Texas System (U)
University of Utah (U)
University of Wisconsin Colleges (U)
University of Wisconsin–Platteville (U)
University of Wyoming (U)
Virginia Polytechnic Institute and State University (N, U)
Walters State Community College (U)
Wayland Baptist University (U)
Weber State University (U)
Western Washington University (U)
West Virginia University (N)
Whatcom Community College (U)
Wichita State University (U)
William Paterson University of New Jersey (N, U)
Winston-Salem State University (U)
Wright State University (U)

Natural resources conservation

Ashworth College (N)
Athabasca University (U)
Goddard College (G)
Lansing Community College (U)
Mount Wachusett Community College (U)
Northern Arizona University (U)
Oregon State University (U, G)
Prescott College (U)
University of La Verne (N)
University of Massachusetts Amherst (U)
Virginia Polytechnic Institute and State University (N)

N–Noncredit; U–Undergraduate; G–Graduate

Natural resources management and protective services

Arkansas Tech University (U)
Athabasca University (U)
Northern Arizona University (U)
Oregon State University (U)
Prescott College (G)
University of Denver (G)
University of Wisconsin–River Falls (G)
Virginia Polytechnic Institute and State University (G)

Nuclear and industrial radiologic technologies

Bismarck State College (U)
Oregon State University (G)

Nuclear engineering

Bismarck State College (N)
The Ohio State University (G)
Oregon State University (G)
University of Missouri–Columbia (U, G)

Nursing

Albuquerque Technical Vocational Institute (U)
Alcorn State University (U)
Allen College (N, U, G)
Arapahoe Community College (U)
Arkansas Tech University (U)
Athabasca University (N, U, G)
Azusa Pacific University (G)
Bishop State Community College (U)
Bloomsburg University of Pennsylvania (U)
Boise State University (U)
Bowling Green State University (U)
Brenau University (U, G)
Brigham Young University (U)
Broward Community College (U)
Bucks County Community College (U)
Butler County Community College (U)
California State University, Chico (U)
California State University, Dominguez Hills (U, G)
California State University, Dominguez Hills (U, G)
California State University, Sacramento (U, G)
Carl Albert State College (U)
Central Connecticut State University (U)
Central Missouri State University (G)
Central Missouri State University (G)
Central Missouri State University (G)
Central Missouri State University (G)
Central Missouri State University (G)
Central Texas College (U)
Charter Oak State College (N, U)
Clarion University of Pennsylvania (U, G)
Cleveland State University (U)
The College of St. Scholastica (U, G)
College of the Siskiyous (U)
Colorado State University-Pueblo (U)
Columbus State Community College (U)
Community College of Denver (U)
Concordia University Wisconsin (U, G)
Connecticut State University System (U)
Cossatot Community College of the University of Arkansas (U)
Culver-Stockton College (U)
Daemen College (U, G)
Danville Community College (U)
Davenport University Online (U)
Delaware County Community College (U)
Dickinson State University (U)
Eastern Kentucky University (G)
Eastern Michigan University (G)
Edison State Community College (U)
Fairleigh Dickinson University, Metropolitan Campus (U, G)
Ferris State University (U)
Florida Atlantic University (U)
Florida Gulf Coast University (U)
Fort Hays State University (U, G)
Georgia Southern University (U, G)
Gonzaga University (U, G)
Gonzaga University (U, G)
Greenville Technical College (N)
Hibbing Community College (U)
Howard College (U)
Illinois State University (U, G)
Immaculata University (U, G)
Indiana State University (U, G)
Indiana University–Purdue University Fort Wayne (U, G)
Ivy Tech State College–Northwest (U)
Jacksonville State University (U, G)
James Madison University (N)
Jefferson College of Health Sciences (N, U)
John Tyler Community College (U)
Kauai Community College (U)
Kent State University (U)
Lewis-Clark State College (N)
Long Beach City College (U)
Lord Fairfax Community College (U)
Loyola University New Orleans (U, G)
Madison Area Technical College (U)
Madonna University (U)
Mansfield University of Pennsylvania (U)
Marshall University (U)
Maui Community College (U)
Maysville Community College (U)
Memorial University of Newfoundland (U, G)
Mesa Community College (U)
Metropolitan State University (U, G)
MGH Institute of Health Professions (G)
Middle Tennessee State University (N, U, G)
Mississippi University for Women (U)
Monroe County Community College (U)
Montana Tech of The University of Montana (U)
Montgomery County Community College (U)
Mountain State University (U, G)
Murray State University (U, G)
National University (U)
Naugatuck Valley Community College (U)
Nebraska Methodist College (U, G)
Northampton County Area Community College (N, U)
Northeastern University (N, U, G)
Northern Arizona University (U)
Northern Kentucky University (U, G)
Northern New Mexico Community College (U)
North Georgia College & State University (U, G)
North Hennepin Community College (U)
Northwestern Michigan College (U)
Northwestern State University of Louisiana (U)
Ocean County College (U)
The Ohio State University (G)
Old Dominion University (U, G)
Pace University (N, U, G)
The Paralegal Institute, Inc. (U)
Pennsylvania College of Technology (U)
Quinnipiac University (G)
Raritan Valley Community College (U)
Rend Lake College (U)
The Richard Stockton College of New Jersey (U, G)
Rockland Community College (N, U)
Ryerson University (U)
Sacred Heart University (G)
Saddleback College (U)
St. Clair County Community College (U)
Saint Joseph's College of Maine (U, G)
Shawnee State University (U)
Slippery Rock University of Pennsylvania (G)
Snead State Community College (U)
South Central Technical College (U)
Southern Illinois University Edwardsville (U, G)
Southwestern College (U)
Southwest Missouri State University (U, G)
Southwest Wisconsin Technical College (U)
Stanly Community College (U)
State University of New York at Plattsburgh (U)
State University of New York Institute of Technology (U, G)

State University of New York Institute of Technology (U, G)
State University of New York Institute of Technology (U, G)
State University of New York Institute of Technology (U, G)
Sullivan University (G)
Tacoma Community College (U)
Tarleton State University (U)
Texas Woman's University (U, G)
Tompkins Cortland Community College (U)
Triton College (U)
The University of Akron (N, U, G)
The University of Alabama (G)
The University of Arizona (G)
University of Arkansas at Little Rock (U)
The University of British Columbia (U)
University of Calgary (U)
University of California, Riverside (N)
University of Central Arkansas (G)
University of Central Florida (U)
University of Colorado at Colorado Springs (U, G)
University of Delaware (U, G)
University of Illinois (G)
University of Illinois at Chicago (N, G)
The University of Iowa (U, G)
University of Maine (U)
The University of Maine at Augusta (U)
University of Maryland (U, G)
University of Massachusetts Amherst (G)
University of Massachusetts Boston (U, G)
University of Minnesota, Twin Cities Campus (U)
University of Missouri–Columbia (U, G)
University of Nebraska–Lincoln (U)
The University of North Carolina at Chapel Hill (N)
The University of North Carolina at Charlotte (N, U, G)
University of North Dakota (U)
University of Northern Colorado (U)
University of North Florida (U)
University of St. Francis (U, G)
University of Saint Francis (U, G)
University of Saskatchewan (U)
University of South Carolina Spartanburg (U)
University of South Carolina Sumter (G)
The University of South Dakota (U)
University of Southern Indiana (U, G)
University of Southern Mississippi (U, G)
The University of Texas at Austin (U)
The University of Texas at Tyler (U, G)
The University of Texas Medical Branch (U, G)
The University of Texas System (G)
University of Tulsa (U)
University of Vermont (U, G)
The University of Virginia's College at Wise (U)
University of Wisconsin–Eau Claire (N, U)
University of Wisconsin–Madison (U, G)
University of Wyoming (U, G)
Valparaiso University (U)
Walters State Community College (U)
Washtenaw Community College (U)
Waubonsee Community College (U)
William Paterson University of New Jersey (U, G)
William Rainey Harper College (U)
Wisconsin Indianhead Technical College (N, U)
Wright State University (U, G)
York Technical College (U)
York University (U)
Youngstown State University (U)
Yuba College (U)

Occupational therapy

St. Ambrose University (G)
Texas Woman's University (U, G)
University of Central Arkansas (G)
University of Minnesota, Twin Cities Campus (U)
University of St. Augustine for Health Sciences (G)
Western Michigan University (U)

Ocean engineering

Florida Atlantic University (U, G)
San Bernardino Valley College (U)
University of Michigan (N)
William Paterson University of New Jersey (U)

Oceanography

Anne Arundel Community College (U)
Baltimore City Community College (U)
Johnson County Community College (U)
Oregon State University (U)
Riverside Community College (U)
Seattle Central Community College (U)
Umpqua Community College (U)
The University of British Columbia (U)
University of Oregon (U)
West Valley College (U)

Ophthalmic/optometric services

Hillsborough Community College (U)
Madison Area Technical College (U)

Optometry (O.D.)

Ferris State University (G)

Organic chemistry

American Academy of Nutrition, College of Nutrition (U)
Illinois Institute of Technology (G)
Mountain State University (U)
The Pennsylvania State University University Park Campus (U)
Sam Houston State University (U)
University of Utah (U)
University of Waterloo (U)

Organizational behavior

Brigham Young University (U)
California Institute of Integral Studies (N, G)
California National University for Advanced Studies (U, G)
Columbus State Community College (U)
Connecticut State University System (U, G)
Duke University (G)
Embry-Riddle Aeronautical University (U)
Kansas State University (U)
Louisiana State University and Agricultural and Mechanical College (U)
Milwaukee School of Engineering (G)
Montana State University–Billings (U)
Mountain State University (U)
Northern Virginia Community College (U)
Oklahoma State University (U)
Park University (U)
Pennsylvania College of Technology (U)
The Pennsylvania State University University Park Campus (U)
Regis University (U, G)
Southern Christian University (N, U, G)
State University of New York Empire State College (U)
Troy University–Florida Region (U)
Troy University Montgomery (U)
University of Delaware (U)
University of Missouri–Columbia (G)
University of Nebraska–Lincoln (U)
University of Toronto (N)
University of Waterloo (U)

Organizational psychology

College of the Southwest (U)
Lawson State Community College (U)
Montana State University–Billings (U)
Old Dominion University (U)
Saint Joseph's College of Maine (U)
University of Colorado at Denver (U)
University of Guelph (U)
University of Houston–Downtown (U)
University of North Dakota (U)
Upper Iowa University (N, U)

N–Noncredit; U–Undergraduate; G–Graduate

Paralegal/legal assistant

Anne Arundel Community College (U)
College of Mount St. Joseph (U)
Johnson County Community College (U)
Manatee Community College (U)

Parks, recreation and leisure facilities management

Acadia University (U)
Arkansas Tech University (U)
North Carolina State University (U)
Northern Arizona University (U)
Prescott College (G)
Saint Joseph's College of Maine (G)
Slippery Rock University of Pennsylvania (G)
United States Sports Academy (N)
University of Mississippi (U)
University of Wisconsin–La Crosse (G)
University of Wisconsin–River Falls (G)

Parks, recreation and leisure studies

Arkansas Tech University (U)
Clemson University (U)
The Community College of Baltimore County (U)
Madison Area Technical College (U)
Prescott College (U)
Seattle Pacific University (G)
Southern Illinois University Carbondale (U)
United States Sports Academy (N)
University of Georgia (U)
The University of North Carolina at Chapel Hill (U)

Parks, recreation, leisure and fitness studies, other

The Community College of Baltimore County (U)
James Madison University (N)
Santa Fe Community College (N)
United States Sports Academy (N, G)
University of La Verne (N)
University of Southern Mississippi (G)
Western Washington University (U)

Pastoral counseling and specialized ministries

Assemblies of God Theological Seminary (G)
Bethany College of the Assemblies of God (U)
Calvin Theological Seminary (G)
Central Baptist Theological Seminary (N, G)
Crown College (U)
Earlham School of Religion (G)
Global University of the Assemblies of God (N)
Hartford Seminary (G)
The King's College and Seminary (N, U, G)
Master's College and Seminary (U)
Mid-America Christian University (N, U)
Regent University (N)
Saint Joseph's College of Maine (N, U, G)
Southern Christian University (N, U, G)
Southwestern Assemblies of God University (U)
Southwestern Baptist Theological Seminary (G)
Summit Pacific College (U)
Taylor University (U)
Taylor University (U)
William and Catherine Booth College (U)

Peace and conflict studies

Caldwell Community College and Technical Institute (N)
California State University, Dominguez Hills (G)
Drake University (U, G)
Earlham School of Religion (G)
Goddard College (U, G)
John F. Kennedy University (G)
Jones International University (G)
Massasoit Community College (N)
Mercy College (G)
Naropa University (N, U)
Prescott College (U, G)
St. Edward's University (G)
Santa Fe Community College (N)
Saybrook Graduate School and Research Center (G)
Sullivan University (G)
Taylor University (U)
University of Bridgeport (U)
University of Missouri–Columbia (U)
University of Waterloo (U)

Personal and miscellaneous services, other

Baltimore City Community College (N)
Gateway Community College (N)
Kansas City Kansas Community College (U)
Lewis-Clark State College (N)
Linn-Benton Community College (N)
Long Island University, C.W. Post Campus (N)
Minnesota State College–Southeast Technical (N)
Pace University (N)
Pasco-Hernando Community College (N)
Texas State Technical College–Waco (N)
University of Missouri–Columbia (N)
Vance-Granville Community College (N)

Petroleum engineering

New Mexico Institute of Mining and Technology (G)
Texas A&M University (G)
Texas Tech University (G)

Pharmacy

Arapahoe Community College (U)
Auburn University (N)
Bossier Parish Community College (U)
Broome Community College (U)
Charter Oak State College (N)
Creighton University (G)
Delaware County Community College (U)
Drake University (U, G)
Ferris State University (G)
Long Beach City College (U)
Northeastern Oklahoma Agricultural and Mechanical College (N)
Northeastern University (G)
Ohio Northern University (U, G)
Randolph Community College (N)
Shenandoah University (U)
Shoreline Community College (U)
The University of Akron (U)
University of Georgia (N)
University of Illinois (G)
University of Illinois at Chicago (N, G)
The University of Montana–Missoula (U, G)
University of Washington (U)
University of Wisconsin–Madison (G)

Philosophy and religion related

Atlantic University (N, G)
Brigham Young University (U)
Brookdale Community College (U)
Broward Community College (U)
Bucks County Community College (U)
Chaminade University of Honolulu (U)
Cleveland State University (U, G)
Community College of Denver (U)
Denver Seminary (G)
Duquesne University (U, G)
East Carolina University (U)
Eastern Kentucky University (U)
Edison State Community College (U)
Fairleigh Dickinson University, Metropolitan Campus (U)
Indiana Wesleyan University (U)
John Wood Community College (U)
Kellogg Community College (U)
Life Pacific College (U)
Louisiana State University and Agricultural and Mechanical College (U)
Manatee Community College (U)
Marylhurst University (U, G)
Mountain State University (U)
Murray State University (U)
New York Institute of Technology (U)
Northern Virginia Community College (U)
Oregon State University (U)

Non-Degree-Related Course Subject Areas
Philosophy and religion related

Park University (U)
Pennsylvania College of Technology (U)
Pierce College (U)
Pitt Community College (U)
Prairie Bible College (U)
Randolph Community College (U)
Regis University (U, G)
Seattle Central Community College (U)
Southeast Community College, Lincoln Campus (U)
Triton College (U)
University of Alaska Fairbanks (U)
University of Colorado at Denver (U)
University of Delaware (U)
University of Idaho (G)
The University of Texas of the Permian Basin (U)
University of Toledo (U)

Philosophy and religion

Alliance University College (U)
American Public University System (U)
Asheville-Buncombe Technical Community College (U)
Assemblies of God Theological Seminary (G)
Athabasca University (N, U)
The Baptist College of Florida (U)
Baptist Theological Seminary at Richmond (N)
Bemidji State University (U)
Bethany College of the Assemblies of God (U)
Bowling Green State University (U)
Brevard Community College (U)
Brunswick Community College (U)
Bucks County Community College (U)
Butler County Community College (U)
California Institute of Integral Studies (N, G)
Central Texas College (U)
Chadron State College (U)
Chattanooga State Technical Community College (U)
Chemeketa Community College (U)
Clatsop Community College (U)
College of DuPage (U)
College of the Canyons (U)
Colorado Christian University (U)
Columbia College (U)
Covenant Theological Seminary (N, G)
Crown College (U, G)
Dallas County Community College District (U)
Darton College (U)
Delaware County Community College (U)
Des Moines Area Community College (U)
East Carolina University (U)
Eastern Michigan University (U)
Edison State Community College (U)
Emmanuel Bible College (U)
Feather River Community College District (N)
Florida Community College at Jacksonville (U)
Global University of the Assemblies of God (N)
Gonzaga University (G)
Hebrew College (N, U, G)
Holy Apostles College and Seminary (G)
Institute for Christian Studies (G)
Inter American University of Puerto Rico, San Germán Campus (U)
Iowa Western Community College (U)
The Jewish Theological Seminary (N, U, G)
John F. Kennedy University (U, G)
John Wood Community College (U)
Lake Superior College (U)
Lamar State College–Port Arthur (U)
Los Angeles Pierce College (U)
Loyola University New Orleans (U)
Marylhurst University (N)
Master's College and Seminary (U)
Maysville Community College (U)
Miami Dade College (U)
Middlesex Community College (U)
MiraCosta College (U)
Moody Bible Institute (U)
Murray State University (U)
Naropa University (N, U)
Northern Arizona University (U)
Northwestern College (U)
Ohio University (U)
Prescott College (U, G)
Rend Lake College (U)
Sacramento City College (U)
Sacred Heart University (U)
St. Edward's University (U)
Saint Joseph's College of Maine (U, G)
Saint Leo University (U)
San Bernardino Valley College (U)
Schoolcraft College (U)
Southern Christian University (N, U, G)
Southwestern Baptist Theological Seminary (G)
Spoon River College (U)
Taylor University (U)
Taylor University (U)
Teikyo Post University (U)
Umpqua Community College (U)
The University of Akron (U)
The University of Alabama (U)
University of Arkansas at Little Rock (U)
University of Bridgeport (U)
University of California, Los Angeles (G)
University of Cincinnati (U)
The University of Findlay (U)
University of Florida (U)
University of Georgia (U)
University of Great Falls (U)
University of Houston (U)
University of Mississippi (U)
University of St. Francis (U)
University of Southern Mississippi (U)
University of the Incarnate Word (U)
University of Waterloo (U)
Upper Iowa University (U)
Wilkes Community College (U)
William Paterson University of New Jersey (U)

Philosophy

Acadia University (U)
Adirondack Community College (U)
Albuquerque Technical Vocational Institute (U)
Allan Hancock College (U)
Alpena Community College (U)
American Public University System (U)
Anne Arundel Community College (U)
Athabasca University (N, U, G)
Bellevue Community College (U)
Bemidji State University (U)
Berkeley College (U)
Berkeley College-New York City Campus (U)
Berkeley College-Westchester Campus (U)
Bismarck State College (U)
Boise State University (U)
Bowling Green State University (U)
Brigham Young University (U)
Broward Community College (U)
Bucks County Community College (U)
Butler County Community College (U)
Butler County Community College (U)
Cape Fear Community College (U)
Carroll Community College (U)
Central Texas College (U)
Central Virginia Community College (U)
Chadron State College (U)
Chaminade University of Honolulu (U)
Charter Oak State College (U)
Chemeketa Community College (U)
Citrus College (U)
Clackamas Community College (U)
Clarion University of Pennsylvania (U)
Coastal Bend College (U)
Coconino Community College (U)
Coleman College (U)
College of San Mateo (U)
College of the Canyons (U)

N–Noncredit; U–Undergraduate; G–Graduate

Colorado Mountain College District System (U)
Columbus State Community College (U)
Community College of Denver (U)
Connecticut State University System (U)
Corning Community College (U)
Dallas County Community College District (U)
Darton College (U)
Delaware County Community College (U)
Delta College (U)
Des Moines Area Community College (U)
East Carolina University (U)
Eastern Michigan University (U)
Eastern Oregon University (U)
East Los Angeles College (U)
Edison State Community College (U)
El Camino College (U)
Everett Community College (U)
Fairleigh Dickinson University, Metropolitan Campus (U)
Feather River Community College District (N)
Fontbonne University (U)
Franciscan University of Steubenville (N, U)
Frederick Community College (U)
Gannon University (U)
Gateway Community College (U)
Goddard College (U, G)
Golden West College (U)
Gonzaga University (U)
Harrisburg Area Community College (U)
Honolulu Community College (U)
Hopkinsville Community College (U)
Horry-Georgetown Technical College (U)
Houston Community College System (U)
Indiana University–Purdue University Fort Wayne (U)
Institute for Christian Studies (G)
Iowa Western Community College (U)
Ivy Tech State College–North Central (U)
James Madison University (U)
Jefferson College (U)
Jefferson College of Health Sciences (U)
The Jewish Theological Seminary (N, U, G)
John Tyler Community College (U)
John Wood Community College (U)
Kansas City Kansas Community College (U)
Lamar State College–Port Arthur (U)
Liberty University (U)
Limestone College (U)
Long Beach City College (U)
Los Angeles Pierce College (U)
Louisiana State University and Agricultural and Mechanical College (U)
Marshall University (U)
Massasoit Community College (U)
Maui Community College (U)
Memorial University of Newfoundland (U)
Metropolitan State University (U)
Middlesex Community College (U)
MiraCosta College (N, U)
Modesto Junior College (U)
Montana Tech of The University of Montana (U)
Montgomery County Community College (U)
Moody Bible Institute (U)
Mountain State University (U)
Mount Saint Mary College (U)
Mount Saint Vincent University (U)
Mt. San Antonio College (U)
Murray State University (U)
Naropa University (N)
New York Institute of Technology (U)
Northampton County Area Community College (U)
North Carolina State University (U)
Northern Arizona University (U)
North Harris Montgomery Community College District (U)
North Hennepin Community College (U)
North Idaho College (U)
NorthWest Arkansas Community College (U)
Northwestern Michigan College (U)
Northwest Missouri State University (U)
Ocean County College (U)
Okaloosa-Walton College (U)
Oklahoma State University (U)
Old Dominion University (U)
Oregon State University (U)
Oxnard College (U)
Palomar College (U)
Patrick Henry College (U)
Peninsula College (U)
The Pennsylvania State University University Park Campus (U)
Quinnipiac University (U)
Riverside Community College (U)
Rockland Community College (U)
Ryerson University (U)
Sacred Heart University (U)
St. Ambrose University (U)
St. Cloud State University (U)
St. Edward's University (U)
Saint Joseph's University (U)
Saint Leo University (U)
St. Petersburg College (U)
San Bernardino Valley College (U)
San Jacinto College District (U)
Santa Rosa Junior College (U)
Shawnee State University (U)
Shippensburg University of Pennsylvania (U)
Shoreline Community College (U)
Southeast Community College, Beatrice Campus (U)
Southern Illinois University Carbondale (U)
Southwestern College (U)
Spring Arbor University (U)
Stephens College (U)
Syracuse University (U)
Taylor University (U)
Teikyo Post University (U)
Temple College (U)
Texas State University-San Marcos (U)
Touro University International (U)
Triton College (U)
Troy University Montgomery (U)
Tunxis Community College (U)
Umpqua Community College (U)
The University of Akron (U)
The University of Alabama (U)
University of Alaska Fairbanks (U)
University of Arkansas at Little Rock (U)
University of Bridgeport (U)
The University of British Columbia (U)
University of Cincinnati (U)
University of Connecticut (U)
University of Florida (U)
University of Georgia (U)
University of Hawaii–West Oahu (U)
University of Idaho (U)
University of Illinois at Springfield (U, G)
University of La Verne (U)
The University of Maine at Augusta (U)
University of Massachusetts Amherst (U)
University of Massachusetts Lowell (U)
University of Minnesota, Twin Cities Campus (U)
University of Mississippi (U)
University of Missouri–Columbia (U, G)
The University of Montana–Missoula (G)
University of Nebraska–Lincoln (U)
University of New Orleans (U)
The University of North Carolina at Chapel Hill (U)
The University of North Carolina at Greensboro (U)
University of Oklahoma (U)
University of Saskatchewan (U)
University of South Carolina (U)
The University of Texas at Austin (U)
University of the Incarnate Word (U)
University of Toledo (U, G)
University of Washington (U)
University of Waterloo (U)
University of West Florida (U)
University of Wisconsin Colleges (U)
Utah Valley State College (U)
Utah Valley State College (U)
Virginia Polytechnic Institute and State University (U)

Washington State University (U)
Wayne State College (U)
Weber State University (U)
Webster University (U)
Westchester Community College (U)
Western Wyoming Community College (U)
West Valley College (U)
Whatcom Community College (U)
Wilfrid Laurier University (U)
William Paterson University of New Jersey (U)
Worcester State College (U)
York Technical College (U)
York University (U)
Youngstown State University (U)

Photography

Fashion Institute of Technology (U)
Houston Community College System (U)
The Richard Stockton College of New Jersey (U)
Sam Houston State University (U)
Sinclair Community College (U)
West Valley College (U)

Physical science technologies

Lord Fairfax Community College (U)

Physical sciences, general

Allen County Community College (U)
American River College (U)
Arkansas Tech University (U, G)
Athabasca University (N, U)
Barclay College (U)
Bethany College of the Assemblies of God (U)
Brevard Community College (U)
Brigham Young University (U)
Broome Community College (U)
Bucks County Community College (U)
Butler County Community College (U)
Caldwell Community College and Technical Institute (U)
Chadron State College (U)
Champlain College (U)
Chemeketa Community College (U)
Chesapeake College (U)
Coleman College (U)
The Community College of Baltimore County (U)
Dallas County Community College District (U)
Darton College (U)
Everett Community College (U)
George C. Wallace Community College (U)
Goddard College (U)
Harrisburg Area Community College (U)
Houston Community College System (U)
Iowa Western Community College (U)
Ivy Tech State College–Columbus (U)
Ivy Tech State College–Northwest (U)
Ivy Tech State College–Southcentral (U)
Ivy Tech State College–Wabash Valley (U)
James Madison University (N)
John F. Kennedy University (U)
John Tyler Community College (U)
John Wood Community College (U)
Kansas City Kansas Community College (U)
Lake Superior College (U)
Lord Fairfax Community College (U)
Louisiana State University and Agricultural and Mechanical College (U)
Massasoit Community College (U)
Mesalands Community College (U)
Middlesex Community College (U)
Mississippi Delta Community College (U)
Moody Bible Institute (U)
Mountain State University (U)
Mount Allison University (U)
Northwestern State University of Louisiana (U)
Okaloosa-Walton College (U)
Oxnard College (U)
Pasco-Hernando Community College (U)
Passaic County Community College (U)
Rockland Community College (U)
Roosevelt University (U)
Sacred Heart University (U)
Saint Leo University (U)
San Bernardino Valley College (U)
Santa Fe Community College (U)
Schiller International University (U)
Shawnee State University (U)
Snead State Community College (U)
Sul Ross State University (U)
Syracuse University (U)
Tarleton State University (U, G)
Taylor University (U)
Treasure Valley Community College (U)
Troy University Montgomery (U)
The University of Akron (U)
University of Arkansas at Little Rock (U)
University of La Verne (U)
The University of Maine at Augusta (U)
University of New Orleans (U)
University of North Dakota (U)
The University of Texas System (U)
University of Waterloo (U)
University of West Florida (U)
University of Wisconsin–Superior (U)
Utah Valley State College (U)
Waubonsee Community College (U)
Wayne State College (U)
Western Baptist College (U)
Worcester State College (U)

Physical sciences, other

Adams State College (G)
Brevard Community College (U)
Chadron State College (U)
Chemeketa Community College (U)
Dallas County Community College District (U)
Iowa Western Community College (U)
James Madison University (N)
Miami Dade College (U)
Mississippi Delta Community College (U)
Mississippi State University (U)
Nassau Community College (U)
The University of Akron (U)
University of Arkansas at Little Rock (U)
University of La Verne (N)
The University of Texas System (U)
University of West Florida (U)

Physical therapy

Northern Arizona University (G)
St. Ambrose University (G)
Texas Woman's University (G)
University of Central Arkansas (G)
University of St. Augustine for Health Sciences (G)
Walters State Community College (U)

Physical/theoretical chemistry

University of Waterloo (U)
William Rainey Harper College (U)

Physics

Acadia University (U)
Boise State University (U)
Brigham Young University (U)
Broome Community College (U)
Butler County Community College (U)
Cecil Community College (U)
Chaminade University of Honolulu (U)
Chattanooga State Technical Community College (U)
Clemson University (U)
Coastal Bend College (U)
College of DuPage (U)
Colorado Mountain College District System (U)
Columbia Union College (U)
Community College of Denver (U)
Danville Area Community College (U)
Davenport University Online (U)
Delaware County Community College (U)
Eastern Oregon University (U)
Edison State Community College (U)
Grantham University (U)
Immaculata University (U)

N–Noncredit; U–Undergraduate; G–Graduate

Indiana University of Pennsylvania (U, G)
Ivy Tech State College–Wabash Valley (U)
Jacksonville State University (U)
James Madison University (N)
Jefferson College (U)
John Tyler Community College (U)
John Wood Community College (U)
Louisiana State University and Agricultural and Mechanical College (U)
Maui Community College (U)
Mississippi State University (U)
Missouri Southern State University (U)
Montana State University–Billings (U)
Montana State University–Bozeman (G)
Mountain State University (U)
New England Institute of Technology (U)
New Jersey City University (U)
North Carolina State University (U)
North Hennepin Community College (U)
Northwestern Michigan College (U)
Oxnard College (U)
The Pennsylvania State University University Park Campus (U)
Pierce College (U)
St. John's University (U)
Shippensburg University of Pennsylvania (U)
Snead State Community College (U)
Southwest Missouri State University (U)
Tacoma Community College (U)
Texas A&M University–Kingsville (U)
University of Colorado at Denver (U)
University of Idaho (U)
University of Minnesota, Twin Cities Campus (U)
University of Missouri–Columbia (U)
University of Nebraska–Lincoln (U)
The University of North Carolina at Chapel Hill (U)
University of North Dakota (U)
University of Oregon (U)
The University of Tennessee (U)
The University of Texas at Austin (U)
University of Utah (U)
University of Waterloo (N, U)
University of Wyoming (U)
Virginia Polytechnic Institute and State University (U)
Wayne State College (U)
Weber State University (U)
Youngstown State University (U)

Physiological psychology/psychobiology
Athabasca University (U)
Colorado Christian University (U)
Eastern Wyoming College (U)
Lord Fairfax Community College (U)
Los Angeles Pierce College (U)
Mesa Community College (U)

Physiology
American Academy of Nutrition, College of Nutrition (U)
Floyd College (U)
Louisiana State University and Agricultural and Mechanical College (U)
Mountain State University (U)
The Pennsylvania State University University Park Campus (U)
University of Utah (U)
University of Waterloo (U)

Plant sciences
Athabasca University (U)
Bismarck State College (N)
James Madison University (N)
John Wood Community College (U)
Nova Scotia Agricultural College (N, U)
Oregon State University (U)
The Pennsylvania State University University Park Campus (U)
Santa Fe Community College (N)
Texas A&M University (G)
Texas Tech University (G)
University of California, Riverside (N)
University of Georgia (U)
University of Missouri–Columbia (U)

Plumbers and pipefitters
Augusta Technical College (N)
Madison Area Technical College (U)

Podiatry (D.P.M., D.P., Pod.D.)
Umpqua Community College (U)

Political science and government
Acadia University (U)
Allan Hancock College (U)
Allen County Community College (U)
Alpena Community College (U)
American Public University System (U)
Arapahoe Community College (U)
Arkansas State University–Beebe (U)
Arkansas Tech University (U)
Athabasca University (N, U, G)
Berkeley College (U)
Berkeley College-New York City Campus (U)
Berkeley College-Westchester Campus (U)
Bethany College of the Assemblies of God (U)
Bowling Green State University (U)
Brazosport College (U)
Brenau University (U)
Bridgewater State College (U)
Brigham Young University (U)
Broome Community College (U)
Butler County Community College (U)
Caldwell College (U)
Campbell University (U)
Carl Albert State College (U)
Carleton University (U)
Cayuga County Community College (U)
Central Texas College (U)
Central Virginia Community College (U)
Central Wyoming College (U)
Chaminade University of Honolulu (U)
Charter Oak State College (U)
Chattanooga State Technical Community College (U)
Chemeketa Community College (U)
Clatsop Community College (U)
Cleveland State University (U)
Coastal Bend College (U)
College of Mount St. Joseph (U)
College of San Mateo (U)
College of the Canyons (U)
College of the Siskiyous (U)
Colorado State University-Pueblo (U)
Columbia Basin College (U)
Columbia College (U)
Columbia Union College (U)
The Community College of Baltimore County (U)
Community College of Denver (U)
Cuyamaca College (U)
Darton College (U)
Davenport University Online (U)
Delta College (U)
Drake University (U, G)
East Arkansas Community College (U)
Eastern Kentucky University (U)
Eastern Michigan University (U)
Eastern Oregon University (U)
Eastern Wyoming College (U)
El Camino College (U)
Evergreen Valley College (U)
Fairleigh Dickinson University, Metropolitan Campus (U)
Florida Atlantic University (U)
Florida Metropolitan University–Brandon Campus (U)
Gateway Community College (U)
Georgia Southern University (U)
Golden West College (U)
Grossmont College (U)
Henry Ford Community College (U)
Hibbing Community College (U)
Honolulu Community College (U)
Houston Community College System (U)
Independence Community College (U)
Indiana State University (G)
Indiana University of Pennsylvania (U)
Indiana University–Purdue University Fort Wayne (U)

Institute for Christian Studies (G)
Iowa Western Community College (U)
Irvine Valley College (U)
Ivy Tech State College–North Central (U)
Jacksonville State University (U, G)
James Madison University (N)
Jefferson Davis Community College (U)
John A. Logan College (U)
John Wood Community College (U)
Judson College (U)
Judson College (U)
Lake Superior College (U)
Lander University (U)
Limestone College (U)
Long Beach City College (U)
Los Angeles Harbor College (U)
Los Angeles Pierce College (U)
Louisiana State University and Agricultural and Mechanical College (U)
Louisiana Tech University (U)
Memorial University of Newfoundland (U)
Mesa Community College (U)
Miami Dade College (U)
Middlesex Community College (U)
Middle Tennessee State University (U)
Mississippi Delta Community College (U)
Missouri Southern State University (U)
Modesto Junior College (U)
Monroe County Community College (U)
Mount Allison University (U)
Mount Wachusett Community College (U)
New Jersey City University (U)
New School University (G)
New York Institute of Technology (U)
North Carolina State University (U)
North Central Texas College (U)
Northeastern Oklahoma Agricultural and Mechanical College (U)
Northeast State Technical Community College (U)
Northern Arizona University (U)
Northern Kentucky University (U)
North Idaho College (U)
Northwest Missouri State University (U)
The Ohio State University (U)
Okaloosa-Walton College (U)
Oklahoma State University (U)
Oregon State University (U)
Oxnard College (U)
Pace University (U)
Park University (U)
Patrick Henry College (U)
The Pennsylvania State University University Park Campus (U)
Pierce College (U)
Pratt Community College (U)
Rend Lake College (U)
Rio Hondo College (U)
Riverside Community College (U)
Rockland Community College (U)
Sacred Heart University (U)
Saddleback College (U)
St. Clair County Community College (U)
St. John's University (U)
St. Joseph's College, Suffolk Campus (U)
Saint Mary-of-the-Woods College (U)
Saint Mary-of-the-Woods College (U)
St. Petersburg College (U)
San Bernardino Valley College (U)
Seton Hill University (U)
Shawnee State University (U)
Southern Illinois University Carbondale (U)
Southwestern College (U)
Southwest Missouri State University (U)
State University of New York at Plattsburgh (U)
State University of New York College at Fredonia (U)
State University of New York Empire State College (G)
Strayer University (U)
Sul Ross State University (U)
Syracuse University (U)
Tacoma Community College (U)
Tarleton State University (U)
Teikyo Post University (U)
Texas A&M University–Texarkana (U)
Texas State University-San Marcos (U)
Touro University International (U)
Troy University Montgomery (U)
The University of Akron (U, G)
The University of Alabama (U)
University of Arkansas at Little Rock (U, G)
University of Bridgeport (U)
University of Central Arkansas (U)
University of Colorado at Denver (U, G)
University of Connecticut (U)
University of Delaware (U)
University of Florida (U)
University of Georgia (U)
University of Hawaii–West Oahu (U)
University of Houston–Downtown (U)
University of Idaho (U)
The University of Maine at Augusta (U)
University of Massachusetts Boston (U)
University of Minnesota, Morris (U)
University of Missouri–Columbia (U, G)
The University of Montana–Missoula (G)
University of Nebraska–Lincoln (U, G)
University of New Orleans (U)
The University of North Carolina at Chapel Hill (U)
University of Northern Colorado (U)
University of Oklahoma (U)
University of Oregon (U)
University of South Carolina (U)
University of South Carolina Spartanburg (U)
The University of South Dakota (U)
University of Southern Indiana (U)
The University of Tennessee (U)
The University of Texas at Arlington (U)
The University of Texas at Tyler (U)
The University of Texas System (U)
University of Toledo (G)
University of Utah (U)
University of Washington (U)
University of West Florida (U)
University of Wisconsin Colleges (U)
University of Wisconsin–Madison (G)
University of Wisconsin–Platteville (G)
University of Wisconsin–River Falls (U)
Upper Iowa University (N, U)
Utah State University (G)
Vance-Granville Community College (U)
Virginia Polytechnic Institute and State University (U, G)
Washington State University (U)
Weber State University (U)
West Los Angeles College (U)
West Valley College (U)
Wilfrid Laurier University (U)
William Paterson University of New Jersey (U)
York University (U)

Polymer/plastics engineering

Lehigh University (N, G)
The University of Akron (U)

Precision metal workers

Central Wyoming College (N)

Precision production trades, other

Bristol Community College (N)
Lord Fairfax Community College (N)

Professional studies

Aspen University (N)
Athabasca University (N, U)
California State University, Hayward (N)
Champlain College (U)
DePaul University (U)
Franklin Pierce College (U)
Jacksonville State University (G)
Manchester Community College (N, U)
North Hennepin Community College (N)
State University of New York at Oswego (N)
Taylor University (U)
University of Saint Francis (G)
University of the Incarnate Word (U)
University of West Florida (G)

N–Noncredit; U–Undergraduate; G–Graduate

Protective services, other

Ashworth College (N)
Jacksonville State University (U, G)
John Jay College of Criminal Justice of the City University of New York (G)
John Wood Community College (U)
Lord Fairfax Community College (N)
Madison Area Technical College (U)
Seminole Community College (N)
The University of Akron (U)

Psychology

Acadia University (U)
Adirondack Community College (U)
AIB College of Business (U)
Albuquerque Technical Vocational Institute (U)
Allen County Community College (U)
Alliant International University (N, G)
Alvin Community College (U)
American Academy of Nutrition, College of Nutrition (U)
American College of Computer & Information Sciences (U)
American Public University System (U)
Arkansas State University–Beebe (U)
Arkansas Tech University (U)
Asheville-Buncombe Technical Community College (U)
Athabasca University (N, U, G)
Athens Technical College (U)
Austin Peay State University (U)
Baltimore City Community College (U)
Barclay College (U)
Beaufort County Community College (U)
Bellevue Community College (U)
Bemidji State University (U)
Berkeley College (U)
Berkeley College-New York City Campus (U)
Berkeley College-Westchester Campus (U)
Bethany College of the Assemblies of God (U)
Bethune-Cookman College (U)
Bishop State Community College (U)
Bismarck State College (U)
Black Hills State University (U)
Boise State University (U)
Bowling Green State University (U, G)
Brazosport College (U)
Brenau University (U)
Brevard Community College (U)
Bridgewater State College (U, G)
Brigham Young University (U)
Bristol Community College (U)
Broome Community College (U)
Broward Community College (U)
Brunswick Community College (U)
Bucks County Community College (U)
Butler County Community College (U)
Butler County Community College (U)
Caldwell College (U)
Caldwell Community College and Technical Institute (U)
California State University, Chico (U)
California State University, Sacramento (U)
Cape Cod Community College (U)
Cape Fear Community College (U)
Capella University (N, G)
Carl Albert State College (U)
Carleton University (U)
Carroll Community College (U)
Casper College (U)
Cayuga County Community College (U)
Cecil Community College (U)
Central Oregon Community College (U)
Central Texas College (U)
Central Virginia Community College (U)
Central Washington University (U)
Central Wyoming College (N, U)
Chadron State College (U, G)
Chaminade University of Honolulu (U)
Champlain College (U)
Charter Oak State College (U)
Chattanooga State Technical Community College (U)
Chemeketa Community College (U)
Chesapeake College (U)
Citrus College (U)
Clackamas Community College (U)
Clarion University of Pennsylvania (U)
Clark College (U)
Clatsop Community College (U)
Cleveland State University (U)
Clinton Community College (U)
Coastal Bend College (U)
Coconino Community College (U)
Coleman College (U)
College of DuPage (U)
The College of St. Scholastica (U)
College of San Mateo (U)
College of The Albemarle (U)
College of the Canyons (U)
College of the Siskiyous (U)
College of the Southwest (U)
Colorado Mountain College District System (U)
Colorado State University (U)
Colorado State University-Pueblo (U)
Columbia Basin College (U)
Columbia College (U)
Columbia Union College (U)
Columbus State Community College (U)
The Community College of Baltimore County (U)
Community College of Denver (U)
Concordia College (U)
Concordia University at Austin (N)
Copiah-Lincoln Community College–Natchez Campus (U)
Corning Community College (U)
Cossatot Community College of the University of Arkansas (U)
County College of Morris (U)
Cumberland County College (U)
Cuyamaca College (U)
Dakota County Technical College (U)
Dakota State University (U)
Dallas Baptist University (U)
Dallas County Community College District (U)
Daniel Webster College (U)
Danville Area Community College (U)
Darton College (U)
Davenport University Online (U)
Dawson Community College (U)
Delaware County Community College (U)
Delaware Technical & Community College, Jack F. Owens Campus (U)
Delaware Technical & Community College, Stanton/Wilmington Campus (U)
Delta College (U)
Des Moines Area Community College (U)
Dickinson State University (U)
Drake University (U, G)
East Carolina University (G)
East Central College (U)
Eastern Illinois University (U)
Eastern Michigan University (U)
Eastern Oregon University (U)
Eastern Shore Community College (U)
East Los Angeles College (U)
Edgecombe Community College (U)
Edison Community College (U)
El Camino College (U)
Elizabeth City State University (U)
Embry-Riddle Aeronautical University, Extended Campus (G)
Emmanuel Bible College (U)
Everett Community College (U)
Evergreen Valley College (U)
Fairleigh Dickinson University, Metropolitan Campus (N, U, G)
Fayetteville State University (U)
Feather River Community College District (N, U)
Florida Community College at Jacksonville (U)
Florida Gulf Coast University (U)
Florida Metropolitan University–Brandon Campus (U)
Fontbonne University (U)
Gannon University (U)
Gaston College (U)

George C. Wallace Community College (U)
Goddard College (U, G)
Gogebic Community College (U)
Golden West College (U)
Grand View College (U)
Grantham University (U)
Harford Community College (U)
Harrisburg Area Community College (U)
Heartland Community College (U)
Heart of Georgia Technical College (U)
Hibbing Community College (U)
Hillsborough Community College (U)
Honolulu Community College (U)
Hope International University (N, U, G)
Hopkinsville Community College (U)
Houston Community College System (U)
Howard College (U)
Howard Community College (U)
Illinois Eastern Community Colleges, Olney Central College (U)
Immaculata University (U)
Indiana Institute of Technology (U)
Indiana State University (U)
Indiana University of Pennsylvania (U)
Indiana University–Purdue University Fort Wayne (U)
Indiana Wesleyan University (U)
Iowa Western Community College (U)
Irvine Valley College (U)
Ivy Tech State College–Eastcentral (U)
Ivy Tech State College–North Central (U)
Ivy Tech State College–Northwest (U)
Ivy Tech State College–Wabash Valley (U)
Ivy Tech State College–Whitewater (U)
Jacksonville State University (U)
James Madison University (U)
Jefferson College (U)
Jefferson College of Health Sciences (U)
Jefferson Community College (U)
John A. Logan College (U)
John F. Kennedy University (U, G)
Johnson County Community College (U)
John Tyler Community College (U)
John Wood Community College (U)
Judson College (U)
Judson College (U)
Kansas City Kansas Community College (U)
Kansas State University (U, G)
Kentucky State University (U)
Lake Region State College (U)
Lake Superior College (U)
Lamar State College–Port Arthur (U)
Lander University (U)
Lansing Community College (U)
Lenoir Community College (U)
LeTourneau University (U)
Lewis-Clark State College (U)
Liberty University (U, G)
Limestone College (U)
Long Beach City College (U)
Lorain County Community College (U)
Los Angeles Pierce College (U)
Louisiana State University and Agricultural and Mechanical College (U)
Louisiana State University at Eunice (U)
Louisiana State University in Shreveport (U)
Madonna University (U)
Marshall University (U)
Martin Community College (U)
Massasoit Community College (U)
Maui Community College (U)
Maysville Community College (N, U)
Memorial University of Newfoundland (U)
Mercy College (G)
Metropolitan Community College (U)
Metropolitan State University (U)
Miami Dade College (U)
Middlesex Community College (U)
Minnesota School of Business–Brooklyn Center (U)
Minnesota School of Business-Richfield (U)
Mississippi Delta Community College (U)
Missouri Southern State University (U)
Moberly Area Community College (U)
Modesto Junior College (U)
Monroe Community College (U)
Monroe County Community College (U)
Montana State University–Billings (U)
Montgomery Community College (U)
Montgomery County Community College (U)
Moody Bible Institute (U)
Mott Community College (U)
Mountain Empire Community College (U)
Mountain State University (U)
Mount Allison University (U)
Mt. Hood Community College (U)
Mount Saint Mary College (U)
Mount Saint Vincent University (U)
Mt. San Antonio College (U)
Mount Wachusett Community College (U)
Naropa University (N, U)
Nassau Community College (U)
National University (U)
Neumann College (U)
New England Institute of Technology (U)
New Hampshire Community Technical College System (U)
Northampton County Area Community College (U)
North Carolina State University (U)
Northcentral University (U)
North Country Community College (U)
North Dakota State University (U, G)
Northeastern Oklahoma Agricultural and Mechanical College (U)
Northeast State Technical Community College (U)
Northern Kentucky University (U)
Northern New Mexico Community College (U)
North Georgia College & State University (U, G)
North Hennepin Community College (U)
North Idaho College (U)
NorthWest Arkansas Community College (U)
Northwestern College (U)
Northwestern Michigan College (U)
Northwestern State University of Louisiana (U, G)
Northwestern Technical College (U)
Northwest Missouri State University (U)
Oakland City University (U)
Ohio University (U)
Okaloosa-Walton College (U)
Oklahoma State University (U)
Oregon State University (N, U)
Owensboro Community and Technical College (U)
Oxnard College (U)
Pace University (U)
Pacific Graduate School of Psychology (G)
Palomar College (U)
Park University (U)
Pasco-Hernando Community College (U)
Patrick Henry Community College (U)
Paul D. Camp Community College (U)
Peninsula College (U)
The Pennsylvania State University University Park Campus (U)
Pierce College (U)
Portland State University (U)
Prairie Bible College (U)
Pratt Community College (U)
Prescott College (U, G)
Pulaski Technical College (U)
Queen's University at Kingston (U)
Randolph Community College (U)
Rappahannock Community College (U)
Raritan Valley Community College (U)
Reading Area Community College (U)
Rend Lake College (U)
The Richard Stockton College of New Jersey (U)
Richland Community College (U)
Rio Hondo College (U)
Riverland Community College (U)
Riverside Community College (U)
Rockland Community College (U)
Roosevelt University (U)

N–Noncredit; U–Undergraduate; G–Graduate

Rowan Technical College (U)
Ryerson University (U)
Sacramento City College (U)
St. Clair County Community College (U)
St. Cloud State University (U)
St. Joseph's College, Suffolk Campus (U)
Saint Leo University (U)
Saint Mary-of-the-Woods College (U)
St. Petersburg College (U)
Salem Community College (U)
San Jacinto College District (U)
Santa Rosa Junior College (U)
Santiago Canyon College (U)
Sauk Valley Community College (U)
Saybrook Graduate School and Research Center (N, G)
Schiller International University (U)
Schoolcraft College (U)
Seminole Community College (U)
Seton Hill University (U)
Seward County Community College (U)
Shawnee State University (U)
Shippensburg University of Pennsylvania (U, G)
Shoreline Community College (U)
Sinclair Community College (U)
Snead State Community College (U)
Southeast Arkansas College (U)
Southeast Community College, Beatrice Campus (U)
Southeastern College of the Assemblies of God (U)
Southeastern Community College (U)
Southwestern Assemblies of God University (U)
Southwestern Baptist Theological Seminary (G)
Southwestern College (U)
Southwestern Oregon Community College (U)
Southwest Missouri State University (G)
Southwest Wisconsin Technical College (U)
Spartanburg Technical College (U)
Spring Arbor University (U)
Stanly Community College (U)
State University of New York at New Paltz (U)
State University of New York at Oswego (U, G)
Stephen F. Austin State University (U, G)
Stephens College (U)
Strayer University (U)
Sul Ross State University (U)
Syracuse University (U, G)
Tacoma Community College (U)
Taft College (U)
Tarleton State University (G)
Taylor University (U)
Taylor University (U)
Teikyo Post University (U)
Temple College (U)
Texas A&M International University (U)
Texas State University-San Marcos (U)
Texas Tech University (U)
Three Rivers Community College (U)
Tompkins Cortland Community College (U)
Touro University International (U)
Treasure Valley Community College (U)
Trinity Western University (U)
Triton College (U)
Tunxis Community College (U)
Umpqua Community College (U)
The University of Akron (U, G)
The University of Alabama (U)
University of Alaska Fairbanks (U)
University of Arkansas at Little Rock (U)
University of Bridgeport (U)
The University of British Columbia (U)
University of California, Los Angeles (G)
University of Central Arkansas (U)
University of Cincinnati (U)
University of Colorado at Colorado Springs (U)
University of Colorado at Denver (U)
University of Florida (U)
University of Georgia (U)
University of Great Falls (U)
University of Hawaii–West Oahu (U)
University of Houston–Victoria (U, G)
University of Idaho (U, G)
University of Idaho (U)
University of Illinois at Springfield (U)
The University of Iowa (U, G)
University of La Verne (U)
University of Maine (U)
The University of Maine at Augusta (U)
University of Maryland University College (U)
University of Massachusetts Amherst (U)
University of Massachusetts Boston (U)
University of Minnesota, Morris (U)
University of Minnesota, Twin Cities Campus (U)
University of Missouri–Columbia (U)
The University of Montana–Missoula (U)
University of Nebraska at Omaha (U)
University of Nebraska–Lincoln (U)
University of Nevada, Reno (U)
University of New Orleans (U)
The University of North Carolina at Chapel Hill (U)
The University of North Carolina at Greensboro (U)
University of North Dakota (U)
University of Northern Colorado (U)
University of Northern Iowa (U)
University of Saskatchewan (U)
University of South Carolina (U)
University of Southern Indiana (U)
The University of Tennessee (U)
The University of Texas at Austin (U)
The University of Texas at Tyler (U)
The University of Texas of the Permian Basin (U)
The University of Texas System (U)
University of the Incarnate Word (U, G)
University of Toledo (U)
University of Utah (U)
The University of Virginia's College at Wise (U)
University of Washington (U)
University of Waterloo (U)
University of Wisconsin Colleges (U)
University of Wisconsin–Platteville (G)
University of Wisconsin–Platteville (G)
University of Wisconsin–River Falls (U)
Upper Iowa University (N, U)
Utah Valley State College (U)
Valparaiso University (U, G)
Vance-Granville Community College (U)
Walden University (G)
Walters State Community College (U)
Washington State University (U)
Washtenaw Community College (U)
Waubonsee Community College (U)
Weber State University (U)
Westchester Community College (U)
Western New England College (U)
Western Washington University (U)
West Los Angeles College (U)
West Valley College (U)
West Virginia University at Parkersburg (U)
Whatcom Community College (U)
Wichita State University (U)
Wilfrid Laurier University (U)
Wilkes Community College (U)
William and Catherine Booth College (U)
William Rainey Harper College (U)
Worcester State College (U)
York Technical College (U)

Psychology, other

Alvin Community College (U)
Athabasca University (U)
Atlantic University (N, G)
Black Hills State University (U)
Bossier Parish Community College (U)
Bristol Community College (U)
Capella University (N, G)
Central Texas College (U)
Chadron State College (U, G)
Chemeketa Community College (U)
Cumberland County College (U)
Delaware County Community College (U)

Drake University (U)
East Carolina University (G)
Eastern Michigan University (G)
Eastern Washington University (U)
Everett Community College (U)
Gaston College (U)
Glenville State College (U)
Goddard College (U, G)
Illinois Eastern Community Colleges, Lincoln Trail College (U)
Immaculata University (G)
Jacksonville State University (U)
Jamestown Community College (N)
Limestone College (U)
Los Angeles Pierce College (U)
Louisiana State University and Agricultural and Mechanical College (U)
Marylhurst University (N)
Massasoit Community College (U)
Master's College and Seminary (U)
Mercy College (G)
Modesto Junior College (U)
Naropa University (N, G)
Nassau Community College (U)
New Hampshire Community Technical College System (U)
Northcentral University (G)
NorthWest Arkansas Community College (U)
Northwestern Michigan College (U)
Raritan Valley Community College (U)
St. Cloud State University (G)
San Bernardino Valley College (U)
Santa Rosa Junior College (U)
Saybrook Graduate School and Research Center (N, G)
Southwestern Baptist Theological Seminary (G)
Southwestern Oregon Community College (U)
Taft College (U)
Tarleton State University (U)
Teikyo Post University (U)
Tompkins Cortland Community College (U)
Umpqua Community College (U)
The University of Akron (G)
University of Arkansas at Little Rock (U)
University of Missouri–Columbia (U)
University of Nevada, Reno (G)
University of Vermont (U)
University of Waterloo (U)
Upper Iowa University (U)
Western Baptist College (U)
York University (U)
Yuba College (U)

Public administration and services, other

American Public University System (G)
Athabasca University (N, G)
College of The Albemarle (N)
Drake University (G)
George Mason University (G)
Georgia Southern University (G)
Hamline University (N, G)
Indiana State University (G)
Jacksonville State University (U, G)
John Tyler Community College (U)
Kent State University (G)
Kentucky State University (U, G)
Mercy College (U)
Northern Arizona University (G)
North Georgia College & State University (G)
Park University (G)
Regis University (G)
Roger Williams University (U)
Royal Roads University (G)
Sullivan University (G)
University of Colorado at Denver (G)
University of Illinois at Chicago (N)
University of La Verne (U)
The University of North Carolina at Charlotte (N)
Upper Iowa University (U)
York University (U)

Public administration

American Public University System (U)
Andrew Jackson University (G)
Athabasca University (N, U, G)
Austin Peay State University (U)
California State University, Dominguez Hills (G)
California University of Pennsylvania (G)
Cleveland State University (U, G)
College of The Albemarle (N)
DeVry University Online (G)
Drake University (G)
Elizabeth City State University (U)
Feather River Community College District (N)
Florida Gulf Coast University (U, G)
Florida Institute of Technology (G)
Fulton-Montgomery Community College (U)
Hamline University (N)
Hudson County Community College (N)
Indiana State University (G)
Jacksonville State University (U, G)
James Madison University (N)
John Jay College of Criminal Justice of the City University of New York (U, G)
Kansas State University (G)
Kent State University (G)
Lander University (U)
Marist College (G)
Metropolitan State University (U)
Mississippi State University (G)
National University (G)
Northcentral University (G)
Northern Arizona University (G)
North Georgia College & State University (G)
Park University (G)
Regis University (U, G)
Roger Williams University (U)
Ryerson University (U)
St. Edward's University (U)
Saint Joseph's College of Maine (G)
Saint Leo University (U)
San Jacinto College District (U)
Texas A&M University–Texarkana (U)
The University of Akron (U, G)
University of Colorado at Colorado Springs (G)
University of Colorado at Denver (G)
University of Delaware (G)
The University of Findlay (G)
University of Florida (U)
University of Hawaii–West Oahu (U)
University of Illinois (N, G)
University of Illinois at Springfield (U, G)
University of La Verne (U)
University of Maine (U)
University of Management and Technology (G)
University of Maryland University College (G)
University of Missouri–Columbia (U)
University of Nebraska at Omaha (G)
University of New Orleans (U)
The University of North Carolina at Pembroke (G)
University of North Dakota (G)
University of Oklahoma (G)
University of South Carolina Sumter (U)
The University of Texas at Tyler (G)
University of Vermont (U, G)
University of Wyoming (G)
Upper Iowa University (N, U)
Utah State University (G)
Virginia Polytechnic Institute and State University (G)
Youngstown State University (G)

Public health

Athabasca University (N, U, G)
Bowling Green State University (U)
Capella University (G)

N–Noncredit; U–Undergraduate; G–Graduate

Cleveland State University (N)
Drake University (G)
Emory University (G)
Harrisburg Area Community College (U)
James Madison University (N)
Jefferson College of Health Sciences (U)
Mercy College (U)
Montana Tech of The University of Montana (G)
New Jersey City University (U, G)
New School University (G)
Northern Arizona University (G)
Oregon State University (G)
Oxnard College (U)
The University of Akron (G)
University of Bridgeport (U)
University of Illinois (N)
University of Illinois at Chicago (N, G)
University of Massachusetts Amherst (G)
University of Minnesota, Twin Cities Campus (U, G)
The University of North Carolina at Greensboro (U)
University of South Carolina Sumter (U)
University of Southern Mississippi (G)
Virginia Polytechnic Institute and State University (N)
William Paterson University of New Jersey (U)
Youngstown State University (G)

Public policy analysis

American Public University System (U)
Athabasca University (N, U, G)
California State University, Sacramento (G)
Elizabeth City State University (U)
Ferris State University (N)
New School University (G)
University of Colorado at Denver (G)
University of Illinois at Springfield (U)

Public relations and organizational communications

Athabasca University (N, U, G)
Brenau University (U)
Florida Metropolitan University–Brandon Campus (U)
Frederick Community College (N)
James Madison University (N)
Jones International University (G)
Minnesota State College–Southeast Technical (N)
Montana State University–Billings (U, G)
Murray State University (U)
Royal Roads University (G)
Ryerson University (U)
St. Edward's University (G)
Santa Fe Community College (N)
Taylor University (N)
University of Massachusetts Amherst (N)
University of Southern Indiana (U)
Worcester State College (N)

Quality control and safety technologies

Asheville-Buncombe Technical Community College (N)
Bismarck State College (U)
California National University for Advanced Studies (N, U)
California State University, Dominguez Hills (U, G)
Capella University (G)
East Carolina University (G)
Eastern Michigan University (G)
Hudson County Community College (N)
Ivy Tech State College–Kokomo (U)
Jacksonville State University (U, G)
James Madison University (N)
Kansas State University (G)
Lakeland Community College (N)
Mitchell Technical Institute (N)
Mott Community College (U)
Murray State University (G)
Okaloosa-Walton College (U)
Southern Illinois University Carbondale (U)
The University of Alabama in Huntsville (G)
The University of Texas at Tyler (G)

Radio and television broadcasting

Athabasca University (N)
Feather River Community College District (N)
James Madison University (N)
Middle Tennessee State University (U)
Oxnard College (U)
San Bernardino Valley College (U)
Southern Illinois University Carbondale (U)
University of Alaska Fairbanks (U)
University of Missouri–Columbia (G)
University of Southern Indiana (U)

Radio/television broadcasting

Adams State College (U)
Cerritos College (U)
Eastern Kentucky University (U)
Lawson State Community College (U)
Missouri Southern State University (U)
Murray State University (U)
Texas A&M University–Commerce (G)
University of Nebraska–Lincoln (U)
University of Southern Indiana (U)

Real estate

Albuquerque Technical Vocational Institute (U)
Bainbridge College (N)
Blackhawk Technical College (N)
Bossier Parish Community College (N)
Bucks County Community College (U)
California State University, Sacramento (U)
Central Texas College (U)
Chadron State College (U)
Chemeketa Community College (U)
Clarion University of Pennsylvania (N, U)
Dallas County Community College District (U)
Darton College (N)
Feather River Community College District (N)
Frederick Community College (N)
Golden West College (U)
Hibbing Community College (N)
Houston Community College System (U)
James Madison University (N)
Jamestown Community College (N)
Johnson County Community College (N)
Lakeland Community College (N)
Madison Area Technical College (U)
Marylhurst University (U)
Maysville Community College (U)
Middle Tennessee State University (N)
MiraCosta College (U)
Mt. San Antonio College (U)
Naugatuck Valley Community College (N)
Oklahoma State University (N)
Orange Coast College (U)
Peirce College (U)
Prairie State College (N)
Rend Lake College (U)
Saddleback College (U)
San Jacinto College District (U)
Santa Rosa Junior College (U)
Santiago Canyon College (U)
Southeast Arkansas College (U)
Southern Illinois University Carbondale (U)
Tarleton State University (N)
Triton College (U)
University of Alaska Fairbanks (U)
University of Idaho (U)
University of Mississippi (U)
University of Missouri–Columbia (N, U, G)
University of Nebraska–Lincoln (U)
University of North Dakota (N)
The University of South Dakota (N)
University of Utah (N)
University of Wyoming (U)
Walters State Community College (U)
Washington State University (U)
William Rainey Harper College (U)

Rehabilitation/therapeutic services

Brenau University (G)
Chesapeake College (U)
Clarion University of Pennsylvania (G)
East Carolina University (G)

Salve Regina University (G)
Southern Illinois University Carbondale (U, G)
University of Arkansas at Little Rock (G)
The University of British Columbia (U, G)
University of Northern Colorado (U)
The University of Texas–Pan American (U)

Religion/religious studies

Andrews University (U)
Assemblies of God Theological Seminary (G)
Atlantic School of Theology (N, G)
Atlantic University (N, G)
Azusa Pacific University (U)
Baptist Bible College of Pennsylvania (G)
Baptist Theological Seminary at Richmond (N, G)
Bethany College of the Assemblies of God (U)
Bethany Theological Seminary (U, G)
Boise Bible College (U)
Briercrest Distance Learning (N, U, G)
Brigham Young University (N, U)
Caldwell College (U)
Calvin Theological Seminary (G)
Cape Fear Community College (U)
Carleton University (U)
The Catholic Distance University (N, U, G)
Central Baptist Theological Seminary (N, G)
Central Texas College (U)
Central Wyoming College (U)
Chaminade University of Honolulu (U, G)
Chattanooga State Technical Community College (U)
Chemeketa Community College (U)
College of DuPage (U)
College of Mount St. Joseph (N, U)
College of the Southwest (U)
Columbia Union College (U)
Community College of Denver (U)
Concordia College (U)
Concordia University at Austin (N, U)
Covenant Theological Seminary (N, G)
Crown College (U)
Delaware County Community College (U)
Des Moines Area Community College (U)
Earlham School of Religion (G)
Emmanuel Bible College (U)
Eugene Bible College (U)
Fontbonne University (U)
Gannon University (U)
Global University of the Assemblies of God (N)
Gonzaga University (U)
Halifax Community College (U)
Hartford Seminary (N, G)
Hebrew College (N, U, G)
Henry Ford Community College (U)
Hope International University (N, U, G)
Immaculata University (U)
The Jewish Theological Seminary (N, U, G)
John Wood Community College (U)
The King's College and Seminary (N, U, G)
La Sierra University (U)
Liberty University (G)
Life Pacific College (N)
Limestone College (U)
Lutheran Theological Seminary at Gettysburg (G)
Madonna University (U)
Master's College and Seminary (U)
Maui Community College (U)
Memorial University of Newfoundland (U)
Mesa Community College (U)
Miami Dade College (U)
Mid-America Christian University (N, U)
Missouri Baptist University (U)
Moody Bible Institute (N, U, G)
Mountain Empire Community College (U)
Mount Allison University (U)
Mt. San Antonio College (U)
Naropa University (N, U)
Neumann College (U)
Northwestern College (U)
Northwest Graduate School of the Ministry (G)
Oakland City University (U)
Okaloosa-Walton College (U)
Patrick Henry Community College (U)
The Pennsylvania State University University Park Campus (U)
Portland State University (U)
Queen's University at Kingston (U)
Rappahannock Community College (U)
Regis University (U)
Riverside Community College (U)
Sacred Heart University (U)
Saint Joseph's College of Maine (N, G)
San Bernardino Valley College (U)
Seton Hill University (U)
Shasta Bible College (U)
Snead State Community College (U)
Southern Christian University (N, U, G)
Southern Illinois University Carbondale (U)
Southwestern Assemblies of God University (U, G)
Southwestern Baptist Theological Seminary (U, G)
Southwestern College (U)
Southwest Missouri State University (G)
Stephens College (U)
Summit Pacific College (N, U)
Syracuse University (U)
Taylor University (N, U)
Taylor University (U)
Trinity Western University (G)
Union University (N, U, G)
The University of Alabama (U)
University of Bridgeport (U)
University of Dubuque (N)
The University of Findlay (U)
University of Georgia (U)
The University of Iowa (U, G)
University of Missouri–Columbia (U)
The University of North Carolina at Chapel Hill (U)
The University of North Carolina at Greensboro (U)
University of North Dakota (U)
University of Northern Iowa (U, G)
University of Saint Francis (U)
University of Saskatchewan (U)
The University of Tennessee (U)
University of the Incarnate Word (U)
University of Toledo (U)
University of Vermont (U, G)
University of Washington (U)
University of Waterloo (U)
University of West Florida (U)
Virginia Polytechnic Institute and State University (U)
Western Baptist College (U)
Western Seminary (N, G)
Wilfrid Laurier University (U)
Wilkes Community College (U)
William Tyndale College (U)
York University (U)

Religious education

Atlantic School of Theology (N, G)
Baptist Theological Seminary at Richmond (N, G)
Bethany College of the Assemblies of God (U)
Bethany Theological Seminary (G)
Boise Bible College (U)
Bossier Parish Community College (N)
Briercrest Distance Learning (U, G)
Brigham Young University (U)
Calvin Theological Seminary (G)
The Catholic Distance University (N, U, G)
Central Baptist Theological Seminary (N, G)
Crown College (U)
Dallas Baptist University (G)
Defiance College (U)
Eugene Bible College (U)
Global University of the Assemblies of God (N)
The Jewish Theological Seminary (N, U, G)
The King's College and Seminary (N, U, G)

N–Noncredit; U–Undergraduate; G–Graduate

Lutheran Theological Seminary at Gettysburg (G)
Marylhurst University (U)
Master's College and Seminary (U)
Moody Bible Institute (U)
Naropa University (N, G)
Newman Theological College (G)
Sacred Heart University (U)
Saint Joseph's College of Maine (U)
Southwestern Assemblies of God University (U, G)
Southwestern Baptist Theological Seminary (U, G)
Summit Pacific College (N, U)
Taylor University (U)
Taylor University (U)
Trinity Western University (G)
Wayland Baptist University (U, G)
Western Seminary (N, G)
William Tyndale College (U)

Religious/sacred music

Atlantic School of Theology (G)
Baptist Theological Seminary at Richmond (G)
Barclay College (U)
Calvin Theological Seminary (G)
Eugene Bible College (U)
Global University of the Assemblies of God (N)
The King's College and Seminary (N, U, G)
Lutheran Theological Seminary at Gettysburg (G)
Naropa University (N)
Northwestern College (U)
Southwestern Assemblies of God University (U)
Southwestern Baptist Theological Seminary (G)
Taylor University (U)

Romance languages and literatures

Bowling Green State University (G)
Brevard Community College (U)
Darton College (U)
Horry-Georgetown Technical College (U)
Houston Community College System (U)
James Madison University (N)
John Tyler Community College (U)
Oregon State University (N)
The Pennsylvania State University University Park Campus (U)
Rio Hondo College (U)
State University of New York College at Potsdam (N)
The University of Alabama (U)
University of Minnesota, Twin Cities Campus (U)
University of Missouri–Columbia (N, U)
The University of Tennessee (U)
University of Toronto (N)

Russian

University of Minnesota, Twin Cities Campus (U)
University of Missouri–Columbia (U)
The University of North Carolina at Chapel Hill (U)
University of Waterloo (U)

School psychology

Athabasca University (N)
Capella University (N, G)
Chadron State College (G)
Eastern Michigan University (G)
Eugene Bible College (U)
Goddard College (G)
Jacksonville State University (U, G)
Liberty University (G)
Mesa Community College (U)
Texas Woman's University (G)
The University of Akron (G)
University of Georgia (U)
University of Massachusetts Boston (G)
University of Missouri–Columbia (G)
Utah State University (G)

Science technologies, other

Athabasca University (N)
Columbus State Community College (U)
Delaware County Community College (U)
Everett Community College (U)
Lorain County Community College (U)
Northeastern University (N, U)
Virginia Polytechnic Institute and State University (U, G)

Science, technology and society

American College of Computer & Information Sciences (U)
Athabasca University (N)
Delaware County Community College (U)
Everett Community College (U)
Oregon State University (U)
Pace University (U)
Pennsylvania College of Technology (U)
The Pennsylvania State University University Park Campus (U)
Teachers College Columbia University (N, G)
University of Illinois at Urbana–Champaign (G)

Sign language interpretation

Eastern Kentucky University (U)
Floyd College (U)
Palomar College (U)
University of Utah (U)
Waubonsee Community College (U)

Social and philosophical foundations of education

Athabasca University (N)
California State University, Monterey Bay (U)
Marylhurst University (N)
The University of Akron (U, G)
University of South Carolina Sumter (U)
University of Southern Mississippi (G)
The University of Texas System (U, G)
Winston-Salem State University (U)

Social psychology

The American College (U)
Andrews University (U)
Anne Arundel Community College (U)
Athabasca University (N)
Beaufort County Community College (U)
Bethany College of the Assemblies of God (U)
Bishop State Community College (U)
Brevard Community College (U)
Brookdale Community College (U)
Bucks County Community College (U)
California Institute of Integral Studies (N, G)
Capella University (N)
Carleton University (U)
Carroll Community College (U)
Charter Oak State College (U)
College of DuPage (U)
College of Mount St. Joseph (U)
College of the Southwest (U)
Collin County Community College District (U)
Colorado Mountain College District System (U)
Delaware County Community College (U)
Eastern Washington University (U)
Florida Metropolitan University–Brandon Campus (U)
Goddard College (G)
Grand View College (U)
Greenville Technical College (U)
Howard Community College (U)
John Tyler Community College (U)
John Wood Community College (U)
Lansing Community College (U)
Lawson State Community College (U)
Liberty University (U)
Limestone College (U)
Long Beach City College (U)
Lorain County Community College (U)
Lord Fairfax Community College (U)
Maui Community College (U)

Mercy College (U)
Middlesex Community College (U)
Missouri Southern State University (U)
Modesto Junior College (U)
Montgomery County Community College (U)
Mott Community College (U)
Mountain State University (U)
New Hampshire Community Technical College System (U)
New York Institute of Technology (U)
North Harris Montgomery Community College District (U)
Odessa College (U)
Old Dominion University (U)
Oxnard College (U)
Park University (U)
Paul D. Camp Community College (U)
Regis University (U)
Richland Community College (U)
Saint Joseph's College of Maine (U)
St. Petersburg College (U)
Saybrook Graduate School and Research Center (G)
Seminole Community College (U)
Sinclair Community College (U)
Southeast Community College, Beatrice Campus (U)
Southwestern Assemblies of God University (U)
State University of New York Empire State College (U)
Tarrant County College District (U)
Taylor University (U)
Teikyo Post University (U)
Texas Tech University (U)
Tompkins Cortland Community College (U)
Triton College (U)
University College of Cape Breton (U)
The University of Akron (G)
University of Bridgeport (U)
University of Central Arkansas (U)
University of Colorado at Denver (U)
University of Guelph (U)
University of Maine (U)
University of Missouri–Columbia (U)
University of South Carolina Sumter (U)
The University of Texas at Austin (U)
University of Utah (U)
University of Washington (U)
University of Waterloo (U)
University of Wyoming (U)
Upper Iowa University (U)
Washington State University (U)
Waubonsee Community College (U)
Western New England College (U)
William Rainey Harper College (U)

Social sciences and history, other

American River College (U)
Anne Arundel Community College (U)
Athabasca University (N, G)
Bellevue Community College (U)
Berkeley College (U)
Berkeley College-New York City Campus (U)
Berkeley College-Westchester Campus (U)
Bethany College of the Assemblies of God (U)
Bishop State Community College (U)
Brevard Community College (U)
Bristol Community College (U)
Brookdale Community College (U)
Bucks County Community College (U)
Central Texas College (U)
Chadron State College (U)
Chemeketa Community College (U)
College of DuPage (U)
Columbia College (U)
Dakota County Technical College (U)
Dallas County Community College District (U)
Delaware County Community College (U)
Des Moines Area Community College (U)
Drake University (U)
Eastern Illinois University (U)
El Camino College (U)
Fort Hays State University (U)
Gogebic Community College (U)
Harford Community College (U)
Honolulu Community College (U)
Hopkinsville Community College (U)
Howard Community College (U)
John Tyler Community College (U)
Jones College (U)
Los Angeles Pierce College (U)
Louisiana State University and Agricultural and Mechanical College (U)
Louisiana State University in Shreveport (U)
Mercy College (G)
Middlesex Community College (U)
Moberly Area Community College (U)
Mountain State University (U)
Murray State University (U)
NorthWest Arkansas Community College (U)
Oregon State University (U)
Pasco-Hernando Community College (U)
Pratt Community College (U)
Rockland Community College (U)
Sacred Heart University (U)
Saddleback College (U)
St. Cloud State University (U)
St. Edward's University (U)
Saint Leo University (U)
Saint Mary-of-the-Woods College (U)
San Bernardino Valley College (U)
San Jacinto College District (U)
Shawnee State University (U)
Southwestern Assemblies of God University (U)
Stony Brook University, State University of New York (G)
Taft College (U)
Taylor University (U)
Troy University–Florida Region (U)
The University of Alabama (U)
University of Alaska Fairbanks (U)
University of Florida (U)
University of Idaho (U)
University of Massachusetts Lowell (U)
The University of Texas System (U)
University of Waterloo (U)
Utah Valley State College (U)
Wake Technical Community College (U)
Waynesburg College (U)
William Paterson University of New Jersey (U)

Social sciences, general

Athabasca University (N, U, G)
Bethany College of the Assemblies of God (U)
Bucks County Community College (U)
Butler County Community College (U)
Caldwell Community College and Technical Institute (U)
California State University, Chico (U)
Cedarville University (U)
Central Texas College (U)
Central Wyoming College (U)
Chadron State College (U)
Charter Oak State College (U)
Chemeketa Community College (U)
College for Lifelong Learning (U)
College of DuPage (U)
College of the Siskiyous (U)
Collin County Community College District (U)
Columbia Union College (U)
Concordia University, St. Paul (N)
Dakota County Technical College (U)
Dallas County Community College District (U)
Delaware County Community College (U)
Des Moines Area Community College (U)
Embry-Riddle Aeronautical University, Extended Campus (U)
Everett Community College (U)
Fort Hays State University (U)
Gateway Community College (U)
Glenville State College (U)

N–Noncredit; U–Undergraduate; G–Graduate

Goddard College (U)
Hibbing Community College (U)
Indiana Institute of Technology (U)
Inter American University of Puerto Rico, San Germán Campus (U)
Iowa Western Community College (U)
Jacksonville State University (U, G)
James Madison University (N)
John Wood Community College (U)
Jones College (U)
Kansas City Kansas Community College (U)
Lewis-Clark State College (U)
Louisiana State University and Agricultural and Mechanical College (U)
Louisiana State University in Shreveport (G)
Massasoit Community College (N)
Maysville Community College (U)
Miami Dade College (U)
Middlesex Community College (U)
Middle Tennessee State University (U)
Monroe Community College (U)
Mountain State University (U)
Murray State University (U)
New York Institute of Technology (U)
Northampton County Area Community College (U)
Northeast State Technical Community College (U)
Northern Arizona University (U)
NorthWest Arkansas Community College (U)
Okaloosa-Walton College (U)
Pennsylvania College of Technology (U)
Raritan Valley Community College (U)
Roosevelt University (U)
Ryerson University (U)
St. Clair County Community College (U)
Saint Mary-of-the-Woods College (U)
Seminole Community College (U)
Shawnee State University (U)
Southeastern Community College (U)
Southwestern Assemblies of God University (U)
Southwestern College (U)
Southwest Wisconsin Technical College (U)
State University of New York Empire State College (G)
Stephens College (U)
Taft College (U)
Tarleton State University (G)
Taylor University (U)
Taylor University (U)
Tri-State University (U)
Triton College (U)
Troy University–Florida Region (U)
The University of Alabama (U)
University of Alaska Fairbanks (U)
University of Bridgeport (U)
University of California, Los Angeles (G)
The University of Findlay (U)
University of Great Falls (U)
University of Hawaii–West Oahu (U)
University of Idaho (U)
The University of Maine at Augusta (U)
University of Maryland University College (U)
University of South Carolina Sumter (U)
The University of Texas at Austin (U)
The University of Texas System (U)
University of Utah (U)
University of Waterloo (U)
University of Wisconsin–Superior (U)
Utah Valley State College (U)
Utah Valley State College (U)
William Paterson University of New Jersey (U)
York University (U)

Social work

Athabasca University (N, G)
Bemidji State University (U)
Bowling Green State University (U)
Brigham Young University (U)
Broome Community College (U)
Capella University (N, G)
Carleton University (U)
Chadron State College (U)
Cleveland State University (U, G)
Coastal Bend College (U)
Columbia College (U)
Connecticut State University System (G)
Eastern Kentucky University (U)
Florida Atlantic University (G)
Fort Hays State University (U)
Indiana State University (N)
Jacksonville State University (U, G)
Kentucky State University (U)
Lake Region State College (U)
Lawson State Community College (U)
Limestone College (U)
Mansfield University of Pennsylvania (U)
Marshall University (U, G)
Maui Community College (U)
Memorial University of Newfoundland (U, G)
Middle Tennessee State University (U)
Mountain State University (U)
Murray State University (U)
Naugatuck Valley Community College (U)
New York Institute of Technology (U)
Northampton County Area Community College (U)
Northern Arizona University (U)
Northwestern State University of Louisiana (U)
The Ohio State University (U, G)
Raritan Valley Community College (U)
Shippensburg University of Pennsylvania (U)
Skidmore College (U)
Southwestern Oregon Community College (U)
Southwest Missouri State University (U, G)
Stephen F. Austin State University (U)
Sullivan University (G)
Texas A&M International University (U)
Texas A&M University–Commerce (U)
The University of Akron (U, G)
University of Alaska Fairbanks (U)
University of Arkansas at Little Rock (G)
The University of British Columbia (U)
University of Calgary (U, G)
The University of Iowa (U, G)
University of Maine (G)
University of Minnesota, Twin Cities Campus (U, G)
University of Missouri–Columbia (U)
The University of Montana–Missoula (U)
University of North Dakota (U, G)
University of Northern Iowa (U, G)
University of Oklahoma (G)
University of South Carolina (U)
University of South Carolina Sumter (G)
University of Southern Indiana (G)
University of Southern Mississippi (U, G)
The University of Texas at Austin (U)
University of Vermont (U, G)
University of Waterloo (U)
University of Wisconsin–Madison (G)
University of Wyoming (G)
Waubonsee Community College (U)
Western Michigan University (U)
Western New England College (U)
Western Washington University (U)
Wilfrid Laurier University (U)
William and Catherine Booth College (U)
William Paterson University of New Jersey (U, G)
Winston-Salem State University (U)
York University (N, U)
Youngstown State University (G)

Sociology

Abilene Christian University (U)
Acadia University (U)
Adams State College (U)
Adirondack Community College (U)
AIB College of Business (U)
Albuquerque Technical Vocational Institute (U)
Allan Hancock College (U)
American River College (U)
Andrews University (U)
Anne Arundel Community College (U)
Arapahoe Community College (U)

Arkansas Tech University (U)
Asheville-Buncombe Technical Community College (U)
Ashland Community and Technical College (U)
Athabasca University (N, U, G)
Austin Peay State University (U)
Baltimore City Community College (U)
Barclay College (U)
Beaufort County Community College (U)
Bellevue Community College (U)
Bemidji State University (U)
Berkeley College (U)
Bethany College of the Assemblies of God (U)
Bishop State Community College (U)
Bismarck State College (U)
Black Hills State University (U)
Boise State University (U)
Bossier Parish Community College (U)
Brevard Community College (U)
Bridgewater State College (U)
Brigham Young University (U)
Bristol Community College (U)
Brookdale Community College (U)
Broward Community College (U)
Bucks County Community College (U)
Burlington County College (U)
Butler County Community College (U)
Butler County Community College (U)
Caldwell College (U)
Caldwell Community College and Technical Institute (U)
California Institute of Integral Studies (N, G)
California State University, Chico (U)
California State University, Fullerton (U)
California State University, Sacramento (U)
Cape Cod Community College (U)
Cape Fear Community College (U)
Carroll Community College (U)
Casper College (U)
Cecil Community College (U)
Cedarville University (U)
Central Texas College (U)
Central Virginia Community College (U)
Central Wyoming College (U)
Cerritos College (U)
Chadron State College (U)
Chaminade University of Honolulu (U)
Champlain College (U)
Charter Oak State College (U)
Chattanooga State Technical Community College (U)
Chemeketa Community College (U)
Chesapeake College (U)
Citrus College (U)
Clackamas Community College (U)
Clatsop Community College (U)
Cleveland State University (U)
Clinton Community College (U)
Clovis Community College (U)
Coastal Bend College (U)
Coconino Community College (U)
Coleman College (U)
College of DuPage (U)
College of San Mateo (U)
College of The Albemarle (U)
College of the Canyons (U)
College of the Southwest (U)
Collin County Community College District (U)
Colorado Mountain College District System (U)
Colorado State University (U)
Columbia Basin College (U)
Columbia College (U)
Columbia Union College (U)
Columbus State Community College (U)
The Community College of Baltimore County (U)
Community College of Denver (U)
Concordia College (U)
Concordia University at Austin (N)
Concordia University, St. Paul (U, G)
Connecticut State University System (U, G)
Copiah-Lincoln Community College–Natchez Campus (U)
Corning Community College (U)
Cossatot Community College of the University of Arkansas (U)
County College of Morris (U)
Cumberland County College (U)
Cuyamaca College (U)
Dakota County Technical College (U)
Dakota State University (U)
Dallas Baptist University (U)
Dallas County Community College District (U)
Daniel Webster College (U)
Danville Area Community College (U)
Darton College (U)
Davenport University Online (U)
Dawson Community College (U)
Delaware County Community College (U)
Delaware Technical & Community College, Jack F. Owens Campus (U)
Delaware Technical & Community College, Stanton/Wilmington Campus (U)
Delta College (U)
Des Moines Area Community College (U)
Drake University (U)
Eastern Kentucky University (U)
Eastern Michigan University (U)
Eastern Shore Community College (U)
Eastern Wyoming College (U)
Edgecombe Community College (U)
Edison Community College (U)
Edison State Community College (U)
El Camino College (U)
Elizabeth City State University (U)
Emmanuel Bible College (U)
Eugene Bible College (U)
Everett Community College (U)
Evergreen Valley College (U)
Fairleigh Dickinson University, Metropolitan Campus (U)
Fairmont State University (U)
Fayetteville State University (U)
Florida Community College at Jacksonville (U)
Florida Metropolitan University–Brandon Campus (U)
Floyd College (U)
Fort Hays State University (U)
Frederick Community College (U)
Fulton-Montgomery Community College (U)
Georgia Southern University (U)
Goddard College (U)
Gogebic Community College (U)
Golden West College (U)
Grand View College (U)
Grantham University (U)
Greenfield Community College (U)
Greenville Technical College (U)
Harrisburg Area Community College (U)
Hartford Seminary (G)
Hillsborough Community College (U)
Hopkinsville Community College (U)
Horry-Georgetown Technical College (U)
Houston Community College System (U)
Howard College (U)
Illinois Eastern Community Colleges, Olney Central College (U)
Immaculata University (U)
Independence Community College (U)
Indiana State University (U)
Indiana University–Purdue University Fort Wayne (U)
Iowa Western Community College (U)
Irvine Valley College (U)
Ivy Tech State College–North Central (U)
Ivy Tech State College–Northwest (U)
Ivy Tech State College–Southcentral (U)
Ivy Tech State College–Wabash Valley (U)
Ivy Tech State College–Whitewater (U)
Jacksonville State University (U, G)
Jamestown Community College (N)
Jefferson College (U)
Jefferson College of Health Sciences (U)

N–Noncredit; U–Undergraduate; G–Graduate

Jefferson Community College (U)
Johnson County Community College (U)
John Tyler Community College (U)
John Wood Community College (U)
Jones College (U)
Judson College (U)
Judson College (U)
Kansas City Kansas Community College (U)
Kansas State University (U)
Kellogg Community College (U)
Kentucky State University (U)
Lakeland Community College (U)
Lake Superior College (U)
Lander University (U)
Lansing Community College (U)
Limestone College (U)
Long Beach City College (U)
Lorain County Community College (U)
Lord Fairfax Community College (U)
Los Angeles Pierce College (U)
Louisiana State University and Agricultural and Mechanical College (U)
Louisiana State University in Shreveport (U)
Loyola University New Orleans (U)
Manatee Community College (U)
Manchester Community College (U)
Mansfield University of Pennsylvania (U)
Marshall University (U, G)
Massasoit Community College (U)
Maui Community College (U)
Maysville Community College (U)
Memorial University of Newfoundland (U)
Mercy College (U)
Mesalands Community College (U)
Metropolitan Community College (U)
Middlesex Community College (U)
Middle Tennessee State University (U)
Mid-State Technical College (U)
Millersville University of Pennsylvania (U)
MiraCosta College (U)
Mississippi Delta Community College (U)
Missouri Southern State University (U)
Moberly Area Community College (U)
Modesto Junior College (U)
Montana Tech of The University of Montana (U)
Montgomery Community College (U)
Montgomery County Community College (U)
Mott Community College (U)
Mountain Empire Community College (U)
Mountain State University (U)
Mount Saint Mary College (U)
Mount Saint Vincent University (U)
Mt. San Antonio College (U)
Mount Wachusett Community College (U)
Murray State University (U)
Nassau Community College (U)
New Hampshire Community Technical College System (U)
New Mexico State University (U)
New York Institute of Technology (U)
Northampton County Area Community College (U)
North Country Community College (U)
North Dakota State College of Science (U)
North Dakota State University (U)
Northeastern Oklahoma Agricultural and Mechanical College (U)
Northern Arizona University (U)
Northern New Mexico Community College (U)
Northern Virginia Community College (U)
North Georgia College & State University (U, G)
North Harris Montgomery Community College District (U)
North Hennepin Community College (U)
North Idaho College (U)
NorthWest Arkansas Community College (U)
Northwestern Michigan College (U)
Northwestern Oklahoma State University (U)
Odessa College (U)
Ohio University (U)
Okaloosa-Walton College (U)
Oklahoma State University (U)
Old Dominion University (U)
Oregon State University (U)
Oxnard College (U)
Pace University (U)
Palomar College (U)
Pasco-Hernando Community College (U)
Patrick Henry Community College (U)
Peninsula College (U)
The Pennsylvania State University University Park Campus (U)
Pitt Community College (U)
Portland State University (U)
Pratt Community College (U)
Queen's University at Kingston (U)
Quinebaug Valley Community College (U)
Randolph Community College (U)
Rappahannock Community College (U)
Raritan Valley Community College (U)
Reading Area Community College (U)
Regis University (U)
Rend Lake College (U)
The Richard Stockton College of New Jersey (U)
Richland Community College (U)
Rio Hondo College (U)
Riverland Community College (U)
Riverside Community College (U)
Rochester Institute of Technology (U)
Roger Williams University (U)
Rowan Technical College (U)
Ryerson University (U)
Sacramento City College (U)
Saddleback College (U)
St. Clair County Community College (U)
St. Cloud State University (U)
Saint Joseph's College of Maine (U)
Salem Community College (U)
Sam Houston State University (U)
San Bernardino Valley College (U)
San Jacinto College District (U)
Santa Fe Community College (U)
Santa Rosa Junior College (U)
Sauk Valley Community College (U)
Schoolcraft College (U)
Seattle Central Community College (U)
Seminole Community College (U)
Shawnee State University (U)
Shelton State Community College (U)
Sinclair Community College (U)
Skidmore College (U)
Snead State Community College (U)
Southeast Arkansas College (U)
Southeast Community College, Lincoln Campus (U)
Southeastern College of the Assemblies of God (U)
Southeastern Community College (U)
Southern Illinois University Carbondale (U)
Southwestern Assemblies of God University (U)
Southwestern College (U)
Southwestern Oregon Community College (U)
Southwest Missouri State University (U)
Southwest Virginia Community College (U)
Southwest Wisconsin Technical College (U)
Spartanburg Technical College (U)
Spring Arbor University (U)
Stanly Community College (U)
State University of New York at New Paltz (U)
State University of New York at Plattsburgh (U)
State University of New York Empire State College (U)
Strayer University (U)
Syracuse University (U, G)
Tacoma Community College (U)
Taft College (U)
Tarrant County College District (U)
Taylor University (U)
Teikyo Post University (U)
Texas A&M University–Commerce (U)
Texas State University-San Marcos (U)
Texas Tech University (U)
Texas Woman's University (U, G)

Tompkins Cortland Community College (U)
Treasure Valley Community College (U)
Trinity Western University (U)
Triton College (U)
Troy University Montgomery (U)
Tunxis Community College (U)
Umpqua Community College (U)
The University of Akron (U)
University of Alaska Fairbanks (U)
University of Arkansas at Little Rock (U)
University of Bridgeport (U)
University of Central Arkansas (U)
University of Central Florida (U)
University of Cincinnati Raymond Walters College (U)
University of Colorado at Colorado Springs (U)
University of Colorado at Denver (U)
University of Connecticut (U)
University of Delaware (U)
The University of Findlay (U)
University of Florida (U)
University of Georgia (U)
University of Great Falls (U)
University of Guelph (U)
University of Hawaii–West Oahu (U)
University of Houston–Downtown (U)
University of Idaho (U)
The University of Iowa (U, G)
University of Maine (U)
The University of Maine at Augusta (U)
University of Maryland University College (U)
University of Massachusetts Amherst (U)
University of Massachusetts Boston (U, G)
University of Massachusetts Lowell (U)
University of Missouri–Columbia (U)
The University of Montana–Missoula (U)
University of Nebraska at Omaha (U)
University of Nebraska–Lincoln (U)
University of Nevada, Reno (U)
The University of North Carolina at Chapel Hill (U)
The University of North Carolina at Greensboro (U)
The University of North Carolina at Pembroke (U)
University of North Dakota (U)
University of Northern Iowa (U, G)
University of North Florida (U)
University of Oklahoma (U)
University of Saint Francis (U)
University of Saskatchewan (U)
University of Sioux Falls (U)
University of South Carolina Sumter (G)
The University of South Dakota (U)
University of Southern Mississippi (U)
The University of Tennessee (U)
The University of Tennessee at Martin (U)
The University of Texas at Arlington (U)
The University of Texas at Austin (U)
The University of Texas at Tyler (U)
The University of Texas of the Permian Basin (U)
The University of Texas System (U)
University of the Incarnate Word (U)
University of Toledo (U)
University of Washington (U)
University of Waterloo (U)
University of Wisconsin Colleges (U)
University of Wisconsin–Platteville (G)
University of Wisconsin–River Falls (U)
Upper Iowa University (N, U)
Utah Valley State College (U)
Valley City State University (U)
Valparaiso University (U, G)
Vance-Granville Community College (U)
Virginia Polytechnic Institute and State University (U)
Walters State Community College (U)
Washington State University (U)
Washtenaw Community College (U)
Waubonsee Community College (U)
Westchester Community College (U)
Western Michigan University (U)
Western New England College (U)
Western Washington University (U)
West Valley College (U)
Whatcom Community College (U)
Wichita State University (U)
Wilfrid Laurier University (U)
Wilkes Community College (U)
William and Catherine Booth College (U)
William Paterson University of New Jersey (G)
William Rainey Harper College (U)
Winston-Salem State University (U)
York Technical College (U)
York University (U)
Yuba College (U)

Soil sciences

Cedarville University (U)
John Tyler Community College (U)
Lakeland Community College (N)
North Carolina State University (U)
Oregon State University (U)
The University of British Columbia (U)
University of Georgia (N, U)
University of Saskatchewan (N)
Washington State University (U)

South Asian languages and literatures

Lakeland Community College (N)
North Carolina State University (U)
University of Toronto (N)

Spanish

Boise State University (U)
Brigham Young University (U)
Broward Community College (U)
Bucks County Community College (U)
Burlington County College (U)
Clovis Community College (U)
College of DuPage (U)
College of San Mateo (U)
Colorado Mountain College District System (U)
Columbus State Community College (U)
Delta College (U)
Evergreen Valley College (U)
Greenville Technical College (U)
Houston Community College System (U)
Louisiana State University and Agricultural and Mechanical College (U)
Montgomery County Community College (U)
Mountain Empire Community College (U)
Nassau Community College (U)
Northern Virginia Community College (U)
Oklahoma State University (U)
Palomar College (U)
The Pennsylvania State University University Park Campus (U)
Queen's University at Kingston (U)
Seattle Central Community College (U)
Southeast Community College, Lincoln Campus (U)
Southwest Virginia Community College (U)
Texas State University-San Marcos (U)
Texas Tech University (N, U)
Triton College (U)
Troy University Montgomery (U)
The University of Iowa (U)
University of Minnesota, Twin Cities Campus (U)
University of Missouri–Columbia (U)
University of Nevada, Reno (U)
The University of North Carolina at Chapel Hill (U)
University of Toronto (N)
University of Waterloo (U)
Virginia Polytechnic Institute and State University (U)
Walters State Community College (U)
Washington State University (U)
West Valley College (U)
Yuba College (U)

Special education

Acadia University (U)
Athabasca University (G)

N–Noncredit; U–Undergraduate; G–Graduate

Baltimore City Community College (U)
Bowling Green State University (G)
Bridgewater State College (U, G)
Brigham Young University (U)
Buena Vista University (U)
California State University, Monterey Bay (U)
California State University, Sacramento (U)
Casper College (U)
Cedarville University (U)
Central Missouri State University (G)
Central Missouri State University (G)
Central Missouri State University (G)
Central Missouri State University (G)
Central Missouri State University (G)
Chadron State College (U, G)
College for Lifelong Learning (U)
Cossatot Community College of the University of Arkansas (N)
Cumberland College (G)
Drake University (U)
East Carolina University (G)
Eastern Kentucky University (G)
Eastern Michigan University (U)
Elizabeth City State University (U)
Fayetteville State University (U, G)
Hamline University (G)
Illinois State University (G)
Indiana State University (G)
Jacksonville State University (U, G)
James Madison University (N, G)
John Wood Community College (U)
Lakeland Community College (N)
Liberty University (G)
Millersville University of Pennsylvania (U, G)
Montana State University–Billings (U)
Mount Saint Mary College (U, G)
Murray State University (G)
National University (G)
New Hampshire Community Technical College System (U)
New Jersey City University (G)
Northampton County Area Community College (U)
North Dakota State University (G)
Northern Arizona University (U)
Northwestern State University of Louisiana (G)
Northwest Missouri State University (G)
The Ohio State University (N)
Oklahoma State University (N)
Oxnard College (U)
Pennsylvania College of Optometry (G)
St. Ambrose University (G)
Saint Mary-of-the-Woods College (U)
Santa Fe Community College (N)
Seattle Pacific University (G)
Southwest Missouri State University (U)
State University of New York at Plattsburgh (G)
Stephen F. Austin State University (U, G)
Tarleton State University (G)
Texas A&M University–Commerce (G)
University of Arkansas at Little Rock (G)
University of Georgia (N, U)
University of Idaho (U)
University of Maine (U)
University of Massachusetts Boston (G)
University of Missouri–Columbia (U, G)
University of Nebraska at Omaha (G)
The University of North Carolina at Greensboro (G)
University of Northern Colorado (U, G)
University of North Florida (G)
University of Phoenix Online Campus (G)
University of Southern Mississippi (U, G)
The University of Tennessee at Martin (U, G)
The University of Texas at Tyler (U, G)
The University of Texas of the Permian Basin (U)
University of Toledo (G)
University of Utah (U)
Utah State University (G)
Wayne State College (U, G)
Western Carolina University (U)
Western Washington University (U)
William Paterson University of New Jersey (U)

Speech and rhetorical studies

Albuquerque Technical Vocational Institute (U)
Asheville-Buncombe Technical Community College (U)
Austin Peay State University (U)
Bellevue Community College (U)
Bowling Green State University (G)
Brevard Community College (U)
Brigham Young University (U)
Butler County Community College (U)
Central Virginia Community College (U)
Chattanooga State Technical Community College (U)
Chemeketa Community College (U)
Clackamas Community College (U)
College of the Canyons (U)
Columbus State Community College (U)
Community College of Denver (U)
Dallas County Community College District (U)
Darton College (U)
Delta College (U)
East Central College (U)
East Los Angeles College (U)
Eugene Bible College (U)
Florida Community College at Jacksonville (U)
Frederick Community College (U)
Grand View College (U)
Honolulu Community College (U)
Iowa Western Community College (U)
James Madison University (N)
Jefferson College (U)
Johnson County Community College (U)
Lansing Community College (U)
Miami Dade College (U)
Mississippi Delta Community College (U)
Moberly Area Community College (U)
Mountain Empire Community College (U)
New York Institute of Technology (U)
Northeast State Technical Community College (U)
Northwestern College (U)
Oxnard College (U)
Pasco-Hernando Community College (U)
The Pennsylvania State University University Park Campus (U)
Rend Lake College (U)
St. Cloud State University (U)
Salem Community College (U)
San Bernardino Valley College (U)
Schoolcraft College (U)
Shippensburg University of Pennsylvania (U)
Snead State Community College (U)
Southeast Community College, Beatrice Campus (U)
Tacoma Community College (U)
Taylor University (U)
Triton College (U)
The University of Akron (U, G)
University of Arkansas at Little Rock (U)
University of Georgia (U)
University of La Verne (U)
University of Minnesota, Twin Cities Campus (U)
The University of Montana–Missoula (U)
University of Southern Indiana (U)
University of Vermont (G)
University of Washington (U)
University of Wisconsin–Platteville (U)
University of Wisconsin–River Falls (U)
Waubonsee Community College (U)
West Los Angeles College (U)
Wichita State University (U)
William Paterson University of New Jersey (U)

Student counseling and personnel services

College of the Siskiyous (U)
Fort Hays State University (U)
Indiana State University (G)

Irvine Valley College (U)
Jacksonville State University (U)
James Madison University (N)
Modesto Junior College (N)
University of Massachusetts Boston (G)

Surveying

Michigan Technological University (U)
University of Maine (U)

Systems engineering

Bristol Community College (N)
California National University for Advanced Studies (N)
Capitol College (G)
Florida Institute of Technology (G)
James Madison University (N)
Mid-State Technical College (U)
Southern Methodist University (G)
The University of Alabama in Huntsville (G)
University of Michigan (N)

Systems science and theory

Capitol College (G)
Florida Institute of Technology (G)
Immaculata University (U)
Nova Southeastern University (G)
Syracuse University (G)

Taxation

Ashworth College (N)
Athabasca University (N, G)
Brenau University (G)
Brevard Community College (U)
Bucks County Community College (U)
Davenport University Online (U)
DeVry University Online (U, G)
Drexel University (U)
Elizabeth City State University (U)
Fairleigh Dickinson University, Metropolitan Campus (U)
Golden Gate University (G)
James Madison University (N)
Jones College (U)
Lakeland Community College (N)
Liberty University (U)
Massasoit Community College (N)
Miami Dade College (U)
Middlesex Community College (U)
Oxnard College (U)
Saint Leo University (U)
Southwest Missouri State University (G)
State University of New York Institute of Technology (G)
State University of New York Institute of Technology (G)
State University of New York Institute of Technology (G)
State University of New York Institute of Technology (G)
Suffolk University (G)
The University of Akron (U)
The University of Maine at Augusta (U)
The University of North Carolina at Charlotte (N)
University of Notre Dame (N, G)
The University of Texas at Dallas (G)
University of Tulsa (G)
University of Wisconsin–Milwaukee (G)

Teacher assistant/aide

Ashworth College (N)
Blue Mountain Community College (U)
Casper College (U)
College of the Siskiyous (U)
Community College of Denver (U)
Education Direct Center for Degree Studies (N)
Fort Hays State University (G)
Grossmont College (N)
Halifax Community College (U)
Heart of Georgia Technical College (U)
John Tyler Community College (U)
Mesalands Community College (U)
Minot State University–Bottineau Campus (U)
Southwestern Oregon Community College (U)
Université Sainte-Anne (N)
The University of Texas System (G)
Vance-Granville Community College (U)

Teacher education, specific academic and vocational programs

Adams State College (G)
Alcorn State University (U)
Alliant International University (N)
Azusa Pacific University (G)
Bemidji State University (U)
Boise State University (U, G)
Bucks County Community College (U)
California State University, Fullerton (N)
Central Missouri State University (U)
Central Missouri State University (U)
Central Missouri State University (U)
Central Missouri State University (U)
Central Wyoming College (U)
Chadron State College (U, G)
Colorado State University (N)
Columbus State University (G)
Community College of Denver (U)
East Carolina University (U)
Eastern Illinois University (U)
Eastern Michigan University (G)
Edgecombe Community College (U)
Elizabeth City State University (U)
Fontbonne University (G)
Fort Hays State University (U, G)
Gaston College (U)
Goddard College (G)
Hamline University (N, G)
Hudson County Community College (N)
Jacksonville State University (U, G)
The Jewish Theological Seminary (N, U, G)
John Tyler Community College (U)
Kirkwood Community College (U)
La Sierra University (U, G)
Lawrence Technological University (G)
Marygrove College (U, G)
Millersville University of Pennsylvania (U, G)
Mississippi State University (U, G)
Missouri Baptist University (U, G)
Montana State University–Bozeman (U, G)
National University (G)
New Hampshire Community Technical College System (U)
New Mexico Institute of Mining and Technology (G)
North Carolina State University (U, G)
North Georgia College & State University (N, U, G)
Oregon State University (G)
Pace University (U)
Quinnipiac University (U, G)
Randolph Community College (U)
St. John's University (G)
Saint Joseph's College of Maine (U, G)
Saint Mary-of-the-Woods College (U)
Salem Community College (N)
Seattle Pacific University (G)
Seminole Community College (U)
Simpson College (G)
South Piedmont Community College (U)
Southwestern Assemblies of God University (U, G)
Southwest Missouri State University (G)
State University of New York at Oswego (U, G)
Sul Ross State University (G)
Tarleton State University (G)
Texas A&M International University (G)
Texas A&M University–Texarkana (U)
Touro University International (G)
Trinity Western University (G)
The University of Akron (U, G)
The University of Arizona (G)
University of Georgia (U)
University of Illinois (G)
University of La Verne (N, U)
University of Maine (U)

N–Noncredit; U–Undergraduate; G–Graduate

University of Maryland University College (G)
University of Minnesota, Morris (U)
University of Missouri–Columbia (G)
University of Nebraska at Omaha (G)
University of North Dakota (U, G)
University of Saskatchewan (N)
University of Southern Indiana (G)
The University of Tennessee at Martin (G)
The University of Texas of the Permian Basin (U, G)
The University of Texas System (U, G)
University of Utah (U)
University of West Florida (N)
University of Wisconsin–River Falls (U, G)
Virginia Polytechnic Institute and State University (U, G)
Wake Technical Community College (N)
Wayne State College (U, G)
Western Washington University (U)
William Paterson University of New Jersey (U)

Teaching English as a second language/foreign language

Athabasca University (N)
Briercrest Distance Learning (U)
Feather River Community College District (N)
Hamline University (N, G)
Irvine Valley College (U)
Lewis-Clark State College (U)
Madison Area Technical College (U)
Murray State University (G)
North Carolina State University (U)
Santa Fe Community College (N)
Seattle Pacific University (G)
Trinity Western University (G)
The University of Akron (U)
University of Maine (U)
University of Massachusetts Boston (G)
University of Nevada, Reno (U)
The University of North Carolina at Greensboro (G)
University of North Dakota (G)
University of Saskatchewan (N, U)
The University of Texas System (G)
Western Washington University (U)

Technology education/industrial arts

Bismarck State College (U)
Bowling Green State University (U, G)
Brigham Young University (U)
Bristol Community College (N)
Central Missouri State University (U, G)
Central Missouri State University (U, G)
Central Missouri State University (U, G)
Central Missouri State University (U, G)
Central Missouri State University (U, G)
Chadron State College (G)
Cleveland State University (N, G)
Colorado Christian University (U)
East Carolina University (U)
Eastern Michigan University (U, G)
Fort Hays State University (U)
Heart of Georgia Technical College (U)
Hudson County Community College (N)
Illinois State University (U, G)
Indiana State University (U, G)
Jacksonville State University (U)
Lesley University (G)
Marquette University (G)
Marshall University (G)
Millersville University of Pennsylvania (G)
National University (G)
Nova Southeastern University (G)
Okaloosa-Walton College (U)
Stevens Institute of Technology (N)
The University of Akron (U, G)
University of Massachusetts Boston (U, G)
University of Missouri–Columbia (G)
University of North Dakota (G)
University of Phoenix Online Campus (U)
The University of South Dakota (G)
The University of Texas at Tyler (U)
University of West Florida (N)
Valley City State University (U)
West Virginia University at Parkersburg (U)

Telecommunications

American River College (U)
Aspen University (G)
Bossier Parish Community College (U)
Bowling Green State University (U)
Bristol Community College (N)
Capitol College (G)
Carl Albert State College (U)
Cayuga County Community College (U)
Champlain College (U)
Cleveland State University (N, U, G)
College of The Albemarle (N)
Dallas County Community College District (U)
Davenport University Online (U)
DePaul University (G)
DeVry University Online (G)
Golden Gate University (U, G)
Hudson County Community College (N)
Illinois Institute of Technology (G)
James Madison University (N)
Jones International University (U, G)
Lord Fairfax Community College (N)
Murray State University (G)
New Hampshire Community Technical College System (U)
New York Institute of Technology (U)
Northeastern University (N)
Pace University (U)
Riverside Community College (U)
Santa Rosa Junior College (U)
Southern Illinois University Carbondale (U)
Southern Methodist University (G)
Stanford University (N)
State University of New York at Oswego (U)
Syracuse University (G)
The University of Akron (U)
The University of Alabama (U)
University of Colorado at Boulder (N, G)
University of Dallas (G)
University of Denver (G)
University of Massachusetts Lowell (U)
University of Nebraska at Omaha (U, G)
The University of Texas System (U)
University of the Incarnate Word (U)
University of Tulsa (G)
University of West Florida (U)

Textile sciences and engineering

North Carolina State University (U, G)
Syracuse University (N)
Texas Tech University (G)

Theater arts/drama

Boise State University (U)
Brigham Young University (U)
Brookdale Community College (U)
Connecticut State University System (U)
Eastern Michigan University (U)
Edison State Community College (U)
Lansing Community College (U)
Louisiana State University and Agricultural and Mechanical College (U)
Montana State University–Billings (U)
Northern Virginia Community College (U)
Northwest Missouri State University (U)
Queen's University at Kingston (U)
Texas Christian University (U)
Triton College (U)
University of Colorado at Denver (U)
The University of North Carolina at Chapel Hill (U)
The University of South Dakota (U)
The University of Texas of the Permian Basin (U)
University of Wisconsin–River Falls (U)

Theological and ministerial studies

Alliance University College (U, G)
Aquinas Institute of Theology (G)
Arlington Baptist College (N, U)
Assemblies of God Theological Seminary (G)
Atlantic School of Theology (N, G)
Azusa Pacific University (G)
Baptist Bible College of Pennsylvania (G)

Baptist Missionary Association Theological Seminary (N, U, G)
Baptist Theological Seminary at Richmond (N)
Barclay College (U)
Bethany College of the Assemblies of God (U)
Boise Bible College (U)
Briercrest Distance Learning (U, G)
Calvin Theological Seminary (G)
The Catholic Distance University (N)
Central Baptist Theological Seminary (N, G)
College of Emmanuel and St. Chad (G)
Columbia Union College (U)
Covenant Theological Seminary (N, G)
Crown College (G)
Denver Seminary (G)
Drew University (G)
Earlham School of Religion (G)
Eastern Mennonite University (G)
Emmanuel Bible College (U)
Franciscan University of Steubenville (N, U, G)
Global University of the Assemblies of God (N)
Institute for Christian Studies (G)
The King's College and Seminary (N, U, G)
Liberty University (G)
Lutheran Theological Seminary at Gettysburg (G)
Marylhurst University (G)
Master's College and Seminary (U)
Mid-America Christian University (N, U)
Moody Bible Institute (N, U, G)
Naropa University (N)
Newman Theological College (U)
North Central University (N, U)
Northwestern College (U)
Northwest Graduate School of the Ministry (G)
Oral Roberts University (N)
Prairie Bible College (U, G)
Sacred Heart Major Seminary (U)
Saint Joseph's College of Maine (G)
Saint Mary-of-the-Woods College (G)
Southeastern Baptist Theological Seminary (G)
Southern Christian University (N, U, G)
Southwestern Assemblies of God University (U, G)
Southwestern Baptist Theological Seminary (U, G)
Summit Pacific College (N, U)
Taylor University (N, U)
Taylor University (U)
Trinity Episcopal School for Ministry (G)
Western Seminary (N, G)
William and Catherine Booth College (U)

Theological studies and religious vocations, other

Assemblies of God Theological Seminary (G)
Atlantic School of Theology (N, G)
Baptist Bible College of Pennsylvania (G)
Baptist Missionary Association Theological Seminary (N, U, G)
Baptist Theological Seminary at Richmond (N)
Boise Bible College (U)
Briercrest Distance Learning (U, G)
Calvin Theological Seminary (G)
The Catholic Distance University (N, U, G)
Central Baptist Theological Seminary (N, G)
College of Emmanuel and St. Chad (G)
Covenant Theological Seminary (N, G)
Earlham School of Religion (G)
Global University of the Assemblies of God (N)
Immaculata University (U)
The King's College and Seminary (N, U, G)
Liberty University (U, G)
Lutheran Theological Seminary at Gettysburg (G)
Master's College and Seminary (U)
Moody Bible Institute (U, G)
Naropa University (N)
North Central University (N, U)
Northwestern College (U)
Northwest Graduate School of the Ministry (G)
Saint Joseph's College of Maine (G)
Saint Mary-of-the-Woods College (U)
Saint Mary-of-the-Woods College (U, G)
Southwestern Assemblies of God University (U, G)
Southwestern Baptist Theological Seminary (G)
Taylor University (U)
Taylor University (U)
Trinity Episcopal School for Ministry (N, G)
Valparaiso University (U, G)
Western Seminary (N, G)

Tourism/travel marketing

Arapahoe Community College (U)
Ashworth College (N)
Bridgewater State College (N)
Central Texas College (U)
Chemeketa Community College (U)
Colorado State University (N)
Colorado State University-Pueblo (N)
Corning Community College (U)
Feather River Community College District (N)
Lakeland Community College (N)
Madison Area Technical College (U)
Massasoit Community College (U)
Naugatuck Valley Community College (U)
Northeastern Oklahoma Agricultural and Mechanical College (N)
Ohio University (U)
Oxnard College (U)
Saint Joseph's College of Maine (G)
Schiller International University (G)
Shenandoah University (U)
State University of New York at Plattsburgh (U)
State University of New York College at Potsdam (N)
Sullivan University (U)
Texas Tech University (U)
The University of Alabama (U)
University of Southern Mississippi (N)
University of Wisconsin–River Falls (G)
West Los Angeles College (U)

Transportation and materials moving workers, other

James Madison University (N)
The Pennsylvania State University University Park Campus (G)
Sullivan University (U)
University of Toronto (U)
University of Wisconsin–Milwaukee (N)

Urban affairs/studies

Cleveland State University (U, G)
Hamline University (N)
James Madison University (N)
The King's College and Seminary (N, U, G)
Marylhurst University (U)
Taylor University (U)
The University of British Columbia (U)
University of Delaware (U, G)
University of Illinois at Chicago (N)
The University of Texas at Arlington (G)
University of Washington (U, G)
Virginia Polytechnic Institute and State University (G)

Vehicle and mobile equipment mechanics and repairers

Bristol Community College (N)
Madison Area Technical College (U)
Maui Community College (U)
Naugatuck Valley Community College (U)

Vehicle/equipment operation

Bristol Community College (N)
Frederick Community College (N)

N–Noncredit; U–Undergraduate; G–Graduate

Veterinary clinical sciences (M.S., Ph.D.)

Lakeland Community College (N)
Virginia Polytechnic Institute and State University (G)

Veterinary medicine (D.V.M.)

Auburn University (N)
University of Georgia (U)
University of Illinois (G)
Virginia Polytechnic Institute and State University (G)
Yuba College (U)

Visual and performing arts

Brevard Community College (U)
Brigham Young University (U)
Delta College (U)
East Los Angeles College (U)
Everett Community College (U)
Frederick Community College (U)
Gonzaga University (U)
Howard Community College (U)
Irvine Valley College (U)
Ivy Tech State College–Columbus (U)
James Madison University (N)
Jefferson College (U)
John F. Kennedy University (G)
Marshall University (U, G)
Maui Community College (U)
Missouri Southern State University (U)
North Harris Montgomery Community College District (U)
North Hennepin Community College (U)
Pace University (U)
The Pennsylvania State University University Park Campus (U)
Prescott College (U, G)
Santa Fe Community College (U)
Santa Rosa Junior College (U)
Shawnee State University (U)
Texas Tech University (G)
Tompkins Cortland Community College (U)
University of Bridgeport (U)
University of California, Los Angeles (G)
The University of Findlay (U)
University of Maine (U)
University of Southern Indiana (U)
The University of Tennessee at Martin (U)
Wilfrid Laurier University (U)

Visual and performing arts, other

Brenau University (U)
Central Virginia Community College (U)
Columbus State Community College (U)
Drake University (U)
Gonzaga University (G)
Ivy Tech State College–North Central (U)
Naugatuck Valley Community College (U)
The Ohio State University (U)
St. Cloud Technical College (N)
University of Oregon (U)

Vocational home economics, other

Hudson County Community College (U)
Northern Arizona University (G)

Wildlife and wildlands management

Lakeland Community College (N)
Middle Tennessee State University (N)
Oregon State University (U, G)
The Pennsylvania State University University Park Campus (N, U)
Prescott College (U, G)
Texas A&M University (G)
University of Massachusetts Amherst (U)
University of Wisconsin–River Falls (G)

Women's studies

Atlantic University (N, G)
Bucks County Community College (U)
California Institute of Integral Studies (N, G)
Cleveland State University (U)
Eastern Michigan University (U)
Eastern Washington University (U)
Kansas State University (U)
Louisiana State University and Agricultural and Mechanical College (U)
Memorial University of Newfoundland (U)
Mount Saint Vincent University (U)
Ohio University (U)
Oregon State University (U)
Queen's University at Kingston (U)
The Richard Stockton College of New Jersey (U)
University of Alaska Fairbanks (U)
The University of British Columbia (U)
University of Illinois at Springfield (U)
The University of Iowa (U, G)
University of Maine (U)
University of Minnesota, Twin Cities Campus (U)
University of Missouri–Columbia (U)
University of Toledo (U)
University of Waterloo (U)
University of Wyoming (U)
Virginia Polytechnic Institute and State University (U, G)
Washington State University (U)
Western Washington University (U)

Woodworkers

Blackhawk Technical College (N)
Madison Area Technical College (U)

Zoology

Brigham Young University (U)
Casper College (U)
Eastern Wyoming College (U)
Maui Community College (U)
Mississippi State University (U)
North Carolina State University (U)
Northwestern State University of Louisiana (U)
The University of Akron (U)
Washington State University (U)
Weber State University (U)

GEOGRAPHICAL LISTING OF DISTANCE LEARNING PROGRAMS

In this index, the page locations of the profiles are printed in regular type and **In-Depth Descriptions** in **bold type.**

U.S. AND U.S. TERRITORIES

Alabama

Alaska

Arizona

Arkansas

California

Colorado

Connecticut

Delaware

District of Columbia

Florida

Georgia

Hawaii

Idaho

Illinois

Oklahoma

Oregon

Pennsylvania

Puerto Rico

Rhode Island

South Carolina

South Dakota

Tennessee

Texas

Utah

Vermont

Virginia

Washington

West Virginia

Wisconsin